Buffets &
Receptions

Buffets & Receptions

Pierre Mengelatte   Walter Bickel   Albin Abelanet

Editor: Michael Small

Assistant Editor: Mabel Quin

VIRTUE & COMPANY LIMITED
London, Dublin and Coulsdon

British Library Cataloguing in Publication Data
Mengelatte, Pierre
  Buffets and receptions. – 4th ed.
  1. Buffets (Cookery)
  I. Title II. Bickel, Walter
  III. Abelanet, Albin
  641.5'68   TX738.5
ISBN 0-900778-20-2

International editions copyright © René Kramer, publisher,
Lugano-Castagnola, Switzerland.
English language editions copyright © Virtue & Company
Limited, 25 Breakfield, Coulsdon, Surrey, England.

This edition first published 1978.
Second edition 1979.
Third edition 1980.
Fourth edition 1983. Reprinted 1984, 1986.

Printed in Great Britain by Ebenezer Baylis & Son Ltd,
The Trinity Press, Worcester, and London.
Colour plates printed by Presses Centrales, S.A., Lausanne,
Switzerland.

FOREWORD

by John Fuller

Quondam Professor of Hotel Management, University of Strathclyde

Each nation and each style of cuisine share features reflecting food's place in celebrating personal and public festal occasions. Of course, not all parties feature elaborate food. Some feast days in some countries may highlight a simple dish like a pancake on Shrove Tuesday. On the whole, however, party fare, elaborate or simple, calls for flair and presentation. Buffets, when party fare both hot and cold, is displayed before the guest, give special opportunity for culinary artistry.

This book embodies kitchen and table lore from many lands to guide the adventurous chef, caterer and cook in creating party fare for every conceivable occasion. Just as parties and buffets themselves are fun; so does this book reflect hospitality with gaiety. Its pages are pleasurable as well as instructive.

The book is certainly pleasurable to the eye, often dubbed the first organ of digestion. The eye must be pleased if appetite and meal enjoyment are to follow and at party time this is doubly important. But this book is primarily designed for the professional caterer. For professional chefs this book's illustrations constitute an essential part of the instructional material. They provide both inspiration and visual guidance for standards of finish. They stimulate imagination and help achieve enhanced effect.

Cookery is a fleeting art form. Perhaps that is why both chefs and their customers have special regard for decorative works, sweet and savoury, which, though impermanent, remain long enough on a buffet for finer points of craftsmanship to be displayed and to be admired.

Salons culinaire where such culinary artistry is exhibited are sometimes criticised because, it is averred, they please chefs more than customers. I doubt whether this is really so. The diner out, and especially the party goer, surely appreciates the compliment of the *pièce montée* and the sense of occasion which a fine buffet engenders. What is, alas, true is that harsh economics, the high cost of the time and labour of the skilled *chef garde manger* or *pâtissier* may reduce the commercial application of high culinary art. Nevertheless, show work for the table will endure as a labour of love for chefs, because spectacular dishes will always have a role in emphasising a celebration. Drama on the buffet table can still mean good business.

Catering for weddings, bar mitzvahs, company and association occasions and many others is an important, and profitable, part of the hospitality industry from the modest pub to the posh hotel. This book, though it highlights some spectacular fare, still affords practical guidance for professionals who aim to achieve profit through pleasing their patrons.

In its style, and especially in its colour presentation, BUFFETS AND RECEPTIONS will worthily partner Pellaprat's MODERN FRENCH CULINARY

ART in providing chefs and caterers with essential knowhow for an essential sector of their work, the pre-booked celebration and the special occasion. This English language version of an authoritative text from international contributors will surely be welcomed by *brigades de cuisine* throughout the English speaking world.

PUBLISHER'S PREFACE

Pellaprat's great work MODERN FRENCH CULINARY ART has become, in the last thirty years or so, a classic of its kind. Chefs and restaurateurs in many countries throughout the world use his book as a ready reference in their work on many occasions.

We believe that BUFFETS AND RECEPTIONS is a worthy companion to Pellaprat's masterpiece for the next generation of professional chefs. Like Pellaprat, BUFFETS AND RECEPTIONS was first published in French by René Kramer, Swiss publisher and gastronome. We are proud to be the publishers of the English language edition, and we are confident that it will rapidly find its way into hotel and restaurant kitchens both great and small, and into the hands of teachers and students alike in catering schools and colleges.

The book was several years in the making and a widely drawn team of experts have contributed recipes, ideas and gastronomic creations to make this book into a truly comprehensive and unique guide to a particular aspect of catering and entertaining.

The French edition was edited and compiled by Pierre Mengelatte, Walter Bickel and Albin Abélanet, eminent names in the field of European gastronomy. The French text was translated by Mrs. Annie Jackson. We are particularly grateful to our Editor, Michael Small, MHCIMA, MICA, already an established author in his own right, for the long hours he spent in preparing the book for publication, and in ensuring that it conforms to the highest standards of culinary craftsmanship. We are also grateful to Professor John Fuller for his help and guidance through the preparation of this book and for the honour he has done us by writing the Foreword for it.

We commend this book to our readers and wish them well with it.

ACKNOWLEDGEMENTS

Contributors

PROF. GENEVIEVE ABELANET, France
COLETTE AUER, France
BETTY BALUGANI, Switzerland
PAOLA BIANCHI, Switzerland
ELLA BIRKENMAYER, Germany
GUNNEVI BONEKAMP, Sweden
EVA MARIA BORER, Switzerland
WINA BORN, Netherlands
ANNA CALANDRA, Switzerland
GERLINDE FASETH, Austria
SUZANNE GARTNER, Germany
COLETTE GUEDEN, France
ANNIE JACKSON, Great Britain
RENATE LÅNGSJØ, Norway
HENNIE LIEF, India
LILY VAN PAREREN-BLES, Tunisia
SANDRA ROSSI, Switzerland
ELSA SCIOLLI-MARTINEZ CALVO, Spain
COLETTE SCYBOZ, Switzerland
EVA TEUBNER, Germany
PROF. GUDRUN KARIN WIRTH, Austria
ALBIN ABELANET, France
MICHEL ABELANET
MASSIMO ALBERINI, Italy
FRITZ BALESTRA, Switzerland
JULIUS G. BANDL, Hungary
ANDRE BEGHIN, Belgium
WALTER BICKEL, Germany
ROLAND BIRKENMAYER, Germany
KARL BRUNNENGRAEBER, Germany
JOSEF BUERGI, Switzerland
GUIDO CALANDRA, Italy
NEREO CAMBROSIO, Switzerland
ERIC CEDERHOLM, Denmark
CLAUDIO CESAROTTO, Germany
LUISITO CLERICETTI, Switzerland
FRANTISEK CZERNY, Czechoslovakia
PROF. DR. LASZLO CZISMADIA, Hungary
WERNER DABERNIG, Austria
MARCEL DERRIEN, France
MAX DICK, Austria
BEN JOUSSEF DJENDOUBI, Tunisia
VEANDRO DOMENECQ, Spain
P. DOSZA, Hungary
EGON EIGEN, Hungary
DR. FELIX ERNI, Austria
CHARLES EULER, France
WILFRED FANCE, Great Britain
PROF. ERNEST FASETH, Austria

EGON VON FODERMAYER, Austria
PROF. JOHN FULLER, Great Britain
ERHARD GALL, Switzerland
JANOS GARACI, Hungary
PIERRE GAERTNER, France
GERARD GARTNER, Germany
PRES. A. GERMA, France
KARL GOETZ, Germany
JAN GRAVENDEEL, Netherlands
PROF. JOSEF GROSS, France
CAV. MARCO GUARNORI, Italy
MAURICE GUILMAULT, France
GYULA GULLNER, Hungary
OTTO GUNTHER, Germany
GEORGES GUTH, Germany
ERIC HAACK, Finland
BJORN HALLING, Sweden
PAUL HEINZ, Germany
FERENC HORVATH, Hungary
JEAN-PIERRE HUBON, France
HANS JOACHIM JEGLITZA, Germany
VICTOR JUZA, Austria
ERNST KAUFMANN, Switzerland
KAROLY KECSKEMETI, Hungary
HARTMUT KEITEL, Japan
LASZLO KENDERESI, Hungary
HANS VAN DER KLINKENBERG,
                              Switzerland
ALEXANDRE KOENE, Netherlands
HELMUT KOLLER, Austria
FRANTISEK KOSTINEK, Czechoslovakia
JIRI KRUPICKA, Czechoslovakia
GOTTFRIED LEITNER, Austria
DIR. EGON LONTAI, Hungary
EDGAR LUDL, Norway
XAVER MAIER, Germany
PROF. DR. ALBANO MAINARDI, Italy
GERFRIED MARSCHALLINGER, Norway
VOLKER MALZ, Norway
VICTOR MARX, Switzerland
EDUARD MAYER, Austria
ANTON MARZWEILER, Austria
ADOLF MEINDL, Austria
PIERRE MENGELATTE, France
CHRISTIAN MEYER, France
FLAVIEN MONOD, France
ANDRE MOREAU, France
KURT MULLAUER, Austria
FRIEDRICH NAGEL, Germany

ROBERT NORMANN, Norway
M. OPARTNIK, Czechoslovakia
RUDOLF PALLA, Austria
BOHUMIL PAVLICEK, Czechoslovakia
LOUIS PELLETIER, Switzerland
FRANÇOIS PERRET, Switzerland
EWALD PLACHUTTA, Austria
OTTO RAMSBACHER, Norway
FELIX REAL, Lichtenstein
ERNEST RICHTER, Austria
KARL RUPPERT, Austria
RUSSIAN EMBASSY, Berne
FERENC SAGODI, Hungary
LUDWIG SCHEIBENPFLUG, Austria
GOTTFRIED SCHELLMANN, Austria
ERNESTO SCHLEGEL, Switzerland
MICHAEL SCHNOEKE, Germany

ADRIANUS SCHRAVEMAKER, Netherlands
HELMUT STADLBAUER, Austria
EMANUEL STEHLE, Germany
ING. MILIVOJ STRICEVIC, Yugoslavia
SUCHARD S. A., Switzerland
HANS THIERY, Austria
TODOR TODOROW, Bulgaria
GABRIELE TOGNETTI, Italy
CARLO TOZZINI, Italy
GEORGE K. WALDNER, USA
HANS WEGER, Germany
FINN WEIRUM, Norway
ERICH WINKLER, Austria
ECKART WITZIGMANN, Germany
ØIVIND WOLD, Norway
J. ZLATOHLAVEK, Austria
FRANZ ZODL, Austria

Photographers
A. S. ARVESCHOUG, Norway
ALICE BOMMER, France
HAN BORN, Roumania
P. DRUSZKO, Czechoslovakia
ELSA DICK, Austria
EDITIONS PINGUIN, Austria
WERNER FINK, Germany
JEAN FROHLICH, Switzerland
BEAT JOST, Switzerland
PREMYSL KARASEK, Czechoslovakia
MARTTI KIRJAVAINEN, Finland
GERHARD KOLLING, Germany
HANS KROGERSTROM, Sweden

J. VON LUHOVOY, Austria
R. MAYERHOFER, Austria
ERIC MULLER-GRUNITZ, Germany
JACQUES PRIMOIS, France
MARIO ROSSI, Italy
MICHAEL SCHETTLING, Germany
FERDINAND SCHREIBER, Austria
BOB STEGEMANN, Netherlands
ED SUISTER, Netherlands
KAROLY SZELENYI, Hungary
CHRISTIAN TEUBNER, Germany
STUDIO WEZATA, Sweden
RAINER WIEDERKEHR, Switzerland

Culinary establishments, hotels and restaurants
LE CYGNE, Autun
DEMEL, Vienna
KRANZLER, Frankfurt
CHRISTIAN MEYER, Strasburg
RYSER, Berne
VOROSMARTY, Budapest
THE HOTEL SCHOOLS of Strasburg,
    Stresa, Vienna
GASTRONOMIC INSTITUTE, Vienna
DES ALPES, Champéry
ASTORIA, Vienna
CALEDONIEN, Kristiansand
DUNA INTERCONTINENTAL, Budapest
EXCELSIOR-RIVIERA, Lugano
GOLDENER HIRSCH, Salzburg
GRITTI PALACE, Venice
HILTON, Amsterdam
HILTON, Berlin

KEYTO PLAZA INTERCONTINENTAL,
    Tokyo
KONIGSHOF, Munich
MEINDELEI, Bayrischzell
OESTERREICHISCHER HOF, Salzburg
PARKHOTEL, Frankfurt
PARKHOTEL, Sandefjord
PITTER, Salzburg
ROYAL, Budapest
SACHER, Vienna
SCHLOSS DURNSTEIN, Durnstein
SCHLOSS KLESSHEIM, Salzburg
SCHWEIZERHOF, Berne
TIHANYI, Tihanyi
L'AEROPORT, Salzburg
AUX ARMES DE FRANCE, Ammerschwihr
CARTHAGE, Amsterdam
CSARDA, Bugac

DREI HUSAREN, Vienna
FISCHERHAUS, Seefelden
GRAVENMOLEN, Amsterdam
GROTTO ANTICO, Bioggio
GUNDEL, Budapest
MOTTI, Helsinki
PETERSKELLER, Salzburg
RITZ, Berlin
E. and G. FASETH, Vienna

TEUBNER, Fussen
WEZATA, Gothenburg
LA MAISON E. LACROIX, Frankfurt
PANNONIA, Budapest
VOLONTE S.A., Lugano
R. KUEHN, Ammerschwihr
A. MARZWEILER, Baden
G. SCHELLMANN, Gumpoldskirchen

Contents

INTRODUCTION

'The world is nothing without life, and all that lives takes nourishment.' So wrote that earliest gourmet, Jean-Anthelme Brillat-Savarin, in *Physiologie du Goût* published in 1825. However, he added, 'Animals feed; men eat: only the man of intellect knows how to eat.'

Throughout the world, food—which is the basis of life itself—very soon became associated with ceremonies, religion and art. From the earliest days hardly any ceremony of whatever nature could take place without eating and drinking, and the birthday cake is only one of the many modern examples. The prehistoric cave paintings of bison and the cubist still-lifes of fruit and wine demonstrate the concern of artists throughout the ages to portray items of food in whatever style and medium they had mastered. The ancient Romans used to foretell the future from the entrails of edible beasts, sacrificed to the gods in complicated religious rites. Before we of the twentieth century claim that this connection between the basic need for food and the deepest need for a religious belief belongs to earlier ages, it is worth reflecting upon the Sacrament of the Christian church. The fact that this also involves the acts of eating and drinking—imbued with particular significance—demonstrates the basic place of food and drink in all forms of ceremony from the profane to the profound.

This book deals with but one aspect of mankind's concern for food and drink—the area of social gatherings, where people meet to share the pleasures of the table—regardless of the reason.

Every occasion in life from the cradle to the grave, every major event—engagements, weddings, Christenings, birthdays, religious festivals, celebrations and business events—all require food and drink. These events can all be termed 'parties' and this book is designed to provide recipes, ideas, inspiration and practical knowledge for the caterer, who is so often called upon to provide the food, drink and expertise needed to cater for buffets and receptions—and other forms of party catering from barbecues to formal dinners.

In the first part of the book, we have tried to give guidelines on the various forms of party.

In the second part of the book, we give guidelines on the eating habits of other countries, with the help of authors from the countries concerned. They have naturally approached the subject in different ways, and it seems only right and proper to let them speak for themselves. In this restless age, when everyone seeks to escape from his or her normal surroundings and seeks the unfamiliar in all its forms, it is easy to travel abroad or to have a meal in a foreign restaurant, but it is more difficult to understand another nation's attitude to food and thus fully appreciate its cuisine.

This is continued in the main part of the book, comprising, as it does, recipes collected from the finest chefs of many lands. These, plus what precedes them, will enable the caterer to produce unforgettable parties featuring exotic foreign dishes with complete confidence. These recipes, which form the main part of the book, are the outcome of three years of research. The most highly qualified experts of the various countries were approached on the spot, and their help was sought to ensure that all the recipes from the most simple to the most elaborate were both sound and authentic, having been repeatedly tested by experienced craftsmen. The photographs showing the results of some of the recipes were also taken on the spot to ensure their authenticity; they furnish ample evidence of the diversity of culinary and artistic ideas. We hope that they will both help and inspire the reader, to the delight of the guests, to produce unforgettable buffets and receptions.

Finally, in this age of mechanisation, when man longs for a sight of the green countryside and the simpler way of life, we have thought it appropriate to include ideas and recipes for catering out of doors.

This introduction opened with a quotation from Brillat-Savarin. Let us also close with one of his aphorisms, 'To entertain a guest is to make yourself responsible for his happiness so long as he is beneath your roof.' Happy catering, and bon appetit!

FUNCTIONS

PARTIES IN GENERAL

To many people giving and attending parties is a genuine pleasure, which is eagerly anticipated, but a badly planned or a badly organised party gives enjoyment to no one, be he guest or host. It is therefore axiomatic that planning and organisation are the essential ingredients in the recipe for a successful party. In order to achieve this vital organisation, close co-operation and mutual understanding are required of the two people concerned—the host or hostess and the caterer or chef. (Although these notes assume that a professional caterer or chef is involved, they will also be useful to a host or hostess planning a party without professional help.)

It occasionally happens that a host is full of enthusiasm for a type of party which the caterer, from his experience, knows to be either impractical or unsuitable for the occasion. In these circumstances, the caterer must guide and advise the host and persuade him to consider a more suitable alternative.

The host and the caterer need to take into account all the many aspects which go to make up a successful party—which is the objective of both. These aspects are listed below.

Guests

To be successful, any party must be planned with the preferences or prejudices of the guests in mind. It is obvious that an occasion which a group of elderly professional people would enjoy would not be at all enjoyable to a group of school children, and 'trendy' teenagers would require something different again. It is difficult to generalise, because many old people are flattered to be invited to a party designed for a younger age group—and some of them actually enjoy themselves! Nevertheless, a knowledge of the type of guests is needed to plan a successful function because, in spite of exceptions, what one group of people enjoy, another group will find too dull or too frantic.

Type of party

A 'party' can be a formal dinner party, a 'tramps' supper', a reception, a cocktail party, a barbecue, a buffet or a cheese and wine party, or any other form of social gathering, and the style can vary widely. The type of party will depend upon the time of the year; the space available (more people can be accommodated for a reception than for a dinner); the type of guests; the aspirations of the host and the depth of his pocket.

Whatever the type of party, the event gains in effect if it is planned round a theme, and this is where both the host and the caterer can give scope to their ingenuity. Ideally, the theme should be reflected in the room and the table decorations as well as in the food and drink. This need not be so expensive as it might at first appear. For example, if the party were to celebrate Burns' Night (the actual date is January 25th, but a Burns' Supper is often held at other times) then the traditional menu could be supported by tartan table mats and napkins, or a tartan travelling rug could be used as a tablecloth, and the room or rooms in which the party takes place could be suitably decorated on a Scottish theme without incurring excessive expense. Every country has its own particular festivals—Hallowe'en, Thanksgiving Day and Bastille Day spring readily to mind—and a party on or near these days becomes much more memorable if it reflects the occasion.

Another thematic idea is to plan the party around the food, drink and customs of a foreign country, and the chapters and recipes in this book will provide ample inspiration and plentiful examples for this type of occasion. Once more, the décor should be appropriate, and again this need not be prohibitively expensive if ingenuity is used. Travel agents, national airlines and tourist boards, embassies and consulates are usually helpful, if given sufficient notice, and will often supply display material on loan. Glossy posters are often a great help in setting the scene.

Receptions, buffets, barbecues, drinks, cheese and wine parties and menu planning for parties are dealt with at greater length in the successive chapters, and a careful perusal of these will enable even the relatively inexperienced to plan a successful party.

Invitations

These must be sent out in good time, so that the people invited have a chance to make whatever arrangements are necessary for them to attend. The circumstances vary, and many people lead such full lives nowadays that three months in advance is by no means too early to invite guests to a formal, sophisticated party. Indeed, many important functions are planned more than twelve months in advance if public figures are to be amongst the guests of honour. If the party is being held in an hotel or public room, it may be necessary to book the room even earlier but, obviously, one would not send out formal invitations that far ahead. In many cases a much shorter period of notice is needed and, for an informal intimate occasion, there is no reason why the invitation should not be made by telephone, a couple of weeks in advance. The timing depends upon the circumstances, and only the host can determine the appropriate time scale. In general, it is better to send the invitations too early rather than too late.

The invitations should indicate clearly what the guests are to expect, because an invitation which does not do so is more likely to be declined, simply because the recipient is not sure if he or she will find the occasion enjoyable. The wise host will eliminate the element of uncertainty by making the type of party, the degree of formality (so that the ladies know what to wear) and the type of meal quite clear on the invitation.

Timing

The timing of a party is important and it is even more important that, once it has been decided upon, the timetable should be adhered to. If the invitations say, for example, '7 for 7.30 pm carriages at 1 am' then the caterer is committed, in writing, to a schedule which is known to all the guests and it would appear highly unprofessional if this were altered.

It is advisable to have everything ready fifteen minutes before the guests are due to arrive—the doorman at his post, the cloakroom staff at theirs, and the reception bars set up and fully stocked and staffed. Not only does this allow any early arrivals to be properly received, it also allows time for a final inspection by the person in charge or by the host.

The meal should be announced promptly at the time stated, and the food for the first course should be ready, even though it takes a few minutes for guests to finish their drinks and take their places at the table. The state of readiness of the succeeding courses will depend upon the numbers of guests and staff and, of course, the menu, and the caterer must steer between the Scylla of delay and the Charybdis of serving food which has been kept hot for too long.

Coming and going

Guests must be respectfully greeted on arrival, and the doorman or porter should wish everyone 'good evening' and smile as he does so. The cloakroom staff should also make each guest feel welcome, as should the bar staff or waiters at the reception. Politeness and deference must not be confused with aloofness. Most guests at a party are anxious to enjoy themselves, and the service must encourage their enjoyment by being always friendly but never familiar.

In this day and age, considerable thought needs to be given to the vexed question of car parking, since if a guest and his lady arrive by car and it proves troublesome to park the car safely then their evening is less pleasant than it should be, and this reflects upon the planning of the host. All guests should know whether car parking is available or not, and be advised of the most convenient way of reaching the venue of the party.

At the end of the party, guests should be tactfully speeded upon their way, because however much they may think they wish to linger on, a party which fizzles out by slow degrees is less enjoyable than one which ends on a high note. In Britain, the singing of 'Auld Lang Syne' and the National Anthem is sufficient to indicate to everyone present that the party is over.

It is difficult to analyse precisely the ingredients of a successful party. There is 'magic' which will make one party more successful than another—an atmosphere which renders one event memorable and another less so. A close perusal of this book will give the guidelines, but the secret can only be learned by experience and practice. The 'secrets'—if secrets there are—can be summarised as a genuine concern for the needs and expectations of the guests, and a scrupulous attention to detail. These, plus the professionalism of the genuine caterer, and a close understanding of the requirements of the host, will normally blend together to produce the indefinable element which ensures the success of the party.

RECEPTIONS

Receptions fall into two main categories—those which are a prelude to a luncheon or dinner, and those which are an event in themselves.

Pre-meal receptions

The real purpose of having a reception before a meal is to allow guests to foregather over a period of time, and to mix and mingle with each other, but it is customary to offer refreshments during this period. (This was not the case in Victorian England, and many a young person dreaded 'the ghastly half hour' before the company went in to their meal. A reference to the history of pre-meal foods is made in the introduction to the section on hors d'oeuvre.)

The type of drinks offered at a pre-meal reception will vary according to the wishes of the host, but in Britain sherry is always offered, and whisky-and-soda and gin-and-tonic are also customary. These can be supported by aperitifs and other spirits and mixers until the range offered is almost that of an ordinary bar. Less usual, but nevertheless acceptable is to offer only a range of wines, or a wine cup, and these are cheaper to serve. Obviously, non-alcoholic drinks must also be available, and fruit juices and fruit squash are the most usual. Nowadays, cocktails are less fashionable than they once were, but a white-coated barman shaking cocktails to guests' requirements is a good idea even if he is asked for a gin-and-tonic more often than anything else. For a small private reception, it is usual to offer one cocktail and nothing else, provided that the proportions of the cocktail can be adjusted to suit the recipient. If, for example, a host were to offer only 'Tequila Sunrise' (a measure of tequila topped up with chilled orange juice, with a dash of grenadine sirop poured in on top, which filters down and colours the orange juice pink to resemble a sunrise) then the amount of tequila could be increased for the gentlemen and reduced for the ladies or even omitted entirely.

Drinks may be offered by waiters and waitresses circulating with trays rather than guests collecting their own drinks from a bar, and not only does this prevent a crowd forming at the bar but it also enables a discreet control to be exercised over the speed at which drinks are consumed, which is often important if there is a limited budget.

At a pre-meal reception of relatively short duration, it is best either to dispense with chairs altogether, or to have very few, since otherwise fixed groups of people will form, and guests will not circulate and meet each other so readily. (Obviously, a chair must be produced immediately for an elderly or disabled person.) On the other hand, plenty of occasional tables and ashtrays are essential, and it is advisable to have staff detailed to keep the ashtrays emptied and the tables clear of used glasses.

It is important that there is sufficient space to allow guests to circulate without jostling or being jostled by other guests. Ideally, a space of about $15\frac{1}{2}$ m by $15\frac{1}{2}$ m (50 ft by 50 ft) is needed for 250 guests, but if the room is of an irregular shape it will hold fewer in comfort.

A pre-meal reception is usually of only half an hour's duration, and invitations indicate this by being phrased '6.30 for 7 pm'. These events can be longer if some guests arrive early or if important guests arrive late but, in general, thirty minutes is as long as most people want to wait before going in to their meal. (Also, since it is usual at a private function not to allow a guest to remain without a drink, a reception which goes on for too long can become rather expensive for the host.)

The food at pre-meal receptions should not be substantial but should only consist of small 'nibbles' which sharpen the guests' appetites and complement the drinks. Nuts, potato crisps, olives, cocktail onions and small 'cocktail biscuits' are usually all that is required, but occasionally canapés and other savoury items are offered. When this is so, care should be taken that the appetite is not dulled by their consumption, and they should be small and piquante. Sweet items are never offered before a meal.

Full reception

A full reception, being an event in itself, is not followed by anything further to eat or drink, and usually lasts between an hour and a half and two hours. It therefore follows that the food, whilst still being finger food, needs to be more substantial than that provided for a pre-meal reception, and a wide variety of hot and cold items are usually provided. In fact, the food often approaches that of a finger buffet in range and quantity. Small hot vol-au-vents, cocktail canapés, various dips and dunks, hot and cold sandwiches and similar items are all appropriate but, generally speaking, it is not usual to provide too many sweet items since they are less suitable to accompany alcoholic drinks.

Many examples of suitable foods to offer will be found in the 'Finger Foods' section of this book, and to read through that section will provide copious inspiration for anyone engaged in catering for a full reception.

Whilst it is usual for 'hard liquor' to be provided at a pre-meal reception, at a full reception it is perfectly normal if guests are only offered wines, as would be the case at a dinner or buffet. A choice of red, sweet white, dry white and rosé wines should be available, each at the correct serving temperature, but the quality of the wine will depend upon the nature of the occasion and the price range. It is also acceptable to offer only a wine cup but, if there is to be no other drink, the wine cup should be a very good one.

BUFFETS

'Buffet' is a fairly loose term, which is applied to many different types of occasion. At one end of the scale, it can mean no more than sandwiches and other finger food whilst at the other end it can mean an elaborate meal of many courses. A buffet can contain both hot and cold dishes, the food can be collected by the guests or served by waiters, and a buffet is not necessarily less formal than a dinner. It will therefore be seen that it is necessary to outline some of the different types of buffet.

Display buffets

Some large restaurants set up a display in the centre of the room to catch the customer's eye. These displays generally include an arrangement of flowers as well as fruit in season, bundles of raw asparagus or other fresh vegetables in season, often cooked shellfish on ice, smoked salmon and other delicacies, and cakes and pastries and other cold desserts. Sometimes an assortment of cheeses and wines and spirits is also included. The sole purpose of the display is to show customers some of the items which the restaurant can offer, and to decorate the room.

Breakfast buffets

Many international hotels offer patrons a buffet breakfast, with a wide selection of dishes organised on a self-service basis with the exception of hot beverages, which are ordered from a waiter. The selection varies widely from one region to another, and from one continent to another. It normally includes a wide selection of bread and rolls, with butter, cheeses, jam and marmalade, cold meats and fish, hot grilled items on hotplates, fresh and stewed fruit and fruit juices, and possibly breakfast cereals. In English country houses, it used to be the custom for house-guests to help themselves to breakfast from a sideboard, and kedgeree, cold York ham and grilled kidneys and bacon were usually available. The practice of providing self-service breakfast is common in commercial hotels, but for reasons of staff economy and speed of service rather than gastronomy, and these breakfasts do not really qualify for the term 'buffet'.

Full buffets

A full buffet is a main meal, only distinguished from a dinner or luncheon because the food is displayed in the dining-room. For a full buffet, tables and chairs are essential for all guests, and these should be fully laid with china, cutlery and glassware. The food is displayed on the buffet table, which gives the chef a chance to demonstrate his skill at decorating and garnishing the dishes. (It must be remembered, however, that if the guests are to collect their own food then the garnishing cannot be over-elaborate, otherwise the last guests are faced with a far from appetizing sight. Simple but effective garnishing is needed, which can either be removed just before the service starts or served to the guests without spoiling the appearance of the dish.)

The buffet table must be clothed right down to the ground on the customers' side and, whilst coloured cloths are sometimes appropriate, nothing displays the food quite so well as a plain white linen tablecloth, set with sparkling silverware and glassware. The buffet itself can be decorated, but again this should not be over-done, the elaborate floral displays of earlier eras are no longer fashionable. A simple but elegant arrangement of flowers is probably the best centrepiece, but a central feature made from 'kitchen materials'—salt, sterine, pulled sugar, ice etc.—is sometimes used, if the chef is able to undertake such work successfully. It must be remembered that although a buffet should be a feast for the eyes it is primarily intended as a feast for the palate, and any decoration should enhance the appearance of the food, not detract from its taste. At a wedding buffet, of course, the cake is all the centrepiece that is needed. Small 'posy bowls' can also be placed on the buffet, provided that the table is large enough to allow this and still leave ample room for the food and plates. It is very important that the table should not look overcrowded.

When possible, it is best if guests simply inspect and admire the buffet before the service begins, but are thereafter served at their tables by waiters, since this avoids the need for guests to queue. However, this is rarely possible, and guests normally collect their own food from the buffet table. In this case, the first course and roll and butter should be placed on the diners' tables in advance, where the menu permits, in order that the arrival of guests at the buffet is 'staggered'. At any but the smallest buffets, it is essential to have sufficient staff to serve the food on to the guests' plates, rather than allowing them to help themselves, since few people have the ability to handle serving and carving cutlery speedily and neatly. It is traditional to have one or more chefs in their whites serving behind the buffet and this has many advantages. It means that fewer staff are needed, it means that the chef can keep an eye on the service, most people like to see the chef or chefs and most chefs like to meet their customers.

It is a pleasant idea to have at least one whole joint or fish to be carved at the buffet, but this should only be considered when the carver is sufficiently expert to keep the correct portion size, and sufficiently speedy to avoid delaying the service. If enough skilled carvers are not available, then the meat must be pre-sliced, and laid out on silver flats, with an appropriate light garnish.

It is also a good idea if there is a menu for guests to see, and this can be either a typed or printed menu placed on the dining-tables, or a poster-sized menu near to the buffet table. It is strange that this is not always provided, since it adds to the guests' enjoyment.

A buffet can take the place of a formal meal, either as an event in itself or at the start of an evening's entertainment, and in these circumstances the preparation and setting up of the buffet presents no extra problems. Difficulties can be experienced, however, if the buffet is to take place during a party or dance, and there is only one room available. The tables need to be set up and clothed before the party starts, but it is not normally possible to set out the food in advance because it will inevitably suffer from being on display in a warm atmosphere for one or more hours. Furthermore, the first course cannot be set out on the dining-tables in advance, either, and hence most of the guests will be queuing for their meal almost before it is announced as being ready. For these reasons, it is advisable not to attempt a buffet in the middle of a party unless two rooms of adequate size are available.

Almost all dishes can be used for a buffet meal, although preference is usually given to dishes of an attractive appearance, since it is the element of display which is so important. Hot dishes are frequently included, in which case both cold and heated plates are required. It is far better to put out only a proportion of each item, and to replace it with a fresh supply, rather than setting out all the food to begin with, since the former arrangement ensures both that the later servings are at the correct temperature and that the appearance has not suffered during the service.

Fork buffets

A 'fork buffet' has been defined as 'a meal which can be eaten standing up, with a plate in one hand and a fork in the other' and these events are ideally suited when space will not permit tables and chairs for everyone. Nevertheless, as many tables and chairs should be provided as is possible, and occasional tables are quite adequate. If guests are also being offered drinks, they will need somewhere to put down their glasses whilst eating, even if they themselves remain standing.

A fork buffet table can look just as attractive as that for a full buffet, but the range of foodstuffs cannot be as wide. It is important to avoid sliced roasted meats, for example, since few people can manage to eat these easily with just a fork, and salads of diced meats are the obvious alternative. (Again, a menu at the buffet is required, since compound dishes are not always easy for guests to identify.) Hot dishes are eminently suitable, and curries, goulashes, sautés and casseroles are all popular. Soup (in cups), fish cocktails, and similar items make ideal first courses, and most sweets are quite suitable. A fork buffet is obviously less formal than a sit-down buffet, but people tend to eat less, possibly because it is less easy to eat without a table. It is important to provide plenty of table-napkins, of good quality and adequate size, and as with any party, plenty of ashtrays are essential.

Finger buffets

This title is self-explanatory, and finger buffets are the least formal type of buffet. Like fork buffets, they are particularly suitable when the host hopes that guests will mingle with each other. This ability to circulate makes a finger buffet particularly suitable for a modest wedding reception, for example, when distant relatives will be attending. A finger buffet can take the place of a main meal, but generally speaking, it is only a snack meal, frequently served at a time of day when guests will not be anticipating a substantial amount of food.

Care must be taken that the food offered really can be eaten without cutlery, and with the exceptions of such items as sandwiches and chicken legs, most food should be in bite-sized pieces. A slice from a large quiche, for example, cannot easily be eaten without a fork, whereas small individual quiches are ideal finger food. With a finger buffet, plenty of large napkins are essential, and finger bowls are a good idea. Although the food can readily be eaten standing up, it is still advisable to have as many chairs and tables available as is possible, if only for the convenience of elderly guests.

Buffets in the home

A cold buffet in a private house is rather different, regardless of whether the food is prepared at home or supplied by an outside caterer. Unlike hotels, few homes have a room large enough to hold both the buffet and the dining-tables for the guests. There is usually no alternative but to use the largest room for the buffet, set up on one long table or several shorter ones of the same height joined end to end, and for guests to take their food in to an adjacent room, containing small tables and chairs. These tables should be clothed, and have a small vase of flowers on each.

The buffet is covered with the most beautiful damask cloth which the hostess possesses, and is decorated with flowers, candelabra, old silver and even porcelain figurines. Combined with tastefully and simply garnished dishes, these add to the attractiveness of the display. The plates, cutlery, bread, and butter can be laid out on a side table, and the drinks set out on the sideboard, with the appropriate glasses and accessories.

Hot and cold buffet in an hotel

MENU PLANNING FOR PARTIES

When there is a selection of dishes from which guests may choose—as with an à la carte menu and most buffets—then menu planning, whilst still being important, is less critical than it is when planning a formal dinner party menu, for which no choice is offered. In these circumstances, the theory behind menu planning becomes of paramount importance, and it can do no harm to give a reminder of this theory here. It has three main aspects—gastronomic, economic and practical.

Gastronomic aspects

The important thing here is that the menu must be planned as a whole, an entity

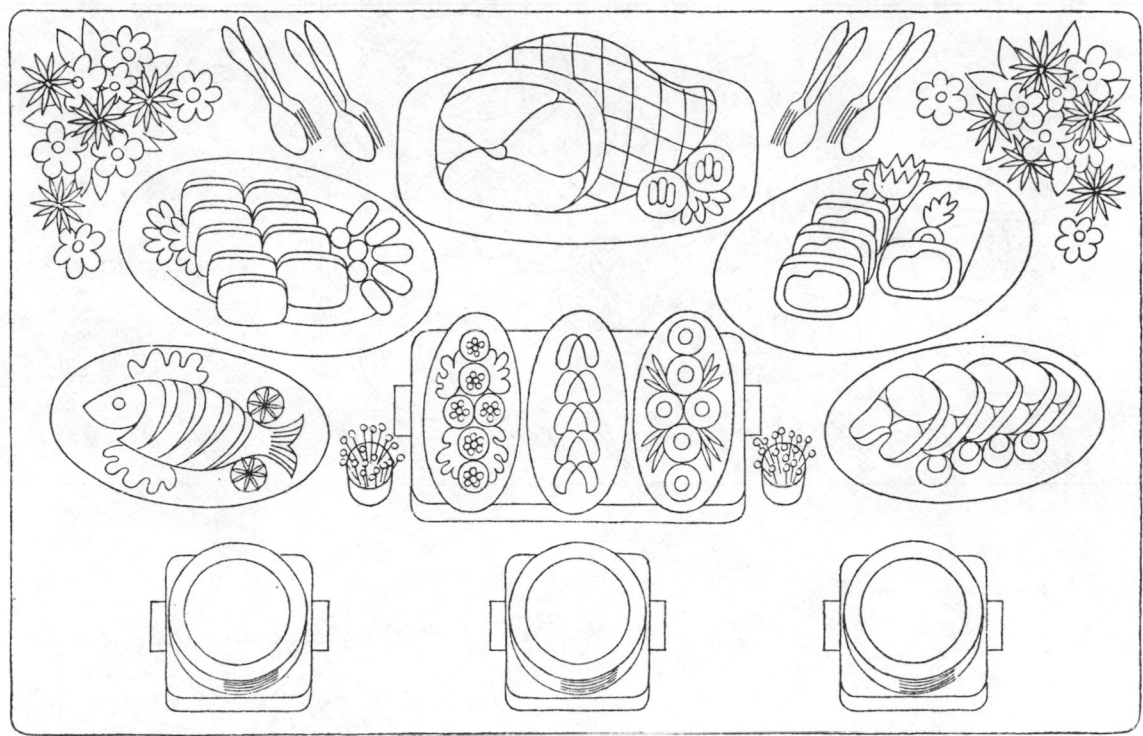

Hot buffet in an hotel

in itself, rather than a succession of independent, unrelated courses. This is achieved by avoiding repetition of colour, ingredients and texture.

If a menu begins with a grapefruit cocktail, then it must not end with a fruit salad, and if it begins with a pâté and toast, then it would be wrong to end with Canapé Diane. These are obvious examples, but there is also a need to avoid using an ingredient as a garnish if it has been a major ingredient of a previous course. If a mushroom soup is featured, for example, then mushrooms should not be used as a garnish for a subsequent dish of grilled meat.

Colour contrast is important. Tomato soup, poached salmon, gammon steaks and strawberry mousse might make a very pleasant menu for a colour-blind person, but for others it would not be successful, because the eye would be bored with red, and the mousse would be received with less enthusiasm than it deserved.

Contrast of texture is perhaps the most important and most often neglected of these factors. After say, a consommé, sole bonne femme, and spaghetti bolognaise the guests would be craving for something crisp and crunchy, and a crème caramel, whilst not being totally unacceptable, would be much less welcome than a firm apple with cheese and biscuits. Conversely, Parma ham, whitebait and entrecote should be followed by a soft pudding, a mousse or a crème—rather than a crisp pastry.

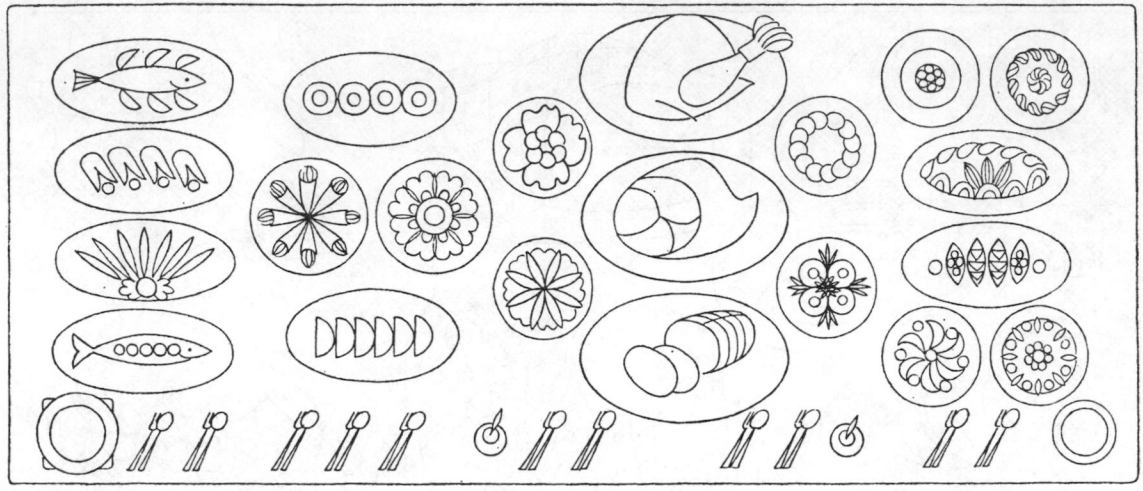

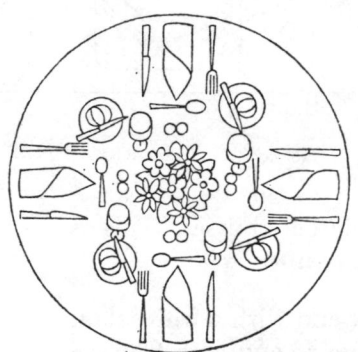

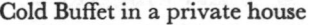

Cold Buffet in a private house

Overall balance is also important. The menu should not be a succession of rich dishes, nor of elaborate, heavily garnished dishes, but a combination of rich and simple dishes, or even a series of plain simple ones. Possibly the best combination is one 'grand piece' supported by less complicated dishes.

One further point to be borne in mind is that, although improved preservation techniques mean that most foods are available all the year round, it is best for a dinner party to use seasonal foods wherever possible.

Economic aspects

Very few menus are now planned without close regard for costs. At whatever price level, the host will have a budget, and the caterer will require a worthwhile profit margin. The menu therefore needs to be costed as it is being planned, and considerable skill is often needed to meet both the gastronomic and economic criteria. This is another reason for avoiding too many elaborate dishes, since time costs money, particularly the time of staff with sufficient skill to produce them properly.

Practical aspects

If the dinner is a large one, then the kitchen equipment may be a governing factor in the choice of menu, for the simple reason that all the covers are served simultaneously, as opposed to being served over a period of time. The menu must also be well within the skills and abilities of the kitchen staff, and it is advisable not to include dishes of which they have little experience. The type of service also needs to be borne in mind when planning the menu, since not all dishes are suitable for all service methods.

For small private parties, the range of dishes is wider, since the constraints of bulk service do not apply, and dishes such as soufflés can be more precisely timed.

The number of courses served will vary from the ordinary two- or three-course menu up to sumptuous feasts of many courses, dependent upon the factors outlined in 'Parties in general'. However, four or five courses are now normal and, generally speaking, the marathon menus of Victorian times went out with the Victorians.

It is generally agreed in Britain that courses are served in the following order:

1. Hors d'oeuvre (or single dish such as smoked salmon or pâté).
2. Soup (usually only a clear soup is offered at dinner).
3. Farinaceous dish (usually only at luncheon).
4. Egg dish.
5. Fish or shellfish dish.
6. Entrée (a small garnished meat dish such as Vol-au-Vent de Volaille, usually served without vegetables).
7. Relevé (a braised joint or bird with vegetables).
8. Sorbet (traditionally accompanied with a Russian cigarette).
9. Roast (a whole joint or bird, frequently game, served with a salad).
10. Cold buffet.
11. Vegetable dish (asparagus or another special vegetable).
12. Sweet.
13. Savoury.
14. Cheese.
15. Dessert.
16. Coffee.

It is not essential to adhere strictly to this order for an informal occasion, but it is customary to do so for formal dinners, with one exception. The continental practice of serving the cheese before the sweet, in order that a red wine may be served with both, is growing in Britain.

Three typical modern menu patterns are:

Soup ⎫	Dry white wine
Fish course ⎭	
Meat course	Red wine
Sweet	
Coffee	

Hors d'oeuvre ⎫	Dry white wine
Fish course ⎬	
Meat course ⎫	Red wine
Cheese ⎭	
Sweet	Sweet white wine
Coffee	

'Starter'	Sherry
Main course	Red wine
Cheese	Red wine
Dessert	Fortified wine

Buffet menus

At a full buffet, it is usual, though not essential, to provide a choice of dishes for each course. There is no reason why hot dishes cannot be successfully served at a buffet (as mentioned in 'Buffets') and hence there is virtually no dish which cannot be used. However, thought must be given to the method of service and to the appearance of the dish, since this is all-important at a buffet.

When there is a choice of dishes, these should be of a contrasting nature. If a soup is offered, then a fish cocktail would make a suitable alternative first course. If one main course is a roast joint, then the other should be in the nature of a mayonnaise or compound salad, and if one sweet is based upon fruit, then there should be no fruit in the other. It is often impossible to avoid repetition of ingredients and colour, but this is of lesser importance when guests have a choice of dishes, even though many of them will sample every dish!

A suitable menu for a large cold buffet would be:

> Chicken liver pâté
> Jellied eggs
>
> Whitstable oysters
> Cold salmon Jack Gauer
>
> Roast beef Liselotte
> Chicken mayonnaise

Lorette salad
Mushroom salad
Celeriac and walnut salad

Pineapple and kirsch cream
Coffee éclairs

Language of the menu

The use of a foreign language on a menu is a topic which always arouses discussion (often heated) amongst both caterers and diners alike. In some circumstances it is traditional, in some it is desirable but in others it is reprehensible.

It must be stated immediately that, unless there are valid reasons, the menu should be written in the language of the reader, and that to translate it into another language without those valid reasons is a pretentious practice with little to recommend it. Such terms as 'Boeuf roti avec pouding Yorkaise' or 'Sardines sur toast' are accurate enough, and would be correct in France, but most English people would find them rather silly.

Where a dish is well known under its foreign name (Spaghetti Bolognaise, for example) then that name should be thought of as international and not requiring translation. To translate 'Welsh Rarebit' as 'Croute gauloise' is no more logical than translating 'Sole Bonne Femme' as 'Sole good woman'. In general, therefore, translation is best avoided altogether whenever possible.

When a whole menu is made up of dishes of one country—a Swedish evening for example—then, obviously, the menu will be written in Swedish. However, unless all the guests are Swedes it is essential to add a note of explanation after each dish, e.g.:

Lattrimmat senapsbrynt revbensspjall
(Devilled salt loin of pork)

Indeed, this practice should be adopted for a set menu in any language other than that of the reader or French.

French is the language of food and eating—as Italian is the language of music—and for a menu the caterer should assume that the diners are familiar with French menu terminology, and not add explanations of the dishes.

Strictly speaking, a menu should be in one language only, and it is a bad practice to mix English and French on a menu. A problem arises when the menu contains both traditional British dishes and one or more of the classical dishes of French cuisine, Poulet sauté chasseur and Scotch woodcock, for example. In these circumstances one of the principles must be broken, since either translating or mixing languages is unavoidable.

Most set menus are written in French, and many pitfalls await the compiler if French is not his mother tongue. Space does not permit a full article on menu French—which would be many pages long, but a short resumé of the more common rules may be useful.

Capital letters are only used at the beginning of a phrase and for proper nouns, e.g. Fillet de sole Waleska.

The definite article can be used throughout the menu, but the practice is optional and best avoided.

When the method of cookery is indicated by a past participle, it must agree with the cut or portion named, not with the meat or fish itself, e.g. Suprême de sole poché (to agree with suprême not pochée to agree with sole).

If the word describing the potatoes is a noun, it always remains singular, e.g. Pommes château, not châteaux.

If the word used to describe the potatoes is a participle or adjective, it must be feminine plural to agree with pommes, e.g. Pommes rissolées.

The phrase 'à la mode' which may refer to a trade (boulangère) or a place (Parisienne) is frequently omitted but the adjective nevertheless must be feminine singular to agree with 'mode' regardless of the gender of the item.

Menu compilation is a mixture of both art and science, and it is a most pleasant and enjoyable task to anyone who really enjoys cooking or eating. With the aid of this book the repertoire of dishes which can be included in the menu is considerably extended.

DRINKS FOR PARTIES

As has already been noted, a 'party' can vary in style from the rigidly formal to the completely casual, and in price from the very expensive to the 'cheap and cheerful'. The type of drinks which can be served cover an equally wide range. The service of drinks can also vary widely from an open sideboard or table where guests simply help themselves from the range of drinks provided, to waiter or bar service and the latter two may dispense drinks without charge, or they may be on a cash only basis. The quantity and quality of the drinks provided will depend upon the occasion, the type of service, the type and age of the guests and the amount of money available.

When drinks are to be paid for by the guests, the caterer need only ensure that an adequate supply of suitable drinks is available, but when they are either included in the price of the ticket or paid for directly by the host, problems of supply and demand can occasionally arise. The caterer must use his judgement to ensure that the range offered avoids any hint of an inadequate supply, and also make sure that all the guests have the chance of an equal amount to drink.

When drinks are not served at a dining-table (at a reception or a fork buffet, for example) they are best served by waiters or waitresses circulating with trays, since not only does this prevent a crowd forming at the bar or service point, but also allows a discreet control to be exercised over the amount consumed. At a reception or other 'stand-up affair' guests will tend to average one drink per fifteen minutes for the first hour, and rather less per hour thereafter.

There is obviously no problem in controlling the quantity of wine served to diners at their tables.

Wine

The study of wine is fascinating—many learned men (and women) have spent years acquiring their knowledge of oenology, and books on the subject abound. In this section of the book it will only be possible to give a brief outline of a few of the less contentious 'rules', for wine is a contentious subject, and not all experts agree! Wine—or at least, its consumption and appreciation—is more of an art than a science and a host or caterer should match the provision of wine to the requirements and understanding of the guests. To use an analogy, many enthusiastic amateur chess players derive great pleasure and satisfaction from games which a grand master would find boring and trite, and conversely cannot appreciate all the subtleties of grand-master play. It is the same with wine—there are many different levels of appreciation. Not every enthusiastic drinker has the palate to appreciate fine vintages, and genuine connoisseurs employ different criteria to those of lesser mortals! However, provided that a wine is sound and honest, it will give pleasure (if not delight) to even the most discerning connoisseur so the uninitiated or those whose purses are limited need not be ashamed to offer good, ordinary wines to their guests. A good wine merchant will always be pleased to advise and guide genuine enquirers as to the quality and characteristics of the wines in his stock, and most will supply wines on a sale or return basis for a private client.

On the understanding that the following can only be a very basic summary, it can be said that the most usual wines to offer with various foods are:

With soup—a dry fortified wine (sherry or Sercial) but quite often no wine is served. (If the soup were thick and chunky, almost a meal in itself, then a light red wine would be quite suitable, but this would be more appropriate at an outdoor event.)

With hors d'oeuvre—a dry white wine, or a dry sherry, but if any item in the hors d'oeuvre contains vinegar, then it is best to offer no wine, since the vinegar makes the wine taste vinegary.

With fish—a light white wine.

With poultry or white meat—a white wine is usually served with these foods, but a red or rosé wine would not be wrong, only unusual.

With red meats—a full-bodied red wine.

With game—a full-bodied red wine.

With the sweet—a sweet white wine.

With cheese—cheese compliments all wine and is flattered by the wine in return. A red wine is usual in France, where the cheese is served before the sweet. In England, port is the accepted drink with the cheese course, which is served at the end of the meal.

It must be reiterated that these are very basic rules and subject to many variations occasioned by local customs and individual taste. Many people prefer Guinness to any white wine with oysters; in Alsace, the home of foie gras, a Riesling or Traminer is drunk with that delicacy and in Bordeaux a Barsac is often served with ripe Brie. The moral appears to be that the 'rules' can be broken if you know what you're doing, but if not it is safest to take them as a guide.

Wines must be served at the correct temperature. Red wine should be at room temperature (chambré) but this must be achieved by leaving the bottle in the room for a couple of hours beforehand so that the temperature is reached gradually. It is quite fatal to a red wine if it is 'warmed up' by being placed near a stove, or in a bain-marie. Most red wines will benefit from having the cork drawn about an hour before being served, to allow the wine to breathe. White wine should be served cool, not cold. There is an unfortunate tendency to overdo this and serve the wine at a temperature so low that the flavour and bouquet are deadened. Wine is best chilled lightly by being immersed for a short time in a bucket of ice and water.

Wine should be served in glasses large enough to allow it to be swirled, to release the bouquet, and a 190 cc glass is normal (approx 6⅔ oz). Stemmed glasses are essential, so that the wine is not affected by the heat of the hand, and coloured glasses should not be used, since they obscure the colour of the wine.

Other drinks

There is scarcely a drink in the world, alcoholic or non-alcoholic, which is not suitable for service at some type of party from the liqueur at the end of a grand banquet to the synthetic cola which so many youngsters seem to find ambrosial.

Beer is a suitable drink for many lively informal parties, particularly if care is taken over its service, and it has the advantage of being relatively cheap. A glass—or more

Cocktail party in an hotel self service

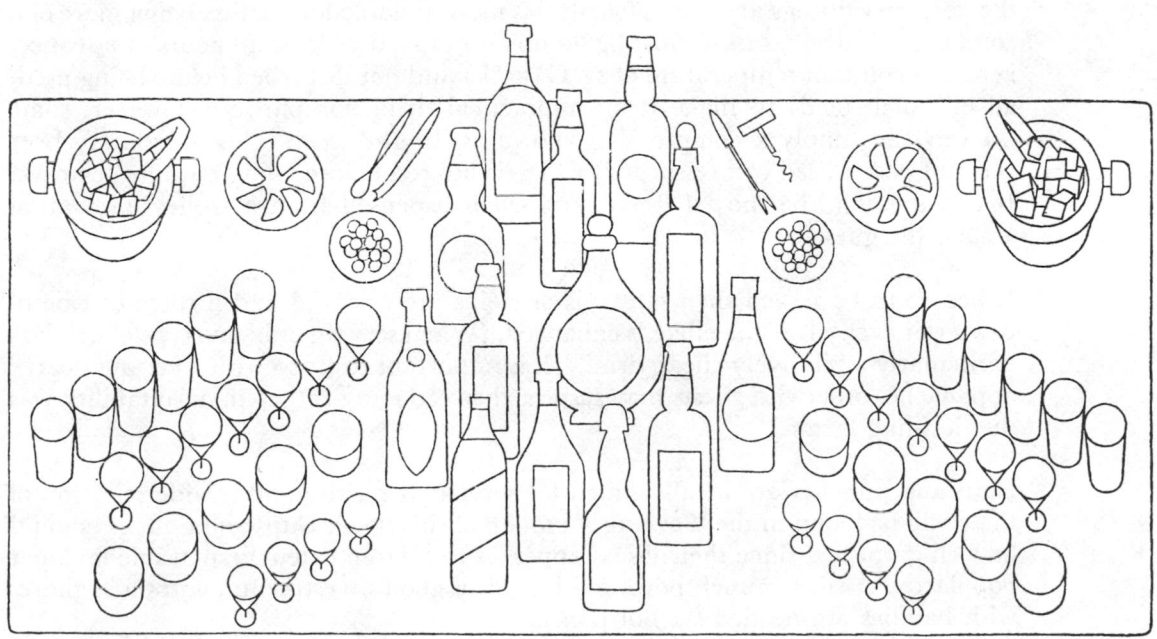

Cocktail party in an hotel with service

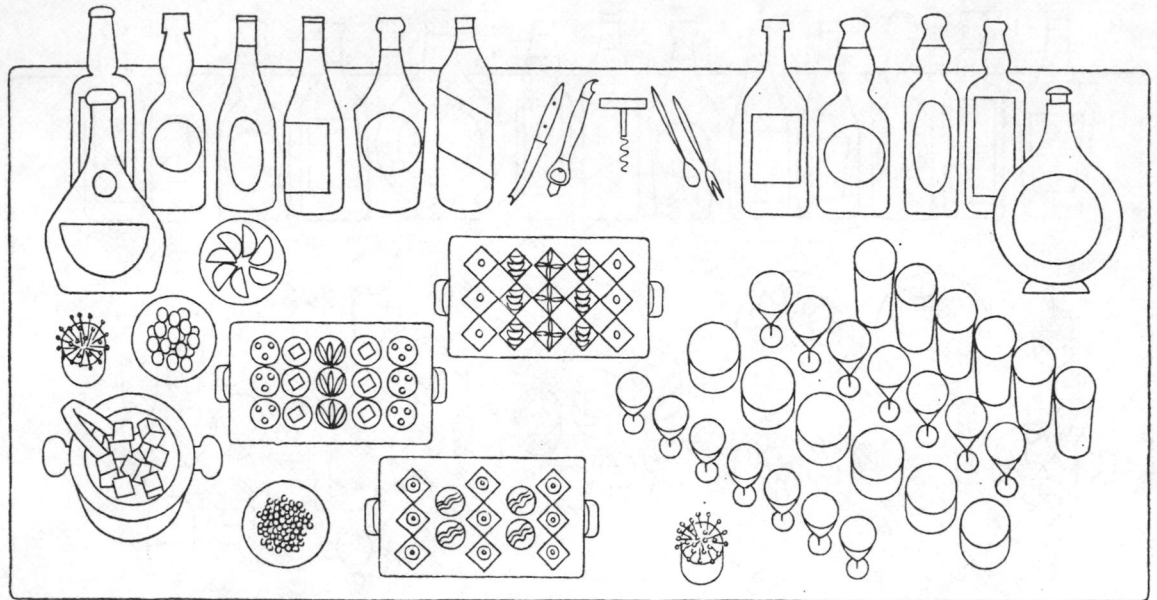

Cocktail party in a private house

—of cool beer is very welcome at a picnic on a hot day, and canned or bottled beer can easily be chilled in a lake or stream. Cask beer is of two types—filtered, 'pasteurised' pressurised beer, dispensed by means of cylinders of carbon dioxide, and 'real' beer, which is not filtered, and which is drawn off by gravity. The former can be set up anywhere, and does not need to settle, and most brewers will supply the necessary fittings and gas. The latter is more suitable for parties, being more of a connoisseur's drink, but it must be set up and tapped at least 48 hours in advance, kept at a constant temperature of 14°C (55°F) and not disturbed before being used, all of which tends to make it an impractical drink for parties. However, some brewers can supply a compromise, known as 'bright' beer. This is ordinary beer (i.e. not pasteurised or pressurised) which is filtered before being put into the cask. It can therefore be moved freely, and even dispensed from a trolley circulating among the guests.

If beer is to be served then tankards or steins are essential and if these can be of pewter or even silver the effect is enhanced. (When serving only one type of drink—particularly a relatively cheap drink—it is important to do so with a certain degree of panache, otherwise guests may suspect that economy rather than suitability was the deciding factor.)

Cups and punches are ideally suited for service at parties and a wide selection of these will be found in the 'Beverages' section of this book. Cups and punches should be well garnished since their visual appeal is to a large extent responsible for their popularity. A silver punch bowl and ladle is a good investment, and punch glasses with handles are needed for hot punches.

After being out of fashion for some years, cocktails are beginning to regain some of

Cocktail party in a private house self service

the popularity which they enjoyed in the 1930s and a wide selection will be found in the 'Beverages' section of this book. Care should be taken to follow the recipes accurately, and obviously no cocktail should be offered unless all the ingredients are available. A mixing jug and stirring spoon and a silver-plated cocktail shaker and strainer are needed, as is a small stainless steel knife and a wooden board, since many cocktails are garnished with a slice of citrus or other fruit.

CHEESE AND WINE PARTIES

Fifteen or twenty years ago, very few buffets or receptions took the form of a cheese and wine party, and an invitation to such an event was novel, unusual and intriguing. Now, cheese and wine parties are one of the most popular ways of entertaining a group of people, and it is interesting to consider some of the reasons underlying this change.

1. A cheese and wine party is an informal affair, and for a great many occasions there is a growing trend towards informality.

2. The food is substantial, and can take the place of a main meal, which means that a cheese and wine party is more of a 'buffet' than a 'reception'.

3. It is simple, and so enables a hostess (or a caterer) to serve a relatively large number of people with less work and worry than would be needed for a buffet.

4. It is relatively cheap, as it does not involve expensive ingredients, nor high labour costs.

5. It offers scope for originality and imagination within a fairly well-defined framework.

6. The people invited know more or less what to expect, and do not need to wonder if the event includes a meal, as is so often the case with an invitation to 'a party'.

7. Most important of all, cheese and wine parties are fun both for the organisers and their guests.

A really wide range of cheeses is essential for a cheese and wine party, and these should include hard and soft cheeses, mild and strong cheeses and cream and blue cheeses. If enough people are attending to make it practical to buy whole cheeses of up to 4½ kg (9 lb) in weight, then these should not be cut up into wedges. A round cheese, with one wedge cut out and placed on top has a much greater visual impact than it would if cut up and distributed on to mixed cheese boards. (The one wedge is cut out both in order to display the colour and texture of the cheese, and to encourage guests, who might be reluctant to broach an uncut cheese.) If whole cheeses are displayed in this way, then it is important to provide suitably large knives since it is not really practical to cut pieces from a large hard cheese using only a table knife.

The next requirements are bread, crispbreads, biscuits and butter, and here again variety is important. White bread, brown bread, wholemeal bread, black bread, pumpernickel, rye bread, soda bread and challah should all be considered, in addition to the essential French bread, and many of these breads can be obtained in different shapes and sizes, which adds interest and again enhances the visual appeal. As with the cheeses, some loaves of bread should be left uncut, in which case bread knives or bread saws should be provided, also some of the wide range of crispbreads now available. It is pleasant if there is both salted and unsalted butter, and the butter can either be left in large pieces, or made into pats, but foil wrapped pats should not be used, since these are not suitable to offer at any sort of party, and should be confined to cafeterias.

A wide variety of garnishes and accompaniments is also desirable. Crisp raw vegetables such as celery, radishes, endive, fennel and carrot strips are ideal; tomatoes and thinly sliced onion rings are also suitable. These items should be dished individually, however, since anything approaching a mixed salad would be out of place. The other ideal partner for cheese is, of course, fresh fruit, and there is no limit to the amount or variety of fresh fruit which can, with advantage, grace the table at a cheese and wine party.

Other 'cheesy' savoury flans and cheesecakes make a welcome addition to the table. It is within this sector that the hostess can add those little extra touches which distinguish one party from another.

Generally speaking, it is not necessary to provide fine wines at a cheese and wine party, which is essentially an informal occasion, and a selection of honest, drinkable wines is usually acceptable. Of course, this does not preclude the provision of fine vintage wines, but most people would feel that these were better saved for a more formal occasion. Guests should have the choice of a full-bodied red wine, a more delicate red wine, a rosé wine, a dry white wine and a sweet white wine. These could be red Burgundy, a red Bordeaux, a white Burgundy, an Anjou and a Sauternes—but it would be a brave man who suggested such a choice in Germany! In any wine-producing country, or area, the wines of the region will normally be served, for reasons of economy as well as local pride. Some non-alcoholic drinks should be provided, fruit juices and mineral waters being ideal. It is usual to serve coffee at the end of the party.

The table for a cheese and wine party should be large enough to allow ample space for guests to put down their plates whilst they serve themselves and it must be remembered that guests tend to stay at the table for a comparatively long time.

The best size of plate is a breakfast plate (20 cm or 8 in) but if these are not available, then a dinner plate (25 cm or 10 in) is more suitable than a side plate (17 cm or 6½ in) since the latter is too small to be really practical.

The amount of cheese and wine consumed will depend upon many factors, the time and length of the party and the age and sex of the guests being the main considerations, but in general between 120–140 g (4 and 5 oz) is sufficient, and guests tend to take one glass of wine every fifteen minutes or so, up to about six glasses per head.

Some popular cheeses

There are so many cheeses made throughout the world (some of which are not available outside their immediate area) that it is only possible to list a few of the better known.

Blue cheeses

Stilton. A creamy-coloured cheese, veined with blue, with a rough textured rind which is considered by many connoisseurs to be the king of cheeses. This cheese used to be served by being scooped out from the centre with a silver cheese scoop or a silver spoon, and the hole thus made filled up with port wine, but this practice is now in disfavour, and real enthusiasts prefer to slice the cheese horizontally. Stilton has a subtle and well-flavoured taste, without being offensively strong.

Gorgonzola. A blue-veined Italian cheese with a strong flavour.

Roquefort. A French cheese, made from ewes' milk, which has the blue veins introduced by a culture grown on mouldy breadcrumbs. It is a pungent, slightly salty cheese with a soft crumbly texture.

Dolcelatte. A variety of Gorgonzola, made with sweet milk, this cheese combines the characteristics of both blue and soft cheeses.

Danish Blue. A sharp, pungent cheese, crumbly in texture which is an imitation of Roquefort.

Soft cheeses

Camembert. A small round flat cheese, which is pale in colour, with a soft white rind. It ripens in flavour as it matures, and is one of the finest of all cheeses.

Brie. A large round flat cheese, which has a pale yellow curd and a whitish-orange rind. This is one of the most loved of all French cheeses.

Boursin. A small cream cheese, often flavoured with chopped herbs and garlic.

Mozzarella. A pale, egg-shaped Italian cheese made from buffalo milk, which needs to be eaten very fresh.

Ricotta. An unsalted Italian cheese made from ewes' milk. It has a creamy flavour, and is eaten when fresh.

Petit Suisse. A very mild soft full cream cheese from France.

Semi-hard cheeses

Tome au Raisin. A bland, slightly rubbery French cheese which has a crust of dried grape skins and pips, instead of rind. Although not an exciting cheese to eat, Tome au Raisin looks well on a cheese table because of its unusual crust.

Bel Paese. A mild flavoured Italian cheese which goes particularly well with grapes.

Port du Salut. A spongy cheese from France, which has a yellow curd and a golden rind.

Edam. A spherical Dutch cheese, with a yellow curd covered in a layer of bright red wax. A mild, pleasant cheese although not very exciting.

Gouda. A Dutch cheese, similar to Edam, but with a yellow rind.

Leyden. A Dutch cheese, very similar to Edam, but flavoured with cumin seeds.

Munster. A German cheese, flavoured with caraway or anise.

Hard cheeses

Cheddar. A fine, straightforward cheese, which becomes stronger as it matures.

Caerphilly. A white mild cheese, with a subtle refreshing flavour.

Cheshire. A mild, slightly salty cheese, Cheshire is available either white or red, the white being slightly sharper in flavour.

Derby. A tangy white cheese, which can also be obtained veined with sage leaves.

Leicester. A red-brown cheese, with a rich tangy flavour.

Dunlop. A Scottish cheese with a close texture, highly rated by connoisseurs.

Gruyère. A Swiss cheese, with many small holes, caused by fermentation.

Emmenthal. A Swiss cheese, ivory-yellow in colour. Irregular holes, golden brown rind, strong distinctive flavour.

Mysost. A Norwegian cheese made from goats' milk, Mysost is dark brown, with a slightly sweet flavour.

ENTERTAINING IN THE OPEN AIR

The pressures of modern life, and increasing urbanisation have resulted in an increase in the popularity of eating and entertaining out of doors. Al fresco meals or snacks do not call for elaborate meals involving time-consuming preparations. On the contrary, basic ingredients made up into simple, tasty dishes are much more compatible with an outdoor setting.

Occasions for outdoor entertaining may be divided into three broad categories—barbecues, picnics and garden parties.

Barbecues

The word 'barbecue' may be used to mean an outdoor charcoal grill, but when used in the sense of 'an outdoor party' the methods of cookery need not be confined to grilling. A barbecue can be a permanent fixture, built into a patio; a portable grill, which can often be quite sophisticated with a mechanically turned spit, or it can be improvised over a camp fire. In the latter case, there is little distinction between a barbecue and a picnic.

The fire can be made of dry hardwood, vine cuttings or charcoal, but whatever fuel is used, cooking takes place over the hot embers not over a blazing fire. A fire of wood therefore needs to be lit well in advance, but if time is short a charcoal fire, lit with a fire-lighter (i.e. a stick of solidified alcohol) produces the correct embers much more quickly. No fuel should be added whilst cooking is in progress. If more heat is needed, the fire should merely be poked.

Grilling is done on a gridiron or metal rack over the embers. Some metal barbecues have a means of adjusting the height of the grill, and hence regulating the heat. On an improvised barbecue, the grill should be set at an angle, higher at the rear, lower at the front so that the degree of heat varies according to where the food is placed. The bars of the grill are well greased or oiled before cooking begins, and the food is handled with tongs, and never pierced with a fork.

Chops, steaks, sausages, chicken joints and various types of brochette and kebab are all ideal barbecue foods, and can be marinaded if suitable. A selection of marinades is given in the section 'Basic Preparations'. The marinade must be drained off before grilling begins otherwise the liquid will drip in to the embers, causing them to flare up, but the food should be carefully basted with the marinade during cooking. The food is brushed with oil (which can be herb-flavoured) and seasoned before being grilled.

Suitable fillets or steaks of firm-fleshed fish, or whole fish such as trout, are also well suited to cooking over an open fire, and many recipes will be found in the 'Meat' and 'Fish' sections of this book.

It is possible to extend the range of suitable foods by wrapping the item in aluminium foil, and all types of food from fish to fruit may be barbecued in this way. It is also possible to enclose a garnish or even a vegetable with the main item, and grill a whole course at once. The foil is oiled or buttered and wrapped round the contents loosely, to allow for expansion, and then the edges are tightly sealed. If a crisp surface is required, the foil is opened out towards the end of the cooking, to expose the contents to direct heat.

Potatoes can be baked in their jackets, in or close to the embers, either directly or each potato wrapped in aluminium foil. After it is cooked and opened out, the centre is garnished either with a compound butter, or with a mixture of cream and chopped herbs.

Spit roasting gives excellent results, and is the simplest and oldest method of roasting. The spit should be made of either iron or a straight branch of hardwood, but willow or acacia should not be used, since they impart a bitter flavour. The spit can be supported at one or both ends in a variety of ways, including simply pushing one end into the ground.

The cooking time depends upon the thickness of the food roasted, the heat of the fire and its distance from the food, the type of meat and personal preferences. For an underdone spit-roasted joint of beef, about 35 minutes should be allowed per

1 kg (2 lb). 5–15 minutes longer will be required if the meat is preferred well done. Pork and veal take longer to cook, an average of 1 hour per 1 kg (2 lb) should be allowed for spit-roasting. Leg or shoulder of lamb takes 1–1½ hours per 1 kg (2 lb) for medium or well-cooked meat.

Ox roasting or roasting whole carcases of pork or lamb is a popular way in Britain of raising money for charity, but it is occasionally undertaken at private parties.

It is usual to build a low brick wall in the direction of the prevailing wind in order to reflect the heat forward, for the beast is roasted in front of the fire rather than over it. Two firm pillars are erected to carry the spit, which is a stout iron bar, with a cartwheel attached to one end, to enable the carcase to be rotated, or held still to expose any particular side to the heat. The carcase must be firmly wired to the spit, otherwise its weight will tend to mean that it does not turn when the spit turns round inside it. The beast must be basted throughout with its own dripping, and very long-handled ladles are needed for this.

The selection of the ox is vital to the success of the operation—it should not be too large to be manageable and must be well hung. An ox weighing 100 kg (220 lb) will take up to 18 hours to spit roast in this way, and will lose up to 40% of its original weight.

When the ox is cooked, the whole spit is removed away from the fire, for the comfort of the carvers, who expertly carve thick juicy slices of beef which are sold in aid of the charity. The spectators enjoy congregating round the fire, eating their beef which, ideally, is washed down with tankards of foaming beer from the wood.

Other methods of outdoor cookery include baking in clay, and stewing in a cauldron suspended over the fire. In Hungary the woodcutters have for centuries cooked their mid-day meal in a special tin, rather like two metal plates, with a hinge at one side and a fastening clip at the other, forming a tightly sealed container. The raw food is placed inside, and left to cook in glowing embers for about an hour.

Picnics

Most of the methods of cookery outlined above can be served at a picnic, provided the site has been prepared, or a portable barbecue brought along in the boot of the car. Otherwise, a selection of cold foods, packed in a hamper, are served to guests who seat themselves on logs or on the ground round a bright checked cloth.

Cold roast joints or birds for carving, pies, pâtés and croûtes are suitable, as are mousses, jellies, gâteaux and fruits. Where possible, the food should be served lightly chilled, since picnics perforce take place in warm or hot weather. Insulated boxes will keep food cold for several hours, and chilled soups or fruit salad and similar items can be transported in small quantities in vacuum flasks. Lettuce and similar green salads should be washed and transported in plastic bags; compound salads in bowls or basins, but 'wet' ingredients such as tomato or cucumber should be carried whole and added on site. Bread, rolls and butter are needed, and the salt, pepper and dressings should not be forgotten.

Wine, beer and minerals can be cooled in a handy pond or stream, or carried in an insulated box (known in Australia as an 'Eskie'—short for Eskimo). A hot beverage is often welcome, and a spirit stove or picnic stove fuelled with a small can of 'camping gaz' is useful, if no fire is lit. With imagination and a little forethought, a picnic can be an exciting and enjoyable open-air meal—sandwiches carried in haversacks are for hikers and climbers only!

Garden parties

In spite of notoriously unreliable weather, garden parties are something of an institution in Britain, and indeed, the Royal garden parties held in the grounds of Buckingham Palace are world famous. However, a garden party can be held in any location, provided the garden is beautiful and well tended, with a sufficiently large expanse of smooth green lawn. A garden party differs from other forms of outdoor catering in that it is an occasion for formal dress, not casual outdoor clothes. (At Buckingham Palace, the gentlemen wear full morning dress, including the grey top hat, and the ladies their best finery. with 'Ascot hats'.)

It follows, therefore, that the food consists of small, dainty items, prettily presented on delicate china. Since garden parties are usually afternoon events, tea and freshly made lemon and orange squash are the only drinks normally served, but any of the cold, non-alcoholic drinks listed under 'Beverages' could also be offered. As guests are not usually provided with tables and chairs, the occasion is a 'finger buffet' and details are given in 'Buffets' as to the type of food which is suitable. At a garden party, however, fresh fruit salad and ice creams are usually served, and strawberries and cream are almost obligatory, when in season.

OUTSIDE CATERING

Not all parties take place in the caterer's own establishment. In fact, catering at the host's premises—'outside catering'—is a large and thriving sector of the party catering business. There are many reasons why the host may require the caterer to come to him, rather than have his guests go to the caterer's establishment, and the type, style and size of the party can vary widely.

One type of party, perhaps the simplest, is when a host and hostess require help for a small dinner party in their own home, and the caterer needs only to supply a chef and a waiter or waitress. (The dining-room staff are traditionally referred to as 'parlour maids' and 'butlers' when the party is in a private house.)

Another type of party, perhaps the most common, is when a caterer is asked to provide a wedding reception (which often includes a full meal, either formal or buffet service) in a marquee on the lawn of the bride's parents' house.

Commercial enterprises also often require the services of an outside catering organisation. These events include the provision of receptions and dinners at the firm's premises, for visiting VIPs, and catering for guests and potential buyers at trade shows and exhibitions. These may be held indoors, in a hall or exhibition centre or they may take place in a field—as in the case with an agricultural show, for example.

Catering of this nature, with the need to provide all the equipment for cooking and serving on site (including tenting and floor covering) and the attendant problems of power, water and drainage, is a specialised field, beyond the scope of this book. Little has been written on the business of outside catering—the expertise remains in the heads of the experts—but, in view of the wide variety of sites, many of which have particular aspects which are not encountered elsewhere, this lack of technical literature is less surprising than it would appear.

The supply of catering services to private houses (which is relevant to this book) used to be largely in the hands of provision merchants. Nowadays, however, it is normally undertaken either by a specialist outside caterer, or as a side-line by an hotelier or *restaurateur*. When this is the case, the outside catering activities represent an additional workload for both management and staff and great care must be taken that this does not result in a lower standard to either the outside client or the regular business.

The most important requirement for catering in private houses is suitably qualified staff who can prepare and serve a meal in the customer's home strictly in accordance with the conditions laid down by him. From the moment the staff arrive until the moment they leave, they are the representatives of their employer's business, and his reputation is in their hands. It goes without saying that not all staff are of equal ability and none of them should be entrusted with a task beyond his or her capacity, particularly when the employer is not present to supervise. News of good service travels fast, but news of a fiasco travels faster, and can mar the reputation of a business.

When asked to cater for an outside party, the first thing the caterer must do is to visit the premises, preferably with the chef or chefs who will be involved. This needs to be done before discussing the menu with the host since the facilities available (and the size of the kitchen) will in many cases determine what food can be offered. It is important that the caterer does not rely on the host's assessment of the adequacy of his kichen, since the host will almost certainly claim that the kitchen is very modern and perfectly adequate. It may well be—for normal family meals— but it does not necessarily follow that the space and equipment are sufficient for a party menu.

A cold buffet is a much less onerous task for the caterer than a hot meal. A buffet can be prepared in his own premises, there is little disturbance in the client's home, only one or two chefs are needed, and the problem of the adequacy of the cooking facilities does not arise. Some dishes can be transported in bulk, and dressed and garnished on site, and some can be individually prepared and garnished before transportation. The chefs will only need to dress the buffet table, garnish the dishes, and carve and serve to the guests.

This does not mean that hot meals are not possible—they are, but they are more difficult to provide, and more complicated to organise. Generally, it is best if all preparation work is undertaken at the caterer's premises, leaving only the actual cooking to be done at the client's home. The practice of cooking at base and re-heating on site is to be treated with caution (even if the menu makes it possible) because of the food hygiene hazards and the deleterious effect upon the quality of the dish.

The chefs who undertake the provision of hot meals in other people's kitchens are craftsmen of the highest order. They must be able to maintain their standards whilst working in unfamiliar kitchens, with unfamiliar equipment, and the chef who will confidently undertake to produce a perfect cheese soufflé in a strange oven is indeed highly skilled! Apart from training and professional ability he also requires inborn talent, artistic sense and the flexibility to adapt to different surroundings.

There are plenty of opportunities for catering in private houses. Family gatherings, anniversaries, weddings and birthdays and the need to entertain business clients at home are all instances of events when the services of a caterer may be required Every meal provided for a customer in his own home brings new difficulties but these can be minimised by a careful and methodical approach, right from the time of the initial approach by the client.

The caterer should ascertain:

The reason for the meal.
The number of guests.
The price per head.
The age of the guests.
The space available.
The need (if any) to supply tableware, glassware, china or linen.
The client's requirements for the supply and service of drinks.
The time when his staff can move in, and the time by which they must be clear of the premises.

Once all these matters have been settled satisfactorily, it would seem reasonable to suppose that the rest could not be so difficult. But the next obstacle has already been reached—discussion of the menu. This discussion with the customer should not be underrated, for it is the foundation on which the whole operation rests. It is no exaggeration to say that it is often more difficult to sell a dinner than to cook it, especially at a price enabling the caterer to demonstrate the culinary achievements of which he is capable and also to make a reasonable profit. Selling cheaply is no feat. If the caterer is obliged to keep timidly within a tight budget, he cannot offer his client very much and has no scope to deploy his skill to the full, which is absolutely essential for success. When accepting an order, and especially when discussing the menu, definite and precise information should be given to the customer to gain his confidence from the start and give him the feeling that he is in good hands.

The correct composition of the menu, whatever the occasion, does not always coincide with eating habits, but for business reasons the host's wishes must be respected. It would be unfair to blame the chef for a badly or wrongly composed menu. Experience has shown that often a menu which was perfectly planned at the outset has been transformed into the worst one imaginable, flouting every culinary principle, through the personal wishes of the host. Here is an example of how this can come about. A client asks a hotel or restaurant with which he is familiar to suggest a few alternative menus for a given number of guests at a function to be held in his own home. After carefully checking the supplies and facilities available, the caterer works out various possible menus, making sure that each is complete in itself. They are then submitted to the customer who, however, has his own ideas. The lady of the house, or even guests whose tastes have to be consulted by the host, would like some dish or other added which simply does not fit in with any of the suggested menus. The caterer then receives one of the menus back, ruined by the addition of unsuitable dishes, with a formal order to proceed. A head-on clash with the customer because he has made nonsense of the menu would serve no useful purpose. While this example is not the general rule it does happen. If it proves impossible to persuade the customer to accept a menu in keeping with sound culinary principles, the consequences may be bad for the caterer too. If an expert, ignorant of the circumstances, happens to see a menu of this kind, he may well doubt his colleague's abilities, even though the latter's failure is solely due to a lack of understanding on the customer's part.

Before taking a few practical examples of outside catering, mention should be made of costing. For every order it is important to know whether to allow normal or generous portions, whether any additional members of the customer's household are also to be catered for, and whether there are any special requirements to be taken into consideration as regards items such as tableware, napery, candle-holders, glasses, cups, table decorations, etc. Efficient catering service also requires proper equipment and lay-out ensuring high productivity. Accurate costing is a prerequisite for profitability. Calculation of quantities for recipes cannot be based on a rough estimate, for frequent changes in market prices are an important factor, necessitating continual checks and comparisons. Pricing should never be confined to a rigid system of fixed charges to cover costs and profit margin, but requires great flexibility, with constant adjustments in the light of prevailing conditions and price fluctuations.

The following four menus are given as examples.

3

Menu 1

Private function in the home of Mr J. Hargreaves, 13 Long Road, Bath
Date: Tuesday 16th May
Time: 7 for 7.30 pm
Covers: 24
Departure: 6 pm
Chef: John Ives

Scotch smoked salmon
Caviar with blinis and sour cream

Cream of asparagus soup
Cheese straws

Saddle of lamb (medium done)
with bacon and fines herbs

Broccoli with Hollandaise sauce
Grilled tomatoes
Croquette potatoes

Hazelnut parfait
Florentine pastries

Work schedule for Menu 1

Salmon—960 g (2 lb 2 oz). Larder chef to make up into 3 services of 8 covers each.
Lemons—6.
Blinis—Veg. chef to make 25, and pack in foil in 5×5.
Caviar—1 kg 250 can (8¾ oz).
Sour cream—1 kg pot (2 lb 3 oz).
Soup—Soup chef to provide 7 l (12½ pt) in covered bain-marie.
Cheese straws—Pastry chef to provide 30, carefully packed.
Saddles—2 joints, ready for roasting, total weight 4 kg 800 (10½ lb).
Gravy—Slightly thickened, 2 l (3½ pt) in covered pan.
Herbs—100 g (4 oz) not chopped too finely.
Bacon—400 g (1 lb) finely diced.
Tomatoes—25 in number.
Broccoli—Veg. chef to provide 25 portions, ready blanched.
Hollandaise—Sauce chef to prepare 2 l (3½ pt) in insulated bowl.
Croquette potatoes—Veg. chef to prepare 80 pieces.
Hazelnut parfait—3 bricks in insulated box.
Cream—½ l (1 pt) send savoy bag.
Florentines—50 pieces, 3 small silver flats, doyleys.

Menu 2

Private function in the home of Mr J. Williams, 8 The Close, Cambridge
Date: Wednesday 6th December
Time: 1 pm
Covers: 16
Departure: 11.45 am
Chef: Charles Bush

Pheasant consommé

Lobster mousse, Carthusian style
Newburg sauce, fleurons

Grilled tournedos
Maître d'hôtel butter
Celery bundles
Château potatoes
Mixed salad

Pear savoury with Roquefort cream sauce au gratin

Praline parfait with hot rose hip sauce

Work schedule for Menu 2

Pheasant consommé—Soup chef to prepare 4½ l (8 pt).
Lobster mousse—Sauce chef to poach for 1½ hours before departure, leave in moulds.
Newburg sauce—Sauce chef to prepare 1½ l (2½ pt) to be finished with butter on site.
Fleurons—Pastry chef to cook and pack 20.
Tournedos—Sauce chef to cut 16 by 140 g (5 oz) and marinade in oil and herbs. Pack portable grill.
Butter—Sauce chef to make 2 rolls. Transport in insulated box.
Celery bundles—Veg. chef to cook, wrapped in bacon. Reheat on site.
Salad—Veg. chef to prepare ingredients for 16 portions. To be assembled on site.
Potatoes—Veg. chef to turn and blanch. Finished on site.
Bread—8 thick slices.
Pears—Pastry chef to prepare Roquefort sauce. Take horseradish; 400 g (14 oz) cranberries; 2 cans pears; grated Parmesan.
Praline parfait—2 bricks in insulated box.
Fresh cream—one savoy bag.
Rose hip sauce—pastry chef to prepare ½ l (1 pt).

Menu 3

Meeting of the Board of Directors, The District Savings Bank, The Avenue,
  London W2
Date: Wednesday 12th April
Time: 6.30 pm
Covers: 21
Departure: 5.15 pm
Chefs: George Davies, Michael Jones.   2 Waiters.
Meal served in small conference room (staff kitchen available from 4 pm)

Lobster ballotines
Crayfish tail salad, Creole sauce

Medallions of veal in tarragon butter
Braised chicory
Saffron rice
Mimosa salad

Cheese board

Lemon sorbet
Fruit salad with gin

Work schedule for Menu 3

Ballotines—Larder chef to make up 3 services of 8 each.
Crayfish tail salad—Larder chef to make up 3 dishes of 7 by 60 g (2 oz) portions
  each.
Creole sauce—Sauce chef to prepare 1 l (2 pt).
Veal medallions—Sauce chef to prepare 42 by 80 g (3 oz) to be cooked on site.
Tarragon butter—Sauce chef to prepare $\frac{3}{4}$ l (1$\frac{1}{4}$ pt).
Chicory—Veg. chef to cook 21 portions.
Saffron rice—Veg. chef to prepare 21 portions, for cooking on site.
Lettuce—4, plus 8 hard-boiled eggs and 1 bottle dressing.
Cheese—1 board for 21 covers.
Lemon sorbet—2 l (3$\frac{1}{2}$ pt) in insulated container.
Fruit salad—2 kg (4$\frac{1}{2}$ lb) with gin added.

Menu 4

Private function for American guests at the home of Dr Butterworth, The Crescent, Edinburgh
Date: Friday 12th May
Time: 8 pm
Covers: 14
Departure: 6.45 pm
Chef: Ian McKay

Melon Lady Drummond-Hay
Toast and butter

Fresh salmon in puff paste
Fennel butter
Cucumber salad in sour cream

Saddle of venison with orange segments Florian
Potato croquettes with almonds

Strawberries Capuchin style

Note: Tableware, cutlery, candelabra, carvers, serving spoons and napkins are to be supplied on hire. Delivery by 10 am.

Work schedule for Menu 4

Melon—7 melons halved, 2 boats ginger sauce by larder chef.
Bread—15 slices for toast.
Butter—500 g (1 lb).
Salmon—Sauce chef to make—1 kg 500 (3¼ lb) skinned and marinaded for 8 hours, enclose in puff paste, bake ¾ hour before departure.
Fennel butter—Sauce chef to make 350 g (12 oz).
Cucumber—Veg. chef to peel and slice 3. 1 carton soured cream, chopped dill.
Saddle of venison—1 saddle prepared for roasting. Allow 220 g (8 oz) per person. Make gravy with trimmings—Sauce chef.
Florian—Veg. chef to make up 14 portions, as per recipe.
Potato—Veg. chef to make 14 portions, ready for frying.
Strawberries—1 kg 200 (2 lb 10 oz), 950 g strawberry pulp, ½ l (1 pt) cream.

QUANTITIES AND TEMPERATURES

The imperial quantities used in this book are not exact equivalents of the metric quantities. Both are expressed in the nearest practical amounts which maintain the correct proportions of the ingredients.

It is essential that either all metric quantities or all imperial quantities are used throughout a recipe since to use imperial for one ingredient and metric for another would affect the overall proportion.

The quantities have been calculated to give correct results in each recipe, therefore the metric/imperial conversion may not correspond in every recipe.

Oven temperature chart

	Electric		Gas	
100°C	200°F	$\frac{1}{4}$	Cool
130°C	250°F	$\frac{1}{2}$	Slow
140°C	275°F	1	Slow
150°C	300°F	2	Slow
170°C	325°F	3	Moderate
180°C	350°F	4	Moderate
190°C	375°F	5	Fairly hot
200°C	400°F	6	Fairly hot
220°C	425°F	7	Hot
230°C	450°F	8	Hot
250°C	500°F	9	Very hot

Metric conversion

Pints		Litres	Ounces		Grams	Pounds		Kilograms
1·761	1	0·568	0·035	1	28·350	2·205	1	0·454
3·521	2	1·136	0·071	2	56·699	4·409	2	0·907
5·282	3	1·704	0·106	3	85·049	6·614	3	1·361
7·043	4	2·272	0·141	4	113·398	8·819	4	1·814
8·804	5	2·840	0·176	5	141·748	11·023	5	2·268
10·564	6	3·408	0·212	6	170·097	13·226	6	2·722
12·325	7	3·976	0·247	7	198·447	15·432	7	3·175
14·086	8	4·544	0·282	8	226·796	17·637	8	3·629
15·847	9	5·112	0·317	9	255·146	19·842	9	4·082

The key figure in the centre column can be read as either metric or the British measure, thus:

$$1 \text{ pint} = 0.568 \text{ litres}$$
$$1 \text{ litre} = 1.761 \text{ pints}$$

CUSTOMS AND TRADITIONS

Every major geographical area of the world has its own culinary habits and technology, originating from the most efficient use of indigenous crops and livestock. These large geographical areas can be subdivided into political and economic areas in which the pattern of eating has been further influenced by other factors including foreign trade and religion. Thus the food of Devonshire for example differs from that of Normandy although both areas are geographically and climatically similar.

The influences which have caused these differences are too diverse and too subtle to be fully analysed but anyone who is enthusiastic about food and drink must be grateful for the wide and fascinating variety of culinary customs and traditions which has resulted.

In this section, we give brief outlines of the gastronomic traditions of a number of countries, as a guide to the successful planning of buffets and receptions.

AUSTRIA

It has been said that there are as many different types of cuisine as there are nations. This is certainly quite correct, with one exception—Austrian cooking. It is not a national cuisine in the strict sense, yet it is 'national' just the same, for the lifestyles of the forty or so peoples under the old Austro-Hungarian monarchy have blended together to make it what it is. As a result of this close relationship between a wide variety of peoples and races, with its mutually enriching effect, Austrian cooking reflects a large number of different influences—Bavarian, Bohemian-Moravian, Italian, Hungarian, Polish, Croatian, Illyrian, Galician, Celtic, Rumanian, Ruthenian, Slovenian, Allemannian, Frankish, French, Jewish and many others. At the same time, it is different from the various national cuisines that have influenced it.

Generations of chefs and housewives throughout the monarchy have created a cuisine which appeals to everyone's palate, having been perfected and refined over the years without becoming 'haute cuisine'. The term 'good plain cooking', an art which is still practised in many restaurants as well as in private households, and which is known as 'Viennese cooking' in many of the so-called succession states, does justice to Austrian cuisine more than to almost any other.

Only this thoroughly baroque country could have been the birthplace of such culinary delights as boiled beef with chive sauce, apple and horseradish sauce with browned potatoes; emperor's schmarren with stewed plums; Viennese apple strudel; semolina dumpling soup; beef soup with milt croûtes; Viennese fried chicken; stuffed halibut; carp with root vegetables; stuffed fogas; stuffed ham; snail mould Sir Sigbert; apples Esterhazy.

It is impossible to ignore the almost unrivalled art of the Viennese confectioners, whose many products include torten, sponge rolls, slices, fancy buns of various kinds and a wide selection of biscuits. Examples of these Viennese creations of the confectioner's art include Napfkuchen Torte, Sacher Torte, Viennese apple strudel, hazelnut torte, curd cheese pastries, hazelnut slices, nut crescents, and snowballs.

Buffet suppers

Many excellent and even famous buffet suppers abound in the Austrian social calendar. At the Salzburg Festival magnificent 'after-concert' buffet suppers are served by candlelight. At the famous Hotel Sacher in Vienna many events are celebrated with buffet suppers. This famous hotel which has witnessed many a historic occasion is an institution and a meeting place for the traditional 'after-theatre' suppers beloved of the Viennese. New Year's Eve is another occasion for celebrating with a sumptuous buffet supper. The Hotel Sacher is also the venue of the most important government reception held in honour of visiting heads of state. Another event, one of the most sparkling and elegant in the international social calender is the annual Viennese Opera Ball.

The Viennese coffee house

This is an institution dating back to the time when Vienna was besieged by the Turks. Here the Viennese meet to read their favourite newspaper or periodical and to drink a cup of coffee (and there are innumerable types of coffee available) or perhaps a cup of chocolate. Here business deals are negotiated, gossip is exchanged or friends get together before or after a concert or play, to discuss the merits or otherwise of a performance. There are many other occasions celebrated with gastronomic events. On Ash Wednesday the 'Heringsschmasus'-Herring feast is celebrated. Every restaurant that prides itself on its cuisine sets up a buffet rich in local produce. This feast commences on Shrove Tuesday to help the participants to survive through Lent.

Feasts

Game weeks, dumpling weeks, steak weeks, pudding weeks, fish weeks and other culinary festivals as well as large and small congresses, and seminars ensure that there is no break in the chain of feasts. Excellent snack meals are a feature of many small town and country events. Such is the wine grower's hospitality to the public where he serves a mixture of wines from his vines.

Sautauz

Then there is 'Sautauz' (hog dance) which is held after a pig has been slaughtered. A very copious amount of food is served at these celebrations and include a wide variety of pork specialities. During the shooting season game lovers gather around richly laden festive tables.

Family celebrations

These include occasions such as christenings, birthdays, confirmations and weddings. Here again a festive table is laden with culinary dishes, rich and satisfying.

Housewives

When Viennese housewives entertain friends in the afternoon, coffee or chocolate with whipped cream (schlagobers) is served together with delicious home-made cakes and biscuits such as gugelhupf, stollen or walnut crescents.

Wines

Austrian wines are prized for their body, flavour, finesse, bouquet and colour and these with the typical apricot spirit (marillengeist) and apricot brandy (marillenlikar) with their lingering fragrance are served in generous amounts at all parties.

BULGARIA

Bulgaria with its mountain ranges and many rivers produces a very rich variety of fauna and flora. It is famous for its fields of roses and rose petal perfume is one of its charming exports. From rose petals, a sweet rose petal jam is made which is used in some of its confiserie. In many of its wilder regions bears, wild boar, and deer are hunted and at festivals to end the hunting season rich dishes made from these meats are a feature. The rivers produce excellent fish—carp and perch in great abundance—and fish dishes are specialities for grand occasions. The wide expanses of plain produce a prodigious variety of vegetables including tomatoes, peppers, aubergines, and various beans. These provide the ingredients for their tasty meat and vegetable dishes such as the typical kebab made with a basis of meat mixed with a variety of vegetables. All the dishes including their goulash are well seasoned with aromatic herbs and spices.

The Turkish influence is seen in the kebabs which are favourite dishes for parties and especially at out-of-door festivals. Bulgaria, claimed to be the home of yoghourt, uses this for many speciality dishes.

With so much fruit available from spring through summer and well into autumn Bulgarians invariably end their meals with fresh fruit such as strawberries, raspberries, cherries, apricots, apples, pears and various melons.

Confectionery in Bulgaria is much influenced by Turkish sweet dishes many of which are soaked in syrup.

CZECHOSLOVAKIA

Many cultural influences can be found in Czechoslovakian cuisine. The Slav contribution can be said to be the sour creams and sour vegetables and pickles while the Hungarian influence can be seen in the goulash dishes so loved for main meals and the many goose dishes also show the same influence. The favourite sauerkraut and dumplings come from Germany and schnitzels from Vienna.

Czechoslovak cooking can be said to be heavy in many respects—such as their bread dumplings—a favourite with many main meals. The heaviness may in part be due to the use of lard where the French would use butter or oil. The slaughtering of a pig is a traditional occasion. Friends join in, in the preparation of a kind of sausage made from the head and offal. In this ritual the broth made from cooking the ingredients is thickened with barley and fresh blood. When this is done the feast is ready. From the pig also comes the famous Prague Ham which is the most regal of all smoked hams.

Game birds, and game such as hare and venison may be roasted or cooked in elaborate sauces.

The national fish is carp from the lakes of southern Bohemia. This is traditionally served at a Christmas feast in a number of variations. The streams of Slovakia abound in trout which are delicious baked in Bohemian style.

Open-air party

In the spring and autumn rambles into the mountains at weekends are occasions for open-air parties. Usually a spot near a shepherd's chalet is chosen for a rest and a meal. If possible to find a pasture near a trout stream is ideal. This provides an opportunity to fish for trout. A camp fire is built and with permission from the shepherd the basic preparation for the main supper meal is carried out inside. A few hours before the actual supper which takes some time to prepare, a light hot meal is eaten. This usually consists of

> Grilled trout
> Brigands barbecue
> White and red wine to drink.

The main supper meal might consist of

> Potato gnocchi with Brimsen cheese
> Barbecued lamb
> Bread
> Pickled cucumber
> Tomatoes
> Pickled onions
> To drink—Moravian grog, gin, slivovitz, vodka and apricot brandy.

Such a party develops into a sing-song going on until after midnight.

Anglers' party

Angling is very popular in Czechoslovakia where the mountain torrents abound with trout and other fish such as carp, salmon, pike, pike-perch, sheat fish and other freshwater fish. The tight-knit community of anglers organises a gastronomic event at the beginning of the fishing season. The food consists of a cold buffet and a modest luncheon. The menus do not consist of fish only but always include a meat dish. It is important to have the right setting decorated with various kinds of fishing nets, old fishing tackle, trophies etc. The buffet table should be covered with a green cloth and a fishing net thrown over the top.

The buffet would consist of

> Carp in aspic
> Fish mousse
> Anglers' salad
> Marinated carp
> Smoked salmon, chive sauce, Wittingau sauce
> Hot ham with horseradish
> Small croissants (mignon)
> To drink—Metropol aperitif, Metropol vermouth and vodka.

The luncheon would consist of

> Baked trout Bohemian style
> To drink—Budweiser beer and white wine (Zernoseky Riesling).

Apart from national festivals a number of celebrations such as birthdays, weddings etc. are occasions for parties. One of these birthday celebrations, separate from and usually taking place before the family event is the Fiftieth Birthday Stag Party, when a group of old friends meet and enjoy happy hours together.

Fiftieth Birthday Stag Party

The birthday cake in this instance is decorated with a motif connected with the guest of honour's occupation or hobby—a musical instrument, a tennis racket, even a typewriter. The evening starts with cocktail savouries and a drink. Then comes the supper of typical Czechoslovak dishes and later in the evening more refreshments are served, with cocktail savouries in the form of canapés and bouchées of cheese, egg, ham and chicken.

Supper menu.
> Breaded carp, horseradish, lemon
> Brochettes hunter's style, mixed salad
> Emmenthal cheese with bread and butter
> Ice cream coupe
> To drink—white wine (Riesling)

Late refreshments.
> Garlic soup
> Potato cakes
> Garlic toast
> Salted almonds
> To drink—vodka, gin, korn (grain spirit)

All country districts of Czechoslovakia hold their own parish festival in late summer or early autumn. Families entertain one another and friends and relatives from the towns join in the merry-making where dancing is an indispensable part of the entertainment. The festival goes on throughout the day starting with a second breakfast, followed by a midday meal, then afternoon coffee and finally an evening meal. Different regions have their own specialities for the festival. The following is an example of such a community celebration.

Southern Bohemian parish festival

A specimen menu could be:

Second breakfast.
> Pork goulash with mushrooms with Budweiser beer

Midday meal.
> Chicken broth with noodles
> Stuffed breast of veal, boiled potatoes

Roast goose with cabbage and dumplings
To drink—Budweiser beer, white wine

Afternoon coffee.
Festival cakes
To drink—for female guests—coffee with milk or cream, kummel, kirsch
for male guests—black coffee, rum, brandy

Evening meal.
Larded haunch of wild boar, potatoes and cranberries
Escalope of pork with potato salad
To drink—red wine, korn

Another occasion for a party is the celebration of the end of the hunting season or it may be during a large shooting party. There is a traditional form for these events which must be in a suitable setting, such as a room with antlers on the walls, guns and other equipment and suitable motifs on tablecloths, glassware etc. The menu is decorated with a hunting motif. In accordance with an old custom glasses are placed on the guests' left, leaving their right hand free for their weapons. There is also a rule by which the place at the head of the table is occupied either by the host or by the hunter who has achieved the largest kill during the previous season. A round table is an essential if all guests are of equal status.

End of season hunters' banquet

After the guests arrive, heralded by a fanfare, they settle to partake of the following dishes and during the meal suitable hunting music is played on the bugle or French horn.

Menu.
Aperitif: Hunter's korn
Soup: Pheasant broth
Entree: Hunter's toast and Pilsner Urquell
Main course: 1. Haunch of venison in wine with stewed cranberries
2. Pheasant Czech style, potato croquettes, red cabbage
To drink—Pilsner Urquell, South Moravian Burgundy
Dessert: Baked apples with cranberries and whipped cream
To drink—Black coffee
Slovakian modrá perla (red wine)
Vodka, brandy

DENMARK

As a major food producing country Denmark is famous for its cuisine and the first thing that springs to mind when considering Danish food is their national speciality

Smørrebrod. Great importance is placed on the appearance of Danish Smørrebrod and each open sandwich is expected to be a work of art which pleases the eye as well as the palate. There is a wide range of Smørrebrod from the simple kind with a flat topping to those built up with an artistic arrangement of various ingredients. Preparing attractive Smørrebrod calls for a good eye and sound taste. Like all sandwiches they are best when freshly made but if a number have to be prepared in advance they can be wrapped in foil and stored under refrigeration, then garnished at the last minute.

The base is generally rye bread, but white bread, toasted or fresh, and crispbread are sometimes used. Occasionally the bread is served separately instead of being topped with the ingredients. Two or three open sandwiches of this type provide an ample meal. The Danes serve Danish lager with them and usually aquavit as well. There are both hot and cold Smørrebrod and an astonishing variety is available in many restaurants. One establishment in Copenhagen offers a selection of over 100 and the Oskar Davidsens restaurant has a menu over a yard long and offering 178 different kinds of Smørrebrod, each with a choice of four different kinds of bread.

Breakfast in Denmark usually consists of coffee or tea, rolls, butter, marmalade or jam. Lunch will probably be Smørrebrod, with meat, fish, cheese and perhaps other cold foods; while the evening meal may include a hot dish.

Danish ham and bacon are excellent and well known in England. Other meats are also of good quality as are poultry.

Fish of all kinds abound in the Danish fish markets and the tiny juicy shrimps are a speciality as are the Limfjord oysters. Danish caviar which is greenish-grey in colour has a delicate taste.

Denmark produces a wide variety of cheeses including the distinctive blue-veined Danish blue and Mycella kind, the light yellow smooth Havanti with its large and small punctured holes, the Samsoe bland and easy to digest and a similar cheese flavoured with caraway seeds. When topping Smørrebrod, fruits, vegetables and nuts are combined with certain of the cheeses which give a delicious taste. Green grapes and strawberries combine well with Mycella for example while purple grapes and walnuts give a delicious added flavour to Danish blue.

Danish pastries are famous as are the small almond cakes, sometimes coated with chocolate for tea parties. They can also be large enough to cut into slices. They appear hot and crisp from the bakery every morning.

Christmas dinner party

Dishes served for Christmas dinner are much like the British except that goose appears to be more popular than turkey. One difference is the serving of rice pudding at the beginning of the meal.

New Year's Eve celebration

Traditionally in Denmark the main course for a New Year's Eve dinner party is boiled cod which may not seem very inspiring but if cooked the Danish way with a choice of spices has a very pleasant flavour.

The round birthday party

This is a great occasion for eating and drinking in Denmark. A round birthday is celebrated in Denmark on each tenth birthday starting at ten years old. When a Dane celebrates his 6oth birthday relatives gather from all over the world to enjoy the event. There is much eating, drinking and merry-making and gifts are presented, but the focal point of the celebration is the huge layer birthday cake. The cake can be served as a dessert, when it is usual to sandwich the layers with fruit and whipped cream. The cake is then frosted with more whipped cream on the top and sides and decorated with fruits, piped cream and chopped nuts.

At all Danish parties aquavit is drunk. It should be served in a small glass which has been kept in the refrigerator with the aquavit. This gives a heavy frosting to the glass. The first aquavit is tossed back and the secret is the coldness which is followed by a fiery feeling. It is followed by a mouthful of beer.

FINLAND

The festivals celebrated in Finland are little different from those in other Scandinavian countries.

New Year's Eve is celebrated among friends at a good dinner, but there are no traditional dishes. At midnight the host offers his guests champagne and the hostess hands round home-made canapés with caviar, smoked salmon, reindeer, etc. The company engages in the practice of tin melting, trying to guess what the future holds from the resulting shapes.

Easter is celebrated as a particularly festive occasion, a custom dating from the time when Finland was a grand duchy of the Russian Empire. The table is always decked at Eastertime with consecrated candles and with painted eggs. The main meal consists of eggs as an hors d'oeuvre, followed by the main course of poached salmon (served with Hollandaise sauce in restaurants) and lastly the traditional dessert 'mammi'. The latter is prepared by all sections of the population and is always served as part of the Easter celebrations.

The eve of May Day and May 1st are celebrated as a spring festival, as Finland remains in the grip of its harsh winter up to this time. The most impressive celebration is the informal and spontaneous ceremony which takes place at midnight by the statue of 'Havis Amanda' in the market place in Helsinki. Towards midnight people gather there and wait patiently for the scene that is about to be enacted. They are all wearing a flower in their buttonhole, carrying balloons and sticks decked with paper plumes, and making a deafening noise with small penny whistles. Suddenly there is silence. A student climbs up over the edge of the fountain to the sweetly smiling 'Havis Amanda' and puts a white Finnish student's cap on her head. At the same time the fountains begin to play again—spring has come. The crowd sings spring songs and people wander through the centre of the Finnish capital in a happy holiday mood until the early hours of the dawn.

Even before the celebrations, almost every housewife begins to prepare 'sima' (mead). It is drunk with 'tippaleipa' which, with its interwoven strands of batter, resembles a bird's nest. 'Sima' and 'tippaleipa' are served everywhere on the morning of May Day, both in restaurants and in private homes.

Another May Day tradition is the 'Silliaamiainen' (herring breakfast) which is eaten with friends and acquaintances; most of those who have stayed up all night are greatly in need of a copious breakfast such as this. It includes various kinds of preserved herring, e.g. herring in vinegar marinade, herring Russian style, and sardines in oil, served with bread and butter. Beer and schnaps are drunk with this meal.

In Finland the period from July to September is called 'the culinary months'. The crayfish season opens on July 21st. There is no lobster, but Finnish crayfish are firm and very tasty. On fine warm summer evenings, friends are entertained at home or in a restaurant—preferably on a terrace—with a dish of Finnish crayfish which, as is well known, are larger and better than anywhere else in Europe. The crayfish, which have been cooked in white wine on the previous day and kept on ice, are served with toast, butter and cheese; the drinks consist of vodka and beer or white wine. Fifteen to twenty crayfish are allowed per person.

In the autumn the gastronomic specialities are roast elk, duck and bear. The menu for a hunting or shooting party generally consists of marinated mushrooms, roast bear—especially bear ham—with a garnish of boiled potatoes, cranberries and rowan jelly, and vanilla ice cream and jam as dessert. The most popular beverages are again vodka and beer; red wine is seldom drunk. On Martinmas (November 10th) the customary meal is black soup made with goose blood followed by roast goose.

Pikkujoulou ('little Christmas') is celebrated at Advent as a sort of preparation for Christmas, with the same food and drink as at Christmas-time. It is the occasion for a works or office party held at an hotel for employees only, without their families. The proceedings begin with hot 'glogi' (mulled wine); the menu consists of ham with peas, carrots and potatoes, followed by 'riisipuuro' (Christmas rice) and 'joulutortut' (plum jam turnovers), a Christmas speciality.

On Independence Day (December 6th) the President of Finland holds a grand ball at the palace. The guests are served coffee with a large variety of cakes, wine cups and cocktail canapés in the form of small aspic moulds.

At Christmas the family and friends gather round the brightly lit Christmas tree for their celebrations. The special dishes served at this time include Baltic herring, dried cod, ham, roast hare, turkey, reindeer tongue purée and Karelian pirogs. 'Riisipuuro' and 'joulutortut' are indispensable desserts. Christmas rice is found on every Finnish table. A small almond is concealed in it and, according to an old tradition, the first unmarried person to find it will be married during the coming year. Apart from these specialities, gingerbread is also an essential part of the Christmas festivities.

FRANCE

Over the centuries French cuisine with its ancient tradition has gained world-wide acceptance and acclaim. The prestige of their chefs and the excellence of their dishes still make French restaurants—be they in New York or in London—the favourite haunts of discriminating diners. Incidentally, cookery has remained one of the only inviolable strongholds of the French language, which is still used for menu composition in the most distant countries.

The tradition of French cooking is centuries-old: one of the first French cookery books, *Le Viandier* by Taillevent, first chef to King Charles V, appeared in the 1370s. He opened the way for cookery to develop into a science with its own laws; ever since then it has formed the subject of a long succession of books and research.

Nostradamus, who was not above devising and writing down recipes for preserves between predictions, Marie-Antoine Carême, Brillat-Savarin, Prosper Montagne, Curnonsky, the prince of gastronomes, and many others: a galaxy of world-famous great names illuminate the history of French cooking or, to be more precise, of the great national cuisine of France. At the same time we should not forget the importance of regional cooking in its richness and variety; though despised for too long, it became known in Paris during the French Revolution, when the deputies representing all the provinces of France introduced their regional specialities into the capital. These made the fortune of some restaurant owners at a time when more and more restaurants were being opened in Paris, several of them by chefs from great private houses whose masters had died or emigrated, and who began to work for the public. Cooking now became simpler, concentrating on taste rather than decoration, which had been overwhelmingly lavish until then. After the period of semi-restrictions during the Revolution, abundance returned with the Napoleonic era. The tables kept by Talleyrand and Cambacérès have remained famous for their sumptuousness, the artistry of their arrangement and the company that gathered round them. It was at this time that Carême—illustrious Carême—appeared on the scene.

Marie-Antonin Carême, who was born in 1784 and died in 1833, built up the art of modern cookery and codified its laws as solidly as Napoleon codified French civil law. France also owes to him the tradition of very elaborate, flower-decked architectural buffets, with the dishes arranged round a large centre-piece, in contrast to the restrained, functional style of buffets in other countries such as Austria or Sweden.

All the great cooks who succeeded him, including Gouffé, Escoffier, Montagne and, later on, Pellaprat and Mengelatte, used his work as a basis for their own in one way or another, although each of them made his personal contribution to the historic edifice of French cooking.

French regional cooking introduced into Paris during the French Revolution has now found a secure place in a wide variety of restaurants. Sometimes however the attempts by London restaurants, for example, to produce regional dishes is far from satisfactory and many so-called Provençal dishes are not the traditional dishes of the region.

Although southern Provence has become a coastal playground much of the northern and western part of the province is very unsophisticated. It retains a great deal of the traditional character of the area and relies on the richness of its own produce of meat, game, vegetables, fruit and cheese. Even the pots, the traditional earthenware ones in which the beef stew is cooked, have some effect on the dish and the delicate care in the use of the herbs and wine make such a dish an experience. The vegetable dishes—never over-cooked—could be succulent French beans, or asparagus and broad beans from the Vacluse. Black truffles essential for some choice dishes are plentiful in the area of Carpentras. In the Basses Alpes, pâtés, sausages and local cured ham are excellent.

Normandy, famous for its soft rich cheeses produces dishes such as chicken or vegetables with rich cream sauces. Such dishes are sometimes enriched with Calvados. Cream and butter are lavishly used in Norman cooking and their Calvados—cider brandy—when used in sauces with pork and veal gives a special taste to the dishes. Meat in the Normandy region whether beef, veal, lamb or pork is of the highest quality. Included in their hors d'oeuvre is usually found a melting potted pork called 'rillettes' and the famous duck pâté is another choice hors d'oeuvre. Numerous duck dishes from the famous Rouennais are very rich and gamey in comparison with the English Aylesbury or the Perigord, and have a very different flavour. Tripe is another dish which is famous and cooked the Normandy way for about 12 hours though now it is usually bought ready-cooked.

The region of Lorraine is famous for its quiche which is copied in many guises but in Lorraine restaurants is cooked fresh for each customer. Various pâtés, brawns and sausages go with highly flavoured salads and there is a variety of cream cheeses.

Alsatian cookery has been influenced by many changes which have happened in the region and various types of Jewish and German dishes have become part of Alsatian cookery. The famous foie gras of Strasbourg studded with truffles or one of the famous pâtés or terrines are served very cold as an hors d'oeuvre. Munster is one of the strong flavoured cheeses of Alsace with its rich creamy texture. The local 'eaux-de-vie' are famous and are made from the local fresh fruit for which Alsace is well known. No meal is complete without wine. The wines of Alsace, the Rieslings, the Traminers, the fruity Gewurtztraminers are excellent with any of the Alsatian specialities.

Brittany with its long coastline abounds in the best possible fish dishes. From the sweet mullet, the sole, mackerel and sardines to the lobsters, scallops, clams, oysters, mussels, and prawns there is no lack of variety along the Breton coast. Lamb from the salt marshes is sweet and tender while poultry—chickens and ducklings served with tiny green peas—are mouth watering.

In the wild districts of the Haute Savoie game plays an important part in the dishes found in the region. Partridges, capercailzies, chamois, hares and rabbits abound. Roasted or in terrines with truffles and aromatic herbs they give a rare richness to any meal.

The cookery of Burgundy brings to mind the full flavoured wines of the region which are used for its many rich sauces. The 'escargots à la Bourguignonne' and 'le boeuf Bourguignon' are among the very many famous dishes of Burgundy. Garnishes of cubes of bacon and glazed buttered onions proclaim a Burgundian dish. Lyonnaise cookery has given a great deal to European dishes and the pig plays an important part in the region's dishes. Famous are the fish dishes and in particular the quenelles which when properly made are delicious.

Bresse to the south of Burgundy is famous for 'poularde de Bresse'.

The Bearnais and Basque region in south-western France unlike most of the regions of France use butter only for pastry making. For all other dishes the rich goose fat is used and the other speciality in so many of Bernaise dishes is the brick red pepper called 'piment basquais'. The coastline of the Basque region provides a vast variety of fish. Fresh sardines, squids, prawns, langoustines and mussels are cooked in similar manner to the paella of Spain. Freshwater fish, especially fine river trout are to be found inland and there is an abundance of wild fowl.

The Perigord with its rich tradition of good cooking is the region of black truffles, Roquefort cheese, walnut oil, pigs and geese. It brings to mind the real country type cooking—in deep casseroles, or roasting on spits.

From the region of Languedoc comes the famous lobster dish about which there is a difference of opinion as to its origin. Claimed to be originally 'langouste niçoise' or a special version 'à la setoise' it is a dish similar to what we now know as 'homard à l'americane'. From Toulouse comes the famous cassoulet with its many variations.

GERMANY

German cooking owes its main features to centuries-old customs stemming partly from courtly and clerical tradition and partly from that of the middle classes and the rural population. In addition, Germany's neighbours, especially her eastern ones, made a strong impact on her cooking, and the Huguenots who were encouraged to settle in Brandenburg in the seventeenth century by the Great Elector Frederick William had an unmistakable influence on its development.

Good food has always been greatly appreciated in the German states, as evidenced by one of the oldest works on cookery, 'Das buch von guter spise' (The Good Food Book), a parchment manuscript written in Wurzburg before 1350. There are delicious specialities all over Germany, such as Black Forest trout, Starnberg vendace, smoked eel, Hamburg chicken, Havel crayfish, smoked breast of goose, Frankfurters, Bavarian knuckle of veal, many tasty varieties of sausage and cheese, and Westphalian ham. The Westphalian ham was already a popular delicacy by about 1400; when the city of Dortmund wanted to make a special gift to Emperor Sigismund, it decided to present him with twelve smoked hams, apparently much to the Emperor's pleasure.

Where else is there so wide a selection of hearty farinaceous dishes such as noodles, dumplings and the like? The many different kinds of Torten, cakes and other flour confectionery are also famous. The Nuremberg Lebkuchen and Mutzen bakers were already well known as confectioners in the Middle Ages. Their recipes are still in use today with very little alteration. The wide range of regional specialities is matched by a great variety of excellent wines, including German champagne, many kinds of beer which are well known throughout the world, and limpid fruit and grain spirits as well as brandies. The various types of bread are also worthy of mention, including pumpernickel; the special way in which the latter is prepared suggests that the old Germanic peoples baked their bread in a similar fashion.

Increasing industrialisation during the nineteenth century brought considerable affluence to a section of the middle classes, which now wanted to make its mark in society by entertaining on a lavish scale, with sumptuous buffets. This led to the introduction of catering firms which supplied complete meals for private functions in the home. Although restaurants delivering cooked meals to private houses had been in existence for a long time, these new caterers did not confine themselves to providing food and the requisite cooks and waiters, but also supplied all the tableware on request. Up to the third decade of the twentieth century the most famous of these caterers was the firm of F. W. Borchardt in Berlin, which supplied gala meals and buffets for European rulers, eastern potentates, South American millionaires and many others.

Over the years many German chefs have specialised in receptions and cold buffets. Nowadays, however, large buffets for special functions are by no means confined to cold dishes; very often a few hot dishes are also requested and these may be kept hot on dish-warmers or served from trolleys. During the winter months a rustic style buffet also includes a nourishing vegetable soup, such as lentil, pea or potato soup.

Old Berlin cooking

Over the years there have often been very great changes in the climate of life in

Berlin, but partiality to palatable, if somewhat substantial food has survived every change. In actual fact, Berlin cooking is by no means as unimaginative or tasteless as it is often maintained to be. The large numbers of people who migrated to the capital from the various provinces of the former Prussian monarchy, especially from the east, and also the many Huguenots who settled there have left their mark on Berlin cooking.

Magnificent restaurants with the finest French and international cuisine have existed for a long time and the large cold buffets set up for special occasions are unsurpassable, but they are not typical of Berlin. Truly characteristic Berlin cooking, especially where cold meals are concerned, has always been found in the city's 'pubs on the corner' and the small homely restaurants frequented by the Berliner.

Recently some large well-known Berlin hotels have also discovered it and have found that an old Berlin evening can be a great success, even with the most demanding of patrons. The following are some of the favourite Berlin dishes:

Jellied eels
Berlin sausages with potato salad
Soused herrings
Jellied goose
Rollmops old Berlin style
Smoked loin of pork with potato salad
Pork chops in aspic
Berlin Napfkuchen

GREAT BRITAIN

'Haute Cuisine' are not the words that come to mind when British cooking is mentioned. Elaborate dishes with rich sauces have not been specialities of British cooking but the excellent quality of the meat available has made British roasts among the world's best. The Aberdeen Angus rib of beef served at home with Yorkshire pudding, and the baron of beef served at the Lord Mayor's Banquet can hardly be bettered anywhere. Saddle of mutton served with fresh vegetables is another excellent main dish whilst leg of Welsh lamb served with new potatoes and mint sauce is one of the delightful early spring dishes.

The famous Aylesbury duckling roasted to crisp tastiness is another excellent main course and a roast saddle of venison is a big occasion dish.

Roast goose followed by plum pudding have always been the favourites on the Christmas dinner table but of recent years fewer geese have been seen and turkeys have taken their place. Although Britain is an island, fish does not appear to hold the place it should on British menus, though fresh salmon poached and served hot or cold or grilled is a great favourite in season. Other fish available include herring, plaice, sole, whiting and mackerel as well as a variety of shell fish.

Tea has always been considered the British beverage but now coffee has become as popular.

Wine with meals has been steadily gaining in popularity but beer still remains the main British beverage, Scotch whisky is the popular spirit, while Drambuie has its place among liqueurs.

Cheeses in Britain are varied in style and taste. Stilton and Cheddar are among the most popular English cheeses while from Wales comes Caerphilly and from Scotland comes Cabec.

Parties in Britain cover a wide range of occasions, from the out-of-doors garden party, and the formal banquet, to the wedding, birthday and other anniversary celebrations catered for in the home by the hostess or undertaken by professional caterers. Of late more and more professional catering is done for events highlighting family life. Outside the home large informal buffets and formal receptions are usually undertaken by professional caterers. Such receptions may take place in an hotel or restaurant or even in a hall suitably decorated for the occasion.

In Britain the breakfast meal has been considered one of the best meals of the day consisting as it does of a cooked meal of porridge, cereal or fruit juice followed by bacon or ham and eggs, perhaps sausages and garnished with tomato and completed with tea or coffee, toast and marmalade. The word 'breakfast', not surprisingly, has therefore been affixed to some celebration meals. The wedding breakfast and the hunt breakfast are examples.

Wedding breakfast

This can be as elaborate a meal as a luncheon in the celebration of a marriage. When such a meal is provided it would consist of a variety of sandwiches, cakes, as well as the wedding cake with possibly ices; drinks would include tea, coffee and claret cup.

Formal wedding reception

When a large number of guests are invited to a more formal wedding reception the lunch is usually served between two and three o'clock in the afternoon and is generally given at an hotel. Only if the wedding is a quiet or small one is the lunch offered at the bride's parents' home.

Light refreshments. When only light refreshments are offered, it is a fork or finger meal. The buffet is set out either in the dining-room or some other convenient place.

Sit-down luncheon. Such a luncheon is served in the dining-room with the arrangement of the tables adapted to the size of the room and number of guests, either one large table in the centre or a number of small tables to seat either 4, 6 or 8 guests. In any case, a table d'honneur in a prominent part of the room is provided for the bridal party of bride and groom, their parents, the 'best man', the bridesmaids and a few of the principle guests.

A wedding luncheon table is laid with plates, silver and glasses in the same style as for any other special occasion except that the wedding cake and the bride's bouquet are placed in the centre of the table before the newly weds.

Buffet luncheon. Arrangements for a stand-up wedding luncheon are simple. A long buffet table is set up at one end of the room. The tablecloth should just touch the carpet in front and at the back should hang a few centimetres only (garlands for example of smilax and vases of flowers may be used to decorate the buffet). The wedding cake is placed prominently on the buffet or else on a table by itself in the middle of the room. As many covers as necessary are laid in front of the buffet close together. This consists of one small plate, one small knife and fork, a dessert spoon, two glasses—one for champagne and the other for any alternative wine. Cups for consommé (if on the menu), tea and coffee and sugar basins are laid on a conveniently sited sideboard. Also placed there are small plates, silver, glasses and fruit plates with their corresponding doyleys and finger bowls.

Cutting the cake. It is customary for the bride to cut the first slice of cake after the actual meal is finished. Large wedding cakes are, as a rule, sent out with a large slice already cut through and fastened round with a white silk ribbon. The bottom layer of cake is usually cut up into finger pieces by the maître d'hôtel and then handed round to guests on silver dishes or on dessert plates.

Hunt breakfasts in the past used to be elaborate meals of five courses with a wide selection of hors d'oeuvre, fish, cold meats and salad, sweets, dessert and coffee. Today the choice would be limited with perhaps one fish dish and a much reduced selection for the main course.

Two events in the British summer calendar are the Henley Regatta in June and the Ascot summer race meeting. A gala buffet at a club for the former would consist of a choice of soup, a cold fish or meat dish, a sweet and dessert. A luncheon menu in the royal enclosure at the Ascot summer meeting would have a choice of cold fish dishes, such as salmon and lobster while strawberries and cream and champagne always appear on the menu.

Alfresco lunches are the order of the day at two other outdoor events—the Eton and Harrow cricket match and Derby Day at Epsom. A luncheon basket would contain a selection of cold meats, fish and pies with salad, with fresh fruit and a selection of cheeses.

Banquets are traditionally splendid occasions held to celebrate important events, to entertain foreign guests, to honour eminent national figures or as in the Lord Mayor's Banquet of the City of London to remind us of the past splendours and authority of the City.

The Lord Mayor's Banquet

The banquet is held in the historic Guildhall after the civic pageant has passed through London during the day. The Lord Mayor with his Lady Mayoress receives his guests usually headed by the Prime Minister in state. V.I.P.s enter the Great Hall, the Lord Mayor leading with the Prime Minister. The Lord Mayor in robes of office with a heavy gold chain round his neck and breast covered with decorations is flanked on either side by people eminent in public life, ministers of the crown, the Lord Chief Justice, ambassadors from other countries, all wearing state dress. At the other end of the Great Hall, the trumpeters in white wigs and scarlet livery embellished with gold, blow fanfares. In contrast at the far end of the hall may be discerned cooks and carvers slicing away at the baron of beef of old England.

Behind the Lord Mayor, the toastmaster in traditional robes announces the toasts during the evening.

By tradition, the menu starts with real turtle soup.

Tea parties

Although modern entertaining has changed a great deal as regards a 'tea' meal the British 'afternoon tea' is still a feature in Britain. It is not a main meal but rather a light refreshment taken between about 3.45 and 5 p.m. It is mainly an institution for home entertaining though afternoon teas are provided in hotels. At home, afternoon tea is served in the lounge or drawing-room and usually consists of dainty sandwiches, bread and butter, toasted goods, preserves (but never marmalade), and small cakes.

Tea parties also form entertainment for children to celebrate birthdays and Christmas. In the case of children's parties the meal would be served around the dining-room table.

HOLLAND

The Dutch are essentially home entertainers and even so-called 'grand occasion' receptions have a homely simplicity. The general practice in Holland is one hot meal a day either at home between 6 and 7 p.m. or in a restaurant between 7 and 9 p.m. The midday meal called 'Kaffiestaffel' is served cold and consists of different kinds of bread, butter, cold meat, cheese and jam served with milky white coffee. Kaffiestaffel however can become a more elaborate meal for special occasions.

Wedding receptions

This can be a luxurious kaffiestaffel. In Brabant and Gelderland magnificent kaffiestaffels in the best rustic traditions are served in country restaurants. Before the meal guests drink little glasses of 'brandewijin', a white spirit distilled from grain. It is not a very strong drink and is sometimes flavoured with lemon or bitter herbs, or served with a lump of sugar.

The table for the reception is laden with a wide variety of foods: whole raw and cooked hams, all kinds of whole smoked sausages, terrines, at least two kinds of cheese, butter, boiled eggs, oven-baked buttered eggs, bacon, cold meat and cold chicken is accompanied by large mugs of coffee with lots of cream and lumps of crystallised sugar. At least four kinds of bread are available: wholemeal, white, rye and currant bread eaten with butter and cheese, preferably very young Gouda while it is still creamy and soft.

Two other famous Dutch specialities for large parties are smoked salmon and smoked eel. Although Dutch salmon due to river pollution has almost disappeared, Scotch and Danish salmon are available. Smoked eels—fat Dutch eels, succulent and rich in flavour—fortunately are still available. They are served in fillets on toast with slices of hard-boiled eggs and lemon.

Entertaining on a canal boat

Canals are a feature of the Dutch scene and entertaining foreign guests on a canal boat is a pleasant surprise for the guests. This type of entertaining takes the form of a fish buffet and could include all kinds of fish from herring to lobster. The most blasé of guests would be impressed by the original presentation of tasty fishes.

The following are some dishes for such a buffet:
Herrings in tomato sauce
Sprats in Royale
Jellied eels
Fried plaice
Herrings in dill cream
Bread rolls baked in fish shapes
Smoked salmon
Smoked mackerel

New Year's Eve

One of the important family celebrations in Holland is on New Year's Eve and as cafés, restaurants and theatres close at 9 p.m. most families have their New Year's Eve party at home where the hostess has been busy all afternoon baking cakes traditionally associated with this festival. These cakes are called 'ollieballen' (currant puff fritters). 'Sulluwbollen' (snowballs) are another speciality and these are similar to our apple fritters. Just before midnight the family sits down to supper and this is the only time supper is eaten in Holland. Well-to-do people drink champagne and feast on such Dutch specialities as oysters, smoked salmon and smoked eel on toast. Humbler parties include on their menu herring salad or salmon salad and drink moselle.

Cheese and wine party

This is the usual informal way of entertaining friends in Holland. When guests arrive (about 8.30 p.m.) they are served a cup of tea or coffee and then pass on to wine and cheese. A selection of cheeses is placed on the table. They will include French, Swiss and Dutch cheeses. A basket contains different kinds of bread—rye, toast, french bread and Swedish crispbread, and small salty biscuits. Butter is always served with the bread. Cheese dips are also popular for these more intimate parties and are served with savoury biscuits.

Indonesian cookery

Holland is said to have two types of cooking—its own and the Indonesian type. Indonesian cookery has indeed a strong influence on Dutch food. For example, at the time of the Dutch East India Company (in the seventeenth and eighteenth century) trade with the tropical spice islands led to departure from traditional ways of seasoning food and, in fact, many tropical spices are still used in Dutch cooking—nutmeg, cloves, cinnamon, curry powder. Dutchmen returning from the tropical islands had lost their taste for the somewhat insipid Dutch food; Chinese immigrants from Indonesia opened Chinese and Indonesian restaurants all over the country and, as a result, Indonesian cooking became very popular in Holland and many families have an 'Indonesian style' dinner once a week. The most spectacular Indonesian meal is the 'Rijsttafel' (rice meal); traditionally this was the meal generally eaten by Dutchmen in Indonesia in colonial times. The preparation of a proper 'Rijsttafel' is very complicated; a large number of ingredients are required, including fruit, vegetables, spices and tropical fish. In Holland there are special shops (called by an Indonesian name, 'toko') where all these fragrant, aromatic, exotic products may be bought. Although it is impossible, especially in countries where Oriental delicacies are not commercially available, for the housewife to make a real 'Rijsttafel' as served in Indonesian restaurants at The Hague or Amsterdam, she can serve a meal very similar to this luxurious, exotic feast.

Rijsttafel
The basic dish is a large bowl of white, dry, fluffy rice. Little dishes containing all the various delicacies are placed round it. Each guest helps himself to a portion of rice, which he puts on his plate (a soup-plate is used); he then surrounds the rice with little portions of the delicacies and condiments. A 'Rijsttafel' is eaten with a spoon and fork; a knife is never used (Illustration p. 366).

The drinks served with a 'Rijsttafel' are beer or iced mineral water.

HUNGARY

Hungarian cooking, like that of every other nation, is closely bound up with the country's history and culture. It is the end product of a long, but by no means steady development, and has been influenced and shaped by many factors, such as geography, methods of production, economic and political development.

Hungarian cooking has a distinctive character connected with the use of lard. Butter or oil is only used for cold dishes, international cookery, special diets and, of course, baked sweets and other flour confectionery. The extensive use of lard is connected with the fact that pig-farming has flourished in Hungary for many years. A Hungarian roux, for example, is made with lard and strong flour, cooked to the appropriate colour (light or dark) with the required flavouring—garlic, paprika, onion, parsley, dill, etc.

When preparing a genuine Hungarian dish, finely chopped onion is first fried until golden or pale brown, and then paprika is added. The frying process releases flavouring substances (essential oils) and the heat produces an attractive red colour. These paprika-flavoured fried onions, often with the addition of green peppers and various seasonings, impart a basic flavour to the goulash, paprikash, porkolt and other typical Hungarian dishes. The use of various types of capsicum is characteristic of Hungarian cooking; a typical example is stuffed peppers with tomato, mushroom or dill sauce. Raw peppers are a popular food rich in vitamin C. But even though peppers and paprika are so extensively used in Hungary, it should not be assumed that they form part of every authentic Hungarian dish. There are many such dishes made without them, such as crisp roast sucking-pig, Transylvanian platter and white cabbage with tomatoes, amongst others.

Another characteristic feature of Hungarian cuisine is found in the actual cooking processes. The view is held that long, steady boiling or stewing of raw foods imparts an inimitable aroma and flavour which make the dishes attractive and appetizing. More often than not, the main course on Hungarian menus consists of a dish prepared in advance, and grills and similar dishes cooked just before they are required play a correspondingly less important part. A good example of this long slow cooking is the preparation of porkolt (braised meat). It is always made in the same way, regardless of the type of meat used—beef, veal, pork or mutton. Finely sliced onions are lightly browned in hot lard, paprika is added, then cut-up meat and salt to taste. The meat is then stewed slowly under cover in very little liquid. When it is half-cooked, tomatoes and sliced fresh green peppers are added and the stewing continues until the meat is tender. Cooking the meat in very little liquid produces a small amount of strong stock in which the flavour and aroma of the meat, fat, onions, paprika, peppers and tomatoes are combined. When properly prepared, a porkolt stimulates the appetite by its appearance, aroma and flavour.

Of course, Hungarian chefs have other flavouring substances at their disposal to produce tasty dishes. A mixture of finely chopped garlic and caraway seeds, for example, lends a characteristic flavour to goulash soup and many other dishes. The amount used is of decisive importance for the harmonious flavour of the dish; the right quantity of flavouring can enhance it, while too much will spoil it. The secret is to use just enough to bring out the basic flavour of the food.

Cream also plays an important part in Hungarian cooking, from soups right through to the sweet course. Fresh and sour cream are used both to flavour and to enrich dishes. The pleasant taste of sour cream combines harmoniously with onions and paprika in a large number of dishes, such as veal paprikash, paprika chicken.

The number of different soups is increasing rapidly. Their basic ingredients may be various vegetables, cereals, fish, meat, giblets, milk, wine or fruit. In the past a substantial thick soup formed an important part of the diet in Hungary, while in other countries soups were mainly light and intended as a means of stimulating the appetite only. There is still a large variety of substantial soups in Hungary and large platefuls are still served today. Some Hungarian soups could even be regarded as nourishing main courses.

Farinaceous foods have an important place in Hungarian cooking. A wide choice awaits the gourmet, from items made with simple noodle or potato paste to cakes and pancakes. The paste is used to make an immense variety of soup garnishes of different shapes—scrolls, squares, pellets and many others. As for the sweet course, there are some delicious creams such as chestnut cream and rainbow cream. Other rich sweets are nut desserts, chocolate baskets and Dobos slices. Yeasted goods such as dumplings with sabayon sauce, fritters or jam doughnuts are almost too substantial to be served as a sweet. The existence of so many variations and varieties is due to local differences.

Hungarian chefs set great store by garnish and decoration, for the dishes are intended to provide a feast for the eye as well as for the palate. A garnish which is both attractive to look at and edible can be made with a few simple ingredients—a lettuce leaf, sweet peppers, tomatoes, cream, paprika-flavoured fat, parsley, etc. The use of different ways of serving the various types of dishes is also of great importance. Goulash or fish soup, for example, is brought to the table in pots on small wrought-iron stands, while wooden platters are used for such dishes as beef steaks of various kinds, pork chops and fillets, and many others. Another example of originality in arranging food for the table is oven-baked whole Balaton fogas, which is placed on a dish in a semicircle with its tail pointing upwards and a piece of lemon in its mouth.

A large number of plants thrive on Hungarian soil. Lakes and rivers are alive with darting fish and forests abound in a wide variety of game. Domestic birds thrive on farms and the favourable climate and privileged geographical position have contributed to stocking Hungarian kitchens with the best raw materials. Foreign trade relations make possible the import of southern and exotic varieties of fruit and vegetables, squid, mussels, lobster, fresh and frozen fish and many other foodstuffs. With all these raw materials, Hungarian chefs can make tempting meals which satisfy even the most pampered gourmet. Hungarian wines with their fragrant bouquet, the appetising appearance of the dishes, courteous service and dashing gipsy music all help to heighten the pleasures of the table.

INDIA

Indian cookery owes its complexity to a wide variety of factors which have influenced its development over the centuries. The climate and customs of the country have, of course, played their part; the food habits of many nations have left their mark and, above all, the precepts of Hinduism and Islam, sometimes based on health considerations, have had a major influence on Indian cookery. Hindus are generally vegetarians; many do not even eat eggs, while Moslems are allowed to eat meat. In the various regions of the country the diet of the population is in strict accordance with ethnic and religious traditions.

Entertainment is generally lavish, both at family gatherings and on the occasion of religious festivals, weddings or receptions in honour of a distinguished guest. Men and women eat separately, seated on rugs. A wide range of cunningly flavoured regional dishes prepared by professional cooks is served in individual portions. Each guest is customarily given a dish with five small metal bowls arranged round it on banana leaves; the bowls contain the various accompaniments to the main dish. The tableware is changed for each course.

Strange as it may seem, Indian cooks never measure or weigh ingredients, but rely on judgment and experience. When making a curry, for example, each cook has his own recipe and uses the different spices to suit his taste. The curry powder sold in many countries is not used in India. Instead the various ingredients are ground separately into a paste with a little water on a curry stone for use on the same day. A good curry powder, in combination with ready-made curry paste if desired, provides a satisfactory alternative.

Apart from stimulating the appetite, curry is said to have a beneficial effect on the digestion. Some of its ingredients have carminative properties; one of them, tamarind, has a slight laxative action.

A classic curry contains the following ingredients:
    fat ('ghee', butter or margarine)
    garlic and onions—these are fried until lightly coloured, but not browned
    limes, tamarind, lemon juice or vinegar to provide acidity
    curry ingredients (or commercial curry powder)—coriander and cumin seed, chillies, mustard seed, ginger, turmeric
    coconut milk—this is made by boiling freshly grated coconut or desiccated coconut in water and extracting the liquid under pressure
    home-made sour curds or yoghurt

It is important to remember that curries should be simmered slowly to extract the full flavour from the ingredients. An Indian curry never contains apples, sultanas or almonds. Flour should never be used to thicken curry; if it is too thin, coconut milk is added to obtain the right consistency.

Patna rice is the best type to use as an accompaniment to curry. It should be served separately, not in the same dish. Curry is eaten with a dessert fork and spoon.

Apart from rice, the classic accompaniments are puppadums (savoury wafers) and chupatties (unleavened bread), chutney, pickles and sambals.

Sambals. These may be compared to hors d'oeuvre, but are served as accompaniments to a main dish. There are countless varieties of sambal.

Chutneys. These are freshly prepared when required. Their pungent flavour is obtained by the use of chillies. The ingredients are pounded in a mortar.

Chupatties. Various types of bread, leavened or unleavened, are eaten in India, forming an important part of the diet, second only to rice. Chupatties may be made of rice flour (in southern India) or wheat flour (in the north).

Samoosas. These are puffs containing different kinds of fillings; they are fried in hot fat. Travellers carry them when making a long journey.

Mulligatawny. In southern India, where food is generally more highly spiced than in the north, the word 'mulligatunny' means 'pepper water'. It is served with some types of curry. The mulligatawny soup served in European countries is of Anglo-Indian origin.

Pillaus (pilafs). These have always been very popular in Eastern cookery. A festival meal without a pillau is unthinkable for Moslems, who prepare this dish with consummate skill. It is a combination of rice and meat or poultry, cooked in fat and flavoured with spices, although there are regional and seasonal variations in the ingredients.

Meetais (sweets). These are not merely eaten for pleasure, but considered essential foods. When guests are invited to a party, they bring home-made sweets with them.

ITALY

Italy gave the other countries of Europe her style—that of the Renaissance. While the Renaissance mainly concerned the arts, architecture and the theatre, it also had an important influence on the manner of life, on fashion and cooking. One of the fullest manifestations of Renaissance civilisation, from the viewpoint of social intercourse, was the banquet.

Its origin dates back to ancient times. During the first centuries of the Roman Empire, when the arts and literature were triumphant, Rome had raised the tradition of banquets and feasts to a high level by transforming the simple meal of cold meat, cheese, olives and black bread (typical of the republican period) into a sumptuous ceremony during which the courses were punctuated by a variety of entertainment—mime, dancing, comic or tragic acting and sometimes even gladiator fights.

After a long interval this form of hospitality reappeared when, following the foreign invasions, feudal domains controlled by landed nobles became firmly established and the great families held receptions in their town residences or on their country estates. They revived and carried further the tradition of interspersing courses with long or short entertainments and lavishly decorating the table to delight the eyes of the guests. In this way the banquet developed into the present-day reception.

The Renaissance banquet brought about a change in rural habits and customs. Greater refinement was introduced in the use of table accessories (as strikingly demonstrated in the paintings of Mantegna) despite the absence of chinaware; forks and spoons were now considered obligatory; the table was covered with several cloths one on top of another, corresponding to the number of courses to be served. Later on napkins were introduced; they were artistically folded and provided additional table decoration.

Some features of the Renaissance banquet are seen in certain Italian present-day functions, such as those at which the princes of industry hold court; they are also called to mind by the pre-theatre gala dinners held on the occasion of state visits (at the Quirinal Palace, for example).

Society gatherings in the nineteenth century

The nineteenth century saw the rise of the middle class, which held the new-born industrial power in its hands. Its members aimed at becoming the leaders of fashion, displaying their wealth by means of social gatherings. They began to entertain at home; they formed groups and clubs which organised gatherings and social evenings frequented by the fashionable world. Guidance for such occasions was sought in a cookery book published in 1837, 'Cucina teorico pratica con corrispondente riposto ad apparecchio di pranzi e cene' by Ippolito Cavalcanti, Duke of Buonvicino, who lived on the fringe of the Bourbon royal court. The book contains valuable advice and sets out all the rules of private entertaining. In Naples the tradition described by Buonvicino has survived to some extent in the 'periodiche' (periodical 'at homes'). These are typical social evenings held regularly in middle-class and less well-to-do homes. The guests foregather round a buffet table holding local gastronomic specialities.

Informal entertaining at home

In Italy, as elsewhere, people enjoy dining out in congenial company. Before proceeding to the restaurant, the group of friends have a drink at the home of the person who suggested the outing. The bottles, glasses, ice cubes, mixing glass, etc. should be ready on a serving table.

While this is not a specifically Italian custom, there is something which has become very popular and would have been unthinkable a few years ago—the ritual of the midnight spaghetti supper after the theatre or a meeting. The invitation is usually issued on the spur of the moment.

The spaghetti are brought in from the kitchen already coated with sauce and sprinkled with cheese on individual plates, for the guests do not sit at a table, but round the room as they please. A glass of light red wine is served with the meal. A pound of spaghetti is sufficient for six persons. The spaghetti should be cooked 'al dente' in 5 l (about 9 pt) salted water. If possible the following sauces should be prepared in advance and kept in the refrigerator: garlic and oil, tomato, quick tomato. Sometimes the spaghetti may be seasoned with pepper.

Special parties

A special theme may be chosen for a party held at cocktail time.

Rustic buffet party. The buffet table is covered with a checked or hand-woven cloth. It holds pottery or wooden dishes containing the following items:

> a large piece of cheese (such as Parmesan);
> a few salami sausages (with knives);
> salads in season;
> artichokes in oil (canned), cepes (flap mushrooms) in oil (canned), and stuffed olives;
> raw vegetables (celery, fennel, etc.) with a sauce-boat of vinaigrette sauce for dipping;
> cheese board;
> country-style brown bread;
> a rustic dessert (apple or curd cheese tart, etc.);
> wines—red, white;
> liqueur—grappa.

Wild flowers and brightly coloured napkins add to the rustic atmosphere (paper napkins and containers should be avoided—they spoil the effect).

Cheese party. This may comprise the following:

> a selection of cheeses with brown and French bread, etc.;
> fresh fruit salad;
> wines—white (pinto gris) and, if possible, a selection of red.

Later in the evening, if the hostess wants her guests to stay on, vegetable soup (e.g. minestrone) or ravioli in tomato sauce may be served.

Ligurian buffet. There are many specialities suitable for a stand-up or sit-down buffet meal:

> focaccia Andrea Doria cut into squares or oblongs;
> vegetable pie ('torta di verdura');
> stuffed breast of veal ('cima alla genovese');
> stuffed courgettes, aubergines, celery and artichokes;
> stuffed peppers and tomatoes;
> tangerine or orange tart;
> wines—Portofino, Gavi, Cinque Terre or similar.

Country reception. Those who own a second home in the country often like to entertain their friends there. The important thing is to create a relaxed atmosphere in which everyone feels at ease. A sham rustic style should be avoided at all costs.

A good time for such a party is in the late afternoon, when the sun has lost much of its heat and the guests can enjoy the garden.

Many of the items for the buffet may be bought ready-made from the local suppliers (pork products, cakes and pastries, etc.). A suitable buffet might be made up as follows:

> a plentiful supply of fresh fruit (washed) in a decorative arrangement;
> a few fried specialities—cheese fritters, rice balls ('arancini');
> regional cakes and pastries;
> regional cheeses;
> pizza;
> sausages and ham;
> mozzarella in carrozza;
> local wines.

If the guests are to stay for the evening, a hot dish should be served at dinner-time (about 8 p.m.)—risotto country style or with flap mushrooms or polenta with chasseur sauce or mushrooms sprinkled with chopped parsley.

Traditional festivals

In Italy, as in other countries, the way of living has changed; family ties have slackened and the former ritual of family gatherings have been disrupted. Nevertheless, some traditions are still upheld.

New Year's Eve. Families still come together to celebrate New Year's Eve and traditional midnight supper parties are still held to see the New Year in, but this is a sad day for true gourmets, for nothing is well cooked in restaurants at this time.

Italians eat a dish of lentils to start the New Year, for lentils remind them of small coins—hence the saying 'Lots of lentils will bring lots of money in the New Year'.

Many families eat a different traditional meal consisting of:

> raw Parma ham, toast and butter;
> macaroni pie;
> orange salad with rum.

Epiphany (January 6th). Celebration of this festival is a French custom which has been adopted in Italy (twelfth cake).

Carnival (Shrovetide). Restaurants and hotels organising dinner parties on this occasion should provide a plentiful supply of carnival specialities. These generally consist of different types of fritters. In Naples carnival-time lasagne are eaten by everyone.

Easter. 'Natale coi tuoi, Pasqua con chi vuoi' (Christmas with your family, Easter with whom you please). There are no typical Easter parties as such, but the traditional Easter dish is roast lamb ('agnello') or kid ('capretto').

Easter Monday is the day for the first picnic ('pic-nic di Pasquetta'). The contents of the hamper include roast chicken, rolls, vegetable pies, cheese, frittata de spaghetti (pieces of omelette containing spaghetti in tomato sauce).

The vintage season. The friends of the fortunate owner of a country house await this season eagerly. An open-air reception is the most appropriate.

The following items may be served:

> grapes;
> biscuits for dipping in the wine;
> sugoli;
> wine from the estate.

All Hallows. This is a day for family gatherings. In Sicily, in particular, it is celebrated as a happy occasion, not a sad one. Special cakes and pastries are served. Sicilian pastrycooks make richly coloured marzipan figures ('pupi') representing the paladins of France, Charlemagne, blackamoors and warriors.

Martinmas (November 11th). 'Per San Martino, castagne e vino' (for Martinmas chestnuts and wine). Guests are entertained at home, in town or in the country; they sit round a fire over which chestnuts are roasted in a perforated frying pan (the chestnuts are first slit with a knife). A good wine (e.g. Chianti) helps to create a cosy atmosphere.

If no fire is available, the chestnuts are boiled in advance, 1 kg (2 lb 3 oz) in 4 l (7 pt) water with a little salt and a pinch of fennel seed.

Christmas. Panettone is without any doubt the traditional feature of the Christmas table.

JAPAN

The conditions set out below apply to any typical Japanese buffet or reception; western-style cooking in Japan and true Japanese cookery which is divided into various specialities, have nothing in common. This means that a Japanese chef with a western training cannot cook typically Japanese dishes and vice versa.

Receptions of all kinds are mostly held in hotels. The buffet is decorated with gigantic flower displays which, in their great variety, have made the Japanese art of flower arranging (ikebana) world famous. Very often, artistically carved ice figures provide additional decoration. In front of them, depending on the season, is a selection of the following on ice: smoked salmon or trout, raw fish (sashimi), finely cut and artistically arranged, and often sliced king-crab's legs which may be up to 2 m (6½ ft) long. Smoked salmon from Hokkaido is a very popular and much sought after delicacy. At any reception or buffet the guests can admire, not only the variety and choice of food, but also the original tableware (lacquer or china bowls, china spoons, artistically shaped and decorated earthenware dishes, etc.). The Japanese have an innate appreciation of food as a 'feast for the eye'. The arrangement of the various hors d'oeuvre for the table is almost a ritual in the Japanese cuisine.

At many buffet functions in Japan, at the host's request, typical speciality food bars are set up at a fixed price, serving such dishes as tempura, sushi, yakitori (grilled chicken on skewers) or onigariyaki. The latter consists of large prawns cut in half, marinated in soya sauce and grilled on skewers, or charcoal-grilled mussels flavoured with herbs. The guests are served at the various bars by chefs who specialise in preparing the foods concerned. This type of reception, where the food is cooked in front of the guests, has an atmosphere all its own and is particularly appreciated by foreign visitors. The dessert mainly consists of fresh fruit, which is cut up by the chefs ready for the guests to eat.

There are, of course, a good many variations. In addition to Japanese dishes, Chinese and Korean specialities are often served. An example of an original form of entertainment is found in the banquets held in tatami rooms on rice straw mats. The guests sit on the floor at small low tables. Part of the meal is already set out on these, and various courses are served later on by geishas or hostesses. Traditional dances and songs performed by the waitresses contribute to the festive mood.

The following are typical breakfast, luncheon and dinner menus:

Breakfast (A)

Kobachi	Cod's roe and radish salad
Tamagoyaki	Folded fried eggs
Takiawase	Braised fish and bamboo shoots
Yakinori	Dried laver
Akadashi	Tofu-miso soup
Gohan	Steamed rice
Kohnomono	Pickles
Ochya	Green tea

Breakfast (B)

Kobachi	Cucumber and crab salad
Yakimono	Baked salmon with boiled egg
Takiawase	Stuffed cabbage oden style
Hasaniage	Stuffed eggplant
Akadashi	Tofu-miso soup
Gohan	Steamed rice
Kohnomono	Pickles
Ochya	Green tea

Luncheon (A)

Sumashijiru	Clear soup
Oyakodonburi	Rice with chicken and egg
Kohnomono	Pickles
Ochya	Green tea

Luncheon (B)

Sumashijiru	Clear soup
Barazushi	Vinegared rice with fish and vegetables
Kohnomono	Pickles
Ochya	Green tea

Dinner (A)

Kozuke	
Taramabushi	Tuna-cod variety
Tsukuri	
Sashimi	Sliced raw fish
Yakimono	

Wakadori Tebayaki	Fried chicken with sesame seeds
Agemono	
Tempura	Mixed fry
Sunomono	
Kyurimomi	Cucumber salad
Mimono	
Awabi no Sobazuyuni	Boiled abalone
Suimono	
Sumashijiru	Clear chicken soup
Gohan	Steamed rice
Kohnomono	Pickles
Ochya	Green tea
Kudamono	Fresh fruit

Dinner (B)

Kozuke	
Tamago-Dofu	Egg royale
Tsukuri	
Sashimi	Sliced raw fish
Yakimono	
Buri No Teriyaki	Grilled yellow-tail
Agemono	
Tatsuta Age	Cut up fried chicken
Sunomono	
Kurage No Sanbaizu	Vinegar-seasoned eel-pout
Suimono	
Hamaguri No Ushio Jiru	Clam consommé
Gohan	Steamed rice
Kohnomono	Pickles
Ochya	Green tea
Kudamono	Fresh fruit

NORWAY

With its sweeping, dense forests, its fjords edged by romantic cliffs, its peaceful, remote lakes and majestic mountains, Norway is a source of delight to every nature lover and a haven of rest and relaxation for the weary. Anyone familiar with the splendours of her scenery, her hospitable people and their way of life, her writers, composers and painters is drawn back to her shores again and again. Nature plays an important part in Norwegian literature; the region of Gudbrandsdal, for example, provided the setting for Henrik Ibsen's *Peer Gynt*.

Norway's cuisine, which is old and rich in tradition, makes full use of the wide variety of natural produce available. The coastal areas are very fertile; the warm sea air, influenced by the gulf stream, creates favourable climatic conditions and in January the black earth is already ploughed up and prepared for sowing. Around Hardanger fjord in the south large fruit plantations yield excellent varieties. Vegetable growing is confined to the summer months, but at this time of year the hours of daylight are so long that everything may confidently be said to grow and ripen twice as fast as usual. Norwegian produce is largely free from chemical fertilisers; the springs are pure and unpolluted, so much so that spring water figures prominently among Norway's exports. Mountain streams, rivers, lakes and the sea provide an incredible abundance of fish and shellfish; in the forests the supply of game is inexhaustible. Where livestock is concerned, sheep-raising is widespread among the farmers. A much prized fruit of the Rubus family, the arctic cloudberry grows in Norway. It is similar to the raspberry, but orange in colour and grows only in Scandinavia. Norway also produces a variety of cheeses, including the typical 'gammel ost' (old cheese) which is not really an 'old' cheese but a young blue-veined cheese, the special mould for which is taken over from one batch to the next. It has a very strong odour and does not suit all tastes. Another variety is a special goat cheese made from the byproduct obtained when casein is precipitated from milk. Goat's cream is added and the mixture is boiled down until fairly thick and caramelised. This cheese has nothing in common with ordinary cheese production, for it contains little protein and does not undergo a ripening process. Its fat content may be as high as 45%. It is usually cut very thinly with a special slicer and eaten on Norwegian 'flat bread'.

The Norwegian housewife is faithful to the national culinary traditions, but hotel and restaurant meals are based on French cuisine. In their homes Norwegians practise the art of plain cooking, trying to preserve and enhance the natural flavour of the ingredients without excessive use of herbs or spices. Home entertaining is a particularly marked feature of the way of life and a friendship once made lasts a lifetime. Hospitality at home includes the pleasures of a festive, well-laden table. Norwegian housewives are adept at providing entertainment which makes a long winter evening round a cosy fire a truly enjoyable experience. The most important family celebrations are weddings, christenings and confirmations. A bereavement is also an occasion for bringing family and friends together in the home.

Norway's National Day

The main event in the culinary calendar is 17th May, Norway's national day. It is celebrated among family and friends either at home or in a restaurant. The salmon season opens at this time and the accent is on special salmon dishes. The accompaniments to poached salmon are parsley butter, Hollandaise sauce and cucumber salad. The favourite dessert is strawberries and cream. Midsummer Eve (24th June) and Olsok Day (29th July) are spent in holiday huts in the mountains or by the sea. Young and old alike celebrate these occasions round bonfires at a time of year when only a light dusk distinguishes night from day. By the sea, lamb is grilled or spit-roasted; the meat is particularly tender and savoury, very like French 'pre-sale'. A popular Norwegian speciality is 'Fenalar', consisting of salted, smoked, air-dried leg of mutton or lamb. It is carved into paper-thin slices and handed round at informal parties. The night of 7th to 8th August marks the opening of the crayfish season; hundreds of people come down to the shores of the lakes to await the event with gaily lit lanterns. But, despite the opening of the season, the law still prohibits the catching of crayfish under 9 cm (3½ in) and lobsters under 21 cm (8½ in) in length. The most popular way of serving crayfish is boiled in dill-flavoured court-bouillon with toast and butter mayonnaise. Shrimps are on sale all the year round. In September the lobster season replaces that of crayfish. At the same time elk and reindeer hunting begins, followed by the wild duck season. Another occasion for celebrations is Martinmas (11th November), the start of the goose season. Goose is served with apple stuffing, red cabbage, glazed chestnuts and red-currant jelly.

In December gourmets really come into their own. From 5th to 20th December the 'Julebord' (Christmas buffet), a national institution, provides a remarkable selection of hot and cold dishes, giving an ambitious, inventive chef ample scope to demonstrate his expertise and imagination. Although nutritionists are making an onslaught on dietary excesses of this kind, no one has yet succeeded in imposing any limitation whatsoever on the pre-Christmas festivities which take place in hotels and restaurants. On New Year's Eve Norwegians like to eat out and large banquets are held to celebrate the occasion. During the months ending in 'R' in Norwegian, a great deal of cod is eaten. Red wine is the drink with boiled cod. The meal ends with cheese or a cheese soufflé.

Easter is spent in the mountains or by the sea when summer huts and boats have to be put in good repair, a sign that spring is on the way.

Norway can still offer nature lovers an unspoilt countryside and quiet mountain valleys. How blissful it is to fish or roam at leisure, to see the midnight sun in the far North, to celebrate with friends, or to join in a hunting or shooting trip as the fancy takes us. Every season has much to offer and provides the visitor to Norway with an unforgettable experience.

RUMANIA

Rumania is a land of fertile plains and high mountain ranges, a land on the Black Sea, which is sometimes more intensely blue than the Mediterranean. At the mouth of the Danube where it enters the Black Sea is a region of solitude often glowing with all the colours of the rainbow, a paradise of wild birds. But Rumania is also the home of a nation which has never lost its sense of humour, even under the most adverse circumstances. Its love of life and its ironical turn of mind may best be seen from its proverbs. A highly typical example of these is 'It is better to lie drunk under the bed than ill inside it'.

The remote ancestors of the Rumanians were the Dacians, a pastoral people who inhabited Wallachia and the Carpathians and engaged in vine-growing long before Roman times. They were so fond of wine that their priests suggested to the legendary King Decebalus that all the vines should be destroyed, as his people were neglecting their religious duties on account of their wine-drinking. Needless to say, good King Decebalus did not take their advice.

In the second century A.D. Dacia was conquered by the Emperor Trajan. He gave the most fertile regions to the veterans of his army for their retirement and they settled in Wallachia and Transylvania, married pretty young Dacian girls, romanised the country and latinised the language. The Rumanian nation was born of the inter-mixture of Romans and Dacians, as a people with a love of life, easily moved, poetically minded and blessed with a hearty appetite.

Country wedding

There is no better opportunity of studying the Rumanian character and learning at first hand about Rumanian cooking than at a country wedding. The favourite month for weddings is October, when the weather is still certain to be clear and pleasant after the heat of summer. The wine is already casked, the Tsuiça (plum brandy) has been distilled, the pigs, geese and turkeys have been fattened, the maize and wheat are in the barns and everything is ready for the festive occasion.

A Rumanian country wedding lasts for three days, from Friday afternoon to midday on Monday. In Moldavia the bridegroom goes to the bride's home on the Friday afternoon to collect the presents, the dowry and the trousseau. The guests are all dressed in their finery and have taken their seats in wagons, the last of which is occupied by gipsies with their musical instruments. When they arrive at the farm where the bride lives, the wagons are loaded with mattresses, pillows (the richer the bride's parents, the more pillows are provided), pots and pans, embroidered cushions, icons and the various household requisites. Meanwhile, the musicians have installed themselves on the verandah of the farmhouse and have begun to play, sometimes just accompanying the 'strigature'. These are improvised four-line ditties making fun of the bride's parents, especially her father, and of everyone else who plays an important part at a wedding, not excluding the priest, who smiles affably behind his black beard. Sometimes the father starts crying, not because he is losing his daughter, but at the thought of having to part with a cow as part of the dowry.

The civil marriage takes place on the Saturday, the marriage service on the Sunday. The Saturday is also the day for preparations. Guests arrive, the tables are laid (always out-of-doors), the soup is made, pigs, geese and turkeys are slaughtered, the house is prepared for the newly-weds, and meanwhile the gipsies play continuously. There is dancing and drinking and everyone has a wonderful time. The climax comes on the Sunday; there are generally 60–70 wedding guests on this day, though even 100–120 are not uncommon.

The most important person at a wedding is neither the bride nor the bridegroom, but the latter's godfather. Wearing a white silk sash and a hat decked with flowers, he receives the guests at the gate. In his hand is a bottle or a carved wooden flask of Tsuiça and each guest takes a pull at it. The whole party escorts him to the church, followed by the gypsies, still playing. The marriage service is conducted according to the rites of the Orthodox Eastern Church. The young couple have golden crowns placed on their heads—in smaller villages the gold is often very faded—and then the priest takes their hands and dances 'Jeremiah's dance' with them, their parents and the godfather, three times around the saint's shrine.

At the end of the ceremony the gypsies are waiting outside the church and the whole party goes to the home of the bride's father, where the long tables are laid ready. In front of each guest's seat a warm welcome awaits him in the shape of ½ l (17½ fl oz) Tsuiça and 1 l (35 fl oz) wine. The wine is a rosé; though slightly sharp and a little turbid, as it is still young, it is very refreshing. The wedding meal traditionally includes giblet soup, mititei (small grilled sausages), piftie (pork brawn), roast goose and turkey, pickled vegetables, boiled eggs and black olives. The gypsies play throughout the meal and when the first stars appear in the sky everyone grows sentimental. At this point, the gypsy leader and his band take up position directly behind the young couple and play old ballads, the second violinist sings and everyone listens in silence. The newly-weds' mother and godparents are hard put to it to choke down their tears, but this is not enough for the gypsies, who play and sing long love ballads to the young couple until they have succeeded in bringing tears to the bride's eyes. And when she finally starts sobbing and lays her head on her husband's chest, the gypsies smile, for they have achieved their purpose. Now the bridegroom puts his arms round his young wife and follows the old tradition by taking her indoors to their marriage-bed. He has to hold his sobbing bride very tight—what a pleasure it is to be able to console her!

For the guests the party is not yet over. They eat, drink and dance till midnight. Next day at noon the young couple make their appearance to say goodbye to the guests (Illustration p. 463).

Festival in commemoration of the dead

This festival is celebrated in the spring in honour of the dead of past generations. The village women bring large baskets of eggs, bread and 'coliva' (see recipe) to the church. The priest conducts a special litany in honour of the dead and blesses the food. In the graveyard wine is poured on the graves. After this ceremony a meal is served for the whole village, including the poor, i.e. the gypsies of the surrounding countryside. The guests often sit at long tables set up alongside the church. The gypsies express their gratitude by playing music for dancing on the village green after the meal.

SPAIN

Spanish cuisine though it cannot claim to be as varied as that of France or even of Italy is certainly not as heavy as that of the Eastern European countries. Throughout Spain oil rather than butter is used for cooking. Each region of Spain has its own specialities and all regions have excellent sea food dishes. There are fish soups, main dishes, and the famous snacks—tapas—which are served throughout the day. Meal times in Spain are much later than in other countries. The two main meals are lunch which can be served any time from 1.30 to 3 p.m. and supper which is rarely served before 9.30 to 10 p.m.

Basque cooking

This is perhaps the richest and considered among the best in Spain. Beef which is not as popular as veal among the Basques can still be very good but their most popular dishes are based on fish or chicken rather than meat. The quality and the amount of fish available is second to none and the sea offers dozens of different kinds of shellfish, sardines, anchovies, bream, hake and tuna. A speciality of the region is salt cod with fresh tomatoes and a luxury winter dish consists of baby eels cooked whole and served in hot olive oil with garlic and hot peppers. Pulses form an important part of the Spanish diet and the Basques have a dish of white or red beans which are cooked with either a peppery red sausage called chorizo or a blood sausage.

In the Aragon region a special dish is lamb's head which is heavily flavoured with garlic and roasted for about two hours. In the mountain districts the lamb is especially fine and the local dish of lamb and red peppers is a delicacy.

Catalonia

This region is known for its many varieties of sauces, in some cases reminiscent of those of Provence. The most pungent is the ali-oli garlic sauce and there is a very hot red sauce—romesco—which is made with tiny red peppers.

Valencia

Valencia cooking has in the past been much influenced by the spices, exotic fruits and many other products of the East which were brought into Spain during the Moorish occupation. Valencia can boast a wide variety of sea food and fine vegetables and is famous as the region where paella first originated. This national dish is at its best when cooked in the open air over a wood fire giving off a most delicious aroma into the fresh air.

Andalusia

The region of fiestas, flamencos—produces some delicious hams and here again as in most of Spain fish plays an important part in the menus. All round the coast there is a wide variety of fish—sardines, bream, skate, whiting, tunny fish, prawns and squids. Many are cooked with rich sauces. Two soups of this region are melon soup which is drunk ice cold in summer and the famous gazpacho.

Galicia

Both sea and freshwater fish abound in this region and among them the best oysters in Spain. Eels, octopus and inkfish—the inkfish either cooked simply in a sauce made of their own ink or stuffed with chopped ham and onion. As in all Spain ham and sausages appear in many dishes. This fertile region produces chestnuts in abundance and excellent marron glacés are made.

Leon

The Leon region has a number of famous dishes. The roast sucking pig is one which can be found in some of the first-class restaurants of Madrid. Known throughout Spain and also in South America are the little cakes and biscuits of Astorga. This is a rich region of fertile land producing excellent game, fruit and vegetables and the rivers have a wealth of good fish.

There is an abundance of fruit throughout Spain. The quinces of Cordoba make excellent quince jelly and quince cheese. Almeria grapes are among the most succulent and in Aragon are such fruits as greengages, peaches, pears, apples, apricots, cherries, and strawberries.

SWEDEN

The Swedes are particularly fond of simple, informal gatherings. They like sitting round the table with a few friends to eat one of their excellent sandwiches, washed down with a glass of beer or wine, or to enjoy the pleasures of a 'smorgåsbord'. When drinking, they love to toast each other frequently, saying 'skål' as they do so. Whatever the occasion, this is a very pleasant way of doing honour to the juice of the grape, which has to be imported into Sweden.

At functions of some importance—larger dinner-parties, the celebration of special occasions such as a fiftieth birthday, etc.—there is an established ritual for drinking toasts. After welcoming all his guests, the host raises his glass and takes wine with each of them and also the lady occupying the seat of honour next to the host, after which they toast each other. Even if no words of welcome are spoken by the host, the guests do not raise their glasses until he has raised his to the lady occupying the seat of honour.

Other customs are closely linked with the calendar or religious festivals. Culinary specialities play an important part in the festivities. A few examples of such traditional Swedish foods are given below.

Christmas

Christmas is primarily a family festival and the meal served on Christmas Eve does justice to the occasion—three or four kinds of pickled herring, meat in aspic, liver pâté and meat balls, with red and green cabbage as accompaniments. A place of honour is occupied by the Christmas ham.

Like all Scandinavians, the Swedes have a passion for dried cod. This is a popular late supper dish on Christmas Eve, when it is eaten before retiring, accompanied by white sauce and boiled potatoes and followed by the traditional Christmas rice porridge.

On Christmas Day, more distant relatives often join the gathering round the family table. The meal begins with a sample of all the Christmas Eve dishes, specially set aside for this purpose. It continues with cabbage soup, usually made with ham broth. The sweet consists of left-over rice porridge mixed with whipped cream and served with thick raspberry jam.

Easter

The Easter table decorated with dainty mats, brightly coloured feathers and young birch shoots makes an effective setting for the many-hued Easter eggs. The predominant colours are blue and yellow. Boiled eggs are the main feature of the Easter meal, which also includes other egg dishes, salads and early vegetables such as fresh spinach or young nettles. Dinner very often begins with a slice of smoked salmon on toast, washed down with a glass of white wine.

After the Easter bonfire it is customary for friends to gather in small groups to drink an egg toddy, consisting of egg yolks, sugar, Cognac and boiling water. Each guest whips up the mixture in his glass until it is light and frothy. The fun of this operation, its simplicity and the pleasure of being in gay company make this drink a great success.

Midsummer's Eve and the midnight sun

The Swedes never miss their 'date' with the famous midnight sun, a splendid occasion which they celebrate with great rejoicing on Midsummer's Eve. The best place to see this festival is its birth-place, the region of Dalarna, or the island of Aland lying halfway between Sweden and Finland, where none of the authentic, old-time character of the festivities has been lost.

A month earlier the village boys and girls join in decorating the Midsummer's Eve tree with dyed sheep's wool, tissue paper and leaves. Just as the sun disappears on the horizon, only to reappear a few moments later, the tree is set up as a signal for the festivities to begin.

The guests sit round a richly laden table, out of doors. The main item is boiled salmon, served with various sauces such as Remoulade sauce and green mayonnaise. The dessert consists of a highly-prized speciality, Småland cheese cake served with whipped cream and thick raspberry jam.

A crayfish party

The Swedes are extremely fond of crayfish. Connoisseurs are said to prefer eating this delicacy out of doors under an August moon in the company of good friends. This no doubt explains why some slight breaches of good manners are permitted, such as using the fingers and making a characteristic sucking noise while eating.

The crayfish are boiled with dill and then left to cool in a cellar—this is essential to give them the strong taste of dill in which the Swedes delight. The crayfish course is followed by a hot dish—a meat gratin—and then by cheese and/or a dessert. The latter will consist of plum blancmange, once a very popular sweet and still considered as the proper ending to a crayfish party.

The drink usually served with crayfish is aquavit. This light fragrant spirit is drunk during the meal, in the middle of the toasts and songs.

Vicknings

After an evening's entertainment at a family party or a large public function, where the guests have eaten, drunk, danced and enjoyed themselves hugely, they discover at about midnight that they feel hungry again, in spite of the copious meal which they consumed only a few hours earlier. A host who is anxious to promote the physical wellbeing of his guests will be mindful of this fact and arrange for a so-called 'Vicknings table' to be provided in good time. At a family gathering this is often just a 'hangover breakfast' with aquavit, beer and strong coffee to round it off. At festivities organised at some distance from a town, which are a less frequent occurrence, the guests are served in most cases with a large cup of broth and cheese patties in addition to the traditional 'vicknings' dishes before starting on the journey home through the cold winter night.

The number and type of 'vicknings' dishes varies according to local circumstances and the size and nature of the gathering. At large receptions or similar functions a special buffet is generally set up with a wide choice of foods. At a family gathering one or two dishes are usually sufficient. All the dishes served on this occasion have one thing in common—their salty taste.

Typical 'vicknings' dishes include the following: herring au gratin, and various other herring dishes; Jansons' temptation; baked herring with butter, chopped eggs and chives; thinly sliced marinated salmon with creamed potatoes; marinated salmon and scrambled egg; pytt i panna (Swedish hash); hot sausages with potato salad; small fried sausages; cold meats; cheese board. A very popular dish is Parisian smörgås (hot minced meat sandwich) served with a fried egg.

In course of time the habit of having a glass of aquavit and a snack before a meal also became popular in the towns. Before sitting down to the actual meal, the first port of call of the male guests was the room where a small table awaited them, laden with pickled salt or marinated herrings, well-matured cheese, bread and butter, a few potatoes boiled in their jackets and—most important of all—a carafe of aquavit. The guests did not care whether any special culinary delights were in store for them after their appetizers and drink—or drinks. They all ate and drank without bothering to wonder whether it was good for them or not. Before long, middle-class restaurants introduced a 'permanent aquavit table' for their patrons. The range of snacks available was constantly enlarged, and soon included not only herring specialities and cheese, but also home-made sausages and pork specialities and small warm dishes, 'småvarmt', and herring au gratin. The centrepiece of the table was an impressive drinks dispenser with four taps for various well-known types of aquavit. Guests helped themselves to food and drink and paid a fixed price appropriate to those days.

Instead of this self-service arrangement, better class restaurants served their patrons at the table with various combinations of traditional hors d'oeuvre or choice delicatessen, either followed by other courses or not. One combination was always found—cheese, bread and butter and herring specialities, with the peculiar name 'SOS'. This was served with well chilled aquavit, first a glassful $7\frac{1}{2}$ cl ($\frac{1}{8}$ pt), then sometimes an extra half glass 4 cl ($\frac{1}{16}$ pt).

This 'smorgåsbord', which was quite modest in quantity and quality, developed over the years into the 'stora smorgåsbord' (large 'smorgåsbord') which is still popular today. In the reception-rooms at large hotels and restaurants, in railway station waiting-rooms, on passenger ships and in catering establishments at winter and summer resorts, there is always a large 'smorgåsbord' with its countless classic and regional specialities. On Sundays and public holidays the large establishments recommend their 'stora smorgåsbord' as a family meal, mainly between 1 and 6 p.m. The self-service system naturally has great advantages as regards the general organisation of the meal, since empty dishes can be replaced very quickly and the overall aesthetic effect is not spoilt. People who, in our modern age, value a healthy diet in accordance with the principles of nutrition can easily find the foods that suit them best among the wide selection available. In this respect, too, the traditional 'smorgåsbord' is keeping up with the times.

Swedish 'smorgåsbord'

The Scandinavian custom—particularly prevalent in Sweden—of having a few appetizers and a glass of aquavit before a meal dates back countless years. The main ingredients are bread and butter, herrings in various marinades and strong cheese, accompanied—last but not least—by one or two glasses of neat spirits. Although other countries have their traditional hors d'oeuvre, the difference is that in Sweden they are no longer just snacks to whet the appetite, but have developed into a proper meal.

Like the rest of Scandinavia, Sweden was once a country of farmers and fishermen; these were the chief occupations. As was the general practice at the time, Swedes produced most of the food they required themselves. In Sweden, as elsewhere, many of the present-day eating habits date back to a time when northern Europe was still a blank on the gastronomic map as far as tourist traffic was concerned. Chance visitors found Swedish manners and customs highly unusual, but the impressions which the traveller gained on these journeys, which must have been extremely tiring, did give him some idea of a natural, simple, even robust type of hospitality. Culinary influences from abroad, especially from France and the southern countries, were mainly confined to the ruling classes and diplomatic circles. But inevitably, immigrant craftsmen and commercial agents, a large number of whom came from Germany, brought their eating and drinking habits with them and made their contribution to Swedish cooking.

Swedish 'smorgåsbord' probably goes back to the time when it was Sweden's ambition to play a leading part in European history. During their marches from the Baltic to the East, most of the soldiers recruited from among the peasants had ample opportunity to observe the manners and customs of other countries and to become familiar not only with their food, but also with their attitude towards alcohol. It is quite possible that these often rough experiences were gradually adapted to conditions at home and became part of the Swedish way of life as time went by. Nowadays a 'smorgåsbord' set up at home is still the central feature of any festivity, especially in the country. The custom, followed at almost all festive gatherings, of 'knocking back' the first drink is also based on an ancient tradition.

The Swedish winter is severe, especially in the northern provinces; the days are short and it is often bitterly cold. On the rare occasions when friends and relatives pay a visit, their host has ample opportunity to entertain them in the traditionally generous manner.

The ingredients for a 'smorgåsbord' naturally depend on seasonal availability. Apart from this, there are some variations between northern and southern Sweden and also at special holiday times. On a Sunday before Christmas, for instance, the traditional 'smorgåsbord' is made up as follows.

On a smaller table in front are placed several kinds of bread, butter, about three varieties of cheese, including Edam, a strongly flavoured and a mild cheese of top quality, sweet-and-sour pickled herring, matjes herring in sour cream with capers, Chef's pickled herring in the jar, pepper herring, herring in dill, herring in sherry, curry herring, sardines in oil or tomato sauce, gaffelbitar, mustard herring, herring au gratin, various Baltic herring dishes, boiled potatoes, etc.

On the main table the dishes include:

marinated salmon with scrambled egg;
marinated buckling fillets with chopped parsley and chopped egg;
salmon mayonnaise with tomatoes and cucumber;
prawn pyramids;

smoked eel;
eel cooked with dill and vegetables;
home-made liver pâté;
home-made liver sausage;
pressed beef with pickled tomatoes;
brawn;
foreloin of pork with prunes;
roast spare ribs of pork with apple salad;
roast beef with pickles;
roast veal garnished with cucumber and tomatoes;
roast mutton with Remoulade sauce;
spring chicken in aspic with garnish;
cold capercailzie with ham and fruit;
home-made Cognac sausage;
various salads.

The imagination may be given free rein in devising a wide variety of other dishes.

The 'småvarmt' (warm table) includes the following:

small meat balls fried in butter (kottbuller);
fried sausages;
smoked salmon with egg custard;
morels, chanterelles and field mushrooms with cream sauce served in
    croustades;
fine ragouts of various kinds, browned;
omelettes filled with asparagus, spinach, ham, prawns or crab meat, country
    style (flat) omelettes;
vegetables in season prepared in many different ways.

In summer there is a preponderance of fresh salad, raw or cooked vegetables, marinated or cooked fish of all kinds and shellfish.

Because of the custom of starting off at the small table with the herring specialities and drinking the first glass of aquavit there this table is placed in front, close to the entrance. The long sides of the main table are reserved for the various cold dishes, which are never over-garnished and are mostly home-made. The appropriate salads, marinated vegetables, sauces and relishes are arranged between the dishes. On both sides there are some hot-plates with small warm dishes. Over the years the 'småvarmt' has become so much part of the Swedish way of life that every guest expects to find it. The quality of an authentic, traditional 'smorgåsbord' lies in the fact that many of the sausage and meat products are home-made and do not give the impression of having been commercially manufactured or canned.

The end of the table is taken up by various cheeses—Camembert, Brie, Roquefort and Swedish varieties—together with crackers, black bread, biscuits, a variety of fresh fruit and sometimes fruit salad. The person responsible for the whole 'smorgåsbord' is the 'kallskankan', the cold table supervisor; her knowledge and ability are very important for this specialised type of work.

In other countries there are many restaurants offering a Swedish 'smorgåsbord', where patrons can eat their fill at a fixed price, but they have never achieved the authentic style of the original.

SWITZERLAND

The puritanical background to Swiss life for many years affected the part women played in society. Many festivities were and in some cases still are confined to men only. Today many Swiss homes have introduced the American style of self-service into their entertaining and hot and cold buffets—sometimes with exotic dishes— are the most popular. Many Swiss specialities can be introduced into such a buffet.

In home entertaining the salad today has become an important part of the meal taking the place of hors d'oeuvre. It is often of crisp raw vegetables. A small party among friends would very likely have the traditional Fondue as a dish and fondues can vary from region to region. Raclette, another speciality, has its place at home or in the small mountain restaurants of the Valais where it is cooked to perfection.

Festivities in Switzerland are many and varied and one of the many standard dishes is the jambon en croûte which is served with an assortment of salads.

One of the traditional festivities is the Harvest Festival of the Bernese Emmenthal. On the table decorated for the occasion are the home-baked plaited tresses of bread. Shining brown and rich in butter and eggs these attractive loaves are a tradition in the farms of the region. Usually the party begins with a pork and veal stew. Real beef soup with finely cut slices of pancake can precede or follow the stew. The well-known Berner dish, Berner Platte, consists of a bed of fresh beans (in summer) or sauerkraut (in winter) on which are placed smoked meats, sausages and often slices of beef used in the soup. The sweet to complete the meal consists of a mound of whipped cream framed by meringues. The coffee is accompanied by a quantity of spirit—usually kirsch.

Another festival in the canton of Fribourg is the Benichon. Originally a religious festival it still today is an important ceremony paying due tribute to the fruits of the earth—blending the plains and the mountains. Famous is the mustard of Benichon which is served with spiced pears and cooked wine. The meal usually begins with a rich bread made in a flat cake shape. It is very fragrant and coloured with saffron. It is served with Benichon mustard and a lump of butter and is fol- lowed with soup garnished with vegetables and marrow bones. A different kind of flavour for a lamb stew is given with large Devia grapes with apple purée and pears caramelised in their own juice. Before going on to the next part of the meal comes a beautiful 'eau de vie' made from fresh apples and then follows ham, saucisson, cabbage and beans. The lamb returns as a leg with garlic potato purée and beetroot salad. Finally there are cheeses—the incomparable Gruyère and the Vacherin, followed by a wealth of desserts—saucers of cream, meringues, mulberries, fritters, croquettes and aniseed cakes. Wines served include the Mon-sur-Ralle, Vully, Fendant of the Sion vineyards, Pinot Noir of the Valais and the Red Faverges of the canton of Fribourg. The meal ends with coffee laced with the 'eau de vie' of the region.

TUNISIA

In general Tunisians eat a great deal, but they eat well and, in some regions, especially in the capital, the art of fine cooking is highly developed. There is what amounts to an unwritten code of gastronomy with its own specific rules of conduct.

If a visitor is invited to a meal by a Tunisian, there is always a possibility of his disliking some of the dishes although he enjoys most of them. In this case, he should try to forget his own eating habits completely and remember what a great honour it is to be invited to a Tunisian's home for a meal. This is not just a polite gesture, but the expression of an attitude of mind, upbringing, and religion according to which everyone is in duty bound to invite a stranger to his table and, if necessary, give him shelter.

For a Mohammedan his home is sacred and inviolable. Consequently any violation involving even the humblest home has been severely punished from time immemorial. Yet a traveller from abroad is welcome in every home and the female members of the household, who keep in the background, take pains to send the best possible dishes to the dining-room for the guest's entertainment. It is the master of the house who entertains the guests, and his wife and daughters are not allowed to be present. Of course, this is not an invariable rule; in a modern household, especially in the towns, the lady of the house may be present. Such cases are still exceptional, however.

Every major event in Tunisian private and religious life has a culinary aspect. For example, the consumption of fish under certain conditions is believed to have a beneficial effect. On the other hand, for hygienic reasons connected with the hot climate of almost all the Mohammedan countries, their religion strictly prohibits the consumption of pork in any form, so that the use of pork in the home is absolutely out of the question.

In Tunisia, family events are occasions for celebration, just as they are all over the world. In addition, Islam provides many opportunities for festive gatherings (for instance, Ramadan and Mouled). It should be borne in mind that Tunisia has been in the process of developing from a feudal state into a modern country for little more than twenty years; this development has by no means been completed. Incidentally, it has only begun to attract tourists in recent years. For all these reasons, apart from any others, receptions and festivities in Tunisia have a character of their own and cannot be compared with those in other countries. Official receptions do, it is true, provide foreign visitors with an opportunity of tasting Tunisian specialities, but these are adapted to suit the visitors' tastes and have generally been prepared without the pungent spices which are so popular with Tunisians. This does not hold true of private entertaining, however. In this case the host entertains his guests in his own home, where they gather round the family table to enjoy the classic and regional specialities. The various dishes are all brought to the table at the same time. They are nearly always dressed with a sauce.

In the modern cities of Tunisia it is quite customary for men and women to sit round the same table to eat the dishes prepared by the lady of the house. It is well known that Islam prohibits the consumption of wine and other alcoholic drinks. But it is quite possible anywhere to be a believer without observing all the precepts of religion. This applies equally to Tunisia, where many people are by no means averse to drinking a little glass of the good local wine on festive occasions. While the consumption of wine is beginning to gain ground a little, it is still limited. Wine is primarily intended for export and is rarely found on the table at an every-day meal in a Tunisian home.

Tunisia, lying in the centre of the Mediterranean basin, has had to submit to a great many conquerors, each having his own culture and eating habits. The fact that the Tunisian cuisine was able to assimilate all these widely different eating habits has made it extremely varied and interesting. Yet it is neither definitely oriental nor European, but a synthesis of several different cultures, with the original national cuisine predominating. As a general rule, the ordinary menu consists of two dishes though it may consist of one dish only or sometimes of several, for example a farinaceous dish, a sauce, and a selection of hors d'oeuvre. Hors d'oeuvre are not served as appetisers, but are eaten throughout the meal.

The principal foods are much the same throughout the country, with only a few regional variations. But apart from the dishes which are common to the whole country, each region has its own specialities.

Soups

There is a wide variety of soups in Tunisia, but they are only served during the winter, that is to say, the first three months of the year. As in most Tunisian dishes, tomatoes are used to give a red colour.

The two commonest soups are 'leblabi' and 'medamess' (or 'mdamess'). 'Leblabi' is made with well-soaked chick-peas boiled in the water used for soaking, flavoured with harissa and other spices, and served with olive oil poured on top. 'Medamess' is prepared in the same way with broad beans instead of chick-peas.

Pâtés and briks

Home-made pâtés, consisting of meat or poultry mixed with vegetables and eggs and flavoured with cheese, are called 'tajine'; this is the name of the dish in which they are cooked. They are always a welcome addition to the menu, especially the delicate tasty pâté known as 'tajine malsouka', which is wrapped in paper-thin pastry before baking. 'Malsouka', the preparation of which requires great skill, is also used in making the famous 'briks'. Tunisian eggs or briks eaten in this way taste delicious.

Hors d'oeuvre

As a Tunisian meal does not consist of courses arranged in any particular order, all the dishes, including the hors d'oeuvre, are served at the same time. The latter comprise all kinds of raw vegetable salads, as well as appetisers such as olives, small bowls of tunny or other fish flavoured with 'harissa', and olive oil to be used by the guests with the various dishes according to individual taste.

Fish

Tunisia has a total coastline of 750 miles. Accordingly, large quantities of fish of all kinds are caught and eaten. Shellfish are not greatly liked; in view of refrigeration problems, they are virtually unknown outside the towns. As they deteriorate even more quickly than other types of fish, they cannot be transported over long distances in very hot weather. Tunisians are very spoilt where fish is concerned and therefore take very little interest in shellfish.

Fish is fried, grilled or used in couscous, which is eaten all the year round. On the islands of Djerba and Kerkenna, where fish is sold by auction, it is the population's staple food. But it is popular everywhere and is found on the humblest tables just as it is on those of the nobility and in luxury hotels. It is imagined to have a beneficial effect and the custom is for bride and bridegroom to step over a large fish on the morning after their wedding. This is supposed to protect their home.

Couscous

The dish which plays the most important part in the Tunisian menu, their famous couscous, has crossed every frontier and made conquests everywhere. It is generally made from semolina but maize meal and barley may be used. Couscous has to be steamed, not cooked over direct heat. This means that special utensils are required for its preparation. The stockpot in which the meat and vegetables are cooked is called the 'marga' and forms the lower half of the steamer. The top half is the perforated colander which allows steam to escape.

Couscous is served in a large dish, topped with choice pieces of meat and garnished with vegetables, and is eaten all the year round. Monotony is avoided by varying the accompaniments constantly: these may be mutton as in the dish chakchouka or tripe, poultry or fish, or vegetables alone. In the spring, fresh buttermilk—often supplemented with a piece of melon—is a popular accompaniment for couscous made either of fine semolina or of coarse barley.

The best beverage to accompany couscous is a Tunisian wine, such as Rossel rosé, Koudiat or Thibar, an excellent wine. Couscous cooked by steaming only and eaten with icing sugar, fresh milk, dates and dried fruit is another favourite dish (mesfauf). Tunisians serve it for their Ramadan night supper after the traditional festivities are over. For Tunisians couscous is a sign of plenty and well-being. In country districts, couscous is always served at weddings with spit-roasted mutton.

Sauces

There are many different sauces in Tunisia, at least as many as there are vegetables, of which there is certainly no shortage. Owing to the Mediterranean climate, there are crops of fresh vegetables all the year round. There are sauces with potatoes or peppers of all kinds, as well as with okra; savoury or semi-sweet American style sauces; red tomato sauces and white sauces prepared in the French or Spanish manner.

A distinction should be made between sauces containing meat, poultry or fish in addition to vegetables and those which have a special name of their own.

Fruit

Tunisian fruit is of exceptional quality. As it can ripen in the sun, it is juicy and has an excellent flavour. There are oranges, clementines, fresh dates and superb grapes, as well as plums, pears, peaches, apples, figs, blackberries, prickly pears and melons, especially the large thirst-quenching water-melons. These are served sliced and chilled in restaurants as an accompaniment to a Tunisian meal.

Sweets

Sweets are extremely popular in Tunisia. They are eaten every day, though there are some specialities which are reserved for holidays. Flour confectionery items include almond, walnut and date cakes, which are either soaked in syrup or honey or else eaten dry. These delicate cakes are usually small. They are made in every conceivable shape to please the womenfolk and children. Although weddings and holidays naturally provide the best opportunity for eating these delicacies, they are obtainable from any pastrycook. There is one, however, which is not on sale— 'assida', a simple cream made with flour or pine kernels and decorated with confectioner's custard and dried fruit. It is an indispensable item for the Mouled festival (the Prophet's birthday). Housewives begin preparing it in the early hours of the morning, as it is customary to send some to friends and relatives.

Anyone who is in Tunisia on the day of the Mouled festival will see men and children in the streets carrying baskets made of dwarf palm leaves and containing 'assida' for friends or relatives. They will feel flattered if a visitor asks to taste their 'assida'.

Dried fruit, almonds, roasted chick-peas and peanuts are popular for nibbling at any time of the day.

Beverages

Tunisians drink water with their meals; mineral water is also frequently served. Water is healthy and simplifies the serving of a meal. Wine is a highly-valued export. At the end of the meal, Tunisians may drink a glass of mint tea, often a cup of coffee, which is made individually for each person. Liquid refreshment is taken at any hour and the precepts of hospitality require a host to offer his guest something, however short the visit. Coffee and tea are imported. There is one beverage in Tunisia which is typical of the country, even though it is not drunk by everyone. This is 'bsissa', made with roasted ground chick-peas and grains of wheat, which are steeped in water and then removed. 'Bsissa' is supposed to have a cleansing effect on the body and to give women a beautiful complexion. The ancient gods on Olympus, it is said, already quenched their thirst with 'Bsissa'.

'Boukha' is a national liqueur and an excellent aperitif distilled from figs and raisins. It is drunk neat. This is a dry liqueur not at all unlike marc-brandy. It is served with a wide variety of dishes, for instance boiled chick-peas or broad beans, whiting, cod, fried red mullet, salad in vinegar dressing, bitter oranges, flans, hard-boiled eggs, and peppers. Apart from 'boukha', there is a very good nut liqueur which has a softer, milder flavour.

JEWISH CUISINE

Many nations have a distinctive and different cuisine, which is what makes the study of national foods and eating habits so fascinating. India, China, Italy and Germany spring immediately to mind when one is thinking of a 'national cuisine'. France is in a unique position since, being the home of western gastronomy, many French dishes have become international and their origins are less geographically obvious.

Jewish catering—or Jewish cuisine—is also international, but for different reasons. It is not based upon any particular nation, nor on any particular geographical area; its origins lie in the complicated dietary laws of a religion which is worldwide. It would be a mistake to imagine that all Jews observe all these laws all the time, since the degree of observance varies widely but, nevertheless, a distinctive culinary tradition has evolved from the need to cater within these restrictions.

The way in which this is achieved varies widely. It is fairly obvious that the food of Jews in the north of Poland will be quite different from the food of Jews in Morocco or Cyprus. In fact, however strictly the dietary laws are observed, the resultant food will also reflect the climate, the availability of ingredients, and the local customs of the area where it is prepared and eaten.

For practical purposes 'Jewish food' as that term is generally interpreted, has derived mainly from colder climates (or, to be more precise, from the Ashkenazic Jews of central and northern Europe) since its main characteristics are generous quantities of—usually hot—substantial food, which is nevertheless both appetising and subtle in flavour.

It is important to distinguish between 'Jewish food' and 'Kosher food'. Jewish food means only that the food is traditionally Jewish, as described above, and this is the type of food listed as Jewish in this book. Challah, gefilte fish, kreplach and latkes are all typically Jewish dishes. 'Kosher' is something quite different. The word means literally 'fit' or 'proper' but when applied to food it means 'prepared according to Jewish dietary laws'. These laws are lengthy and fairly complex, but are only of concern to those wishing to observe the Jewish faith, or those interested in Judaism.

For students of food, the most important rules can be summarised as:

1. Only meat or by-products from four-footed, cloven-hooved animals which chew the cud can be used, and then only if the animal is slaughtered according to the religious ritual of the Jewish faith.

2. During preparation, all blood must be removed from the meat as far as possible, and the meat should stand in salt for an hour, and be soaked in water for half an hour.

3. Creatures that crawl are taboo.

4. Birds of prey and wild fowl also are taboo.

5. Shellfish are taboo.

6. Only fish with fins and scales may be eaten.

7. Meat and milk or dairy products may not be eaten within six hours of each other and different utensils should be used for the storage, cooking and serving of meat and dairy produce.

In practice meals in Jewish homes are either 'meat meals' or 'fish meals' (as are meals at functions) and most Jewish restaurants do not serve any dishes involving milk or other dairy produce, which explains the Jewish predilection for taking black tea with lemon, since this, or black coffee, can be taken after a meat meal.

As well as explaining why pork and pork products are taboo, the dietary laws also explain why milk and cream play a relatively insignificant part in Jewish cuisine, since dishes containing dairy foods can only be served at a non-meat meal. Chicken fat is a common substitute for lard in many recipes and a Jewish goulash will differ from a Hungarian goulash because the latter contains sour cream. In spite of these restrictions, however, Jewish cooking is flexible and readily adapts and adopts recipes from other sources. Jewish pizza and Jewish sweet-and-sour fish are both perfectly feasible.

For many centuries, Jews were amongst the poorer sections of whatever community they settled in, and this too is reflected in many traditional Jewish recipes which produce appetising and sustaining dishes from relatively cheap ingredients.

Cooking and eating have always played an important part in Jewish life and Jews tend to hold and attend many parties and functions. One occasion peculiar to Jews is the Bar mitzvah, a ceremony which occurs when a Jewish boy attains the age of thirteen, and is counted as a man in religious affairs. It is almost always followed by a party—at which a meal of many courses is usually served. Jewish hosts are extremely generous; they usually provide plenty of food and drink and guests are constantly urged to eat and drink a little more. (Consumption of alcohol at Jewish functions is less than would be the case at an equally lavish Gentile affair, however.) For a guest not to eat a little too much is sometimes thought to be an adverse reflection upon the quality of the refreshment provided by the host—but no Jewish host would be happy to provide anything less than too much!

RECIPES

BASIC PREPARATIONS
(Fonds de Cuisine)

The recipes in this section have two aspects. First they represent a degree of elementary skill and elementary knowledge without which more elaborate recipes should not be attempted. Secondly they are what professional chefs know as 'mise-en-place', that is to say basic preparations which are normally prepared in bulk and kept on hand to be used in the creation or construction of other dishes. Thus, in a professional kitchen, these basic preparations are thought of as ingredients rather than dishes, and a chef making for example, a cold chicken pie would not need to make the jelly or the pastry just for that dish, since these would be part of the normal mise-en-place.

STOCKS AND MARINADES

Stock is one of the most important ingredients in many 'wet-cooked' dishes and without good stock it is impossible to achieve good results. It follows, therefore, that care should be taken when making stocks and that the ingredients should be of good quality. Stock should simmer gently since vigorous boiling will result in a cloudy stock and, generally speaking, stock is seasoned only lightly (if at all) since it may need to be reduced before being used.

Marinades are used both to impart flavour to meat and to tenderise it. It is for the latter reason that they always contain an acid ingredient, usually wine, lemon juice or vinegar.

White stock

Yield: 2 litres (3½ pints)   Cooking time: 4–5 hours

2 kg	beef bones	4 lb
100 g	leeks	3 oz
200 g	carrots	6 oz
200 g	onions	6 oz

100 g	celery	3 oz
	1 clove garlic	
	1 bouquet garni	
3 l	water	5 pt

Chop the bones and bring slowly to the boil with the water, skimming frequently. (Add a little cold water occasionally, in order to slow down the process, and help to expel the scum more thoroughly.) Add the chopped vegetables, garlic and bouquet garni and simmer slowly for 4 to 5 hours, skimming as necessary. Strain into a clean cold pot and carefully remove all the fat from the top.

Brown stock

Yield: 2 litres (3½ pints)   Cooking time: 5–6 hours

2 kg	beef bones	4 lb
100 g	pork rind	3 oz
200 g	carrots	6 oz
200 g	onions	6 oz
100 g	celery	3 oz
25 g	fat	1 oz
	1 clove garlic	
	1 bouquet garni	
3 l	water	5 pt

Chop the bones into small pieces, wash and chop the vegetables. Cook the bones, vegetables and pork rind through the oven with the fat until brown. Place in a large pot and bring slowly to the boil, add the bouquet garni and garlic and simmer gently for 5 to 6 hours. Strain into a clean cold pot and carefully remove all the fat.

Chicken stock

Yield: 2 litres (3½ pints)   Cooking time: 3 hours

2 g	raw chicken bones and/or giblets	4 lb
200 g	carrots	6 oz
200 g	onions	6 oz
100 g	leeks	3 oz
100 g	celery	3 oz
	1 clove garlic	
	1 bouquet garni	
3 l	water	5 pt

Bring the bones or giblets slowly to the boil skimming well. Add the chopped vegetables and simmer gently for 3 hours. Strain into a clean cold pot and carefully remove all fat.

Game stock

Cooking time: 1½–2 hours

500 g	game bones and scraps (hare, roe deer, wild rabbit, pheasant, etc.)	1 lb
1 l	brown stock	1¾ pt
1 dl	white wine	⅙ pt
	1 medium carrot	
	half an onion	
	1 parsley root	
	1 sprig thyme	
	a quarter of a bay leaf	

Chop up the bones and scraps finely and dice the carrot and half onion. Spread on a buttered roasting-tin, add the bay leaf, thyme, and parsley root and roast in the oven until lightly browned. Pour off the fat, transfer to a large stew pan, rinse out the tin with the white wine, scraping well to dissolve the caramelised residue, and pour into the pan. Add the brown stock, together with a crushed tomato if desired. Season very lightly with salt, simmer gently, then pass through a conical strainer and remove the fat.

France

Veal stock

Yield: 2 litres (3½ pints)   Cooking time: about 3½ hours

1 kg	knuckle of veal	2¼ lb
500 g	gelatinous veal bones	1 lb
600 g	shoulder of veal	1¼ lb
100 g	fresh pork skin	4 oz
	set chicken giblets	
300 g	onions	¾ lb
300 g	carrots	¾ lb
	1 bouquet garni	
	2 cloves of garlic	
20 g	fat	1 oz
10 g	salt	½ oz
3 l	water	5¼ pt

Tie the shoulder of veal, saw up the knuckle and chop the bones into small pieces. Dice the pork skin and the vegetables coarsely. Roast all these ingredients in the oven for about 20 minutes, or until the bones and meat are browned. Pour off the fat, pour in the water, boil up, then transfer to a large stew pan, add the salt, garlic and bouquet garni and simmer gently, skimming continually. When the meat is cooked it may be removed and used elsewhere. Strain the stock, allow to stand for a while, then remove all fat and adjust the seasoning, but be sparing with the salt so that the stock may be boiled down if necessary. If the yield is more than 2 litres (3½ pints) reduce to this quantity. Strain through a cloth. The liquid should be clear, pale brown and free from fat. It should set to a jelly when cold.

France

Fish stock

Yield: about 2 litres (3½ pints)   Cooking time: 30–40 minutes

500 g	white fish-bones (from sole, whiting, turbot or pike-perch)	1 lb
	1 small bouquet garni	
100 g	sliced onions	3 oz
50 g	mushroom peelings	1½ oz
	10 peppercorns	
4 dl	white wine	⅔ pt
	juice of half a lemon	
2 l	water	3½ pt
12 g	salt	½ oz

Wash and chop up the bones and place in a pan with the other ingredients. Cook slowly for 30–40 minutes and strain, first through a conical strainer and then through a cloth.

France

Red wine marinade

½ l	red wine	¾ bottle
	1 measure brandy	
125 ml	olive oil	¼ pt
	½ clove garlic	
120 g	onions	4 oz
120 g	carrots	4 oz
120 g	celery	4 oz
	1 sprig thyme	
	1 crushed bay leaf	
	12 crushed peppercorns	

Finely chop or mince all the vegetables and mix all the ingredients together in a glass or china bowl.

White wine marinade

½ l	dry white wine	¾ bottle
120 g	onions	4 oz
120 g	carrots	4 oz
120 g	celery	4 oz
125 ml	olive oil	¼ pt
	12 crushed peppercorns	
120 g	fennel	4 oz
	1 sprig tarragon	
	juice of 2 lemons	

Finely chop or mince all the vegetables and mix all the ingredients together in a glass or china bowl.

Exotic marinade

125 ml	olive oil	¼ pt
	1 measure gin	
25 g	mustard	1 oz
125 ml	pineapple juice	¼ pt
125 ml	wine vinegar	¼ pt
120 g	brown sugar	4 oz

Mix all the ingredients thoroughly in a glass or china bowl. Many variations of this marinade are possible. The recipe given is particularly suitable for roast or grilled ham and pork.

Herb marinade (For beef, veal, lamb or poultry)

Mix 1 tablespoon mild mustard, 3 tablespoons olive oil, 1 tablespoon finely chopped mixed herbs (rosemary, basil, thyme, marjoram, fennel, sage and savory), 2 chopped cloves of garlic and freshly ground white pepper. The meat is spread with the marinade, wrapped in aluminium foil and refrigerated for at least an hour.

Exotic marinade (For pork or sausages)

Mix 2 tablespoons wine vinegar, 2 tablespoons soya sauce, 1 tablespoon honey, 1 tablespoon cornflour, 2 chopped cloves of garlic, freshly ground white pepper and a dash of tabasco. The marinade is spread on to the meat or sausages several times 5–10 minutes before the end of the cooking time.

Marinade for beef (For roast, steak, châteaubriand, rump, etc.)

Marinade made up of a little mustard, oil, mixed herbs and a liberal amount of pepper. The meat is brushed with the marinade several hours before cooking and refrigerated until required. Salt is added when the meat is half-cooked.

ASPIC JELLIES

Light aspic jelly

Yield: about 3½ litres (6 pints)   Cooking time: 6 hours

1 kg	lean beef (shin)	2 lb
500 g	knuckle of veal	1 lb
	2 calf's feet	
1 kg	beef bones	2 lb
200 g	pork skin without fat	½ lb
150 g	carrots	¼ lb
	2 large onions	
	2 leeks	
	1 stick celery	
	1 bouquet garni	
	2–3 cloves of garlic	
	10 crushed peppercorns	
	1 clove	
5 l	water	8¾ pt

Split the calf's feet in two and blanch for 4–5 minutes with the pork skin. Place in a large pan with the beef bones and the water, bring to the boil, skim, add the beef and the knuckle of veal (tied), the vegetables, herbs and spices and simmer gently, skimming repeatedly. As soon as the beef, knuckle of veal and vegetables are cooked, remove and use for other purposes. When the aspic stock has cooked long enough, strain and remove all the fat.

N.B.—Veal bones may be used instead of beef bones.

France

Clarification of aspic jelly

Cooking time: 10 minutes

100 g	very lean chopped or minced beef	4 oz
	3 egg whites	
	few sprigs chervil	
	green part of 1 small leek	
	few tarragon leaves	
2 l	aspic jelly	3½ pt

Place the meat in a large pan with the finely sliced leek, the chervil, tarragon and egg whites. Mix well with ¼ litre (½ pint) cold liquid aspic jelly. Pour in the rest of the jelly, which should be hot, stirring constantly with a wire whisk until boiling point is reached. Now simmer gently without stirring, season very well—the liquid should taste slightly salty while still hot—draw aside, cover and allow to stand for a few moments. The egg whites will form a crust on top. Strain through a napkin which has been damped and wrung out, then remove all traces of fat from the top with tissue paper. The aspic should now be absolutely clear. Allow to cool for a short time, then add wine or spirits as desired.

France

Dark aspic jelly

This is prepared in the same way as light aspic jelly, but the vegetables, bones and meat (except for the calf's feet and pork skin) are first browned in fat, which is then poured off.

France

Aspic flavoured with Champagne, Madeira, etc.

Some dishes require aspic flavoured with wine or spirits. These are not added until the jelly is almost cold. They should be allowed for in measuring the total amount of liquid to be used in preparing the jelly, especially if it is being made with gelatine only. The maximum quantities of wines and spirits per litre (1¾ pints) aspic jelly are as follows:

1 dl	Champagne	⅙ pt
7 cl	Curaçao	⅛ pt
1 dl	Madeira	⅙ pt
1 dl	port	⅙ pt
1 dl	sherry (dry)	⅙ pt
7 cl	whisky	⅛ pt

France

CULINARY
TECHNIQUES

Centrepiece for a special buffet, sculptured in butter, margarine or sterine.

Medallions of turbot chaud-froid as presented by the Société mutualiste des Cuisiniers de Paris.

Paupiettes of sole, simply presented for a family buffet.

Exhibits from the Salon Culinaire 'WIKA', Vienna.

Stuffed saddle of veal.

Chaud-froid of chicken with a basket of truffles en surprise. (Balls of foie gras rolled in finely chopped truffles.)

Ham, Hawaiian style.

Saddle of venison.

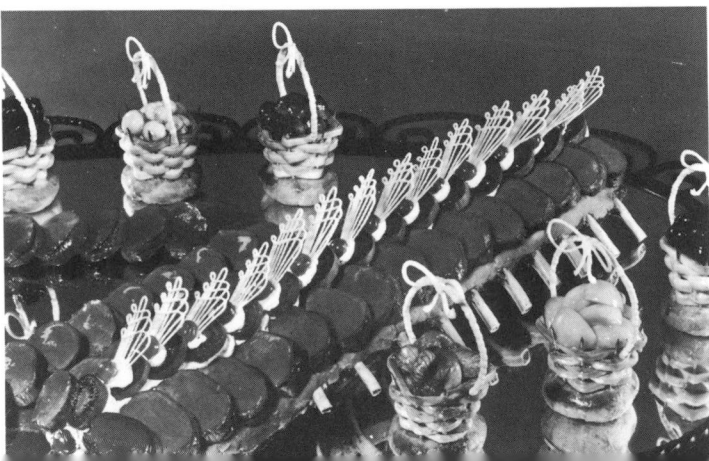

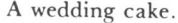

A wedding cake.

Small cakes for a children's party.

Fancy Sandwiches

Pinwheel sandwiches (see recipe pages 259, 260).
Remove the crust from a sandwich loaf and cut horizontally into long thin slices.

Spread the slices with a suitable filling or fillings.

Roll them up, chill thoroughly and cut into slices when cold.

Butter slices of bread, and cover with slices of tongue, ham, cold chicken, liver pâté or other suitable filling.

Assemble strips of white bread and rye bread as shown using either butter or cream cheese.

Before these special sandwiches are cut, they must be tightly wrapped in foil and thoroughly chilled.

Louis XV or surprise loaf (see recipe p. 262)

Cut vertically round a brioche or round loaf, as shown, without piercing the bottom crust.

Insert a thin knife near the base of the loaf and cut through the crumb without cutting the crust.

Remove the cylinder of bread, with the aid of a knife . . .

. . . leaving a hollow shell of crust.

Cut the crumb into regular slices, taking care not to damage the top crust.

The slices laid out.

Making the filling of butter, finely chopped herbs and calvados. (Other fillings are suitable.)

Spread the filling on the slices . . .

. . . and cover each with another slice.

Cut each sandwich into eight triangles.

Fill the shell neatly with the
sandwiches, replace the lid, decorate
with a bow of ribbon and present on
a lace doyley.

Croissants and small rolls (see
recipes pp. 835, 836)

After the dough has risen, cut it into
150g (5oz) pieces.

Divide each piece into eight.

For small rolls, roll each piece into a
ball, place on a greased baking tray
and sprinkle lightly with salt.

For croissants, roll the 150g (5oz) pieces of dough into thin circles and cut into eight segments.

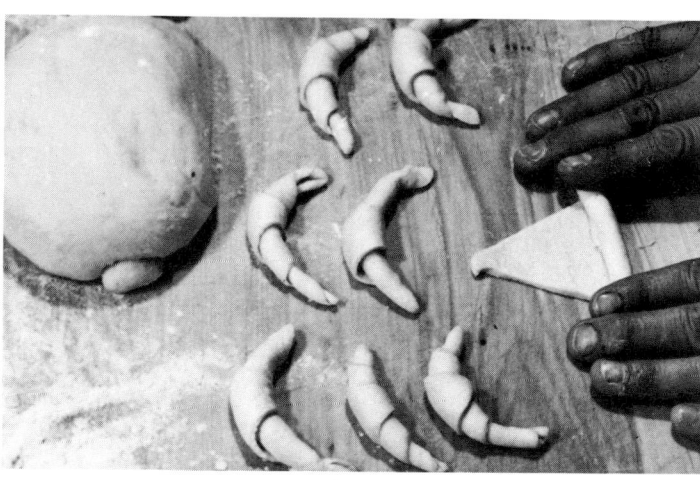

Roll these from the base to the point, and shape into crescents.

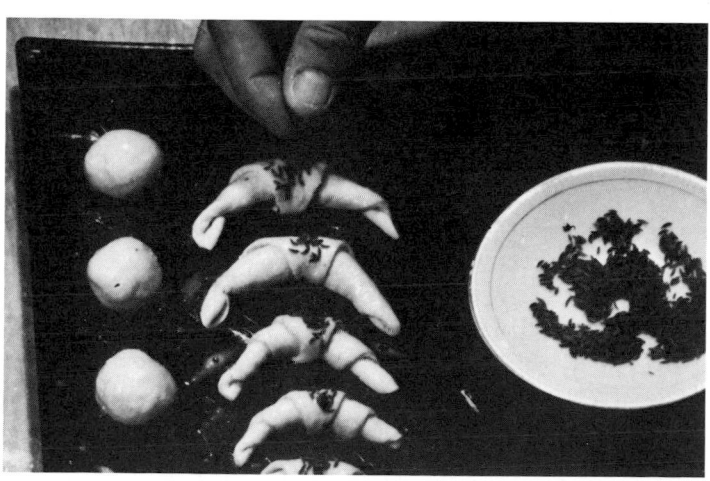

Put onto a greased baking sheet and leave to prove for 1½ hours. Egg wash, and sprinkle with cumin or poppy seeds.

Goose greave puffs (see recipe p. 679)

Make a bay in the flour, and add all the ingredients except the greaves.

Work the paste well on a floured table, beating it until it does not stick.

Stretch out the paste.

Cover with the minced greaves and work the paste well.

Fold as for puff pastry, and give one turn . . .

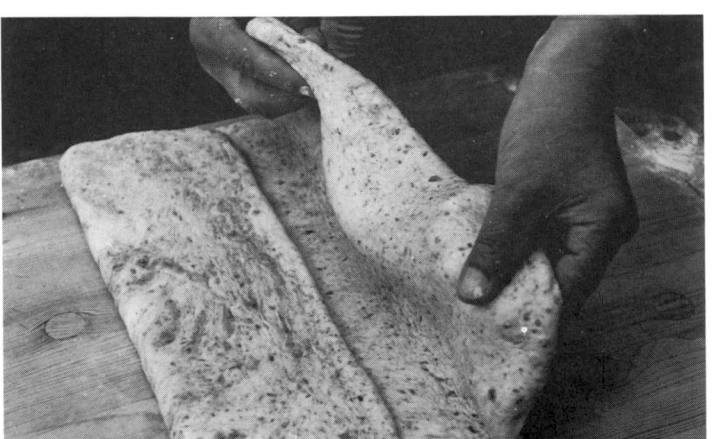

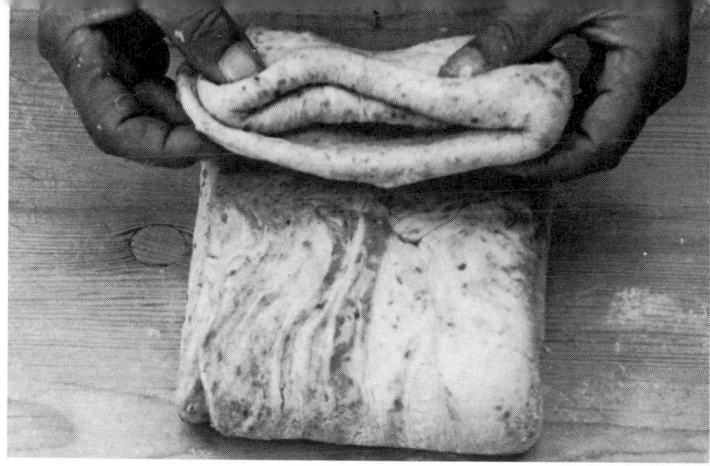

. . . then a second turn . . .

. . . and a third.

Pin out to a disc about 4cm (1½in) thick and mark with a knife.

Cut into small discs with a plain cutter.

Glaze with egg yolk and bake.

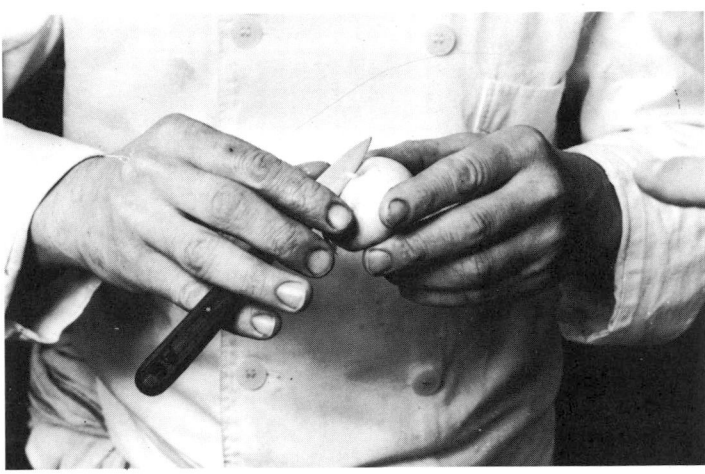

Turning mushrooms

Trim the end of the stalks and wash the mushrooms thoroughly. Using a sharp knife cut one groove in the head.

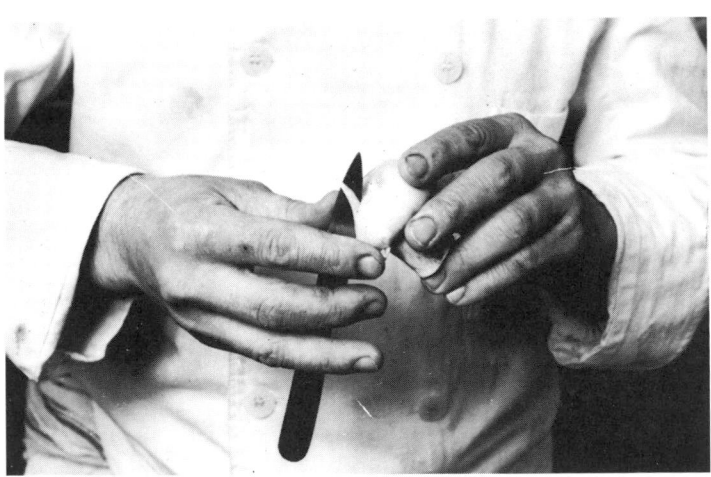

And continue cutting spiral grooves . . .

. . . all round the mushroom.

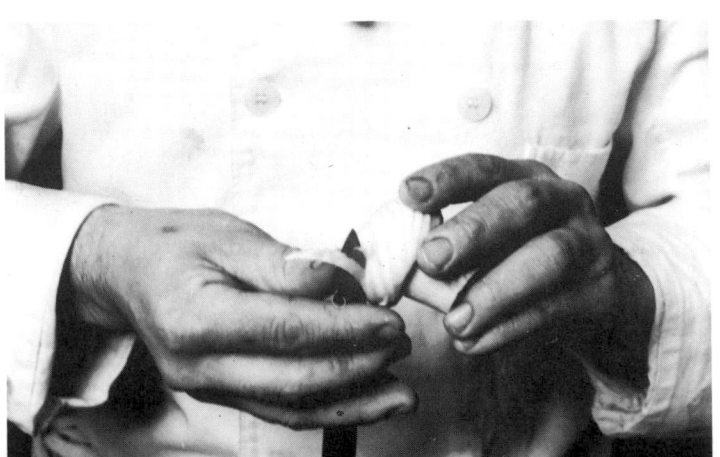

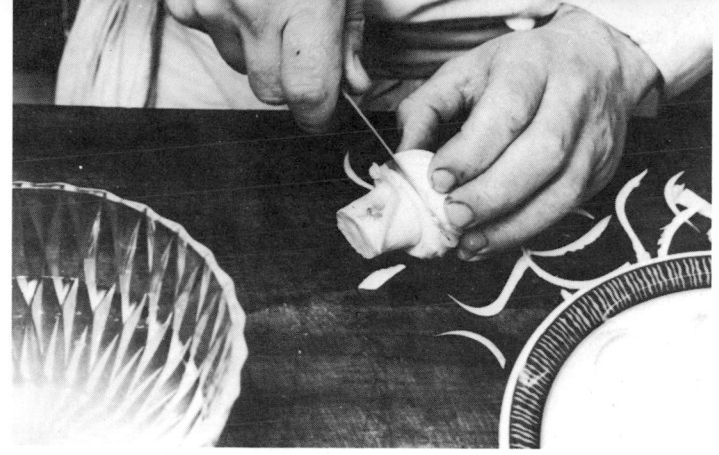

Cut off the decorated part . . .

. . . and keep in acidulated water until required.

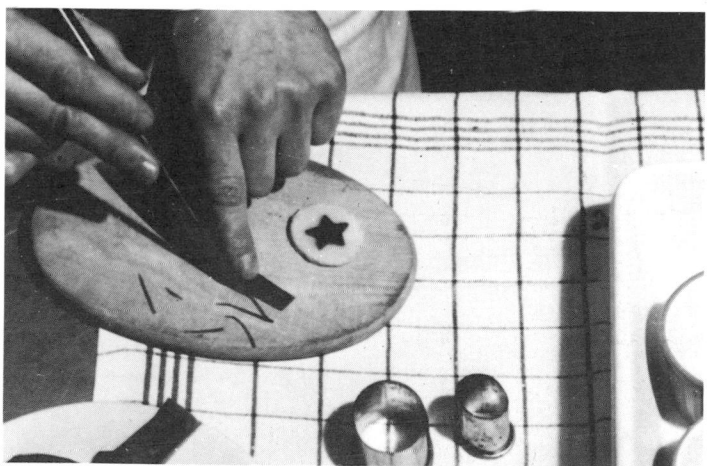

Jellied eggs (see p. 415 and colour illustration p. 811)

Chill the cocotte dishes, or other moulds, add a little liquid aspic jelly and tilt the mould so that it is evenly coated with jelly. Place in a refrigerator. Prepare the decoration (sprigs of tarragon, cut out pieces of ham, leek, truffle etc.).

When the jelly in the moulds is set, stick the decoration to it, using a little melted jelly and cover with a very thin layer of jelly. Poach the eggs, cool them in iced water, drain on a napkin and trim them.

Place the trimmed eggs carefully into the moulds and fill with jelly on the point of setting. Chill until fully set.

Pass the moulds quickly through hot water and unmould the eggs carefully onto a suitably dainty plate.

Vine leaf strudel (see recipe p. 328)

Make a well in the flour, add the oil and knead.

Add the luke warm water in small quantities and work the dough thoroughly.

Stretch the dough and continue working it.

Form into a ball.

Brush the dough with oil.

Place the dough on a floured cloth, flour the hands and very carefully stretch the dough to beyond the edge of the table.

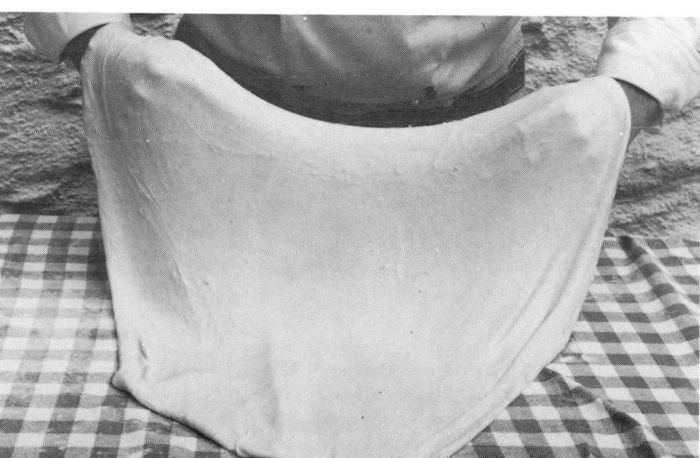

I

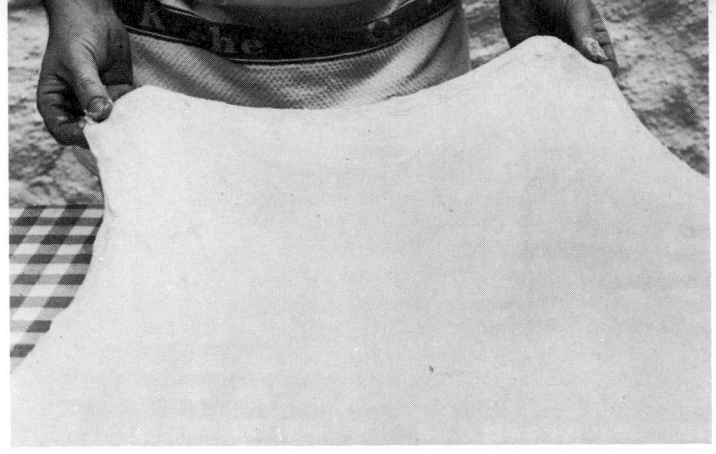

The same process. Stretch the dough to a rectangle.

Place a layer of drained vine leaves down the centre.

Lay the sliced ham on top, then the slices of cheese.

Add the anchovy fillets at regular intervals, then the bean sprouts.

Add the hard boiled eggs cut in six.

Put the lychees between the eggs, and sprinkle with green peppercorns.

Trim the edges to make a regular rectangle.

Fold the edges over the filling, and using the cloth, roll up the strudel.

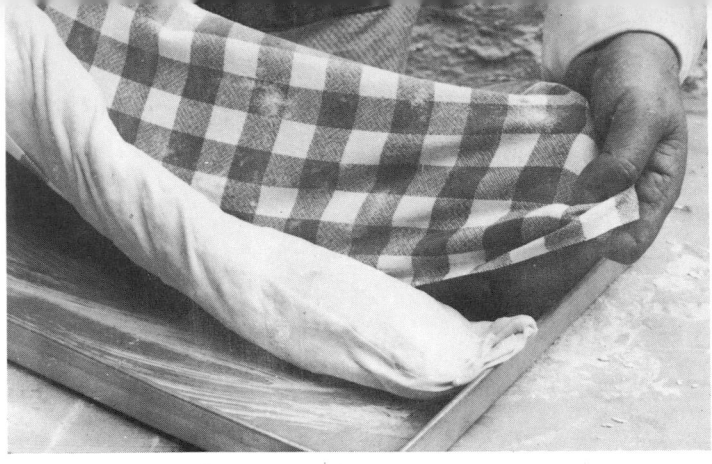

Using the cloth, turn the strudel onto a buttered baking sheet.

Turban of fillets of sole (see recipe p. 454)

Butter a savarin mould and line with alternate fillets of sole and slices of smoked salmon.

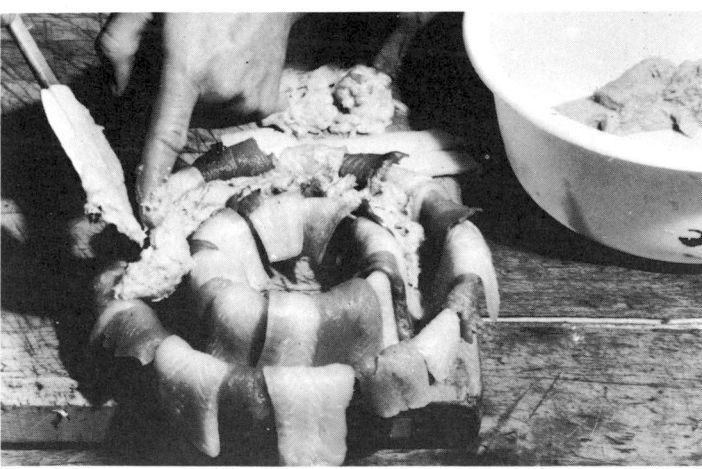

Fill the centre with a fish stuffing (or a mixture of minced sea food).

Fold the fillets over the filling.

Cook through the oven in a bain-
marie, unmould onto a dish and
coat with an appropriate sauce.

Cold stuffed turbot

(See recipe p. 456, which describes a
slightly different method using
halibut, colour illustrations pp. 691,
812).

Cut down the spine of the fish, and
lay back the fillet as shown without
removing it completely.

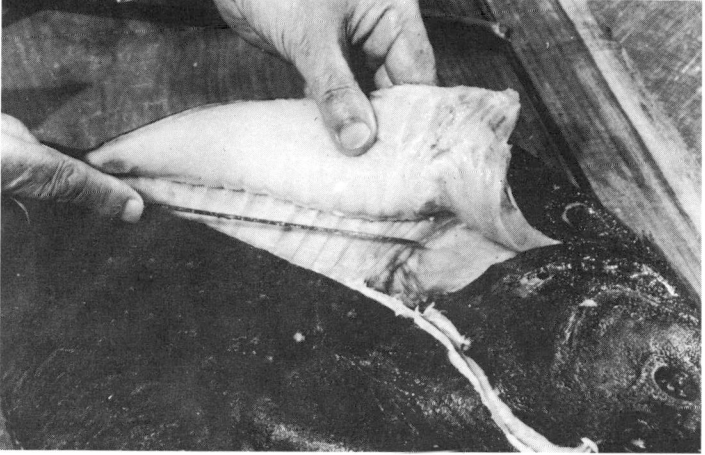

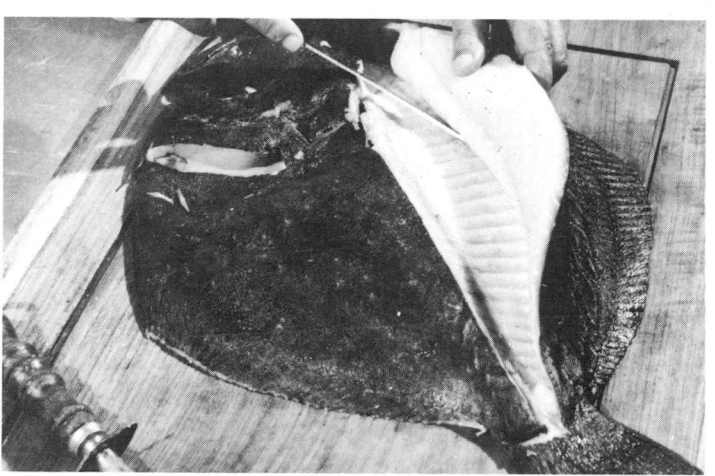

Repeat the process on the other side.

Cut the back bone at the head and
tail and remove the whole bone.

Lay back the fillets and fill the centre with the stuffing.

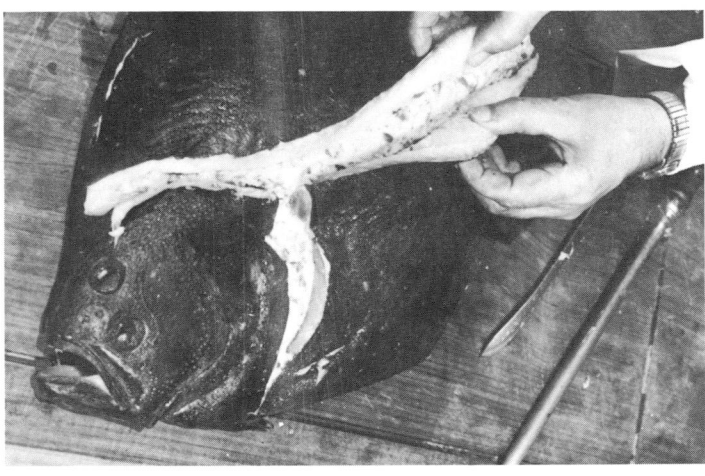

Fold the fillets back over the stuffing and secure with small skewers or cocktail sticks.

Cook the fish on a drainer plate in a fish kettle, using a good court-bouillon.

When the fish is cold and drained, coat with a white sauce chaud-froid. Remove one fillet and cut it into slices.

Replace the slices neatly in the same order, decorate and glaze the whole fish.

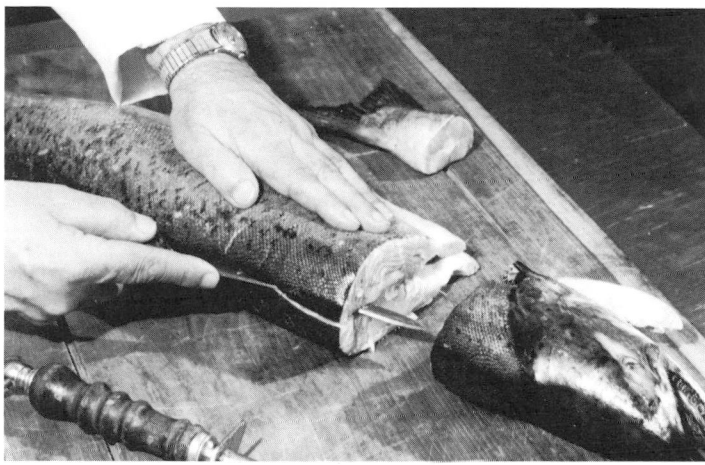

Salmon or trout for a cold buffet
(Recipe p. 510. colour illustration p. 699)

Clean, gut and wash the fish, cut off the head and tail, then cut down the back to the backbone.

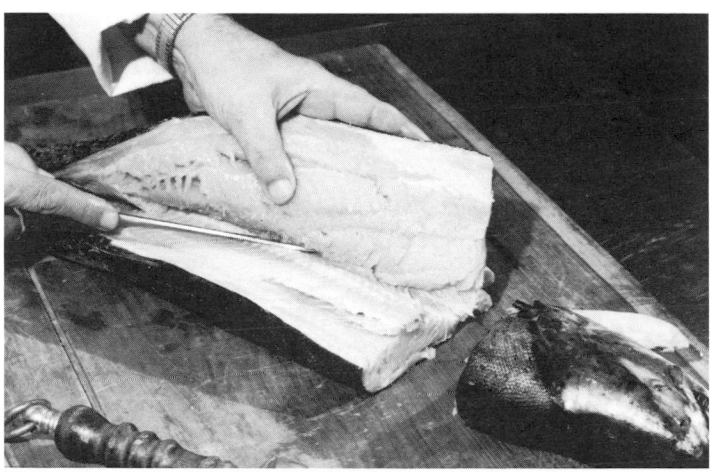

Remove the two fillets.

Put the fillets, the head and tail and suitable vegetables into a fish kettle and poach in a court-bouillon. Allow to cool in the liquid.

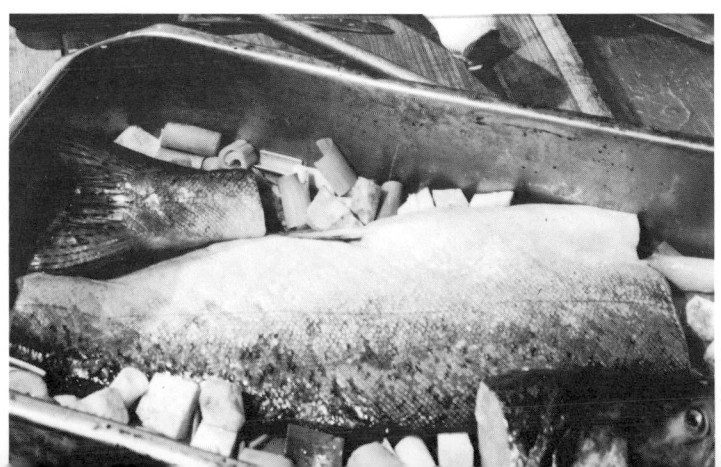

When cold, drain the fillets well,
chill them, coat with a white chaud-
froid sauce, allow to set and slice
into portions.

Put the vegetable salad on a long
dish, place the head and tail of the
salmon at either end, arrange the
slices neatly on top, garnish the dish
and lightly glaze the slices and head
and tail with aspic jelly.

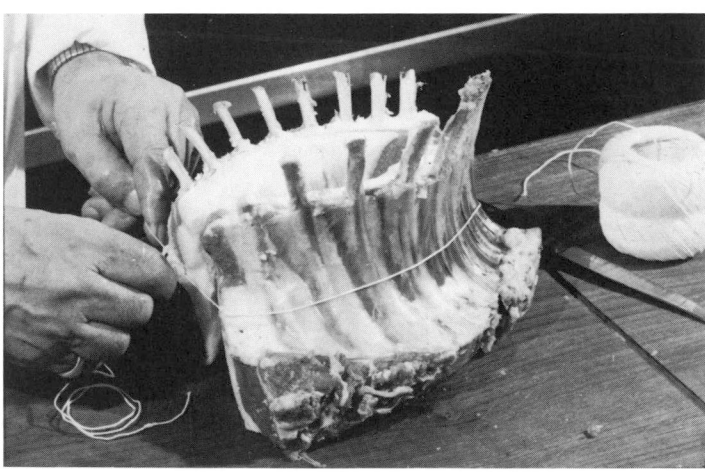

Preparing a crown of lamb (recipe
p. 601)

Trim the cutlet bones neatly,
remove any excess fat.

Tie the joints round an empty tin
(not visible in the photograph) to
the shape of a crown. The meat is
then ready for roasting.

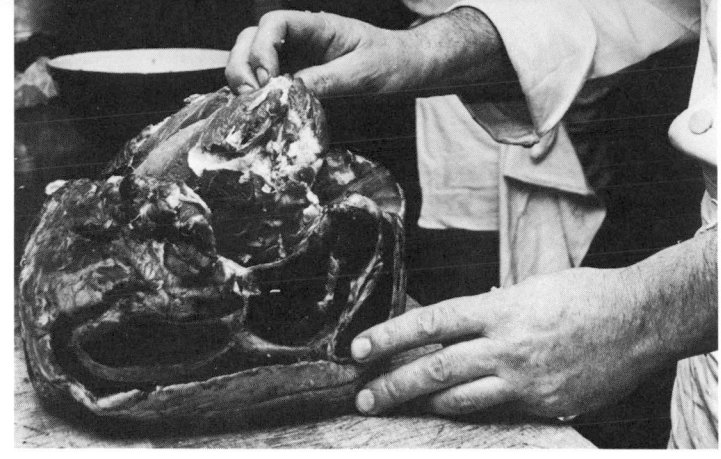

Stuffed ham 'four seasons' (recipe p. 640)

To make a cavity in the ham, use a small sharp knife . . .

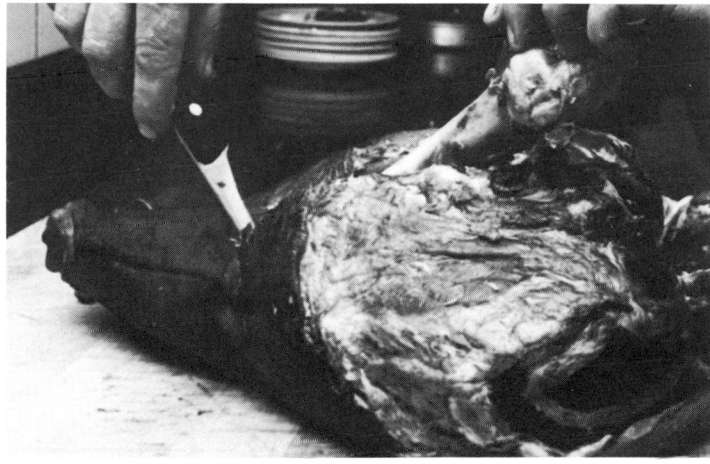

. . . and cut round the thigh bone.

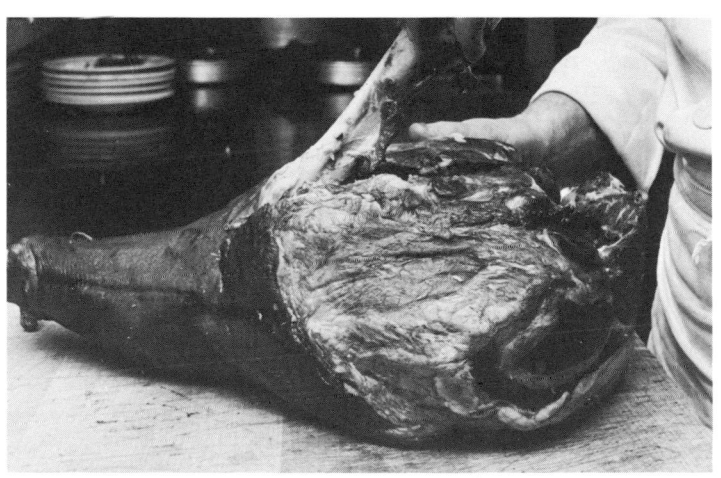

Pull away the bone.

Put some ham in the resulting pocket to shape it evenly, pour in the madeira and leave to marinate.

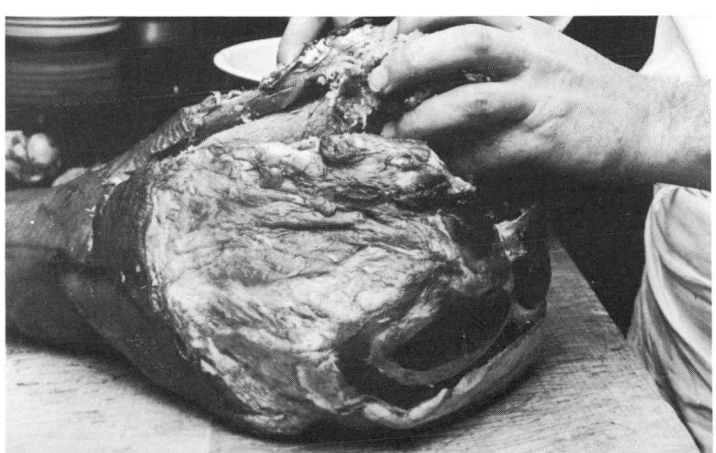

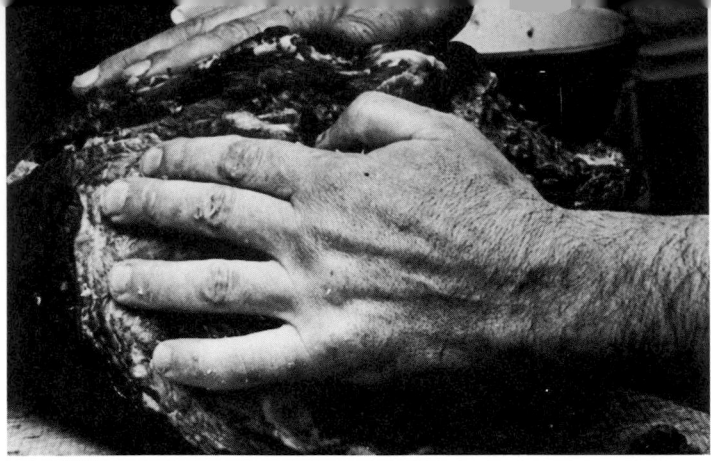

Stuff the ham with forcemeat, filling it well to give a good rounded shape.

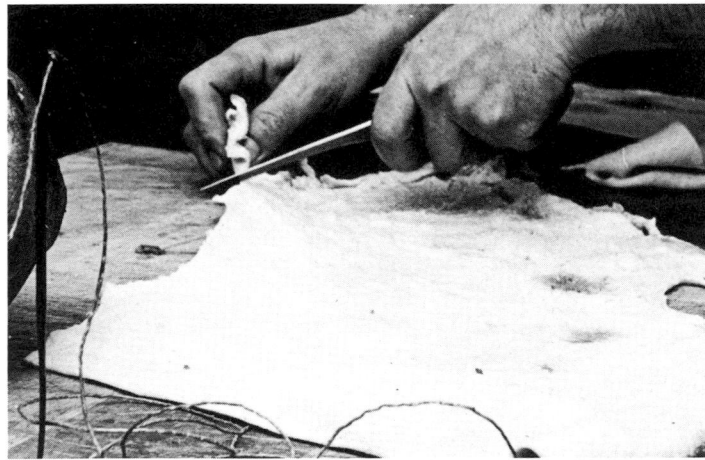

Cut a piece of pork skin to fit the open side.

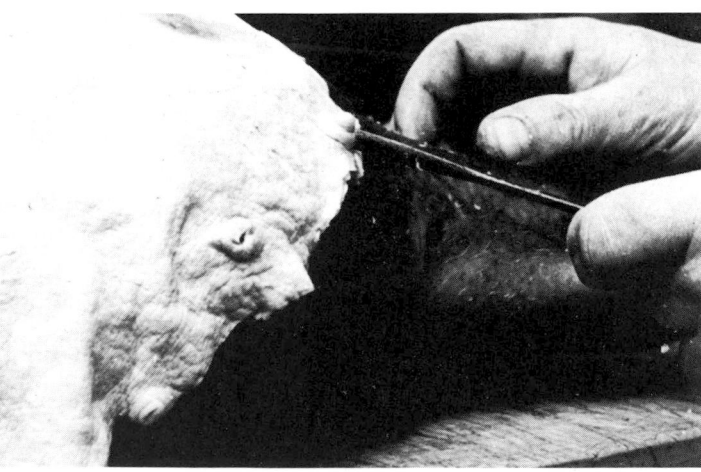

Sew one edge of the skin on to the ham.

Sewing the skin.

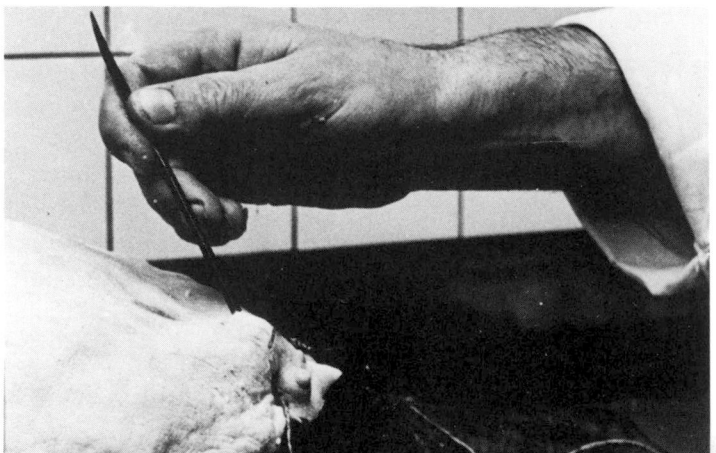

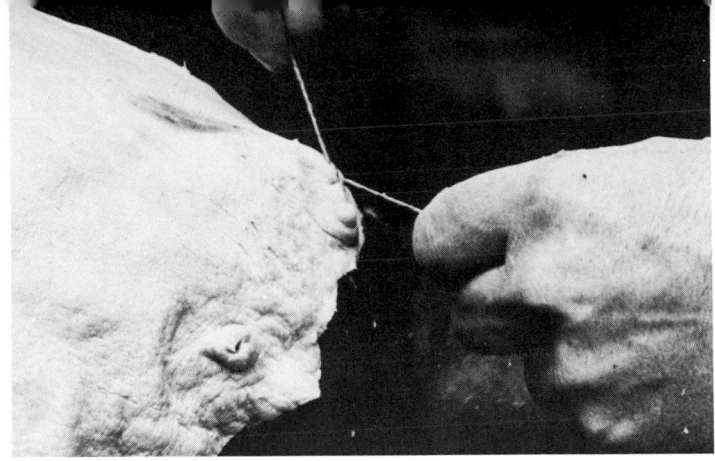

Knotting the string.

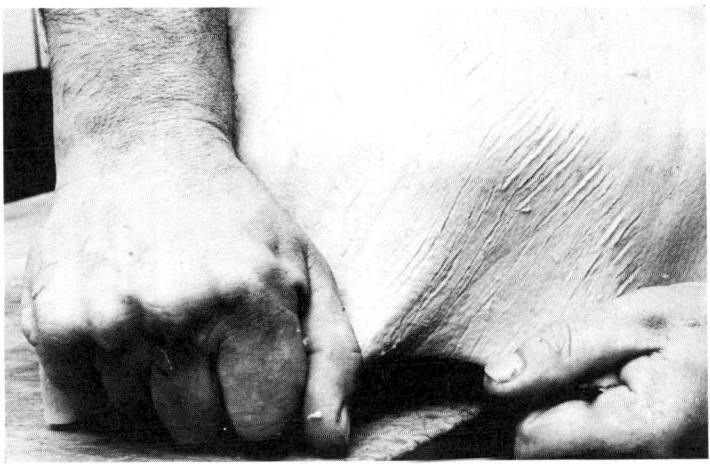

Stretch the skin evenly over the
stuffing . . .

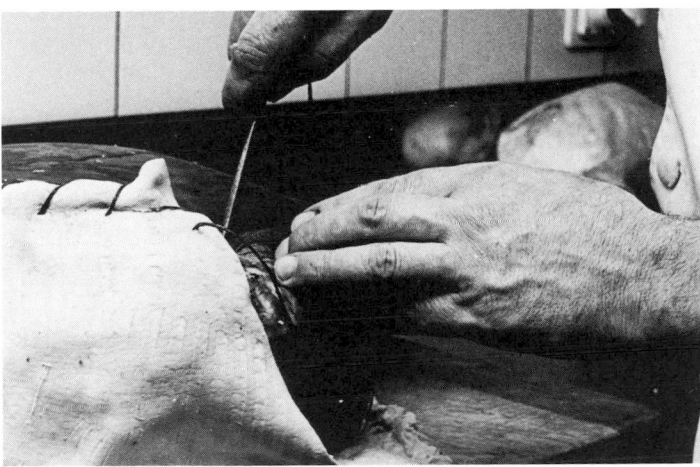

. . . and continue sewing.

Make sure the stuffing is in position.

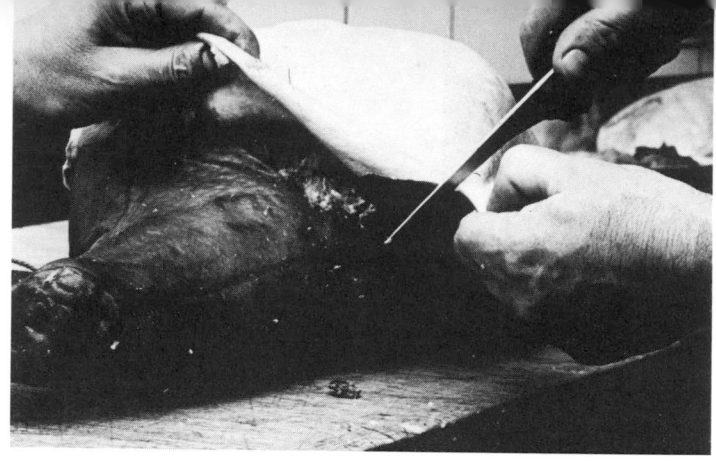

Trim off any excess skin.

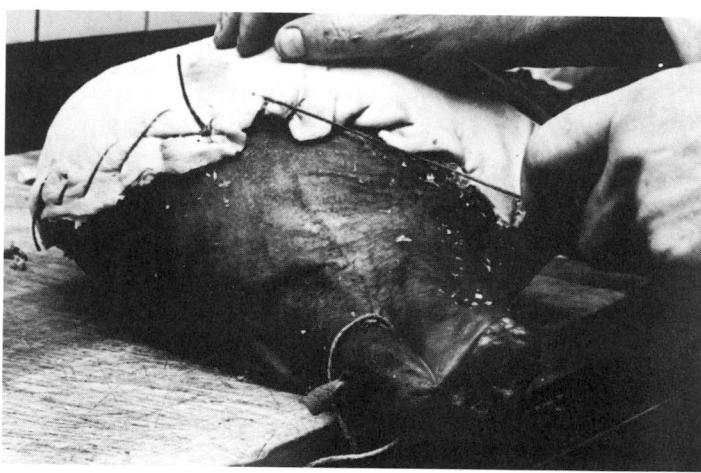

Press the skin down to pack the stuffing tightly, and tie off the string.

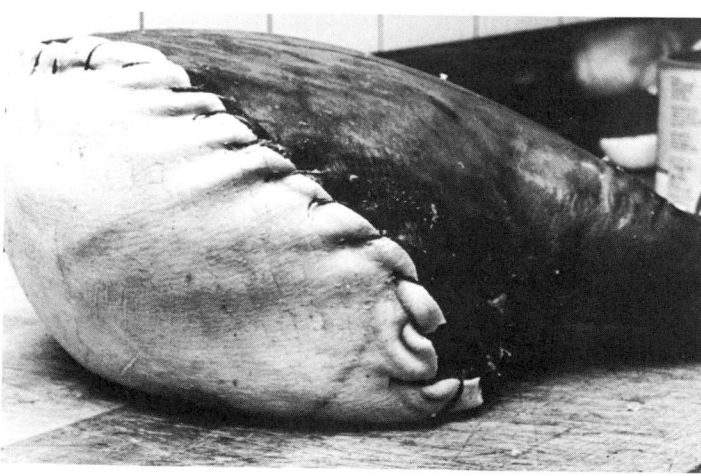

The sewing completed.

Tie the ham, as for a galantine.

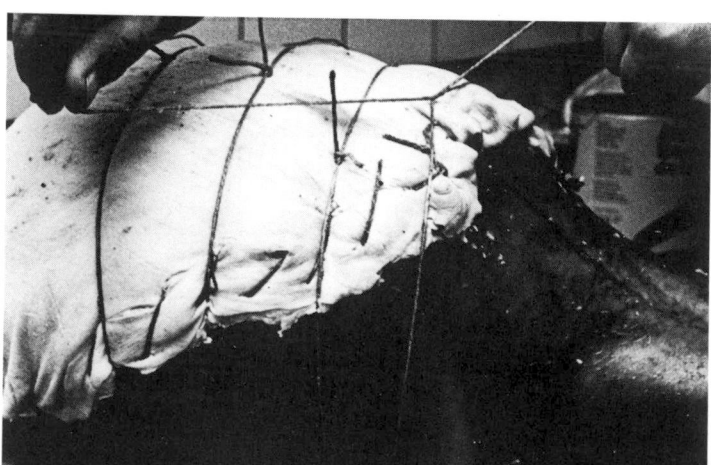

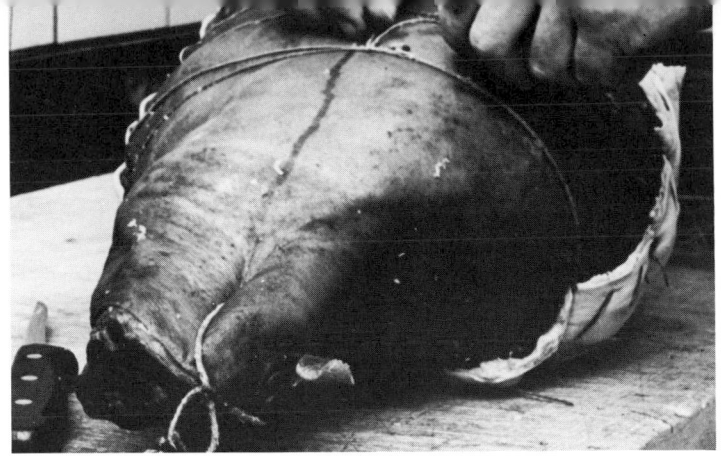

Tying the ham.

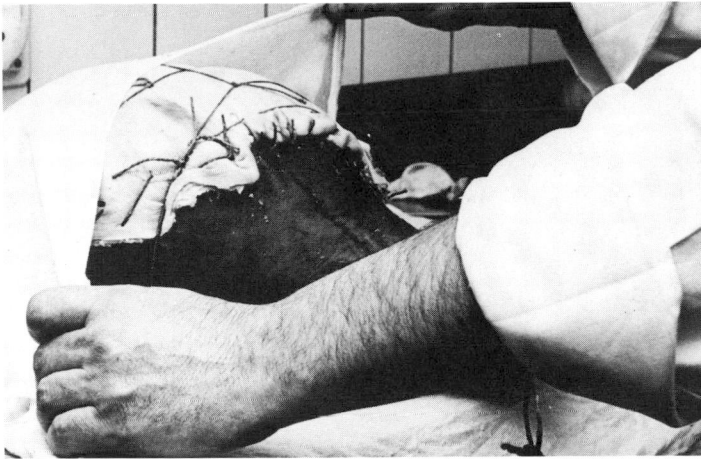

Wrap the ham in a cloth . . .

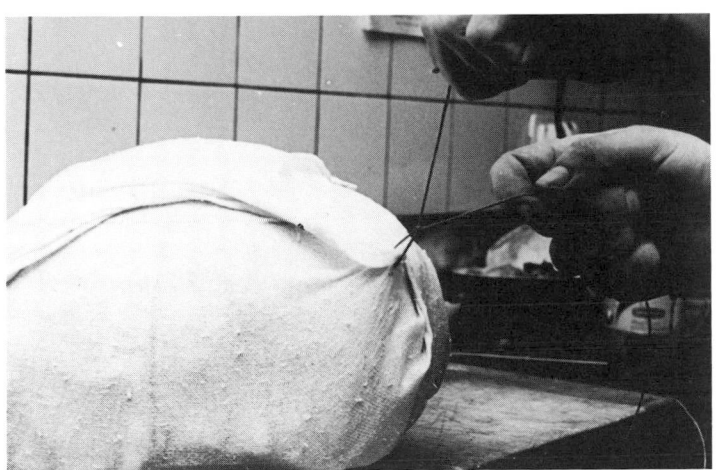

. . . and tie the ends together.

Carving breast of turkey (recipe p. 676)

Carefully cut both breasts cleanly off the breast bone.

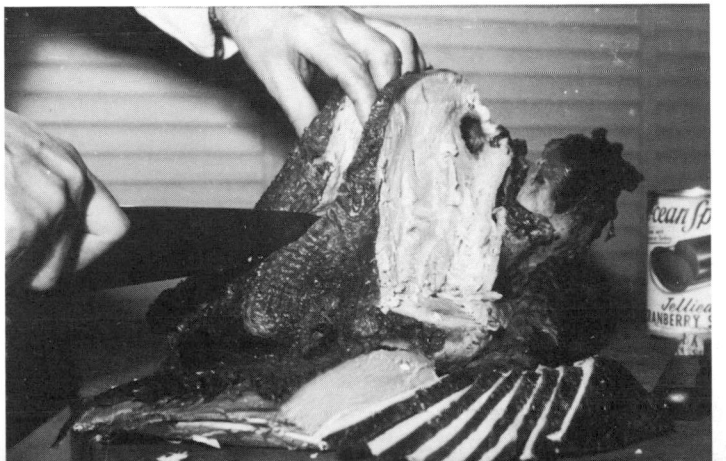

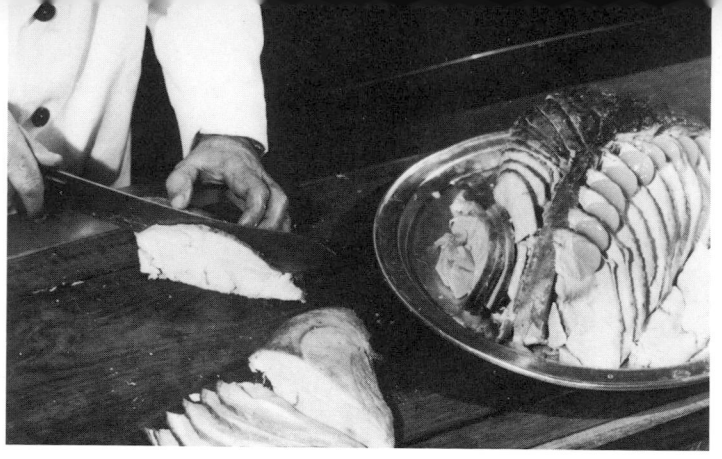

Carve one breast in slices.

The breast sliced.

Replace the slices on the carcase, in the correct order.

The re-built joint.

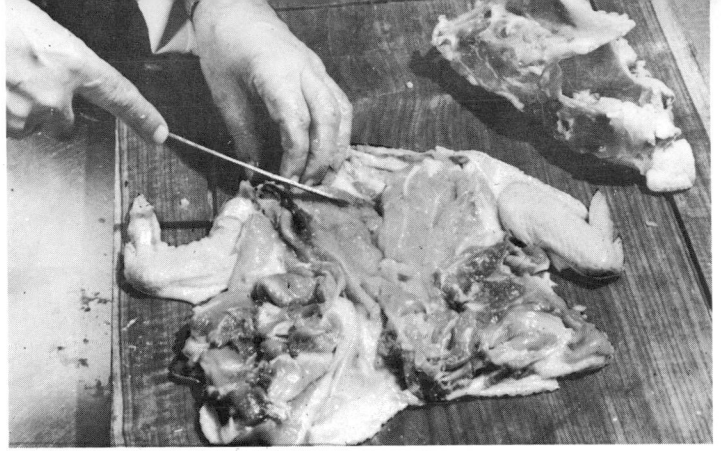

Chicken galantine (recipe p. 754)
(colour illustration p. 924)

Cut the chicken down the back and
bone it out completely, (the carcase
is shown on the right) without
damaging the skin.

Spread the boned bird with the
forcemeat, sprinkle with the
pistachio nuts and arrange strips of
tongue, foie gras and truffle on top.
(Here the truffle is shown wrapped
in thin rashers of fat bacon.)

Roll the bird up round the filling.

Roll tightly in a cloth and tie
securely.

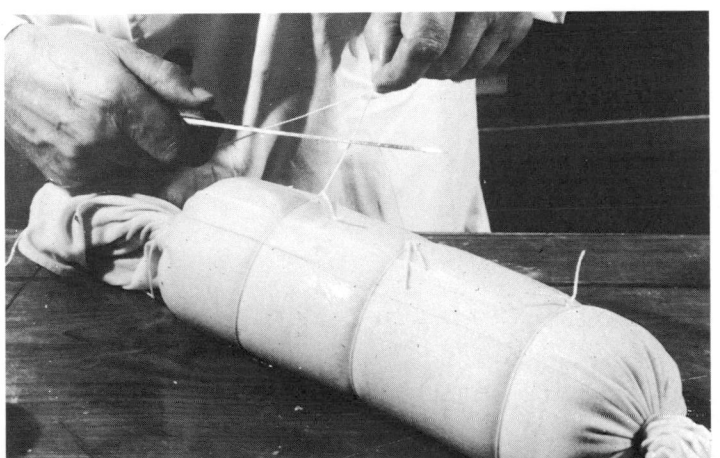

When cold, coat the galantine . . .

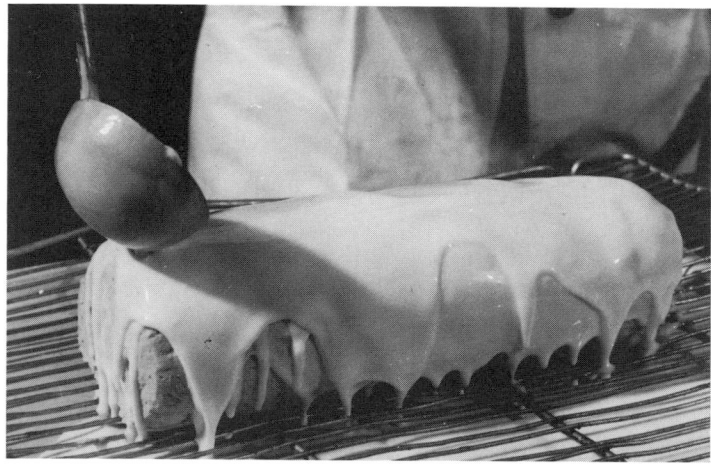

. . . . with chaud-froid sauce, and glaze with aspic.

Slicing the finished galantine.

Family pie (recipe p. 739)

Pin out the pastry to a rectangle and lay slices of fat bacon or fat pork on it. Cover with a layer of forcemeat, then strips of tongue (or other suitable meat).

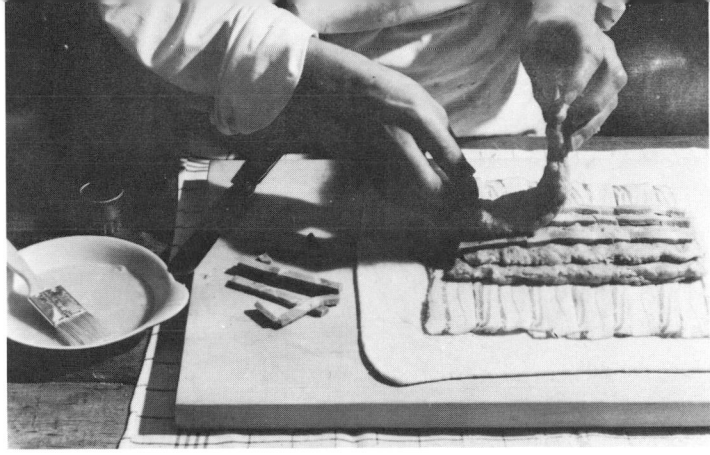

Cover this with a layer of forcemeat.

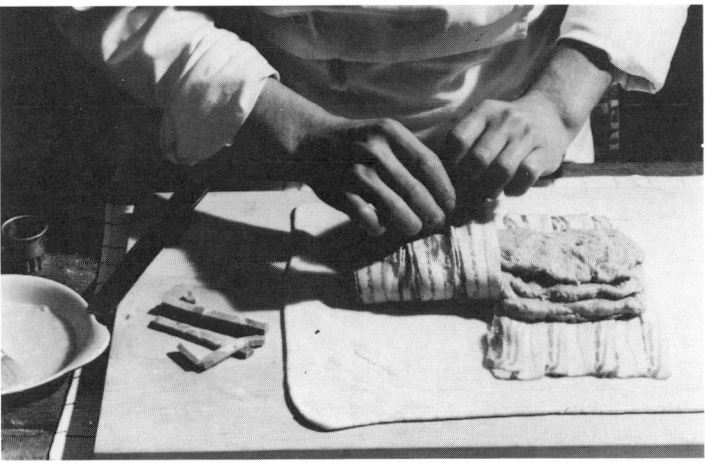

Wrap over the slices of bacon.

Damp the edges of the pastry with a little water to make them stick . . .

. . . and turn the pie over.

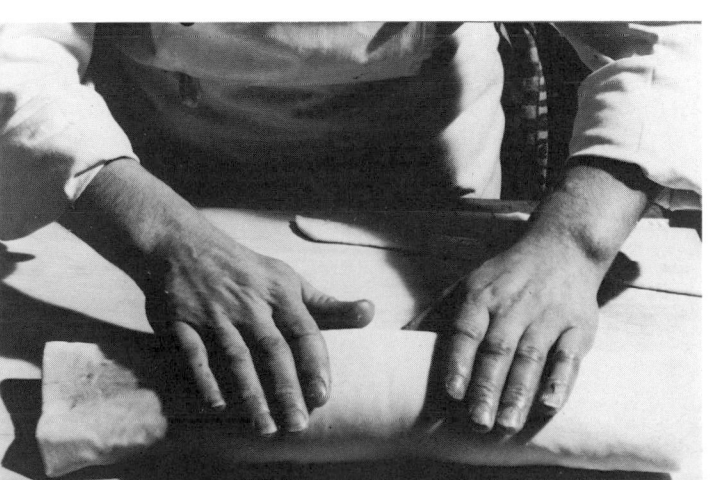

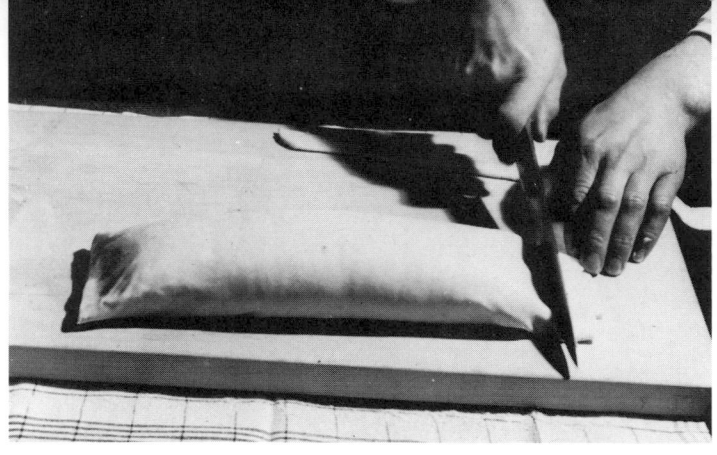

Trim the ends.

Decorate the top in a simple way.

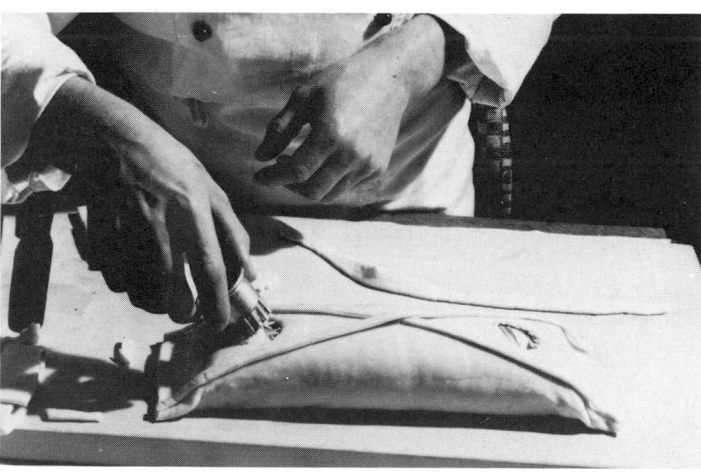

Glaze with beaten egg, and cut one or two steam vents, bake for 50–60 minutes.

The pie ready to be served, hot or cold.

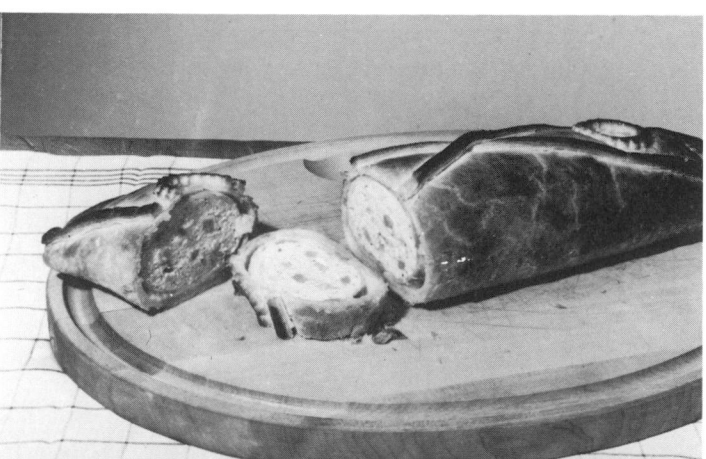

(colour illustrations pp. 993, 1027, 1028)

Decorating moulds for vegetables in aspic or mousses

Line a savarin mould with jelly and decorate with slices of truffle cut with a fluted cutter, and dipped in jelly. Then line the mould with white chaud-froid sauce. Set in the refrigerator, and then fill with the chosen mixture.

An alternative method: use a charlotte mould or a carefully opened tin, and decorate with truffle motifs. Line the sides with asparagus and then fill with vegetable salad in aspic mayonnaise.

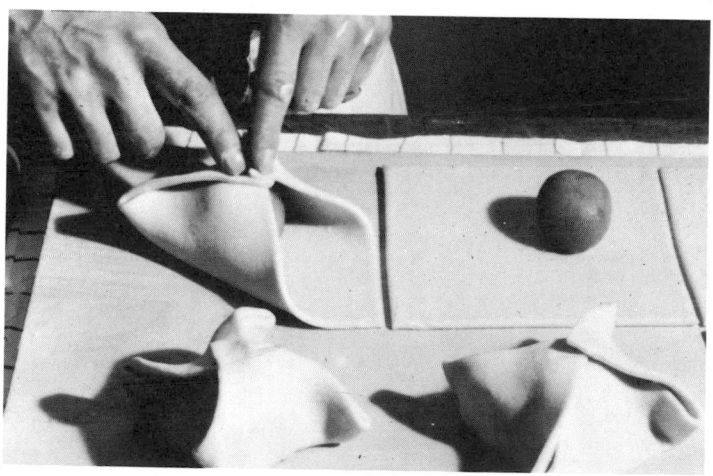

Baked tomato 'Dumplings'
(The same method for fruits — Apple, Apricot etc.)

Remove the core from the tomatoes, blanch and refresh quickly, skin them and remove the seeds. Pin out the puff paste and cut into squares. Place on the tomatoes and season with salt, pepper and herbs. Damp the edges of the paste and enclose the tomato.

Seal well, and cover the top with a round piece of pastry. Egg-wash and bake. Serve hot.

Viking ship (see recipe p. 262)

Remove the crust from a large loaf and cut to the shape of a boat.

Cut around the side, without cutting through the base.

Cut parallel to the base along one side.

Remove the centre.

The shell of the boat thus obtained.

Slice the centre lengthwise and make into sandwiches.

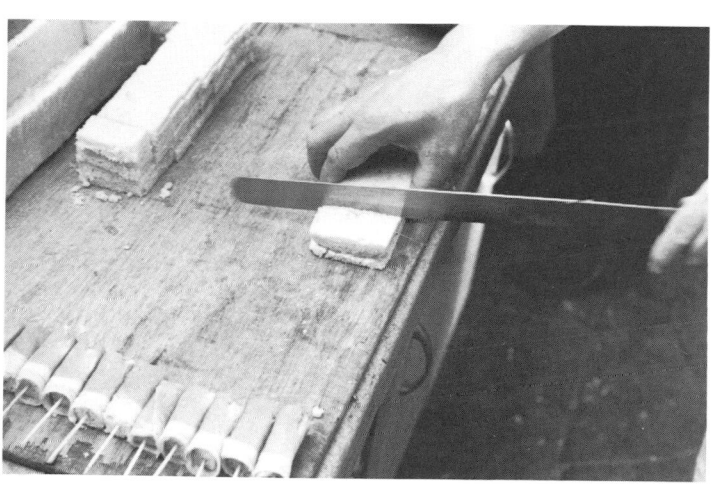

Cut into small, regular sandwiches.

Make the exterior of the boat from gold coloured cardboard, stapled at each end, and fit over the bread shell.

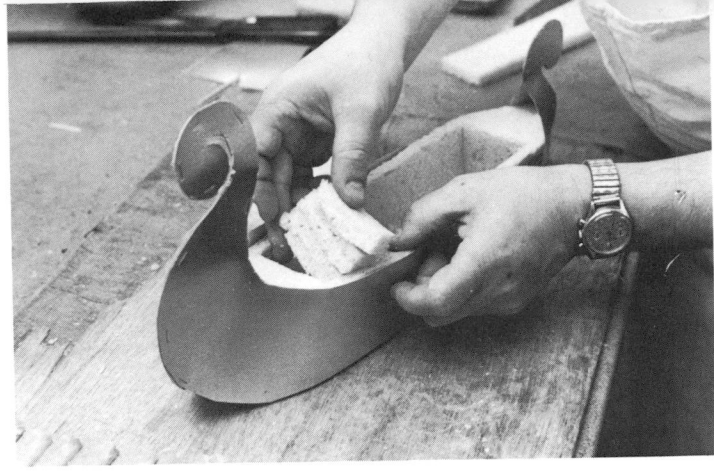

Fill the shell with the sandwiches.

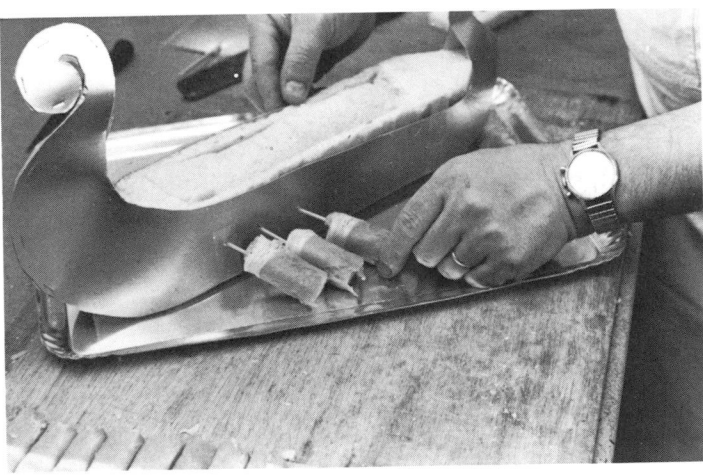

Roll slices of ham round small pieces of bread and fix to the shell with cocktail sticks, to represent oars.

Fix small salami canapes, to represent shields.

Put small brioches in the centre and tartelettes at each end, and add a sail made from the same gold card.

Open air cookery

Hungarian Bread—skewer some pieces of bacon and grill in front of a fire. When the fat begins to melt let it drip on to slices of wholemeal bread. When the bread has absorbed plenty of fat, season it with salt, pepper and a sprinkling of paprika, garnish with onion rings and serve with a glass of wine or a tankard of beer.

Barbecued fish, Hungarian style—(Recipe p. 432)—gut and scale the fish thoroughly and wash well. Spit on to a wooden skewer, through the mouth and down the backbone.

Season the fish inside and outside with salt, pepper and a sprinkling of paprika. (Alternatively, insert sprigs of fennel into the cavity.)

Cut some rectangular pieces of bacon fat, and thread them on a skewer, with an onion, if liked. Score the bacon with a sharp knife, hold both skewers over the embers, one in each hand. When the fat begins to melt, let it drip onto the fish. Heat up the fat again and repeat the process until the eyes of the fish stand out from its head, a sign that it is perfectly cooked.

Hungarian Woodcutter's
Casserole—assemble the ingredients:
meat, bacon, potatoes, tomatoes,
onions, peppers, salt, pepper and
paprika.

Line the base and lid of the
casserole with oiled paper, or grease
well with lard. Cut the ingredients
into small pieces.

Fill the casserole.

Cook in embers for 50–60 minutes.

Fruit dumplings (apricots, plums etc)
(Recipe p. 908)

Assemble the ingredients.

Peel and grate the jacket potatoes.

Add the flour, eggs and salt.

Add the melted butter and work quickly to a smooth paste.

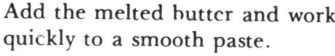

Stone the plums and insert a lump of sugar into each.

Pin out the dough to a thickness of 1cm ($\frac{1}{2}$in) on a floured table.

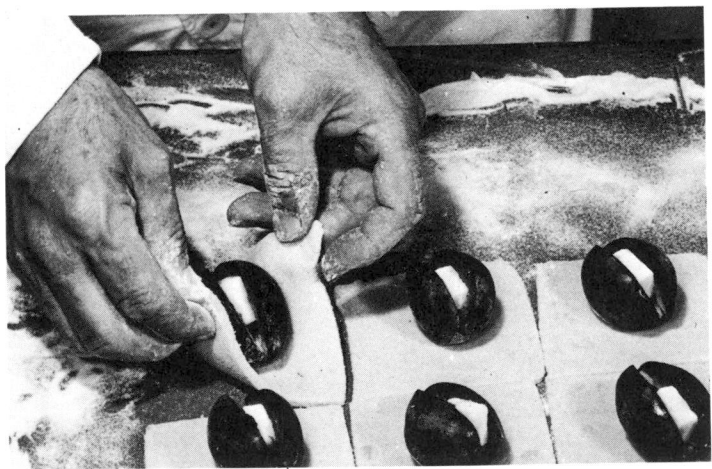

Cut the dough into squares and put a plum in the centre of each.

Enclose the plums in the dough and shape into dumplings.

Poach in lightly salted boiling water.

Drain on a rack.

Roll the dumplings in breadcrumbs fried in butter and dust with caster sugar.

Apple strudel (recipe p. 1161)

Prepare the dough as for vine leaf strudel (p. 110 and p. 328). Mould into a ball and brush with oil, pin out on a floured cloth.

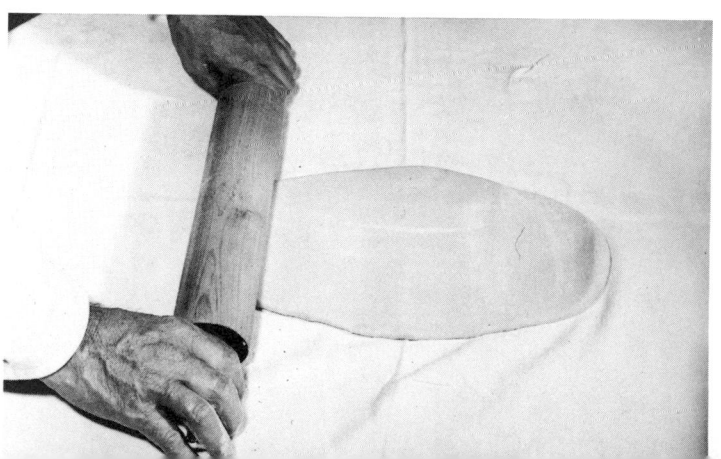

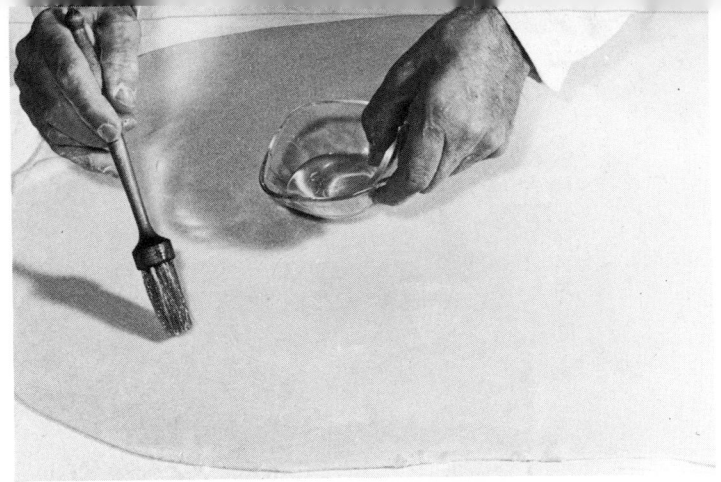

Brush with oil to prevent sticking when the dough is stretched.

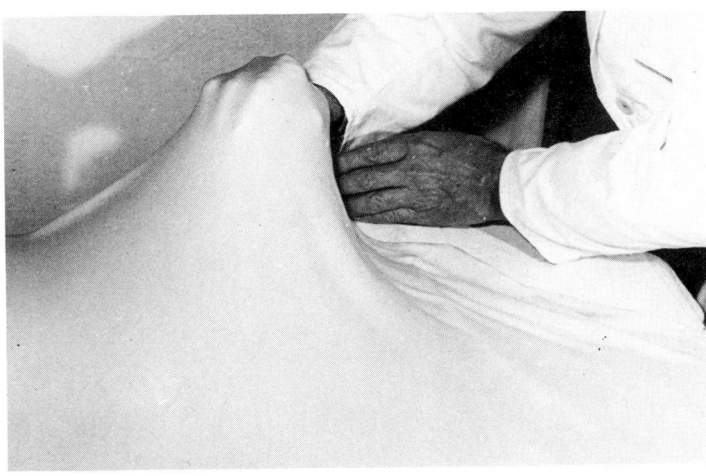

Flour the hands, and stretch the dough . . .

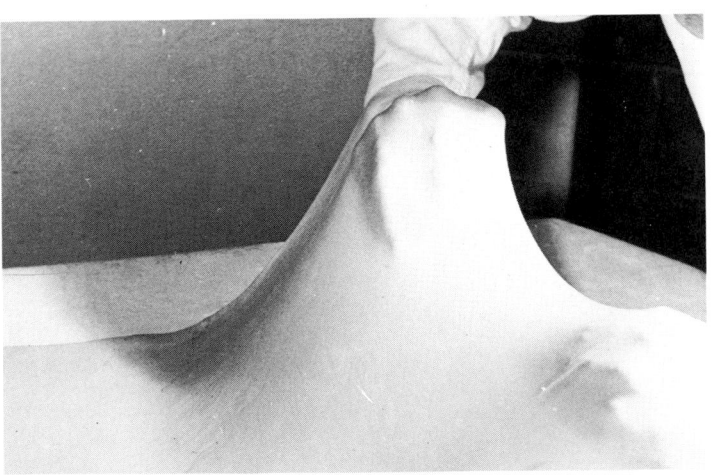

. . . until it is paper thin . . .

. . . and overhangs the edge of the table.

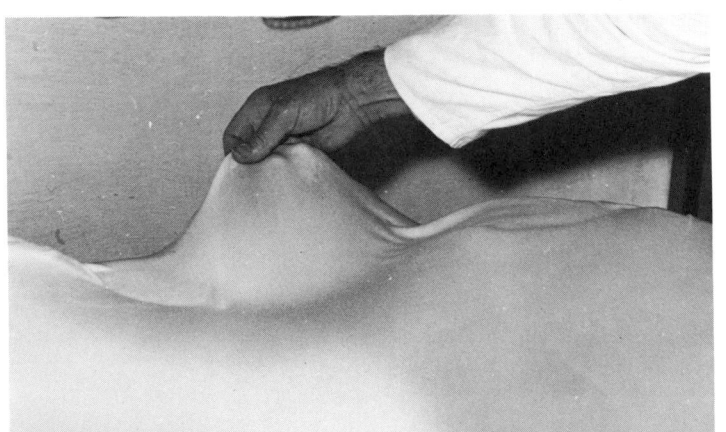

Sprinkle half the dough with the breadcrumbs browned in butter.

Put the sliced apples on top.

Distribute the apples evenly.

Sprinkle with sugar and flavour with rum.

Sprinkle with half the currants, the ground cloves and the cinnamon.

Add the rest of the currants and the lemon juice.

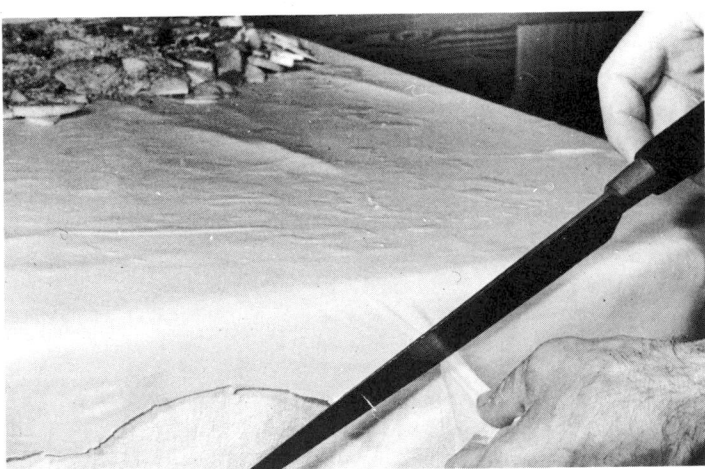

Trim the dough to a rectangle.

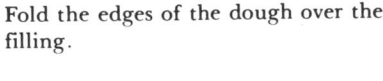

Fold the edges of the dough over the filling.

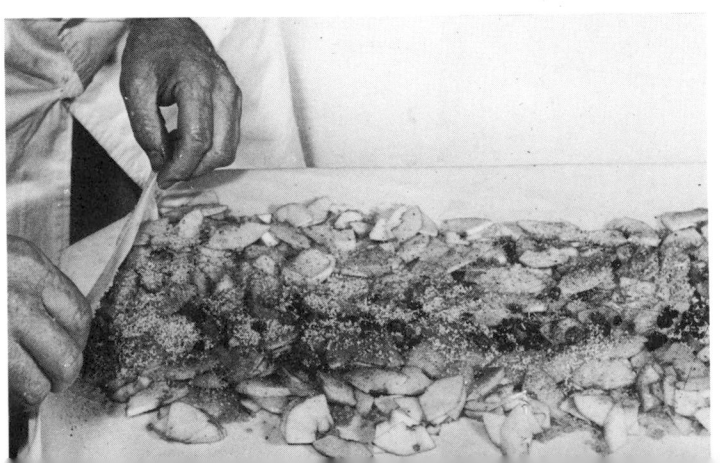

Roll up with the help of the cloth.

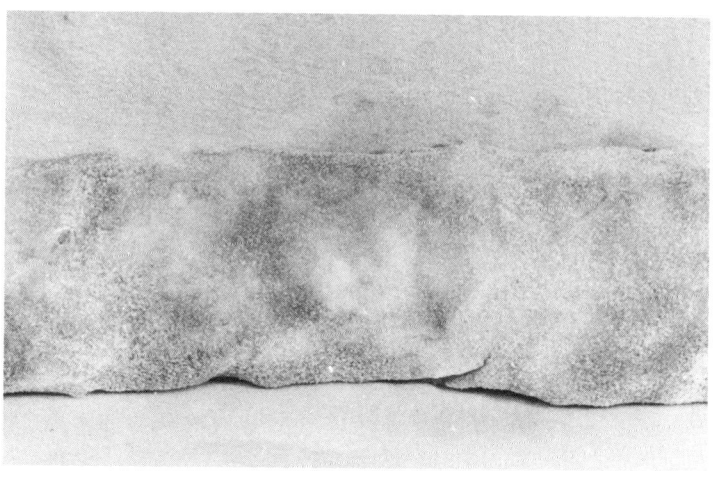

The completed roll.

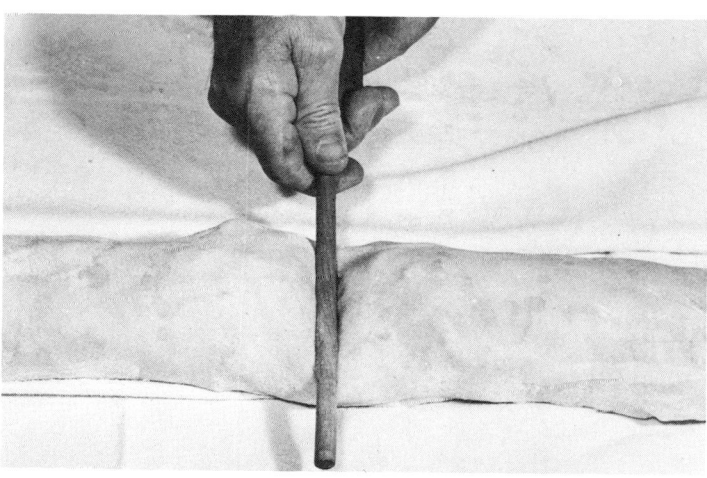

Divide the strudel with the handle of a wooden spoon.

Place on a buttered baking sheet and brush with melted butter.

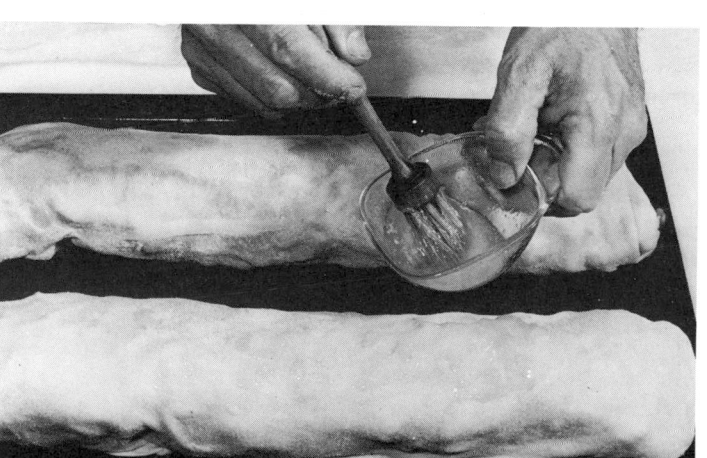

Gumpoldskirchner strudel with various fillings (recipe p. 889)

The ingredients for the dough.

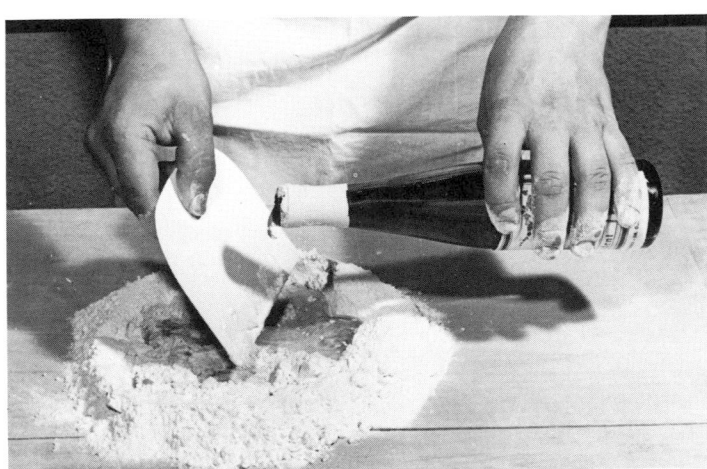

Add the egg yolks and the vinegar.

Work to a smooth dough.

Mould into a ball.

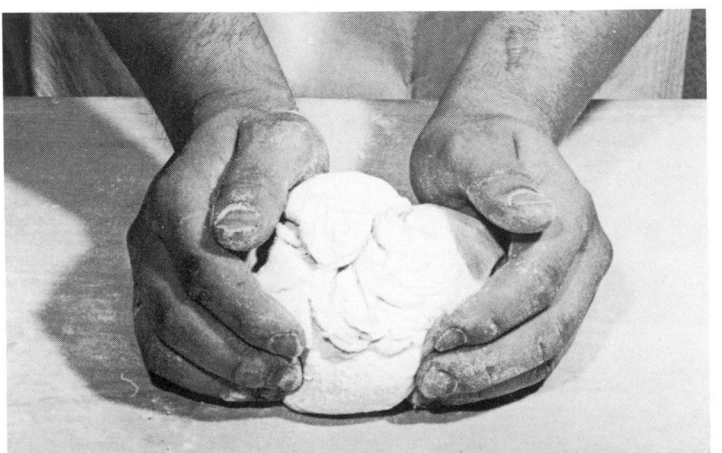

Brush with melted butter or lard, and leave to rest for 25 minutes.

Mince the leaf fat and mix with a little flour.

Shape into a rectangular block.

Pin out the dough on a floured board.

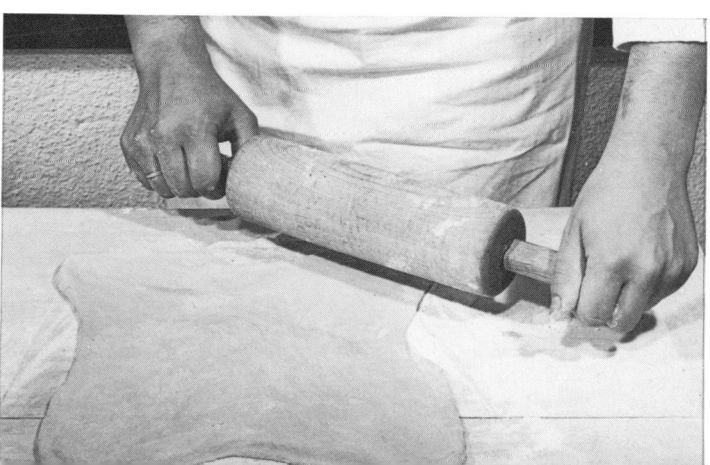

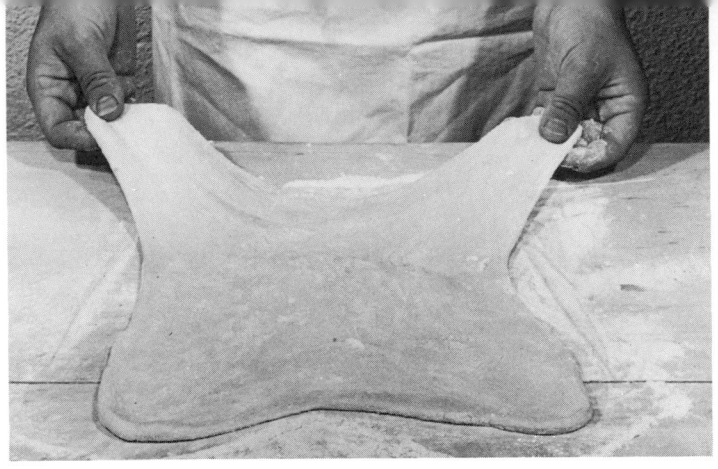

Stretch the dough a little, to make the edges thinner than the centre.

Put the block of fat in the centre . . .

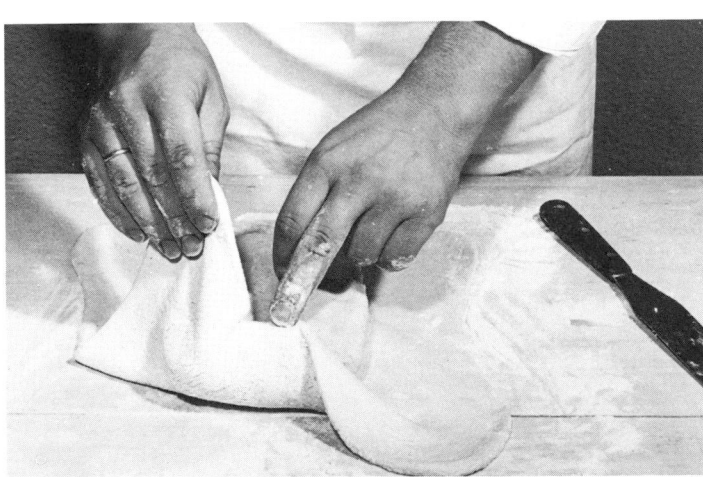

. . . and fold the edges over . . .

Brush off any excess flour.

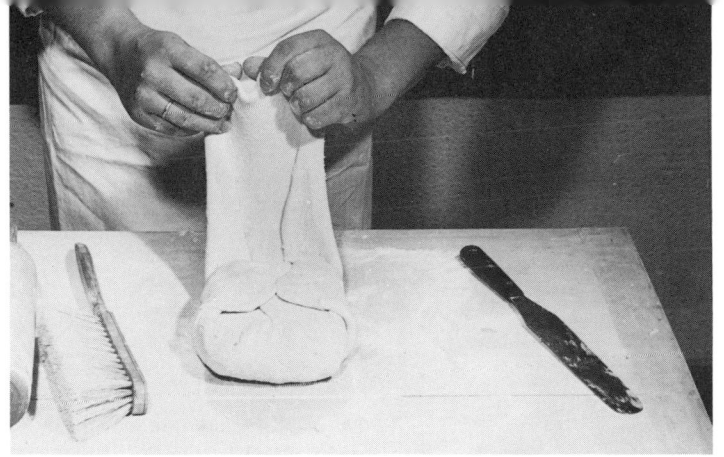

Continue folding, until the fat is completely enclosed.

Pin out the paste . . .

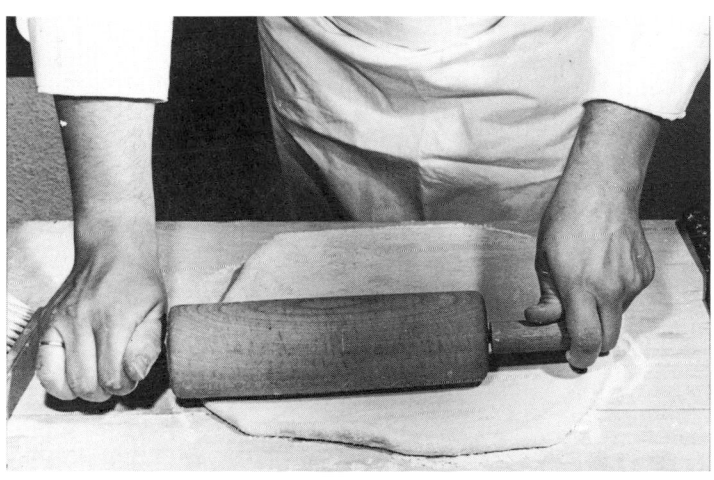

. . . to a rectangular shape.

Brush off excess flour.

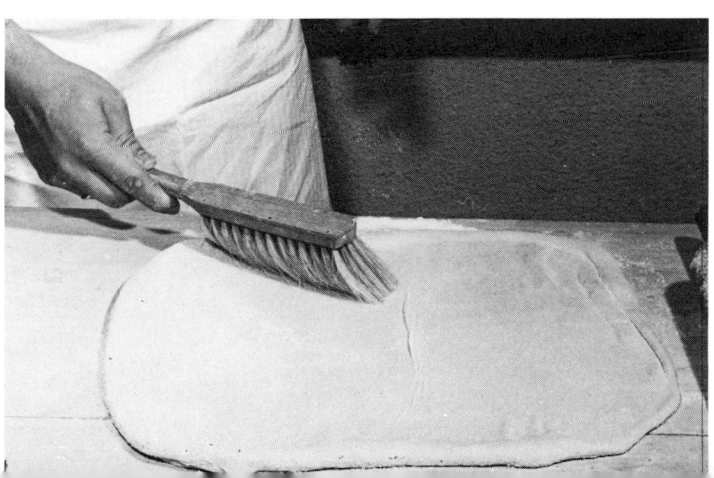

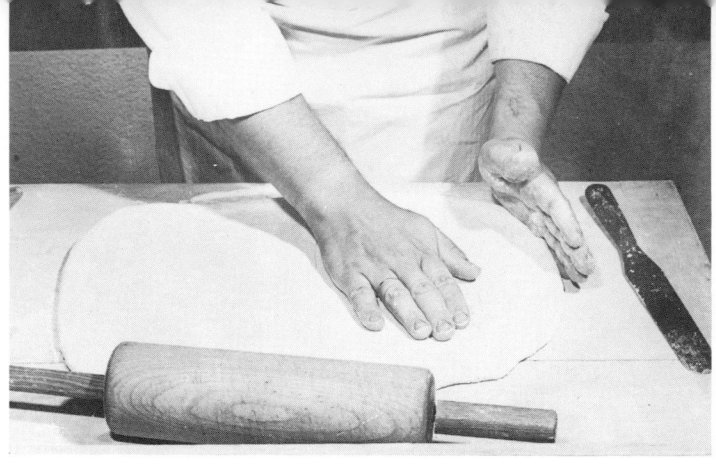

Make sure the rectangle of dough is a regular shape . . .

. . . and fold . . .

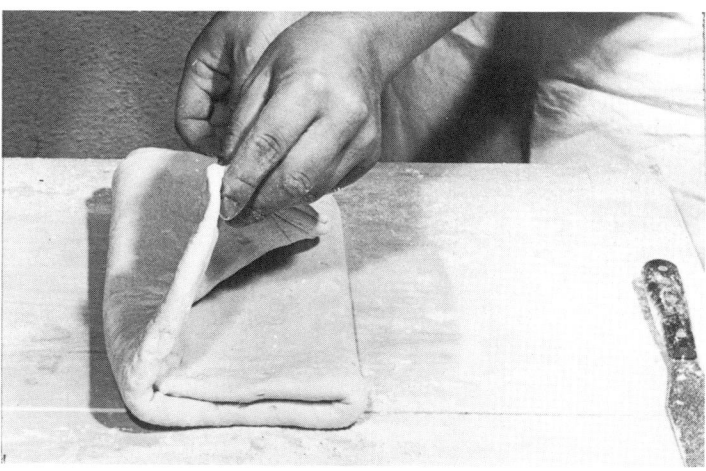

. . . into three.

After allowing it to rest for 10 minutes, pin out again and fold . . .

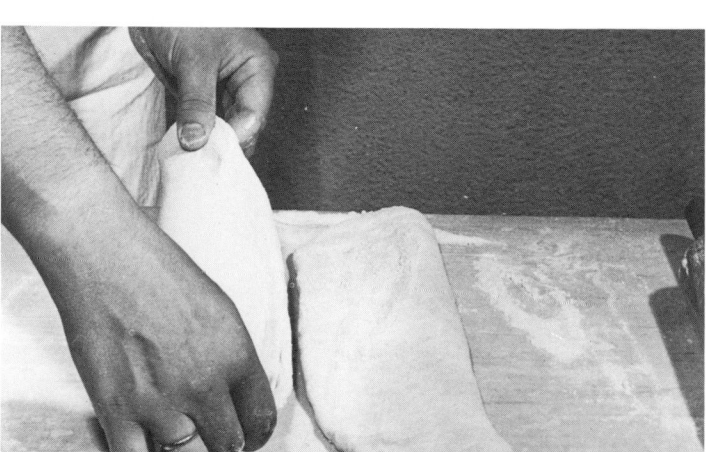

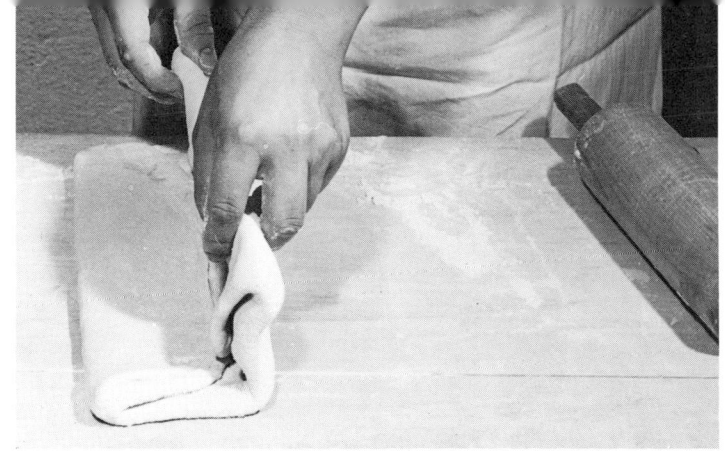

. . . into four and rest in the refrigerator.

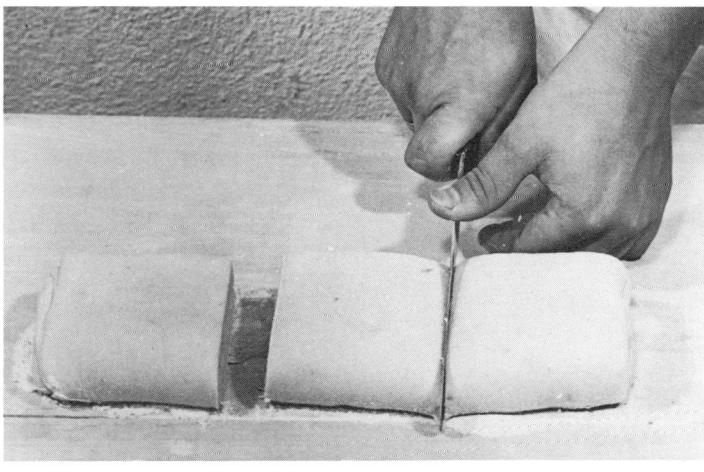

Cut the dough into three equal pieces.

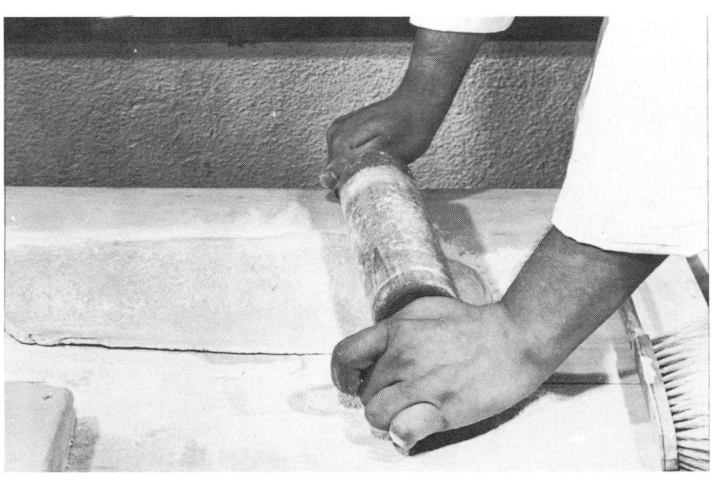

Pin out each piece separately.

Mix the finely sliced apples with the currants, cinnamon and sugar.

Place on one strip of pastry and dampen the edges.

Fold the dough over the filling . . .

. . . enclosing it completely.

Place on a buttered baking sheet, with the sealed side down.

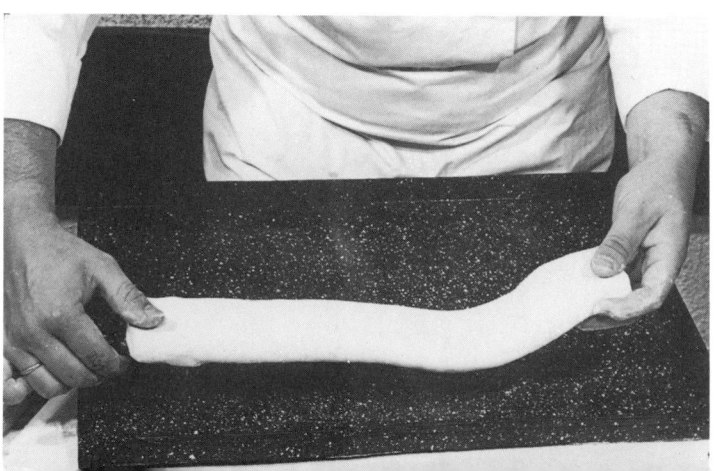

Moisten the minced nuts and sugar with rum.

Spread the filling onto the second piece of dough and proceed as shown on the preceding page.

Make the third strudel with redcurrant jam.

And proceed as shown on the previous page.

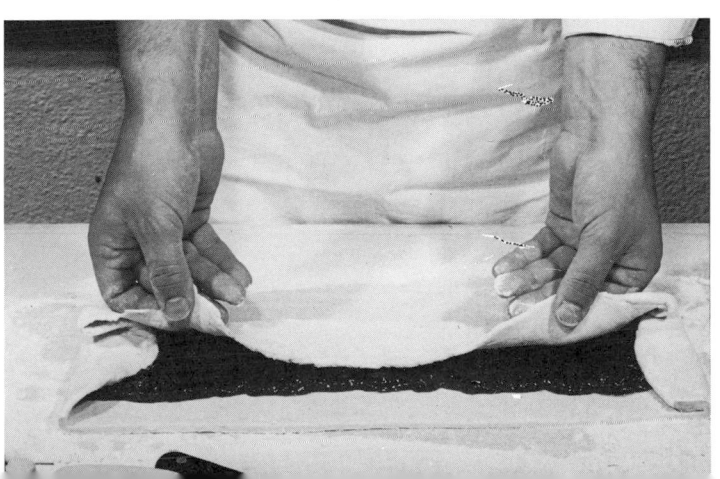

Brush with beaten egg and sprinkle with sugar.

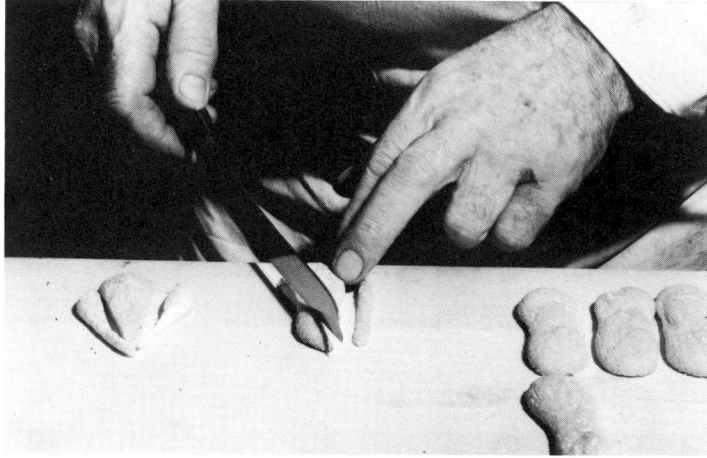

Charlotte russe

Cut sponge fingers to shape.

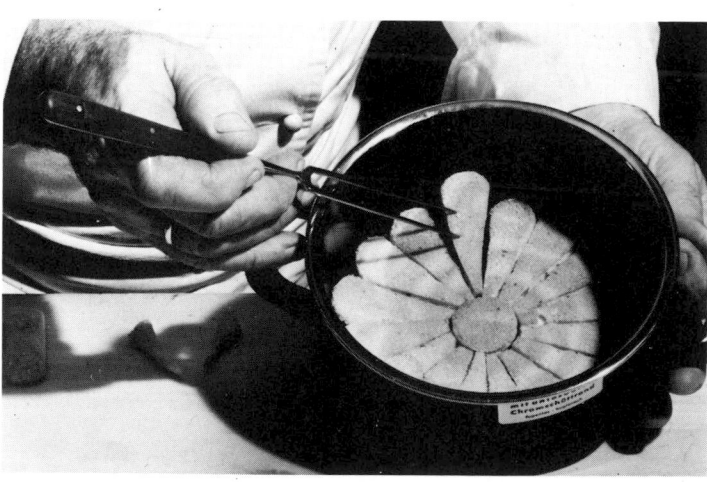

And line the bottom of a mould as shown.

Place more sponge fingers round the sides of the mould and fill with a Bavarian cream (recipe p. 864).

150

Harlequin tart

With the aid of a stencil, cut out the base shape from a sheet of puff paste or short paste. Prick well with a fork. Pipe choux paste through a plain tube to form the sections. Brush with beaten egg and bake blind. Spread Creme St. Honoré in the bottom of each section.

Fill with either well drained canned fruit or suitable fresh fruit. Glaze with jelly or apricot jam, according to the fruit used.

Strawberry gateau

Bake a base of sweet paste in a flan ring. Spread with confectioners' custard flavoured with Grand-Marnier.

Glaze with fruit flavoured jelly with Grand-Marnier and kept liquid in a bain-marie.

Coat the sides with toasted almond flakes.

Dobos torte (see recipe p. 1001)

Sandwich the first four slices together with buttercream.

Coat the sides with buttercream and mark with a comb.

Cover the fifth slice with warm caramel, and immediately cut into sections with an oiled knife. Place these on top of the torte.

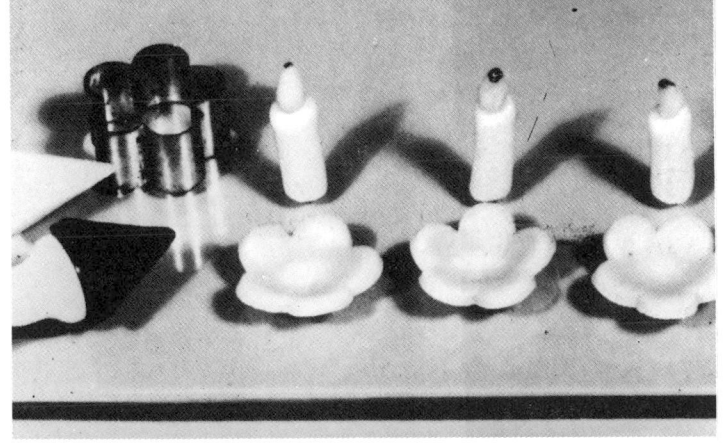

Birthday cake (also for engagements etc)

Make the candles and the flowers from almond paste. Stick the candles on to the flowers with a little melted chocolate.

Fill the sponge cake with buttercream and brush the surface with melted apricot jam. Cover the cake with almond paste. Decorate with buttercream, using a piping bag and put the candles on top.

Cherry cream croustades (see recipe p. 982)

Pin out short pastry to a thickness of 6mm (¼in.) cut into rounds about 5cm (2in.) and bake lightly. Lightly grease the outside of plain round patty pans and stand them upside down on a baking sheet. Cover with a round of short paste and pipe on a trellis of sieved choux pastry. Bake at 190°C and remove from the pans whilst still warm.

When cold, dredge with icing sugar, and fill with well drained, stoned poached cherries.

Pipe over the cherries with cherry cream, covering them completely.

Decorate with a cherry and a choux paste ornament.

Kermesse cakes (see recipe p. 1017)

Divide up the dough.

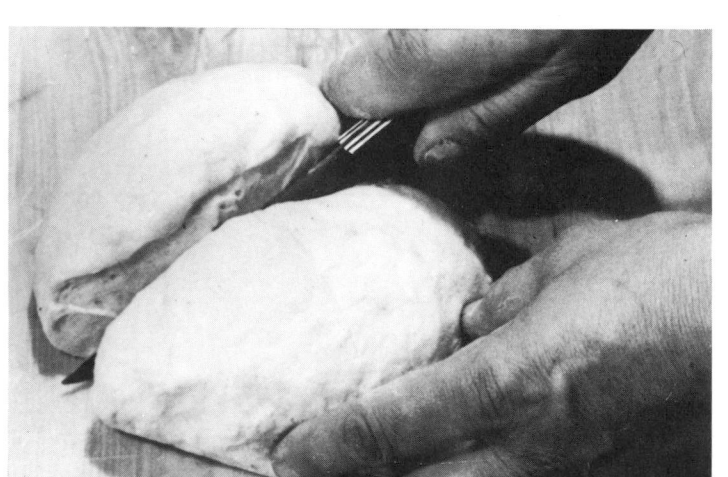

Cut into 50g (2oz) pieces.

Roll these into balls and place on a greased baking sheet.

Let them rise a little, then make a hollow in the centre.

Fill the hollow with one of the listed fillings and top with a glacé cherry or almond nibs.

Brush the dough with eggwash.
When cooked, dust with icing sugar.

Fruit baskets

The picture shows a honeydew
melon cut in half zig-zag fashion,
and grapefruit cut into baskets.

Chestnut vermicelli meringues
(recipe p. 983)

Pipe out the chestnut purée with the
special press shown (or a savoy bag
with a fine plain tube) and
refrigerate.

When cold, cut into discs of a
suitable size with a plain cutter.

Pipe a little whipped cream into the cases and put a small meringue on top.

Fill up with whipped cream and . . .

. . . place the disc of chestnut vermicelli on top.

Mocha fondant cubes

Split and sandwich a Genoise sponge with coffee buttercream. Chill, and brush the top with melted apricot jam and cover with a layer of coffee icing. When the icing is set, cut into cubes and coat the sides of each cube with melted buttercream, using a fork as shown.

Roll the cubes in finely chopped grilled almond flakes.

Carefully remove the fork.

Pipe a rosette of buttercream onto each piece.

Brussels sticks (see recipe p. 976)

Pipe out the Brussels sticks as shown and bake.

158

Sandwich the cooked biscuits together with a little apricot jam with apricot brandy added.

Once assembled, the tops are decorated with three lines of chocolate couverture and a little gold leaf in the centre.

Marbled biscuits (see recipe p. 1026)

Sandwich the two colours of paste together alternately, as shown, then roll out, roll in greaseproof paper and refrigerate until firm.

When firm, cut carefully into slices, with a sharp knife.

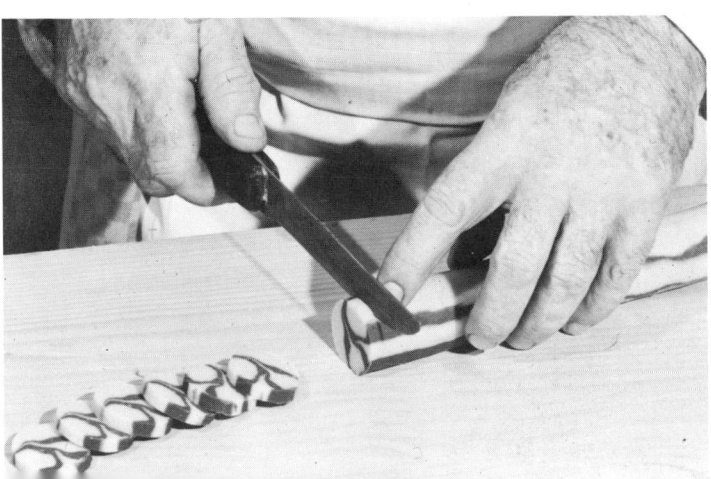

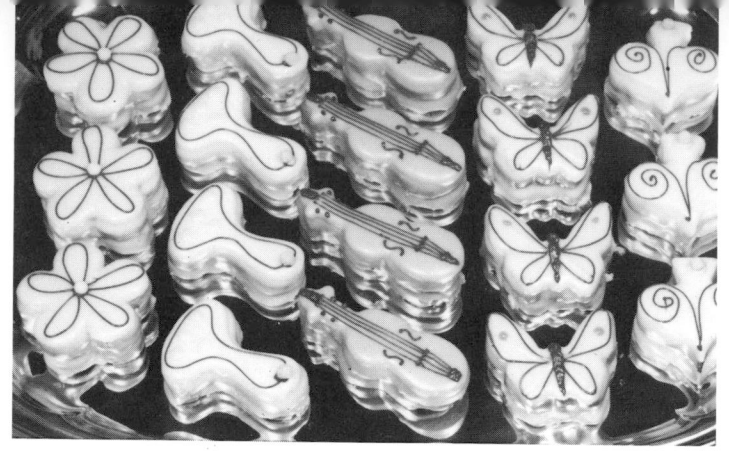

Iced petits fours

Cut the petits fours from a sheet of genoise sponge, using a variety of fancy shaped cutters. Brush with melted apricot jam and glaze with fondant icing. Decorate with chocolate couverture.

Marzipan tea confections (see recipe p. 1018)

Pin out the Konigsberg marzipan between two strips of wood. Cut out with the special cutter.

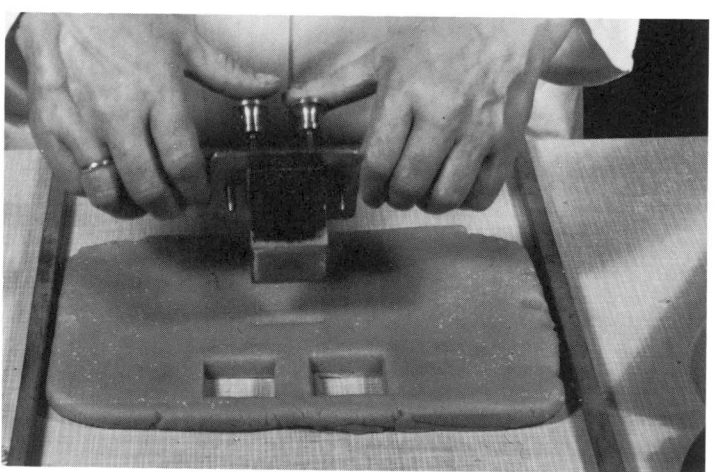

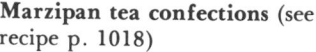

The cut out marzipan pieces are ejected by pressing the two knobs.

The finished product. The cases have been left to dry for 24 hours, flashed through the oven or under the salamander, glazed with gum arabic, filled with kirsch flavoured fondant and decorated with small pieces of crystallized fruit.

Game flavoured aspic

Cooking time: 40 minutes

2½ l	dark aspic jelly	4½ p
750 g	game bones (venison, hare, etc.)	1¾ lb
	1 old lightly roasted partridge or old pheasant, depending on purpose for which the aspic is to be used (if available)	
	butter	

Chop up the bones as small as possible and brown together with the partridge or pheasant, then pour off all the fat. Place the bones and the bird in a large stew pan, rinse out the pan in which they were browned with a little of the aspic jelly and pour into the large pan together with the rest of the aspic jelly. Bring to the boil, skim, simmer gently, strain and clarify in the usual manner.

N.B.—The browned bird may be added when clarifying if desired.

France

Fish aspic

Yield: about 2 litres (3½ pints)   Cooking time: 25–30 minutes

2½ l	fish stock	4½ pt
100 g	chopped fish (cod, whiting, etc.)	4 oz
	4–5 egg whites	
25 g	chervil	1 oz
	green part of 1 small leek	
32–35 g	gelatine	1–1¼ oz

Soak the gelatine and squeeze dry. Using a wire whisk, mix the chopped fish with the egg whites, the coarsely cut chervil and leek, the gelatine and ¼ litre (½ pint) cold fish stock. Pour in the rest of the fish stock, which should be warm but not boiling-hot, and bring to the boil, stirring constantly. Simmer gently, draw aside, cover and allow to stand for 5–10 minutes before straining through a napkin.

N.B.—If the fish stock has been made with very gelatinous fish-bones and scraps of fish such as turbot, the amount of gelatine should be reduced by 4–5 g (about ⅙ oz).

France

7

Quick aspic

Cooking time: 10 minutes

2½ l	beef or chicken consommé	4½ pt
150 g	chopped lean beef	5 oz
	2 egg whites	
100 g	leek (green part only), sliced	3 oz
	a little chervil	
	36–40 sheets gelatine	

Mix the beef thoroughly with the egg whites, leek and chervil, the gelatine which has been soaked and squeezed dry, and ½ litre (⅞ pint) cold consommé. Heat the rest of the consommé and gradually stir in. Bring slowly to the boil, then simmer gently without stirring until the liquid is quite clear. Draw aside, cover, leave for a few minutes, then strain through a fine cloth.

Cold dishes which are not turned out, but served in glass or other moulds, require only half the usual amount of aspic, or the same amount made with only half as much gelatine as usual.

France

Ready-made aspic

Aspic jelly may be bought ready-made in a wide variety of forms. The best one is probably the canned sterilised preparation. The jelly is also available in powdered and tablet form. The directions for use should be followed carefully. There is no harm in adding a little Madeira, sherry or port.

Ready-made aspic can sometimes be very helpful, as it saves a great deal of time and may be kept in store until required, although it is by no means as delicate as traditional aspic jelly.

France

COURTS-BOUILLON

These preparations are used for poaching either whole fish or fish fillets, because the cooking time for such dishes is so short that the flavour needs to be extracted from the vegetables first.

Court-bouillon I

Yield: about 3½ litres (6 pints)   Cooking time: 30 minutes

2 l	white wine	3½ pt
2 l	water	3½ pt
200 g	carrots	8 oz
200 g	onions	8 oz
	1 large bouquet garni	
	10 peppercorns	
40 g	salt	1½ oz

Slice the carrots and onions finely and cook slowly with the other ingredients. Pass through a conical strainer.

France

Court-bouillon II

Yield: about 3½ litres (6 pints)   Cooking time: 30 minutes

3½ l	water	6 pt
4 dl	wine vinegar	⅔ pt
200 g	carrots	8 oz
200 g	onions	8 oz
	1 large bouquet garni	
	10 peppercorns	
40 g	salt	1½ oz

Procccd as for Court-bouillon I.

France

STUFFINGS, FORCEMEATS AND FARCES

Panada (basic recipe)

Cooking time: 5–6 minutes

¼ l	milk	½ pt
150 g	flour	5¼ oz
	4 egg yolks	
100 g	melted butter	3½ oz
	salt	
	pepper	
	grated nutmeg	

Mix the flour with the egg yolks. Season with salt, pepper and a small pinch of grated nutmeg and add the melted butter. Gradually blend with the boiling milk and cook until smooth, without allowing the mixture to boil, stirring constantly. Before using place in a bowl, dot the top with butter to avoid skinning and allow to cool completely.

A panada is used to bind other ingredients to make a stuffing.

France

Fish mousseline forcemeat

500 g (net weight)	fish (pike, whiting, salmon or sole, etc.)	1 lb
	2–3 egg whites	
½ l	dairy cream	⅞ pt

Work the fish to a fine purée in the blender with a little egg white and rub through a sieve. Transfer the purée to a pan, place in a bowl full of ice and chill well. Using a spatula, gradually work in the cream and the rest of the egg whites a little at a time, then season with salt and pepper. Store in a cool place until required.

N.B.—As the amount of egg white required is variable, the consistency of the mixture should be tested before all the egg white has been used. A small ball of forcemeat is dropped into boiling water; if it is too soft to hold together, a little more egg white should be added; if it is too firm, a little more cream is required.

France

Gratin forcemeat

Yield: about 500 g (1 lb 1½ oz)

125 g	belly of pork (or streaky bacon)	4 oz
125 g	boneless veal	4 oz
125 g	chicken livers (or, if not available, calf's liver)	4 oz
25 g	mushrooms	1 oz
20 g	chopped shallots	1 oz
	1 sprig thyme	
	quarter of a bay leaf	
1 dl	Madeira	⅛ pt
50 g	butter	2 oz
	2 egg yolks	

	1 tablespoon well-reduced	
	veal stock	
15 g	lard	1 oz
8 g	salt	¼ oz

Dice the belly of pork and brown lightly in the lard. Remove, place the diced veal in the pan, brown lightly and remove. Slice the livers, place in the same pan and fry lightly in the hot fat until firm. Return the belly of pork and the veal to the pan, add the shallots, the sliced mushrooms, a few truffle peelings (if available), the bay leaf and thyme and mix well. Season with salt and pepper, pour in the Madeira, cover and cook gently for about 5–6 minutes. Strain off the liquid, but set aside the fat. Remove the thyme and bay leaf and pound the meat or work to a fine purée in the blender, then add the butter, egg yolks and veal stock without switching off and lastly blend in the fat which has been set aside. Mix the forcemeat thoroughly, check the seasoning and rub through a fine sieve. Work a little longer, place in a basin, cover with buttered paper and store in the refrigerator if not required at once.

N.B.—If the forcemeat is intended for game birds, the veal should be replaced by scraps or trimmings from the same type of bird or, if not available, the same amount of livers of game birds.

France

Herb stuffing

125 g	breadcrumbs	4 oz
60 g	chopped suet	2 oz
	1 tablespoon chopped parsley	
	½ teaspoon chopped	
	mixed herbs	
	nutmeg	
	grated rind of ½ lemon	
	salt and pepper	
	1 beaten egg	

Mix together all the ingredients and season to taste.

Sage and onion stuffing

250 g	onions	½ lb
	8 young sage leaves (rubbed)	
125 g	breadcrumbs	4 oz
60 g	butter	2 oz

1 egg
salt
black ground pepper

Sauté onions in butter and add to the breadcrumbs. Add sage, salt, pepper and beaten egg.

Chestnut stuffing

1 kg	chestnuts	2 lb
1 kg	sausage meat	2 lb
250 g	breadcrumbs	½ lb
	1 teaspoon salt	
	1 teaspoon poultry seasoning	
40 cl	Cognac	1½ fl oz

Cut gashes in the convex side of chestnuts with a sharp-pointed knife. Place chestnuts in a saucepan with water to cover and bring to boiling point. Remove from heat. Remove chestnuts one at a time from the water and peel off shells and inner skins while nuts are hot. Cook in chicken stock (covering nuts) for ½ hour, or until chestnuts are barely soft. Drain and chop. Add to remaining ingredients. Mix well.

Lemon and tarragon stuffing

120 g	fresh white breadcrumbs	4 oz
60 g	butter	2 oz
30 g	finely chopped onion	1 oz
30 g	chopped fresh tarragon	1 oz
30 g	chopped fresh parsley	1 oz
	1 lemon	
	1 egg	

Blend together the breadcrumbs, butter, onion and herbs and season to taste. Add the grated zest of the lemon, and moisten with the beaten egg and lemon juice.

Great Britain

HOT SAUCES

Béchamel sauce

½ l	milk	1 pt
60–75 g	butter	2 oz

60 g	flour	2 oz
	1 onion	
	1 bay leaf	
	2 cloves	

Pin the bay leaf to the onion with the cloves and simmer in the milk for 5 or 6 minutes. Melt the butter, stir in the flour and cook gently for 4 or 5 minutes without allowing the flour to colour (this is a white roux). Let the roux cool for a few minutes then gradually stir in the hot milk a little at a time, beating out any lumps. Simmer the sauce for at least 10 minutes, then strain.

Béchamel sauce may be stored for a few days in the refrigerator. The top should be dabbed with butter to prevent skinning.

France

Mornay sauce

½ l	Béchamel sauce	1 pt
	2 egg yolks	
75 g	grated Gruyère cheese	3 oz

Thicken the Béchamel sauce with the egg yolks. Stir in the cheese without heating.

This sauce may be stored in the same way as Béchamel sauce.

France

Aurore sauce

Cooking time: 2–3 minutes

½ l	Béchamel sauce	1 pt
1 dl	dairy cream	¼ pt
5 cl	tomato sauce	3 tablespoons

Mix together the Béchamel and tomato sauce, bring to the boil, allow to boil gently for 2–3 minutes and finish off with the cream.

France

Nantua sauce

½ l	light Béchamel sauce	1 pt

1 dl	dairy cream	¼ pt
50 g	crayfish butter	2 oz

Let the Béchamel sauce boil gently for a few moments, then stir in the cream with a spatula. As soon as the sauce is thick enough to coat the spatula, pass it through a conical strainer. Without returning to the heat, add the crayfish butter in small knobs while stirring with a spatula to keep the sauce smooth and prevent skinning. Adjust the seasoning.

France

Velouté sauce

Cooking time: 30 minutes

½ l	veal stock	1 pt
50 g	flour	2 oz
100 g	butter	4 oz

Proceed as for Béchamel sauce, but use veal stock instead of milk.

France

Fish velouté sauce

Cooking time: 20–30 minutes

½ l	concentrated fish stock	1 pt
70 g	butter	2 oz
50 g	flour	2 oz

Proceed as for Béchamel sauce, but use concentrated fish stock instead of milk.

France

Joinville sauce

½ l	fish velouté made with white wine	1 pt
5 cl	mushroom cooking liquid	1/12 pt
	3 tablespoons dairy cream	
75 g	shrimp or prawn butter	3 oz

Add the mushroom cooking liquid to the fish velouté, bring to the boil and allow to boil gently for a few moments. Blend in the cream with a spatula. The sauce should be of a smooth and creamy coating consistency. Pass through a conical strainer. Without returning to the heat, add the shrimp or prawn butter in small knobs while stirring with a spatula to keep the sauce smooth and prevent skinning. Adjust the seasoning.

France

Chicken velouté

Proceed as for Béchamel sauce, but use rather strong well-skimmed chicken broth instead of milk.

Velouté sauces are finished off with double cream when about to serve. They are boiled gently for a moment, then 30–40 g (1–1½ oz) butter is blended in a little at a time after removing from the heat.

France

Suprême sauce

Cooking time: 30 minutes

125 g	butter	4½ oz
60 g	flour	2 oz
1 l	chicken stock	1½ pt
½ l	dairy cream	½ pt
	2 egg yolks	

Melt 75 g (3 oz) butter, stir in the flour with a whisk and cook over very gentle heat for 4–5 minutes without colouring. As soon as the mixture begins to froth, add the chicken stock and stir until boiling. Simmer gently without stirring. When cooked, skim and remove from the heat. Thicken with the egg yolks and cream, then add the rest of the butter a little at a time.

France

Hollandaise sauce

250 g	butter	8 oz
	3 egg yolks	
	3 tablespoons white wine vinegar	
	lemon juice	
	cayenne pepper	

Whisk together the egg yolks and vinegar in a saucepan which is deeper than it is wide. Stand the saucepan in a very hot—but not boiling—bain-marie and whisk constantly, taking care to keep the mixture away from the sides of the pan. After a time the mixture should thicken to a creamy foamy consistency (it is difficult to gauge the length of time required, as this depends on the heat). It should be possible to place a finger in the mixture without its being scalded. Now whisk in the butter which has been melted in a bain-marie, pouring it into the pan in a thin stream and being careful to keep back the whey. For this operation the saucepan may be left in the bain-marie or stood over very gentle heat. If the sauce becomes too thick while working, add a few drops of lukewarm water. Season with salt, pepper and a dash of cayenne pepper. Sharpen with a few drops of lemon juice. Keep the sauce hot in a moderately hot bain-marie.

France

Béarnaise sauce

To the above quantity of Hollandaise sauce add:

> 1 tablespoon tarragon vinegar
> 1 teaspoon chopped fresh parsley
> 1 teaspoon fresh tarragon
> 1 teaspoon fresh chervil

Mousseline sauce

This is Hollandaise sauce with the addition of varying amounts of whipped cream, up to a maximum of one-third of the volume of the Hollandaise sauce.

3 tablespoons whipped cream may be used for the quantities given in the recipe for Hollandaise sauce.

France

Choron sauce

4 dl	Béarnaise sauce	$\frac{1}{2}$ pt
	3 soup spoonfuls	
	concentrated tomato purée	

Prepare the Béarnaise sauce without the addition of chopped chervil and tarragon and add the tomato purée.

Espagnole sauce

250 g	roux made with butter	8 oz
5 l	light brown stock	$8\frac{3}{4}$ pt

50 g	butter	2 oz
125 g	carrots	4½ oz
75 g	onions	3 oz
125 g	mushroom peelings	4½ oz
	sprig thyme	
	1 bay leaf	
5 cl	white wine	1/12 pt
1 kg	fresh tomatoes	2¼ lb

Bring the stock to the boil, bind with the prepared roux. Bring to the boil again, add the mirepoix of vegetables well coloured in hot shallow butter and deglazed with white wine. Allow to cook for 2 hours over a low heat. Strain, allow to reduce for a further 2 hours, adding the fresh tomatoes. Strain.

Demi-glace sauce

4 dl	Espagnole sauce	½ pt
4 dl	brown meat stock	½ pt
	2 tablespoons sherry	

Combine Espagnole sauce and meat stock in a saucepan. Simmer until the mixture is reduced by half. Remove from heat and stir in the sherry.

Madère sauce

Cooking time: 15 minutes

2 dl	Madeira	¼ pt
½ l	demi-glace	1 pt
25 g	meat glace	1 oz
25 g	butter	1 oz

Place Madeira and meat glace in a casserole and reduce to half the volume. Add 1 pint (½ litre) demi-glace, boil for a few minutes. Remove from heat, season and stir in butter.

Chasseur sauce

½ l	demi-glace	1 pt
25 g	minced shallot	1 oz
250 g	sliced mushrooms	½ lb

¼ l	white wine	½ pt
250 g	fresh tomato purée	½ lb
60 g	butter	2 oz
25 g	chopped parsley and tarragon	1 oz

Melt the butter and add the shallots. Cook gently and then add the mushrooms. Add the white wine and reduce by half. Add 1 pint (½ litre) demi-glace and the tomato purée and boil for a few minutes. When cooked, add butter and the chopped parsley and tarragon.

Diable sauce

	2 shallots	
2 dl	dry white wine	¼ pt
	1 teaspoon tomato purée	
½ l	demi-glace	1 pt
	chopped chervil	
	Worcestershire sauce	
	cayenne pepper	

Brown the chopped shallots lightly in butter. Add the wine and reduce by half, slowly. Add the demi-glacé and the tomato purée. Cook for 5 minutes. Season with a generous dash of Worcestershire sauce, cayenne pepper and a little chopped chervil.

Curry sauce

25 g	butter	1 oz
25 g	flour	1 oz
50 g	chopped onions	2 oz
	2 medium sized, peeled, cored and chopped apples	
12 g	curry powder	½ oz
	1 crushed clove garlic	
	1 tablespoon concentrated tomato purée	
½ l	stock	1 pt
25 g	grated coconut	1 oz

Fry onion in butter until pale brown. Sprinkle flour on top and cook for few minutes. Add curry powder and apple. Cook briefly. Stir in the stock. Add tomato purée, garlic and coconut. Salt lightly and cook slowly for 35 to 40 minutes. Do not strain.

Tomato sauce

1 l	brown stock	2 pt
3 dl	tomato purée	½ pt
50 g	butter	2 oz
50 g	flour	2 oz
100 g	onion	¼ lb
100 g	carrot	¼ lb
100 g	celery	¼ lb
50 g	bacon trimming	2 oz
	1 bay leaf	
	1 sprig thyme	

Make a mirepoix with the onions, carrots, celery, bacon trimmings, bay leaf and thyme. Add the flour and cook over low heat for 5 minutes stirring constantly. Add tomato purée and stir well. Add the stock, cover and cook slowly for 1 hour, if possible in the oven. Strain, season lightly. Add a pinch of sugar and the butter. If too thick, thin with a little stock.

White wine sauce (For fish)

5 dl	fish velouté sauce	1 pt
3 dl	fish stock	½ pt
250 g	butter	8 oz
	juice of 1 lemon	
	dry white wine	

Add fish stock to the velouté sauce. Reduce over high heat to ½ litre (1 pint). Remove from heat. Blend in butter and lemon juice. Add white wine until sauce is desired consistency. Strain and butter the surface.

Lobster sauce

½ l	fish velouté	1 pt
1 dl	cream	¼ pt
125 g	lobster butter	¼ lb
60 g	diced lobster	2 oz
	1 teaspoon paprika	

Reduce velouté cream and paprika to ½ litre (1 pint), strain, remove from heat. Beat in the butter and diced lobster.

Spaghetti sauce I—garlic and oil

	2 cloves garlic	
5 cl	olive oil	$\frac{1}{12}$ pt
	1 small bunch parsley,	
	finely chopped	
	1 small hot red pepper,	
	finely chopped	
	grated Parmesan cheese	

Heat the oil in a frying pan, add the garlic and fry either lightly or well, according to taste. Remove from the pan and discard. Drain the cooked spaghetti well, pour the oil from the pan over and sprinkle with the chopped red pepper (or freshly ground black pepper), the chopped parsley and grated Parmesan cheese. Serve at once, leaving the guests to mix the spaghetti with the sauce.

This sauce is mainly served in southern Italy at midnight; it is supposed to aid digestion.

Italy

Spaghetti sauce II—raw tomato sauce

	4 large very ripe tomatoes	
1 dl	olive oil	$\frac{1}{6}$ pt
	1 small bunch basil	
	grated Parmesan cheese	

Skin the tomatoes, scoop out the seeds and juice, dice the flesh and rub through a sieve. Place the purée in a basin, mix with salt, freshly ground black pepper and the finely chopped basil and stir in the oil. Drain the cooked spaghetti, serve on to soup plates in individual portions, coat with the sauce and serve at once. Hand grated Parmesan cheese separately.

Italy

Spaghetti sauce III—quick tomato sauce

	1 large can skinned tomatoes	
30 g	butter	1 oz
3 cl	olive oil	3 dessertspoons
	few fresh basil leaves	
	or 1 small bunch parsley,	
	finely chopped	
	1 medium onion	
	diced oregano	
	freshly ground black pepper	
	grated Parmesan cheese	

Heat the oil and butter in a pan, add the onions and fry gently until golden. Add the tomatoes and the juice from the can, season with salt and freshly ground black pepper, flavour with oregano and cook briskly for 5 minutes. Drain the pasta, place in a serving dish or on individual plates, coat with the sauce and sprinkle with parsley or basil. Hand the grated Parmesan cheese separately.

Italy

CHAUD-FROID SAUCES

These sauces are extensively used for decorated cold dishes. The dish to be coated is placed on a wire rack when very cold, and the sauce is spooned or ladled over when just on the point of setting. The decoration is then stuck on with aspic jelly, and the whole piece lightly glazed with jelly.

Chaud-froid sauce can be kept under refrigeration but obviously it needs to be re-heated before use. It is essential that the sauce is allowed to boil when it is re-heated.

Chicken chaud-froid sauce

Cooking time: 20 minutes

½ l	chicken aspic jelly	1 pt
40 g	butter	2 oz
30 g	flour	1 oz
15 cl	double cream	¼ pt
	cayenne pepper	
	lemon juice	

Make a roux with the butter and flour. Draw aside and, while stirring with a whisk, add the boiling-hot jelly a little at a time. When thoroughly blended, cook over gentle heat, skimming now and again. After 20 minutes, add the cream and boil gently for a moment. Remove from the heat, add a few drops of lemon juice and pass through a conical strainer or a tammy cloth. Stir until cold to prevent skinning. Season well and use at once or store in a refrigerator.

France

Brown chaud-froid sauce, household type

Cooking time: 20 minutes

½ l	veal gravy	⅞ pt

½ l	aspic jelly	⅞ pt
40 g	flour	1½ oz
40 g	butter	1½ oz
	1 level tablespoon	
	tomato purée	
3 cl	Madeira	3 dessertspoons

Make a brown roux as follows. Melt the butter, stir in the flour with a whisk and cook over very gentle heat for about 10 minutes, stirring frequently, until the roux is light brown. Pour in the hot veal gravy a little at a time, blending it in with a whisk over very gentle heat. Add the tomato purée and simmer for 10–12 minutes, skimming several times. Stir in the aspic jelly a little at a time with a spatula while keeping the mixture on the boil. Reduce to three-fifths of its volume, i.e. 7–8 dl (about 1¼ pints), stirring constantly meanwhile. Adjust the seasoning, pass through a conical strainer, add the Madeira and stir until the sauce is cold to prevent skinning.

Argenteuil chaud-froid sauce

Prepare chicken chaud-froid sauce and add 100 g (4 oz) white asparagus tips which have been cooked, dried over gentle heat under cover and passed through a fine sieve. Mix the asparagus into the sauce, bring to the boil and pass through a tammy cloth.

France

Aurore chaud-froid sauce

Prepare chicken chaud-froid sauce. Add 25 g (1 oz) tomato concentrate and a dash of paprika.

France

Belle de Lauris chaud-froid sauce

Proceed as for Argenteuil chaud-froid sauce, but use green instead of white asparagus tips. Add a little vegetable green to improve the colour.

France

Game chaud-froid sauce

This sauce is made in exactly the same way as brown chaud-froid sauce, except that it is based on concentrated stock made from the game bird concerned, e.g. pheasant stock if required for coating a pheasant.

France

Game chaud-froid sauce, household type

Cooking time: 20 minutes

½ l	strong game stock	1 pt
½ l	game aspic jelly	1 pt
40 g	flour	2 oz
40 g	butter	2 oz
3 cl	Madeira	3 dessertspoons

Proceed as for brown chaud-froid sauce household type.

France

Lobster chaud-froid sauce

½ l	sauce as for lobster American style	1 pt
1 dl	double cream	¼ pt
3 dl	fish or meat aspic jelly	½ pt

Gradually blend the cream and then the jelly into the sauce over brisk heat while stirring with a spatula. Reduce to two-thirds of its volume and strain through a tammy cloth. Adjust the seasoning with a pinch of salt and cayenne pepper.

If the American sauce is prepared specially for this recipe, it should be reduced before being thickened with the creamy parts of the lobster.

France

Occitane chaud-froid sauce

Prepare chicken chaud-froid sauce and add 100 g (4 oz) sweet red peppers which have been cooked and passed through a fine sieve. Strain the sauce through a tammy cloth. Add a tiny drop of carmine to improve the colour.

France

Quick brown chaud-froid sauce

Cooking time: 20 minutes

½ l	consommé	1 pt
	1 level tablespoon tomato purée	
30 g	flour	1 oz
40 g	butter	1 oz

| 10 g | powdered gelatine | ½ oz |
| 3 cl | Madeira | 3 dessertspoons |

Dissolve the gelatine in the hot consommé and slowly bring to the boil. Skim and add the tomato purée. Cook for a few minutes, skimming meanwhile, and proceed as for brown chaud-froid sauce household type.

France

Quick chicken chaud-froid

½ l	chicken broth	1 pt
10 g	powdered gelatine	½ oz
30 g	flour	1 oz
40 g	butter	1 oz
15 cl	double cream	¼ pt
	lemon juice	
	cayenne pepper	

Dissolve the gelatine in the very hot chicken broth. Boil up over medium heat and skim. Now proceed as for ordinary chicken chaud-froid sauce.

France

Sevillian chaud-froid sauce

Proceed as for Occitane chaud-froid sauce, adding a little cayenne pepper and a little tomato concentrate to deepen the colour.

France

COLD SAUCES

Mayonnaise sauce

Yield: about ½ litre (⅞ pint)

½ l	oil	1 pt
	4 egg yolks	
	1 teaspoon mustard (optional)	
	1 tablespoon vinegar	

Place the egg yolks, the mustard and a dash of cayenne pepper in a basin. Season with salt, mix well and add the vinegar. Whisk in the oil drop by drop. Should the mayonnaise become too thick, add a little vinegar. Lastly stir in a spoonful of boiling water.

Mayonnaise should be soft and not, as some people wrongly believe, 'firm enough to cut with a knife'; if it is as firm as this, it is indigestible and unattractive. Should curdling occur, put a spoonful of hot vinegar in a clean basin and whisk in the curdled mayonnaise gradually.

France

Aspic mayonnaise

Yield: 6 dl (1 pt)

½ l	mayonnaise	1 pt
1 dl	aspic jelly	¼ pt

Blend the lukewarm aspic jelly into the mayonnaise, which should be stiff. This mayonnaise may be stored in the refrigerator.

France

Apple and horseradish sauce

10 portions

500 g	apple purée	1 lb
100 g	freshly grated horseradish	4 oz
	juice of half a lemon (about)	

Mix the apple purée with the horseradish and add lemon juice to taste.

Austria

Barbecue sauce

	12 bottles chilli sauce	
2 dl	each	⅓ pt
	9 bottles tomato ketchup,	
2 dl	each	⅓ pt
	12 finely chopped cloves of garlic	
800 g	brown sugar	1 lb 12 oz
1 l	sweet soya sauce	1¾ pt
	1 bottle Worcestershire sauce	
	1 small bottle Tabasco sauce,	
1·2 cl	each	2½ teaspoons

6 dl	oil	1 pt
½ l	vinegar	⅞ pt
6 l	water	10½ pt

Mix all the ingredients together well and store in an airtight container. The sauce may be used for a wide variety of food, which should be marinated for 24–48 hours before grilling.

The above quantities are sufficient for 150 portions, that is, 50 half-chickens, 50 pork cutlets, 50 hamburgers (lightly fried beforehand).

Chantilly sauce

Yield: 6 dl (1¼ pt)

½ l	mayonnaise	1 pt
100 g	whipped cream	¼ pt

Blend the whipped cream into the mayonnaise.

France

Green sauce

Yield about ½ litre (1 pint)

½ l	mayonnaise	1 pt
30 g	tarragon	1 oz
30 g	parsley	1 oz
30 g	chervil	1 oz
	2 spinach leaves	

Blanch the spinach and herbs, starting with the spinach. Allow to boil for a few minutes, then refresh, squeeze dry and pass through a fine sieve. Mix with the mayonnaise and adjust the seasoning.

France

Hatzfeld sauce

300 g	rose hip preserve	10 oz
300 g	red-currant jelly	10 oz
3 dl	red wine	½ pt

100 g	mustard	4 oz
	zest of 1½ to 2 green lemons	
	lemon juice	

Mix the mustard thoroughly with the rose hip preserve and the red-currant jelly. Add the wine and blend to a smooth sauce. Now add the lemon zest, stir well and allow to stand for a time. Stir in lemon juice to taste.

Austria

Marseillaise sauce for fish

Yield: about ½ litre (1 pint)

½ l	mayonnaise	1 pt
	6 sea urchins	

Pass the yellow part of the sea urchins through a fine sieve and mix with the mayonnaise.

France

Marseillaise sauce for cold meat I

Yield: about ½ litre (1 pint)

½ l	mayonnaise	1 pt
	1 tablespoon well-reduced	
	concentrated tomato sauce	

Mix the tomato sauce with the mayonnaise.

France

Marseillaise sauce for cold meat II

½ l	mayonnaise	1 pt
100 g	fresh tomatoes	4 oz

Skin the tomatoes, remove the seeds, press out the moisture well and chop coarsely. Press again to dry, then mix with the mayonnaise and adjust the seasoning.

France

Morgonnaise sauce

Yield: about ½ litre (1 pint)

¼ l	Morgon	½ pt (approx.)
½ l	Chantilly sauce	1 pt
	2 shallots	

Chop the shallots and place in a pan with the wine. Reduce until the wine has boiled away almost completely; then leave until cold and mix with the Chantilly sauce.

France

Rémoulade sauce

Yield: about ½ litre (1 pint)

½ l	mayonnaise	1 pt
75 g	capers and gherkins (mixed)	4 oz
	1 rounded tablespoon chopped chervil and parsley	

Chop the capers and gherkins very finely and dry in a cloth. Mix with the herbs and add to the mayonnaise.

France

Sharp sauce

10 persons

	2 hard-boiled egg yolks	
	2 raw egg yolks	
	pinch of salt	
	dash of paprika	
	2 teaspoons French mustard	
	2 tablespoons vinegar	
4 dl	whipped cream	⅔ pt

Mash the hard-boiled egg yolks and mix with the raw yolks. Season with salt, paprika and mustard and blend in the vinegar. Mix well with the whipped cream.

Sweden

Tartare sauce

Yield: about ½ litre (1 pint)

½ l	oil	1 pt
	2 raw egg yolks	
	2 hard-boiled egg yolks	
	1 tablespoon vinegar	
	1 teaspoon mustard	
	1 tablespoon chopped chervil and parsley	
75 g	chopped capers and gherkins	4 oz
20 g	chopped onion	1 oz

Mash the hard-boiled egg yolks with the addition of the raw yolks and the mustard. Season with salt, pepper and a dash of cayenne pepper. Mix well, add the vinegar, then proceed as for mayonnaise. Lastly work in the herbs, capers and gherkins as for Rémoulade sauce.

France

Viennese chive sauce

10 portions

	10 egg yolks	
200 g	white bread without crusts	8 oz
½ l	oil	1 pt
100 g	finely cut chives	4 oz
	vinegar	
	salt	
	sugar	

Carefully cook 5 egg yolks in water containing a little vinegar. Soak the bread in water containing a little vinegar, squeeze dry and rub through a fine wire sieve together with the cooked yolks. Place in a bowl, add the 5 raw egg yolks, salt, a pinch of sugar and a little vinegar and beat in the oil a little at a time with a wire whisk in the same way as for mayonnaise. Adjust the seasoning if necessary (the sauce should have a sweetish-sourish taste) and sprinkle liberally with cut chives.

Austria

Vinaigrette dressing

Yield: sufficient for 3–4 portions of salad

3 tablespoons oil

1 tablespoon wine vinegar
½ teaspoon mustard

Place the wine vinegar and mustard in a salad bowl with the addition of salt and pepper. Mix until the salt is dissolved, then add the oil.

France

Vinaigrette dressing with cream

Use cream instead of oil and lemon juice instead of vinegar.

France

Vinaigrette dressing with herbs

Mix the vinaigrette dressing with 1 tablespoon of mixed chopped herbs—chervil, tarragon, parsley and chives.

France

Apple sauce

A slightly sweetened apple purée seasoned with cinnamon.

Aioli sauce

	6 cloves of garlic	
	2 egg yolks	
3 dl	oil	½ pt
	salt	
	pepper	
	lemon juice	

Pound garlic very finely in a mortar, add salt, pepper and egg yolks. Add the oil very gradually as for mayonnaise and from time to time add a few drops of lemon juice. Finally stir in a teaspoonful of boiling water to prevent sauce curdling.

Cumberland sauce

250 g	red-currant jelly	½ lb
	2 chopped shallots	
	zest of ½ orange	
	½ lemon cut in fine julienne	

2 tablespoons port
juice of $\frac{1}{2}$ orange
juice of $\frac{1}{4}$ lemon
$\frac{1}{8}$ teaspoon mustard powder
pinch of ground ginger
pinch of cayenne pepper

Blanch the zest and shallots for 3 minutes and drain. Pass the jelly through a sieve, and mix with the port, orange and lemon juice and season with mustard, ground ginger and cayenne pepper. Finally add shallots and julienne and leave to stand for several hours.

Horseradish sauce

4 dl	whipped cream	$\frac{3}{4}$ pt
	3 tablespoons grated horseradish	
	pinch of sugar, salt and paprika	
	2 teaspoons vinegar	
	1 teaspoon made mustard	
60 g	breadcrumbs	2 oz

Mix horseradish with vinegar and breadcrumbs. Season with sugar, salt and paprika and gently fold in whipped cream.

Mint sauce

90 g	freshly chopped mint	3 oz
30 g	sugar	1 oz
4 dl	vinegar	$\frac{3}{4}$ pt
3 dl	water	$\frac{1}{2}$ pt

Pour vinegar over chopped mint and allow to stand. Add cold water and sugar.

Soufflé mayonnaise sauce

Proceed as for ordinary mayonnaise sauce, but make the sauce slightly thicker. Finally, gently fold in the stiffly whipped whites of the eggs used.

This makes a lighter sauce and avoids wasting the egg whites, if there is no other use for them.

COMPOUND BUTTERS

These consist of best quality butter mixed with various ingredients which impart flavour and often colour. They are used for spreading on bread, canapés, etc., or for decoration, and should be of a soft, creamy consistency. They should not be made up a long time before they are required, for they undergo changes in colour and slight fermentation due to the fact that they are mixtures.

A spatula or knife is used to spread the butters on canapés, etc. For decoration they are piped through a savoy bag fitted with a fine plain or star pipe.

There are two essential prerequisites for making compound butters successfully—firstly, the absolute freshness and fine quality of the ingredients and, secondly, the use of these ingredients in the right proportions. The butters should be tasted repeatedly during preparation.

COLOURED BUTTERS

These are butter mixtures coloured by the flavouring ingredient incorporated in them. They are listed below with the names of the compound butters to which reference should be made. All the butters are, of course, arranged in alphabetical order.

Black   —   truffle butter

Cream   —   lightly worked salted butter

Green   —   Montpellier or herb butter

Grey   —   truffle butter (made with only a little truffle) or caviar butter

Pale green —   Lauris or pistachio butter

Pink   —   crayfish, ham, paprika or tomato butter

Red   —   lobster butter II

White   —   salted butter

Yellow   —   egg butter; the depth of colour depends on the amount of hard-boiled egg yolk

It is possible to colour butters by adding vegetable colours, but these are tasteless and should be avoided. Their use is only justified if there is absolutely no alternative, or if the natural colour of a butter mixture is not bright enough. In the latter case they should be used very sparingly to avoid producing a gaudy effect in the worst possible taste. The object is always to imitate natural colouring, not to create excessively vivid colour schemes.

All the recipes for compound butters which follow use 100 g (4 oz) of butter and only the added ingredients are named. Unless otherwise stated, the ingredients are crushed or pounded to a purée and mixed with the butter which is then passed through a fine sieve.

Almond butter I

50 g (2 oz) blanched almonds.

Almond butter II

50 g (2 oz) ground almonds.

Anchovy butter

50 g (2 oz) drained anchovy fillets.

Asparagus butter

100 g (4 oz) cooked green asparagus tips.

Caviar butter

24–50 g (1–2 oz) caviar; one drop of lemon juice.

Cayenne butter

a dash of cayenne; a pinch of salt.

Chervil butter

50 g (2 oz) chervil, blanched and refreshed.

Chivry butter

25 g (1 oz) chervil; 15 g (½ oz) chives; 30 g (1 oz) parsley; 15 g (½ oz) burnet; 15 g (½ oz) savoury. All blanched and refreshed. (Other herbs can be used, but no one flavour should predominate.)

Crayfish butter I

| 100 g | butter | 4 oz |
| | 8 heads and shells of crayfish cooked Bordeaux style | |

Split the crayfish heads in two and dry inside. Pound 100 g (4 oz) of the heads and shells. When quite cold, add the butter and pound again. Pass through a hair sieve or, preferably, a tammy cloth. Adjust the seasoning. If necessary, add a little carmine to deepen the colour.

France

Crayfish butter II

| 100 g | butter | 4 oz |
| | 8 boiled crayfish heads and shells | |

Place the crayfish heads and shells in a pan, cover and stand over low heat until any remaining court-bouillon has boiled away. Pour in a spoonful of Cognac and ignite. Allow to cool, then pound with the butter and pass through a hair sieve. This butter is inferior to crayfish butter I.

France

Curry butter

25 g (1 oz) chopped onion cooked in 2 dessertspoons white wine; 1 level teaspoon curry powder.

Egg butter

25–40 g (1–1½ oz) hard-boiled egg yolk.

Emmenthal butter

75 g (3 oz) grated Emmenthal; 10 g (½ oz) mustard; 2 egg yolks; a pinch of cayenne. Not sieved.

Garlic butter

25–50 g (1–2 oz) garlic, boiled for 2 minutes.

Glarus butter

75 g (3 oz) grated Schapzieger (Glarus) cheese; 50 ml (2 fl oz) double cream.

Goms butter

100 g (4 oz) grated Goms cheese; 1 hard-boiled egg; 1 dessertspoon Kirsch.

Gruyère butter

As for Emmenthal butter above.

Gruyère and ham butter

50 g (2 oz) grated Gruyère cheese; 75 g (3 oz) finely chopped ham; 50 ml (2 fl oz) sour cream; pinch paprika. Not sieved.

Ham butter

100 g (4 oz) lean cooked ham. (This butter should be covered with foil as soon as prepared, to prevent discolouration.)

Hazelnut butter

50 g (2 oz) hazelnuts, roasted in a frying pan and skinned by rubbing in a damp cloth.

Herb butter

25 g (1 oz) each of spinach leaves, watercress leaves and lettuce leaves, all blanched and refreshed. (This is not such a good butter as Chivry butter above.)

Herring butter

50 g (2 oz) pickled herring fillets.

Horseradish butter

25 g (1 oz) grated horseradish.

Lauris butter

As asparagus butter above.

Lobster butter I

100 g	butter	4 oz
100 g	lobster cooked American style (head only)	4 oz

Pound the lobster as finely as possible. Add the butter and pound again. Pass first through a fine sieve, then through a tammy cloth.

France

Lobster butter II

100 g	butter	4 oz
100 g	coral and berries of lobster cooked in court-bouillon	4 oz
	Cognac	

Pound the lobster coral and berries very finely. Mix with the butter, adding a few drops of very good Cognac. Pass through a tammy cloth. Deepen the colour with a little carmine.

France

Maître d'hôtel butter

1 heaped teaspoon chopped parsley, a little lemon juice. Not sieved.

Montpellier butter

125 g	butter	4 oz
	2 anchovy fillets	
	1 tablespoon capers	
10 g	chervil leaves	$\frac{1}{2}$ oz
5 g	chives	$\frac{1}{2}$ oz
	1 medium-size gherkin	
5 g	sound young spinach leaves	$\frac{1}{2}$ oz
5 g	tarragon leaves	$\frac{1}{2}$ oz
	2 hard-boiled egg yolks	
10 g	parsley leaves	$\frac{1}{2}$ oz
1 dl	oil	3 fl oz
	1 teaspoon vinegar (tarragon if possible)	

Bring some water to the boil in a small copper pan (not tin-lined). Drop in the spinach leaves and boil for 2 minutes. Add the chervil, chives, tarragon and parsley and boil for a further 2 minutes. Drain and refresh quickly, then dry in a cloth. Pound with the anchovy fillets, capers and gherkin to obtain a very fine paste. Work in the egg yolks one at a time, then the butter. Cream well. Add the vinegar and oil alternately a little at a time, starting with the vinegar. Adjust the seasoning and add a dash of cayenne pepper. Pass through a fine sieve.

France

Mustard butter

½ a hard-boiled egg yolk; 1 tablespoon Dijon mustard.

Printanier butter

50 g (2 oz) green asparagus tips; 50 g (2 oz) green peas; 50 g (2 oz) french beans. All cooked separately.

Ravigote butter

As for Chivry butter with the addition of 10 g (½ oz) pounded gherkin.

Roe butter I

150 g	butter	6 oz
100 g	red herring roes	4 oz

Remove excess salt from the roes by soaking well in water or milk, which should be changed several times. Clean and dry the roes, then mix with the butter, working vigorously. Season lightly with pepper. Check the taste and add a little salt if necessary.

France

Roe butter II

100 g	butter	4 oz
150 g	raw roes of very fresh carp, herring, mackerel or other fish	6 oz
1 dl	white wine	3 fl oz

Clean, wash and dry the roes. Arrange in a lightly buttered shallow fireproof dish, pour in the white wine and season with salt and pepper. Heat gently to simmering point, then poach for 3–6 minutes, depending on the size of the roes, without allowing the liquid to boil. Leave in the cooking liquid until cold, drain and dry. Pound to a fine paste, mix with the butter and season well.

France

Roquefort butter

50 g (2 oz) Roquefort cheese; 2 dessertspoons Cognac; 2 tablespoons half-whipped cream; pinch of cayenne.

Salmon butter I

75 g (3 oz) smoked salmon scraps.

Salmon butter II

50 g (2 oz) poached salmon scraps.

Sardine butter

50 g (2 oz) sardines, little lemon juice.

Sbrinz butter

225 g (8 oz) grated Sbrinz cheese; 10 g (½ oz) mustard; 35 ml (1½ fl oz) white wine; grated nutmeg. Not sieved.

Shallot butter

50 g (2 oz) shallots, boiled for 2 minutes.

Shrimp or prawn butter

100 g	butter	4 oz
50 g	shrimps or prawns (or trimmings)	2 oz

Pound the butter with the shrimps or prawns or trimmings (heads and shells). Pass through a sieve. Season with a little salt, pepper and a dash of cayenne pepper.

Prawns give a more delicate colour and flavour than shrimps. The heads and shells only may be used where the tails are required for garnish or decoration without affecting the quality of the butter.

France

Tarragon butter

50 g (2 oz) blanched tarragon leaves.

Tomato butter

100 g	butter	4 oz
50 g	fresh tomato pulp	2 oz
	(2 tomatoes)	

Skin the tomatoes, remove the seeds and squeeze in a cloth. Pound lightly and mix with the butter. Pass through a hair sieve and mix again. Season well.

France

Truffle butter

75 g (3 oz) grated truffles or truffle peelings.

Tuna butter

75 g (3 oz) tuna in oil (drained).

Walnut butter

50 g (2 oz) green walnuts.

Watercress butter

100 g (4 oz) watercress leaves.

FINGER FOOD

The dishes in this section are all suitable for 'stand-up buffets' and most of them can be eaten without the aid of cutlery. They are mainly used for cocktail parties, receptions and informal buffets, but many of these dishes are also suitable for a dinner, either as a first course or as a savoury (which is often taken as a last course in Britain).

When a selection of small items is served, it should include as many different types of savoury and as great a variety of ingredients as is practical. The items should all be small and dainty, and should be attractively arranged on large silver flats, as shown on pages 579, 580.

BARQUETTES AND BOUCHÉES

These are particularly useful items, since the fillings can be more moist than those of other finger foods. There is almost no limit to the variety possible, since a small dice of any savoury item usually served in a sauce makes a suitable filling for a bouchée or a barquette. The fillings listed may be used for either.

PUFF PASTE FOR BOUCHÉES (Pâté feuilletée)

200–250 g	butter	7–8 oz
250 g	flour	8 oz
5 g	salt	$\frac{1}{6}$ oz
approx. 15 cl	water	$\frac{1}{4}$ pt approx.

There are three steps in making puff pastry—the 'détrempe', folding the dough round the butter, and turning, which involves giving six turns.

1. The 'détrempe'. Make a bay in the flour and pour in four-fifths of the water, in which the salt has been dissolved. Mix in the flour, drawing it in towards the centre and kneading briskly with one hand only. Sprinkle with a little of the remaining water from time to time if the flour will not all mix smoothly. Work the

dough a little and mould into a ball. It should not stick to the fingers; it should look smooth and its consistency should be neither too hard nor too soft. To test the consistency, press a finger into it; the mark should remain. (If it does not, and the dough springs back like rubber, this means that the dough has been worked too much. In this case, allow it to rest longer than indicated below.) Place the ball of 'détrempe' on a floured plate and cut a cross in the top. Cover with a cloth and allow to rest in a cool place for 20 minutes.

2. Folding the dough round the butter. Squeeze the butter in a cloth, beat and work with the hand to expel any water or buttermilk and to make it pliable, though still firm. Now place the 'détrempe' (dough) on the lightly floured slab and flatten it with the palm of the hand to form a disk 2½–3 cm thick (about 1 in). Shape the butter into a square slab 2 or 3 cm (about 1 in) thick and place it in the middle of the dough, leaving about 4 cm (1½ in) of dough showing all round. Fold the four edges of the dough inwards to encase the butter, stretching them a little, and press them together without leaving a ridge. Straighten the sides of the resulting square by pressing them lightly with a rolling pin. Lightly flour the slab and the top of the square of paste and increase the size of the latter a little, while still keeping it square, by gently tapping it with the rolling pin, first in one direction and then in the other. Allow to rest in a cool place for 10 minutes.

3. Turning. Lightly flour the slab, the rolling pin and the paste. (Dust with flour again several times during this operation.) Place the rolling pin in the centre of the paste and push it forwards with firm, but not excessive, pressure, the hands being kept flat on the rolling pin on either side of the paste. Roll out to a thickness of about 2 cm (¾ in), repeating the above procedure several times if necessary, always starting in the centre of the paste, pushing the rolling pin forwards and *never working in the opposite direction*. When the first side has been rolled out, bring it towards you by turning the pastry so that the end nearest you is now furthest away. Pin out the other half of the pastry in the same way, always working away from you and never in the opposite direction, to make an even strip 50–60 cm (20–24 in) long and 2 cm (¾ in) thick. Now fold one end of the strip two-thirds of the way towards the other end and tap with the rolling pin to stick the fold down. Fold the opposite end over to cover the first fold and tap it down in the same way. Straighten the sides of the paste by pressing lightly with the rolling pin to make as even a rectangle as possible. This is called 'giving one turn'. For the second turn, begin by turning the pastry half-way round so that the smooth fold (the one that looks like the spine of a book) is on the right. Now roll out and fold in the same way as for the first turn, remembering that the paste should always be folded in the same manner. Wrap in a barely damp cloth and allow to rest in a cool place for 10–15 minutes. After this time, give two more turns and allow to rest again for 10–15 minutes before giving the last two turns (making six in all). Allow to rest for a further 15–20 minutes. If the paste is made on the day before it is required, only the first four turns should be given at that time, leaving the last two until shortly before the paste is to be used.

After the six turns and the resting period, the pastry may be rolled out and shaped as desired, bearing in mind that it should be baked upside down (the side which was nearest the slab during the pastry-making operation being on top during the baking process). Allow the pastry pieces to rest for 10 minutes before baking. The baking sheet should be lightly moistened beforehand. Bake in a hot oven (200–225°C).

The flour used for puff pastry should be of finest quality. The butter should be firm and well worked; it should contain no water or buttermilk. The amount of water required may vary slightly according to the quality of the flour, but the quantity shown in the formula should never be exceeded by more than one small teaspoon. It is advisable to work in a cool place, preferably using a marble slab.

France

SHORT PASTE (UNSWEETENED)

For tartlets, barquettes, and croustades.

Sufficient to line 10–12 moulds about 5 cm (2 in) in diameter or length.

125 g	flour	4 oz
65 g	butter	2 oz
	good pinch of salt	
approx. 5 cl	water	$\frac{1}{12}$ pt approx.

Make a bay in the flour and place the salt, water and slightly softened butter in it. Mix and work with the tips of the fingers. Knead with the palm of the hand (once in summer, twice in winter). Mould the paste into a ball and wrap in a damp cloth. Leave to rest in a cool place for at least an hour before using.

Make this pastry on the day before it is required.

France

American boats

Fill with spiny lobster in American sauce. Serve hot.

France

Anchovy boats

Fill with egg butter, using a savoy bag fitted with a star pipe. Decorate with rolled anchovy fillets stood on end and place a spot of tomato on each anchovy. Serve cold.

France

Angela boats

Fill with tomato butter. Decorate with anchovy fillets across the top and with sliced green olives. Serve cold.

France

Beetroot boats

Fill with finely diced well-drained cooked beetroot salad. Decorate with chopped parsley. Serve cold.

France

Bigorre boats

Fill with tarragon butter and a piece of salmon trout. Decorate with blanched tarragon leaves and glaze with aspic. Serve cold.

France

Bouchées financier

Fill with diced lambs' sweetbreads, foie gras and green olives in Madeira sauce. Serve hot.

France

Bouchées Gayolle

Fill with diced cooked ham, mushrooms and Gruyère cheese in Béchamel sauce seasoned with cayenne pepper. Serve hot.

France

Bouchées Montglas

Fill with diced calves' sweetbreads, mushrooms and truffles in demi-glace sauce flavoured with Madeira. Serve hot.

France

Bouchées Perigord

Fill with diced foie gras and truffles in demi-glace sauce flavoured with Madeira. Serve hot.

France

Bouchées à la Reine

Fill with diced chicken breast, mushrooms and truffles in chicken cream velouté sauce. Serve hot.

France

Bouchées St Hubert

Fill with diced game (any type of ground- or winged game) and truffles in venison sauce. Serve hot.

France

Bouchées Toulouse

Fill with diced lambs' sweetbreads, cocks' combs, cocks' kidneys, mushrooms and truffles in chicken velouté sauce. Serve hot.

France

Bouchées York

Fill with diced York ham in very strong tomato-flavoured veal stock. All the above fillings are also suitable for barquettes. Serve hot.

France

Breton boats

Fill with scallops in white wine sauce. Serve hot or cold.

France

Cambacérès boats

Fill with cucumber salad in cream and lemon dressing. Decorate with chopped parsley.

The cucumber may be cut into balls or small olive shapes with a vegetable scoop; alternatively, it may be finely diced or just thinly sliced. Serve cold.

France

Celeriac boats

Fill with finely diced celeriac which has been blanched for 2 minutes and dressed with vinaigrette or mayonnaise. Decorate with chopped parsley. Serve cold.

France

Clamart boats

Fill with very small garden peas which have been cooked in salted water and dressed with vinaigrette or mayonnaise. Serve cold.

Dublin Bay prawn boats

Fill with Dublin Bay prawns which have been cut into pieces and rolled in cream mayonnaise flavoured with chopped parsley and chervil. Serve cold.

France

Dieppe boats

Fill with small mussels in white wine sauce. Serve hot.

France

Favourite boats

Fill with young French beans which have been boiled uncovered in salted water, refreshed, cut into dice or lozenges and dressed with vinaigrette. Decorate with chopped parsley. Serve cold.

France

Glazed lobster boats

Fill with a lobster or spiny lobster medallion, garnish with truffle and coat with fish aspic flavoured with Champagne. Serve cold.

France

Greek vegetable boats

Fill with vegetables cooked in the Greek manner and cut into small dice, balls or olive shapes. Drain the vegetables thoroughly before use and do not fill the boats until the last minute. Serve cold.

France

Game purée bouchées

10 persons

10 puff pastry cases
5 cm (2 in) in diameter

350 g	game purée (any game may be used)	12 oz
1 dl	well-reduced game or poivrade sauce	¼ pt
	10 disks truffle or fluted poached mushrooms	
3 cl	Cognac or sherry	3 dessertspoons

Warm the game purée, bind with the hot well-reduced sauce, flavour with Cognac or sherry and season well. Fill into the hot pastry cases and cover with a disk of truffle or a mushroom cap instead of a pastry lid. Serve very hot.

Germany

Ham boats Caledonian style

8 persons

Pastry

300 g	flour	10 oz
	1 egg	
	1 egg yolk	
150 g	melted butter	5 oz
	a little water	
6 g	pinch of salt	

Mousse

250 g	lean ham	8 oz
1 dl	thick Béchamel sauce	¼ pt
	4 sheets gelatine	
1 dl	half-whipped dairy cream	3 fl oz
	forcemeat spices	
	pinch of cayenne pepper	
	leek (green part only) blanched	
	hard-boiled egg white	
	sliced truffle	
	aspic jelly	

Prepare the pastry for lining the boats with the egg, egg yolk, flour, butter, salt and a little water, then allow to rest for several hours. Pin out to about 4 mm (⅛ in) thick. Line small boat moulds with the pastry and bake blind, but only until pale golden. Cut out 8 thin slices of ham to fit the top of the boat moulds and set aside. Mince the rest of the ham as finely as possible, mix with the Béchamel sauce and rub through a sieve. When cold, stir in the gelatine which has been soaked, squeezed dry and dissolved, flavour to taste with the spices and fold in the cream. Fill into the pastry cases at once and smooth the top. Cover each one with a slice of ham and decorate with leek, truffle and hard-boiled egg white cut into diamond shapes. Glaze with aspic and arrange on a round dish to resemble the petals of a flower. Serve with horseradish cream.

(Illustration, p. 581)   Norway

Joinville boats

Fill with picked shrimps in Joinville sauce. Serve hot.

France

Lobster boats (hot)

Fill with lobster meat in American sauce. Serve hot.

France

Lobster boats (cold)

Fill with diced lobster in aspic mayonnaise. Garnish the ends of the boats with chopped lobster coral. Serve cold.

France

Lobster boats Marseilles style

Fill with diced lobster in Marseillaise sauce. Decorate with half-moons of green olive. Serve cold.

France

Lobster tartlets

Cut cooked lobster meat into small cubes and mix with well-flavoured savoury mayonnaise. Fill into tartlet cases that have been baked blind, garnish with a thin slice of lobster tail and a tiny disk of truffle, and glaze lightly with aspic. Serve cold.

Austria

Marius boats

Fill with anchovy butter. Garnish alternately with anchovy fillets and coarsely chopped tomato cooked in the Greek manner. Serve cold.

France

Mascot boats

Fill with diced cooked artichoke bottoms in oil and lemon dressing. Decorate with chopped chervil, parsley and tarragon. Serve cold.

France

Mikado boats

Fill with Japanese artichoke salad dressed with lemon juice. Decorate with chopped hard-boiled egg yolk or a small slice of egg yolk. Serve cold.

France

Mushroom boats

Fill with white button mushrooms which have been peeled and either very finely diced or thinly sliced. Dress with oil seasoned with salt and white pepper. Serve cold.

(Illustration, p. 689)   France

Nantua boats

Fill with pieces of crayfish tail in Nantua sauce. Serve hot.

France

Nivernaise boats

Fill with finely diced very young carrots in oil and lemon dressing. Serve cold.

France

Paprika Dublin Bay prawn boats

Fill with shelled Dublin Bay prawns in cream sauce well seasoned with paprika. Serve hot.

France

Prawn boats

Fill with three or four shelled prawns in aspic mayonnaise and place a spot of tomato in the centre. Serve cold.

France

Rosalind boats

Fill with crisp julienne of bacon in Mornay sauce, garnished with bacon grilled until brown and then crumbled over the top. Serve hot.

Great Britain

Russian salad boats

Fill with Russian salad. Serve cold.

Salmon boats Béarn style

Fill with tomato butter and salmon fillets. Decorate with tarragon butter. Serve cold.

France

Shrimp boats Marseillaise

Fill with picked shrimps in Marseillaise sauce stiffened with aspic. Decorate with half-moons of green olive. Serve cold.

France

Tomato boats

Fill with skinned, seeded and coarsely chopped tomatoes in vinaigrette dressing. Decorate with chopped parsley and tarragon. Serve cold.

Undine boats

Fill with sole fillets in white wine sauce. Serve hot.

France

Vegetable salad tartlets country style

Salad

　　　　　1 part each carrots, turnips,
　　　　　　　French beans, peas,
　　　　　　　beetroot
　　　　　2 parts potatoes
　　　　　mayonnaise
　　　　　vinegar
　　　　　ground pepper
　　　　　salt

Short pastry

250 g	flour	8 oz
125 g	butter	4 oz
5 g	pinch of salt	
approx. 1 dl	water	3 fl oz approx.

The vegetables should preferably be cooked whole to preserve their flavour and colour. Shell the peas and string the beans. Wash all the vegetables well in running water and cook in salted water. The beetroot will keep its colour better if cooked in the oven. After cooking, peel as required and cut up evenly into small pieces. Mix well, season with salt and pepper, add a few drops of vinegar and dress liberally with mayonnaise.

Line tartlet pans with short pastry and bake blind (filling with dried haricot beans). Allow to cool and remove from the pans. Fill with the salad to a dome shape, smooth over with a knife or spatula, coat with mayonnaise and decorate.

If desired any of the following may be added to the salad: cold poached fish, mussels, raw or cooked ham, poached or roast chicken or meat, hard-boiled eggs, capers. Suitable garnishes for decoration include anchovy fillets, caviar on slices of hard-boiled egg, cooked mushroom caps, pieces of red pepper, gherkins, etc.

Spain

Roquefort barquettes Jules Guyat

10 persons

350 g	unsweetened short paste	12 oz
150 g	butter	5 oz
150 g	Roquefort cheese	5 oz
5 cl	port	2 fl oz
	1 large ripe raw pear	
	a pinch of paprika	
	3 tablespoons whipped cream	
2 dl	port-flavoured aspic	$\frac{1}{4}$ pt

Line boat-shaped pans about 8·5 by 4 cm ($3\frac{1}{2}$ by $1\frac{1}{2}$ in) with the short paste and bake blind. Cream the butter, mix with the sieved Roquefort and the port, and season with the paprika. Add the pear, peeled, cored and very finely diced. Lastly fold in the whipped cream. Fill the pastry cases with the cheese cream, using a savoy bag and star pipe. Place in the refrigerator until firm and glaze lightly with the aspic.

TARTLETS

Anchovy and olive tartlets

Yield: 10 tartlets   Baking time: 7–8 minutes

500 g	bread dough	1 lb
1·5 kg	onions	3 lb
	2 cloves of garlic	
	small bouquet garni	
	20 stoned black olives	
	10 anchovy fillets	
2 dl	olive oil	⅓ pt

Slice the onions finely and cook gently in hot oil without colouring, together with the garlic and bouquet garni. Allow to cool. Divide the dough equally into 10 portions and mould round, then pin out into disks 5–7 cm (2–3 in) in diameter. Turn up the edges to make a rim. Fill the tartlets with the cooked onions and make a cross on top of each with an anchovy fillet cut in half lengthwise. Place half a black olive in each of the four spaces. Prove for about a quarter of an hour. When the dough has almost doubled in volume, bake in a hot oven. Serve warm or cold.

France

Mireille tartlets

Yield: 40–45 tartlets   Cooking time: 8–10 minutes

500 g	scrap puff paste (*or* unsweetened short paste for lining tarts)	1 lb
600 g	tomatoes	1 lb 4 oz
100 g	green peppers	4 oz
100 g	Arles sausage	4 oz
100 g	grated Parmesan or Gruyère cheese	4 oz

Skin the tomatoes, cut in half and squeeze out the seeds and liquid as well as possible. Chop finely and squeeze well again in a cloth. Remove the seeds from the green pepper, cut into very small thin slices, mix with the tomatoes, together with the finely sliced sausage, and season well. Line deep plain tartlet tins 5 cm (2 in) in diameter with the pastry pinned out to about 4 mm ($\frac{1}{8}$ in) thick, fill with the tomato mixture and sprinkle with grated cheese. Bake in a hot oven.

N.B.—Raw ham may be used instead of Arles sausage.

France

Parisian tartlets

500 g	scrap puff paste (*or* short paste for lining tarts)	1 lb
800 g	tomatoes	1 lb 4 oz
100 g	grated Parmesan or Gruyère cheese few cultivated mushrooms	4 oz

Proceed as for Mireille tartlets, but omit the green peppers and the sausage. Before sprinkling with cheese, place 2 or 3 slices of mushroom on top of each tartlet.

France

Provençal tartlets

Proceed as for Parisian tartlets, but flavour the filling with chopped basil to taste.

France

CANAPÉS

It would almost be possible to make up a whole buffet out of canapés; there are countless different ways of decorating them and an infinite variety of ingredients may be used for their toppings.

Canapés are small slices of bread, often toasted, covered with a topping and a decorative finish. This broad definition leaves scope for individual taste and imagination. Consequently, the list of recipes for canapés given below cannot be restrictive, nor is it intended to be.

Canapé bases may be plain or toasted bread—white, rye, black, brown or brioche—or cut out of short or puff pastry. Biscuits and crispbreads can also be used as bases.

The name by which a canapé is known, and which does not really matter much, usually relates to the topping or its origin. Here again, everyone is free to invent new types of canapés and choose appropriate names for them, while taking care to avoid too violent a contrast between the different flavours of the ingredients used. Another point to be borne in mind is the need for tastefully discreet decoration; variety is achieved, not by over-decorating each individual canapé, but by the general effect of an assortment of canapés of alternating shapes and colours.

Canapés are a very good example of a product depending far more on painstaking work, patience and good taste than on vast financial or technical resources.

SHAPE AND SIZE OF CANAPÉS

The bases should be thin; as their name implies, they are only intended to serve as a foundation for the toppings. Generally speaking the bread should not be more than 3–4 mm ($\frac{1}{8}$ in) thick. Canapés can be square, rectangular, triangular, diamonds, stars, round, oval or crescent shaped but should be small enough to be eaten in one or two bites. About 5 or 6 cm (2 or $2\frac{1}{2}$ in) is a suitable size.

BREAD FOR CANAPÉS

Whatever the type of bread used, it should not be too new. It may be bought fresh, wrapped in a cloth and stored for two or three days in a dry fairly cool place. The crusts are always removed before using for canapés, and the shape of these will depend on the shape of the loaf.

Pumpernickel is black bread made from a mixture of rye and wheat flours; it is found all over Germany and may be bought sliced or unsliced. It is quite easily digested in spite of its black close-textured appearance.

As for white bread, rectangular or cylindrical loaves are most commonly used for canapés.

Cutting White Loaves
Cutting a cylindrical loaf is quite straightforward. The crusts may be left on if they are soft and thin.

A rectangular loaf which has not been machine sliced is cut into long strips without crust as described below. The operation requires some skill.

First of all the crust is cut off at one end of the loaf, then it is removed from the top and the two long sides, leaving only the bottom and one end still covered with crust. The bread is then spread with butter or butter mixture right along the top. It is held in the left hand while a horizontal cut is made about 3–4 mm ($\frac{1}{8}$ in) down, using a long flexible knife which is moved to and fro with the blade slightly on the slant like a saw held flat. When the first slice has been cut off in this manner, the part of the loaf which is now on top is again spread with butter and the operation is repeated for each slice. The end crust at right angles to the blade of the knife protects the hand.

MAKING CANAPÉS IN SERIES

Some canapés of a simple angular shape (square, oblong, triangle, diamond) can be prepared a whole strip at a time and then cut. A long slice of bread which has been buttered and cut from a rectangular white loaf as described above is placed on a board or table. It is then covered along its whole length with a topping prepared according to any recipe which lends itself to this procedure. The topping is pressed down with the blade of a knife and the bread is then cut carefully into canapés as shown in the diagrams below.

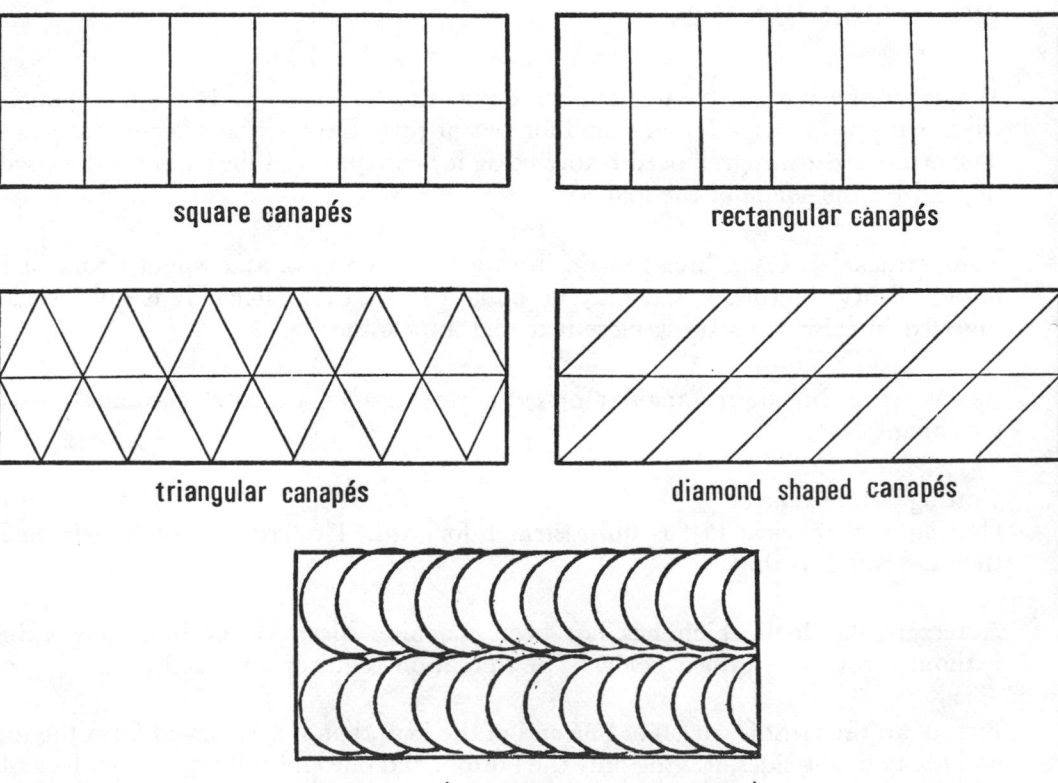

square canapés   rectangular canapés

triangular canapés   diamond shaped canapés

crescents (cut with a round cutter)

Pastry cutters may be used for curved or star-shaped canapés.

Bread which has been sliced in the usual manner (either at home or by machine) may of course be used for canapés.

Each of the recipes that follow starts off with the type of bread, the recommended shape and the butter or butter mixture to be used. The recipes for butter mixtures will be found in the chapter on 'Compound Butters', page 186.

CHARCUTERIE CANAPÉS

Ardennes canapés

White bread; oval; fresh butter.
Cover with Ardennes ham.

France

Arlesian canapés

White bread; round; fresh butter.
Cover with a slice of Arles sausage.

France

Bayonne canapés

White bread; square or oblong; fresh butter.
Cover with Bayonne ham and pipe on butter in decorative motifs.

France

Berry canapés

White bread; oval; fresh butter.
Cover with Berry ham and decorate with small dots of butter.

France

Canapés Gâtinais style

White bread; triangular; chicken liver pâté.
Decorate with blanched tarragon leaves which have been dipped in aspic (optional).

France

Foie gras canapés I

White bread; triangular or oval; fresh butter.
Cover with a very thin slice of foie gras, decorate with truffles and brush with aspic jelly to glaze.

France

Foie gras canapés II

White bread; oblong; foie gras purée.
To make the purée, mix together equal parts of foie gras and butter until well blended, then pass through a fine sieve. Flavour with a few drops of Cognac and season with salt and pepper. Work thoroughly before spreading on the bread. Decorate with truffles.

France

Liver pâté canapés

White bread; oblong; pig's liver pâté.
Decorate with capers or gherkin.

France

Lyons canapés

White bread; round; fresh butter.
Cover with a thin slice of skinned Lyons sausage and decorate with butter.

France

Mortadella canapés

White bread; triangular or oval; mustard butter.
Cover with a thin slice of Mortadella sausage and decorate with capers or gherkin.

France

Paris ham canapés

White bread; square or oblong; fresh butter.
Cover with a thin slice of Paris ham. Decorate with capers, gherkin or butter.

France

Paris sausage canapés

White bread; round or oval; fresh butter.
Cover with a thin slice of skinned Paris sausage. Decorate with gherkin or with
Montpellier butter. This sausage should be used sparingly; it contains a little garlic.

France

Parma ham canapés

White bread; diamond-shaped; fresh butter.
Cover with a thin slice of Parma ham.

France

Salami canapés

White bread; round or oval; fresh butter.
Cover with a thin slice of skinned salami and decorate with butter.

France

Saveloy canapés

White or rye bread; round, fresh butter.
Cover with a slice of skinned saveloy and decorate with motifs piped on with
horseradish, caper or gherkin butter.

France

Tongue canapés

White bread; oblong or oval; fresh butter.
Cover with a thin slice of pickled tongue and decorate with butter.

France

Tours canapés

White bread; oblong or oval; Tours rillettes.
Serve without further garnish.

France

Westphalia ham canapés

Brown bread; square; fresh butter.
Cover with a thin slice of Westphalia ham. Using a savoy bag, pipe on butter to
make a St Andrew's cross.

France

York ham canapés

White bread; square or oblong; fresh butter.
Cover with a thin slice of York ham. Decorate with capers, gherkin or butter.

France

CHEESE CANAPÉS

Canapés Bavarian style

Pumpernickel; square; demi-sel cheese with fine herbs. Serve without further garnish.
If preferred, the bread may be spread with paprika-flavoured demi-sel, or the cheese may be left plain and decorated with slices of radish.

France

Curd cheese canapés

White bread; square or oblong; fresh butter.
Spread with curd cheese seasoned with salt and pepper. Smooth the top or decorate with the point of a knife.

France

Curd cheese and fine herb canapés

White bread; square or oblong; fresh butter.
Spread with curd cheese seasoned with salt and pepper and mixed with chopped parsley, chervil and chives.

France

Gruyère canapés

White bread; oblong; salted butter.
Cover with a thin slice of Gruyère cheese and decorate with pink butter.

France

Pink and white canapés

White bread; square.
Spread with a triangle of demi-sel and a triangle of cream cheese tinted pink with a little paprika.

France

Port Salut canapés

White bread; oblong; salted butter.
Cover with a slice of Port Salut cheese and decorate with red butter.

France

Roquefort canapés

White bread; oval; fresh butter.
Spread with Roquefort mixed with an equal amount of butter.

France

Rosette canapés

White bread; round; fresh butter.
Spread with curd cheese seasoned with salt and white pepper. Decorate with slices of radish.

France

EGG CANAPÉS

Canapés Belle Muguette

White bread; oval; tarragon butter.
Cover with a slice of hard-boiled egg cut lengthwise. Decorate with a lily of the valley motif on top of the yolk, using blanched tarragon leaves for the stem and leaves, and hard-boiled egg white for the flowers. Glaze with aspic.

France

Canapés with hard-boiled egg only

White bread; square; salted butter.
Cover with a round slice of hard-boiled egg and decorate the centre with a rosette of green butter.

Many other types of hard-boiled egg canapés can be devised. Any tasteful variation is permissible and the judicious use of the imagination is even recommended. It should, however, be borne in mind that the butter or butter mixture used for decoration must form a contrast with that used for spreading on the base; in addition, the bright yellow of the egg yolk has to be taken into account in selecting the colours.

France

Canapés Mandelieu

White bread; oblong; tarragon butter.
Cover with sieved hard-boiled egg seasoned with salt and pepper, pressing it down on to the butter well with the blade of a knife. Draw a letter X on top with the back of a knife, sprinkle it with a mixture of chopped chives, parsley and gherkin and place a spot of tomato in the centre.

France

Canapés Spanish style

White bread; oblong; cayenne butter.
Beat up an egg as for an omelette and season with pepper. Fry in very hot oil for a few seconds and remove with a skimmer. Drain on a cloth and season lightly with salt and cayenne pepper. Place on the base and garnish the centre with a little skinned, seeded and coarsely chopped tomato.

Canapés Titian

White bread; square; Provençal purée.
Cover with chopped hard-boiled egg, pressing it down well. Decorate with a slice of olive stuffed with tomato.

France

Frivolous canapés

White bread; round; mustard butter.
Cover with a slice of hard-boiled egg cut out with a plain cutter. Garnish the centre of the yolk with a tiny spot of tomato or sweet red pepper and surround it with a star-shaped arrangement of small tarragon leaves which have been blanched and dipped in aspic jelly.

France

Prelate's canapés

White bread; round; lobster butter.
Cover with cold firm scrambled egg mixed with coarsely chopped tomato. Season with cayenne pepper.

France

Rose canapés

White bread; triangular; Montpellier butter.
Cover with a slice of hard-boiled egg. Decorate with a neat arrangement of chervil leaves interspersed with a few small spots of tomato. Glaze with aspic.

France

FISH CANAPÉS

Anchovy canapés I

White bread; oblong; fresh or anchovy butter.
Garnish with well-drained anchovy fillets in oil.

France

Anchovy canapés II

White bread; oblong; fresh or anchovy butter.
Cut anchovy fillets into fine strips and arrange on the base lattice fashion.

France

Anchovy canapés III

White bread; oblong; fresh or anchovy butter.
Arrange the anchovy fillets to make a St Andrew's cross and garnish the triangular spaces in between with egg yolk and white chopped separately.

France

Anchovy canapés IV

White bread; oblong; fresh or anchovy butter.
Garnish the centre of the canapé with a rolled half anchovy fillet and place half a green olive on top. Surround with a star-shaped arrangement of half anchovy fillets.

France

Baltic canapés

Black bread; oblong; plain butter.
Cover with soft roe and apple purée. Garnish with small strips of herring fillet arranged lattice fashion. The garnish for these canapés is made from soft-roed smoked herrings, which are filleted, soaked for at least an hour, skinned and cut into small strips. For the purée, equal amounts of soft roe and raw apples are chopped together finely and the seasoning is adjusted.

France

Botargo canapés

White or brown bread; oblong or oval; mustard butter.
Cover with thin slices of botargo (pressed dried roe of grey mullet or tuna) which
have been dressed with oil and vinegar or with lemon juice and well drained.
Decorate with chopped parsley or crescents cut out of sweet red peppers.

France

Canapés Brillat-Savarin

White bread; oblong; crayfish butter.
Garnish with boiled crayfish tails, using two half tails for each canapé. Decorate
with truffle and glaze by brushing with aspic.

France

Canapés Claire

White or brown bread; oblong; lemon butter.
Cover with slices of smoked salmon and caviar arranged alternately.

France

Canapés Livonian style

Black bread; oblong; horseradish butter.
Garnish with strips of well-drained pickled herring fillet alternating with oblong
pieces of raw apple. Brush lightly with oil and decorate with chopped chives.

France

Canapés marinière

Black bread; oblong; lemon butter.
Garnish with well-drained cooked mussels and decorate with chopped parsley and
chervil.

France

Canapés Monseigneur

White bread; oblong or oval; anchovy butter.
Garnish with a thin slice of well-drained tuna in oil and decorate with anchovy
butter.

France

Canapés Muscovite I

Black bread; square or round; horseradish butter.
Pipe on an edging of lobster butter.

France

Canapés Muscovite II

Black bread; square or round; horseradish butter.
Garnish the centre with caviar and decorate with prawn tails.

France

Canapés Nederland

White bread; oval, mustard butter.
Make an oblong cavity in the centre of the base. Spread with butter and garnish
with a large mussel which has been cooked in white wine, trimmed, rolled in cream
vinaigrette sauce well flavoured with mustard, and decorated with finely diced
celery. The mussels should be drained a little before use.

France

Canapés Nice style

White bread; round or oval; anchovy butter.
Garnish with a thin slice of tomato. Cut a well-drained half anchovy fillet in oil
into two and arrange on the tomato to make a cross. Place a small slice of raw
onion in each space and sprinkle all over with chopped parsley.

France

Canapés Ondine

White bread; diamond-shaped; tarragon butter.
Garnish with a diamond-shaped piece of sole fillet poached in white wine. Coat
with fish chaud-froid sauce flavoured with tarragon. Decorate with tarragon
leaves and glaze with aspic.

France

Canapés Collioure style

White bread; oblong or diamond-shaped; anchovy butter.
Garnish with anchovy fillets and small tomato balls.

France

Canapés Danish style

Black bread; oblong; horseradish butter.
Cover with small thin slices of smoked salmon alternating with slices of smoked herring. If desired, separate the slices by alternating lines of dots of caviar and chopped chive.

France

Canapés Douarnenez style

Brown bread; oblong; salted butter.
Cover with well-drained sardine fillets in oil and decorate with lemon peeled down to the pulp.

France

Canapés Dutch style

White bread; square, oblong or oval; roe butter.
Garnish with a criss-cross arrangement of well-drained small pickled herring fillets. Fill the spaces alternately with chopped hard-boiled egg yolk and chopped chive.

France

Canapés Irish style

White or brown bread; horseradish butter.
Garnish with a thin slice of smoked cod liver. Decorate with a triangle of lemon, peeled down to the pulp.

France

Canapés J. Guérot

White bread; diamond-shaped; printanier butter.
Cover with a thin slice of poached fresh salmon. Decorate with a lily of the valley motif, using hard-boiled egg white for the flowers and blanched tarragon leaves for the stem and leaves. Glaze with Champagne jelly and edge with a narrow border of printanier butter.

France

Canapés Jutland

Black bread; oval; horseradish butter.
Garnish with an oblong slice of smoked salmon arranged lengthwise and decorated with a line of caviar. Surround with a border of strips of herring fillet.

Scandinavia, Russia

Canapés La Fayette

White bread; oblong; fresh butter.
Cover with a thin slice of lobster. Coat with lobster chaud-froid sauce, decorate with truffle and glaze with aspic.

France

Canapés Phileas Gilbert

White bread; round; shrimp or prawn butter lightly seasoned with cayenne pepper.
Garnish with a thin slice of turbot cheek braised in Chablis. Coat with fish chaud-froid sauce, decorate with truffle and glaze by brushing with aspic. Turbot cheek is the fleshy part of the head on the white side. It is the most delicate part of the fish and tastes very good when served cold. If not available, thin slices of turbot fillet may be used.

France

Canapés Swedish style

Brown bread; oblong; horseradish butter.
Garnish with smoked sprat fillets.

France

Caviar canapés

White bread; square or oblong; fresh butter.
Garnish with caviar and decorate with small triangles of lemon peeled down to the pulp.

France

Fresh salmon canapés

White bread; oblong or triangular; green butter.
Cover with thin slices of poached fresh salmon. Decorate with a few spots of aspic mayonnaise and with blanched tarragon leaves.

France

Herring canapés I

White bread; oblong; mustard butter.
Cover with well-drained pickled herring and decorate with chopped hard-boiled egg white.

France

Herring canapés II

White bread; triangular or square.
Place a piece of fat herring on the unbuttered base and insert a cocktail stick in the centre.

Israel

Kerling canapés

White or brown bread; round; fresh butter.
Spread with kerling.

Scandinavia

Lobster canapés

White bread; round; lobster butter.
Garnish with a lobster medallion, decorate with chervil and spots of tomato, and glaze by brushing with aspic.

France

Oyster canapés

White bread; oblong; shallot butter.
Cover with an oyster poached in white wine and well drained. Sprinkle with chopped parsley, hard-boiled egg and chives.

France

Oyster canapés English style

White bread; oval; horseradish butter.
Cover with a Marennes oyster poached in white wine. Add a few drops of ketchup and sprinkle with chopped parsley.

France

Phocaean canapés

White bread; round; lemon butter.
Cover with a salpicon of red mullet fillets which have been baked in olive oil and sprinkled with a dash of lemon juice. Decorate with fresh tomato.

France

Red caviar canapés

White bread; round or oval; fresh butter.
Garnish with red caviar.

France

Rollmop canapés

Brown bread; square; horseradish butter.
Garnish with a rollmop, decorate with a small slice of pickled onion and place a thin disk of carrot in the centre.

Scandinavia

Sardine canapés

White bread; oblong, diamond-shaped or oval; horseradish or mustard butter.
Cover with mashed fresh sardine and decorate with capers.

France

Sea urchin canapés

Brown bread; salted butter.
Cover with the pink creamy part of the sea urchins. Decorate with triangles of lemon peeled down to the pulp. These canapés are prepared at the very last minute. The sea urchins must be absolutely fresh.

France

Shrimp canapés

White bread; round; shrimp butter.
Garnish with picked shrimp tails arranged in a rose pattern and decorate the centre with a spot of yellow butter.

France

Sigui canapés

Brown bread; fresh butter.
Cover with a thin slice of sigui. Decorate with butter. Sigui is a Baltic fish which has been dried and smoked.

Russia

Smoked eel canapés

White or rye bread; oblong, triangular or oval; fresh or horseradish butter.
Cover with a thin slice of smoked eel and decorate with small dots of butter.

France

Smoked salmon canapés

White bread; oblong or oval; fresh butter.
Cover with a thin slice of smoked salmon and decorate with butter.

France

Spiny lobster canapés

White bread; oval; spiny lobster butter.
Garnish with a spiny lobster medallion. Decorate both ends with spiny lobster berries dressed with lemon juice and oil and well drained. Place dots of truffle on the medallion and glaze with aspic.

France

Vikings canapés

Brown or white bread; oblong; horseradish butter.
Cover with thin slices of cucumber which have been sprinkled with salt and allowed to drain. Decorate lattice fashion with smoked salmon purée and sprinkle with chopped hard-boiled egg.

Northern Europe

GAME CANAPÉS

Canapés Souvaroff

Brown bread; foie gras purée.
Cover with a thin slice of pheasant. Decorate with truffle and glaze with aspic.

France

Partridge canapés I

White bread; oblong or oval.
Cover with a thin slice of partridge. Coat with brown chaud-froid sauce containing

partridge essence. Decorate with hard-boiled egg white and truffle. Glaze by brushing with aspic.

France

Partridge canapés II

White bread; oblong; horseradish butter.
Cover with a thin slice of young partridge. Decorate with chervil leaves.

France

Pheasant canapés

White bread; oblong.
Cover with a thin slice of pheasant. Coat with brown chaud-froid sauce made with concentrated pheasant stock. Decorate with truffle and glaze with aspic.

France

Venison canapés

Rye or black bread; oval; horseradish butter.
Cover with a thin slice of fillet of roe deer.

France

LETTUCE SHELL CANAPÉS

For these canapés, a small lettuce heart leaf is fixed on top of a lightly hollowed-out oblong of white bread.

Canapés Brillat-Savarin

Spread the bread with truffle butter. Fill the lettuce shells with finely diced truffles, potatoes and russet apples in a light mayonnaise dressing. Sprinkle with chopped chervil and walnuts.

France

Canapés Dandy

Spread the bread with fine herb butter. Fill the lettuce shells with prawn tails and green asparagus tips bound with mayonnaise. Sprinkle with chopped hard-boiled egg yolk and truffles.

France

Canapés gipsy style

Spread the bread with mustard butter. Fill the lettuce shells with julienne strips of ham, pickled tongue, truffles and chicken breast in a light mayonnaise dressing.

France

Canapés Joinville

Spread the bread with shrimp or prawn butter. Fill the lettuce shells with small pieces of shelled shrimp or prawn tails and very finely diced raw mushrooms flavoured with lemon juice in mayonnaise dressing lightly flavoured with tomato.

France

Canapés royal style

Spread the bread with truffle butter. Fill the lettuce shells with finely diced chicken breast, truffles and hard-boiled egg yolk and white, in cream mayonnaise dressing.

France

Canapés Scottish style

Spread the bread with salmon butter. Fill the lettuce shells with truffles and potatoes cut into tiny triangles and dressed with vinaigrette sauce. Place a thin slice of smoked salmon on top.

France

POULTRY CANAPÉS

These canapés should be made with the breasts only, cut in thin slices. The skin and all fat should be removed before slicing. The slices of breast are flattened very slightly and placed on buttered bread, then trimmed to fit the bread with a sharp knife. Chervil or tarragon leaves, a tiny piece of skinned tomato or red pepper, or other similar garnishes are used for decoration. Finally, the canapés are brushed with aspic jelly which is just beginning to set.

Preparation of chaud-froid canapés

Cut the bread to the desired shape, butter and refrigerate for 15 minutes to harden the butter. Cut the poultry breasts to fit the bread exactly, mask very lightly with chaud-froid sauce on the point of setting, leave until firm, then decorate. Brush very lightly with aspic to glaze, and place on the bread. When set, trim evenly all round with scissors. Refrigerate until required.

Chicken canapés Aurora

Base: toasted or untoasted white bread, any shape, with fresh butter.
Butter the bread and cover with a small slice of chicken breast masked with Aurora chaud-froid sauce. Decorate as desired and glaze with aspic.

France

Chicken canapés Belle de Lauris

Base: toasted or untoasted white bread with green asparagus butter.
Butter the bread and cover with a small slice of chicken masked with asparagus chaud-froid sauce. Decorate with a green asparagus tip and glaze with aspic.

France

Chicken canapés Burgundy style

Base: white bread, oval with shortened ends (to make the canapés barrel-shaped), with fresh butter.
Butter the bread and cover with a small slice of chicken masked with Burgundy chaud-froid sauce. Decorate with a slice of truffle and glaze with aspic.

France

Chicken canapés domino

Base: toasted or untoasted white bread, rectangular, with fresh butter.
Butter the bread and cover with a small slice of chicken masked with white chicken chaud-froid sauce. Decorate with dots of truffle to resemble a domino and glaze with aspic.

France

Chicken canapés Laguipière

Base: brioche bread, oval or diamond-shaped, with truffle butter.
Butter the bread and place a round slice of chicken breast in the centre. Sprinkle both ends alternately with chopped truffle and pickled tongue and edge all round with the same garnish.

France

9

Chicken canapés Marseilles style

Base: white bread, rectangular, with fresh butter.
Butter the bread and cover with a small slice of chicken masked with Marseilles sauce reinforced with aspic.

France

Chicken canapés with mayonnaise

Base: white bread, any shape, with fresh butter.
Butter the bread and cover with a small slice of chicken masked with firm mayonnaise.

France

Chicken canapés Oriental style

Base: white bread, triangular or half-moon shape, with fresh butter.
Butter the bread and cover with a small slice of chicken masked with Oriental chaud-froid sauce. Decorate with red pepper cut to a half-moon or star shape, depending on the shape of the canapé, and glaze with aspic.

France

Chicken canapés Parisian style

Base: white bread, rectangular, with chervil butter.
Butter the bread and cover with a small slice of chicken masked with firm mayonnaise. Decorate with truffle and blanched tarragon and glaze with aspic.

France

Chicken canapés Pompadour

Base: white bread, rectangular, oval or round, with fresh butter.
Butter the bread and cover with a small slice of chicken masked with Aurora chaud-froid sauce. Decorate with a small sprig of chervil and place tiny disks of tomato between the leaves. Glaze with aspic.

France

Chicken canapés pompon rose

Base: white bread, rectangular, round or oval, with fresh butter.
Butter the bread and cover with a small slice of chicken breast masked with white

chicken chaud-froid sauce. Decorate in the same way as chicken canapés Pompadour.

France

Chicken canapés verdurette

Base: white bread, any shape, with maître d'hôtel butter.
Butter the bread and cover with a small slice of chicken breast masked with firm herb mayonnaise.

France

Chicken canapés demi-deuil

Base: white bread, square, with fresh butter.
Butter the bread and cover with a small slice of chicken masked with chicken chaud-froid sauce. Decorate with hard-boiled egg white and small slices of truffle. Glaze with aspic.

France

Chicken canapés white lady

Base: toasted or untoasted white bread, rectangular, with fresh butter.
Butter the bread and cover with a small slice of chicken masked with chicken chaud-froid sauce. Glaze with aspic.

France

Duck and cherry canapés

Base: toasted or untoasted white bread, rectangular, round or oval, with fresh butter.
Butter the bread and cover with a small slice of duck breast masked with brown duck chaud-froid sauce. Decorate with a stoned stewed morello cherry and glaze lightly with aspic.

France

Duck canapés Gedeon

Base: white bread, rectangular, with fresh butter.
Butter the bread and cover with a purée consisting of 2 parts duck and 1 part foie gras. Decorate with crossed strips of duck and glaze with aspic.

France

Duck and orange canapés

Base: toasted white bread, rectangular or oval, with fresh butter.
Butter the bread and cover with a small slice of duck breast which has been masked with brown duck chaud-froid sauce flavoured with Curaçao. Decorate with small triangles of skinned orange.

France

Duck canapés Rouen style

Base: toasted or untoasted white bread, triangular, with fresh butter.
Butter the bread and coat with brown chaud-froid sauce flavoured with duck essence. Decorate with a small slice of truffle and glaze with aspic.

France

Guinea-fowl canapés

Any recipes for pigeon canapés can be used for guinea-fowl. The birds should be young and very tender.

France

Guinea-fowl canapés A. Guerot

Base: white bread, square, with truffle butter.
Butter the bread and cover with a small slice of breast of guinea-fowl masked with brown chaud-froid sauce. Decorate with a small cap of fresh butter topped with a blanched tarragon leaf on the slant.

France

Guinea-fowl canapés English style

Base: white bread, any shape, with printanier butter.
Butter the bread, cover with a small slice of guinea-fowl and decorate with printanier butter.

France

Guinea-fowl canapés Gascon style

Base: white bread, oval, with fresh butter.
Butter the bread and cover with a purée consisting of 2 parts well-seasoned guinea-fowl to 1 part foie gras. Decorate with a tiny disk of truffle and glaze with aspic.

France

Pigeon canapés I

Base: white bread, rectangular, with watercress butter.
Butter the bread and cover with a small slice of pigeon breast. Decorate with blanched watercress leaves and glaze with aspic.

France

Pigeon canapés II

Base: white bread, oval, with shallot butter.
Butter the bread and cover with a small slice of pigeon breast. Decorate with tomato butter seasoned with cayenne pepper.

France

Pigeon and paprika canapés

Base: white bread, diamond-shaped, with paprika butter.
Butter the bread and cover with a small slice of pigeon breast. Decorate the centre with a star of paprika butter.

France

Turkey canapés Prosper Montagne

Base: white bread, oval, with tomato butter.
Butter the bread and cover with a small slice of turkey breast masked with Occitan sauce. Decorate with red pepper and glaze with aspic.

France

VEGETABLE CANAPÉS

Blood-red and gold canapés

White bread; half-moon shaped.
Cover with a small wedge of tomato (without seeds) seasoned with salt and pepper. To decorate, pipe on yellow butter lightly seasoned with cayenne pepper, using a savoy bag fitted with a star pipe.

France

Canapés Beaulieu

White bread; round; salted butter.
Cover with a round slice of tomato seasoned with salt and pepper. Garnish the centre with half a black olive.

France

Canapés Cambacérès

White bread; oblong; salted butter.
Cover with half-moons of cucumber dressed with lemon vinaigrette. The cucumber should be well drained before use.

France

Canapés Lutetia

White bread; round; mustard butter.
Cover with lightly salted finely shredded lettuce. Garnish the centre with a small slice of tomato seasoned with salt and white pepper.

France

Canapés mascot

White bread; oblong; Montpellier butter.
Cover with thin slices of artichoke bottom dressed with vinaigrette. Garnish the centre with a slice of potato.

France

Mushroom canapés I

White bread; oblong; salted butter.
Cover with thin slices of firm white button mushrooms dressed with lemon and fine herb vinaigrette. The mushrooms should be well drained before use.

France

Mushroom canapés II

White bread; oblong; salted butter.
Wash button mushrooms well and cook in very little water well sharpened with lemon juice and lightly seasoned with salt and pepper. Allow to cool and slice thinly. Dress with lemon vinaigrette and drain thoroughly. Arrange the slices on the base one overlapping another and decorate with chopped parsley or with chervil leaves.

France

Pink radish canapés

White bread; square; salted butter.
Cover with slices of radish and decorate as desired.

France

Tomato canapés

White bread; round; salted butter.
Cover with slices of tomato seasoned with salt and white pepper.

France

VARIOUS CANAPÉS

Canapés Beatrice

Base: white bread, rectangular or oval, with chervil butter.
Butter the bread and cover with two paper-thin slices of dried sausage with a slice of hard-boiled egg in between. Decorate with dots of tomato butter.

France

Canapés Bordeaux style

Base: white bread, oval, with shallot butter.
Butter the bread and cover alternately with thin overlapping slices of cooked preserved flap mushrooms (boletus) and Bayonne ham.
N.B.—Use the shallot butter sparingly as it has a very strong smell.

France

Canapés buttercup

Base: white bread, round, with watercress butter.
Butter the bread and cover with blanched watercress leaves. Decorate with egg yolk paste.

France

Canapés Chantereine

Base: white bread, triangular, with fresh butter.
Butter the bread and leave until the butter is firm. Cover half the bread with ham mousse and the other half with chicken mousse. Place a tiny disk of truffle on the latter and a tiny disk of hard-boiled egg white on the ham mousse.

France

Canapés Creole style

Base: white bread, rectangular, with fresh butter.
Butter the bread, cover with a thin slice of Emmenthal cheese and decorate with two thin slices of banana.

France

Canapés Dolomites style

Base: pumpernickel or black bread, square, with fresh butter.
Sieve 100 g (3½ oz) curd cheese and mix well with 30 g (1 oz) softened butter, a teaspoonful of chopped chives, a few caraway seeds, salt and pepper. Spread the bread with this paste.

France

Canapés Grenoble style

Base: white bread, round, with walnut butter.
Butter the bread, place half a walnut in the centre and surround with a border of finely diced Gruyère cheese.

France

Canapés Hamburg style

Base: white or light rye bread, rectangular, with fresh butter.
Butter the bread, cover with a thin slice of Hamburg smoked meat and decorate with thin slices of gherkin.

France

Canapés Harlequin style

Base: white bread, rectangular or diamond-shaped, with mustard, horseradish, paprika, watercress or tomato butter.
Spread the bread with any of the above savoury butters. Cover with chopped or, preferably, finely diced chicken, pickled tongue, hard-boiled egg white or yolk, truffle, etc. and surround with a ring of the savoury butter used for spreading.

France

Canapés Helvetia

Base: pumpernickel or black bread, rectangular, with fresh butter.
Cream 100 g (3½ oz) butter and mix well with 100 g (3½ oz) grated Emmenthal cheese, 2 sieved hard-boiled egg yolks, 1 teaspoon grated celeriac, 2 tablespoons dairy cream, salt and pepper. Spread the bread with this paste.

France

Canapés Jodler

Base: small rounds of toast with fresh butter.
Butter the toast, cover with grated radish and place a small round of pumpernickel in the centre. Top this with a small cube of processed Emmenthal cheese and decorate with salted peanuts.

France

Canapés Lulli

Base: white bread, square, with fresh butter.
Butter the bread and cover with chicken mousse. Decorate the centre with truffle cut to represent a note of music.

France

Canapés Monselet

Base: white bread, oval, with egg yolk butter seasoned with cayenne pepper.
Butter the bread and cover alternately with half-moons of chicken breast, truffle and pickled tongue. Surround with a border of egg yolk butter.

France

Canapés Ninon

Base: white bread, oval, with printanier butter.
Butter the bread and cover with half-moons of chicken breast and York ham. Decorate with a dot of the same savoury butter.

France

Canapés Pellaprat

Base: white bread, round, with fresh butter.
Butter the bread and cover with salmon mousse. Pipe on a narrow border of watercress butter.

France

Canapés Swiss domino

Base: pumpernickel or black bread, square, with fresh butter.
Butter the bread and cover with a small slice of Emmenthal cheese. Decorate with small dots of pumpernickel, fixed in position with butter, to imitate a domino.

France

Canapés Tilsit style

Base: pumpernickel or black bread, square, with fresh butter.
Butter the bread and cover with a thin slice of salami. Place a slice of Tilsit cheese on top.

France

Graubündner dried meat canapés

Base: white bread, square, with watercress butter.
Butter the bread, cover with a thin slice of the dried meat and decorate with watercress butter.
N.B.—The dried meat is cut paper-thin with the aid of a special cutter.

France

Horseradish canapés

Base: black bread, rectangular, with butter flavoured with English mustard and chopped chives.
Butter the bread and sprinkle with grated horseradish. Edge with chopped hard-boiled egg yolk.

France

Ogourzi canapés

Base: rye bread with fresh butter.
Butter thick slices of rye bread and cover with slices of pickled dill cucumber.

France

Pickled tongue canapés

Base: white bread, star-shaped, with cayenne butter.
Butter the bread and cover with a thin, star-shaped slice of pickled ox tongue.

France

Walnut canapés

Base: white bread, oval, with fresh butter.
Butter the bread and sprinkle with coarsely chopped walnuts.

France

Watercress canapés

Base: white bread, rectangular, round or oval, with watercress butter.
Butter the bread and cover with blanched watercress leaves.

France

INTERNATIONAL CANAPÉS

AUSTRIAN CANAPÉS

From right to left:

Steak tartare on rye bread with caviar in the centre (Moscovites).

Shrimps on dill butter.

Canapés spread with Cumberland butter, topped with a small disk of foie gras purée and a piece of pineapple.

Leaf spinach with fried onion rings.

Ham purée with Cumberland sauce.

Mixed chopped egg white and yolk, chopped cocktail onions, capers, parsley and gherkins.

Smoked salmon on horseradish cream, topped with capers.

Anchovy butter, a slice of hard-boiled egg, a rolled anchovy fillet, parsley.

Gervais mixed with butter, dairy cream, chopped eggs, gherkins and cocktail onions, seasoned with paprika, salt and pepper and sprinkled with chopped egg yolk.

Smoked ham on horseradish cream.

Gervais seasoned with red paprika and sprinkled with chopped green peppers.

Small pieces of smoked trout on horseradish cream.

With the exception of the steak tartare, all the canapés are made with white bread.

(Illustration, p. 579)

ITALIAN CANAPÉS (TARTINE)

Italian canapés are made with the following kinds of bread:

1. White bread (tin or sandwich loaf) without crust, measuring 6 cm × 4 cm × 6 mm ($2\frac{1}{2}$ × $1\frac{1}{2}$ × $\frac{1}{4}$ in), for chicken salad, fish or shellfish.

2. Rye bread without crust (same measurements as above) for smoked salmon, caviar, vegetable salad, herring, smoked foods of various kinds.

3. Brown bread without crust (same measurements as above) for salami, ham, corned beef, roast beef and canapés garnished with capers or pickled cucumbers.

4. French sticks with crust, thinly sliced, for roast beef, cheese, sardines, etc.

5. Round or square crackers, used for any kind of topping.

The most popular canapés:

1. Smoked salmon. Here never use savoury butter.

2. Caviar with a wedge of lemon. Here never use savoury butter.

3. Pickled ox tongue garnished with slices of pickled cucumber and cocktail onions.

4. Cooked Parma ham. (These canapés are not made up until just before serving, as Parma ham dries up quickly.)

5. Vegetable salad garnished with mussels, lightly fried in butter and trimmed.

6. Salami with peppers or cocktail onions.

7. Lettuce leaf and chicken salad.

8. Roast beef, cold roast pork or veal or roast turkey.

9. Small rounds of cold pork sausage, garnished with piccalilli, on bread spread with mustard butter.

10. Tomato with a criss-cross garnish of anchovy fillets.

11. Slices of minced meat loaf with pickled cucumber.

12. Cheese.

13. Lettuce leaf, sardine in oil and finely chopped onion.

SPANISH CANAPÉS

Chorizo canapés

24 canapés

	24 rounds caviar bread 4 cm (1½ in) in diameter and 5 mm (about ⅛ in) thick	
250 g	best quality chorizo	about 8 oz
250 g	ripe tomatoes	about 8 oz
	1 clove of garlic, peeled	
	1 bay leaf	
	half a teaspoon sugar	
15 cl	oil	¼ pt

Fry the garlic in part of the oil until lightly coloured, add the tomatoes cut into small pieces and cook gently till all the liquid has evaporated. Add the sugar, season with salt and pepper, reduce until thick and pass through a sieve. Cook the chorizo in the oven, allow to cool and cut into 24 slices. If preferred, slice while still raw and fry in oil. Toast the bread lightly. Place a small spoonful of the tomato purée on each round of toast, cover with a slice of chorizo and fix in place with a toothpick without crushing the purée.

Cocktail canapés (Cariacias)

Cut oblongs 5 cm × 3 cm × 7 mm (2 × 1¼ × ¼ in) from a day-old sandwich loaf and toast on one side only. Allow to cool, then butter the toasted side and cover with a slice of semi-soft cheese 7 mm (¼ in) thick to fit the bread exactly. Glaze with cold melted butter and place 4 half Muscat grapes (peeled and seeded) on each canapé.

FINNISH CANAPÉS (HOHDOKKAAT. ALKUPALAT)

Oil a metal tray with a rim lightly and cover with thin slices of bread without crusts or with fairly thick slices of hard-boiled egg. Depending on the number of canapés required, a separate tray may be used for each type.

1. Spread with a layer of liver purée about 3 cm (1¼ in) thick. Cover with a thin round of roast turkey-cock and decorate with a disk of truffle. Pour a liberal amount of aspic jelly over and refrigerate.

2. Roll up a thin slice of salmon, leaving a small opening, poach and allow to cool. Fill the centre with horseradish cream stiffened with a little gelatine, pour aspic jelly over and refrigerate.

3. Fill the centre of a small rolled-up poached fillet of sole with a trimmed mussel, pour aspic jelly over and refrigerate.

4. Spread with a layer of calves' liver purée about 3 cm (1¼ in) thick and decorate with a cocktail onion. Pour aspic jelly over and refrigerate.

5. Mix finely sieved cheese with chopped mushrooms, spread on to the bread or sliced egg to a thickness of about 3 cm (1¼ in), pour aspic jelly over and refrigerate.

May also be prepared in the same way as No. 2.

6. Proceed as for No. 3.

7. Pipe foie gras purée on to slices of egg, using a savoy bag fitted with a star pipe, and pour aspic jelly over.

When quite cold, the various canapés are cut out with a round cutter and a toothpick is inserted into each one.

Instead of this complicated and costly procedure, it is advisable to place the toppings and garnish in individual moulds which have been masked with aspic jelly. The moulds are then filled up with jelly. When set, each one is turned out on to a small slice of fried bread or a slice of egg.

In addition to the above Finnish canapés, the types of canapés that are well known in other countries are also often served.

(Illustration, p. 588)

NORWEGIAN CANAPÉS

Slice pumpernickel or other good-quality rye bread, cut into rounds, butter and garnish as follows.

1. Chop smoked salmon trimmings finely, compress, spread on bread to a domed shape and decorate with half a cocktail onion.

2.   1 part finely chopped marinated herring fillets
             1 part finely chopped peeled and cored apples
             1 part finely chopped pickled beetroots
             thick mayonnaise (one-third of the total weight
                of the above ingredients)
             sprigs of dill

Mix the herring with the apples and beetroots, bind with the mayonnase, adjust the seasoning and pile on to bread in a dome. Decorate each canapé with a small sprig of dill.

3.　　　　　　　fresh raw herring fillets
　　　　　　　marinade consisting of 1 part water and
　　　　　　　　　1 part 7% vinegar
　　　　　　　salt
　　　　　　　sugar
　　　　　　　finely chopped cucumber
　　　　　　　small julienne strips of cucumber

Place the herring fillets in a marinade of water, vinegar, salt and sugar and stand aside for 24 hours. Remove, dice as finely as possible, mix with a little finely chopped cucumber, adjust the seasoning and pile on to bread in a dome. Sprinkle lightly with cucumber cut into julienne strips.

4.　　500 g　　　picked shrimps　　　　　1 lb
　　　100 g　　　mayonnaise　　　　　　　4 oz
　　　　　　　　lemon slices
　　　　　　　　dill leaves

Chop the shrimps finely, mix with the mayonnaise, season well and pile on to bread in a dome. Decorate each canapé with a quarter of a slice of lemon and a dill leaf.

5.　　　　　　　Smoked eel trimmings without skin or bones
　　　　　　　　sliced stuffed olives

Chop the eel finely, compress and spread on rye bread to a dome shape. Decorate each canapé with a slice of stuffed olive.

6.　　　　　　　Smoked lake trout trimmings without skin or bones
　　　　　　　　small black olives, stoned and cut in half

Chop the trout finely, season with pepper, compress and spread on bread to a dome shape. Decorate each canapé with half a black olive.

7.　　　　　　　spiced herring fillets
　　　　　　　　whipped sour cream
　　　　　　　　chopped chives

Cut the herring into rounds the same size as the bread. Place one of these on each slice of bread, pipe on whipped sour cream, using a savoy bag fitted with a plain pipe, and sprinkle with chopped chives.

8.
    whale meat
    paprika
    Chablis
    very small onion rings
    beluga caviar

Scrape the whale meat finely, season with salt, freshly ground pepper and paprika and mix well with sufficient Chablis to give the desired consistency. Shape into a small flat-topped ball and place a tiny ball on each slice of bread. Garnish with a small onion ring and fill the centre of this with caviar.

Glaze all the canapés with fish aspic.

(Illustration, p. 702, from front to back)

JAPANESE CANAPÉS

Trim thin slices of white bread so that the various sizes can be assembled in the shape of a fan. Toast them very lightly, assemble with mustard butter and spread with the same butter. Garnish as follows from top to bottom:

1. Black caviar decorated with rings of stoned green olive.

2. Sieved cream cheese seasoned with salt and pepper, flavoured with lemon juice and decorated with steamed leek cut to resemble a bamboo leaf.

3. Red caviar ('ikura' in Japanese).

4. Steamed leek decorated with red pepper.

5. Cover the bottom part with smoked cheese and decorate with leek shaped like a pine needle.

Use cream cheese alone for the centre part of the fan and decorate the middle with red caviar to make the 'good luck' sign 'kotobuki' (this is used at weddings in particular).

(Illustration, p. 590)

HOT CANAPÉS

These are among the most popular delicacies as they can be served anywhere at any time. They are not at all complicated to make and may be prepared at home just as easily as in a restaurant. They are especially popular as snacks after the theatre or with drinks served at home.

▶ A Celebration Buffet at 'Der Konigshof' Hotel, Munich, pp. 273, 274, 716, 734
▶▶ A Reception in honour of the Mayor of Berne at the Hotel Schweizerhof, Berne

◀ ▲ Buffet for a meeting of the Chaine des Rotisseurs at La Residence, Salzburg

245

▲ A dinner party at the Hotel Schweizerhof, Berne

246 ▶ A farewell dinner at the Hotel Fischerhaus, Lake Constance, Germany, pp. 488, 673

▼ A hunting dinner at the Drei Husaren Restaurant, Vienna

There is no need to specify quantities in the recipes, as each of these may be adjusted to national habits or individual tastes.

White bread for toasting can be bought wrapped and sliced; alternatively, the bread may be bought unsliced and cut to the thickness desired. Black bread is also used for these hot savouries. First of all the crusts are removed and each slice is cut square. The bread is then toasted or fried in fat.

Angels on horseback

12 oysters
few thinly cut rashers of bacon
finely minced sweet herbs
pepper
12 rounds of bread (fried)
little lemon juice

Trim bacon into squares large enough to roll round an oyster. Sprinkle with herbs and pepper. Put an oyster on each square and squeeze a drop of lemon juice over. Roll them up. Skewer and fry until bacon is cooked. Place an oyster on each round of fried bread. Serve hot.

Great Britain

Canapé Diane

4 portions

	2 slices white bread	
150 g	chicken liver	6 oz
50 g	rashered streaky bacon	2 oz

'Spread' the bacon rashers until very thin. Lightly sauté the chicken livers. Roll the livers in the bacon and thread on to skewers. Grill until the bacon is crisp and the liver just cooked and serve on toast.

France

Calf's brains on toast (Toust s mozeckem)

Toast slices of white bread. Fry the soaked and blanched brains in butter, cut up a little, mix with capers, season with salt and sharpen with lemon juice. Spread on the toast and sprinkle with a little gravy.

Czechoslovakia

◀   Aperitif time at De Gravenmolen Restaurant, Amsterdam, pp. 261, 566

Calf's kidney on toast

Remove the fat and skin surrounding the kidney, clean well, fry and then season with salt. Cut on the slant into 2–3 slices, depending on size. Wrap each slice in thinly sliced ham and fry for a few moments longer. Toast slices of white bread and cover each one with a slice of calf's kidney wrapped in ham.

Czechoslovakia

Chicken on fried bread

Fry slices of white bread on both sides in butter until golden. Cover each one with a neat piece of chicken (boneless) and garnish with a few hot asparagus tips. Brush over lightly with melted butter.

Czechoslovakia

Chicken livers on fried bread

Fry a slice of black bread in fat. Cut the chicken livers in thick slices, fry in a little fat, keeping them slightly underdone, season with salt and pepper and place on the fried bread. Cover with a slice of fried ham and moisten very lightly with gravy.

Czechoslovakia

Club sandwich

Cut 2 slices of white bread into triangles and toast lightly. Spread one with chicken mayonnaise and place 2 slices of hot fried bacon or ham on top. Cover with the second triangle of toast and serve hot.

USA

Cucumber toast

Toast 4 slices of bread on both sides and butter one side. Spread with a very thin layer of hot mustard and lay a slice of cooked ham on each. Slice half a cucumber fairly thickly and cover the ham with the slices. Sprinkle lightly with garlic salt, cover with a slice of Emmenthal or Appenzell cheese and place under the grill for a moment. Garnish with a sprig of dill.

Germany

Devils on horseback

12 plump poached prunes
12 salted almonds
a few trim rashers of streaky bacon

pepper
lemon juice
3 slices toast

Replace the stone in each prune by a salted almond, roll each prune in bacon, skewer and grill. Serve 4 prunes on a slice of buttered toast.

Great Britain

Goose liver on fried bread

Fry a slice of black bread in fat. Cover with a fairly large slice of goose liver fried in goose fat or butter and top with a peeled, cored and fried slice of apple and a thin slice of fried bacon.

Czechoslovakia

Hunter's toast

10 portions   Cooking time: 10–15 minutes

	5 cooked pheasants (used to make the broth)	
150 g	mushrooms	5 oz
100 g	flour	3 oz
1 dl	oil	⅛ pt
½ l	red wine	1 pt
1 dl	Cognac	1 measure
100 g	tomato purée	3 oz
	2 lemons	
	Worcestershire sauce	
	chopped parsley	

Cut the meat off the pheasants, skin and dice finely. Prepare blond roux with the oil and flour, blend in the wine, add the diced cooked mushrooms, the tomato purée and the Cognac, season with salt and pepper, flavour with Worcestershire sauce and simmer gently. Add the meat, boil up once, check the flavour, pile on to white toast and garnish with slices of lemon and chopped parsley.

Czechoslovakia

London toast

Toast 4 slices of bread on both sides, spread with a thin layer of hot mustard on one side and sprinkle with chopped parsley. Lay a slice of cold roast veal weighing about 80 g (about 3 oz) on each. Drain a small can of mushrooms, cut these in half and arrange on the veal. Cover with a slice of Emmenthal cheese, place in the oven for a moment, and garnish with a sprig of parsley.

Germany

Mussel toast

Chop 1 large or 2 small onions finely and fry lightly with 80 g (2¾ oz) diced smoked bacon. Add 2 small cans mussels after draining off the brine. Brown well on all sides.

Toast 4 slices of bread on both sides, butter thinly on one side, sprinkle each one with a teaspoon chopped chives and a little powdered garlic, then cover with the mussels. Top with a slice of Cheshire cheese cut into two triangles and finish off in the oven or under the grill. Sprinkle with chopped chives.

Germany

Pig's kidneys on fried bread

Fry slices of black bread in fat. Skin and core the pig's kidneys, cutting them in half, wash them, season with salt and pepper and fry until half-cooked only. Wrap each half kidney in a very thin rasher of bacon, fry until cooked, place on the fried bread and spread lightly with mustard.

Czechoslovakia

Roast beef on fried bread

Fry slices of black bread in fat and spread with mustard. Cover with a slice of hot roast beef and garnish with 2 slices of fried tomato.

Czechoslovakia

Salami toast

Toast 4 slices of white bread on both sides. Butter one side and place 4 slices of salami on each. Melt 40 g (1½ oz) butter in a pan and lightly fry 4 tablespoons chopped canned mushrooms in it. Add 4 eggs and half a teaspoon salt, stir as for scrambled eggs and, when lightly cooked, cover the salami with the mixture. Top with a slice of fried tomato and sprinkle with chopped parsley.

Germany

Scotch Woodcock

Cover a square of buttered toast with lightly cooked scrambled egg and arrange strips of anchovy fillet on top in a lattice pattern. Place a caper in each space and serve at once.

(Illustration, p. 588)   Great Britain

Scrambled egg and anchovies on toast

Toast slices of white bread, cover with hot lightly set scrambled egg, garnish with rings of anchovy fillet and sprinkle with chopped parsley.

Czechoslovakia

Scrambled egg and tunny fish on toast

Toast a slice of white bread, cover with a layer of scrambled egg and top with a slice of fried tunny fish (canned). Sprinkle with chopped parsley.

Czechoslovakia

Spinach and cheese toast

Toast 4 slices of white bread on both sides. Wash 250 g (8 oz) spinach and cook under cover with a knob of butter, a little salt and pepper. Butter the toast thinly, cover with a thin slice of ham and top with the spinach. Drain off the liquid from a small can of mushrooms, slice the latter and arrange on the spinach. Lastly, cover with a fairly thick slice of Emmenthal cheese. Finish off in a pre-heated oven or under the grill and sprinkle with paprika.

Germany

Sweetbreads on fried bread

Soak, blanch and cook the sweetbreads in the usual manner. Fry slices of black bread in fat and cover each one with 2 slices of sweetbread. Coat lightly with thickened gravy mixed with sliced sauté mushrooms and place a fairly large slice of fried ham on top.

Czechoslovakia

Venison on fried bread

Fry 2 round slices of black bread lightly in fat. Cut medallions from a haunch of venison, fry lightly, keeping them pink, season with salt and pepper and place on the bread. Cover one medallion with a slice of pineapple lightly stewed in butter and the other with a slice of peeled stewed orange.

Czechoslovakia

Welsh rarebit

200 g	Cheshire cheese	7 oz
3 cl	beer	3 dessertspoons
	English mustard	
	cayenne pepper (optional)	
	buttered toast	

Dice the cheese and place in a pan with the beer and a little mustard. Stir over low heat to a smooth paste, pour over the toast and glaze the top lightly in a very hot oven or under a salamander.

Great Britain

SANDWICHES

Sandwiches are named after John Montagu, the 4th Earl of Sandwich who, in the eighteenth century, had slices of meat placed between slices of bread and brought to him at the gaming table so that he could continue gambling whilst he ate. (This was a necessary expedient, since we are told he did not leave the table for twenty-four hours!) From this simple beginning, sandwiches have rapidly established themselves in many different circumstances, and many variations of size and style have evolved.

RECEPTION SANDWICHES

The sandwiches referred to here are not, of course, the substantial ones which are sometimes eaten instead of a meal, but dainty ones suitable for a cocktail party or small cold buffet. They consist of two thin slices of bread enclosing a filling and are generally cut from a white tin or sandwich loaf to make square, oblong, triangular or other shapes. They may also be made with long brioche-type rolls. Brown and rye bread are less commonly used, but everyone is quite free to experiment. The sandwiches are 5–8 cm (2–3 in) in length and should not be larger than this. Except where otherwise stated, the bread is buttered.

For instructions on slicing a tin or sandwich loaf and cutting the bread into various shapes, and also for details of suitable sizes, see page 208 (canapés).

Here is a selection of sandwiches. There are, of course, many other possible fillings.

All sandwiches which are not required immediately are stacked and tightly wrapped to prevent the bread from curling up at the corners, and stored in a refrigerator until needed. Sandwiches are normally presented on a flat dish or plate with a doyley, and garnished with parsley, cucumber or mustard and cress.

American sandwiches

1. White bread sandwiched with ham mousse and cut into half-moons.

2. Bread sandwiched with a mixture of tongue mousse and chopped hard-boiled egg and cut into triangles.

3. Buttered slices of sandwich loaf, sandwiched with thin slices of cooked ham and wafer-thin slices of cucumber and cut into diamonds.

4. Thinly buttered white bread, covered with thinly sliced chicken, seasoned, spread with mayonnaise and cut into squares.

5. Three thin slices of pumpernickel sandwiched with a mixture of sieved Roquefort cheese, butter and a little port and cut into triangles.

6. Heart-shaped slices of white bread, thinly buttered and covered with small thin slices of turkey breast coated with mayonnaise.

7. Oblongs of white bread with a filling of paper-thin slices of cooked ham, cheese and hard-boiled egg.

8. Buttered bread sandwiched with hard-boiled egg and chopped pickled cucumber and cut into triangles.

Anchovy sandwiches I

Fill with 2 or 3 pieces of anchovy fillets in oil which have been well drained.

France

Anchovy sandwiches II

Spread with anchovy butter.

France

Bayonne ham sandwiches

Fill with Bayonne ham.

France

Canadian sandwiches

Cover with watercress, place a slice of smoked salmon on top and cover this with watercress.

Cheshire cheese sandwiches

Fill with very thinly sliced Cheshire cheese.

Club sandwiches

Cover with slices of tomato, trimmed lettuce leaves and a light coating of mayonnaise. Place thinly sliced chicken breast on top and cover with more sliced tomato, lettuce, mayonnaise and also sliced hard-boiled egg. Instead of chicken, all kinds of meat or poultry may be used.

France

Demi-sel cheese sandwiches

Spread with demi-sel cheese lightly tinted pink with a little paprika.

France

Fish sandwiches

Spread with Provençal purée and fill with thin slices of fish—hake, turbot, sole fillet, whiting, etc.

France

Foie gras sandwiches I

Fill with thin slices of plain or truffled foie gras.

France

Foie gras sandwiches II

Spread with plain or truffled foie gras purée, consisting of 2 parts foie gras to 1 part butter lightly seasoned with salt and pepper. Do not butter the bread.

France

Game sandwiches

Fill with thin slices of cooked game.

France

Gruyère cheese sandwiches

Spread with salted butter and fill with thinly sliced Gruyère cheese.

France

Ham sandwiches I

Fill with York or Paris ham.

France

Ham sandwiches II

Fill with ham purée consisting of 2 parts lean ham mixed with 1 part butter, seasoned with salt and pepper. Do not butter the bread.

France

Hard-boiled egg and tomato mayonnaise sandwiches

Fill with sliced hard-boiled egg lightly coated with mayonnaise and covered with sliced tomatoes.

France

Lamb and onion sandwiches

Spread with horseradish butter. Fill with thin slices of roast leg of lamb and sliced onions.

France

Lettuce, chicken and tomato sandwiches

Spread with tarragon butter. Garnish alternately with shredded lettuce, thin slice of chicken breast, sliced tomato, seasoning lightly with salt.

France

Lettuce and Gruyère sandwiches

Spread with lemon butter. Fill with shredded lettuce and thin slices of Gruyère cheese lightly sprinkled with salt.

France

Lettuce and roast beef sandwiches

Spread with mustard butter. Fill with shredded lettuce and thin slices of roast beef lightly sprinkled with salt.

France

Liver paste sandwiches

Spread with pig's liver paste.

Port Salut cheese sandwiches

Fill with slices of Port Salut cheese.

France

Poultry sandwiches

Fill with thinly sliced poultry breast.

France

Rhineland sandwiches

Butter a slice of pumpernickel, cover with a slice of white bread, butter this and cover with another slice of pumpernickel.

France

Roquefort cheese sandwiches

Spread with Roquefort butter (2 parts Roquefort to 1 part butter mixed together with the aid of a fork).

France

Sardine sandwiches I

Fill with thin sardine fillets sprinkled with a few drops of lemon juice.

France

Sardine sandwiches II

Spread with sardine butter. Do not butter the bread.

France

Sausage sandwiches

Fill with a slice of any sausage, first removing the skin.

France

Smoked eel sandwiches

Fill with thin slices of smoked eel.

France

Smoked salmon sandwiches

Fill with thin slices of smoked salmon.

France

Tongue sandwiches

Fill with pickled tongue.

France

Tuna sandwiches

Proceed as for sardine sandwiches, using tuna in oil instead of sardines.

France

Veal and tomato sandwiches

Fill with thin slices of veal lightly coated with mayonnaise and covered with sliced tomato.

France

FANCY SANDWICHES

Pinwheel sandwiches

These are made with a tin or sandwich loaf which is one or, at most, two days old. The loaf is sliced lengthwise as described for making canapés (see p. 208). Each slice is buttered, covered with filling and rolled up. The rolls are then individually wrapped in greaseproof paper, then in a muslin or other cloth. They are stored in the refrigerator overnight, or for at least 4 hours. They are then unwrapped, cut across into 2 or 3 mm (about $\frac{1}{10}$ in) slices, arranged on a disk covered with a napkin or fancy paper and kept cool until required.

Harlequin pinwheel sandwiches

Spread with mustard butter. Cover alternately with strips of pickled tongue, truffle and green pepper along the whole length of the slice of bread.

France

Pinwheel sandwiches Armorican style

Spread with lobster butter and dot with spiny lobster coral.

France

Pinwheel sandwiches Catalonian style

Spread with butter lightly seasoned with cayenne pepper. Cover alternately with strips of egg butter and tomato.

France

Pinwheel sandwiches Clairette

Spread with cayenne butter and sprinkle with a mixture of chopped spiny lobster coral and truffle.

France

Pinwheel sandwiches Muscovite style

Spread with plain butter and cover with caviar.

France

Pinwheel sandwiches Périgord style

Spread with truffle butter and cover with strips of foie gras.

France

Pinwheel sandwiches D. Pinaudier

Spread with watercress butter and cover with strips of cooked sweet red pepper.

France

Pinwheel sandwiches Riviera style

Spread with anchovy butter and cover with strips of green olive and tomato.

France

Smoked salmon pinwheel sandwiches

Spread with plain butter and cover with a thin slice of smoked salmon.

France

American pinwheel sandwiches

1. Thinly buttered bread spread with a mixture of cream cheese and redcurrant jelly and rolled up tightly.

2. Thinly buttered bread spread with a mixture of well-seasoned cream cheese and lightly roasted finely chopped nuts and rolled up tightly.

3. As above, but the cream cheese is mixed with finely chopped green olives instead of nuts.

4. Same as No. 2 but the cream cheese is mixed with mint jelly instead of nuts.

5. Same as No. 2 but the cream cheese is mixed with sufficient sieved apricot jam to flavour well instead of nuts.

(Techniques, p. 100.)

Cheese zebras

	6 slices black bread	
100 g	butter	4 oz
	4 hard-boiled egg yolks	
50 g	grated Parmesan	2 oz
	dash of cayenne pepper	

Make a smooth cream with the butter, the sieved egg yolks, the Parmesan and a dash of cayenne pepper. Spread on thin slices of black bread and sandwich these together in threes so that there are two thick layers of cheese/butter/egg paste in between. Wrap in foil and refrigerate for a few hours, then slice thinly; each slice will be striped black and white like a zebra.

(Illustration, p. 248)   Holland

Olmertz sticks

Mix 1 part creamed butter with 1 part sieved Roquefort cheese and spread on to a slice of pumpernickel or black bread. Cover with a second slice of bread, spread this with a mixture of cream cheese and paprika butter (2 parts cheese to 1 part butter) and top with a third slice of bread. Refrigerate for at least 1 hour and, when firm, cut into sticks 2 cm ($\frac{3}{4}$ in) wide.

France

Open cheese sandwiches for a children's party

Cut 1 cm ($\frac{1}{2}$ in) thick slices from a sandwich loaf into various shapes, e.g. birds, fish, sailing boats. Cover with a slice of cheese cut to the same shape and decorate as follows:

Birds. Use a gherkin cut in the shape of a fan for the wing and tail, a caper for the eye and curly-leaved parsley for the crest.

Fish. Use sliced radishes or gherkins for the scales and a caper for the eye.

Sailing boats. Use thin strips of gherkin and tomato for the bottom of the boat.

Punch heads. Use half a slice of hard-boiled egg for the eyes, a gherkin for the nose and a strip of tomato for the mouth. Make the hair out of curly-leaved parsley, triangles of salami or slices of Frankfurter sausages.

Switzerland

Louis XV or surprise loaf

A country-style round loaf at least a day old is used for this purpose.

Remove the crumb as follows. Insert a flexible knife just inside the crust so that the tip almost reaches the bottom of the loaf and cut all round. Now insert the knife into the base of the loaf just above the bottom crust, holding it slightly on the slant so that the tip reaches the crust on the opposite side without penetrating it. Pivot the loaf round the blade so that the crumb is removed in one piece, leaving a hollow shell of crust. Make small sandwiches from the crumb of the loaf, place them inside the crust, cover with the top crust and decorate with a bow of ribbon.

The sandwiches may be made with brown or other bread if desired.

(Techniques, p. 101.)

Viking ship

1. Cut the crusts off a sandwich loaf and trim to the shape of a ship.

2. Insert a knife in the top and make a rectangular cut.

3. Make an incision in the base.

4. Insert the knife into the centre rectangle and remove.

5. The remaining forms the hull of the ship.

6. Cut the rectangle of bread into strips and spread with savoury butters.

7. Cut the strips into small sandwiches.

8. Make the outer shell of the ship from gilt cardboard cut to size and stapled at both ends.

9. Insert the hull into the outer shell.

10. Fill with the sandwiches.

11. Wrap pieces of ham round small fingers of bread cut from a sandwich loaf, insert a toothpick and fix into the lower part of the ship to simulate oars.

12. Make round salami canapés and fix into the sides of the ship above the oars.

13. Place small filled brioches on top of the ship.

14. Arrange filled tartlets at both ends.

15. Cut the sail out of gilt cardboard and fix in position in the centre.

(Techniques, pp. 130, 131.)

Cut-out sandwiches

These are made by making a sandwich with one slice of white bread and one of brown, cutting a fancy shape out of the centre with a pastry cutter and replacing it the other way up.

HOT SANDWICHES

Cheese croûtes Basle style

10 croûtes

	10 slices bread (sandwich loaf) without crusts,	
40 g	each weighing	1½ oz
	10 slices Gruyère cheese,	
60–70 g	each weighing	2 oz
80 g	butter	3 oz
300 g	onion rings	10 oz
	paprika	

Butter the slices of bread thinly, cover with the slices of cheese, dust with paprika, arrange on a baking-sheet and bake until well coloured. Meanwhile fry the onion rings in butter until light brown and crisp. Place a small heap of onion rings on each cheese croûte to serve.

Switzerland

Cheese croûtes Zug style

10 croûtes

	10 slices bread (sandwich loaf) without crusts,	
40 g	each weighing	1½ oz
250 g	grated Emmenthal cheese	8 oz
250 g	grated Sbrinz cheese	8 oz
2 dl	milk	⅓ pt
2 dl	kirsch	2 dessertspoons
	4 eggs	
	butter	

Mix the grated cheese, egg yolks, milk and kirsch together and fold in the stiffly whipped egg whites. Spread on the bread in a thick layer, arrange on a lightly buttered baking-sheet and place in the oven or under a salamander until the cheese topping has melted and is well-browned.

Switzerland

Fried Mozzarella sandwiches (Mozzarella in carrozza)

10 portions

	20 slices white bread (tin loaf) without crust	
700 g	Mozzarella cheese (3 medium-size pieces)	1 lb 8 oz
¼ l	milk or cream	½ pt
	3 eggs	
	3 tablespoons flour	

Cut the Mozzarella cheese into neat, even pieces, if possible of the same size as the bread, and make 10 sandwiches with the slices of cheese as a filling. Fasten the edges with toothpicks. Beat the eggs well, mix with the milk and season lightly with salt. Sprinkle the sandwiches all over with flour, dip in the egg/milk mixture and soak well. Remove, drain well and fry in hot fat until golden. The sandwiches will swell a little while frying. Remove the toothpicks, arrange on a hot dish and garnish with parsley. Warm dessert plates and dessert cutlery will be required when serving.

Italy

Bikinis

These are savouries for receptions where wine or spirits are being served.

Cut white bread (sandwich loaf) in slices 1 cm (about ½ in) thick and toast lightly on both sides. Butter one slice and cover with a slice of cooked ham of the same size. Place a slice of semi-soft cheese on a second round of toast and stand in a hot oven or under a salamander for a short time to melt the cheese a little. Place one round of toast on top of the other with the cheese and ham on the inside and serve very hot on warmed plates.

Spain

Croque-Monsieur

For one portion, take a slice of bread 6 by 9 cm (about 2½ by 3½ in) and cover with a thin slice of Gruyère cheese then with a slice of ham of the same size. Top this with another slice of cheese and a slice of bread. Press down very carefully and fry in clarified butter until brown and crisp.

(Illustration, p. 588)

France

Cheese Dreams

Place several very thin slices of cheese between two thin well buttered slices of bread. Remove the crusts, and then press the sandwich heavily and grill slowly until crisp. (It is important to press the sandwich so that the cheese is melted by the time the bread is toasted.)

Great Britain

FILLED ROLLS

These are not normally thought of as 'party food' but if the rolls are small, they are quite suitable to be served with canapés and other Finger Food at a reception.

Sandwiches made with brioche rolls

Very small brioche rolls are cut open on one side and filled with foie gras mousse or a suitable purée.

Brioche rolls with chicken mousse

Fill the rolls with chicken mousse.

France

10

Brioche rolls with foie gras I

Mix 2 parts sieved foie gras with 1 part creamed salted butter, season with pepper and spread the rolls with this paste.

France

Brioche rolls with foie gras II

Fill the rolls with truffled foie gras paste.

France

Brioche rolls with game mousse

Fill the rolls with any game mousse desired.

France

Brioche rolls with ham mousse

Fill the rolls with ham mousse.

France

Filled French rolls

Long French rolls may be split and used for open sandwiches, but may also be served filled. In this case, a piece is sliced lengthwise off the top about a quarter of the way down and the crumb is removed from the remainder. The rolls now resemble a boat or a small oval box with a lid. They may be filled with most of the fillings used for barquettes and small pies or patties. The top is then replaced and pressed down lightly. Depending on the recipe selected, the rolls may be served either hot or cold, dished on a napkin.

France

Filled rolls Bigourdan style

Spread the hollow base of each roll with a little tarragon butter and fill with flaked, boned and skinned salmon trout.

France

French rolls with lobster filling Marseilles style

Fill with diced lobster in Marseilles sauce.

France

French rolls with prawn filling

Fill with picked prawns in aspic mayonnaise and replace the top.

France

Filled rolls Warsaw style

Fill with vegetable salad and small cubes of herring fillet in mayonnaise.

France

Pan bagna

Slice rolls in half and remove some of the crumb, leaving a boat shape. Rub the bottom of the cavity with garlic and sprinkle with olive oil. Cover alternately with slices of tomato, anchovies, slices of onion and capers. Add very little salt on account of the saltiness of thc anchovies. Season with pepper.

French bread cut into short lengths may be used instead of rolls.

Italy

OPEN SANDWICHES

Open sandwiches can vary from small, dainty items, suitable for a cocktail reception to substantial knife and fork meals, suitable for a manual worker's lunch. However, given a little common sense, a caterer can adapt the size of an open sandwich to suit the occasion and the needs of his customers.

Open sandwiches can be made on a variety of bases: white, brown or black bread, bread rolls ('bridge rolls' are often used in Britain) and various types of crispbreads. It is a moot point as to precisely where canapés end and open sandwiches begin, since two rolled pieces of ham placed upon a slice of French bread and garnished with tomato and cucumber could be thought of as either. Generally speaking, however, open sandwiches are more heavily garnished than canapés.

SMØRREBROD

In Denmark, open sandwiches, called 'smørrebrod' are something of a national institution! They are usually hearty knife and fork dishes, and examples are found in the fish and meat sections of this book. Those listed here could be adapted for receptions.

Landing-stage sandwich

6 persons

	6 slices white bread cut lengthwise	
150 g	butter	4 oz
300 g	liver pâté aspic jelly	10 oz
150 g	caviar wedges of lemon	4 oz
300 g	smoked eel scrambled egg	10 oz
300 g	smoked salmon dill	10 oz
300 g	steak tartare capers horseradish	10 oz
300 g	peeled shrimps mayonnaise	10 oz

Butter the bread and garnish one slice with liver pâté and aspic, the second with caviar and wedges of lemon, the third with small pieces of skinned smoked eel covered with scrambled egg, the fourth with thin slices of smoked salmon decorated with dill leaves, the fifth with steak tartare, capers and horseradish, and the sixth with peeled shrimps decorated with a mayonnaise stripe. Cut each slice evenly into 6 and dish.

Denmark

Rye bread with salami, onion rings, aspic and cress

6 persons

300 g	salami	10 oz
	1 onion	
½ l	aspic jelly cress	¾ pt
	3 slices rye bread (6 half slices)	
90 g	butter or lard	3 oz

Spread the bread with the butter or lard. Cover with thin slices of salami and decorate with onion rings, aspic jelly and cress.

Denmark

Rye bread with smoked eel and scrambled egg

6 persons

500 g	smoked eel	1 lb
	3 eggs	
	3 tablespoons dairy cream	
	3 slices rye bread	
	(6 half slices)	
90 g	butter	3 oz
	finely cut chives	

Skin and bone the eel and cut the fillets evenly in 12 pieces. Prepare lightly scrambled egg with the eggs, the cream and seasonings. Butter the bread, place 2 pieces of smoked eel on each portion, cover with scrambled egg and sprinkle with chives.

Denmark

Rye bread with smoked ham, scrambled egg and chives

6 persons

450 g	cooked ham	1 lb
	3 eggs	
	3 tablespoons dairy cream	
	chives	
	3 slices rye bread	
	(6 half slices)	
	or 6 slices white bread	
90 g	butter	3¼ oz

Butter the bread and cover with slices of cooked ham. Pile cold scrambled egg on top and sprinkle with chives.

Denmark

Rye or white bread with liver pâté, bacon and mushrooms

6 persons   Cooking time: 1 hour

500 g	pig's liver	1 lb
250 g	smoked fat pork	8 oz
	4 anchovies	
	1 onion	
	salt, pepper and allspice	

¼ litre	dairy cream	½ pt
approx. 250 g	flour	8 oz approx.
300 g	mushrooms	10 oz
	12 rashers bacon	
	3 slices rye bread	
	(6 half slices)	
	or 6 slices white bread	
90 g	butter	3 oz

Mince the liver, fat pork, onion and anchovies three times, using the finest cutter, season with salt, pepper and allspice and work to a smooth forcemeat with the flour and the cream. Fill into a greased mould and poach in a medium oven in a bain-marie. When cold, turn out, slice and place on fairly thick slices of buttered bread. Garnish with fried rashers of bacon and mushrooms. Serve at once.

Denmark

'Sour' bread with marinated salmon

6 persons

1 kg	salmon (raw)	2¼ lb
	1 tablespoon crushed	
	peppercorns	
	2 tablespoons salt	
2 dl	oil	⅓ pt
	several bunches fresh	
	green dill	
	6 slices 'sour' bread	
90 g	butter	3 oz

Fillet the salmon, but do not skin. Rub well with the salt and pepper, lay in a dish of suitable size on a thick bed of finely cut dill mixed with oil and cover with the dill mixture. Cover the dish with a cloth and marinate for 3–4 days, turning the fish once or twice a day. Remove from the marinade, wipe dry, cut in thin slices, arrange on the buttered bread and cover liberally with fresh dill leaves.

Denmark

Toast with chicken breast, asparagus and mayonnaise

6 persons

	3 poached and skinned	
	half chicken breasts	
250 g	asparagus tips	8 oz

100 g	mayonnaise	3 oz
	lettuce hearts	
	cress	
	6 slices white bread	
90 g	butter	3 oz

Toast the bread, spread with butter, cover with lettuce heart leaves and place thin slices of chicken breast on top. Mask with well-flavoured mayonnaise and decorate with asparagus tips and cress.

Denmark

Vet's supper

6 persons

300 g	liver pâté	10 oz
300 g	pickled veal	10 oz
	3 slices rye bread	
	(6 half slices)	
90 g	lard	3 oz
½ l	aspic jelly	¾ pt
12 g	gelatine	½ oz

Spread the rye bread with lard and cover with liver pâté and sliced pickled veal. Decorate with aspic jelly cut out in shapes as desired.

Denmark

White bread with fresh shrimps

6 persons

1 kg	live shrimps	2 lb
	6 lettuce hearts	
	6 lemon wedges	
	6 slices white bread	
90 g	butter	3 oz

Drop the shrimps in boiling salted water, cook for a short time, leave until cold, then pour off the water and drain the shrimps well. Sprinkle lightly with salt, then peel them. Butter the bread, cover with shrimps and garnish with a lettuce heart, also a wedge of lemon if desired.

Denmark

White bread with shrimp salad

6 persons

300 g	peeled shrimps	10 oz
150 g	thick mayonnaise	5 oz
150 g	cooked asparagus	5 oz
	1 lemon	
	lettuce hearts	
	6 slices white bread	
120 g	butter	4 oz

Flavour the mayonnaise with paprika and a little asparagus liquor. Mix with the shrimps and the cold asparagus which has been well-drained and cut in pieces. Butter the bread, arrange the shrimp salad on top and garnish with a slice of lemon, lettuce hearts and asparagus tips.

Denmark

White bread with smoked fillet of pork and chives

6 persons

300 g	smoked fillet of pork	10 oz
	finely chopped chives	
	6 slices white bread	
90 g	butter	3 oz

Cut the fillet of pork into very thin slices, place on the buttered bread and sprinkle with chives.

Denmark

White or 'sour' bread with crayfish and dill mayonnaise

6 persons   Cooking time: 8 minutes

	36 crayfish	
100 g	mayonnaise	3 oz
	3 small bunches fresh dill	
	6 small lettuce hearts	
	6 slices bread	
90 g	butter	3 oz

Boil the crayfish in salted water with dill and cumin seeds, allow to cool, then remove the shells and the intestinal tube. Butter the bread, cover with lettuce heart leaves, arrange the crayfish on top and mask with mayonnaise mixed with chopped dill.

Denmark

White or 'sour' bread with smoked salmon

6 persons

300 g	smoked salmon (uncut)	10 oz
	6 small lettuce hearts	
	6 slices white or 'sour' bread	
90 g	butter	3 oz
	fresh dill	

Remove the bones from the smoked salmon, then slice very thinly. Butter the bread, cover liberally with smoked salmon and decorate with dill leaves. Garnish with the lettuce hearts.

Denmark

SMALL CHAUD-FROIDS

Chaud-froids of turbot with shrimps

12 chaud-froids

	500 g	turbot without skin or bones	1 lb
		2 egg whites	
	¾ l	double cream	1¼ pt
approx.	¾ l	white fish chaud-froid sauce	1¼ pt
		1 tablespoon chopped herbs	
		1 small truffle	
approx.	½ l	aspic jelly	¾ pt approx.
approx.	500 g	shrimps	1 lb

Reduce the turbot to a very fine purée, mix with the egg whites, season with salt and pepper and rub through a fine sieve. Chill thoroughly, then gradually blend in the cream. Check the taste—the mixture should be well-seasoned—and transfer to a buttered metal tray with a rim or a fireproof dish of suitable shape and size. Cover with buttered paper and poach slowly in the oven. When cold, cut into ovals, place these on a wire rack and mask with the chaud-froid sauce mixed with the chopped herbs. When the sauce has begun to set, decorate each oval with a tiny disk and a very thin strip of truffle and glaze with aspic jelly.

Coat a round serving dish thinly with aspic jelly and allow to set. Arrange the chaud-froids on it in a ring and fill the centre with the picked pink shrimps which have been lightly marinated in a lemon juice–oil mixture.

(Illustration, p. 241)   Germany

Chicken chaud-froids

Mix salpicon of chicken with a little white chicken chaud-froid sauce and pile on to small rounds of chicken breast to a dome shape. Mask with white chicken chaud-froid sauce. When set, decorate with a truffle motif and glaze with chicken aspic.

(Illustration, p. 241)   Austria

Small chaud-froids of giant crab

10 persons

150 g	giant crab meat (net weight)	6 oz
	10 small pieces of crab for decoration	
50 g	mayonnaise	2 oz
	1 tablespoon tomato ketchup	
½ l	aspic	¾ pt approx.

Line 10 small dariole moulds with aspic and allow to set. Place a small piece of crab in the bottom of each mould and fix into position with aspic. Chop the crab meat very finely, bind with the mayonnaise mixed with a little aspic, flavour with tomato ketchup, adjust the seasoning, fill into the moulds and leave to set. Do not turn out until very firm.

Austria

Lobster chaud-froid

6 persons   Cooking time: 15–20 minutes

500 g	3 lobsters each weighing	1 lb approx.
9 dl	lobster chaud-froid sauce	1½ pt
	(see p. 177)	
	lettuce	

Pull the heads off the live lobsters without cutting. Cook in the same way as lobster American style. Split the tail shells lengthwise and remove the flesh. Shell the claws. Coat the pieces of lobster with chaud-froid sauce, set aside for 5 minutes and coat again, then refrigerate until set. Decorate with hard-boiled egg white and yolk, truffles and chervil. Glaze with fish aspic and dish surrounded with lettuce leaves.

Lobster cooked in court-bouillon may be dressed in the same way with left-over American sauce.

France

CHEESE SAVOURIES

HOT CHEESE SAVOURIES

Burgundian cheese ring

6–8 persons   Baking time: 12–15 minutes

150 g	flour	5 oz
75 g	butter	3 oz
¼ l	water	½ pt approx.
	3–4 large eggs	
90 g	Emmenthal cheese, very finely diced	3 oz
50 g	Emmenthal cheese, cut in very small thin slices	2 oz
	beaten egg	
	pinch of cayenne pepper	

Prepare fairly firm choux paste with the flour, butter, water and eggs. Remove from the heat and add the diced cheese. Pipe out in a ring on a lightly greased baking-sheet, using a savoy bag and a large plain pipe. Wash with beaten egg, cover evenly with the sliced cheese and bake at 200–220°C. Serve immediately. Although the cheese ring is usually served hot, it may also be served cold.

Cheese and ham crescents

Yields 10 crescents   Baking time: 10–12 minutes

400 g	cheese puff paste	14 oz
250 g	cheese cream (see p. 292)	8 oz
75 g	lean cooked ham, finely chopped	3 oz
	beaten egg	

Stir the chopped ham into the cheese cream, season well and allow to cool. Pin out the puff paste to 4 mm (⅛ in) thick and cut into 7–8 cm (3 in) triangles. Place a small spoonful of cheese cream in the centre of each and roll up to make a crescent with the point of the triangle in the centre. Arrange on a baking-sheet, pressing the ends down a little, egg wash and bake at about 200°C. Serve warm or cold.

(Illustration, p. 589)

Cheese fritters

10 persons

175 g	flour	6 oz
100 g	butter	3 oz
125 g	grated Emmenthal or Parmesan cheese	4 oz
3½ dl	water	⅔ pt approx.
3 g	pinch of salt	
	pinch of cayenne pepper	
	5 eggs	

Prepare choux paste with all the ingredients except the cheese, remove from the heat and stir in the cheese. Shape into fritters with a dessertspoon and deep fry in hot fat. Drain well, dish on a paper napkin and serve very hot.

(Illustration, p. 589)

Cheese pie

Baking time: 50 minutes

125 g	butter	4 oz
150 g	full fat cheese (Gruyère, Emmenthal, Fontine), finely diced	5 oz
250 g	cooked ham, diced	8 oz
250 g	flour	8 oz
	3 eggs	
1 dl	dairy cream	⅙ pt
	1–2 teaspoons mustard	
	1 teaspoon chopped parsley or basil	
	1 tablespoon baking powder	
	salt, pepper, nutmeg	

Whisk the butter and eggs together, add the mustard and salt, pepper and nutmeg to taste, then stir in the herbs and mix well. Now stir in the ham and cheese, the flour which has been sieved with the baking powder and lastly the cream. The mixture should be smooth and fairly thick. Fill into a buttered cake tin and bake in a medium oven. Turn out and serve very hot.

Switzerland

Cheese pudding

6 persons   Baking time: about 20 minutes

	6 slices bread (sandwich loaf) without crusts	
	6 slices Emmenthal cheese about 6 mm (¼ in) thick and the same size as the bread	
	1 egg yolk	
	3 eggs	
6 dl	milk	1 pt
50 g	butter	2 oz
	salt, pepper, grated nutmeg	

Cut the bread and the cheese in half. Butter an oval pie dish lightly and arrange the bread and cheese in it alternately with the slices overlapping. Beat the eggs and egg yolk, stir in the milk and season with salt, pepper and nutmeg. Strain through a conical sieve and gradually pour into the pie dish, allowing the bread to absorb the custard. Dot with butter and bake at 200°C.

Cheese sacristans

          cheese puff paste
          grated cheese
          paprika
          beaten egg

Pin out the puff paste 4 mm (⅛ in) thick and cut into strips 12 cm (5 in) wide. Cut across at intervals of 1–1½ cm (about ½ in), brush with egg, sprinkle with grated cheese and dust lightly with paprika. Hold each piece by both ends and twist into a spiral. Place on a baking-sheet splashed with water and press the ends down firmly. Bake in a hot oven for 6–8 minutes and serve hot or cold.

Cheese semelles

Baking time: 8 minutes

          puff paste
          grated cheese
          paprika

Pin out virgin or scrap puff paste to 4 mm (about ⅛ in) thick. Cut into rounds with a 5 cm (2 in) fluted cutter. Sprinkle a table or marble slab thickly with grated cheese mixed with a little paprika and pin out each round of pastry to an oval shape. Arrange on a baking-sheet splashed with water, placing the cheese-covered side uppermost, and bake at 200°C.

Cheese straws

Pin out cheese puff paste or short paste to 3 cm (⅛ in) thick, brush with egg and sprinkle with grated cheese. Cut into strips 10 cm (4 in) wide and cut each one into sticks about 5 mm (¼ in) wide. Arrange on a lightly greased baking-sheet and bake quickly in a hot oven until golden-brown.

Cheese straws are usually made with Parmesan or Gruyère. They are mostly used as a garnish for clear soup.

Cheese tit-bits

Baking time: about 10 minutes

500 g	scrap puff paste	1 lb
100 g	Gruyère cheese, grated or finely diced	4 oz
2 dl	Mornay sauce	⅓ pt

Mix the cheese with the cold Mornay sauce and season with a good pinch of cayenne pepper. Pin out the puff paste to 2 mm (about 1/10 in) thick and cut out with a 4 cm (1½ in) fluted cutter. Brush half the rounds lightly with beaten egg, place a bulb of the cheese sauce the size of a hazelnut in the centre of each and cover with another round of pastry. Seal the edges well, place on a baking-sheet splashed with water, egg-wash and bake in a hot oven. Serve hot.

France

Cheshire cakes

10 persons   Baking time: 6–8 minutes

200 g	flour	8 oz
200 g	butter	8 oz
200 g	grated Cheshire cheese	8 oz
	3 large egg yolks	
	paprika	
	salt	
	Cheshire cheese cream	

Make a fairly firm dough with the flour, butter, cheese, egg yolks, a few drops of water, paprika and a good pinch of salt. Allow to rest for 2 hours in a cool place. Pin out to barely 1 cm (½ in) thick and cut into rounds with a fluted cutter 4–5 cm (2 in) in diameter. Arrange on a baking-sheet and bake at 180°C until pale brown. While still hot, sandwich in pairs with hot Cheshire cheese cream (see p. 292). Serve hot.

Alternatively, serve cold with other cheese savouries. In this case the cheese cream should be lighter than usual.

Cheshire cheese cream buns

10 persons   Baking time: about 10 minutes

250 g	flour	8 oz
100 g	butter	4 oz
3 dl	water	½ pt
3 g	pinch of salt	
	5 eggs	
30–40 g	grated Cheshire cheese	1–1½ oz
	beaten egg	
	Cheshire cheese cream	
	(see p. 292)	

Prepare choux paste in the usual manner with the flour, water, butter, salt and eggs. Using a savoy bag and plain tube, pipe out in bulbs about 4 cm (1½ in) across on to lightly greased and floured baking-sheets. Egg wash, sprinkle with grated cheese and bake at 220°C until dry. While still hot, cut open on one side and pipe in hot Cheshire cheese cream. Serve very hot.

If preferred, allow the buns to cool, fill with cold cheese cream and serve cold. In this case, fold a little more half-whipped cream into the cheese cream.

Cheshire duchesses

10 persons   Baking time: 12–14 minutes

	choux paste	
	(see p. 830)	
	beaten egg	
40 g	grated cheese	1½ oz
	Cheshire cheese cream	
	(see p. 292)	

Using a savoy bag and coarse star tube, pipe the paste on to a lightly greased and floured baking-sheet to make wave-like finger rolls about 7 cm (3 in) long and 4 cm (1½ in) wide. Egg wash, sprinkle with grated cheese and bake at 200°C until crisp. Remove from the oven, slit open on one side, pipe in hot Cheshire cheese cream and serve at once.

Cheshire eclairs

Using the same choux paste as for petits choux (see p. 830), pipe finger shapes about 8 cm (3 in) long and 2 cm (¾ in) wide on to a lightly greased, floured baking-sheet. Bake at 220°C. On removing from the oven, make a slit in one side, fill with Cheshire cheese cream (see p. 292) and serve hot.

Alternatively, serve cold on a dish of assorted cheese savouries.

Cheshire soufflé

8–10 portions   Baking time: about 20 minutes

80 g	butter	3 oz
60 g	flour	2 oz
3½ dl	milk	⅔ pt
125 g	grated Cheshire cheese	4 oz
	5 egg yolks	
	6 egg whites	
	paprika	
	grated nutmeg	
	salt	

Melt the butter, mix with the flour and cook for a moment to make a blond roux. Blend in the cold milk, boil up in the same way as Béchamel sauce and season with paprika, grated nutmeg and salt. Remove from the heat, stir in the grated cheese, add the egg yolks and mix until smooth. Lastly fold in the egg whites whipped to a stiff snow. Thinly butter a large soufflé dish, sprinkle with grated cheese and threequarters fill with the mixture. Bake at about 180°C, dish and serve at once.

If preferred, the mixture may be baked in individual ramekin dishes. In this case, the baking time is about 10 minutes.

Chester cakes

50 g	flour	2 oz
60 g	grated Cheshire cheese	2 oz

	1 egg	
30 g	cayenne butter	1 oz

Filling

30 g	butter	1 oz
30 g	grated Cheshire cheese	1 oz

Work the flour, cheese, butter and egg to a paste. Do not add salt, as the cheese is salt enough. Leave in a cool place for a good hour, then pin to a thickness of about 2 mm ($\frac{1}{10}$ in) and cut out with a plain 3 or 4 cm ($1\frac{1}{2}$ in) cutter. Arrange on a lightly buttered baking-sheet, prick with a fork and bake in a hot oven, checking from time to time.

To make the filling, mix the butter and cheese together well. Sandwich the biscuits in pairs with a small knob of the filling, press down lightly and return to the oven for a few minutes only. Serve warm or cold.

France

Cottage cheese pirojky

20 small pies   Baking time: 20 minutes

600 g	plain unsweetened brioche dough	1¼ lb
250 g	well-drained cottage cheese	8 oz
100 g	flour	3 oz
150 g	butter	5 oz
	1 egg	

Line the bottom and sides of buttered dariole moulds with brioche dough. Cream the butter and flour together until fairly soft. Add the cheese and the egg, together with salt and pepper. Fill this mixture into the moulds and cover with a disk of brioche dough, moistening the edges lightly to seal. Prove for 30–35 minutes covered with a cloth. Bake in a hot oven, remove from the moulds and serve hot.

Russia

Ewe cheese savoury

1 portion   Cooking time: 15 minutes

100 g	ewe cheese	4 oz
	2 tomatoes	
	half a pimento	
20 g	butter	1 oz

Skin the tomatoes, cut them in half, remove the seeds and slice. Melt the butter in a small fireproof dish, cover with the tomato slices, sprinkle lightly with salt and cook for a moment. Place the cheese on top and garnish with half a pimento after removing the seeds. Cover and cook in a moderate oven until the cheese is soft (about 15 minutes). Serve very hot.

Bulgaria

Fried Balkan hard cheese (Kaschkaval)

1 portion

100 g	Balkan hard cheese	3½ oz
	1 egg	
	flour	
	breadcrumbs for coating	

Cut the cheese in one slice 1½ cm (about ½ in) thick. Dip in cold water, shake off the excess and toss in a little flour. Coat with beaten egg, dip in breadcrumbs, then coat with egg again. Fry for about 10 minutes in deep fat, which should not be too hot, then drain well and dish. Serve with fried potatoes and mixed salad.

Alternatively, coat the cheese with thin batter before frying. In this case, do not dip it in water before coating.

Bulgaria

Grilled Balkan hard cheese

1 portion   Grilling time: approx. 10 minutes

100 g	Balkan hard cheese	3½ oz
	flour	
	oil	

Cut the cheese in one slice 1½ cm (about ½ in) thick. Dip in cold water, shake off the excess, coat with flour, sprinkle with oil and grill for about 10 minutes, brushing with oil occasionally and turning the cheese as soon as one side is soft. Serve with fried potatoes and mixed salad.

Bulgaria

Grilled cheese

1 portion

100 g	cheese	3½ oz
20 g	butter	1 oz
3 g	pinch of paprika	
	half a pimento	

Cut a piece of greaseproof paper large enough to wrap round the cheese and spread thickly with butter. Place the cheese on it and sprinkle with the paprika. Cut the pimento in half, remove the seeds and place one half on the cheese. Fold the paper over the top and pinch the edges together. Dip in cold water to prevent the paper burning, and cook on a charcoal grill. Dish in the paper, which is not removed until after serving. Accompaniments: fried potatoes and mixed salad.

Bulgaria

Parmesan matchsticks

Baking time: 6–8 minutes

Parmesan puff or short paste
beaten egg
grated Parmesan cheese

Pin out the paste 4–5 mm (about ¼ in) thick and cut into strips 8 cm (3 in) wide. Brush with egg, sprinkle with grated cheese and cut into sticks 1 cm (about ½ in) wide with a sharp knife. Place on a baking-sheet splashed with water and bake at 200°C.

The matchsticks are mainly used hot as a garnish for clear soup. Cheshire matchsticks may be made in the same way, using Cheshire instead of Parmesan cheese.

Pear savoury with Roquefort cream sauce

10 persons

	10 slices sandwich loaf	
200 g	cooked ham	7 oz
250 g	stewed cranberries, drained	9 oz
180 g	fresh grated horseradish	6 oz
	10 pear halves (canned)	
350 g	Roquefort cheese	12 oz
	2 egg yolks	
	3 tablespoons dairy cream	
2 cl	kirsch	2 dessertspoons

Cut the bread to the shape of the pears, toast and cover with a thin slice of ham cut to the same shape. Mix the cranberries and horseradish together and place a teaspoonful on each slice of ham. Warm the pear halves, drain thoroughly, dry and place on the cranberries with the rounded side uppermost.

Sieve the Roquefort, mix to a thick sauce with the egg yolks, cream and kirsch, pour over the pears and brown under a salamander.

Germany

Ramekins I

30 small buns	Baking time: 10–12 minutes	
250 g	choux pastry	8 oz
100 g	Gruyère cheese	3 oz

Mix the choux pastry with 30 g (1 oz) grated Gruyère cheese and 30 g (1 oz) finely diced Gruyère. Deposit on a baking-sheet in walnut-size bulbs, using a teaspoon or a savoy bag fitted with a plain pipe. Wash with egg and place a thin slice of Gruyère on top of each bulb. Bake in a moderate oven.

France

Ramekins II

6–8 persons	Baking time: about 10 minutes	
150 g	flour	5 oz
75 g	butter	$2\frac{1}{2}$ oz
$\frac{1}{4}$ l	water	$\frac{1}{2}$ pt approx.
125 g	grated Emmenthal cheese	4 oz
60 g	finely diced Emmenthal cheese	2 oz
	3–4 eggs	
	beaten egg	

Prepare fairly firm choux paste with the flour, butter, water and eggs. Remove from the heat and add the grated cheese. Using a savoy bag and plain tube, pipe small choux no larger than an apricot on to a lightly greased baking-sheet. Egg wash, sprinkle evenly with the diced cheese and bake at about 200°C. Serve very hot.

(Illustration, p. 582)

Roquefort pancakes

6–8 persons   Cooking time: 3–4 minutes

150 g	flour	5 oz
	3 eggs	
approx. ¼ l	milk	½ pt approx.
60 g	sieved Roquefort cheese	2 oz
40 g	melted butter	1½ oz
	clarified butter	

Mix the sifted flour with the egg yolks and milk to make a fairly thick batter. Add a good pinch of paprika and strain. Stir in the Roquefort, then add the melted butter and lastly fold in the stiffly whipped egg whites. Brush small omelette pans with clarified butter, pour in a spoonful of batter, spread over the base of the pan and cook on both sides until golden-brown. Serve very hot.

Schopski cheese savoury

1 portion

50 g	2 slices Bulgarian cheese, each	2 oz
	2–3 ripe tomatoes	
40 g	butter	1½ oz
	1 egg	

Place the cheese in water to remove excess salt. Skin the tomatoes, slice, remove the seeds and fry lightly in the butter. Transfer to a suitable fireproof dish and cover with the well-drained slices of cheese. Grill for about 7–10 minutes under a salamander. Remove from the heat, make a hole in the centre large enough for the egg, break the egg into it and place in a moderate oven until the egg is set on the outside, but still soft inside.

Bulgaria

FONDUE

There are many different recipes for this famous traditional Swiss dish, but certain procedures are common to them all. Fondue is always eaten with a piece of bread impaled on a fork, which is twirled in the mixture as it is kept warm over a low flame at the table. Fondue dishes are usually made of ovenproof earthenware, or enamelled cast iron, and a 'fondue set' often has special forks as well as the essential spirit stove.

The fondue is given a stir each time, with the fork, which helps to prevent the mixture from separating. As a general rule, mature cheeses are most suitable for a fondue as they melt more easily than newer ones. A dry white wine is used for making the fondue and Neuchatel, Côte Valois, Yvorne, Pouilly Fumé and white Chianti are amongst the many which are suitable.

The ideal companion for fondue is also white wine, which is drunk both before and during the meal. (It is a tradition that anyone who allows their cube of bread to fall into the fondue must buy the company another bottle of wine.) Aerated drinks, such as beer, mineral waters or lemonade should never be drunk before, during or after a fondue meal, as they can have a serious congestive effect, and those who cannot take wine or spirits should stick to tea.

A few fondue recipes are given below. If a fondue is too liquid, a little extra cheese, or a little cornflour, should be stirred in; if it is too thick, a little lukewarm white wine stirred slowly in will rectify matters, but experts in making fondue never use thickening agents.

Fribourg Vacherin fondue

This is the speciality of the Canton of Fribourg. At least three differently flavoured types of fondue Vacherin are used, one of them always being a very mature cheese, and the fondue will not really be successful if it is made with Vacherin cut from one cheese only. A cheesemonger should know the difference between Vacherin for table use, and that for use in a fondue.

4 persons

800 g	Fribourg Vacherin cheese for fondue	1¾ lb
	1 clove of garlic	
600–800 g	cubes of bread	1¼–1¾ lb
	pepper	
	nutmeg	
	salt	
	hot water	

Cut the cheese into small cubes and place in the fondue dish which has been well rubbed with garlic. Pour in half a cup of hot water and warm over a very gentle heat (very important) while stirring constantly until the cheese is perfectly smooth and creamy. If necessary, add a spoonful of hot water from time to time to give the fondue the desired consistency. Some people like this fondue fairly thick, whilst others prefer it more liquid. Season with pepper and nutmeg, and a pinch of salt if desired. Important note: on no account should Vacherin fondue be allowed to boil; and the flame of the spirit stove should be adjusted accordingly (a hot-plate warmed by candles can even be used). This fondue is never hot.

Half-and-half fondue

In Fribourg, half-and-half fondue is extremely popular. It is mild and creamy, being made with equal quantities of Gruyère and special Fribourg Vacherin cheese for fondue. It can be made stronger in flavour by increasing the proportion of Gruyère. It is important not to exceed 1 dl ($\frac{1}{8}$ pt) wine to 200–250 g (7–9 oz) Gruyère.

4 persons

400 g	grated Gruyère cheese	14 oz
400 g	grated Fribourg Vacherin cheese for fondue	14 oz
	1 clove of garlic	
2 dl	white wine	$\frac{1}{3}$ pt
	2–3 level tablespoons cornflour*	
	1 liqueur glass kirsch	
	pepper	
	nutmeg	
600–800 g	cubes of bread	$1\frac{1}{4}$–$1\frac{3}{4}$ lb

Mix the cheeses together, and proceed as for the recipe above. Melt the cheese slowly, stirring constantly and reducing the heat as the cheese melts. Lastly season with pepper and nutmeg. During the meal, stand the dish over a low flame; this fondue should not boil because it contains Vacherin.

Switzerland

* Experts only use thickening agents if absolutely necessary.

Neuchâtel fondue

4 persons

500 g	grated Gruyère cheese	1 lb
300 g	grated Emmenthal cheese	10 oz
3 dl	Neuchâtel semi-sparkling white wine	$\frac{1}{2}$ pt
	1 teaspoon fresh lemon juice	
	4 level teaspoons cornflour	

Rub the inside of the fondue dish with a clove of garlic, and leave it in the dish, either whole or chopped. Put all the other ingredients into the dish and cook over a fierce heat while carefully stirring with a wire whisk. Finish off with a little nutmeg, freshly-ground pepper and a small glass of kirsch.

Switzerland

Tomato fondue (without alcohol)

4 persons

	8–10 tomatoes, skinned, seeded and coarsely chopped	
	1–2 cloves of garlic	
400 g	grated Gruyère cheese	14 oz
400 g	grated Emmenthal cheese	14 oz
	4 level teaspoons cornflour	
	pepper	
	wild marjoram	
	dairy cream	

Place the tomatoes and the finely crushed garlic into the fondue dish and cook slowly under a lid until the resultant purée is well reduced. Pass through a conical strainer and make up to 3½ dl (⅔ pt) with canned tomato juice. Stir in the grated cheeses and the cornflour (if used). Cook over a good heat, stirring constantly. Season with pepper and wild marjoram. If desired, a tablespoonful of dairy cream can be added just before serving.

This fondue is sometimes served with small new potatoes boiled in their jackets instead of the usual cubes of bread. They are impaled on a fork and twirled in the fondue in the same way as bread.

Switzerland

Vaud fondue

4 persons

	1 clove of garlic	
3–4 dl	Vaud white wine, 'Dorin' quality (Epesses, Dozaley, St Saphorin, Aigle, etc.)	½–⅔ pt
	1 teaspoon fresh lemon juice	
800 g	grated Gruyère cheese	1¾ lb
	4 teaspoons cornflour*	
	1 small glass kirsch	
	freshly ground pepper	
	grated nutmeg	
	butter	

* Experts in making fondue do not use thickening agents, but for the inexperienced these ensure that the ingredients will bind together.

Chop the garlic finely and fry in the fondue dish in a little butter until lightly coloured. Add the white wine, the lemon juice and the grated Gruyère (which should be cut from several different cheeses). Stir with a spatula. Blend the flour with the kirsch, add pepper and nutmeg to taste and stir into the fondue. Cook for a minute or two and add a little kirsch to enhance the aroma when bringing to the table. Serve with cubes of French bread.

Switzerland

RACLETTE

In the Swiss Canton of Valais, where raclette originated, it is usually served out of doors. A creamy valley cheese is cut in half, and the cut surface is held in front of a brightly flaming fire. The melted cheese is scraped off on to a plate which is then filled up with small potatoes boiled in their jackets, gherkins and small white pickled onions. It is seasoned with a turn of the pepper mill. Raclette should be eaten hot, so it is customary for the guests to start eating without waiting until everyone has been served. The 'scraper' has an important task (see illustration). He looks after the fire, exposes the cheese to the heat and, holding it on a slant, skilfully scrapes it on to a plate with the back of a knife or a spatula.

Ideally, half a cheese should be used for raclette but, failing this, a quarter will suffice. Valais cheeses, such as those of Bagnes and Conches are ideal for this Valais speciality. They are creamy, fat and relatively mild, they melt at a fairly low temperature and do not harden on cooling. The usual quantity to allow for raclette, which is a meal in itself, is 200–300 g (7–10 oz) per person.

Some ingenious electric grills and ovens have been designed to allow raclette to be prepared in restaurants and private homes, which helps to explain its growing popularity in other countries. If these are not available, the cheese may be cut into slices 3–5 mm ($\frac{1}{8}$–$\frac{1}{4}$ in) thick and cooked at the top of a preheated oven on a fireproof plate. The result is an imitation raclette which tastes very much like the real thing and has the added advantage that it can be made with other cheeses such as Tilsit, Fontine, Appenzell or even soft cheeses such as Camembert. It is important for the cheese to melt quickly, consequently the heat should be fierce and evenly distributed.

(Illustration, p. 586) Switzerland

COLD CHEESE SAVOURIES

Balkan hard cheese (Kaschkaval)

Cut the cheese into small, thin fingers, pile them on a dish criss-cross fashion and serve as an hors d'oeuvre or entrée.

Bulgaria

Brie mille-feuilles

10 persons   Baking time: 5–6 minutes

400 g	puff paste	14 oz
250 g	ripe Brie without rind	8 oz
150 g	butter	5 oz
	3 rounded tablespoons unsweetened whipped cream	
4 cl	Cognac	4 dessertspoons
	paprika	
150–175 g	roasted hazelnuts, crushed and coarsely sieved	5–6 oz

Pin out the puff paste to 4 mm (about ⅛ in) thick. Cut into 5 cm (2 in) rounds, dock lightly and bake in a fairly hot oven until crisp. Cream the butter with the sieved cheese, season with salt and paprika, add the Cognac and lastly fold in the whipped cream. Sandwich the rounds of pastry in fours with the cheese cream and leave in the refrigerator under light pressure until set. Trim neatly, coat the sides with the cheese cream and mask with the hazelnuts. Decorate the top with a whirl of the cheese cream, using a star tube, and serve cold.

Camembert spirals

6 persons

250 g	cheese puff paste	8 oz
40 g	grated Emmenthal or Parmesan cheese	2 oz
	beaten egg to egg wash	
	Camembert cheese cream (see p. 292)	

Pin out virgin or scrap cheese puff paste to 3 or 4 mm (about ⅛ in) thick and cut into strips 2 cm (¾ in) wide and 15–16 cm (about 6 in) long. Roll each strip round a lightly moistened cream horn tin so that each turn overlaps the previous one and press the end down firmly. Wash with egg, sprinkle lightly with grated cheese and arrange on baking-sheets. Bake for 8 to 10 minutes in a hot oven and remove from the tins while still warm. When cold, fill with cold Camembert cheese cream.

Cheese balls

	3 egg yolks	
	pepper and salt	
180 g	grated cheese	6 oz
120 g	butter	4 oz
300 g	flour	10 oz

Make a smooth paste with all the ingredients, leave in the refrigerator for half an hour, then cut the paste into pieces the size of a walnut, shape each one into a ball and bake in a hot oven for 15 to 20 minutes.

Holland

Cheese biscuits

10 persons   Baking time: 6–8 minutes

200 g	flour	7 oz
200 g	cornflour	7 oz
200 g	finely grated Emmenthal cheese	7 oz
150 g	butter	5 oz
7 g	baking powder	$\frac{1}{4}$ oz
7 g	salt	$\frac{1}{4}$ oz
approx. 2 dl	water	$\frac{1}{3}$ pt
	poppy or caraway seeds	
	beaten egg	

Sieve the flour with the cornflour and baking powder, rub in the butter, add the salt and mix to a paste with the water. Shape into a ball and allow to rest for at least 1 hour. Pin out to 3 mm ($\frac{1}{8}$ in) thick and cut into the desired shapes with a cutter or knife. Egg wash, sprinkle with poppy or caraway seeds and bake at about 180°C.

Cheese choux

Fill petits choux with a mixture of butter and grated Parmesan cheese.

(Illustration, p. 582)   Holland

Cheese cream

1 dl	thick Béchamel sauce	⅛ pt
75 g	butter	3 oz
	1 egg yolk	
75 g	grated Parmesan, Emmenthal, Comte, Dutch or Cheshire cheese	3 oz
100 g	*or* ripe Brie or Camembert cheese (without rind)	4 oz
	2 tablespoons dairy cream, half-whipped	
	paprika	
	grated nutmeg	

Prepare the Béchamel sauce, remove from the heat and, while still hot, thicken with the egg yolk. Allow to cool, stirring repeatedly, then beat in the cheese and butter. Add paprika and grated nutmeg, as well as a pinch of salt if required, and lastly fold in the cream.

Germany

Cheese crispies

These are individual Cheshire or Gruyère cheese biscuits made as for Chester cakes.

France

Cheese frivolities I

1. Fill tiny choux with cheese cream, dip in thin cheese cream and roll in grated pumpernickel.

2. Cut tinfoil to make tiny tartlet cases, line with fine pie pastry, bake blind and leave until cold. Pipe in paprika-flavoured cheese cream, using a star pipe, and top with a tiny piece of lemon peel (mustard pickle).

3. Pin out puff pastry to about 4 mm (⅛ in) thick, brush with egg and sprinkle with grated cheese mixed with paprika and a pinch of salt. Cut out in half-moon shapes, bake in a brisk oven, split and sandwich with cheese cream.

4. Cut curd cheese palatschinken (Austrian pancakes) into tiny oblongs. Pipe on a line of cheese cream, using a plain pipe, place an eighth of a fresh fig on top and glaze with wine jelly.

5. Bake tiny fine pie pastry cases, fill with cheese cream, using a plain pipe, and top with a glacé cherry.

6. Drain a small poached half apricot well and place it on a small slice of toasted brioche. Sprinkle with sieved Roquefort cheese and paprika and brown under a salamander.

7. Pipe out choux paste into tiny éclairs, bake, slit on one side and fill with cheese cream. Pipe on a line of cheese cream, using a plain pipe, and sprinkle with finely chopped pistachio nuts.

(Illustration, p. 587) Germany

Cheese frivolities II

1. Pipe out tiny bulbs of choux paste, bake, fill with cheese cream mixed with grated pistachio nuts, dip in thin cheese cream and roll in chopped pistachio nuts.

2. Cut tinfoil to make tiny tartlet cases, line with fine pie pastry and bake blind. Fill with Gervais cream and decorate with half a yellow cherry (mustard pickle).

3. Pin out puff pastry, brush with egg, sprinkle with grated Parmesan cheese and paprika, cut into rounds and bake. Split with a sharp knife and sandwich with cheese cream.

4. Cut curd cheese palatschinken (Austrian pancakes) into small oblongs. Pipe on a rosette of cheese cream, decorate with a red glacé cherry with its stalk and glaze with wine jelly.

5. Cover small evenly shaped pieces of canned pineapple well with sieved Roquefort cheese, sprinkle with curry powder and brown quickly under a salamander.

6. Using a coarse star tube, pipe cheese cream into and on top of tiny puff pastry cases, dust lightly with paprika and top with half a pistachio nut.

7. Pin out puff pastry to 3 mm (about $\frac{1}{10}$ in) thick, brush with egg, sprinkle with grated cheese and cut in strips. Roll round small sticks (shaping them in a similar fashion to cream horns) and bake. Remove the sticks, fill the hollows with cheese cream and mask the ends with roasted nibbed almonds.

(Illustration, p. 587) Germany

Cheese palmiers

Pin out some puff paste and give it two turns, sprinkling the paste each time with grated cheese (Parmesan, Emmenthal, Dutch, hard Cheddar, etc.). Pin out to a rectangle, fold towards the centre twice, press down a little with the rolling pin, and chill well. Using a sharp knife, cut in 1 cm (about $\frac{1}{2}$ in) slices, bend the ends outwards a little and arrange cut side down on a baking-sheet splashed with water. Bake for about 10 minutes at 190–200°C, turning once with a palette knife.

Cheese petits fours French style

It is not possible to specify the ingredients; these will depend on individual taste, and the information given below is merely intended as a suggestion.

Depending on the type of cheese, sieve or finely grate each variety separately. Mix with creamed butter, flavour with suitable spirits (gin, cognac, pear or other brandy, calvados, etc.) or sweet wine (sherry, port) and add paprika, finely chopped ham or olives, pine kernels and other nuts, roasted and ground if desired. Depending on consistency, pipe or mould into small tinfoil cups. Decorate with a small piece of the ingredient used for flavouring, e.g. a slice of stuffed olive, a quarter of a walnut, etc. Use white or rye bread, pumpernickel, crackers, etc. for the bases, depending on the type of cheese.

Cheese plaits

Baking time: 8–10 minutes

> cheese puff paste
> grated cheese
> beaten egg

Cut the puff paste in $\frac{1}{2}$ cm ($\frac{1}{4}$ in) strips and make into plaits. Brush with egg, sprinkle with grated cheese, cut to the desired length and bake at 200°C.

Cheese pretzels

Baking time: 6–7 minutes

> cheese puff paste
> grated cheese
> beaten egg
> paprika
> rock salt

Prepare cheese puff paste and pin out to 4 mm ($\frac{1}{8}$ in) thick. Cut into strips barely 1 cm ($\frac{1}{2}$ in) wide and about 18 cm (7 in) long. Shape into pretzels, egg wash, sprinkle with grated cheese, paprika and a few salt crystals and bake in a hot oven.

Cheese roll

6–8 persons   Baking time: about 8 minutes

100 g	butter	3½ oz
	6 eggs	
165 g	sieved flour	6 oz
100 g	finely grated Parmesan cheese	3½ oz
	pinch of salt	
	paprika	
	grated nutmeg	
	any desired cheese cream	
	(see p. 292)	

Cream the butter, beat in the egg yolks a little at a time and season with salt, paprika and grated nutmeg. Gently fold in the stiffly whipped whites together with the flour and the grated cheese. Spread evenly about 8 mm (⅓ in) thick on to lightly greased and floured paper. Bake on a baking-sheet at about 200°C until pale golden and still soft. Cool very slightly, remove the paper, spread the underside with cheese cream and roll up at once. Wrap in very thinly buttered paper, refrigerate until firm and unwrap. Cut into slices 1 cm (about ½ in) thick and dish as desired, possibly with other cheese savouries.

The cheese roll may be coated thinly with cheese cream and rolled in finely chopped roasted almonds or hazelnuts before slicing.

Cheese swans

10 persons

750 g	unsweetened choux paste	1 lb 10 oz
	(see p. 830)	
	cheese cream (see p. 292)	

Pipe most of the paste on to baking-sheets in oval shapes 5 mm (2 in) long and about 3 cm (1 in) thick, using a savoy bag and coarse plain pipe. Bake for about 12 minutes until dry and crisp. To make the head and neck pieces, pipe out the rest of the paste through a small plain pipe into 'S' shapes about 4 cm (1½ in) long and barely 1 cm (½ in) thick. Bake for about 5 minutes until dry and crisp. When cold, make an incision in the tops of the oval pieces, pipe in any desired cheese cream filling and insert an 'S' piece in each one for the head and neck.

Cheese tartlets Duquinha

10 persons

| | 10 tartlet cases | |
| | (Emmenthal cheese | |

	short paste or scrap cheese puff paste, baked blind)	
	3 Gervais	
	10 green olives, stoned, blanched and chopped	
	2–3 stuffed olives	
	½ teaspoon paprika	
	juice of 1 large orange	
1 dl	half-whipped cream	⅙ pt
2 dl	aspic	⅓ pt

Sieve the Gervais into a basin and mix with the orange juice. Season with salt and the paprika, stir in the finely chopped green olives and fold in the half-whipped cream. Fill the tartlets with the mixture, using a savoy bag and star pipe. Place a slice of stuffed olive in the centre of each. Chill well and lastly glaze with aspic.

Cheese truffles

150 g	mushroom-flavoured cheese	6 oz
100 g	butter	4 oz
	salt and pepper	
	pumpernickel crumbs	

Pound the cheese and butter to a smooth paste and season with a little salt and pepper. Shape into small balls, roll in pumpernickel crumbs and leave in the refrigerator until hard.

(Illustration, p. 582)   Germany

Edam crackers

Cut fairly thick slices of Edam cheese and cut these into triangles. Impale on cock-tail sticks between salted cracker biscuits with a piece of preserved pimento. The flavour may be enhanced by a little strong mustard placed between the cheese and the crackers.

(Illustration, p. 582)   Germany

Emmenthal cubes

Cut small cubes of Emmenthal cheese. Melt a little butter in a frying pan and lightly fry the cheese cubes for a moment without allowing them to melt. Roll in chopped walnuts until coated all round. Fix a grape on each one with a cocktail stick.

(Illustration, p. 582)   Germany

Ewe or white cheese

This cheese is sold in cans. It is heavily salted for prolonged preservation. After opening the can, immerse the cheese in warm water for 10–15 minutes to dissolve out the excess salt, which would spoil the flavour. The cheese may then be either sliced or moulded. It is served cold as an hors d'oeuvre or entrée, but never at the end of a meal as it is too sharp in flavour.

                                                                            Bulgaria

Gervais tit-bits

> 3 parts Gervais
> 1 part butter
> 1 part half-whipped dairy cream
> salt

Sieve the Gervais. Cream the butter, mix with the Gervais, season and fold in the cream. This paste may be mixed with other ingredients such as grated pumpernickel chopped dill, paprika, chives, etc.

From right to left:

1. Gervais on pumpernickel with a shelled walnut.

2. Sieved Gorgonzola mixed with butter, spread on pumpernickel and dusted with paprika.

3. Slices of pumpernickel sandwiched with Gervais and cut into strips.

4. Balls of Gervais rolled in chopped chives.

5. Balls of Gervais rolled in grated pumpernickel.

6. Wedges of Gervais on pumpernickel.

7. A rosette of Gervais coloured pink with paprika, piped on the pumpernickel and topped with a grape.

8. A rosette of Gervais piped on to pumpernickel and topped with a roasted hazelnut.

11

9. Slices of pumpernickel sandwiched with pink Gervais.

10. Achleitner Schloss cheese on pumpernickel with caraway seeds.

11. Gervais mixed with dill spread on pumpernickel, with a cocktail onion rolled in paprika in the centre.

12. Slices of pumpernickel sandwiched with Gervais and chives.

13. Pink Gervais piped on to pumpernickel and topped with a roasted almond.

14. Gervais piped on to pumpernickel and topped with a black grape.

15. Balls of Gervais rolled in paprika.

(Illustration, p. 590)   Austria

Polish cheese crispies

100 g	curd cheese	4 oz
	2 chopped anchovy fillets	
30 g	butter	1 oz
	1 teaspoon chopped onion	
	1 teaspoon chopped fine herbs	
	few caraway seeds	
	10 chopped capers	

Mix the ingredients together well and season with salt, pepper and paprika. Sandwich the cheese crispies in pairs with a little of this filling.

                                                                   France

Sbrinz horseshoes

6 persons   Baking time: 6–8 minutes

250 g	Sbrinz puff paste	8 oz
50 g	grated Sbrinz cheese	2 oz
	beaten egg	

Cut out puff paste horseshoes with a cutter or cut the pastry into strips 1 cm (about ½ in) wide and shape into horseshoes. Egg wash, sprinkle with grated Sbrinz and bake in a hot oven.

Sbrinz sticks

6 persons   Baking time: 6–8 minutes

250 g	Sbrinz puff paste	8 oz
50–60 g	grated Sbrinz cheese	1½–2 oz
	caraway or poppy seeds	
	beaten egg	

Pin out the pastry to about 4 mm (⅛ in) thick, brush with egg and sprinkle with grated Sbrinz cheese and caraway or poppy seeds. Using a pastry wheel, cut into strips 12 cm (5 in) wide and cut these across into 1 cm (about ½ in) sticks. Place on a baking-sheet splashed with cold water and bake in a hot oven.

Villalon cheese fingers

These are made with the same dough as midnight savoury rolls. Divide the dough into smaller pieces than for midnight rolls and shape into fingers with rounded ends. Arrange on baking-sheets, prove, egg wash and bake in a hot oven. When cold, split the fingers and spread with creamed butter. Sandwich each one with a small slice of Villalon or other cheese about 3 mm (⅛ in) thick and large enough to project slightly beyond the edges.

Spain

DIPS (FRI-FRI)

Dips have become very popular for cocktail parties, drinks before dinner or similar occasions.

A dip is a hot or cold sauce or a softish mixture into which the guests 'dunk' small items such as cubes of grilled meat or prawns, raw vegetables, etc.

A small bowl containing the dip is stood on a cake dish or a small tray covered with a paper doyley. The 'dunks' are impaled on toothpicks and arranged round the bowl.

Suitable combinations include the following: cubes of cold grilled fillet or entrecote steak with Tartare sauce; diced prawns with Andalusian sauce; sprigs of raw cauliflower with Gribiche sauce; cubes of cold pork fillet with cold tomato and anchovy sauce.

Bacon and cheese dip

Mix some cream cheese as desired with double cream or softened butter, small strips of fried bacon and grated radishes.

Holland

Chicken dip

5 persons

Bone a plump raw chicken weighing about 800 g (1 lb 12 oz) and cut the meat in 3 cm (1¼ in) cubes. Season with a mixture of salt, pepper and paprika. Egg-and-crumb the cubes of chicken in the usual way (by dipping in flour, then in beaten egg and lastly in breadcrumbs). Fry in salad oil until golden-brown.

For the dip, make the following Hollandaise sauce. Add 2 cc (a dash) white wine and a pinch of salt to two egg yolks and stir over very gentle heat until thick. Now stir in 160 g (5¾ oz) melted butter drop by drop (using the same procedure as when making mayonnaise) and finish off with the juice of a quarter of a lemon, chopped parsley and chopped tarragon.

A secret tip—add a small dash of Pernod.

Pour the dip into a bowl and place it in the centre of a round dish. Arrange lettuce leaves all round the bowl and cover with the chicken cubes impaled on cocktail sticks. Decorate if desired with slices of lemon or with lemon segments shaped into baskets and containing sprigs of parsley.

Holland

Cream cheese dip

Mix some cream cheese (such as Gervais) with grated cheese, paprika, parsley and chives to taste.

Holland

Guacamole

	2–3 avocado pears	
200 g	cream cheese	8 oz
	1 small onion	
	2 tablespoons diced green pepper	
	¼ teaspoon paprika	
	2 tablespoons lemon juice	

Peel the avocados and sieve them, then blend them with the sieved cream cheese and lemon juice. Add the finely diced onion, the finely diced green pepper, a dash of tabasco and season to taste.

Mexico

Roquefort cheese dip

100 g	Roquefort cheese	4 oz
100 g	butter	4 oz
	1 tablespoon Cognac	
	1 tablespoon ground walnuts	

Soften the butter, mix with the cheese and add a few drops of Cognac and the ground walnuts.

Holland

Fri-fri Behague style

Cut small fairly thick pieces off a leg of 'baby' lamb and season with salt, pepper and a pinch of cayenne pepper. Fry quickly in a pan of hot fat, impale on cocktail sticks and serve hot.

Pork fri-fri

Proceed as above, using tender pork cut from the back (without fat) or fillet.

France

SAVOURY GÂTEAUX AND TARTS

Ducks' tongue gâteau Pompeian style

1 gâteau (12 portions)   Baking time: 45 minutes

400 g	unsweetened short pastry	1 lb
1 kg 800	1 duck weighing	4 lb
50 g	sweet almonds, blanched	2 oz
100 g	skinned peanuts	4 oz
25 g	stoned black olives	1 oz
25 g	stuffed green olives	1 oz
	30–40 ducks' tongues	
50 g	truffled foie gras	2 oz
5 dl	Cordial-Médoc	¾ pt

Braise the duck, adding a little Cordial-Médoc to the cooking liquid, and allow to cool. Remove all skin and bones, then mince the meat, using the finest cutter, and work to a creamy purée with the cooking liquid which has been reduced and strained.

Line a flan ring of suitable size with the pastry to make a case with a 2 cm (¾ in) rim. Mix the duck purée with the almonds, half the peanuts, the black olives and a few green olives, fill into the pastry case and bake in a very moderate oven. Clean and trim the ducks' tongues, braise in Cordial-Médoc in the same way as the duck, allow to cool, and arrange neatly side by side on the gâteau once it has cooled. Prepare aspic jelly with ¼ litre (½ pt) Cordial-Médoc and 6 sheets gelatine, allow to cool and use to glaze the gâteau. Decorate with peanuts, sliced stuffed olives and the foie gras.

(Illustration, p. 364)   Germany

Focaccia Andrea Doria

10–12 persons   Baking time: 35–40 minutes

1 kg 200	bread dough	2½ lb
400 g	semolina	12 oz
3 dl	olive oil	½ pt
1 kg	onions, peeled and sliced	2 lb
1 kg	fresh ripe juicy tomatoes	2 lb
	or canned tomatoes	
	10 anchovies in brine	
200 g	brined black olives	8 oz
	5 cloves of garlic	
	1 tablespoon dried oregano	

Work the semolina into the bread dough, add 1 dl (⅛ pt) oil and a little salt, knead well, mould into a ball, wrap in a cloth and set aside. Place the rest of the oil in a pan, fry the sliced onions in it lightly without colouring, add the tomato flesh without the skin, juice or seeds and cook over brisk heat. Wash the salt off the anchovies, fillet and cut in small pieces. Soak the olives.

Pin out the dough to 2 cm (about ¾ in) thick and lay on a large baking-sheet. Raise the edges a little to make a rim as for pizza. If any dough is left over, use a second baking-sheet. Cover evenly with the onion/tomato mixture, decorate at regular intervals with anchovies, drained olives and pieces of garlic, and sprinkle with oregano. Preheat the oven, prove the dough, then bake at about 180°C until the rim is golden-brown. Serve lukewarm, first removing the garlic.

Italy

Gourmet's brioche (Panettone gastronomico)

1 kg 500	unsweetened (salted) brioche dough	3¼ lb
200 g	soft butter	8 oz
50 g	smoked salmon	2 oz
100 g	cooked smoked ham	4 oz
50 g	Gorgonzola or other blue-veined cheese	2 oz
	juice of a quarter of a lemon	

Bake the brioche dough to the shape of a traditional panettone and leave until cold.

1. Cut up the smoked salmon, rub through a sieve, mix well with 100 g (4 oz) soft butter and sharpen with lemon juice.

2. Chop the ham finely, rub through a sieve, mix with 50 g (2 oz) soft butter, flavour with Dijon mustard, mix well again and add more mustard if required.

3. Cream the rest of the butter, mix with the finely cut cheese, rub through a sieve, mix well again and flavour with a few drops of port if desired.

Using a saw-toothed knife, first cut the domed top off the brioche and set aside, then cut the rest across evenly into very thin slices and sandwich as follows: spread one slice with salmon butter, cover with a second slice and refrigerate. Proceed in the same manner with the ham and cheese butter until all the slices have been used up. When well chilled, place the sandwiched slices one on top of another, alternating the colours, then cut right through into 8 or 16 portions in the same way as a cake. Cover with the domed top and wrap the sides in aluminium foil. If not required immediately, wrap in greaseproof paper and refrigerate.
To serve, remove the paper and foil and place in the centre of the cocktail buffet. At a self-service function the guests can easily help themselves to the triangular sandwiches as they please.

Italy

Quiche Lorraine

For 6 persons   Cooking time: 25 minutes

300 g	unsweetened short crust pastry	¾ lb
150 g	blanched bacon	6 oz
50 g	Gruyère cheese	2 oz
	3 eggs	
½ l	milk	¾ pt
	salt and pepper	

Place a lightly buttered flan ring on a baking sheet and line with unsweetened short pastry. Prick the bottom with a fork and cover with very thin slices of grilled bacon. Cover the bacon with thin slices of cheese and on top of this the well-beaten eggs and milk, to which have been added salt and pepper. Place in a hot oven. Bake and serve hot. Instead of milk, half milk and half cream can be used.

(Illustration, p. 457)

Rhodes tomato cream gâteau

12 portions   Baking time: 15 minutes

	3 egg whites	
60 g	flour	2 oz
20 g	packet tomato soup	$\frac{3}{4}$ oz
200 g	cooked ham	8 oz
50 g	tomato ketchup	2 oz
500 g	fresh tomatoes, skinned, cut in half and seeded	1 lb
	Worcestershire sauce	
$\frac{1}{2}$ l	whipped dairy cream	$\frac{3}{4}$ pt
500 g	fresh tomato purée	1 lb
	10 sheets gelatine	
	finely cut chives	
	fresh green pepper	
	1 small onion, chopped	
	half a clove of garlic, crushed	
	roasted nibbed almonds	
	gin	

Whip the egg whites to a stiff snow, fold in the flour and the packet tomato soup, fill into a greased gâteau mould, bake and allow to cool. Chop 200 g (7 oz) of the skinned tomatoes coarsely and mix with the chopped onion and crushed garlic. Split the baked gâteau base evenly into three layers. Cover the bottom one with cooked ham, spread with tomato ketchup and place the second layer on top. Splash this layer well with gin, cover with the rest of the skinned halved tomatoes, press down and flavour with Worcestershire sauce. Prepare tomato mousse with the fresh tomato purée, 8 sheets gelatine, the whipped cream, salt and pepper and spread one-third on the halved tomatoes. Cover with the third layer of gâteau base and coat the top and sides of the gâteau with the rest of the mousse. Stiffen the chopped tomato mixture wih 2 sheets of gelatine and use to make a border round the top of the gâteau. Finish off with a ring of cut chives inside this border and a haphazard sprinkling of fresh green pepper in the centre. Mask the sides with roasted nibbed almonds.

(Illustration, p. 364)   Germany

Rustic pizza

6–8 persons	Baking time: 20–25 minutes	
350 g	flour	12 oz
150 g	butter	5 oz
	3 eggs	
300 g	curd cheese	10 oz
250 g	smoked sausage or salami, finely diced	8 oz
100 g	grated Parmesan cheese	3 oz
	3 tablespoons dairy cream	
	1 tablespoon chopped parsley	

Prepare a paste with the flour, 140 g (5 oz) butter, 2 eggs and a little salt, using the rub-in method and working lightly. Shape into a ball, wrap in aluminium foil and refrigerate. Sieve the curd cheese or beat well until smooth, add the cream, the remaining egg and the Parmesan and work to a light soft cream. Stir in the diced sausage and the chopped parsley and season to taste with salt and pepper. Pin out the pastry to about 3 mm ($\frac{1}{10}$ in) thick. Set aside one-quarter for the lid and line a pie tin 23 cm (about $9\frac{1}{2}$ in) in diameter with the remainder. Fill with the curd cheese cream, cut a lid out of the rest of the pastry, moisten the inside edge, lay on top and press the edge down firmly with the fingers or pastry pincers. Brush the top with the rest of the butter which has been melted, and make two slits in the lid for the escape of steam. Bake at 175°C. Do not leave in the oven too long— a needle inserted into the filling should remain dry when withdrawn. Serve luke-warm or cold.

The rustic style of the pizza is enhanced by the addition of diced Provolone (smoked cheese) and coarsely crushed black pepper.

Italy

Savièse tart

8 persons	Cooking time: $1\frac{1}{4}$ hours	
850 g	leeks	2 lb
$2\frac{1}{2}$ dl	bouillon	$\frac{1}{2}$ pt
25 g	flour	1 oz
30 g	butter	1 oz
800 g	puff paste	2 lb
200 g	bacon	8 oz
300 g	raclette cheese or Gruyère	10 oz
200 g	potatoes (raw)	8 oz

Line a 30 cm (12 in) tart mould with puff paste so that the paste projects 2 cm
($\frac{3}{4}$ in) beyond the edge of the mould. Cover the bottom with the potatoes which
have been cut into slices 2 mm ($\frac{1}{10}$ in) thick. Cut the leeks into about 3 cm ($1\frac{1}{4}$ in)
lengths, blanch well in salted water for 10 minutes and drain, but do not refresh.
Make a roux with the flour and butter, blend in the bouillon, cook for a few minutes
and mix at once with the leeks. Cover the potatoes with this mixture, then top with
the thinly sliced cheese. Arrange very thin rashers of bacon on top. Cover with a
puff paste lid, seal the edges together with beaten egg, turn them up and mark with
pincers. Decorate the cover with strips of puff paste cut with a pastry wheel. Bake
in a hot oven, making sure that the bottom of the tart does not burn and
protecting the top with aluminium foil.

(Illustration, p. 592)   Switzerland

Savoury sandwich gâteau

12 portions

Bake 500 g (1 lb 1$\frac{1}{2}$ oz) roll dough for 30 minutes at 250°C in a greased large round
cake tin. Allow to cool, then split twice. Blend 6 packets Philadelphia cheese to a
smooth paste with 6 tablespoons yoghurt. Divide in half and season one half with a
little pepper and garlic powder. Divide the other half in two portions; mix one with
4 tablespoons chopped herbs and salt, and the other with 100 g (3$\frac{1}{2}$ oz) very finely
chopped ham, 1 tablespoon tomato purée and a small teaspoon paprika. Season
with salt and add a pinch of sugar. Spread one base with the red paste, place a
second one on top, spread this with the herb-flavoured paste and cover with the
third base. Blend the rest of the paste with 2 heaped tablespoons horseradish, spread
over the top and sides of the gâteau and pipe a bulb on each portion. Mask the
sides with flaked almonds, place a triangular slice of Gruyère cheese on each portion
and sprinkle with 50 g (1$\frac{3}{4}$ oz) diced raw ham and 1 tablespoon pistachio nuts.

(Illustration, p. 587)   Germany

Seafood flan

200 g	flour	8 oz
50 g	margarine	2 oz
50 g	lard	2 oz
	$\frac{1}{2}$ teaspoon salt	
50 g	prawns (shelled)	2 oz
	10 mussels (cooked)	
	2 scallops (cooked)	
	1 slice smoked salmon	
250 ml	cream	$\frac{1}{2}$ pt
	4 egg yolks	
	chopped parsley	

Make a short crust pastry and line a flan tin. Bake blind for 10 minutes and leave to cool. Dice the seafood, cut the smoked salmon in strips and fill into the case. Beat the cream and egg yolks together with the parsley and season to taste. Pour into the flan and bake gently 20–25 minutes.

Spanakopitta

1 kg	fresh spinach	2 lb
500 g	filo*	1 lb
	7 eggs	
250 g	feta†	½ lb
	1 onion	
	olive oil	
	butter	
	salt	
	pepper	

Trim and wash the spinach and tear the leaves into small pieces, whilst sprinkling heavily with salt. When the spinach is reduced to a quarter of its bulk, wash the salt off and drain. Beat the eggs and add to the spinach with the crumbled feta cheese and mix together. Chop and sauté the onion in olive oil, add to the spinach and season well.

Well butter a large casserole. Brush each sheet of filo with melted butter and fit into the casserole, letting the edges hang out irregularly, reserving two or three sheets. Pour in the filling and fold the ends of the pastry over the top. Butter the remaining sheets, fold them to the size of the dish and place on top. Cut through the lid with a sharp knife down to the filling in about three places and bake for 50 minutes at 180°C (350°F). Serve hot.

Greece

* filo—a Greek puff-type pastry, bought ready made in large thin sheets.
† feta—a white, crumbly, salty Greek cheese.

Spinach and cream cheese quiche

200 g	flour	8 oz
50 g	margarine	2 oz
50 g	lard	2 oz
	½ teaspoon salt	
200 g	spinach	8 oz
250 ml	cream	½ pt
	4 egg yolks	
200 g	cream cheese	4 oz

Proceed as for seafood flan (above). Fill the case with the cooked leaf spinach and the egg yolks, cream and cream cheese beaten together. Bake gently for 20–25 minutes.

Torta di verdura

10 persons   Baking time: 45 minutes

700 g	flour	1½ lb
	3 eggs	
1 dl	olive oil	3 fl oz
1 kg	spinach	2 lb
	10 young artichokes (spiny-leaved Riviera variety)	
200 g	curd cheese	8 oz
50 g	butter	2 oz
100 g	grated Parmesan cheese	4 oz
	1 tablespoon chopped parsley	
	2–3 chopped marjoram leaves	
	coarsely ground pepper	

Prepare a paste with the flour, 2 eggs, 5 cl ($\frac{1}{12}$ pt) olive oil, salt and a little water if required. Work very lightly. Shape into a ball, wrap in a cloth or aluminium foil and allow to rest in a cool place for a few hours. Clean the spinach, blanch in salted water, drain, refresh and squeeze lightly. Place in a pan of foaming butter, season and cook over gentle heat for 5 minutes. Cut the stalks off the artichokes level with the leaves, remove the hard outside leaves, cut into small pieces and wash in water containing a little lemon juice. Heat the rest of the oil, place the artichokes in it, season lightly with salt, cook gently for 20 minutes and sprinkle with the parsley. Place the curd cheese in a bowl, mash with a fork, add the artichokes and spinach, the grated Parmesan, the chopped marjoram, 1 beaten egg, the ground pepper and a little salt, then work well with a spatula to amalgamate the ingredients.

Pin out the paste to about 3 mm ($\frac{1}{10}$ in) thick. Line a flan ring or case with two-thirds of the paste, pressing it against the sides firmly. Fill with the vegetable and cheese mixture, smooth the top and cover with a lid made with the rest of the pastry, moistening the edge first. Press down well round the edge to seal. Prick the top once or twice to allow the escape of steam and bake at 180°C. Serve hot or cold.

The pastry may be replaced by puff paste if desired.

Italy

SAVOURY PUFF SLICES

Pin out scrap puff pastry into strips about 6 mm (2½ in) wide and 2 mm ($\frac{1}{10}$ in) thick. Place the strips on a baking-sheet splashed with water. Wash half of them with egg, dock them all well and bake in a very hot oven for 4 or 5 minutes. Cool on a rack. Spread mousse or savoury butter on to the strips which have not been egg-washed, then cover with the remaining strips, placing the egg-washed side uppermost. Press down lightly and cut across into 2 or 3 cm (about 1 in) slices.

France

Anchovy puff slices

Spread with anchovy butter.

France

Savoury puff slices Alenais style

Spread with watercress butter and fill with blanched watercress leaves.

France

Savoury puff slices Caprice

Spread with truffle butter and fill with pheasant mousse.

France

Savoury puff slices Coquin

Spread first with tarragon butter, then with tomato butter and lastly with celery butter.

France

Savoury puff slices Joinville

Spread with shrimp butter and fill with picked shrimps.

France

Savoury puff slices Nantes style

Spread with sardine butter.

France

Savoury puff slices Parisian style

Fill with ham mousse.

France

Savoury puff slices Périgord style

Fill with truffled foie gras mousse.

France

Savoury puff slices Pompadour

Spread with tarragon butter and fill with finely diced York ham.

France

Savoury puff slices Printanier

Spread with printanier butter.

France

Savoury puff slices Queen's style

Fill with chicken mousse.

France

Savoury puff slices Rhine style

Fill with salmon mousse.

France

Savoury puff slices Strasbourg style

Fill with foie gras mousse.

France

OLIVETTE TOMATOES

These are made from firm tomatoes, cut in half if large or with the bottom sliced off if small. In each case the inside is scooped out and the cases sprinkled inside with a little salt and then inverted on to a wire rack to drain for half an hour before filling.

Olivettes Armorican style

Stuff with very finely diced lobster and coral bound with mayonnaise which has been flavoured with tomato ketchup.

France

Olivettes Canoness

Fill with tuna mousse and glaze with aspic.

France

Olivettes caprice

Stuff with a fine truffled ham mousse.

France

Olivettes Gâtinais style

Fill with finely diced chicken breast bound with mayonnaise. Decorate with truffle and glaze with aspic.

France

Olivettes Greek style

Fill with vegetables cooked Greek style (but no leeks or onions).

France

Olivettes Gustave Ninlias

Fill with small pieces of cock's kidney and diced truffles and cooked artichoke bottoms bound with cream mayonnaise lightly flavoured with tomato.

France

Olivettes Imperial style

Fill with ham mousse, decorate with truffle and glaze with aspic.

France

Olivettes jardinière style

Fill with finely cut mixed cooked vegetables bound with mayonnaise.

France

Olivettes Joinville

Fill with shrimp mousse, decorate with picked shrimps and glaze with aspic.

France

Olivettes Maria Theresa

Fill half of each barquette with ham mousse and the other half with chicken mousse. Decorate the ham mousse with a small heart made of truffle and the chicken mousse with a small heart made of lean ham. Glaze with aspic.

France

Olivettes Marmande

Fill with tomato mousse, decorate with chervil leaves and glaze with aspic.

France

Olivettes Masséna

Fill with diced truffles and artichoke bottoms bound with cream mayonnaise.

France

Olivettes Montpellier

Stuff with Montpellier butter.

France

Olivettes Montreal

Stuff with salmon butter.

France

Olivettes Nantua

Stuff with crayfish butter.

France

Olivettes Queen's style

Stuff with chicken mousse.

France

Olivettes Russian style

Stuff with Russian salad.

France

Olivettes Rouget-rouge

Stuff with diced pickled tongue in Andalusian sauce.

France

Olivettes Scottish style

Fill with salmon mousse and glaze by brushing with aspic.

France

Olivettes Var style

Fill with asparagus mousse.

France

Olivettes with prawns

Fill with shelled prawns bound with light mayonnaise. Sprinkle with fine herbs.

France

COCKTAIL SAVOURIES

These include all kinds of small hot or cold savouries which may be served at a cocktail party, as an appetiser, with a drink at the bar or at home. The main thing is that they should be very piquant, attractively served and easy to eat.

Anchovy sticks I (Allumettes aux anchois)

Pin out puff pastry to 2 mm (about $\frac{1}{10}$ in) thick. Cut into strips 8 cm (3 in) long and 2–3 cm (about 1 in) wide. Moisten the edges slightly. Place a well-drained anchovy fillet in oil in the centre of each strip of pastry, cover with a strip of the same size and seal the edges well. Brush with egg and bake in a hot oven for about 12 minutes. Serve hot.

Anchovy Sticks II

Pin out puff pastry to 3–4 mm ($\frac{1}{8}$ in) thick and cut into strips 8 cm (3 in) long and 2–3 cm (about 1 in) wide. Egg wash, score crosswise with the point of a knife and allow to stand for 15 minutes. Bake for about 5 minutes in a hot oven and leave until cold. Carefully lift off the top, pipe a line of anchovy butter on to the base, using a savoy bag and plain pipe, replace the top and press down lightly. Arrange on a dish covered with a paper napkin and serve cold.

Anchovy tit-bits

Proceed as for cheese tit-bits (p. 278), but place a rolled anchovy fillet in the centre of each round of pastry instead of cheese sauce. Serve hot.

France

Assorted savoury biscuits

300 g	flour	10 oz
150 g	butter	5 oz
	3 egg yolks	
5 cl	single cream	2 fl oz
	grated nutmeg	
8 g	salt	$\frac{1}{2}$ teaspoon

Set aside 50 g ($1\frac{3}{4}$ oz) flour for dusting the table. Sieve the rest on to the table, make a bay and place the egg yolks and cream in the centre together with the slightly softened butter, the salt and grated nutmeg. Knead until all the flour has been absorbed, but do not work the paste too much. Allow to recover for 15 minutes. Pin out to the required thickness on a lightly floured table.

The shape of the biscuits varies according to the garnish. They should be made no more than 3 cm ($1\frac{1}{4}$ in) in size; they will shrink a little while baking.

Type I. Pin out the pastry to 5 mm ($\frac{1}{5}$ in) thick. Cut into squares and oblongs with a knife or into rounds or other shapes with a pastry cutter. Egg wash and top with an almond, a hazelnut, a walnut, 2 or 3 skinned peanuts or blanched pine kernels, a stoned olive, etc. Bake in a fairly hot oven. Other possible garnishes include small rolled anchovy fillets, sliced cooked sausage, diced ham or hard cheese, small pieces of choriza or tuna in oil, small clams or picked shrimps.

Type II. Divide the pastry in half and pin out more thinly than for Type I into 2 squares of the same size and thickness. Spread one square thickly with liver purée, chorizo or black pudding paste, mashed sardine or tuna in oil. Cover with the other square of pastry, egg wash, sprinkle with grated cheese and cut with a knife into various shapes. Bake in a medium oven.

Type III. Pin out the pastry thinly and prepare little ravioli or pasties, using various types of purée as a filling (liver, game, ham, chorizo, black pudding, sardine, anchovy, etc.). Egg wash before baking.

Type IV. Pin out the pastry into an oblong, spread with one of the above fillings and roll up. Egg wash and make a wavy design on top with a fork. Slice and bake in a fairly hot oven.

If the savouries are to be served with drinks before a meal, they should preferably be made with puff pastry.

Spain

Bagatelles

These may be made with a wide variety of ingredients—in fact, with anything edible. They include 1 cm ($\frac{1}{2}$ in) cubes of ham, pickled tongue, sausage, cheese, cocktail sausages and all kinds of other items. Stoned green or black olives or small radishes may also be used. Each cube is fixed on to a small square of buttered white bread 5 mm (about $\frac{1}{4}$ in) thick by means of a toothpick or cocktail stick. These cubes are then fixed, alternating the different colours, into a grapefruit, orange, large tomato, red cabbage, etc. with a flat base, so that they look like the spines on a hedgehog.

A savoury butter (see 'Savoury Butters') may, of course, be used instead of ordinary butter. If desired, two different items may be fixed on to the same square of bread, or the bread may be omitted.

A few possible combinations are given below:

A folded anchovy fillet, a stoned olive, buttered bread.
Saveloy, capers, buttered bread.
Chorizo (piquant Spanish sausage), sweet pepper.
Cheshire cheese, chicken breast.
Preserved goose (confit d'oie), pickled sweet pepper, buttered bread.
Roast pork, gherkin, Gruyère cheese.
Foie gras, buttered bread.
Bayonne ham, buttered bread.
York ham, round slice of pickled cucumber, Gruyère cheese.
Pickled tongue, slice of pickled cucumber, buttered bread.
Stuffed olives.
Salami, slices of radish, buttered bread.
Salami, stoned olive, Gruyère cheese.
Slice of dried sausage, Gruyère cheese, buttered bread.
Parisian sausage, round slice of pickled cucumber, Gruyère cheese.

France

Blinis I (Russian yeast pancakes)

Yield: about 50 pancakes   Cooking time: 2–3 minutes

150 g	wheat flour	5 oz
150 g	buckwheat flour	5 oz
20 g	yeast	$\frac{3}{4}$ oz
	4 egg yolks	
	4 egg whites	
approx. 8 dl	milk	1$\frac{1}{3}$ pt approx.
40 g	melted butter	2 oz
	2 heaped tablespoons	
	unsweetened whipped cream	
	butter for frying	

Prepare a ferment with the yeast, 50 g (1$\frac{3}{4}$ oz) wheat flour and 3 dl ($\frac{1}{2}$ pt) lukewarm milk. Cover with a cloth and leave to rise for about 1 hour in a warm place. Mix the rest of the wheat flour with the buckwheat flour, the egg yolks and a pinch of salt. Add the ferment and enough lukewarm milk to make a batter of the same consistency as ordinary pancake batter. Fold in the whipped cream, the stiffly whisked egg whites and the melted butter, then leave to rise for a further 30 minutes or so. Fry in tiny pancake pans shortly before the blinis are required. Serve very hot.

N.B.—Blinis are served as an accompaniment to caviar. If no buckwheat flour is available, they may be made with wheat flour only. They are always served with smetana (sour cream) and melted butter.

Russia

Blinis II

10 persons

500 g	buckwheat flour	1 lb
500 g	wheat flour	1 lb
40 g	yeast	1$\frac{1}{2}$ oz
$\frac{1}{4}$ l	sour cream	$\frac{1}{4}$ pt
	3 eggs	
$\frac{1}{8}$ l	whipped cream	$\frac{1}{4}$ pt
8 g	salt	$\frac{1}{2}$ teaspoon
	milk	
	butter	

Sieve the wheat and buckwheat flour together, place in a bowl and make a bay. Disperse the yeast in lukewarm milk, pour into the bay, add a pinch of sugar and the salt, work in the flour and leave to ferment. When well developed, add the beaten eggs, the sour cream and, lastly, the whipped cream to make a smooth batter. Heat small blini pans, brush with melted butter, pour a spoonful of batter in each one and fry. When the underside is brown, turn over to fry the other side.

Russia

Blinis III

600 g	wheat flour	1¼ lb
	1 tablespoon sugar	
50 g	butter	2 oz
25 g	good pinch of yeast	
	1 egg	
4 g	salt	⅛ oz
approx. 8 dl	milk	1⅓ pt
4–5 cl	olive oil	2 fl oz approx.

Warm 6 dl (1 pt) milk to 30–35°C and disperse the yeast in it. Mix with half the sugar, the salt, the egg yolk, the melted butter and half the flour and beat well. Cover with a cloth and leave in a warm place to rise. After 1½–2 hours, when the dough has doubled in volume, blend in the rest of the milk which has been heated to 50°C, the rest of the flour and sugar and the egg white whipped to a stiff snow. Knock back and leave to rise for a further 3 hours. The batter should be of the same consistency as very thick unwhipped cream; if it is too thin, add a little flour.

Brush small frying pans with oil, heat and pour in a small ladleful of batter. When the underside is brown, brush the top with oil and turn over to fry the other side. Now brush with oil again, place in a pot and wrap in a cloth. Do not stir the batter while frying.

N.B.—Blinis are also made with buckwheat flour, or with equal proportions of wheat flour and buckwheat.

Russia

Blinis with anchovies

Place small pieces of anchovy fillet (fresh if possible) in the hot buttered pancake pans, pour the batter on top and fry.

Russia

Blinis with hard-boiled egg

Cut up hard-boiled eggs in small pieces. Place a few pieces in the bottom of the hot buttered pancake pans, pour in a little batter and cover with a little more hard-boiled egg. Fry on both sides and serve with thick smetana and melted butter.

Russia

Blinis with sprats

Proceed as above, using small pieces of skinned smoked sprat fillet.

Russia

CAROLINES

Carolines are small éclairs made of fairly fine choux paste. They are filled with various types of mousse. Often they are coated with chaud-froid sauce; in this case they are impaled on a cocktail stick.

Basic recipe

Baking time: 15 minutes

Pipe out choux paste on to a buttered baking-sheet in finger shape, not more than 5 cm (2 in) long, using a savoy bag fitted with a plain $\frac{1}{2}$–1 cm ($\frac{1}{4}$–$\frac{1}{2}$ in) pipe and leaving a space of about 2 cm ($\frac{3}{4}$ in) in between. Wash with egg and bake in a hot oven until fairly dry. Cool on a wire rack, then slit along one side with scissors and pipe in a mousse of the type preferred. If desired, coat with a suitable chaud-froid sauce.

France

Carolines Diana

Fill with game mousse and coat with chaud-froid sauce prepared with concentrated game stock.

France

Carolines Gâtinais style

Fill with chicken mousse and coat with chicken chaud-froid sauce.

France

Carolines Joinville

Fill with shrimp mousse and coat with Joinville chaud-froid sauce.

France

Carolines Landes style

Fill with foie gras mousse or with a mixture of 4 parts sieved foie gras to 1 part butter. Check the seasoning before use.

France

Carolines Lyon style

Fill with pike mousse and coat with fish chaud-froid sauce flavoured with Chablis.

France

Carolines Marmande style

Fill with tomato aspic mousse.

France

Carolines Murat

Fill with artichoke mousse.

France

Ham carolines

Fill with ham mousse and coat with port jelly.

France

Lobster carolines

Fill with lobster mousse and coat with American chaud-froid sauce.

France

Salmon carolines

Fill with salmon mousse and coat with Champagne jelly.

France

Chipolata sausage rolls

Baking time: 7–8 minutes

Grill or fry chipolata sausages briskly, skin them and allow to cool. When quite cold, place them 1 cm (about $\frac{1}{2}$ in) apart on puff pastry which has been pinned out to a thickness of $2\frac{1}{2}$ mm ($\frac{1}{10}$ in). Moisten the pastry all round the sausages and cover with a second strip of pastry of the same thickness. Press down well to seal the two strips of pastry all round each sausage. Wash with egg and cut right through the pastry between the sausages. To decorate, draw a few lines on top of each sausage roll with a fork. Bake in a hot oven and serve hot.

France

Cocktail chipolatas

Tiny chipolata sausages each weighing about 10 g ($\frac{1}{3}$ oz) are fried over brisk heat and served very hot on cocktail sticks.

France

Cumin sticks

Proceed as for golden sticks, but flavour the Mornay sauce with cumin seeds at the rate of 1 tablespoon cumin to $\frac{1}{4}$ litre ($\frac{1}{2}$ pint) sauce.

France

Fried scampi

Marinate shelled scampi tails for 30 minutes in lemon juice with the addition of fine herbs and a little cayenne pepper. Drain and dip into batter, then fry in deep fat.

Italy

Fritots of brains

Soak calves' brains in cold water, remove any clots of blood, pull off the skin and poach in lightly salted water containing a little vinegar, then allow to cool. Drain well, cut into small pieces and marinate in lemon juice with finely chopped herbs and a little paprika. Coat with fritter batter and deep-fry in hot fat. Impale on cocktail sticks and serve hot.

France

Frankfurters in brioche

Roll out brioche dough thinly and wrap round cooked skinned Frankfurter cocktail sausages to enclose completely. Place on a buttered baking-sheet, egg wash, prove and bake at about 200°C. Arrange the little rolls on a paper napkin and serve hot.

N.B.—Frankfurter cocktail sausages are sold ready cooked in jars or cans.

France

Game pirojky

12–15 small pies   Baking time: 12–15 minutes

250 g	virgin puff pastry	8 oz
	or puff pastry cuttings	
250 g	minced cooked game	8 oz
	4 hard-boiled eggs	
125 g	cooked rice	4 oz
½ litre	veal gravy or game sauce	¾ pt
25 g	onion, very finely chopped	1 oz

Cook the onion in a little butter. Add the minced game and the veal gravy or game sauce and cook for 3 or 4 minutes. Allow to cool, then add the cooked rice and the chopped hard-boiled eggs. Adjust the seasoning. Pin out the puff pastry 5 mm (¼ in) thick and cut out with a plain 5 cm (2 in) cutter. Place a spoonful of the game filling in the centre of half the disks and cover with the other half, moistening the edges lightly and pressing down well to seal. Wash with egg and bake in a hot oven. Serve hot on napkins or patterned paper.

Russia

Golden sticks

Remove the crusts from a tin loaf and cut into slices 2–3 mm (1/10 in) thick. Spread half the slices with lukewarm Mornay sauce, cover each one with a plain slice, press down lightly and refrigerate. Cut in 15 mm (½ in) strips, dip in beaten egg, coat with white breadcrumbs and deep-fry in hot fat until golden (2–3 minutes). Drain well on paper, dish on a paper napkin and serve very hot.

France

Ham sticks

Proceed as for golden sticks, but mix the Mornay sauce with small cubes of lean cooked ham at the rate of 2 tablespoons ham to ¼ litre (½ pint) sauce.

France

Karelian pirogs

6–8 persons   Baking time: 10–12 minutes

250 g	rye flour	8 oz
2 dl	water	⅓ pt
	rice porridge or mashed	
	potatoes	
	salt	
	milk	
	or a mixture of	
	butter and water:	
1 dl	hot water	⅙ pt
50 g	butter	2 oz
	egg butter:	
	2 hard-boiled eggs	
100 g	butter	4 oz

Mix the flour, a good pinch of salt and the water to a smooth dough and knead well. Care should be taken in adding the water, as rye flours differ in the amount of water they will carry. Allow the dough to recover for a short time, then pin out until barely 1 cm (½ in) thick and cut out pieces 10–15 cm (4–6 in) long. Place 1–2 tablespoons rice porridge or mashed potato in the centre of each pirog, depending on size, turn the ends in to the centre, notch lightly with the back of a knife and bake in a hot oven. After removing from the oven, dip at once into hot milk or a hot water/butter mixture and serve hot with egg butter.

To make the egg butter, either chop the hard-boiled eggs finely or rub them through a sieve, mix with the butter which has been well creamed and season with salt and white pepper.

The pirogs are usually served with milk or coffee.

(Illustration, p. 589)   Finland

Lobster medallions

Prepare a salpicon of lobster trimmings and mix with very little cocktail sauce. Spread on salty cracker biscuits and cover with a lobster medallion to fit each biscuit exactly. Decorate with a truffle motif and glaze with fish aspic.

(Illustration, p. 580)   Austria

Mini-pizzas

30 pizzas   Baking time: about 12 minutes

1 kg	pizza dough	2¼ lb
3 dl	well-reduced cold tomato sauce	½ pt
300 g	diced Mozzarella cheese	10 oz
1 dl	olive oil	⅙ pt
	10 anchovy fillets, soaked and cut into three	
	good pinch dried oregano	

Pin out the dough to 5 mm (¼ in) thick and cut into rounds 5 cm (2 in) in diameter. Stretch each one a little with both thumbs and roll the edges up to make a small rim while turning constantly. Cover with a cloth to prevent drying. Using a table-spoon, cover each pizza with a little tomato sauce, avoiding the rim. Sprinkle with a few cubes of Mozzarella cheese, place a piece of anchovy fillet on top and add a pinch of oregano. Arrange on a baking-sheet and bake at 200°C until the rims are golden-brown. Serve very hot on a dish covered with a napkin.

Italy

Pancake roll Stresa

10–12 persons

Pancake batter

50 g	flour	2 oz
	2 eggs	
2 dl	milk	⅓ pt
	grated nutmeg	
	butter for frying	

Blend the eggs and flour together, add the milk, season with salt and flavour with grated nutmeg, then pass through a conical strainer. Make 3 very thin pancakes from the batter, cooking them on both sides in a pancake pan and making sure that they do not dry out. Place one on top of another and leave until cold.

Fillings

Foie gras purée

300 g	foie gras	10 oz
50 g	butter	1½ oz
50 g	double cream	1½ oz

3 cl	Marsala	3 dessertspoons
2 cl	Cognac	2 dessertspoons
	a little black truffle	
	cayenne pepper	

Season the foie gras with salt and pepper, place in a terrine, pour in the Marsala, cover and cook slowly. When cold, rub through a sieve. Cream the butter and gradually add the sieved liver, the cooking liquid, the cream, the Cognac and a good pinch of cayenne pepper. Beat until light and frothy, then draw in the chopped truffle and adjust the seasoning.

N.B.—The raw foie gras may be replaced by ready-made foie gras paste.

Ham purée

300 g	cooked ham	10 oz
50 g	butter	1½ oz
50 g	double cream	1½ oz
5 cl	velouté or Béchamel sauce	2 fl oz
2 cl	Cognac	2 dessertspoons
	a little sweet red pepper, finely chopped	
	cayenne pepper	
3 cl	Marsala	3 dessertspoons

Mince the ham, using the finest blade of the mincer, mix with the velouté or Béchamel sauce and rub through a sieve. Cream the butter, add the ham, cream, Marsala and Cognac, season with salt and cayenne pepper and beat until light and frothy. Lastly stir in the chopped red pepper.

Pheasant purée

800–900 g	hen pheasant weighing	2 lb
70 g	butter	3 oz
50 g	double cream	2 oz
3 cl	Marsala	3 dessertspoons
2 cl	Cognac	2 dessertspoons
	cayenne pepper	
	a little finely chopped pistachio nuts	

Stew the pheasant, seasoning it lightly with salt, then brown in 20 g (¾ oz) butter, cool, bone and skin. Mince the meat, using the finest blade of the mincer, add the cooking stock and rub through a sieve. Cream the butter, gradually add the pheasant, cream, Marsala and Cognac, season with salt and a good pinch of cayenne pepper, beat until light and frothy and add the chopped pistachio nuts.

Garnish and decoration

2 dl	brown chaud-froid sauce	⅓ pt
1 dl	aspic jelly	⅛ pt
	2 hard-boiled eggs, chopped	
	salt	

Spread one of the pancakes with foie gras purée, the second one with ham purée and the third with pheasant purée. Place one on top of another in the following order: foie gras purée at the bottom, then ham purée, and lastly pheasant purée. Roll up together tightly, wrap in oiled paper to make a firm roll and refrigerate for at least 2 hours. Unwrap, coat the pancake roll with chaud-froid sauce on the point of setting, sprinkle with the chopped eggs and glaze with aspic. Refrigerate for a further 2 hours before using, then slice with a lukewarm knife.

Italy

Parmesan sticks

Proceed as for golden sticks, but make the Mornay sauce with Parmesan cheese.

France

Pineapple medaillons with Roquefort cheese

6 persons

	1½–2 slices fresh pineapple (depending on size) or, if not available, canned pineapple	
35 g	Roquefort cheese	1½ oz
50 g	butter	2 oz
2 cl	port	2 dessertspoons
	aspic jelly lightly flavoured with port	

Reduce the Roquefort to a purée, cream with 30 g (1 oz) butter and flavour with port and a good pinch of paprika. Trim the pineapple slices neatly and cut out the core—this has already been done with canned slices—then drain well, fry quickly on both sides in the rest of the butter until golden-brown, then allow to cool. Split each slice with a sharp knife, sandwich with the Roquefort butter and refrigerate until firm. Cut the whole slice into four and the half slice into two triangles and glaze each piece with the aspic jelly.

Germany

Pirojky Muscovite style

15 small pies   Baking time: 20 minutes

500 g	plain unsweetened brioche dough	1 lb
250 g	cooked fish (pike, bass, hake or grey mullet) without skin or bones	8 oz
	5 hard-boiled eggs	
25 g	vesiga (dried spinal marrow of the sturgeon)	1 oz

Soak the vesiga in cold water for 5 hours. Simmer under cover in 1½ litres (2½ pints) salted water for 3½–4 hours, allow to cool and drain thoroughly. Chop together with the cooked fish and the hard-boiled eggs. Season well with salt, pepper, a dash of celery salt and chopped parsley.

Pin out the brioche dough and cut into ovals 5 cm (2 in) long and 3 cm (1¼ in) wide. Place a spoonful of the fish filling in the centre of each, moisten the edges and fold over to enclose the filling. Press together lightly to seal. Now proceed as for cottage cheese pirojky.

                                                            Russia

Poached oyster in turtle jelly

Remove the 'beard' from choice even-sized raw oysters, cover with turtle jelly and allow to set. Cut into rounds and arrange on cracker biscuits.

Turtle jelly: clear turtle soup, strained and stiffened with 16–18 sheets gelatine per litre (1¾ pints). Do not boil the soup, but warm to 80°C only, then add the gelatine which has been soaked and squeezed dry. Allow to cool, then flavour to taste with Madeira.

(Illustration, p. 580)   Austria

Polenta oblongs

20 oblongs

300 g	coarse maize meal	10 oz
½ l	milk	¾ pt
¼ l	water	½ pt
200 g	pork sausage (for frying)	8 oz
20 g	butter	1 oz
5 cl	white wine	2 fl oz

Place the milk and water in a pan and bring to the boil. Pour in the maize meal slowly and cook while stirring constantly until the polenta is smooth and thick, but not hard (about 45 minutes). Pour on to a lightly oiled marble or plastic slab. Using an oiled brush or palette knife, spread evenly to a thickness of 1 cm (about ½ in). When cold, cut into 5 × 3 cm (2 × 1¼ in) oblongs and remove from the slab. Arrange on a wire rack and either bake in the oven at 200°C or fry in butter or oil until golden-brown.

Meanwhile melt the butter in a pan, add the sausage, prick several times with a fork, cover and cook lightly. Pour in the white wine after a few minutes and cook until all the wine has boiled away. Cut the sausage into 20 slices. Arrange the polenta oblongs on a hot dish and fix a slice of sausage on each one with a toothpick or plastic cocktail stick. Serve very hot. Small plates and forks are required for serving.

Italy

Provençal sticks

Proceed as for anchovy sticks (Recipe II), but pipe in Provençal purée instead of anchovy butter.

France

Prunes and bacon

Soak prunes for 2 or 3 hours, then cook in good white stock or consommé, keeping them firm. Drain thoroughly and stone. Fry thin rashers of bacon over brisk heat until lightly browned, allowing one rasher per prune. Wrap a rasher round each prune to leave only a quarter of the prune showing, or insert the bacon into the slit through which the stone was removed. Fix in position with a cocktail stick. Keep hot until required.

France

Rabbie's savoury puff

6 persons   Cooking time: 10 minutes

	6 puff pastry cases	
450 g	1 haggis weighing	1 lb
225 g	mashed turnips	8 oz
450 g	duchesse potatoes	1 lb

Place purée of turnips on the bottom of each vol-au-vent case, then a layer of haggis. Pipe a rosette of duchesse potato on each and brown in the oven.

Great Britain

Rastegais

15 small pies	Baking time: 20 minutes	
600 g	plain unsweetened brioche dough	1¼ lb
250 g	salmon (raw) without skin or bones	8 oz
	5 hard-boiled eggs	
25 g	vesiga	1 oz
25 g	chopped onion	1 oz
	1 tablespoon chopped parsley	

Colbert sauce:

100 g	maître d'hôtel butter	4 oz
	2 tablespoons strong veal gravy	

Dice the salmon, season with salt and pepper and fry quickly in very hot butter until the flesh is just firm, then remove from the pan at once. Cook the onion separately in a little butter without colouring. Chop the hard-boiled eggs and the vesiga which has been prepared as directed for pirojky Muscovite style, then mix with the salmon, onion and chopped parsley. To make the pies, proceed as for pirojky Muscovite style, but make a steam vent by cutting a small hole in the top and inserting a tube of greaseproof paper. Bake in a hot oven. After removing from the oven, pour in the Colbert sauce through the hole in the top and remove the paper. Serve on a napkin.

To make Colbert sauce, heat the veal gravy, remove from the heat and add the maître d'hôtel butter a little at a time.

Russia

Vine leaf strudel

18 persons

Strudel paste

750 g	flour	1½ lb approx.
	oil	
	lukewarm water	

Filling

	⅓ tin of vine leaves	
600 g	cooked ham	1¼ lb
900 g	cheese (Gruyère, Fontina etc.)	2 lb

600 g	bean sprouts	1¼ lb
30 g	anchovy fillets	1 oz
	8–10 hard-boiled eggs,	
	cut into 6	
	green peppercorns to taste	
	2 tins lychees, stoned	

Make the strudel dough in the usual way, and stretch out on to a floured cloth. Place down the centre first the drained vine leaves, then the thinly sliced cheese. Place the anchovy fillets at regular intervals then add the bean sprouts. Add the wedges of hard-boiled egg and the lychees, and sprinkle with green peppercorns. Trim the edges of the dough and use the cloth to roll up the strudel. Place on a greased tray and bake.

(Techniques, p. 110)   Germany

Rice balls

30 balls

300 g	rice (preferably Vialone)	10 oz
75 g	butter	3 oz
1 l	light meat broth	1¾ pt
	1 small onion	
100 g	grated Parmesan cheese	4 oz
	2 eggs	
150 g	minced veal	5 oz
5 cl	white wine	2 fl oz
	breadcrumbs	

Melt 50 g (1¾ oz) butter in a stew-pan. Add the onion, finely sliced, fry lightly without colouring, then add the rice and fry until transparent. Gradually stir in the broth a little at a time and cook until the grains of rice are tender but not sticky (about 15 minutes). Season to taste, stir in the Parmesan with a fork, remove from the heat and leave until lukewarm. Now stir in the beaten eggs carefully. Melt the rest of the butter in a pan, add the veal, pour in the white wine and season with salt and pepper. Cook until all the wine has boiled away.

Flour the hands. Using a tablespoon, place a little risotto in the palm of the hand and shape into a ball the size of a walnut. Make a hollow in the centre with the index finger of the right hand, fill with minced veal and squeeze the ball of risotto to enclose the filling completely. Roll each ball once or twice in breadcrumbs and fry until golden in hot oil or vegetable fat. Impale the little balls on cocktail sticks or toothpicks, arrange on a dish covered with a folded napkin and serve very hot.

Italy

Roe-deer medallions

Place a very thin skinned and seeded orange slice on each cracker biscuit. Cover with a lightly fried round of roe-deer brushed with game glaze. Pipe on a rosette of foie gras mousse, using a star tube, and decorate with half a cherry, half an almond and a strip of angelica. Lastly, glaze with aspic jelly.

(Illustration, p. 580)   Austria

Roe deer medallions

6 persons

120 g	fillet of roe deer	4¼ oz
60 g	foie gras purée	2 oz
	6 stoned morello cherries	
	wine jelly	

Fry the meat, keeping it pink, cut on the slant into 6 slices of equal size and trim to a slightly oval shape. Pipe on the foie gras purée, using a plain pipe. Place a cherry in the centre of each medallion and refrigerate until the foie gras purée is half set, then glaze with wine jelly.

Germany

Savoury petits choux

Using a savoy bag and small plain tube, pipe out choux paste in small bulbs about 4 cm (1½ in) in diameter on to lightly greased baking-sheets. Brush with egg and bake at about 180°C until crisp. Cool on a cake rack. When quite cold, make a small slit in one side or a small hole in the bottom, so that the petits choux can be filled with the help of a small plain pipe. All kinds of mousses and purées may be used as a filling, e.g.: foie gras paste, shrimp or prawn mousse, chicken mousse, lobster or crayfish mousse, purée of fresh salmon with fish velouté, purée of smoked salmon with horseradish cream, ham mousse, purée of game with Cumberland sauce, etc.

The petits choux may be glazed with aspic, or the tops may be coated with a suitable chaud-froid sauce and then glazed with aspic.

France

Savoury sardine biscuits

6 persons

400 g	flour	14 oz
	3 eggs	
10 g	baking powder	$\frac{1}{3}$ oz
	4 tablespoons oil	
	6 large sardines in oil	
150 g	butter	5 oz
	3 tablespoons tomato purée	

Make a bay in 350 g (12$\frac{1}{4}$ oz) flour and place in it 2 eggs, the baking powder, the oil, 5 g ($\frac{1}{6}$ oz) salt and a good pinch of pepper. Mix with the hand, adding enough water to make a smooth paste of medium firmness. Mould into a ball, cut a cross on top, cover with a floured cloth and stand aside for at least 30 minutes.

Skin the sardines, remove the bones, rub through a fine sieve and mix with the creamed butter and the tomato purée. Season well.

Pin out the paste on a floured table to a thickness of 3–4 mm (about $\frac{1}{8}$ in) and cut into rounds with a 4 cm (1$\frac{1}{2}$ in) cutter. Arrange on a baking-sheet, brush with beaten egg and bake in a hot oven. When cold, sandwich in pairs with the sardine and tomato butter, taking care not to use too much or too little.

Spain

Small pizzas

10 pizzas   Baking time: 6–7 minutes

500 g	bread dough	1 lb
	10 soaked anchovy fillets	
	10 stoned black olives	
	3 small tomatoes	
50 g	grated Parmesan cheese	2 oz

Divide the bread dough evenly into 10 portions and mould round. Pin out into disks 4–5 cm (1$\frac{1}{2}$–2 in) in diameter. Place 2 small wedges of tomato and 2 half anchovy fillets on each disk. Press an olive lightly into the centre. Transfer the pizzas to a baking-sheet and prove for about a quarter of an hour. When the dough has almost doubled in volume, bake in a medium oven. Serve warm or cold.

The following may be used instead of plain bread dough: puff pastry trimmings, pie pastry, ordinary short pastry for lining tarts or unsweetened short pastry made with 250 g (8$\frac{3}{4}$ oz) flour and 6 cl ($\frac{1}{10}$ pt) olive oil. If any of these except puff pastry is used, baking powder should be added at the rate of 1 g to 250 g ($\frac{1}{2}$ teaspoon to $\frac{1}{2}$ lb) flour.

France

Small quiches Lorraines

25 small quiches   Baking time: 20 minutes

250 g	fine unsweetened short pastry or scrap puff pastry	8 oz
	2 eggs	
	2 egg yolks	
$\frac{1}{4}$ l	milk or dairy cream	$\frac{1}{2}$ pt
100 g	bacon, blanched and finely diced	4 oz
100 g	Gruyère cheese, diced	4 oz

Line tartlet moulds about 4 cm ($1\frac{1}{2}$ in) in diameter with the pastry. Cover the bottom with the diced bacon and cheese. Beat the eggs in a basin, adding salt, pepper and nutmeg. Blend in the cream or cold boiled milk. Pour this custard into the tartlets and bake in a hot oven. Serve hot or cold.

The cheese is optional; Lorrainers omit it.

(Illustration, p. 589)   France

Smoked sturgeon with caviar

Chop equal parts of smoked sturgeon and hard-boiled egg, mix with butter which has been well creamed and season to taste. Spread on salty cracker biscuits and cover with a thin disk of smoked sturgeon. Glaze with fish aspic and place about a quarter of a teaspoonful of caviar in the centre.

(Illustration, p. 580)   Austria

Snacks for the bar

500 g	chorizo from Estremadura	1 lb
500 g	cooked ham (with fat)	1 lb
500 g	very ripe tomatoes, skinned, seeded and chopped	1 lb
	1 hard-boiled egg	
50 g	flour	2 oz
150 g	breadcrumbs	5 oz
	1 egg (raw)	
	1 clove of garlic, finely chopped	
	salt	
	sugar	

	oil	
$\frac{1}{4}$ l	bouillon	$\frac{1}{2}$ pt
	chopped parsley	

Slice the ham, then cut into small pieces and fry in oil. Remove, pour off the oil and set the ham aside. Pour 5 cl ($\frac{1}{12}$ pt) olive oil into the same pan and fry the garlic in it for a moment. Before it turns brown, add the chopped tomatoes and a good pinch of sugar and season with salt. Cook gently until all the liquid has evaporated and the tomatoes are beginning to fry. Now add the bouillon and the pieces of ham. Cook for 10 minutes, check the seasoning and keep hot. Cut the chorizo into 3–4 mm (about $\frac{1}{8}$ in) slices, remove the skin, dip in flour and beaten egg, then coat with breadcrumbs. Fry in hot oil until golden-brown. Arrange on small plates, allowing 2 or more slices for each one; cover with a little of the tomato and ham sauce and sprinkle with chopped hard-boiled egg and chopped parsley. Serve with small cocktail-forks or pierce each slice with a picker.

Spain

Spanish rissoles

10–12 persons

Pastry

500 g	flour	1 lb
1 dl	oil	$\frac{1}{6}$ pt
approx. 2 dl	white wine	$\frac{1}{3}$ pt
10 g	baking powder	$\frac{1}{3}$ oz
5 g	pinch of salt	

Filling

250 g	white fish, skinned and boned	8 oz
200 g	chopped onions	8 oz
200 g	ripe tomatoes, skinned, seeded and chopped	8 oz
	1 large pepper, skinned and seeded	
	1 clove of garlic, chopped	
1 dl	oil	$\frac{1}{6}$ pt
	1 tablespoon chopped parsley	
2 dl	white wine	$\frac{1}{3}$ pt

Sieve the flour on to a table and make a bay. Place the oil, wine, baking powder and salt in the centre and add enough water to make a fine paste of medium firmness which does not stick to the table. Cover and set aside for at least 10 minutes. Heat the oil in a pan and fry the chopped onions and garlic in it until they begin to turn brown, add the tomatoes, continue cooking until the liquid has evaporated, then add the wine and chopped parsley and season with salt and pepper. When the wine is reduced to half its volume, add the fish which has been cut into small pieces and the finely diced pepper. Cook until all the wine has boiled away, then allow to cool.

Pin out the paste to a rectangle and give it two single turns. Allow to rest for 10 minutes, then pin out to a thickness of 3 mm ($\frac{1}{10}$ in). Cut out with a round cutter of any size desired and press lightly with the rolling-pin to shape into ovals. Place a heaped teaspoonful of the filling in the centre of each oval and brush the edge lightly with water. Fold over to make a half-moon shape, press the edges together and mark with a fork to seal well and decorate. Fry in oil over moderate heat or arrange on baking-sheets, egg wash and bake. Serve hot or cold.

The rissoles may be filled with egg, meat, vegetables or a salpicon or, if they are to be served as pastries, with jam, custard, etc. Scrap puff paste is used to make those which are baked in the oven.

Spain

Spiced water-melon rind

Cooking time: 1–1$\frac{1}{2}$ hours

1 kg	water-melon pieces	2$\frac{1}{4}$ lb
$\frac{1}{8}$ l	wine vinegar	$\frac{1}{4}$ pt
$\frac{1}{8}$ l	maple syrup	$\frac{1}{4}$ pt
	2 tablespoons honey	
$\frac{3}{4}$ l	water	1$\frac{1}{4}$ pt
200 g	sugar	7 oz
	6 cloves	
	1 small piece cinnamon quill	
	zest of 1 lemon	

Cut the melon open, scoop out the flesh and use for fruit salad. Cut the rind, with any red flesh left on it, into pieces about 3 cm (1 in) square, or alternatively into thick strips. Bring the water, sugar, vinegar and remaining ingredients to the boil, skim, add the melon rind and boil for 30 minutes. Remove the pieces of rind with a ladle and reduce the liquid to half its volume. Return the rind to the pan and cook until soft. The process may be repeated to obtain a thicker syrup. Remove the melon rind, strain the syrup over and leave until cold. Seal up in cellophane wrapping and store in a cool place.

Spiced water-melon rind is served as an appetizer or as an accompaniment to hot or cold chicken dishes.

USA

Stuffed tomato

Select fairly small even-sized tomatoes, skin them, cut in half and scoop out the centre. Mix together boiled rice, picked shrimps and chopped mango chutney. Fill the half tomatoes with this mixture and invert on to cracker biscuits so that the cut side is underneath. Decorate with a small disk of egg white and glaze with aspic jelly.

(Illustration, p. 580)   Austria

Surprise golden eggs

Mould butter to the shape of a pigeon's egg. Leave in the coldest part of the refrigerator for at least an hour. When quite firm, coat three times to prepare for frying, as follows. Roll lightly in flour, dip into beaten egg, drain and roll in fresh breadcrumbs if possible, otherwise in oven-dried breadcrumbs. Repeat twice, omitting the flour coating. Place the coated butter 'eggs' in a wire basket and immerse in a pan of very hot fat. As soon as the breadcrumbs have changed colour (this will take about 1 minute) drain carefully on a cloth. Cut off one end of each egg very carefully and set aside. Drain off the butter, which may be used again. This leaves the breadcrumb 'eggs' ready for filling. Leave until cold, pipe in a suitable filling and replace the end which was cut off. Arrange on small round or square canapés which have been hollowed out a little to make the eggs stand securely. Alternatively, pile the eggs up in a pyramid in a nest of potato straws or wafer chips, or on a napkin.

If the eggs are to be served cold, they may be filled with any cold fish, meat or vegetable mousse. If they are to be served hot, the filling consists of a vegetable or chicken purée. These are also known as cassolettes.

France

Tit-bits Périgord style

Proceed as for cheese tit-bits, but replace the cheese sauce by diced truffles which have been marinated under cover for 2 hours, seasoned with salt and pepper, in old Cognac. Use one cube of truffle for each tit-bit.

France

Trianon custard flan

Baking time: 10–12 minutes

500 g	short paste for lining tarts or scrap of puff paste	1 lb 2 oz

100 g	skinned and seeded tomatoes coarsely chopped	4 oz
100 g	diced mushrooms cooked in butter	4 oz
	4 eggs	
	2 egg yolks	
100 g	finely diced Gruyère cheese	4 oz
4 dl	dairy cream or milk	⅔ pt

Line tartlet tins about 4 cm (1½ in) in diameter with the pastry and bake blind. Cover the bottom of each with equal amounts of tomatoes, mushrooms and cheese. Beat the eggs and egg yolks together, mix with the cream or milk, season with salt and pepper, add a pinch of grated nutmeg, pour through a conical strainer to fill the tartlets, then bake in a moderate oven.

France

Truffled foie gras medallion in Madeira jelly

Cut truffled foie gras into rounds barely 1 cm (½ in) thick and place on cracker biscuits. Cover with a round of Madeira jelly of the same size.

(Illustration, p. 580)   Austria

Veal medallions with mushrooms

Cut thin medallions of fillet of veal, season, fry quickly in butter, keeping the meat pink, and allow to cool. When cold, trim evenly and brush with meat glaze. Mix thinly sliced sauté mushrooms with a little aspic mayonnaise lightened with a little whipped cream and spread on the veal medallions. Place each medallion on a cracker biscuit, cover with a mushroom cap, top with a tiny disk of truffle and glaze with aspic jelly.

(Illustration, p. 580)   Austria

HORS D'OEUVRE

The term 'hors d'oeuvre' means literally 'outside the work' and dates from the time when these items were fairly simple and were served in an ante room before guests went in to dinner. They were the responsibility of the dining-room staff, not the kitchen staff and hence, to the chefs they were outside the work.

Nowadays, of course, the first course of a dinner is taken in the dining-room and hors d'oeuvre are prepared by the kitchen staff. Only such 'nibbles' as olives, crisps and nuts are offered with pre meal drinks and these are set out by the bar staff or the waiters. Thus the wheel has turned full circle, but the term 'hors d'oeuvre' has acquired a new meaning since the nibbles offered with pre meal drinks are indeed 'outside the work' of the kitchen but are no longer called hors d'oeuvre!

First courses are now often called 'starters' which is a useful term since it includes soups, hors d'oeuvre, fruit juices and, in fact, any item taken as a first course.

There are three main types or categories of hors d'oeuvre: mixed hors d'oeuvre, single items, and made-up dishes.

Mixed hors d'oeuvre are what most people understand by the term hors d'oeuvre, that is, a variety of different items eaten as a first course. In most good restaurants, a wide selection of items is offered to a diner, usually from a specially designed hors d'oeuvre trolley, but a smaller selection is often used for a dinner party or function. Any restricted selection of mixed hors d'oeuvre should include contrasts of colour, flavour and texture and normally includes:

Something fishy —sardines, prawns, etc.

Something meaty—salami, pâté, etc.

Something spicy —pickled cucumber, vegetables à la Grecque, etc.

Something bland —egg mayonnaise, potato salad, etc.

Something crisp —celery, radishes, etc.

Something raw —cole-slaw, olives, etc.

337

A suitable 'mini-selection' for a dinner party could be: tomato salad, olives, radishes, potato salad, pickled herrings, anchovies, pâté and sliced raw ham.

Single items used for hors d'oeuvre include fruits such as avocado pear, melon and grapefruit, various types of pâté and smoked meats, smoked fish such as smoked salmon and smoked trout and such luxuries as oysters and caviar.

There is almost no limit to the range of made-up dishes which can be served as a first course, and some are included in this section. However, small portions of many fish, pasta and egg dishes are frequently served and suitable recipes are to be found in the appropriate sections. The section on Finger Food also contains both ideas and recipes which could be used for hors d'oeuvre dishes.

Artichoke bottoms with vinaigrette dressing

Make a thick vinaigrette dressing with 1 part vinegar to 2 parts oil, very finely chopped onions, chopped parsley, chervil, tarragon and chives. Season with salt and pepper. Fill into the artichoke bottoms and garnish with small pieces of skinned tomato.

Austria

Avocado pears vinaigrette

Split the pear in half lengthwise and remove the stone. Fill the centre of the pear with vinaigrette dressing as above, seasoning with salt and pepper.

Avocado pears with prawns

> 3 ripe avocados
> 3 tablespoons shelled prawns
> 3 tablespoons french dressing
> 3 tablespoons red tomato sauce
> 1 teaspoon Tabasco sauce

Split the avocados in half lengthwise and remove the stones. Combine the french dressing with the tomato sauce and Tabasco sauce. Bind the prawns with the sauce and fill each avocado half with the mixture.

Banderillas

Practically any cold food may be used for banderillas and served as an hors d'oeuvre.

1. A 3 cm (1¼ in) square of potato omelette, an olive stuffed with sweet pepper and a thick skinned slice of chorizo (garlic sausage) threaded on a toothpick.

2. An anchovy fillet wrapped round a stuffed olive, a peeled prawn and a small piece of hard-boiled egg threaded on a toothpick.

3. A square of Mortadella or foie gras pâté, a square of cheese and a square of cooked Bayonne ham threaded on a toothpick.

Spain

Caviar

Caviar must be served very cold and the jar or glass dish must be surrounded by crushed ice. Approximate portions about 15 g (½ oz). Thinly sliced brown bread and butter or toast are served with the caviar. Lemon, hard-boiled egg and finely chopped onions are also served.

Cauliflower à la grecque

Cut a medium sized cauliflower into florets. Blanch in boiling salted water for about 10 minutes. Drain off the water and add to the cooking liquor made with 15 cl (¼ pt) white wine, 50 cl (2 fl oz) olive oil, 1 sprig parsley, 15 cl (¼ pt) water, juice of 1 lemon, 1 small bay leaf, 6 peppercorns, 1 teaspoon salt, bringing these ingredients to the boil before adding the cauliflower. Cook 10–15 minutes and cool in the liquor. Other vegetables, artichokes, celery, mushrooms, fennel can be cooked in same way.

Chicken breasts with egg salad

Cut the breast of a plump cold roast chicken into thin even slices and arrange on the following salad. Cut hard-boiled eggs and pickled cucumbers into thin julienne strips and bind with curry mayonnaise. Glaze the slices of chicken lightly with chicken aspic.

Austria

Egg mayonnaise

	4 egg yolks	
½ l	olive oil	1 pt
	salt and pepper	
	1 small tablespoon vinegar	
	1 teaspoon English mustard	
	12 hard-boiled eggs	

Whisk the egg yolks in a bowl with salt, pepper, mustard and half the vinegar. Add the oil drop by drop, then in a thin stream as the sauce begins to bind, stirring vigorously. Add a few drops of vinegar from time to time together with the oil. Then add remainder of the vinegar continuing to stir until all the oil has been added and the sauce is thick and smooth. Lemon juice may be used instead of vinegar. Halve the hard-boiled eggs and serve on a dish. Coat with the mayonnaise.

Fried cocks' combs with chicory salad

6 persons   Frying time: 10 minutes

18 fresh cocks' combs

Savoury paste

	flour	
	chicken dripping	
300 g	onions, finely chopped	10 oz
30 g	tomato purée	1 oz
50 g	chicken dripping	2 oz
15 g	anchovy paste	½ oz
50 g	mushrooms, finely grated	2 oz
	1 tablespoon chopped parsley	
	good pinch of basil	
	pinch of chili powder	
900 g	chicory	2 lb
	chopped parsley	
	chopped dill	
	mayonnaise	
	flour	
	chicken dripping	

Fry the onions lightly in the chicken dripping, add the mushrooms, cook without colouring until soft, stir in the chopped parsley, tomato purée, anchovy paste, basil and chili powder and reduce to a thick paste. Rub through a sieve, boil down again to 250 g (about 8 oz) and allow to cool.

Soak, blanch and skin the cocks' combs, cut a pouch 1–1½ cm (about ½ in) deep, fill the cavity with savoury paste and level off. Season the cocks' combs, coat with flour and fry until brown in chicken dripping. Dress the chicory salad with salt, pepper, a light mayonnaise, chopped parsley and dill and dish the hot cocks' combs on the cold salad. It should be noted that the French for chicory is 'endive' and the French for endive is 'chicoree'.

(Illustration, p. 591)   Germany

Fillet steak with foie gras

For each portion, cut a tiny round slice of fillet steak weighing 50 g (1¾ oz), fry until pink and juicy in the middle and allow to cool. Cover with a round slice of foie gras pâté or parfait and glaze with Madeira-flavoured aspic.

Austria

Fried turtle eggs

12 persons   Cooking time: 10 minutes

	24 turtle eggs	
500 g	Chinese cabbage	1 lb
75 g	kemiri nut butter*	3 oz
	sesame oil	

When heated, the whites of turtle eggs do not remain firm like those of hens' eggs, but become unpleasantly glassy. To remedy this drawback, prepare the eggs as follows: mix equal parts of loess, chaff, potash and water to a semi-liquid paste and warm to 36°C. Place the eggs in this paste and store at this temperature for 8 days. After removing from the paste, wash well, cut open with scissors, fry in a small pan brushed with kemiri butter and allow to cool.

Cut the Chinese cabbage into strips and dress with vinegar, sesame oil, salt and pepper. Arrange the cold turtle eggs on the salad.

(Illustration, p. 364)   Germany

* Kemiri: an Indonesian nut resembling the chestnut, with a flavour somewhere between a walnut and an almond.

Grapefruit

Cut the grapefruit in half, and cut in between the sections. Cut round the outside, slipping the knife under the central core and removing any pips. Take the core between finger and thumb, lift out gently when the side membranes will come with it. Lightly dust the grapefruit with caster sugar.

Grilled grapefruit

Prepare the grapefruit as above. Add a tablespoon of dry sherry to each half. Dust liberally with caster sugar and set under a pre-heated grill. Leave until the sugar has caramelized slightly. Remove and serve.

Pâté de Campagne

500 g	minced pork	1 lb
500 g	minced veal	1 lb
250 g	minced ham or bacon	½ lb
200 g	minced pork fat	6 oz
250 g	pig's liver	½ lb
	2 cloves garlic	
	salt	
	pepper	
	allspice	
	1 glass brandy	
	slices of fat	
	unsmoked bacon	
	bay leaf	
	clarified butter	

Combine the minced meats and fat. Remove all skin and ducts from liver and chop very finely. Season with freshly ground black pepper and allspice. Crush the garlic with salt and add with the brandy. Line a terrine with the fat bacon. Press in the mixture, place a bay leaf on top and then the lid. Seal down with a flour and water paste and cook in a bain-marie for about 1½ hours in a moderate oven. Press lightly until cold. Cover with a layer of clarified butter.

Peanuts with coconut

4 spoonsful shelled, skinned
    peanuts
2 tablespoons grated coconut
salt
sugar
grated lemon zest
good pinch of red pepper

Mix all the ingredients together and brown in a small oiled pan.

Indonesia

Grapefruit cocktail

4 portions

	2 large sweet grapefruit	
100 g	sugar	4 oz
	4 maraschino cherries	
	1 tablespoon kirsch	

Frost the rims of 4 goblets by dipping into egg white and then caster sugar. Peel the grapefruit and divide into segments, free of membrane. Mix with the sugar and kirsch and place in the goblets. Top with a cherry just before serving.

Game purée mock eggs

	4 slices brown bread	
	4 thin rashers bacon	
200 g	game purée	8 oz
	sliced truffle	
¼ l	aspic	½ pt

Mask 4 small egg moulds with aspic and garnish with a truffle motif. Fill with game purée and refrigerate until firm. Cut each slice of bread to make a base, cover with strips of bacon and turn out a mock egg on each one.

Austria

Kipper pâté

4 portions

	3 fat kippers approx.	
	200 g (8 oz) each	
300 g	unsalted butter	12 oz
	nutmeg	
	cayenne pepper	
	lemon juice	

Pour boiling water over the kippers, and leave to stand for 10 minutes. Melt the butter gently until just liquid. Skin and bone the kippers and blend in a liquidizer with the butter. Season to taste (do not omit a little nutmeg) pack into a terrine and chill thoroughly.

Great Britain

Marinated salmon Norwegian style

5–6 kg	1 side fresh salmon weighing	11–13 lb
250 g	sugar	8 oz
200 g	fine salt	7 oz
200 g	crushed white peppercorns	7 oz
2 dl	oil	⅓ pt
2 dl	brandy	⅓ pt
	juice of 2 lemons	
1 kg	fresh dill	2¼ lb

Clean the salmon, remove all the bones, but do not skin, and place on a rustproof metal tray with a rim. First cover with the peppercorns, lemon juice, oil and brandy, then sprinkle with about 750 g (1 lb 10 oz) coarsely chopped dill mixed with the sugar and salt. Cover with a cloth and marinate for 4–5 days, turning every 12 hours. Remove, wipe dry, cut in thin slices and serve as a first course.

If used as a main course, serve with the following accompaniments: dill potatoes— boil diced potatoes, keeping them fairly firm, drain off the water, bind with thin Béchamel sauce and mix with a generous amount of chopped dill; dill sauce— mix 6 egg yolks with 1 teaspoon powdered English mustard and 1 teaspoon sweet mustard, then stir in as much oil as the egg yolks will absorb (about 1 litre—1¾ pints). Add a pinch of sugar and salt and pepper to taste, and stir in a generous amount of finely chopped dill.

Norway

Melon

Slice the melon. Chill well. Remove seeds. Dress on crushed ice sprinkled with caster sugar. It can be served soaked in fortified wine.

Melon cocktail

4 portions

600 g	melon balls	1¼ lb
	mint leaves	

Cut the melon balls from both a green fleshed and a pink fleshed melon, using a Parisian cutter. (Alternatively, frozen ready-cut melon balls can be used.) Frost the rims of 4 glasses by dipping first into egg white then into caster sugar and fill with melon balls. Place a sprig of fresh mint on top. (The cocktail can be enhanced by a sprinkling of Crème de Menthe.)

Great Britain

Melon Lady Drummond-Hay

10 persons

	5 ripe first-size cantaloup or Charentais melons	
700 g	red-currant jelly	1 lb 8 oz
5 cl	port	$\frac{1}{12}$ pt
4 cl	kirsch	4 dessertspoons
	2 pieces preserved ginger	

Cut the melons in half horizontally and remove the seeds.

Sieve the red-currant jelly, mix to a thick sauce with the port and kirsch and stir in the ginger which has been cut in small thin julienne strips. Serve the melon well chilled on crushed ice, with the hollow in the centre half-full of ginger sauce.

Germany

Melon Victoria

4 portions

600 g	melon balls	1¼ lb
3 dl	whipped cream (unsweetened)	½ pt
	½ teaspoon powdered ginger	
	1 piece crystallized ginger	

Fold the powdered ginger into the cream. Stir in the melon balls and place in goblets. Sprinkle with crystallized ginger chopped very finely.

Great Britain

Pickled tongue pouches

Yield: 6

120 g	pickled ox tongue	4 oz
	1 large hard-boiled egg	
10 g	red peppers, skinned	½ oz
10 g	green peppers, skinned	½ oz
20 g	mayonnaise	1 oz
	6 small new carrots	
	3 gherkins	
	chopped dill	
	mustard	
	Madeira jelly	

Cut 6 even slices out of the middle of the tongue and trim neatly. Prepare a fine salpicon with the hard-boiled egg and the peppers, mix with the mayonnaise, season with mustard and stir in a little chopped dill. Place a teaspoonful of the salpicon on one half of each slice of tongue and fold the other half over the filling. Decorate each slice with finely sliced new carrots and gherkins which have been dipped in Madeira jelly, and coat with jelly. Chill well before use.

Germany

Potted shrimps

12 dl	fresh shrimps	1 quart
120 g	fresh butter	¼ lb
	cayenne	
	pounded mace	
	little salt	

Boil and shell the shrimps. Pound to a paste in a mortar with the butter and seasoning. Rub through a fine sieve, press into small pots, cover with clarified butter. When cold tie down closely.

Great Britain

Pâté Maison

300 g	chicken liver	8 oz
120 g	butter	4 oz
	1 medium onion	
	1 small bouquet garni	
	1 clove garlic	
	1 tablespoon brandy	
	seasoning	

Chop the onion and garlic finely and soften in 1 oz of the butter until just turning colour. Add the liver, herbs and seasoning and fry together for about 3 minutes. Cool, then chop very finely. Pass through a fine sieve and work in the remaining butter well creamed. Add the brandy. Put in a china pot. Smooth the top and cover with a layer of clarified butter.

Rissoles Murcia style

Pastry

500 g	flour	1 lb
1 dl	oil	¼ pt
	1 glass white wine	
10 g	baking powder	⅓ oz
	pinch of salt	

Filling

250 g	skinned fish fillets (e.g. whiting, angler, bass, sea bream, etc.), boiled, grilled or marinated and trimmed	8 oz
200 g	onions	8 oz
200 g	ripe tomatoes *or* a small quantity of tomato purée	8 oz
	1 large red pepper (fresh or canned)	
	1 clove of garlic	
1 dl	oil	⅛ pt
	1 glass white wine	
	parsley	
	freshly ground pepper	
	salt	
	oil for frying	

Sieve 400 g (14 oz) flour on to the table and make a bay. Pour the oil and wine in the centre, add the baking powder, the salt and sufficient water to make a fairly firm paste. Work until all the ingredients are well blended and the paste does not stick to the table or the hands. Cover with a cloth and leave to rest for 15 minutes.

To make the filling, heat the oil in a frying pan, add the finely chopped onion and the garlic and fry until lightly coloured. Add the tomatoes which have been scalded, skinned, seeded and coarsely chopped and continue frying. Pour in the wine, add the chopped parsley and a little salt and pepper. When the wine is reduced to half its volume, stir in the flaked fish and the red pepper which has been grilled, skinned, seeded and finely cut. Brown lightly until almost dry, then fry well.

Pin out the pastry into an oblong and give two turns as for puff pastry, lightly flouring the table. Allow to recover for 10 minutes and pin out again to a thickness of 8 mm (⅛ in). Cut into rounds with a plain cutter of the desired size. Extend them to an oval shape. Place a good spoonful of filling near the centre of each, moisten the edges with a little water and fold over to a half-moon shape. Using a fork, score the edges lightly to decorate and to seal well. Fry in moderately hot oil or arrange on a baking-sheet, egg wash and bake in a medium oven. Serve hot or cold.

The rissoles may be made with scrap puff pastry. Meat rissoles are prepared in the same way.

Spain

Salmon medallions with dill mayonnaise

Poach some slices of fresh salmon, keeping them very juicy, and cut into rounds when cold. Mix a generous amount of chopped dill with thick mayonnaise and fold in a little whipped unsweetened cream. Mask the salmon medallions with the mayonnaise, place a thin round of smoked salmon on each one, decorate with dill leaves and glaze with fish aspic. Cover cracker biscuits with a paper-thin slice of fresh cucumber and place a salmon medallion on each.

(Illustration, p. 579)   Austria

Smoked eel

600 g	smoked eel	24 oz
	1 lemon	
	lettuce leaves	

Skin and fillet the eel. Cut into slices of about 6 cm (2 in) in length. Dress them on lettuce leaves with a fan of gherkins. Serve quarters of lemon, toast and butter.

Smoked trout

Loosen the skin and remove the lateral and dorsal bones. Re-form the skin. Serve on lettuce leaves accompanied by hard-boiled egg and a fan of gherkin decorated with small slices of lemon. Serve horseradish cream separately and thin slices of brown bread and butter.

Smoked salmon

For 6 servings

18–24 very thin slices
of smoked salmon
6 quarters of lemon
leaf parsley

Garnish the salmon with quarters of lemon and leaf parsley. Serve separately toast and butter. Freshly milled black pepper and horseradish cream can be served.

Seafood cocktail

150 g	shelled shrimp tails	5¼ oz
150 g	cooked lobster meat	5¼ oz
150 g	crab meat	5¼ oz
	12 large raw mushrooms	
	1 lettuce	
	6 round slices lemon	
25 g	caviar	1 oz
	1 small clove garlic	
	olive oil	
	vinegar	

Place in each cocktail glass a small spoonful of julienne of lettuce. Arrange on top a salpicon of lobster, crab, minced mushrooms and shrimp tails. Sprinkle with a marinade of oil, vinegar, salt, pepper and crushed garlic. Garnish with a round slice of lemon and place a little caviar in the middle. Serve separately croûtons browned in butter.

Snails Burgundy style

	48 prepared snails	
250 g	butter	8 oz
25 g	garlic	1 oz
6 g	chopped parsley	¼ oz
	2 small chopped shallots	
	pinch of pepper	
	pinch of salt	

Mix the slightly creamed butter very thoroughly with the very finely grated garlic, the finely chopped shallot, the parsley, salt and pepper. Put the prepared snails in the cleaved shells, close the opening with the prepared butter and put in refrigerator for butter to harden. Serve the snails on snail plates, or on a baking-sheet covered with salt, with opening upwards. Bake in a hot oven, until the butter in the shells starts to melt. Serve at once.

Snail fritters

6 persons

144 Spanish (very small) snails
or 72 French (Burgundy) or
other large edible snails
6 chopped shallots

	1 clove of garlic, chopped	
	1 egg yolk	
	3 egg whites	
150 g	flour	5 oz
1 dl	sherry	3 fl oz
	1 tablespoon chopped parsley	
	allspice	
	oil	

First clean and cook the snails, take them from the shells and remove the intestine. Fry lightly in a little hot oil with the garlic and shallots, sprinkle with salt and a little allspice, toss in chopped parsley and leave in a cool place. Sieve the flour, make a bay, pour in 4 tablespoons oil, the egg yolk, the sherry and salt, together with a little water if required, and mix to a fairly thick batter with the hand. Fold in the stiffly whipped egg whites and add the snails without working the batter too much. Take 3 or 4 Spanish snails (or 1 or 2 French ones) at a time in a thin coating of batter and deep fry in hot oil until crisp and golden. Dish on small plates, allowing 3–4 fritters (depending on size) per person.

Spain

Snail mould Sir Sigbert

350 g	snail flesh	12¼ oz
¾ l	Schilcher (rosé) wine	1¼ pt
	2 bay leaves	
	5 juniper berries	
	5 peppercorns	
	1 small teaspoon coriander seeds	
	1 tablespoon onion rings	
	pinch of marjoram	
	pinch of grated nutmeg	
	8 sheets gelatine	
	20 pistachio nuts	
¼ l	whipped dairy cream	½ pt

Clean the snail flesh thoroughly and marinate under cover for 5 days in ½ litre (⅞ pint) Schilcher together with the juniper berries, bay leaves, peppercorns, coriander seeds, onion rings, nutmeg and marjoram. Do not cook the marinade beforehand. After 5 days, cook the snails in the marinade until tender, adding wine to make up for evaporation so that there is still ¼ litre (½ pint) liquid left at the end of the cooking time. Set aside 250 g (8¾ oz) of the best snails. Mince the remainder three times, as finely as possible, then rub through a hair sieve. Strain the cooking liquid and dissolve 4 sheets gelatine in it. Beat the sieved snail flesh with a wire whisk and mix to a smooth, thick paste with the cooking liquid. Allow to cool until almost setting, then season with salt, pepper and crushed coriander seeds.

Chop half the reserved snails with the pistachio nuts, stir into the snail paste and fold in the whipped cream. Mask a wetted mould with Schilcher wine jelly and decorate with sliced truffles or as desired. Cover with half the snail mixture, arrange the remaining snails on it in a row running right across the mould and top with the rest of the snail mixture. Chill well before use.

Serve with a small teaspoon chopped Schilcher wine jelly per portion, little balls of butter, toast and preserved flap mushrooms (boletus).

To make the wine jelly, soak 4 sheets gelatine in water and squeeze dry, heat $\frac{1}{4}$ litre ($\frac{1}{2}$ pint) Schilcher, stir in the gelatine and add a pinch of salt and a little sugar. If the jelly is required for garnishing and not only for lining the mould, the quantities given should be doubled.

(Illustration, p. 694)   Austria

Small rice timbales

15 timbales

350 g	Vialone rice	12 oz
100 g	butter	4 oz
1 l	light meat broth	1$\frac{3}{4}$ pt
	1 small onion	
100 g	grated Parmesan cheese	4 oz
	1 egg, beaten	
250 g	minced veal	8 oz
100 g	cooked ham, finely diced	4 oz
	3 tablespoons tomato sauce	
50 g	small peas (canned)	2 oz
5 cl	white wine	3 fl oz
	breadcrumbs	

Prepare a risotto with the chopped onion, 50 g (2 oz) butter, the rice and the broth, keeping the grains of rice firm, allow to cool a little and stir in the Parmesan and the egg. Heat the rest of the butter in a pan until foamy, add the veal and the white wine and cook until all the wine has boiled away. Add the diced ham, the tomato sauce and the peas, mix well and season; the mixture should be well-flavoured and of the same consistency as a thick stew. Butter small timbale moulds, sprinkle with breadcrumbs and shake off the excess. Line the moulds with risotto, using a table-spoon and pressing it against the sides with the hand, fill the centre with the veal mixture and cover with risotto. Bake in the oven at 175°C until the top is crusted over. Run a small knife round the edge of each mould to loosen, turn out on to a hot dish and serve at once.

                                                                              Italy

Snails Madrid style

Cooking time: about 1¼ hours

2 kg	cooked and drained snails	4½ lb
1 dl	oil	3 fl oz
200 g	raw ham or ham scraps	8 oz
2 dl	dry white wine	7 fl oz
	2 large cloves of garlic	
	1 large red pepper, skinned and seeded	

Tomato sauce

1 kg	ripe tomatoes	2¼ lb
100 g	bacon rind or ham trimmings	4 oz
50 g	onions	2 oz
	1 large clove of garlic	
	1 small teaspoon allspice	
1 dl	olive oil	3 fl oz
	1 medium carrot	
	1 bay leaf	
	1 sprig thyme	
	1 stalk celery	
50 g	flour	2 oz
	2 small lumps sugar	
1¼ l	bouillon	2¼ pt

Fry 2 large cloves of garlic in 1 dl (3 fl oz) oil until they begin to turn brown, then remove and discard. Fry the diced ham and red pepper in the oil until the ham begins to change colour, then stir in the white wine and add the snails. Cover the pan and cook until the wine has boiled away, shaking the pan from time to time, then pour in the hot tomato sauce and simmer for 1 hour. If the sauce is too thick, add a little bouillon. Adjust the seasoning, making sure the sauce is well-flavoured. Serve very hot, preferably in individual ramekin dishes.

To make the tomato sauce, lightly fry the bacon rind, onions, carrots and garlic, which have been finely cut, in the oil. When they begin to turn brown, add the thyme and bay leaf, sprinkle with the flour and cook until lightly coloured. Add the cut-up tomatoes, the finely cut stalk of celery, the allspice and a little pepper and cook gently for a short time. Pour in about 1¼ litres (2¼ pints) bouillon and simmer gently, adding salt and sugar, until the sauce is reduced to half its volume. Strain through a conical strainer, check the flavour, bring to the boil again and pour over the snails.

Spain

Stuffed grapefruit Skagerak style

6 persons

	3 medium-sized grapefruit	
150 g	peeled shrimps	6 oz
120 g	crab meat	4 oz
	6 lobster medallions	
	24 mussels, poached and trimmed	
	2 tablespoons tomato ketchup	
200 g	mayonnaise	7 oz
	2 tablespoons sherry	
	2 tablespoons white wine	
	half an orange	
	1 lemon	
	1 round lettuce	
	dill	

Cut the grapefruit in half lengthwise, remove the outer skin intact from each half, then remove the inner skin and cut round the sections of pulp to loosen from the pith. Set aside 6 of the best lettuce heart leaves, cut the remainder in julienne strips and place inside the half grapefruit shells. Cover with the sections of grapefruit pulp and fill up with the shrimps, mussels, and flaked crab meat. Mask with cocktail sauce and decorate with a lettuce heart leaf, a lobster medallion, half a slice of lemon and dill

To make the cocktail sauce, mix the mayonnaise with the tomato ketchup, orange juice, sherry, white wine, lemon juice and a few drops of Tabasco sauce, adding salt and pepper as required. The sauce should be of coating consistency.

(Illustration, p. 699)   Norway

Swallows' nests Madagascan style

12 persons   Cooking time: about 1½ hours

	9 fresh birds' nests	
500 cc	green corn mash*	1 pt
3 dl	santan†	½ pt

* Corn mash. Remove the outside leaves from 5 to 6 green unripe corn cobs which are still tightly closed and cut the cobs into pieces the width of a finger. Crush in a mortar or mince coarsely. Mix with 1 tablespoon sugar and 1 coffeespoon wheat flour and pour on 1 litre (1¾ pints) warm water and ¼ litre (½ pint) white wine. Transfer to a wooden container and stand in a warm kitchen for eight days, then filter.

† Santan (coconut cream). Open a fresh coconut and collect the milk. Remove the brown skin, scrape off about 1 cupful of the flesh very finely and grate the rest. Add boiling water to the coconut milk to make it up to ¾ litre (1¼ pints) and pour over the grated coconut flesh. Leave to steep at 80°C for half an hour. Pass through a fine sieve, stand aside for 1 hour to settle, then carefully skim off the top layer with a spoon. Mix this with a very small amount of the thin liquid and the cupful of scraped coconut flesh.

| 100 g | roasted coconut chips | 4 oz |
| | 1 fresh pig's caul | |

Clean the nests carefully, removing all feathers, and smoke for 3 days in a mixture of sandalwood, crushed pepper, cloves and cardamom, making sure that they keep their colour. Line the bottom of a pan with the pig's caul, arrange the nests on top, cover and steam well. When cooked, transfer eight of the nests at once to a glass bowl of suitable depth and refrigerate.

Sieve 300 cc (12½ fl oz) of the remaining corn mash under pressure, mix with the santan and season with salt. When on the point of setting pour over the eight nests. Place the ninth nest in the centre and decorate the edge of the bowl with a border of roasted coconut chips.

Smoked cod's roe pâté

4 portions

200 g	smoked cod's roe	½ lb
100 g	white bread	¼ lb
	1 clove garlic	
3 dl	olive oil	½ pt
	1 lemon	

Soak the roe for an hour, and remove the skin. Soak the bread in a little water; finely crush the garlic and blend these, the oil and the juice of the lemon into a smooth purée. Serve chilled.

Middle East

Terrine Maison

	6 rashers streaky bacon	
250 g	pig's liver	½ lb
	1 small onion	
	1 clove of garlic	
250 g	sausage meat	½ lb
250 g	minced fat pork	½ lb
	2 chopped hard-boiled eggs	
	1 teaspoon chopped herbs	
250 g	veal or game	½ lb
	seasoning	
	1 bay leaf	

Line the sides and bottom of a small earthenware terrine with bacon. Mince the liver with the onion and garlic and add to the sausage meat and minced pork.

Season well. Add chopped eggs and herbs, and put a layer of the mixture on the bottom of the terrine.

Cut the veal or game into five strips. Arrange in layers with the rest of the mixture until the terrine is full and the top layer is the mixture. Place the bay leaf on top. Put the lid on and seal round the edge with a paste of flour and water. Stand in a bain-marie or a roasting tin full of water and cook in a moderate oven for 1 to $1\frac{1}{2}$ hours. Take out, remove the lid and put a weight of about 2 lb on top. Leave until next day. Then fill up the sides of the terrine with good jellied stock. Leave until quite set and then turn out.

Terrine of eels with herbs

1 kg	small eels	$2\frac{1}{4}$ lb
	$\frac{1}{2}$ bottle lylit beer or white wine	

	1 large handful chiffonade
	    of fresh sorrel, parsley,
	    chives, burnet, sage,
	    tarragon and chervil	

65 g	butter	2 oz
	juice of 1 lemon	
	15 coffeespoons potato flour	

Skin the eels, cut in 5 cm (2 in) pieces and stiffen in butter. Add the herbs. Cook them for a minute and add just enough beer or wine to cover everything. Season with salt, pepper, bay leaf and thyme and cook slowly until done. Make a thickening of 3 egg yolks mixed with lemon juice, potato flour and a little water. Use to thicken the stock boiling up once only. Pour into a terrine at once.

Foie gras terrine

10–12 persons   Cooking time: 35–40 minutes

700 g	1 foie gras weighing	1 lb 8 oz
300 g	fine forcemeat	10 oz
5 cl	Cognac	$\frac{1}{12}$ pt
50 g	truffles	2 oz
	thin strips of pork	
	back fat	
	salt	
	pepper	
	spices	

Clean and trim the liver, removing all fibres. Stud with pieces of truffle, season with salt, pepper and a dash of cayenne pepper, place in a dish, pour the Cognac over and marinate under cover for at least 2 hours. Mix the sieved liver trimmings with the forcemeat, season well and add the Cognac used to marinate the liver. Line a terrine with thin strips of pork back fat and cover the bottom with a thin layer of forcemeat. Place the foie gras on top, making it fit the dish, fill up the spaces with forcemeat and also cover with a layer of forcemeat. Lay a piece of pork fat on top, add half a bay leaf and cover with the lid. Seal with flour and water paste and cook in a moderate oven in a bain-marie. When cooked, remove the lid and replace by a small board with a 2 kg (4 lb) weight. Allow to cool. Refrigerate for at least 6 hours before cutting.

France

Ural pelmeni

4 persons   Cooking time: 10–15 minutes

Pastry

300 g	flour	10 oz
approx. 1½ dl	water	¼ pt approx.
	1 egg	

Filling

180 g	lean beef	6 oz
180 g	lean pork	6 oz
120 g	mutton	4 oz
60 g	butter	2 oz
2 g	pinch of grated nutmeg	
50 g	onions, finely chopped	
	2–3 tablespoons dairy cream	

Sauce

3–4 cloves of garlic
2 tablespoons butter
3 tablespoons vinegar

Work the flour, egg and water with a pinch of salt to a fairly firm paste (as for noodles), cover and stand aside for 20–30 minutes. Mince the beef, pork and mutton with the butter twice, using the finest cutter, season with salt and pepper and gradually blend in the cream. Lastly stir in the finely chopped onions.

Shape the pastry into a roll and cut into rounds; alternatively, pin out 5–6 mm (¼ in) thick and cut with a plain round cutter. Place a teaspoonful of filling in the centre of each round, moisten the edges lightly, fold over to a half-moon shape and press the edges together firmly. Arrange on a floured baking-sheet until required, then poach or steam for 10–15 minutes and serve with the sauce. To make the sauce, crush the garlic finely, mix with the butter and vinegar and season with salt and pepper.

Russia

SOUPS

The number of soups is countless and the number of variations is limited only by the imagination and skill of the cook. Soups range from delicate consommés, served as a first course at a formal dinner to robust casseroles full of chunky meat and vegetables which are almost meals in themselves.

SOUP GARNISHES

Many clear and some cream soups are garnished with items which are not an integral part of the soup but which are served separately (croûtons, for example) added to the soup just before serving (royales, for example) or cooked in the soup (dumplings, for example).

Austrian dumplings

Cooking time: 40 minutes

500 g	rolls, finely diced	1 lb
	5 eggs	
approx. $\frac{1}{2}$ l	milk	$\frac{7}{8}$ pt
	butter	
	nutmeg	
	salt	
	pepper	

Mix the eggs, milk, salt, pepper and grated nutmeg together and pour over the diced rolls. Stand aside for a time, then roll in a buttered napkin, tie up securely and boil in salted water. To serve, remove the dumpling from the napkin, cut into slices and spread with melted butter.

Austria

Bavarian liver dumplings

100 g	ox liver	4 oz
	half a roll, grated	
	1 egg	
	garlic powder	
	marjoram	
	milk	

Soak the grated half-roll in milk and squeeze dry. Mince the liver, mix well with the soaked crumbs and the egg, and season with salt, freshly ground pepper, garlic powder and a pinch of marjoram. Shape into four large dumplings and cook in salted water. Drain and serve in clear soup.

Germany

Cheese dumplings

$\frac{1}{8}$ l	water	$\frac{1}{4}$ pt
30 g	butter	1 oz
100 g	flour, sieved	4 oz
	2 eggs	
100 g	Emmenthal cheese	4 oz

Place the water in a pan with the butter, a pinch of salt and a little grated nutmeg, and bring to the boil. Pour in the flour all at once and cook like choux paste, i.e. until the paste comes away from the sides of the pan. Transfer to a basin, allow to cool slightly, then beat in the eggs one at a time. Lastly, stir in the diced cheese, shape into small dumplings with a damp teaspoon and fry until brown in hot deep fat.

Germany

Croûtons I

Cut bread into small cubes and quickly fry in hot fat. Serve separately with cream soups.

Croûtons II

Dice some French bread and pour over some of the fat from the bouillon. Toast or brown in the oven. Serve with a pot-au-feu soup.

Dumplings

120 g	flour	4 oz
60 g	suet (shredded)	2 oz
	salt	
	water	

Mix all the ingredients to make an elastic dough, and roll into 12 balls. Poach with the meat for 20 minutes until they swell up and float on the top.

Great Britain

Farfel

	1 egg	
about 150 g	flour	5 oz approx.
	salt	

Beat the egg with a pinch of salt, then work in enough flour to form a very stiff dough. Roll this into small balls and allow to dry, then grate on a course grater, and again allow to dry (shaking occasionally). When required, add to the boiling soup and cook for 10 minutes.

Jewish

Ham dumplings

20 g	butter	1 oz
20 g	flour	1 oz
2 dl	evaporated milk	⅓ pt
30 g	chopped onion	1 oz
100 g	cooked ham	4 oz
	1 tablespoon chopped parsley	

Make a blond roux with the butter and flour, gradually add the milk and boil up to make a thick paste. Lightly brown the finely chopped onion with the diced ham, pour off the fat and add the parsley. Mix all the ingredients together very well and allow to cool. Shape into small dumplings with a damp teaspoon, drop into boiling-hot salted water and poach gently.

Germany

Herb quenelles

Proceed as for quenelles for soup, p. 377, but mix the forcemeat with 2 heaped tablespoons of very finely chopped herbs (parsley, chervil and tarragon).

France

Knaidlach dumplings

	2 eggs	
	4 tablespoons chicken fat	
5 dl	water	2 fl oz
200 g	matzo meal	½ lb

Beat together the eggs, fat, water and salt and add enough matzo meal to make a fairly firm dough. Chill for an hour, then mould into balls and cook for 30 minutes in clear soup.

Israel

Kreplach stuffed soup dumplings

Noodle paste

400 g	flour	1 lb
	2 eggs	
	1 tablespoon iced water	
	½ teaspoon salt	

Filling

200 g	minced beef	8 oz
100 g	diced onion	4 oz
	1 tablespoon chicken fat	
	salt	
	pepper	

Work the eggs, water and salt into the unsifted flour and knead to a smooth dough. Roll out as thinly as possible and cut into 5 cm (2 in) squares.

Fry the meat and onions in the fat for about 10 minutes, then season and allow to cool. Place a little of the filling on to each square of paste, moisten the edge with water, fold into a triangle and seal well.

Poach the kreplach in a clear soup for about 20 minutes.

Israel

Nockerl dumplings

	2 eggs	
5 dl	water	2 fl oz
	1 teaspoon salt	
100 g	flour	4 oz
	½ teaspoon baking powder	

364 ▲ Buffet supper at the Ritz Restaurant, Berlin, pp. 301, 304, 341

▲ 'Brunch' at the Amsterdam Hilton
◄ A Tunisian buffet at the Carthago Restaurant, Amsterdam, pp. 432, 599, 602, 609

▼ Lunch at the Amsterdam Hilton

▲ A Bavarian buffet at the Brasserie Lowenbrau, Munich

370 ▶ A rustic buffet at the Grotto Antico, Bioggio, Switzerland

▼ A fish buffet on a boat in Amsterdam harbour

▲ A buffet during the hunting season at the Hotel Duna Intercontinental, Budapest
◄ Local desserts at the Grotto Antico, Bioggio, pp. 901, 934, 957
▼ A display of Old Berlin specialities, at the Berlin Museum, West Berlin, p. 53

374 ▲ Martinmas dishes at the Czarda Restaurant, Duna Intercontinental Hotel, Budapest, pp. 678–681, 895

Beat together the eggs, water and salt, beat in the dry ingredients. Drop teaspoonfuls of the batter into boiling soup and cook until the nockerl rise to the surface.

Israel

Potato dumplings

	2 eggs	
	1½ teaspoons salt	
25 g	chopped onion	1 oz
50 g	potato flour	2 oz
25 g	matzo meal	1 oz
400 g	potatoes	1 lb

Grate the raw potato finely and drain well. Mix all the ingredients together and mould into balls. Poach in clear soup for 20 minutes.

Israel

Royales

¼ litre	consommé	½ pint
	1 whole egg	
	3 egg yolks	

Beat the cold consommé, egg and yolks together and then strain into a buttered mould. Poach through the oven, standing the mould in a container of water, which must not be allowed to boil, for about ½ hour, or until set. Allow to cool, then cut into diamonds which are added to a clear soup immediately before serving.

France

Soup quenelles

Cooking time: 2–3 minutes

250 g	raw chicken	8 oz
	(white meat only)	
2 dl	dairy cream	⅓ pt
	2 egg whites	

Work the chicken to a very fine purée in the blender (veal may be used instead if no chicken is available). Rub through a fine sieve, then place in a sauté pan, surround with ice and chill well. Stir in the egg whites a little at a time and gradually fold

◀ Christmas table in a private Swedish home, p. 638

13

in the cream. Season with salt, pepper and a very small pinch of nutmeg. If preferred, the egg whites may be added while working the chicken in the blender, but the machine should be switched off from time to time to avoid overheating.

Test the consistency of the forcemeat by dropping a small ball into boiling lightly salted water. If the ball of forcemeat is too soft to hold together, add a little more egg white; if it is too firm, add a little more cream. To make the quenelles, pipe the forcemeat in tiny finger shapes on to a thinly buttered metal tray with a rim, using a savoy bag fitted with a small plain pipe. Pour on some boling lightly salted water and poach very gently. If not required at once, remove with a ladle and store in the refrigerator in cold consommé.

France

Quenelles Verdi

Proceed as for quenelles for soup, but mix the forcemeat with 50–60 g (about 2 oz) very green leaf spinach cooked in butter and rubbed through a fine sieve.

CLEAR SOUPS

Beef soup with milt croûtes

8 persons

2 l	beef bouillon	3½ pt
150 g	grated milt	5 oz
100 g	calf's liver, finely sieved	4 oz
	2 eggs	
30 g	butter or margarine	1 oz
	1 small white loaf (Vienna)	
	breadcrumbs	
	chopped chives	
	fat for frying	

Cream the butter and mix with the eggs, the milt and the liver. Season with salt and pepper, flavour with grated nutmeg and a pinch of rosemary, and add sufficient breadcrumbs to make the mixture hold together. Slice the bread and fry in fat on one side until golden-brown. Spread the milt and liver paste on to the fried side, then fry in fat again on both sides. Sprinkle the soup liberally with chopped chives and either add the croûtes or serve them separately.

Austria

Clear chicken soup

4 persons

	2 chicken legs with the bones	
$\frac{3}{4}$–1 l	water	$1\frac{1}{4}$–$1\frac{3}{4}$ pt
250 g	radish	8 oz
100 g	carrots	4 oz
	3 tablespoons saké or white wine	
	$1\frac{1}{2}$ teaspoons salt	
	1 spring onion (green top only)	
	aji-no-moto (see p. 384)	

Divide the chicken legs into 8 pieces (preferably with a saw, to avoid splintering) and wash thoroughly. Place in a saucepan, pour in the water and bring to the boil. Reduce the heat and remove the scum and fat. Slice the peeled carrots and radish thinly with a vegetable cutter, add to the soup together with the saké, the salt and about half a teaspoon aji-no-moto and simmer until the chicken is cooked and the liquid has been reduced by one-third. Season well and sprinkle with very finely sliced spring onion to serve.

Japan

Clear turtle soup*

Yield: 2 litres ($3\frac{1}{2}$ pints)   Cooking time: $1\frac{1}{2}$–$1\frac{3}{4}$ hours

100 g	dried turtle meat	4 oz
$\frac{1}{2}$ l	white chicken stock	1 pt
2 l	chicken consommé	$3\frac{1}{2}$ pt
	1 packet turtle herbs	
20 g	arrowroot	1 oz
1 dl	dry sherry	4 fl oz

Soak the turtle meat for 24 hours. Drain, place in the stock and cook gently until tender—about $1\frac{1}{2}$ hours. Strain the stock into the consommé and set aside the turtle meat. Meanwhile infuse the turtle herbs in $\frac{1}{2}$ litre ($\frac{7}{8}$ pint) hot chicken consommé for 15 minutes, then strain through a cloth into the rest of the consommé. Thicken very slightly with arrowroot, add the sherry and serve with a garnish of finely diced turtle meat.

Great Britain

* Traditionally served at the Lord Mayor's banquet.

Consommé

Ordinary unclarified consommé is a soup made with the stock from fresh meat and chicken giblets. 'Double' or clarified consommé has a richer flavour due to the process of clarification. The consommés served at buffets or suppers are always clarified; the basic recipe is given below.

Consommé double

8–10 persons   Time required for clarifying: 10–18 minutes

2½ l	ordinary unclarified consommé	4½ pt
300–400 g	lean minced beef	10½–14 oz
	1 leek (green part only)	
	a little chervil	
	2 egg whites	

To clarify the consommé proceed as follows. Mix together the beef, the finely sliced leek, the chervil and the egg whites. Add 1 litre (1¾ pints) cold consommé and beat well until thoroughly blended. Heat the rest of the consommé and add very gradually to prevent the egg white from setting. Bring to the boil over gentle heat, stirring from time to time. As soon as boiling point has been reached, stop stirring and reduce the heat until the consommé is barely simmering, then continue simmering for 10–18 minutes. Adjust the seasoning and carefully strain through a damp cloth. Remove the fat, first with a skimmer, then with a ladle and lastly with tissue paper, changing the paper several times until there is no fat left on the surface. Deepen the colour with a little caramel or with a commercial food colour.
Serve hot or cold in a tureen or in individual cups.

Consommé should always be served very hot or very cold; there is nothing worse than tepid consommé.

France

Chicken consommé

This is clarified consommé made with chicken broth. Two sets of chicken giblets which have been coarsely chopped, lightly browned in the oven and drained of all fat are added when clarifying. The consommé should be very pale in colour. It is served hot or cold.

France

Consommé Belle Aurore

Prepare consommé Madrilène. Just before serving, thicken with a little tapioca and pass through a fine conical strainer.

France

Consommé with cheese straws

This is clarified consommé served with cheese straws.

France

Consommé with devilled cheese straws

This is clarified consommé served with devilled cheese straws.

France

Consommé with herb quenelles (Consommé Prairial)

This is clarified consommé with a garnish of small soup quenelles made with chicken and flavoured with chopped parsley, tarragon and chervil.

France

Consommé Madrilène

Add 500 g (1 lb) very ripe tomatoes when clarifying. Small pieces of skinned tomato cooked in consommé may be placed in the tureen or the individual cups when serving. A few drops of carmine may be added, if desired, to improve the colour.

France

Consommé Monte Carlo

This is clarified consommé served with small disks of plain genoese which are sprinkled with cheese, toasted and handed separately.

France

Consommé Primrose

This is consommé Madrilène with a garnish of pearl barley.

France

Consommé velours

| $2\frac{1}{2}$ l | clarified consommé | $4\frac{1}{2}$ pt |
| | 3 level tablespoons tapioca | |

Sprinkle the tapioca into ¼ litre (½ pint) consommé and cook until very soft. Pass through a conical strainer into the rest of the consommé, which should be hot. Stir carefully until well blended. Serve hot.

France

Consommé Viveurs

A duck flavoured consommé, turned deep red with the addition of beetroot juice, and garnished with a julienne of celery.

Consommé with sherry

Cooking time: 1 hour

125 g	raw lean minced beef	4 oz
	1 egg white	
	a few spoons cold water	
100 g	root vegetables, thinly sliced	4 oz
	half an onion, chopped	
½ l	bouillon (without fat)	1 pt
5 cl	sherry	2 fl oz

Mix the meat thoroughly with the egg white, the root vegetables and a little water. Gradually add the cold bouillon and slowly bring to the boil. Brown the onion, add to the meat, season and simmer very gently. The consommé should be clear and a pale golden colour. Strain through a tammy cloth, adjust the seasoning, re-heat and finish off with the sherry.

Austria

Consommé with Tarragon

Add a small bunch of tarragon when clarifying.

France

Garlic soup (Česneková polevka)

10 portions

3 l	strong beef bouillon	5 pt
30 g	garlic	1 oz
	3 eggs	
300 g	black bread	10 oz
1½ dl	oil	¼ pt
	marjoram	

Season the bouillon with salt and pepper and flavour with a little marjoram. Add the beaten eggs and the garlic which has been very finely grated and boil up. Dice the bread, fry in the oil, drain well and add to the hot soup when serving.

Czechoslovakia

Giblet soup

10 persons   Cooking time: about 4 hours

1 kg	goose giblets	1 lb approx.
1 kg	turkey giblets	1 lb approx.
750 g	cleaned root vegetables (carrots, celeriac, onions, leeks)	1½ lb
	2 cloves of garlic	
½ l	sauerkraut liquor	1 pt approx.
	1 tablespoon chopped parsley	
	1 tablespoon chopped dill	

Clean the giblets thoroughly, place in a pan with 5 litres (8¾ pints) cold water, bring to the boil and skim. Add the vegetables and garlic and simmer gently until the giblets are very tender. Strain the soup, remove the meat from the wing bones and cut the giblets, including the gizzards, into small pieces. Return these to the strained soup, adding a little cooked chicken if required. Bring to the boil, taste for flavour and add salt if necessary, then pour in the sauerkraut liquor. Sprinkle with chopped dill and parsley to serve.

Rumania

Hungarian goose giblet soup

Cooking time: about 2 hours

	2 sets of giblets, except for the necks	
300 g	carrots	12 oz
300 g	parsley roots	12 oz
100 g	celeriac	4 oz
50 g	onion	2 oz
	1 clove of garlic	
	peppercorns	

Place the giblets in a pan with about 4 litres (7 pints) water and a little salt, bring to the boil, skim well, add the vegetables, garlic and a few peppercorns and simmer gently. Remove the vegetables as soon as they are cooked. When the soup is ready, adjust the seasoning, making sure it is well-flavoured, remove the fat, strain and garnish with the finely diced vegetables.

Hungary

Semolina dumpling soup

10 portions   Cooking time: 25 minutes

2 l	strong clear beef stock	3½ pt
	2 large eggs	
100 g	butter	4 oz
250 g	semolina	10 oz
	grated nutmeg	

Cream the butter well, using a wire whisk, and add the eggs one at a time. Season with grated nutmeg and salt, stir in the semolina and leave to stand for 1 hour. Using a small teaspoon, shape into 2–3 cm (about 1 in) dumplings and place in water which is just on the boil. Simmer very slowly, remove and drain well. The above quantities will yield about 20–25 dumplings.

Add 2 or 3 dumplings to each plate of hot soup and sprinkle with chopped chives.

Austria

Tofu-Miso soup

4 persons

	½ piece bean curd (tofu)	
	3 tablespoons oil	
½ l	bouillon	1 pt
approx. 600 g	bean paste (miso)	1¼ lb
5–10 g	good pinch of aji-no-moto*	
50 g	spinach	2 oz

Wrap the bean curd in a cloth and press to remove all the excess water, then cut into about 1 cm (½ in) cubes. Heat the oil in a frying pan, drop the cubes into it, toss for a few moments, then drain well in a bamboo basket.

Boil up the bouillon and drop in the cubes of bean curd. Blend the bean paste with a little bouillon and add to the soup.

Cut the spinach into coarse julienne strips, add to the soup and bring to the boil. Season with aji-no-moto, also a little salt if required, skim, remove all fat and serve in individual soup bowls.

Japan

* aji-no-moto: a seasoning based on monosodium glutamate.

CREAM SOUPS

Avocado soup

6 persons

$\frac{1}{4}$ l	hot chicken broth	$\frac{1}{2}$ pt
	3 avocados	
$\frac{1}{4}$ l	fresh cream	$\frac{1}{2}$ pt
$\frac{1}{8}$ l	sour cream	$\frac{1}{4}$ pt
$\frac{1}{8}$ l	dry white wine	$\frac{1}{4}$ pt
	juice of half a lemon	

Scoop out the avocado flesh, cut half the flesh from one of them in strips and set aside, and reduce the rest to a very fine purée with the hot chicken broth, then allow to cool. Blend in the fresh and sour cream and the wine, season well with salt and pepper, add the lemon juice and pass through a hair-sieve. Chill well and garnish with the strips of avocado flesh to serve.

Germany

Avgolemono (egg and lemon soup)

4 servings

1 l	well flavoured clear chicken stock (made with fresh bones, giblets and vegetables)	$1\frac{3}{4}$ pt
50 g	rice	2 oz
	2 eggs	
	2 lemons	
5 dl	single cream	2 fl oz

Cook the rice in the stock, then strain out. Beat the eggs thoroughly with the juice of the lemons and beat in some of the stock. Beat this mixture into the stock and heat until the soup thickens, without letting it boil. Replace the rice. Allow the soup to get quite cold, then carefully stir in the cream and serve cold. A little chopped mint can be sprinkled over, as garnish.

Middle East

Boula-Boula I

6 portions

	6 cans turtle soup each containing	
$\frac{1}{8}$ l		$\frac{1}{4}$ pt
$\frac{1}{8}$ l	fresh green pea soup	$\frac{1}{4}$ pt

	4 egg yolks	
5 cl	dry sherry	2 fl oz
⅛ l	whipped dairy cream	¼ pt

Place the turtle soup in a bain-marie until very hot and mix well with the warm pea soup and the egg yolks. Remove from the bain-marie, flavour with the sherry and carefully stir in the whipped cream. Fill into preheated cups and brown the top under a salamander or in an oven with good top heat.

Austria

Boula-Boula II (palm wine soup)

12 persons

800 g	shin of beef	1¾ lb
500 g	mirepoix	1 lb
	small piece of cinnamon	
	a little cardamom	
	1 small bay leaf	
	few allspice berries	
	1 sprig thyme	
½ l	palm wine	1 pt
300 g	fresh tomatoes	12 oz
2 dl	fresh cream	6 fl oz

Prepare strong, concentrated broth—1½ litres (2½ pints) at the most—with the shin of beef, the mirepoix, the herbs and spices, salt and pepper, then refrigerate and remove the fat. Skin the tomatoes, remove the seeds and reduce to a purée.

Mix the broth with the palm wine and tomato purée, heat until just below boiling point, then stir in the cream to enhance the flavour.

Germany

Cream of artichoke soup

10 persons   Cooking time: 40 minutes

	10 fresh artichoke bottoms	
125 g	butter	4 oz
150 g	flour	5 oz
1½ l	milk	2½ pt
1½ l	chicken broth	2½ pt
	4 egg yolks	
¼ l	dairy cream	½ pt

Boil the artichoke bottoms until tender, keeping them white, and set aside 2–3 of the best ones to garnish the soup. Prepare a white roux with the butter and flour, gradually add the milk and broth, mix thoroughly, add the artichoke bottoms, season with salt, flavour with a little mace and simmer for 30 minutes. Rub through a fine sieve, re-heat and thicken with the egg yolks which have been blended with the cream. Adjust the seasoning and lastly add the remaining artichoke bottoms which have first been diced.

Germany

Gazpacho cream soup (cold)

	1 fairly large cucumber	
250 g	tomatoes (as red as possible)	8 oz
	2 medium-size sweet peppers	
	1 clove of garlic	
125 g	white breadcrumbs	4 oz
	½ teaspoon cumin seeds	
	3–4 tablespoons thick mayonnaise	
1 l	cold bouillon or water	1¾ pt
	4 tablespoons vinegar	
	ground pepper	
	salt	

Wash the peppers, tomatoes and cucumber, but do not peel. Cut up and work in the mixer. Place in a fairly deep bowl and add the breadcrumbs (these will thicken the bouillon). Refrigerate for 1–2 hours. Pound the cumin seeds and the peeled garlic to a paste in a mortar, then stir in the mayonnaise and vinegar. Mix well with the refrigerated vegetables and the cold bouillon (or water). Rub through a conical sieve. Adjust the seasoning, adding salt and pepper to taste.

The finished soup should be pale pink; this is why very red tomatoes should be used. If they are not red enough, a teaspoonful of good quality paprika may be added when pounding the cumin and garlic.

Serve very cold, stirring well before filling the cups so that the thickest ingredients do not settle at the bottom. Hand vegetables and bread separately.

Spain

Gazpacho garnishes

	1 small cucumber, peeled
	3 medium-size firm red
	tomatoes, skinned and
	crushed to remove the
	seeds

	1 medium-size onion, peeled	
	1 medium-size sweet pepper, skinned	
100 g	day-old bread (crumb only)	4 oz

Cut up the prepared vegetables finely and serve in separate little dishes with the gazpacho. Cut the bread into small pieces and toast lightly.

To skin the pepper, expose it to fierce heat until black (but not cooked), then hold under running water and rub off the skin.

Spain

Mushroom soup with oysters

6 persons

	12 fresh mushrooms	
50 g	each weighing	2 oz
	12 fresh oysters	
9 dl	well-seasoned veal bouillon	1½ pt
12 cl	dairy cream	¼ pt
70 g	flour butter (beurre manié) consisting of:	2 oz
	40 g (1 oz) flour	
	30 g (1 oz) butter	
75 g	fresh butter	3 oz

Clean the mushrooms and carefully twist off the stalks without damaging the caps. Spread the inside of the caps thinly with flour, butter, insert an oyster into each, after trimming off the 'beard', cover with the rest of the flour butter and refrigerate.

When ready to use, heat the fresh butter in a pan, slice the mushrooms and fry lightly in the butter. Pour in the veal bouillon, heat until almost boiling, then thicken with the cream.

(Illustration, p. 592)

Germany

Pumpkin soup

Cooking time: 45 minutes

500 g	pumpkin	1 lb
30 g	butter	1 oz
½ l	milk	1 pt

Cut the pumpkin into small pieces and cook in salted water. Rub through a fine sieve with the liquor, then add the heated milk in order to give the soup a creamy consistency. Season and add a little sugar. Put some fairly thick slices of bread in the soup and simmer for 6 minutes. Remove from heat, and add butter.

Tomato soup

Cooking time: 45 minutes

	1 medium-size onion	
	1 medium-size carrot	
650 g	fresh tomatoes	1¼ lb
50 g	butter	2 oz
50 g	cooked rice	2 oz
	1 bouquet garni	
1½ l	stock	2½ pt
50 g	cream	2 oz
	salt and sugar	
50 g	flour	2 oz
50 g	bacon	2 oz

Cut bacon, onion and carrot into small dice. Fry lightly, and add flour, stirring until brown. Cut the ripe tomatoes in quarters and add to the roux. Pour in the stock, stir well and season with a pinch of salt and sugar. Add the bouquet garni. Cook slowly for 45 minutes. Put through a sieve, boil up again. If too thick thin with a little stock. Bind with the cream. Garnish with boiled rice.

Vichyssoise soup

10 persons   Cooking time: 40–50 minutes

	4 large leeks	
	(white part only)	
50 g	onion	2 oz
60 g	butter	2 oz
450 g	peeled potatoes	1 lb
¾ l	milk	1 pt
½ l	water	1 pt
¼ l	double cream	½ pt
	chopped chives	

Slice the leeks, onion and potatoes finely and cook gently in the butter without browning until softened. Pour in the water, then the milk, season with salt and pepper and simmer gently until the vegetables are well cooked. Pass through a fine sieve, then through a tammy cloth if possible. Chill well, stirring frequently, then add the cream and adjust the seasoning. The soup should have the consistency of fairly thin sauce; if it is too thick, add a little single cream. Serve well chilled with a sprinkling of chopped chives.

France

POTAGES

Beetroot soup (cold) (Bortsch)

4 persons

450 g	beetroots	1 lb
$\frac{1}{8}$ l	sour cream	$\frac{1}{4}$ pt
	4 hard-boiled egg whites	
300 g	cucumber	10 oz
	1 lettuce	
45 g	spring onions	2 oz
20 g	dill	$\frac{3}{4}$ oz
20 g	parsley	$\frac{3}{4}$ oz
	sugar	
$1\frac{1}{2}$ l	beetroot stock	$2\frac{1}{2}$ pt
	citric acid	

Cook the beetroots until tender in very lightly salted water containing a little citric acid. Remove them from the water and strain the latter through a cloth. Leave the beetroots until cold, then skin them carefully and grate into the strained cooking liquid. Add the chopped hard-boiled egg whites and the very finely cut spring onions, together with the shredded lettuce. Add sugar to taste, then the cucumber which has been peeled, seeded and finely diced, and lastly the sour cream. Chill well and sprinkle with chopped dill and parsley before serving.

Russia

Bortsch

8 persons   Cooking time: about $2\frac{3}{4}$ hours

800 g	lean beef (topside or fresh silverside)	2 lb
600 g	raw beetroots	$1\frac{1}{4}$ lb
400 g	white cabbage	1 lb
	2 carrots	

	2 parsley roots	
	3 medium onions	
	4–5 tomatoes or	
	2 tablespoons tomato purée	
	2 small teaspoons vinegar	
	4 tablespoons vegetable oil	
	2 tablespoons salt	
2 dl	smetana (sour cream)	⅓ pt
	chopped parsley	
	finely cut dill	

Place the beef in a pan with about 3½ litres (6 pints) water, a little salt and 2 bay leaves, bring to the boil and cook until tender but still fairly firm. Remove the meat and strain the broth. Chop the cleaned beetroots, carrots, parsley roots and onions, place in a stew-pan of suitable size together with the vegetable oil, add the tomatoes or purée and 1 dl (⅛ pt) broth, cover and cook gently for 25 minutes, stirring from time to time. Add the cabbage, finely shredded, 1 dl (⅛ pt) broth and sugar, salt and pepper to taste. Mix well, pour in the rest of the broth and the vinegar, then cook for a further 10–15 minutes. To serve, place a small slice of meat in each plate, pour the soup over, top with a spoonful of smetana and sprinkle with chopped parsley and cut dill. The meat may be carved and served separately or omitted and used for other purposes.

Russia

Bortsch Romanoff

8 persons   Total cooking time: about 70 minutes

approx. 1 kg 800	1 duck	4 lb approx.
600 g	rindless streaky bacon	1 lb 4 oz
500 g	white cabbage hearts	1 lb
600 g	young beetroots	1 lb 4 oz
	2 carrots	
	2 parsley roots	
	1 tablespoon tomato purée	
	1 tablespoon sugar	
	2 medium onions, cut in half, then finely sliced	
	1 tablespoon vinegar	
50 g	butter	2 oz
3 l	lightly salted beef broth	5 pt
¼ l	smetana (sour cream)	½ pt
	1 dessertspoon chopped dill	
	1 dessertspoon chopped parsley	

Clean and prepare the duck, sprinkle lightly with salt inside and outside, truss, brown in butter in a brisk oven, then remove. Blanch the bacon for 15 minutes and refresh. Cut 200 g (7 oz) beetroots, the carrots and parsley roots into fairly coarse julienne strips. Fry the sliced onions lightly in butter without colouring, add the julienne and a ladleful of beef broth, cover and cook gently for 25 minutes. Stir in the tomato purée, add the bacon, the cabbage, finely shredded, the duck, salt and a good pinch of sugar, pour in the rest of the broth and simmer gently. As soon as the bacon and the duck are cooked, remove from the pan and keep hot in a little broth. Grate the rest of the beetroots finely and press through a cloth completely. Mix the juice with the vinegar. Cut the duck breast off the bone, then cut the meat and the bacon into small thin slices and arrange on a dish. Pour the beetroot juice and the smetana into sauce-boats. When the soup is ready, adjust the seasoning, pour into a tureen while boiling-hot and sprinkle with parsley and dill. Serve into plates, leaving each guest to add beetroot juice and smetana as desired. Serve the sliced duck and bacon at the same time, together with piroshky.

Russia

Botwinja imperial style

10 persons

250 g	young beet leaves	8¾ oz
250 g	sorrel	8¾ oz
350 g	spinach	12¼ oz
approx. 1½ l	kvass	2½ pt approx.
	4 cucumbers	
	1 heaped tablespoon coarsely chopped dill	
	salt	
10 g	sugar	⅓ oz
750 g	fillet of sturgeon or salmon, skinned	1 lb 10 oz

Cook the spinach, sorrel and beet leaves in their own juice, adding only a few drops of water or a small knob of butter and a pinch of salt, and leaving the pan uncovered. When soft, mash through a fine sieve and dilute to the required consistency with kvass. Add salt and sugar to taste, mix with the cucumbers which have been peeled, seeded and diced (or, preferably, cut into balls with a small vegetable scoop) and refrigerate. Meanwhile wrap the fish fillet in buttered greaseproof paper or aluminium foil and poach for a short time, leaving the fish very juicy. Cool under light pressure, unwrap and cut on the slant into 10 slices. Serve the soup, place a small cube of ice in each plate of soup and sprinkle with chopped dill. Serve the fish separately, lightly sprinkled with chopped dill, on a small plate. Grated horseradish is often served with sturgeon.

Russia

Calf's foot broth (Hargma)

4 persons   Cooking time: 3–4 hours

	1 calf's foot	
	1 tablespoon harissa	
	(see p. 427)	
	½ teaspoon tabel	
	(see p. 427)	
	½ teaspoon chili powder	
	½ teaspoon black peppercorns	
	1 tablespoon vinegar	
2 l	water	3½ pt

Singe the calf's foot to burn off the remaining hairs, scrape well, brush and wash. Saw into four pieces, place in a pan of cold water, add the spices, bring to the boil and simmer gently, adding a dash of vinegar from time to time. When the calf's foot is tender, remove from the pan, cut off the meat and cut it up into small pieces. Strain the broth, add the meat, together with a little salt if required, and lastly stir in 1 tablespoon vinegar. Serve very hot and hand small slices of dried bread as an accompaniment.

Tunisia

Chervil soup

6 persons   Cooking time: 45 minutes

	1 large carrot	
	1 parsley root	
	1 small onion	
	1 stick celery	
	3 medium floury potatoes	
1 l	bouillon	1¾ pt
60 g	smoked bacon	2 oz
30 g	butter	1 oz
	generous amount of	
	fresh chervil	

Dice all the vegetables finely. Fry the onion lightly in the butter, add the diced bacon and the other vegetables excepting the potatoes and cook for a few moments. Stir in the bouillon and simmer for 30 minutes. Blanch the potatoes and add to the soup, season with salt and pepper and cook for a further 15 minutes. Adjust the seasoning and add a generous amount of freshly chopped chervil.

Austria

Chicken broth with noodles

5 portions   Cooking time: 1–1¼ hours

800 g	chicken (boneless)	1¾ lb
50 g	celeriac	2 oz
50 g	carrots	2 oz
50 g	onions	2 oz
50 g	parsley roots	2 oz
3 l	water	5¼ pt
	salt	

Noodle dough

100 g	flour	4 oz
	2 eggs	
	salt	

Place the chicken in a pan of cold water with the vegetables and a little salt, bring to the boil, skim and simmer gently.

Make a firm dough with the flour and eggs, cover and allow to rest for a time. Pin out as thinly as possible, cut into strips, fold, then cut into very fine noodles and boil in salted water.

When the chicken is tender, remove and cut into cubes. Strain the broth, reduce a little if necessary, adjust the seasoning and serve in cups or plates with the chicken and noodles, sprinkled with chopped parsley.

Czechoslovakia

Cock-a-Leekie

To yield 1 litre (1¾ pints)

2 l	chicken stock	3½ pt
2 kg	1 fowl	4½ lb **approx.**
30 g	boiled rice	1 oz
	12 large stewed prunes	
250 g	julienne of white leek	8 oz
	1 bouquet garni	
	butter	

Joint the fowl as for sauté and fry to a golden brown in butter. Add the fowl to the stock, bring to the boil and skim. Add the bouquet garni and simmer till the fowl is cooked. Strain the liquid. Cut the fowl into small pieces, removing the bones. Stew the leeks in butter, pour the stock over and cook for 20 minutes. Add the boiled rice and chicken to the soup; remove all fat and season. Add the stewed prunes just before serving.

Great Britain

French onion soup

Cooking time: 15 minutes

800 g	onions	2 lb
100 g	butter	4 oz
	1 clove garlic	
2 l	water	3½ pt
90 g	Gruyère cheese	3 oz
40 g	flour	1½ oz

Slice the onions thinly. Fry slowly in the butter with the crushed garlic until golden. Dust with flour and add the water. Season with salt and pepper. Simmer until the onions are soft. Remove fat. Place small slices of bread and the cheese cut in thin small slices in a soup tureen or in soup bowls. Pour in the boiling hot soup, cover and allow to stand 5–6 minutes before serving.

Georgian soup

4 persons   Cooking time: about 1½ hours

500 g	mutton	1 lb
100 g	onions	4 oz
	1 tablespoon oil	
25 g	flour	1 oz
	2 egg yolks	
	½ teaspoon saffron	
	2 tablespoons vinegar	
	chopped parsley	

Cut the meat into 12–16 pieces, place in a pan of cold water, bring to the boil and cook for about 1½ hours, skimming occasionally. Remove the meat from the pan and strain the stock through a conical strainer. Dice the onions, fry lightly in the oil without colouring, add the flour and brown. Blend in the hot stock, add the meat which has been trimmed and boned, flavour with the saffron, season with salt and pepper and bring to the boil. Boil up the vinegar separately, add to the soup and boil up again. Shortly before serving, beat the egg yolks with a little bouillon, add to the soup, heat without boiling to prevent the egg yolk from curdling, and sprinkle with chopped parsley to serve.

Russia

Kharcho soup (Georgian)

4 persons   Cooking time: about 2 hours

500 g	breast of mutton	1 lb
	2 fairly large cloves of garlic	
100 g	onions	4 oz
	2 tablespoons tomato purée	
	or 2–3 fresh tomatoes	
50 g	rice	2 oz
	½ jar sour bottled plums	
	dill, parsley	
	1 tablespoon fat	

Leave the meat on the bone and cut into 12–16 pieces. Place in a pan of cold water, bring to the boil, then simmer gently, skimming occasionally. After 1–1½ hours, add the diced onions, the grated garlic, the rice, plums, salt and pepper and simmer for a further 30 minutes. Lightly fry the skinned, seeded and diced tomatoes or the tomato purée in the fat and add to the soup 5–10 minutes before it is ready. Sprinkle with chopped dill and parsley before serving.

Russia

Minestrone

100 g	fat bacon	4 oz
100 g	lean bacon	4 oz
	1 large onion	
	2 carrots	
	1 small turnip	
	white of 2 leeks	
100 g	white cabbage	4 oz
	2 potatoes	
200 g	fresh tomatoes	8 oz
50 g	shelled peas	2 oz
100 g	french beans	4 oz
	1 large clove garlic	
50 g	spaghetti	2 oz
100 g	grated cheese	4 oz

Place diced fat bacon in a saucepan, add diced lean bacon and fry pale yellow with the thinly sliced onion. Slice thinly all vegetables except the beans, peas and tomatoes. Add to the soup with a pinch each of basil and thyme and half a bay leaf. Fry until vegetables at bottom of the pan turn yellow. Add 2 litres (3½ pints) water, the peeled and diced deseeded tomatoes, the peas, sliced beans, and broken spaghetti. Season and cook slowly for 45 minutes. Crush the garlic into the soup and serve with chopped chervil sprinkled on top. Serve grated cheese separately.

Italy

Mulligatawny

2 l	brown stock	3½ pt
50 g	butter	2 oz
50 g	flour	2 oz
	1 tablespoon tomato purée	
	2 medium-size onions	
	1 large cooking apple	
10 g	curry powder	½ oz
	1 level tablespoon chutney	
25 g	boiled rice	1 oz
	3 tablespoons cream	
	seasoning	

Fry the chopped onion gently in butter. Mix in the curry powder and cook for a few minutes. Mix in the flour to make a roux and add the tomato purée. Add the stock and add the chopped apple and chutney. Bring to the boil, skim, and then simmer for 40 minutes. Strain, season and finally add the cream. Garnish with the rice, boiled separately.

Great Britain

Okroshka

8 persons

500 g	roast meat (and/or leftovers—beef, veal, cooked tongue)	1 lb
2½ l	kvass	4½ pt
	2 fresh cucumbers	
150 g	spring onion	5 oz
	3 hard-boiled eggs	
	1 teaspoon mustard	
	chopped parsley	
	chopped dill	
2 dl	smetana (sour cream)	⅓ pt

Slice the meat thinly. Peel the cucumbers, remove the seeds and cut in thin slices. Chop the spring onions finely until moist and slice the hard-boiled egg whites. Mash the egg yolks well, mix with the mustard, smetana, spring onions, egg whites and kvass and add salt and sugar. Carefully stir in the sliced meat and cucumbers and chill. When serving, sprinkle with chopped parsley and dill and place a small cube of ice in each plate. The meat should be completely free from fat. The soup may be made with small slices of game or poultry if desired.

Russia

Pea soup

(A winter soup)

500 g	split peas	1 lb
500 g	leeks	1 lb
	1 celeriac	
	1 head of celery	
200 g	salt pork	8 oz
	1 knuckle of pork	
250 g	smoked sausage	8 oz
	salt and pepper	
	2 potatoes	
	parsley	
approx. 4 l	water	7 pt

Wash the split peas, place them in a saucepan with the water, the salt pork and knuckle of pork (or a pig's trotter), season with salt and simmer very gently for 3 hours. Add the prepared leeks, celeriac and celery cut in pieces. Bring to the boil, stirring meanwhile to prevent burning (the peas are cooked to a pulp by now), then turn down the heat as low as possible. Add the sausage and cook for a further half an hour. Grate the potatoes into the soup to thicken well. Cut the sausage into small slices and return to the soup. Slice the salt pork and place on buttered slices of black bread. Season with salt and pepper, sprinkle with parsley and serve very hot with the black bread, and mustard.

Holland

Petite Marmite

225 g	silverside of beef	½ lb
225 g	flank of beef	½ lb
	1 small boiling chicken with giblets	
	1 marrow bone	
	1 large carrot	
	½ small turnip	

	1 white leek	
	1 onion	
	½ head of celery	
	½ small cabbage	
2½ l	beef bouillon	4½ pt

Brown the chicken for about 20 minutes. Drain well. Put in a marmite or large casserole together with the meat, bone and bouillon. Bring to the boil slowly and allow to simmer. Meanwhile shape the carrots and turnip like small olives. Slice the leek, celery and cabbage. Add to the pot and continue to cook. Take out the meat when tender and cut into small cubes. Slice the chicken meat and discard giblets. Return the meats to the pot. Skim off the fat and season. The marrow bone may be served in the pot. Serve with thin slices of toast.

Pheasant broth

10 portions   Cooking time: 2–2½ hours

	5 old pheasants	
20 g	onions	1 oz
20 g	carrots	1 oz
20 g	celeriac	1 oz
20 g	parsley root	1 oz
	6 allspice berries	
	8 peppercorns	
	2 cloves	

Draw and clean the pheasants and place in a pan containing 4 litres (7 pints) cold water, together with the vegetables, the spices and a little salt. Bring to the boil, skim and cook slowly to keep the broth clear. Skim again from time to time and reduce to about 1½ litres (2½ pints). Adjust the seasoning, strain and serve in soup cups holding 1–1½ dl (¼ pt).

Czechoslovakia

Sajaur Lodeh

1 kg	vegetables (cauliflower,	2¼ lb
	carrots, french beans,	
	if possible a tin of	
	bamboo shoots)	
	1 onion	
	2 cloves of garlic	
	1 red pepper	

	3 walnuts	
	1 teaspoon coriander seeds	
	1 bay leaf	
	salt	
	sugar	
	1 cup coconut milk	
1 l	bouillon	1¾ pt

Pound the onion, garlic, red pepper, walnuts, coriander and bay leaf in a mortar. Clean the vegetables and cut them into fairly thin slices. Cook the vegetables and spices in the bouillon over gentle heat until the vegetables are almost soft ('al dente', as the Italians say). Add the coconut milk or, if not available, some tamarind or tomato juice.

Holland

Sauerkraut soup

8 persons   Cooking time: broth 2–3 hours; soup 40–45 minutes

400 g	beef bones	1 lb
800 g	meat for boiling	1¾ lb
1 kg 500	sauerkraut	3 lb
	4 carrots	
	6 parsley roots	
	4 medium onions	
	6 tablespoons tomato purée	
	6 tablespoons wheat flour	
200 g	butter	6 oz
2 dl	smetana (sour cream)	⅓ pt

Chop up the bones, place in a pan with the meat, 4 litres (7 pints) water and a little salt and simmer until completely cooked, then strain the broth. Cut the carrots and parsley roots in coarse julienne strips and cook the flour in a frying pan without butter until light brown. Chop the onions, brown lightly in butter, stir in the tomato purée, mix thoroughly with the flour, the rest of the butter, the sauerkraut, carrots and parsley roots, cover and cook in a moderate oven. Remove, pour in the broth, bring to the boil and season well. Hand smetana and chopped parsley separately.

This soup tastes better if warmed up after 24 hours.

Russia

Snert

Cooking time: 60–70 minutes

250 g	celery	8 oz
250 g	leeks	8 oz
250 g	carrots	8 oz
150 g	bacon rinds	4 oz
500 g	pig's trotters	1 lb
1 kg	dried peas	2 lb
175 g	lard	6 oz
500 g	cooked mashed potatoes	1 lb
6 l	bouillon	10 pt

Soak the peas overnight. Cut the celery, leeks and carrots in coarse dice and fry in the lard without browning, together with the bacon rinds. Add the drained peas, pour in the bouillon and add the pig's trotters, chopped up and tied in a cloth. Cook slowly. As soon as the peas are soft and begin to split open, remove the bacon rinds and the pig's trotters. Pass two-thirds of the soup through a strainer or mincer, add the rest of the soup and stir in the mashed potatoes. Season with salt and freshly ground pepper, re-heat and serve, adding some slices of sausage if desired.

Holland

Solianka

8 persons   Cooking time (meat): 2–3 hours

1 kg	meat for boiling (half beef, half veal)	2 lb
200 g	fried calf's kidneys	8 oz
200 g	boiling sausage	8 oz
200 g	cooked ox tongue	8 oz
	4 medium onions	
	4 tablespoons tomato purée	
	8 salted cucumber	
	4 tomatoes	
	8 stoned prunes	
	8 stoned olives	
120 g	butter	4 oz
	1 lemon	
	1 tablespoon capers	
	1 bay leaf	
	chopped parsley	
	chopped dill	
2 dl	smetana (sour cream)	⅓ pt

Place the meat in a pan with 3 litres (5¼ pints) water and a little salt, bring to the boil and simmer until the meat is completely cooked and all the nutrients and flavour have been extracted from it, then strain the broth. Chop the onions and fry in half the butter until lightly coloured. Add the tomato purée, the rest of the butter and two tablespoons broth, stir well and simmer under cover for 3–5 minutes. Peel the cucumbers, remove the seeds and slice. Cut the kidneys, sausage and tongue in small slices, skin the tomatoes, remove the seeds, chop coarsely and add to the onion mixture in the pan together with the prunes which have been stewed but kept fairly firm, the sliced cucumbers and the capers. Pour over the hot broth, season with salt and pepper, add the bay leaf and simmer over gentle heat for 5–10 minutes. Transfer to a tureen and serve with a slice of lemon, an olive and a spoonful of smetana. Sprinkle the slices of lemon with chopped parsley and dill. If preferred, the smetana may be handed separately, instead of being added to the soup when serving.

Russia

Soup au gratin Vallée d'Illiez style

8 persons   Cooking time: 30 minutes

800 g	bread	1½ lb
300 g	onions	¾ lb
2½ l	strong bouillon	4½ pt
350 g	dry alpine cheese or old Gruyère	¾ lb
100 g	butter	4 oz

Slice the onions thinly and cook until soft in the butter without colouring. Fill an ovenware soup-tureen successively with a thin layer of onion, a layer of slices of bread 1 cm (about ½ in) thick and a layer of grated cheese. Repeat until the tureen is three-quarters full. Pour in the piping-hot bouillon which has been lightly flavoured with nutmeg. Press the solid ingredients down with a ladle until the bouillon has soaked right through. When the top is covered with bouillon to a depth of a few centimetres (an inch or two) sprinkle with grated cheese and place in a hot oven. Serve piping-hot.

Switzerland

Vegetable soup with meat balls

6 cups

1½ l	bouillon (preferably made with shin of beef)	2½ pt
50 g	vermicelli	2 oz

100 g	minced meat (half beef, half pork)	4 oz
	salt	
	pepper	
	grated nutmeg	
	1 tablespoon white bread (without crusts)	
	milk	
	mixed vegetables (carrots, cauliflower, peas, leeks, chervil, celery leaves)	
	parsley	

Soak the bread in a tablespoonful of milk and squeeze dry. Mix the minced beef and pork with the bread, season with salt, pepper and grated nutmeg, then shape into tiny balls the size of a hazelnut. Clean the vegetables and cut the carrots into thin slices, the cauliflower into small sprigs and the leeks into thin rounds; chop the chervil and celery. Place the vegetables, the broken vermicelli and the meat balls in the bouillon and cook over gentle heat for about half an hour. Sprinkle with chopped parsley.

Holland

Westland vegetable soup

Yields 30 cups   Cooking time: 60 minutes

250 g	cleaned carrots	8 oz
250 g	cleaned leeks	8 oz
250 g	cleaned celery	8 oz
250 g	tomatoes	8 oz
125 g	vermicelli	4 oz
4 l	bouillon	7 pt
150 g	onions	6 oz
	2 sprigs parsley	
60 g	fat	2 oz

Meat balls

250 g	lean boneless veal	8 oz
250 g	lean boneless pork	8 oz
	2 eggs	
	4 grated rusks	
	nutmeg	
	salt	
	pepper	

Dice the onions, leeks and other vegetables, but not too finely, and lightly cook separately in a little chicken fat. Mix together in the pan, pour in the bouillon and simmer until the vegetables are cooked but still fairly firm. Season well. Skin the tomatoes, remove the seeds and cut into dice. Add to the soup together with the vermicelli and simmer gently for a further 15 minutes. Adjust the seasoning. Serve in cups with one or two meat balls in each.

To make the meat balls, mince the meat finely and mix well with the eggs and the grated rusks. Add salt, pepper and grated nutmeg to taste and shape into small balls each weighing about 10 g (about ⅓ oz). Poach gently, preferably in the bouillon to be used for the soup.

Holland

FISH SOUPS

Fisherman's soup Paks style

10 persons

3 kg 500	carp	8 lb
600 g	onions	1½ lb
120 g	red paprika	4 oz
20 g	small hot red peppers	1 oz
250 g	letcho (thin home-made noodles)	8 oz

Scale, gut and wash the fish; set aside the roes. Slice the onions thinly and place in a large saucepan. Cut off the fish heads and tails, and cut the rest of the fish into pieces two fingers thick. Without washing the fish again, lay the heads and tails in the saucepan and place the other pieces of fish on top. Pour in enough water to cover, allowing 1–1½ litres for each kg of fish (1–1¼ pints to 1 lb fish). Season with salt, bring quickly to the boil and skim. Add the red paprika, letcho and small hot red peppers. Boil over brisk heat for 30–40 minutes, adding the roes shortly before the end of the cooking time. If preferred, part of the paprika may be added at the beginning and the rest stirred in just before serving.

Serve the gelatinous soup first with boiled noodles, followed by the boiled carp as a separate course.

Hungary

Fisherman's soup Tisza style

10 persons

2 kg	carp	4½ lb
1 kg	sheat-fish	2½ lb
500 g	sturgeon	1 lb
500 g	bleak, crucian, etc.	1 lb
600 g	onions, chopped	1¼ lb
100 g	mild red paprika	4 oz
250 g	letcho	8 oz

Clean and wash all the fish thoroughly. First prepare strong stock with the chopped onions, the small fish and the heads and tails of the large fish, using a little water only. Pass through a fine sieve. Transfer to a large saucepan and pour in enough water to cover the fish. Season with salt to taste and add the paprika and letcho. Cut the carp, sheat-fish and sturgeon into 3–4 cm (about 1½ in) pieces and place in the saucepan. Simmer gently to prevent the pieces of fish from breaking up. The stock should gradually thicken to the consistency of a thick sauce while cooking.

Hungary

Manhattan clam chowder

35 persons   Cooking time: about 40 minutes

30 g	lean smoked bacon	1 oz
125 g	butter	4 oz
300 g	finely chopped onions	10 oz
750 g	potatoes, peeled and diced	1½ lb
250 g	green peppers, diced	8 oz
5 l	fish stock *or* clam juice (if using canned clams)	8 pt
125 g	tomato purée	4 oz
	2 crushed cloves of garlic	
50 g	flour	2 oz
1 kg 500	clams	3½ lb
1 kg	tomatoes, skinned, seeded and coarsely chopped	2¼ lb

Dice the bacon and fry lightly to render the fat. Add the butter, then the chopped onions and cook these until transparent. Add the tomato purée and garlic and continue cooking gently for a few moments. Now add the potatoes and peppers. Sprinkle with the flour, cook for a few moments, stir in the fish stock or clam juice, bring to the boil and simmer for 20 minutes. Add the chopped tomatoes and the clams and simmer for a further 5 minutes. Season well and serve very hot.

Ucha is riba (fish soup)

8 persons   Cooking time: 2 hours

1 kg 500	small freshwater fish	3½ lb
	(perch, gudgeon, etc.)	
500 g	pike-perch or eel-pout	1 lb
	2 small bay leaves	
	4 medium onions	
	1 parsley root	
	10 peppercorns	
	chopped parsley	
	chopped dill	

Gut the small fish, wash very well and divide into three portions. Place one portion in a pan with 3 l (5¼ pt) water and very little salt, bring to the boil and simmer for 30 minutes. (Do not scale the small fish.) Strain the cooking liquid, simmer the second portion of small fish in it very gently, strain again, cook the rest of the small fish in the same liquid, then strain again. Peel the onions, but do not cut up; cook them very slowly in the strained fish stock for 15–20 minutes, then add the boned skinned pike-perch or eel-pout cut in 8 pieces, also the bay leaves, black peppercorns, parsley root and salt if required. Simmer until the fish is cooked. Diced potatoes may be added to the soup at the same time as the onions if desired. Before serving, sprinkle the soup with chopped parsley and dill.

It is advisable to remove the pieces of fish from the pan with a ladle and to strain the soup over them.

Russia

Clam consommé

4 persons

	about 30 live clams	
9 dl	water	1½ pt
	2 teaspoons salt	
	1 tablespoon saké	
	(dry rice wine)	
	1 teaspoon aji-no-moto	
	(monosodium glutamate)	

Wash the clams thoroughly in running water, brushing the edges well to remove any sand or grit. Place the clams in a pan, pour in the water and heat until the clams open. Discard any which fail to open. Do not simmer for long after the clams have opened, or they will become hard and tasteless. Season with the salt and aji-no-moto, flavour with the saké and serve without removing the clams from their shells.

Japan

EGGS

Eggs may be cooked in many ways, but not all of these are suitable for serving at a buffet or reception. Omelettes, oeufs sur la plat, fried eggs and scrambled eggs are dishes best suited to an à la carte menu, since they are impossible to keep hot and difficult to produce for large numbers of people simultaneously. Egg dishes are particularly useful for a first or second course at a dinner party and for inclusion among the smaller items at a cold buffet.

BOILED EGGS

COLD DISHES

Barrel eggs

12 persons

	12 hard-boiled eggs	
	18 anchovy fillets	
	12 croûtons	
$\frac{1}{2}$ l	mayonnaise	$\frac{3}{4}$ pt
	gherkins	
	capers	
	watercress	

Cut a slice of the white off each end of the eggs to give them a barrel shape, then cut them in half lengthwise and keep the two halves of each egg together so that they may be subsequently re-assembled. Remove the yolks and pass through a sieve with six anchovy fillets. Transfer to a basin and mix to a fairly soft paste with a little mayonnaise. Season well and spread on the croûtons, using the remaining paste to fill 12 half eggs to a dome shape. Cover with the other 12 half eggs, making sure that they are edge to edge and pressing down lightly. Place the stuffed eggs lengthwise on the croûtons. Lay two strips of anchovy fillet round each egg to simulate the hoops of a barrel. Place a small caper on top, in the centre (the bung) and fix a small piece of gherkin on to one side (the spigot). Arrange on a serving dish with a border of watercress. Hand the mayonnaise separately if desired.

Any other stuffing suitable for eggs may be used.

France

Eggs Aurore style

12 persons

	12 hard-boiled eggs	
100 g	smoked salmon	4 oz
50 g	butter	2 oz
$\frac{1}{2}$ l	aspic jelly	$\frac{3}{4}$ pt

Cut the eggs in half, remove the yolks and pass through a fine sieve together with the smoked salmon. Mix with the butter and season well, then fill into the whites and smooth off to a dome shape. Refrigerate, then coat with half-set aspic. Serve on a bed of chopped aspic. If desired, the eggs may be decorated with tomato before glazing.

France

Egg bombe

$1\frac{1}{2}$ l	aspic	$2\frac{1}{2}$ pt
	10 eggs boiled to a waxy consistency	
	2 tomatoes, diced and blanched	
	1 bunch dill	
1 kg	loaf of bread	2 lb
	3 thin slices of pressed ham	
	3 rashers bacon	
	sliced truffles	

Mask a hemispherical mould with aspic, sprinkle with coarsely chopped dill, allow to set, then line with an irregular arrangement of diced tomatoes dipped in liquid aspic. Place the eggs in the mould and fill up with aspic. Cut the bread to the size of the mould to make a base, cover with strips of bacon and ham, wrapping these round it where required, decorate with slices of truffle and coat with aspic. When set hard, turn the egg bombe out on to the bread. If there is a border of bread projecting beyond the bombe, cover with chopped aspic.

(Illustration, p. 811)   Austria

Eggs Fantasio

12 persons

	12 medium-boiled eggs	
	12 fried croûtons	
100 g	anchovy butter	4 oz

Salad

300 g	picked shrimps	12 oz
250 g	potatoes cooked in their jackets	8 oz
50 g	truffles	2 oz
¼ l	aspic mayonnaise	½ pt

Tomato aspic

750 g	fresh tomatoes	1¾ lb
¼ l	aspic jelly	½ pt
	1 tablespoon chopped onion	
	salt	
	pepper	
	pinch of sugar	
	1 clove of garlic	
	small bouquet garni	

Spread the croûtons with anchovy butter and cover with the medium-boiled eggs, which should be quite cold. Coat several times with half-set tomato aspic. Mix the shrimps with the diced potatoes and the truffles and dress with the aspic mayonnaise. Arrange to a dome shape in the centre of a round dish and surround with the eggs on croûtons. Keep cool until required.

To make the tomato aspic, cook the onions in butter without colouring and add the tomatoes after squeezing out the liquid and cutting into pieces. Cook until soft with the addition of salt, pepper, a pinch of sugar, the garlic and the bouquet garni. Pass through a fine sieve into a small saucepan and reduce until the purée has thickened a little while stirring with a spatula. Gradually add the aspic jelly which has been reduced to half its volume, strain through a tammy cloth and allow to cool, but not to set.

France

Eggs Felix Ziem

12 persons

	12 hard-boiled eggs	
250 g	lean ham	8 oz
	2 gherkins	
	1 tablespoon chopped shallot	
	1 tablespoon chopped fine herbs	
	1 truffle	
¼ l	mayonnaise	⅛ pt

Cut the eggs in half lengthwise and rub the yolks through a sieve. Dice the ham finely, chop the gherkins and mix with the egg yolks, the shallot and the herbs (parsley, chervil, tarragon). Bind with the mayonnaise and adjust the seasoning. Fill into the whites and smooth off to a dome shape. Decorate with three lozenges of truffle and ham. Serve on a bed of shredded lettuce or place each half egg in the centre of a small lettuce heart leaf.

France

Eggs florist style

12 persons

	12 hard-boiled eggs	
	3 carrots	
	3 turnips	
100 g	French beans	4 oz
¼ l	mayonnaise	⅛ pt
	6 small tomatoes	

Cut the eggs in half across and cut a thin slice off each end to make them stand securely. Rub the yolks through a sieve and mix to a fairly soft smooth paste with well-seasoned mayonnaise. Cut the carrots, turnips and French beans into small sticks and cook separately in boiling salted water. Refresh and drain well on a cloth. Dice the egg white trimmings and place in the bottom of the whites, then fill up with the egg yolk paste, using a savoy bag fitted with a star pipe. Stud all round with sticks of carrot, turnip and French bean, alternating the vegetables. Stand each half egg in half a tomato which has been seeded, well dried and seasoned. Arrange on a dish with a border of watercress. A little mayonnaise may be served separately.

Any other stuffing suitable for eggs may be used.

Eggs gipsy style

12 persons

	12 hard-boiled eggs	
	12 white bread canapés	
100 g	pickled tongue	4 oz
100 g	chicken breast	4 oz
25 g	truffle	1 oz
$\frac{1}{4}$ l	Andalusian sauce	$\frac{1}{3}$ pt
	stiffened with aspic	
$\frac{1}{4}$ l	aspic jelly	$\frac{1}{3}$ pt
50 g	butter	$1\frac{1}{2}$ oz

Cut the eggs in half lengthwise, remove the yolks and pass through a sieve. Mix with the butter, season well with a good dash of cayenne pepper and sharpen with a few drops of lemon juice. Spread the canapés with this paste. Cut the tongue, truffle and chicken into julienne strips, bind with the Andalusian sauce and fill at once into half the egg whites to a dome shape. Cover with the unfilled egg whites, press down lightly so that the sauce will seal the edges together when it sets, and wipe off any sauce which has run out. Place the eggs on the canapés, decorate with tongue or truffle, coat with half-set aspic, arrange on a dish and surround with watercress. The eggs may be stuffed with shrimps, lobster, ham, salmon, etc.

France

Eggs Niçoise

12 persons

	12 hard-boiled eggs	
	6 large tomatoes	
250 g	French beans	8 oz
250 g	cooked potatoes	8 oz
$\frac{1}{2}$ l	mayonnaise	$\frac{3}{4}$ pt
$\frac{1}{2}$ l	aspic jelly	$\frac{3}{4}$ pt
	tarragon leaves	

Dice the French beans and cook uncovered for about 15 minutes in boiling salted water (preferably in an untinned copper pan). When cooked, refresh at once and drain thoroughly. Cut the eggs in half lengthwise. Decorate the convex side with tarragon leaves, coat several times with aspic and keep cool. Dice the potatoes. Cut the tomatoes in half and squeeze out the seeds gently. Cut away the pulp, leaving a little round the sides. Pass a third of the pulp through a fine sieve and drain in muslin for at least 1 hour, then squeeze gently to remove as much water as possible. Add the drained pulp to the mayonnaise, which should be very firm. Adjust the seasoning. Coarsely chop the rest of the tomato pulp and drain. Mix with the French beans and the potatoes and dress with the tomato-flavoured mayonnaise. Fill the half tomatoes with this salad and place the decorated half eggs on top. Serve the rest of the mayonnaise separately.

France

Glazed eggs

12 persons

	12 hard-boiled eggs	
100 g	butter	4 oz
100 g	tunny in oil	4 oz
	1 tablespoon Béchamel sauce	
1 l	port jelly	1½ pt

Cut the eggs in half lengthwise. Remove the yolks and rub through a sieve. Soften the butter, pass the tunny through a sieve and mix with the yolks and the Béchamel sauce until well blended. Season well, adding a dash of cayenne pepper. Fill into the whites, level off the top and invert on a wire rack. Decorate the convex side with tarragon, chervil, tomato, truffle, ham, etc., first dipping each item of garnish in liquid jelly. Refrigerate until set, then coat two or three times with half-set jelly, allowing each layer to set in a cold place before proceeding. Dish on a bed of chopped jelly.

The stuffing may be made with sardines, ham, foie gras, anchovies, smoked salmon or game purée instead of tunny.

France

Hard-boiled eggs Navacerrada style (cold)

Cut the hard-boiled eggs in half lengthwise and remove the yolks without damaging the whites. Mix the yolks and equal amounts of creamed butter and foie gras purée to a smooth paste, adding a few spoonsful of dairy cream if too thick. Season with salt and a pinch of ground pepper. Fill into the whites to the original shape of the eggs.

Fill the centre of a round dish with fairly firm country-style vegetable salad and smooth to a cone shape. Cover the upper part of the cone with slices of ham cut into isosceles triangles or semi-circles, overlapping them fan-wise, with the narrowest part pointing towards the centre of the cone. Place a stuffed egg in the centre. Glaze the ham by brushing with half-set aspic jelly. Arrange the rest of the stuffed eggs round the salad. Refrigerate. Pour a spoonful of Chantilly sauce over each egg at the last minute.

Country-style vegetable salad. Finely cut cooked vegetables (carrots, turnips, peas, French beans, potatoes and a few beetroots) in a dressing of salt, a little vinegar, tarragon and mayonnaise.

Chantilly sauce. Just before serving, add 1 dl (¼ pt) whipped cream to ½ l (¾ pt) mayonnaise. Adjust the seasoning.

Spain

Water-lily eggs I

12 persons

	18 hard-boiled eggs	
	12 medium-size artichokes	
1 dl	mayonnaise	¼ pt
	6 anchovy fillets	

Cut off the top half of the artichokes and cut the edges of the outside leaves zigzag fashion. Cook in boiling salted water; do not use a lid, but make sure the artichokes are well covered with water to preserve their colour. As soon as they are tender, refresh and drain. Remove the centre leaves and the choke. Marinate the base of the artichokes for at least 1 hour in the stock used for cooking vegetables Greek style. Cut each hard-boiled egg into six lengthwise. Remove the yolk and rub through a sieve with the anchovy fillets. Mix with the mayonnaise to obtain a smooth well-seasoned paste. Drain the artichokes and fill with the paste, smoothing it off to a dome shape. Stick the pieces of egg white into the paste all round with the tips pointing upwards.

France

Water-lily eggs II

Cut small artichokes into wedges, trim neatly and cook in boiling salted water. Refresh, then drain between two cloths. Marinate for at least 1 hour in the stock used for cooking vegetables Greek style. Cut large tomatoes in half, remove the seeds, press out the liquid and season. Fill with the same paste as in recipe I and smooth off to a dome shape. Decorate the top with a ring of artichoke wedges and a ring of egg white.

France

HOT DISHES

Egg curry

3 persons

	1 onion, finely chopped	
	1 clove of garlic, finely chopped	
20 g	fat	1 oz
	1 dessertspoon ground corianders	
	1 teaspoon ground turmeric	

	1 teaspoon ground ginger	
	½ teaspoon powdered chillies	
	1 teaspoon ground cumin seed	
½ l	coconut milk or curds	¾ pt
	6 hard-boiled eggs	
	2 tablespoons yoghurt	
	juice of 1 lemon	

Lightly fry the onion and garlic in the fat. Add the spices and stir. Blend in the coconut milk or curds and simmer until the mixture begins to thicken. Add the hard-boiled eggs cut in half. Thicken with the yoghurt if necessary. Season with salt and sprinkle with lemon juice. Dress on a bed of pilaf rice.

Eggs in piquant sauce

> 4 hard-boiled eggs
> 1 onion
> 1 clove of garlic
> 1 red pepper
> 2 tablespoons soya sauce
>   ('ketjap')
> 1 bay leaf
> zest of 1 lemon
> salt
> sugar
> tomato juice
> oil

Cut up the onion and garlic finely, pound in a mortar with the red pepper, bay leaf and lemon zest, and fry to a golden colour in a spoonful of oil. Add the eggs, cut in half, then a cup of water, the soya sauce, 1 spoonful of tomato juice, salt and pepper and cook for a few moments over gentle heat.

Holland

POACHED EGGS

Cooking time: 4–4½ minutes

The eggs, which should be 4 or 5 days old at the most, are poached in water containing vinegar at the rate of 2 cl (1 tablespoon) vinegar to 1 l (1¾ pt) water. 10 g (⅓ oz) salt is also usually added for each litre (1¾ pt) water to counteract the insipid taste of the eggs, although not everyone recommends this practice.

Bring the water to the boil in a shallow sauté pan, break the egg into a saucer and slide it in level with the surface of the water at the point where it is boiling hardest. Repeat in quick succession with the remaining eggs. If there is too long an interval in between, the eggs will not all be cooked after the same length of time; the first one will be too hard and the last one too soft. Six to eight eggs at a time is a maximum for anyone who is not very experienced. The cooking time for eggs weighing 55–65 g (about 2 oz) is 4½ minutes in lightly but steadily boiling water. After this time, the poached eggs are carefully removed with a skimmer and placed in cold water. When cold, they are trimmed to a neat ovoid shape.

Eggs required for hot dishes are poached for about 1 minute less.

France

COLD DISHES

Eggs and ham in aspic

12 persons

	12 poached eggs	
	3 slices ham	
	tarragon leaves	
1 l	port jelly	1½ pt

Mask the bottom of oval moulds or small china cocottes with port jelly to a thickness of 5 mm (¼ in). Leave in a cool place to set. Decorate with a few blanched tarragon leaves. Cover carefully with a slice of ham to fit the mould and top with a poached egg, which should be very cold. Fill up with half-set jelly, refrigerate until set and turn out. Dish on lettuce or mixed vegetable salad.

(Techniques, p. 109)
(Illustration, p. 811)

France

Eggs Madrid style

12 persons

	12 poached eggs	
	12 slices cooked ham	
½ l	Andalusian chaud-froid	¾ pt
	sauce well flavoured	
	with tomato	
1 l	Madeira jelly	1½ pt

Place the eggs on a wire rack and coat with half-set Andalusian chaud-froid sauce. Refrigerate until set. Mask the bottom of a glass bowl with jelly and allow to set. Trim the slices of ham neatly and arrange in the bowl alternately with the eggs. Decorate these with blanched tarragon leaves and fill up the bowl with jelly.

France

Harlequin eggs

12 persons

	12 poached eggs	
	12 unsweetened short pastry or puff pastry barquetttes	
¼ l	chicken chaud-froid sauce	⅓ pt
¼ l	Aurore chaud-froid sauce well flavoured with tomato	⅓ pt
	1 truffle	
	2 slices pickled tongue	
250 g	mixed vegetable salad in mayonnaise	8 oz

Cover the bottom of each pastry case with vegetable salad. Place a poached egg on top and coat half of it with chicken chaud-froid sauce and the other half with Aurore chaud-froid sauce. Sprinkle the white sauce with finely diced tongue and the red sauce with chopped truffle.

France

Poached eggs Raquel

Poach the eggs, cool and trim. Prepare 1 cooked artichoke bottom for each egg. Make potato, artichoke and celery salad as follows, allowing 1 part celery to 2 parts potatoes and 2 parts artichoke bottoms. Boil the potatoes in their skins, cool, peel and cut into small sticks. Cook the artichoke bottoms and slice thinly. Cut young celery hearts into fine julienne strips. Mix these ingredients together, season and dress with oil, vinegar and mayonnaise. Place the salad in the centre of a round or oval dish and smooth the top to make a base. Cover with mayonnaise, arrange the whole cooked artichoke bottoms on top and place a poached egg on each. When about to serve, coat the eggs with fairly thick mayonnaise. Decorate the top with a small disk of sweet pepper. Place a few even-sized asparagus tips between the artichoke bottoms and round the salad, decorating them with strips of sweet pepper arranged like the sails of a windmill. Hand mayonnaise separately.

If this dish has to be made in advance, aspic mayonnaise should be used.

Poached egg tartlets

	4 cold poached eggs, neatly trimmed	
	4 pie pastry tartlets, baked blind	
	4 tablespoons French salad	
	4 tablespoons tomato purée	
¼ l	aspic	⅓ pt

Fill the tartlets with the salad. Coat the eggs with the tomato purée, thickened with aspic, allow to set, then place on the salad and surround with chopped aspic.

French salad (Viennese style): cooked diced potatoes, celery and carrots, cooked peas and diced gherkins in aspic mayonnaise.

Austria

Tarragon eggs

12 persons

	12 poached eggs	
1 l	tarragon-flavoured aspic jelly	1½ pt
	tarragon leaves	

Mask the bottom of small oval cocottes or moulds with aspic jelly to a thickness of 5 mm (¼ in). Keep in a cool place until set. Decorate with blanched tarragon leaves, place a poached egg in each mould, slowly pour in half-set jelly to fill the mould and refrigerate until set. To turn out, hold the mould in hot water for a moment. Serve on a dish garnished with shredded lettuce.

France

HOT DISHES

(See Poached eggs, p. 414, for basic recipe.)

Bulgarian poached eggs

1 portion   Cooking time: 4 minutes

3 eggs
water and vinegar

60 g	firm ewe cheese	2 oz
20 g	butter	¾ oz
	paprika	

Cut the cheese in thin slices and place on a warmed plate. Poach the eggs in water containing a little vinegar, trim, drain well and place on the slices of cheese. Pour a little melted butter over and sprinkle with a little paprika.

Poached eggs Benedict

Place the poached eggs on toast covered with a slice of fried ham and coated with Hollandaise sauce. Decorate with truffle slices.

Poached eggs with flap mushrooms hunter's style

Cooking time: about 20 minutes

500 g	flap mushrooms (boletus)	1 lb
60 g	butter	2 oz
50 g	onion, finely chopped	2 oz
	1 small clove of garlic	
40 g	flour	1½ oz
¼ l	sour cream	½ pt
	chopped parsley	
	grated Parmesan cheese	
	6 large fresh eggs	

Poach the eggs in the usual manner, trim neatly and keep hot in warm salt water. Clean and wash the mushrooms carefully. Fry the onion in butter until golden, add the mushrooms, coarsely sliced, season with salt and stew gently for 15 minutes. Blend the flour with the sour cream and mix with the cooked mushrooms and onion. Finish off with a little garlic and some chopped parsley and adjust the seasoning. Transfer to a fireproof dish, arrange the well-drained eggs on top, sprinkle liberally with grated Parmesan, then sprinkle with melted butter and brown quickly under a salamander or in the oven with fierce top heat.

Poached eggs Florentine

Place the poached eggs on tartlets filled with spinach sautéd in butter. Coat with cheese sauce. Sprinkle with grated cheese and glaze.

Poached eggs opera

6 portions

	6 fresh eggs	
	6 rounds white bread	
80 g	butter	3 oz
	2 small bundles green	
	asparagus	
approx. ⅛ l	light Hollandaise sauce	½ pt approx.
	6 round slices truffle	

Prepare the asparagus in the usual manner, tie the tips in bundles and cut the edible parts of the stalks in 1 cm (½ in) lengths. Cook in salted water, drain, season the cut stalks and toss them lightly in butter. Break the eggs into cups, slide them into salted water containing a little vinegar, making sure the water is just on the boil, and poach for 4 minutes. Remove, trim and keep hot in lightly salted water. Fry the rounds of bread in butter on both sides until crisp and arrange in a ring on a round dish. Top each one with a poached egg which has been well drained and wiped dry, coat thinly with Hollandaise sauce and decorate with a slice of truffle. Place the cut asparagus stalks in the centre of the dish, arrange the bundles of tips on top and brush very lightly with melted butter.

Austria

STUFFED EGGS

Eggs stuffed with anchovy paste

	4 hard-boiled eggs	
200 g	egg yolk paste	7 oz
40 g	anchovy fillets, previously	2 oz
	soaked	
	sliced and blanched carrots	
	leek (green part only),	
	blanched	
	sliced truffle	

Cut the eggs in half lengthways, remove the yolks and use these to make the paste. Rub the anchovy fillets through a sieve, blend with the paste. Fill the eggs and put together again. Decorate with a flower motif made from small slices of carrot, leek and truffle and glaze with aspic.

(Illustration, p. 811)

Austria

Eggs stuffed with aspic mayonnaise

4 persons

	6 hard-boiled eggs	
$\frac{1}{8}$ l	mayonnaise	$\frac{1}{4}$ pt
$\frac{1}{4}$ l	aspic	$\frac{1}{2}$ pt
	sliced truffles	

Cut two eggs in half across the width and serrate the edges. Remove the yolk whole without damaging it from each of the remaining four eggs. Mix the mayonnaise with an equal amount of aspic, season well, coat the egg yolks with it and, when firm, place on the serrated half-eggs. Garnish with a small slice of truffle and glaze with aspic.

(Illustration, p. 811)   Austria

Eggs stuffed with caviar paste

4 persons

	4 hard-boiled eggs	
200 g	egg yolk paste	7 oz
50 g	caviar	$1\frac{3}{4}$ oz
$\frac{1}{4}$ l	aspic	$\frac{1}{2}$ pt
	parsley	
	lemon juice	
	leek (green part only), blanched	

Cut the eggs in half lengthwise, remove the yolks and use these for the paste. Sieve the caviar, mix with the egg yolk paste, flavour to taste with lemon juice, fill into the half-eggs and put these together again. Decorate with a motif made of parsley, strips of leek and caviar to depict a vine shoot. Glaze with aspic.

(Illustration, p. 811)   Austria

Eggs stuffed with egg yolk paste

4 persons

2 tomatoes
4 hard-boiled eggs
4 tarragon leaves

$\frac{1}{4}$ l	aspic	$\frac{1}{2}$ pt
60 g	butter	2 oz
	mustard	
	Worcestershire sauce	
	pepper	
	salt	

Cut the tomatoes in half and scoop out the centres. Cut the eggs in half horizontally, remove the yolks and rub through a sieve. Cream the butter, work in the egg yolks, season with salt, pepper, mustard and Worcestershire sauce, and fill the whites with this paste. Stand the stuffed eggs in the half-tomatoes with the whites uppermost, garnish with a tarragon leaf and glaze with aspic.

(Illustration, p. 811)　　　　　　　　　　　　　　　　　　　　　　　　Austria

Eggs stuffed with ham purée

4 persons

	4 hard-boiled eggs	
200 g	ham purée	8 oz
$\frac{1}{8}$ l	mayonnaise	$\frac{1}{4}$ pt
$\frac{1}{4}$ l	aspic	$\frac{1}{2}$ pt
250 g	spinach	8 oz
	sliced truffles	

Blanch the spinach, squeeze dry and rub through a nylon sieve. Cut the eggs in half lengthways, scoop out the centre, fill the half-eggs with ham purée and put together again. Mix the mayonnaise with the spinach and a little aspic. When almost setting, pour over the eggs. Using a fine plain tube, pipe on a 'cap' and place a small slice of truffle in the centre. Glaze with aspic and place in paper cases.

(Illustration, p. 811)　　　　　　　　　　　　　　　　　　　　　　　　Austria

Eggs stuffed with liver paste

4 persons

	2 hard-boiled eggs	
100 g	liver pâté	3 oz
50 g	butter	1 oz
	4 tangerine segments	
	4 half glacé cherries	
	aspic	

Cut the eggs in half lengthwise. Cream the butter, mix with the sieved liver pâté, season with salt and pepper and add a dash of Cognac. Pipe this liver paste into each half-egg; when firm, decorate with a tangerine segment and half a cherry and glaze with aspic.

(Illustration, p. 811)   Austria

Eggs stuffed with lobster paste

4 persons

	4 hard-boiled eggs	
	1 small can lobster	
⅛ l	mayonnaise	¼ pt
	4 tablespoons tomato	
	ketchup	
200 g	egg yolk paste	7 oz
¼ l	aspic	½ pt

Cut the eggs in half lengthwise, remove the yolks (use these for the paste), fill the half-eggs with the egg yolk paste mixed with finely chopped lobster meat and put them together again. Mix the mayonnaise with the tomato ketchup and enough aspic to make it set and pour over the eggs. When firm, decorate with a small piece of lobster meat which has been set aside and with a small disk of truffle. Glaze with aspic. Place in paper cases.

(Illustration, p. 811)   Austria

Eggs stuffed with oyster paste

4 persons

	2 hard-boiled eggs	
50 g	butter	2 oz
	10 oysters	
	dill leaves	
	aspic	

Cut the eggs in half and remove the yolks. Mix the sieved yolks well with the creamed butter and 6 sieved oysters, season and pipe into the half-eggs. Garnish each one with a trimmed oyster and a dill leaf and glaze with aspic.

(Illustration, p. 811)   Austria

Eggs stuffed with smoked salmon paste

4 persons

	4 hard-boiled eggs	
150 g	egg yolk paste	4 oz
75 g	smoked salmon, sieved	2 oz
¼ l	aspic	½ pt
	sliced truffles and smoked salmon for decoration	

Cut the eggs in half lengthwise, remove the yolks (use these for the egg yolk paste) and fill with the sieved smoked salmon mixed with the egg yolk paste. Put the half-eggs together in pairs, decorate with a small piece of smoked salmon and small slices of truffle and glaze with aspic.

(Illustration, p. 811)   Austria

Eggs stuffed with tongue purée

4 persons

	4 hard-boiled eggs	
100 g	butter	4 oz
100 g	pickled tongue, cooked and very finely minced	4 oz
	2 slices pickled tongue	
	2 large olives	
	sliced truffles	
¼ l	aspic	⅓ pt

Cream the butter, mix with the minced tongue, season well and rub through a sieve if necessary. Cut the eggs in half lengthways, scoop out the centres, fill with the tongue purée and put together again. Decorate with a mosaic of diamond-shaped pieces of tongue, olive and truffle and glaze with aspic.

(Illustration, p. 811)   Austria

OTHER EGG DISHES

Egg royale (Tamago-Dofu)

Cooking time: 25 minutes

	6 large eggs	
3½ dl	clear bouillon	⅔ pt
	⅔ teaspoon salt	
	1 teaspoon mirin	
	⅔ teaspoon usukuchi*	
	pinch of aji-no-moto	

Sauce

1½ dl	bouillon	¼ pt
	¼ teaspoon salt	
	2–3 drops soya sauce	
	pinch of aji-no-moto†	
	2 slices lemon or lime	
	cut into 4	

Beat the eggs lightly, mix with the bouillon and add salt, mirin, aji-no-moto and usukuchi. Cover 4 small moulds with a piece of muslin and slowly pour in a quarter of the mixture, straining it through the muslin by twisting the ends. Remove the scum from the top, cover with a cloth, place a lid on top, leaving it slightly open and cook gently in a steamer. Alternatively, poach the custard in a bain-marie in a moderate oven, but do not cover with a cloth. When cooked, stand aside for a short time, then turn out and cut in half. Serve hot or cold with the sauce poured over and garnished with slices of lemon or lime.

This dish may be varied by adding finely pounded pink shrimps or mashed green peas to the savoury custard and thinly sliced shrimps to the sauce.

Japan

* usukuchi: light soya sauce.
† aji-no-moto: a Japanese seasoning based on monosodium glutamate which brings out the flavour of foods.

Folded fried eggs (Tamagoyaki)

4 persons

	5 eggs	
50 g	sugar	2 oz
5 cl	water	1½ fl oz
	⅓ teaspoon salt	
	pinch of aji-no-moto	
75 g	grated radish	3 oz
	4–5 tablespoons soya sauce	
	oil	

Place the sugar and water in a pan, heat and stir until the sugar is completely dissolved. Add the salt and allow to cool. Beat up the eggs in a bowl and mix with the cold syrup. Brush the bottom and sides of a frying pan with oil, heat the pan, allow to cool a little and pour in a quarter of the egg/syrup mixture. Cook over moderate heat while constantly pricking the top with chopsticks. When cooked, fold both sides together, then fold into three and push to one side of the pan. Brush the pan with oil again and repeat the operation until the remaining egg mixture has been cooked. Place the folded eggs one on top of another on a carving board, press into a square, allow to cool and cut into four. Serve with the grated radish which has been mixed with the soya sauce and aji-no-moto.

Japan

Stuffed goose eggs

	10 goose eggs	
200 g	cooked spinach	8 oz
75 g	butter	2 oz

Boil the eggs until hard, shell, cut in half lengthwise and carefully remove the yolks. Rub through a fine sieve together with the cooked spinach which has been pressed dry, mix well with the butter, season with salt, pepper and a pinch of grated nutmeg and pipe into the half eggs, using a savoy bag.

Hungary

Eggs Villamanrique

6 persons

250 g	Andalusian ham	8 oz
200 g	calf's, lamb's or chicken liver	8 oz
	2 medium potatoes	
	5 ladles cooked peas	
	5 ladles cooked young beans (small if possible)	
100 g	chorizo (best quality)	4 oz
	1 medium onion	
	6–8 eggs	
200 g	pork fat	8 oz
	1 fairly large clove of garlic	
500 g	ripe tomatoes	1 lb
	1 wine-glass sherry	

a little dried saffron
nutmeg
salt
pimentón
(Spanish paprika)

Render down half the pork fat in a pan, add the diced ham and the liver cut in small pieces and fry well. Stir in the onion and garlic which have been finely chopped. When the onion begins to colour, add the tomatoes which have been scalded, skinned, crushed to remove the seeds and very finely chopped. Continue frying and pour in the sherry. When the sherry is reduced to half its volume, stir in the cooked peas and beans, the chorizo which has been skinned and finely sliced and the potatoes which have been peeled, washed, finely diced and fried in the rest of the fat. Mix well, flavour with the saffron and a little grated nutmeg and season with a little paprika and with salt as required. Reduce over gentle heat for about 10 minutes and transfer to a wide flat-bottomed earthenware casserole, spreading the mixture evenly. Place the eggs on top, first breaking each one into a small dish separately. Sprinkle with a little chopped parsley and bake in the oven until the whites are set and a thin skin has formed over the yolks. Remove from the oven and serve at once in the casserole.

Spain

Tunisian eggs (Brik à l'oeuf)

1 person   Cooking time: 3–4 minutes

1 fresh egg
1 sheet malsouka*
finely chopped onions
finely chopped parsley
lemon juice
oil for frying

Mix the chopped onions and parsley together, cook in a little salted water until soft, drain well and add ground black pepper. Lay a sheet of malsouka on a deep plate and place about half a teaspoonful of the onion and parsley mixture in the centre. Break the egg on top and fold the malsouka over to enclose the egg completely, sealing well. Slide off the plate into very hot oil and turn almost at once to brown the other side. Remove from the oil immediately, drain well on paper and serve very hot sprinkled with lemon juice.

Tunisia

* Malsouka: paper-thin sheets of pastry. To make these, work fine wheat flour and fine semolina to a tight dough with water and salt. Invert a round copper mould over an open fire, cover it very thinly with the dough, using the hand, and allow to dry without baking off completely.

Tunisian egg and meat dish (Kaftaji Dyari)

4 persons

200 g	lean meat (beef or lamb)	8 oz
	1 slice liver	
	4 eggs	
2 dl	olive oil	⅓ pt
	3–4 potatoes, peeled	
250 g	red gourd or courgettes	8 oz
	3–4 fresh tomatoes	
	2–3 sweet peppers	
	few fresh hot peppers	
	2–3 cloves of garlic	
	½ teaspoon harissa*	
	2 teaspoons ground black pepper	
	2 tablespoons ground red pepper	
	2 tablespoons tabel†	

Chop (or mince) the meat and season with a pinch of pepper and ground tabel. Add salt to taste and shape into balls the size of a hazelnut. Cut the liver into small pieces and season in the same way. Peel the red gourd or courgettes and slice finely. Wash the peppers, make a small incision on one side with the point of a knife and sprinkle inside with a little fine salt and ground tabel. Heat the oil and fry the meat balls, then the pieces of liver and then the potatoes, cut into chips, and the vegetables. When all these are cooked, fry the eggs and keep hot together with the meat and vegetables. Prepare a sauce with the remaining oil, the tomatoes which have been reduced to a purée, the finely cut cloves of garlic, the harissa and a few drops of water. Season with the ground red pepper, salt and tabel.

Place one or two spoonfuls of sauce on each plate with a fried egg in the centre. Surround with a few slices of gourd or courgette, a few chips and the peppers which have been seeded and cut into julienne strips. Add a few meat balls and pieces of fried liver and serve very hot.

Tunisia

* Harissa: a paste made of fresh or dried hot red peppers, which are pounded to a very fine purée in a mortar with garlic, olive oil and a little coriander, and well mixed.
† Tabel is Tunisian coriander.

Eggs en cocotte

A variation of poached eggs. Each egg is placed in a small fireproof dish or cocotte and poached in cream, bouillon or other liquid. Heat the liquid, allowing 1 tablespoon for each egg, and pour into the heated cocotte. Break in the egg and place the cocotte in a roasting tin or sauté pan with lid which has water to come halfway up each cocotte. Heat for 2 or 3 minutes with the water at simmering point. Cover and place in the oven to complete cooking at 190°C (375°F). Total cooking time approximately 8 minutes. The white should be set while the yolk is soft. Each cocotte is dried and served on a napkin.

Many varieties of this dish are possible.

Portuguese eggs

	4 large tomatoes	
	4 eggs	
50 g	white breadcrumbs	2 oz
50 g	melted butter	2 oz
	chopped parsley	
	finely crushed garlic	

Cut the tops off the tomatoes, scoop out the centres, season lightly and carefully break an egg into each. Mix the breadcrumbs with chopped parsley, crushed garlic, salt and freshly ground black pepper, and cover the eggs. Pour the melted butter over, and bake in a moderate oven for 15 minutes.

Portugal

Scotch eggs

	4 eggs	
500 g	sausage meat	1 lb

Hard boil the eggs, shell them and mould 125 g (4 oz) of the sausage meat round each egg, keeping them egg shaped. Coat in egg and breadcrumbs and deep fry until golden brown. Scotch eggs can be served hot and cold, and look best when sliced in half lengthways.

Great Britain

Spanish eggs (Huevos al Plato Barcino)

	6 eggs	
125 g	minced pork	4 oz
250 g	tomatoes	8 oz
	1 onion	
	1 clove of garlic	
¼ l	meat stock	⅓ pt
50 g	butter	2 oz
	1 bay leaf	

Finely chop the onion and garlic and sweat gently in the butter, until just beginning to take colour. Add the minced pork and continue to fry gently. Add the skinned, seeded and coarsely chopped tomatoes and the bay leaf and simmer. Add the stock and simmer until the sauce is reduced to a thick, moist purée. Turn it into a large oven-proof dish, and make six hollows in the purée with the bowl of a ladle. Carefully break an egg into each hollow and cook in a moderate oven until the eggs are set. Serve in the dish.

Spain

Plovers' eggs, gulls' eggs, etc.

These are hard boiled, and offered as an hors d'oeuvre, usually surrounded by cress or lettuce in the shape of a nest.

Great Britain

FISH

Fish come in such a variety of shapes and sizes that to list them all, from sardine to whale would be an impossible task, and furthermore this variety of species is reflected in a profusion of recipes. Most fish can be cooked in many different ways, which could create confusion. However, no cook is likely to use a coarse fish to be poached and served with a delicate wine sauce, nor to use a freshly caught trout to make a fish pie. The following basic recipes can be used for many different fish.

BASIC FRIED FISH IN BREADCRUMBS

Flour the fillets of fish and pass them through beaten egg. Season with salt and pepper and cover with breadcrumbs. Put into very hot fat and cook until a golden colour. Drain the fillets and arrange on a serving dish with quarters of lemon.

BASIC FRIED FISH IN BATTER

For the batter

125 g	flour	4 oz
2 dl	water	$\frac{1}{3}$ pt
	2 spoons olive oil	
	2 egg whites	
	pinch salt	

Mix together pinch of salt, oil and tepid water in a bowl. Mix in the flour carefully to prevent elasticity. Leave for 1 hour. Fold in the stiffly beaten egg whites when required for use.

Wipe the fish dry, dip in the batter and pass through hot fat. Drain and arrange on a napkin and garnish with fried parsley.

BASIC FISH MEUNIÈRE

Smaller fish such as sole and trout are fried whole in clarified butter in a pan. Large fish are cut in slices or darnes. Whole fish not above 1½ kg (3½ lb) can **also be** cooked meunière using half oil and half clarified butter.

Season the fish with salt and pepper and pass through flour. Lay the fish in the pan containing the hot clarified butter or the oil and butter. When golden on both sides, drain and arrange on a dish. Sprinkle with lemon juice, chopped parsley and noisette butter.

BASIC GRILLED FISH

Choose medium sized or cut fish. Incise the whole fish for the heat to penetrate. Fish which dry quickly are floured beforehand and oiled or brushed with butter. Oily fish—salmon, mackerel, herring and trout—can be grilled after simply passing through oil. Grilled fish are accompanied by a savoury butter or a sauce.

BASIC POACHED FISH

This method of cooking can be applied to sole, turbot, brill, halibut and fillets of other fish.

Butter a fireproof dish, fish tray or shallow pan. Place on it the fish. Salt lightly and sprinkle with fish stock and mushroom cooking liquor or dry white wine. Cover with buttered paper and cook in a medium oven. The cooking liquor is reduced and added to the appropriate sauce accompanying the fish.

BASIC COURT BOUILLON

2½ l	water	4¼ pt
1 dl	vinegar	⅛ pt
20 g	salt	1 oz
300 g	minced carrots	10 oz
200 g	chopped onion	8 oz
50 g	parsley stalks	2 oz
	1 bay leaf	
	crushed peppercorn	

Flute the carrots and cut into roundels. Cut the onions into rings. Fill the fish kettle with the water adding the vinegar, carrots, onion, bay leaf, parsley stalks, salt and crushed peppercorns. Cook for 1 hour and then pass through a conical strainer or muslin.

BASIC FRYING BATTER

125 g	flour	4 oz
	2 spoons olive oil	
2 dl	water	$\frac{1}{3}$ pt
	2 egg whites	
	pinch of salt	

Mix in a bowl the oil and tepid water. Mix in the flour. Add a pinch of salt. Leave for 1 hour and when required for use fold in the stiffly beaten egg whites.

BARBECUED FISH

Prepare the fresh fish in the usual manner, i.e. remove the scales, cut off the fins, gut and wash. Season with a mixture of salt and pepper and flavour with lemon juice. Impale each fish on a stick 1 m ($3\frac{1}{4}$ ft) long and 4 mm (about $\frac{1}{8}$ in) thick, inserting it into the mouth of the fish and pushing it through the body by passing several times to the left and right of the backbone. Fix the end of the stick into the ground so that the fish is over the glowing charcoal. The distance required between the fish and the fire will depend on the heat of the glowing embers. The fish should roast slowly for about 30–40 minutes, during which time it should be turned repeatedly. (Techniques p. 133)

SEA FISH

HOT DISHES

Baked cod

1 kg	cod (fresh or frozen)	2 lb
15 g	salt	$\frac{1}{2}$ oz
30 g	margarine	1 oz

Rub the fish with salt and arrange in a buttered shallow fireproof dish. Cover with aluminium foil and bake for 40 minutes at 200°C. Pour off the cooking liquid. Serve with peas and Béchamel sauce seasoned with freshly ground white pepper.

Sweden

Baked mullet

4 persons   Baking time: 30 minutes

| | 1 large mullet | |
| 750 g | peeled potatoes | $1\frac{1}{2}$ lb |

1 lemon
ground black pepper
salted butter
pinch of saffron

Scale the fish, which should be very fresh, make a small slit along the abdomen and remove the entrails, then wash the fish very thoroughly. Score lightly with a sharp knife, season inside and outside with salt and black pepper and place a little salted butter inside the abdomen. Cut the potatoes in slices about 1 cm ($\frac{1}{2}$ in) thick and sprinkle lightly with salt. Place the fish in an oval fireproof dish of suitable size and surround with the sliced potatoes. Sprinkle the lemon juice and pour in just enough water to cover after dissolving the saffron in it. Cover with buttered paper, bake at about 180°C and serve at once in the baking dish.

(Illustration, p. 368)   Tunisia

Black Sea turbot cheeks Nikolajev

6 persons   Cooking time: 10 minutes

	12 fresh turbot cheeks	
1–1 kg 500	round country loaf	2$\frac{1}{4}$–3$\frac{1}{4}$ lb
200 g	onions	8 oz
300 g	fresh beetroots	10 oz
1 kg	white cabbage	2$\frac{1}{4}$ lb
200 g	fresh butter	8 oz
	3 egg yolks	
100 g	sweet almonds, blanched	4 oz
100 g	soft pink flesh of	4 oz
	Achatina snails*	
	carrots	
	leeks	
	mushrooms	
	1 fresh lemon leaf	
	thyme	
	lemon juice	
	white wine	

Place the turbot cheeks on a bed of finely sliced mushrooms, leeks, carrots and onions, season lightly with salt and pepper, pour in white wine, cover with buttered paper and poach in the oven. Cut the top off the loaf, scoop out the crumb and grate. Shred the cabbage and prepare in the same way as Bavarian cabbage, but keep it very crisp. Towards the end of the cooking time, stir in the

* Achatina margina: a tropical land snail weighing about 500 g (1 lb) and greatly in demand as a delicacy.

beetroots cut into strips and cook under cover for a further 10 minutes. Mix well with the breadcrumbs.

Instead of the caviar sauce which is usually served with this dish, prepare Achatina snail sauce as follows. Pound the soft pink snail flesh and the almonds to a very fine purée in a mortar, mix with the fresh butter and warm to about 45°C. Beat the egg yolks in a bain-marie together with 2 tablespoons well-reduced vinegar sauce (as used to make Hollandaise sauce). Work in the snail butter a little at a time, sharpen with lemon juice and season with salt, pepper and a good pinch of cayenne pepper.

Braised fish and bamboo shoots (Takiawase)

4 persons

500 g	fillets of white fish	1 lb
200 g	cooked bamboo shoots (canned)	8 oz
1½ dl	water	¼ pt
7 cl	mirin (sweet rice wine)	⅛ pt
5 cl	saké (dry rice wine)	2 fl oz
25 g	sugar	1 oz
	4 tablespoons soya sauce	
125 g	green beans without threads, boiled in salted water until just tender	4 oz
7 cl	bouillon, mixed with 1 teaspoon each soya sauce, mirin and sugar	⅛ pt

Cut the fish evenly into 8 pieces. Arrange in a suitable pan, pour in the water, mirin and saké, cover and bring to the boil. Turn down the heat, add the sugar and poach for 4–5 minutes. Now add half the soya sauce and poach for a further 7–8 minutes. Pour in the rest of the soya sauce, boil up once, turn off the heat and remove the fish from the pan. Cook the bamboo shoots for 2–3 minutes in the fish stock.

Place the beans in the flavoured bouillon, bring to the boil, remove from the heat and allow to cool.

Dish the fish with the bamboo shoots and the beans which have been cut in half, and pour over the liquid in which the fish and the bamboo shoots were cooked.

Japan

Buckling au gratin

4 persons   Cooking time: about 15 minutes

	10–12 skinned buckling fillets	
	2 medium yellow onions, chopped	
50 g	red caviar	2 oz
2 dl	single cream	$\frac{1}{3}$ pt
	1 heaped tablespoon chopped dill	
60 g	butter	2 oz
	breadcrumbs	

Cook the chopped onions gently in a little butter without browning. Butter the bottom of an oval fireproof dish and sprinkle first with the onions, then with the dill. Arrange the buckling fillets on top and cover with the caviar blended with the cream. Sprinkle with breadcrumbs, dot with butter and brown in the oven at 275°C.

Sweden

Casserole of salt cod Pil-Pil

6 persons   Cooking time: about 1 hour 10 minutes

1 kg	salt cod cut from the narrow part of a large fish	$2\frac{1}{4}$ lb
3–4 dl	olive oil (depending on amount of sauce required)	$\frac{1}{2}$–$\frac{2}{3}$ pt
	4 cloves of garlic, peeled and chopped	

Wash the fish, cut into 2 or 3 pieces and soak for 24 hours, changing the water twice. Clean thoroughly and cut each piece lengthwise into even strips 5 cm (2 in) wide. Place in a saucepan, cover with cold water, heat to 65°C (taking care that the water does not boil) and poach at this temperature for 1 hour. Allow to cool and remove the bones, making sure the strips of fish keep their shape. Heat the oil in a fireproof earthenware casserole, drop in the chopped garlic and fry lightly without colouring. Place the strips of fish in the casserole skin side down, allow the oil to cool a little and turn the strips over, keeping them flat. Serve very hot in the casserole, in the same way as young eels, without stirring the oil or shaking the casserole.

Alternatively, the fish may be served in a creamy sauce if preferred. When the fish is almost ready, add a few small spoonfuls of the water in which it was poached and which has been allowed to cool. Shake the casserole gently to blend the water, the fish juices and the oil together.

Spain

Creamed haddie

6 persons

1 kg	lightly salted smoked haddock	2¼ lb
1 l	milk	1¾ pt
1 l	Béchamel sauce	1¾ pt
	4 hard-boiled eggs, coarsely chopped	
	1 teaspoon black peppercorns	
	2–3 pimentos	
	juice of 1 lemon	
100 g	grated cheese	4 oz
	1 tablespoon finely chopped chives	

Soak the smoked haddock in milk for 24 hours. Meanwhile prepare a creamy Béchamel sauce. Place the fish and milk in a pan, heat slowly to boiling point and carefully remove the skin and bones. Place the fish in the Béchamel sauce, add the lemon juice and carefully stir in the eggs, the chives and the seeded, diced pimentos. Transfer to a fireproof dish, sprinkle with the cheese and brown as desired.

Great Britain

Cod's roe Danish style

6 persons

500 g	cod's roe	1 lb
	flour	
150 g	Remoulade sauce	4 oz
	1 lemon	
	3 slices rye bread (6 half slices)	
90 g	butter	4 oz
	butter for frying	

Season and flour the cod's roe and fry in butter. Dish with slices of lemon and serve rye bread and butter separately.

Denmark

Fillet of turbot Norwegian style

4 persons   Cooking time: about 18–20 minutes

	2 fillets of turbot	
250 g	each weighing	8 oz
150 g	salmon	5 oz
50 g	picked prawns	2 oz
50 g	mussels, removed from the shells, trimmed and poached	2 oz
½ l	white wine	¾ pt
1 l	dairy cream	1½ pt
50 g	butter	2 oz
	2 eggs	
	4 lobster medallions	
	4 slices truffle	
30 g	breadcrumbs for coating	1 oz
	fish stock	
	lemon	

Rub the salmon through a sieve and mix on ice with salt, pepper and the egg yolks. Chill well and gradually stir in enough cream to make light, rather soft forcemeat— about 2¼ dl (⅖ pt) cream will be required. Skin the fillets of turbot, flatten slightly and season. Spread each fillet with salmon forcemeat to a thickness of 1 cm (about ½ in), fold over and arrange in a well-greased fireproof dish. Pour in the white wine and a little fish stock, cover with buttered paper and poach in the oven. When cooked, remove and keep hot in a little stock, covered with buttered paper. Reduce the rest of the stock and cream to a thick sauce, flavour with lemon juice, check the taste and strain through a cloth. Drain the fish, cut in slices, coat with sauce and garnish with the lobster medallions and truffle slices. Coat the mussels and prawns with egg white and breadcrumbs, deep-fry in hot fat until golden, and serve separately.

Norway

Fish Sambal

Coat poached fish with Sambal sauce. Sprinkle with grated coconut, chopped parsley and lemon juice.

Sambal sauce

1 onion, finely minced
2 fresh chillies, finely minced

1 clove of garlic, finely minced
½ teaspoon ground ginger
½ teaspoon ground cumin seed
1 teaspoon ground turmeric
pinch of powdered red chillies

Fry the onion lightly in a little fat without browning. When cooked to a soft paste, blend with coconut milk or curds, using a whisk.

India

Fried fresh Baltic sprats

6 persons   Frying time: 8–10 minutes

600 g	sprats	1¼ lb
100 g	fresh unroasted	4 oz
	sesame seeds	
	1 egg, beaten	
	2 bunches curly parsley	
	sesame oil	

Cut off the heads of the sprats, slit along the abdomen, clean out the entrails, wash the fish thoroughly and dry. Dip in beaten egg seasoned with salt and pepper, coat with sesame seeds and fry in sesame oil over moderate heat. Drain well, dish, and garnish with fried parsley.

(Illustration, p. 591)   Germany

Fried whitebait with lemon

Wash the fish and dry in a cloth. In a dry cloth put 3 tablespoons of flour and toss the whitebait in it, a few at a time. Place the fish in a frying basket. Have ready a pan of hot fat and fry the whitebait until crisp and lightly browned—2–3 minutes. Drain the fish and serve at once, sprinkled with salt and garnished with quarters of lemon.

Great Britain

Grilled yellow-tail (Buri no Teriyaki)

4 persons

100 g	4 fillets of yellow-tail, each weighing	4 oz

	4 tablespoons soya sauce	
	4 tablespoons mirin	
	(sweet rice wine)	
	4 tablespoons saké	
	(dry rice wine)	
	1 lotus root	
1 dl	vinegar	3 fl oz
50 g	sugar	2 oz
	½ teaspoon salt	
	¼ teaspoon aji-no-moto	
	(monosodium glutamate)	

Marinate the fish fillets for 30 minutes in the mirin and saké mixed with the soya sauce. Cut the lotus root into 6 mm (¼ in) slices and at once pour over the vinegar. Cut a small cone-shaped piece out of the centre of each slice, then cut the edges to a flower shape. Boil for 3 minutes in water containing 1 tablespoon vinegar, then drain. Place 5 cl (1/12 pt) vinegar in a pan with the sugar, salt, aji-no-moto and barely 1 dl (⅛ pt) water, bring to the boil, allow to cool, pour into a basin, add the cooked lotus root and marinate for 30 minutes. Grill the fish under medium heat. When it is about two-fifths cooked, turn and brush with the marinade. Continue grilling for a short time, then turn the fish again and baste with the marinade until the latter has evaporated completely. Arrange the fish fillets on a dish and garnish with the lotus root.

Japan

Little soldiers from Pavia

3–4 persons   Cooking time: about 10 minutes

500 g	salt cod, boned and	1 lb
	skinned	
	1 small lemon	
	1 clove of garlic,	
	peeled	
	½ teaspoon allspice	
	pepper	
	oil	

Coating batter

250 g	flour (medium)	8 oz
10 g	yeast	⅓ oz
2–3 cl	brandy	2–3 dessertspoons
	a little powdered saffron,	
	lightly browned	

	pinch each of salt	
	and pepper	
approx. 2 dl	lukewarm water	$\frac{1}{3}$ pt approx.

Cut the salt cod into strips 5 cm (2 in) long and 1 cm (about $\frac{1}{2}$ in) wide. Soak for 12 hours, changing the water twice. Dry thoroughly and place in a bowl which has been rubbed with garlic. Add a few drops of olive oil, the allspice, pepper and the juice of 1 small lemon and marinate for at least 30 minutes, stirring carefully from time to time. Coat each piece of cod well with the prepared batter (see below) and deep fry in hot oil until golden-brown. Drain well and dish on hot plates, allowing 4–6 fritters per person.

To make the batter, sieve the flour into a bowl, make a bay and add the saffron, the brandy, the crumbled yeast, the salt and pepper and the lukewarm water. Mix to a smooth coating batter a little thicker than Béchamel sauce. Cover and leave to rise in a warm place, then use at once. The batter should be deep yellow in colour.

Spain

Skate with black butter

For the court bouillon

1$\frac{1}{4}$ l	water	2 pt
	1 dessertspoon salt	
	1 wine glass vinegar	
	1 medium onion (sliced)	
	1 bouquet garni	
	6 peppercorns	

Put all ingredients in a pan; bring to the boil, simmer for 5 minutes and allow to cool.

Prepare the wing of skate weighing about 675–900 g (1$\frac{1}{2}$–2 lb). Cut into portions and place in a shallow stewpan. Strain over the court bouillon. Bring slowly to the boil, and then barely simmer for 25 to 30 minutes. Take out the fish and drain thoroughly. Skin both sides and arrange in a dish.

For the black butter

40 g	butter	2 oz
	2 tablespoons wine vinegar	
	salt and pepper	
	1 dessertspoon capers	
	1 teaspoon chopped parsley	

Heat a frying pan. Drop in the butter and cook gently to a deep nut brown. Pour over the fish. Add the vinegar to the pan and the seasoning. Reduce to half. Sprinkle capers and parsley over the fish and pour over the reduced vinegar.

Sliced raw fish (Sashimi)

4 persons

400 g	raw tuna (about 3 pieces cut into fillets)	1 lb
15 cm	white Japanese radish	6 in
	2 cucumbers	
	few small carrots	
20 cm	Japanese yams	8 in
	vinegar	
	shungiku (edible chrysanthemum leaves)	
	2 squids	
	1 sheet of nori (dried laver seaweed)	
	horseradish*	
	soya sauce	

Pare the radish, cut into thin strips and soak in sufficient water to remove the smell. Cut the cucumbers into 5 cm (2 in) slices, then into strips of the same size as the radish. Cut up the carrots in the same way, then soak all these ingredients in water and drain thoroughly. Cut the yams into 7 cm (3 in) lengths, peel them, soak in water containing a little vinegar, drain and cut into thin rectangles. Wash the shungiku well and set aside. Cut the tuna into thin oblongs 5 cm (2 in) long, 3 cm (1 in) wide and 5 mm ($\frac{1}{4}$ in) thick. The pieces of raw fish are served in a fanwise arrangement on ice or on lacquer, plain wooden, china or earthenware dishes, often on a bed of fresh raw seaweed or julienne strips of daikon (Japanese radish).

Cut off the arms of the squids, remove the entrails and skin, then score the surface, spacing the cuts 1 cm (about $\frac{1}{2}$ in) apart. Wrap in a sheet of nori of suitable size and cut into rings. Arrange all the ingredients neatly on a dish.

Sashimi is served with soya sauce mixed with powdered wasabi* (Japanese horseradish). Each guest dips the raw fish into the sauce before eating it. Ordinary horseradish may be used instead of wasabi.

Japan

* The horseradish root only is grated; it yields a greenish powder.

15

Sole Bonne Femme

1 kg 500	3 soles	3 lb approx.
1½ dl	white wine	¼ pt
250 g	mushrooms	8 oz
	Hollandaise sauce	
	made with 2 egg yolks	
	and 150 g (6 oz) butter	
	parsley	
30 g	finely chopped shallots	1 oz

Fillet the soles and lay the fillets in a buttered fireproof dish with the shallots and sliced button mushrooms. Season, and poach with the white wine and an equal quantity of fish stock made from the bones. Remove the fillets and reduce the liquid almost to a glaze. Add the Hollandaise sauce and the chopped parsley, coat the fillets with the sauce and glaze quickly under a hot grill.

France

Sole Colbert

For 6 persons

	6 soles	
200 g	each weighing	½ lb
	2 eggs	
	fresh breadcrumbs	
150 g	beurre maître hôtel	5 oz
	milk	
	flour	

Remove the black skin and scale the white skin. On the skinned side make an incision right along the bone and partially lift the fillets without removing them. Break the bone at the head and tail to facilitate removal of backbone after cooking. Leave the fillets folded back. Dip in milk, flour, egg and breadcrumbs and deep fry in hot fat. Drain well. Carefully remove the bone and fill the cavity with beurre maître hôtel.

France

Sole Veronique

For 6 persons

	12 fillets of sole	
1 dl	white wine	⅙ pt

1 dl	fish fumet	⅙ pt
5 cl	curaçao	2 fl oz
200 g	peeled and seeded muscat grapes	8 oz
75 g	butter	3 oz

Fold the fillets and poach them in the white wine, fish fumet and curaçao. Arrange them on a serving dish, with the grapes. Reduce the cooking liquor almost to a glaze and whisk in the butter. Coat the fish and grapes with this sauce and glaze under a hot grill. Place a grape on each portion.

France

Sole Waleska

For 6 persons

	12 fillets of sole	
	12 escalopes of cooked lobster tail	
	12 thin slices of truffle	
2 dl	fish fumet	⅓ pt
25 g	butter	1 oz
4 dl	Sauce Mornay	⅔ pt

Poach the fillets flat in the fish fumet. Arrange them on a buttered gratinating dish. Place on each an escalope of lobster with a slice of truffle. Coat with the Sauce Mornay, and glaze.

Squid Roman style

6 persons   Cooking time: 6–7 minutes

600 g	cleaned prepared squid	1¼ lb
	2 lemons	
	flour	
	2–3 beaten eggs	
	oil for frying	
	mayonnaise	

Cut the squid into rings and marinate for at least 1 hour in lemon juice, salt and pepper. Coat with flour, shake off the excess, dip in beaten egg and fry until golden in hot oil. Drain well on paper, dish and hand the mayonnaise separately.

Spain

Squid in yellow batter

6 persons   Cooking time: 6–8 minutes

600 g	cleaned prepared squid (body only), medium-sized	1¼ lb
	2 lemons	
	flour	

Batter

	1 large clove of garlic	
250 g	flour, sieved	8 oz
10 g	yeast	⅓ oz
	3 tablespoons oil	
	little white wine	
	few drops vegetable yellow	

Cut the squid into rings, marinate in lemon juice, salt and pepper, coat with flour, shake off the excess and dip in the batter. Fry in hot oil until golden. Allow at least 5 rings per person.

To make the batter, sieve the flour into a bowl and make a bay. Place the crumbled yeast, a little white wine, the oil, salt, pepper and the vegetable yellow in the centre and mix with sufficient lukewarm water to make a smooth coating batter. Cover with a cloth and leave to rise for a time before using.

                                                                                Spain

Tuna-cod variety (Taramabushi)

4 persons

	1 can tuna	
	1 cucumber	
	½ teaspoon salt	
20 g	dried cod or Katsuobushi*	1 oz
	1½ tablespoons soya sauce	
	monosodium glutamate	
	mustard powder	

Flake the tuna, cut the cucumber into thin slices, sprinkle these with salt, leave to stand under pressure, then wrap in a cloth and press well. Grill the dried cod, break up into tiny pieces and set aside.

* Katsuobushi: dried thinly shaved bonito (a type of tuna).

Place the tuna, cucumber and cod or katsuobushi in a bowl and mix thoroughly with the soya sauce, monosodium glutamate and a little mustard powder.

Japan

Tunny fish mousse

Proceed as for salmon mousse, using well-drained canned tunny fish in oil.

France

Tunny fish croquettes (Chulaponas)

6–8 persons   Frying time: 5–6 minutes

1 l	milk	1¾ pt
180 g	flour	6 oz
100 g	butter	3 oz
	or half butter and half oil	
50 g	onions, chopped	2 oz
250 g	tunny fish in oil or marinade	8 oz
	3 hard-boiled eggs	
	3 raw eggs	
	juice of 1 small lemon	
5 cl	dry sherry	2 fl oz
250 g	breadcrumbs	8 oz
	nutmeg	
	oil for frying	

Heat the butter in a saucepan and fry the chopped onions in it lightly without colouring. Add 100 g (3½ oz) flour, mix well, cook for a few moments, remove from the heat and gradually blend in the hot milk with a wire whisk. Cook for a few minutes while stirring constantly until the sauce is as thick as confectioner's custard. Add the flaked tunny fish and the coarsely chopped hard-boiled eggs, season with salt and pepper, flavour with a good pinch of nutmeg, mix well with a wooden spoon and continue cooking for a few minutes longer. Check the taste. Mix 3 egg yolks, the sherry and the lemon juice together in a small basin. Stir into the hot croquette mixture to bind it, then transfer to a clean metal tray with a rim and leave in a cool place. When quite cold, shape into small rolls on a floured table, cut off small pieces and shape these into cylinders, then dip into the 3 whole eggs which have been lightly beaten and coat with breadcrumbs. Pat the cylinders into shape and deep fry in hot oil until golden. Depending on the size of the croquettes, allow 4–6 per person.

Spain

Turbot kedgeree

6 persons

300 g	rice	10 oz
500 g	cooked, skinned and filleted turbot	1 lb
$\frac{1}{2}$ l	thick Béchamel sauce	$\frac{3}{4}$ pt
$\frac{1}{4}$ l	dairy cream	$\frac{1}{2}$ pt
	4 sliced hard-boiled eggs	
	1 good teaspoon curry powder	
50 g	butter	2 oz

Cook the rice until the grains are tender but still firm. Rinse in hot water and drain well. Flake the fish and warm in a moderate oven in a little butter. Spread the rice out, add the rest of the butter, mix with a fork and dry in the oven. Add the cream to the Béchamel sauce and boil down a little without allowing to become too thick. Add the curry powder, adjust the seasoning and strain. To serve, arrange in a hot dish in alternate layers of rice, fish, rice, eggs, etc. with a little hot sauce in between. Coat the top with sauce and serve very hot.

The turbot may be replaced by haddock, cod, halibut or any other fairly firm white fish.

Germany

COLD DISHES

Bass en Bellevue

12–15 persons   Cooking time: $1\frac{1}{4}$ hours

2 kg 500	1 bass	$5\frac{1}{2}$ lb
4 l	court-bouillon	7 pt
$\frac{3}{4}$ l	mayonnaise	$1\frac{1}{4}$ pt

Clean, gut, scrape and wash the fish. Poach and allow to cool in the court-bouillon. Drain and dry gently. Decorate and glaze with aspic, then arrange on a dish with any garnish desired.

Bass is a fish with an excellent flavour and an attractive-looking skin which does not need to be removed before serving. It may be cooked according to any recipe for salmon, with the exception of those requiring the use of red wine in the cooking liquid.

France

Fillets of mackerel in vinegar

6 persons

1 kg	very fresh mackerel	2¼ lb
1 l	vinegar	1½ pt
100 g	onions, finely chopped	4 oz
	2 bay leaves	
	16 peppercorns	
	4 cloves	
	few sprigs of parsley	
15 g	salt	½ oz

Clean, gut and fillet the mackerel; cut any large fillets in half. Arrange side by side in an oval fireproof dish. Place the fish heads and bones in a pan with the chopped onions, the bay leaves, peppercorns, cloves, parsley and salt, pour the vinegar over and cook slowly for 5–10 minutes. Strain over the fish fillets, boil up, remove from the heat and leave in a cool place. Serve the fish cold in the cooking liquid. Alternatively, remove and pour a light vinaigrette sauce or mayonnaise over the fish to serve.

Fresh anchovies or sardines and other small fish may be prepared in the same way.

Spain

Fillets of sole in aspic

8 persons   Cooking time: 8–10 minutes

	4 soles	
400–500 g	each weighing	14–18 oz
2 dl	concentrated fish stock	⅓ pt
	flavoured with	
	white wine	
	1 lemon	
1½ l	fish aspic flavoured	2½ pt
	with Champagne	
750 g–1 kg	Russian salad	1¾–2¼ lb
½ l	mayonnaise or green	¾ pt
	sauce	

Prepare the fillets as for glazed fillets of sole Ninon. Fold each fillet in half and poach. Drain on muslin and cool under pressure. Mask a deep chimney mould with half-set aspic. Arrange the sole fillets all round the sides of the mould with their tips pointing downwards or top to bottom. Fill up with half-set aspic. Keep in a cool place until set. To serve, turn out on a thick bed of Russian salad. Hand mayonnaise or green sauce separately.

The sole fillets may be decorated with truffle motifs, but in this case the aspic used to fill the mould should be firm enough to avoid spoiling the decoration.

France

(Illustration, p. 689)

Fillets of sole in aspic with pink and white garnish

8 persons   Cooking time: 12–15 minutes

	2 soles	
800 g	each weighing	1 lb 12 oz
2 dl	concentrated fish stock	⅓ pt
	flavoured with	
	white wine	
	1 lemon	
	fish aspic	
	barquettes	
	salmon mousse	
	sole mousse	

Fillet the soles and sprinkle with lemon juice on the inside. Roll up and tie round twice with twine. Cook, allow to cool, dry and refrigerate. Mask a small chimney mould with half-set clear aspic. Cut the rolled fillets into 1 cm (½ in) slices and stand them on end in the mould in layers while filling the spaces with half-set aspic. Refrigerate for 2 hours before unmoulding. Garnish with small barquettes filled half with salmon mousse and half with sole mousse.

France

Fillets of sole Oceanic style

8 persons

	8 sole fillets	
75 g	each weighing	3 oz
	8 large crayfish	
approx. 250 g	finely cut vegetable	8 oz approx.
	brunoise (carrots,	
	mushrooms, fennel,	
	onions)	
½ l	dry white wine	¾ pt
1 l	gelatinous fish stock	1½ pt
350 g	fresh salmon	12 oz
¼ l	dairy cream	½ pt
50 g	truffles	1½ oz

	veloute	$\frac{1}{3}$ pt
2 dl	3 sheets gelatine	
	hard-boiled egg white	
	aspic jelly	
	butter	

Cook the vegetables under cover in butter. Prepare fine forcemeat with the crayfish and the vegetables, spread on the sole fillets which have been well flattened, and fold over. Poach in white wine and fish stock and allow to cool under light pressure. When cold, dry well, decorate as desired with truffle, hard-boiled egg, etc., and glaze with aspic. Arrange the fillets in a ring on a large round or rectangular dish with the tip of each fillet inserted into a crayfish shell. Fill the centre of the dish with salmon mousse on an ornamental base made of rice. Place the cracked crayfish claws in between the sole fillets and finish off with an edging of finely chopped aspic jelly.

Salmon mousse: poach the salmon in very gelatinous fish stock and allow to cool in the stock. Drain and sieve finely. Transfer to a bowl, add the veloute and the gelatine which has been soaked, squeezed dry and dissolved. Mix thoroughly, adjust the seasoning and fold in the half-whipped cream. Mask a charlotte or hemispherical mould with aspic, decorate with truffle and hard-boiled egg white, fill with the salmon mousse and finish off with aspic. Refrigerate until set, then turn out.

(Illustration, p. 701) France

Fillets of sole in Pernod jelly

Yield: 6 pieces, 3 servings

120 g net	fillets of sole, trimmed	$4\frac{1}{2}$ oz
	fish stock	
	juice of $\frac{1}{4}$ lemon	
40 g	hard-boiled egg yolk	2 oz
20 g	soft butter	1 oz
	1 level teaspoon chopped dill	
	6 small even-sized mushroom caps, poached	
	6 small disks of truffle	
	fish aspic flavoured with Pernod	

Poach the sole fillets in fish stock with the addition of salt, pepper and lemon juice, keeping the flesh firm, then cool under light pressure. Wipe dry and cut into 6 neat even-sized diamond shapes. Sieve the egg yolk finely (adding the poached fish trimmings if desired), mix well with the butter, season with salt and pepper and stir in the chopped dill. Pipe evenly on to the fish, cover with a mushroom cap and top with a tiny disk of truffle which has been dipped in aspic. Refrigerate until the egg yolk paste is firm, then glaze with Pernod-flavoured fish aspic.

Germany

Glazed fillets of sole Ninon

8 persons   Cooking time: 12–15 minutes

	2 soles	
800 g	each weighing	1 lb 12 oz
2 dl	concentrated fish stock flavoured with white wine	$\frac{1}{3}$ pt
$\frac{1}{2}$ l	Chantilly sauce	$\frac{3}{4}$ pt

Mousseline forcemeat

200 g	raw salmon, boned and skinned	8 oz
15 cl	dairy cream	$\frac{1}{4}$ pt
	1$\frac{1}{2}$ egg whites	

Decoration

1 l	fish aspic flavoured with Champagne	1$\frac{1}{2}$ pt
	1 lemon	
	1 tomato	

Fillet the soles and sprinkle the inside with a little lemon juice. Flatten on a board or marble slab with the skin side uppermost. Prepare mousseline forcemeat with the salmon, cream and egg white, spread on the fillets and fold them over. Trim the ends so that each fillet forms a neat double triangle. Place in a well-buttered fireproof dish, pour in the fish stock, cover with buttered paper and poach, then allow to cool and refrigerate for 2 hours. Dry the fillets between 2 cloths. Decorate with small heart shapes cut out of the tomato. Glaze with aspic and dish on a bed of chopped aspic. Surround with a border of deckle-edged half slices of lemon and place a spot of tomato in the centre of the straight edge of each one. Hand the sauce separately.

France

Glazed stuffed fillets of sole Miraflore

8 persons   Cooking time: 10–12 minutes

	2 soles	
800–900 g	each weighing	1¾–2 lb
2 dl	concentrated fish stock	⅓ pt
	flavoured with	
	white wine	
	1 lemon	
	8 tomatoes	
200 g	small asparagus tips	8 oz
150 g	prawn mousse	6 oz
	24 prawns	
½ l	aspic jelly	¾ pt
½ l	Chantilly sauce or	¾ pt
	Marseillaise sauce	
	for fish	

Wash and flatten the sole fillets, sprinkle the inside with a little lemon juice and season with salt and white pepper. Roll each fillet with the skin side inside round small buttered wooden cylinders about 2 cm (¾ in) in diameter. Place them with the join undermost in a well-buttered sauté pan just large enough to hold them. Cook and allow to cool in the cooking liquid. Carefully remove the wooden cylinders, drain the fish fillets on a cloth and keep cool. Skin the tomatoes, cut off the top third of each and remove the seeds. Season inside with salt and pepper, then drain on a rack for 30 minutes. Cook the asparagus, allow to cool and dry well in a cloth, then dip into half-set aspic and leave in a cool place until set. Fill up the cavity in the centre of the fish fillets with prawn mousse. Place them in the tomatoes and surround with the asparagus, the tips pointing upwards. Top each fillet with three prawns, preferably with their tails shelled, sticking them firmly into the mousse. Glaze with aspic. Dish on napkins and serve the sauce separately.

France

Glazed turbot Floralies

15 persons   Cooking time: 1½ hours

4 kg 200–4 kg 500	1 turbot	9¼–10 lb
1½ l	fish aspic	2½ pt
¾ l	mayonnaise, Andalusian	1¼ pt
	or green sauce	

Place the fish on the drainer of a turbot kettle with the dark skin underneath. Cover with water containing boiled milk (1 part milk to 10 parts water) and season with salt at the rate of 10 g per litre (⅛ oz per pint). Add 2 slices of lemon peeled down to the pulp. Poach the fish and allow to cool in the cooking liquid. Drain and remove the dark skin, sliding the fish gently across the drainer to facilitate skinning. Wipe the white skin carefully and decorate with a floral motif made up of green leek, blanched tarragon, chervil, radishes, etc. Glaze with aspic. Slide the fish on to a board of the same shape covered with a white napkin (if no suitable board is available, use a serving dish). Surround the fish with a brightly coloured garnish arranged on small lettuce heart leaves or shredded lettuce. Hand the sauce separately.

Warning—the flesh of cold turbot is particularly firm.

France

Hake Parisian style

10–12 persons   Cooking time: 1¼ hours

	2 kg 500	1 hake	5½ lb
Garnish			
		10–12 small tomatoes	
	500 g	Russian salad	1 lb
		6 hard-boiled eggs	
		lettuce	
	½ l	mayonnaise	¾ pt

Clean and gut the fish, scrape off the scales and wash. Poach in court-bouillon or in water with the addition of vinegar, seasoning, thyme, bay leaf, parsley and sliced onions. Leave in the cooking liquid until cold, then drain and skin carefully. Decorate and glaze with fish aspic. Place on a dish and surround with lettuce heart leaves. Fill these alternately with wedges of hard-boiled egg and tomatoes stuffed with Russian salad. Stick a small sprig of watercress into the lid of each tomato to simulate leaves. Hand the mayonnaise separately.

France

Hake cutlets Parisian style

Cooking time: 10–12 minutes

Cut the fish into slices (cutlets). Poach and allow to cool in the cooking liquid. Drain and remove the skin carefully, together with the black membrane inside the fish. Wipe the surface, decorate and glaze with aspic. Dish surrounded with the garnish.

France

Hake fillets Parisian style

Cooking time: 12 minutes

Fillet the fish and remove the skin before cooking. Cut up the fillets and poach, then allow to cool in the cooking liquid. Decorate the top, glaze with aspic and dish surrounded with the garnish.

France

Red mullet Oriental style

6 persons   Cooking time: 10 minutes

1 kg	small red mullets	2¼ lb
1 kg 250	fresh tomatoes	2¾ lb
25 g	onion, finely chopped	1 oz
	1 bouquet garni	
	(thyme, fennel,	
	chervil, parsley,	
	¼ bay leaf)	
	pinch of saffron	
	20 coriander seeds	
	1 clove of garlic	

Remove the gills and wipe the fish, but do not gut. Season with salt and pepper, then coat with flour. Heat a little oil in a frying pan until it begins to smoke, lay the fish in it side by side and brown for about 1 minute on each side over brisk heat. Arrange in an oiled fireproof dish. Cook the onion in oil without colouring. Skin the tomatoes, remove the seeds and chop coarsely. Place the liquid from the tomatoes in a pan, season with salt and pepper, add a pinch of sugar, the bouquet garni, the crushed garlic, the saffron and coriander, the chopped tomatoes and the chopped onion. Simmer until three-quarters of the liquid has evaporated. Remove the garlic and the bouquet garni and adjust the seasoning. Spread on the fish, cover with oiled paper and bring to the boil. Cook in the oven, allow to cool and dish. Decorate with slices of lemon peeled down to the pulp and garnish each slice with chervil leaves.

France

Red mullet Provençal style

8 persons   Cooking time: 10 minutes

1 kg	small red mullets	2¼ lb
1 kg	tomatoes	2¼ lb
	30 stoned black olives	

25 g	chopped onion	1 oz
	1 bouquet garni	
	(thyme, bay leaf,	
	parsley)	
	1 clove of garlic	

Prepare the fish as for red mullet Oriental style, brown in oil and place in a fire-proof dish. Skin, seed and coarsely chop the tomatoes. Cook the onion in oil without colouring. Add the tomatoes and olives. Spread on the fish, season with salt and pepper, add the bouquet garni and the crushed garlic, then cook in the same way as red mullet Oriental style. (If the fish are large, fillet after cooking and serve coated with sauce.)

France

Turban of sole fillets black and white

Proceed as for turban of sole fillets in aspic, but spread the fillets with whiting mousseline forcemeat containing chopped truffles. To serve, turn out and surround with small barquettes filled with a salpicon of truffles and sole fillets bound with cream vinaigrette.

France

Turban of sole fillets in aspic

This is prepared with fillets of sole as for glazed fillets of sole Ninon. Instead of glazing and dishing on a bed of aspic, arrange the fillets to overlap slightly in a ring mould masked with aspic, then fill up with half-set aspic and refrigerate. To serve, turn out and surround with small barquettes containing any filling desired.

(Techniques, p. 114)   France

Shark medallions

Yield: 6 pieces

120 g	shark, boned, skinned and trimmed	4 oz
60 g	egg yolk and pistachio purée consisting of:	2 oz
	35 g (1½ oz) hard-boiled egg yolk	
	15 g (½ oz) butter	
	10 g (½ oz) pistachio	

nuts, finely chopped
or ground
12 crayfish tails or shrimps
fish aspic

Prepare the egg yolk and pistachio purée. Cut 6 shark medallions and poach in lemon juice with the addition of a knob of butter and seasonings as required, keeping the fish white. Allow to cool, then wipe the medallions dry and pipe on the egg yolk purée, using a plain pipe. Decorate each one with 2 small crayfish tails, chill well and glaze with fish aspic.

Germany

Sprats in Royale (savoury custard)

6 persons

36 fresh sprats of
equal size
lemon juice
Worcestershire sauce
salt and pepper

Royale

200 g	diced onions	8 oz
	5 eggs	
$\frac{1}{2}$ l	milk	$\frac{3}{4}$ pt
200 g	tomatoes	8 oz
	2–3 sage leaves	
	coarsely chopped parsley	
	oil	
	nutmeg	

Clean and draw the sprats and bone in the same way as herrings. Season with salt and freshly ground pepper, flavour with Worcestershire sauce and lemon juice, and roll up with the skin outside, starting at the tail end. Arrange the rolled sprats one next to the other on an oiled baking sheet or in an ovenproof dish with a 3 cm (1¼ in) rim.

To make the Royale, cook the diced onions, chopped sage and chopped parsley over gentle heat until soft. Beat the eggs, add the milk and mix well, add to the cooked onions away from the heat, stir in the tomatoes after skinning them, removing the seeds and chopping coarsely, and add salt and grated nutmeg. Pour over the sprats and poach for about 30 minutes at 100°C. Leave until quite cold before cutting.

Holland

Stuffed halibut

20–25 portions   Cooking time: about 50 minutes

2 kg 500	1 halibut	5½ lb
300 g	pike, skinned and boned	10 oz
300 g	frangipane panada	10 oz
	2 eggs	
	2 egg yolks	
50 g	truffle	2 oz
	1 small red pepper, skinned and seeded	
	1 small green pepper, skinned and seeded	
100 g	prawn tails	4 oz
	5 hard-boiled eggs	
75 g	butter	3 oz
	1 tablespoon mayonnaise	
	10 slices cucumber, cut on the slant and well blanched	
	10 balls skinned tomato flesh the size of a cherry	
	10 small asparagus tips	
	10 small narrow strips smoked salmon	
	10 slices truffle	
	fish stock	

Prepare forcemeat with the pike, the panada, the eggs and the egg yolks. Season with salt and flavour with grated nutmeg and a good pinch of cayenne pepper. Cut up the prawns and chop the truffle and peppers coarsely, then mix with the forcemeat. Make an incision lengthwise in the dark skin of the halibut and detach the flesh just enough to remove the centre bone. Cut back the fins to within a short distance of the flesh, but do not remove completely or the fish may split open after stuffing. Now stuff the fish with the forcemeat, but do not fill too tightly, to avoid bursting. Sew up the incision and wrap the halibut in buttered greaseproof paper or oil and then in a buttered cloth, making sure that it keeps its shape. Place on a rack in a turbot-kettle with the dark skin side underneath, pour in fish stock and poach gently, then allow to cool. When cold, remove, drain well and press lightly, making sure that the fish keeps its shape. Before slicing, remove the remaining fin bones with a pair of tweezers.

For the garnish, cut the hard-boiled eggs in half, sieve the yolks and work to a well-flavoured paste with the butter, the mayonnaise and seasoning as required. Decorate the slices of cucumber with some of this paste, using a savoy bag and star pipe and

▶   Wine tasting with Quiche Lorraine at M. Keuhn's cellars, Ammerschwiehr, France, p. 303
▶ ▶ A 'Hangover Breakfast' of herrings, bacon and onion flan and beer at the Meindeler Hotel, Bayrischzell, Germany
▶ ▶ ▶ Fondue at the Hôtel des Alpes, Champéry, Switzerland, p. 285
▶ ▶ ▶ ▶ A connoisseurs' cheese and wine party

place a ball of tomato on top. Stuff the half whites with the rest of the paste, cover with a slice of truffle and decorate with an asparagus tip and a strip of smoked salmon.

(Illustration, p. 812)   Austria

Stuffed whalemeat

2 kg	whalemeat	4½ lb
250 g	boned spare rib	8 oz
250 g	boned shoulder of veal	8 oz
250 g	whalemeat trimmings	8 oz
	5 egg whites	
½ l	dairy cream	¾ pt
	(30% butter fat)	
	1 reindeer tongue	
	1 truffle	
	crayfish claws	
	hard-boiled egg white	
	Madeira jelly	

Season the whalemeat with salt and pepper, brown lightly and roast at 180°C for 45 minutes. Cool and refrigerate.

Mince the pork, the veal and the whalemeat trimmings three times, using the 2 mm ($\frac{1}{10}$ in) blade of the mincer. Season well with salt and pepper and flavour with a little nutmeg and forcemeat herbs and spices. Work in the egg whites a little at a time. Chill well, then beat in the cream and add a little finely chopped truffle and the reindeer tongue which has been cooked and finely diced. Fill into a greased mould, poach in a bain-marie at about 110°C and cool for at least 1½ hours.

Slice the whalemeat evenly and neatly. Cut out the centre of each slice with a round cutter. Slice the forcemeat, cut out disks to fit the holes in the slices of whalemeat, place one in the centre of each slice and glaze with jelly.

Cut 8 medallions out of the remaining forcemeat, place them on a metal tray with a rim, decorate with a half-moon of truffle and a crayfish claw and fill up the tray with Madeira jelly. Allow to set and cut out with a round cutter. Fill 8 small moulds with firm Gordon gin tomato. After turning out, decorate with hard-boiled egg white and truffle.

Arrange the whalemeat on a dish and garnish with the Gordon gin tomato moulds and the forcemeat medallions.

NB—If the meat is obtained from whales caught off the Norwegian coast, these should be no more than 1000 kg (1 ton) in weight. The meat from larger whales is coarse-fibred and less suitable.

◄ ◄ ◄ ◄   At the Casle Durnstein Hotel, Durnstein, Austria
◄ ◄ ◄   Roumanian specialities, Pork Brawn p. 631 : Coliva p. 873
◄ ◄   A Roumanian wedding lunch p. 72
◄   Local specialities at Da Ivo, Ascona, Switzerland, Osso bucco, p. 566

Gordon gin tomato is tomato juice laced with Gordon gin and set with gelatine as for aspic jelly.

Norway

HERRING DISHES

SALTING

The herrings should be freshly caught. To prepare for salting, slit the throat, remove the gall, but do not clean. Preserve at once in 3 parts salt to 1 part sugar, sprinkling the herrings with powdered sandalwood to enhance the flavour. The fish should be laid side by side on their back, belly uppermost. Store for a maximum of 6 months.

FILLETING

Soak the fish for at least 24 hours, depending on size and saltiness; only a slightly salty taste should remain after soaking. Pour off the water, place the herrings in a colander between two cloths and refrigerate for several hours. The herrings cannot be filleted immediately as they are too soft; they would fall to pieces and turn grey in the marinade. They should have the same consistency in the marinade as they do in the sea. Extremely careful handling is of the utmost importance.

After chilling, fillet the fish, cut into 2 cm ($\frac{3}{4}$ in) pieces and marinate or coat with the marinade.

Norway

Basic marinade

300 g	sugar	10 oz
6 dl	water	1 pt
11·3 dl	wine vinegar (7%)	2$\frac{1}{4}$ pt
	5 bay leaves	
	1 teaspoon mustard seed	
	1 teaspoon black peppercorns	
	6 cloves	

Place all the ingredients in a pan, bring to the boil, then simmer very gently for 5 minutes. Allow to cool, strain, pour into bottles and store in a cool place until required.

Norway

FRESH HERRINGS

Preparation

Herrings no larger than 10 cm (4 in) should be used fresh. Twist off the head, run the thumb along the backbone, remove the bones, wash the fillets thoroughly and leave to dry on a clean cloth. Sprinkle the inside (flesh side) with salt and roll up with the skin outside, starting at the head end.

Brush a fireproof dish lightly with oil, arrange the herring rolls in it side by side, packing them tightly, and pour over basic marinade or one of the following marinades.

Marinade for fresh herrings

2 dl	water	$\frac{1}{3}$ pt
1 dl	wine vinegar	$\frac{1}{6}$ pt
100 g	sugar	$3\frac{1}{2}$ oz

First sprinkle the herring rolls with salt and pepper, then pour the marinade over. Cover with aluminium foil, bring to the boil, remove from the heat, leave to stand for 24 hours and serve cold.

Red wine marinade

3 dl	red wine	$\frac{1}{2}$ pt
5 cl	vinegar (7%)	$\frac{1}{12}$ pt
	1 tablespoon sugar	
1 dl	water	$\frac{1}{6}$ pt
	3 crushed bay leaves	
	2 cloves	

Sprinkle the rolled herring fillets with salt and sugar, place in a fireproof dish and add the bay leaves and cloves. Pour the water and vinegar over, cover with aluminium foil and bring to the boil. Do not add the red wine until the liquid has boiled, in order to preserve the flavour of the wine. Remove from the heat, leave to stand for 24 hours and serve cold.

White wine marinade

Proceed in exactly the same way as for red wine marinade, but use white wine instead of red.

Bornholm sandwich

6 persons

	6 smoked herrings	
	1 round lettuce	
	radishes	
	2 small onions, chopped	
	6 egg yolks	
	6 slices white bread	
90 g	butter	4 oz

Skin and fillet the herrings, taking care to remove all the bones. Butter the bread, cover with herring fillets and place a raw egg yolk in the centre. Surround the egg yolk with chopped onions, shredded lettuce and sliced radishes.

Denmark

Baked salt herring with butter, chopped eggs and chives

4 persons   Baking time: 10–15 minutes

	4 Icelandic herrings, well	
	soaked and filleted	
	2 hard-boiled eggs,	
	finely chopped	
60 g	butter	2 oz
	2 tablespoons chopped chives	

Butter the bottom of an oval fireproof dish and arrange the fillets in it. Sprinkle with the finely chopped eggs and the chives, then dot the top with butter. Cover with aluminium foil and bake in the oven. Serve with jacket potatoes.

Sweden

Ceramic herring

4 persons   Cooking time: 15 minutes

	4 filleted Scotch herrings	
	2 red onions, finely	
	chopped	
50 g	butter	2 oz
2 dl	dairy cream	⅓ pt
	breadcrumbs	

Soak the herring fillets well, then dry them. Butter a shallow oval ceramic baking dish. Sprinkle the bottom with the chopped onions and arrange the herring fillets on top. Pour in the cream, sprinkle with breadcrumbs and dot with butter. Cover with aluminium foil and bake at 250°C.

Sweden

Chef's pickled herring

4 persons

> 4 large salt Icelandic herrings
> marinade as for pickled salt
>   herring (see p. 478)
> red onion rings
> coarsely cut dill

Clean the herrings, remove the heads and trim, but do not skin or fillet. Soak for at least 12 hours and drain well. Cut across into 1 cm (about ½ in) pieces and place in a suitable glass container (there are special small glass jars for the purpose in Sweden). Pour in the marinade, cover and marinate for 24 hours. Garnish with red onion rings and sprinkle liberally with coarsely cut dill.

Sweden

Clear dill herring

Prepare herring rolls as described earlier and arrange in an oiled fireproof dish. Sprinkle liberally with chopped dill, season with salt and pepper and pour over the following marinade:

2 dl	water	⅓ pt
1 dl	vinegar (7%)	⅙ pt
50 g	sugar	1¾ oz

Cover with aluminium foil, poach in the oven and leave for 24 hours before using.

(Illustration, p. 698) Norway

Curry herring

100 g	mayonnaise	4 oz
	2 tablespoons curry powder	
100 g	sugar	4 oz
	3 tablespoons double cream	
1 dl	pear juice	⅙ pt

Mix together all the ingredients carefully.

Cut the herring fillets into pieces 2 cm ($\frac{3}{4}$ in) wide and pour the marinade over.

Fried Baltic herrings (Suolasilakat)

4 persons   Cooking time: 10–12 minutes

1 kg	salted Baltic herrings	2$\frac{1}{4}$ lb
60 g	butter	2 oz
	rye flour	

Clean and gut the herrings, then soak for 24 hours, changing the water several times. Dry thoroughly, coat with rye flour and fry in the butter on both sides. Dish and serve with boiled potatoes and onion sauce.

Finland

Herring Andalusian style

Prepare the herring fillets in the usual manner, season with salt and pepper and cover with onion rings and strips of red and green pepper. Pour the following marinade over the fillets:

2 dl	water	$\frac{1}{3}$ pt
1 dl	vinegar (7%)	$\frac{1}{6}$ pt
50 g	sugar	2 oz

Cover the dish with aluminium foil, poach in the oven and leave for 24 hours before serving.

(Illustration, p. 698)   Norway

Herring au gratin Swedish style

4 persons   Cooking time: 10–15 minutes

	2 large herrings, soaked and filleted	
	4 medium potatoes cooked in their skins	
	2 medium onions, cut in half and thinly sliced	
	breadcrumbs	
60 g	butter or margarine	2 oz

Cook the sliced onions gently in half the butter without colouring. Peel the potatoes when cold and slice thinly lengthwise. Cut the herring fillets in half lengthwise. Butter a shallow oval baking dish and pack as tightly as possible with the various ingredients arranged in alternate rows. Sprinkle all over with melted butter and a generous amount of breadcrumbs. Place in the oven at 225°C and leave until a light brown crust has formed on top.

Herring with bacon

Fillet fresh herrings, taking care to remove all the bones, wash carefully and drain well. Roll up, starting at the head end, and wrap in thin rashers of streaky bacon. Arrange side by side in an oiled fireproof dish, pour over equal quantities of marinade and single cream, sprinkle with salt, cover with aluminium foil and poach in the oven. Chill well before serving.

(Illustration, p. 698)   Norway

Herring with Cognac

Leave the herrings to stand for 24 hours in a marinade consisting of 2 parts vinegar to 1 part water. Remove, dry well with a clean cloth and slice in the same way as salt herring.

Arrange the pieces of herring in a glass bowl, sprinkle with Cognac and mix with small pieces of canned pineapple and dill. If the herring is too dry, pour a little of the canned pineapple syrup over.

Herring Italian style I

	12 soaked herrings, sliced	
2 dl	tomato ketchup	$\frac{1}{3}$ pt
	$\frac{1}{2}$ can tomatoes, skinned and coarsely chopped	
	2 cloves of garlic, finely cut	
	1 teaspoon chopped fresh mint	
	1 teaspoon marjoram leaves	
	1 teaspoon ground white pepper	
	$\frac{1}{2}$ teaspoon paprika	
	salt to taste	

Mix all the ingredients for the marinade thoroughly, then mix with the pieces of herring and leave to stand.

Herring Italian style II

	12 soaked herrings	
	6 tomatoes, skinned, seeded and diced	
2 dl	tomato ketchup	⅓ pt
	2 cloves of garlic, crushed	
	1 teaspoon oregano	
	1 teaspoon rosemary	
	a little ground white pepper	

Mix together all the ingredients for the marinade. Cut the herrings into pieces 2 cm (¾ in) wide, place in the marinade, stir well, cover and leave to stand for 24 hours before serving.

Herring in Ravigote sauce

Add a little fresh cream to Ravigote sauce to enhance the flavour. Pour over the fresh herring rolls, season with salt and white pepper, cover with aluminium foil, poach and leave until cold before serving.

(Illustration, p. 698)   Norway

Herring with red caviar

Prepare in the same way as dill herring, omitting the dill and spreading the herring rolls with red caviar.

(Illustration, p. 698)   Norway

Herring rolls in dill

	fresh herring rolls	
	1 green pepper	
	1 red pepper	
	1 shallot	
	generous amount of fresh dill	
2 dl	water	⅓ pt
1 dl	vinegar (7%)	⅙ pt
100 g	sugar	3½ oz

Break up the dill into small pieces with the fingers, so that no juice is lost through cutting with a knife. Remove the seeds from the peppers. Chop the peppers and the shallot and sprinkle over the herring rolls together with the dill. Pour over a marinade consisting of the water, vinegar and sugar, cover the dish with aluminium foil, bring to the boil, cool and leave to stand.

Norway

Herring rolls with salted anchovies

Soak some anchovies, dry them and dice finely together with an equal amount of onions. Sprinkle the fresh herring rolls with salt, arrange in a dish and fill the spaces with the diced anchovies and onions. Pour fresh cream over and poach in the oven. Do not use a marinade for this dish.

(Illustration, p. 698)

Norway

Herring rolls with shrimps

Cover the herring rolls with canned shrimps, pour the liquid from the can over, sprinkle with broken-up dill, cover with aluminium foil and poach. Flavour at once with sherry, white or red wine to taste, replace the foil and leave for 24 hours before using.

(Illustration, p. 698)

Norway

Herring salad I

100 g	soaked salt herring fillets (including end pieces)	4 oz
250 g	pickled ox tongue	8 oz
100 g	onions	4 oz
125 g	apples	4 oz
	4 medium-sized cucumbers	
	4 medium carrots	
	basic marinade	

Peel the carrots. Peel the cucumbers and remove the seeds. Peel and core the apples Peel the onions. Dice all these ingredients together with the herring fillets and the tongue, then mix well. Dress with basic marinade.

Norway

Herring salad II

5 portions

100 g	soaked salt herring fillets	4 oz
	1 medium onion, diced	
	1 apple, peeled and cored	
	1 cooked beetroot	
	1 cooked potato	
1 dl	beetroot juice	$\frac{1}{6}$ pt
	2 tablespoons English mustard	

Dice all the ingredients fairly finely. Make up the mustard powder with the beetroot juice and mix well with the diced ingredients. Chill and leave to stand for some time before use.

Norway

Herring salad III

2 soaked salt herring fillets
2 large onions, peeled
2 pickled cucumbers
2 beetroots
1 tablespoon mustard

Dice the herring, onions, cucumbers and beetroots finely, add the mustard and mix thoroughly.

Norway

Herring salad IV

6 persons

750 g	firm waxy potatoes	1 lb 10 oz
	3 salted herrings	
	1 large sour cucumber	
	1 gherkin	
	4 ripe slightly tart apples	
	cooked beetroot	
	1 large onion, finely chopped	
	1 heaped tablespoon mustard	
1 dl	oil	$\frac{1}{6}$ pt
1 dl	wine vinegar	$\frac{1}{6}$ pt
	salt and pepper	

Garnish

> 3 hard-boiled eggs
> 1½ tablespoons capers
> 1½ tablespoons chopped
> parsley

Clean the herrings well and soak overnight, preferably under a slowly running tap. Boil the potatoes in their skins, peel and dice finely. Skin and fillet the herrings, peel the apples, cucumbers and cooked beetroot, then dice all these ingredients finely. Add the chopped onion and mix carefully. Prepare a dressing with the mustard, salt, pepper, vinegar, oil and a few spoonsful of hot bouillon (or hot water). Toss the salad in the dressing and adjust the seasoning to give a piquant flavour. Stand aside for 2–3 hours, check the taste again and pile in a salad bowl to a dome shape. Garnish with chopped egg yolk and white, chopped parsley and, if desired, chopped beetroot. Sprinkle all over with capers.

If preferred, the oil may be replaced by herring roes mixed with dairy cream.

Germany

Herring salad V

	2 salted herrings	
	1 pickled herring	
300 g	cooked potatoes	10½ oz
	1–2 cooked beetroots	
	apples	
	1 onion	
	a few gherkins	
	4 tablespoons oil	
	2 tablespoons vinegar	
	mayonnaise	
	hard-boiled eggs	
	lettuce	

Soak the salted herrings in water for an hour to remove excess salt. Cut the herrings into fillets, then slice these finely. Keep back a few neat pieces for decoration. Dice the potatoes, beetroot, apples and gherkins, and chop the onion. Keep back a little of the diced beetroot and gherkins, and mix the rest with the herrings and the other vegetables and fruit. Add the oil and vinegar. Arrange some lettuce leaves on a large dish and place the herring salad on top. Pour mayonnaise over and decorate with the herring fillets and diced beetroot and gherkins which have been set aside, and also with slices of hard-boiled egg.

Holland

Herrings in sour milk sauce

Select herrings 15 cm (6 in) long, fillet them, but do not marinate. Starting at the head end, roll up with the skin outside. Arrange the rolls on a dish, and bake until just cooked. Garnish with sliced onion and serve with boiled potatoes and the following sauce:

Dilute 100 g (3½ oz) mayonnaise with 5 tablespoons sour milk or buttermilk and mix with finely chopped chives. If the sauce is too thin, add some cream which has been soured with lemon juice.

Norway

Herrings in sweet pepper marinade

	12 herring fillets	
	1 red pepper	
	1 green pepper	
	1 large shallot	
½ l	basic marinade	¾ pt

Cut the peppers open at the stalk end, remove all the seeds and cut into fairly coarse julienne strips. Chop the shallot finely, mix with the peppers and add the basic marinade.

Cut the herring fillets in pieces, pour the marinade over and leave to soak until well flavoured.

Norway

Herrings in tomato sauce I

Fillet fresh herrings, taking care to remove all the bones, wash well, drain and roll up, starting at the head end. Arrange in a lightly oiled fireproof dish and pour over the following marinade:

2 dl	tomato ketchup	⅓ pt
1 dl	water	⅙ pt
1 dl	vinegar (7%)	⅙ pt
50 g	sugar	2 oz

Season with salt, cover with aluminium foil, bring to the boil and leave to stand for 24 hours before using.

Norway

Herrings in tomato sauce II

6 persons   Cooking time: 15 minutes

	6 fresh herrings	
200 g	tomato purée	8 oz
	1 bottle tomato ketchup	
100 g	diced onions	4 oz
1 dl	vinegar	⅙ pt
½ l	fish or meat stock	¾ pt
	1 teaspoon mustard seed	
1 dl	oil	⅙ pt
	salt	
	sugar	
	pepper	

Fillet the herrings and arrange in layers on an oiled baking sheet with the skin side uppermost. Cook the tomato purée in the oil over gentle heat for some time to remove the acid. Flavour with the vinegar and add the stock and ketchup, then the mustard seeds, freshly ground pepper, and 1 part salt to 2 parts sugar. Boil up once. Pour over the herrings and bake in a medium oven.

(Illustration, p. 698)   Holland

Herrings in dill cream

6 persons   Total cooking time: 30 minutes

	6 fresh herrings	
	1 large bunch dill	
1 dl	oil	⅙ pt
¼ l	white wine	½ pt
¼ l	dairy cream	½ pt
25 g	flour	1 oz

Fillet the herrings and cut each fillet in half, so that each herring is divided into four. Arrange on an oiled baking sheet with the skin side uppermost. Make a white roux with the oil and flour, blend in the white wine and cream, season with salt and pepper, cook slowly for 15 minutes and add the chopped dill. Pour over the herring fillets and poach in a moderate oven for 15 minutes. Serve cold with hot boiled potatoes.

Holland

Marinated Baltic herrings

8 persons   Cooking time: 8 minutes

2 kg	Baltic herrings	4½ lb
	2 medium onions,	
	cut in rings	
	juice of 1 lemon	

Marinade

2 dl	wine vinegar	⅓ pt
1 dl	oil	⅙ pt
8 g	salt	¼ oz
	10 white peppercorns	
	3 sprigs thyme	
	1 small bunch dill	
	1 small bay leaf	
	1 clove of garlic	

Place the ingredients for the marinade in a pan and simmer for 8 minutes. Remove the heads from the fresh herrings, gut and clean them and place in a suitable earthenware dish. Sprinkle with the lemon juice, cover with the onion rings and strain the marinade over. Cover the dish and marinate for at least 3–4 days before using. Serve with potatoes in their jacket.

(Illustration, p. 812)   Finland

Pickled salt herring

4 persons

	4 large salt Icelandic	
	herrings	

Marinade

2 dl	strong vinegar	⅓ pt
4 dl	water	⅔ pt
150 g	sugar	5 oz
	1 teaspoon allspice	
	4 bay leaves	
	1 medium yellow onion,	
	sliced	
	1 small carrot, finely	
	sliced	
	1 tablespoon finely cut dill	
	1 leek (white part only),	
	cut into rings	
	crushed allspice and cloves	
	cut dill	

Clean and fillet the herrings, taking care to remove all the bones, and soak for at least 12 hours. Mix all the ingredients for the marinade together in a pan, simmer for 15 minutes and allow to cool. Drain the herring fillets thoroughly, place them in a suitable dish, pour the marinade over and leave for 24 hours. Remove the fillets, cut into 1 cm (about ½ in) strips and arrange in an oval glass dish or an hors d'oeuvre dish. Garnish with rings of leek, sprinkle with crushed allspice and cloves, pour over a little marinade and sprinkle with cut dill.

Sweden

Rollmops I

4 persons　　　Cooking time (fish): 5 minutes

1 kg	Baltic herrings	2¼ lb
	dill	

Marinade

4 dl	water	⅔ pt
1½ dl	wine vinegar	¼ pt
	1 small bay leaf	
	1 medium onion, sliced	
	4 black peppercorns	
	8 white peppercorns	
10 g	sugar	½ oz
5 g	pinch of salt	

Clean the herrings, remove the head, fillet and sprinkle the inside with salt, then set aside. Meanwhile combine and simmer the ingredients for the marinade. Wipe the herring fillets well to remove most of the salt and roll up each one round a small bunch of dill. Insert a small wooden skewer into each roll, place in a suitable pan, pour the marinade over and cook for 5 minutes. Allow to cool in the marinade, cover and leave for at least 24 hours before using.

(Illustration, p. 812)　　　　　　　　　　　　　　　　　　　　Finland

Rollmops II

fresh herring fillets

Marinade I

2 dl	water	⅓ pt
1 dl	vinegar (7%)	⅙ pt
50 g	salt	1¾ oz

Marinade II

2 dl	water	⅓ pt
1 dl	vinegar (7%)	⅙ pt
50 g	sugar	1¾ oz
	strips of cucumber and onion	
	strips of red or green pepper	
	onion rings	
	pepper rings	
	sliced salted cucumber	
	fresh dill	

Wash the herring fillets carefully and leave in marinade I (which has been prepared without heating) for 24 hours. Remove and drain thoroughly, cover the flesh at the head end with strips of cucumber, red or green pepper and onion, roll up and secure with a toothpick. Arrange in a glass bowl and garnish with red onion rings, pepper rings, slices of salted cucumber and fresh dill. Pour marinade II over, leave to stand for 24 hours and serve.

Norway

Rollmops old Berlin style

6 persons

	6 choice salted herrings	
	3 pickled cucumbers	
	4 chopped shallots (or finely chopped onions)	
	1 tablespoon mustard	
	2 lemons	
	1½ tablespoons mustard seed	
	10 peppercorns	
1 l	wine vinegar	1½ pt
	2 medium onions	
	4–6 herring roes	

Gut and scale the herrings, clean thoroughly and soak for at least 12 hours in equal parts of milk and water. Cut off the head, tail and fins, then cut each fish in half lengthwise and remove the bones. Spread the skin side lightly with mustard, sprinkle with chopped shallots, place a small slice of pickled cucumber on top, then roll up with the skin inside and fasten with a small wooden skewer. Place in an earthenware pot and add the peppercorns and mustard seed, 1 bay leaf, slices of lemon and the sliced onions. Shred the roes finely and mix well with very light wine vinegar—diluted with a little water if too strong—and pour over the rollmops to cover completely. Marinate for 5–6 days. Dish with a little of the marinade poured over and serve with slices of light rye bread ('stullen'), either plain or buttered. If preferred, the rollmops may be drained and served with a light mayonnaise or Remoulade sauce.

Germany

Rye bread with salt herring in sherry

6 persons

	3 salt herrings preserved in brine with herbs	
½ l	mild vinegar	¾ pt
1 dl	sherry	3 fl oz
150 g	sugar	5 oz
	4 cloves	
125 g	onions	4 oz
	fresh green dill	
	crushed peppercorns	
	3 slices rye bread (6 half slices)	
90 g	butter	3 oz

Cut the head off the herrings, clean out, wash and soak for 1 hour. Drain well, then marinate for 1–2 days in the vinegar and half the sherry with the sugar, cloves, crushed peppercorns and dill. Remove from the marinade, dish, pour the rest of the sherry over and garnish with onion rings and a liberal amount of fresh dill leaves. Serve the bread and the butter separately.

Denmark

Rye bread with smoked herring and egg yolk

6 persons

	6 smoked herrings	
	6 egg yolks	
	6 onion rings	
	lettuce hearts	
	10 radishes	
	3 slices rye bread (6 half slices)	
90 g	butter	3 oz

Skin the herrings and remove all the bones. Butter the bread, cover with lettuce leaves, arrange the herrings on top and finish off with a raw egg yolk surrounded by an onion ring. Decorate with sliced radishes.

Denmark

Sherry herrings

3 dl	ketchup	$\frac{1}{2}$ pt
150 g	sugar	5 oz
5 cl	wine vinegar	2 fl oz
$\frac{1}{4}$ l	dry sherry	$\frac{1}{2}$ pt
50 g	onions, finely chopped	2 oz

Mix all the ingredients together.

Cut the herring fillets into pieces 2 cm ($\frac{3}{4}$ in) wide, pour the marinade over, stir lightly and leave to stand.

Norway

Soused herrings

6 persons   Cooking time: 8–10 minutes, depending on size

	6 large or 12 small fresh herrings	
60 g	fat for frying	2 oz
	flour	
	5 small bay leaves	
	3–4 medium onions, sliced	
	1–2 lemons	
1 l	very light wine vinegar	1$\frac{1}{2}$ pt
$\frac{1}{4}$ l	water	$\frac{1}{2}$ pt
	2 sprigs thyme	
	10 allspice seeds	
10 g	good pinch of salt	

Gut and scale the herrings, wash very thoroughly, dry, season lightly, coat with flour and shake off the excess. Fry on both sides until brown, then pack into an earthenware pot with the bay leaves and half the sliced onions. Place the vinegar and water in a pan with the rest of the sliced onions, the salt, herbs and spices and simmer for 6–7 minutes. Leave until cold, then pour this marinade over the herrings. Cover the pot tightly with cellophane and marinate for at least two days under refrigeration before use. Dish the herrings with a little of the marinade and with slices of onion and lemon. They will keep for 8 days if stored in the marinade in a cool place. The herrings are usually served with fried potatoes.

Germany

Tyrolean herring

	12 herring fillets	
	2 medium tomatoes	
	1 medium cucumber	
½ l	basic marinade	¾ pt

Skin the tomatoes, cut them in half and remove the seeds. Peel the cucumber, cut in half and remove the seeds. Dice the tomatoes and cucumber finely and mix with the basic marinade. Add the herring fillets cut in 2 cm (¾ in) pieces and mix.

Norway

FRESH WATER FISH

HOT DISHES

Baked trout southern Bohemian style

10 portions   Cooking time (trout): 10 minutes

150 g	10 trout prepared for cooking, each weighing	5 oz
2 dl	oil	⅓ pt
100 g	butter	3 oz
	10 eggs	
150 g	onions, finely chopped	5 oz
500 g	cooked potatoes	1 lb
100 g	flour	3 oz
	3 lemons	
	parsley	

Season the trout with salt, coat with flour and brown lightly on both sides in hot oil. Bake in the oven until cooked, then remove and keep hot. Pour off the oil, place the butter in the pan, cook the onions lightly in it without colouring, then add the diced potatoes and brown lightly. Beat the eggs, season with salt and pepper and pour into the pan. Cook until the eggs are only partly set. Place the fish on a serving dish or individual plates and cover with the egg mixture. Garnish with slices of lemon and parsley to serve.

Czechoslovakia

Barbecued trout mountain style

5 portions   Cooking time: about 15 minutes

1 kg	trout	2¼ lb
100 g	bacon	4 oz
100 g	onions	4 oz
100 g	peppers	4 oz
1 dl	oil	¼ pt

Gut the trout, wash well and season lightly with salt. Cut the bacon and onions in small slices, together with the peppers from which the seeds have been removed. Fill into the trout and secure with a thin skewer. Cook in hot oil over an open fire and serve with bread.

Czechoslovakia

Bisse trout in foil

1 person   Cooking time: 15 minutes

	1 river trout	
200 g	weighing about	7 oz
35 g	butter	1 oz
	2 tarragon leaves	
	a pinch of chopped parsley	
	a sprig of thyme	
	1 very small sorrel leaf	
	salt	
	pepper	
	1 fir-tree bud	
	4 dessertspoons (1 liqueur glass)	
	Fendant or dry white wine	

Use a live trout if possible. After gutting it, fill with the butter which has been creamed with the chopped herbs and a pinch of salt and pepper. Place a small fir-tree bud in the mouth of the fish. Season outside with salt and pepper and place on a piece of aluminium foil. Fold over both sides and one end of the foil carefully to enclose the fish and seal well, then pour in the white wine and fold over the other end of the foil, sealing tightly. Bake on a dish in a hot oven. Serve with a boiled potato, and also with Hollandaise sauce if desired.

Switzerland

Barbecued trout Szalajka style

10 persons

	10 live trout	
250 g	each weighing	½ lb
1 kg	fat bacon	2¼ lb

Seasoning mixture

50 g	salt	2 oz
20 g	pepper	½ oz
100 g	paprika	4 oz

Kill the trout just before they are required. Gut quickly, wash thoroughly inside and outside, and allow to drain. Hold the fish in the left hand with its belly uppermost and its head pointing inwards. Take a wooden spit with a flattened point in the right hand and, holding it vertically, insert this point into the mouth of the fish, then pass it through the neck. Continue working the spit down through the back bone as far as the tail, passing it in and out three more times, so that the spit snakes through the fish, but do not allow the spit to project beyond the tail. Holding the trout with the belly uppermost, sprinkle the inside and then the outside evenly with the seasoning mixture. Impale about 100 g (3½ oz) bacon on a separate spit for each trout and make deep incisions in the top to expose the fat well to the heat.

Cook the trout and bacon over hot glowing embers, preferably of hard wood. Hold the bacon and the fish close to the fire, with the fish a little higher than the bacon, and turn the spits constantly. When the bacon fat begins to melt, allow it to drip on to the fish until well greased, then hold the fish closer to the fire and turn the spit faster and faster. When the eyes are white and protruding, the fish is cooked.

Hungary

Barbecued salmon

8 persons

2 kg	salmon	4 lb 6 oz

Cut the head off the salmon, split the fish in half and remove the bones. With the aid of a few steel nails, fix on to a suitable oak or hickory board with a long handle. Make a high glowing wood fire in the open air and hold the board in front of it to cook the fish. When cooked, dish with a garnish of lemon wedges and parsley and serve with spinach and boiled potatoes. This dish is usually eaten out of doors. The board, which is generally scorched, may be used again.

Finland

Breaded carp with horseradish and lemon

10 portions   Cooking time: 12–15 minutes

1 kg 500	carp	3½ lb
¼ l	oil	½ pt

	2 eggs	
1 dl	milk	3 fl oz
100 g	flour	4 oz
250 g	white breadcrumbs	8 oz
	2 lemons	
100 g	grated horseradish	4 oz

Divide the carp into 10 portions, scale and wash well, then sprinkle lightly with salt. Dip first in flour, then in beaten egg and coat well with breadcrumbs. Fry slowly on both sides in the hot oil. Drain on paper or on a cloth before serving. Garnish with slices of lemon each covered with a small spoonful of horseradish.

Czechoslovakia

Fish paprikash

10 persons

	fillets of carp	4½ lb
2 kg	fillets of carp	4½ lb
100 g	lard	4 oz
200 g	onions	8 oz
250 g	green peppers	8 oz
150 g	tomatoes	5 oz
	or	
250 g	letcho	8 oz
30 g	mild red paprika	1 oz
	salt	

Carefully remove any remaining bones from the fish fillets, wash and cut into pieces the thickness of two fingers. Cut up the onions finely, fry in the lard until golden, sprinkle with a third of the paprika and remove from the heat. Add the fish, pour in a little water and cook slowly. Season with salt, add the seeded diced peppers and the tomatoes which have been skinned, seeded and cut into quarters, then continue cooking. Do not add the rest of the paprika until about an hour before the end of the cooking time.

Instead of carp, sturgeon, eel, pike or sheat-fish may be used for this dish. The fish should be carefully cleaned and filleted.

Freshly boiled potatoes or dumplings make a suitable accompaniment.

Hungary

Fish platter

2 persons

120 g	fogas fillet	4 oz
120 g	carp fillet	4 oz
120 g	sheat-fish fillet	4 oz
	2 pairs frogs' legs	
100 g	mushroom caps, cleaned	4 oz
60 g	smoked bacon	2 oz
50 g	flour	2 oz
	1 egg	
	white breadcrumbs	
100 g	frying batter made with beer	4 oz
	1 large bunch parsley	
	2 portions potato straws	
	1 portion Tartare sauce	
	1 portion Remoulade sauce	
	salads in season	

Cut each fish fillet in half. Toss the frogs' legs, sheat-fish and mushrooms in flour and coat with seasoned beaten egg and breadcrumbs, dip the fogas in the frying batter and deep-fry all these ingredients in hot fat. Roll the carp in breadcrumbs, sprinkle with oil, then grill. Fry the parsley in the hot fat. Arrange the potato straws in a pile in the middle of a wooden platter, cover with the fish fillets, the mushrooms and the rashers of bacon which have been fried or grilled, and shape into a pyramid. Surround with the fried parsley. Garnish round the edge with salads in season and, if desired, whole tomatoes and sweet peppers. Serve the sauces separately.

Hungary

Fried pike-perch

10 persons

3 kg–3 kg 500	1 pike-perch	7 lb approx.
$\frac{3}{4}$ l	Tartare sauce	1$\frac{1}{4}$ pt
	flour	
	paprika	

Scale and gut the fish, remove the gills, wash thoroughly, dry well and score at intervals of 2 cm ($\frac{3}{4}$ in). Coat with flour mixed with paprika and deep fry until crisp. Serve with Tartare sauce and buttered potatoes.

Hungary

Fried shad Coriana style

approx. 3 kg	1 large shad	7 lb approx.
150 g	flour	5 oz
	1 teaspoon cumin seeds	
	1 teaspoon wild marjoram	
	2 teaspoons Extremadura or	
	Murcia pimenton (paprika)	
	2 large cloves of garlic	
20 g	cooking salt	1 oz
½ l	good wine vinegar	¾ pt
	oil for deep frying	
	1 large lemon	
	parsley	

Wash the shad well in running water, cut into thin slices and place them in a glazed earthenware or china dish. Pound the cumin seeds, wild marjoram, garlic and salt in a mortar; when well blended, add the paprika mixed with the vinegar (if the vinegar is too strong, add a little cold water). Cover the pieces of fish with this mixture and marinate for 10–12 hours, turning twice to make sure that all the pieces are well steeped in the marinade.

Half an hour before the fish is to be served, heat the oil in a pan. Remove the fish from the marinade, dry with a cloth and coat with flour. Fry the pieces to a good golden colour in the oil, which should remain hot. Serve at once dished on a napkin and garnished with 6 slices of lemon and with fried parsley.

Spain

Lake trout St. Peter

4 persons

	4 lake trout	
200–225 g	each weighing	7–8 oz
100 g	maître d'hôtel butter	4 oz
	pinch of turtle herbs	
1 dl	dry white wine	3 fl oz
20 g	butter	1 oz

Clean the fish carefully and stuff with very good maître d'hôtel butter mixed with the herbs. Season with salt and pepper, wrap each fish in buttered foil and pour a little white wine over before sealing tightly. Cook in a medium oven or on a charcoal grill.

(Illustration, p. 247)

Germany

Salmon in puff paste

20 persons   Baking time: 45–50 minutes, depending on size

	1 salmon,	
4 kg	gross weight about	8½ lb
	2 lemons	
¼ l	oil	½ pt
150 g	chopped herbs	5 oz
2 kg	puff paste	4½ lb
	2 eggs	

Remove the head from the salmon, cut the fish in half lengthwise and remove the skin and bones. Marinate for 20 hours in lemon juice, oil, chopped herbs, salt, pepper and a pinch of sugar. Pat dry, place the two halves together, enclose in puff paste and egg-wash. Decorate with puff paste trimmings, egg-wash again, bake in a hot oven for a short time, then reduce the heat a little and bake off.

Hand fennel butter and cucumber salad in sour cream separately.

Germany

Salmon pudding

4 persons   Cooking time: about 30 minutes

300 g	marinated salmon, thinly sliced	10 oz
	6 medium potatoes cooked in their skins	
	2 yellow onions, finely chopped	
	1 tablespoon chopped dill	
	2 eggs	
2 dl	single cream	⅓ pt
50 g	butter	2 oz
	breadcrumbs	

Soak the salmon in milk for a short time to remove excess salt. Fry the chopped onions in a little butter until lightly coloured. Peel and slice the cooked potatoes when cold. Prepare an unsweetened custard mixture with the cream and eggs. Butter the bottom of a baking dish and sprinkle with the onions and dill. Arrange the salmon and sliced potatoes on top in rows and pour the custard mixture over. Cover with breadcrumbs, dot with butter and bake at about 225°C.

Sweden

Smoked trout Swedish style

10 persons

	10 smoked trout	
250 g	each weighing	8 oz approx.
	10–20 eggs	
	butter	

Accompaniments

spinach cooked in butter
steamed potatoes

Wrap each trout in buttered aluminium foil and bake for 15 minutes at 200°C. Scramble the eggs meanwhile.

To serve, open the foil cases and arrange the fish on a serving dish. Place the scrambled eggs, the spinach and the potatoes in separate dishes.

(Illustration, p. 690)   Sweden

Baked salmon with boiled egg

4 persons   Cooking time: 15–20 minutes

320 g	salmon fillet, skinned	11 oz
	4 hard-boiled eggs	
	5 tablespoons saké	
	2 teaspoons salt	
	1 teaspoon aji-no-moto	
	2 lemons	
	soya sauce	

Cut the fresh salmon fillet into four pieces and marinate for at least 5 minutes in the saké seasoned with the salt and aji-no-moto. Shell the eggs, cut both ends off each one, then cut in half lengthwise.

Place each piece of fish on a square of aluminium foil, cover with 2 half eggs and a slice of lemon, turn up the edges of the foil, pour a little of the seasoned saké over the fish, fold the foil over, sealing tightly, and bake in a medium oven. Remove from the foil, garnish with slices of lemon to serve and hand soya sauce sharpened with lemon juice separately.

N.B.—This dish may be made with any white fish or with shrimps instead of salmon. The baked fish may be dressed with mayonnaise or vinaigrette sauce and served as an hors d'oeuvre.

Japan

Stuffed fogas

Cooking time: 40 minutes

1 kg 500	1 fogas	3¼ lb approx.
300 g	fogas fillets, skinned	10 oz
100 g	white bread without crusts	4 oz
	4 egg whites	
2 dl	dairy cream	⅓ pt
	1 good tablespoon chopped herbs (parsley, chervil, tarragon)	
	little salmon to colour the forcemeat (optional)	

Soak the white bread in the cream. Mash the fogas fillets with the bread, add three egg whites, season with salt and pepper, rub through a hair-sieve and add the chopped herbs. Wash and dry the whole fish, slit down the back, cut away as much of the bone as necessary and remove the entrails. Wash well inside, dry and brush with the remaining egg white. Fill with the forcemeat, tie evenly, poach in good fish stock and make sure the fish does not burst open or lose its shape.

Austria

Trout au bleu

Per person

150 g	1 trout weighing approx.	5 oz

For this recipe live trout are necessary. Kill at the last minute before cooking. Clean quickly without scraping or wiping as it is the film of mucosity covering the trout that gives them the blue colour. Put the trout into well-salted boiling water, bring to the boil and poach until cooked (about 7 minutes), without allowing the water to boil. Serve on a napkin. Garnish with parsley and lemon. Serve separately melted or creamed butter or sauce Mousseline.

Young eels in casserole

10 portions in individual dishes   Cooking time: about 12 minutes

1 kg 250	young eels (elvers) indispensable minimum 6 cm (3 in) length	2¾ lb
½ l	olive oil	¾ pt
	10 large cloves of garlic	
	1 large hot red pepper	

Peel the cloves of garlic, cut them in half and remove the green centres. Cut the red pepper into 10 pieces of equal size. Divide the oil between 10 individual fireproof dishes, heat and drop 2 half cloves of garlic in each. When they begin to turn brown, place a piece of red pepper and 125 g (4½ oz) lightly salted eel in each dish. Stir and mix well with two forks (preferably wooden ones), working from the sides to the bottom and centre of the dish to make the eels absorb the oil. Remove from the heat, allow to stand until the dishes are cool enough to handle, but still hot, and serve.

Spain

COLD DISHES

Carp in aspic

10 portions   Cooking time: about 15 minutes

2 kg	carp	4¼ lb approx.
2 l	water	3½ pt
2 dl	vinegar	⅓ pt
100 g	pot-herbs (celery, carrot, onion, parsley root)	4 oz
20 g	salt	1 oz
	allspice	
	peppercorns	
	1 bay leaf	
	juice of 1 lemon	
200 g	tomatoes	8 oz
	3 lemons, sliced	
	1 lettuce	
	2–3 egg whites	
	24 sheets gelatine	

Prepare a court-bouillon with the water, vinegar, salt, pot-herbs, a few allspice berries and peppercorns, the bay leaf and the lemon juice. Divide the carp (without the head) into 10 portions and poach in the court-bouillon. When cooked, bone the fish and arrange the portions 3 cm (1¼ in) apart in a dish of suitable size or on a metal tray with a rim. Strain the court-bouillon, remove all fat, dissolve the gelatine in it after soaking and squeezing dry and clarify with the egg whites. Check the taste of the jelly, which should be well flavoured, then strain. Garnish the portions of carp with slices of lemon and sliced vegetables cut into various shapes, leave in a cool place and coat with the cold jelly before it has begun to set. When firm, cut with a knife or cutter to separate the portions, dish and garnish with tomatoes and lettuce.

Czechoslovakia

Carp with root vegetables

10 portions   Cooking time: 20 minutes

approx. 1 kg	leather carp fillets	2¼ lb approx.
	1 bouquet garni	
	2 carrots	
75 g	onions	3 oz
	a little vinegar	
400 g	julienne of carrots, celeriac, leeks and onions	1 lb
	3 hard-boiled eggs	
30 g	butter	1 oz
½ l	fish aspic	¾ pt
	sweet pepper salad	

Prepare a court-bouillon with water, a dash of vinegar, a bouquet garni, sliced onions and carrots and salt to taste. Cook the julienne of vegetables in the butter and a little water with a pinch of salt. Place 10 carp fillets, each weighing 100–120 g (about 3½ to 4 oz) in the boiling court-bouillon, bring to the boil again, then poach gently and allow to cool in the court-bouillon. Remove the fish from the pan, bone, drain very well and dish. Sprinkle with the drained julienne and glaze with fish aspic. Garnish with sliced hard-boiled eggs and sweet pepper salad.

Austria

Cold fogas Belvedere style

10 persons   Cooking time: 10 minutes

1 kg 600	fogas fillets, skinned	3½ lb
1 kg 200	vegetable salad	2¾ lb
1 l	fish aspic	1¾ pt
	egg yolk stuffing	
	gherkins	
	radishes	
	stuffed eggs	
	court-bouillon	

Place the fogas fillets in boiling court-bouillon, poach gently for about 10 minutes and leave in the court-bouillon until cold. Remove carefully, drain, coat the inside with aspic and chill thoroughly. Cut in slices ½ cm (about ¼ in) thick and arrange these on a triangular base of vegetable salad in overlapping rows. Pipe on egg yolk stuffing, decorate with sliced gherkins and radishes and glaze with aspic. Garnish with stuffed eggs.

Austria

Cold fogas with crayfish sauce

10 persons   Cooking time: 20–25 minutes

3 kg	1 fogas	6¾ lb
50 g	onions	2 oz
50 g	carrots	2 oz
50 g	parsley roots	2 oz
	bay leaf	
	1 bunch celery leaves	
1 dl	tarragon vinegar	3 fl oz
3 g	a few peppercorns	
3 g	a little tarragon	
50 g	crayfish tails	2 oz
	7 hard-boiled eggs	
1 kg 500	Russian salad	3¼ lb
200 g	peas	8 oz
400 g	butter	1 lb
1 l	aspic jelly	1¾ pt

Sauce

	5 egg yolks	
1 dl	lemon juice	3 fl oz
3 cl	Cognac	3 dessertspoons
5 dl	crayfish oil	¾ pt

Prepare strong court-bouillon with the sliced root vegetables, 1 bay leaf, peppercorns, celery leaves, tarragon vinegar, water and salt, then strain. Gut and scale the fish, wash well, place in the boiling court-bouillon, belly side down, and poach over moderate heat. Allow to cool in the court-bouillon, remove, chill well in the refrigerator and skin carefully. Remove the flesh carefully from the backbone, place the head and backbone on a board and fill the belly cavity with the Russian salad. Replace the fillets to give the fish its original shape and decorate with tarragon leaves, crayfish tails, peas and egg yolk paste. Chill well and glaze with aspic. Cut the hard-boiled eggs in half, carefully remove the yolks, sieve, cream with the butter and season with salt, pepper and a pinch of nutmeg. Use part of this paste to decorate the fish and pipe the remainder into the half whites, using a savoy bag and star pipe. Chill, then glaze with aspic. Carefully arrange the fish on a dish and garnish with the stuffed eggs and cubes of aspic jelly. Hand crayfish mayonnaise separately.

To make the mayonnaise, beat the egg yolks with a little lemon juice or Cognac, adding a pinch of salt and pepper, then blend in the crayfish oil a little at a time, proceeding in the same way as for ordinary mayonnaise. While blending in the crayfish oil, dilute from time to time with a little lemon juice. Lastly, flavour with the Cognac.

Crayfish oil

Fry the crayfish shells in 5 dl ($\frac{7}{8}$ pt) oil, colour with powdered paprika, add a little water (about 1 dl ($\frac{1}{8}$ pt)), cook well, allow to cool, then collect the oil which has risen to the top.

Hungary

Cold salmon Jack Gauer

45 persons   Cooking time: 12–15 minutes

4 kg	1 salmon weighing about	8$\frac{3}{4}$ lb
700 g	unsweetened short paste	1$\frac{1}{2}$ lb
	20 shelled crayfish tails	
	40 shelled crayfish claws	
300 g	cucumber balls	10 oz
600 g	melon balls	1 lb 4 oz
	tomatoes, skinned, cut in quarters and seeded	
	quails' eggs	
	egg yolk paste	
	sliced truffle	
	lemon juice	
	oil	
	chopped parsley and tarragon	
	fish aspic	

Fillet and skin the salmon. Place in a pan of cold court-bouillon, bring to simmering point, poach gently and allow to cool. Carefully lift out of the pan, drain well and slice evenly with a sharp knife. Poach the head and tail and allow to cool. Bake an oval short paste croustade. Marinate the crayfish and the melon and cucumber balls in oil and lemon juice with the addition of chopped parsley and tarragon, then fill into the cold croustade.

Coat a rectangular dish with aspic jelly. Place the croustade in the centre, edge with the quarter tomatoes and glaze with aspic. Decorate each slice of salmon with half a cucumber ball and a third of a quails' egg stuffed with egg yolk paste, then glaze with aspic. Arrange the slices symmetrically round the croustade and place the head and tail at either end.

(Illustration, p. 696)   Switzerland

Cooked salt eel

6 persons   Cooking time: 10–12 minutes

750 g	1 eel	1¾ lb
150 g	coarse salt	5 oz
	2 sliced onions	
	4 bay leaves	
	2 tablespoons vinegar	
	10 peppercorns	
	3 slices rye bread	
	(6 half slices)	
90 g	butter	4 oz

Kill the eel, gut, clean thoroughly and cut into pieces about 5 cm (2 in) long. Rub salt into each piece all round, then leave to stand for 24 hours. Place in a pan with the vinegar and just enough water to cover, add the peppercorns and bay leaves, bring to the boil and simmer until cooked, then leave in the cooking liquid until cold. Drain, dish and serve with rye bread and butter.

Denmark

Fillet of perch maison

8 persons   Cooking time: 8 minutes

	8 fillets of perch,	
	each weighing	4 oz
120 g		
25 g	butter	1 oz
1 dl	white wine	3 fl oz
4 dl	fish velouté	⅔ pt
	3 tablespoons Hollandaise	
	sauce	
	2 tablespoons whipped	
	dairy cream	
	8 small lobster claws	
30 g	caviar	1 oz
	8 small lightly cooked	
	tomatoes stuffed with	
	white asparagus tips	
	parsley	

Butter a fireproof dish, arrange the perch fillets in it, season lightly with salt and pepper, pour in the wine, cover with buttered paper and poach in the oven. Remove from the oven, dish and keep hot. Reduce the poaching liquid and mix with the velouté. Add the Hollandaise sauce and the cream and pour over the fish fillets. Decorate each one with a small lobster claw and a tiny bulb of caviar and garnish with the stuffed tomatoes and parsley.

Germany

Fillets of pike-perch Tihany

10 persons   Cooking time: 12 minutes

1 kg 800	fillets of pike-perch	4 lb
3 dl	white wine	½ pt
50 g	flour	2 oz
5 cl	oil	2 fl oz
2 dl	water	⅓ pt
	2 egg whites	
1 dl	dairy cream	⅙ pt
1 dl	aspic jelly	⅙ pt
500 g	mayonnaise	1 pt
5 g	2 sprigs tarragon leaves	
100 g	firm tomatoes	4 oz
	5 hard-boiled eggs	
150 g	butter	5 oz
10 g each	dill, chervil, tarragon, and parsley	total 2 oz approx.
50 g	sorrel	2 oz
50 g	spinach	2 oz
	1 shallot, finely chopped	
750 g	Russian salad	1½ lb

Cut the fish fillets into lozenge shapes. Make a panada with 50 g (2 fl oz) oil, 50 g (2 oz) flour, about 2 dl (⅓ pt) water and a pinch of salt, proceeding as for choux paste, then allow to cool. Blend the fish trimmings, the egg whites and the cold panada to a fine purée in the liquidiser, rub through a sieve, lighten with the cream and season with salt, pepper and a pinch of nutmeg. Spread this forcemeat on the fish lozenges to a thickness of ½ cm (about ¼ in), fold over, arrange in a buttered fireproof dish, pour in the wine, cover with buttered paper and poach in the oven. When cold, drain on a wire rack and coat with aspic mayonnaise (200 g (8 oz) mayonnaise, 100 g (4 oz) aspic jelly). When half-set, decorate with thin slices of skinned tomato or with tarragon leaves and glaze with aspic. Cut the hard-boiled eggs in half, remove the yolks, sieve, mix with 100 g (4 oz) creamed butter, season, pipe into the whites using a star tube, and glaze with aspic. Arrange the fish fillets on a base of Russian salad and garnish with the stuffed eggs and cubes of aspic jelly. Serve with green sauce.

To make the green sauce, blanch the herbs, sorrel and spinach for 4–5 minutes, press out all the water and reduce to a very fine purée in the liquidiser. Mix with the rest of the mayonnaise and season well.

Hungary

Fish mousse

10 portions

1 kg	carp scraps and edible internal parts (e.g. roes) of various fish	2¼ lb
500 g	butter	1 lb
2 dl	dairy cream	⅓ pt
50 g	onions	2 oz
	5 eggs	
	3 lemons	
150 g	sour cucumbers	5 oz
	1 lettuce	
	4 tomatoes	

Cook the fish and roes in salted water containing sliced onion and lemon and a few peppercorns. Drain well, remove any skin or bones and mince several times, using the finest cutter. Cream the butter, mix well with the fish, add the cream, season with salt and pepper and sharpen with lemon juice. Fill into individual moulds, allow to set, then turn out. Garnish with hard-boiled eggs cut into quarters, tomatoes, slices of lemon and small lettuce leaves.

Czechoslovakia

Glazed salmon in Chambertin

12–15 persons   Cooking time: 1¼ hours

2 kg 500	1 salmon	5 lb 8 oz
	concentrated fish stock	
	Chambertin	
¾ l	mayonnaise or green sauce	1¼ pt

Clean, wash and dry the salmon. Place it on a salmon kettle drainer and cook in concentrated fish stock mixed with an equal amount of Chambertin. Check the taste before adding salt, as the fish stock may be salty enough. Make aspic jelly with the cooking liquid. Dress and garnish in the same way as salmon Parisian style.

France

Glazed salmon in Champagne

Proceed as for glazed salmon in Chambertin, but substitute Champagne for the Chambertin.

France

Glazed salmon cutlets

12–15 persons   Cooking time: 12–15 minutes

| 2 kg 250–2 kg 500 | 1 salmon court-bouillon | 5–5½ lb |

Garnish

| 750 g | Russian salad lettuce | 1½ lb |
| ¾ l | mayonnaise or green sauce | 1¼ pt |

Clean the salmon and cut into slices weighing about 130–140 g (4½–5 oz). Poach and allow to cool in the cooking liquid, then drain. Carefully lever out the centre bone with the tip of a knife. Decorate each cutlet and glaze with aspic. Arrange on a dish with a border of small lettuce leaves filled with Russian salad. Hand mayonnaise or green sauce separately.

France

Glazed salmon imperial style

12–15 persons   Cooking time: 1¼ hours

| 2 kg | 1 salmon court-bouillon | 4½ lb |

Garnish

	12 hard-boiled eggs	
100 g	cooked truffles	4 oz
	15 trussed crayfish cooked in court-bouillon	
	lettuce	
1½ l	fish aspic flavoured with Champagne	2½ pt
¾ l	mayonnaise	1¼ pt

Poach, skin and decorate the salmon as for salmon Parisian style. Coat a dish with clear aspic and allow to set. Carefully place the fish on top and surround with the eggs which have been stuffed with truffles, alternating with the trussed crayfish (see p. 540), their heads pointing outwards. Edge the dish with slices of lemon which have been cut in half, fluted and topped with small disks of tomato in the centre of their straight edge. Hand mayonnaise separately.

France

Jellied eels I

6 persons   Cooking time: 15–18 minutes

1 kg 200–1 kg 600	eels	2½–3½ lb
75 g	onions	3 oz
	1 bay leaf	
	8 allspice seeds	
	8 peppercorns	
	good dash of vinegar	
	8–10 sheets gelatine	
	per litre (1¾ pt)	
	cooking liquid	

Select fairly thick eels, skin them, wash thoroughly and remove all the blood inside near the bone. Cut the fish into pieces 5–6 cm (about 2 in) long and place in a pan with the sliced onions, the herbs, spices and vinegar and enough lightly salted water to cover. Simmer gently until tender, then remove the fish from the cooking liquid and arrange in a glass bowl. Strain the cooking liquid, remove all the fat, add the gelatine which has been soaked and squeezed dry, bring to the boil and check the taste. The amount of gelatine indicated is sufficient as the eel stock is already gelatinous. If a completely clear jelly is required, clarify with a whipped egg white and strain through a cloth. After adjusting the seasoning, set the jelly aside until it begins to set, then pour over the eels and refrigerate until firm.

Germany

Jellied eels II

8 persons   Cooking time: 30 minutes

600 g	2 eels each weighing	1¼ lb
	1 bottle dry white wine	
¾ l	water	1¼ pt
250–300 g	carrots cut in small stars	8 oz
250–300 g	leeks (green part)	8 oz
	cut in thick strips	
	1 large bunch coarsely	
	cut dill	

Make a court-bouillon with the white wine, water, carrots and leeks. Season with salt and pepper. Prepare the eels in the usual way, cut into pieces 6 cm (about 2½ in) long and wash thoroughly. Drain, then cook slowly in the court-bouillon until tender. Transfer to an earthenware dish and refrigerate. The stock will set when cold.

Holland

Jellied eels Harlequin style

6 persons   Cooking time: 30 minutes

900 g	2 eels each weighing	2 lb
	10 hard-boiled eggs	
	1 can skinned red peppers	
	2–3 truffles	
2 l	fish aspic	3½ pt
	finely chopped parsley	
	fish stock	
100 g	cooked lobster	4 oz
100 g	cooked carrots	4 oz
100 g	pickled cucumbers	4 oz
100 g	small garden peas	4 oz
approx. 200 g	mayonnaise	7 oz approx.

Clean the eels thoroughly, cut off the heads and tails, skin the fish and fillet carefully, working from the back. Beat the fillets lightly along their whole length to make them of uniform thickness as far as possible. Place on a board and spread with a thin layer (about 2–3 mm ($\frac{1}{10}$ in) thick) of semi-liquid fish aspic mixed with a liberal amount of chopped parsley. Starting at the head end, roll up the fillets, taking care not to displace the parsley filling, and shape into a roll 5–5½ cm (about 2 in) in diameter. Wrap the roll tightly in tinfoil, making sure it is watertight, then tie in a cloth, poach in fish stock and leave in the stock until cold. Remove from the stock and refrigerate for at least 5 hours before proceeding. Have ready 2 rectangular tins 30 cm (12 in) long, 10 cm (4 in) wide and 8 cm (3 in) deep, with sloping sides. Proceed as follows:

Figure 1, stand the first tin in a container almost full of iced water and mask the bottom with aspic jelly to a thickness of 2 cm (¾ in). As soon as it has set, place the second tin, filled with iced water, inside the first (Fig. 2) and fill up the space between the sides of the two tins with aspic jelly. As soon as the jelly on the sides of the first tin has set, remove the ice from the second (inside) tin, fill this up with lukewarm water and remove without damaging the aspic lining the sides of the first tin (Fig. 3). Refrigerate until the aspic in the first tin has set uniformly (Fig. 4). The second tin may be put away, as it is no longer required. Decorate the bottom of the masked tin neatly with a mosaic of blanched green leek and hard-boiled

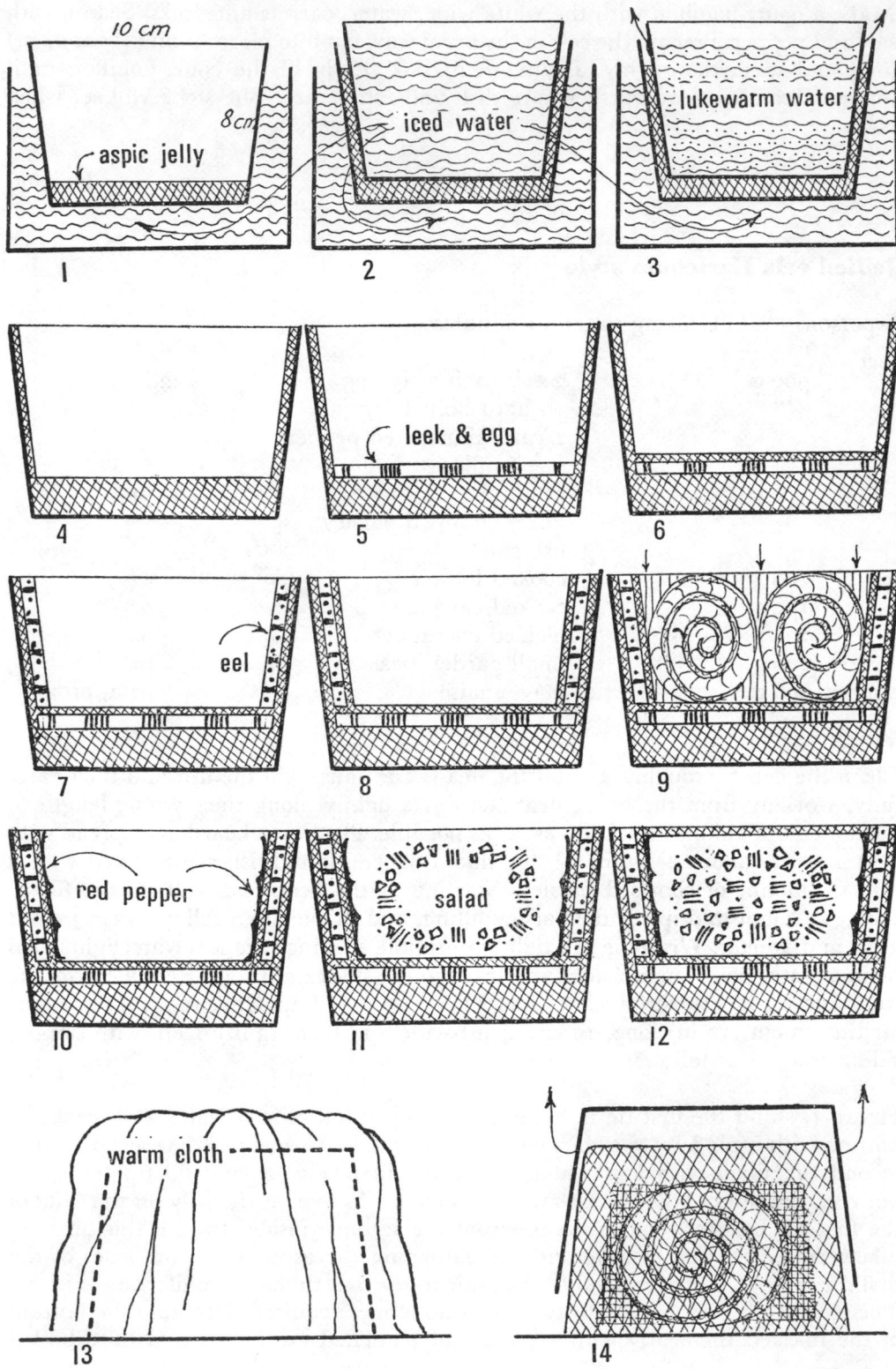

egg white cut in diamond shapes; cover very thinly with aspic (Figs. 5 and 6). Unwrap the eels, wipe dry and, using a sharp knife, cut evenly into slices 5–6 mm (¼ in) thick, taking care to keep the parsley off the white eel flesh. Brush each slice very lightly with semi-liquid aspic jelly and fix at once on to the sides of the tin to avoid the formation of air bubbles and to ensure that all the slices will adhere firmly to the sides. The best side of each slice should face outwards. Place 5 slices along each of the longer sides of the tin and 1 slice at each end (Fig. 7). Cover all the slices with another thin layer of aspic jelly (Figs. 8 and 9). Place thin slices of red peppers along the tin, especially in the spaces between the slices of eel (Figs. 9 and 10), so that the filling will be completely hidden. Cut the carrots, pickled cucumbers, truffles and lobster in small cubes, mix well with the peas, marinate, drain and bind with the mayonnaise. Fill up the tin with this vegetable salad, stand aside for a short time, then cover with a thin layer of aspic jelly which is just beginning to set and refrigerate until firm (Figs. 11 and 12).

Turn out in a refrigerated room. Invert the tin and stand upside down on a stainless steel or plexiglass tray. Cover the tin for a moment with a cloth which has been dipped in hot water and wrung out, then lift off, holding the tin at the same time, leaving the jellied eels behind. The water should not be too hot, or the aspic lining the sides of the tin will liquefy (Figs. 13 and 14).

After thorough chilling, the jellied eel mould may be placed on a rectangular serving dish which has been coated with aspic. No further decoration is required but, if desired, it may be garnished with truffles.

(Illustration, p. 697)

Marinated carp I

10 portions

2 kg	carp	4½ lb
50 g	carrots	2 oz
50 g	celeriac	2 oz
50 g	onions	2 oz
50 g	peas	2 oz
50 g	pickled cucumbers	2 oz
50 g	sugar	2 oz
1 kg	mayonnaise	2 lb
	3 lemons	
4 dl	white wine	⅔ pt
	Worcestershire sauce	

Cut the carrots, celeriac and onions into very fine julienne strips, blanch and drain well. When cold, add the pickled cucumber which has been seeded and cut into julienne strips, together with the cooked peas. Mix with the mayonnaise, wine and lemon juice, season with salt and pepper, add the sugar and flavour with Worcestershire sauce. Cook the carp, remove the skin and bones, cut into portions and place in the above marinade. Allow to stand for several hours before use.

Czechoslovakia

Marinated carp II

10 persons   Cooking time: 25–30 minutes

5–6 kg	carp	11–13 lb
250 g	onions, finely sliced	8 oz
500 g	tomatoes, skinned and seeded	1 lb
	1 tablespoon tomato purée	
	3 lemons	
	1 bay leaf	
½ l	dry white wine	¾ pt
	flour	
	paprika	
	sunflower seed oil	

Scale and gut the carp, remove the head, wash the fish well, cut in half lengthwise and divide into 10 portions. Season with salt and paprika, dust with flour and fry lightly in oil on both sides. Fry the sliced onions in oil until pale golden, add the diced tomatoes, the wine mixed with the tomato purée, the juice of 1 lemon, the bay leaf and a little salt. Bring to the boil, then transfer the pieces of carp to a fireproof dish, top with the onion and tomato mixture, cover and cook in the oven. Leave until cold, remove the bay leaf, place a slice of lemon on each piece of carp and serve very cold.

Rumania

Marinated salmon Swedish style

3 kg	fresh (preferably North Sea) salmon	6½ lb
1 kg 500	fine salt	3¼ lb
	1 tablespoon white pepper	
	1 tablespoon sugar	
500 g	fresh dill, coarsely cut	1 lb
	1 lemon	

Scale and gut the salmon, remove the head, cut in half lengthwise and remove all the bones. Cut off the tip of the tail and the fat flaps round the belly, but do not skin. Wipe the fish clean, but do not wash, then rub with lemon juice inside and outside. Mix the salt with the pepper, sugar and dill. Spread half the mixture on a clean metal tray with a rim. Place the salmon on top, skin side uppermost, and cover with the rest of the mixture. Cover the tray with aluminium foil and keep in cold storage overnight. Now turn the fish, then marinate for a further 2 days (making a total of 56 hours), turning several times. Dry thoroughly. The salmon will keep for some time if wrapped in a cloth and stored in the refrigerator.

To serve, cut the salmon off the skin in paper-thin slices and dish with a garnish of lemon wedges, lettuce leaves and dill.

Sweden

Marinated salmon with spinach or scrambled egg

The marinated salmon, prepared as directed (see p. 504), is served with fluffy scrambled egg or sieved spinach. Hot creamed potatoes are another popular accompaniment.

Sweden

Poached, decorated and garnished salmon

30–32 persons	Cooking time: salmon on the bone, 30 minutes; fillet, 12–15 minutes	
4 kg	1 salmon	8¾ lb

Court-bouillon

3½ l	water	6 pt
½ l	white wine	¾ pt
200 g	carrots, sliced	8 oz
200 g	onions, sliced	8 oz
	1 bouquet garni	
	8 peppercorns	
	salt	

Vegetable salad

200 g	carrots, diced	8 oz
200 g	celeriac, diced	8 oz
200 g	sweet peppers, diced	8 oz
200 g	French beans, diced	8 oz
200 g	garden peas	8 oz
200 g	mayonnaise	8 oz
	juice of 2 lemons	
	5–6 sheets gelatine	

Chaud-froid sauce

½ l	fish velouté	¾ pt
	4 sheets gelatine	
1 dl	dairy cream	¼ pt
1 l	fish aspic jelly	1¾ pt

Stuffed eggs

	12 hard-boiled eggs	
50 g	mayonnaise	2 oz
50 g	cream cheese	2 oz
	½ teaspoon dry mustard	
	little Worcestershire sauce	

Decoration

skinned, blanched red pepper
blanched leek (green part)
truffles

Accompaniment

thousand island dressing

Scale and gut the salmon and wash thoroughly. Using a sharp knife, cut a fillet off the backbone, leaving the head and tail attached to the bone. Poach the salmon slowly in the court-bouillon, keeping it firm, and allow to cool in the court-bouillon. Thoroughly chill the fish with the head and tail attached, wipe dry and place on a suitable dish thinly coated with aspic. Season the vegetables for the salad with salt, add the lemon juice and bind with the mayonnaise mixed with the gelatine which has been soaked, squeezed dry and dissolved. Adjust the seasoning and fill into the cut side of the salmon to give the fish its original shape. Smooth over the top and refrigerate until firm. Carefully mask the salmon with the chaud-froid sauce, leaving the head and tail uncovered. When firm, decorate with a Mexican motif, e.g. a Mexican boy with a donkey, and neatly brush with aspic.

If using a salmon fillet, season the fillet lightly, wrap in buttered greaseproof paper or in aluminium foil, poach in a little court-bouillon until cooked but still very moist, allow to cool and place in the refrigerator for several hours until firm.

Unwrap salmon fillet, dry well, cut into 18–20 slices with a sharp knife, place on a wire rack, glaze thinly with aspic, decorate with a colourful motif in keeping with the Mexican setting and glaze again. Garnish the salmon with the decorated slices and the stuffed half-eggs, also with moulded vegetables or, better still, moulded shrimps if desired. Hand the dressing separately.

Stuffed eggs: cut the eggs in half horizontally, carefully remove the yolks and level off the whites underneath to make them stand securely. Sieve the yolks and the cream cheese, add salt, dry mustard and a dash of Worcestershire sauce and bind with the mayonnaise. Pipe into the whites using a star tube, decorate as desired and glaze with aspic.

Thousand island dressing

500 g	mayonnaise	1 pt
	1 tablespoon chilli sauce	
50 g	chopped green peppers	2 oz
50 g	chopped red peppers	2 oz
	1 tablespoon chopped green olives	
	1 teaspoon grated horseradish	

Mix the mayonnaise with the other ingredients. If too thick, dilute with a little hot water.

USA

Poached trout in wine jelly

16 persons   Cooking time: 15–18 minutes

425–450 g	6 trout each weighing	1 lb
300 g	boned and skinned pike	10 oz
	2 egg whites	
¼ l	dairy cream	½ pt
	1 level tablespoon chopped dill	
	1 level tablespoon chopped parsley	
	white wine court-bouillon	
	fish aspic jelly	
	butter	

Choose trout which have been killed several hours previously, clean thoroughly, wash and remove the backbone. Mince the pike, using the finest blade of the mincer, season with salt and pepper, mix with the egg whites and rub through a sieve. Chill well in a bowl stood on ice or in the refrigerator, then draw in the cream a little at a time and adjust the seasoning. Test a little of the forcemeat in boiling water; while it should not be too firm, it should hold together. Add the very finely chopped parsley and the dill, then wipe the trout well inside and stuff with the forcemeat. Close up the slit in the belly to hold the stuffing in place, wrap each fish separately in buttered greaseproof paper or in aluminium foil, tie lightly, poach carefully in the court-bouillon and leave in the cooking liquid until quite cold. Unwrap, skin carefully, place on a wire rack, glaze very lightly with wine jelly (made with the court-bouillon) and refrigerate. Decorate each fish with a flower motif made up of tomato, egg white, tarragon, etc., bearing in mind that the fish is to be cut up. Glaze with jelly again and chill well again.

Coat a serving dish of suitable size with a thin layer of aspic jelly. Using a very sharp knife, cut each trout in three and arrange on the coated dish to its original shape. Garnish with sprigs of parsley, wedges of lemon and diced jelly. If desired, the fish may also be garnished with stuffed half-eggs or tomatoes and Dublin Bay prawns.

USA

River salmon with mixed vegetable salad

20–22 portions   Cooking time: 12–15 minutes

3 kg 500	1 river salmon	7 lb
3 l	court-bouillon	5 pt
500 g	vegetables for salad (celeriac, carrots, green peppers, peas, tomatoes, all finely diced and cooked)	1 lb
	2 lemons	
	oil	
100 g	thick mayonnaise	4 oz
	3 sheets gelatine	
1 l	fish aspic made with white wine	1¾ pt
	12 hard-boiled eggs	
50 g	butter	2 oz
50 g	mayonnaise	2 oz
50 g	cream cheese	2 oz
	Worcestershire sauce	
	20–22 cucumber baskets	
	carrots cut matchstick size	
	vinegar	

Scale the salmon, remove the head and fillet the fish. Wrap the fillets up in buttered or lightly oiled paper, arrange in a shallow tin, pour court-bouillon over and poach, keeping the flesh very moist. Carefully remove from the court-bouillon and press lightly until quite cold. Unwrap, skin, chill well again, then slice evenly with a sharp knife.

Cut the eggs in half, remove the yolks, sieve, work to a paste of piping consistency with the creamed butter, the cream cheese and the mayonnaise, and add salt, pepper and Worcestershire sauce to taste. Fill the whites with this paste using a savoy bag and star pipe. Drain the vegetables well, marinate in oil, lemon juice, salt and pepper, then bind with the mayonnaise mixed with the gelatine which has been soaked and dissolved in a bain-marie. Blanch the cucumber baskets for 1 minute at the most, drain well, marinate and fill with carrot sticks dressed with vinegar, oil, salt, pepper and chopped parsley.

Decorate the slices of salmon with dill, leek, radishes, red peppers, truffles or other garnishes and glaze with fish aspic. Coat a dish of suitable size with fish aspic, allow to set, then cover with a bed of well-flavoured vegetable salad to fit the slices of salmon. When the vegetable salad is firm, carefully arrange the slices of salmon on top, spacing them evenly. Garnish with the stuffed eggs and cucumber baskets, parsley, slices of lemon and diced or chopped fish aspic.

(Illustration, p. 699)   USA
(Techniques, p. 117)

Salmon mousse

400 g	cooked fresh salmon, skinned and boned (net weight)	16 oz
15 cl	thick fish velouté	$\frac{1}{4}$ pt
4 dl	fish aspic reduced to half	$\frac{2}{3}$ pt
3–3$\frac{1}{2}$ dl	dairy cream	$\frac{1}{2}$ pt

Reduce the salmon to a fine purée in the blender with a little fish velouté. Place in a bowl, stir in the rest of the velouté with a spatula and add the cold liquid aspic a little at a time. Check the seasoning, tint lightly with a little permitted food colour and fold in the whipped cream.

France

Salmon Parisian style

12–15 persons   Cooking time: 1$\frac{1}{4}$ hours

2 kg 500	1 salmon court-bouillon	5$\frac{1}{2}$ lb

Garnish

	15 tomatoes	
	8 hard-boiled eggs	
750 g	Russian salad	1$\frac{1}{2}$ lb
$\frac{3}{4}$ l	mayonnaise	1$\frac{1}{4}$ pt

Clean the salmon and poach in court-bouillon. Allow to cool in the cooking liquid, then drain. Skin carefully, starting a short distance below the head and finishing a short distance above the tail. The correct procedure is as follows. Make a cross-cut through the skin near the head and tail, then a lengthwise cut down the back along the backbone. Now remove the skin, working from the back of the fish towards the belly. Decorate as desired with coloured butter mixtures, truffle motifs, tomatoes, hard-boiled egg yolk or blanched tarragon. Glaze with fish aspic. Surround with the tomatoes stuffed with Russian salad, and with the hard-boiled eggs. Hand the mayonnaise separately.

The decorated salmon may be served without a garnish; in this case green sauce is handed as an accompaniment.

France

Salmon steaks modern style

12 persons   Cooking time (salmon): 15 minutes

2 kg 500–2 kg 800	fresh salmon without head or tail end	5½ lb approx.
approx. 3 l	court-bouillon	5 pt
1 l	fish aspic	1¾ pt
	12–14 tomatoes	
	6 hard-boiled eggs	
	cucumbers	
	fish salad	
	truffle slices	
	salmon mousse	
	white fish chaud-froid sauce	
	peeled shrimps	
	red and green peppers	
	egg yolk and chopped herb paste	

Fillet the salmon carefully, removing all the bones. Poach the salmon in well-flavoured court-bouillon containing a little oil and leave in the court-bouillon until cool, but not quite cold. Remove, skin carefully, wrap each side of salmon in lightly oiled aluminium foil and chill well under light pressure. Remove from the foil, cut into slices 1 cm (about ½ in) thick with a sharp knife, trim evenly and glaze each slice with aspic. Use the scraps and trimmings for the mousse.

Mask a round mould with fish aspic and decorate with a truffle motif as desired. When set, coat with white chaud-froid sauce, leave until firm, then fill up with salmon mousse which is on the point of setting. Peel some of the cucumbers, cut up evenly, hollow out a little, marinate, drain, stuff with horseradish cream, decorate with a small disk of tomato and pipe on a border of the same cream lightly stiffened with aspic jelly. Cut the hard-boiled eggs in half across the middle, scoop out the yolks, stuff with egg yolk and herb paste and top with a small ball of carrot. Place the shrimps in aspic jelly in very small savarin moulds. Skin the tomatoes, scoop out the seeds from the stalk end, stuff with fish salad, decorate with a tiny disk of egg white and glaze with aspic. Cut the unpeeled cucumbers into 2–2½ cm (about 1 in) pieces, hollow out and stuff with fish mousse mixed with small cubes of red and green pepper and truffle.

(Illustration, p. 698)   Austria

Sliced fresh salmon with scampi

12 portions   Cooking time: salmon, 15 minutes;
                   pike pâté, 20 minutes (approx.);
                   scampi, 6 minutes

1 kg 500	1 side of fresh salmon (boned) weighing	3½ lb
	24 raw scampi	

Bombe

800 g	poached salmon trimmings	1¾ lb
200 g	diced cooked celeriac	8 oz
150 g	diced poached mushrooms	5 oz
	1 red pepper	
350 g	mayonnaise	12 oz
	2 truffles	
½ l	aspic mayonnaise	¾ pt

Garnish

	8 hard-boiled eggs	
50 g	caviar	2 oz
70 g	butter	2 oz
	2 stuffed olives	
	8 unpeeled slices cucumber 1½ cm (about ½ in) thick, lightly blanched	
450 g	pike pâté	1 lb

Made with:

250 g	pike, skinned and boned	8 oz
150 g	choux paste	5 oz
	1 egg	
	1 egg yolk	

	herbs, blanched and sieved	
	a large amount of spinach, blanched and sieved	
approx. 3⅓ l	aspic jelly	5½ pt approx.

Poach the salmon (without skinning) in good fish stock, then allow to cool completely under light pressure. Mince the pike as finely as possible, mix with the cold choux paste, the egg, egg yolk and seasoning as required, rub through a fine sieve, then divide into three. Colour one-third pale pink, leave one-third as it is and mix the remainder with the finely sieved herbs and spinach. Fill three lightly buttered moulds with the three pâtés, poach and allow to cool. Lay the cold poached side of salmon flat, trim neatly and evenly and skin carefully. Transfer to a wire rack and glaze with aspic. Leave in a cold place to facilitate cutting, then slice evenly and glaze each slice with aspic. Cook the scampi, peel when cold, cut away the intestines, decorate with blanched chives and glaze with aspic.

Mask a bombe mould about 18 cm (7 in) in diameter with aspic. Decorate the bottom with a truffle motif. When set, line with aspic mayonnaise. Fill with salad consisting of the salmon trimmings, finely diced celeriac, mushrooms and red pepper, dressed with the mayonnaise which has been reinforced with 3 dl (½ pt) aspic and well seasoned. Refrigerate.

Cut the tops of the hard-boiled eggs zig-zag fashion, carefully remove the yolks, sieve, cream with butter and season to taste. Half fill the egg whites with caviar, pipe on the egg yolk paste, decorate each with a slice of stuffed olive and glaze with aspic.

Slice the pike pâtés and cut out small rounds. Cover each slice of cucumber with one disk of plain and one disk of pink pâté and glaze. Use the green pike pâté to decorate the slices of salmon.

(Illustration, p. 692)   Austria

Smoked eel medallions

Yield: 6

120 g	smoked eel, skinned and boned	4 oz
20 g	soft butter	1 oz
35 g	hard-boiled egg yolk	1 oz
	good dash of tomato ketchup	
	3 stuffed Spanish olives	
	white wine jelly or fish aspic	

Cut 6 eel medallions of equal size. Rub the egg yolk through a fine sieve and mix with the butter, seasoning with salt, paprika and the tomato ketchup. Pipe this paste on to the medallions and decorate each with half an olive. Refrigerate, then glaze with fish or white wine jelly.

Germany

Smoked salmon with piquant sauces

10 persons

2 kg	smoked salmon	4½ lb

Place the smoked salmon on a large board with a carving knife and fork next to it so that guests can help themselves. Prepare the following sauces and leave close to the fish.

Chive sauce

700 g	mayonnaise	1½ pt
	1 lemon	
1 dl	white wine	¼ pt
300 g	finely cut chives	10 oz

Mix the mayonnaise well with the juice of the lemon and the wine, then stir in the chives. Season with pepper and salt and add Worcestershire sauce to taste. Chill well before use.

Wittingau sauce

600 g	tomato sauce	1¼ pt
100 g	mayonnaise	¼ pt
200 g	onions, finely chopped	8 oz
20 g	garlic, finely grated	1 oz

Mix all the ingredients together, season with salt and pepper, flavour with Worcestershire sauce to taste and chill well before use.

Czechoslovakia

17

Smoked salmon rolls

Yield: 6

120 g	fresh smoked salmon	4 oz
60 g	thick horseradish cream	2 oz
	3 boiled quails' eggs	
	12 large capers	
	fish aspic	

Trim the smoked salmon, cut evenly into 6 thin slices and spread with horseradish cream. Roll up and decorate each roll with half a quail's egg and 2 capers. Chill well and glaze with fish aspic.

Germany

Sturgeon rolls Vladivostok

12 persons   Poaching time: 15 minutes

1 kg 200	sturgeon (flesh from the back of the fish only)	$2\frac{1}{2}$ lb
240 g	sturgeon's liver	8 oz
35 g	vesiga (dried)	2 oz
120 g	caviar	4 oz
7 dl	fresh cream	$1\frac{1}{4}$ pt
	$1\frac{1}{2}$–2 egg whites	
$2\frac{1}{2}$ cl	Cognac	2 dessertspoons
$2\frac{1}{2}$ cl	Madeira	2 dessertspoons
	white wine	
	dill	

Soak the vesiga in cold water for at least 5–6 hours, then cook for 3–$3\frac{1}{2}$ hours, cool and drain. Dice the sturgeon's liver finely and marinate in the Cognac and Madeira. Prepare mousseline forcemeat with 350 g ($12\frac{1}{4}$ oz) sturgeon, the egg whites and cream, salt and pepper. Stir in the diced liver and the vesiga which has been finely chopped.

Cut the rest of the sturgeon (which may be lightly frozen to facilitate cutting) into thin slices 12 cm (5 in) long, 9 cm ($3\frac{1}{2}$ in) wide and 100 g ($3\frac{1}{2}$ oz) in weight. Spread each one evenly with forcemeat, arrange 10 g ($\frac{1}{3}$ oz) caviar in a line down the centre, roll up, pack side by side in a thinly buttered sauté pan and poach gently in white wine. When cold, cut each roll in half diagonally, then arrange the halves neatly in a circle on a round dish and decorate with an edging of dill.

Germany

Trout in aspic

12 persons   Cooking time: 10–12 minutes

140–150 g	12 trout each weighing	5 oz approx.
1 l	fish aspic	1¾ pt
	1 lemon	
½ l	green sauce or mayonnaise	⅞ pt

Clean the trout, wash quickly, dry and poach in court-bouillon. Allow to cool in the cooking liquid, then drain and skin carefully. Decorate and coat with half-set aspic. Dish with a border of deckle-edged half slices of lemon and place a small parsley leaf or a spot of tomato in the centre of the straight edge of each half slice.

France

Trout in aspic Morgonnaise

Use Morgon instead of white wine for the court-bouillon. Make the aspic jelly with the cooking liquid. Hand Morgonnaise sauce separately.

France

Trout in aspic Rhine style

Make the aspic with white Moselle.

France

SHELLFISH

HOT DISHES

Crab au gratin

For 6 persons

	6 small crabs	
4 dl	Mornay sauce	⅔ pt
50 g	grated cheese	2 oz
50 g	butter	2 oz
	brown breadcrumbs	

Cook the crabs, extract the meat and the creamy parts and pound them with a little butter. Pass through a hair sieve. Mix the flaked meat with half the sauce and garnish the shells with it. Mask with Mornay sauce to which the creamy parts have been added. Sprinkle with the grated cheese, brown breadcrumbs and melted butter. Brown in a hot oven.

Fried prawns

Select large raw prawns, remove the shells and heads (use for soup if desired) and marinate for 20 minutes in lemon juice seasoned with salt and pepper. Using a fork, dip each one in Spanish coating batter* and deep fry in hot oil until golden. Remove, drain thoroughly and sprinkle with fine salt before serving.

*Spanish coating batter

250 g	flour	8 oz
10 g	yeast	$\frac{1}{2}$ oz
	few drops olive oil	
	1 clove of garlic, finely grated	
approx. $\frac{1}{4}$ l	water	$\frac{1}{2}$ pt approx.

Sieve the flour, add the yeast which has been dispersed in a little sherry or white wine, the olive oil and the garlic. Season with salt and pepper, pour in the water and mix to a smooth batter of coating consistency. Allow to stand for at least 15 minutes before using.

Spain

Garlic prawns

In some places prawns are sold ready boiled; elsewhere, freshly caught raw ones are obtainable. They may be prepared in two ways:

Raw prawns: select large ones, remove the antennae only and marinate for 10 minutes in a mixture of lemon juice, a few drops of oil, salt and pepper. Sprinkle a clean baking-sheet with a little oil, place the prawns on it and brown lightly on both sides, making sure that they do not become dry and shrivelled. When lightly browned, arrange in a fireproof dish and pour over a little boiling-hot oil containing chopped garlic to taste. Brown the prawns in the oil for a moment, making sure that the garlic does not burn.

Boiled prawns: place the boiled shelled prawns in small earthenware casseroles and arrange these on a baking-sheet. Pour a dash of oil into each casserole, adding 6 to 8 or more prawns (according to size) as soon as the oil is hot. Flavour with chopped garlic to taste, turn the prawns a few times with a fork and make sure that the garlic does not burn; this can best be avoided by adding the garlic last of all. Raw prawns may be shelled and then cooked in small casseroles in the same way as ready boiled ones. They are seasoned with salt and pepper, and flavoured with garlic at the last minute.

Spain

Lobster Américaine

For 6 persons

600 g	3 live lobsters, each weighing	1¼ lb
4 cl	Cognac	4 dessertspoons
3 dl	white wine	10 fl oz
4 dl	fish stock	14 fl oz
5 cl	oil	2 fl oz
	4 chopped shallots	
100 g	tomatoes, skinned, pipped and diced	4 oz
	2 soupspoons tomato purée	
100 g	butter	4 oz
	1 coffeespoon meat glaze	
	1 small crushed clove of garlic	
	1 coffeespoon chopped parsley, chervil and tarragon	

Sever the head from the trunk and cut the tail into troncons. Crack the claws to facilitate extraction of meat after cooking, and split the head in two lengthwise. Reject the sac containing sand. Retain creamy parts and the coral. Add 40 g of butter to the oil and heat in a plat a sauter. Sauté the lobster troncons in this until the shell becomes a bright red colour. Drain the oil. Flame in the cognac, moisten with white wine and fish stock. Add the chopped shallot, the tomato, the tomato purée, the garlic, the meat glaze and a pinch of cayenne pepper. Allow to cook with the lid on for 15–20 minutes. Remove the troncons and extract the meat from them and from the claws. Arrange in a timbale; place the two halves of head on top. Reduce the cooking liquor by half. Bind it with the creamy parts and the coral mixed with a little butter and cook for a moment. Pass through a fine strainer, heat without boiling and incorporate the rest of the butter. Adjust the seasoning and consistency and pour over the lobster. Sprinkle with chopped parsley, chervil and tarragon. Serve separately a pilaf of saffroned rice.

Lobster kedgeree

6 persons

300 g	rice	10 oz
500 g	finely sliced lobster meat	1 lb
	4 hard-boiled eggs, sliced	
50 g	lobster butter	2 oz
⅛ l	dairy cream	¼ pt
	chopped parsley	

Cook the rice in salted water until the grains are tender but still firm. Rinse in hot water and drain well. Warm the lobster meat in the lobster butter. Carefully mix the rice, lobster and sliced hard-boiled eggs with the cream and heat in a bain-marie. Sprinkle with chopped parsley when about to serve.

Germany

Lobster Newburg

4 persons

500 g	2 lobsters each weighing	1 lb
50 g	butter	2 oz
5 cl	brandy	2 fl oz
10 cl	Madeira	4 fl oz
⅛ l	thick cream	¼ pt
	2 egg yolks	

Boil lobsters for 20 minutes. Remove flesh from claws and tails, remove inedible parts and cut flesh into not too thin slices. Heat the butter, toss the flesh in it, flame with brandy, add Madeira, reduce. Simmer for a few minutes in the wine, add the cream, simmer a little longer and boil down. Season with salt and pepper, remove from heat and thicken the sauce with the egg yolks mixed with 2 spoonfuls of cream kept back for this purpose. Do not boil again. Arrange in a deep dish and serve with rice Creole.

Lobster Thermidor

For 4 persons

	2 cooked lobsters	
600 g	each	1¼ lb
1 dl	sauce Béchamel	¼ pt
2 dl	sauce Bercy	½ pt
	1 teaspoon English mustard	
50 g	grated Parmesan cheese	2 oz

Remove the claws and legs, split the lobsters in two lengthwise. Remove the tail meat and cut into neat round slices; remove and dice the claw meat. Mix the two sauces, and season with the mustard. Place a little of the sauce into each shell, bind the diced meat with sauce and add to the shells, arrange the sliced meat neatly on the top, mask with sauce, sprinkle with Parmesan cheese and place in a hot oven for 10 to 15 minutes to glaze.

Moules Marinière

3 l	mussels	5 pt
2 dl	white wine	7 fl oz
	2 chopped shallots	
50 g	chopped onion	2 oz
	6–8 parsley stalks	
1 dl	fish velouté	3 fl oz
50 g	butter	2 oz
	1 soupspoon chopped parsley	

Cook the mussels in white wine with parsley stalks, chopped shallot and onion, and a little milled pepper. Drain, and keep only one shell. Arrange in a timbale. Pass and decant the cooking liquor, reduce it by two-thirds. Add the velouté and the butter, and bring to the boil once or twice. Pour over the mussels and sprinkle with chopped parsley.

Mussel and mushroom stew

6 persons

3 l	mussels	5 pt
	when not in season use	
450 g	1 can weighing	1 lb
	plus	
225 g	1 can weighing	8 oz
300 g	small button mushroom caps	10 oz
75 g	butter	3 oz
80 g	flour	3 oz
1½ dl	milk	¼ pt
	2 egg yolks	
1 dl	dairy cream	⅙ pt
	juice of half a lemon	
40 g	grated Gruyère cheese	2 oz

If using fresh mussels, wash and scrub them thoroughly, then poach with the usual herbs and seasoning until the shells open. Remove from the shells, cut away the 'beard', and strain the liquid. If canned mussels are used, drain well and reserve the liquor. Dry the mussels, coat with flour and fry lightly in butter until pale golden. Drain the mushrooms (either fresh or canned) and toss in butter until pale golden. Make a blond roux with 30 g (1 oz) butter and 40 g (1½ oz) flour. Gradually add the milk and the same quantity of mussel liquor which has been strained through a cloth. Mix well, season with pepper and add a little salt if required. Cook slowly for at least 10 minutes. Thicken with the egg yolk and cream which have been whisked together, and flavour with the lemon juice. The sauce should be fairly thick. Carefully mix the mussels and mushrooms with the sauce and fill into lightly greased individual fireproof dishes or mussel shells. Sprinkle with grated cheese and brown for 5 minutes in an oven with good top heat.

(Illustration, p. 703)   Germany

Mussels Spanish style

6 persons   Cooking time: 8–10 minutes

4 kg	mussels	8½ lb
2 dl	best quality wine vinegar	⅓ pt
2 dl	olive oil	⅓ pt
	4 bay leaves	
	2 large cloves of garlic	
	12 white peppercorns	
	1 coffeespoon chilli powder	
1 dl	white wine	3 fl oz

Scrub the mussels clean, wash them and drain. Place in a saucepan with the wine and cook over brisk heat until the shells open. Remove from the heat at once, pour off the cooking liquid and set aside, take the mussels out of the shells and cut away the 'beard'. Heat half the oil in another pan, add the mussels and the cooking liquid and simmer for a few minutes until cooked. Drain, set aside the liquid and place the mussels in an earthenware or glass dish. Heat the rest of the oil in the second pan, add the thinly sliced garlic and fry until lightly coloured, then add the bay leaves, peppercorns and chilli powder and immediately stir in the vinegar. Pour in the cooking liquid, reduce by half and strain through a conical strainer. Cook gently for a further 5 minutes, strain through a cloth, allow to cool and pour over the mussels.

Spain

Paella

6 persons

3 l	mussels	5 pt
400 g	rice	1 lb

40 g	onion	1½ oz
	1 clove of garlic	
¼ l	olive oil	½ pt
2 g	pinch of saffron	
	1 cooked pimento	
	cut in strips	

Clean the mussels and cook them on a quick fire in 1 l of water. When the mussels are well open—about 5–8 minutes—drain them and retain the liquor. Remove half the mussels from their shells and keep the others hot in their half shells with a little cooking liquor. Colour the chopped onion and garlic in the oil, add the rice, the saffron, and stew for 5 minutes, stirring constantly. Moisten with the previously decanted cooking liquor, add the mussels which were removed from their shells, pour all into a large gratinating dish and, without stirring, cook in a moderately hot oven. Before serving, stick the mussels left in half-shells, in a crown on the rice, the shell side in the rice. Garnish the centre with the strips of red pimento.

Prawn crackers

'Kroekpoek' is an Indonesian speciality which is on sale in all food stores in Holland and which is indispensable for a 'Rijsttafel'. It is a very hard fermented prawn paste. Small pieces are dropped in boiling oil; they swell while frying and become crisp and crunchy. 'Kroekpoek' has not much taste, but it is fun to munch and makes a pleasant change from all the highly-seasoned dishes.

Holland

Prawns or scampi with whisky

6 persons

	24 large prawns or	
	fairly small scampi	
3 cl	Scotch whisky	3 dessertspoons
4 dl	dairy cream	⅔ pt
50 g	butter	1¾ oz

Cook this dish in front of the guests. After shelling the prawns or scampi and removing the heads, season lightly with salt and pepper. Heat the butter in a copper pan over a spirit stove, add the prawns or scampi and cook for a few moments. Pour in the whisky, ignite, reduce and add the cream. Cook gently to a coating consistency, without allowing the sauce to become too thick. Dish on small warmed plates, allowing 4–6 prawns or scampi per portion, depending on size, and coat with the well-flavoured sauce.

Prawn pilau

10 persons

	1 onion, finely chopped	
150 g	butter or margarine	5¼ oz
	1 dessertspoon Korma mixture (a mixture of spices)	
1 dl	curds or yoghurt	⅙ pt
300–500 g	cooked shelled (or canned) prawns (or as many as desired)	10½–18 oz
	pilau rice (for quantity, see recipe, p. 789)	

Fry the onion lightly in the butter or margarine, add the Korma mixture and cook for a further 4–5 minutes. Stir in the curds or yoghurt, add the cooked or canned prawns and simmer for 5 minutes. Season with salt and add the pillau rice. Cover the pan until ready to serve.

India

Scallops in cheese sauce

6 persons

	6 large scallops	
300 g	pommes duchesse mixture	10½ oz
4 dl	Mornay sauce	⅔ pt
50 g	grated cheese	2 oz
40 g	butter	2 oz

Shell the scallops and cook them in a court-bouillon with white wine. Drain and cut into slices slantwise. Mask the bottom of each deep shell, edge with pommes duchesse mixture by using a piping bag with fluted tube. Place a soupspoonful of Mornay sauce on the bottom of the shell and the scallops on top. Mask with Mornay sauce, sprinkle with grated cheese and melted butter and brown.

Scallops and bacon on skewers

Detach the scallops from their shell carefully separating the membrane and the beards surrounding the scallops, as well as the coral. Clean scallop and coral in water to remove any trace of sand.

Cut slices of bacon into small rectangles of the same size as the scallops and the coral. Skewer alternately scallops, coral and bacon and grill.

Great Britain

Stuffed clams

	48 clams	
120 g	mushrooms	4 oz
	4 slices bacon	
	chopped parsley	
	breadcrumbs	
60 g	butter	2 oz
	salt	
	pepper	

Cook the bacon until crisp, then crush it and mix with the finely diced raw mushrooms. Open the clams, reserving the liquor, and arrange them on a base of salt in an oven dish. Mix the mushrooms, bacon and parsley with the breadcrumbs and clam juice to make a moist stuffing, and cover the clams with this. Dot with butter and bake in the oven until brown and bubbling hot. Serve immediately.

USA

Oysters in Chablis 'Old Geneva'

6 persons

	36 Belon oysters	
	½ bottle Chablis	
¼ l	dairy cream	½ pt
	3 good-size grey shallots,	
	chopped	
¼ l	Hollandaise sauce	½ pt

Open 6 oysters per person. Remove from the shells and place the oysters in a pan with their own liquid. Add the Chablis and poach for 3 minutes, but do not allow to boil. Drain on a tammy cloth. Trim the 'beards' off the oysters. Wash and dry the shells. Return the oysters to the shells and keep warm. Add the chopped shallots to the liquid in which the oysters were cooked and reduce, then pour in the cream and reduce to the desired consistency. Remove from the heat and add the Hollandaise sauce. Adjust the seasoning. Pour over the oysters and glaze under a salamander. Serve very hot.

Switzerland

Oysters Rockefeller

	24 oysters	
120 g	butter	4 oz
	4 tablespoons breadcrumbs	

4 tablespoons watercress, chopped
2 tablespoons celery leaves, chopped
2 tablespoons parsley, chopped
2 tablespoons chervil, chopped
2 tablespoons tarragon, chopped
1 measure Pernod
salt
pepper

Arrange the oysters on a bed of salt (to hold them steady during cooking). Pound the butter, herbs and Pernod to a smooth paste and place a little on each oyster. Bake in a hot oven for 5 minutes and serve immediately.

Tempura mixed fry

4 persons

	12 medium-size prawns	
300 g	fillets of white fish	10 oz
	1 large bunch of parsley	
	sheets of nori*	
	4 small aubergines cut into slices or sticks	
50 g	grated radish	2 oz
	2 tablespoons grated ginger root	

Tempura batter

	1 egg	
200 g	flour	7 oz
$\frac{1}{4}$ l	ice-cold water	$\frac{1}{2}$ pt
	oil for frying (in Japan sesame oil is used)	

Tempura sauce

2 dl	bouillon	$\frac{1}{3}$ pt
	5 tablespoons soya sauce	
	$3\frac{1}{2}$ tablespoons mirin (sweet rice wine)	
	aji-no-moto (monosodium glutamate)	

* Nori: purple laver, a black seaweed dried in thin sheets in Japan.

Remove the heads and shells of the prawns, leaving the tails intact. Make a cut in the underside with a sharp knife to keep the prawns straight while frying. Wash the parsley and cut off the stalks. Cut the sheets of nori into four rectangles. Beat the egg, add the ice-cold water, sift the flour and stir in lightly to make a smooth batter. Dip the prawns and the fish, which has been sliced on the slant, into the batter and fry in oil at 175–180°C, stirring with a chop-stick to brown the fish evenly. Coat the parsley, aubergines and nori less thickly with batter, fry and drain on paper. Use as a garnish for the fish. Serve with tempura sauce. To make the sauce, mix together the bouillon, soya sauce and mirin, flavour with aji-no-moto and stir in the grated ginger root and radish.

Other vegetables suitable for tempura are raw asparagus cut into small sticks, small sweet peppers or large ones cut into sticks, and shitake, a strongly flavoured large flat mushroom which is very popular.

Japan

COLD DISHES

Boiled abalone

4 persons

	1 medium-size abalone*	
	3 tablespoons saké†	
5 cl	soya sauce	$\frac{1}{12}$ pt
5 cl	mirin	$\frac{1}{12}$ pt
	aji-no-moto	

Scrub the surface of a fresh abalone with salt and water, wash, place in a pan with the saké and hot water to cover, and boil until tender, adding water two or three times if required. When the flesh is cooked, remove it from the shell. Flavour the cooking liquid with the mirin, the soya sauce and $\frac{1}{4}$ teaspoon aji-no-moto, pour over the abalone flesh and cook over moderate heat for a further 20 minutes. The liquid should be well reduced. Allow to cool and cut the flesh into 1 cm ($\frac{1}{2}$ in) slices, allowing 2 per person. Arrange in the shell and pour over the cold stock, which should have been reduced until it barely covers the slices of fish.

Japan

---

* Abalone, awabi or ear-shell (Latin *haliotis vulgaris*): a genus of gastropod molluscs with a flat ear-shaped shell. There are about seventy species of different size in the hot and temperate zones.
† Saké: dry rice wine.

Boiled crayfish

Per person

8–10 crayfish
2 tablespoons salt per litre (1¾ pt)
water
large bunch of fresh dill

Wash the crayfish in cold running water. Place sufficient water in a pan to cover the crayfish, add the salt and part of the dill and bring to the boil. Plunge the first portion of crayfish into the boiling water, bring to the boil again and add the next portion with a generous amount of dill. Repeat the process with the remaining portions, finishing up with dill. Cover the pan and cook for 5 minutes. Allow the crayfish to cool in the cooking liquid, then drain and arrange in a pyramid.

(Illustration, p. 690)   Sweden

Boiled crayfish in court-bouillon

10 persons   Cooking time: 12–15 minutes

	40 crayfish	
50–60 g	each weighing	2 oz
	2 small carrots	
	5 small onions	
	1 shallot	
	a few parsley roots	
	half a bay leaf	
¾ l	dry white wine	1 bottle
½ l	water	¾ pt
1 dl	Cognac (optional)	3 fl oz
20 g	salt	1 oz

Finely slice the carrots, onions and shallot. Place the vegetables and herbs in a pan, pour in the wine, water and Cognac, and add the salt together with a little pepper and a dash of cayenne pepper. Simmer until the vegetables are tender, then drop in the crayfish and simmer until cooked. Serve either lukewarm or cold in the cooking liquid.

To remove the intestine from live crayfish, grasp the middle tail fin between the thumb and the first finger, twist and pull gently; the intestine should come away.

France

Crayfish parfait Don Juan

10–15 portions

5 kg	medium-sized crayfish	11 lb
1 l	white wine	1¾ pt
1 l	dairy cream	1¾ pt
1 l	white stock	1¾ pt
	20 egg yolks	
	14 mushroom caps,	
	neatly shaped	
	6 hard-boiled eggs	
	dill leaves	
120 g	caviar	4 oz
4 cl	Cognac	4 dessertspoons
	cumin and dill seeds	
	truffles	
	saffron	
	lemons	
	butter	
1 l	aspic jelly flavoured with	
	white wine	1¾ pt

Plunge the crayfish into a large pan of boiling salted water to kill them. Remove after 2 minutes and cool thoroughly in cold water. Select 10–12 of the best ones, cook in salted water with a little white wine, cumin and dill for 10 minutes and allow to cool. Remove the tails, claws and shells from half the remaining (almost raw) crayfish. Poach the other half (with shells on) in white wine with a little dill for 8 minutes.

Set aside 10–15 of the best head shells. Pound all the other shells, including the claw shells, as finely as possible in a mortar. Cook in butter for a moment in a sauté pan, pour in the Cognac and ignite, detach the cooking juices with the white stock and the cream, then simmer for about 1 hour. Press through a sieve, reduce by half and allow to cool. Gut the shelled crayfish and mash as finely as possible together with the claws and the egg yolks, adding small amounts of the sauce prepared from the shells. Season this crayfish cream with salt and pepper, flavour with Cognac and pour into a mould which has been lined with aluminium foil and buttered. Poach in a moderate oven in a bain-marie until just beginning to set. Now insert truffles along the length of the mould, pressing them in until they are about halfway down, and continue poaching until firm enough to slice. Leave this parfait until cold, then mask another mould with aspic jelly, decorate with crayfish claws and small disks of truffle, place the parfait in it and fill up with aspic.

Mask a ring mould with aspic, decorate with small disks of truffle and arrange about 24 of the poached tails evenly all round. Fill with aspic and refrigerate. Poach the shaped mushroom caps in butter and lemon juice with a little saffron.

Cut the hard-boiled eggs in half, decorate with dill leaves and glaze with aspic. Mask small moulds with aspic and fill with caviar and crayfish claws. After turning out, place on slices of lemon. When firm, arrange the parfait, the ring of crayfish tails in aspic and the small moulds on an oblong dish.
(Illustrations, p. 591)   Austria

Crayfish bombe with sliced fresh salmon

10–12 portions	Cooking time: salmon, 15 minutes; crayfish, 10 minutes	
	1 side of fresh salmon (boned, without skinning)	
1 kg 500	weighing	3¼ lb
	45 crayfish	
100 g	poached mushrooms	4 oz
200 g	cooked celeriac	8 oz
½ l	aspic mayonnaise	¾ pt
	2 truffles	
	1 teaspoon chopped dill	
	1–2 tablespoons tomato ketchup	
	1 apple, peeled and cored	
200 g	mayonnaise	8 oz
2½ l	aspic jelly	4½ pt

Poach the salmon (without skinning) in good fish stock, then allow to cool completely in the stock under light pressure. Cook the crayfish, remove the tails, gut, and set aside 20 of the best ones. Take the salmon out of the stock, dry well, remove any bones which may have been left behind, lay on a wire rack and skin carefully. Glaze lightly with aspic and chill well to facilitate cutting. Slice evenly and glaze each slice with aspic.

Mask a bombe mould about 16 cm (6½ in) in diameter with aspic jelly, decorate the bottom with a truffle motif, allow to set, then line thinly with the aspic mayonnaise. Dice the mushrooms and celeriac, the apple and the 25 crayfish tails, mix with 200 g (7 oz) mayonnaise and 2 dl (⅓ pt) aspic jelly, season with salt and pepper as required, flavour with tomato ketchup and the dill, then fill into the bombe mould and refrigerate.

To dish, hold the bombe in hot water for a moment, turn out on one side of a round dish and surround with the 20 remaining crayfish tails, lightly glazed with aspic. Arrange the slices of salmon in a semicircle round the bombe.

(Illustration, p. 693)   Austria

Crayfish bush

Boiled crayfish are drained, dried and arranged in a pyramid to serve.

Crayfish bush is a very attractive, decorative dish for a buffet, but the crayfish are difficult to eat. At the very least finger-bowls and paper napkins must be provided.

Crayfish mousse

Proceed as for salmon mousse, using 400 g (14 oz) crayfish tails and claws. (Weighed when shelled.)

France

Dressed crab

Crabs are poached in either court-bouillon or in salted water (enough salt to float an egg in the brine) for 15 minutes for the first 450 g (1 lb) and 10 minutes per 450 g (1 lb) thereafter.

When the crab is cold, twist off the claws and legs. Lay the body on its back and lever off the central part of the underside. Press down on the small mouth part which will snap off easily. Discard the stomach sack (located behind the mouth) and the filters or fronds (often called 'dead men's fingers'). Scoop out the soft brown flesh from the body and pass this through a sieve. (This can be 'extended' with a small quantity of fresh white breadcrumbs if necessary, and is sometimes seasoned with a very small dash of Worcestershire sauce.) Tap the rim of the hole in the body with the handle of a knife until it breaks away at the line which runs round it, leaving a neat shell, which is thoroughly scrubbed, and rubbed with a little oil to give it a good appearance.

Crack the claws and legs with the back of a heavy knife and remove all the white flesh, taking great care not to include any small flakes of bone. Cut in half the central part, removed from the body, and extract all the white meat, with the aid of a trussing needle.

Place a little finely shredded lettuce into the shell, place the flaked white meat at each side, and the brown meat down the centre. Decorate lightly with sieved hard-boiled egg white, sieved egg yolk and a few capers.

Serve with a mayonnaise sauce and brown bread and butter.

Great Britain

Glazed spiny lobster Nice Style I

12 persons

	2 spiny lobsters	
2 kg 200	each weighing	4¾ lb
6 dl	fish aspic	1 pt
¾ l	mayonnaise	1¼ pt

Mousse

400 g	1 sole weighing	1 lb
	2 anchovy fillets	
2 dl	whipped cream	⅓ pt
1 dl	concentrated fish stock	⅙ pt
	2 hard-boiled egg yolks	
1 dl	fish aspic	

Garnish

	8 hard-boiled eggs	
	12 small artichoke bottoms (cooked)	
	3 small bundles asparagus tips (cooked)	
	12 small tomatoes	
150 g	tunny in oil	5 oz
200 g	potatoes cooked in their jackets	8 oz
	sprigs of curled parsley	
	tarragon	
	12 small short pastry barquettes	

Prepare and dress the spiny lobsters in the same way as for spiny lobster en Bellevue. To make the mousse, fillet the sole, cook in the fish stock and pound or reduce to a purée in the mixer together with the spiny lobster trimmings, the hard-boiled egg yolks and the anchovy fillets which have been soaked. Pass through a fine sieve. Stand on ice and gradually work in the fish aspic and then the whipped cream. Adjust the seasoning—the mousse should be well flavoured. Fill into the barquettes. Fill the artichoke bottoms with the asparagus tips dressed with vinaigrette. Stuff the tomatoes with a salpicon of tunny, well soaked anchovy fillets and potatoes in aspic mayonnaise. Cut the hard-boiled eggs in half, decorate with blanched tarragon leaves and glaze with aspic. Arrange the garnishes alternately round the spiny lobsters on a bed of curled parsley. Hand the mayonnaise separately.

France

Glazed spiny lobster Nice style II (lyre-shaped arrangement)

Cut the spiny lobsters in half lengthwise, remove and slice the flesh, decorate with blanched tarragon leaves and glaze with aspic. Wipe the inside of the half-shells, fill with the same mousse as the preceding recipe, smoothing the top, and refrigerate, then place the slices of spiny lobster meat on top, overlapping them a little. Arrange the half-shells on a dish facing one another to the shape of a lyre, with their backs towards the edge of the dish. Surround with the garnish. Hand the mayonnaise separately.

France

Lobster ballottines

10 persons   Cooking time: 25 minutes

	10 large firm tomatoes (or 2 smaller ones per person)	
200 g	boneless chicken	8 oz
600 g	1 lobster weighing about	1¼ lb
40 g	pistachio nuts	2 oz
	1 small truffle	
100 g	mushrooms	4 oz
	3 egg whites	
approx. ¼ l	dairy cream	½ pt
1 cl	brandy	1 dessertspoon

Prepare forcemeat with the chicken, the lobster meat, the raw egg whites, salt and pepper and rub through a fine sieve. Chill well, add the cream and stir in the finely diced meat from the lobster claws which have been boiled and allowed to cool, together with the diced truffle, mushrooms, brandy and pistachio nuts. Carefully scoop out the centre of the tomatoes, working from the stalk end, fill with forcemeat and wrap tightly in aluminium foil. Stand on a rack in a suitable pan containing water, making sure that the tomatoes are clear of the water, and steam at 80°C. Remove from the pan with the rack, unwrap, dish, coat with light lemon sauce* and garnish with neatly shaped stewed pieces of cucumber and with fleurons. Serve as an hors d'oeuvre with a spoonful of crayfish tail salad, first glazing with aspic jelly. Hand cold Creole sauce separately.

Creole sauce

	3 eggs	
¾ l	oil	1¼ pt
	1 tablespoon curry paste	

* Lemon sauce. Prepare mayonnaise in the usual manner, but use lemon juice instead of vinegar and add a little finely grated lemon zest to the egg yolk. Finish off with 1 tablespoon whipped unsweetened cream to 250 g (8 oz) mayonnaise.

	juice of 1 lemon	
200 g	tomato ketchup	7 oz
1½ dl	sour cream or yoghurt	¼ pt

Using a mixer, prepare a sauce with all the ingredients except the sour cream or yoghurt in the same way as mayonnaise. Season with salt and pepper and finish off with the sour cream or yoghurt.

(Illustration, p. 695)   Germany

Lobster and coral in aspic

6 persons   Cooking time: 20–25 minutes

	3 live lobsters	
500–600 g	each weighing	1¼ lb approx.
approx. 250 g	1 live lobster	½ lb approx.
1 l	concentrated fish stock	1¾ pt
	2 tomatoes	
	1 level tablespoon chopped shallot	
3 cl	Cognac	1 measure
1 dl	Bordeaux	3 fl oz
	small bunch tarragon	
10 g	gelatine	⅓ oz
	2 green leek leaves	
	2–3 sprigs chervil	
	2 egg whites	
½ l	cream and herb mayonnaise	¾ pt

Drop the 3 large live lobsters into boiling court-bouillon, cook and allow to cool in the cooking liquid, then drain. Scrub one of them with a brush and remove the soft membrane under the tail, cutting it away with a pair of scissors right along the shell without detaching the tail from the head. The shell will now be intact with an opening large enough for the flesh to be removed without breaking it up. Set aside the empty shell with the claws for use in decorating the dish. The claw flesh may be removed more or less undamaged by making a cut in the underside of the claw shells. Split the other 2 large lobsters lengthwise and remove the 2 halves of the tail from the shell. Crack the claws carefully and remove the flesh intact. Set aside the red coral which lies in the head. Cover all the lobster meat and coral with damp muslin and refrigerate until required.

To make the aspic jelly, pull the tail of the small live lobster hard to detach it from the head. Split the head lengthwise, discard the gritty sac lying near the eyes, then cut the head into pieces. Drop these, together with the whole tail and the cracked claws, into a pan containing a tablespoonful of smoking-hot oil. Season with salt and pepper and cook only until the lobster turns red, stirring meanwhile. Remove the tail and set aside with the other lobster tails. Drain away all the oil. Add the chopped shallot and stir for a minute or two over low heat. Pour in the Cognac, heat, but do not ignite. Add the white wine and boil up for a moment. Now add the crushed tomatoes, the tarragon and the fish stock. Season with a dash of cayenne pepper, salt and freshly ground pepper, taking care not to use too much salt as the fish stock already contains some. Simmer for 15 minutes, skimming repeatedly. Pass through a fine conical strainer, allow any sediment to settle, then pour into a clean pan. Prepare aspic jelly (see p. 95) with this concentrated lobster stock, the leek, chervil, gelatine and egg whites.

Place the lobster tail and claw meat on a rack standing on a dish. Coat with half-set aspic and sprinkle the top immediately with finely chopped or sieved coral. Refrigerate until set, then coat with aspic again and refrigerate. Line the bottom of a serving dish with the rest of the half-set aspic jelly, sprinkle with the rest of the coral and allow to set. Place the intact empty lobster shell at one end of the dish and arrange the glazed tail and claw meat on the coating of coral in aspic. Hand cream and herb mayonnaise separately.

Lobster in court-bouillon

1 person	Cooking time: 18 minutes	
350 g	1 lobster weighing	¾ lb
or 2 persons	Cooking time: 20–25 minutes	
500–600 g	1 lobster weighing	1¼ lb

Boil the lobster in vinegar court-bouillon well seasoned with cayenne pepper and allow to cool in the cooking liquid. Split from head to tail, crack the claws halfway through their shell without spoiling their appearance and dish on a bed of curled parsley without further garnish. Serve with mayonnaise, green sauce or any other suitable cold sauce.

Lobster may be prepared according to any recipe for spiny lobster.

Lobster Miramare

Cooking time (lobsters): 18–20 minutes

450 g	10 lobsters each weighing	1 lb
	disks of truffle	
	egg yolk paste	
	10 short pastry tartlet cases, baked blind	
approx. 1½ dl	thick fish velouté	¼ pt approx.

approx. 1½ dl	half-whipped cream	¼ pt approx.
	Cognac	
	caviar	
	10 large green	
	asparagus tips	
	1 red pepper	
	curled parsley	

Boil the lobsters and leave in the cooking liquid until cold. Crack open the tails and claws. Remove the claw meat. Detach the tail meat, working from underneath, and cut each tail into 10 medallions. Arrange these in a row along the shell so that they overlap and fix in position with a little egg yolk paste. Decorate each one with a disk of truffle.

Reduce the claw meat to a fine purée and mix with cold fish velouté and aspic jelly (1½ dl (¼ pt) velouté and 1 dl (⅙ pt) jelly to 400 g (14 oz) claw meat). Add a dash of Cognac, season with salt and a good pinch of cayenne pepper and lastly fold in the cream. Pipe into the tartlet cases, using a plain pipe, decorate with a little caviar and glaze with aspic. Decorate the asparagus tips with a thin strip of red pepper and coat with aspic.

Line a round dish with aspic. Stand the lobster heads, which have been levelled off underneath and glazed with aspic, in a ring in the centre and fill up the space in the middle with curled parsley. Arrange the very lightly glazed tails all round with one end resting against the heads, and place a tartlet and an asparagus tip in each space between two tails.

(Illustration, p. 701)   Switzerland

Lobster mousse

350 g	cooked lobster	12 oz
	(net weight)	
50 g	lobster coral, cooked	2 oz
4 dl	aspic jelly reduced to half	⅔ pt
3 dl	dairy cream	½ pt
15 cl	cold thick Béchamel sauce	¼ pt

Reduce the lobster and the coral to a very fine purée, then proceed as for salmon mousse, page 509.

France

Lobster mousse Carthusian style

15 persons   Cooking time: 45–60 minutes, depending on size of mould

400 g	pike without skin	14 oz
	or bones	
400 g	boneless chicken (raw)	14 oz

	3 lobsters	
500 g	each weighing	1 lb
80 g	pistachio nuts	3 oz
	1 large truffle	
150 g	fresh mushrooms	5 oz
approx. ½ l	dairy cream	¾ pt approx.
	6 egg whites	
150 g	thick white onion purée	5 oz
	1 cucumber	
⅛ l	Noilly Prat vermouth	4 fl oz
1 cl	brandy	1 dessertspoon
	pike quenelles	
	asparagus tips	
	tomatoes, skinned, seeded	
	and cut in quarters	
	chopped lobster coral	

First prepare fairly firm (but not hard) forcemeat with the pike, 2–3 egg whites, about ¼ l (½ pt) dairy cream, salt, pepper and brandy, and add the onion purée. Retain 20% forcemeat for the pike quenelles.

Now prepare slightly softer forcemeat with the chicken, 400 g (14 oz) raw lobster, the remaining egg whites and cream, the Noilly Prat, salt and pepper. Boil the rest of the lobsters, including the claws, and allow to cool. Mix the chicken and lobster forcemeat with coarsely cut cooked lobster, pistachio nuts, mushrooms and finely diced truffle. Line a round mould with a thin layer of pike forcemeat, fill with the chicken and lobster forcemeat, finish off with the rest of the pike forcemeat and cover with oiled aluminium foil. Poach in the oven in a bain-marie at 80°C, then stand aside under light pressure for 10 minutes.

To serve, turn out and garnish with pike quenelles, poached mushrooms, asparagus tips, small neatly shaped stewed pieces of cucumber, and a few bright red lobster claws. Sprinkle with chopped coral for final decoration.

(Illustration, p. 806)   Germany

Prawn mousse

Proceed as for salmon mousse, page 509, using 400 g (14 oz) picked prawns.
France

Pyramid of jumbo shrimps

18 persons

	36–40 jumbo shrimps	
	(Dublin Bay prawns)	
1 kg	total weight	2¼ lb

⅛ l	white wine	5 fl oz
	2 egg whites	
	16 sheets gelatine	

Court-bouillon

1½ l	water	2½ pt
150 g	onions, finely sliced	5 oz
150 g	carrots, finely sliced	5 oz
20 g	parsley stalks	1 oz
	1 sprig thyme	
	1 bay leaf	
1 dl	vinegar	3 fl oz
12 g	salt	½ oz
	10 peppercorns	

Vegetable salad

500 g	diced cooked carrots, celeriac, green peppers, garden peas	1 lb
200 g	mayonnaise	8 oz
	salt	
	pepper	
	Worcestershire sauce	
	6 sheets gelatine	

Cocktail sauce

4 dl	chilli sauce	⅔ pt
4 dl	tomato ketchup	⅔ pt
100 g	grated horseradish	4 oz
	few drops Tabasco sauce	

Simmer the ingredients for the court-bouillon for 1 hour. Ten minutes before straining, add 10 peppercorns. Boil the prawns for a short time in the court-bouillon and cool before removing. Prepare aspic jelly with 1 l (1¾ pt) strained court-bouillon and 16 sheets of gelatine which have been soaked beforehand. Clarify the jelly with the egg whites which have been lightly beaten with the white wine, strain and adjust the seasoning. Shell the prawns and clean well, taking care not to damage the vein down the middle of the back. Mix the vegetables for the salad with the mayonnaise, add salt, pepper and Worcestershire sauce to taste, and stiffen with 6 sheets of gelatine which have been soaked, squeezed dry and dissolved.

Mask a ring mould with aspic jelly and decorate. When half-set, fill with vegetable salad and chill well. Turn out on a large round silver dish. Fill up the centre of the moulded salad with the rest of the vegetable salad smoothed to a dome shape and refrigerate for a few hours. Cover the dome symmetrically with rows of prawns arranged lengthwise until all the prawns are used up and glaze neatly with aspic.

The dome may be topped with a small vegetable mould or a fancy skewer. Garnish the dish with diced aspic and sprigs of parsley. The dome of vegetable salad may be replaced by a dome of lobster or shrimp mousse.

To make the sauce, mix the chilli sauce with the ketchup, stir in the horseradish and add a few drops of Tabasco sauce. Hand separately.

USA

Spiny lobster en Bellevue

12 persons   Cooking time: 35–40 minutes

	2 spiny lobsters	
1 kg 200	each weighing	2½ lb
½ l	fish aspic	¾ pt
	chervil	
	white bread (tin loaf)	
¾ l	mayonnaise	1¼ pt

Garnish

	12 small short pastry barquettes	
500 g	Russian salad	1 lb
	12 small tomatoes	
	6 hard-boiled eggs	
	lettuce	

Wash and scrub the spiny lobsters, which should be alive. Tie them on to a small board from head to tail and drop them into a large pan of boiling water containing vinegar (1 part vinegar to 20 parts water), a large bouquet garni, salt and a little cayenne pepper. The liquid should cover the spiny lobsters completely. Cook and allow to cool in the cooking liquid, then drain. Insert the tip of a knife between the eyes and press downwards a little to drain out the cooking liquid. Scrub the shell with a wet brush. Cut the twine. Remove the tail meat in one piece as described for lobster and coral in aspic. Cut into medallions 6–7 mm (¼ in) thick, trim slightly and remove the intestine lying in the centre with the aid of the tip of a knife. Set aside the trimmings and any pieces unsuitable for medallions.

Decorate the medallions with truffle motifs or with neatly arranged sprigs of chervil interspersed with tiny dots of deep red tomato. Glaze with aspic, then refrigerate until set. Cut up the trimmings finely (increasing their bulk, if desired, by adding diced mushrooms cooked in the Greek manner) and bind with mayonnaise. Fill into the barquettes and sprinkle with the coral from the spiny lobsters. Hollow out the tomatoes and fill with Russian salad. Cut the hard-boiled eggs in half and stuff with the yolks which have been rubbed through a sieve and bound with mayonnaise. Decorate with a small spot of tomato or truffle.

Make a stand with the bread and arrange the spiny lobsters on it facing one another, with their antennae pointing upwards. Insert a skewer (or knitting needle) into the top of each head and push it right down into the bread to fit the shellfish securely in position. Conceal the top of the skewer by impaling a small tomato and a lettuce heart on it. Arrange the medallions along the spiny lobsters, making them overlap slightly. Surround with the garnish on a bed of shredded lettuce.

France

Spiny lobster La Baule style

	2 choice spiny lobsters	
approx. 2 kg 500	weighing	5½ lb
	2 crabs	
600 g	each weighing	1¼ lb
1 kg	large mussels	2¼ lb
1 kg	scampi	2¼ lb
200 g	prawns	8 oz
	mayonnaise	
	green sauce	

Tie each spiny lobster on to a small board and cook in court-bouillon. Cook the crabs and scampi in the same way. Allow to cool.

Cook the mussels until the shells open as for mussels marinière. Cut away the membrane under the tail of the spiny lobsters and remove the flesh in one piece. Cut the flesh into medallions, coat with mayonnaise, decorate and glaze with aspic jelly.

Remove the crab meat from the shell, chop it coarsely and mix with a few finely chopped shallots which have been gently cooked under cover in dry white wine. Bind with a few spoonfuls of American sauce to make a smooth, well-blended forcemeat. Check the seasoning.

Shell the scampi tails and set aside the heads.

Remove the 'beard' from the mussels and set aside 12 choice shells. Stuff the scampi heads with the crab forcemeat and top each one with a scampi tail which has been decorated and glazed with aspic. Fill the mussel shells with the same forcemeat. Coat with green sauce. Place a choice mussel on top, decorate and glaze with aspic. Shell the prawn tails and glaze with aspic.

To dish, decorate an oblong tray with a mosaic of vegetables. Arrange two slightly sloping pedestals in a V shape in the centre of the tray and place the two spiny lobster tails on top so that they meet at the point of the V. Stand one of the shells on top at this point. Decorate with the medallions of spiny lobster flesh, fixing them in place with a little softened butter. Surround with the mussels, scampi and prawns arranged alternately to form circles. Serve green sauce separately.

(Illustration, p. 704)   France

Spiny lobster medallions in green sauce

Proceed as for spiny lobster medallions Russian style, but coat the medallions with green sauce which has been stiffened with aspic instead of mayonnaise. Decorate with blanched tarragon leaves. Add pieces of stuffed cucumber to the garnish. Hand green sauce separately.

France

Spiny lobster medallions Russian style

12 persons   Cooking time: 35–40 minutes

1 kg 200	2 spiny lobsters each weighing	2½ lb
½ l	mayonnaise	¾ pt

Garnish

1 kg 500	Russian salad	3¼ lb
	6 hard-boiled eggs	
	6 tomatoes	
¾ l	aspic mayonnaise	1¼ pt

Prepare and cook the spiny lobsters as for spiny lobster en Bellevue. Cut the tail meat into medallions and coat each one with aspic mayonnaise. Decorate the top and glaze with aspic. Remove the shells from the heads and claws and cut up the flesh and the coral. Bind with aspic mayonnaise and fill into the tomatoes which have been cut in half, hollowed out, sprinkled inside with salt and well drained.

Arrange the medallions on a base of Russian salad corresponding in shape to the serving dish. Surround with the stuffed tomatoes and wedges of hard-boiled egg on lettuce heart leaves. Hand the mayonnaise separately.

France

Spiny lobster Moscow style

12 persons   Cooking time: 35–40 minutes

1 kg 200	2 spiny lobsters each weighing	2½ lb
¾ l	cream mayonnaise flavoured with paprika	1¼ pt
½ l	fish aspic	¾ pt

Garnish

	12 small cooked artichoke bottoms	
	6 hard-boiled eggs	
150 g	caviar	5 oz
	3 small bundles of asparagus tips (cooked)	
100 g	anchovies	4 oz
2 dl	whipped cream	$\frac{1}{3}$ pt
	lettuce hearts	

Prepare and dress the spiny lobsters in the same way as for spiny lobster en Bellevue, decorating the medallions with truffle only before glazing with aspic.

Soak the anchovies to remove excess salt, pound or reduce to a purée in the mixer and rub through a fine sieve. Beat with a spatula for a few moments and blend in the whipped cream. Fill into the artichoke bottoms and round off the top. Cut the hard-boiled eggs in half across, slice off the ends to make them stand securely, remove the yolk and fill with caviar. Glaze the bundles of asparagus tips with aspic. Cut the lettuce hearts into four or six.

Arrange the garnish on the dish round the spiny lobsters. Hand the mayonnaise separately.

France

Trussed crayfish

Fold back the claws, handling them gently as they break off easily, and insert one of the tips of each into the tail through the shell after having removed the spinal cord by twisting the centre fin of the tail and pulling firmly. Drop the crayfish into boiling court-bouillon (as for boiled crayfish) and simmer until cooked. Allow to cool in the cooking liquid, then drain and wipe dry before using.

France

MEAT

However much people enjoy the other parts of a meal—the soups and savouriest puddings and desserts—the heart of the meal is the main course, and to most people the main course usually means meat.

Meat is one of the oldest foods known to man, since our remote ancestors were hunters before they were either herdsmen or farmers. Meat is also one of the most natural and nutritious of foods. Not only is it rich in proteins, but meat proteins contain the amino acids essential for adequate nutrition in more suitable combinations than other protein sources such as dairy foods and pulses.

Meat can be cooked in any of the basic methods of cookery. It can be fried, grilled, baked, roasted, boiled, braised and steamed, depending upon the particular cut.

Different nations all have their own specialities, and recipes for many of these will be found in the following pages.

In many parts of the world, meat has long been considered a luxury, to be eaten only on rare occasions, because of its relatively high price, and these countries have evolved a wide variety of recipes which enable small quantities of meat to serve large numbers of people, and which make imaginative use of the cheaper cuts of meat. Now that meat prices have risen to an unprecedented high figure in the western world, these recipes are increasing in popularity.

For the really important occasion, however, there is no substitute for one of the extravagant set-pieces of classical cuisine.

BEEF

HOT DISHES

Boiled beef

10 portions   Cooking time: about 2 hours

      2 kg 500   top rump   5½ lb

1 kg 500	raw beef bones	3¼ lb
50 g	ox milt	2 oz
50 g	carrots	2 oz
80 g	parsley roots	3 oz
50 g	celeriac	2 oz
100 g	chives	4 oz
50 g	parsley and celery leaves	2 oz
	2 cloves of garlic	
	1 small bay leaf	
	8 peppercorns	
	salt	

Place the bones, milt, vegetables, herbs and seasonings in a pan with 5 l (8¾ pt) water, bring to the boil and cook slowly to make bouillon. Strain, return to the pan and, while the bouillon is still hot, add the beef and simmer very slowly until cooked. Remove from the pan, carve into portions, sprinkle with chopped chives and dish with a little of the bouillon poured over.

Serve with Viennese chive sauce (see recipe, p. 183), apple and horseradish sauce (see recipe, p. 179), and browned potatoes (see recipe, p. 780).

Austria

Boiled silverside and dumplings

2 kg	salted and pickled silverside	4 lb
	4 onions	
	4 carrots	
	3 leeks	
	1 turnip	
	3 sticks celery	
	bouquet garni	
	salt	

Soak the meat for 3 or 4 hours, then rinse. Cover with water and bring slowly to the boil, and remove any scum. Simmer gently for 3½ hours, add the cleaned vegetables, and simmer a further ¾ hour.

Barbecued beef brochettes

10 persons

1 kg 500	fillet of beef	3½ lb
300 g	bacon	10 oz

300 g	medium-size firm onions	10 oz
	salt	
	pepper	
	mustard	
	oil	

If possible, marinate the beef with oil and mustard before use, proceeding as follows: remove any skin, spread the meat with the marinade and leave in the refrigerator in a covered dish for 4–6 days. When ready to use, cut the meat into pieces about 3 cm (1 in) thick; dice the bacon and cut the onions into slices thick enough to hold together. Sprinkle the meat with salt, also a little pepper if required, and thread on to skewers alternately with the onion and bacon, but do not pack too tightly. Individual portions may be cooked out-of-doors over a charcoal fire, as for a barbecue. For indoor cooking, all the ingredients may be threaded on to a long spit and grilled.

To keep the meat very juicy, wrap the prepared brochettes in greased aluminium foil and twist wire round the ends to seal. Remove the foil before the meat has finished cooking and turn the skewers over the glowing hot charcoal for a moment to brown.

Hungary

Barbecued sweet sour brisket of beef with horseradish

20 persons   Total cooking time: about 2½ hours

3 kg	pickled brisket of beef	6 lb approx.
500 g	pot vegetables	1 lb
	1 bay leaf	
	3 cloves of garlic	
	5–6 cloves	

Barbecue sauce

100 g	brown sugar	4 oz
	4 tablespoons vinegar	
	1 tablespoon dry mustard	
	2 tablespoons honey	
	½ teaspoon ground black pepper	
1 dl	Espagnole sauce	¼ pt

Horseradish sauce

200 g	grated horseradish	8 oz
300 g	mayonnaise	12 oz
	3 tablespoons whipped cream	

Cover the boned brisket with water, but do not add salt, bring to the boil and skim. Add the vegetables, bay leaf, garlic and cloves and simmer gently until tender but still firm enough to carve. Remove from the water, drain well, cut off all fat, then dry. Mix the Espagnole sauce well with the brown sugar, vinegar, mustard, honey and pepper and spread on the meat to cover. Roast for 30 minutes in a hot oven with good top heat, or brown lightly under a salamander or grill on a barbecue. Carve the brisket thinly and serve hot or cold. Blend the horseradish well with the mayonnaise, season well and fold in the whipped cream. Hand separately. If the brisket is served hot, a green vegetable is a suitable accompaniment.

USA

Beef bourguignon

Cooking time: 3 hours

1 kg	chuck steak	2¼ lb
70 g	butter	2½ oz
	some seasoned flour	
10 g	unseasoned flour	½ oz
	2 tablespoons oil	
	5 tablespoons brandy	
120 g	bacon	4 oz
120 g	button onions	4 oz
	1 crushed clove of garlic	
	1 tablespoon tomato purée	
½ l	red wine	¾ pt
	water	
	salt and pepper	
120 g	button mushrooms	4 oz
	1 dessertspoon sugar	

Cut the meat into cubes and roll them in the seasoned flour. Using 60 g (2 oz) of the butter and the oil, fry the meat all over until brown. Add the brandy and ignite. When the flame dies out transfer the meat to a casserole. Fry the bacon, onions and garlic until golden brown and add to the meat. Add the tomato purée, the mushrooms and the wine, and enough water to just cover. Add salt and pepper. Cook in moderate oven for 2¼ hours. Cream the remaining butter and the unseasoned flour and whisk into the casserole and cook for a further ¾ hour. Finally add the sugar and chopped parsley.

Beef pörkölt Bugac style

10 persons   Cooking time: 1½–2 hours, depending on cut

1 kg 400	beef (rump or shin)	3 lb
200 g	lard	8 oz

400 g	onions, sliced	1 lb
	2 cloves of garlic, crushed	
30 g	red paprika	1 oz
2 g	pinch ground cumin	
100 g	tomatoes, skinned and seeded	4 oz
200 g	peppers, skinned and seeded	8 oz
2 dl	red wine	⅓ pt

Fry the onions in the hot lard until pale golden, add the paprika and, immediately afterwards, the meat cut into about 3 cm (1¼ in) cubes. Brown the meat well, stirring constantly, turn down the heat, season with salt, add the garlic and cumin and cook gently, pouring in a little red wine from time to time. The meat should stew in its own juices and a little wine or water should only be added if required. When the meat is half-cooked, add the tomatoes and peppers which have been coarsely diced.

When dishing, sprinkle with rings of green pepper if desired. Serve boiled potatoes, fried potatoes with fried onions, or spätzle as an accompaniment.

N.B.—Beef is replaceable with mutton, veal or pork.

Hungary

Calcutta beef curry

4 persons

600 g	lean beef, cut into cubes and boiled	1 lb 4 oz
100 g	fat	4 oz
	2 onions, finely chopped	
	2 cloves of garlic, finely chopped	
	1 tablespoon ground corianders	
	½ teaspoon ground turmeric	
	½ teaspoon ground cumin seed	
	½ teaspoon powdered chillies	
	freshly ground black pepper	
	ground ginger	
½ l	coconut milk or yoghurt	¾ pt
	juice of 1 lemon	

Blend the spices into a paste with a little coconut milk. Lightly fry the onions and garlic in the fat. Stir in the paste, then add the meat and a little of the bouillon in which it was cooked. Bring to the boil and stir in the coconut milk. Season with salt and sprinkle with lemon juice.

India

Corned beef hash

18 persons

3 kg 300	corned beef cuttings	7¼ lb
	2 cloves of garlic	
1 kg	onions	2¼ lb
300 g	tomato purée	10 oz
3 kg	potatoes	6¾ lb
2 l	beef broth	3½ pt
25 g	potato flour	1 oz
	12 eggs	
200 g	butter	8 oz

Dice the onions, crush the garlic and fry lightly in butter without browning. Add the tomato purée and cook lightly to make it less acid, then add the diced beef together with the diced potatoes. Pour in the beef broth, season with salt and pepper, sprinkle in the potato flour and simmer until cooked. Allow to cool, then shape into individual steaks and fry until crisp. Cover each steak with a fried egg and serve with pickled cucumber.

Germany

Fried meat balls

300 g	cooked meat	10 oz
	(beef or veal)	
60 g	butter	2 oz
50 g	flour	2 oz
4 dl	bouillon	⅔ pt
	salt	
	pepper	
	grated nutmeg	
	curry powder	
	1 egg	
	browned breadcrumbs	

Make a very thick sauce with the butter, flour and bouillon, then add salt, pepper, grated nutmeg and a small pinch of curry powder, together with the meat cut in very small pieces. Allow to cool, then shape the mixture into little balls the size of a walnut. Coat twice with egg and breadcrumbs and deep-fry in very hot fat. Serve hot with mustard.

Holland

Fillet of beef Colbert

Cooking time: 30–40 minutes, depending on size

3 kg 500–4 kg	fillet of beef in one piece (gross weight)	7¾–8¾ lb
4 kg	white cabbage	8¾ lb
	1 pig's caul	
	fat for roasting	

Duxelles

250 g	onions, finely chopped	8 oz
750 g	mushrooms, finely chopped	1½ lb
80 g	chopped parsley	3 oz
30 g	oil	1 oz
30 g	butter	1 oz
40 g	white breadcrumbs	2 oz
$\frac{1}{16}$ l	white wine	3 fl oz
$\frac{1}{8}$ l	demi-glace	¼ pt

Garnish

600 g	pie pastry	1 lb 4 oz
	beaten egg	
400 g	Brussels sprouts	1 lb
	10 new carrots	
	10 young corn cobs	
	10 small tomatoes	
$\frac{1}{8}$ l	green sauce (sauce verte) with aspic	¼ pt
	10 slices truffle	
500 g	mushroom salad	1 lb

Remove the cabbage leaves from the stumps, cut away the leaf ribs, wash, blanch, refresh and drain well. Trim the joint of beef neatly, tie, season with salt and brown in hot fat for 5 minutes, turning repeatedly. Prepare the duxelles in the usual manner. Spread out the pig's caul on a cloth and cover very evenly with the cabbage leaves. Season with salt and pepper, flattening repeatedly. Cover with the duxelles and place the beef on top after allowing it to cool and untying it. Roll up tightly by lifting the cloth, tie evenly, place in hot fat, roast in a hot oven at first for a short time, then in a slow one.

Cook the Brussels sprouts, carrots and corn on the cob separately in salted water, drain and marinate. Line 10 small fireproof dishes or tartlet moulds neatly with pie pastry, bake blind, remove, egg-wash inside and outside and return to the oven for a short time. When cold, fill with the marinated vegetables.

Skin the tomatoes, cut off the tops, scoop out the seeds, marinate and drain well. Stuff with mushroom salad and decorate with a small disk of stiff green sauce and a small disk of truffle.

(Illustration, p. 807)   Austria

Fillet of beef Wellington

10 persons   Baking time: 30–35 minutes

1 kg 800	fillet of beef, trimmed	4 lb
350 g	dry duxelles	12 oz
400 g	truffled foie gras purée	14 oz
approx. 1 kg	puff paste	$2\frac{1}{4}$ lb approx.
1 l	Madeira sauce	$1\frac{3}{4}$ pt
30 g	butter	1 oz
	1 egg	

Season the beef with salt and pepper and roast at 200°C for about 15 minutes to brown on all sides. If the joint is long and thin, roast for a short time only. Allow to cool. Meanwhile, pin out the puff paste to a rectangle 4 mm (about ⅛ in) thick. Spread the beef with the cold foie gras purée to cover completely and place in the centre of the pastry. Top with the duxelles and wrap the pastry round it to enclose completely. Egg-wash and decorate with strips of pastry. Egg-wash again and bake in a hot oven. The beef should remain pink in the centre. Dish and serve the Madeira sauce separately.

The foie gras purée may be omitted if not available, but the duxelles should then be brought to a spreading consistency with a little tomato flavoured demi-glace sauce.

Hamburgers

Bone fresh leg or shoulder of beef and mince finely. Shape into flat round cakes each weighing 150 g (5¼ oz). Fry or grill quickly so that the hamburgers remain juicy. Split round milk rolls, toast, sandwich each one with a hamburger and garnish with small lettuce leaves, sliced onion, tomatoes and pickled cucumber. Serve with tomato ketchup, chilli sauce, horseradish, barbecue sauce and mustard relish.

Germany

Meat balls I

300 g	minced beef	10 oz
300 g	minced pork	10 oz
	1 egg	
	1 teaspoon mustard	
	salt	
	peppercorns	
60 g	dry breadcrumbs	2 oz
2 dl	dairy cream	⅓ pt
	1 onion, finely chopped	
	margarine or butter	

Mix the minced meat with the egg and season with mustard, salt and freshly ground pepper. Soak the breadcrumbs in the cream and add to the meat together with the chopped onion. Shape into small balls and brown evenly in margarine or butter.

Sweden

Meat balls II

4 persons

200 g	best lean beef	8 oz
50 g	lean pork	2 oz
50 g	fine breadcrumbs	2 oz
	1 teaspoon potato flour	
	1 tablespoon very finely chopped onion	
1 dl	double cream	3 fl oz
1 dl	milk	3 fl oz
50 g	butter	2 oz
	1 tablespoon oil	

Mix together the breadcrumbs, potato flour, onions and cream, season with salt and pepper and leave until the breadcrumbs are well soaked. Add the meat which has been minced as finely as possible, mix thoroughly, check the taste and adjust the consistency with the milk. Test the consistency and flavour by frying a little of the mixture before proceeding. With the help of a teaspoon repeatedly dipped in hot water, shape the mixture into balls the size of a hazelnut. Place these on a lightly oiled plate so that they will slide easily into the pan. Heat the butter and oil, slide in the meat balls off the plate and brown evenly, shaking the pan constantly. When cooked, transfer them to a warmed serving dish and pour the fat from the pan over.

Sweden

Minced meat sandwich

4 persons

	4 slices white bread (sandwich loaf) without crusts	
200 g	scraped (or minced) beef	8 oz
	4 egg yolks	
5 cl	dairy cream	2 fl oz
	2 tablespoons cooked potatoes, very finely diced	
	2 tablespoons pickled beetroots, very finely diced	
	2 tablespoons finely chopped onions	
	2 tablespoons chopped capers	
50–60 g	butter or margarine	2 oz

Mix the meat, egg yolks and cream to a smooth paste, season with salt and freshly ground pepper and work in a little water if required to bring the mixture to a spreading consistency. Stir in the potatoes, beetroots, onions and capers. Brown the bread lightly in butter on one side. Spread the paste evenly on the browned side, making sure that it does not project over the edges. Place the bread with the meat side down in a frying pan containing hot butter and fry slowly without cooking right through. Lastly, turn the bread and brown the other side, which will absorb the rest of the butter. Arrange on a hot dish and serve at once.

Sweden

Ox-tail farmhouse style

	1 large ox-tail	
400 g	ripe tomatoes	14 oz

500 g	small potatoes	1 lb 1½ oz
	1 large onion	
	3 fairly large green peppers	
	1 large clove of garlic	
	1 bay leaf	
	small bunch of thyme	
	1 teaspoon Murcia or Extremadura pimentón (paprika)	
¼ l	olive oil	½ pt
¼ l	good white wine	½ pt
	a little dried saffron	
	nutmeg	
	salt	
	pimentón (paprika)	
	parsley	

Cut the ox-tail into even-sized pieces and season with salt and paprika. Place in an earthenware dish and add the onion, the peppers which have been washed and cut into fairly large pieces, the tomatoes which have been scalded, skinned, seeded and coarsely chopped, the chopped garlic, the herbs, the Murcia or Extremadura pimentón (or paprika), the crushed saffron, a little grated nutmeg, the wine and the oil. Mix thoroughly, then transfer to a stew pan and heat until the liquid is boiling fast. Cover and cook over gentle heat until the ox-tail is tender. Now add the potatoes which have been peeled, washed and drained, but left whole. Adjust the seasoning and add hot water if required for the potatoes to cook right through. When they are soft, remove the stew pan from the heat and stand aside for a few minutes. There should be just enough liquid left in the pan to serve as gravy. Sprinkle a little chopped parsley on top and serve in the pan, after removing the herbs.

Spain

Pilaf with beef

10 persons

750 g	lean boneless beef	1¾ lb
750 g	rice	1¾ lb
150 g	chopped onions	5 oz
1½ dl	sunflower seed oil	¼ pt
2 l	bouillon or bone stock	3½ pt
50 g	butter	2 oz

Fry the chopped onions in the oil until pale golden, add the rice and cook gently until almost transparent, stirring repeatedly. Pour in the bouillon or bone stock, season with salt and pepper and cook gently for a short time. Transfer to a fireproof dish, cover with the beef, finely diced, sprinkle with salt, black pepper and a little melted butter and cook in the oven until the rice is soft and the meat browned.

Rumania

Pot goulash

10 persons

1 kg 500	beef (fillet trimmings, shin, neck)	3½ lb
100 g	lard	4 oz
400 g	onions	¾ lb
10 g	garlic	⅓ oz
30 g	mild red paprika	1 oz
2 g	pinch of caraway seeds	
200 g	letcho, or an equivalent amount of green peppers and tomatoes	8 oz
2 kg	potatoes	4½ lb

Trim the beef and cut into smaller cubes than when making pörkölt. Chop the onions and fry lightly in the lard in a large saucepan. Remove from the heat, sprinkle with the paprika and pour in a little water. Return to the heat; as soon as the onions begin to fry again, add the pieces of meat, season with salt, mix thoroughly and cook gently without adding any more water, stirring repeatedly. When the meat is half cooked, pour in about 3 dl (½ pt) water per person and flavour with the caraway seeds and the crushed garlic. Add the potatoes which have been peeled, washed and evenly diced, together with diced seeded green peppers and skinned seeded tomatoes cut into quarters. Simmer until all the ingredients are cooked. Waxy potatoes which do not break up easily should be used for this dish.

Hungary

Roast ribs of beef, Yorkshire pudding

3 kg	ribs of beef	6 lb
60 g	dripping	2 oz
	salt	
	pepper	

Season the beef and roast in a fierce oven for 10 minutes, to seal the surface. Reduce the heat to 350°C and roast for a further 2 hours, basting occasionally.

Yorkshire pudding

120 g	flour	4 oz
125 ml	milk	¼ pt
125 ml	water	¼ pt
	1 egg	
	salt	

Sieve the flour and salt, add the egg and gradually beat in the remaining liquid until a smooth batter is made. (It is advantageous to make this well in advance.) Put a little lard into a baking tin and heat in the oven until smoking hot. Pour in the batter and bake in a hot oven for 40 minutes. (The batter may be cooked in individual pattie tins, and the resulting small puddings are known as 'Popovers'.)

Great Britain

Roast sirloin of beef

Sirloin of beef is roasted as ribs of beef, above, but for a shorter time.

Small grilled sausages: Mititei

10 persons   Cooking time: 6–8 minutes

1 kg	lean fresh-killed beef (neck)	2¼ lb
	4 cloves of garlic, finely grated	
2 dl	hot bouillon	⅓ pt
	pinch of bicarbonate of soda	
	dried thyme stripped off the stalks	
	ground allspice	

Mince the meat while still warm, using the medium blade of the mincer. Season with salt and pepper and flavour with thyme, allspice and garlic. Strain the bouillon (hot) over the meat and mix quickly and thoroughly. Add a pinch of bicarbonate of soda and work well again. Shape into small skinless sausages about 8 cm (3 in) long and 2½ cm (1 in) thick. Cook on both sides on a greased charcoal grill and serve hot with pickled green peppers.

Rumania

Stuffed steak with flap mushrooms

8 persons   Total cooking time: 1½ hours

	8 rib steaks	
150 g	each weighing	5 oz

Stuffing

150 g	lean boneless beef	5 oz
150 g	pork	5 oz
	2 rolls (crumb only), soaked in milk	
	1 egg	
	1 tablespoon chopped parsley	
500 g	fresh flap mushrooms (boletus)	1 lb
40 g	oil	2 oz
¾ l	bouillon	1¼ pt
50 g	onions, diced	2 oz
40 g	butter	2 oz
¼ l	dairy cream	½ pt
40 g	flour	2 oz
	1 clove of garlic	
	1 tablespoon chopped parsley	
40 g	fat	2 oz

To make the stuffing, mince the pork, the beef, the rolls which have been squeezed dry and half the mushrooms, previously stewed and allowed to cool. Put the above ingredients through the mincer twice, using the finest cutter. Bind with the egg, season with salt and pepper, add a little chopped parsley and mix well. Flatten the steaks well, season with salt and pepper, spread with stuffing, roll up and tie or fix in place with toothpicks. Fry lightly in fat until golden brown on all sides, arrange in a fireproof dish or pan of suitable size, pour in a little bouillon and cook for about 30 minutes, basting well so that the meat is roasted and not stewed. When cooked, remove the meat and keep hot. Clean the rest of the mushrooms and cut into slices. Cook the diced onions lightly in the butter without colouring, add the mushrooms, the crushed garlic and the chopped parsley, season with salt, pepper and grated nutmeg and cook until all the liquid has evaporated. Pour the rest of the bouillon into the dish or pan in which the steaks were cooked, boil up to detach the juices, thicken with the flour blended with the cream, boil for a short time and strain. Add half the mushrooms and adjust the seasoning. Remove the thread from the steak rolls, arrange on a silver dish, pour the sauce over and sprinkle with chopped parsley.

N.B.—If desired, the cleaned mushroom stalks may be chopped finely, stewed and used in the stuffing, keeping the caps for the sauce.   Austria

Swedish hash

4 persons

300–350 g	left-over meat (boiled or roast)	12 oz approx.
300–350 g	raw potatoes, finely diced	12 oz approx.
50 g	onions, finely chopped	2 oz
50 g	butter	2 oz
	4 eggs	

Blanch the potatoes very well and drain thoroughly. Cut the meat in small thin slices. Melt the butter in a frying pan, fry the onions in it lightly without colouring and add the potatoes and meat. Toss over brisk heat until the meat is dry without crusting over and the potatoes are cooked. Season with a little salt and freshly ground pepper. Serve raw egg yolks or fried eggs as an accompaniment.

Though this is a simple dish, it is much appreciated when properly prepared.

Sweden

Steak Rosemary

1 person

1 fillet or strip sirloin steak
equal quantities of roughly crushed
pepper and rosemary
fresh butter

Rough the surface of the steak with a fork, season with salt, cover both sides with the pepper and rosemary mixture, press well in. Grill and serve with a plain knob of butter.

Great Britain

Tenderloin of beef Teriyaki

20 persons

2 kg	trimmed fillet of beef	4¼ lb
500 g	fresh mushrooms	1 lb
	2–3 medium onions	
	2 medium sweet peppers, seeded	
5 cl	sesame oil	2 fl oz

50 g	butter	2 oz
1 dl	sherry	3 fl oz
	¼ teaspoon garlic powder	
	1 teaspoon powdered ginger	
	2 teaspoons sugar	
½ l	beef stock	¾ pt
	2 tablespoons cornflour	

Cut the meat into small even-sized pieces, brown quickly in the sesame oil and set aside. Cut the onions and peppers in half, then in slices, slice the mushrooms and fry together in hot butter until lightly browned. Pour in the beef stock, season with salt and pepper, add the powdered garlic and ginger, the sugar and sherry, cook until soft and thicken with the cornflour. Add the meat and keep warm until required.

This dish may also be made with small hamburgers or cut-up chicken. Serve with plain rice, cooked until the grains are tender but well-separated, or with curry rice.

USA

COLD DISHES

Cold fillet of beef

12 persons (buffet meal) or 8 persons (table service)   Cooking time: 15 minutes

1 kg	fillet of beef	2¼ lb
100 g	pork back fat	4 oz
1 l	Madeira or port jelly	1¾ pt
	bouquet garni	

Trim the fillet of beef (middle cut) so that it will cook evenly and may be carved into slices of equal size. Lard the surface with the pork fat and place the joint in a casserole on a bed of carrots and onions cut into fairly thick slices. Season with salt and pepper, add the bouquet garni, cover and cook in a hot oven. Allow to cool, carve, glaze each slice by brushing with jelly and arrange on a dish to the original shape of the joint. Coat with half-set jelly and garnish the dish with decorative motifs made of jelly.

If desired, the jelly may be mixed with the cooking liquid from which all fat has been removed.

France

Cold fillet of beef Parisian style

After placing the joint on a serving dish and coating with jelly, surround it with Parisian aspic moulds turned out on to small lettuce heart leaves.

France

Home-made liver sausage

Cooking time: 30 minutes

1 kg	fresh ox liver	2¼ lb
300 g	fresh fat pork	10 oz
	5 anchovy fillets, well rinsed	
	2 tablespoons finely chopped onions	
1 dl	dairy cream, mixed with	3 fl oz
	1 tablespoon potato flour	
	3 teaspoons salt	
	½ teaspoon white pepper	
	½ teaspoon ground ginger	

Wash the liver well and soak for 15 minutes. Mince several times together with the anchovy fillets. Blanch the fat pork, then cook for 30 minutes, cool and mince. Chill all the above ingredients well, then work thoroughly for about 15 minutes with the salt, pepper, ginger and cream. Pack firmly into wide casings, tie and rinse in cold water. Place the sausages in a pan of hot water with a few peppercorns, a bay leaf and a little salt, making sure that the water is not too hot. Prick well with a fine needle and poach without boiling. Remove after 30 minutes and place in cold water. When quite cold, dry well and store in the refrigerator.

Sweden

Lucca eyes

6 persons

600 g	lean beef without gristle, minced or finely chopped	1 lb 4 oz
150 g	caviar (Danish)	4 oz
	6 trimmed oysters	
	6 large slices white toast	
90 g	butter	3 oz

Butter the toast and spread evenly with the seasoned raw minced beef (steak tartare). Make a hollow in the centre, fill with caviar and place an oyster on top.

Denmark

Ox tongue Ruster Riesling

12 persons

	2 pickled ox tongues	
	8 tomatoes	
	2 cucumbers	
	1 leek	
½ l	whipped dairy cream	¾ pt
	little grated horseradish	
	48 grapes, skinned and seeded	
1 kg	scorzonera, cleaned and blanched	2¼ lb
	1 lemon	
approx. 500 g	pie pastry	1 lb approx.
500 g	vegetable salad in aspic	1 lb
	mayonnaise	
1½ l	aspic	2½ pt
	little velouté	
	vinegar	
	olive oil	
	small disk of truffle	

Line a hemispherical mould with aspic and place a small disk of truffle in the centre. Line with long triangles of boiled pickled ox tongue and fill the spaces with an irregular arrangement of tomato wedges. Coat with a thin layer of aspic; when set, fill the mould with the vegetable salad in mayonnaise reinforced with a little aspic and leave until quite firm. Make horseradish cream with the whipped cream, a little grated horseradish lightly sprinkled with vinegar, a pinch of salt, a pinch of sugar and a little aspic. Prepare tongue mousse with scraps of tongue, velouté, a little aspic and the appropriate seasoning.

Line the bottom of a rectangular mould 30 × 16 × 4 cm (12 × 6½ × 1½ in) with thick slices of pickled tongue and spread with half the horseradish cream. When beginning to set, cover with the tongue mousse. Leave until quite firm, then cover with the rest of the horseradish cream and thick slices of tongue. Glaze lightly with aspic, chill well and cut as shown on the illustration. To garnish, mark the scorzonera, previously marinated, into 12 even portions, cut into pieces of exactly the same length and arrange in bundles decorated with strips of blanched leek and tongue. Peel the cucumbers, cut up evenly, scoop out the centre, blanch and marinate. Drain well, fill with tongue mousse and top with a round of blanched leek.

Pin out the pie pastry to about 4 mm ($\frac{1}{8}$ in) thick and cut out vine leaves with a cutter or stencil. Notch these and egg wash lightly. Line lightly greased shell moulds with the pastry leaves to give them a concave shape and bake slowly. When cold, fill with the grapes and glaze with aspic.

(Illustration, p. 816)   Austria

Pressed beef

Cooking time: $2\frac{1}{2}$ hours

2–3 kg	salt brisket of beef strong aspic jelly made with beef stock	$4\frac{1}{2}$–$6\frac{1}{2}$ lb

Soak the salt beef in cold water overnight, then place in a pan with sufficient cold water to cover, bring to the boil and cook gently. Place the brisket in a press while still hot and apply the pressure. When well-chilled, remove from the press, trim and glaze with several layers of aspic jelly.

Great Britain

Ribs of beef bouquetière

About 26 persons   Total roasting time: about 3 hours

approx. 15 kg	joint of beef comprising 8 ribs and weighing	33 lb approx.
Vegetable garnish		
	fine French beans carrots sprigs of cauliflower peas mushrooms Brussels sprouts, etc. depending on season brown chaud-froid sauce aspic jelly	
$1\frac{1}{2}$ l	Rémoulade sauce	$2\frac{1}{2}$ pt

Remove excess fat from the meat, tie securely and place in a large roasting tin rib side down. Season well with salt and roast in a hot oven (about 230°C) for $1\frac{1}{2}$ hours, basting frequently with the dripping from the joint. Remove from the oven, pour off all the dripping in the tin, reduce the heat to 175°C and continue roasting for a further 1½ hours. Leave to cool near the stove for 1 hour, until cold enough to store in the refrigerator. Next day, trim the joint neatly and coat with brown chaud-froid sauce. When it has set, cut the joint in half through the middle. Place the thick half at one end of a serving dish and garnish with marinated well-drained vegetables or vegetable timbales. Carve the other half neatly and arrange the slices at the other end of the dish to the shape of a fan or as desired. Glaze all over with aspic jelly and serve the Rémoulade sauce separately.

USA

Roast beef Liselotte

Roasting time (on the bone): 1 hour

4 kg	thin cut of sirloin on the bone	8¾ lb
40 g	tiny onions	2 oz
40 g	stewed chanterelles	2 oz
40 g	blanched cauliflower sprigs	2 oz
40 g	carrots, shaped round	2 oz
40 g	celeriac	2 oz
40 g	courgettes	2 oz
	vinegar	
	oil	

Garnish

	10 artichoke bottoms	
100 g	grain-separate cooked rice	3 oz
20 g	soaked currants	1 oz
40 g	sweet corn (canned)	2 oz
20 g	sweet peppers, skinned and finely diced	1 oz
	1–2 tablespoons mayonnaise	
	triangles of courgette, peeled and blanched	
	small corn cobs	

Marinate the onions, chanterelles, cauliflower, carrots, celeriac and courgettes in oil and vinegar seasoned with salt and pepper. Roast the sirloin on the bone, keeping it slightly underdone, allow to cool, then bone, trim and carve part of the joint. Fill a 19 cm (7½ in) ring mould with aspic jelly and allow to set. Cut the artichoke bottoms in half and marinate. Mix together the rice, currants, sweet corn and diced pepper and marinate separately from the artichoke bottoms, then dress lightly with mayonnaise and stuff the half artichoke bottoms with this mixture.

Coat a rectangular silver dish with aspic jelly and turn out the aspic ring mould in the centre towards the front of the dish. Cover the ring of aspic with thin over-lapping slices of roast beef and fill the centre with the vegetable salad. Place the uncut part of the joint behind the aspic mould and decorate with blanched courgette triangles and small corn cobs. Arrange overlapping slices of roast beef in a quarter circle on either side, with the stuffed artichoke bottoms in front of them.

(Illustration, p. 807)   Switzerland

VEAL

HOT DISHES

Calves' liver crépinettes

10 persons

1 kg	calves' liver	2¼ lb
500 g	bacon	1 lb
1 kg 500	fresh spinach	3¼ lb
300 g	firm tomatoes	¾ lb
	1 large pig's caul	
	2 eggs	
5 cl	rum	2 fl oz
600 g	apples	1¼ lb
	nutmeg	
	port-flavoured gravy	
	butter	

Remove any pipes from the liver and cut it into cubes. Cut the spinach in coarse julienne strips. Skin, seed and dice the tomatoes. Dice the bacon, blanch and dry. Mix all these ingredients together, add salt, pepper and grated nutmeg, moisten with the rum and place on the pig's caul in small separate heaps. Roll up into small round or oval crépinettes, each wrapped in a piece of pig's caul, arrange in a fire-proof dish and bake in the oven. Peel and core the apples, cut each one into four or eight, depending on size, shape a little with a knife and fry in butter. Dish the crépinettes with the apples and serve slightly thickened port-flavoured gravy separately.

                                                                   Germany

Escalopes of veal Agaune

1 person

	2 small escalopes of veal cut from the best end,	
80 g	each weighing	3 oz
	1 firm ripe tomato	
60 g	Gruyère cheese	2 oz
	1 egg	
	breadcrumbs for coating (made by crushing pale golden oven-dried bread)	
	salt	
	pepper	
	1 slice cooked ham	

Flatten the escalopes lightly. Slice the tomato and select the three best slices. Arrange these down the centre of the slice of ham and cover with the thinly sliced cheese. Roll up the ham carefully and place between the two escalopes which have been seasoned with salt and pepper. Dip in beaten egg, coat with the breadcrumbs and fry slowly in butter until golden brown.

A good fresh green vegetable may be served as an accompaniment.

Switzerland

Escalope of veal Cordon Bleu

For 1 person

2 small escalopes
1 slice of ham
1 slice Swiss cheese
flour
1 egg
breadcrumbs
butter

Flatten the escalopes and place in between a small thin slice of the cheese and one of ham. Dip in flour, egg and breadcrumbs and fry in butter until golden.

Escalope of veal Holstein

Shallow fry the escalope in butter. Place on top a fried egg sprinkled with capers. Garnish with sippets of sardine, smoked salmon and anchovy fillet. Serve separately, beetroot salad, gherkins and fried potatoes.

Escalope of veal Viennoise

For 1 person

Flatten the escalope. Dip in flour, egg and breadcrumbs and fry in lard. Serve dry with wedges of lemon and sprig of parsley.

Fillet of veal Oscar

4 persons

600 g	fillet of veal	1¼ lb
30 g	butter or margarine	1 oz
	salt	
	freshly ground white pepper	
200 g	asparagus tips	8 oz
170–200 g	lobster or crab meat (canned)	6 oz
2 dl	Béarnaise sauce	⅓ pt

Cut the veal into medallions 1½ cm (about ½ in) thick. Heat the butter or margarine and fry the meat in it quickly and lightly. Arrange on a serving dish and cover first with the asparagus tips and then with the lobster or crab meat cut into small pieces. Coat with Béarnaise sauce.

Sweden

Fillet of veal Todor

1 portion   Total cooking time: about 30 minutes

180 g	fillet of veal	6 oz
	1 tablespoon oil	
10 g	butter	½ oz
50 g	coarsely diced onions	2 oz
40 g	sweet peppers	2 oz
30 g	fresh mushrooms	1 oz
20 g	lean bacon	1 oz

30 g	coarsely chopped tomato	1 oz
2 cl	white wine	2 dessertspoons
50 g	canned pineapple	2 oz
	2 glacé cherries	
1 cl	rum	1 dessertspoon
100 g	rice	4 oz
5 g	pinch of chopped parsley	
3 g	pinch of chopped mint	

Trim the fillet of veal and cut into three pieces of the same size. Cook the rice in slightly salted water until soft but not mushy, drain very well, toss in the butter and flavour with the rum. Fry the diced onions in oil until lightly coloured, add the bacon and sweet pepper cut in julienne strips, together with the mushrooms, cook for a moment and mix with the tomato. Stir in the white wine, add the chopped parsley and mint, together with a little veal stock, cover and simmer until cooked. Season the fillets of veal, fry lightly on both sides until cooked but not too dry, and dish on top of the rice. Coat with the sauce, which should be fairly thick, and garnish with thin segments of pineapple and halved glacé cherries. Serve with mixed salad.

Bulgaria

Fillet of veal Vreteno

1 portion

180 g	fillet of veal (knuckle end)	6¼ oz
20 g	mushrooms	¾ oz
10 g	ground walnuts	⅓ oz
	1 small coarsely chopped tomato	
15 g	butter	½ oz
	oil	

Trim the veal neatly, make a lengthwise incision through the middle without detaching completely, open up and beat very well until quite thin. Season both sides lightly with salt and pepper, lay out flat, brush with melted butter, sprinkle with the nuts, cover with the finely sliced mushrooms and top with the chopped tomato. Roll up and insert a skewer to hold the filling in place. Brush with oil and grill. Garnish with slices of lemon and serve with sauté potatoes.

Bulgaria

Goulash

For 5 persons

1 kg	shoulder of veal	2¼ lb
250 g	chopped onions	½ lb
	1 teaspoon paprika	
	salt	
	1 tablespoon tomato purée	
¼ l	sour cream	⅓ pt
25 g	flour	1 oz
100 g	lard	4 oz

Fry the chopped onions in the lard until golden. Pour off the excess fat. Add the veal cut into cubes and dusted with paprika. Moisten with a little water and season with salt. Cook gently in a closed casserole. When the meat is half cooked add the sour cream blended with the flour. Add the tomato purée.

Matelote of veal

10 persons   Cooking time: 1¾ hours

1 kg 750	boneless veal (cut from the shoulder or breast)	4 lb
	4 onions cut in quarters	
	1 bouquet garni	
50 g	fat	2 oz
40 g	flour	2 oz
	1 crushed clove of garlic	
	20 small glazed onions	
	30 sauté mushroom caps	
¾ l	red wine	1¼ pt
½ l	bouillon	¾ pt
4 cl	Cognac	4 dessertspoons

Cut the meat into 60 g (2 oz) cubes, brown in the fat together with the 4 onions which have been cut in quarters, then pour off the excess fat. Add the Cognac and ignite the pan. When the flames have died down sprinkle with the flour, cook gently for a few moments, pour in the red wine and the bouillon, season with salt and pepper, add the bouquet garni, stir well and bring to the boil. Add the garlic, cover and cook slowly in a medium oven for 1½ hours. Remove from the oven, take the meat out of the pan and transfer to a clean one, then add the sauté mushroom caps and the small glazed onions. Strain the cooking liquid, check the taste and consistency (if too thin, reduce a little), pour over the meat and simmer gently for a short time until cooked. Serve with a garnish of small heart-shaped croûtons fried in butter.

Meat croquettes

Yields 50 croquettes

600 g	butter	1¼ lb
600 g	flour	1¼ lb
4½ l	bouillon	8 pt
½ l	dairy cream	¾ pt
1 kg 600	cooked veal	3½ lb
95 g	potato flour	4 oz
	Worcestershire sauce	
	grated nutmeg	

Make a blond roux with the butter and flour and gradually stir in the bouillon. Season with salt, freshly ground pepper and grated nutmeg and cook for 20 minutes. Blend the potato flour with the cream, pour into the pan and simmer for 5 minutes. Stir in the coarsely minced veal, flavour with Worcestershire sauce, adjust the seasoning and transfer to an oiled baking sheet. When cold, shape into small cylinders or balls, egg-and-crumb and deep fry in hot fat. Serve with strong mustard.

(Illustration, p. 248)   Holland

Osso bucco

	5 slices of knuckle of veal	
	sawn straight	
	through the bone,	
200 g	each weighing approx.	6 oz
	2–3 tablespoons olive oil	
	1 large onion	
	1 carrot	
	2 cloves of garlic	
	1 tablespoon flour	
300 g	ripe tomatoes	¾ lb
	chopped	
	1 teaspoon tomato purée	
	1 glass white wine	
2 dl	stock	⅓ pt
	bouquet garni	

Brown the ossi bucci in hot oil in a large stewpan. Draw aside and take them out. Slice onion and chop the garlic. Add to the pan, cover and sweat for 4–5 minutes. Stir in the flour, add the tomatoes, purée, wine and stock. Season and bring to the boil. Put in the veal, add the bouquet garni, cover and cook slowly for 1½ hours. Keep the slices flat in order to retain the bone marrow which is what makes this dish unusual. Dish the ossi bucci, strain the sauce and reduce if necessary so there is just enough to cover the meat. Serve with rice or pasta.

(Illustration, p. 464)

Ragoût Premonstratensian style

10 portions   Cooking time: about 60 minutes

600 g	boneless veal (cut from the leg)	1¼ lb
200 g	fresh mushrooms	8 oz
1 dl	dairy cream	3 fl oz
1 dl	white wine	3 fl oz
	2 lemons	
60 g	flour	2 oz
100 g	smoked ham	4 oz
50 g	onions, diced	2 oz
120 g	asparagus	4 oz
90 g	butter	3 oz
	zest of half a lemon	
200 g	grated cheese	6 oz
	Worcestershire sauce	
	sliced lemon	

Cut the veal into small cubes and cook under cover for 45 minutes with the diced onions and a little salt. Make a blond roux with the butter and flour, blend in the veal stock (adding a little bouillon if necessary) and boil to a very thick sauce. Blend in the cream and stir in the juice of 1 lemon, salt, pepper, the lemon zest and a little Worcestershire sauce. Cook the mushrooms under cover in a little lemon juice with a pinch of salt, add to the sauce together with the cooking liquid and the cooked veal, then cook for 5 minutes, stirring constantly. To serve in individual portions, cover the bottom of small fireproof dishes with a slice of ham weighing 10 g (⅓ oz), place 100 g (3½ oz) ragoût on top and decorate with small pieces of asparagus. Sprinkle liberally with grated cheese and brown well in a hot oven or under a salamander. Serve in the dishes garnished with a slice of lemon.

Czechoslovakia

Ragoût of veal jardinière

10 persons   Cooking time: about 1¾ hours

1 kg 750	boneless veal (cut from the shoulder, breast, etc.)	4 lb
	1 diced carrot	

	2 diced onions	
	1 bouquet garni	
50 g	fat	2 oz
40 g	flour	2 oz
	1 crushed clove of garlic	
	bouillon	
100 g	cauliflower sprigs, cooked until tender but firm	4 oz
100 g	cooked small round carrots	4 oz
100 g	freshly cooked peas	4 oz
100 g	freshly cooked French or runner beans cut diagonally	4 oz

Cut the meat into cubes weighing 60 g (2 oz) and brown lightly in the fat together with the carrot and onions. Pour off the surplus fat, dust with the flour, cook gently for a moment, pour in enough bouillon to cover, season with salt and pepper, add the bouquet garni and the garlic, cover and cook slowly in the oven for 1½ hours. Remove the meat and transfer to a clean pan, skim the fat off the cooking liquid, check the taste, then strain over the meat. Add the sprigs of cauliflower and the remaining fresh vegetables, cook for a few moments, then serve in small individual fireproof dishes.

Germany

Saddle of veal Duchess

8 persons   Cooking time: 40 minutes

2 kg–2 kg 500	saddle of veal	4¼–5½ lb
	rosemary	
	fresh white breadcrumbs	
120 g	butter	4 oz
	8 puff paste bouchées	
	young garden peas	
	new carrots	
	8 small artichoke bottoms	
approx. 50 g	1 truffle weighing	2 oz
5 cl	Madeira	2 fl oz
	little veal stock	
	2 goose livers (when not in season, use preserved foie gras)	

Trim the joint of veal (comprising both loins), rub with a little rosemary, salt and pepper, tie and roast, keeping the meat juicy. Remove from the oven, allow to stand for a short time, cut the meat off the bone, slice and replace on the carcase. Cover completely with the breadcrumbs, dot with butter and brown under a salamander. Prepare well-seasoned foie gras purée with the livers and the truffle and pipe into the artichoke bottoms. Pour off the butter in the pan used to roast the veal, rinse out the pan with veal stock to detach the cooking juices, reduce, flavour with truffle liquor and Madeira and strain. Dish the veal and garnish with the stuffed artichoke bottoms. Toss the carrots in butter and serve separately, also the bouchées filled with garden peas and the gravy, which should be very hot.

Germany

Sauté of veal with mushrooms

10 persons   Cooking time: about $1\frac{3}{4}$ hours

1 kg 750	boneless veal (cut from the shoulder, breast, etc.)	4 lb
50 g	fat	2 oz
1 l	brown stock	$1\frac{3}{4}$ pt
$\frac{1}{2}$ l	tomato-flavoured demi-glace sauce	$\frac{3}{4}$ pt
1 dl	oil	3 fl oz
750 g	mushrooms	$1\frac{1}{2}$ lb

Brown the meat well in oil, then pour off all the oil. Add the stock and the demi-glace sauce, cover and cook slowly in the oven for $1\frac{1}{2}$ hours. Remove the meat from the gravy, transfer to a clean pan, strain the gravy and reduce to the required consistency. Toss the mushrooms in oil, season, add to the meat, strain the reduced sauce over, then simmer for a few minutes longer. Sprinkle with chopped parsley when serving.

Germany

Stuffed breast of veal

5 portions   Cooking time: $1\frac{1}{2}$–2 hours

1 kg	breast of veal	$2\frac{1}{4}$ lb
150 g	white bread or rolls	5 oz
100 g	ham (cooked)	4 oz
15 cl	milk	$\frac{1}{4}$ pt
150 g	butter	5 oz
	3 eggs (separated)	
	mace	
	chopped chives	

Bone the breast of veal and slit open with a long knife. Dice the bread; soak for a short time in a little milk. Cut up the ham finely. Cream barely half the butter, gradually work in the egg yolks, stir in the bread, ham and chives, mix to a fairly firm paste with a little milk, season with salt and pepper, add a little mace, then fold in the stiffly whipped egg whites. Fill the cavity in the breast with this forcemeat and skewer or sew in place. Season the meat with salt, dot with butter, pour a little water into the roasting-tin and roast in a medium oven. Serve with boiled potatoes.

Czechoslovakia

Tripe Andalusian style

6 persons   Cooking time: about 3 hours

1 kg	calf's tripe	2¼ lb
1 kg	calf's muzzle	2¼ lb
1 kg	calves' feet	2¼ lb
150 g	raw ham, diced	5 oz
	4 chorizos	
500 g	chick-peas	1 lb 2 oz
	1 medium onion, chopped	
	3 large very ripe tomatoes	
	3 large cloves of garlic	
	2 bay leaves	
	1 small sprig fresh mint	
	1 coffee-spoon chilli pepper	
½ l	white wine or sherry	¾ pt
100 g	lard	4 oz
	little saffron	
	1 coffee-spoon cumin	
	6 white peppercorns	
	2 cloves	
50 g	butter	2 oz

Soak the chick-peas overnight in lukewarm salted water, drain and cook in boiling water containing a dash of olive oil, but do not add salt until halfway through the cooking process.

Cut the prepared tripe and the muzzle into small squares, blanch together with the bones from the calves' feet, skim, pour off the water, place in a pan of fresh water, adding a ham bone if desired, season lightly with salt and bring to the boil, then simmer gently. Fry the garlic in the lard until golden, remove and set aside. Add the diced ham, the chopped onions and the bay leaf and mint which have been tied together. When the onion is lightly coloured, add the finely cut tomatoes and the chilli pepper. Cook for a few moments, stir in the wine and reduce by half. Meanwhile, cook the chorizos in the tripe stock. Add the ham, onions and tomatoes in their wine sauce to the pan in which the tripe is cooking, making sure that the stock has not boiled away. When the tripe is almost cooked, remove the bones from the calves' feet and the herbs and add the cooked chick-peas and the following paste: place the saffron, cumin, peppercorns, cloves and lightly fried garlic in a mortar with a round of white toast and pound to a fine paste, mix with 3 tablespoons oil and dilute with the strained tripe stock, then check the flavour. Cook the mixture for a further 10 minutes over gentle heat, transfer to small individual earthenware dishes, garnish each one with 2 large slices of chorizo and 2 fresh mint leaves and serve very hot.

Spain

Tripe Madrid style

6 persons   Cooking time: calf's tripe, about 3 hours;
                          ox tripe, 5–6 hours

1 kg	calf's or ox tripe	$2\frac{1}{4}$ lb
500 g	calf's or ox muzzle	1 lb
	1 calf's foot	
100 g	liver sausage	4 oz
200 g	hard chorizo or other pork sausage	8 oz
100 g	raw ham	4 oz
200 g	onions	8 oz
	1 large leek	
100 g	carrots	4 oz
	2 cloves of garlic	
$\frac{1}{2}$ l	tomato purée	$\frac{3}{4}$ pt
$\frac{1}{2}$ l	white wine	$\frac{3}{4}$ pt
	1 tablespoon flour	
	1 level teaspoon allspice	
	2 cloves	
	12 peppercorns	
1 dl	oil	3 fl oz
	1 bay leaf	

Have the tripe (preferably calf's) prepared by the butcher. Cut it into small squares, together with the prepared muzzle, and place in a pan with the calf's foot which has been cleaned and split into two. Blanch for 5 minutes, skim, pour off the water, cover with fresh water and bring to the boil, adding the bay leaf, wine, peppercorns, allspice, cloves and salt. Simmer gently for 3 hours or until the tripe is tender, adding a little water if required, to keep the tripe covered with liquid. Remove the tripe, place the liver sausage and chorizo in the stock and simmer until three-quarters cooked. Take the sausage and the calf's foot out of the stock and blend in the flour. Heat the oil in a frying pan, brown the finely diced ham in it, then add the chopped onions, carrots, leek and garlic and fry until lightly coloured. Add the tomato purée, cook for a moment, then stir in the stock containing the flour. Pour this sauce over the tripe, add the sausage and simmer for another hour or so, but remove the liver sausage and chorizo as soon as they are cooked, to prevent their splitting open, and cut into slices. Transfer the tripe with the sauce to a serving dish and garnish with the slices of sausage one overlapping another.

Spain

Veal medallions with spring vegetables

Cooking time (veal): 4–5 minutes

	6 round slices fillet of veal,	
60 g	each weighing	2 oz
100 g	butter	3 oz
	asparagus tips	
	leaf spinach, blanched and	
	pressed dry	
	young carrots	
	early garden peas	
	2 half-tomatoes	
	cooked rice	

Trim the slices of veal neatly, beat a little to flatten, season with salt and fry in clarified butter, keeping the meat very juicy. Arrange on a long dish and garnish with the vegetables which have only been tossed in butter and seasoned and with the fried half-tomatoes.

If desired, the meat may be supplemented with fried sliced calf's kidneys or sweetbreads.

Austria

Veal paprikash

10 persons

2 kg	veal	4¼ lb
200 g	lard	6 oz
200 g	onions	6 oz
25 g	mild paprika	1 oz
200 g	green peppers	6 oz
100 g	fresh tomatoes	4 oz
½ l	sour cream	¾ pt
4 dl	fresh cream	½ pt
50 g	flour	2 oz

Bone the meat, wash and cut into cubes. Cut up the onions finely, brown lightly in the lard, remove from the heat and stir in the paprika. Add the meat, the seeded, diced peppers and the skinned, seeded, diced tomatoes. Braise gently without adding liquid. When the meat is half cooked, add the sour cream into which the flour has been blended, and continue cooking until the meat is tender. Transfer to a heated dish and pour the fresh cream over. Dumplings are the most suitable accompaniment.

Hungary

Veal rolls

1 portion

180 g	veal (cut from the leg or back)	6 oz
15 g	butter	$\frac{1}{2}$ oz
	1 egg	
20 g	mushrooms	1 oz
30 g	Bulgarian ewe cheese (or, if not available, crumbly Roquefort or Gorgonzola)	1 oz
20 g	smoked ham cut in julienne strips	1 oz
	flour	

Cut a slice of veal for each portion. Beat it well until very thin. Season with salt and pepper and place the butter, the finely sliced mushrooms and the ham in the centre. Sprinkle the crumbly cheese on top and fold the edges over to enclose the filling. Coat lightly with flour, dip carefully in beaten egg and fry in deep oil until golden in colour. Dish with fried parsley and a grilled tomato.

Bulgaria

Veal rosettes country style

4 persons

	8 small rounds fillet of veal,	
75–80 g	each weighing	3 oz
	8 artichoke bottoms	
400 g	vegetables in season	14 oz
50 g	smoked bacon	2 oz
80 g	butter	3 oz
	thickened veal gravy	

Shape the vegetables neatly and cook in a little butter and water with a pinch of salt until lightly glazed. Cook the artichoke bottoms in butter, cut the bacon in small strips and fry until crisp. Lard the slices of veal, season lightly with salt and pepper, fry in butter for 4 minutes, leaving them very juicy, and arrange on the artichoke bottoms. Pour off the butter, rinse out the pan with veal gravy to detach the juices and pour over the veal. Garnish with the vegetables and sprinkle with the fried bacon.

Austria

COLD DISHES

Best end of veal Boris

Roasting time: 50 minutes

2 kg 500	best end of veal with trimmed bones	5½ lb
200 g	raw carrots	8 oz
300 g	celeriac	10 oz
	vinegar	
	oil	
approx. 150 g	thick mayonnaise	5 oz approx.
	cress	

Garnish

	20 small slices courgette,	
10 g	blanched, each weighing	½ oz
300 g	finely diced tomatoes,	10 oz
	marinated and seasoned	
	fine julienne strips of truffle	
	20 small boat shapes cut from green peppers	
	finely diced marinated radishes	
	aspic jelly	

Roast the veal, keeping it juicy, and allow to cool, then neatly cut the meat off the bones and trim. Meanwhile marinate in oil and lemon the carrots and celeriac which have been cut into julienne strips, then drain and mix with the mayonnaise. Spread this salad on the veal bones. Coat a rectangular silver dish with aspic jelly, allow to set, and place the veal bones in the centre towards the back edge. Arrange the thinly sliced meat on the bones to cover the vegetable salad, glaze with aspic and top with a little cress. Any slices of veal which are left over should be placed in front of the bones. Arrange the pepper boats, filled with the diced radishes, in a semicircle on either side of the meat and edge the front of the dish with the blanched slices of courgette which have been lightly marinated, decorated with the diced tomatoes and sprinkled with strips of truffle.

(Illustration, p. 810)   Switzerland

Cold veal with tunny fish I

6 persons

1 kg	cushion of veal	2¼ lb
200 g	tunny fish in olive oil	8 oz
	6 anchovy fillets	
50 g	capers	2 oz
	2 small lemons	
	2 eggs	
2 dl	olive oil	⅓ pt
	½ carrot	
	½ onion	
	1 clove of garlic	
	1 bay leaf	
2 dl	dry white wine	⅓ pt
	1 small spoon Dijon mustard	
	salt	
	white peppercorns	

Season the veal with salt and pepper, then place in a saucepan with a spoonful of oil. Add the carrot, onion, bay leaf and garlic. Cover and cook slowly over gentle heat until the meat is lightly browned on both sides. Remove the garlic, add the tunny fish and the anchovy fillets, cover the saucepan again and continue cooking for a few minutes. Now pour in the white wine and cook over very gentle heat for about 2 hours, stirring occasionally. If the pan becomes too dry, add a little water or consommé. When cooked, remove the veal from the pan and allow to cool.

Meanwhile make mayonnaise with the eggs, the lemons, the mustard and the oil. Pass the cooking stock and vegetables through a fine sieve, allow the resulting purée to cool, then add it to the mayonnaise a little at a time. When the meat is cold, carve it and dip each slice in the mayonnaise. Arrange the slices on a plate one overlapping another and coat with the rest of the mayonnaise. Garnish with capers and slices of lemon. Decorate with slices of hard-boiled egg and place a little Dijon mustard on each one.

Cold veal with tunny fish II

(Recipe of the Stresa Hotel School)

Proceed as for cold veal with tunny fish I, but make the mayonnaise with only 1 egg and 1 dl (⅙ pt) olive oil.

Whisk 200 g (7 oz) butter until light. Gradually add the cooking stock and vegetables which have been finely sieved, together with the mayonnaise. Season with salt and pepper; add mustard to taste. The mixture should have the consistency and appearance of a mousse.

Carve the veal, cover each slice with the mousse and assemble to the original shape of the joint. Mask the top with mousse, smooth over with a spatula and leave until firm. Decorate as desired with slices of hard-boiled egg and glaze with aspic. Leave in a cold place for 6 hours before serving.

Italy

Jellied veal

2 kg	veal on the bone (neck, breast, etc.)	4½ lb
2 l	water	3½ pt
15 g	salt	½ oz
	10 white peppercorns	
	5 cardamom seeds	
	1 bay leaf	
	2 cloves	
	1 onion	
	freshly ground white pepper	
	1 tablespoon wine vinegar	
	2 sheets gelatine (soaked and squeezed dry)	

Trim the meat, place in a pan with the water, bring to the boil and skim. Add the onion and the seasonings, cover and cook for 1½ hours. Remove the meat and allow to cool. Cut the meat off the bone, remove any gristle and cut into cubes. Strain the broth through a conical strainer, return to the pan, add the cubes of meat and bring to the boil. Allow to boil for a moment, adjust the seasoning and add the gelatine, stirring well. Pour into moulds and allow to set.

Sweden

►   Macaroni Pie, p. 738

▲ Austrian hors d'oeuvre, p. 348
◄ Cream cheese and spinach pie
▼ A selection of canapés, p. 235

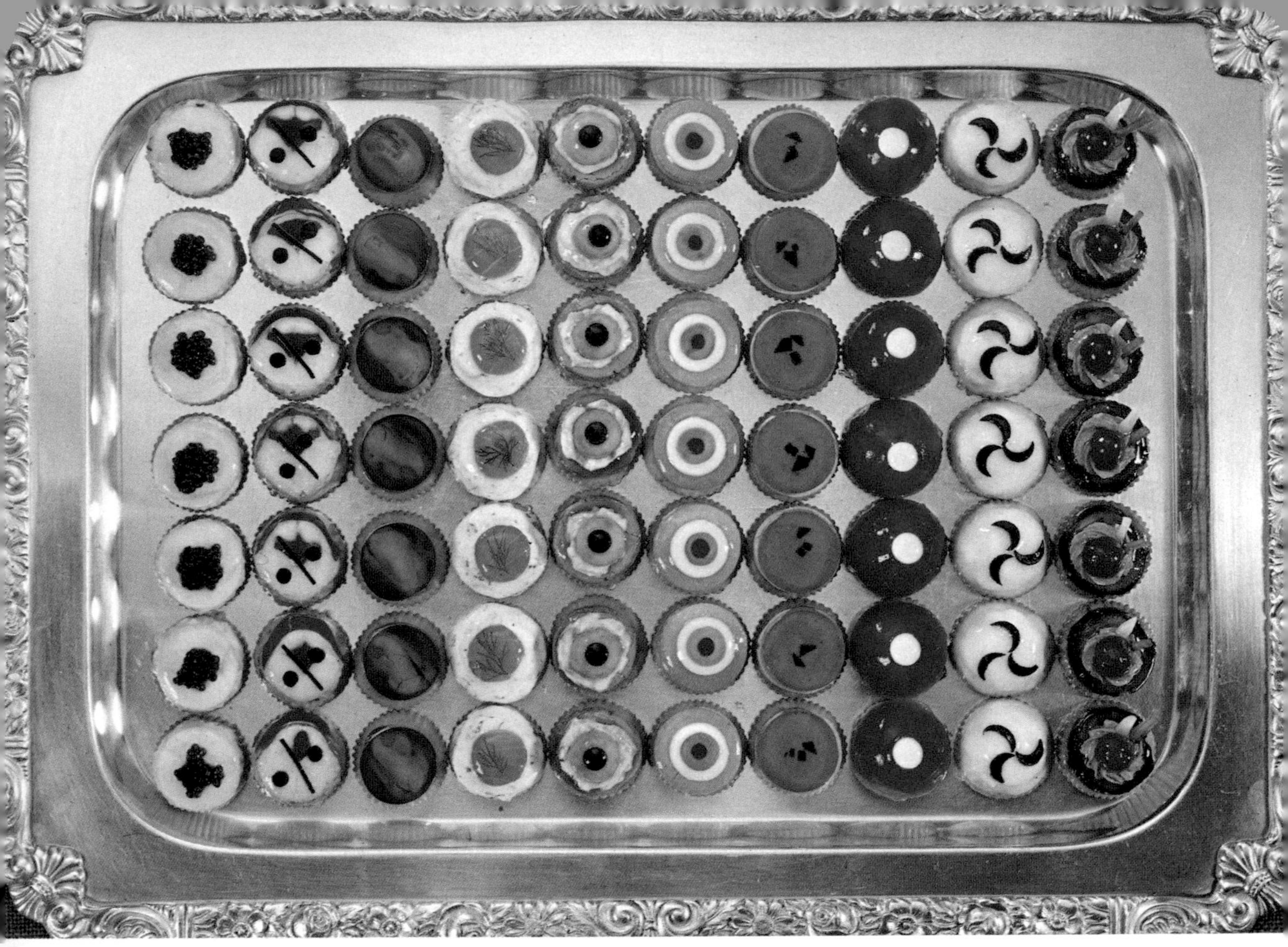

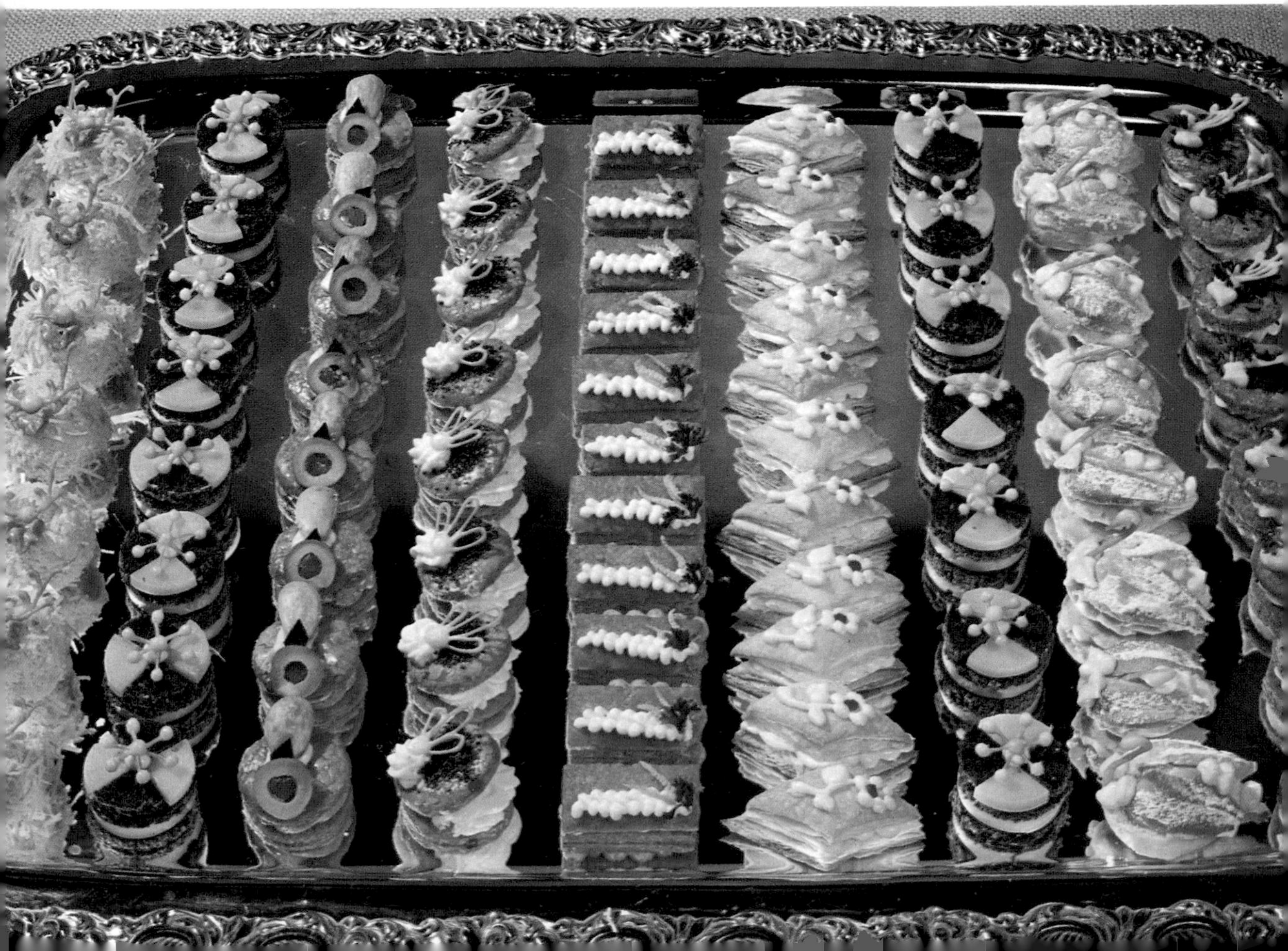

◄ A selection of small cocktail savouries, pp. 322, 326, 330, 332, 335, 336, 348

◄ Small cheese savouries

► Ham boats, Caledonian style, p. 200

▼ A Hungarian cheese selection, with stuffed peppers

▲ A barbecue party, arranged by a Dutch caterer
◄ Cheese choux, p. 291, cheese truffles, p. 296, ramequins, p. 284, Emmenthal cubes, p. 296, Edam crackers, p. 296
▼ A barbecue in a Hungarian garden

583

▲ Buffet du Valais at the Hôtel des Alpes, Champéry, Switzerland
◀ Waiting for the guests of a barbecue, Bugac, Hungary
▼ Buffet for a country wedding, Baden, Austria

586 ▲
▼ Raclette at the Hôtel des Alpes, Champéry, p. 289

▲ Cheese frivolities, pp. 292–3
▼ Savoury sandwich gateau, p. 306

588
▲ Finnish canapés, p. 237–8
▼ Scotch woodcock, p. 252, Stilton corks, little Croque Monsieur, p. 265, fried Camembert

▲ Karelian pirogs, p. 322
▼ Cheese savouries, pp. 275–6, 332

590   ▲   Japanese canapés, p. 240
       ▼   Gervais tit-bits, p. 297

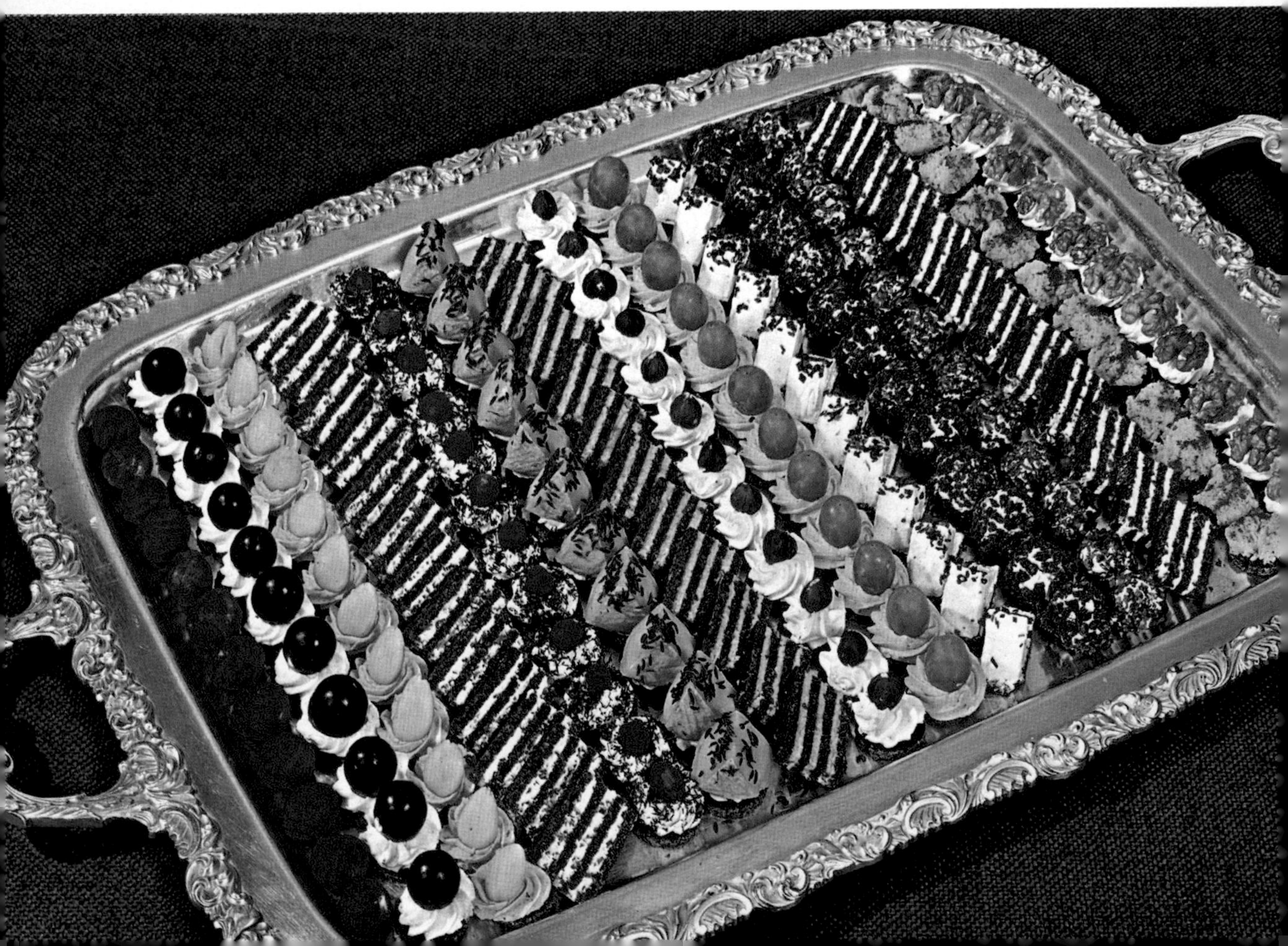

▲ Parfait of crayfish Don Juan, p. 527

▼ Fried sprats and fried coxcombs, pp. 340, 438

592 ▲ Saviese Tart, p. 305

▼ Mushroom soup with oysters, p. 388

Saddle of veal with golden pans

12 persons	Cooking time (galantines): 80 minutes	
2 kg 500	saddle of veal	$5\frac{1}{2}$ lb
500 g	veal without sinews	1 lb
500 g	fat pork	1 lb
200 g	panada	8 oz
	or	
300 g	veal	10 oz
300 g	lean pork	10 oz
400 g	fresh pork back fat	14 oz
$\frac{1}{8}$ l	dairy cream	$\frac{1}{4}$ pt
3 cl	Cognac	3 dessertspoons
200 g	smoked bacon	7 oz
400 g	raw spinach	14 oz
300 g	pickled tongue (tip)	10 oz
60 g	bay salt	2 oz
	pie pastry	
	small corn cobs	
	preserved cherries	
	carrots and cucumber	
	cut into balls	
	peas	
	stoned black and green	
	olives	
	12 hard-boiled eggs	
	red and green peppers	
	veal bones	
	root vegetables, onions	
$1\frac{1}{2}$ l	aspic jelly	$2\frac{1}{2}$ pt
	forcemeat flavouring	

Cut the saddle fillets off the bone neatly and remove all skin and sinews. Roast the carcase, allow to cool, then trim neatly. Cut each fillet open, cover with a wet plastic sheet and flatten gently. Place in a brine bath consisting of 3 l ($5\frac{1}{4}$ pt) water and the bay salt, and refrigerate for 2 days. Mince the pork and veal together finely, mix well with the panada and the cream, add the Cognac and season to taste with salt and forcemeat flavouring. Cut the spinach, pickled tongue and smoked bacon into julienne strips and mix with the forcemeat. Remove the fillets from the brine, dry well and stuff each one with the forcemeat shaped into a roll, making sure that the two ends of the fillet meet exactly. Wrap each galantine in a wet napkin and tie in the usual manner. Meanwhile prepare strong stock with the veal bones, root vegetables, onions and seasonings. Strain the stock, poach the

19

galantines in it and remove them when cool but not quite cold. Unwrap, tie up firmly again and leave until cold. Cut into slices and glaze each one with aspic.

Make four pie pastry cases with handles to resemble frying pans and bake blind. Cut the eggs in half, stuff with a fine mixture of the egg yolks and mayonnaise or butter, then assemble in pairs so that the filling is visible. Marinate the vegetables with which the pastry pans will be filled.

Invert the veal carcase, cover each side (i.e. the inside of the carcase) with overlapping slices of galantine, pipe a light mousse down the centre and top this with a row of spiced cherries. Cut a small slice off the bottom of each stuffed egg to make it stand securely, decorate with red and green pepper drops, glaze with aspic and arrange in front of the carcase. Fill the pastry pans with the marinated vegetables, arranging them to contrast the colours. Place on the serving dish with a row of overlapping slices of galantine on either side.

(Illustration, p. 801)   Austria

Stuffed breast of veal Genoese style

12 persons   Cooking time: about 2 hours

approx. 2 kg	breast of veal, boned	$4\frac{1}{2}$ lb
	1 calf's sweetbread, well washed and soaked	
150 g	cushion of veal	5 oz
150 g	loin of pork	5 oz
50 g	butter	2 oz
	$\frac{1}{2}$ onion, finely chopped	
	1 clove of garlic	
5 cl	milk	2 fl oz
5 cl	white wine	2 fl oz
50 g	white breadcrumbs	2 oz
100 g	pickled tongue	4 oz
100 g	canned peas	4 oz
60 g	grated Parmesan cheese	2 oz
	9 eggs	
	salt	
	pepper	
	nutmeg	
	marjoram	

Bone the breast of veal with a sharp knife, taking care not to pierce the flesh. Cut an opening in the centre and slit across to make a long, wide pocket, leaving the sides and the back of the pocket intact. Boil 5 eggs until hard, then allow to cool. Fry the chopped onion lightly in the butter until golden, together with the clove of garlic, which should be removed as soon as it is golden.

Dice the tongue finely. Mince the loin of pork, the cushion of veal and the sweet-bread, using the finest blade of the mincer. Add all the remaining ingredients except the peas and the hard-boiled eggs. Mix and work well to a smooth forcemeat. Add the peas and leave in a cool place for several hours.

Stuff the pocket with the forcemeat, placing the hard-boiled eggs side by side in the centre, and sew up the opening. Roll the breast of veal in a damp cloth, tie to the shape of a galantine and cook slowly under cover in salted water for about 2 hours. To improve the flavour, the following may be added to the cooking water: 1 onion, 1 carrot, 1 stick celery, 2 bay leaves, 6 basil leaves, 6 peppercorns and a few veal bones.

Remove the saucepan from the heat and stand in a cold place, allowing the meat to cool in the stock. Cover with an oval plate and stand a weight on top to shape the meat evenly. Remove after 24 hours, drain and unwrap. Serve cold, cut into thin slices. Glaze with aspic if desired.

All kinds of cooked or raw salad vegetables make suitable accompaniments.

Italy

Stuffed saddle of veal

approx. 8 kg	1 saddle of veal weighing	17¾ lb
1 kg	veal forcemeat	2¼ lb
300 g	diced pickled tongue	10 oz
200 g	diced pork back fat	8 oz
200 g	diced ham	8 oz
150 g	diced truffles	5 oz
150 g	blanched pistachio nuts	5 oz
	4 small fillets of veal, lightly blanched	
	4 thin slices fat bacon	

Garnish

1 l	aspic jelly	1¾ pt
	quails' eggs	
	artichoke bottoms	
	hard-boiled eggs	
	red and green peppers cut into julienne strips	
	truffles	
	cucumber cut into ½ cm (⅕ in) slices	
	sweet corn	
	tomato balls	

Mix the forcemeat with the tongue, ham, pork back fat, truffles and pistachio nuts. Cut off the saddle fillets neatly and spread with half the forcemeat. Wrap the blanched fillets of veal in the slices of fat bacon and arrange on the saddle fillets, then cover with the rest of the forcemeat. Fold the flaps on either side of the saddle over to enclose the stuffed saddle fillets, making a neatly shaped joint, sew in place and tie the ends securely. Tie the whole saddle evenly, season and roast slowly, keeping the meat juicy. Allow to cool, re-tie and stand aside under light pressure. Coat a suitable silver dish thinly with aspic jelly. Arrange the saddle on it, carving part of the joint only. Decorate the top of the uncut part with quails' eggs and glaze with aspic.

For the garnish, cut hard-boiled eggs into six and place two pieces on the artichoke bottoms. Fill the centre with red and green peppers cut into fine julienne strips, together with truffles and hard-boiled egg white. Cover slices of cucumber with sweet corn to a dome shape and top with tomato balls. Glaze all the items with aspic.

(Illustration, p. 815)   Austria

Veal chaud-froid

12 persons   Cooking time: 40 minutes

1 kg	cushion of veal	2¼ lb
½ l	light chaud-froid sauce	¾ pt
1 l	port jelly	1¾ pt
	truffles (optional)	

Trim the joint evenly and roast or cook in the oven under cover. Leave until cold, carve, brush each slice with jelly and arrange to the original shape of the joint. Coat very thinly with chaud-froid sauce. Decorate with pickled tongue, truffles or hard-boiled egg white and yolk cut into fancy shapes. Glaze with jelly.

Artichoke bottoms filled with mixed vegetable salad or cucumber balls are suggested as a garnish.

France

Veal medallions

6 persons

120 g	fillet of veal, trimmed	4¼ oz
60 g	truffled foie gras purée	2 oz
	6 fluted mushroom caps	
	Madeira jelly	

Fry the veal, keeping it juicy, cut out 6 medallions and trim evenly. When cold, pipe on the foie gras purée, using a plain pipe, and place a small fluted mushroom cap on top. Refrigerate until the foie gras purée is half set, then glaze with Madeira jelly.

Germany

Veal medallions with palm hearts

10 medallions

60–75 g	10 veal medallions each weighing	2–2¾ oz
	choux paste	
	1 large can palm hearts	
	half a red pepper	
	little chopped truffle	
	cooked sieved rice	
	whipped cream	
	aspic jelly	
	butter	

Fry the veal medallions in butter, keeping them juicy, and allow to cool. Cut 10 thin neat slices off the palm hearts and set aside, then drain the rest well. Mix the choux paste with a little thick sieved rice, the palm hearts which have been finely chopped, very finely diced truffle and red pepper and a little whipped cream. The mixture should be firm enough to poach. Fill into a synthetic sausage casing, poach and leave until cold. Remove from the casing, slice and cover with a slice of palm heart. Place these palm heart mousselines on the veal medallions, glaze over with aspic jelly and arrange on a round serving dish coated with aspic.

Germany

LAMB OR MUTTON

HOT DISHES

Barbecued English lamb chops Shikar style

4 persons   Cooking time: 15–20 minutes

	4 large lamb chops, thickness of each	
2 cm	at least	¾ in
	4 rashers rinded back bacon to wrap round chops	

Marinade

> 1 crushed clove of garlic
> 1 tablespoon curry powder
> 2 crushed cardamom seeds
> small sliver of ginger
> ¾ cup soy sauce

Mix together the ingredients for the marinade. Lay the lamb chops in the marinade for at least 4 hours before required, turning them after an hour. Grill the marinated chops in the usual style over the barbecue. Serve with mango chutney.

Great Britain

Barbecued lamb

Cooking time: 1–1½ hours

> 1 young lamb
> oil

Sprinkle the lamb with salt, brush with oil, fix on to two spits and roast over a moderate fire while rotating constantly. When tender, cut into portions and serve with bread, tomatoes, peppers, pickled cucumber and mustard.

Czechoslovakia

Chakchouka

4 persons   Cooking time: about 1 hour

	few small pieces of quadid*	
	or	
	a few Merguez sausages†	
500 g	tomatoes	1 lb
250 g	fresh peppers	8 oz
1 dl	olive oil	3 fl oz
	2 medium onions	
	½ tablespoon harissa	
	½ tablespoon ground red pepper	

* Quadid: mutton which has been seasoned with salt, black pepper, thyme and mint, air-dried for at least 10 days and stored in olive oil in earthenware or glass jars.

† Merguez: sausage made of mutton and mutton fat, sometimes also containing liver, heart or lights, flavoured with harissa, basil, mint, thyme and parsley. Each one weighs about 50 g (1¾ oz).

Peel the onions, cut each one in eight and fry lightly in the olive oil. Add the quadid or Merguez sausages, the tomatoes which have been seeded and cut up, the harissa, the red pepper and a little salt. Pour in enough water to cover and simmer gently until the quadid is cooked. Add the peppers which have been seeded and coarsely cut, then cook for a further 15 minutes. Check the seasoning, adding a little more salt if required, and serve very hot.

Tunisia

Couscous and mutton

4 persons   Cooking time: $1\frac{1}{4}$–$1\frac{1}{3}$ hours

500 g	lean boneless mutton	1 lb
	walnut-size knob of salted butter	
750 g	couscous	1 lb 8 oz
	2–3 sweet peppers	
	3–4 onions	
	2–3 carrots	
	2 turnips	
	1 tablespoon harissa (see p. 427)	
	$\frac{1}{2}$ tablespoon ground black pepper	
	good pinch of ground dried rosebuds	
	1 slice mutton fat	
$1\frac{1}{2}$ dl	olive oil	3 fl oz
	1 slice red gourd	
	2 hot red peppers	
	3–4 potatoes	
	4 fresh tomatoes	
	1 tablespoon red pepper (ground)	
	pinch of cinnamon	
50–75 g	chick-peas	$1\frac{3}{4}$–$2\frac{3}{4}$ oz

Cut the meat and mutton fat into even pieces. Season with salt and pepper and brown in hot oil for a few minutes together with a diced onion. Add the ground red pepper, the tomatoes which have been reduced to a purée, the harissa blended with a little water, and the chick-peas which have been soaked for 24 hours. Now add 2 small peeled onions, 3–4 whole potatoes, the carrots cut in half lengthwise and the turnips cut in quarters. Pour in 2 l ($3\frac{1}{2}$ pt) water, season lightly with salt, bring to the boil, then reduce the heat. Moisten the couscous* with a little fresh water and place it in the couscous colander† without crushing. Stand the colander on the marga‡ containing the meat and vegetables and cover with a lid that is permeable to steam. Cook for 40 minutes from the time when the steam from the marga reaches the colander. Transfer the couscous to a dish, sprinkle well with fresh water and loosen the grains with a fork or wooden spoon. Peel and cut up the slice of red gourd, and add it to the marga together with the sweet and hot peppers. Return the couscous to the colander, stand it on the marga again and cook for a further 30 minutes.

Transfer the couscous to a large dish. Using a ladle, remove the fat from the bouillon in the marga, then blend the fat with the salted butter, the cinnamon and the ground dried rosebud. Pour over the couscous, mix thoroughly and level off. Garnish with the meat and vegetables and pour over the rest of the bouillon after adjusting the seasoning.

Leave to stand for a few minutes before serving.

The most usual method of making couscous is as follows. Two different kinds of semolina are required, the fine commercial grade and a coarser variety. The coarse semolina is poured into a bowl and lightly moistened with a little water. A little fine semolina is sprinkled on top and rubbed with the palm of the hand; the moisture makes it stick to the coarser grains. The semolina is rubbed between the palms of the hands until it forms tiny pellets roughly the size of poppy seeds, then passed through a coarse sieve to make the couscous evenly granular, and lastly spread on a cloth to dry. Only a small amount of couscous should be made at a time, otherwise it is difficult to work. Once the quantity required has been dried a little, it is placed in the colander for steaming. It should be transferred to a bowl and worked to loosen the grains at least twice during the steaming process.

(Illustration, p. 368)   **Tunisia**

---

* Couscous: all over North Africa couscous—with mutton, poultry, or vegetables alone—is one of the most popular dishes. It is generally made from semolina, but maize meal and barley are not infrequently used.
† Couscous colander: the upper half of the couscous steamer; its perforations allow the steam to escape. It may be used with a permeable plaited straw or bamboo cover instead of a lid.
‡ Marga: the stockpot in which the meat and vegetables are cooked, and which forms the lower half of the couscous steamer.

Epigrammes of lamb

500 g	breast of lamb	1 lb
	1 carrot	
	1 onion	
	1 bouquet garni	
	white breadcrumbs	
	1 egg	

Poach the breast of lamb in water with the aromatics until cooked. Remove the bones and excess fat whilst still warm and press until cold. When cold cut into diamond shapes, coat in egg and breadcrumbs and shallow fry until crisp and golden brown. Serve with a piquant tomato sauce.

Garnished lamb crown

6–8 persons   Cooking time: about 1¼ hours

	2 pieces of best end of neck of lamb, each with 6–8 cutlets	
250 g	mirepoix	8 oz
	2 cloves of garlic	
	1 teaspoon rosemary	
	1 tablespoon potato flour	
	12 small tomatoes	
250 g	green beans	8 oz
250 g	young carrots, cut into small sticks	8 oz
	1 small cauliflower	
	peas	
	small mushroom caps, fluted and poached	
¼ l	water	½ pt
	butter	

Chine the joints, cut away any excess fat and trim the cutlet bones neatly. Season lightly, then roll the joints round a ½ kg (1 lb) size can, tie round securely and wrap aluminium foil round the cutlet bones to prevent burning. Baste with melted butter and roast in a moderate oven, adding the mirepoix, rosemary and crushed garlic. After removing from the oven, keep hot for a short time before untying and removing the foil. Pour off the fat in the roasting-tin, pour in water or stock to detach the cooking juices, boil well, thicken with potato flour, bring to the boil again and strain. After scooping out the centres of the tomatoes and stewing them gently, fill them alternately with finely sliced cooked green beans, carrot sticks or mushroom caps. Arrange the lamb crown on a dish, place a cutlet frill on the end of each bone, garnish the top with the cauliflower, arrange a border of peas round the bottom and surround with the tomatoes. Serve the gravy separately.

(Techniques, p. 118)   Great Britain

Haricot of mutton

15 persons   Cooking time: 2 hours

2 kg	shoulder of mutton	4½ lb
200 g	streaky bacon	½ lb
	20 small glazed onions	
400 g	haricot beans, half cooked	1 lb
40 g	flour	2 oz
	2 crushed cloves of garlic	
50 g	fat	2 oz
	1 tablespoon tomato purée	
	1 bouquet garni	

Bone the meat and cut into pieces weighing about 50 g (1¾ oz). Brown in the hot fat, then pour off the excess fat. Sprinkle with the flour, cook gently for a moment, add the crushed garlic and the tomato purée, mix well and cook a little longer. Pour in a good litre (1¾ pt) of water, stir well, season with salt and pepper, add the bouquet garni, cover and braise in a medium oven for 1 hour. Dice and blanch the bacon, drain well and brown lightly. Remove the meat from the oven, transfer to a clean pan without the gravy and add the onions, diced bacon and haricot beans. Remove the fat from the gravy and strain over the meat and vegetables. Cover and continue braising in the oven until cooked. Skim off the fat, check the taste and serve in individual fireproof dishes.

This dish is only suitable for serving with a cold buffet at lunch-time.

Germany

Lamb's head

Per person

> ½ lamb's head
> ½ lamb's brain
> 1 lamb's tongue
> freshly ground pepper

Split the lamb's head through the middle and remove the brain. Season with salt, freshly ground pepper and cumin, and place in the oven in a fireproof dish; do not add any fat as lambs' brains are fat enough. Cook the head and brain in a moderate oven for 2 hours, or a little less if the brain is from a small young lamb. It is easy to tell when the brain is cooked by its colour.

Cook and serve the tongue separately.

(Illustration, p. 368)   Tunisia

Lamb pilau

6–10 persons

1 kg	boned and sliced loin of lamb or mutton	2¼ lb
400 g	fat	14 oz
	2 onions, finely chopped	
	2 cloves of garlic, chopped	
	1 stick cinnamon	
	8 cardamoms	
	6 cloves	
	1 level teaspoon finely chopped green ginger	
600 g	rice	1¼ lb
100 g	sultanas	4 oz
100 g	blanched almonds	4 oz

Boil the meat until tender. Lightly fry the onions and garlic in the fat. Add the spices and continue frying for 4 minutes while stirring. Stir in the rice and add the meat bouillon, which should cover it well. If there is not sufficient bouillon, add boiling water. Season with salt, cover the pan and simmer until the water is absorbed and the rice cooked. Now add the slices of meat and work in the sultanas and almonds which have been lightly fried in fat. Dish and garnish with fried sliced onions.

India

Lamb stew

4 persons　　Cooking time: 1¼–1½ hours

500 g	lamb	1 lb
	knob of salted butter	
1 dl	olive oil	3 fl oz
	1 small onion	
	1 bunch of parsley	
	1 lemon	
	1 small teaspoon tomato purée	
	1 small teaspoon harissa (see p. 427)	
	½ small teaspoon ground black pepper	

Cut the meat into small cubes, season with salt and ground pepper and fry lightly in the hot oil for a few minutes. Add the tomato purée and harissa, together with just enough water to cover, place a lid on the pan and braise slowly. When the meat is tender, check the flavour, stir in the butter and dish on individual plates. Sprinkle with very finely chopped onions, chopped parsley and lemon juice.

Tunisia

Navarin of mutton

15 persons   Cooking time: 2 hours

2 kg	mutton (shoulder, breast, neck)	4½ lb
60 g	fat	2 oz
500 g	ripe tomatoes	1 lb
	1 crushed clove of garlic	
	1 bouquet garni	
40 g	flour	2 oz
	1 level teaspoon caster sugar	
	20 small glazed onions	
	30 potatoes, trimmed to the shape of large olives and blanched	
	chopped parsley	

Bone the meat and cut into pieces weighing about 50 g (1¾ oz). Brown in the hot fat, season with salt and pepper and sprinkle with the sugar (which will caramelise and give the gravy a good colour). Now pour off almost all the fat, sprinkle the meat with the flour and continue cooking until the flour is lightly coloured. Add the tomatoes, cut up small (if not available, 1 tablespoon tomato purée), the garlic and the bouquet garni. Pour in enough water to cover all the ingredients well— about 1¼ l (2½ pt)—stir and bring slowly to the boil. Braise for 1 hour, if possible in the oven, which should not be too hot. Remove the meat, transfer to a clean pan and add the glazed onions and the potatoes. Skim the fat off the gravy in which the meat was cooked and strain into the clean pan. Cover and cook in the oven for a further hour. Remove, skim off the fat again, check the taste and keep hot. Sprinkle with chopped parsley when serving.

Germany

Navarin of mutton spring style

15 persons

2 kg	mutton	4½ lb
60 g	fat	2 oz

500 g	ripe tomatoes	1 lb
	1 crushed clove of garlic	
	1 bouquet garni	
40 g	flour	2 oz
	1 teaspoon caster sugar	
	20 small glazed onions	
	30 small round new carrots	
	30 small potatoes, trimmed	
	to the shape of large olives	
	and blanched	
125 g	fresh peas	4 oz

Prepare the navarin as above. After transferring the meat to a clean pan, add the onions, carrots and potatoes and braise until cooked. Cook the peas separately in salted water, also (if desired) a few French or runner beans sliced diagonally, and do not add to the navarin until the last moment, after the fat has been skimmed off, to prevent their discolouring.

N.B.—For hot dishes to be served at a cold buffet, the meat used in a navarin or stew should always be boneless.

Germany

Potato and mutton stew

4 persons   Cooking time: 60–65 minutes

	a few Merguez sausages	
	(see p. 598)	
	4 eggs	
1 dl	olive oil	3 fl oz
	3–4 potatoes	
	1 tablespoon tomato purée	
	1 tablespoon harissa	
	2–3 cloves of garlic	
	$\frac{1}{2}$ teaspoon cumin	
	$\frac{1}{2}$ tablespoon ground	
	red pepper	

Heat the oil and add the tomato purée, the harissa mixed with a little water, the garlic which has been finely pounded with the cumin, the red pepper and the diced potatoes. Add sufficient water to cover and simmer gently for 45 minutes. Add the sausages either whole or cut in half and continue for a further 15 to 20 minutes. Season with salt, break in the eggs, mix well, remove from the heat and serve at once.

Tunisia

Rosette of Scotch lamb

6–8 persons   Cooking time: $1\frac{1}{4}$–$1\frac{1}{2}$ hours

1 kg 350	saddle or best end of lamb	3 lb
	cooking fat	

Forcemeat

120 g	pork sausage meat	4 oz
80 g	white breadcrumbs	3 oz
60 g	chopped suet	2 oz
	1 egg	
	1 teaspoon chopped parsley	
	pinch of mixed herbs	
	pinch of mixed spices	
	1 tablespoon apple purée	
	1 tablespoon chestnut purée	

Bone the meat, open out and sprinkle with salt. Mix together the ingredients for the forcemeat, season with salt and pepper and spread on the inside of the meat. Roll up and fasten securely. Season the outside and roast in hot fat in the usual way. Serve in thick slices.

Great Britain

Saddle of lamb with herbs

10 persons   Roasting time: 30 minutes, plus 10 minutes to brown topping

	1 saddle of lamb	
2 kg 500	weighing	$5\frac{1}{2}$ lb
150 g	chopped fresh herbs (parsley, marjoram, basil, rosemary)	5 oz
	pinch of powdered sage	
500 g	bacon, cut in thin strips	1 lb
200 g	white bread, cut in thin strips	8 oz
	mustard	
1 dl	oil	3 fl oz

Trim the saddle of lamb well, season with salt, flavour with sage, sprinkle with oil and marinate for 3–4 hours. Roast in a medium oven 20–30 minutes before using, depending on size; the meat should be medium done. Fry the strips of bacon and bread in oil until lightly coloured only. Cool a little, then mix with the chopped herbs and a few finely chopped juniper berries. Cut off the saddle fillets, slice and return to the carcase which has been spread with a little mustard. Sprinkle with the savoury topping mixture and brown in the oven for about 10 minutes.

Germany

Salt air-dried mutton

6 persons   Cooking time: 1–1½ hours, depending on quality

2 kg 400	mutton (salted in the same way as salt pig's trotters)	5¼ lb
1 kg	peeled swedes	2¼ lb
300 g	peeled potatoes	¾ lb

Soak the meat for 6 hours, dry and cut in pieces about 10 cm by 2 cm (4 in by ¾ in). Place small pieces of birch-wood in a cooking pot to a thickness of about 5 cm (2 in) and pour in enough water barely to cover the wood. Place the meat on top and steam until it comes away from the bone, adding water from time to time, but making sure that the meat remains above the level of the water and does not come in contact with it. Cut up the swedes and potatoes, boil together until soft, drain off the water and steam until dry. Rub through a sieve and mash well with the remaining cooking liquid, which should not be too salty.

The most suitable cut of mutton is best end. This speciality is found in every home at Christmas time.

Norway

Barbecued stuffed lamb Bugac style

10 persons   Roasting time: 1½–2 hours

15 kg	1 whole lamb, live weight	33 lb
500 g	tomatoes	1 lb
500 g	hot yellow Hungarian peppers	1 lb
3 g	peppercorns	1 teaspoon
	2 large bunches of parsley	
400 g	fat bacon (or smoked pork)	1 lb

After the lamb has been prepared and slit open on the belly side, season it with salt inside and outside. Fill the belly cavity with the whole tomatoes, peppers, peppercorns and parsley, insert a spit in the centre, sew up the belly, cover the lamb in several places with slices of fat bacon, especially over the leg hollows, and tie firmly to the spit. Rotate the lamb slowly on the spit while roasting. Garnish with the tomatoes and peppers which were cooked inside the belly and with other vegetables in season as desired.

Hungary

Stuffed baby lamb

Cooking time: 2 hours

1 baby lamb, boned

Forcemeat

all kinds of vegetables
all kinds of whole shelled nuts
couscous or steamed rice
dried fruit
palm hearts
skinned, seeded, chopped
    tomatoes
orange segments
very little goat cheese

Garnish

vine leaves
sprigs of parsley
oranges
tomatoes
peppers
sprigs of cauliflower

Mix the rice or couscous with the dried fruit which has been soaked, the chopped tomatoes, the palm hearts, orange segments and sieved goat cheese. Season with salt to taste. Slit open the belly of the lamb, stuff with the forcemeat and sew up. Roast at 220–230°C and place on a heated dish. Fix the garnish on to the lamb with small skewers or sticks.

Tunisia

Stuffed tripe Bedouin style

4 persons   Cooking time: about 3 hours

	lamb or beef tripe	
	lamb's or ox liver	
	1 lamb's or ox heart	
	1 tablespoon chopped parsley	
100 g	boiled rice	4 oz
	½ teaspoon harissa	
	(see p. 427)	
	½ teaspoon cumin	
	couscous sauce	
	(see p. 600)	

Clean the tripe thoroughly, wash and boil for 2 hours in salted water. Remove, drain very well and cut into 32 cm (13 in) squares. Prepare forcemeat with very finely chopped raw lamb's or ox liver and lamb's (or ox) heart, the rice and the chopped parsley. Season with salt and pepper and add the harissa and cumin. Place a ball of forcemeat in the centre of each square of tripe, wrap the tripe round it and sew up to keep in place. Place the stuffed tripe in couscous sauce, which should not be too thick, and cook slowly over moderate heat for at least ¾ hour. When cooked, remove, dish, garnish with slices of orange, lettuce leaves and parsley and serve the sauce separately.

(Illustration, p. 368)   Tunisia

COLD DISHES

Stuffed saddle and leg of mutton

7 persons   Cooking time: forcemeat, 40 minutes; leg, 80 minutes; saddle,
                 50 minutes

2 kg 800	saddle of mutton, boned	6¼ lb
2 kg 100	leg of mutton without	4¾ lb
	the knuckle bone	
	mint	
	rosemary	
	bay leaf	
	marjoram	
	peppercorns	
½ l	white wine	¾ pt
	parsley	
¼ l	dairy cream	½ pt

	3 eggs	
	2 egg yolks	
75 g	diced truffles	3 oz
100 g	diced cooked ham	4 oz
100 g	diced pickled tongue	4 oz
50 g	pistachio nuts	2 oz
1 l	aspic jelly	1¾ pt

Garnish

artichoke bottoms stuffed
    with marinated French
    beans
skinned tomatoes stuffed
    with chanterelle salad
    and quails' eggs
celeriac stuffed with parsley,
    dill, red peppers,
    mushroom caps and
    artichoke hearts

Steep the boned meat for 1–2 days in an uncooked marinade made with the white wine, mint, marjoram, rosemary, bay leaf and peppercorns. Brown the bones and meat trimmings lightly, cook for a long time, strain and reduce to a glaze. Chop the pieces of meat left after boning the leg and saddle—about 1 kg 800 (4 lb)—with salt, pepper, chopped parsley and mint, flavour with Worcestershire sauce and aromatic seasoning, add the cream, 1 dl (3 fl oz) white wine, the eggs and egg yolks and 250 g (8 oz) ice cubes. Blend well, using a cutter. Adjust the seasoning and mix with the truffles, ham, pickled tongue and pistachio nuts. Wrap the forcemeat in a cloth or caul, shaping it into a long roll, and poach at 75°C. Allow to cool, then unwrap, trim and divide into three rolls. Roll up two of these in the saddle spiral fashion. Slide the third one into the cavity in the leg. Tie in place, roast and allow to cool under light pressure. When quite cold, carve the saddle and leg evenly, leaving a portion of each whole as a showpiece, and brush the latter with the glaze.

Coat an oblong serving dish with aspic jelly and place the two showpieces near the top end. Arrange the slices of meat in front, one slightly overlapping another, and garnish with the stuffed artichoke bottoms, tomatoes and celeriac.

Garnish
Artichoke bottoms. Stuff canned artichoke bottoms with blanched marinated French beans. Glaze with aspic.

Stuffed tomatoes
Skin the tomatoes, scoop out the seeds and pulp, and season with salt. Fill with chanterelle salad and cover with a hard-boiled quail's egg decorated with truffles.

Stuffed celeriac

Mix together chopped parsley (with its juice), chopped dill, finely diced mushroom caps, red peppers, artichoke hearts, salt and aromatic seasoning to taste, 2 dl ($\frac{1}{3}$ pt) white wine and $\frac{1}{4}$ l ($\frac{1}{2}$ pt) aspic jelly. Hollow out the centre of the celeriac, poach, line inside with thinly sliced truffles and fill with the stuffing. Cut each slice in half when quite cold.

Austria

PORK

HOT DISHES

Barbecued Hawaiian sweet and sour spare ribs

15 persons   Total cooking time: about $1\frac{1}{2}$ hours

2 kg	spare ribs	$4\frac{1}{4}$ lb
	1 carrot	
	1 onion	
	1 parsley root	
	1 bay leaf	
	little allspice (whole)	

Barbecue sauce

	2 crushed cloves of garlic	
50 g	finely chopped onion	2 oz
	1 tablespoon English mustard (dry)	
	2 tablespoons wine vinegar	
	1 teaspoon salt	
	2 tablespoons maple syrup	
	2 tablespoons honey	
	2 tablespoons Espagnole sauce	
	2 tablespoons tomato purée	
	$\frac{1}{2}$ teaspoon thyme leaves	
	few drops Worcestershire sauce	
40 g	brown sugar	$1\frac{1}{2}$ oz
	white breadcrumbs	

Place the pork in a pan of lightly salted warm water, bring to the boil, skim, add the pot-herbs, bay leaf and allspice, simmer for half an hour and leave in the cooking liquid until cold. Meanwhile thoroughly mix together all the ingredients for the barbecue sauce. Drain the spare ribs, dry and coat liberally with the sauce. Sprinkle with very fine white breadcrumbs to coat well and roast in a moderate oven until cooked and well-coloured; if necessary, finish browning under a salamander, or cook on a barbecue. Cut up and serve hot without delay.

USA

Barbecued pork chop Gowrie

4 persons   Cooking time: about 20 minutes

	4 pork chops	
	4 pineapple rings	
	4 tomatoes	
	2 peaches	
350 g	potatoes	$\frac{3}{4}$ lb
	parsley	
	1 tablespoon brown sugar	
	2 cloves	
	chutney	
	mixed spice	

Season the chops lightly with salt and grill for 10 minutes. Remove, sprinkle with mixed spice, place in a greased pan together with the sugar and glaze on both sides, adding the cloves meanwhile. Garnish with straw potatoes, grilled tomatoes and pineapple rings, fried parsley and the peaches which have been skinned, halved, stoned, filled with chutney and then heated under the grill.

Great Britain

Brigands' barbecue

5 portions   Cooking time: 20–25 minutes

250 g	pork	8 oz
250 g	leg of veal	8 oz
250 g	fillet of beef	8 oz
250 g	streaky bacon	8 oz
250 g	onions	8 oz
200 g	peppers (without seeds)	7 oz
	4 bay leaves	
$1\frac{1}{2}$ dl	oil	$\frac{1}{4}$ pt

Cut the meat evenly into fairly thick slices and thread on a spit alternately with pieces of streaky bacon, slices of onion, peppers and bay leaves. Sprinkle with salt, brush with oil and wrap in a double layer of oiled aluminium foil. Roast over a moderate fire, rotating constantly. Remove from the spit, unwrap and serve in small bowls with bread, pickled cucumber, tomatoes and mustard.

The spit in its foil wrapping may be placed in glowing embers to cook this dish if desired.

Czechoslovakia

Barbecued brigands' brochettes

10 persons

1 kg 500	fillet of pork	3½ lb
400 g	bacon	¾ lb
200 g	green peppers	½ lb
300 g	onions	¾ lb
400 g	potatoes	1 lb
40 g	mustard	1½ oz
6 g	pinch of ground pepper	
	salt	

Remove any skin from the pork, cut into 4–5 cm (about 2 in) pieces and flatten a little. Slice the bacon and onions thinly; peel the potatoes and cut into slices 3–4 mm (about ⅛ in) thick. All the slices should be round and of the same size; this also applies to the green peppers. Sprinkle the meat with salt and spread with mustard or rub with garlic if preferred. Thread the pieces on to skewers alternately with the bacon, peppers, onion and potatoes, then sprinkle with salt and pepper (the meat has already been salted). Wrap in greased aluminium foil and cook over a charcoal fire.

Sweet red peppers may be used instead of green ones, as long as they are thick. Brochettes containing raw potatoes should always be wrapped in aluminium foil so that the potatoes are sufficiently cooked by the time the meat is ready.

Hungary

Braised pork with soya sauce

500 g	pork (not too lean)	1 lb
	4 onions	
	8 cloves of garlic	
	1 teaspoon ground ginger	
	1 tablespoon vinegar	
	4 tablespoons soya sauce ('ketjap')	
	1 tablespoon ginger in syrup (cut up)	
	salt and pepper	

Cut the meat into small cubes. Place in a pan with a few spoonfuls of water, the onions and garlic (cut up), the vinegar, ground ginger and preserved ginger. Braise over very gentle heat for at least an hour. Add the 'ketjap', salt and pepper.

Holland/Indonesia

Christmas sausage

3 kg	lean boneless pork	6½ lb
1 kg	bacon or fat pork	2¼ lb
30 g	salt	1 oz
30 g	freshly ground white pepper	1 oz
1½–2 l	bouillon	2½–3½ pt
5 m	sausage casings	5½ yd

Mixture for rubbing in

60 g	salt	2 oz
30 g	sugar	1 oz
7 g	saltpetre	¼ oz

Cut up the pork and bacon and mince several times, using the finest cutter. Season, add a little flour and knead. Work in the bouillon a little at a time, mixing thoroughly. Adjust the seasoning. Cook a little of the mixture; if it is not firm enough, add some flour; if it is too stiff, add bouillon as required. Fill into the casings and tie to shape into sausages. Dip into cold water and dry. Rub in the salt/sugar/saltpetre mixture and allow to stand overnight.

If the sausages are to be stored for some time, they should be kept in deep freeze or in the refrigerator under vacuum.

Sweden

Home-made Cognac sausage I

3 kg	lean beef (thick flank or topside) without sinews	6½ lb
1 kg	lean pork	2¼ lb
2 kg	pork back fat	4½ lb
125 g	salt	4 oz
	2 tablespoons freshly ground pepper	
10 g	saltpetre	⅓ oz
3 dl	beer	½ pt
2 dl	Cognac	6 fl oz
	2 tablespoons sugar	

Thoroughly chill the back fat, which should be firm, dice very finely and chill again. Mince the well-chilled beef and pork five times, keeping the meat very cool. Work for about 30 minutes with the fists or a suitable implement. Now season, add the beer, then the Cognac and knead for a further 15 minutes or so. Lastly work in the diced fat thoroughly. Adjust the seasoning—the mixture should be well-flavoured—then pack tightly into large casings with the fat side outermost and tie firmly. Rub very well with a mixture of 1 tablespoon salt, 1 tablespoon saltpetre and 2 tablespoons sugar and leave in the refrigerator for 24 hours. Compress the sausage meat well in the casings—it may have shrunk a little—and re-tie, then smoke for 2 to 4 days, depending on size, at 20° to not more than 30°C.

Sweden

Home-made Cognac sausage II

1 kg	best beef without sinews	2¼ lb
1 kg	lean pork	2¼ lb
1 kg	pork back fat, finely diced	2¼ lb
500 g	cooked potatoes	1 lb 2 oz
3 dl	beer	½ pt
2 dl	Cognac	6 fl oz
	1 tablespoon salt	
	1 teaspoon white pepper	

Mixture for rubbing in

	1 tablespoon salt
	1 tablespoon saltpetre
	2 tablespoons sugar

Proceed in exactly the same way as for home-made Cognac sausage I, but use narrower casings. Smoke for 2 to 4 days at 20 to 30°C.

Sweden

Devilled salt fore loin of pork

8 persons   Cooking time: about 1½ hours, plus about 20 minutes in the oven

1 kg 500	fore loin of pork without fat, rind or backbone	3¼ lb
100 g	salt	4 oz
	1 tablespoon sugar	
	good pinch of saltpetre	
	1 carrot	
	1 onion studded with cloves	
	1 egg yolk	
	1 tablespoon syrup	

1 tablespoon potato flour
4 tablespoons made yellow
    mustard
breadcrumbs

Rub fine salt into the pork. Place the salt, sugar and saltpetre in a pan containing 1 l (1¾ pt) water, bring to the boil and allow to cool. Leave the pork in this brine for 24 hours. Remove, blanch and cook with the carrot and the onion until just tender. Allow to cool in the cooking liquid. Blend the egg yolk, syrup, potato flour and mustard to a smooth paste. Dry the pork well, place it on a rack, spread the meat evenly with the mustard paste, sprinkle with breadcrumbs, place in the oven at about 200°C and leave until the paste has dried into a light-brown crust. Serve hot or cold with Brussels sprouts, boiled potatoes and prunes.

Sweden

Escalope of pork with potato salad

5 persons   Cooking time: 8 minutes

750 g	leg of pork	1½ lb
2 dl	oil	⅓ pt
	2 eggs	
	flour	
	white breadcrumbs	

Cut the meat into 5 neat even slices, beat well to flatten, and season with salt. Toss in a little flour, dip in beaten egg, then coat well with breadcrumbs. Fry on both sides in hot oil until golden-brown. Dish and serve the potato salad separately.

Potato salad

750 g	potatoes	1¾ lb
150 g	chopped onions	6 oz
100 g	cooked carrots	4 oz
100 g	cooked celeriac	4 oz
100 g	cooked peas	4 oz
100 g	cooked haricot beans	4 oz
	1 teaspoon mustard	
1 dl	oil	3 fl oz
	vinegar	
	ground pepper	

Boil the potatoes in their skins, then peel, allow to cool and dice finely. Drain the cooked vegetables well, dice the celeriac and carrots finely and mix all the vegetables with the potatoes. Dress with the mustard dispersed in vinegar, oil, salt and pepper and stand aside in a cool place. Before serving, add a little more vinegar, also salt, pepper and mustard if required.

Czechoslovakia

Fillet of pork and salted cucumbers with rye bread

6 persons

300 g	trimmed fillet of pork	10 oz
	3 large onions	
150 g	butter	5 oz
	salted cucumbers	
	3 slices rye bread	
	(6 half slices)	

Cut the fillet of pork into 6 slices, flatten, season and fry in butter. Slice the onions thinly and fry in the rest of the butter until golden. Dish the slices of pork, cover with the fried onions and pour over the butter used for frying. Serve the bread and salted cucumbers separately.

Denmark

Fore loin of pork with prunes

8 persons   Cooking time: about $1\frac{1}{2}$ hours

1 kg 800	fairly thick fore loin of pork, without fat, rind and backbone	4 lb
	stoned prunes	
	1 large onion	
	1 large apple	
	ground ginger	
	or	
	mustard powder	
	butter	

Remove the ribs and all other bones from the pork. Using the point of a sharp knife, make slanting cuts 1 cm (about $\frac{1}{2}$ in) deep from top to bottom. Insert halved prunes into the cuts until they are completely covered by the meat. Season with salt and pepper and flavour with ground ginger or mustard powder. Place the meat on a bed of chopped-up bones, prunes and thickly sliced onions and apples. Pour melted butter over and brown briskly. Turn down the heat, pour in a little water, cover with aluminium foil and cook until tender. Remove all fat from the cooking liquid, thicken with a little potato flour and strain. Serve with Brussels sprouts, red cabbage, broccoli or mixed vegetables, boiled or château potatoes and salted cucumber.

Sweden

Fricadelles

400 g	finely minced veal	1 lb
50 g	minced pork fat	2 oz
	1 small onion	
	1 teaspoon chopped thyme	
125 g	stale white bread	5 oz
	without crust	
	milk	
$\frac{1}{8}$ l	cold water	$\frac{1}{4}$ pt

Soak the bread for half an hour in enough milk to cover. Squeeze dry and crumble into a bowl. Chop the onion very finely and add together with the veal, fat, and thyme. Season and work thoroughly together, adding the water by degrees. Season well with salt, pepper and paprika. Shape into small balls—about the size of a marble—roll lightly in flour, and fry quickly in oil or butter until brown. Lay in a deep fireproof dish and spoon over tomato sauce enough to cover. Cook in the oven for 15–20 minutes. Add 2–3 tablespoons of sour cream to the sauce without stirring too much so as not to break the fricadelles.

Frying sausages

2 kg	pork pieces	$4\frac{1}{4}$ lb
	little lukewarm water	
24 g	salt	$\frac{3}{4}$ oz
8 g	pepper	$\frac{1}{4}$ oz
20 g	red paprika	$\frac{3}{4}$ oz
	5–6 cloves of garlic	
	crushed juice of 2 lemons	

Mince the pork coarsely. Add the seasonings, the garlic and a little lukewarm water, mix well and mince again. Add the lemon juice and work well to a compact mixture. Fill into pig's small intestines which have been carefully cleaned and soaked, press down firmly and tie off. If desired, the sausages may be smoked and air-dried.

Austria

Hawaiian luau

At almost every luau (feast) in Hawaii a whole pig is cooked in an earth oven. It is possible to hold a luau in other countries, too, though on a smaller scale. A small 'imu' made of clay and stones is required (see illustration); this home-made oven is lined with banana leaves, which are obtainable from the larger horticultural suppliers.

12 persons   Cooking time: 4 hours

approx. 3 kg	1 leg of pork weighing	6½ lb approx.
300 g	sweet potatoes	10 oz
300 g	black beans	10 oz
300 g	broccoli stalks	10 oz
300 g	red lentils	10 oz
150 g	translucent noodles	4 oz
200 g	fresh pineapple	8 oz
50 g	jaggery syrup	2 oz
300 g	mackerel, skinned and filleted	10 oz
	1 fresh mango or avocado	
250 g	mango chutney	8 oz
250 g	tomato ketchup	8 oz
	honey	
	Cognac	
7 cl	coconut oil	2 fl oz
	banana leaves	
	bay salt	

Remove the end bone from the leg of pork. Pull the middle bone apart as far as the knee from the inside. Rub with freshly ground pepper, salt, honey and Cognac. Press the cut surfaces together firmly and sew up with strong twine to hold the edges of the rind together.

Take a large number of stones the size of the hand and heat them very well in the oven. Use part of them to line the bottom of the 'imu'. Cover the stones with several layers of banana leaves which have been moistened with a saline solution (8 g (¼ oz) bay salt to 1 l (1¾ pt) fresh water). Place the prepared leg of pork in the centre and fill up all the available space with the various accompaniments, wrapped in banana leaves—the sweet potatoes, the black beans which have been soaked overnight, the broccoli stalks which have been lightly fried, the red lentils which have been soaked and then lightly browned in lard, and the pineapple which has been cut up and mixed with the fried noodles and the jaggery syrup. For the small accompaniments, such as beans and lentils, it is best to shape banana leaves into small bags.

Cover over well with moistened banana leaves and place the rest of the hot stones on top. To speed up the cooking process, cover with thick cloths, but reheat the top stones several times.

Sauces

1. Mix the tomato ketchup and mango chutney with roughly chopped, skinned and seeded tomatoes.

2. Typical Polynesian fish sauce. Mash the mackerel well with a fork, then add a ripe mango or avocado, mash well again, pour on the hot coconut oil, season with salt, pepper and cayenne pepper and work to a smooth sauce. If it is too thick, dilute with a little milk or cream.

(Illustration, p. 925)

Hungarian pork stew

10 persons   Cooking time: about 1½ hours

2 kg–2 kg 250	shoulder of pork	4½–5 lb
200 g	finely chopped onions	8 oz
	1½ tablespoons paprika	
	2 crushed cloves of garlic	
	6 green peppers, seeded and cut in strips	
	3 large tomatoes, skinned, seeded and cut in quarters	
60–70 g	lard	2–2½ oz

Cook the onions in the lard until very lightly coloured and sprinkle with the paprika. Add the meat, cut into cubes, brown lightly, season with salt, add the tomatoes and pour in a little water. Add the garlic, cover and cook slowly, adding a little water from time to time. As soon as the meat is three-quarters cooked, add the strips of green pepper and continue cooking until tender. Serve with small dumplings made by boiling pieces of noodle dough, or alternatively with butter dumplings.

Butter dumplings

	2 large eggs	
100 g	butter	4 oz
100 g	flour	4 oz
	salt	

Cream the butter, work in the eggs and the flour, season with salt and stand aside for 20 minutes. Shape into small dumplings with a teaspoon, drop in boiling bouillon or lightly salted water and simmer gently. Drain very well before serving. If desired, the noodle or butter dumplings may be mixed with the stew at the last minute.

Germany

Pork cutlets in foil

150 g	2 pork cutlets each weighing	5 oz
	2 slices cooked ham	
50 g	mushrooms	2 oz
	1 tablespoon chopped onion	
	1 small teaspoon chopped parsley	
	oil for frying	
	1 firm tomato, skinned, sliced and seeded	
	2 slices Emmenthal or Gruyère cheese	

Accompaniments

	4 large floury potatoes	
40 g	butter	2 oz
	salt	
	4 tablespoons sour cream	
	chopped chives	

Beat and season the cutlets, fry lightly and place on greased aluminium foil. Fry the onion lightly, add the finely chopped mushrooms and continue frying for a few moments, then flavour with the parsley. Spread the cutlets with this mixture, cover each one with a slice of ham, a slice of cheese and sliced tomato, fold the foil over to enclose, seal well and cook in a hot oven for 10 minutes.

Wash the potatoes well without peeling, wrap each one in foil and bake in the oven for about an hour, depending on size. Cut the foil, insert a spoon into the top of each potato to open, season with salt, pour in butter and sour cream and finish off with a liberal sprinkling of chives.

Austria

Pork kebab

1 portion   Grilling time: about 10 minutes

180 g	pork (fillet or boned fore loin)	6 oz
20 g	oil	1 fl oz

40 g	onions	2 oz
120 g	tomatoes	4 oz
60 g	peppers (half red, half green)	2 oz
	marjoram	
	chopped parsley	
2 cl	white wine	2 dessertspoons

Base

20 g	chopped onions	1 oz
10 g	butter	½ oz
50 g	boiled potatoes	2 oz
30 g	sweet peppers	1 oz
	1 medium tomato (coarsely chopped)	
5 cl	white wine	2 fl oz
5 cl	beef broth	2 fl oz

Cut the pork in cubes, season and fry lightly in hot oil. When brown on all sides, add button onions or larger onions cut in coarse dice, the red and green peppers cut in squares and the tomatoes (3 each weighing 40 g (about 1½ oz)). When only half-cooked, flavour with marjoram, pour in the white wine and simmer for 2 minutes. Remove from the heat and thread on to a skewer in the following order: meat, tomato, meat, sweet pepper, meat, onion, and so on. Grill and dish on the following base: fry the chopped onions lightly in the butter without browning, add the sliced potatoes, the finely diced pepper and the tomato, and moisten with the broth to prevent burning. Flavour with cubriza, add the white wine and simmer for 2–3 minutes. Transfer to a serving dish to form a bed for the skewer.

Bulgaria

Kebabs vine-grower style for a vineyard setting

4 persons   Cooking time: 8 minutes

350 g	trimmed fillet of beef	12 oz
350 g	trimmed fillet of pork	12 oz
	8 mushroom caps	
160 g	streaky bacon	5 oz
50 g	oil	2 oz
	salt	
	pepper	
	grill spices	

Cut the meat and bacon evenly into coarse dice. Thread cubes of beef and pork on to skewers alternately with the bacon, finishing off with the mushroom caps. Sprinkle with salt, pepper and grill spices; brush with oil and grill.

Serve with chipped potatoes, pepper salad, finely chopped onions and mustard.

Austria

Pork goulash with mushrooms

5 portions   Cooking time: $1\frac{1}{4}$–$1\frac{1}{2}$ hours

750 g	shoulder of pork	$1\frac{1}{2}$ lb
1 dl	oil	3 fl oz
200 g	onions	8 oz
50 g	mushrooms	2 oz
	a little cumin	

Cut the meat into small cubes and cook slowly in the hot oil with the onions (chopped) and the mushrooms, adding salt, pepper and a little cumin. Pour in a little water whenever the meat becomes dry and begins to fry. Serve with boiled potatoes or with bread.

Czechoslovakia

Pork pörkölt

10 persons

1 kg 500	pork (shoulder, leg, lean fore loin, tail, with a small piece of belly)	$3\frac{1}{4}$ lb
150 g	lard	5 oz
400 g	onions	1 lb
	1 large clove of garlic	
40 g	mild red paprika	$1\frac{1}{2}$ oz
	caraway seeds	
	pepper	
	tomato purée	
	letcho	
	dried sweet peppers	
	1–2 green peppers	

The amount of lard required will depend on the fattiness of the pork; if the latter is fat enough, little or no lard need be added for cooking.

Cut the pork into cubes and fry lightly in its own fat or a little lard until the pan is dry. Slice the onions finely and fry separately in a little lard until golden, then blend in the paprika and add to the meat. Season with salt to taste and add the crushed clove of garlic, tomato purée to taste, letcho or a few fresh tomatoes, a little ground caraway, pepper, 1–2 dried sweet peppers and 1–2 green peppers cut into rings. Pour in a little water and simmer until the meat is tender. Serve with freshly boiled potatoes, pasta pellets or white bread, also pickled peppers and tomatoes or melon.

Hungary

Roast leg of pork with apple sauce

Score the rind of the pork at ½ cm (¼ in) intervals and rub well with oil and salt. Place on a rack in a roasting tin at a temperature of 220°C (425°F) and cook allowing 25 minutes per pound plus 25 minutes.

Apple sauce

	2 cooking apples	
50 g	butter	2 oz
	sugar	
	lemon juice	

Peel, core and slice the apples and cook to a pulp in 2 tablespoons of water. Beat until smooth and add the butter. A little sugar may be added if wished but a tart sauce is the best accompaniment for pork.

Roast spare ribs

10 persons   Roasting time: 1½ hours

1 kg	lean spare rib	2¼ lb
	½ teaspoon powdered mustard	
	salt	
	freshly ground white pepper	
3 dl	meat broth	½ pt
	3 apples	
	red-currant jelly	

Score the pork, trim and rub with salt, pepper and mustard. Place in a roasting tin with the fat uppermost, pour in the broth and roast at 175°C until the meat comes away from the bone. Remove, carve into portions and arrange on a dish. Surround the meat with the apples filled with red-currant jelly. To prepare the apples, peel them, cut in half, remove the core and poach for 5 minutes in water flavoured with lemon juice, then drain well and fill the centre with red-currant jelly.

Sweden

Roast sucking pig

Lay the whole pig on a wire tray keeping the legs apart by a wooden skewer fastened through the hind feet. Wrap the ears and tail in greased paper to prevent burning. During roasting brush constantly with butter or oil and keep covered with greased paper, changing it several times. Prick with a needle the bubbles in the skin caused by the fat. Average roasting time is about 1½–2 hours according to size, adding 15 minutes for every pound of stuffing. Usual English stuffing is sage and onion.

Sage and onion stuffing

	4 large onions	
	6 fresh sage leaves	
	or	
	dried sage to taste	
120 g	breadcrumbs	¼ lb
	1 teaspoon salt	
60 g	butter	2 oz

Blanch the onions; throw away the first water and boil in fresh water until tender. If fresh sage is used cook with the onions for the last five minutes. Drain well and chop. Mix with the rest of the ingredients. If dried sage is used mix with the dry breadcrumbs, before the final mixing.

Sateh

500 g	pork	1 lb
	1 clove of garlic	
	1 teaspoon brown sugar	
	salt	
	1 tablespoon soya sauce	
	('ketjap' in Indonesian)	

Mix together the crushed garlic, sugar, salt and 'ketjap', cut the meat in small cubes and marinate for two hours. Thread the pieces of meat on small skewers (preferably made of bamboo and well-moistened) and grill over a charcoal fire.

Holland/Indonesia

Stuffed cabbage Oden style

4 persons   Cooking time: 15–20 minutes

	8 large white cabbage leaves	
200 g	radish	7 oz

20

60 g	carrots	2 oz
	4 dried Japanese mushrooms (kinoko)	
250 g	lean pork or boned chicken	8¾ oz
	oil	
18 cm	kampyo*	7 in
7½ cm	carrots	3 in
	1 piece grilled bean curd	
½ l	bouillon	⅞ pt
	1 teaspoon soya sauce	
	1½ teaspoons salt	
	1 teaspoon mirin	
	½ teaspoon sugar	
	1 teaspoon aji-no-moto	
	kombu†	
	mustard	

Soak the dried mushrooms and cut into strips, together with the radish, 60 g (2 oz) carrots and the chicken or pork. Season lightly with salt and fry in oil for a few moments. Cut away the hard cabbage stalks, blanch the leaves well, drain and dry thoroughly with a paper napkin. Stuff each leaf with one-eighth of the fried meat and vegetable mixture, roll up, turn in the sides and secure with thread. Cut the rest of the carrots into flower shapes 1 cm (½ in) thick and boil. Dice the bean curd coarsely. Wipe the kombu with a damp cloth and place in a saucepan. Cover with the cabbage rolls, the bean curd and the flower-shaped carrots, pour in the bouillon with the addition of the soya sauce, salt, mirin, sugar and aji-no-moto and cook over moderate heat. Serve with made-up mustard.

Japan

* Kampyo: dried gourd.
† Kombu: kelp seaweed, used for flavouring.

Roast sucking pig with vegetable salad tartlets

Cut open a 3-week-old sucking pig weighing 3 kg 500–4 kg (7 lb 11 oz–8 lb 12 oz), working from the tail end but leaving the head intact. Wipe with a cloth inside and outside. To shorten the roasting time, make small cuts all the way up the back on both sides of the spine, or split the pig in half through the spine. Season with salt and, if desired, a little paprika.

If the pig is to be roasted whole, make two parallel cuts along the neck and insert the front legs, wedge the back legs apart with a small wooden skewer and protect the ears and tail with oiled paper or several thicknesses of damp paper. Place the pig on a bed of bay branches stripped of their leaves in a flat earthenware dish of suitable size or a roasting tin with fairly high sides. Pour in a little water to prevent the skin from sticking to the dish. Coat the pig inside and outside with lard well mixed with finely crushed garlic. Roast in a medium oven at an even temperature. When brown on one side, turn and brush with the dripping to brown the other side. Prick frequently with a needle to prevent blistering. When the pig is cooked— the skin should be well browned and crisp—remove from the dish or tin and brush with butter to glaze. Pour off part of the dripping in the roasting dish, add about 1½ dl (¼ pt) white wine, reduce to half its volume, pour in a ladleful of bouillon, boil for a few minutes and pass through a fine strainer. Serve the sucking pig in the earthenware dish, handing the gravy separately, with mixed vegetable salad tartlets or a suitable salad in season as an accompaniment.

Spain

COLD DISHES

Black pudding

Cooking time: 35–40 minutes

1 kg	lean pig's head meat	2¼ lb
100–150 g	pork rinds	3–5 oz
100 g	cooked bacon	4 oz
250 g	onions, browned	8 oz
250 g	pig's intestine fat, rendered down to make greaves	8 oz
	3 rolls	
2 dl	pig's blood	⅓ pt
25 g	salt	1 oz
2 g	pinch of pepper	
2 g	pinch of crushed allspice	
2 g	pinch of paprika	
	pinch of marjoram	
	little bouillon to moisten if required	
	pig's large intestines	

Cook the meat and pork rinds until tender and reduce to a purée in the blender. Cut the bacon into 1 cm (about ½ in) cubes. Dice the rolls, pour the blood over, add to the meat and pork rinds together with the onions, seasonings and spices and whirl in the blender again for a moment. Squeeze the greaves dry, add to the mixture together with the diced bacon and blend all the ingredients together well. If too dry, moisten with a little bouillon. Fill into the intestines which have been thoroughly cleaned and washed, tie up and cook gently for 35 to 40 minutes in water at 80°C.

Austria

Brawn and beetroot

6 persons   Cooking time: $1\frac{1}{2}$–$1\frac{3}{4}$ hours

> half a pig's head
> 2 carrots
> 2 onions
> 1 leek
> half a head of celeriac
> 4 bay leaves
> 10 peppercorns
> mustard
> pickled beetroot
> 6 slices rye bread

Blanch the half pig's head, rinse, then cover with fresh water, add the root vegetables, bay leaves, peppercorns and salt as required and simmer until cooked. Remove the meat from the bone, cut it into 1 cm (about $\frac{1}{2}$ in) cubes, place in a saucepan, strain over enough of the cooking liquid to cover well and boil up again. Transfer to an oblong or other tin, cover with the cooking liquid and refrigerate. Turn out, slice and serve with rye bread (without butter), mustard and pickled beetroot.

Denmark

Boiled belly of pork with rye bread

6 persons   Cooking time: 1–$1\frac{1}{2}$ hours

1 kg	lean belly of pork, boned	$2\frac{1}{4}$ lb
	2 carrots	
	1 leek	
	2 onions	
	$\frac{1}{2}$ head of celeriac	
	2 bay leaves	
	10 peppercorns	
	mustard	
	3 slices rye bread (6 half slices)	
90 g	butter	3 oz

Boil the pork with the bones which have been removed, the vegetables, bay leaves, peppercorns and salt as required. Leave in the cooking liquid until cold, then remove, carve, cover with the strained cooking liquid and decorate with bay leaves and onion rings. Serve the bread, butter and mustard separately.

Denmark

Fricadelles and cucumber salad with rye bread

6 persons

250 g	pork	8 oz
	1 egg	
35 g	flour	1 oz
	half an onion, finely chopped	
15 cl	dairy cream	¼ pt
	1 large cucumber	
1 dl	vinegar	3 fl oz
5 cl	water	2 fl oz
	salt	
	sugar	
	pepper	
	3 slices rye bread	
	(6 half slices)	
90 g	butter	4 oz
	fat for frying	

Mince the pork, but not too finely, mix with the onion, egg, flour and cream and season with salt and pepper. Shape into flattened balls or ovals, notch with the back of a knife, and dry in hot fat for 5 minutes on each side. Serve lukewarm with rye bread, butter and a salad of thinly sliced cucumber dressed with the vinegar, diluted with water, and salt, pepper and sugar.

Denmark

Fore loin of pork, red cabbage, cucumber salad and beetroot with rye bread

6 persons

1 kg	fore loin of pork	2¼ lb
	red cabbage	
	vinegar	
	sugar	
	pepper	
	pickled beetroot	
	3 slices rye bread	
	(6 half slices)	
90 g	butter	3 oz
	1 cucumber	

Leave some of the fat on the pork, score it and sprinkle with salt, then roast and allow to cool. Slice the cucumber thinly and dress with vinegar, a little water, salt, pepper and sugar. Prepare the red cabbage in the usual manner. Butter the bread, cover with slices of roast pork, garnish with cucumber salad and beetroot, and serve the red cabbage separately.

Denmark

Pork brawn

2 kg 500	½ pig's head weighing	5½ lb
1 kg	fat pork or bacon	2¼ lb
1 kg	veal on the bone	2¼ lb
	(breast, neck, etc.)	
	1–2 bacon or pork rinds	

Bouillon seasonings per litre (1¾ pt) water

15 g	salt	½ oz
	5 white peppercorns	
	5 juniper berries	
	½ bay leaf	
	1 clove	

To make up dish

	thin slices of pork fat or	
	fat bacon	
	4 sheets gelatine (soaked)	
15 g	salt	½ oz
	1 teaspoon crushed white	
	pepper	
	1 teaspoon crushed coriander	
	½ teaspoon crushed cloves	

Clean, scrape and wash the pig's head well. Soak in cold water for 12 hours, changing the water fairly frequently. Place the head in a large pan together with the fat pork (or bacon), the rinds and the veal. Cover with water (for the bouillon) and bring to the boil, then skim. Add the bouillon seasonings, cover the pan and cook for 1–1½ hours. Remove the meat and allow to cool. Carefully cut the rind from the head. Cut the meat into small pieces.

To make up the dish, first mix the salt and spices. Wring out a linen cloth in hot water, line an earthenware bowl with it and cover the cloth with thin slices of pork fat or fat bacon. Fill up with alternate layers of lean and fat meat, sprinkling each layer with salt and spice mixture and covering with a sheet of gelatine before adding the next layer. Top with pork fat or fat bacon to cover. Fold the cloth over the top and tie the ends together. Cook in the bouillon for 20 minutes, standing the bowl on a rack if necessary. When cooked, place the brawn between two plates, weighted down to press into shape, and leave in the refrigerator for 10 hours.

Sweden

Pork brawn Rumanian style

10 persons   Cooking time: about 5 hours

> 10 pig's trotters
> 10 pig's ears
> 2–3 cloves of garlic
> 1 lemon
> pickled vegetables,
>   e.g. cauliflower, red and
>   green peppers, cucumber,
>   carrots, etc.
> allspice
> peppercorns
> 1 bay leaf

Clean the trotters well, split lengthwise and place in a pan with the pig's ears, the garlic, allspice, a few peppercorns, a bay leaf, a little salt and 3 l (5¼ pt) water. Bring to the boil and simmer gently until the trotters and ears are tender. Remove from the cooking liquid, bone, cut the meat into pieces and arrange in a suitable mould or bowl with the pickled vegetables, alternating the colours. Skim all the fat off the cooking liquid, sharpen with lemon juice, taste for flavour, adjusting the seasoning if necessary, strain, pour over the meat and vegetables and refrigerate. When firm, turn out on to a serving dish. The general effect should be similar to a mosaic.

(Illustration, p. 462)   Rumania

Pork chops in aspic

6 persons   Cooking time (meat): about 1½ hours

> 1 joint fore loin of pork
>   with 6 ribs (chined)
> 2 calf's feet
> 1 carrot
> 2 fairly small onions
> 1 bay leaf
> 8 allspice seeds
> 8 peppercorns
> 3 cloves
> 2 egg whites

¼ l   wine vinegar   ½ pt

Garnish

3 hard-boiled eggs
3 gherkins
a few capers
blanched tarragon leaves

Wash the calf's feet well, split lengthwise, blanch for 10 minutes, then return to the pan with fresh water, the carrot, onions, bay leaf and spices and a little salt, bring to the boil and simmer gently for 1½ hours. Add the meat and continue simmering until cooked, making sure that the meat remains firm and in one piece. Cool in the cooking liquid, then remove the meat and simmer the stock for a further hour, strain and skim off all the fat. Add the vinegar, clarify with the egg whites, strain through a cloth and adjust the seasoning.

Cut the joint, which will have cooled meanwhile, into 6 even chops, remove the bones and trim each chop neatly. Mask the bottom of special chop moulds thinly with the aspic jelly, leave to set, then decorate with slices of hard-boiled egg, carrot and gherkin, tarragon leaves, capers, etc. Place the chops in the moulds and fill up with aspic jelly which is just beginning to set. If no special moulds are available, place the trimmed chops in a shallow dish, pour a little aspic jelly over and decorate individually before the jelly has completely set, to keep the garnish in place. Now cover well with jelly and refrigerate until firm. Cut the chops out of the aspic carefully so that they keep their shape. If chop moulds have been used, hold each one in hot water for a moment, then turn out. Garnish with the remaining aspic jelly and serve with fried potatoes or light rye bread and butter.

N.B.—Glass or tin moulds for chops in aspic are on sale in some shops specialising in kitchen utensils.

Germany

Pork medallions

Yield: 6 pieces

120 g	juicy roast fillet of pork (cold)—net weight	4 oz
60 g	foie gras purée	2 oz
	½ Californian peach	
	6 half pistachio nuts, blanched	
	white wine jelly	

Cut 6 pork medallions of equal size and pipe on foie gras purée, using a savoy bag fitted with a plain pipe. Cut the peach half into 6 and place 1 piece on each medallion, together with half a pistachio nut. Lastly glaze with white wine jelly.

Germany

Pressed sausage

2 pig's heads, hearts and
    tongues
4 pig's hocks
few large pieces of pork rind
little bouillon
salt and pepper
allspice
marjoram
3–4 cloves of garlic
few spoons pig's blood
dash of vinegar
pig's stomach, well soaked

Cut the pig's heads, hearts and tongues in half. Place in a pan with the hocks and pork rind and barely cover with water. Simmer until tender. Remove the meat from the bones and cut into fairly large pieces together with the pork rind. Moisten with a little bouillon, add the seasoning, allspice, marjoram, crushed garlic and a little pig's blood mixed with a dash of vinegar, and blend all the ingredients together thoroughly. Fill the pig's stomach with the mixture, sew up well and cook in hot water at about 75°C for roughly 1½ hours. When cold, press well between weighted boards.

Austria

Rolled belly of pork, onion rings and aspic with rye bread

6 persons

2 kg	boned belly of pork	4¼ lb
500 g	boneless pork	1 lb
250 g	pork fat	8 oz
	2 onions	
	allspice	
	aspic jelly	
	cress	
	3 slices rye bread	
	(6 half slices)	
	or 6 slices white bread	
90 g	butter or lard	3 oz

Beat the belly of pork with the inside uppermost and shape into a square. Sprinkle lightly with salt, pepper and allspice and cover with a layer of pork fat 5 mm (¼ in) thick. Cut the boneless pork into broad strips and arrange on top, season again, cover with a thin layer of pork fat and roll up. Sew up the join well and leave for

6 days in dilute brine (not more than 18%). After removing, rinse, cook for 1–1½ hours and leave under light pressure for 1 day. Spread the bread with butter or lard, cover with slices of rolled belly of pork and garnish with onion rings, cress and aspic jelly.

Denmark

Saddle of pork Swedish style

10–12 persons   Cooking time: 80 minutes

1 kg 300	boned saddle of pork	2 lb 14 oz
200 g	lean boneless pork	7 oz
200 g	veal without gristle	7 oz
100 g	fresh pork back fat	3½ oz
200 g	cooked smoked tongue (tip)	7 oz
200 g	stoned prunes	7 oz
⅛ l	dairy cream	¼ pt
¾ l	aspic jelly	1¼ pt
4 l	white pork stock	7 pt
	pie pastry	
	red apples	
	horseradish cream	
	chopped pistachio nuts	
	brunoise	
	sweet corn	
	green peppers	
	vegetable salad	
	cucumber cut into balls	
	assorted vegetables in	
	contrasting colours	
	forcemeat flavouring	
	powdered cumin	

Cut the saddle fillets open lengthwise, cover with a moistened plastic sheet and flatten gently, but evenly. Prepare forcemeat with the pork, veal and back fat, season with salt and pepper, add forcemeat flavouring and powdered cumin to taste, and stir in the cream. Dice the cooked tongue coarsely and add to the forcemeat, together with the stoned whole prunes. Place a roll of forcemeat on each pork fillet and fold the ends of the fillets over to enclose the forcemeat completely. Wrap the galantines in a damp cloth, tie and poach in the pork stock. While still warm, unwrap, rinse out the cloth, wrap up again, tie tightly and chill well under light pressure. Cut into fairly thin slices and glaze each one with aspic.

Bake a fancy pie pastry case resembling a casserole, fill with a colourful assortment of vegetables, previously marinated, and place at the top end of the serving dish, in the centre. Arrange the glazed slices of galantine one overlapping another in two rows along the length of the dish close to the edges. Fill up the space between the two rows with unpeeled cored apple slices stuffed with horseradish cream and sprinkled with chopped pistachio nuts, sweet corn and brunoise, and with green peppers cut in half, levelled off underneath, stuffed with vegetable salad and covered with vegetables in contrasting colours.

(Illustration, p. 816)

Smoked loin of pork with potato salad

6 persons   Cooking time: 45–50 minutes

1 kg 200–1 kg 500	lightly pickled and smoked fore loin of pork ('Kasseler')	2 lb 10 oz–3 lb 5 oz
	1 large carrot, coarsely diced	
	1 large onion, coarsely diced	
	1 bay leaf	

Place the meat in a hot oven in a roasting tin containing a little water. As soon as the water has evaporated, add the carrot, onion and bay leaf, but no salt. Reduce the heat and roast the meat slowly until tender. Remove, allow to cool, cut off the bone, carve evenly into neat slices and dish. Serve with potato salad (for method of preparing, see Berlin sausages).

N.B.—'Kasseler' pickled and smoked pork is not named after the German town of Kassel, but after a master butcher called Casel who traded in Friedrichstadt, on the southern outskirts of Berlin, during the first thirty years of the nineteenth century, and who was the first to produce this type of salt pork. Over the years, the name 'Casel' became 'Cassel' or 'Kasseler'.

Germany

Stuffed loin of pork

20 portions   Cooking time: 2 hours

2 kg 500	loin of pork, chined	5½ lb
200 g	lightly pickled veal forcemeat	8 oz
200 g	lightly pickled pork forcemeat	8 oz
150 g	pickled tongue, diced	5 oz
100 g	cooked ham, diced	4 oz
100 g	smoked fat pork (or bacon), blanched and diced	4 oz
80 g	diced truffles	3 oz
50 g	blanched pistachio nuts	2 oz

oblong slices of well-blanched
celeriac 1 cm ($\frac{1}{2}$ in) thick
diced, skinned and seeded
tomatoes
thick slices of blanched
cucumber
very small marinated
vegetables or mixed pickles
stewed prunes
forcemeat flavouring
Cognac

The loin of pork should be lightly pickled and smoked. Cut a piece off on the same side as the short bone. Make a cavity right in the centre of the cutlet meat by means of a horizontal incision, which should be fairly large, to leave sufficient room for the forcemeat. Push a stick through the cavity and beat lightly to enlarge it. Flavour the forcemeat with Cognac, herbs and spices, add the diced tongue, ham, fat pork (or bacon) and truffles together with the pistachio nuts, then pack tightly into the cavity, using a savoy bag without a tube. Wrap in a cloth, tie firmly, poach at about 80°C, allow to cool in the cooking liquid, then press lightly. Marinate the celeriac, diced tomatoes and slices of cucumber. Stone the cold prunes.

For the garnish, cover the oblongs of celeriac with the diced tomatoes and sprinkle with a little chopped parsley. Top the slices of cucumber with a mound of mixed marinated vegetables or mixed pickles and arrange the prunes in the shape of a star. Trim the loin of pork neatly, stripping the ends of the rib bones, carve part of it and decorate the remainder with mixed vegetables.

(Illustration, p. 808)   Austria

HAM

WHOLE HAMS

Baked ham spring style

20–25 persons   Cooking time: 1$\frac{1}{2}$ hours, plus 1 hour in the oven

4–5 kg   1 smoked ham weighing   8 lb 12 oz–11 lb

Chaud-froid sauce

$\frac{1}{2}$ l	strong veal or chicken velouté	$\frac{7}{8}$ pt
	6 sheets gelatine	
2 dl	dairy cream	$\frac{1}{3}$ pt

Decoration

	green and red peppers, blanched leek, truffles, egg white, etc.	
1 l	aspic jelly	$1\frac{3}{4}$ pt

Soak the ham for 6 hours. Place in a pan of cold water with the usual herbs and spices, bring to the boil and simmer gently for $1\frac{1}{2}$ hours. Take out of the water, remove the end bone and shorten the knuckle-bone a little. Bake in a medium oven for 1 hour. Skin, cut off any surplus fat and chill well overnight. Cut off the smaller side and set aside. Coat the rest of the ham with chaud-froid sauce and allow to set, then coat again and refrigerate. Decorate with a basket motif made with threads of truffle and a flower arrangement consisting of red pepper and leek, then glaze with aspic jelly. Carve the piece of ham which was set aside into very thin slices (use a little extra ham if required). Arrange the slices from top to bottom round the decorated ham and glaze them with aspic. Garnish with baked half-apples stuffed with red-currant jelly, stuffed eggs, tomatoes stuffed from underneath, fluted mushroom caps, or as desired.

(Illustrations p, 924)   USA

Baked Virginia ham

Cooking time: 20–25 minutes per 500 g (per lb)

6 kg	1 Virginia ham weighing approx.	$13\frac{1}{4}$ lb
	6 medium onions	
$\frac{1}{4}$ l	sherry	$\frac{1}{2}$ pt
250 g	brown sugar	8 oz
	cloves	

Place the ham in a saucepan of suitable size and barely cover with water. Add the sliced onions and the sherry and bring to the boil. Skim, then simmer gently. The ham is cooked when the small hock-bone comes away easily. Allow to cool overnight in the water in which it has simmered. Next morning, remove the skin, lightly score the fat criss-cross fashion, cover with the brown sugar and stud closely with cloves. Bake at 220°C until well glazed. Slice very thinly to serve.

Germany

Christmas ham

10–15 persons

3 kg	1 cured ham weighing	6 lb 10 oz
	1 egg	
	2 tablespoons mustard	
	1 tablespoon sugar	
	2 tablespoons dry breadcrumbs	

Place the ham on an oven rack or in a large saucepan with the skin side uppermost. Insert a meat thermometer into the thickest part. Heat the oven to 125°C, then bake the ham, allowing 1 hour per kg (2 lb 3 oz). When the thermometer shows 77°C and the ham is tender, remove from the oven and skin. Set aside the cooking juices. Mix together the egg, mustard and sugar and spread this coating on the ham. Sprinkle with the breadcrumbs. Raise the oven temperature to 250°C and bake the ham for a further 10 minutes to brown the top.

(Illustration, p. 376)   Sweden

Hot ham with horseradish

The cooked ham should be carved in the presence of the guests and served with horseradish or mustard according to individual preference. Bread or salty rolls should be handed as an accompaniment.

Czechoslovakia

Stuffed ham

60–70 portions   Cooking time: 5 hours at 80°C

	1 mild lightly smoked	
7–8 kg	long ham, weighing	15½–18 lb
500 g	pickled veal forcemeat	1 lb
500 g	pickled pork forcemeat	1 lb
400 g	pickled ox tongue	1 lb
200 g	hard back pork fat, blanched	8 oz
150 g	truffles	5 oz
150 g	pistachio nuts	5 oz
400 g	diced ham (including trimmings from the whole ham to be stuffed)	1 lb
approx. 2 kg	aspic	3½ pt
	12 tomatoes of equal size	
750 g	very ripe tomatoes	1¾ lb

40 g	butter	2 oz
	2 tablespoons velouté	
	2 sheets gelatine	
2 dl	whipped dairy cream	$\frac{1}{3}$ pt
approx. 1 kg	French salad	$2\frac{1}{4}$ lb
	asparagus tips	
	marinated vegetables	
	(small corn cobs, small	
	artichoke hearts, French	
	beans, sprigs of	
	cauliflower)	
	forcemeat flavouring	
	Madeira	
	Cognac	
	lemon juice	

The ham for stuffing should be cut off the loin at the thigh bone. Carefully cut away the chump-end bone, as well as the bone up to the knuckle end, then carefully remove the cushion bone. Cut away the thick portions inside to leave sufficient space for the forcemeat. Pour in Madeira and marinate for a few hours. Dice the pickled tongue, the pork fat, the truffles and the ham trimmings and stir into the forcemeat together with the pistachio nuts. Flavour well with forcemeat herbs and spices and Cognac and insert into the hollow in the ham. Wrap the ham carefully in a cloth, sew up, place in a pan of boiling water, bring to the boil again, then poach gently until cooked. Allow to cool in the cooking liquid, then tie round again and press lightly. Refrigerate for 8–10 hours before carving and dishing.

Garnish

Mask a ring mould with aspic, but not too thinly. Cut even-sized cooked asparagus stalks in half and place the top ends in the mould with the tips downwards. Fill up the mould with French salad bound with aspic and chill for a few hours. Turn out and fill the centre of the ring with the marinated vegetables.

Skin the 12 tomatoes carefully, cut open at the stalk end, scoop out the seeds, season inside with salt and pepper and drain well. Skin and seed the remaining tomatoes, chop finely and stew in the butter until the liquid has evaporated. Mix with the velouté, rub through a fine sieve and mix with the gelatine which has been soaked, squeezed dry and dissolved. Before the mixture sets, fold in half as much whipped cream, add salt, lemon juice and a good pinch of cayenne pepper and pipe at once into the hollow tomatoes, using a savoy bag and a plain pipe. Chill very well, decorate each one with a star of egg white and glaze with aspic. Wait until the aspic has set before cutting a wedge out of each one.

(Illustration, p. 809)   Austria

Stuffed ham four seasons

Cooking time: 1 hour per kg (2 lb 3 oz) at 85°C

	1 ham with chump end,	
7 kg	weighing not more than	15½ lb
1 kg 200	finely minced pork	2¼ lb
500 g	cooked pickled pig's tongues	1 lb
150 g	blanched pistachio nuts	5 oz
75 g	dried flap mushrooms (boletus), soaked	3 oz
75 g	dried morels, soaked	3 oz
50 g	truffle trimmings	2 oz
50 g	chopped onions	2 oz
50 g	butter	2 oz
2 dl	Madeira	⅓ pt
	a little marjoram	

Cut the ham with the chump-end bone off the hind loin. Cure without cutting away the skin and smoke for 45 minutes. Remove the bone as far as the hock, leaving a fairly large pocket. Shape this pocket evenly by applying the meat to the part of the joint between the middle bone and the hock. Pour the Madeira into the pocket, cover the ham and marinate for a few hours. To make the forcemeat, heat the butter to a light yellow colour in a sauté pan, add the chopped onions and cook lightly, then add the soaked flap mushrooms and morels and the truffles. Cook for a short time, then pour in the Madeira used to marinate the ham, flavour with a little marjoram, add the pig's tongues cut in small dice and allow to cool. Mix with the minced meat together with the pistachio nuts, season to taste and pack tightly into the cavity in the ham. Sew a piece of skin from lean belly of pork (or a piece of streaky bacon rind) round the open side, wrap the ham tightly in a cloth of suitable size, tie round firmly and place in sufficient warm water to cover well. Cook at a constant temperature of 80–85°C checking with a thermometer to make sure that the temperature of the water does not rise above 85°C.

For a cold buffet, allow the ham to cool in the cooking water, unwrap and arrange on a dish of suitable size, placing some slices which have been cut off beforehand in front. If desired, coat the dish with aspic first and glaze the sliced ham with aspic. Serve with suitable salads in season.

(Techniques, p. 119)   Switzerland

Stuffed ham in puff pastry

About 20 persons   Baking time: 90 minutes

1 kg 600	cooked ham	3½ lb

500 g	boneless veal	1 lb
500 g	boneless fat pork	1 lb
350 g	pig's liver	¾ lb
	2 eggs	
50 g	blanched pistachio nuts	2 oz
50 g	diced truffles	2 oz
100 g	fatted goose liver, coarsely diced	4 oz
1 dl	Madeira	3 fl oz
500 g	puff paste	1 lb
	pepper	
	rose paprika	
	ground nutmeg and cloves	
	pinch of marjoram	
	2 chopped shallots	
30 g	butter	1 oz

It is best to use a round cooked ham. Remove the skin, cut the ham through lengthwise and distribute the layer of fat evenly. Marinate under cover in the Madeira for 1 to 2 hours. Mince the veal and pork as finely as possible. Dice the pig's liver, sprinkle with forcemeat spices, toss lightly in butter with the chopped shallots, allow to cool completely and mince. (The liver and meat may be minced together.) Add 1 egg and the Madeira used as a marinade, season, using very little salt, mix well and stir in the pistachio nuts, truffles and goose liver. Pin out barely half the puff paste to make a rectangle about 5 mm (¼ in) thick, place on a baking-sheet and spread with a 1 cm (½ in) layer of the forcemeat to fit the ham exactly. Make sure that at least 3 cm (a good inch) of pastry is left uncovered all round to provide a tight seal when the pastry cover is placed on top. Place the ham on the forcemeat flat side down, cover with the rest of the forcemeat, spread it evenly and press down lightly, making sure that the ham is completely covered. Pin out the rest of the puff pastry a little more thinly, cover the ham with it and seal the edges firmly. Make two vents at the top as for a pie; prick all the way round three-quarters of the way up, preferably with the blunt end of a trussing needle, to make air holes. Brush all over with egg, score lightly with a fork and bake at about 200°C with even top and bottom heat. Serve either cold as a buffet dish or warm with Madeira sauce, any desired vegetable and potatoes.

Germany

Stuffed ham Strasbourg style

40–45 persons

3 kg 500–4 kg	1 York ham weighing	7¾–8¾ lb
1 kg	foie gras mousse	2¼ lb
3 l	port jelly	5 pt
50 g	truffles	2 oz

Trim the ham, leaving a cone-shaped piece of skin at the knuckle bone end and cut the edge of the skin zigzag fashion. Carefully cut out the centre kernel of meat without touching the knuckle bone. This will leave a rounded cavity. Finely slice the ham which was cut out and trim each slice to an oblong shape 10 cm (4 in) long and 4–5 cm (1½–2 in) wide. Brush with cold liquid jelly. Using a savoy bag fitted with a coarse tube, pipe on a roll of foie gras mousse 2 cm (¾ in) from the edge. Roll the slices up and tie round once. Pack the rolls into a dish just large enough to hold them. Decorate the top with a truffle motif. When firm, untie and pack into the cavity in the ham. Glaze with jelly and refrigerate for at least an hour. Decorate the edges of a serving dish with jelly and place the ham in the centre with a frill round the knuckle bone.

France

Stuffed ham York style

40–45 persons

3 kg 500–4 kg	1 York ham weighing	7¾–8¾ lb
1 kg	ham mousse	2¼ lb
50 g	chopped truffles	2 oz
3 l	aspic jelly	5 pt

Trim and dress the ham as for stuffed ham Strasbourg style, but use ham mousse mixed with chopped truffles to stuff the slices of ham.

France

York ham in aspic

50 persons   Cooking time: 20 minutes per 500 g (pound)

3 kg 500–4 kg	1 York ham weighing	7¾–8¾ lb
2 l	port jelly	3½ pt

Loosen the flesh round the chump-end bone. Soak the ham in a large bowl of cold water for 24 hours, changing the water two or three times. Transfer to a large pan of unsalted water, bring to the boil and simmer gently until cooked, then allow to cool in the cooking liquid. Remove the skin, the chump-end bone and any excess fat. Slice and arrange the slices on a serving dish to the original shape of the ham. Decorate and glaze with port jelly. Garnish the edges of the dish with jelly cut into fancy shapes. Place a frill round the knuckle bone. Store in a cold place.

France

HAM DISHES

Cassolettes of ham in aspic

4 persons

	8 slices ham	
	8 slices Lyons sausage	
	2 hard-boiled eggs	
	2–3 gherkins	
6–8 dl	aspic jelly	1–1$\frac{1}{3}$ pt

Mask cassolettes or waxed carton cups with aspic jelly to a thickness of $\frac{1}{2}$ cm (about $\frac{1}{4}$ in) and allow to set. Fill with alternate layers of ham and Lyons sausage, pouring a little liquid jelly which is on the point of setting, between the layers. Finish off with a round slice of ham. Place a slice of hard-boiled egg on top, decorate with a gherkin rosette or a colourful motif and cover with a thin layer of jelly. As the moulds are not turned out, the jelly can be very light. Serve with toast and butter. Other suitable accompaniments are poppy seed rolls, black radishes, or cucumber in mustard pickle.

Switzerland

Ham and asparagus au gratin

5 portions

250 g	Prague ham	8 oz
100 g	butter	4 oz
250 g	asparagus (canned)	8 oz
50 g	white breadcrumbs	2 oz
100 g	grated cheese	4 oz

Fry fairly thick slices of ham in a third of the butter. Place in a buttered fireproof dish of suitable size and arrange the asparagus on top. Sprinkle with the breadcrumbs, grated cheese and the rest of the butter (melted) and brown in a hot oven or under a salamander.

Ham may be prepared in the same way with artichoke bottoms, sliced mushrooms or cooked leeks.

Czechoslovakia

Ham Biedermeier style

12 persons

2 l	ham mousse well stiffened with aspic jelly	3½ pt
1 kg	cooked ham on the bone	2¼ lb
	12 slices cooked ham	
¾ l	whipped dairy cream	1¼ pt
	2 tablespoons grated horseradish	
1½ l	aspic jelly	2½ pt
100 g	chopped walnuts	4 oz
	cucumbers	
	egg yolk paste	
	tomatoes	
	Gervais cream	
	cooked round slices of celeriac	
	truffles	
	carrots cut into small balls	
	peas	
	pistachio nuts	
	red peppers	

Line a round mould with aspic jelly, fill with ham mousse, allow to set, then turn out on a glazing rack. Cut the ham off the bone in thin even-sized slices and arrange evenly, one overlapping another, to cover the mousse. Chill well and pour over aspic jelly to glaze. Shape the rest of the slices of ham cut off the bone into cones and set aside. Mix the whipped cream with the horseradish and chopped walnuts and add a pinch each of salt and sugar. Pipe on to the 12 slices of ham, using a savoy bag without a pipe, roll up and glaze with aspic. Fill the ham cones with the same cream, decorate with a dot of red pepper, glaze with aspic and arrange in a ring on top of the mousse.

Level off the cucumbers lengthwise, remove the seeds from the centre with a vegetable scoop and pipe in egg yolk paste, using a savoy bag. When firm, cut in slices and glaze. Skin the tomatoes, scoop out the seeds, working from the stalk end, and fill with Gervais cream mixed with chopped pistachio nuts, diced truffles and small cubes of red pepper. Refrigerate, then cut out a quarter of each tomato and glaze the remainder with aspic. Cut the slices of celeriac into neat rounds and decorate with small marinated carrot balls, egg yolk paste, peas and small disks of truffle and red pepper.

(Illustration, p. 809)   Austria

Ham with chicken liver and mushrooms

5 portions

250 g	cooked Prague ham	8 oz
100 g	mushrooms	3 oz
150 g	chicken livers	5 oz
100 g	butter	3 oz
2 cl	brandy	2 dessertspoons

Cook fairly thick slices of ham in a little stock or bouillon. Slice the mushrooms and cut the livers into pieces. Toss the mushrooms in butter, remove, then toss the livers in butter, stir in the brandy and season with salt and pepper. Cover each portion of ham with liver and mushrooms and sprinkle the ham with a little gravy.

Czechoslovakia

Ham cones Basque coast style

8 persons

	4 slices Bayonne ham	
200 g	rice	8 oz
	4 green peppers	
750 g	fresh tomatoes	1 lb 12 oz

Cut out 8 triangles of lean ham, each measuring 7 cm (3 in) along the base and 9 cm (3½ in) high. Dip in half-set aspic jelly and roll up into cones, which may be placed inside decorating pipes so that they keep their shape while the jelly is setting. Refrigerate.

Skin the peppers, set aside half of one of them for decoration and dice the remainder finely. Cook in 2 tablespoons oil over low heat, add the rice and mix well. Pour in twice as much water or, preferably, chicken broth from which all fat has been removed. Season with salt and pepper, cover with oiled paper and cook for 18 minutes, or until all the liquid has boiled away, without stirring. Cool until the rice is barely lukewarm, then dress with vinaigrette, stirring it in with a fork. Transfer at once to a chimney mould and pack fairly tightly. When quite cold, turn out on to a round serving dish. Skin the tomatoes, remove the seeds, chop very roughly, drain well and dress with vinaigrette. Pile the tomato salad in the centre of the ring of rice. Stand the ham cones on their tips round the base of the tomato salad, steadying them against the rice. The cones may be filled with a little rice if desired. Decorate the top of the tomato salad with strips of green pepper.

France

Ham forester style

5 portions

250 g	Prague ham	8 oz
50 g	butter	2 oz
50 g	bacon fat	2 oz
150 g	flap mushrooms (boletus)	5 oz
5 cl	red wine	2 fl oz
5 cl	tomato ketchup	2 fl oz
	maître d'hôtel butter	

Fry fairly thick slices of ham in butter for a few moments. Cut the mushrooms in quarters, fry in the rendered bacon fat, stir in the wine, add the ketchup and cook gently. Pour over the slices of ham and place a knob of maître d'hôtel butter on top. Serve with stewed cranberries garnished with slices of orange as an accompaniment.

Czechoslovakia

Ham gipsy style

5 portions

250 g	cooked Prague ham	8 oz
150 g	fat smoked bacon	5 oz
100 g	onions, diced	3 oz
150 g	flap mushrooms (boletus)	5 oz
300 g	peeled potatoes (raw)	10 oz
100 g	peppers	3 oz
	1 clove of garlic	
	crushed paprika	

Dice the bacon, render the fat and brown the diced onions in it lightly. Remove the seeds from the peppers, cut into strips and add to the onions in the pan, together with the diced mushrooms and potatoes and the garlic. Season with salt and paprika and pour in a little ham stock. Cook gently until the potatoes are soft. Lastly add the diced ham, mix well and cook gently in the oven for a further 10–15 minutes.

Czechoslovakia

Ham medallions with artichoke hearts

Yield: 6

180 g	lean cooked ham	6 oz
60 g	foie gras paste	2 oz
	3 small artichoke hearts	
	6 small salted almonds	
	Madeira jelly	

Cut out 12 oval ham medallions 5½ cm (2 in) long. Pipe a thin layer of foie gras paste on to 6 of them, cover with the other 6 and press down lightly. Decorate each double medallion with half an artichoke heart and place a salted almond on top. Chill thoroughly and coat with Madeira jelly.

Germany

Ham medallions Jeannette

12–15 persons

	30 York ham medallions	
	5 cm (2 in) in diameter	
350 g	chicken mousse	12 oz
1 l	port jelly	1¾ pt

Spread half the ham medallions with chicken mousse and cover with the other half. Decorate the top with truffles, hard-boiled egg white, tarragon, chervil, tomato or pistachio nuts. Glaze with jelly and arrange on a dish with a border of chopped jelly. Serve with mayonnaise if desired.

France

Ham medallions Royal style

	30 York ham medallions	
	5 cm (2 in) in diameter	
350 g	truffled foie gras mousse	12 oz
1 l	port jelly	1¾ pt

Proceed as for ham medallions Jeannette, but use foie gras mousse instead of chicken mousse.

France

Ham and pineapple

5 portions

250 g	Prague ham	8¾ oz
50 g	butter	1¾ oz
	5 slices pineapple	
5 cl	whipped cream	1/12 pt
50 g	roasted almonds, chopped	1½ oz
50 g	icing sugar	1¾ oz

Heat up fairly thick slices of cooked ham in butter and a little canned pineapple juice. Brown the sugar to the amber caramel stage, stir in the pineapple juice, reduce and heat the slices of pineapple in this syrup. Place a slice of pineapple on each slice of ham and coat with the syrup blended with the whipped cream. Sprinkle with the chopped almonds and serve, preferably with curry rice.

Czechoslovakia

Ham roll Gervais

10 persons

200 g	pressed ham (10 slices)	7 oz
500 g	Gervais	1 lb 2 oz
125 g	butter	4 oz
1 dl	sour cream	4 fl oz
	1 level tablespoon grated horseradish	
	1 level tablespoon chopped chives	

Cream the butter, mix with the sieved Gervais, the sour cream, horseradish and chives and season to taste with salt and pepper. Place the slices of ham on grease-proof paper, spread with the Gervais cream, roll up and refrigerate. Trim the ends, cut up the roll and dish.

Austria

Ham roll Hawaii style

2 persons   Baking time: 8 minutes

100 g	raw or cooked ham	4 oz
80 g	veal	3 oz
20 g	ham fat	1 oz
	1 slice pineapple, chopped	
	3 chopped pistachio nuts	
	Cognac	
	paprika	

Pastry

60 g	flour	2 oz
30 g	fat	1 oz
	pinch of salt	
	little cold water	
	egg yolk	

Prepare forcemeat with the veal and ham fat, season to taste with paprika and salt, flavour with Cognac and stir in the pineapple and the pistachio nuts. Trim the slice of ham, which should be 2 mm (about $\frac{1}{10}$ in) thick, spread with the forcemeat and roll up. Work the flour, fat and salt to a paste with a little cold water, pin out, wrap round the ham roll, brush with egg yolk and bake at about 220°C.

The ham roll may be made in any desired size and either served hot or allowed to cool and decoratively cut. The pastry should be allowed to rest before use.

Germany

Ham rolls with pickled melon

	28 thin slices cooked ham	
20 g	each weighing	1 oz
1 kg	pickled melon	$2\frac{1}{4}$ lb
	$\frac{1}{2}$ melon	
	15 sheets gelatine	
	small semicircles of cooked ham	
	small disks of truffle	
	finely diced pineapple sprinkled with very fine green pepper	
	julienne, on small bases of finely chopped prunes	
	skinned, seeded tomato slices filled with finely diced green asparagus sprinkled with fine red pepper julienne	
	boat shapes of skinned seeded tomato filled with a melon ball topped by a tiny dot of truffle	
	aspic jelly	

Reduce the pickled melon* to a purée and mix with the gelatine which has been soaked, squeezed dry and dissolved. When on the point of setting, pipe part of the purée on to a metal tray to a thickness of barely $1\frac{1}{2}$ cm ($\frac{1}{2}$ in), using a savoy bag fitted with a plain pipe, smooth off and refrigerate until set. Remove the flesh from the half melon without damaging the skin. Place a cutter of suitable size just inside the melon shell, fill with the rest of the melon purée and refrigerate until set. Carefully remove the cutter so that the melon resembles a soufflé, cover the top with a ring of ham semicircles decorated with tiny disks of truffle and glaze with aspic. Detach the piped melon purée from the metal tray and cut into pieces $8\frac{1}{2}$ cm ($3\frac{1}{2}$ in) long. Place one of these on each slice of ham, which should be 13 cm ($5\frac{1}{2}$ in) long and $8\frac{1}{2}$ cm ($3\frac{1}{2}$ in) wide, and roll up.

Coat a large round dish with aspic jelly and allow to set. Place the half melon in the centre and surround with the tomato boats. Arrange the ham rolls to a rhomboid shape and edge the dish on one side with the prune bases covered with pineapple, and on the other with the stuffed tomato slices. Brush the ham rolls lightly with aspic jelly which is on the point of setting.

* Pickled melon:

1 kg	small melons	2¼ lb
⅛ l	white wine vinegar	¼ pt
¼ l	water	½ pt
310 g	sugar	12 oz
15 g	English mustard powder	1 teaspoon

Place the vinegar, water, sugar and mustard powder in a pan, bring to the boil and allow to cool. Pour over the melons which have been cut into four and seeded, then leave to stand for 24 hours. Drain on a colander and reduce the liquid until thick enough to form large drops. Add the melons and reduce the liquid again until a thick syrup is obtained. Place the melons in an earthenware jar and pour in the syrup to cover completely.

(Illustration, p. 810)   Switzerland

Ham and shrimps

5 persons

250 g	ham	9 oz
200 g	picked shrimps	7 oz
100 g	butter	3 oz
30 g	chopped onion	1 oz
50 g	tomato ketchup	2 oz
250–300 g	fresh tomatoes	8–10 oz
	chopped dill or parsley	

Cut the ham into 5 thick slices and brown lightly in butter. Fry the chopped onion without colouring, add the picked shrimps, brown lightly, then add the ketchup and cook slowly under cover. Skin the tomatoes, cut them in half, remove the seeds and chop coarsely. Cook gently under cover in butter until all the liquid has boiled away, then add salt to taste and a pinch of sugar. Cover the slices of ham with the shrimps, garnish with a little cooked tomato pulp and sprinkle with chopped dill or parsley.

Czechoslovakia

Ham stuffed with scrambled egg and brains

5 portions

250 g	ham	8 oz
50 g	fat bacon	2 oz
	5 eggs	
150 g	calf's brains	5 oz
150 g	hard cheese	5 oz
25 g	butter	1 oz
	tomato purée	
	1 tablespoon chopped parsley	

Dice the bacon and render the fat. Add the brains which have been soaked, blanched, cleaned and chopped, and brown them in the fat for a short time. Pour in the beaten eggs, season with salt, add the chopped parsley and cook until the eggs are lightly set, stirring meanwhile. Cut the ham into very thin slices, spread with the scrambled eggs, roll up and place in buttered individual fireproof dishes. Top with a thin slice of cheese covered with a little tomato purée. Stand the dishes in a hot oven or under a salamander for a few moments, until the cheese has melted.

Czechoslovakia

Ham Znojmo style

5 portions

250 g	Prague ham	8 oz
100 g	butter	3 oz
150 g	Znojmo pickled cucumbers	5 oz
50 g	mushrooms	$1\frac{3}{4}$ oz
	2 egg yolks	
$\frac{1}{4}$ l	dairy cream	$\frac{1}{2}$ pt
	chopped dill	

Fry fairly thick slices of ham in a third of the butter. Peel the cucumbers and cut into small strips, slice the mushrooms and toss in the rest of the butter over gentle heat. Pour in 2 dl ($\frac{1}{3}$ pt) cream, add 1 tablespoon chopped dill and cook gently until soft. Beat the rest of the cream and the egg yolks together and blend with the cucumber and mushroom mixture to thicken. Check the flavour, adding seasoning to taste, and pour over the slices of ham.

Czechoslovakia

Montanchez ham Pepe-Hillo style

4 persons

	4 thin slices lean Montanchez (salted) ham cut from the	
100 g	centre, each weighing	4 oz
	8 slices day-old brown bread, 1 cm (about $\frac{1}{2}$ in) thick	
	2–3 eggs	
500 g	ripe tomatoes	1 lb
	1 clove of garlic	
500 g	potatoes	1 lb
200 g	shelled peas	8 oz
$\frac{1}{4}$ l	sherry or Manzanilla	$\frac{1}{2}$ pt
$\frac{3}{4}$ l	olive oil	$1\frac{1}{4}$ pt
$\frac{1}{4}$ l	milk	$\frac{1}{2}$ pt
	salt	

Cut each slice of ham in half evenly. Steep in milk for 30 minutes to remove excess salt (though the ham is just sufficiently salted to be eaten as it is). Soften the slices of bread a little with the milk in which the ham has been steeped, then dip in beaten egg and fry in oil on both sides.

Scald and skin the tomatoes, remove the seeds and chop coarsely. Place 80 g ($2\frac{3}{4}$ oz) finely diced fat cut from the same ham in a frying pan with a little oil and fry until it changes colour, then add the tomatoes, season with salt, stir in a spoonful of sugar to make the sauce less acid and fry until well reduced. Stir in the remaining egg to make a thick concentrated sauce and spread on the fried bread.

Peel and wash the potatoes and dice them fairly coarsely. Fry until soft and golden-brown, then drain. Cook the peas, drain at once and toss in a sauté pan in the oil left over after frying the bread. Mix with the fried potatoes and season with salt.

When about to serve, fry the 8 slices of ham on both sides over fierce heat. Remove, pour the wine into the fat remaining in the pan and reduce to half its volume. Add $\frac{1}{4}$ l ($\frac{1}{2}$ pt) meat gravy or bouillon and reduce for a few seconds. Arrange the 8 slices of bread covered with tomato sauce in a ring on a warmed round or oval dish and place a slice of fried ham on each. Pile the peas and potatoes in the centre. Coat the ham with the rest of the sauce. Serve at once.

Spain

Small dumplings with ham and green salad

8 persons   Cooking time: 10–12 minutes

600 g	flour	1¼ lb
	3 eggs	
approx. ½ l	milk	¾ pt approx.
30 g	melted butter	1 oz
200 g	cooked ham	8 oz
40 g	butter for frying	2 oz

Sift the flour. Beat the milk well with the eggs, the melted butter and as much salt as required. Add the flour and beat to make a smooth batter. Drop into boiling salted water either through a special 'Nockerl' sieve or with the aid of two teaspoons. Simmer for 5 minutes and rinse in cold water. Cut up the ham finely and brown lightly in the butter. Drain the dumplings well and add, season with a little salt, toss in the fat, transfer to a fireproof dish and place in a hot oven for a few minutes to heat right through. Serve with green salad in season.

N.B.—If desired, the chopped ham may be worked into the dumpling batter.

Austria

York ham cones Lucullus

8 persons

	4 slices York ham	
300 g	foie gras mousse	10 oz
½ l	aspic jelly	¾ pt
20 g	truffles	1 oz
750 g	Russian salad	1½ lb
	1 hard-boiled egg	

Shape the ham into cones. Fill with foie gras mousse and smooth down. Decorate the mousse with tiny crescents of truffle and hard-boiled egg white which have been dipped in half-set jelly, alternating the colours to make an attractive design. Keep in a cool place.

Shape the Russian salad into a round base in the centre of a dish. Coat the rest of the dish with aspic jelly. When set, place the ham cones on the base with their tips meeting in the centre. Stand small lozenges of York ham round the edge of the base with a small disk of truffle at the top of each.

France

York ham cones Russian style

8 persons

	4 slices York ham	
1 kg	Russian salad	2 lb 3 oz
	2 tomatoes	
¼ l	aspic jelly	½ pt

Shape the ham into cones, fill with Russian salad and smooth down. Shape the rest of the Russian salad into a round base on a serving dish. Place the ham cones on top with their tips pointing towards the centre. Glaze the top of the cones by brushing with half-set aspic jelly. Edge the dish with slices of tomato and arrange a sprig of chervil next to these, spreading the leaves out well.

France

POULTRY

CHICKEN

HOT DISHES

Ballottines White Russian style

4 persons   Cooking time: 18–20 minutes

	4 chicken legs	
	4 slices white bread	
4 cl	milk	2 tablespoons
50 g	chicken liver	2 oz
50 g	onions, diced	2 oz
30 g	butter	1 oz
	4 teaspoons sour cream	
	grated nutmeg	

Skin the drumsticks, but leave the skin attached at the end. Chop off the bone with the flesh on it, then cut the flesh off and mince, using the finest cutter. Soak the bread in the milk and mince twice, using the finest cutter. Fry the onion in the butter until lightly coloured, add the chicken liver which has been blanched in hot water for a moment and drained, and fry slowly for 5 minutes. Allow the liver to cool, chop finely and mix with the minced chicken, adding the onion and bread. Season with salt and pepper, flavour with grated nutmeg, mix well again, fill into the drumstick skins and sew up. Spread with the sour cream and roast in the oven at about 180°C.

Russia

Boned stuffed chicken

4 persons   Cooking time: 1½ hours

	1 medium-sized chicken
	1 hard-boiled egg

655

freshly cooked garden peas
grilled sweet peppers, skinned,
    seeded and finely cut
grilled tomatoes, skinned,
    seeded and chopped
raisins
pistachio nuts
almonds
peanuts
onions
parsley

Sauce

butter
paprika
red pepper
ground aniseed

Bone the chicken, working from the back and being careful not to damage the skin. Blanch the parsley to remove its rather bitter flavour, squeeze dry and chop together with the raisins, almonds, pistachio nuts, peanuts and onions. Mix with the tomatoes, peppers and peas and keep hot. Add salt to taste, mix well again, place the hard-boiled egg (shelled) in the centre and mould into a ball. Fill into the chicken and sew up.

Mix all the ingredients for the sauce, add salt to taste, then cook the chicken in the sauce for 30 minutes, basting frequently. Baste well again, then cook in the oven for a further hour at about 180°C with even top and bottom heat. Serve at once garnished with various vegetables and with hard-boiled eggs.

Tunisia

Braised chicken

1 chicken
½ cup vinegar
2 cups water
2 cups sliced onions
5 slices ginger
or
2–3 small spoons ground ginger
5 peppercorns
5 coriander seeds
a little mace
salt, oil

Cut up the chicken and boil in the water and vinegar. Remove the pieces of chicken and brown in oil. Add the bouillon, onions and spices and braise over very gentle heat.

Holland/Indonesia

Chicken curry

4 persons

	1 chicken, jointed	
	1 onion, finely minced	
	2 cloves of garlic, finely minced	
	3–4 fresh or canned chillies, cut lengthwise	
	1 teaspoon ground turmeric	
	1 dessertspoon ground coriander	
½ l	coconut milk, curds or yoghurt	¾ pt
	3 tablespoons yoghurt	
15 g	butter or margarine	1 oz
	lemon juice	

Melt the butter or margarine and add all the remaining ingredients except the chicken, coconut milk, yoghurt and lemon juice. Fry for 3 minutes, then add the chicken and the coconut milk. Simmer gently until the chicken is tender. Add the yoghurt, salt and lemon juice and simmer for a further 5 minutes. The pan should be uncovered throughout.

Commercial curry powder may be substituted for the curry spices.

India

Chicken Georgian style

4 persons   Cooking time: 20–30 minutes

	4 small chickens	
	8 cloves of garlic	
50 g	melted butter	2 oz
	4 tomatoes	
100 g	spring onions	4 oz
2 dl	Tkemali sauce (made with sour plums)	⅓ pt
	or garlic sauce	
	dill	
	parsley	

21

Clean, draw and wash the chickens. Cut open down the back, open out flat and dry well. Rub well on both sides with garlic, season with salt and pepper and place in a frying pan containing hot butter. Cover with a weighted lid to keep the chickens flat. When well browned on one side, turn and brown on the other side. Garnish with parsley and dill and serve the tomatoes, spring onions and Tkemali or garlic sauce separately.

To make garlic sauce, crush 3–4 cloves of garlic, pour over 1 dl ($\frac{1}{6}$ pt) hot meat or chicken stock and leave to stand for 2–3 hours.

Russia

Chicken goulash Szeged style

15 persons

3 kg 500	chicken	7$\frac{1}{2}$ lb
200 g	lard	8 oz
300 g	onions	12 oz
	1 large clove of garlic	
35 g	mild paprika	1 oz
50 g	tomato purée	2 oz
200 g	letcho	8 oz
100 g	carrots	4 oz
100 g	celeriac	4 oz
100 g	leeks	4 oz
1 kg 500	potatoes	3$\frac{1}{4}$ lb
	caraway seeds	

Cut up the chicken as for fricassée and add the livers together with the cut-up gizzards. Slice the onions and garlic finely; dice the carrots, leeks and celeriac. Fry the onions in the lard until lightly coloured, add the garlic and flavour with caraway seeds. Remove from the heat, sprinkle with the paprika, add the pieces of chicken, season with salt, stir well and fry lightly. Now stir in the diced vegetables, the tomato purée and letcho and, lastly, the finely diced potatoes. Pour in sufficient water to leave 3 dl ($\frac{1}{2}$ pt) per person at the end of the cooking time, then simmer until cooked. Adjust the seasoning before serving.

It is customary to add a few small squares of pasta when cooking this dish.

Hungary

Chicken à la king

6 persons

750 g	boned poached breast of chicken	1 lb 8 oz

	2 green peppers	
200 g	raw button mushrooms	8 oz
3 dl	dairy cream	½ pt
50 g	butter	2 oz
	3 egg yolks	
⅛ l	dry sherry	5 fl oz
	1 small truffle (optional)	
	paprika	

Skin the breast of chicken and cut on the slant into small thin slices. Cut the green peppers in half, remove the seeds and cut into fairly thick strips (they should preferably be lightly grilled and skinned beforehand). Soften in butter in a sauté pan, add the cleaned and finely sliced mushrooms, sprinkle lightly with salt and cook until soft. Pour in ¼ l (about ⅓ pt) cream and reduce slightly. Add the sliced chicken, season with paprika and heat without allowing the liquid to come to the boil. Mix the egg yolks with the sherry and the rest of the cream and stir into the pan after removing from the heat. Do not cook any longer. Transfer to a fireproof dish, and serve with rice Creole, or dish on slices of toast. Sprinkle with strips of truffle if desired.

There are many variations of this dish, but it is always thickened with egg yolks, sherry and cream.

Germany

Chicken Maryland

	4 suprêmes of chicken
	1 small tin sweet corn
	2–3 tablespoons thick
	sauce Béchamel
	2 eggs
	white breadcrumbs
	4 small tomatoes
	4 very small bananas
	4 rashers of bacon
	parsley
	horseradish sauce
	flour

Flatten the suprêmes slightly and dip in flour, beaten eggs and breadcrumbs. Drain the sweet corn, bind with thick sauce Béchamel, add an egg yolk, and season with salt and pepper. When the mixture is cold, shape into small flat croquettes, dip in beaten egg and coat with breadcrumbs. Skin and halve the bananas and sauté them in butter. Grill the tomatoes. Fry the chicken pieces in deep oil until golden and arrange on a dish. Garnish with the corn fritters, bananas, fried bacon and grilled tomatoes. Serve the horseradish sauce.

Chicken Mexican style

15–16 persons   Cooking time: about 40 minutes

	3 young roasting chickens	
1 kg	each weighing	2¼ lb
50 g	flour	2 oz
	2 medium onions, chopped	
1 dl	oil	3 fl oz
50 g	butter	2 oz
	3 ripe tomatoes	
100 g	raisins	4 oz
100 g	stuffed olives	4 oz
	1 piece cinnamon quill	
	3–4 cm (1½ in) long	
	chicken broth	

Cut each chicken into 10 pieces. Prepare 1 l (1¾ pt) chicken broth from the giblets and the usual pot-herbs. Season the pieces of chicken with salt and pepper, coat with flour, removing any excess, and brown in hot oil. Remove from the pan, pour away the oil, add the butter and fry the chopped onions in it until lightly coloured. Return the chicken to the pan, add the raisins which have been soaked and drained, the peeled, seeded and chopped tomatoes, and the stuffed olives. Pour in just enough chicken broth to cover, place a lid on the pan and cook slowly until tender. Add the cinnamon shortly before the end of the cooking time and remove before serving. Transfer the chicken, the well-reduced stock and the remaining ingredients to a heatproof dish and keep hot. Serve rice with mushrooms, or sweet corn, and avocado and black olive salad as accompaniments.

USA

Chicken paprikash with sour cream

10 persons

4 kg	chicken (about 4 birds)	8½ lb
200 g	lard	8 oz
200 g	onions	8 oz
30 g	mild paprika	1 oz
200 g	green peppers	8 oz
100 g	tomatoes	4 oz
½ l	sour cream	¾ pt
3 dl	fresh cream	½ pt
50 g	flour	2 oz
	little bone stock	

Draw the chickens, wash thoroughly and cut up as for fricassée. Slice the onions finely, fry in the lard until golden, remove from the heat and stir in the paprika. Add the pieces of chicken, mix well, season with salt and fry for a moment. Add the seeded diced peppers, together with the skinned and seeded tomatoes cut into quarters, and stir well over the heat. Pour in a little bone stock or water and simmer. When the chicken is nearly tender, remove from the cooking liquid, pour in the fresh and sour cream into which the flour has been blended, return the chicken to the pan and continue cooking for a short time. Serve with freshly boiled dumplings.

Hungary

Chicken pörkölt

10 persons

2 kg	2 cocks (old) each weighing	$4\frac{1}{2}$ lb
300 g	lard	10 oz
300 g	onions	10 oz
	1 large clove of garlic	
40 g	mild red paprika	$1\frac{1}{2}$ oz
	few tomatoes	
	little letcho	

Clean, draw and joint the birds. Cut up the legs, breast and back evenly, season with salt and brown lightly in lard. Slice the onions thinly, fry lightly in lard in a large saucepan without colouring, remove from the heat and sprinkle with the paprika. Add the pieces of chicken, the garlic, a few tomatoes cut up finely and a little letcho. Braise slowly without adding liquid. Cock is drier than other types of chicken, but the juices obtained from it are thicker and meatier.

Hungary

Fried chicken

4 persons

750 g	chicken, cleaned and drawn	1 lb 10 oz

Marinade

4 tablespoons soya sauce
1 tablespoon sugar
2 tablespoons saké
3 tablespoons cornflour
vegetable oil for frying
sansho* or mustard

* Sansho: Japanese spice made from the leaf of the prickly ash.

Bone the chicken completely, remove the skin and cut the flesh into 4 cm (1½ in) pieces. Pour the marinade over and leave for 30 minutes. Remove the chicken from the marinade, roll in the cornflour and deep fry until crisp in vegetable oil at 190°C (this will take about 3 minutes). Serve with sansho or mustard.

Japan

Fried chicken with sesame seeds

2 persons

200–300 g	boned chicken wings	7–10 oz
	2 tablespoons saké	
	½ teaspoon salt	
	oil	
	1 teaspoon sesame seeds	
	2–3 lettuce leaves	
	ginger or celery	

Cut open the chicken wings at the thickest point and marinate for 15 minutes in the saké to which the salt has been added. Heat the oil in a frying pan, brown the wings in it on both sides and remove from the pan. Heat the sesame seeds in a pan and sprinkle on the fried wings. Dish on lettuce leaves with a garnish of fresh young ginger shoots or celery.

Pork or beef may be used instead of chicken wings.

Japan

Grilled chicken

Remove the entrails from the chicken and split down the centre of the breast bone with a very sharp knife. Remove the breast bone. Flatten the chicken to give it a regular shape and more even surface. Insert the drumsticks into the skin. Brush the chicken with melted butter or oil, sprinkle with salt and pepper and put on a greased grid. Cook under a moderate heat for 15 minutes turning to other side for a further 15 minutes or until tender. Serve garnished with watercress.

Rice with chicken and egg

4 persons

250 g	raw chicken, skinned and boned	8 oz
	4 dried mushrooms	
	3 spring onions	
	4 eggs	

	1 large sheet nori*	
	4 tablespoons saké	
5 cl	soya sauce	2 fl oz
50 g	sugar	2 oz
	3 tablespoons mirin	
1½ dl	water	¼ pt
	cooked rice	

Soak the mushrooms in water, wash and cut into strips. Dice the chicken. Remove the green part of the spring onions and cut each one into four. Place the saké, soya sauce, sugar, mirin and water in a saucepan, heat almost to boiling point and draw aside. Place enough chicken, mushrooms and onion for 1 person in a small pan and pour over a quarter of the saké sauce. Simmer for a few minutes until the sauce becomes frothy. Add 1 beaten egg and a little salt, cover and poach gently until cooked. Repeat for each portion. To serve, fill donburi bowls† with cooked rice, cover with the chicken and egg mixture and sprinkle with thin strips of nori.

Japan

* Nori: purple laver, a dried edible black seaweed.
† Donburi: deep china bowl with lid in which individual portions are served.

Roast chicken with stuffing

Wash the inside of the chicken and dry thoroughly. Fill at the neck end with stuffing. To add flavour an onion or a wedge of lemon can be put in the body of the bird or a knob of butter. Brush the chicken with melted butter or oil and sprinkle with salt and pepper. Put in a shallow roasting tin in a fairly hot oven. A few strips of streaky bacon can be put over the breast to prevent dryness during cooking. Allow 20 minutes to each pound plus 20 minutes. The chicken can be wrapped in foil before roasting, joining the foil at the top so it can be opened for the final 20 minutes for the bird to brown.

Stuffing

120 g	fresh breadcrumbs	4 oz
60 g	bacon or ham chopped	2 oz
	1 teaspoon chopped parsley	
60 g	suet	2 oz
	rind of ½ lemon grated	
	½ teaspoon mixed herbs	
	salt and pepper	
	beaten egg	

Mix all the dry ingredients together and add the beaten egg to bind the mixture.

Sliced chicken oriental style

4 persons   Cooking time: 4–5 minutes

600 g	raw breast of chicken, skinned	1¼ lb
200 g	rice	6 oz
100 g	diced tomatoes	3 oz
100 g	tiny onions	3 oz
100 g	butter	3 oz
½ l	curry sauce	¾ pt
	3 egg yolks	
6 cl	dairy cream	2 fl oz

Either boil the rice until the grains are tender but still firm, or cook as for risotto. Season the diced tomatoes and cook in a little butter. Glaze the onions in butter with a pinch of sugar. Cut the chicken in small thin slices, toss in hot butter over fierce heat for 4 or 5 minutes, then season lightly with salt. Place the rice in a fireproof dish of suitable size and arrange the sliced chicken on top. Cover with the diced tomatoes and the glazed onions. Heat the curry sauce and thicken with the egg yolks mixed with the cream. Pour some sauce over the chicken and the garnish and brown in a brisk oven or under a salamander. Serve the rest of the sauce separately.

Austria

Spatchcocked chicken

1 kg	spring chicken	2¼ lb
100 g	butter	4 oz
	breadcrumbs	
25 g	maître d'hôtel butter	1 oz

Draw and singe the chicken. Chop off the feet above the joint. Cut the breast through the thickest part, starting at the point of the breast and stopping at the wings, so that it is not completely cut through. Flatten the chicken with a heavy knife. This will give it the shape of a toad about to jump. Fix it on a skewer to keep it open. Cook it in butter in a hot oven for about 30 minutes. Coat with butter and breadcrumbs and grill. Arrange on a hot dish, cover with maître d'hôtel butter. Garnish with watercress and straw potatoes.

Barbecued stuffed chicken Bugac style

10 persons   Roasting time: 40–50 minutes, depending on size

3 kg 500	young chickens	7½ lb
200 g	lard, oil or butter	8 oz
300 g	fresh mushrooms	12 oz
150 g	foie gras	4 oz
150 g	tomatoes, skinned and seeded	6 oz
150 g	peppers, seeded	6 oz
300 g	cooked rice	12 oz
200 g	cooked peas	8 oz
100 g	onions, diced	4 oz
	4 eggs	
	2 tablespoons chopped parsley	
400 g	fat bacon (or smoked pork)	1 lb

Fry the onions in the fat until pale golden, add the finely diced mushrooms, tomatoes, peppers and foie gras and fry well. Mix with the cooked rice and peas, season with salt and pepper, add the chopped parsley and, when cold, the beaten eggs. Loosen the chicken skin, pipe in the forcemeat in the usual manner and draw the skin over to enclose it. Sprinkle the chickens with salt, truss, lard with fat bacon, impale on a spit and roast slowly over a glowing hot fire, rotating constantly.

Hungary

Viennese fried chicken

10 persons   Cooking time: about 15 minutes

	5 young chickens	
800 g–1 kg	each weighing	1¾–2¼ lb
	chopped parsley	
	lemon juice	
	flour	
	5 eggs	
500 g	white breadcrumbs	1 lb approx

Garniture

	wedges of lemon	
	parsley	
	fat for frying	

Cut each chicken into quarters, skin, but do not bone. Wash, dry well, season with salt, chopped parsley, lemon juice, then coat with flour, lightly beaten egg and white breadcrumbs. Fry slowly to a light golden colour in fat which should not be too hot. Drain well, arrange on a paper-lined dish and garnish with wedges of lemon and fried parsley. If desired, the chicken livers and the gizzards, previously blanched, may be coated and fried as well to make up the portions. Serve with fresh green salad, especially cabbage lettuce.

(Illustration, p. 926)   Austria

Yakitori

1 cockerel, its liver and gizzard
leeks cut into 3 cm (1 in) lengths
bamboo skewers

Yakitori sauce

500 g	sugar	1 lb
9 dl	mirin (sweet rice wine)	1½ pt
9 dl	soya sauce	1½ pt
15–20 g	cornflour	½–1 oz

Boil the sugar until it caramelises, add the rice wine to obtain the caramel, thicken with the cornflour and blend in the soya sauce.

Bone the cockerel and cut into small pieces without skinning. Cut up the liver and gizzard and skewer separately. Thread alternate pieces of chicken and leek on to skewers. Grill slowly over charcoal, dipping the skewers into the special sauce from time to time to give the chicken an attractive gloss.

Japan

COLD DISHES

Capon Pepita Jimenez style

	1 large capon	
300 g	lean boned veal (as white as possible)	10 oz
750 g	cooked ham	1¾ lb
	1 thin slice fat bacon for larding	
	4 tablespoons tomato concentrate or reduced tomato purée	

½ l	sherry	¾ pt
	4 eggs	
	3 large fleshy sweet peppers	
3 dl	half-whipped cream	½ pt
150 g	threaded egg	5 oz
	1 fairly large truffle	
	12–14 large very red candied morello cherries	
	1 lemon	
100 g	white breadcrumbs	4 oz
	3–4 tablespoons thick Béchamel sauce	
100 g	butter	4 oz
	1 tablespoon flour	
	few mint leaves	
	nutmeg	
	ground pepper	
	salt	

Aspic jelly

	sheet gelatine	
	consommé	
250 g	minced beef	8 oz
	few vegetables	

Trim the capon and cut through the wishbone and the breast bone to separate the two halves of the breast. Cut up the veal and remove any sinews. If necessary, soak in cold water to whiten, then drain well. Mince twice and add 150 g (5¼ oz) cooked ham cut into pieces, together with the breadcrumbs which have been soaked in sherry. Mix to a very fine forcemeat, season with salt, pepper and grated nutmeg and work in 2 egg yolks and 1 sweet pepper cut into fine julienne strips. Mix well with a spatula to a smooth, fairly soft consistency; if the forcemeat is too stiff, adjust with a few spoons of half-whipped cream. Sew up the tail end of the bird, fill with the forcemeat, truss and lard with the bacon. Place in a deep stew pan, cover with bouillon and add a little celery, a glass of sherry and a few mint leaves. Simmer gently until the capon is tender, then allow to cool in the bouillon.

Set aside part of the bouillon for the sauce, strain the rest and use to make fine aspic jelly with the minced beef, a few vegetables, egg white and gelatine. Pour in a small glass of sherry when the jelly is beginning to set.

To make the mousse for the garnish, cut up the rest of the cooked ham, pound in a mortar, mix with the Béchamel sauce and pass through a sieve. Place in a fairly deep glazed dish standing on crushed ice. Add the rest of the peppers, previously chopped (setting aside 10–12 thin rings of pepper for the garnish), half the tomato concentrate, chopped truffle trimmings, a little pepper, about 2 dl (⅓ pt) liquid jelly and most of the cream (keeping a little back for the sauce). Work to a piping consistency. Stand 10–12 small dariole moulds on a fairly deep tray covered with crushed ice. Mask the moulds with aspic jelly and pour a spoonful of jelly into each one. When set, lay a thin ring of sweet pepper on the jelly and place a disk of truffle in the centre. (The rest of the sweet pepper and truffle is chopped and added to the mousse.) Pour a little jelly on top to hold in position. Using a savoy bag fitted with a fairly large plain tube, pipe the ham mousse into the moulds. Fill up with half-set jelly and refrigerate until set.

To make the sauce, melt 70 g (2½ oz) butter in a small pan, add the flour and cook to a blond roux. Add the rest of the bouillon in which the capon was cooked (about ½ l (⅞ pt)), after removing all fat and straining, together with some of the aspic jelly, 2 sheets gelatine previously soaked in cold water, the rest of the tomato concentrate and a little pepper and grated nutmeg to make a very fine sauce. Simmer for 15 minutes, then remove from the heat and stir in 2 egg whites blended with a little lemon juice and the rest of the cream. Strain through a tammy cloth and adjust the seasoning.

To decorate the capon, skin it when cold, cut off the breast, slice it thinly and replace on the carcase to the original shape of the bird. Coat two or three times with cold sauce, allowing each coat to set before proceeding. When firm, decorate the breast and legs with thin slices of truffle dipped in cold liquid jelly. Mark the divisions between the slices of breast with a line of threaded egg. Lastly glaze the capon all over by brushing with cold jelly.

To dish, coat the bottom of an oval silver tray with a 1 cm (½ in) layer of jelly and leave until cold. Place the capon on the tray and mark down the centre with a line of threaded egg. Arrange 6–8 half morello cherries along this line, spacing them evenly.

Turn out the ham mousse moulds and place them round the capon, alternating them with small heaps of threaded egg decorated with half a morello cherry. Finish off with half-moons or triangles of aspic jelly as desired. Refrigerate for at least 15 minutes before serving.

Large chickens, pullets and turkeys are prepared in the same way.

Spain

Chicken Belle de Mai

8 persons   Cooking time: about 50–60 minutes

2 kg 500–3 kg	1 plump pullet weighing	5½–6½ lb
500 g	chicken giblets	1 lb
1 kg	fresh ripe tomatoes	2¼ lb
1 dl	white wine	4 fl oz
	3 eggs	

50 g   foie gras purée   2 oz
                        3 sheets gelatine
                        5–6 tablespoons whipped cream
                        white chaud-froid sauce
                        tomato-flavoured chaud-froid
                              sauce
                        chicken aspic

Prepare concentrated stock with the giblets and strain. Truss the chicken in the usual manner, poach in the stock and allow to cool. Use half the stock to make aspic and the other half for the chaud-froid sauce. When the chicken is cold, remove the skin, cut away the breast on the bone, then remove the two halves of the breast from the bone, cut evenly into 8 slices and trim neatly. Coat the slices with chaud-froid sauce lightly flavoured with tomato, decorate with a lily of the valley motif, using blanched leek for the stalk and hard-boiled egg white for the flowers, and glaze with aspic. Mask the chicken legs and carcass with white chaud-froid sauce, fill the breast cavity with tomato mousse and smooth to a dome shape. Decorate the legs with a simple design and the tomato mousse with a small bunch of lilies of the valley. Glaze the chicken all over with aspic; when it has set, dress the chicken on a large oval or rectangular dish on an ornamental base made of rice. Arrange the slices of breast fanwise in front and place a semicircle of tiny skinned tomatoes (the size of a cherry) stuffed with foie gras behind the chicken, first glazing them with aspic. Edge the dish with chopped aspic and insert an ornamental skewer between the chicken legs.

Tomato mousse

Fry 1 tablespoon finely chopped onion in butter until lightly coloured, pour in 1 dl ($\frac{1}{6}$ pt) white wine and reduce to half its volume. Skin 300 g ($10\frac{1}{2}$ oz) tomatoes, remove all the seeds, chop the flesh and add to the pan, together with salt, pepper and a small bouquet garni (parsley, 1 sprig thyme, half a bay leaf). Cover and simmer gently for 25 minutes. Now add 4 tablespoons velouté and 3 tablespoons light aspic jelly (if not available, 3 sheets gelatine which have been soaked and squeezed dry) and cook for a further 3–4 minutes. Strain through a tammy cloth, check the flavour, allow to cool and blend in 5–6 tablespoons whipped cream.

Chaud-froid sauce

Add 3–4 sheets gelatine and 1 dl ($\frac{1}{6}$ pt) cream to $\frac{1}{2}$ l ($\frac{7}{8}$ pt) well reduced chicken velouté.

Tomato-flavoured chaud-froid sauce

Add 2 tablespoons finely sieved reduced tomato purée to white chaud-froid sauce.

(Illustration, p. 926)   France

Chicken medallions

6 pieces

120 g	breast of fat pullet	4 oz
60 g	ham purée	2 oz
5 g	chopped pistachio nuts	1 teaspoon
	1 seedless orange	
	Calvados-flavoured aspic jelly	

Fry or roast the chicken breast, keeping it juicy, cut into 6 medallions of equal size and trim evenly. Mix the ham purée with the chopped pistachio nuts, pipe on to the medallions, using a plain pipe, and place an orange segment on each one. Refrigerate and glaze fairly thickly with the jelly.

Germany

Cold chicken with fruit

4 persons   Cooking time (chicken): about 50 minutes

1 kg 500–1 kg 800	1 plump pullet weighing	3¼–4 lb
500 g	Waldorf salad	1 lb
	stewed fruit	

Roast the pullet in butter until brown and juicy and allow to cool. When quite cold, remove the meat from the bones and cut up as required. Dish on a base of Waldorf salad and garnish with stewed fruit. Glaze with aspic if desired.

Austria

Suprême of chicken Strasbourg style

12 pieces

breast of a roast pullet
2 parts foie gras parfait
1 part cold sauté chicken livers
chicken chaud-froid sauce
    enriched with white wine
    and dairy cream truffles
chicken aspic jelly

Cut the cold chicken breast into fairly thick slices and then into ovals. Prepare a purée with the foie gras parfait and the chicken livers, season well and spread on the ovals of chicken to a dome shape. When half-set, mask with the chaud-froid sauce and decorate with a truffle motif. When the sauce has set, glaze with aspic and arrange on a round serving dish coated with aspic.

Germany

Suprême of chicken with goose liver medallions

15–16 persons   Cooking time: 50 minutes

	2 fat pullets	
1 kg 500–1 kg 750	each weighing	3¼–5 lb
	pot-herbs	
	1 bouquet garni	
300–400 g	foie gras purée	10–14 oz
	1 small can truffles	
	10–12 round slices foie gras	
	parfait in Madeira jelly	
100 g	butter	4 oz
1 dl	whipped cream	3 fl oz

Chaud-froid sauce

50 g	flour	2 oz
50 g	butter	2 oz
¼ l	chicken broth	½ pt
¼ l	milk	½ pt
⅛ l	dairy cream	¼ pt
	4 sheets gelatine	
5 cl	dry sherry	2 fl oz

Aspic jelly

1 l	chicken broth	1¾ pt
	1 glass white wine	
	16 sheets gelatine	
	2 egg whites	

Poach the pullets and leave in the broth until cold. Prepare white chaud-froid sauce with the strained broth, after removing all fat, the butter, flour, milk and gelatine, seasoning with salt and pepper as required, then strain and finish off with the cream and the sherry. Prepare aspic jelly in the usual manner with 1 l (1¾ pt) chicken broth, the gelatine which has been soaked and squeezed dry, the white wine and the egg whites, and season well; the jelly should be quite clear. Skin the birds and cut off the breasts neatly. Carve 15–16 neat slices off the breast of one bird, trim evenly, spread lightly with foie gras purée and glaze with aspic. Cut away the breastbone of the other bird, fill the cavity with foie gras purée, smoothing it to a dome shape, replace the breast after cutting each half into 6–7 slices, and mask the whole bird, including the legs, with cold chaud-froid sauce.

When half-set, decorate the breast with a truffle motif and neatly glaze the whole bird with aspic. Place on a serving dish of suitable size and surround with a semi-circle of foie gras-coated slices of breast and foie gras medallions. Garnish with diced aspic jelly.

To make the foie gras purée, cream the butter, mix with the purée, season with salt, flavour with pâté spices, adding a little Madeira if desired, and fold in the whipped cream. A richer purée may be made by using twice as much cream; in this case it is advisable to add 2 sheets of gelatine which have been soaked and dissolved.

USA

Suprême of chicken Jeannette

Cold poached suprêmes of chicken, set upon slices of pâté de foie gras, coated with white chicken chaud-froid sauce decorated with tarragon leaves and glazed.

DUCK, GOOSE AND TURKEY

Duck with orange sauce

4–5 persons

1 kg 400–1 kg 500	duckling	3–3½ lb
	8 oranges	
6 dl	demiglace	1 pt
	½ lemon	
	2 lumps sugar	
	few drops vinegar	

Brown the duck, pour off the fat, and cook, covered, in a hot oven and moistened with demiglace. When it is cooked, skim off the fat and strain the sauce. Add the juice of 2 oranges, the juice of half a lemon, the sugar burnt to a caramel, and the rind of 3 oranges, cut into julienne and blanched for 3 minutes in boiling water. Arrange the duck on a long dish, cover with sauce and garnish with orange segments without seeds or skin. Serve the rest of the sauce in a sauce boat. The orange segments may be filled in half oranges, scooped out and serrated.

Duck medallions

Yield: 6 pieces

½ juicy roast duck breast (cold)
½ slice pineapple

60 g	truffled foie gras purée	2 oz
	6 small split salted almonds	
	Madeira jelly	

Cut 6 neat medallions out of the duck breast. Dry the slice of pineapple, glaze on both sides, allow to set and cut evenly into six.

Pipe the foie gras purée on to the duck medallions, using a plain pipe. Cover with a piece of pineapple and place a split salted almond on top. Chill well and glaze with Madeira jelly.

Germany

Duck in melon

4 persons

700 g	1 honeydew melon weighing	1 lb 8 oz
	1 duck, plucked and drawn,	
1 kg 600	weighing	3 lb 8 oz
	1 medium onion	
	1 tablespoon apple purée	
$\frac{1}{4}$ l	dry sherry	$\frac{1}{2}$ pt
$\frac{1}{4}$ l	dry white wine	$\frac{1}{2}$ pt
$\frac{1}{2}$ l	duck giblet stock	$\frac{7}{8}$ pt
	Duchesse potatoes	

Cut the top off the melon, remove the seeds and fibres and half fill with the sherry. Replace the top, place in a pan of suitable size, pour in the wine and cook in the oven. Meanwhile roast the duck briskly, cut off all the meat and cook the bones in the stock for a short time, then reduce the liquid. Fill the melon with the sliced duck, cover and keep hot. Fry the duck liver very lightly and rub through a sieve. Chop the onion and brown lightly in the duck fat remaining in the pan. Pour off the fat, add the stock, stir well to detach the juices, strain, thicken with the liver purée and the apple purée and season well. Dish the melon and decorate with large shaped mushroom caps on a skewer, a truffle or a morel. Hand the sauce and the potatoes separately. When serving, each slice of duck should be accompanied by a little melon.

(Illustration, p. 247) Germany

Honey glazed roast duck

1 kg 500	duck	3 lb
120 g	honey	4 oz
60 g	brown sugar	2 oz
50 ml	white vinegar	2 fl oz

Stab the duck all over with a fork (to allow the fat to come out more easily) and roast in the normal way. Boil the other ingredients, and use to baste the duck during the last 30 minutes of roasting.

Pressed duck

The roast duck, blood rare, is sent to the dining-room together with a purée of the slightly sautéd liver. Legs and breasts are removed from the bones, the breasts cut into thin slices and placed on a warm chafing dish. The legs are sent back to the kitchen to be grilled. The juice and blood of the carcase are extracted in a special duck press. It is warmed up with the mashed liver in a chafing dish seasoned with orange juice, brandy, Madeira or port, salt and a pinch of cayenne pepper but not allowed to boil. Pour over the breasts and warm up until they are sufficiently done. Serve immediately.

Barbecued Aylesbury duckling

Clean a duckling and cut into quarters, trimming away neck, backbone and wing tips. Place on the barbecue about 45 cm (18 in) above glowing embers. Cook steadily for 15 minutes, then turn and cook for a further 15 minutes. About 5 minutes before completing the cooking, baste with Buckinghamshire barbecue sauce.

Jellied goose

6 persons	Cooking time: about 1½ hours	
3 kg	1 goose weighing	6½ lb
	1 medium carrot	
	1 medium onion	
100 g	celeriac	4 oz
	1 bay leaf	
	3 cloves	
	10 allspice seeds	
	8 peppercorns	
15 cl	wine vinegar	¼ pt

Clean the goose very well, singe and draw. Reserve the giblets for use elsewhere. Cover the goose with lightly salted cold water and bring to the boil. Skim well, add the vegetables, vinegar, bay leaf and spices, simmer gently until tender but still firm and allow to cool in the broth. When cold, remove the goose, cut into pieces and bone completely. Strain the broth, skim off the fat and, while still lukewarm, add 12 g (½ oz) gelatine, previously soaked and squeezed dry, per litre (1¾ pt) of broth. Beat up an egg white with a few spoonfuls of broth, pour in the rest of the broth and bring to the boil, beating constantly. Boil up once, cover and draw aside. As soon as the egg white has formed a crust on the top and the jelly has been cleared, carefully strain through a cloth. Arrange the pieces of goose in a glass bowl and cover completely with the jelly as it begins to set, after first checking the taste and adjusting the seasoning. Refrigerate until firm. Serve with fried potatoes, also light rye bread and butter if required.

Germany

Roast goose with cabbage and dumplings

5 portions   Cooking time: geese, 90 minutes; dumplings, 20 minutes

| 1 kg 500–1 kg 800 | 2 geese each weighing | 3¼–4 lb |
| 20 g | flour | 1 oz |

Bread dumplings

750 g	flour	1 lb 10 oz
50 g	butter	2 oz
290 g	white bread	10 oz
	1 egg yolk	
6 dl	milk	1 pt
15 g	baking powder	½ oz

Cabbage

1 kg 500	white cabbage	3¼ lb
50 g	fat or dripping	2 oz
100 g	chopped onions	4 oz
20 g	flour	1 oz
5 cl	vinegar	2 fl oz
	cumin	

Singe and clean the geese well, draw them, season with salt inside and outside, sprinkle with cumin, place in a roasting-tin with a little water and roast until golden-brown. Pour off almost all the dripping, add the flour, cook for a few moments, blend in ½ l (⅞ pt) water, stir well, scraping the sediment off the tin, simmer for about 30 minutes, then strain.

To make the dumplings, sieve the flour with the baking powder and a little salt, then work to a smooth paste with the egg yolk and milk. Add the bread cut into small cubes. Working on a floured table, shape the mixture into oblong rolls weighing 400–500 g (about 1 lb). Poach in boiling salted water, remove, drain well, cut into 2 cm (about ¾ in) slices, arrange in a heated dish and coat with warm melted butter.

Shred the cabbage finely, place in a pan with the chopped onions, salt, vinegar, a little cumin and water, cover and stew until cooked. Pour off the surplus water, prepare a blond roux with the fat and flour and mix with the cabbage. Season to taste with salt, vinegar and a pinch of sugar.

Carve the geese and hand the dumplings, cabbage and sauce separately.

Czechoslovakia

Roast goose with sage and onion stuffing

10 persons

3 kg 500	goose	8 lb
	2 eggs	
700 g	onions	1¾ lb
½ l	apple sauce	1 pt
600 g	fresh breadcrumbs	1½ lb
½ l	stock	1 pt
50 g	butter	2 oz
	watercress	
25 g	sage	1 oz
	milk	
	salt and pepper	

Sauté the chopped onions in butter, mix into the breadcrumbs, previously moistened with milk and squeezed dry. Add the chopped sage, butter and eggs. Add salt, pepper and ½ teaspoon mace, mix well and stuff the goose. Truss the goose, season, and roast in a moderate oven for 2–3 hours. When cooked skim away the fat. Blend flour with the stock and add to the pan residue. Stir and cook until thickened. Season with salt and pepper. Boil and strain. Garnish the goose with watercress. Serve the apple sauce and gravy in sauceboats.

Turkey with chestnut stuffing

12 persons

6 kg	turkey	14 lb
600 g	soft breadcrumbs	1½ lb
800 g	chestnuts	2 lb
	salt and pepper	
800 g	sausage meat	2 lb
5 cl	Cognac	2 fl oz

Make an incision on the convex side of the chestnuts, cover with water and bring to boiling point. Draw pan aside and remove chestnuts one at a time and peel off shells and skins while the chestnuts are hot. Cook in chicken stock for half an hour or until just soft. Drain and chop. Add to the other ingredients and mix well. Stuff the turkey with the forcemeat, truss and roast in a warm oven. Serve with gravy and watercress.

(Techniques, p 123)

Stuffed breast of turkey

14–15 persons

	½ boned turkey breast	
1 kg 500–1 kg 750	weighing	3¼–4 lb
200 g	turkey (white meat only)	8 oz
200 g	lean boned veal	8 oz
200 g	suet (calf's)	8 oz
⅛ l	dairy cream	¼ pt
	1–2 egg whites	
	1 pig's caul	
4 cl	Cognac	4 dessertspoons
	1 bay leaf	
	a few tarragon leaves	
	rosemary	
	forcemeat herbs and spices	
	grated nutmeg	
	green peppers, skinned and cut in half	
	button mushroom caps, marinated	
	stewed peaches	
	preserved chestnuts	
50 g	tongue (tip)	2 oz
50 g	truffles	2 oz
50 g	bacon, blanched	2 oz
50 g	blanched pistachio nuts	2 oz
	butter for roasting	

Trim the turkey breast neatly, carefully removing any tendons, and open out to a long slightly tapering shape by cutting halfway through the thickness of the meat. Beat a little to flatten, place in a bowl with salt, pepper, tarragon leaves, rosemary, a chopped bay leaf and the Cognac, cover and marinate for 2 hours.

Chop the white turkey with the veal and the suet, after removing any gristle, work in the blender, season with salt, grated nutmeg and forcemeat herbs and spices, flavour with the Cognac used for the marinade and bind with 1 or 2 egg whites as required. Do not work in the blender too long or the mixture will curdle. Stir in the diced tongue, truffles, bacon and the pistachio nuts. Stuff the turkey breast with this forcemeat, shape neatly and wrap in the pig's caul which has been well cleaned and soaked. Tie with twine, but not too tightly. Roast at about 180°C for 1½ hours, basting frequently. Remove from the oven, allow to stand for 30 minutes, then weight the top a little and keep under refrigeration overnight.

To serve, cut the stuffed turkey breast into even slices and garnish with halved green peppers, stuffed with marinated button mushroom caps, and wedges of stewed peach topped with preserved chestnuts. If desired, glaze the sliced meat and the garnish with aspic.

Stuffed turkey

15 persons   Cooking time: about 1½ hours

5–6 kg	1 turkey weighing	11–13 lb
150 g	lean pork	5 oz
200 g	green bacon	7 oz
50 g	goose or chicken liver	2 oz
100 g	diced ham	4 oz
100 g	pickled tongue (tip)	4 oz
50 g	pistachio nuts	2 oz
50 g	diced truffle	2 oz
	forcemeat herbs and spices	

Work the pork, bacon and liver in the blender (not too long, or the forcemeat will curdle) and season to taste with salt and forcemeat herbs and spices. Add the diced ham, tongue and truffle as well as the pistachio nuts. Clean the turkey carefully and cut open the breast from the front. Pipe in the forcemeat, using a savoy bag. Season, truss and bard the turkey and roast at 220–250°C. When cold, cut the stuffed breast off the carcase, remove the breastbone, fill with rice salad, etc. and replace the breast cut into even slices. Glaze with aspic if desired.

Austria

MARTINMAS GOOSE DISHES FROM HUNGARY

Martinmas goose

20 persons

6 kg	2 geese each weighing	13 lb 4 oz

Pluck and prepare the geese, clean them thoroughly, draw, wash well and set the giblets aside.

Fried goose liver

600 g	goose liver	1 lb 5 oz
	1 onion	
	1 clove of garlic	

Trim the liver to leave sufficient cuttings for the purée. Fry slowly in its own fat with a little water, the onion and the garlic. When the water has evaporated, make sure that the liver is evenly browned on all sides.

Goose greave puffs

20 puffs

1 kg	flour	2¼ lb
¼ l	milk	½ pt
100 g	yeast	3 oz
	2 eggs	
100 g	goose fat	3 oz
	goose fat greaves	

Make a ferment with the yeast, 50 g (1¾ oz) flour and a little lukewarm milk. Leave to rise, then work to a dough with 800 g (1 lb 12 oz) flour, the eggs, the rest of the milk, the goose fat, salt and pepper and knead well. Stand aside for 15 minutes, then pin out to 1 cm (about ½ in) thick. Mince the greaves, work to a paste together with the fat from them and 150 g (5¼ oz) flour and shape into an oblong. Enclose this in the rolled-out yeast dough, pin out, fold as for puff paste, pin out again, then refrigerate for 1 hour. Repeat the rolling and folding operation, cut out and bake at 240°C.

(Illustration, p 374)

(Techniques, p. 105)

Goose liver purée

200 g	goose liver trimmings	7 oz
200 g	butter	7 oz
	1 small onion	
	goose fat	
	2 bananas, poached but	
	still firm	
	4 stewed cherries	
½ l	chaud-froid sauce	⅞ pt
	sliced truffle	
	hard-boiled egg white	
	aspic jelly	

Slice the onion and fry in goose fat with the goose liver trimmings. Rub through a sieve, work in the butter and season to taste with salt and forcemeat flavouring. Chill well, then mould. Coat with chaud-froid sauce, decorate with egg white cutouts and small slices of truffle, and glaze with aspic jelly. Arrange small thin slices of banana on top of the small moulds in the centre of the dish and top with a stewed cherry.

Goose sausages

> the legs of both geese
> goose fat
> cornflour
> paprika
> goose fat

Skin and bone the legs, remove the sinews, mince the flesh as finely as possible and work to a smooth forcemeat with cornflour, a crushed clove of garlic, eggs, paprika, salt and pepper. Clean the entrails thoroughly and pack with the forcemeat, using a special mini-filler. Twist into small sausages and fry in goose fat.

(Illustration, p 374)

Matzo dumplings

400 g	matzos	14 oz
250 g	goose fat	8 oz
	2 eggs	
	1 tablespoon chopped parsley	

Crumble the matzos. Mix half of them with the goose fat and the eggs, add the parsley and season with salt, pepper and grated nutmeg. Work well, then add the rest of the matzos. If too stiff, stir in a little lukewarm water. Allow to stand for half an hour, then shape into dumplings. Cook in the soup.

Minced goose breast loaf

	breast of 1 goose	
	2 white rolls	
50 g	diced onion	2 oz
	1 tablespoon chopped parsley	
	1 clove of garlic	
	2 eggs	
	white breadcrumbs	
	goose fat	
	marjoram	

Cut the breast off the goose and mince finely. Mix well with the rolls which have been soaked and squeezed dry. Fry the diced onion lightly in goose fat until pale golden and add to the minced goose breast, together with the crushed garlic and the eggs. Season with salt and pepper, flavour with marjoram and the chopped parsley and mix well. If the mixture is too soft, add some white breadcrumbs. Shape into a loaf, brush with egg and cook in the oven at 180°C, basting frequently.

Goose giblet soup

Cooking time: 2 hours

	2 sets of giblets except for the necks	
300 g	carrots	12 oz
300 g	parsley roots	12 oz
100 g	celeriac	4 oz
50 g	onion	2 oz
	1 clove of garlic	
	peppercorns	

Place the giblets in a pan with about 4 l (7 pt) water and a little salt; bring to the boil, skim well, add the vegetables, garlic and a few peppercorns and simmer gently. Remove the vegetables as soon as they are cooked. When the soup is ready, adjust the seasoning, make sure it is well flavoured, remove the fat, strain and garnish with the finely diced vegetables.

Roast breast of goose

breast of the 2nd goose, boned
goose fat
marjoram
thyme

Season the outside of the breast with salt and sprinkle inside with marjoram and thyme. Roast slowly in the same tin as the goose breast loaf.

Stuffed goose neck

Pluck out any feathers remaining in the skin of the necks, remove the skins, wash well and clean thoroughly. Fill with minced goose and cornflour forcemeat (as for goose sausages), sew up both ends or fix in place with toothpicks, and roast slowly together with the goose breast loaf.

FOIE GRAS

Apricots with foie gras parfait

120 g	foie gras parfait	4 oz
60 g	chopped truffles	2 oz
	6 firm medium-sized apricot halves (canned)	
	or	
	6 ripe fresh apricot halves	
	Madeira jelly	

Shape the foie gras parfait into 6 balls of equal size and roll in the chopped truffles to cover completely. Place each ball in the centre of a well-drained apricot half and chill thoroughly. Lastly glaze with Madeira jelly.

Germany

Brioche slices Strasbourg style

These are slices of foie gras in brioche on a dish covered with a napkin or paper doyley. The foie gras in the centre of each is decorated with truffle and glazed with aspic.

France

Foie gras in aspic

Mask individual moulds or a large fancy mould with sherry-flavoured aspic jelly. Decorate the bottom and sides, place cooked truffled foie gras in the mould and fill up with half-set jelly. Refrigerate before unmoulding.

The jelly should be absolutely clear and very pale in colour.

(Illustration, p. 919)

France

Foie gras in brioche I

20–25 persons   Cooking time: about 45 minutes

800 g–1 kg	1 foie gras weighing	1¾–2¼ lb
700 g	plain brioche dough	1½ lb
½ l	port jelly	¾ pt

Prepare and cook the foie gras as directed in the recipe for foie gras in port jelly, but poach for only 15–18 minutes and leave until quite cold before using. Pin out the brioche dough and cut out 2 ovals a little longer than the foie gras. Place one of them on a baking-sheet, put the foie gras in the centre, cover with the rest of the dough and seal the edges. Trim neatly, prove, wash the top with egg and bake in a medium oven. Cool on a rack. Cut a hole in the top and pour in half-set port jelly. Refrigerate for at least an hour. Serve sliced or whole on a napkin or fancy paper.

The foie gras may be cooked in a buttered mould lined with brioche dough.

France

Foie gras in brioche II

Shape the brioche dough into a long loaf, or deposit in a cylindrical tin, and bake. Refrigerate a can of foie gras for 2 or 3 hours, then open and leave the foie gras in a cool place. Cut the brioche and the foie gras into slices of equal thickness. Cut out the centre of each slice of brioche (using the empty foie gras can if desired) and fill the cavity with a slice of foie gras. Coat the foie gras only with jelly.

France

Foie gras medallions Tosca

Yield: 6

120 g	foie gras parfait	4 oz
120 g	cooking apples	4 oz
	3 morello cherries	
	pistachio nuts	
	aspic jelly	
	Calvados	
	sugar	
	cinnamon	
	lemon juice	
	white wine	

Peel and core the apples and cut out 6 round slices 4½ cm (1¾ in) across and 1 cm (½ in) thick. Poach in white wine with the addition of a pinch of sugar and cinnamon and a little lemon juice, keeping the slices fairly firm, and allow to cool in the cooking liquid.

Cut out 6 rounds of foie gras parfait of equal size. Drain the apple slices well, wipe dry and place a foie gras medallion on each. Decorate with half a morello cherry and a strip of pistachio nut arranged close beside it on the slant. Glaze each medallion with Calvados-flavoured jelly and chill well.

Germany

Foie gras mousse

250 g	cooked foie gras	8 oz
15 cl	Madeira or port jelly	¼ pt
1 dl	dairy cream	3 fl oz
5 cl	unboiled milk	1 fl oz

Rub the foie gras through a fine sieve and blend in the jelly which has been reduced to 1 dl (⅙ pt) and left until cold but still liquid. Beat well on ice with a spatula and fold in the whipped cream together with the milk. Season to taste with salt and white pepper. Keep cool.

France

Foie gras mousselines I

Mask small dariole moulds with aspic jelly. Decorate the bottom of the moulds with truffle, chervil or tarragon motifs, cover with a thin layer of jelly and refrigerate until set. Fill with foie gras mousse and cover with half-set jelly. Return to the refrigerator and unmould when about to serve.

(Illustration, p. 919)   France

Foie gras mousselines II

Mould the cold mousse to the shape of eggs with the aid of a dessertspoon repeatedly dipped into hot water. Decorate and glaze with aspic. Serve in a glass bowl on a bed of aspic or lettuce leaves.

The aspic jelly for mousselines may be flavoured with sherry.

France

Foie gras in port jelly

Approx. 20 persons   Cooking time: 25–30 minutes

800 g–1 kg	1 foie gras weighing	$1\frac{3}{4}$–$2\frac{1}{4}$ lb
50 g	truffles	2 oz
2 dl	Cognac	$\frac{1}{3}$ pt
2 l	very strong port jelly	$3\frac{1}{2}$ pt
	1 pig's caul	

Clean and trim the liver, removing the fibres. Stud with pieces of truffle. Season with salt, pepper and a dash of cayenne pepper. Place in a dish, pour the Cognac over, cover and marinate for at least 2 or 3 hours. Drain the liver and wrap in the caul, compressing the liver a little, then wrap somewhat more tightly in muslin. Tie the ends securely as close to the liver as possible. Simmer gently in the jelly at about 95°C. Allow to cool a little in the jelly, then remove the muslin and replace, compressing the liver at both ends. Return to the pan containing the jelly and leave until quite cold, then remove and refrigerate for about 10 hours. Unwrap and trim the liver slightly. Slice and arrange the slices to the original shape of the liver on a serving dish or in an oval glass bowl. Clarify the jelly in which the liver was cooked and coat the liver with it. Decorate with truffles.

This dish is sometimes called 'Delice des Landes'.

France

Foie gras shells

Cut foie gras into shell shapes, using a sharpened spoon dipped in hot water. Arrange on a bed of diced Madeira jelly with a few neat slices of truffle in between.

Switzerland

Foie gras terrine

(see p. 355)

Foie gras Yugoslav style

Cooking time: about 45 minutes

	1 large fatted goose liver	
1 kg 500	weighing	$3\frac{1}{4}$ lb
1 kg	lard	$2\frac{1}{4}$ lb
	milk for soaking	
$\frac{1}{2}$ l	milk	$\frac{7}{8}$ pt

Prepare the liver by removing all gall stains, nerves and blood clots and pulling out the bundle of nerve fibres. Leave it in milk overnight, compressed to its original shape, making sure that the milk covers it completely. Remove, dry well in a cloth and fry lightly in the lard, pressing it down well on to the base of the pan. Pour in the $\frac{1}{2}$ l ($\frac{7}{8}$ pt) milk and cook slowly until there is no trace of blood when a needle is inserted. Leave in the lard until cold and serve as it is. This dish is always served cold.

If desired, a little garlic may be added to the lard when frying the liver.

Yugoslavia

Fresh foie gras tart 'Parc des Eaux-Vives'

6–8 persons   Baking time: about 20–25 minutes

300–400 g	short pastry for lining tarts	10–14 oz
100–150 g	fresh truffles, finely sliced	3–5 oz
approx. 500 g	fresh duck foie gras	1 lb approx.
100 g	morel duxelles	4 oz
	quiche filling made with 3 eggs and 4 dl ($\frac{2}{3}$ pt) dairy cream, and flavoured with truffle liquor	

The day before they are required, poach the duck livers in very good, slightly oxidised dry white wine, together with a very finely cut mirepoix, a small bouquet garni, salt and peppercorns. Simmer very gently at about 80°C for 15 minutes. Allow to cool in the cooking liquid.

Next day, line a tart mould with the pastry, spread with the duxelles and place the sliced truffles on top. Cover with the foie gras cut into fairly thick slices and pour the quiche filling over. Bake for about 20–25 minutes.

Switzerland

GAME

VENISON

HOT DISHES

Brochettes hunter's style

20 portions   Cooking time: 6–8 minutes

2 kg	haunch of venison	4¼ lb
1 kg 500	breast of pheasant	3¼ lb
1 kg	larding bacon or pork fat	2¼ lb
100 g	truffles	4 oz
8 dl	oil	1¼ pt
300 g	maître d'hôtel butter	10 oz
1 l	cream sauce	1½ pt
	bay leaves	

Remove all the sinews from the haunch of venison and cut 4 fairly small medallions per portion. Lard, season with salt and pepper and marinate in oil for a short time. Cut 3 pheasant breast medallions per portion, making them the same size as the venison medallions, stud them with strips of truffle, season with salt and pepper and spread with maître d'hôtel butter. Wrap the venison medallions in paper-thin slices of bacon and thread on to skewers alternately with the pheasant medallions and a few bay leaves. Fry quickly on all sides in hot oil, remove, drain off the oil and cook for a few minutes in the maître d'hôtel butter. Serve the cream sauce and mixed salad separately.

Czechoslovakia

Haunch of venison in wine with stewed cranberries

10 portions   Cooking time: about 90 minutes

3 kg	1 haunch of roc-deer weighing	6½ lb

688

▲ Fillets of sole in aspic, p. 447

▼ Fish Bouchée, Mushroom Bouchée, p. 202

690
▲ A Swedish dinner party, p. 490
▼ Summer buffet in Sweden, Crayfish with dill, p. 526

▲ Decorated cold salmon

▼ Cold stuffed turbot, p. 115

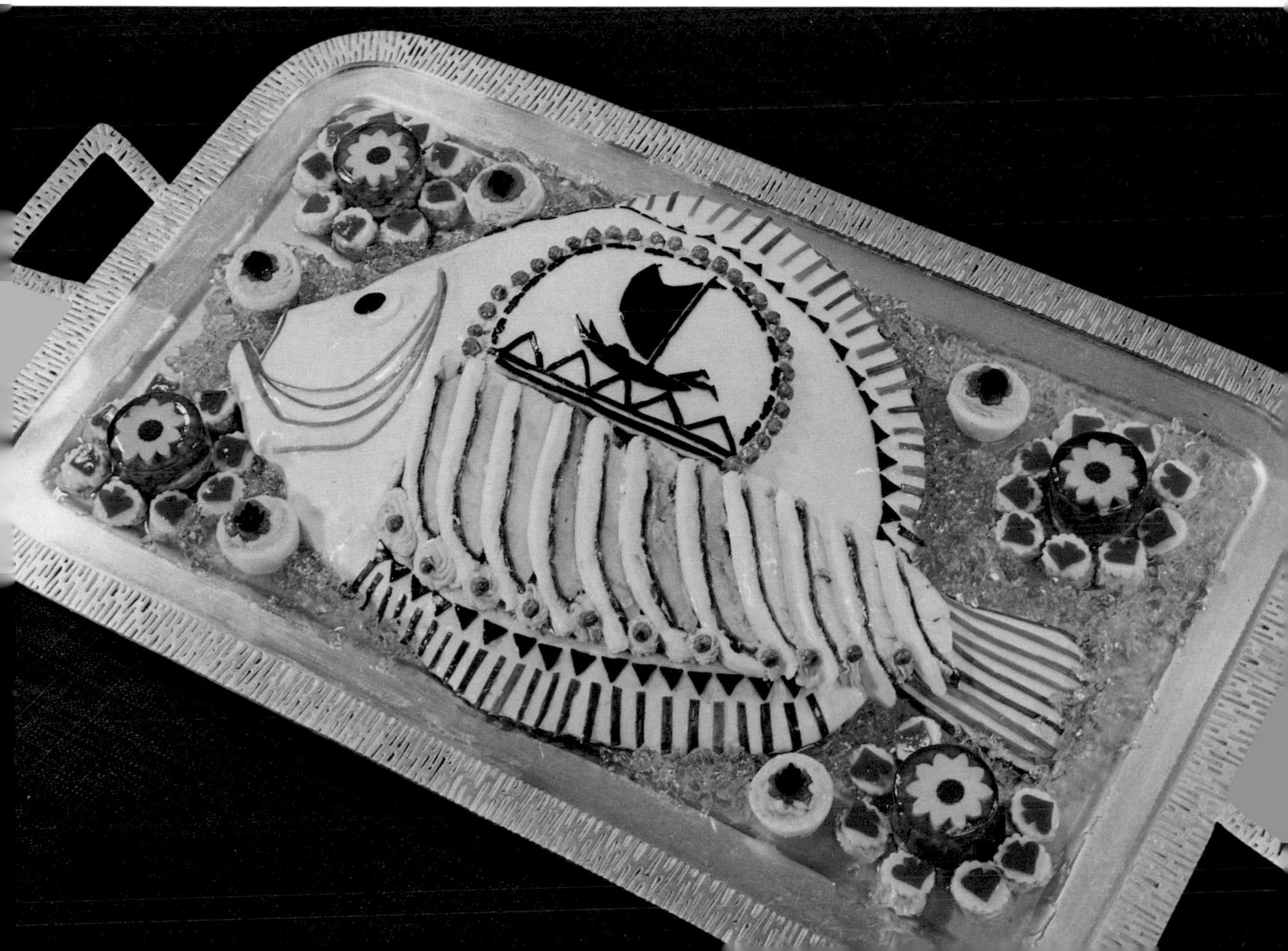

692 ▲ Salmon mousse pie Neptune
▼ Poached salmon with scampi, p. 511

▲ Cold salmon with Crayfish Bombe, p. 528
▶ Snail mould Sir Sigbert, Snail salad, Snails in butter, p. 350
▼ Trout en Bellevue, WIKA 1974

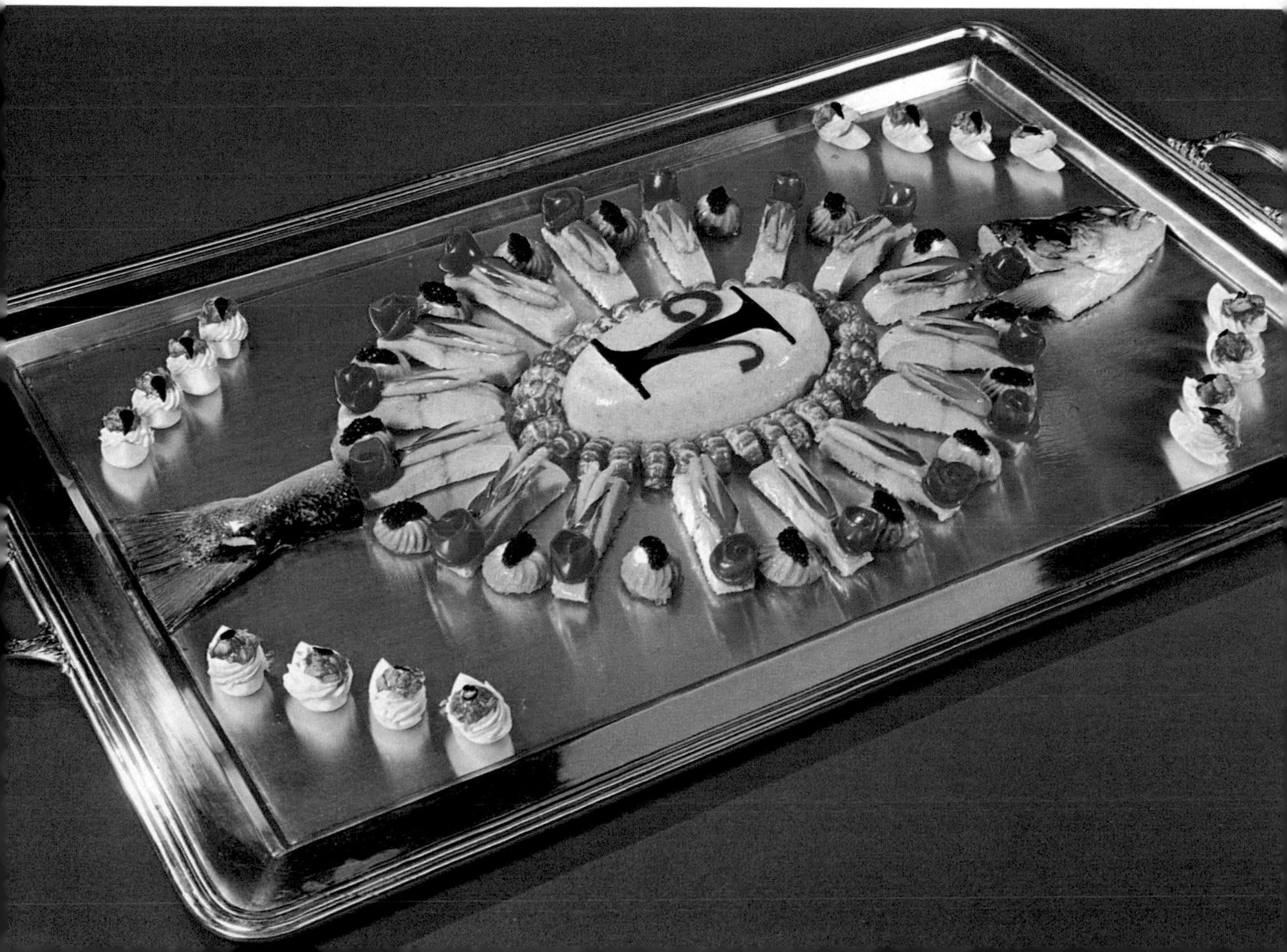

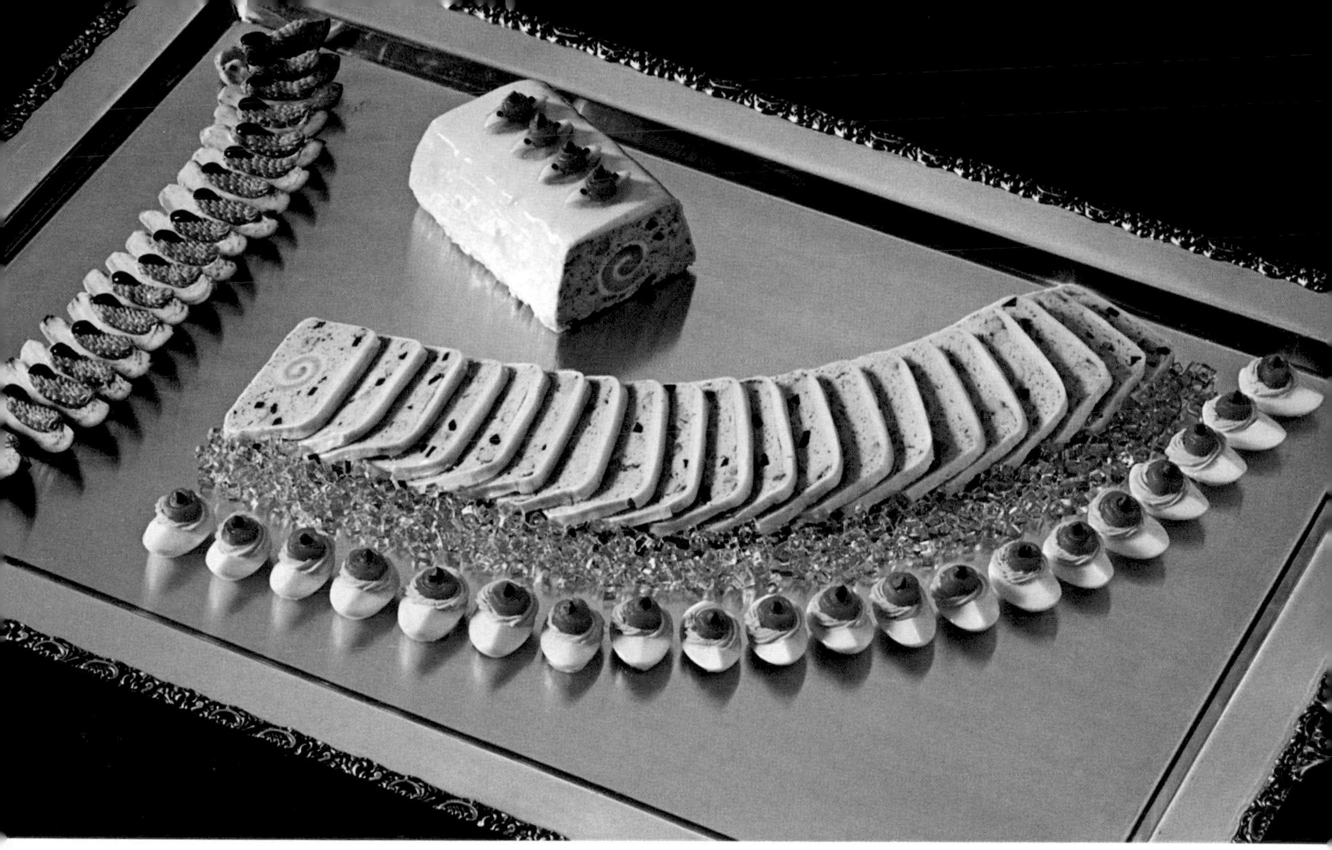

▲ Fish Terrine Jean Jacques
▼ Jellied eels Harlequin style, p. 502

698 ▲ A selection of herring dishes, pp. 469–473, 477
     ▼ Salmon steaks à la moderne, p. 510

▲ Sliced river salmon with vegetable garnish, p. 508

▼ Stuffed grapefruit, Skagerak style, p. 353

▲ Chaud-froid of salmon. Garnish: aspic of vegetables; stuffed eggs; artichoke bottoms, filled with fish-mousse decorated with peas, carrots and a mushroom

700

▼ Trout in Riesling sauce: stuff with fish or lobster forcemeat and braise in Riesling. Stir stock into lobster sauce. Decoration: slice of lobster, slice of truffle, a mushroom

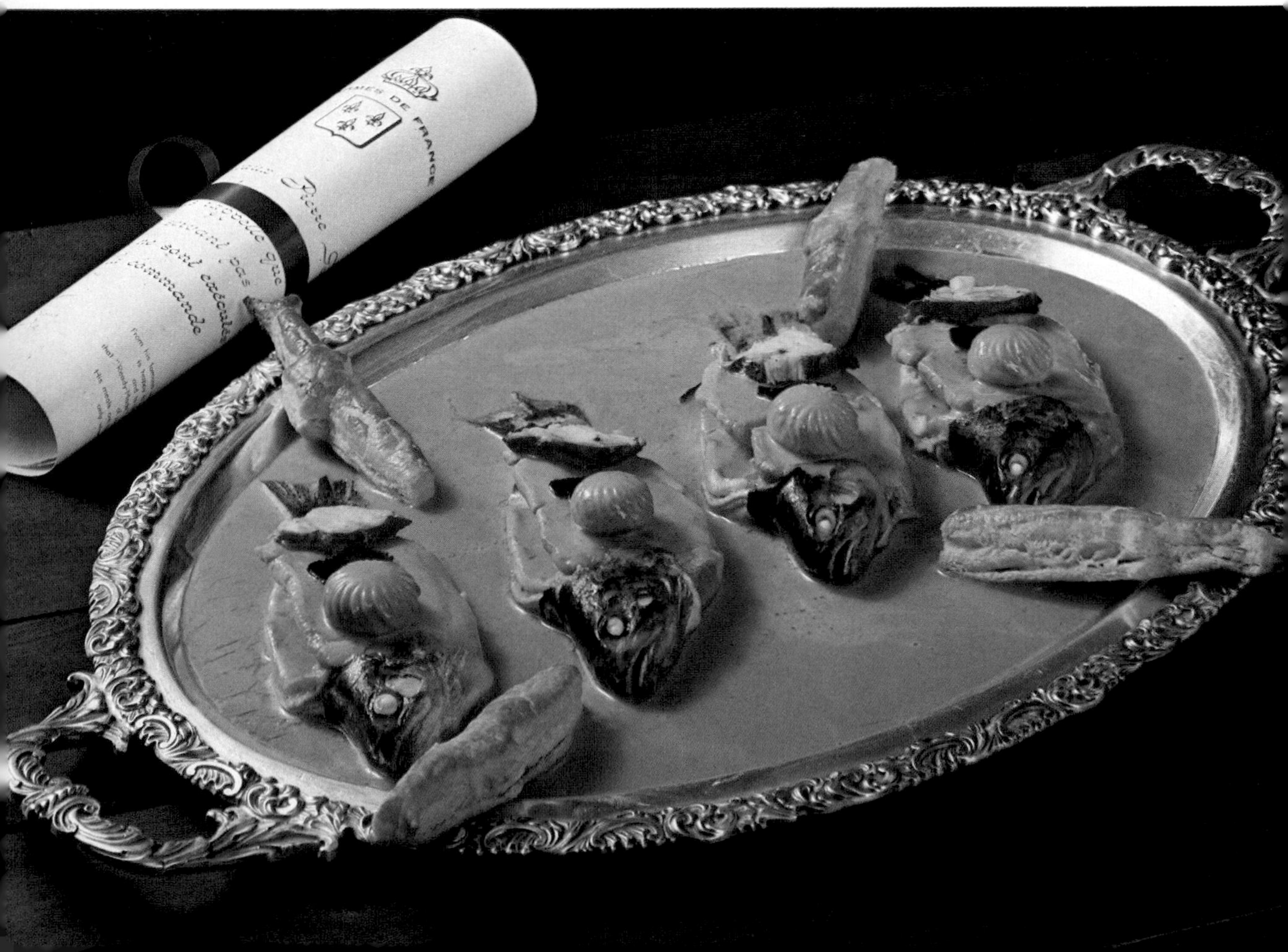

▲ Fillets of sole Oceanic style, p. 448
▼ Lobster Miramare, p. 533

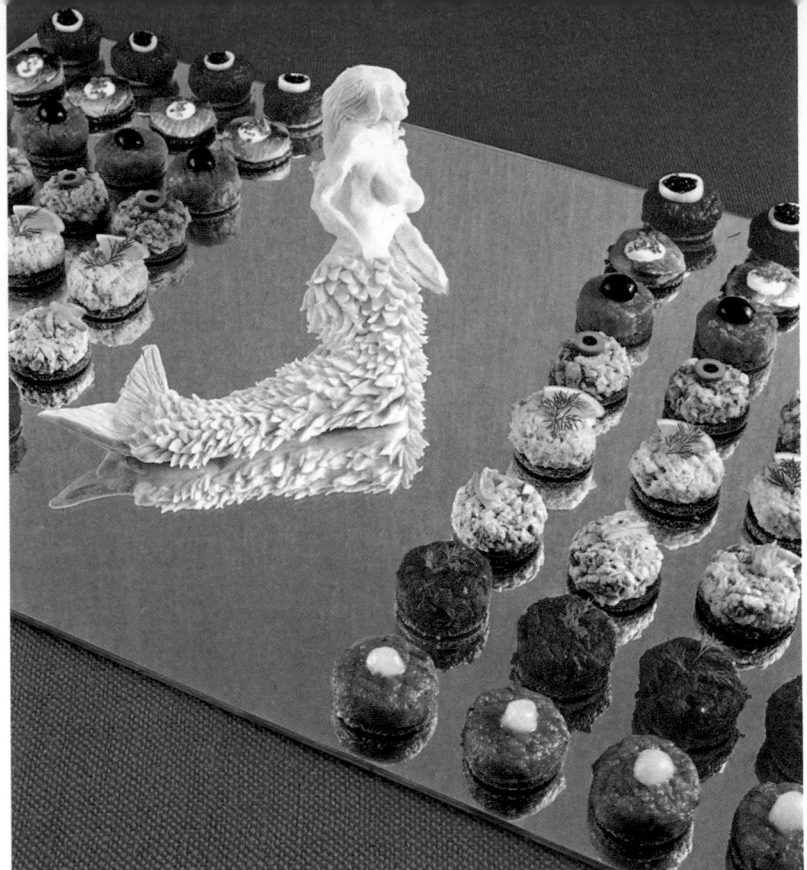

▲ Fish canapés, pp. 238–9

► Mussel and mushroom casserole, p. 519

▼ Crayfish, Bordeaux style, fillets of sole au gratin

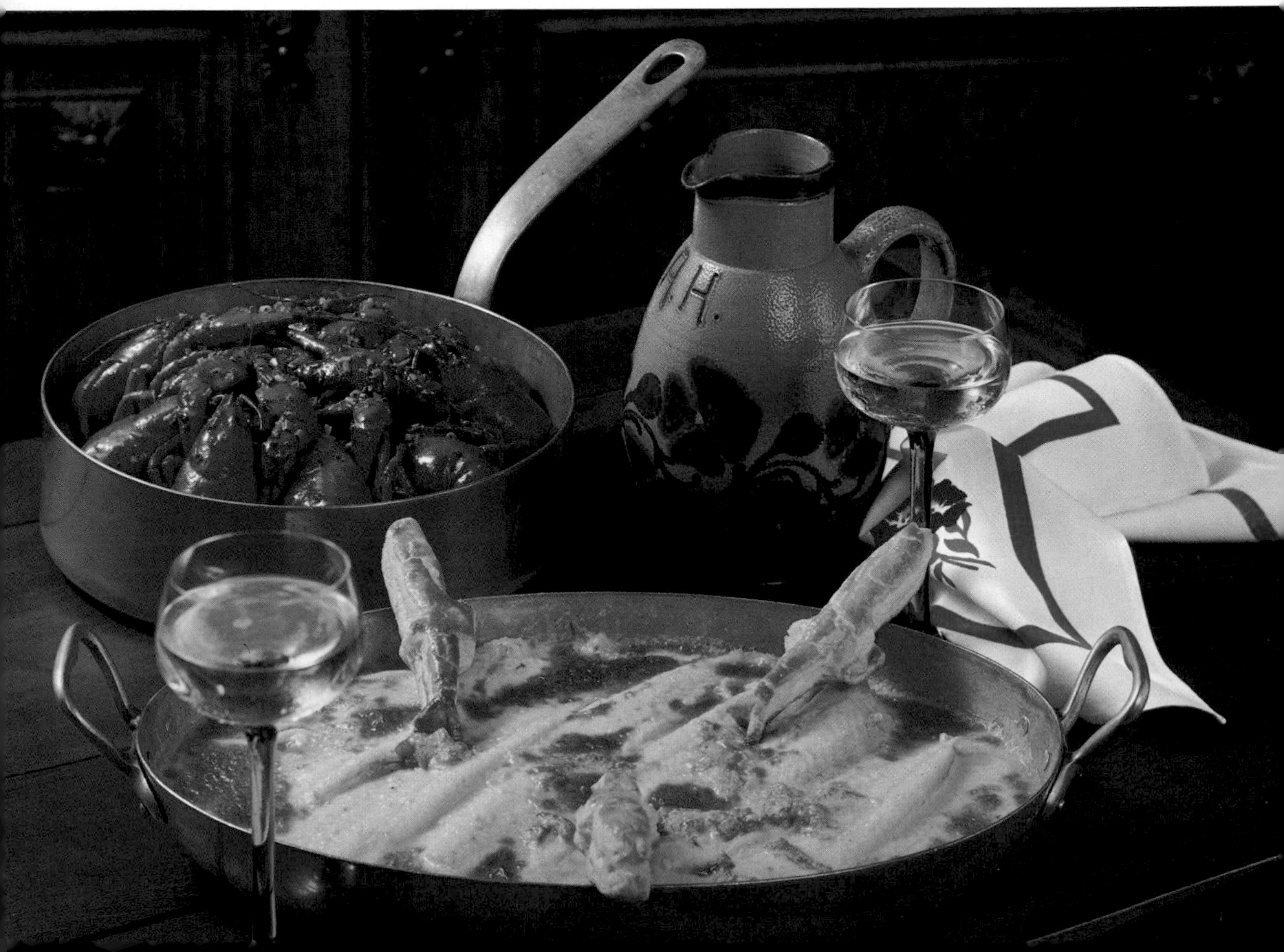

704

▲ Seafood salad in pastry: black olives, shrimps, green olives stuffed with tomato, cooked mussels, scampi, peas, oil, lemon juice and salt

▼ Crawfish La Baule style, p. 538

150 g	larding bacon	5 oz
1 dl	oil	3 fl oz
100 g	sugar	4 oz
1 dl	vinegar	3 fl oz
1 l	stock or bouillon	1¾ pt
150 g	butter	5 oz
100 g	flour	4 oz
4 dl	red Burgundy	⅔ pt
150 g	cranberries	5 oz
	1 lemon	
50 g	carrots	2 oz
50 g	onions	2 oz
50 g	celeriac	2 oz
50 g	parsley roots	2 oz

Prepare dark brown caramel with the oil and sugar and cook the thinly sliced vegetables in it for a few moments. Pour in the vinegar, stir to detach the cooking juices, then add the stock. Bone the haunch of roe-deer, remove the sinews, lard the joint, then season with salt and pepper, tie and brown in butter on all sides. Place on the vegetables, cover and cook slowly in the oven. When the meat is tender, remove and keep hot. Thicken the stock containing the vegetables with a roux made from the flour and the rest of the butter, pour in the wine and cook until thick. Add salt and lemon juice to taste.

Carve the meat, spread each slice well with the vegetables, place a slice of lemon on top and finish off with a small spoonful of stewed cranberries.

Czechoslovakia

Larded saddle of venison with sour cream sauce

6 persons   Roasting time: 20 minutes

	1 fairly small saddle of venison (roe-deer)	
	larding bacon	
	mirepoix	
	a few peppercorns	
	6–8 juniper berries	
	1 bay leaf	
½ l	red wine	¾ pt
2 l	bouillon or game stock	3½ pt
½ l	sour cream	¾ pt
70 g	flour	3 oz
	2 tablespoons cranberries	
	juice of 1 lemon	
	fat for roasting	

22

Fry the venison trimmings lightly in fat with some bacon rinds. Add the mirepoix, peppercorns and bay leaf and fry well. Stir in the wine, pour in the bouillon or game stock, season lightly with salt and simmer for $1\frac{1}{2}$ hours. Thicken with the flour, blended with the sour cream, add the cranberries and lemon juice, cook well, adjust the seasoning and strain.

Lard the venison, season with salt and pepper, cover with crushed juniper berries and roast in a brisk oven, removing when the flesh is still pink. Allow to stand for a few moments, cut the meat off the bone, slice, replace on the carcase, coat lightly with sauce and serve the rest of the sauce separately. If desired, garnish with slices of orange and cranberries. Serve dumplings boiled in a napkin separately.

Austria

Ragoût of game with flap mushrooms

10 persons   Cooking time: $1\frac{1}{4}-1\frac{1}{2}$ hours

2 kg 500	shoulder of venison	$5\frac{1}{2}$ lb
	weak vinegar marinade	
	1 large carrot	
	2 medium onions	
	8 crushed juniper berries	
	1 bouquet garni	
50 g	fat	2 oz
40 g	flour	2 oz
$\frac{3}{4}$ l	strong red wine	1 bottle
600 g	cleaned flap mushrooms (boletus)	$1\frac{1}{4}$ lb
30 g	butter	1 oz
	1 tablespoon oil	
600 g	small potatoes, trimmed to the shape of large olives and blanched	

Leave the venison in the marinade for $1\frac{1}{2}$ days together with the thickly sliced onions and carrot and the juniper berries, turning twice. Remove, wipe dry, bone and cut the meat into cubes. Strain the marinade and brown the meat, carrot and onions in the fat. Pour off most of the fat, sprinkle the meat with the flour and cook gently for a few moments. Season with salt and pepper, pour in the red wine and enough water or bouillon to cover well, add the juniper berries and the bouquet garni and bring to the boil. Cover and cook slowly in the oven for 1 hour. Remove the meat from the pan, transfer to a clean one and add the well-blanched potatoes. Skim the fat off the cooking liquid, strain over the meat, check the taste and return to the oven until cooked. Dice the flap mushrooms, fry in equal amounts of butter and oil, season, add to the meat, cook for a moment longer and serve hot.

Germany

Stuffed saddle of venison Hotel Sacher

6 portions   Cooking time: forcemeat, 10 minutes; venison, 15 minutes

1 kg 500	saddle of venison, skinned (roe-deer)	3¼ lb
150 g	larding bacon	5 oz
3–4 cl	gin	3–4 dessertspoons
	6 juniper berries	

Forcemeat

200 g	venison (roe-deer), boned	8 oz
50 g	pork	2 oz
50 g	green bacon	2 oz
100 g	panada	4 oz
40 g	pistachio nuts	2 oz
	1–2 egg whites	
$\frac{1}{16}$ l	dairy cream	⅛ pt
3 cl	Madeira	3 dessertspoons
	forcemeat herbs and spices	

Garnish

6 half-apples, stewed and
    stuffed with cranberries
slices of orange

To make the forcemeat, mince the venison, pork and bacon as finely as possible and mix well with the panada. Rub through a sieve and leave in a cool place for 12 hours. Bind with the egg white and cream and add the pistachio nuts, salt, white pepper, herbs, and spices, and the Madeira. Place a sheet of oiled paper on a napkin, spread the forcemeat on it, roll up and tie securely. The roll should be thin enough for the saddle fillets to be wrapped round it. Poach the forcemeat in strong game stock.

Cut the raw saddle fillets off the bone, score on the inside and flatten very slightly. Lard the outside. When the forcemeat is cold, lay it on the fillets so that these can be wrapped round it and tie in position. Season with salt and pepper and roast slowly in butter until pale pink. Shortly before the meat is cooked, pour the gin over and ignite. Remove the meat from the pan, rinse out with brown stock to detach the cooking juices, add the crushed juniper berries, reduce to make well-flavoured gravy, then strain. Roast the carcase separately. To dish, untie the saddle fillets, carve on a slant and replace on the carcase. Coat lightly with gravy, garnish with the stuffed apples and slices of orange and serve the rest of the gravy and Berny potatoes separately.

Austria

Venison pörkölt with red wine

10 persons

3 kg	venison on the bone	6½ lb
500 g	onions	1 lb
500 g	lard	1 lb
5 g	good pinch ground pepper	
100 g	mild paprika	3 oz
5 g	good pinch hot paprika	
½ l	tannic red wine	¾ pt
150 g	pritamin*	5 oz

Bone the venison and cut into dice (these should include some pieces with skin attached). Slice the onions finely, fry in the lard until lightly coloured, remove from the heat and add two-thirds of the mild and hot paprika. Stir in the meat and cook gently for about an hour without adding liquid, stirring repeatedly. When the meat is tender, season with salt, add the pritamin and 2 dl (⅓ pt) wine, season with the rest of the paprika and continue cooking for a short time. Shortly before serving, pour in the rest of the wine and bring to the boil. Serve with freshly boiled potatoes, fresh home-baked bread made with potato flour, and mixed pickles or pickled peppers stuffed with red cabbage.

Hungary

* Pritamin: Hungarian pepper purée sold in cans.

COLD DISHES

Cold larded saddle of venison

10 persons   Roasting time: 25–30 minutes

	1 saddle of roe-deer	
3 kg	weighing about	6½ lb
100 g	larding bacon or pork fat	4 oz
300 g	carrots	10 oz
300 g	parsley roots	10 oz
200 g	onions	8 oz
	10 peppercorns	
	1 sprig of thyme	
15 cl	oil	¼ pt
400 g	goose or duck livers	14 oz
200 g	butter	8 oz
½ l	aspic jelly	¾ pt

Trim the saddle neatly, remove all skin and tendons, stud the surface with thin strips of fat bacon or pork and rub with salt and pepper. Clean the root vegetables and cut into round slices together with the onions, then cover the bottom of a roasting tin or other fireproof dish with the slices, adding the peppercorns and thyme. Place the saddle on top, pour the oil over and roast briskly, basting frequently. Allow the saddle to cool, fry the root vegetables with the livers which have been cut up small and mince three times, using the finest cutter. Cream the butter lightly, add the liver purée, season with salt, pepper and a pinch of grated nutmeg and work thoroughly. Cut off the two saddle fillets with a sharp knife. Chop away the centre bone of the saddle and spread the carcase with the liver purée. Cut the fillets on the slant into thin even slices and replace on the carcase. Fill up the spaces with liver purée. Decorate and garnish as desired and glaze with aspic jelly.

(Illustration, p. 918)   Hungary

Cold saddle of roebuck with fruit

8 persons   Cooking time: forcemeat, 20 minutes; saddle fillets, 8½ minutes

	1 saddle of roebuck	
2 kg 500	weighing about	5½ lb
800 g	foie gras	1¾ lb
	4 truffles	
150 g	pork	5 oz
150 g	veal	5 oz
200 g	fresh pork back fat	7 oz
3 cl	Cognac	3 dessertspoons
6 cl	Madeira	6 dessertspoons
6 cl	dairy cream	6 dessertspoons
	forcemeat flavouring	
	finely crushed juniper berries	

Garnish for carcase

Waldorf salad
8 cherries
40 tangerine segments
8 greengages, cut in half
16 stoned Canadian prunes

Other garnish

	8 poached apple slices, cut with a fluted cutter	
	8 round slices chicken galantine	
	8 balls of foie gras rolled in chopped pistachio nuts	
	8 small pears, peeled, poached and stuffed with red-currant jelly	
500 g	peeled white grapes	1 lb
	oil	
	aspic jelly	

First skin and trim the foie gras, and cut into strips about 2½ cm (1 in) thick. Stud with truffles cut in quarters and marinate overnight in the Madeira and Cognac, covering the dish. Prepare forcemeat with the pork and veal, the foie gras trimmings, the Cognac and Madeira used as a marinade, the cream, forcemeat flavouring and salt as required. Using a savoy bag, shape the forcemeat into a long roll about 3 cm (1¼ in) across on an oblong of heatproof wrapping material (synthetic sausage skin cut open) and press in the marinated strips of foie gras along its length. Roll up tightly, tie, then poach, keeping the forcemeat slightly pink. Remove the skin and tendons from the saddle of venison cut off the fillets, open them out by means of a lengthwise incision, make further cuts as required and flatten lightly to obtain two rectangles measuring about 18 × 40 cm (7 × 16 in). Sprinkle lightly with salt, pepper, forcemeat flavouring and finely crushed juniper berries, cover with the foie gras and forcemeat roll after unwrapping, roll in oiled greaseproof paper and tie round. Brown in oil briskly for about 5 minutes, place on a rack and stand in the oven for another 3½ minutes. Roast the carcase and allow it and the stuffed fillets to cool. Place the carcase at the top end of the serving dish, fill with Waldorf salad, level off the top and decorate with the fruit, starting at the bottom. Cut the rolled fillets into slices, glaze with aspic and arrange along the length of the serving dish in two rows on either side of the carcase. Fill the centre with grapes and glaze with aspic. Arrange the stuffed pears on one side and the apple slices on the other, covering these first with a slice of galantine and then with a ball of foie gras. Remove any surplus or spilt aspic from the dish and coat the bottom lightly with fresh aspic.

Austria

Cold saddle of venison

12 persons   Cooking time: about 25 minutes after browning

4 kg	saddle of venison	8¾ lb

approx. 2 kg 500	Waldorf salad	5½ lb
300 g	firm foie gras mousse	10 oz
1½ l	aspic jelly	2½ pt
¾ l	Madeira jelly	1¼ pt
2 cl	gin	2 dessertspoons
	cored poached apple slices	
	cut with a fluted cutter	
	smoked ham	
	candied fruit	
	puff pastry cut into leaf	
	shapes and baked	
	sliced peaches	
	large choice strawberries	
	foie gras mousse for decoration	

Trim the saddle of venison neatly, cut off the fillets and remove all the sinews. Season with salt and pepper, brown on both sides in a little oil in a hot oven, pour off some of the oil, add the gin and ignite, then roast, basting frequently and keeping the meat pink. Reduce the heat after browning, otherwise the meat may turn grey on carving. Insert a metal rod into the carcase and roast separately. Refrigerate, together with the fillets of venison, which should be under slight pressure. Stiffen the Waldorf salad with well-reduced rather firm aspic jelly, spread on the carcase, shape neatly and refrigerate. Cut the fillets of venison into thin slices and arrange evenly, one slightly overlapping another, to cover the Waldorf salad on the carcase. Refrigerate, then pour aspic jelly over to glaze, making sure it is free from air bubbles. Spread the firm foie gras mousse on a flat metal tray to a thickness of about 5 mm (¼ in), allow to harden, then cut out medallions 3 cm (1¼ in) in diameter. Coat a rimmed metal tray to a thickness of 2 mm (about $\frac{1}{10}$ in) with Madeira jelly, refrigerate until set, then arrange the medallions on top, leaving a little space between them. Cover with a second layer of Madeira jelly about 2 mm ($\frac{1}{10}$ in) thick, allow to set, then cut out the medallions with a 3½ cm (1½ in) cutter so that each one has a narrow border of jelly.

Place the saddle on a silver serving dish of suitable size, remove the medallions from the tray of jelly and arrange them in a row along the top of the saddle, one over-lapping another. Decorate the spaces with a little left-over foie gras mousse and pipe on a border of the same mousse. Place a row of poached apple slices, stuffed with smoked ham and candied fruit, along each of the long edges of the dish. Fill the space on either side of the saddle with leaf shapes made of puff pastry, spread with foie gras mousse and topped with a large strawberry and a slice of peach.

(Illustration, p. 913)   Austria

Fillets of fallow deer Montrose

10 persons   Roasting time: about 30 minutes

3 kg 500	saddle of fallow deer	7½ lb
	10 ripe purple figs	
	10 round apple slices	
	1½ cm (½ in) thick and	
	5 cm (2 in) in diameter	
200 g	foie gras en bloc	8 oz
125 g	butter	4 oz
	1 pinch of pâté spices	
	10 half walnuts, skinned	
2 dl	dry port	⅓ pt
¾ l	game aspic	1¼ pt
	1 lemon	
5 cl	dry white wine	2 fl oz

Cut the two fillets off the saddle, remove the skin and sinews, season and wrap in buttered aluminium foil. Chop up the carcase and use in making the aspic jelly. Place the fillets in a brisk oven for 5 minutes, then reduce the heat considerably and roast for a further 25 minutes or so, making sure that the meat remains underdone in the middle. Remove from the oven, unwrap and leave until cold.

Poach the figs in the port and allow to cool in the cooking liquid. Core the apple slices, place in a pan with lemon juice, white wine and a little water and cook gently so that they keep their shape, then leave in the cooking liquid until cold. Rub the foie gras through a sieve, then work to a paste of piping consistency with barely half its weight of creamed butter, the cooking liquid from the figs, previously strained and reduced, a pinch of pâté spices and salt to taste. Dry the apple slices well, pipe a rosette of the foie gras paste on each one, using a star pipe, top with half a walnut and glaze with aspic jelly. Dry the figs gently and also glaze with aspic.

Line the bottom of a rectangular silver dish with a thin coat of aspic. Trim the fillets neatly and evenly, cut into slightly slanting slices, spread out a little, making sure they are evenly arranged, glaze with aspic, allow to set, then arrange on the coated dish in two parallel rows 6–7 cm (2½–3 in) apart. Place the figs between the two rows, arrange the apple slices on the outside of each row and garnish at the top and bottom with cubes of aspic.

Germany

Roe-deer medallions

6 pieces

120 g	fillet of roe-deer	4 oz
60 g	foie gras purée	2 oz
	6 stoned morello cherries	
	wine jelly	

Fry the meat, keeping it pink, cut on the slant into 6 slices of equal size and trim to a slightly oval shape. Pipe on the foie gras purée, using a plain pipe. Place a cherry in the centre of each medallion and refrigerate until the foie gras purée is half set, then glaze with wine jelly.

Germany

Stuffed fillets of roe calf

20–25 portions   Cooking time: 20–30 minutes

	2 trimmed joints of fillet of	
1 kg	roe calf, each weighing	2¼ lb

Galantine

300 g	veal forcemeat	10 oz
100 g	diced ham	4 oz
100 g	diced pickled tongue	4 oz
50 g	smoked fat pork (or bacon), diced and blanched	2 oz
	1 diced truffle	
40 g	pistachio nuts	2 oz
	forcemeat flavouring	
	Cognac	

Forcemeat for covering joints

250 g	boneless veal	8 oz
250 g	boneless lean pork	8 oz
500 g	fresh pork fat	1 lb
100 g	pimentos	4 oz
100 g	blanched pistachio nuts	4 oz
50 g	truffles	2 oz
25 g	seasoned salt	1 oz
	2 undamaged pig's cauls	
approx. 1½ l	Madeira-flavoured aspic jelly	2½ pt

20–25 marinated artichoke
bottoms
small cooked marinated
chanterelles

Mix the veal forcemeat with the diced ham, tongue, smoked pork fat (or bacon) and truffle, add the pistachio nuts and flavour with forcemeat herbs and spices, and with Cognac. Tie in two cloths in the same way as any galantine; each should be of the same length as the joints of roe calf. Poach, allow to cool in the cooking liquid, tie in clean cloths and press very lightly.

Prepare fine forcemeat with the veal, pork and fresh pork fat. Add seasoned salt to taste and work in the chopped pimentos, truffles and pistachio nuts.

Make a horizontal incision through the centre of the two joints of roe calf with a long thin knife. Unwrap the galantine, wipe it dry and push it into the cavity. Cover the joints all round to a thickness of 1 cm ($\frac{1}{2}$ in) with the prepared forcemeat and carefully wrap each one in a pig's caul. Roast with particular care to keep the meat pink. The oven temperature and the time required will depend on the thickness of the joints.

To dish, coat an oblong silver tray with aspic. Place a piece of roast saddle of roe calf (carcase only) at one end. Stuff with game mousse and arrange to the original shape of the saddle. Decorate the centre with a double row of fruit in mustard pickle in a branch-like pattern. Place a row of black grapes, each stuck with half an almond, on either side and edge with a row of honeydew melon balls. Glaze with aspic. Slice the stuffed joints of roe calf and lay the slices overlapping down the tray in two rows, one on either side of the carcase. Stuff the artichoke bottoms with the chanterelles, glaze with aspic and arrange in rows between the two rows of sliced roe calf.

(Illustration, p. 914)   Austria

Stuffed saddle of venison Père Salice

45 persons

	1 saddle of venison (roe-deer)	
600 g	fresh mushrooms, finely chopped	1¼ lb
10 g	soaked dried morels, finely chopped	½ teaspoonful
2 dl	game chaud-froid sauce	⅓ pt
150 g	foie gras purée	5 oz
2 cl	brandy	2 dessertspoons

Garnish

16–18 tiny short pastry boats
3–4 apples
peaches
strawberries
hazelnuts
grapes
white wine
lemon juice
truffle
small mushroom caps
aspic jelly

Trim the saddle of venison, cut off the fillets and beat out to a rectangular shape between sheets of plastic. Season the underside with salt and pepper and brown lightly. Tie each fillet round a long tube, placing the browned side underneath, season and roast until cooked through but still juicy. Chill thoroughly, then carefully pull out the tubes. Stew the mushrooms and morels, bind with the chaud-froid sauce, add the foie gras purée, flavour with brandy and season well. Pipe this stuffing into the fillets, using a savoy bag only, and chill thoroughly. Brown the saddle carcase and allow to cool. Cut the stuffed fillets into even-sized slices, arrange these on the carcase so that they overlap and fill the space between the two rows with mushroom caps each decorated with a dot of truffle. Brush the pastry boats inside with butter, refrigerate, fill with diced peach and decorate with a quarter strawberry and slices of hazelnut. Peel and core the apples and poach in a little water and white wine, with the addition of sugar and lemon juice. When cold, decorate with a seeded black grape and half a pistachio nut.

Coat a rectangular dish with aspic jelly. Glaze the decorated saddle with aspic, place it in the centre of the dish and garnish with the filled pastry boats and the apples.

(Illustration, p. 920)   Switzerland

Stuffed saddle of venison with venison medallions

Cooking time: saddle about 15 minutes; medallions, 5–6 minutes

	1 saddle of venison	
2 kg 500–3 kg	(roe-deer) weighing	$5\frac{1}{2}$–$6\frac{1}{2}$ lb
400 g	hard pork fat (fresh)	1 lb
300 g	lean pork	$\frac{3}{4}$ lb
100 g	goose liver trimmings	4 oz
	sliced truffles	

	blanched pistachio nuts	
	foie gras purée	
	forcemeat flavouring	
	sliced fillet of roe-deer	
	Cognac	
	red wine	
750 g	fresh very white mushrooms	1¾ lb
50 g	butter	2 oz
¼ l	dairy cream	½ pt
	game flavouring	

Cut the fillets of meat off the saddle and shorten by one-quarter below the neck tendons. Open out each fillet to an oblong shape by means of a lengthwise incision and flatten a little. Prepare fine forcemeat with the pork fat, pork and goose liver trimmings, add salt, forcemeat flavouring and a little Cognac and stir in blanched pistachio nuts. Cover the prepared fillets with slices of truffle and spread with the forcemeat, leaving an even margin so that the edges meet neatly after rolling up. Season lightly, wrap each fillet in foil, tie in position, but not too tightly, and brown quickly with the carcase. Roast for 10–12 minutes, turning repeatedly, then allow to cool. Trim the carcase neatly and spread with foie gras purée. Remove the fillets from the foil, cut into slices 1 cm (about ½ in) thick and arrange on the carcase. Decorate with peeled grapes or as desired and glaze lightly with aspic.

For the garnish, cut the slices of roe-deer into small rounds 2 cm (about ¾ in) thick, season, fry quickly so that the meat remains pink, rinse out the pan with Cognac and red wine to detach the juices, and allow the meat to cool. Clean the mushrooms well, dry thoroughly, fry in the butter for a moment, pour in the cream, add a little salt and cook until soft, reducing the liquid in the pan at the same time. Work in the blender, allow the purée to cool, then adjust the seasoning. Cut the medallions of meat open in the centre, fill with mushroom purée, decorate as desired or alternatively spread first with the stock boiled down with a little aspic and glaze lightly with aspic.

Austria

Venison chops Prince Rupert

12 portions   Cooking time: 6–7 minutes

12 double roe-deer chops
game essence
egg yolk paste
chopped tarragon
watercress
game aspic
butter

Trim the chops neatly, especially the bones, season with salt and pepper, then fry them, keeping the meat pink. Allow to cool on a wire rack and glaze with game essence. Using a savoy bag fitted with a plain tube, pipe a border of egg yolk paste mixed with chopped tarragon on to each chop. When firm, fill the centre with watercress leaves and glaze each chop with aspic. Coat a round serving dish with aspic, place a frill on each bone and arrange on the dish with the frills in the centre.

(Illustration, p. 241)   Germany

Venison medallions

Yield: 6

120 g	medium done roast saddle or fillet of venison	4¼ oz
60 g	truffled foie gras purée	2 oz
	2 Chinese gooseberries (caramboles), skinned	
	port jelly	

Cut out 6 venison medallions. Pipe on the foie gras purée, using a savoy bag fitted with a plain pipe, and decorate each medallion with a slice of very green Chinese gooseberry. Chill well and glaze with port jelly.

Germany

WILD BOAR

Boar's head

Bone the head and stuff with forcemeat—diced ox tongue, goose liver, truffles and pistachios. Tie the head in a cloth and boil. When cooled decorate with imitation tusks, eyes, etc. Garnish with aspic jelly. Serve with Cumberland sauce.

Jugged young wild boar

10 persons   Cooking time: about 1½ hours

2 kg	young wild boar (shoulder or leg), without bone or sinews	4¼ lb
	2 fairly small onions	
	1 carrot	
	2 small cloves of garlic	

	1 bouquet garni	
	3–4 juniper berries, crushed	
500 g	mushroom caps	1 lb
4 cl	brandy	4 dessertspoons
4 dl	light red wine	⅔ pt
1 dl	pig's blood	3 fl oz
	1 tablespoon vinegar	
	6 crushed peppercorns	
40 g	butter	2 oz
40 g	flour	2 oz

Cut the meat into pieces each weighing about 50 g (1¾ oz) and marinate for 24 hours in the red wine and 2 dl (⅓ pt) water with the sliced onions and carrot, the garlic, bouquet garni, peppercorns and juniper berries. Drain the meat and vegetables well, dry the meat and brown it with the vegetables. Stir in the brandy, dust with flour, cook gently for a few moments, pour in the strained marinade, add the bouquet garni, cover and braise slowly in the oven. After an hour, transfer the meat to a clean casserole, add the mushroom caps, strain in the stock and braise slowly until cooked. Remove from the oven, thicken the sauce with the pig's blood mixed with the vinegar and re-heat without boiling. Season well, dish and sprinkle with chopped parsley.

Germany

Larded haunch of wild boar

5 portions   Cooking time: 1¼–1½ hours

1 kg	haunch of wild boar	2¼ lb
100 g	larding bacon	4 oz
5 cl	oil	2 fl oz
150 g	onions	5 oz
100 g	celeriac	3 oz
	allspice	
	peppercorns	
	1 bay leaf	
50 g	butter	2 oz
50 g	tomato ketchup	2 oz

Lard the meat, season with salt and brown lightly in butter, together with the vegetables, cut into thick slices. Add the bay leaf and a few allspice berries and peppercorns, and pour in a little bouillon or water. Cover and cook in the oven, adding a little liquid from time to time. When tender, remove the meat, strain the stock, skim off all the fat and flavour with tomato ketchup. Carve the meat, pour the well-reduced stock over and serve with boiled potatoes and cranberries.

Czechoslovakia

Saddle of wild boar with orange segments Florian

20 persons   Roasting time: 35 minutes

6 kg	saddle of wild boar	13 lb
	10 seedless oranges	
4 dl	Cumberland sauce	⅔ pt
½ l	red wine	¾ pt
	mirepoix	
	sugar	

Trim the joints neatly and roast, keeping them very juicy. Stand aside for a short time, then cut off the saddle fillets, slice and arrange in oval fireproof dishes. Pare off the zest of several oranges thinly, cut in small julienne strips, cook until soft and drain. Peel the oranges, cut the skin away from each segment and squeeze out any juice remaining in the skins. Spread the slices of meat thinly with Cumberland sauce and cover with the orange segments. Sprinkle lightly with sugar and glaze under a salamander. Prepare a kind of Grand-Veneur sauce from the bones and trimmings, mirepoix and red wine, strain, flavour with the squeezed-out orange juice and mix with the strips of orange zest.

Serve with a Florian garnish, consisting of small corn cobs tossed in butter, tomatoes stuffed with leaf spinach, and large mushroom caps stuffed with cranberries and grated horseradish, sprinkled with breadcrumbs and grated cheese and baked in the oven. Hand the sauce separately.

Germany

Smoked wild boar rolls with horseradish cream

10 portions

1 kg	smoked haunch of wild boar	2¼ lb
3 dl	whipped cream	½ pt
100 g	horseradish	4 oz
200 g	salted cucumbers	8 oz
150 g	tomatoes	5 oz
	1 lettuce	

Cut the cooked smoked haunch into thin slices each weighing 50 g (1¾ oz). Mix the whipped cream with the horseradish and add paprika, a pinch each of salt and sugar and a few drops of vinegar. Spread on the slices of meat, roll up, arrange on a serving dish on lettuce leaves and garnish with wedges of tomato and slices of salted cucumber.

Czechoslovakia

Wild boar's head brawn with pistachio nuts

This dish is generally made with a pig's head, wild boar's head being used only on special occasions.

The animal should be freshly killed. Split the head in half, singe and clean thoroughly. (Use the brains elsewhere.) To salt it, place in a deep container and allow 50 g (1¾ oz) saltpetre to 1 kg (2 lb 3 oz) common salt, well mixed together. Leave in a cool place for 8 days. Two or three pig's tongues may be added if desired. After pickling, wash the head in running water to remove the salt. Soak overnight in cold water. Next day, place in a deep saucepan or stock pot, cover well with water and add some whole washed vegetables (onions, carrots, leeks and celery), a few peppercorns, cloves, thyme and savory. Bring to the boil, skim and simmer slowly and steadily until the meat is tender enough to leave the bone. Remove from the cooking liquid and allow the head to cool slightly, then bone it and cut the meat into pieces 3 cm (1¼ in) thick. Skin the tongues and cut into thin narrow strips. Slice the ears in the same way.

Pour ½ l (⅞ pt) Madeira into a sauté pan (this is sufficient for a medium-size head), reduce to half its volume, add ½ l (⅞ pt) of the cooking liquid and reduce the liquid in the pan to about one-third of its volume. Now add the pieces of head and tongue, 2–3 sheets of isinglass which have been soaked and drained, a few blanched pistachio nuts, salt, freshly ground pepper and grated nutmeg. Stir well and, while still hot, pour into an oblong mould lined either with a pig's caul which has been soaked in warm water or with very thin slices of salted pork fat. After filling the mould, cover the top with a caul, place a wooden board of the same size on top and weight until the next day. To turn out, dip the mould in hot water for a moment. Dish on a napkin; garnish the top and sides with pieces of jelly. Alternatively, cover with fine breadcrumbs and brown lightly and evenly in the oven before serving.

Spain

HARE

Jugged hare

	1 hare, jointed	
	1 tablespoon dripping	
	2 onions	
	2 carrots	
	1 stick celery	
	bouquet garni	
1 l	stock	1½ pt
	1 tablespoon red-currant jelly	
	glass of port wine	
	forcemeat balls	

Wipe the pieces of hare and reserve the blood. Brown the pieces in the hot dripping in a stewpan. Remove from heat and keep warm. Slice the vegetables, add to the pan, cover and cook slowly for 6–7 minutes. Replace the hare; add seasoning and stock. Cover the pan and braise gently in the oven for 2–3 hours or until tender. Remove the joints and place in a deep casserole for serving. Strain the stock. Return to pan with the jelly and port. Simmer for 5 minutes. Adjust seasoning. Draw aside and add the blood. Re-heat, stirring well but do not boil. Strain the sauce over the hare, cover and place the casserole in a slow oven for 15–20 minutes. Send to the table with forcemeat balls arranged on top.

Great Britain

Finnish Easter hare

4 persons   Roasting time: 30 minutes

	1 saddle of hare	
50 g	larding bacon or pork fat	2 oz
75 g	butter	3 oz
	2 onions cut in quarters	
15 cl	sour cream	¼ pt
	1 tablespoon flour	
	juice of 1 lemon	

Remove all sinews from a large saddle of hare and lard the flesh. Heat the butter in a roasting tin, sprinkle the hare lightly with salt, toss in the butter, add the onions and roast in a brisk oven for 20 minutes, basting occasionally. Reduce the heat a little, pour the sour cream over and roast for a further 10 minutes. Remove from the tin and keep hot. Blend the flour to a paste with a little water, add to the cooking liquid in the tin, stir well and scrape off the sediment, add the lemon juice, adjust the seasoning and strain. Garnish the saddle of hare with fried mushrooms and hand the sauce separately. Serve red whortleberry jam, pickled cucumber and sauerkraut as accompaniments.

Finland

Hare soufflé in aspic

10 persons

450–500 g	2 hare legs each weighing	1–1 lb 2 oz
200 g	Béchamel sauce	6 oz
4 dl	aspic jelly	⅔ pt
3 dl	half-whipped cream	½ pt
40 g	butter	2 oz
	1 carrot	
	1 onion	
	2–3 crushed juniper berries	

	1 bouquet garni	
2 dl	red wine	⅓ pt
3 cl	Cognac	3 dessertspoons
	sliced truffle	

Remove all the sinews from the legs, fry lightly with a mirepoix of carrot and onion and add salt and 2–3 crushed juniper berries. Pour in the Cognac, ignite, then add the red wine and an equal amount of water, together with the bouquet garni. Cover and braise in the oven until very tender. Cut all the meat off the bones, strain the stock and reduce almost to a glaze. Mince the meat, using the finest cutter, mix with the Béchamel sauce and the reduced stock, and rub through a sieve. Transfer to a pan, stand on ice and chill well. Meanwhile, fasten a strip of stiff paper or cardboard round a soufflé dish so that it projects about 2 cm (¾ in) above the top edge. Season the well-chilled hare purée with salt to taste and flavour lightly with pâté spices. Mix with 2 dl (⅓ pt) aspic jelly, then fold in the cream. Fill into the soufflé dish up to 1 cm (about ½ in) below the top edge of the paper, decorate with a ring of truffle disks and refrigerate. When half set, cover with a thin layer of aspic jelly and refrigerate until set. Do not remove the strip of paper until the jelly is quite firm.

Germany

Roast hare Finnish style

8 persons   Roasting time: 40 minutes

2 kg	1 skinned hare weighing	4½ lb
150 g	larding bacon or pork fat	5 oz
¼ l	sour cream	½ pt
	1 large onion	
100 g	butter	4 oz

Lard the skinned hare, season lightly with salt, pour melted butter over and roast in a brisk oven, basting very frequently. Dice the onion coarsely and add shortly before the hare is cooked. Pour in the sour cream just before serving. To serve, joint the hare, arrange on a dish, strain the cream over and garnish with stewed tomatoes, cranberries and marinated mushrooms in a croustade. Hand boiled potatoes separately.

(Illustration, p. 917)   Finland

Roast saddle of hare

Take the back of the hare from the haunch to the first ribs. Skin the meat and lard it well. Roast rare. Hare meat which is dry is much improved if marinated overnight and only a young hare should be used for roasting.

REINDEER, BEAR AND ELK

Reindeer tongue purée in aspic

10 persons	Cooking time (tongues): 15–20 minutes	
	2 smoked reindeer tongues	
	5 fresh reindeer tongues	
250 g	butter	8 oz

Aspic jelly

1 l	consommé	1¾ pt
½ l	red whortleberry juice	¾ pt
	20 sheets gelatine	
	1–2 egg whites	

Cook the tongues until tender, skin and allow to cool completely. Mince, then rub through a sieve or whirl to a fine purée in the blender. Cream the butter, mix thoroughly with the purée and season to taste with salt and white pepper. Spread to a thickness of 1 cm (about ½ in) on a greased metal tray with a rim or other suitable tray, smooth the top and refrigerate. Meanwhile make aspic jelly from the consommé, red whortleberry juice and gelatine, clarify with the egg white and strain through a cloth.

Cut the reindeer tongue purée into rounds 10 cm (4 in) in diameter, coat evenly with the aspic jelly, which should be cold and just beginning to set, then refrigerate until firm. Dish with a garnish of diced aspic and serve with a fresh green salad.

Finland

Roast bear ham

8–10 persons	Roasting time: about 2 hours	
3 kg	bear ham	6½ lb
4 dl	oil	⅔ pt
2 dl	vinegar	⅓ pt
	2 bottles beer	
	1 large onion, sliced	
	2 carrots, sliced	
	½ leek, finely cut	
	¼ celeriac, fincly cut	
	10 sprigs parsley	
	1 cluster rowan berries	
	2 sprigs marjoram	
	10 peppercorns	

Prepare a marinade with the oil, vinegar, beer, vegetables, herbs, berries and peppercorns. Place the bear ham in it, cover with a clean cloth and refrigerate. Marinate for 48 hours, or up to 60 hours if the ham is from a fairly old animal, turning the ham twice a day. After removing, drain thoroughly, wrap in buttered aluminium foil, brown quickly in a hot oven, then reduce the heat and roast until cooked. Serve with boiled potatoes, rowan jelly and cranberries.

A ham from a young bear may be steeped in milk instead of a marinade for 48 hours.

Finland

Roast elk

10 persons

2 kg 500	boned leg of elk	$5\frac{1}{2}$ lb
150 g	butter	5 oz
2–3 dl	bouillon	$\frac{1}{3}$–$\frac{1}{2}$ pt
4 dl	double cream	$\frac{2}{3}$ pt
	2 tablespoons wheat flour	

Marinade

4 dl	beer	$\frac{2}{3}$ pt
2 dl	vinegar	$\frac{1}{3}$ pt
5 dl	water	$\frac{3}{4}$ pt
	1 bay leaf	
	5 cloves	
	6 white peppercorns	
	1 onion	

Prepare a cooked marinade with the beer, vinegar, water, bay leaf, spices and sliced onion, then allow to cool. Wash and dry the meat, place it in the marinade, cover with a cloth and leave to soak for 4–5 days, turning it once a day. After removing, dry thoroughly, season with salt and pepper, place on a rack, pour a liberal amount of melted butter over and roast slowly at 200°C, basting frequently. When cooked, remove from the tin, pour in the bouillon to detach the cooking juices, add the cream blended with the flour, boil and adjust the seasoning to give a well-flavoured gauce. Carve the meat and serve with boiled or noisette potatoes, cranberries and sreen salad. Strain the sauce, pour some of it over the meat and hand the rest separately.

Finland

Saddle of reindeer Christian IV (cold)

8 persons   Cooking time: about 15 minutes

800 g	saddle fillets of reindeer, without tendons	1¾ lb
200 g	boneless reindeer meat	8 oz
200 g	foie gras roll without truffles	8 oz
50 g	1 can truffles weighing	2 oz
½ l	double cream	¾ pt
	2 egg yolks	
	2 tablespoons oil	
	butter	
	aspic jelly	

Slit each of the two fillets on one side so that it will open out to a rectangle when flattened slightly. Prepare fine forcemeat with the boneless reindeer meat, the egg yolks and the cream, standing the bowl on ice to mix. Season with salt and pepper. Lay the two fillets on oiled greaseproof paper and spread evenly with the forcemeat. Cover each one lengthwise with a foie gras roll or parfait studded with thinly sliced truffles and corresponding in size to the dimensions of the rectangle. Roll up the fillets with the foie gras filling inside so that the ends meet and sew up the join lightly to hold in position. Wrap each fillet in the oiled greaseproof paper and tie round lightly in the same way as smoked ham. Roast in a hot oven for a short time, then reduce the heat a little. Roast the saddle carcase at the same time. Leave the fillets in the paper until quite cold, then cut into 1 cm (about ½ in) slices. Spread the carcase lightly with foie gras purée (made with the foie gras trimmings, butter and seasonings) and arrange the stuffed slices of fillet on top after untying. Decorate with melon balls, walnuts and peeled grapes, then glaze with aspic. Coat a rectangular silver dish with aspic and arrange the carcase with the sliced fillets on it. For the garnish, cut peeled and cored apples in thick slices, poach in white wine and fill the centre with pieces of pineapple. Glaze with well-reduced apricot syrup and leave until cold before arranging on the dish. Hand Cumberland sauce separately.

(Illustration, p. 917)   Norway

Sauté of reindeer

6 persons   Cooking time: 10 minutes

1 kg	deep-frozen boneless reindeer	2 lb 3 oz
250 g	smoked fat bacon	8¾ oz

Shred the reindeer meat while still frozen into pieces 2 mm ($\frac{1}{10}$ in) thick. Shred the bacon in the same way, then fry lightly in a suitable pan, add the meat and brown over fierce heat. Season lightly with salt, cover the pan and cook over brisk heat. Dish and serve with mashed potatoes and cranberries.

Finland

FEATHERED GAME

HOT DISHES

Hazel hen soufflé

7–8 persons   Cooking time: about 40 minutes

	3 hazel hens	
300 g	boneless veal	10 oz
1 $\frac{1}{10}$ l	double cream	2 pt
	2 egg whites	
1 dl	white wine	3 fl oz
2 dl	brown stock	$\frac{1}{3}$ pt
	1 small onion	
	1 bay leaf	
	1 sprig thyme	
	1 tablespoon Cognac	
	pinch of quatre-épices*	

Prepare the hazel hens, cut the flesh off the bones, remove the skin and mince several times together with the veal (which has been well trimmed), using the finest blade of the mincer. Transfer to a sauté pan, stand on ice and chill thoroughly. Season lightly with salt, mix well with a wooden spoon, then leave to stand for a short time. Now stir in the egg whites a little at a time. If a very fine mixture is required, rub through a fine sieve. Return to the pan, chill again on ice for a short time, then gradually fold in 1 l (1¾ pt) cream. When half the cream has been added, blend in the rest with a wire whisk to make the mixture smooth and silky. Season to taste with pepper, 'quatre-épices' and more salt if required, then test the consistency by placing a little of the mixture in the oven in a small mould; it should be very light, but firm. If it is too soft, stir in an additional egg white. Fill a thinly buttered soufflé mould not quite to the top with the mixture and poach in the oven in a bain-marie at about 180°C, taking care that the water remains below boiling point.

Meanwhile, chop up the carcases and brown lightly together with the veal trimmings and the coarsely diced onion. Pour the white wine into the pan to detach the cooking juices. When reduced, add the brown stock and seasoning, stir in the rest of the cream and simmer gently for 15 minutes. Strain through a fine sieve, reduce if too thin, then check the seasoning. Dish the soufflé on an unfolded napkin and hand the sauce separately.

Sweden

* Quatre-épices: the ground fruit of a tropical tree. May be replaced by equal parts of ground ginger, white pepper, nutmeg and cloves.

Pheasant Czech style

10 portions   Cooking time: 50–60 minutes

	10 pheasants	
600 g	net weight of each	1¼ lb
100 g	larding bacon or pork fat	4 oz
50 g	smoked bacon	2 oz
200 g	butter	8 oz
200 g	onions	8 oz
	1 bay leaf	
	8 allspice berries	
	10 peppercorns	
50 g	flour	2 oz
1 l	stock or bouillon	1¾ pt

Wash and dry the pheasants, then lard them, season with salt, place in a braising pan on a bed of chopped onions, bay leaf, allspice and peppercorns, and pour the melted butter over. Cover and start cooking in a hot oven, then turn down the heat a little, pour in a little water or stock if required, and braise slowly until tender. When cooked, remove the pheasants from the pan, thicken the cooking liquid with the flour blended with a little water, pour in the stock or bouillon, add the smoked bacon which has been finely cut and lightly browned, reduce to the required consistency, adjust the seasoning and serve without straining.

Serve potato croquettes and red cabbage cooked with red wine as accompaniments.

Czechoslovakia

Braised pigeons

	2–4 pigeons depending on size	
50 g	butter	2 oz
	6 small onions	
¼ l	clear beef stock	½ pt
⅛ l	water	¼ pt
25 g	butter	1 oz
12 g	flour	½ oz

Brown the pigeons very slowly on all sides in the 50 g (2 oz) butter. Remove and keep warm. Brown the onions. Return pigeons to pan, pour over the stock, season, and bring to the boil. Cover and cook in very moderate oven for 1 hour. After 40 minutes baste the pigeons well and add the water to the pan. Continue cooking until tender. Split the pigeons in half, cut away the backbones and arrange in a serving dish. Thicken the gravy with 25 g (1 oz) butter and 12 g ($\frac{1}{2}$ oz) flour kneaded together. Adjust seasoning and spoon over the birds.

Roast capercailzie

6 persons

	1 young capercailzie	
2 kg 500–2 kg 800	weighing	5$\frac{1}{2}$–6$\frac{1}{4}$ lb
100 g	fat bacon	4 oz
2 l	dairy cream	4 pt
100 g	butter	4 oz
	3 choice, slightly tart apples	
$\frac{1}{4}$ l	white wine	$\frac{1}{2}$ pt
	6 tablespoons red-currant jelly	
	6 lettuce hearts	
	1 lemon	
	icing sugar	
600 g	potatoes, trimmed to the shape of large olives and boiled	1$\frac{1}{4}$ lb

Pluck the capercailzie carefully, to avoid damaging the skin, then draw the bird, wash inside and outside, dry and season with salt and pepper. Lard with thin slices of bacon and truss. Set aside the heart and liver. Brown the bird lightly in hot butter, then roast at 250°C, keeping it juicy. Baste repeatedly with the butter while roasting and remove the bacon early enough to brown the breast. When cooked leave to stand for 8 minutes, cut off the breast and legs and bone the bird completely. Wrap in foil and keep hot. Chop up the bones and carcase, pour off the butter in the roasting tin, then place the bones in the tin. Pour in the cream and cook slowly over moderate heat to obtain a thick sauce. Season well, strain and finish off with the heart and liver which have been fried and very finely chopped. Cut up the breast and legs, dish and coat lightly with sauce. Serve the rest of the sauce separately, also the boiled potatoes and the lettuce hearts in a dressing of lemon juice and icing sugar. Cut the apples in half, core them and poach in white wine, keeping them firm. Drain well, fill the hollows with red-currant jelly and use as a garnish for the capercailzie.

Norway

Roast grouse

Grouse may be eaten without hanging. Choose a young bird. Truss the bird, lard well and roast in a hot oven for about 25 minutes according to size. Serve with bread sauce and game chips.

Roast partridge

Choose a young bird and hang for 3–4 days. Truss and lard well. Roast for about 30 minutes basting frequently with hot butter. A few minutes before serving remove the bacon, dredge with flour and baste well to give a pale brown appearance. Dish on toast and serve gravy and bread sauce separately.

Roast pheasant

Truss the pheasant in the same way as a chicken but leave the head on. Cover the breast with slices of bacon or lard it with strips of fat bacon and roast in a moderate oven from 40–50 minutes according to size. Baste frequently with hot butter. After the bird is about three-quarters cooked remove the bacon, dredge the breast lightly with flour to give a light brown appearance. Remove the trussing strings and serve on a hot dish, garnished with watercress. Serve separately the gravy and bread sauce.

Roast quail

After plucking remove the head, neck and stomach but do not draw. Truss each bird and brush over with warm butter. Cover each breast with a vine leaf and tie a piece of bacon over the leaf. Attach them to a long skewer running it through the body of each bird and roast for 12–15 minutes basting frequently with hot butter. When cooked remove skewers and string. The bacon and vine leaves may be served with the birds after being brushed over with warm glaze. Serve the birds on pieces of toast previously put into the dripping tin to catch the trail as it drops from the birds. Garnish with watercress and serve the gravy separately.

Roast snipe

Dress the bird but do not draw. Truss but skin the head and leave it on—the long beak being passed through the legs and body instead of a skewer. Brush the bird with warm butter and tie a thinslice of fat bacon over the breast. Have ready a piece of toast for each bird and plac e the dripping tin to catch the drippings from the trail. Baste frequently with warm butter and roast for about 15 minutes. Dish on the toast and garnish with watercress. Serve the gravy separately.

Roast woodcock

After plucking very carefully as the skin is very tender, truss, but skin the head and leave on the bird passing the beak through the legs and body in place of a skewer.

Brush the bird with warm butter and tie a thin slice of fat bacon over the breast. Put slices of toast in the dripping tin to catch the trail drippings. Roast for about 15 minutes or a little less if liked underdone. Garnish with watercress and serve the gravy separately.

COLD DISHES

Cold capercailzie in aspic with ham

8 persons   Cooking time: 1–1½ hours

	1 capercailzie (young cock or hen)	
	8 slices cooked ham, trimmed square	
	cored sliced apples, poached in white wine and lemon juice	
	glacé cherries	
	slices of truffle or stuffed olives	
100 g	butter for roasting	4 oz
1½ l	Madeira-flavoured game aspic	2½ pt
	pork fat or bacon for larding	

Pluck, singe and draw the bird very carefully, then cut away the thin neck bone with the point of a very sharp knife. Push the breast out well, sprinkle with salt inside and outside, truss, lard and roast, making sure the oven is not too hot and keeping the bird a little underdone. Allow to cool, cut off and skin the drumsticks, trim, cut the meat off the thighs and slice. Skin the breast and flatten it underneath so that it will stand on the board. Meanwhile, coat a suitable silver dish with aspic. Cut 8 thin slices off each half breast parallel with the breastbone and place on a wire rack in the same order. Chill well, glaze thinly with aspic jelly and decorate each slice with a slice of truffle or olive. Glaze again and chill well. Arrange the trimmed drumsticks on the aspic-lined dish to make a base and cover with the sliced thigh meat. With the help of a fork, arrange the slices of breast on either side to simulate feathers. Cover the centre completely with the apple slices, each decorated with half a glacé cherry and glazed with aspic. On either side of the bird, arrange 4 slices of ham which have been curved to a slightly convex shape, glazed with aspic and well chilled. Use cubes of aspic jelly as an additional garnish.

Sweden

Cold roast pheasant and partridge

10 persons   Roasting time: pheasants, 25 minutes; partridges, 18 minutes

	2 large pheasants	
	2 large partridges	
300 g	smoked bacon (fat)	10 oz
250 g	carrots	8 oz
250 g	parsley roots	8 oz
200 g	onions	8 oz
	1 sprig thyme	
300 g	butter	10 oz
400 g	goose or duck livers	14 oz
2 cl	Cognac	2 dessertspoons
1 dl	Béchamel sauce	$\frac{1}{4}$ pt
$\frac{1}{2}$ l	white chaud-froid sauce	$\frac{3}{4}$ pt
	noodle dough	
	sour cream	
	truffles	
	red currants	
	fruit	
$1\frac{1}{2}$ l	aspic jelly	$2\frac{1}{2}$ pt

Clean the game birds thoroughly, draw, wash and dry them, season with salt, truss and lard with thin slices of fat bacon (or pork fat). Place on a bed of root vegetables (carrots, parsley roots and onions), pour hot butter over and roast briskly, basting frequently and removing the larding fat in time for the breasts to brown well. After removing from the oven, fry the root vegetables lightly together with the goose or duck livers which have been cut up small. The livers should remain rather underdone. Mince three times, using the finest cutter, and mix with the creamed butter. Season with salt, pepper and a pinch of grated nutmeg.

Cut the two halves of the breast off each bird carefully and spread the carcases with the purée. Cut the breasts on the slant into thin slices and replace on the carcases. Decorate as shown in the illustration, glaze with aspic jelly and arrange on a mirror base or a silver tray coated with aspic.

For the garnish, sieve the scraps from the pheasants and partridges with a little Béchamel sauce, mix with the rest of the liver purée, the Cognac and a little aspic jelly, season with salt and pepper, fill into small moulds and refrigerate until set. Turn out, mask with chaud-froid sauce, decorate with tiny dots of truffle and red currants, and glaze with aspic. The leaves consist of firm noodle dough mixed with very little butter and sour cream, and baked until golden. Other items which may be used to garnish this dish include apricots, cherries, green almonds and red currants.

(Illustration, p. 915)   Hungary

Hazel hen Veronica

8 persons   Cooking time: breast, 12–15 minutes; legs, 6–8 minutes

	8 hazel hens	
	1 small can truffles	
	2 egg yolks	
¼ l	dairy cream	½ pt
200 g	mushrooms	7 oz
	2 tablespoons oil	
	grapes	
approx. ½ l	white chaud-froid sauce	⅞ pt approx.
¾ l	aspic jelly	1¼ pt
	butter	

Pluck the hazel hens carefully without damaging the skin, draw, and wipe out the inside thoroughly. Cut through each bird vertically to separate the breast from the legs. Remove the breast halves, working from the back to keep them in one piece. Cut off the breast fillets, place the breast halves on oiled paper and flatten them lightly. Prepare forcemeat with the breast fillets, the egg yolks and the cream, season with salt and pepper, chill well and divide in two. Slice the truffles thinly and cut 40–50 tiny heart shapes out of the slices. Chop the rest of the truffles and the trimmings and mix with half the forcemeat. Fill the breast halves with the truffled forcemeat, fit together in pairs to meet, sew together lightly and roll in thinly buttered greaseproof paper. Roast carefully in a hot oven and allow to cool. Place the legs in moulds of even size and shape, and roast very lightly in butter. Season the birds' hearts and livers, fry, cut into small cubes and mix with the mushrooms which have also been fried and diced. Add to the remaining forcemeat (not containing truffles) and check the taste, making sure the forcemeat is well-seasoned. Fill into the leg halves, making the top slightly rounded, smooth over, roast in the oven for 6–8 minutes, then cool. When quite cold, mask with white chaud-froid sauce, decorate with the truffle hearts, leave until firm, then glaze with aspic. Slice the stuffed breasts evenly and glaze lightly with aspic. Arrange with the stuffed legs on a rectangular dish which has been coated with aspic and garnish with peeled white grapes.

Norway

Pheasant breasts vintager style

8 persons   Roasting time: 12–15 minutes

4 plump pheasant breasts
bacon for larding
mirepoix
a few peppercorns
6–8 juniper berries

	1 bay leaf	
120 g	butter	4 oz
	2 large ripe apples	
250 g	grapes, peeled and seeded	8 oz
	2 oranges	
$\frac{1}{8}$ l	red wine	$\frac{1}{4}$ pt
$\frac{1}{2}$ l	game aspic	$\frac{3}{4}$ pt

Bone and skin the pheasant breasts, season lightly with salt and pepper, wrap in thin slices of bacon and lay on a bed of mirepoix and spices. Pour melted butter over and roast at 250°C, leaving the meat slightly pink inside. Near the end of the cooking time pour in the red wine and baste well. When the pheasant breasts are cooked, remove from the oven, allow to cool and remove the bacon. Peel the apples, cut four neat even slices from each of them, core these and fry in butter, taking care to keep them whole. Cut each breast in half and place on a slice of apple. Decorate with peeled, seeded slices of orange and peeled grapes and glaze lightly with game aspic.

Austria

Pheasant medallions

Yield: 6

	$\frac{1}{2}$ lightly roasted breast of	
	pheasant (cold)	
60 g	foie gras or game purée	2 oz
	6 tiny marrons glacé	
	port jelly	

Cut out 6 pheasant breast medallions of equal size and thickness. Decorate with foie gras or game purée, using a star pipe, and place a marron glacé in the centre. Refrigerate, then glaze with port jelly.

Germany

Quail barquettes

10 barquettes   Cooking time: quails, 15–20 minutes

10 plump quails
10 puff pastry barquettes
foie gras purée
fresh morels
fresh white breadcrumbs
eggs

approx. 1 l	game chaud-froid sauce	1¾ pt approx.
	game aspic	
	10 truffle slices	
	10 poached fluted mushroom	
	caps	
	butter	

Bone the quails, but leave the leg bones in place. Clean the morels well, chop finely, fry lightly in butter, mix with fresh white breadcrumbs or with white bread which has been soaked and squeezed dry, bind with egg and season well. Stuff the quails with this forcemeat, sew up and restore each bird to its original shape. Roast slowly in the oven, then leave until quite cold. Transfer to a wire rack, mask with chaud-froid sauce, allow to set, decorate with a slice of truffle and glaze with game aspic. Garnish each quail with a fluted mushroom cap and a tiny ball of truffle impaled on a fancy skewer. Fill the barquettes with foie gras purée and place a quail on each one.

(Illustration, p. 241)   Germany

Quails Castel Snagow

10 persons   Cooking time: 12–15 minutes

	10 plump quails	
400–500 g	gratin forcemeat for game	1 lb approx.
	50–60 black grapes	
	1 small onion	
	1 small carrot	
¾ l	veal stock	1¼ pt
	2 small egg whites	
2 dl	dry sherry	⅓ pt
	10 sheets gelatine	

Skin the grapes, carefully remove the pips without damaging the grapes and macerate in half the sherry for 1–2 hours under cover. Remove the breastbones from the quails, stuff each quail with gratin forcemeat and wrap in aluminium foil. Cover the bottom of a sauté pan with the breastbones and the onion and carrot, thinly sliced, and lay the quails on top close together. Pour in the hot veal stock, cover with buttered paper, then with a lid, and poach slowly in the oven. Meanwhile, slowly heat the grapes and sherry to 80°C, drain thoroughly and collect the liquid. When the quails are cooked, remove from the stock and drain thoroughly. Strain the stock and add the gelatine which has been soaked and squeezed dry. Beat the egg whites well with the liquid drained from the grapes, pour in the warm stock while whisking, then bring to the boil, whisking constantly. Remove from the heat at once and cover. When the egg white has formed a grey crust on top and the jelly is quite clear, strain through a cloth. Check the taste.

When the jelly is completely cold, add the rest of the sherry. The jelly should be very delicate and well-flavoured.

Unwrap the quails, dry well, arrange in a porcelain pan (roaster) and surround with the grapes. Wait until the jelly is beginning to set, then pour over the quails and grapes to cover completely. Place the lid on the pan and leave in a cool place until ready to use.

Germany

Stuffed quail on chestnut rice

10 persons   Cooking time: 10 minutes

	10 plump quails	
200 g	foie gras	8 oz
100 g	white bread without crusts	4 oz
1 dl	dairy cream	3 fl oz
	chestnut rice	
	1 game mousse bombe, decorated as desired	
	10 small moulds foie gras loaf	
	red cabbage leaves without stalks, stewed in red wine	
	sliced cucumber	
	rashers of fat bacon	
	butter	
	aspic	

Prepare fine forcemeat with the foie gras, the quail livers, the white bread soaked in the cream, salt and forcemeat flavouring. Remove the breastbone from the quails, stuff with the forcemeat, season, truss, wrap in fat bacon and roast in a brisk oven. When cold, decorate as desired, glaze with aspic and arrange on a bed of chestnut rice. Place on a rectangular dish and garnish with the game mousse bombe, small moulds of foie gras loaf and stewed red cabbage leaves rolled into balls on slices of cucumber.

(Illustration, p. 913)   Austria

Wild duck parfait

10–15 persons   Cooking time: 40 minutes

	3 wild ducks	
1 l	dairy cream	1¾ pt
300 g	white bread	10 oz
200 g	smoked bacon	7 oz
50 g	currants	2 oz

a little wild duck blood
chicken stock
2 small bay leaves
6–8 juniper berries
1 onion
thin rashers of fat bacon
grated nutmeg
paprika

The wild ducks should preferably be skinned before use. Cut away the breasts. Draw and wash the ducks, blanch the carcases and legs, pour off the water, then cook in chicken stock with the onion, the bay leaves and the juniper berries until soft enough to disintegrate. Pass through a sieve, reduce to 1 l (1¾ pt), add the cream and again reduce to 1 l (1¾ pt). While still boiling hot, pour over the white bread and allow to cool. Remove all tendons from the wild duck breasts, which have been skinned beforehand, whirl in the blender with the white bread, gradually add the rendered bacon fat and the currants, and season with salt, grated nutmeg and paprika.

Line a pâté mould with thin rashers of bacon, cover the bottom and sides with two-thirds of the pâté mixture, darken the remainder with a little wild duck blood and fill into the centre of the mould. Weight the top a little and poach, making sure that the water does not boil. When cold, turn out, decorate as desired, glaze with Madeira aspic and garnish as desired.

(Illustration, p. 919)   Austria

PIES

Chicken pie 1

12 persons   Baking time: about 1 hour

1 kg 200	1 young chicken weighing	2½ lb
300 g	lean pork	10 oz
600 g	pork back fat	1¼ lb
250 g	foie gras	8 oz
100 g	pickled tongue	4 oz
	1 large truffle	
approx. 1 kg	pie paste	2¼ lb

	thin slices of pork fat	
	(or fat green bacon)	
30–35 g	seasoned salt	1 oz
½ l	Madeira-flavoured jelly	¾ pt
5 cl	Cognac	2 fl oz

Skin the chicken and bone it completely. Cut the breast flesh into strips a good 15 mm (⅝ in) thick, clean and trim the foie gras and cut into strips, season the truffle and marinate all these ingredients under cover in the Cognac for 2 hours. Mince the rest of the chicken, the pork, the back fat and the foie gras trimmings, using the finest blade of the mincer, then rub through a sieve. Add the seasoned salt and the Cognac, stir in the diced truffle and tongue and mix well. Line an oblong pie mould with pie pastry pinned out 7 mm (about ¼ in) thick and press down well all round. The pastry should come about 2 cm (¾ in) above the top edges of the mould. Line the bottom and sides with thin slices of pork fat (or fat bacon) and then with a thick layer of forcemeat. Lay strips of chicken breast and foie gras on the forcemeat, cover with another layer of forcemeat, then a second layer of chicken and foie gras, and finish off with the rest of the forcemeat. Smooth the top, cover with a slice of pork fat, turn in the edges of the pastry, moisten lightly and place a pastry lid on top. Make 2 small holes in the top and insert a small tube of greased paper in each as a steam vent. Egg wash, decorate as desired with scraps of pastry and brush with egg again. To bake, start off in a hot oven, then reduce the heat, cover with a damp sheet of thick paper, if necessary, to prevent excessive browning of the top, and bake off in a moderate oven. When the pie is cooked, remove the tubes of paper from the vents and cool on a wire rack. When quite cold, pour in the cold liquid jelly through a funnel inserted into one of the vents. Chill well for 12 hours before cutting.

(Illustration, p. 922)   Germany

Chicken pie II

2 persons   Baking time: about 50 minutes

	1 young cockerel	
900 g	weighing about	2 lb
125 g	small raw mushrooms	4 oz
	10–12 small onions	
75 g	lean bacon	2 oz
	1 clove of garlic	
60 g	butter	2 oz
	2 chopped shallots	
¼ l	red wine	½ pt
	pinch of thyme	
	1 tablespoon flour	
250 g	rough puff pastry	½ lb
	1 egg	

Divide the cockerel into joints, season with salt and pepper and lightly brown in butter. Remove from the pan and brown the diced bacon, the well-cleaned mushrooms and the onions in the butter. Return the chicken pieces to the pan, add the shallots, the crushed garlic and the thyme, dust with the flour, cook for a moment, pour in the red wine and mix well. Adjust the seasoning, allow to cool a little and transfer to a pie dish. Cover with the pastry, make a vent in the centre, wash with beaten egg, decorate with leaves cut out of the pastry, brush with egg again and bake in a moderate oven. Serve hot.

Germany

Macaroni pie

10 persons   Baking time: 45 minutes

400 g	fine flour	14 oz
300 g	butter	10 oz
250 g	sugar	8 oz
	4 eggs	
200 g	chicken hearts and gizzards	7 oz
150 g	sweetbreads (calves')	5 oz
	2 small chicken breasts, skinned	
	2 tablespoons Marsala	
1 dl	rum	3 fl oz
½ l	milk	¾ pt
400 g	small macaroni	14 oz
	grated Parmesan cheese	

Work the flour, 250 g (8 oz) butter, 200 g (7 oz) sugar and 2 egg yolks to a paste, shape into a ball, wrap in a cloth and refrigerate. Clean the chicken giblets, blanch and skin the sweetbreads and cut into small pieces, together with the chicken breasts. Heat 25 g (1 oz) butter in a pan, add the giblets, sweetbreads and chicken breasts, toss lightly in the butter, stir in the Marsala, add a little bouillon if required and cook to a thick stew, reducing the liquid well. Place 2 egg yolks in a stew-pan, mix well with a small spoonful of flour, the rest of the sugar and the rum, heat while stirring with a wire whisk, pour in the milk and beat over gentle heat without allowing to boil, to make a liquid custard. Stand aside to cool, stirring from time to time to prevent skinning. Cook the macaroni 'al dente' in 4 l (7 pt) boiling salted water, then pour off the water and drain well.

Line a timbale mould at least 10 cm (4 in) deep with strips of paste, setting aside enough paste for a lid and decoration. Place the macaroni in a basin, mix with the stew, the custard and grated Parmesan cheese and fill into the mould. Cover with a pastry lid, decorate as desired with pieces of pastry, seal the edge of the pie with a rope of pastry and press down well. Brush the top with butter and bake at 180°C until golden-brown and crisp. Stand aside for a short time before removing from the mould and do not cut until about to serve.

This recipe dates from Renaissance times, before tomatoes were known in Europe and before Béchamel sauce was invented. Rum was introduced into Italy during the Crusades. The pastry must be sweet.

(Illustration, p. 577)   Italy

Meat pie (family pie)

10–12 persons   Baking time: 50–60 minutes

250 g	lean boneless pork	8 oz
250 g	veal	8 oz
500 g	pork back fat	1 lb
100 g	pickled tongue	3 oz
	1 small truffle	
150 g	fat unsmoked belly of pork	5 oz
	(or green bacon)	
approx. 500 g	pie paste	1 lb
	thin slices of pork fat	
	(or fat bacon) for lining	
25 g	seasoned salt	1oz

Mince the pork, veal and back fat twice, using the finest cutter, and rub through a fine sieve. Season well with seasoned salt and add a little Cognac. Mix with the belly of pork (or green bacon) which has been blanched and diced, the diced tongue and the coarsely chopped truffle, adding a few blanched pistachio nuts if desired. Line the bottom and sides of a broad shallow tin (or pie case made of strong aluminium foil) with very thin slices of pork fat (or fat bacon) and fill with the forcemeat. Lay some more thin slices of pork fat on top and cover with a lid of pie pastry. Score with a fork, cut a hole in the centre as a steam vent and insert a small tube of greased paper. Egg wash the pastry and bake in a medium oven. Chill well before cutting.

Alternatively, pin out the pastry to a large rectangle, line the bottom with slices of pork fat (or fat bacon), cover with forcemeat, lay some more slices of pork fat on top and fold the sides and ends of the pastry over to enclose the filling completely, giving the pie a somewhat flattened oblong shape. Egg wash, score with a fork, make a steam vent and bake in a fairly hot oven. Cover with a damp sheet of thick paper, if necessary, to prevent excessive browning of the top.

(Techniques, p. 126)   Germany

Pheasant pie

15–18 persons		Baking time: 70–75 minutes	

approx. 3 kg	2 pheasants, total weight	6½ lb
250 g	boned veal	8 oz
250 g	lean pork	8 oz
1 kg	pork back fat	2¼ lb
200 g	foie gras	8 oz
350 g	fat bacon	12 oz
	2 truffles	
	4 eggs	
50 g	spiced salt	1½ oz
4 cl	Cognac	4 dessertspoons
¾ l	game aspic	1¼ pt
1 kg	pie paste	2¼ lb
2 cl	Madeira	2 dessertspoons
	beaten egg to egg wash	

Prepare and skin the pheasants. Cut all the flesh off the bones, brown these and use in making the aspic. Remove all sinews from the leg meat and add trimmings from the breasts to make up to 500–550 g (about 1 lb 2 oz–1 lb 4 oz). Cut the breasts into strips the size of the little finger, cut the foie gras into strips and blanch 200 g (7 oz) bacon. Marinate the breasts, foie gras and blanched bacon under cover together with the truffles cut in quarters for at least 2–3 hours in the Cognac with pâté spices, thyme, a small bay leaf, salt and pepper. Mince the leg meat and breast trimmings, pork, veal and back fat 2 or 3 times, using the finest blade of the mincer. Season with the spiced salt, flavour with the Cognac from the marinade, mix well with the eggs, check the taste and rub through a fine sieve if necessary.

Pin out the pie paste 4 mm (about ⅙ in) thick and use to line the bottom and sides of a long rectangular pie tin or 2 oval pie dishes. Cover the bottom and sides with thin rashers of fat bacon and spread to the thickness of a finger with the well-worked forcemeat. If using a rectangular tin, fill with alternate layers of forcemeat, strips of pheasant breast, foie gras, bacon and truffles, ending with a slightly dome-shaped layer of forcemeat. Cover with a thin piece of bacon and place a small bay leaf and a little thyme on top. Cover over with a lid of pie paste and seal the edges all round with the help of pastry pincers. Cut 2 round holes in the lid for the escape of steam and insert a vent made of greased paper. Score a cross in the pastry lid, egg wash, decorate as desired with scraps of pastry and egg wash again. Place in a hot oven for a short time, then turn down the heat and bake off in a medium oven. To bake off, the pie may be covered with aluminium foil or oiled paper to avoid excessive browning. If oval or round pie dishes are used, the filling (pheasant breast, foie gras, truffles, etc.) may be diced and mixed with the forcemeat.

When the pie is quite cold, fill with cold liquid Madeira-flavoured jelly through the holes in the top. Wait 24 hours before cutting.

Germany

Pork pie 'Raxo' Galician style

400 g	plain bread dough	1 lb
	5 eggs	
1 dl	olive oil (cold) or melted lard	3 fl oz
	flour	
	1 small glass white wine	

Forcemeat

250 g	finely sliced pork	8 oz
200 g	onions	7 oz
	2 large sweet peppers	
100 g	lean ham or chorizo, diced	3 oz
1 dl	oil	3 fl oz
	2 cloves of garlic	
	2 tablespoons tomato purée	
	½ glass white or red wine	
	a little powdered saffron	
	ground pepper	
	salt	

Place the bread dough in a glazed bowl and add 4 eggs, 1 dl (⅙ pt) oil, the small glassful of white wine and a pinch of salt. Mix well and work to a smooth, fairly slack dough, adding a little water or sieved flour, as the case may be, to bring to the right consistency. Cover with a cloth and allow to recover for 15–20 minutes.

To make the forcemeat, sprinkle the sliced pork with a little salt and fry in the oil, together with the diced ham or chorizo. When lightly coloured, add the chopped onions and garlic. Fry until the onions begin to colour, then add the tomato purée and wine. Season with the saffron and a little paprika. Reduce until almost dry. Lastly stir in the peppers cut into fairly large squares or strips and adjust the seasoning. Allow to cool.

When the dough has recovered, divide it into two equal pieces. Pin out one piece to 5 mm (⅕ in) thick and line a lightly buttered mould. Fill evenly with the cold forcemeat and cover with a lid of thinly pinned-out dough, moistening the edges to seal. Turn up the edges to give a neat finish. Cut the remaining dough into stars, leaves or small rings and fix on to the top of the pie with beaten egg. Prick with a fork to allow the release of steam. Egg wash and bake in a medium oven.

Spain

Veal, ham and egg pie

10–12 persons   Cooking time: about 2 hours

600 g	cushion of veal	1¼ lb
600 g	raw ham	1¼ lb
30 g	finely chopped onion	1 oz
	4 hard-boiled eggs	
300 g	thinly sliced rindless streaky bacon	½ lb
	8 sheets gelatine	
¼ l	white stock	½ pt
	puff pastry	
	beaten egg	

Line a large pie dish with the thinly sliced streaky bacon. Cover with a layer of thin escalopes of veal. Add a layer of ham and a layer of sliced hard-boiled egg. Arrange further layers of veal, ham and egg, seasoning lightly and sprinkling the layers with the finely chopped onion. When the dish is filled, place the soaked gelatine leaves on top, pour the white stock over, and cover with puff paste rolled out to about 4 mm (⅛ in) thickness. Crimp the edges, wash with egg, decorate with leaves of paste, egg wash again and bake at 220°C for 15 minutes, then reduce the heat to 150°C and bake for a further 1½ hours or so. Allow to cool before serving.

Great Britain

Venison pie

15–18 persons   Baking time: 70–75 minutes

	3 fillets (filets mignons) of roebuck	
500 g	roebuck, boned, skinned and free from tendons	1 lb
250 g	foie gras	8 oz
450 g	lean pork	1 lb
1 kg	pork back fat	2 lb
	2 truffles	
	thin slices of fresh pork fat (or green bacon)	
approx. 750 g	pie paste	1½ lb approx.
5 cl	Madeira	1½ fl oz
5 cl	Cognac	1½ fl oz
	seasoned salt	
approx. ½ l	Madeira-flavoured jelly	¾ pt approx.

Skin the fillets carefully, clean the foie gras, trim and cut up lengthwise. Sprinkle lightly with salt and pepper, place in a basin, pour in the Cognac and Madeira, add a few crushed juniper berries and marinate for at least 2 hours. Prepare fine forcemeat with the boned and skinned roebuck, the pork, the back fat and the foie gras trimmings. Add 30 g (1 oz) seasoned salt per kg (2 lb 3 oz) and stir in the Cognac and Madeira used as a marinade (without the juniper berries). Line the bottom and sides of an oblong pie mould with pie pastry pinned out about 7 mm (¼ in) thick and press down well. Now line with thin slices of pork fat (or green bacon), then with forcemeat. Place one of the roebuck fillets on the bottom, fill the spaces at the sides with forcemeat, cover with the strips of foie gras and the truffles cut in quarters, then add the remaining 2 fillets, fill up all the spaces with forcemeat and cover with a final layer of forcemeat slightly rounded in the middle. Fold the left-hand and right-hand edges of the pastry inwards, cover with a pastry lid and seal well with the help of pastry pincers. Make 2 steam escape holes, egg wash, notch the sides with the pincers, decorate along the top as desired and egg wash again. To bake, start off in a hot oven, then finish baking in a moderate oven. Cover with a damp sheet of thick paper, if necessary, to prevent excessive browning of the top. When cooked, cool on a wire rack. When quite cold, fill with the cold liquid jelly through a funnel inserted into the vents. Chill well for at least 12 hours before using.

(Illustration, p. 922)   Germany

Raised pork pie

500 g	flour	1 lb
125 g	lard	4 oz
	2 teaspoonfuls salt	
125 ml	water	¼ pt
750 g	lean pork	1½ lb
	1 egg	
125 ml	stock	¼ pt
	chopped parsley	
	1 small onion	
	salt and pepper	
	jellied stock	

Sieve the flour and salt into a bowl. Boil the water and lard together and pour into the flour. Mix quickly to a fairly soft dough. Turn on to a floured board, and knead to a smooth dough. Mould the pie in the usual way, reserving ¼ of the paste for the lid. Mince the pork and mix with the parsley, seasoning, stock and chopped hard-boiled egg, and fill the pie. Cover with the lid and seal well. Decorate the lid, leaving a steam vent. Tie a band of foil around the pie and bake in a moderate oven for 1½–2 hours. When cooked, and still warm, fill up with warm jelly stock, through the vent hole.

Great Britain

Steak and kidney pie

750 g	chuck steak	1½ lb
100 g	kidney	4 oz
	seasoned flour	
	1 onion peeled and chopped	
100 g	flaky pastry	4 oz
	beaten egg	

Trim the meat and cut into 5 cm (2 in) cubes. Skin, core and slice the kidney. Toss both in seasoned flour. Simmer the meat and onion for about 1½ to 2 hours in very little water, or until almost cooked. Allow to cool. Place in a pie dish filling the dish so that the crust is supported. Add some gravy from the meat.

Roll out the pastry allowing about 2½ cm (1 in) more than the size of the pie dish all round. Wet the rim of the pie dish and place a 2 cm (¾ in) wide strip on it cut from round the pastry. Damp the pastry rim. Cover the pie with pastry pressing the edges on the damp rim. Trim and scallop the edges. Any remaining trimming can be cut into leaves to decorate the pie. Brush with beaten egg and bake near the top of the oven for about 15 minutes or until pastry is well risen and light brown. Reduce the oven to moderate heat and continue cooking for another 30–40 minutes. With good quality meat the preliminary stewing is unnecessary. The meat can be prepared and put straight into the pie dish and cooked as above allowing 2 hours after reducing the oven to moderate heat.

PÂTÉS AND TERRINES

Liver pâté

500 g	pig's liver	1 lb
250 g	fat pork or bacon	½ lb
	1 red onion	
	6 salted anchovy fillets	
	1 teaspoon ground cloves	
	1 teaspoon freshly ground black pepper	
15 g	salt	½ oz
	2 eggs	
50 g	margarine or butter	1½ oz
50 g	flour	1½ oz
4 dl	milk	⅔ pt

Mince the liver and the fat pork (or bacon) several times, using the finest blade of the mincer, then mince the onion and the anchovy fillets. Separate the eggs. Mix the yolks, the salt and the spices with the minced liver and pork, add the onion and anchovy fillets and work thoroughly. Make a blond roux with the flour and the margarine or butter, whisk in the milk and cook for 4–5 minutes. Allow to cool, blend with the liver mixture and fold in the stiffly whipped egg whites. Fill into a buttered mould and bake in a bain-marie for 1 hour at 200°C.

Sweden

Quail terrine Schweizerhof

45 persons   Cooking time: about 1¼ hours

	8 quails	
4 cl	Cognac	4 dessertspoons
	8 small pieces goose liver	
	8 small rashers larding bacon	
	fat bacon for lining terrine	
	white chaud-froid sauce	

745

Forcemeat

800 g	pork back fat	1 lb 12 oz
800 g	lean pork	1 lb 12 oz
200 g	veal	8 oz
150 g	foie gras	5 oz
	1 egg	
1 dl	Cognac	3 fl oz
1 dl	Noilly Prat vermouth	3 fl oz
35 g	spiced salt	1 oz
100 g	chopped truffles	3 oz
100 g	chopped pistachio nuts	3 oz

Garnish

20 slices of orange
celeriac salad
20 cocktail cherries
20 quarter pears
sieved figs

Bone the quails completely, starting from the back. Marinate in the Cognac for 24 hours.

Mince the back fat, pork, veal and foie gras, using the 5 mm ($\frac{1}{4}$ in) blade of the mincer, then mince again through the 2 mm ($\frac{1}{10}$ in) cutter. Work well with the egg, Cognac, Noilly Prat and spiced salt. Stuff the quails with a small piece of goose liver wrapped in larding bacon and 50 g ($1\frac{3}{4}$ oz) of the forcemeat, then truss the birds to their original shape. Mix the remaining forcemeat with the chopped truffles and pistachio nuts.

Line a King Cake mould with thin slices of fat bacon and spread with forcemeat. Place the stuffed quails in the mould, fill up with forcemeat, cover with thin slices of fat bacon and place a bay leaf on top. Cover with a lid and poach in a bain-marie in the oven at about 220°C. Cool under light pressure, then coat with white chaud-froid sauce and decorate the top with truffles to depict the Schweizerhof emblem.

Garnish with slices of orange topped with celeriac salad and a cocktail cherry, and also with poached quarter pears (with stalks) and small cones of sieved figs.

(Illustration, p. 920)   Switzerland

Terrine of pheasant

Cooking time: 60–70 minutes

	2 medium-size pheasants, drawn and cleaned	
100 g	pork	4 oz
100 g	veal	4 oz
500 g	hard back pork fat	1¼ lb
200 g	foie gras	7 oz
80 g	truffles	2 oz
300 g	gratin forcemeat	10 oz
	rashers of bacon	
	1 bay leaf	
	1 sprig thyme	
5 cl	Cognac	1½ fl oz
	forcemeat flavouring	

Bone and skin the pheasants. Prepare a small quantity of strong stock with the carcase and a mirepoix which have been lightly browned together. Trim the pheasant breasts, cut up lengthwise and marinate in the Cognac under cover for at least 2 hours together with the truffles and the coarsely diced foie gras. Prepare fine forcemeat with the flesh from the legs, the trimmings, the pork, veal, gratin forcemeat and back fat. Add salt, pepper, forcemeat flavouring and the Cognac used as a marinade. Line the terrine with thin rashers of bacon and then with forcemeat. Fill up alternately with forcemeat, strips of pheasant breast, diced foie gras and cubes of truffle. Cover with a rasher of bacon and place a bay leaf and a sprig of thyme on top. Place the lid on the terrine and seal with flour and water paste. Cook in the oven in a bain-marie, the temperature of which should not exceed 90°C. To find out whether the terrine is cooked, test with a larding needle in the same way as a meat pie. Another indication that cooking is completed is to be found in the appearance of the fat which rises to the surface; if it is absolutely clear and limpid, with no traces of blood, the terrine may be removed from the oven. After removing, pour off the surplus fat, place a small board of suitable size on top and fix in position with a weight of not more than 1½ kg (3 lb 5 oz). When completely cold, remove the pâté from the dish and wipe dry. Clean the dish and mask the bottom lightly with fairly concentrated well-flavoured aspic jelly prepared from the pheasant stock. When set, replace the pâté in the dish, coat with the same aspic and fill up the spaces at the sides with aspic. Either cover with the lid or decorate the top as desired. Chill well for at least 12 hours before cutting.

(Illustration, p. 927)   Germany

Terrine of wild duck

12 persons   Cooking time: about 1¼ hours

	3 young wild ducks,	
2 kg 400–2 kg 700	total gross weight	5½–6 lb
400 g	lean pork	¾ lb
900 g	fresh fat belly of pork	2 lb
250 g	large flap mushrooms (boletus), canned	8¾ oz
150 g	chicken livers	5¼ oz
approx. 300 g	fat bacon	10½ oz approx.
1 dl	sherry	⅛ pt
1 dl	Cognac	⅛ pt
	4 eggs	
	1 onion	
	1 carrot	
	1 bay leaf	
	thyme	
50 g	butter	1¾ oz
approx. 60 g	spiced salt	2 oz
¾ l	aspic jelly	1¼ pt

Pluck, draw and skin the ducks. Set aside the livers after removing the gall. Cut all the flesh off the carcases and remove the sinews. Chop the bones up small, brown well together with the diced carrot and onion, pour in water to cover, simmer gently for 3 hours, strain, remove all the fat and reduce to a glaze. Cut 200 g (7 oz) of the duck breast meat into 1½ cm (½ in) cubes and fry lightly in butter. Transfer to a bowl, add the drained flap mushrooms and 150 g (5¼ oz) blanched bacon which have been cut into cubes of the same size, pour in the Cognac, sprinkle with a little spiced salt, cover and marinate for 2–3 hours.

Toss the chicken livers and the duck livers quickly in butter, keeping them underdone. Remove, rinse out the pan with the sherry to detach the sediment and add to the livers. Mince the remaining duck meat, the pork and fat belly of pork and the livers in their stock as finely as possible or whirl in the blender until finely reduced. Mix thoroughly with the eggs, the Cognac used as a marinade and the glaze, then season well with the spiced salt. Lastly work in the diced duck, flap mushrooms and bacon.

Line two oval terrines with thin rashers of fat bacon and pack with forcemeat. Lay an oval piece of fat bacon on top, add a bay leaf and a little thyme, cover and poach in a medium oven in a bain-marie. To test whether the forcemeat is cooked, insert a cold trussing needle; it should feel uniformly warm when held to the mouth. Alternatively, examine the fat rising to the surface; when it no longer contains traces of blood, the forcemeat is cooked.

After removing from the oven, cover with a thin board and a light weight to compress slightly. When quite cold, remove all fat and clean the terrine. Coat the bottom with a thin layer of aspic jelly, allow to set, then return the pâté to the terrine and pour in sufficient cold liquid jelly to cover completely. Place the lid on the terrine and leave for 24 hours before cutting.

If this dish is to be stored for some time, return the pâté to the cleaned terrine after removing the fat and pour in sufficient cold melted lard to cover completely. When the lard has solidified, place an oval piece of aluminium foil on top, cover with the lid and store in the refrigerator until required.

Germany

Chicken liver pâté

4–6 persons

100 g	butter	4 oz
	1 small chopped onion	
	4 bay leaves	
	pinch dried thyme	
900 g	chicken livers	2 lb
	salt and pepper	

Melt the butter in a pan. Add the onion, bay leaves and thyme. Cook gently for 2–3 minutes. Prepare the chicken livers; cut each into 2–3 pieces. Add to the pan and simmer for 5–7 minutes, or until the liver is cooked. Remove bay leaves. Mince the liver twice or put in a blender until smooth. Season well and place in a serving dish. Fork the top and chill before serving.

Chopped liver

500 g	chicken liver	1 lb
120 g	onion	4 oz
	2 hard-boiled eggs	
60 g	fresh white breadcrumbs	2 oz
	chicken fat	

Wash and trim the livers and drain them well. Fry gently in chicken fat until cooked but not dried out. Mince the liver and onion and hard-boiled eggs, add the breadcrumbs and blend to a smooth paste with a little melted chicken fat.

Jewish

Chicken liver pâté in brioche

10–12 persons   Baking time: 35–40 minutes

700 g	chicken livers	1 lb 8 oz
250 g	boneless veal	8¾ oz
300 g	green bacon	10½ oz
50 g	truffles	1¾ oz
50 g	blanched pistachio nuts	1¾ oz
1 cl	Cognac	1 fl oz
5 cl	Madeira	1½ fl oz
50 g	butter	1¾ oz
	pâté spices	
½ l	Madeira jelly	⅞ pint
400 g	unsweetened brioche dough	14 oz

(English edition page 828, but without sugar.)

Cut away the nerve fibres and greenish flesh from the livers, sponge them dry and toss quickly but very lightly in hot butter; they should remain pink and rare inside. Season and place in an earthenware dish. Rinse out the cooking pan with the Madeira and pour over the livers. Cover and marinate for at least 2 hours.

Pulp the veal, bacon and livers in the blender, rub through a sieve, flavour with the pâté spices, moisten with the marinade (cooking juices and Madeira) and the Cognac. Mix well and adjust the seasoning if necessary. Add the diced truffles and the pistachio nuts.

Lightly butter a kugelhopf mould and line evenly with brioche dough to a thickness of 7 mm (about ¼ inch). Fill up with the prepared forcemeat, cover with brioche dough and pinch the edges together firmly. Prove for half an hour and bake at 200°C (392°F). Leave until quite cold. Make a tiny hole in the top and pour in the half-set jelly. Hand Cumberland sauce separately.

(Illustration, p. 921)   Germany

GALANTINES

Chicken galantine medallions with crayfish tails

Yield: 6

120 g	chicken galantine	4 oz
60 g	foie gras purée	2 oz
	6 crayfish tails	
	white wine jelly	

Cut out six oval medallions of chicken galantine. Neatly pipe on the foie gras purée, using a star pipe, and cover with a crayfish tail split lengthwise, placing the red side uppermost. Chill well and glaze with white wine jelly.

Germany

Decorated chicken galantine

10–12 persons   Cooking time: 1 hour

	1 plump young chicken	
1 kg 500–2 kg	weighing	3½–4½ lb
200 g	veal	8 oz
800 g	pork back fat	1¾ lb
	1 teaspoon forcemeat flavouring	
	3 eggs	
2 dl	Cognac	6 fl oz
300 g	pickled tongue	10 oz
200 g	foie gras	8 oz
200 g	fat bacon	8 oz
75–100 g	truffles	3 oz about
75 g	pistachio nuts	3 oz
2 l	chicken stock (made from the carcase)	3½ pt
½ l	chicken chaud-froid sauce	¾ pt
1 l	chicken aspic	1¾ pt

751

truffles to decorate
8 stuffed tomatoes
jelly moulds
Cumberland sauce

Bone the chicken completely, cutting it open down the back and being careful not to damage the skin. Set the two breast fillets aside and mince the rest of the flesh twice with the veal and the pork back fat, using the finest blade of the mincer. Then rub through a fine sieve and work to a fine forcemeat with the eggs, the Cognac, the forcemeat flavouring, salt and pepper, after first using the Cognac and flavouring as a marinade for the tongue, foie gras and chicken breast, all cut into pencil strips, the truffles and the fat bacon. These ingredients should be left in the marinade under cover for at least 2 hours. Open the stripped chicken skin out flat and spread with a thick layer of forcemeat. Arrange the strips of tongue and foie gras down the centre together with the truffles cut into four or eight, the strips of chicken breast and bacon and the pistachio nuts to make a mosaic design, filling up the spaces with a little forcemeat. Cover with forcemeat and roll up in a napkin. Fasten the ends with twine and also tie round in the centre to keep in place. Poach and allow to cool in the chicken stock. When cold, remove, tie in a clean napkin, place a lightly weighted board on top and refrigerate overnight.

Remove all fat from the chicken stock and reduce, then use to make the white chaud-froid sauce and the aspic jelly. Season well.

Remove the galantine from the napkin, wipe dry, place on a wire rack, coat with the well-flavoured chaud-froid sauce, allow to set and decorate with truffles. When half-set, mask neatly with aspic.

Coat a rectangular dish with aspic. Arrange the galantine on it, cutting off 6–8 slices, and garnish with stuffed tomatoes and jelly moulds. If desired, hand Cumberland sauce separately.

(Illustration, p. 924)   USA

(Techniques, p. 125)

Galantine of breast of veal bourgeois style

12 persons   Cooking time: 2 hours

1 kg 400	boned breast of veal	3 lb
200 g	lean pork	8 oz
200 g	veal without gristle	8 oz
200 g	fresh pork back fat	8 oz

	2 large fillets of veal without gristle	
300 g	cooked pickled pig's tongues	10 oz
250 g	larding bacon	8 oz
⅛ l	dairy cream	¼ pt
¾ l	aspic jelly	1¼ pt
	meat glaze	
	1 truffle	
	12 tomatoes	
	hard-boiled eggs	
	cooked ham	
	asparagus tips	
	spinach medallions	
	unsweetened short paste	
	assorted vegetables	
3 cl	Cognac	3 dessertspoons
	forcemeat flavouring	
4 l	white veal stock	7 pt

Trim the boned breast of veal neatly, open out flat and lay it on the table with the inside uppermost. Mince the veal, pork and back fat together finely and blend well, rubbing through a fine sieve if necessary. Mix with the cream, add the Cognac, flavouring and salt to taste, and refrigerate. Lard the fillets of veal, brown lightly, allow to cool and wrap in thin slices of bacon. Dice the tongue tips and the rest of the bacon and add to the forcemeat, together with the coarsely chopped truffle. Spread the breast of veal with the forcemeat to a thickness of 3–3½ cm (1¼–1½ in). Arrange the tongues (whole) on top on one side and the larded veal fillets on the other. Cover with the rest of the forcemeat and fold the ends of the breast of veal over to enclose the filling, making sure the ends meet. Wrap the galantine in a cloth in the usual manner, tie firmly, poach slowly in the veal stock and leave until cold. Remove, unwrap, rinse out the cloth, tie up the galantine firmly again and press lightly.

Meanwhile, prepare short pastry cases and lids in the shape of shells and bake blind. Marinate the mixed vegetables.

Unwrap the galantine, trim if necessary, and coat with meat glaze mixed with a little aspic jelly. Cut most of it in thin slices, but leave the remainder as a showpiece. Carefully glaze the individual slices with aspic, either leaving them whole or cutting them in half according to the way in which they are to be arranged.

To dish, decorate the stuffed tomatoes with a slice of egg, a spinach medallion and an asparagus tip and glaze with aspic. Fill the short pastry shells with the marinated vegetables and half cover each one with a pastry lid.

(Illustration, p. 808)   Austria

Galantine of chicken

12–15 persons   Cooking time: 35 minutes per kg (2 lb 3 oz)

	1 plump young chicken	
2 kg	weighing	4½ lb
150 g	lean ham	5 oz
150 g	smoked fat belly of pork (or fat bacon)	5 oz
150 g	pickled tongue (tip)	5 oz
350 g	foie gras	12 oz
40 g	pistachio nuts (blanched)	2 oz
	2 fairly small truffles	
5 cl	Cognac	1 glass
5 cl	Madeira	1 glass

Forcemeat

approx. 250 g	flesh from the chicken legs	8 oz approx.
350 g	pork	12 oz
350 g	veal	12 oz
950 g	hard back pork fat	2 lb
	2 eggs	
40 g	spiced salt	1 oz approx.

After drawing and cleaning the chicken in the usual manner, cut off the wings above the first joint. Turn the bird on its front and, using a small sharp knife, cut through the back skin right down to the bone, starting at the top of the neck and stopping just short of the tail end. Cut the flesh off the carcase in one piece, then remove the leg and wing bones without cutting into the flesh. Tuck in the skin of the legs to give the finished galantine a better shape. Spread out the boned chicken skin side down and level out the flesh, cutting off the small breast fillets and distributing them over the bare areas of skin. Scrape the flesh off the legs and use for the forcemeat.

Stud the foie gras with a truffle cut into quarters, season with salt and pepper and marinate under cover in the Cognac and Madeira for 2 hours. Mince the flesh from the chicken legs, the veal, pork and back fat twice, using the finest cutter, then rub through a fine sieve or work in the blender until smooth. Mix well with the eggs, the marinade used for the foie gras and the spiced salt, then check the seasoning. Dice the remaining truffle, the ham, pickled tongue and smoked belly of pork (or bacon) and add to the forcemeat together with the pistachio nuts. Spread the boned chicken with a thick layer of forcemeat, cover with the foie gras cut lengthwise, then with the rest of the forcemeat. Instead of being diced, the tongue, ham, belly of pork and one truffle may be cut into strips and arranged round the foie gras with the other (quartered) truffle and the pistachio nuts, alternating the colours. Roll the chicken skin up round the forcemeat and wrap first in a very thin slice of pork fat (or fat bacon), then in a napkin or tammy cloth. Tie the ends securely, then tie round in several places with fairly thin thread. Meanwhile prepare strong chicken stock with the chopped-up carcase, the usual root vegetables and seasonings, then strain. Place the galantine in the hot stock, bring to the boil, poach slowly and allow to cool in the stock. When barely luke-warm, remove from the napkin, wipe well, then wrap (not too tightly) in the same napkin which has been rinsed and wrung out. Tie securely, cover with a board of suitable size, place a fairly light weight on top and leave under slight pressure until cold. Next day, unwrap, wipe well and either glaze the whole galantine with chicken aspic or cut off a few slices and glaze individually. Alternatively, the galantine may be coated with chicken chaud-froid sauce and decorated when the sauce is firm. It is then glazed with chicken aspic and garnished as desired.

(Illustration, p. 928)   Germany
(Techniques, p. 125)

ASPICS

Meat in aspic

4 persons

200–300 g	left-over cold meat	7–10 oz
100 g	small peas (canned)	4 oz
	truffle or gherkin cut into	
	star shapes	
	or small disks of red pepper	
6 dl	aspic jelly	1 pt
	1 lettuce	

Stand small moulds in ice or iced water and mask with aspic jelly. Decorate the bottom with a truffle star or a motif of red pepper or gherkin as desired, and fix in position with a little aspic. Cut the meat in pea-size pieces (saveloy or other sausage, pickled tongue, etc. may be used), mix with the peas and fill into the moulds. Fill these up to the top with liquid aspic jelly which is on the point of setting, then refrigerate until firm. Turn out on to a round glass dish shortly before serving. Place a prepared lettuce heart in the centre and fill with celery salad flavoured with a little lemon juice and dressed with cream mayonnaise.

Switzerland

Jellied tongue ring mould

4 persons

	12 thin slices pickled ox tongue	
	1 can asparagus tips	
150 g	cooked ham, cut in thin strips	5 oz
100 g	salami	3 oz
	red pepper	
	or thinly sliced pickled	
	cucumber	
1 l	aspic jelly	1½ pt
	1 lettuce heart	

756

Stand a ring mould on ice, mask with aspic jelly and leave until almost set. Arrange thin slices of pickled cucumber or disks of red pepper all round and stand pairs of asparagus tips upright in the mould at regular intervals, after cutting them into 5 cm (2 in) lengths and dipping them in aspic jelly which is about to set. Also dip the slices of tongue in jelly and arrange round the mould one overlapping another. Let the jelly set. Fill up the mould with aspic jelly which is on the point of setting. Sprinkle in the strips of ham, tongue trimmings and strips of pickled cucumber and stir lightly to distribute them through the aspic. Refrigerate until firm, turn out on to a round glass dish and fill the centre with salami cones and a lettuce heart. Serve with vegetable salad, toast and butter.

Ox tongue in aspic

4 persons

200 g	cold cooked pickled ox tongue, skinned	8 oz
	2 hard-boiled eggs	
	1 pickled cucumber	
	a little mayonnaise mixed with equal amount of soft butter	
	1 slice truffle or red pepper	
1 l	aspic jelly	1½ pt

Slice the tongue very thinly. Place a round mould of suitable size on ice and mask with cold aspic jelly to a thickness of ½ cm (about ¼ in). When the edge is quite firm, pour off the surplus.

Using a greaseproof paper bag, decorate the bottom with mayonnaise butter piped on in a symmetrical design, preferably a flower motif. Alternatively, thin slices of pickled cucumber and hard-boiled egg white may be arranged in a flower shape, or a similar motif may be made with truffle and red pepper; this decorative garnish is fixed in position with a little jelly.

When the bottom has been decorated, half-slices of hard-boiled egg which have been dipped in semi-liquid jelly to prevent their slipping are arranged all round.

When the mayonnaise butter (or the decorative garnish) is firm, cover with a layer of overlapping slices of tongue, pour over some liquid aspic jelly which is about to set, cover with another layer of slices of tongue and fill up with jelly.

Chill well in the refrigerator, dip in warm water for a moment, then turn out on to a glass dish.

(Illustration, p. 925)   Switzerland

Vegetable aspic

Line a deep cake tin about 30 cm (12 in) in diameter with well flavoured aspic. Marinate an assortment of vegetables for a short time, together with skinned and seeded tomato wedges. Drain very well and arrange on the bottom of the cake tin in a symmetrical pattern. Coat lightly with aspic and cover with a second layer of vegetables when set. Fill up with well seasoned vegetable salad mixed with a little aspic, or with more vegetables. Pour in aspic which is on the point of setting to fill up the tin and refrigerate for a few hours until firm.

(Illustration, p. 1027)   Austria

Asparagus mousse timbale

6–10 persons

2 kg 500	green asparagus	5 lbs 8 oz
3 dl	dairy cream	½ pint
½–1 l	aspic jelly	⅞–1¾ pints
1 l	Aurora chaud-froid sauce	1¾ pints
50 g	red peppers	1¾ oz
	cayenne pepper	

Scrape the asparagus and poach in salted water, bringing the water to the boil before adding the asparagus to keep the latter green. Cool and drain well. Select about 500 g (1 lb) even-sized spears and cut off the green tips. Set aside a further 9 choice tips for decoration and 18 to be tied into small bundles (3 per bundle and per person).

To make the mousse, drain the remaining asparagus thoroughly and pass through a fine sieve. Stir in the whipped cream, season with salt and cayenne pepper and add about ½ l (⅞ pint) aspic jelly which is on the point of setting. Mask a timbale mould with aspic and line with the asparagus tips which have been set aside, arranging them side by side. Fill the centre with the asparagus mousse and refrigerate until set.

Chill a round serving dish, cover with Aurora sauce and allow to set. Turn out the timbale in the centre of the dish. Decorate the top with a concentric motif made up of the 9 choice asparagus tips and the same number of small diamond shapes cut out of the red pepper. Pipe a rosette of butter right in the centre. Arrange the small bundles of asparagus round the timbale.

(Illustration, p. 993)   Italy

VEGETABLES

There are many, many varieties of vegetable in the world which are eaten from choice (or sometimes from necessity) by the people of the areas where they grow or are grown. Vegetables can be cooked in most ways, steamed, poached, boiled, braised, stewed, baked, roast and fried. They can be served as a dish in their own right, as an accompaniment to a main course, or as a garnish.

Artichoke bottoms

Yield: 6

	6 small artichoke bottoms (as fresh as possible)	
60 g	fresh smoked salmon, trimmed	3 oz
30 g	horseradish cream	1 oz
30 g	shrimps (12)	1 oz
	fish aspic flavoured with white wine	
	vinegar and oil marinade	

Marinate the artichoke bottoms very well and drain thoroughly. Dice the smoked salmon finely, mix with the horseradish cream and season well. Fill into the artichoke bottoms and decorate each one with 2 small picked shrimps. Chill well and glaze with fish aspic.

Germany

Artichoke hearts with sour cream

10 persons

	40 artichoke hearts	
$\frac{1}{2}$ l	white wine	$\frac{3}{4}$ pt
$\frac{1}{4}$ l	olive oil	$\frac{1}{2}$ pt

	small onions	
	3 cloves of garlic	
	1 tablespoon chopped parsley	
	1 tablespoon chopped dill	
¾ l	sour cream	1 pt
	lemon juice	
200 g	walnuts	8 oz

Prepare the artichoke hearts in the Greek style with the white wine, oil, onions, garlic, salt and pepper. Chill very well and place in glasses or small dishes with the chopped parsley and dill. Coat with the sour cream which has been sharpened with lemon juice and seasoned with salt and paprika. Sprinkle with the coarsely chopped walnuts to serve.

Germany

Asparagus gratin Valais style

4 persons (as an entrée)

1 kg 200	Valais asparagus	2½ lb
	5 large tomatoes	
50 g	butter	2 oz
50 g	flour	2 oz
50 g	concentrated tomato purée	2 oz
	1 bouillon cube	
	salt	
	pepper	
	cayenne pepper	
	Cognac	
1 dl	whipped cream	¼ pt

Clean and scrape the asparagus. Cook in salted water for 25–30 minutes, then drain. Return the cooking liquid to the pan, reduce well and add the bouillon cube.

Make a blond roux with the butter and flour and blend in 4 dl (⅔ pt) of the asparagus cooking liquid. Add the tomato purée, a few drops of Cognac, a dash of cayenne pepper and lastly the whipped cream.

Skin the tomatoes, remove the seeds, dice finely and fry lightly in butter. Season, then transfer to the bottom of a shallow fireproof dish. Arrange the asparagus on the bed of tomato in layers with their tips out of alignment. Coat with the sauce, then brown under a salamander or infra-red grill.

Switzerland

Aubergine risotto Sicilian style

4 persons

300 g	Arborio rice	10 oz
	3 medium-sized aubergines	
200 g	Mozzarella, finely sliced	7 oz
100 g	raw ham	4 oz
	2 spoons olive oil	
	½ onion, chopped	
1 dl	tomato sauce	¼ pt
1 l	chicken consommé	1½ pt
50 g	butter	2 oz
50 g	grated Parmesan cheese	2 oz
	6 basil leaves	
	frying oil for aubergines	
	salt	
	pepper	

Peel the aubergines and slice them finely. Sprinkle the slices with salt and leave them for 30 minutes to draw out the water, then wipe dry and fry in oil.

Chop the ham finely, fry lightly in the olive oil, add the onion and fry until lightly coloured. Pour in the tomato sauce, add salt and pepper, moisten with a little hot water and cook over very gentle heat for 30 minutes. Remove 2 ladlefuls of the sauce from the pan and set aside. Place the rice in the pan and mix with the remaining sauce. Now pour in the hot consommé and cook the risotto in the usual way, stirring well. Before removing from the heat add the butter and part of the grated Parmesan cheese.

Butter a shallow fireproof dish. Cover the bottom with a layer of rice, place a layer of aubergines on top and cover with the rest of the rice. Arrange the slices of Mozzarella on top, coat with the sauce and sprinkle with the rest of the Parmesan cheese. Brown in a hot oven for 15 minutes.

Italy

Bavarian cabbage

	1 white cabbage	
125 g	bacon, finely diced	4 oz
	1 teaspoon caraway seeds	
	salt	
	dash of vinegar	
1 dl	white wine	¼ pt
	1 tablespoon sugar	
	pinch of pepper	
	½ tablespoon flour	

Remove the coarse outer leaves from the cabbage, cut away the stump and any thick leaf ribs, then shred the leaves or cut into julienne strips. Fry the bacon until crisp, then add to the cabbage with the remaining ingredients and cook gently under cover. If desired, the shredded leaves may be blanched before cooking, by pouring boiling water over and draining at once.

N.B.—For serving with turbot cheeks the blanched cabbage should only be lightly fried in butter, seasoned with salt and pepper, flavoured with a dash of vinegar and a little sugar, and cooked under cover in a little white wine.

Germany

Boston baked beans

20–24 portions   Baking time: 3–4 hours

1 kg	haricot beans	2¼ lb
	salt belly of pork,	
500 g	net weight	1 lb approx.
	2 tablespoons dry mustard	
⅛ l	treacle	¼ pt
100 g	brown sugar	4 oz
	2 medium onions	
	1 leek	
	8 cloves	
250 g	tomato purée	8 oz
	2 bay leaves	
2 l	water	3½ pt

Soak the beans overnight and drain off the water on the next day. Place them in an earthenware pot of suitable size and mix thoroughly with the mustard, water, treacle and two-thirds of the brown sugar. Add one of the onions which has been sliced, the sliced leek, the bay leaves and the other onion studded with the cloves. Place the salt pork on top. Make sure that the beans are completely covered with liquid. Season lightly, cover with a lid and seal the edges tightly with bread dough. Bake in a very moderate oven. Half an hour before the beans are cooked, remove the lid, sprinkle the pork with brown sugar and increase the top heat to brown the surface of the meat well. The beans are generally served in small individual dishes with a small piece of browned salt pork on top.

USA

Cardoon or celery boats with stuffed vegetables

10–12 persons   Cooking time: 1 hour

1 large head cardoon or celery

	12 very small artichokes	
	12 medium onions	
	3 eggs	
25 g	dried boletus (flap mushrooms), soaked	1 oz
1½ dl	olive oil	¼ pt
100 g	grated Parmesan cheese	4 oz
100 g	canned tunny fish	4 oz
	breadcrumbs	
	1 tablespoon chopped parsley	

Cut 12 boat shapes about 10 cm (4 in) long out of the lower part of the cardoons or celery stalks. Blanch for 15 minutes in salted water, drain and dry on a cloth. Cut off the tops of the artichokes and onions. Hollow out the onions with the help of a small knife and a teaspoon. Place the soft inside leaves of the artichokes in water sharpened with lemon juice, after removing the choke, and sprinkle the inside of the artichokes with salt. Prepare a basic stuffing mixture with the breadcrumbs, Parmesan, chopped parsley and olive oil, adding salt as required. After soaking the flap mushrooms, drain, chop and fry lightly in oil. Chop the cardoon or celery heart and the artichoke leaves very finely. Divide the basic stuffing mixture in three. Add the finely chopped cardoon or celery heart to the first part, together with half the flap mushrooms. Mix the second part with the chopped onions and the flaked tunny. Add the chopped artichoke leaves and the rest of the flap mushrooms to the remaining part. The three mixtures should be fine, well flavoured and fairly firm. Fill the hollowed-out onions with the artichoke stuffing, the cardoon or celery boats with the tunny stuffing and the artichokes with the onion stuffing. Arrange in oiled fireproof dishes, sprinkle with a little oil and cook in a moderate oven. Serve lukewarm or cold.

Italy

Cauliflower with shrimps

6 persons   Cooking time: 16–18 minutes

1 kg 500	cauliflower	3¼ lb
600 g	picked pink shrimps	1¼ lb
1¼ l	Cardinal sauce	2¼ pt
150 g	butter	5 oz
	1 bunch dill	
	12–18 thin slices truffle	

Cook the cauliflower, keeping it very firm, then drain thoroughly and arrange on a dish. Spread with 50 g (1¾ oz) creamed butter and coat with Cardinal sauce. Decorate with slices of truffle and surround with the shrimps which have been tossed in butter and dill and seasoned with salt and pepper. Serve the rest of the sauce separately.

(Illustration, p. 806)   Germany

Cauliflower cheese

	1 medium cauliflower	
	salt and pepper	
30 g	butter	1 oz
30 g	flour	1 oz
¼ l	milk	½ pt
100 g	grated cheese	4 oz
	1 tablespoon dry breadcrumbs	

Trim most of the leaves from the cauliflower. Cut a cross in the base of the stem. Wash the cauliflower. Cook it upright in boiling salted water until just tender (20–30 minutes according to size). Drain. Place in an ovenproof dish and keep warm. Meanwhile make a white sauce with the butter, flour and milk. When it has thickened stir in 90 g (3 oz) of the cheese and some salt and pepper. Pour the sauce over the cauliflower and sprinkle the top with the rest of the cheese and the breadcrumbs. Place under a medium grill to brown, or it can be browned in the oven.

Kale

2 kg	kale	4½ lb
1 l	meat or ham broth	1½ pt
30 g	butter or margarine	1 oz
2 dl	dairy cream	⅓ pt
	freshly ground white pepper	
	salt	
	sugar	

Cut the kale into quarters. Remove the stump and any thick leaf ribs, wash and cut up the leaves. Blanch them in the broth, drain and chop. Brown lightly in the butter or margarine and mix with the cream. Add salt, pepper and sugar to taste.

Sweden

Marinated mushrooms

6 persons

750 g	mushrooms	1¾ lb
	2 medium red onions	
2 dl	wine vinegar	⅓ pt
1 dl	oil	⅙ pt
2 dl	water	⅓ pt

10 g	little sugar	
8 g	little salt	
	1 small bay leaf	
	6 white and 6 black peppercorns	
	1 large bunch dill	

Clean the mushrooms thoroughly. Leave the very small ones whole and cut the large ones in thick slices. Cut the onions into rings and place on top of the mushrooms. Combine the vinegar, water, oil, salt, sugar, herbs and spices, simmer gently for 6–8 minutes, allow to cool very slightly and pour this marinade over the mushrooms. When cool, cover and leave to marinate in a cold place for 24 hours before using. Dish, pour part of the marinade over the mushrooms and either garnish with dill leaves or sprinkle with chopped dill.

Finland

Mushrooms with bread dumplings

6 persons   Cooking time: mushrooms, about 30 minutes; dumplings, 15–20
minutes

1 kg	chanterelles or mixed mushrooms	2¼ lb
60 g	chopped onion	2 oz
	1 heaped tablespoon chopped parsley	
	¼ teaspoon caraway seeds	
50 g	butter	2 oz
	flour (optional)	

Dumplings

	12–15 stale rolls	
50 g	chopped onion	2 oz
	1 tablespoon chopped parsley	
½ l	warm milk	¾ pt
	5 eggs	
approx. 150 g	flour	5 oz approx.
50 g	butter	2 oz approx.

Fry the onion and parsley very lightly in the butter, add the cleaned mushrooms, a little salt and the caraway seeds, cover and cook slowly without adding any liquid. When nearly cooked, sprinkle with a little flour to thicken if desired. By the end of the cooking time the mushrooms should be almost dry.

To make the dumplings, slice the rolls and pour the warm milk over. Lightly brown the chopped onion and chopped parsley in a little butter and add to the soaked rolls. Now add the eggs and enough flour to make a fairly slack paste. Season with salt and pepper. Shape into small balls, drop into boiling water and simmer until cooked. Remove, drain very well, dish and pour a little brown butter over. The dish of mushrooms may be garnished with the dumplings, but these are preferably handed separately.

Germany

New Year's lentils

6 persons   Cooking time: 2 hours

400 g	lentils	1 lb
5 cl	olive oil	2 fl oz
	1 small onion	
	1 small sprig rosemary	

Soak the lentils for at least 12 hours, changing the water several times. Cut the onion in quarters and cook lightly in the oil in a stewpan without colouring. Add the lentils, the rosemary and enough water to cover. Cook briskly, adding water if required, until the lentils are tender, but still whole. At the end of the cooking time all the liquid should have been absorbed. Serve hot with cotochino (pork sausage) or zampone (stuffed pig's trotter) poached in water.

This is the traditional midday meal at the New Year.

Italy

Radish and cucumber cocktail

6 persons

350 g	large radishes	12 oz
350 g	peeled cucumber	12 oz
	(net weight after removing seeds)	
	juice of half a lemon	
	2 tablespoons olive oil	
	1 medium-size onion	
250 g	tomatoes	8 oz
	1 crushed clove of garlic	
	2–3 tablespoons tomato ketchup	

Cut the radishes (peeled if desired) and the cucumber in small strips and marinate for a few minutes only in olive oil, lemon juice, salt and a pinch of sugar. Meanwhile chop the onion finely, skin the tomatoes, remove the seeds and chop coarsely, and mix with the garlic and tomato ketchup to make a fairly thick sauce. Mix the marinated radishes and cucumber well, fill into champagne goblets or cocktail glasses and cover with the sauce.

(Illustration, p. 367)   Holland

Red cabbage

1 kg–1 kg 500	1 red cabbage weighing	2¼–3¼ lb
	1 large onion, finely chopped	
50 g	margarine	2 oz
	3 apples, cut into pieces	
	5 peppercorns	
	5 cloves	
	1 teaspoon salt	
	2 tablespoons stock syrup	
	2 tablespoons wine vinegar	
	ham cooking juices	

Cut the cabbage into quarters and remove the stump, then cut the leaves into fine julienne strips. Fry lightly in the margarine, add the remaining ingredients and cook under cover for 1 hour. Stir occasionally, adding cooking liquid from the ham as and when required. Season with salt and vinegar. Serve with Christmas ham.

(Illustration, p. 376)   Sweden

Red cabbage on apple slices

6 persons   Cooking time: 1 hour

750 g	shredded red cabbage	1¾ lb
	2 apples, peeled and cored	
¼ l	red wine	½ pt
	juice of 1 orange	
	juice of 1 lemon	
	salt	
	pepper	
	caraway seeds	
60 g	butter	2 oz
60 g	sugar	2 oz
	1 medium onion, sliced	
	6 slices of peeled, cored and	
	poached apple	
	bouillon	

Marinate the shredded cabbage in the red wine, orange and lemon juice with the 2 apples, finely sliced, salt, pepper and caraway seeds. Leave for a few hours. Fry the sugar until golden, add the onions, then the cabbage and a little bouillon and cook until soft, making sure that all the liquid has evaporated. Season well, place the cabbage on the poached apple slices, use as a garnish for the roast venison and serve any remaining cabbage separately.

Austria

Sauerkraut croquettes

1 kg	sauerkraut	2¼ lb
60 g	butter	2 oz
50 g	flour	2 oz
½ l	veal or light beef broth	¾ pt
	salt and pepper	
	2 eggs	
	flour and breadcrumbs for coating	

Squeeze the sauerkraut dry and chop up small. Make a blond roux with the butter and flour, blend in the broth, season lightly with salt and pepper, and cook to a very thick sauce. Mix with the sauerkraut and spread on a baking sheet to cool. When cold, shape into small cylinders weighing 75 g (about 3 oz) if the croquettes are to be served as a separate dish or 50–60 g (about 2 oz) if they are to be used as a garnish. Coat with flour, dip in beaten egg and roll in breadcrumbs, then fry in hot fat for 5 minutes. Drain well.

When used as a separate course, serve 3 croquettes per person with fresh salad.

Germany

Stuffed aubergines

10 persons

	5 even-sized longish aubergines	
500 g	field mushrooms	1 lb
500 g	chanterelles	1 lb
500 g	flap mushrooms (boletus)	1 lb
	1 clove of garlic	
5–6 cl	oil	2 fl oz about

Cut the aubergines in half lengthwise and score the cut surfaces criss-cross fashion with the point of a sharp knife. Deep fry in oil until soft. Allow to cool for a short time, then scoop out the flesh without damaging the skins. Cut up the mushrooms and chanterelles which have been well cleaned, washed and dried, and fry in hot olive oil in a large frying pan. Season with salt and freshly ground pepper, mix well and toss with the crushed garlic and the aubergine flesh, fill into the skins, place in the oven for a moment, and sprinkle with chopped parsley.

(Illustration, p. 367)   Holland

Stuffed cabbage leaves

10 portions   Cooking time: about 50 minutes

1 kg	white cabbage (either fresh or pickled whole)	2 lb
100 g	oil	3 oz
400 g	minced veal	1 lb
400 g	minced pork	1 lb
100 g	chopped onions	3 oz
100 g	rice	3 oz
	10 tomatoes	
	chopped parsley	
	marjoram and basil	

Sauce

50 g	butter	1½ oz
50 g	flour	1½ oz
100 g	chopped onion	3 oz
50 g	tomato purée	1½ oz
200 g	dairy cream	8 fl oz

Separate the cabbage into leaves, remove the hard centre rib and blanch in heavily salted water and drain. Lay the leaves on a napkin, squeeze the stalk dry and beat until soft or cut away with a knife. Lightly cook the onion in the oil without colouring, add the rice and cook until glassy in appearance. Add the tomatoes, previously skinned and coarsely chopped without the seeds. Moisten with water (1½ parts water to 1 part rice), season, cover, cook in the oven, then allow to cool. Stir in the minced meat, add salt and pepper to taste, flavour with marjoram and basil, add a little chopped parsley and mix well. Stuff the cabbage leaves with the mixture, roll each one up, place in a fireproof dish of suitable size, pour a little water over, weight down with a plate and cook in the oven.

To prepare the sauce, lightly cook the onion in the butter without colouring, stir in the flour, add the tomato purée, cook for a moment, then pour in the cooking

24

liquid from the stuffed cabbage leaves. Simmer for 5–8 minutes, season to taste, strain and finish off by adding the cream. Pour over the stuffed cabbage leaves to serve.

Bulgaria

Stuffed courgettes

6 persons   Cooking time: 25–30 minutes

	6 courgettes of equal size	
	half a green pepper (chopped)	
225 g	cooked flageolet beans	8 oz
75 g	chopped walnuts	2 oz
100 g	dry wholemeal or rye breadcrumbs	4 oz
3 dl	olive oil	1¼ pt
	2 tablespoons unwhipped dairy cream	
	¼ teaspoon celery seed or powdered celery	
	1 egg	
½ l	dry white wine	¾ pt

Cut off the ends of the courgettes. Push a sawn-off sharp metal cooking spoon through the centre of each one to expel the seeds and fibres, leaving the flesh in place. Mix the beans with the green pepper, walnuts, breadcrumbs, 2 tablespoons olive oil, the unwhipped cream and the beaten egg. Season with salt and pepper and add the celery seed or powdered celery. Fill the courgettes smoothly with the mixture and arrange in a shallow stewpan, if possible side by side. Pour the wine and the remaining oil over, cover tightly and cook over gentle heat.

Germany

Stuffed courgettes and aubergines

10–12 persons

	24 courgettes 10 cm (4 in) long	
	12 small aubergines	
300 g	lean minced veal	10 oz
200 g	minced pork	7 oz
	3 eggs	
200 g	canned tunny fish	7 oz
100 g	butter	3 oz

200 g	curd cheese	7 oz
1 dl	olive oil	3 fl oz
25 g	dried flap mushrooms (boletus), soaked	1 oz
	breadcrumbs	
	marjoram	
	oregano	

Cut off the ends of the courgettes and aubergines. Split the courgettes lengthwise and scoop out the flesh with a small teaspoon to make boat shapes; set the flesh aside. Proceed in the same way with the aubergines, but discard the flesh; sprinkle inside with salt and invert on a wire rack to drain.

Melt 50 g (1¾ oz) butter in a pan, add the veal and pork and fry lightly, stirring well meanwhile. Add the courgette flesh and 1 beaten egg, season to taste and fill into the courgettes. Mash the tunny fish, flavour with marjoram, add 1 beaten egg and enough breadcrumbs to bind and mix with the olive oil. Work the curd cheese to a paste with 25 g (1 oz) soft butter, the mushrooms which have been chopped and tossed in butter, the remaining egg (beaten) and breadcrumbs, adding salt and oregano to taste. Mix thoroughly with the tunny fish mixture and check the seasoning—the mixture should be well-flavoured. Fill into the aubergine boats.

Brush a fireproof dish of suitable size with oil, arrange the stuffed courgettes and aubergines in it and cook in a moderate oven until the top is lightly browned, sprinkling with water from time to time.

Italy

Stuffed green peppers Andalusian style

12 persons   Cooking time: 40–50 minutes

	6 medium-sized green peppers	
400 g	lean minced meat	14 oz
100 g	cooked rice	4 oz
	2 eggs	
	½ teaspoon chilli powder	
	4 medium onions, chopped	
4 cl	sesame oil	4 dessertspoons
½ l	tomato juice	¾ pt
	2 cloves of garlic	
	1 teaspoon cornflour	

Cut off the stalk end of the peppers, remove the seeds, drop in deep hot fat for a moment, remove quickly and skin. Invert and drain well. Mix the minced meat with the cold cooked rice, 2 chopped onions which have been lightly fried, the beaten eggs, the chilli powder and salt to taste, and stuff the peppers with this mixture. Stand the peppers in an oiled pan, pour in a little tomato juice, cover and simmer gently until cooked. Remove from the pan, pour off the cooking liquid and set aside. Fry 2 chopped onions and the crushed cloves of garlic in the sesame oil until lightly coloured, add the tomato juice, the cooking liquid which has been set aside, salt and pepper and boil for a moment. Blend the cornflour with a little water, stir into the sauce and bring to the boil. Cut each pepper in quarters with a sharp knife, arrange in a heatproof serving dish, pour the sauce over after adjusting the seasoning and keep hot.

USA

Stuffed mushroom caps

Yield: 6

	6 mushroom caps	
25 g	each weighing	1 oz
90 g	ham purée or paste	3 oz
60 g	green, yellow and red peppers, finely chopped	2 oz
	white wine jelly	
	butter	
	lemon juice	

Select very fresh mushroom caps of equal size, prepare in the usual manner and poach for 5 minutes in a little lemon juice with a knob of butter and a pinch of salt, but do not add any water. Allow to cool in the cooking juices, covering the pan tightly with paper. Shape the ham purée or paste into 6 balls and roll in the chopped peppers to cover completely. Drain the mushroom caps well, wipe dry, place a ham ball in the hollow side of each one, glaze all over with white wine jelly and chill well.

Germany

Stuffed sauerkraut leaves

10 persons   Cooking time: about 2–2½ hours

	2 white cabbages salted whole	
500 g	minced beef	1 lb
500 g	minced pork	1 lb
150 g	chopped onions	5 oz
50 g	pork fat	2 oz
100 g	rice, parboiled and well drained	4 oz

½ l	sauerkraut liquor	¾ pt
½ l	tomato juice	¾ pt
	or the corresponding amount of	
	tomato purée mixed with	
	water or bouillon	
	little bouillon	
	1 large piece pork skin	
½ l	thick sour cream	¾ pt

Fry the onions in the fat until pale golden and allow to cool. Mix the minced meat well with 50 g (1¾ oz) onions and the rice, and season with salt and pepper. Separate the cabbage leaves and cut away the thick ribs of the large ones. Arrange the leaves to make 30 oblongs about 12 ×6 cm (5 ×2½ in). Place about 40 g (1½ oz) meat stuffing on each oblong, roll up and tuck in the ends. Shred the remaining leaves finely in the same way as sauerkraut and line a well-greased casserole with them. Place the stuffed leaves on top and cover with any remaining shredded sauerkraut; if there is not sufficient, use additional fresh sauerkraut. Pour the sauerkraut liquor, tomato juice and bouillon over, sprinkle with the rest of the fried onions and cover with the pork skin. Place a lid on top and cook slowly in the oven. Remove the stuffed leaves and dish on the shredded sauerkraut which has been well drained. If desired, reduce the stock and pour over the stuffed leaves. Hand the sour cream separately, leaving each guest to pour it over the stuffed leaves.

N.B.—The casserole is usually lined with coarsely chopped, not shredded sauerkraut and coarsely chopped remaining leaves.

Rumania

Stuffed peppers

6 persons   Baking time: 45–50 minutes

	6 large red peppers	
120 g	celery (with leaves) chopped	4 oz
300 g	onions finely chopped	10 oz
350 g	walnuts finely chopped	12 oz
350 g	cooked tomato pulp	12 oz
	2 tablespoons grated beetroot	
	2 eggs	
100 g	rusk crumbs	4 oz

To make the stuffing, mix the beaten eggs well with the onions, celery, walnuts, tomato pulp and grated beetroot. Season with salt and pepper, add a little grated nutmeg or marjoram and stir in the rusk crumbs. Cut the peppers open at the stalk end, carefully remove all the seeds and fibres, rinse well and invert to drain. Fill with the stuffing, stand side by side in an oiled fireproof dish, cover the stuffing with a sheet of oiled paper and bake at 175°C.

(Illustration, p. 367)   Holland

Tomatoes stuffed with scrambled egg

1 portion

140 g	medium-size tomatoes	5 oz
	2 eggs	
10 g	butter	1 pat
	chopped parsley	
	stuffed olives	
	or	
	rinsed rolled anchovy fillets	

Cut the tops off the tomatoes, scoop out the seeds, sprinkle inside with salt, leave for a while, then invert to drain off the liquid. Scramble the eggs, mix with chopped parsley, allow to cool and fill into the tomatoes. Garnish with a stuffed olive or a rolled anchovy fillet.

Bulgaria

Vegetable curry

Make a macedoine of cooked vegetables.

Lightly fry finely chopped onion and garlic in fat, then add the usual curry spices or commercial curry powder. Cook to a thick sauce with coconut milk or curds, leaving the pan uncovered and keeping the heat low. Add the vegetables and season with salt.

India

Vegetable pilau

6 persons

500 g	macedoine of vegetables	1 lb
500 g	rice	1 lb
150 g	butter	5 oz
	2 onions, finely chopped	
	2 cloves of garlic, finely chopped	

8 cloves
1 stick cinnamon
8 cardamoms
1 teaspoon ground turmeric

Lightly fry the onions, garlic and spices in the butter. Add the rice and cook until lightly coloured, stirring meanwhile. Pour in sufficient boiling water to cover the rice. Season with salt. Cover the pan and cook over gentle heat until all the water has been absorbed. If any water remains when the rice is sufficiently cooked, remove the lid and simmer for a few moments longer. Add the blanched vegetables and, if desired, 100 g (3½ oz) sultanas and 100 g (3½ oz) blanched almonds which have been lightly fried in butter.

India

Gado-gado

selection of finely sliced
     cooked vegetables
     (cauliflower, cabbage,
     carrots, French beans)
1 red pepper
few prawns
salt
juice of 1 lemon
sugar

Place the cold vegetables on a dish. Remove the seeds from the red pepper, heat it, then pound with the prawns, salt and sugar; add the lemon juice. Pour this sauce over the vegetables.

Holland/Indonesia

Tomato sambal

Sprinkle sliced tomatoes with finely chopped onion and green chillies, and with freshly grated or desiccated coconut. Season with salt and pepper and flavour with lemon juice.

Stuffed eggplant

4 persons

6 eggplants (aubergines)
1 medium onion, chopped

	3 tablespoons chopped hard cheese	
160 g	minced chicken	5 oz
30 g	white breadcrumbs	1 oz
	1 tablespoon water	
	cornflour	
	1 ginger root	
	soya sauce	
	oil	

Cut off the stalks of the eggplants, split them open down the middle without cutting right through and soak in salted water. Fry the chopped onion in oil until lightly coloured and mix well with the minced chicken, the breadcrumbs and the water, adding salt as required. Lastly stir in the cheese, then divide the mixture into 6 portions. Wipe the eggplants dry inside and outside and sprinkle the inside surfaces with cornflour. Stuff each one with a layer of the chicken mixture and dust the stuffing with cornflour. Deep fry in oil for 4–5 minutes over brisk heat, then reduce the heat and fry until the stuffing is cooked. Leave to drain on a cloth and serve with grated ginger root and soya sauce.

Japan

Jerez arranque

	4–5 eggs	
	6 medium-sized ripe tomatoes	
	2–3 fairly large green peppers	
	2 cloves of garlic	
600 g	white breadcrumbs made from day-old bread (crumb only)	1¼ lb
	3–4 ladles wine vinegar	
	olive oil	
10 g	cooking salt	1 teaspoonful

Set aside a piece of raw green pepper for pounding, brush the rest of the peppers lightly with oil and bake in glowing embers or in the oven. When cooked, skin them, remove the seeds and cut into thick strips. Season with salt and dress with a little oil and a dash of vinegar.

Boil the eggs for 10 minutes, leave until cold and shell.

Peel the garlic and place in an earthenware pot (as used in the Andalusian countryside for making gazpacho) together with the salt and the piece of raw pepper. Pound well and leave to stand for a few minutes. Meanwhile scald and skin the tomatoes. Mix them with the other ingredients in the pot, pounding well.

Now add the breadcrumbs, amalgamate thoroughly with the mixture in the pot and pour in sufficient oil to make a fairly firm paste. Add the vinegar, keeping the paste thick. Adjust the seasoning with salt. Bring to the boil slowly and remove from the heat after 15 minutes. Slice the hard-boiled eggs or cut them into quarters and arrange on top together with the strips of cooked green pepper.

Spain

La bagna caôda

In Piedmont friends and acquaintances often gather round the table to enjoy 'bagna caôda' ('hot sauce'), a dish which is pre-eminently conducive to a gay, relaxed and friendly atmosphere. A glass of Barbera, Gattinara or Barolo (typical Piedmontese wines) helps to give a festive note to the gathering.

'Bagna caôda', which has a strong, pungent taste, is served in an earthenware dish or silver-lined copper pot standing on a spirit stove in the centre of the table. The guests help themselves, dipping pieces of vegetable into the hot sauce. Large pieces —celery, cardoon, strips of sweet pepper, fennel, etc.—are held in the hand; for vegetables which are cut up small (cauliflower, courgettes or carrots cut into small sticks, etc.) a long-handled fork is used (as for fondue). The vegetables should be well washed in running water, dried on a cloth and served on individual plates.

A suggested recipe for 10 persons is given below.

2 kg	green, yellow and red peppers cut into strips	4 lb
1 kg	celery hearts cut into 10 cm (4 in) lengths	2 lb
500 g	Jerusalem artichokes	1 lb
4 dl	olive oil	$\frac{2}{3}$ pt
150 g	butter	4 oz
200 g	anchovies in brine	6 oz
	10 cloves of garlic	

Chop the garlic very finely, reducing the quantity if a less strongly flavoured sauce is preferred. Wash the anchovies in running water and mash well with a fork. Melt the butter, stir in the garlic and the anchovy purée and lastly the oil. Heat for a few minutes without allowing the oil to come to the boil, then place the dish on a spirit stove in the centre of the table. Each guest dips the vegetables into the sauce, which must be kept hot and should be stirred constantly. The vegetables, soaked in sauce, are then eaten as they are.

In some restaurants 'bagna caôda' is served in individual dishes.

Italy

POTATOES

Anna potatoes

Trim potatoes into cylinders and then slice into very thin rounds. Well grease a Pommes Anna mould with clarified butter and arrange an overlapping layer of potato in the bottom. Fill the mould with layers of potato slices, seasoning and adding dabs of butter as the mould fills up. Bake in a hot oven for 40 minutes, pressing the potato down a few times. Turn out of the mould to serve.

Alsatian potatoes

500 g	potatoes	1 lb
120 g	button onions	4 oz
60 g	bacon	2 oz
30 g	butter	1 oz

Turn the potatoes into small barrel shapes, and bake in the oven with the button onions and lardons of bacon, stirring frequently. Sprinkle with chopped parsley and serve in the same casserole.

Baked soufflé potatoes

10 persons   Total baking time: about 40 minutes

	10 potatoes of equal size	
200–225 g	each weighing	7–8 oz
	3 egg yolks	
	3 egg whites	
	2 tablespoons whipped cream	
	grated nutmeg	

Wrap the potatoes in aluminium foil and bake at 200°C. When cooked, remove the foil, cut off the top of each potato evenly a third of the way down and scoop out

778

the inside, leaving the skin intact. Mash well with a fork, mix with the egg yolks and the whipped cream and add salt and nutmeg to taste. Fold in the egg whites whipped to a stiff snow. Fill the skins with the mixture and smooth the top to a dome shape. Return to the oven and bake for about 5 minutes at 250°C.

(Illustration, p. 366)   Holland

Berny potatoes I

Cooking time: 5–6 minutes

600 g	peeled potatoes	1¼ lb
60 g	chopped truffles	2 oz
	4 egg yolks	
	1 egg	
40 g	butter	1½ oz
	very finely nibbed almonds	

Boil the potatoes in salted water, drain, return to the pan and dry well, then mash through a sieve at once. While still hot, stir in the 4 egg yolks and the butter, season with salt, pepper and a pinch of grated nutmeg and add the chopped truffles. Allow to cool, shape into balls the size of a small apricot, pass through beaten egg, coat with nibbed almonds and deep-fry in hot fat for 5 or 6 minutes. Dish on a napkin.

Berny potatoes II

Cooking time: 5–6 minutes

600 g	peeled potatoes	1¼ lb
60 g	fine diced ham	2 oz
	and chopped parsley	
	4 egg yolks	
	1 egg	
40 g	butter	1½ oz
	very finely nibbed almonds	

Boil the potatoes in salted water, drain, return to the pan and dry well, then mash through a sieve at once. While still hot, stir in the 4 egg yolks and the butter, season with salt, pepper and a pinch of grated nutmeg and add the diced ham and chopped parsley. Allow to cool, shape into balls the size of a small apricot, pass through beaten egg, coat with nibbed almonds and deep fry in hot fat for 5 or 6 minutes. Dish on a napkin.

Boulangère potatoes

500 g	potatoes	1 lb
250 g	onions	½ lb
	white stock	
	salt	
	pepper	
30 g	butter	1 oz
	chopped parsley	

Thinly slice the potatoes and onions, mix them and place in a casserole with a layer of potato on top. Add white stock (but not to cover the top layer) brush the top layer with melted butter and cook in a medium oven until the top is brown, the potatoes cooked and the stock almost evaporated. Sprinkle with chopped parsley.

Browned potatoes

1 kg	peeled potatoes	2 lb
	(weighed after peeling)	
100 g	butter	3 oz
	salt	

Boil the potatoes, allow to cool, then tear to pieces with two forks. Toss in hot butter in a frying pan and sprinkle with salt. Press flat, brown well underneath, turn and brown the other side.

Austria

Dauphine potatoes

Combine ⅔ duchesse potato mixture and ⅓ unsweetened choux paste and form into 50 g (2 oz) cylinders. Deep fry—without a coating of crumbs.

Duchesse potatoes

Boil 1 lb potatoes and dry thoroughly, then pass through a sieve or ricer. Beat in 1 egg and 30 g (1 oz) of butter and pipe out through a star pipe, into mounds about 5 cm (2 in) high on to a buttered tray. Lightly egg wash and brown in a hot oven.

Dauphinoise potatoes

500 g	potatoes	1 lb
250 ml	boiled milk	½ pt

	1 egg	
60 g	finely diced Gruyère cheese	2 oz
	1 clove garlic	
30 g	butter	1 oz

Rub an earthenware casserole with garlic and grease it with butter. Thinly slice the potatoes and mix the milk, egg and nearly all the cheese. Season, put in the casserole, sprinkle with the rest of the cheese and cook in a moderate oven for 45 minutes.

Jacket potatoes with sour cream and chives

6 persons   Baking time: about 30 minutes

	6 large even-sized potatoes	
220–225 g	each weighing	7–8 oz
approx. 2 dl	thick sour cream	⅓ pt
	chopped chives	

Scrub and wash the potatoes thoroughly (a floury variety is best). Wrap completely in aluminium foil and bake on coarse salt on a baking sheet. To test whether they are cooked, insert a fork; the potato should come away from the fork at once. Cut a deep cross on top through the foil and squeeze the sides with both hands. Fill the centre of each with a little thick sour cream, sprinkle with chopped chives and serve hot.

Lyonnaise potatoes

⅔ sautées potatoes and ⅓ fried onions, mixed after cooking.

Mr. Janson's temptation

4 persons   Cooking time: 45 minutes

120 g	salted anchovy fillets	4 oz
100 g	butter	2 oz
1 kg	potatoes	2 lb
300 g	onions	10 oz
3 dl	fresh cream	½ pt
	breadcrumbs	

Soak the salt out of the anchovy fillets thoroughly. Dry them. Peel the potatoes and cut them in julienne. Stew them lightly in butter. Slice the onions thinly, colour them lightly in butter. Butter a gratinating dish and line it with a layer of potatoes. Garnish this layer with anchovy fillets, cover with the onions and finish off with a layer of potatoes. Spread the rest of the butter over the potatoes, sprinkle with the cream and last, with breadcrumbs. Allow 45 minutes for cooking at 250°C.

New potatoes with cream cheese sauce

6 persons   Cooking time (potatoes): about 18 minutes

1 kg 500	new potatoes	3 lb
	1 teaspoon caraway seeds	
250 g	hard cheese	8 oz
60 g	butter	2 oz

Sauces

1 kg	cream cheese	2 lb
	1 small bunch radishes	
80 g	chopped onions	3 oz
	1 tablespoon freshly chopped herbs (dill, chives, parsley)	
	1 finely chopped clove of garlic	
	mustard	
	curry powder	
	1 large white herring fillet, skinned and finely diced	
	1 tablespoon finely diced apple	
	1 tablespoon onion rings	
	1 teaspoon capers	
	pinch of cayenne pepper	
	1 small teaspoon paprika	
	1 good tablespoon tomato ketchup	

Boil the potatoes in their jackets with the caraway seeds and a little salt. When cooked, remove the skins and dish, adding a knob of butter and a large slice of cheese for each person. Hand one or more of the following sauces separately.

Sieve the cream cheese with a little salt or beat it until very creamy, then divide in four. Use each quarter of 250 g (8 oz) as a basis for one of the sauces given below.

Herb sauce. Mix the cream cheese with about 20 g (1 oz) chopped onion, the finely sliced radishes and the chopped herbs. Season with pepper.

Curry sauce. Mix the cream cheese with 20–30 g (about 1 oz) chopped onion and the garlic. Season well with mustard and curry powder.

Herring sauce. Season the cream cheese with pepper and stir in the diced herring and apple, together with the onion rings. Sprinkle with the capers to serve.

Red sauce. Mix the cream cheese with about 20 g (1 oz) chopped onion and season well with salt, a pinch of cayenne pepper, the paprika and the tomato ketchup.

Germany

Potato cakes

10 portions

1 kg	potatoes	2 lb
30 g	garlic	3 cloves
200 g	flour	6 oz about
1 dl	milk	3 fl oz
	3 eggs	
	marjoram	
3 dl	oil	½ pt

Peel and grate the potatoes (raw) and pour off some of the water. Add the beaten eggs, the flour and the milk and work to a batter. Add salt, pepper, marjoram and finely grated garlic. Drop into hot oil in fairly small amounts and fry on both sides until crisp and golden-brown. Serve at once, otherwise the potato cakes will lose their good colour and flavour.

Czechoslovakia

Potato gnocchi

5 portions   Cooking time: 10 minutes

1 kg	peeled potatoes (raw)	2 lb
500 g	flour	1 lb
150 g	streaky bacon	5 oz
500 g	Brimsen cheese	1 lb
	2 eggs	

Grate the potatoes and pour off the water. Add the flour and eggs, season with salt and pepper and quickly mix to a dough. Using a spoon, cut out knobs of dough and drop into boiling water. Simmer gently, drain well and mix with finely diced rendered bacon. Dish and sprinkle liberally with Brimsen cheese to serve.

Sour ewe's milk is drunk as a speciality with this dish.

Czechoslovakia

Potato omelette Spanish style

For one standard size omelette

	4 eggs	
200 g	peeled potatoes	8 oz
1 dl	olive oil	⅛ pt

Wash the potatoes, dry well and cut into very thin slices, then fry in the hot oil until golden. Beat the eggs, season with salt, pour into the pan and stir with a fork until they begin to thicken. Turn and fry on the other side. The omelette should be golden-yellow on both sides and about 3 cm (1¼ in) thick.

The omelette is placed on a round dish, cut in the guests' presence and served with drinks before a meal. It is cut into squares and used in the making of banderillas, a classic Spanish speciality.

Spain

Potatoes Brava style

	large even-sized potatoes	
	oil for frying (or half oil and half lard)	

Sauce

150 g	ripe tomatoes	5 oz
	1 small clove of garlic	
	6 dried hot peppers	
	10 roasted blanched almonds	
¼ l	oil	½ pt
⅛ l	vinegar	¼ pt
	12 white peppercorns	

Peel, wash and dry the potatoes, then cut into strips as for chipped potatoes but slightly thicker. Half cook in deep hot oil (or half oil and half lard) in the usual manner, then fry until crisp and golden-brown just before they are required. Drain well, season with fine salt and arrange in pairs criss-cross fashion on small plates (6 to 8 per portion, depending on size). Hand the following sauce separately. Cut the tomatoes into small pieces. Cook the tomatoes, pepper and garlic separately, making sure that the peppers do not burn (special care is required as they are dried). Place the peppercorns and the peppers in a mortar, pound these, then pound in the almonds and garlic and lastly add the tomatoes and pound all these ingredients together well to make a paste. Blend in the oil and vinegar and season with salt. Mix well, set aside for 5 to 6 hours, then rub through a sieve and check the taste.

Instead of using chipped potatoes for this dish, whole potatoes may be baked in the oven, cut in half lengthwise and topped with a spoonful of the sauce. They are also called 'potatoes Brava style'.

Spain

Potato sambal

Sprinkle diced cooked potatoes with finely chopped green chillies and chopped onions. Season with salt and pepper and dress with lemon juice and oil.

Sautées potatoes

Wash, but do not peel the potatoes. Steam them in their skins then peel them and slice them 0·5 cm (¼ in) thick. Quickly fry in shallow fat until crisp and brown.

CEREALS AND PASTA

Boiled rice Indian style

Wash the rice well in cold water, changing the water frequently. Drain and drop the rice into boiling salted water, stir to prevent it sticking to the pan and boil rapidly for 10–12 minutes. Transfer to a colander (not a sieve) and pour a little cold water over the rice to separate the grains. Drain and stir lightly with a spoon. Rice cooked in this way does not require drying.

India

Semolina gnocchi

½ l	milk	1 pt
50 g	butter	2 oz
180 g	semolina	6 oz
	salt	
	pepper	
	nutmeg	
	2 egg yolks	

Boil the milk, butter, salt and pepper and a little grated nutmeg. Sprinkle in the semolina and beat well to avoid lumps. Cook gently for 10–15 minutes, stirring constantly. Cool slightly then beat in the egg yolks. Turn on to a greased dish, and spread to 1 cm (½ in) thick and allow to get cold. When cold, cut into crescents with a 7 cm (3 in) cutter. These gnocchi can be sautéd, or grilled, and served with any sauce suitable for spaghetti.

Italy

Fried gnocchi

500 g	flour	1 lb 2 oz
5 g	bicarbonate of soda	1 teaspoonful
	water	
	salt	

786

Work the flour, bicarbonate of soda, salt and water to a dough similar to a noodle dough. Roll out to about 8 mm ($\frac{1}{3}$ in) thick and cut into squares, oblongs, triangles or diamonds with a pastry wheel. Fry in deep fat. Keep hot in the oven at 100°C until ready to serve. The gnocchi will swell considerably while in the oven. Serve with ham, salami or cheese.

Alternative recipe

When making the dough, add 20 g ($\frac{3}{4}$ oz) butter, lard or dripping, or 50 g ($1\frac{3}{4}$ oz) finely diced ham. Proceed as above, but roll out to about 1 cm ($\frac{1}{2}$ in) thick. These gnocchi will swell less, but will remain crisper.

Italy

Kobs Mbassis

2 kg 500	fine semolina	5 lb 8 oz
1 dl	olive oil	$\frac{1}{8}$ pt
	1 small slice mutton fat	
200 g	yeast	7 oz
	2 tablespoons sesame seeds	
	1 tablespoon aniseed	
	1 egg	
	approx. 1 tablespoon salt	

Render the mutton fat in the oil. Make a bay in the semolina and pour in the fat and oil, together with the salt dissolved in a little water. Mix quickly, make a bay again, gradually add the yeast dispersed in 1 l ($1\frac{3}{4}$ pt) water and knead well for 15–20 minutes to make a smooth dough. Cover with a cloth and set aside for 1–1$\frac{1}{2}$ hours. Add the sesame and aniseed, knead again for 20–25 minutes, scale and shape into loaves as desired, then prove for 2 hours. Bake at 230–240°C.

Tunisia

Lasagne Neapolitan style

8–10 persons

600 g	lasagne	1$\frac{1}{4}$ lb
300 g	Mozzarella cheese	10 oz
300 g	curd cheese	10 oz
500 g	lean boneless pork or veal	1 lb
350 g	frying sausage	12 oz
	3 eggs	
150 g	grated Parmesan cheese	5 oz
	1 tablespoon tomato purée	

60 g	butter	2 oz
	1 onion	
¼ l	white wine	½ pt
	breadcrumbs	

Dice the onion, fry in 50 g (1¾ oz) butter until lightly coloured, add the meat, fry and stir in the white wine. As soon as the wine has boiled away, add the tomato purée blended with about 1 dl (⅛ pt) water and bring to the boil. Remove the meat and set the sauce aside. Mince the cooked meat twice, mix with 2 beaten eggs and half the Parmesan, season to taste and shape with the hands into balls the size of a hazelnut. Roll in breadcrumbs, deep-fry, remove and keep hot. Sieve the curd cheese and mix with the rest of the Parmesan. Blanch the sausage for a few minutes in boiling water, skin and slice. Slice the Mozzarella, then cut into small cubes. Cook the lasagne 'al dente' in boiling salted water. Drain and dry on a cloth.

Butter an ovenproof glass or china dish. Place a layer of lasagne in the bottom and cover with curd cheese, Mozzarella and slices of sausage. Cover these with a second layer of lasagne, sprinkle a few of the fried meat balls on top and pour a little sauce over. Proceed in the same manner until all the ingredients have been used up; the last layer but one should consist of Mozzarella and curd cheese, with lasagne as the final, top layer. Cook in a slow oven for 15 minutes. After removing, wait a few minutes before serving.

By way of a change, the filling may be made with diced ham, diced smoked cheese and sliced hard-boiled egg.

Italy

Maize meal porridge

10 persons   Cooking time: 15–20 minutes

400 g	fine maize meal	14 oz
30 g	salt	1 oz
4 l	water	7 pt

Add the salt to the water, bring to the boil and pour in the maize meal in a steady stream. Simmer gently while stirring constantly until the mixture is fairly thick and smooth. Serve with poached eggs coated with melted butter, or with ewe's milk cheese and sour cream.

To make mamaliga as an accompaniment to meat dishes, use the following quantities:

600 g	fine maize meal	1¼ lb
36 g	salt	1 oz
4 l	water	7 pt

Proceed as above, but cook until very thick. Turn out on to a wooden platter with a nail inserted in the centre to which a long piece of thread has been attached. The thread is used to divide the mamaliga into even portions.

Rumania

Rice with chicken and egg

4 persons

250 g	raw chicken, skinned and boned	8¾ oz
	4 dried mushrooms	
	3 spring onions	
	4 eggs	
	1 large sheet nori*	
	4 tablespoons saké	
5 cl	soya sauce	$\frac{1}{12}$ pt
50 g	sugar	1¾ oz
	3 tablespoons mirin	
1½ dl	water	¼ pt
	cooked rice	

Soak the mushrooms in water, wash and cut into strips. Dice the chicken. Remove the green part of the spring onions and cut each one into four. Place the saké, soya sauce, sugar, mirin and water in a saucepan, heat almost to boiling point and draw aside. Place enough chicken, mushrooms and onion for 1 person in a small pan and pour over a quarter of the saké sauce. Simmer for a few minutes until the sauce becomes frothy. Add 1 beaten egg and a little salt, cover and poach gently until cooked. Repeat for each portion. To serve, fill donburi bowls† with cooked rice, cover with the chicken and egg mixture and sprinkle with thin strips of nori.

Japan

* Nori: purple laver, a dried edible black seaweed.
† Donburi: deep china bowl with lid in which individual portions are served.

Pilau rice

4–6 persons

600 g	Patna rice	1¼ lb
100 g	butter or margarine	4 oz
	1 medium-sized onion, finely chopped	
	2 cloves of garlic, finely chopped	

	½ teaspoon saffron	
	12 cloves	
	12 cardamoms	
	2 sticks cinnamon	
400 g	sultanas	¾ lb
250 g	blanched almonds	8 oz

Wash the rice well and soak it in cold water for 2 hours. Steep the saffron in half a cup of boiling water. Lightly fry the onion, garlic and spices in the butter or margarine for 5 minutes, stirring meanwhile. Add the saffron and the water in which it was steeped, season with salt and stir well. Now stir in the well-drained rice. Pour in sufficient boiling water to cover the rice well. Cook under cover over gentle heat until all the water has been absorbed, lifting the rice with a spoon from time to time to separate the grains. Lastly stir in the sultanas and almonds which have been lightly fried in butter.

India

Peanut loaf

6 persons   Baking time: 45 minutes

300 g	ground roasted peanuts	10 oz
250 g	cooked unpolished rice	8 oz
300 g	grated raw carrots	10 oz
300 g	skinned coarsely chopped tomatoes (net weight without seeds)	10 oz
100 g	wholemeal breadcrumbs	3 oz
	2 teaspoons chopped parsley or chives	
	1 level teaspoon salt	
	butter	

Mix all the ingredients together well and adjust the seasoning. Fill into a well-greased cake tin, smooth down and bake at 175°C. After removing from the oven, allow to stand for a short time before turning out. Serve with tomato sauce.

Germany

Risi and bisi

350 g	shelled green peas	12 oz
50 g	ham	2 oz
50 g	butter	2 oz

1¾ l	chicken stock	3 pt
	2 cupfuls rice	
	Parmesan cheese	
	1 small onion	

Gently sweat the finely chopped onion and ham in ½ oz (15 g) butter. Add the peas and sweat for a few moments. Add ½ pt (⅓ l) of stock and bring to a slow boil. Add the rice. Cook gently without stirring, adding more stock as it is absorbed. When the rice is cooked, stir in the rest of the butter, and some grated Parmesan cheese.

Savoury rice

4–6 persons

100 g	fat	3 oz
	1 medium-sized onion	
	1 clove of garlic	
	2 cloves	
15 g	ground turmeric	½ oz
10 g	ground cumin seed	⅓ oz
600 g	rice	1¼ lb

Heat the fat (butter or margarine) in a pan and lightly fry the finely chopped onion and garlic and the cloves. Add the ground turmeric and cumin seed and continue frying for a moment. Stir in the rice which has been well washed and drained, season with salt and cook for 5 minutes. Pour in sufficient boiling water to cover the rice well (the level of the water should be about 1–2 cm (¾ in) above the rice). Cover the pan and simmer until the rice is cooked, lifting it with a spoon from time to time to prevent it from sticking.

India

Sushi

To prepare rice for sushi, cook it and allow to cool, then add vinegar containing a little monosodium glutamate and mix well, using a spatula. Line small shallow wooden boxes or rectangular moulds (up to 2 cm (¾ in) deep) with oiled paper, pack in the rice and press down well. Leave in a cool place until firm, then turn out and remove the paper. Cover the top with thinly sliced raw or smoked fish or ham and cucumber cut into narrow lengths. Cut the sushi into bite-size squares with a sharp knife.

Instead of packing the rice into moulds, it may be moulded into balls with the hands, lightly pressed and garnished as above.

Japan

Vinegared rice with fish and vegetables

4 persons

500 g	rice	1 lb 2 oz

Seasoned vinegar

	5 tablespoons vinegar	
50 g	sugar	2 oz
	2 tablespoons salt	
	5–6 medium horse-mackerel	
400 g	*or* shrimps	14 oz
	green beans	
	2 slices ginger root (optional)	
	3 tablespoons seeds of beefsteak plant (optional)	
	1 tablespoon sesame seeds (optional)	

Wash the rice very well and drain in a colander for 1 hour. Place in a saucepan with the same amount of water as that used for soaking, bring to the boil and allow to boil for 30 seconds. Reduce the heat and cook until the water has almost evaporated. Turn up the heat for a further 30 seconds, then remove, cover and leave to stand for 12–13 minutes. While the rice is still hot, sprinkle it with the seasoned vinegar, mix well and cool. Cut the beans in strips, boil in salted water and drain. Clean the fish, open out and remove the bones. Sprinkle with salt and leave to stand for 15 minutes, then wash and marinate in vinegar for 10 minutes. Remove the skin and slice the fish thinly. If shrimps are used instead of horse-mackerel, boil them in salted water in their shells, cool, remove the shells and marinate in vinegar.

Cut the ginger root into coarse julienne strips, sprinkle with salt and soak in vinegar. Soak the seeds of the beefsteak plant in water and squeeze out the moisture. Roast and chop the sesame seeds.

Mix the horse-mackerel or shrimps, the ginger and the beefsteak plant seeds with the rice, sprinkle with the sesame seeds and garnish with the beans.

Japan

SALADS

A salad can be simple or compound—an accompaniment to a course; a course in itself; or a meal on its own. The ingredients of a salad can be raw or cooked or a combination of both and a salad can be served 'au naturel' or dressed with mayonnaise or one of many salad dressings. At one end of the scale is the classic french lettuce salad comprising simply fresh, crisp lettuce torn into pieces and tossed with olive oil, wine vinegar, sea salt and freshly ground black pepper; whilst at the other end are those hearty combinations of vegetables and meat or fish which with a little wine and some coffee to follow make a satisfying luncheon.

All salads, however, have one thing in common: the ingredients must be fresh, and of the very best quality.

Anglers' salad

10 portions

500 g	cooked fish, skinned and boned	1 lb
500 g	tomatoes	1 lb
	5 lettuces	
150 g	cooked celeriac	5 oz
100 g	mayonnaise	3 oz
1 dl	whipped cream (unsweetened)	$\frac{1}{6}$ pt
	5 hard-boiled eggs	
	5 lemons	

Cut the cooked fish into small pieces or chop finely. Mix with the shredded lettuce, the finely cut tomatoes and celeriac, bind with the mayonnaise, fold in the whipped cream, season with salt and pepper and flavour with lemon juice and Worcestershire sauce. Arrange in a bowl and garnish with hard-boiled eggs cut in half or into quarters and slices or wedges of lemon.

Czechoslovakia

Appetizer salad

Grill 150 g (5 oz) pimentos, remove the skin and seeds, cut into strips and dress with oil and vinegar. Arrange on a plate in a star shape and sprinkle with a mixture of chopped parsley and chopped garlic.

Bulgaria

Bohemian meat salad

5 portions

250 g	braised beef	8 oz
300 g	tomatoes	10 oz
100 g	onions	3 oz
1 dl	oil	$\frac{1}{6}$ pt
	1 tablespoon mustard	
	1 tablespoon chopped parsley	
	vinegar	
	1 lemon	

Cut the cold beef into small slices or strips and the tomatoes and onions into thin slices. Toss in a dressing of mustard, a little vinegar, the oil, ground pepper and chopped parsley, adding salt to taste. Dish each portion on a lettuce leaf and garnish with parsley and a slice of lemon.

Czechoslovakia

Bratislava salad

5 portions

100 g	cooked celeriac	4 oz
100 g	asparagus	4 oz
100 g	red or green peppers (without seeds)	4 oz
100 g	ham	4 oz
50 g	carrots	2 oz
50 g	mushrooms	2 oz
1 dl	whipped cream	$\frac{1}{6}$ pt

Garnish

	asparagus tips	
	red peppers	

Cut the celeriac, carrots, peppers and ham into fine strips. Add small pieces of asparagus and sliced or diced mushrooms. Mix well, season with salt and pepper and bind with the whipped cream. Dish, garnish with asparagus tips and red peppers and chill lightly before serving.

Czechoslovakia

Brjanski salad

10 persons

350 g	tender roast ground-game (boned)	12 oz
250 g	calf's head, cooked until tender	9 oz
200 g	pickled cucumbers, peeled and seeded	7 oz
500 g	slightly tart apples	1 lb
	5 hard-boiled eggs	
	1 tablespoon chopped herbs (parsley, chervil, tarragon)	
	wine vinegar	
	oil	
300 g	mustard mayonnaise	10 oz
	2 tablespoons unsweetened whipped cream	

Cut the game, calf's head, cucumbers and the peeled cored apples into short fairly thick strips and marinate for a few hours in wine vinegar (or lemon juice), oil, salt and pepper. Shortly before using, mix well, drain thoroughly and arrange in a salad bowl to a dome shape. Sprinkle with the chopped herbs and decorate all round with the hard-boiled eggs cut into quarters. Fold the whipped cream into the mustard mayonnaise and dress the salad with it when serving.

Czechoslovakia

Caprice salad

chicory
vinaigrette dressing

Mix the chicory with julienne strips of pickled tongue, ham, truffle and young raw artichoke bottoms.

France

Carlsbad veal salad

5 portions

100 g	roast leg of veal	4 oz
100 g	Emmenthal cheese	4 oz
100 g	pineapple	4 oz
1 dl	lemon marinade	$\frac{1}{6}$ pt
1 dl	whipped cream	$\frac{1}{6}$ pt
	1 lettuce	
30 g	flaked roasted almonds	1 oz

Cut the veal, the cheese, the pineapple and half the lettuce into strips and add half the almonds. Dress with the lemon marinade, add the whipped cream and mix well.

Chill slightly, sprinkle with the rest of the almonds and garnish with lettuce heart leaves.

Czechoslovakia

Carp salad Trebon

5 portions

300 g	carp (gutted and with head removed)	10 oz
1 dl	oil	$\frac{1}{6}$ pt
100 g	carrots	4 oz
100 g	onions	4 oz
50 g	celeriac (preserved)	2 oz
100 g	mushrooms	4 oz
100 g	tomatoes	4 oz
50 g	tomato ketchup	2 oz
1 dl	white wine	$\frac{1}{6}$ pt
	1 lemon	

Remove all the bones from the carp, dice fairly coarsely, fry lightly in oil, season with salt and remove from the pan. Cut the onions into rings and fry lightly in the rest of the oil, then add the sliced mushrooms. Cut the celeriac and carrots in strips, place in the pan, brown for a few moments, add the ketchup, pour the wine over and cook gently. Stir in the carp and the diced tomatoes, continue cooking gently for a short time and season to taste with salt.

Chill lightly and garnish with slices of lemon.

Czechoslovakia

Carrot and banana salad

5 portions

250 g	cleaned carrots	8 oz
100 g	apples, peeled and cored	3 oz
150 g	bananas	5 oz
1½ dl	whipped cream	¼ pt
	2 lemons	

Grate the carrots, cut the apples into strips and the bananas into slices. Flavour the cream with the lemon juice and mix with the carrots, apples and bananas. Chill well and dish in glass bowls.

Czechoslovakia

Catalonian salad

endive or lettuce
vinaigrette dressing

Mix with sliced tomatoes and potatoes, onion rings and julienne strips of sweet pepper.

A crust of bread rubbed with garlic may be added if liked.

France

Celeriac and walnut salad

5 portions

250 g	celeriac	8 oz
100 g	carrots	4 oz
100 g	apples	4 oz
100 g	walnuts	4 oz
	1 lemon	
50 g	mayonnaise	2 oz
1 dl	whipped cream	⅙ pt
	lettuce leaves	

Cut the celeriac and carrots into julienne strips, blanch well in salted water and drain thoroughly. Flavour with lemon juice, add the apples, peeled, cored and finely cut, together with the walnuts, mix well and bind with the mayonnaise and the whipped cream. Add a little salt or sugar according to taste, dish on lettuce leaves and garnish with walnuts.

Czechoslovakia

Chicken and fruit salad

5 portions

150 g	roast breast of chicken	6 oz
100 g	peeled oranges	4 oz
100 g	bananas	4 oz
50 g	pineapple	2 oz
100 g	seeded grapes	4 oz
	half a lettuce	
	juice of 1 small lemon	
1 dl	whipped cream	⅛ pt
	sugar	

Slice the chicken, bananas and oranges, cut the pineapple and lettuce into strips, add the grapes, mix well and marinate in the lemon juice. Bind with the whipped cream and add sugar to taste if required.

Chill slightly and serve in glass goblets garnished with a small piece of chicken breast and a tiny lettuce leaf.

Czechoslovakia

Chicory salad

2 persons

Cut 2 heads of chicory in half lengthwise and remove the bitter heart, which should be discarded. Wash and cut in thin rings. Dice 2 peeled apples and oranges and mix with the chicory. Whip ⅛ l (¼ pt) dairy cream, add sugar and lemon juice to taste, and pour over the salad. Lastly sprinkle with 50 g (1¾ oz) coarsely chopped hazelnuts and serve at once.

(Illustration, p. 994)   Germany

Classic Andalusian salad

2–3 heads of lettuce
   (depending on size)
1 cucumber
1 onion
2–3 ripe but firm tomatoes
1 green pepper
3 eggs
1 clove of garlic
½ teaspoon cumin seeds

1 dl	oil	⅛ pt
5 cl	vinegar	1/12 pt
	cooking salt	

Boil the eggs for 10 minutes, leave until cold and shell.

Prepare the lettuce by discarding the outer leaves. Place the hearts in cold water with the tomatoes to freshen them up, then cut each lettuce heart into 4 or 6 and arrange in a salad bowl. Peel and slice the onion and cucumber; slice the green pepper, the tomatoes and the hard-boiled eggs. Arrange these ingredients round the edge and on top of the lettuce. Pound the cumin seeds, garlic and salt in a mortar, add the oil and vinegar and mix well. Pour this dressing over the salad and serve.

Spain

Cod's roe and radish salad

4 persons

175 g	cod's roe	6 oz
300 g	Japanese radish (daikon)	10 oz
	2 tablespoons soya sauce	
	1 tablespoon saké (rice wine)	
	4 tablespoons vinegar	
	1 tablespoon mirin	
	(sweet rice wine)	
	½ teaspoon salt	
	pinch of monosodium	
	glutamate	

Wash the roe thoroughly. Mix together the soya sauce and saké, pour over the roe and marinate for 30 minutes. Remove the skin from the roe if this has not already been done. Peel the radish, grate very finely, drain and squeeze out any remaining juice. Mix together the vinegar, salt, mirin and a little monosodium glutamate, pour over the radish and mix well. Break the cod's roe into small pieces, mix gently with the radish and serve.

Japan

Cucumber salad

	1 cucumber	
	1 tablespoon white sesame seeds	
	1 teaspoon salt	
7 cl	vinegar	⅛ oz

25 g	sugar	1 oz
	2 tablespoons light soya sauce	
	½ teaspoon monosodium glutamate	

Wash the cucumber and slice without peeling into paper-thin rounds. Salt lightly, transfer to a colander and place a plate or bowl on top of the cucumber to press out some of the liquid. Leave to stand for 15 minutes, then pat the slices of cucumber dry with a clean cloth.

Mix together the vinegar, sugar, soya sauce and monosodium glutamate, pour over the cucumber and mix lightly. Roast the sesame seeds in a dry frying pan until they begin to jump. Remove from the heat and crush in a mortar or by any other means, then sprinkle over the cucumber salad.

Japan

Cucumber and crab salad

4 persons

	1 cucumber	
250 g	crab	8 oz
5 cl	vinegar	2 fl oz
	½ teaspoon salt	
	1 tablespoon light soya sauce	
25 g	sugar	1 oz
	½ teaspoon aji-no-moto	
2½ cm	piece of fresh ginger root (optional)	1 in

Wash and dry the cucumber and slice without peeling into thin rounds. Sprinkle with salt, leave to stand under pressure to remove some of the liquid, then dry well with a cloth. Break the crab meat into small pieces, making sure there are no fragments of shell remaining. Mix together the vinegar, salt, soya sauce, sugar and aji-no-moto. Place the cucumber and crab in a bowl, pour the dressing over, mix well and leave to marinate in a cool place until required. When serving, drain away excess dressing. If desired, sprinkle with ginger root cut into fine julienne strips.

Japan

Dutch salmon salad

	1 large tin of salmon
	3 hard-boiled eggs

▲ Stuffed saddle of lamb Innocenti

▼ Saddle of veal with golden pans, p. 593

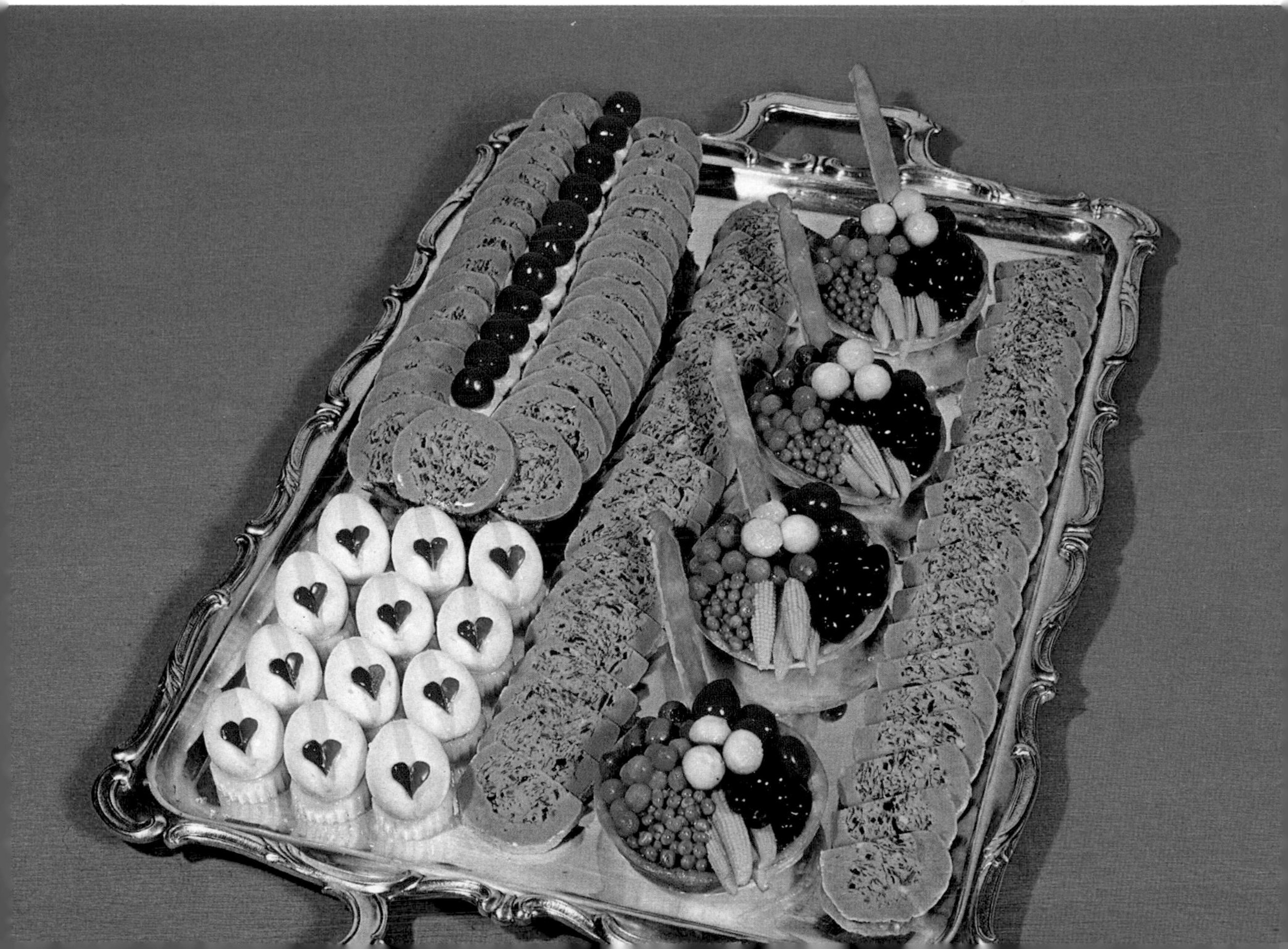

802   ▲   Barbecued saddle of lamb
      ▼   Leg of lamb en croûte

▲ Apples with Bavarois cream, p. 864
▼ Gâteau for an engagement party, p. 1085

► Cold lobster at the Park Hotel, Frankfurt, Germany

▲ Pancake Hussar style, p. 898

804

▲ Fruit tarts, choux buns, p. 988, truffles, p. 1158

▼ Macaroons, p. 1024, florentines, p. 1007, pistachio cornets, p. 1048, espagnoles, langues de chat, 980

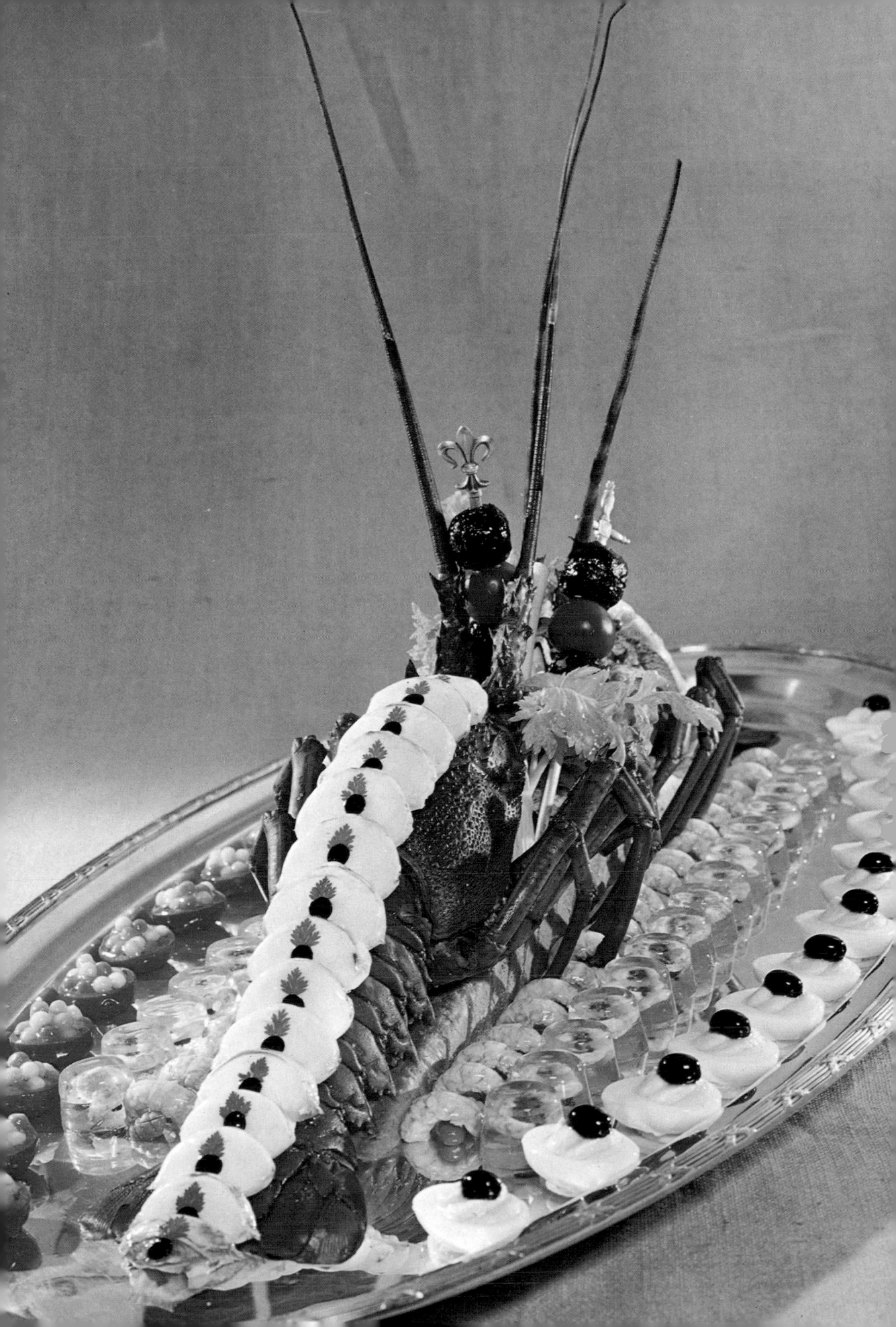

806

◀ Cauliflower with shrimps, p. 763

▼ Lobster mousse Carthusian style, p. 534

▲ Fillet of beef Colbert, p. 547
▼ Roast beef Liselotte, p. 560

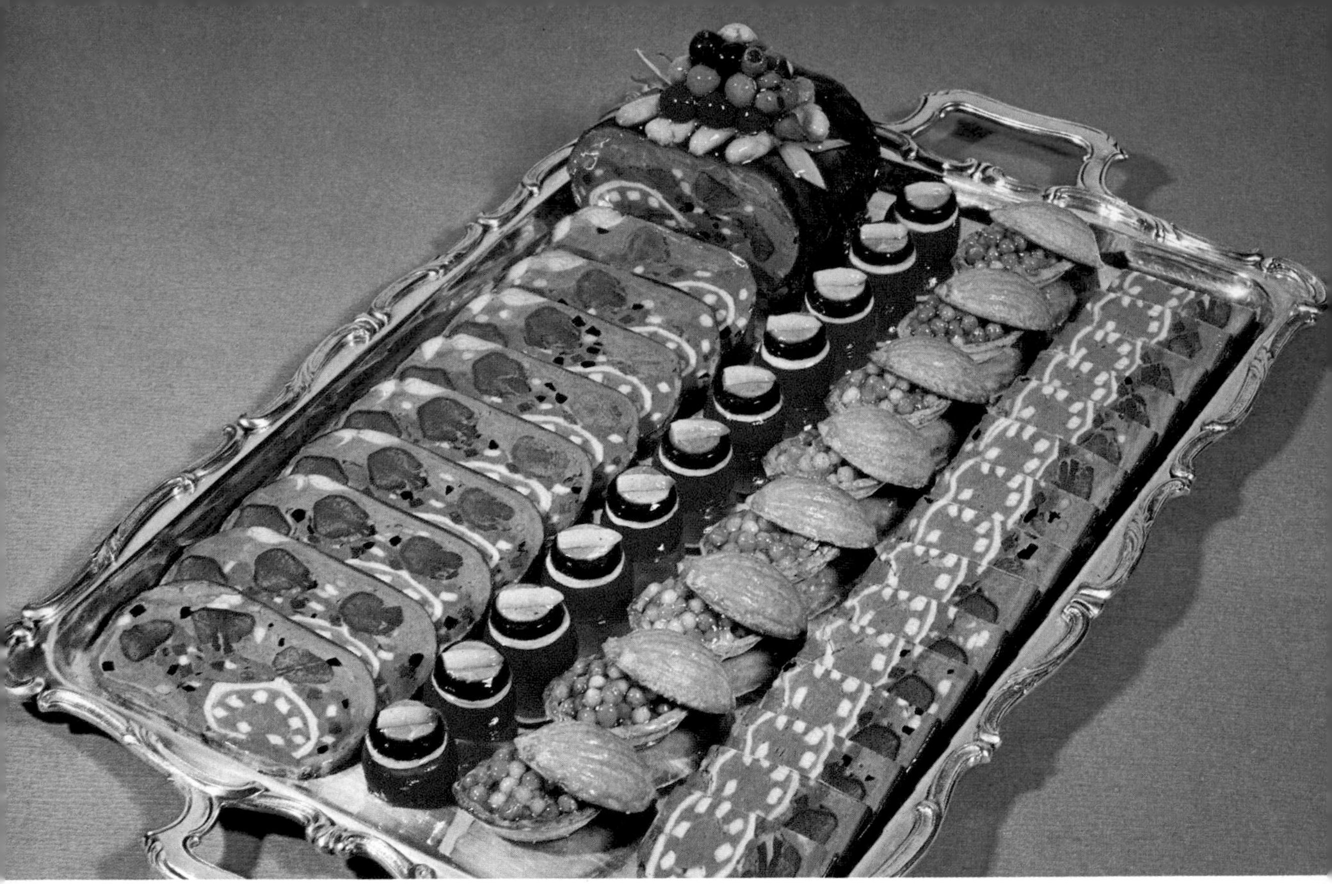

808 ▲ Galantine of veal, p. 752
▼ Stuffed loin of pork, p. 635

▲ Stuffed ham, p. 638
▼ Ham Biedermeier style, p. 644

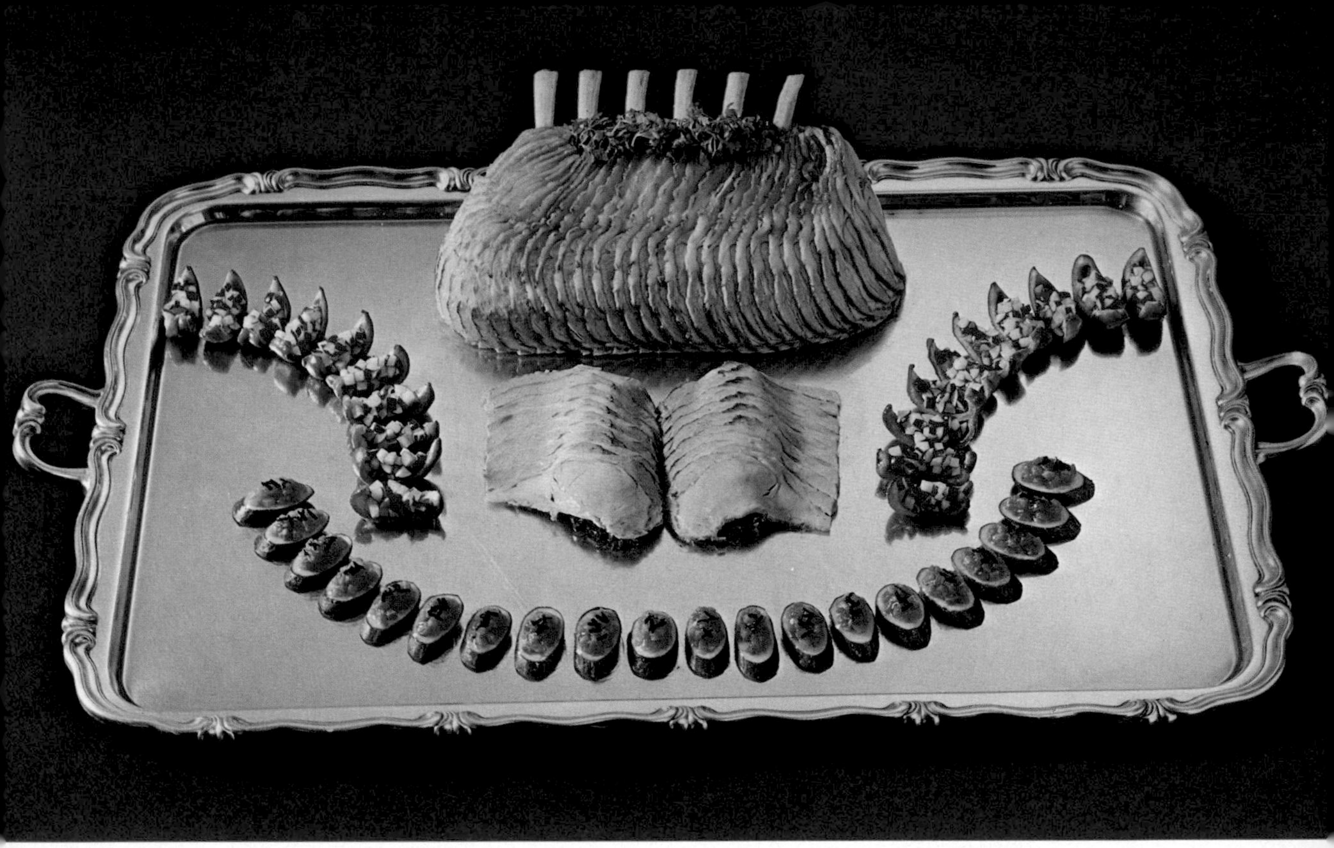

▲ Best end of veal Boris, p. 574

▼ Ham rolls with melon, p. 649

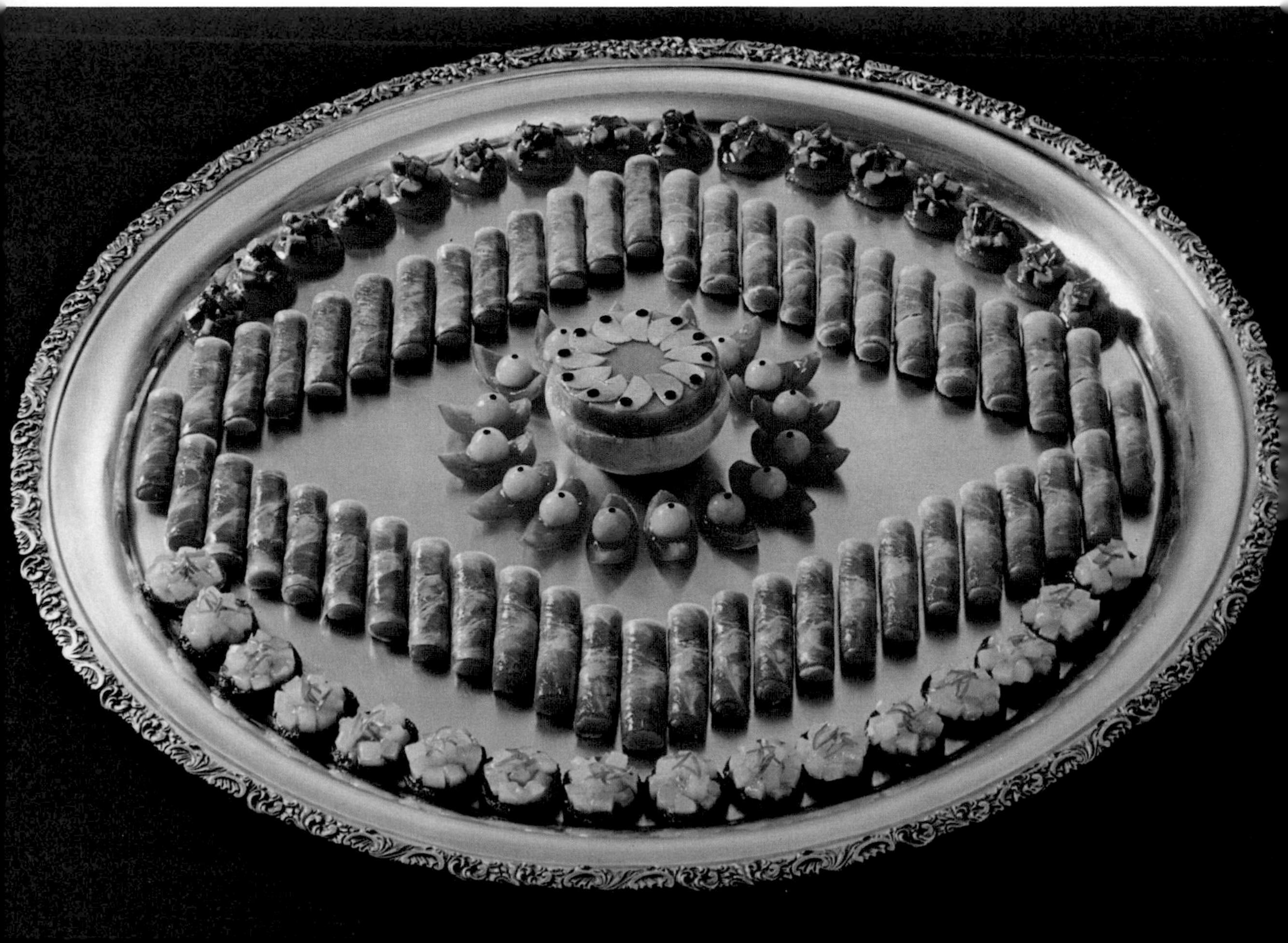

▲ Poached eggs in Jelly with Parma Ham, p. 415

▼ Stuffed eggs and egg bombe, pp. 419–423, 408

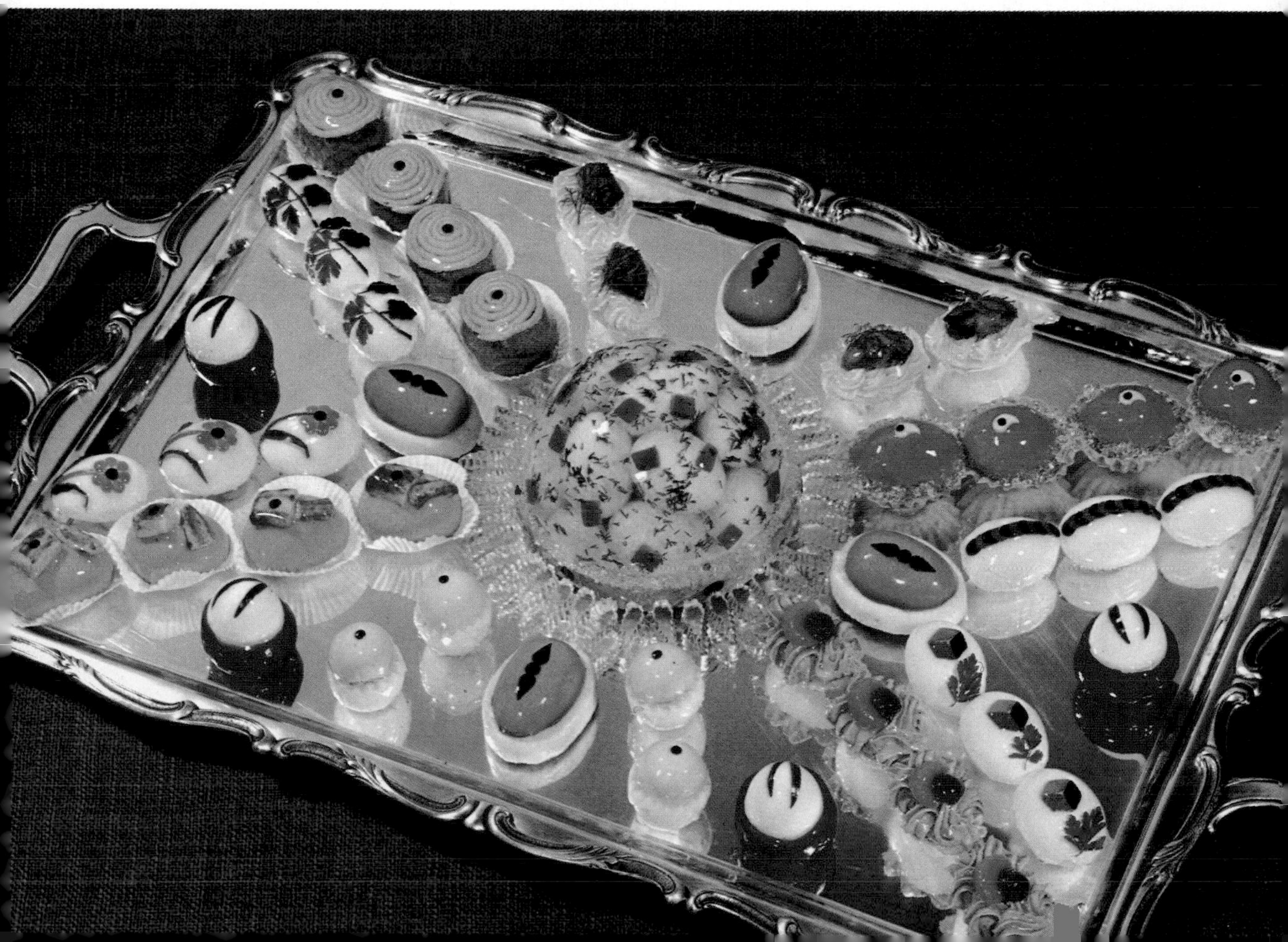

812 ▲ Marinated herrings, grilled herrings, rollmop herrings, pp. 478–9
▼ Stuffed halibut, p. 456

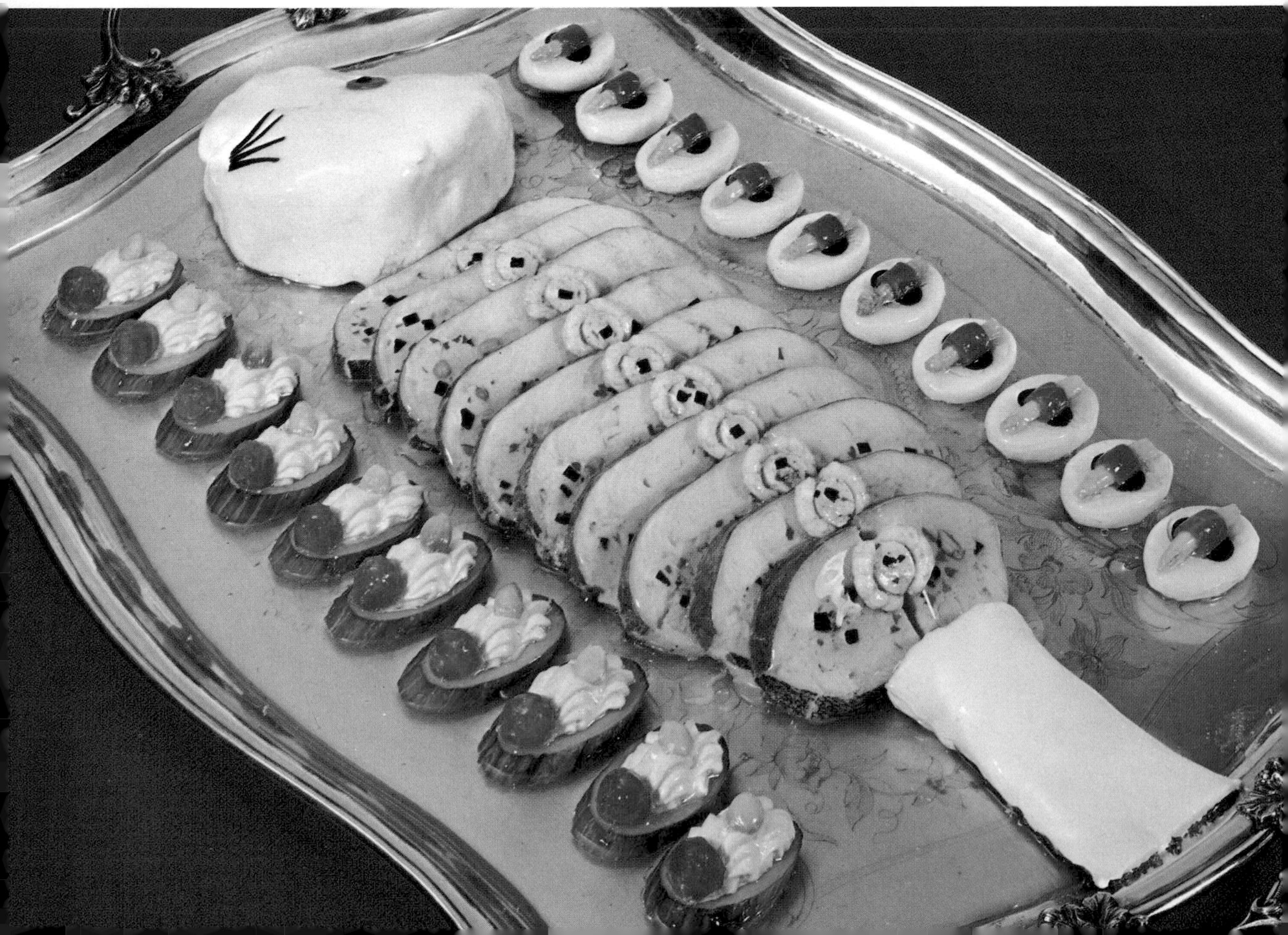

▲ Chocolate baskets, p. 985

▲ Chocolate maces, p. 986

▼ Rainbow desserts, p. 911

▼ Noisettines

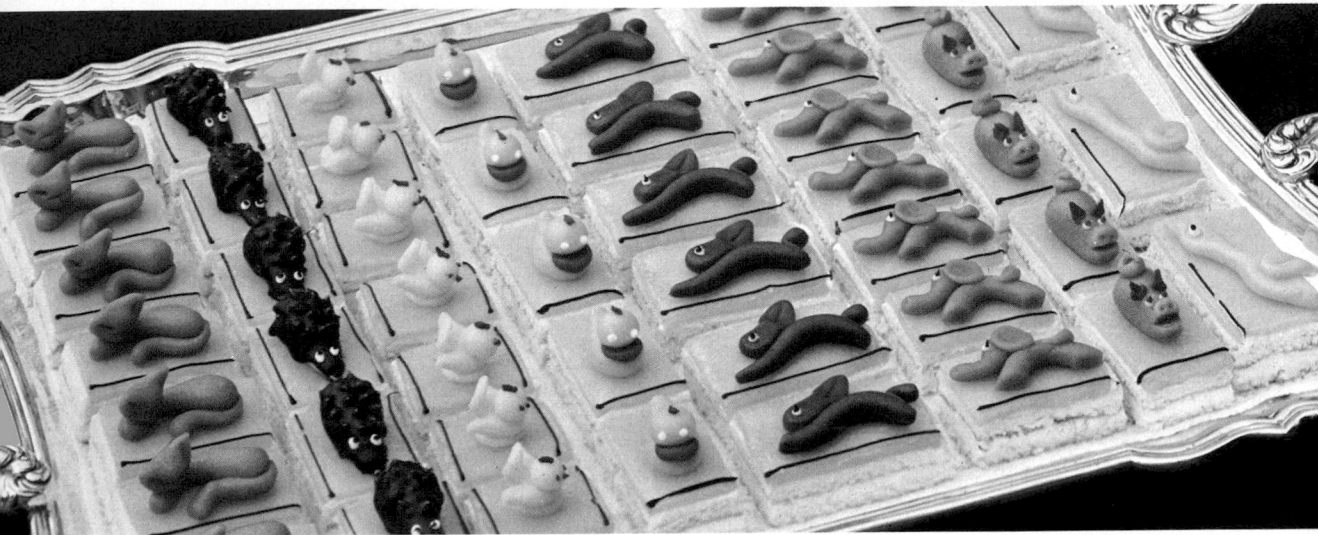

814　▲　Children's party fancies, p. 984

▲　Stuffed bananas, p. 933

　　▶　Stuffed saddle of veal, p. 595

◀　Chocolate log and marzipan train

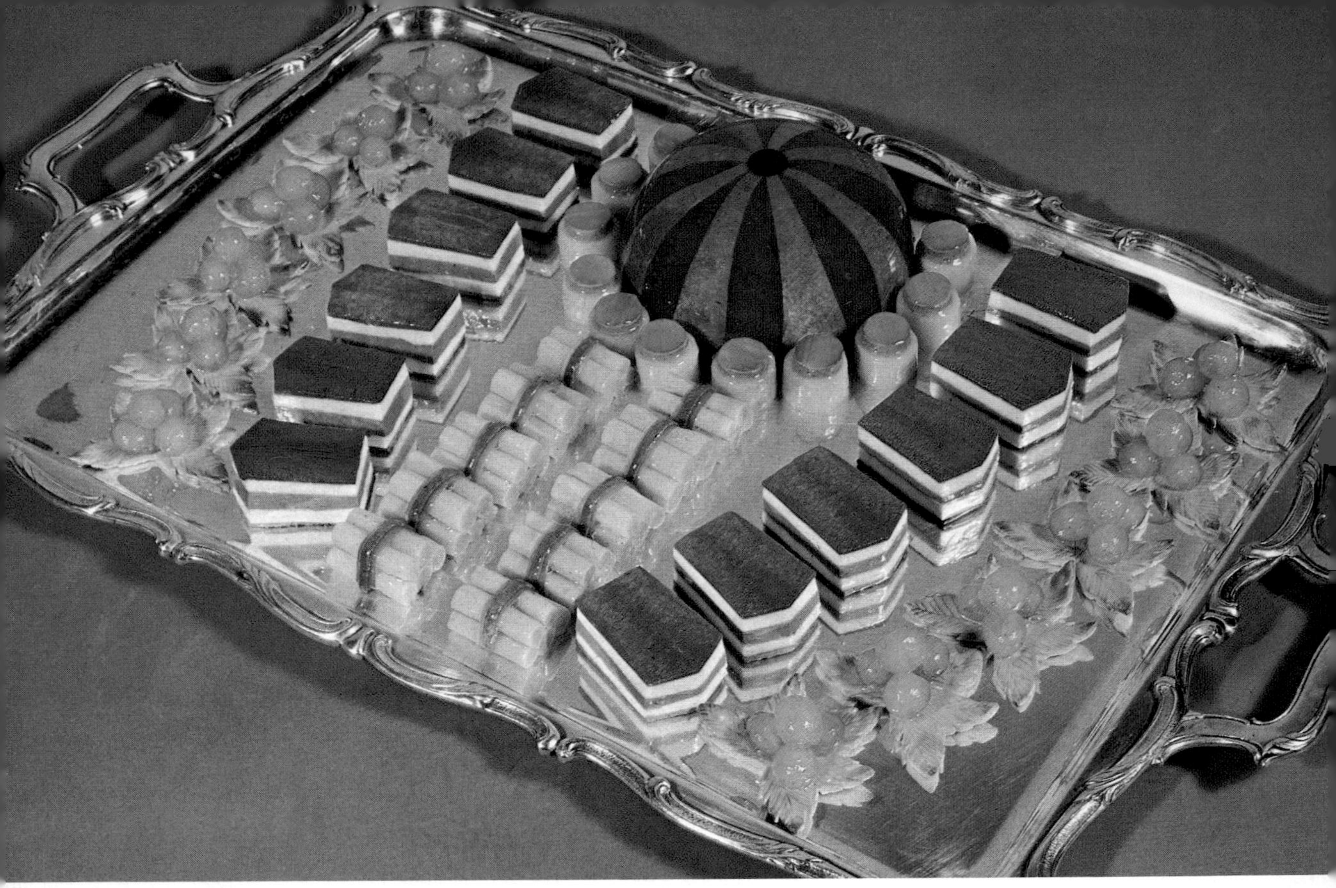

▲ Ox tongue Ruster Riesling. p. 558
▼ Swedish style saddle of pork, p. 634

250 g	cooked potatoes	9 oz
	gherkins	
	mayonnaise	
	lettuce	

Dice the potatoes and crumble two of the eggs finely. Dice the salmon after removing the bones and skin. Dice a few gherkins. Mix the salmon, potatoes, crumbled eggs and diced gherkins with a few spoonfuls of mayonnaise. Arrange some lettuce leaves on a dish and place the salmon salad on top. Garnish with mayonnaise, the third egg cut in slices, some small gherkins cut into fan shapes, little onions, tomatoes, asparagus, etc.

Holland

Ermine salad

chicory
cream vinaigrette dressing

Mix with white celery and potatoes cut into small sticks.

France

Fennel salad

4 persons

String 4 heads of fennel and remove the outer leaves. Cut in half, wash, cut in narrow strips, blanch and drain. Mix with 1 finely chopped onion and the juice of 1 lemon. Make a dressing with oil, vinegar, salt, pepper and a little powdered garlic, and pour over the salad. Sprinkle with chopped fresh chives and refrigerate for about 1 hour before serving.

(Illustration, p. 994)   Germany

Gallic salad

endive
cream vinaigrette dressing

Mix with julienne strips of russet apples and celery. Sprinkle with roughly chopped walnuts.

France

Gipsy salad

endive
vinaigrette dressing

Sprinkle with julienne strips of pickled tongue, lean ham, truffle and chicken breast.

France

Harlequin salad

very white escarole
vinaigrette or cream vinaigrette
dressing

Sprinkle with small lozenges of lean ham, pickled tongue and truffle.

France

Herring salad

4 persons

	2 salt Icelandic herrings	
	3 potatoes cooked in their skins	
	5 pickled beetroots	
	2 apples	
	1 small pickled cucumber	
100 g	cooked meat	3½ oz
	2 tablespoons chopped onions	
1 dl	beetroot liquid	⅛ pt
1 dl	whipped unsweetened cream	⅛ pt
	chopped hard-boiled egg	
	chopped chives	

Fillet and soak the herrings. Peel the potatoes and apples. Dice all the ingredients, add the chopped onions, moisten with the beetroot liquid and leave to steep in the refrigerator for a few hours. Before dishing, blend in the whipped cream, season to taste with freshly ground pepper and add a little salt if required. Garnish with chopped egg and chives.

Sweden

Jardinière salad

1 portion

25 g	tomato	1 oz
30 g	cucumber	1 oz
20 g	peas	¾ oz
20 g	canned white asparagus tips	¾ oz
	chopped parsley	
	1 hard-boiled egg	
	olives	
	sprigs of parsley	
	oil and vinegar	

Skin the tomato and remove the seeds. Dice all the ingredients excepting the egg and olives. Dress with salt, pepper, oil and vinegar and add the chopped parsley. Arrange in a dome shape on a plate and lay the slices of hard-boiled egg on top in a ring. Garnish with olives and sprigs of parsley.

Bulgaria

Jellied cucumber salad

	1 large cucumber	
	½ lemon (juice only)	
	½ shallot (juice only)	
15 g	gelatine	½ oz
	1 lettuce	
	mayonnaise for service	

Soak the gelatine in a little cold water. Peel the cucumber and coarsely grate or chop it. There should be sufficient to fill a ⅓ l tumbler. Gently press to remove excess liquid then add the juice of half a lemon and the juice from the half shallot and the soaked gelatine. Bring to the boil and simmer for 3 or 4 minutes. Colour cautiously with sap green. Cool and when nearly set turn into a mould or for preference a number of individual moulds, turn out when set. Serve on a bed of lettuce accompanied by mayonnaise or any cream-type salad dressing.

Great Britain

Lorette salad

celery and beetroot	
vinaigrette dressing	

Cut the vegetables into small sticks.

France

Mandelieu salad

> lettuce heart
> vinaigrette dressing made
> with olive oil

Sprinkle with chopped hard-boiled egg yolk and roughly chopped tomatoes.

France

Mechwija salad

4 persons

100 g	tunny fish in oil	4 oz
	2 hard-boiled eggs	
1 dl	olive oil	$\frac{1}{6}$ pt
200 g	tomatoes	8 oz
250 g	peppers	10 oz
	2–3 hot red peppers	
	1 small onion	
	1 tablespoon capers	
	1 small pickled lemon	
	1 fresh lemon	

Lightly brown the tomatoes, peppers and onions over glowing hot charcoal, then remove the skins and seeds. Cut up finely, mix with the sliced pickled lemon, the capers and the juice of the fresh lemon, and season to taste with salt. Dish, pour the olive oil over the salad and garnish with small pieces of tunny and sliced hard-boiled egg.

Tunisia

Mimosa salad

> lettuce
> vinaigrette dressing

Sprinkle with chopped hard-boiled egg yolk and with chervil.

France

Mixed vegetable salad

250 g	carrots	$\frac{1}{2}$ lb

250 g	turnips	½ lb
250 g	French beans	½ lb
250 g	green peas	½ lb
250 ml	mayonnaise	½ pt

Dice the carrots and turnips neatly, cut the French beans into diamonds. Cook all the vegetables lightly, separately, in boiling salted water and drain well. Blend with the mayonnaise when cold. (Sweetcorn, cauliflower sprigs and swedes are sometimes also added.)

Moravian salad

5 portions

100 g	smoked meat	4 oz
100 g	lean roast pork	4 oz
100 g	cucumber	4 oz
	1 hard-boiled egg	
	half a lettuce	
1 dl	whipped cream	⅙ pt
	2 apples, peeled	
	2 lemons	
	1 tablespoon chopped dill	

Dice the smoked meat and the pork, the cucumber which has been peeled and seeded and the hard-boiled egg. Cut the apples in strips, sprinkle with lemon juice, shred the lettuce and mix with the above ingredients, together with the dill. Bind with the whipped cream, mix well and season to taste with salt and pepper. Chill lightly and garnish with slices of lemon to serve.

Czechoslovakia

Motley salad

4 persons

Wash 1 small cucumber, 2 bunches of radishes and 4 tomatoes, then slice finely. Peel 4 carrots and 2 radishes, grate coarsely and mix with the sliced vegetables. Blend ¼ l (½ pt) sour cream with 250 g (about 8 oz) curd cheese and 1 bunch each of freshly chopped chives, parsely and dill (the latter is optional). Add salt, pepper, mustard and lemon juice, then pour over the salad.

(Illustration, p. 994)

Germany

Mushroom salad

2 persons

Remove the stalks of 500 g (1 lb) large mushrooms, wash the caps and slice these finely. Cover with a well-seasoned dressing made with vinegar, oil, lemon juice, salt and pepper, sprinkle with chopped parsley and mix well before serving.

(Illustration, p. 994)   Germany

Nitra salad

5 portions

200 g	raw sauerkraut	7 oz
150 g	carrots	5 oz
100 g	green or red peppers	3 oz
50 g	onions	$1\frac{1}{2}$ oz

Cut the sauerkraut finely, grate the carrots, chop the onions, remove the seeds from the peppers and cut into strips. Mix all these ingredients with oil, season with salt and freshly ground pepper and add a little sugar if required.

Czechoslovakia

Oriental salad

rice
vinaigrette dressing flavoured
    with paprika
chopped chervil

Cook the rice in salted water, refresh and drain well. Add wedges of tomato, stoned black olives and sweet peppers which have been skinned and diced.

France

Parisian salad

mixed vegetable salad
mayonnaise

Mix the vegetable salad with diced spiny lobster and truffles. Arrange in a shell of lettuce leaves or serve in a glass bowl.

France

Pineapple and carrot salad

16–18 persons

	2 fresh pineapples (or, if not available, 2 large cans)	
500 g	young carrots	1 lb
	2 lettuces	
200 g	sultanas	7 oz
150 g	chopped hazelnuts	5 oz
	1 teaspoon sugar	
	3 tablespoons sour cream	
100 g	mayonnaise	3 oz
	vinegar	

Peel the pineapple and cut into strips. Clean the carrots and cut in fine julienne strips. Place in a bowl, add the sultanas, season with salt and pepper, add the sugar and a little vinegar and dress with the mayonnaise and sour cream. Dish on choice lettuce leaves and sprinkle with the chopped hazelnuts.

USA

Prague ham salad

5 portions

150 g	cooked ham	5 oz
100 g	celeriac (preserved)	3 oz
100 g	apples, peeled and cored	3 oz
	1 lettuce	
1½ dl	cream salad dressing (whipped cream flavoured with lemon juice)	¼ pt
	1 hard-boiled egg	
	walnuts	

Squeeze out a lemon and mix the juice with the whipped cream. Cut the ham, celeriac, apples and lettuce into strips. Mix with about half the cream dressing, add salt to taste, chill lightly and decorate with the rest of the cream dressing and with sliced hard-boiled egg and half walnuts.

Czechoslovakia

Russian salad

Proceed as for Parisian salad but, instead of spiny lobster and truffles, add diced lean ham and pickled tongue bound with highly-seasoned mayonnaise. Serve in a bowl. The salad may be decorated with beetroot motifs, but these should not be added until the last minute, otherwise the beetroot will stain the other ingredients.

France

Salad Prague butchers' style

5 portions

100 g	cooked ham	4 oz
100 g	smoked pork Debrecen style*	4 oz
50 g	smoked ham	2 oz
50 g	smoked pork roll gipsy style†	2 oz
100 g	mushrooms or flap mushrooms (boletus)	4 oz
100 g	small pickled onions	4 oz
50 g	grated horseradish	2 oz

Cut all the meat into strips and mix well with the onions and mushrooms. Garnish the individual portions with grated horseradish.

Czechoslovakia

* Roast pork coated with paprika and smoked, which makes the surface dark red.
† Two pieces of roast pork rolled up, well coated with blood and smoked, which makes the surface black.

Salt cod salad Condalesa

6 persons

1 kg	salt cod in one piece, preferably the thick middle cut	2¼ lb
	3 ripe medium-sized tomatoes	
200 g	black olives	8 oz
	2 hard-boiled eggs	
	chopped parsley	
	oil	
	vinegar or lemon juice	

Skin the tomatoes, remove the seeds and chop coarsely. Place the fish on a baking sheet, brown lightly in the oven and allow to cool. Cut into 3 or 4 pieces, remove the skin and bones, then cut into long thin strips. Wash these thoroughly in cold water, changing the water several times and squeezing the fish to remove most of the salt, but do not continue too long or the fish will be tasteless. Drain it well, place in a deep bowl, dress with oil, white pepper and a little vinegar or lemon juice and mix with the chopped tomatoes. Transfer to a serving dish, taking care not to break up the strips of fish too much. Garnish with the eggs, each cut into eight, and the olives and sprinkle with chopped parsley.

Spain

Schopska salad

10 portions

400 g	tomatoes	1 lb
400 g	cucumber (peeled)	1 lb
200 g	onion	8 oz
50 g	chopped parsley	2 oz
500 g	sweet peppers	1 lb
40 g	pimento (optional)	$1\frac{1}{2}$ oz
300 g	grated cheese	6 oz
	oil and vinegar	

Grill the sweet pepper, remove the skin and seeds and cut into fairly thick small strips. Peel the onion and cut in thin half-rings. Skin the tomato, remove the seeds and cut in small dice. Dice the cucumber finely. Mix all the above ingredients, add the chopped parsley and dress with salt, pepper, oil and vinegar. Add the pimento if desired. Arrange on a plate in a dome shape, sprinkle with the grated cheese and garnish with olives and a tomato cut to the shape of a rose.

Bulgaria

Slovakian meat salad

5 portions

100 g	roast leg of pork	4 oz
50 g	cooked smoked tongue	2 oz
100 g	red peppers (without seeds)	4 oz
50 g	pickled cucumber	2 oz
100 g	pickled mushrooms or flap mushrooms (boletus)	4 oz
100 g	mayonnaise	4 oz
5 cl	whipped cream	2 fl oz
	1 tablespoon tomato ketchup	
	1 heaped teaspoon mustard	
5 cl	oil	2 fl oz
	vinegar	
	Worcestershire sauce	

Cut the meat, the peppers and the cucumber into strips, and slice the mushrooms finely. Season with salt and pepper and mix with the ketchup, oil, mustard, mayonnaise and whipped cream. Add vinegar to taste, dish on lettuce leaves and garnish with strips of red pepper.

Czechoslovakia

Small Madrid salad

1 kg	large potatoes	2 lb
500 g	carrots	1 lb
1 kg	fresh French beans	2 lb
250 g	*or* canned French beans	8 oz
	1 large lettuce	
100 g	tomato pulp	3 oz
250 g	mayonnaise	8 oz
	olive oil	
	vinegar	

Boil the potatoes in their skins, dry well over low heat, peel, allow to cool and dice finely. String the beans, cook in salted water, drain, rinse in cold water and dice. Clean the carrots, cook, allow to cool and dice. Wash the lettuce, remove any outer leaves which are too green and cut the heart in fine julienne strips. Place all the above ingredients in a large bowl, season with salt and pepper and marinate for a short time in a little oil and vinegar. Mix the mayonnaise with the tomato pulp, bind the salad with this dressing and check the taste. Serve in small individual bowls or on special salad plates, accompanied by grissini.

Spain

Spring salad

5 portions

100 g	radishes	4 oz
50 g	green peppers	2 oz
100 g	cucumber	4 oz
150 g	tomatoes	6 oz
150 g	Roquefort cheese	6 oz
50 g	onions	2 oz
5 cl	oil	2 fl oz
	vinegar	
	lettuce leaves	

Slice the radishes and cucumber without peeling. Remove the seeds from the peppers, cut these and the onions in slices and cut each tomato into eight. Dress all these ingredients with salt, pepper, vinegar and oil, dish on lettuce leaves and sprinkle with grated Roquefort cheese.

Czechoslovakia

Tomato salad

> tomatoes
> vinaigrette dressing

Skin, seed and slice very firm tomatoes. Add a few slices of young onion if desired.

France

SWEETS

BATTERS, DOUGHS, PASTES

Brioche dough

Ordinary. For large and small ordinary sweet brioches, brioche rings and bases for sweets.

250 g	flour	8 oz
175 g	butter	4 oz
6 g	yeast (in summer)	¼ oz
8 g	(in winter)	¼ oz
15 g	sugar	¼ oz
7 g	pinch of salt	
	2 eggs	
5 cl	milk	3½ fl oz

Mousseline. For tea-time, as an accompaniment to creams and other sweets.

The same procedure is used to make all three types of brioche dough. It consists of six stages—making the ferment, making the dough, incorporating the butter, incorporating the ferment, fermenting the finished dough, shaping.

1. The ferment. Take a quarter of the flour and make a bay. Into the centre of this well, pour part of the lukewarm milk and disperse the yeast in it. Gradually work in the flour, adding a little more milk if necessary, to make a fairly soft dough. Knead and shape into a ball, make an incision in the form of a cross on top, place in a basin and cover with a cloth. Set aside in a draught-free place at a temperature of 25–30°C. Leave to rise for at least 1½ hours. The ferment should double in volume.

2. The dough. Make a bay in the rest of the flour and pour in a tablespoon of lukewarm milk. Dissolve the sugar and salt in it. Add 1 egg (for plain brioche dough) or 2 eggs (for the other two types). Mix in the flour and manipulate vigorously to give the dough body, i.e. elasticity, beating it by picking it up with the tips of the fingers held close together and slapping it down hard on to the table. When the

828

dough is really elastic, make a hole in it and beat in the remaining egg (for plain brioche dough).

3. Incorporating the butter. Soften the butter to the same consistency as the dough, then blend the two together as follows: slip both hands under the dough with the fingers outstretched and place the thumbs on top. Hold the dough tightly, pull, tear and work in again; repeat until the butter has been thoroughly blended with the dough.

4. Incorporating the ferment. Spread the ferment on the dough and mix together, proceeding in the same way as for the butter.

5. Fermenting the finished dough. Place the dough in a floured basin and cover with a cloth. Set it aside in a draught-free place at a temperature of 20–25°C. Leave to rise for 5 or 6 hours, then knock back by lifting the dough and dropping it on the floured table several times until it has been compacted to its original volume. Place it in the floured basin again and leave to rise for a further 2 hours or so.

6. Shaping. Knock back again in the same way as during fermentation. Butter the patty pans well or moisten the baking sheet, as the case may be. Two-thirds fill the patty pans. Prove under the same conditions as above until the dough has expanded by one-third. Brush the top with melted butter and bake in a moderate oven (160–180°C). The baking time is 15 minutes for small brioches and 30 or 35 minutes for the largest size. Make sure they are properly cooked by inserting a knitting or trussing needle; it should come out perfectly clean and dry. If the brioches are browned too quickly, cover with lightly moistened white paper.

France

Butter sponge

30 minutes in a slow oven

125 g	flour	5 oz
100 g	butter	4 oz
75 g	sugar (caster)	3 oz
	4 eggs	
	pinch of ground vanilla	

Whisk the egg yolks and sugar in a basin until they have almost doubled in volume, then add the flour and vanilla. Whisk the egg whites to a very stiff snow, stir a quarter of this into the egg/sugar/flour mixture to make it easier to work, then fold in the rest of the snow, working to keep the mixture light. Add the melted butter, which should be barely lukewarm, but pour away any buttermilk it may contain. Pour into a buttered and floured sponge mould, which should only be filled to within 1½ cm (about ½ in) of the edge. Bake, allow to rest for 2 minutes after removing from the oven, and turn out on a wire rack to keep the sponge firm.

N.B.—There are two ways of making sure that the cake is cooked:

1. It will be seen to have shrunk away a little from the sides of the mould;
2. When it is lightly pressed with the finger-tip, a slight crackling will be heard.

France

Choux paste

125 g	flour	5 oz
75 g	butter	3 oz
¼ l	water	½ pt approx.
	4 eggs	
5 g	sugar	1 teaspoon
3 g	pinch of salt	

Boil the water in a pan with the salt, sugar and butter. As soon as the water boils and the butter is completely melted, reduce the heat, wait until the mixture has come off the boil, add the flour all at once and stir it in with a spatula. When smoothly mixed, turn up the heat and stir quickly until the mixture forms into a ball, leaving the sides of the pan clean. At this point the mixture should sweat a little and should not stick to the fingers. Remove from the heat and beat for 2 or 3 minutes. Beat in the eggs one at a time, making sure each one is completely absorbed before adding the next one. The paste should now be quite smooth. It may be stored in a cool place for a few days, covered with lightly oiled paper, but the longer it is stored, the less it will rise when baking.

For larger quantities the first 2 eggs may be beaten in together, followed by the remaining ones 4 at a time.

France

Fine choux paste

125 g	flour	5 oz
85 g	butter	3 oz
¼ l	milk	½ pt approx.
	4 eggs	
5 g	sugar	1 teaspoon
	pinch of ground vanilla	
1 cl	*or* liqueur (optional)	1 dessertspoon
3 g	pinch of salt	

Proceed as for ordinary choux paste. If flavouring is desired, add vanilla or liqueur together with the flour. Never exceed one dessertspoon of liqueur for the quantities given in the formula.

Frying batter I

For small entrées, vegetables, fish, etc.

100 g	flour	4 oz
	pinch of salt	
	1 tablespoon oil	
	1 whole egg	
	1 egg white	
2 dl	lukewarm water	⅓ pt approx.

Place the flour in a basin and make a large well in the centre. Pour the whole egg into it, add the salt and blend together well. Now begin to draw in the flour gradually with a spatula or whisk. As soon as the batter begins to thicken a little, add some water, then continue adding flour and water alternately until the batter is free-flowing. Let it all run down into the bottom of the basin, wipe the sides of the latter and cover the surface of the batter with the oil. Leave to rest in a warm place for at least an hour (the batter will keep for 36 hours at this stage). Just before using, mix the oil into the batter. Whisk the egg white to a very stiff snow and carefully fold into the batter without beating or stirring.

France

Frying batter II

For fritters, including fruit fritters

100 g	flour	4 oz
	pinch of salt	
	good pinch of sugar	
	1 tablespoon oil	
	2 eggs	
2 dl	water or beer	⅓ pt approx.

Proceed as for Formula 1, adding the sugar and 1 extra egg yolk at the beginning.

N.B.—The amount of liquid required to give the correct consistency may vary slightly with the quality of the flour, but the quantity shown in the formula should never be exceeded by more than 1 dessertspoon.

France

Frying batter III

120 g	flour	4 oz
125 ml	water	$\frac{1}{4}$ pt
7 g	oil	$\frac{1}{4}$ oz
15 g	sugar	$\frac{1}{2}$ oz
4 g	yeast	$\frac{1}{8}$ oz
	pinch salt	

Cream the yeast with a pinch of sugar and a little tepid water. Mix all the other ingredients together (the water must be tepid) then whisk in the yeast and leave for at least one hour before using.

Genoese

30 minutes on average in a medium oven

250 g	flour	$8\frac{3}{4}$ oz
250 g	sugar	$8\frac{3}{4}$ oz
125 g	butter	$4\frac{1}{2}$ oz
	good pinch of ground vanilla	
	6 eggs	

Whisk the eggs, sugar and vanilla together for 4 or 5 minutes, then place over gentle heat or in a bain-marie and continue whisking until the sponge is warm and falls like a ribbon from the whisk. Remove from the heat, sift the flour into the sponge and fold it in carefully, together with the butter, previously warmed and drained of buttermilk. Proceed quickly without working the mixture too much. Bake on a genoese baking-sheet or in a small mould, which should be only two-thirds filled.

France

Fine genoese

250 g	flour	$8\frac{3}{4}$ oz
250 g	sugar	$8\frac{3}{4}$ oz
250 g	butter (best)	$8\frac{3}{4}$ oz
	6 eggs	
1 cl	liqueur or other preferred flavouring	1 dessertspoon

Proceed as for ordinary genoese, adding the liqueur or other flavouring with the flour and butter.

France

Pancake batter

15 pancakes (diameter of pan 12–15 cm (5–6 in))

125 g	flour	4 oz
15 g	sugar	½ oz
	pinch of salt	
	2 eggs	
¼ l	cold boiled milk	½ pt approx.
	1 tablespoon liqueur	
	as desired	
30 g	butter	1 oz

Place the flour in a basin and make a large well in the centre. Pour in the eggs, add the salt and sugar, mix together and begin to draw in the flour. When the batter begins to thicken, add a little milk, then draw in some more flour, add some more milk and continue in the same manner. Pour through a fine strainer. Melt the butter in a frying pan and cook until nut-brown, then quickly whisk it into the batter. Leave to rest for an hour before using. Do not add the liqueur until the last minute.

France

Puff paste (see p. 194)

Savarin dough

250 g	flour	8 oz
8 g	baker's yeast (in summer)	¼ oz
10 g	*or* (in winter)	⅓ oz
	4 eggs (medium size)	
100 g	butter	3 oz
7 g	salt	¼ oz
15 g	sugar	½ oz
1 dl	milk	3 fl oz

Place the flour in a warmed basin and make a bay. Warm the milk slightly, pour a good part of it into the centre of the bay and disperse the yeast in it. Add the eggs one at a time, drawing in the flour and adding milk if necessary. Work the dough for 4 or 5 minutes by beating it with the hand. Divide the well-softened butter into small pieces and cover the dough with these. Cover the basin with a cloth and allow to rest at a temperature of 18–20°C until the dough has more or less doubled in volume. Now add the salt and work in the butter, then beat with the hand in the basin for 6 or 7 minutes, until the dough is smooth and elastic and can be lifted up without tearing, then add the sugar.

To gain time, double the amount of yeast may be used, but the quality will be inferior.

France

Savoy sponge

35–40 minutes

125 g	sugar	5 oz
60 g	flour	2 oz
50 g	cornflour	2 oz
	4 eggs	
	good pinch of ground vanilla	

Proceed in the same way as for butter sponge (recipe see page 829). Bake in a Savoy sponge mould and dust with icing sugar.

Short paste (slightly sweet)

For sweet tartlets and barquettes: 10–12 tartlets 5 cm (2 in) in diameter, or barquettes 5 cm (2 in) long

125 g	flour	4 oz
65 g	butter	2 oz
10 g	sugar	$\frac{1}{2}$ oz
	pinch of salt	
6 cl	water	2 fl oz about

Make a bay in the flour and place the sugar, salt, water and slightly softened butter in it. Mix thoroughly with the tips of the fingers and mould into a ball. Wrap in a damp cloth and leave to rest in a cool place for at least an hour before using.

Make this pastry on the day before it is required.

France

Sweet paste

For fine fruit tartlets and barquettes, biscuits and petits fours: 12–15 tartlets 5 cm (2 in) in diameter or barquettes 5 cm (2 in long)

125 g	flour	4 oz
75 g	butter	2 oz
60 g	sugar	$1\frac{1}{2}$ oz

	pinch of salt	
	1 egg yolk (optional)	
5 cl	water or milk	2 fl oz about

Method 1. Make a bay in the flour and place the sugar, salt, butter and egg yolk in the centre. Mix the four latter ingredients together well, then gradually draw in the flour, while sprinkling with the milk (boiled and left until cold) or water and working the paste constantly. Knead the paste with the palm of the hand and mould into a ball. Wrap in a cloth and leave in a cool place for at least 2 hours before using.

Method 2. Mix the flour and sugar together. Make a bay and place the salt, egg yolk, slightly softened butter and the milk or water in it. Mix well, knead and proceed as for Method 1.

Make this pastry on the day before it is required.

France

BREAD AND ROLLS

Brioche-type bread or rolls

8–10 minutes for rolls, otherwise according to size

250 g	flour	9 oz
75 g	butter	3 oz
	1 egg	
1 dl	water	$\frac{1}{6}$ pt
10 g	salt	$\frac{1}{3}$ oz
8 g	yeast	$\frac{1}{4}$ oz

This dough is made in the same way as brioche dough and baked in well-greased tins or shaped into round or long rolls, which are placed on a greased baking-sheet and washed with beaten egg. They are proved before baking.

France

Challah

450 g	flour	1 lb
15 g	sugar	$\frac{1}{2}$ oz
approx. 240 ml	warm water	$\frac{1}{2}$ pt approx.
15 g	salt	$\frac{1}{2}$ oz
	2 eggs	
	1 egg yolk	
	2 tablespoons oil	
	poppy seeds	

Cream the yeast with a little water and the sugar. Sift the flour and salt into a warm bowl and beat in the eggs, the yeast mixture, the oil and most of the water to obtain a smooth dough. Knead this well, until it is smooth and shiny, then cover and leave to prove for 1 hour. Knock back, and prove again, until double in size. Divide the dough into two pieces, one slightly larger than the other. Divide the large piece into three, and roll into strips, then form a fat, even plait. Repeat with the smaller piece, and place this plait on top of the first. Cover with a cloth and allow to rise for $\frac{1}{2}$ hour, in a warm place. Brush with the egg yolk and sprinkle heavily with poppy seeds. Bake in a medium oven for about $\frac{3}{4}$ hour.

Jewish

Croissants

12–15 minutes in a hot oven

250 g	flour	9 oz
100 g	butter	$3\frac{1}{2}$ oz
30 g	sugar	1 oz
$1\frac{1}{2}$ dl	lukewarm milk	$\frac{1}{4}$ pt
5 g	baker's yeast	$\frac{1}{8}$ oz

Place the flour in a basin and make a bay. Pour in part of the warm milk and disperse the yeast in it. Add the sugar and a little salt. Mix to a fairly firm dough, using as much of the remaining milk as required. Scrape down the sides of the basin. Cover with a cloth and allow to rest in a cool place for about 10 hours. Flatten the dough with the fist on a marble slab. Cover with the butter, which should be firm but pliable, and fold the dough over to enclose the butter as for puff paste. Give two turns, allow to rest for 15 minutes, then give a final third turn. Allow to rest again for 15 minutes before shaping into croissants. To shape, pin out the dough to a thickness of 2–3 mm (about $\frac{1}{10}$ in) and cut into 7–8 cm (3 in) triangles. Roll up each triangle, starting at the base, and curl the ends round to form a crescent. Place on a baking-sheet with the point of the rolled triangles on top. Cover with a cloth and prove for $1\frac{1}{2}$ or 2 hours in a moderately warm place. Wash with beaten egg before baking.

(Techniques, p. 104)

France

French loaf

30 g	fresh yeast	1 oz
	1 teaspoon sugar	
55 ml	warm water	2 fl oz
325 ml	warm milk	12 fl oz

110 ml	warm water	4 fl oz
	2 teaspoons salt	
1 kg	plain flour	2 lb
	1 teaspoon salt	
110 ml	water	4 fl oz

Cream the yeast and sugar with 55 ml (2 fl oz) warm water. Pour warm milk, 110 ml (4 fl oz) warm water and salt into a bowl. Stir in the yeast mixture. Slowly add the flour a little at a time. Mix with a wooden spoon until the mixture becomes a medium firm dough. Knead well on a slightly floured surface for at least 10 minutes. Sprinkle the surface with more flour if the dough becomes sticky. Place the dough in a bowl, cover with a damp cloth and leave to rise in a warm place until double in size (about 60 minutes). Knock back. Leave to rise for 40 minutes. Divide dough into 3 equal portions. Shape into 3 loaves as long as your baking-tray. With a sharp knife cut diagonal slashes about 1 cm ($\frac{1}{2}$ in) deep at 5 cm (2 in) intervals on top of the loaves. Dissolve salt in warm water and brush glacé on to loaves. Let the loaves rise until double in bulk. Place loaves on baking-tray in the oven. Bake in pre-heated oven 220°C (425°F) for 15 minutes. Reduce heat to 190°C (375°F) brushing loaves again with salt solution. Repeat after 10 minutes. Bake for another 15–20 minutes until crisp. Remove from oven and cool on wire tray.

France

Milk rolls

8–10 minutes in a hot oven

250 g	flour	9 oz
100 g	butter	$3\frac{1}{2}$ oz
	1 egg yolk	
$1\frac{1}{2}$ dl	milk	$\frac{1}{4}$ pt
10 g	sugar	$\frac{1}{3}$ oz
5 g	salt	$\frac{1}{6}$ oz
10 g	baker's yeast	$\frac{1}{3}$ oz

For the ferment, make a bay in 75 g ($2\frac{3}{4}$ oz) of the flour, disperse the yeast in 4 or 5 cl (about $\frac{1}{12}$ pt) lukewarm water and pour into the bay. Gradually draw in the flour, adding just enough water to make a rather slack dough. Mould into a ball and cut a cross in the top. Place in a floured basin, cover with a cloth and allow to rise in a warm place until it has doubled in volume. (For much quicker fermentation, immerse the ferment in a pan of lukewarm water, then drain carefully before using.) Mix the rest of the flour with the butter, sugar, salt and egg yolk, gradually adding the milk until the dough is fairly slack, but not liquid. Beat on the table in the same way as brioche dough. Now mix with the ferment and allow to rise for 3 or 4 hours in a basin covered with a cloth. Knock back on a floured table or slab until the dough is de-gassed. Divide into pieces the size of a small egg and shape into rolls. Place these on a baking-sheet and prove in a warm place. Wash with beaten egg before baking.

France

Pumpernickel

30 g	fresh yeast	1 oz
140 ml	warm water	¼ pt
½ l	warm milk	1 pt
55 g	margarine	2 oz
60 ml	molasses	⅛ pt
	1 beaten egg	
	1 teaspoon salt	
¾ kg	rye flour	1½ lb
	2 tablespoons caraway seeds	

Dissolve the yeast in the water. Heat the milk and melt the margarine in it. Cool until lukewarm. Sir in the molasses, beaten egg, salt and yeast mixture. Add 225 g (½ lb) rye flour and the caraway seeds and beat until smooth. Leave to rise for ½ hour. Stir in 225 g (½ lb) rye flour, cover with a damp cloth and leave to rise for another ½ hour. Stir in the rest of the flour and knead well for 10 minutes using more rye flour if the dough seems sticky. Shape into 2 oval loaves and prove them in a greased baking tin, covered with a dry cloth, for 1 hour. Bake at 200°C (400°F) for about 40 minutes. Brush with cream 10 minutes before the end of baking time. Leave to cool and slice very thinly.

Rye bread

¾ kg	wholemeal rye flour	1½ lb
½ kg	plain white flour	1 lb
	4 teaspoons salt	
	sour dough paste made with 3 tablespoons rye flour mixed to a smooth paste with some warm milk and left covered for 2 days until it smells sour	
115 g	melted fat	4 oz
½ l	warm milk	1 pt
15 g	fresh yeast	½ oz
	cream for glazing	

Put the flour and salt into a bowl. Make a well in the centre, and pour in the sour dough paste, the warm melted fat, the warm milk and the creamed yeast (to cream fresh yeast sprinkle 15 g ($\frac{1}{2}$ oz) of yeast on to 60 ml ($\frac{1}{8}$ pt) warm water or milk). Mix up well. Knead into a smooth elastic dough for about 15 minutes. Put into a bowl and cover with a damp cloth. Leave to rise in a warm place for 60–90 minutes. Knock back by kneading the dough for about 5 minutes. Cut the dough into equal portions and shape as long as the baking tins. Place each loaf into the greased baking tins and cut a slit on top with a sharp knife. Bake the loaves in a hot oven (220°C) for 30 minutes. Remove from the oven and brush with cream to give a glossy finish. Put back in a cooler oven (180°C) for at least another $\frac{1}{2}$ hour.

Sandwich loaf

About 1 hour in a very hot oven

600 g	flour	1$\frac{1}{4}$ lb
4 dl	lukewarm milk	$\frac{2}{3}$ pt
20 g	salt	$\frac{3}{4}$ oz
25 g	baker's yeast	1 oz

Place one-third of the flour in a warmed basin. Make a well in the centre with the fist so that the bottom of the basin can be seen, place the salt and yeast in the well and mix with part of the warm milk. Work in the flour to make a fairly slack dough. Cover the basin with a cloth, set aside in a warm place and allow to rise until the dough has doubled in volume; this may take up to 2 hours, depending on the surrounding temperature. Work in the remaining flour and milk, kneading vigorously for about 10 minutes. Two-thirds fill a lightly greased sandwich loaf tin with the dough. Prove in a warm place until the dough has risen a further 2 or 3 cm (about 1 in). Cover the tin, set in the oven and bake for $\frac{3}{4}$ hour before opening the oven door. Turn out on to a wire rack.

There are special round tins which may be used for this type of bread if it is intended for canapés. In this case the baking time is shorter—only 30–45 minutes according to size. Alternatively, a cast iron casserole with a tight fitting lid may be used; the inside should be greased and the lid weighted down to make sure that it remains tightly closed while the bread is baking.

France

Wholemeal bread

50 g	yeast	2 oz
850 ml	water	1$\frac{1}{2}$ pt
1 kg 200 g	wholemeal flour	3 lb
	2 tablespoons caster sugar	
	2 tablespoons salt	
25 g	lard	1 oz

Prepare tins as required.

Blend the yeast with $\frac{1}{4}$ l ($\frac{1}{2}$ pint) of water. Mix together the flour, sugar and salt. Rub in the lard. Stir the yeast liquid into the dry ingredients, adding sufficient of the remaining water to make a firm dough that leaves the bowl clean. Turn the dough on to a lightly floured surface and knead by folding the dough towards you, then pushing down and away from you, with palm of the hand only. Give the dough a quarter-turn, and repeat the kneading, developing a rocking rhythm, until the dough feels firm and elastic and no longer sticky. Shape the dough into a round ball, place in a large, greased polythene bag and close it. Leave the dough to rise until it is double in size and springs back when pressed lightly with a floured finger.

When the dough is risen, turn it on to a floured surface and knead again until firm. Divide into two or four and flatten each piece firmly with the knuckles to knock out air bubbles.

To make a tin loaf, shape each piece by folding into three or rolling up like a Swiss roll, and tuck in the ends. The moulded pieces should fit the tins exactly—900 g or 450 g (2 lb or 1 lb). Brush the tops with salted water, put each tin inside a greased polythene bag and tie lightly. Put aside until the dough rises to the top of the tins— about 1 hour at room temperature. Bake the loaves in the centre of a very hot oven 232°C (450°F) for 30–40 minutes. Cool on a wire rack.

ALMOND PRODUCTS AND MERINGUES

Almond meringue

	4 egg whites	
175 g	caster sugar	6 oz
125 g	ground almonds	4½ oz
	little vanilla	

Whisk the egg whites to a very stiff snow. Mix the almonds, sugar and vanilla together and sift into the whites. Now proceed as for Swiss meringue.

France

Almond paste I

250 g	almonds	8 oz
650 g	sugar	1 lb 7 oz
50 g	glucose	1¾ oz
	pinch of ground vanilla	
5–6 cl	water	2 fl oz about

Blanch the almonds, wash them in cold water and drain, then grind them gradually adding the cold water, to make a softish paste. Boil the sugar to the crack degree and pour on to the ground almonds, mixing with a wooden spatula and working until the mixture becomes sandy. Grind again until the paste is lukewarm. Transfer to a marble slab and knead with the palm of the hand until the paste is of the same consistency as short pastry for lining tarts. Wrap in damp muslin and store in a cool place in a covered basin.

This almond paste will keep for 8 days.

France

Almond paste II

250 g	very dry blanched almonds	9 oz
200 g	fondant	7 oz
	pinch of ground vanilla	

Grind the almonds in the mixer, add the vanilla, then mix the ground almonds and fondant together by hand. Knead 5 or 6 times with the palm of the hand. Wrap in damp muslin and store in a cool place in a covered basin.

France

Almond paste III

350 g	icing sugar	12 oz
350 g	ground almonds	12 oz
	½ lemon	
	1 egg	

Sieve the sugar, mix in the almonds and beaten egg and enough lemon juice to make a smooth, stiff paste.

Almond paste using ground almonds

250 g	ground almonds	½ lb
250 g	caster sugar	½ lb
250 g	icing sugar	½ lb
	3 egg yolks	
30 g	orange flower water	1 oz

Mix together into a pliable paste.

Italian meringue

	4 egg whisked to very stiff snow	
250 g	sugar	9 oz
1 dl	water	⅙ pt

Method I. Dissolve the sugar in the water and boil to the large ball degree, then pour at once into the whites in a thin stream, whisking vigorously meanwhile.

Method II (same formula, but omitting the water). Sift the sugar through a hair-sieve and whisk with the egg whites for a few moments. Place over gentle heat or in a hot bain-marie. Whisk until firm enough to stick to the whisk. This meringue will keep for some time. Place it in a basin and cover the top of the meringue with a sheet of greaseproof paper.

France

Swiss Meringue

	4 egg whites	
200–250 g	fine caster sugar	7–9 oz

Whisk the egg whites to a very stiff snow. Sift in the sugar and fold in with a spatula, occasionally turning the bowl a quarter of the way round to blend the ingredients together quickly and thoroughly.

Never stir or beat at this stage, otherwise the meringue will liquefy.

France

SUGAR AND SUGAR COMPOUNDS

SYRUPS—CARAMEL—FONDANT

The best utensil for sugar boiling is a small unlined copper pan or, failing this, an aluminium saucepan. Enamel pans should never be used. Other equipment required consists of an earthenware or china basin, a small cloth pad, a tablespoon and a skimmer.

The ingredients used are very white sugar, a little water and, optionally, some glucose (at the rate of 1 tablespoon to 500 g (1 lb 1½ oz) sugar) to prevent graining.

The density of a syrup may be accurately measured by means of a saccharometer, but a sugar syrup of the desired density may be made without using a saccharometer on the basis of the following principle:

One degree on the saccharometer corresponds to 25 g sugar dissolved in 1 l water (1 oz sugar dissolved in 2 pt water). If we simply multiply the number of degrees desired by 25, this will give the amount (in grammes) of sugar which has to be used to arrive at the desired density.

For example,

if syrup at 10° is required, multiply 10 by 25, which gives 250 g sugar per litre of water;

if syrup at 28° is required, 28 × 25 = 700 g sugar must be used per litre of water.

If smaller amounts are required, the sugar and water should be proportionately scaled down.

The reading for a syrup which has been allowed to cool will be two or three degrees higher than for the same syrup when it is hot. This is due to the fact that its density increases as the water evaporates.

France

Sugar syrup

Place the sugar and water in a pan, using 1 dl water to 500 g sugar ($\frac{1}{6}$ pt water to 1 lb 1$\frac{1}{2}$ oz sugar). When the sugar is dissolved, add one tablespoon glucose (this is optional). Bring to the boil. Skim off the scum which rises to the surface as the solution comes to the boil. Once it is boiling fast, crystals begin to form round the sides of the pan at the top. These sugar crystals have to be removed and prevented from falling back into the boiling solution, where they would cause graining. Wash down the sides of the pan either with the index finger previously dipped in cold water or with a small cloth pad which has been wetted and then well wrung out.

The density of the sugar solution changes fairly quickly. There are six degrees of sugar boiling:

1. thread
2. blow
3. small ball
4. large ball
5. small crack
6. large crack

The sugar then turns into light and dark caramel, after which it begins to burn and turns black.

The above degrees may be recognized as follows:—

Thread. If a drop of sugar is taken between the thumb and forefinger and a thin thread is formed when they are separated, then the sugar is boiled to the thread degree.

Blow. If the skimmer is dipped into the solution and then held up vertically, small bubbles will form which can be burst by blowing through them.

(For the remaining tests, dip the fingers in cold water before dipping the fingertips in the sugar.)

Small Ball. This stage has been reached when the sugar which sticks to the tip of the finger when it is dipped into the solution and quickly dipped in cold water can be rolled into a small, fairly soft ball.

Large Ball. When the above test is repeated, the ball of sugar will be firmer.

Small Crack. If the same test is repeated and the sugar sticks to the teeth slightly when bitten, it has reached the small crack degree.

Large Crack. At this stage, the sugar breaks when bitten, without sticking to the teeth.

A few moments later it caramelises.

France

Syrup for soaking babas and savarins

400 g	sugar	14 oz
$\frac{1}{2}$ l	water	$\frac{7}{8}$ pt
	good pinch of ground vanilla	
3 dl	rum	$\frac{1}{2}$ pt

Bring the syrup to the boil and continue boiling for 2 or 3 minutes. Allow to cool slightly before adding the rum. The amount of rum can be reduced or rum essence can be used, but this produces a very inferior result.

France

Caramel sugar

150 g	sugar	6 oz
3 cl	water	3 dessertspoons

Place the sugar and water in a small pan over gentle heat to dissolve slowly. As soon as the sugar has completely dissolved, raise the heat and boil until the solution turns brown. To ensure uniform colour, tilt the pan in all directions until the solution is well mixed, or stir with a stainless steel fork. Pour the caramel into the mould to be used for cooking a sweet.

France

Caramel sauce

Add 3 or 4 drops of lemon juice and 2 dl ($\frac{1}{3}$ pt) water to the caramel, first drawing the pan to the side of the stove. If the sauce is still rather thick, add water until the desired consistency is reached.

France

Vanilla sugar

This is made by putting two vanilla pods in an airtight jar with about $\frac{1}{2}$ kg (1 lb) of caster sugar, and leaving for a week or so, during which time the sugar will absorb the vanilla flavour. When sugar is taken from the jar, more sugar can be added.

Flavouring sugar

Lemon flavoured sugar

Wipe the lemon well. Rub it with a lump of sugar. As soon as the sugar is saturated, grate the damp part on to a small plate. Repeat until the whole lump of sugar has been used up. One lemon is enough for two or three lumps.

Orange flavoured sugar

Proceed as for lemon flavoured sugar.

Tangerine flavoured sugar

Proceed as for lemon flavoured sugar.

Fondant

Fondant is either used plain or mixed with all kinds of ingredients and flavourings before use. Soften the amount of fondant required over gentle heat, stirring with a wooden spatula. As soon as the fondant is tepid, add the flavouring essence or liqueur, together with a few drops of water to adjust the consistency so that the fondant will coat the spatula without being too firm or too liquid. It should never be allowed to become more than lukewarm. It is difficult to state exactly how much essence or liqueur should be added; this will depend on the degree of concentration of the fondant and on the quality of the product used. If liqueur is used, never exceed a dessertspoonful per 100 g ($3\frac{1}{2}$ oz) fondant.

As soon as the fondant is ready for icing, the small cakes (eclairs, choux, etc.) are dipped in it, or else they are iced by spreading a little of the prepared fondant on top and smoothing it over with a metal spatula. For an attractive gloss, the fondant must be at the right temperature and must dry quickly.

Plain fondant

Boil the sugar to the blow degree and continue boiling for 2 or 3 seconds. Now pour steadily, but very slowly, on to a slightly moistened marble slab (indispensable). If metal bars are available, form a square on the slab with four of them to hold the sugar; it may be poured out more quickly in this case. Allow to cool until the sugar solution no longer sticks to the fingers when the centre of the square is touched. Using a special spatula shaped like a palette knife, bring the edges of the square of syrup towards the centre so that its area is smaller and the heat is evenly distributed through it. Work the syrup by sliding the knife shaped spatula forward under it, then turning it over like a pancake and rubbing it against the slab with the spatula as the latter is drawn back to its original position. Continue working backwards and forwards in this manner until the sugar grains, i.e. becomes sandy and whitish. Be sure to work all the syrup well in this way, otherwise it will be lumpy. Now mould into a ball and knead briskly until smooth. Shape into a ball again and store in an airtight jar or tin, where the fondant will keep for a long time.

France

Chocolate fondant

200 g	fondant	8 oz
50 g	chocolate	2 oz

Soften the chocolate over gentle heat. Add the fondant and warm slightly, working with a spatula meanwhile. Add a few drops of water until the required consistency is reached.

France

Coffee fondant

Add a few drops of coffee essence to the fondant.

France

Coloured fondants

Tint the fondant with *minute* amounts of commercial food colours, adding these when the fondant has the consistency of thick cream. The colour may be selected to match the flavouring used.

France

Liqueur flavoured fondants

Soften the fondant over gentle heat. Using a spatula, blend in a dessertspoonful of the selected liqueur.

France

NOUGAT, PRALINE, ICING

Chocolate nougat

50 g	almonds or hazelnuts roasted until golden	2 oz
50 g	sugar	2 oz
10 g	milk couverture	$\frac{1}{4}$ oz

Boil the sugar to the crack degree and add the almonds or hazelnuts. Grind down to a smooth fairly thick paste. Add the couverture and grind lightly again.

Germany

Parisian nougat

Basic recipe

300 g	caster sugar	10 oz
250 g	chopped almonds the almonds should be very dry and well sieved to remove any fragments that are too small	8 oz
	5 or 6 drops lemon juice	

Melt the sugar in a small pan (preferably a copper one) without adding any water, stirring with a spatula meanwhile. Start cooking over very moderate heat. When the sugar has reached the pale caramel stage (see sugar syrup) turn down the heat until very low and add the lemon juice and almonds. The almonds should be warmed beforehand. Mix well with a spatula. Pour on to a lightly oiled baking-sheet and keep warm until required.

As long as it is hot, nougat is pliable and may be shaped as desired. Moisten the fingers slightly with water before manipulating it, but be careful not to use too much water or the nougat might become soggy. To pin out, use an oiled or damped rolling pin. Cut with a knife or cutter.

For large items, lay the pinned-out nougat on top of oiled moulds and press down by hand on to the sharp edges of the moulds, working as fast as possible and taking care to avoid the formation of folds or bumps. Trim the edges evenly with a knife. To shape small items, either follow the same procedure or place a piece of hot nougat the size of a walnut in the centre of the mould and spread as evenly as possible. For deep or cylindrical moulds, use a rounded stick or a spatula handle.

France

Praline I

| 100 g | sugar | 4 oz |
| 50 g | unblanched almonds | 2 oz |

Boil the sugar to the light brown caramel degree and add the almonds. Tilt and shake the pan to mix well, but do not remove from the heat. Pour on to an oiled baking-sheet or marble slab and leave until cold, then reduce to powder.

Store in an airtight container.

Praline II

| 100 g | sugar | 4 oz |
| 200 g | unblanched almonds | 8 oz |

This praline is of better quality. It is made in the same way as Formula I.

Royal icing

1. For coating cakes and petits fours

| 200 g | icing sugar | 7 oz |
| | 1 egg white | |

Sift the icing sugar into a basin through a silk sieve. Beat in the egg white a little at a time with a wooden spatula until the icing falls like a ribbon from the spatula. The amount of egg white required may vary; if the icing is too thick, more may be added, but only a little at a time. Use in the same way as fondant.

2. For final decoration (piped designs or lettering on cakes)

200 g	icing sugar	7 oz
	1 egg white	
	5 or 6 drops lemon juice	

Proceed as for 1. Add the lemon juice at the end; it makes the icing whiter and more compact, and helps it to dry more quickly.

France

Coloured royal icing

Tint with good colours in the same way as fondant. Add the colour as soon as the ribbon stage has been reached and mix well. If a marbled effect is desired, however, the icing should barely be stirred after adding the colour.

France

Spun sugar

Used to decorate gâteaux.

Boil the sugar to the large crack degree until it is about to turn into caramel. Allow to cool for a moment so that it becomes a little thicker. Now dip a fork in it and lift it out over an oiled rolling pin, the ends of which are resting on the backs of two chairs. Move the fork to and fro quickly above the rolling pin, throwing thin threads of sugar on to it; these will form a kind of veil. (Place a sheet of white paper under the rolling pin to catch any threads that may fall down.) Cut the veil of spun sugar with scissors to the shape required. Must be kept dry.

N.B.—Do not confuse with sugar boiled to the thread degree.

Glacé icing

| 100 g | icing sugar | 4 oz |
| | little cold water | |

26

Sieve the icing sugar. Add a little cold water very slowly to the sugar to form the correct coating consistency at the same time adding the flavouring. Warm it very slightly. If the icing becomes too liquid when warmed up add some icing sugar. Use to ice cakes and petits fours.

American frosting

200 g	sugar	7 oz
	1 egg white	
	4 tablespoons water	

Gently heat the sugar in the water, stirring until dissolved. Then without stirring heat to 125°C (240°F). Beat the egg white stiffly. Remove sugar syrup from the heat and when the bubbles subside pour it on to the egg white, whisking the mixture continuously. When it thickens and is almost cold pour it quickly over the cake.

CREAMS, CUSTARDS AND SWEET SAUCES

Basic buttercream I

Yields 250–260 g buttercream (about 9 oz)

2 dl	vanilla custard	⅓ pt
135 g	butter (best quality)	4 oz

Cream the butter in a basin until soft and smooth. Blend in the custard, which should be at a temperature of 20–25°C.

France

Basic buttercream II

2 dl	confectioner's custard	⅓ pt
100 g	butter	3 oz

Cream the butter in a basin until soft and smooth. Rub the confectioner's custard through a fine sieve and blend into the butter.

France

Almond buttercream

1 part almond paste
(half almonds and half sugar)
2 parts vanilla buttercream

Soften the almond paste with as much water as required, then mix with the buttercream.

Austria

Chocolate buttercream

Add 60 g (2 oz) cocoa or cold melted chocolate.

France

Coffee buttercream

Add a few drops of coffee essence.

France

Liqueur buttercream

For liqueur flavoured mousseline buttercream, add 1 tablespoon liqueur to the egg yolks before pouring in the sugar solution. Omit the vanilla. For the other types of buttercream, add the liqueur to the custard or confectioner's custard before blending into the butter.

France

Meringue buttercream

125 g	butter	5 oz
	2 egg whites	
100 g	sugar	4 oz
	good pinch of vanilla	

Whip the egg whites to a very stiff snow and sift in the sugar while stirring with a spatula. Blend this meringue into the creamed butter. Serve at once.

France

Mousseline buttercream

Yields 250 g buttercream (8¾ oz)

125 g	fresh butter (good quality)	4 oz
50 g	sugar 3 egg yolks good pinch of vanilla	2 oz
5 cl	water	2 fl oz

Dissolve the sugar in the water and boil to the thread degree. Beat the egg yolks with the vanilla for a few moments. Pour the boiling sugar solution very slowly on to the yolks, while stirring with a whisk. Place over gentle heat and whisk for 3 or 4 minutes, then cool, still whisking constantly. Blend gradually into the butter until soft and creamy.

Sometimes the custard is not completely absorbed by the butter, in which case it curdles. If this should happen, take a piece of butter, cream it and blend the curdled custard into it. In cold weather, or if the custard is too cold when it is blended into the butter, it may become grainy. If it does, warm the bowl slightly and whisk the buttercream; it should become smooth, but if it fails to do so, warm another basin, place a little soft, almost liquid butter in it and whisk in the buttercream. Keep in a fairly warm place.

France

Praline buttercream

Add 50 g (1¾ oz) praline, to either basic recipe or to chocolate or coffee butter-cream.

France

Chantilly (whipped) cream

2 dl	very fresh double cream	⅓ pt
2 dl	unboiled milk	⅓ pt
50 g	caster sugar lightly flavoured with vanilla	2 oz

Leave the milk and cream in a cool place for at least 2 hours before use. Whisk together on ice until the cream sticks to the whisk slightly or takes on a dome shape when spooned up. (Excessive whisking will turn it into butter.) Fold in the sugar, using a whisk. Keep in a cool place until ready to use.

Whipped cream will not keep for long and must be used quickly. It should remain white. As soon as it takes on a yellowish tinge, it may be expected to 'turn'.

Marshmallow cream

30 g	gelatine	1 oz
150 g	water	5 oz
500 g	granulated sugar	16 oz
200 g	glucose	7 oz
150 g	water	5 oz
8 g	tartaric acid	$\frac{1}{4}$ oz
	flavour	

Boil the sugar, glucose, one amount of water and acid to 116° C (240°F) and cool to 93°C (200°F) and add the gelatine that has been soaked in the second amount of water. Whisk until light.

Great Britain

Stock marshmallow

250 g	granulated sugar	6 oz
125 g	glucose	4 oz
150 g	water	5 oz
90 g	egg whites	3 oz
4 g	agar-agar	$\frac{1}{8}$ oz
	cream of tartar	

The agar-agar is soaked for some hours in the water and then brought to the boil. To make certain that the agar is properly dispersed, strain the solution. The sugar is then added and when properly dissolved it is taken to 107°C (225°F) when the warmed glucose is run in. The solution is then boiled to 118°C (245°F) washing the sides of the saucepan down from time to time.

Have ready the egg whites, to which have been added the cream of tartar, beaten to a stiff snow. Whilst the machine is running, carefully pour in the boiling solution and continue beating until cool.

To use, add 150 g (5 oz) of egg whites to each 500 g (1 lb) of stock marshmallow and beat it well. It can be coloured and flavoured.

Great Britain

Lemon curd

Yield: sufficient to fill 35 tartlets

180 g	butter	6 oz
350 g	sugar	12 oz
240 g	whole eggs	8 oz
	juice of 2 large lemons	

Melt the butter in a pan. Add the sugar, the beaten eggs and the lemon juice. Cook over low heat, stirring continuously until thick and smooth. Pour into warmed pots and allow to cool, then cover tightly with greaseproof paper or cellophane and store in a cool place until required.

Great Britain

Caramel custard

	4 egg yolks	
125 g	sugar	4 oz
½ l	milk	1 pt
50 g	caramel	2 oz

Crush the caramel finely and dissolve in the milk. Then proceed as for vanilla custard.

France

Chocolate custard

	4 egg yolks	
100 g	sugar	4 oz
75 g	grated chocolate	3 oz
½ l	milk	1 pt

Dissolve the chocolate in the milk before use. Then proceed as for vanilla custard.

France

Coffee custard I

Add a few drops of coffee essence to the custard.

Coffee custard II

(Very good flavour.) Roast 125 g (4½ oz) green coffee. While still very hot, drop into ½ l (⅞ pt) boiling milk. Cover at once and allow to infuse over gentle heat without boiling for 10–15 minutes. Strain the milk through a very fine cloth. Then proceed as for vanilla custard.

Coffee custard III

Place 150 g (5¼ oz) roasted coffee in the oven and heat to the temperature which it would reach in a roaster. Drop in the boiling milk, cover and allow to infuse over gentle heat for 10–15 minutes. Then proceed as for vanilla custard.

France

Confectioner's custard

125 g	sugar	4 oz
60 g	flour	2 oz
	4 egg yolks	
½ l	milk	1 pt
	good pinch of vanilla	

Whisk the egg yolks with the sugar for 5 minutes, then blend in the flour and vanilla. Add the hot milk a little at a time, beating constantly. Boil up for a moment while whisking briskly in all directions. Transfer to a basin and dab the surface lightly with butter to prevent skinning.

This custard may be improved by adding 25–50 g (1–1¾ oz) very fresh butter after removing from the heat.

France

Almond flavoured confectioner's custard

Proceed as for ordinary confectioner's custard, adding 50 g (1¾ oz) ground almonds at the same time as the flour. The amount of flour may be reduced from 60 g (2 oz) to 50 g (1¾ oz).

France

Chocolate flavoured confectioner's custard I

Before cooking, add 75 g (3 oz) cocoa to the confectioner's custard.

Chocolate flavoured confectioner's custard II

Boil 80 g (3 oz) chocolate for 2 or 3 minutes in the $\frac{1}{2}$ l (1 pt) milk with which the confectioner's custard is to be made. The amount of sugar may be reduced by 25 g (1 oz) if desired.

France

Coffee flavoured confectioner's custard

Proceed as for ordinary confectioner's custard, with the addition of a few drops of coffee essence. For an even better flavour, roast 125 g (5 oz) green coffee; while still very hot, drop it into the boiling milk, cover and allow to infuse over gentle heat for 10–15 minutes. Strain the milk through a very fine cloth.

France

Praline flavoured confectioner's custard

After cooking the custard, add 60–75 g (2–3 oz) praline.

France

Tutti-frutti confectioner's custard

125 g	sugar	4 oz
60 g	flour	2 oz
	4 egg yolks	
$\frac{1}{2}$ l	milk	1 pt
	good pinch of vanilla	
75 g	finely diced candied fruit macerated in kirsch	3 oz

Proceed as for ordinary confectioner's custard, adding the candied fruit after cooking.

France

Frangipane custard

100 g	sugar	4 oz
75 g	flour	3 oz
$\frac{1}{2}$ l	milk	1 pt
	1 egg	
	3 egg yolks	
30–50 g	butter	1–2 oz
	3 macaroons	
	good pinch of vanilla	

Beat the eggs with the sugar until pale in colour, then add the vanilla and flour. Pour on the hot milk a little at a time, while stirring with a whisk. Bring to the boil and continue boiling for a moment or two, while stirring constantly with the whisk. Remove from the heat, cool slightly, then add the butter in small knobs and the finely crushed macaroons. Mix well. Transfer to a basin and dab the top with butter to avoid skinning.

France

Gelatine custard

	4 egg yolks	
125 g	sugar	4 oz
	good pinch of vanilla	
10–15 g	gelatine	½ oz about
	(depending on the temperature)	
½ l	milk	1 pt

This is made in the same way as ordinary custard, the gelatine (previously soaked if in leaf form) being added after beating the egg yolks with the sugar. The procedure is now the same as for the first recipe.

The custard should be well stirred at the bottom of the pan, where the gelatine tends to settle, especially at the start of the cooking process.

France

St. Honoré custard I

75 g	sugar	3 oz
	4 egg whites whipped to a stiff snow	
	2 egg yolks	
30 g	flour	1 oz
¼ l	milk	½ pt approx.
	good pinch of vanilla	

Beat the sugar and egg yolks together for 3–5 minutes, then blend in the flour and vanilla. Add the hot milk while stirring with a whisk. Boil up for a moment or two, then remove from the heat and briskly whisk in the egg whites.

St. Honoré custard II

Custard

$\frac{1}{4}$ l	milk	$\frac{1}{2}$ pt approx.
60 g	sugar	2 oz
15 g	flour	$\frac{1}{2}$ oz
	good pinch of vanilla	

Meringue

125 g	sugar	4 oz
	5 egg whites whipped	
	to a stiff snow	

Make the custard as in formula I. Then make the meringue by boiling the sugar to the ball degree and pouring slowly and steadily on to the whipped whites, while whisking vigorously. Fold gently into the very hot custard.

France

Vanilla custard

	4 egg yolks	
125 g	sugar	4 oz
	good pinch of vanilla	
$\frac{1}{2}$ l	milk	1 pt

Beat the egg yolks and sugar together until pale in colour.

Gradually pour in the boiling vanilla flavoured milk, stirring with a whisk meanwhile. Return to the pan in which the milk was boiled and stir constantly over gentle heat with a wooden spatula, moving it backwards and forwards until the custard thickens and will coat the spatula. A white froth will form on top of the custard; when it subsides and disappears completely, the custard has been cooked long enough. Hold the spatula up flat and check that it is lightly coated with custard. Strain through a very fine strainer. Continue stirring while cooling to speed up the cooling process and prevent the custard from clotting.

The custard should never be allowed to boil, which would cause it to curdle.

France

Ganache

1 dl	double cream	⅙ pt
120 g	chocolate (very good quality)	4 oz

Ganache is used for spreading on cakes, etc.

Soften the chocolate over gentle heat or in a bain-marie. Bring the cream to the boil and, while still hot but not boiling, whisk into the chocolate. Continue whisking until quite cold. Will keep for a few days in a cool place.

Chocolate sauce

200 g	chocolate (good quality)	8 oz
1 dl	fresh cream	⅙ pt
	a knob of butter (optional)	
½ litre	water	1 pt

Melt the chocolate in the water and boil fairly fast for about a quarter of an hour. Add the cream and the knob of butter at the last minute. The sauce should coat the spatula.

France

Fresh strawberry sauce

Rub some very ripe strawberries through a fine sieve. Thin down with cold syrup at 15°. Add a little kirsch.

Jam sauce

Pass the jam through a sieve and thin down with stock syrup or water. Boil up and pass through a fine-meshed conical sieve. When about to serve add about 1 tablespoon kirsch to ¼ l (½ pt) sauce.

Noisette sauce

½ l	custard	1 pt
50 g	praline	2 oz

Gradually blend the custard, either hot or cold, with the praline.

Raspberry sauce I

Proceed as for fresh strawberry sauce.

Raspberry sauce II

250 g	raspberries	9 oz
75 g	caster sugar	3 oz

Choose sound, very ripe raspberries. Hull them, place in a glass bowl and sprinkle with sugar. Stir so that all the fruit absorbs the sugar. Cover and leave in a cool place overnight, then strain through muslin, squeezing lightly; do not exert too much pressure, or the syrup will be cloudy. Flavour with kirsch.

Rum flavoured chocolate sauce

Proceed as for chocolate sauce, adding 2 or 3 spoonfuls of rum when about to serve.

Sabayon sauce

150 g	caster sugar	5 oz
	4 egg yolks	
2 dl	first-rate sweet	⅓ pt
	and soft white wine	
	or madeira	
	or champagne	
	or port	
	3 dessertspoons Cognac	
	or rum but only if white	
	wine is used	

Whisk the egg yolks and sugar together in a basin until thick enough to fall from the whisk in a ribbon. Add the wine and mix well. Whisk over gentle heat or in a bain-marie. The sauce is cooked when it is almost three times its original volume and has a frothy, creamy consistency. Add the Cognac or rum at the last minute. Keep until ready to use in a warm bain-marie, whisking occasionally. To serve cold, remove from the heat and whisk until quite cold; a little of the delicate flavour will be lost.

DESSERTS

Apple salad

6 persons

	3 medium-size coconuts	
100 g	9 apples each weighing	4 oz
150 g	walnuts	6 oz
150 g	strip almonds	6 oz
75 g	glacé cherries	3 oz
40 g	pistachio nuts	2 oz
90 g	sugar	4 oz
	juice and zest of three-quarters of a lemon	
	2 tablespoons honey	
5 cl	arrack	2 fl oz
	good pinch of cinnamon	
	2 tablespoons desiccated coconut	

Peel the apples, cut in quarters, core and slice thinly. Add the walnuts cut in pieces, the almonds, the glacé cherries cut in pieces and the thickly sliced pistachio nuts. Mix the sugar with the lemon juice and zest, arrack, honey and cinnamon. Pour over the apples, nuts and cherries, stir, cover and macerate for 1–2 hours in a cool place. Saw through the coconuts exactly halfway up and level off the bases to make the half-shells stand firmly. Scoop out some of the flesh (which may be grated and used) and fill the half-shells with the apple salad mixed with the desiccated coconut. The top may be sprinkled with grated coconut or chopped pistachio nuts; if the latter are used, they should be omitted from the salad.

(Illustration, p. 1098)

Germany

Apricot coupe

8 persons

¾ l	milk	1¼ pt
	7 egg yolks	
150 g	sugar	5 oz

⅛ l	apricot brandy	5 fl oz
½ l	whipped dairy cream	¾ pt
	poached apricots	
	8 sheets gelatine	

Whisk the egg yolks, sugar and milk together in a bain-marie until light and creamy. Add the gelatine, previously soaked and squeezed dry, remove from the bain-marie and continue whisking until cold. Fold in the whipped cream and the apricot brandy carefully and immediately fill into ice cream coupes or glass goblets. To serve, top with a firm well-drained poached apricot and decorate with whipped cream.

Austria

Apricots Empress style

48 half apricots

	48 small apricot halves
	(either cooked or very ripe
	raw ones, or canned ones)
	rice Empress style
	(the same amount as in the recipe)

Drain the apricots well and fill the hollows with rice Empress style to a dome shape. Serve on a plate.

France

Apricots Toulouse style

About 20 half apricots

250 g	small raw apricots	8 oz
75 g	sugar	3 oz
1 dl	double cream	3 fl oz
1 dl	unboiled milk	3 fl oz
10 cl	kirsch	3 fl oz
	10 crystallised	
	toulouse violets	

Peel the apricots and cut them in half. Place the halves in a salad bowl and sprinkle with the kirsch and 25 g (1 oz) sugar. Cover and macerate for 6 hours, stirring occasionally. Whip the double cream and the unboiled milk with the rest of the sugar until stiff, then add 5 finely crushed violets. Pipe the cream into the hollows of the half apricots, using a star tube. Place a small piece of violet on each one and serve on a plate.

France

Baked apples and cream

10 portions   Baking time: 30 minutes

	10 choice apples (Boskop or Jonathan)	
approx. 75 g	butter	3 oz approx.
100 g	ground hazelnuts	4 oz
75 g	sugar	3 oz
150 g	red-currant or quince jelly	5 oz
½ l	whipped cream	¾ pt
	icing sugar	

Peel the apples, remove the cores without cutting right down to the base and stand the apples in a buttered fireproof dish, packing them tightly. Stuff the centre of each apple with a little butter, ground hazelnuts mixed with sugar, and red-currant or quince jelly. Dust with icing sugar. Bake at about 180°C until the apples are soft but not broken up. Cool slightly, dish and pipe whipped cream round each one, using a savoy bag fitted with a star pipe.

Germany

Baked apples with cranberries

10 portions   Cooking time: about 15 minutes

	10 apples	
300 g	cranberries	10 oz
200 g	butter	7 oz
20 g	sugar	1 oz
200 g	ground walnuts	7 oz
3 dl	whipped cream	½ pt

Peel and core the apples and fill the centre with cranberries. Stand them in a buttered fireproof dish, pour melted butter over and bake until cooked but still firm. Sprinkle with sugar, allow to cool and decorate with whipped cream and ground walnuts.

Czechoslovakia

Banana puffs

Mash bananas and mix with an equal amount of grated coconut. Flavour with rose essence or rose water. Blend well.

Pin out puff paste, cut into rounds and place banana filling in the centre. Fold the pastry over the filling, seal the edges and fry in oil or margarine. Serve hot.

India

Bavarian cream

12 persons

	6 egg yolks	
½ l	milk	¾ pt
200 g	sugar	7 oz
12–15 g	gelatine	½ oz or a little less
	depending on the temperature	
½ l	whipped cream made with	¾ pt
1½ dl	double cream	¼ pt
	and	
1½ dl	unboiled milk	¼ pt
	flavouring as desired pinch of vanilla or orange—or lemon— flavoured sugar	
	or	
100 g	chocolate powder	3 oz
	or	
4 cl	liqueur	4 dessertspoons
	or	
100 g	chestnut purée	3 oz

Make a custard with the ½ l (⅞ pt) milk. While still hot, add the gelatine (as it is if in powdered form, or previously soaked in cold water for 10 minutes if in leaf form') Flavour as desired. Whip the double cream with the unboiled milk. When the custard is cold, but has not yet set, fold in the whipped cream. Pour into a wetted or lightly oiled mould and place in the refrigerator or on ice for 1½ hours. Stand in lukewarm water before turning out on a napkin or doyley.

(Illustration, p. 803)   France

Bavarian Cream Recreatio

Prepare vanilla flavoured Bavarian cream in the usual manner. After turning out, cover liberally with bilberries Recreatio and a little of the syrup. Decorate as desired.

Switzerland

Bilberries Villa Recreatio

1 kg	freshly picked bilberries	2¼ lb
1 kg	sugar	2¼ lb
1 l	plum brandy (Quetsch, pflumliwasser or slivowitz), kirsch, mirabelle or alcohol	1¾ pt

Clean and wash the bilberries very carefully. Dry thoroughly, place in a suitable glass jar or similar container, add the sugar slowly and mix carefully. Fill up with alcohol and cover. Stir carefully with a long wooden spoon every day for a week to make sure that the sugar dissolves in the alcohol. Seal the container and leave in a cool, dry, dark place for 5 months.

The bilberries are used to make delicious desserts.

Switzerland

Blairgowrie raspberry foam

6 persons

225 g	raspberry purée	8 oz
225 g	sugar	8 oz
	3 eggs	
15 g	gelatine	½ oz
	1 lemon	
3 dl	whipped unsweetened cream	½ pt

Soak the gelatine in cold water, squeeze dry then dissolve in the warmed lemon juice. Whisk the egg yolks and sugar to the ribbon stage over warm water. Add the lemon juice and gelatine, together with the raspberry purée. Allow to cool. When cold and on the point of setting, fold in the whipped cream and then the stiffly whipped egg whites. Pour at once into a soufflé mould and decorate as desired.

Great Britain

Bohemian pancakes

10 portions, 4 pancakes each   Cooking time: 10 minutes

750 g	flour	1 lb 10 oz
40 g	yeast	1½ oz
260 g	icing sugar	8 oz
	1 egg	
	4 egg yolks	
¼ l	milk	½ pt
	zest of 1 lemon	
	1 tablespoon rum	
	pinch of vanilla sugar	
	pinch of salt	
500 g	jam	1 lb
70 g	butter	3 oz
¼ l	oil	¾ pt

Disperse the yeast in the lukewarm milk. Make a bay in the flour, add the yeast and milk, the butter, which should be soft, the whole egg and yolks, 60 g (2 oz) icing sugar, the salt, vanilla sugar, lemon zest and rum, then work to a smooth dough. Allow to ferment for 1 hour, knock back and pin out to a thickness of 1 cm (about ½ in). Cut into small rounds, place a little jam in the centre of half of them, moisten the edges lightly, cover with the other half and press the edges together well to seal then prove for 20 minutes. Fry in hot oil until golden brown, drain on absorbent paper, dust liberally with icing sugar and serve hot.

Czechoslovakia

Bulgarian Custard

10 persons

1 l	milk	1½ pt
200–250 g	sugar	7–8 oz
16 g	gelatine	½ oz
	7 eggs	
250 g	quince, cherry, apricot or peach jam	8 oz
	2 small packets vanilla sugar	
150 g	sponge fingers	5 oz

Separate the egg yolks and whites. Bring the milk and sugar to the boil. Beat the egg yolks and vanilla sugar together, gradually stir in the milk and add the gelatine, previously soaked and squeezed dry. Stir over gentle heat until the custard will coat the spoon, then allow to cool. As soon as it begins to set, fold in 2 dl (⅓ pt) whipped cream or 4 egg whites whipped to a stiff snow. Rinse a mould with water, cover the bottom with a layer of custard and sprinkle with diced sponge fingers. Cover with the jam and fill up with the rest of the custard. Allow to set, turn out on a round dish and decorate as desired with whipped cream, glacé cherries, sponge fingers or stewed fruit.

Bulgaria

Carnival cookie fritters

240 g	flour	10 oz
20 g	butter	1 oz
20 g	icing sugar	1 oz
	2 eggs	
	1 tablespoon aquavit	
	or kirsch	
	pinch of salt	

Work all the ingredients together well to a paste and stretch in the same way as noodle dough. Using a pastry wheel, cut into oblongs, triangles, squares, diamonds or other shapes as desired, and deep-fry in hot oil or vegetable fat until golden. Drain well, dust with vanilla flavoured icing sugar and serve hot.

In Emilia and southern Italy this paste is used to make ravioli, which are filled with jam or fruit purée and deep fried.

Italy

Carnival fritters

10–12 persons

400 g	flour	1 lb
150 g	sugar	6 oz
	2 eggs	
	1 tablespoon baking	
	powder	
$\frac{1}{4}-\frac{1}{2}$ l	milk	$\frac{1}{2}-\frac{3}{4}$ pt
	water	

Sieve the flour with the baking powder, add the sugar and a pinch of salt and mix to a smooth semi-liquid paste with the milk, adding a little water if required. Stand aside for 2–3 hours. Beat the eggs and add one at a time, then stand aside for a further 30 minutes. Heat a pan of oil or lard, drop in the batter a tablespoonful at a time and deep fry, turning the fritters to colour evenly. When cooked, remove, drain well and dust with icing sugar. Dish on a paper napkin and serve hot.

Variations

1. Peel 4 large russet apples, cut in quarters, core, slice thinly and mix with the batter.

2. Add 5 cl ($\frac{1}{12}$ pt) rum, Cognac, kirsch or any liqueur desired to the batter.

3. Macerate 100 g ($3\frac{1}{2}$ oz) currants in rum, add 50 g ($1\frac{3}{4}$ oz) finely diced candied fruit and stir into the batter.

4. Flavour the batter with the zest of 1 lemon.

Always serve fritters at a Shrovetide reception.

Italy

Charlotte Chocotine

16–18 persons, or 2 portions each for 8 persons

Strawberry cream

500 g	unsweetened strawberry pulp	1 lb
$\frac{1}{2}$ l	whipped dairy cream	$\frac{3}{4}$ pt
	2 egg yolks	
5 cl	stock syrup at 30°B	2 fl oz
150 g	sugar	5 oz
	4 sheets gelatine	

Chocolate cream

200 g	fondant chocolate	7 oz
1 l	whipped dairy cream	$1\frac{3}{4}$ pt

Decoration

30–40 sponge fingers	
milk and plain couverture	

Dip 15 sponge fingers in milk couverture and 15 in plain couverture, then allow to set. Place a flan ring on a dish and line all round with the sponge fingers, alternating the milk and plain chocolate and placing the coated side on the outside.

To make the strawberry cream, beat up the egg yolks and stock syrup, warming the mixture, remove from the heat and continue beating until cold. Stir in the gelatine which has been soaked and dissolved, mix quickly with the strawberry pulp and sugar, then fold in the whipped cream. To make the chocolate cream, melt the chocolate in a bain-marie, allow to cool and, while still liquid, blend with the whipped cream. Fill the ring alternately with strawberry and chocolate cream, arranging a few sponge fingers between the layers. Chill thoroughly before removing the flan ring and decorate with whipped cream or as desired. The charlotte may be served with chocolate sauce.

Switzerland

Charlotte Old Salzburg

18–20 persons

Swiss roll

	9 eggs	
200 g	sugar (caster)	7 oz
200 g	flour	7 oz
	apricot purée	

Vanilla custard cream

½ l	milk	¾ pt
	4 egg yolks	
60 g	custard powder	2 oz
150 g	sugar	5 oz
50 g	butter	2 oz
	8 sheets gelatine	
200 g	roasted ground blanched almonds	7 oz
120 g	finely chopped arancini (candied bitter oranges)	4 oz
3 cl	rum	3 dessertspoons
½ l	slightly sweetened whipped dairy cream	¾ pt
	marzipan	
	sugar flowers	

Whisk the eggs and the caster sugar to a stiff sponge, fold in the flour, spread on paper and bake at about 216°C without allowing to become too dry. Remove from the paper, spread with apricot purée, roll up and allow to cool.

To make the vanilla custard cream, prepare a custard with the milk, egg yolks, custard powder, sugar and butter. While still hot, add the gelatine, previously soaked. When cold, stir in the ground almonds, the chopped arancini and the Swiss roll trimmings, cut into dice and moistened with the rum. Lastly fold in the whipped cream.

Line a large hemispherical mould and a few small ones with slices of Swiss roll and brush very thinly inside with apricot purée. Fill with the vanilla custard cream and chill well. Turn out, glaze with hot apricot purée, decorate the base of each one with a rope of marzipan and top with a sugar flower.

(Illustration, p. 1099)   Austria

Charlotte Schonbrunn

6 persons

¼ l	milk	½ pt
80 g	sugar	3 oz
	2 egg yolks	
	¼ vanilla pod	
12 g	gelatine	½ oz
125 g	diced candied fruit	4 oz
6 cl	rum	2 fl oz
	stock syrup	
	30 sponge fingers	
¼ l	half whipped dairy cream	½ pt
	whipped cream, strawberries and angelica to decorate	

Steep the vanilla in the milk. Soak the gelatine in water and squeeze dry. Make a custard with the egg yolks, the sugar and the milk, cook gently until thick enough to show the mark of the spatula, add the gelatine, strain and allow to cool. Soak the sponge fingers in the rum mixed with the stock syrup, but keep back a few for decoration. Stir the custard frequently while cooling; before it sets, add the diced candied fruit and then fold in the half whipped cream. Fill a wetted mould with alternate layers of soaked sponge fingers and custard cream and chill well in the refrigerator. Turn out and decorate with unsoaked sponge fingers, whipped cream, strawberries and tiny leaves made out of angelica.

Austria

Cherries Kyoto

10–15 persons

1 kg	unstoned stewed cherries	2¼ lb
3 dl	saké	½ pt
150 g	sugar	5 oz
5 g	ground ginger	½ teaspoon
	juice of 1 lemon	
50 g	cornflour	2 oz

Lemon cream

	8 egg yolks	
50 g	cornflour	2 oz
	juice of 1–2 lemons	
2 dl	water	$\frac{1}{3}$ pt
6 dl	saké	1 pt
200 g	sugar	7 oz
50 g	butter	2 oz

Drain the cherries, place in a pan with the ginger, sake and lemon juice and bring to the boil, then thicken with the cornflour and allow to cool.

To make the lemon cream, place the water, saké, sugar and butter in a pan and bring to the boil. Beat the egg yolks and lemon juice, blend in the cornflour, add to the mixture in the pan and cook while whisking constantly.

Half fill individual glass dishes or goblets with the stewed cherries. Cover with the lemon cream and allow to set. Decorate each with a dried cherry blossom and glaze with sake jelly.

Japan

Chestnut cream

10 glasses

8 dl	sweetened whipped cream	$1\frac{1}{3}$ pt
250 g	chestnut purée	$8\frac{3}{4}$ oz
5 cl	rum	$\frac{1}{12}$ pt
3 dl	milk	$\frac{1}{2}$ pt
50 g	cocoa	$1\frac{3}{4}$ oz
60 g	sugar	2 oz
	1 egg yolk	
100 g	plain chocolate	$3\frac{1}{2}$ oz

Mix the egg yolk well with the sugar and cocoa powder, beat in the lukewarm milk, cook to a custard and allow to cool. Using a paper bag, pipe drops of tempered couverture on to the inside of each glass, then allow to set. Flavour the chestnut purée with the rum and mix with the whipped cream. Cook the chocolate to a semi-liquid paste with a little water and sugar. Divide the chestnut cream evenly between the 10 glasses, chill well, cover with the chocolate and top with the custard.

(Illustration, p. 1106)Hungary

Chestnut dessert

16 portions

100 g	chestnut purée	4 oz
¾ l	whipped cream	1¼ pt
50 g	sugar	2 oz
50 g	scraped couverture	2 oz
	4 sheets gelatine	
2 cl	rum	2 dessertspoons
	8 tablespoons cold chocolate sauce, meringue crumbs, chocolate shavings, grated chestnuts	

Soak the gelatine, squeeze dry and dissolve in a few drops of water in a bain marie. Mix the chestnut purée to a smooth paste with the sugar and rum, stir in the dissolved gelatine and fold in the whipped cream and the couverture. Cover the bottom of individual cocottes with half a tablespoon of cold chocolate sauce and sprinkle with a few meringue crumbs. Pipe in the chestnut cream, using a large star pipe, insert 3 chocolate shavings into the top of each and sprinkle with a little grated chestnut.

Germany

Christmas rice (Riisipuuro)

6 persons   Cooking time: 40 minutes

150 g	rice	6 oz
100 g	butter	4 oz
¼ l	water	½ pt
approx. 1¼ l	milk	2¼ pt approx.
	2 blanched almonds	
	sugar and cinnamon	

Blanch the rice in hot water and drain. Heat the water and butter with a pinch of salt, add the rice and bring to the boil. Pour in a little of the milk which has been brought to the boil and stir the rice vigorously. Repeat this process 5 or 6 times until all the milk has been used and the rice resembles porridge. After boiling for 10 minutes, add the almonds and simmer very gently for 30 minutes. Sprinkle with sugar and cinnamon and serve warm.

This dish forms an indispensable part of the Christmas meal.

Finland

Clotildes

7–8 minutes in a hot oven

> savarin dough
> St. Honoré custard
> rum
> apricot jam flavoured
>   with rum
> rum fondant
> syrup for soaking savarins

Half fill well greased, small boat shaped tins with savarin dough, prove, bake and soak in syrup. Drain, then slit each one three-quarters of the way up without cutting right through. Gently lift the top and pipe in St. Honoré custard, using a savoy bag fitted with a star pipe and filling up so that the top is wedged open and the custard can be seen. Brush the top with rum flavoured apricot jam.

France

Coliva

Old recipe of Roman origin.

Cook wheat grains to a thick paste in water with salt, sugar, lemon zest, chopped walnuts and a little cinnamon. Allow to cool and shape into a pyramid on a round serving dish, preferably a silver one. Dust with icing sugar, decorate with walnuts and candied fruit and fix a candle in the centre.

This dish is served, not at a wedding, but at the festival in commemoration of the dead.

(Illustration, p. 462) Rumania

Creams in paper cases

These delicious creams are easy to make and may be stored for a few days under refrigeration, covered with aluminium foil or plastic wrapping. They are decorated shortly before use and look very attractive when finished. They are served in various kinds of containers—strong paper cases 7 cm (3 in) in diameter and holding 100 cc (about $\frac{1}{5}$ pt), small china moulds, glasses or goblets.

Germany

Creams—basic recipe

20 portions

1 l	milk	$1\frac{3}{4}$ pt

200 g	sugar	7 oz
60 g	custard powder	2 oz
	4 egg yolks	
	16 sheets gelatine	
$\frac{3}{4}$ l	whipped cream	$1\frac{1}{4}$ pt
	flavouring (vanilla,	
	orange or lemon zest, etc.)	

Flavour $\frac{3}{4}$ l ($1\frac{1}{4}$ pt) milk as desired and bring to the boil. Blend the egg yolks with the remaining milk, the custard powder and the sugar, pour into the hot milk and stir with a whisk until boiling. Remove from the heat at once and add the gelatine which has been soaked and squeezed dry. Transfer to a clean basin and allow to cook, stirring occasionally. When about to set, fold in the whipped cream and immediately fill into the paper cases, moulds, glasses or goblets.

This is the basic recipe for all the creams given below.

Germany

Cream pots

Basic recipe

Yields 15 individual moulds about 10 cm (4 in) across   20–25 minutes

1 l	milk	$1\frac{3}{4}$ pt
250 g	sugar	8 oz
	4 whole eggs	
	4 egg yolks	
	flavouring (lemon,	
	orange or vanilla)	

Steep the zest of a lemon or orange or half a vanilla pod in the milk. Beat the eggs and sugar together and pour in the hot milk, stirring well. Strain, then set aside for 2 or 3 minutes and remove the white froth which will have formed on top. Pour into individual fireproof ramekin dishes and poach under cover in a bain marie in a medium oven. The water in the bain-marie should only come three-quarters of the way up the dishes and must not be allowed to boil.

France

Chocolate cream pots

Cook 125 g ($4\frac{1}{2}$ oz) chocolate in the milk for 5–6 minutes.

France

Coffee cream pots

Make 2 dl (⅓ pt) very strong coffee and add to 8 dl (1⅓ pt) milk.

Coffee extract or essence may be used.

France

Whisky cream pots

Use only 9 dl (1½ pt) milk. Add 1 dl (⅙ pt) whisky after straining the custard.

France

Crêpes Suzette

	pancake batter flavoured with Curaçao	
40 g	butter	2 oz
20 g	orange or tangerine flavoured sugar	1 oz
	1 small teaspoon ground almonds	
	Curaçao and Fine Champagne brandy	

Prepare Suzette butter by mixing the butter, orange flavoured sugar and almonds together, using a fork. Place a knob of Suzette butter in the centre of each pancake before folding it in four. Splash with Curaçao mixed with an equal amount of Fine Champagne brandy and set alight.

France

Croustadines Marquise

Yields about 15

150 g	chocolate	6 oz
75 g	sugar	3 oz
	3 egg yolks	
75 g	butter	3 oz
	cigarette biscuit mixture	

Dissolve the chocolate in a tablespoonful of water (do not exceed this amount). Mix the egg yolks with the sugar and stir briskly into the lukewarm liquid chocolate. Heat almost to boiling point, stirring constantly, then add the butter a little at a time. Dab the top with butter and leave in a cool place. Use very cold to fill the croustadines, piling it up to a dome shape. Smooth the top with a small metal spatula, previously warmed, or with the handle of a teaspoon. Decorate, if desired, with a tiny rosette of sweetened, whipped cream in the centre of the dome.

France

Curd cheese dumplings

10 portions   Cooking time: 12 minutes

450 g	curd cheese	1 lb
150 g	butter	5 oz
250 g	semolina	8 oz
	5 eggs	
	salt	

Crumb coating

75 g	butter	3 oz
200 g	white breadcrumbs	7 oz

Cream the butter, add the egg yolks a little at a time, stir in the sieved cheese and the semolina, add a pinch of salt, mix well and stand aside for 30 minutes. Fold in the egg whites whipped to a stiff snow, shape into 60–70 small dumplings and simmer in salted water. When cooked, drain thoroughly, roll in crumb coating and serve hot. To make the coating, melt the butter and fry the breadcrumbs in it. The dumplings may be dusted with icing sugar before serving.

Czechoslovakia

Currant puff fritters

500 g	flour	1¼ lb
30 g	yeast	1 oz
½ l	lukewarm milk	¾ pt
200 g	mixed raisins, currants	
	and citron peel	8 oz
	1 chopped apple or grated	
	zest of 1 lemon as desired	
	pinch of salt	

Disperse the yeast in half a cup of milk. Place the flour in a bowl, pour the dispersed yeast in the centre, add the salt and the rest of the milk and beat to a smooth batter. Add the raisins and currants, the finely diced citron peel, the chopped apple and lemon zest. Cover and leave to rise for 45 minutes. Heat some oil in a pan; when it is hot, but not too hot, drop small portions of batter into it with the aid of two spoons. To check whether the puffs are cooked, pierce them with a knitting needle —it should come out dry. Drain on filter paper and dust with icing sugar.

Holland

Custard soufflé

5 persons   15–20 minutes in a hot oven

$\frac{1}{2}$ l	milk	$\frac{3}{4}$ pt
60 g	flour	2 oz
125 g	sugar	4 oz
	4 egg yolks	
	6 egg whites	
	pinch of vanilla	

Beat the egg yolks and sugar together in a basin until pale in colour. Stir in the flour, then gradually pour in the boiling milk flavoured with vanilla. Boil up for a moment, constantly stirring with a whisk meanwhile. Transfer to another basin of fairly large diameter and allow to cool a little, stirring from time to time. Whip the egg whites to a very stiff snow and fold lightly into the custard. Pour into a mould which has been greased and sprinkled with sugar. Smooth over the top and decorate with a few spirals drawn with the point of a knife. Bake at 180°C. Just before baking is completed, dust with icing sugar. This will caramelise to give a glossy finish. Serve on hot plates.

France

Emperor's Schmarren with stewed plums

Baking time of Schmarren: 15 minutes   Cooking time of plums: about 30 minutes

Schmarren

	12 eggs	
90 g	sugar	3 oz
approx. $\frac{3}{4}$ l	milk	$1\frac{1}{4}$ pt approx.
360 g	flour	12 oz
90 g	raisins	3 oz
	pinch of salt	
	butter	

Stewed plums

1 kg	quetsche plums	2¼ lb
500 g	sugar	1 lb
	little water	

To make the Schmarren, prepare a smooth batter with the flour, egg yolks, sugar, salt and milk. Fold in the egg whites whipped to a stiff snow. Melt the butter in a pan; when hot, pour in the batter, cook lightly on one side, sprinkle with raisins, turn and bake in the oven. Tear into small pieces, return to the oven in the buttered pan for a short time, dish and sprinkle with sugar.

Stone the plums, cut them in quarters and stew gently with the sugar and very little water until lightly jellied. Avoid frequent stirring as far as possible while the plums are cooking.

Austria

Eton mess

Crush hulled strawberries with a fork and mix with an equal quantity of half whipped cream. Add a little sugar to the strawberries as required.

Great Britain

Fancy pans Hotel Pitter

Pastry

300 g	flour	10 oz
20 g	icing sugar	1 oz
	5 egg yolks	
	1 large egg	
100 g	butter	4 oz
	zest of half a lemon	
	vanilla	

Caramel cream

130 g	sugar	4 oz
160 g	butter	3 oz
75 g	ground blanched almonds	2 oz
½ l	dairy cream	¾ pt
	apricot purée	
	marzipan	
	couverture	
	sugar roses	

Work the flour, icing sugar, egg yolks, whole egg, butter, lemon zest and vanilla to a paste and allow to rest before use. Line small pancake pans (with handles) with the pastry, using 50 g (1¾ oz) pastry for each one, allow to rest for at least 30 minutes and bake blind. Spread the inside of the pastry cases carefully with melted couverture and fill with caramel cream. To make the caramel cream, cook the sugar to a pale golden colour, add the butter and ground almonds, pour in the cream and stir well. Chill thoroughly for at least 12 hours, then beat up. After filling the pastry cases, cover the caramel cream with a very thin disk of marzipan brushed with apricot purée, coat with a thin film of icing and finish off with a sugar rose and lettering piped on with couverture.

Austria

Filled pancakes

Various types of filling may be placed on the pancakes before they are folded, e.g. jam, candied fruit mixed with jam, confectioner's custard, bourdaloue cream, chestnut purée, thick apple purée, diced juicy pears macerated in kirsch, pineapple, etc. Filled pancakes may be set alight if desired.

France

Flambé pancakes

Grease and heat a serving dish. Place the pancakes on it. Heat the liqueur in a small pan and pour on to the hot dish. Set alight.

France

Fresh fruit salad

15 persons

250 g	cherries	8 oz
250 g	strawberries	
	(preferably wild ones)	8 oz
250 g	pears	8 oz
250 g	white grapes	8 oz
250 g	peaches	8 oz
250 g	apricots	8 oz
250 g	plums	8 oz
	2 bananas (optional)	
350 g	sugar	12 oz
1 dl	kirsch	4 fl oz
	a few flaked fresh almonds	

Peel the pears and peaches, stone the cherries and plums. Cut all large fruit in quarters. Sprinkle with sugar, mix carefully and leave in a cool place for at least an hour. Transfer to the serving bowl, adding the sliced bananas at the last moment. Sprinkle the top with the flaked almonds. If the fruit salad is too dry, add some stock syrup.

France

Fresh fruit salad with Champagne

Proceed as for fresh fruit salad, but add 2 glasses of Champagne.

France

Fresh fruit salad Old Provençal style

12 persons

500 g	pears	1 lb
250 g	white grapes	8 oz
250 g	black grapes	8 oz
500 g	figs	1 lb
200 g	sugar	7 oz
	1 bottle chilled	
	Blanquette de Limoux	
	or 1 bottle Champagne	
5 cl	Cognac	2 measures
½ l	sweetened whipped cream	1 pt

(Recipe devised by Prosper Montagne, a great champion of the Old Provençal language)

Peel the pears and cut in slices lengthwise. Peel the figs and cut into rounds. Mix the sliced pears and the grapes together in a glass bowl and arrange the sliced figs on top. Sprinkle with sugar and Cognac and macerate for half an hour with the bowl covered. Now pour the Blanquette de Limoux over. Cover with sweetened, whipped cream and decorate with black and white grapes.

France

Fresh strawberries Capuchin style

10 persons

800 g	strawberries	1¾ lb
¾ l	vanilla ice cream	1¼ pt
approx. ½ l	kummel sauce	¾ pt

100 g	grated pumpernickel	4 oz
2 cl	kirsch	2 dessertspoons
½ l	whipped cream	¾ pt
	vanilla sugar	

Sprinkle the strawberries with vanilla sugar and macerate for a short time. Shape the ice cream into a ball, cover with the strawberries and coat with the sauce. Decorate with small bulbs of whipped cream which has been mixed with the pumpernickel moistened with kirsch.

To make the kummel sauce, add sufficient kummel to thick vanilla custard sauce to flavour well.

Germany

Flummery

6–8 persons   Cooking time: 20 minutes

6 dl	water	1 pt
250 g	sugar	8 oz
	juice of 4 lemons	
	zest of 1 lemon	
	8 egg yolks	
5 dl	sherry	¾ pt
60 g	gelatine	2 oz

Boil the water, sugar and grated lemon zest to a thin syrup. Add the lemon juice and the gelatine which has been soaked and squeezed dry. Place the egg yolks and sherry in a basin and whisk together over heat in a bain-marie, gradually adding the syrup and whisking until the mixture begins to thicken. Remove from the heat and continue whisking until cool. Pour into moulds and allow to set, then unmould.

Great Britain

Fried choux for carnival time

Prepare choux paste as for Lombardy Carnival Fritters.

Variations

1. Add 3 cl (3 dessertspoons) liqueur or spirits (Strega, Cointreau, rum, kirsch, etc.) to the paste.

2. Take larger spoonfuls of paste than for Lombardy carnival fritters.

27

Arrange on a warm dish and sprinkle with liquid honey to serve. If desired, the fried choux may be stuck together with honey to the shape of a croquembouche.

Italy

Fried crullers

Yield: 25

	3 eggs	
30 g	sugar	1 oz
1¾ dl	dairy cream	¼ pt
210 g	flour	8 oz
	grated zest of half a lemon	
	icing sugar	
	fat for deep frying	

Beat up the eggs, add the sugar and continue beating for a few minutes, then add the cream, flour and lemon zest. Heat the fat to 210°C. Make a piping bag out of thick paper and cut off the tip to leave a small hole. Pipe the batter into the hot fat in coils so that a compact lattice 8 cm (3 in) across is formed for each cruller. Brown on both sides and drain on tissue paper. Dredge with icing sugar before serving.

Sweden

Fructidor dessert

10 persons

Profiteroles

Choux pastry

100 g	butter	4 oz
100 g	water	4 fl oz
10 g	sugar	½ oz
3 g	pinch of salt	
100 g	flour	4 oz
	3 egg yolks	

Filling

2 dl	tokay	⅓ pt
	2 egg yolks	
20 g	flour	1 oz
100 g	whipped cream	4 oz
50 g	sugar	2 oz

Caramel

500 g	cube sugar	1 lb
5 cl	vinegar	1 tablespoon
	water, green colour	

Tokay cream

3 dl	tokay	½ pt
	2 egg yolks	
10 g	flour	½ oz
10 g	dairy cream	½ oz
50 g	sugar	2 oz

To make the profiteroles, prepare choux pastry in the usual manner, pipe out in small bulbs and bake without steam.

To make the filling, beat the egg yolks and sugar, add the flour and stir in the wine which has been brought to the boil. Heat until boiling, then allow to cool. Pipe into the profiteroles and leave in a cool place.

To make the caramel, boil the sugar with the vinegar, a little water and a little green colour to the large crack degree.

Dip the profiteroles into the caramel and leave on an oiled marble slab until quite cold. Arrange them to simulate a bunch of grapes on vine leaves made of green almond paste, then add a few tendrils made of pulled sugar. Serve with disguised fruits (see below) and hand Tokay cream separately. To make the cream, beat the egg yolks and sugar, add the flour and stir in the wine which has been brought to the boil. Heat until boiling, allow to cool and add the dairy cream.

(Illustration, p. 1093)

Disguised fruits (bananas, oranges, greengages, plums, lemons)

	3 egg whites	
	3 egg yolks	
60 g	sugar	2 oz
60 g	flour	2 oz
300 g	buttercream (equal parts of butter and sugar)	10 oz
50 g	greengages	2 oz
50 g	plums	2 oz
100 g	bananas	4 oz
100 g	oranges	4 oz
100 g	lemons	4 oz
	a little triple sec	
300 g	almond paste	10 oz
	colours as required	

Whip the egg whites and sugar to a stiff snow and fold in the yolks and flour lightly. Using a savoy bag, pipe on to a sheet of white paper to the shape of the various fruits. Bake in a medium oven. Hollow out the centre and pipe in buttercream flavoured with the appropriate fruit which has been mashed to a pulp. A little triple sec is added to the orange buttercream to enhance the flavour.

Pin out the almond paste very thinly and wrap round the fruits, then colour with the help of a small brush. If the bristles are brushed away from the fruit, they will flick forwards and spray the colour on. An orange stick with cotton wool round the tip may also be useful for applying colour. The bananas are first wrapped in yellow almond paste and then tinted green.

(Restaurant Gundl Budapest)   Hungary

Fruit Bavarian cream

8 persons

4 dl	fruit purée made with very ripe raw fruit	⅔ pt
2 dl	water	⅓ pt
150 g	sugar juice of 1 lemon	5 oz
3 dl	whipped cream made with	½ pt
1 dl	double cream *and*	¼ pt
1 dl	unboiled milk	¼ pt
15–18 g	gelatine, or a little more depending on the temperature	½ oz

Make a syrup with the sugar and water and dissolve the gelatine in it. (If the gelatine is in leaf form, first soak in water for 10 minutes.) Allow to cool. Add the fruit purée and lemon juice. Cool quickly on ice, stirring with a spatula. Whip the double cream with the unboiled milk. Blend into the custard as soon as it thickens, but before it sets. Pour into a mould and then turn out in the same way as Bavarian cream.

France

Butter sponge

For about 35 desserts

4 eggs
3 egg yolks

125 g	sugar	4 oz
80 g	fine wheat flour	3 oz
50 g	cornflour	2 oz
40 g	butter	2 oz

Mix the egg yolks, whole eggs and sugar together thoroughly. Whisk over a bain-marie, remove from the heat and continue beating until cold. Stir in the flour which has been sieved with the cornflour and lastly blend in the melted lukewarm butter. Spread on paper to a thickness of about ½ cm (¼ in) and bake at about 180°C.

Austria

Vanilla custard (coating custard)

For about 35 fruits

½ l	milk	1 pt
150 g	sugar	6 oz
60 g	vanilla custard powder	2 oz
	4 egg yolks	
⅛ l	kirsch	¼ pt
approx. ¼ l	whipped dairy cream	½ pt approx.
	or a little unwhipped	
	dairy cream	

Make a custard with the milk, sugar, custard powder and egg yolks. Remove from the heat and add the kirsch immediately. When quite cold, pass through a hair or nylon sieve and bring to a coating consistency with a little unwhipped cream. If the whipped cream is folded in instead, the custard will be lighter and more delicate.

Austria

Apples Esterhazy

Fill the centre of the apples with vanilla custard flavoured with kirsch and mixed with finely ground roasted almonds and a little whipped cream. Mask with strawberry custard, pipe on spirals with piping chocolate and run a small knife through them at intervals from top to bottom to give a feathered effect.

(Illustration, p. 1100)

Austria

Apples Wachu style

Fill the centre of the apples with sweetened whipped cream and slices of stewed apricots. Mask with coating custard containing finely sieved apricot pulp.

(Illustration, p. 1100)

Austria

Woodruff apples

Fill the centre of the apples with whipped cream flavoured with chocolate and mask with coating custard which has been flavoured with woodruff liqueur or essence.

Austria

Stuffed peaches

Fill the centre of the peaches with vanilla custard mixed with hazelnut nougat, flavoured with rum and lightened with a little whipped cream. Stand on a rack, glaze with hot apricot jelly and place half a pistachio nut on top.

(Illustration, p. 1100)   Austria

As soon as the fruits have been filled, place each one on a round slice of butter sponge and press down lightly. After masking, decorate with small almond wafer leaves, whipped cream and chocolate stalks.

(Illustration, p. 1100)   Austria

Pears Romanoff

Fill the centre of the pears with finely cut strawberries and sweetened whipped cream lightly flavoured with kirsch. Mask one half with white custard and the other half with red. To make the red custard, mix basic vanilla custard with finely sieved strawberry pulp.

(Illustration, p. 1100)   Austria

Pears St. Helena

Fill the centre of the pears with morello cherries and whipped cream flavoured with chocolate. Mask with tempered couverture well mixed with a more or less equal amount of stock syrup and a few drops of rum. If the couverture sets too early, warm slightly in a bain-marie and stir.

(Illustration, p. 1100)   Austria

Pears White Lady

Fill the centre of the pears with vanilla custard flavoured with kirsch, mixed with chopped pineapple and lightened with whipped cream. Mask with white coating custard and decorate with piping chocolate.

(Illustration, p. 1100)   Austria

Fruit salad with gin

Blend well boiled sieved apricot jam with sufficient gin to make a thick fruit sauce. Add diced stewed fruit in harmonising colours and also fresh red fruit in season, bananas and pineapple. Serve with lemon ice.

Germany

Fruit soufflé

15 minutes (rather tricky to prepare)

100 g	thick fruit purée	4 oz
125 g	sugar	5 oz
	3 egg whites	

Boil the sugar to the crack degree. Add the fruit purée and boil again until the hard ball degree is reached. Stand aside to cool slightly, then pour on to the egg whites whipped to a very stiff snow. Bake at 160°C in a mould which has been greased and sprinkled with sugar. Serve at once.

France

Ganache barquettes

Line small boat-shaped tins with sweet pastry and three parts fill with frangipan mixing as above. Bake at 180°C (360°F). When cool, spread rum flavoured ganache on top of each leaving a ridge along the centre. Dip into chocolate and finish with crushed rose petals or red coralettes.

Gooseberry fool

10 persons

750 g	gooseberries	2 lb
250 g	sugar	12 oz
1 dl	water	3 fl oz
	juice of 1 lemon	
½ l	dairy cream	¾ pt

Top and tail the gooseberries, wash, drain and place in a pan with the water, lemon juice and sugar. Bring to the boil and cook slowly to a thick purée. Pass through a fine sieve and leave until cold. Whip the cream until medium stiff and fold in the purée. Fill the glass coupes and decorate each with a whirl of whipped cream. Serve with finger biscuits.

Great Britain

Other fools

Apple, raspberry and strawberry fools are made in the same way as gooseberry fool, using the appropriate fruit.

Great Britain

Grapefruit lido

Fill empty grapefruit shells with a sufficient quantity of grapefruit ice cream or sherbert. Place on top stewed, cold morello cherries.

(Illustration, p. 1093)   Italy

Green tea caramel custard 'Chawan'

12 persons

Custard

1 l	milk	2 pt
	6 eggs	
250 g	sugar	8 oz
10 g	instant green tea powder	2 teaspoons

Caramel

500 g	sugar	1 lb
2 dl	water	$\frac{1}{3}$ pt
50 g	glucose	2 oz

Decoration

Angelica

To make the custard, heat the milk and dissolve the tea powder in it. Beat the eggs with the sugar, blend in the milk and pass through a conical strainer.

For the caramel, place the sugar, water and glucose in a pan and boil to the caramel degree. Coat buttered individual moulds with the caramel, fill with the custard and poach in a medium oven in a bain-marie. Allow to cool, turn out and decorate with pieces of angelica.

In Japan the custard is moulded in tea bowls (cups) and served without turning out. The top is decorated with angelica.

Japan

Gumpoldskirchner strudel

When a pig was to be slaughtered, the Gumpoldskirchner wine growers used to extend an invitation to all their relations. After all working together, they joined in a real family celebration. On these occasions, which were called 'hog dances', pork specialities were served and housewives tried to surprise each other with special recipes. This is how 'Gumpoldskirchner Schmerstrudel' originated. It is made from fine puff pastry prepared with leaf fat (pig's abdominal fat) and a variety of fillings.

Baking time: 25 minutes

400 g	leaf fat (pig's abdominal fat)	14 oz
500 g	flour	1 lb 2 oz
	2 egg yolks	
	pinch of salt	
approx. $\frac{1}{8}$ l	as much wine as the flour will absorb	$\frac{1}{4}$ pt approx.
	sliced apples, nut filling or red currant jelly	
	beaten egg	

Carefully remove the fine membranes from the leaf fat, mince finely twice and knead with 180 g (6 oz) flour until it can be moulded into a compact rectangular block. Place in the refrigerator and allow to rest. Prepare a smooth strudel dough with the rest of the flour, the egg yolks, a pinch of salt and as much white wine as the flour will absorb. Allow to rest, then stretch with the hands, fold round the block of fat and roll and fold in exactly the same way as puff paste. Allow to rest again, then stretch again, cover with apple slices, nut filling or red currant jelly, roll up, wash with egg and bake in a medium oven.

For a special effect, prepare three strudels each with a different filling and serve a slice of each per portion.

(Techniques, p. 142)

Austria

Harrowgate cream

26–27 portions

Ingredients in basic recipe for 20 portions

300 g	stale sponge or other cake	10 oz
200 g	macaroons	6 oz
1 dl	sherry	4 fl oz

To decorate

4 dl	whipped cream	⅔ pt
200 g	roasted flaked almonds	7 oz
	26–27 red glacé cherries	

Prepare the cream according to the basic recipe with a little lemon zest. Dice the stale cake, crumble the macaroons fairly finely and soak the cake and macaroons in the sherry. Fold into the cream when it begins to set, fill into the containers, smooth the top and refrigerate. Sprinkle with roasted flaked almonds, pipe a whirl of whipped cream in the centre and finish off with a red glacé cherry.

Germany

Honey glazed pink grapefruit

6 persons

3 large pink grapefruit
3 tablespoons honey
6 glacé cherries

Cut the grapefruit in half across the sections. Loosen each section from the surrounding skin with a small knife, but leave in place. Brush with honey and glaze slowly (for about 15 minutes) under moderate top heat. Dish with a glacé cherry in the centre of each.

Germany

Hungarian log

Shape a thin sheet of sponge into a cylinder and fill with the same cream as chocolate maces, but flavour it with orange zest. When the filling is firm, cut into 9 cm (about 3½ in) lengths and then cut each length in half diagonally. Cover the diagonally cut surface with a thin sheet of sponge. Dip each one into chocolate, allow to set, then mask the slanting side with white buttercream. Decorate this surface with rings like those on a tree trunk, using cutters of various sizes dipped in cocoa powder. Chill well before serving.

Hungary

Jam pancakes

10 persons

	5 eggs	
50 g	sugar	2 oz
280 g	flour	10 oz
6 dl	milk	1 pt
4 g	salt	1 teaspoon
80 g	melted butter	3 oz
350 g	jam (any flavour desired)	12 oz
50 g	icing sugar for dusting	2 oz
	syrup as desired	
	candied or stewed fruit	

Beat the eggs well with the sugar, add the salt and flour and stir in the milk a little at a time to make a smooth batter. Strain and set aside for 1–2 hours before using. Heat the pan (or pans), brush with butter and pour in a spoonful of batter to cover the base of the pan in a thin film. When cooked on one side, toss and cook on the other side. Turn out at once, spread with jam and fold or roll up. Dust with icing sugar. Divide evenly into four and arrange the pieces in a star shape on a warmed dish or plate with the fruit in between. Pour some syrup over and serve hot.

Bulgaria

Jamaica cream

25–26 portions

Ingredients in basic recipe for 20 portions

200 g	stoned red cherries	7 oz
200 g	sultanas	7 oz
1 dl	rum	3 fl oz

To decorate

4 dl	whipped cream	⅔ pt
	chocolate shavings	
	icing sugar	

Soak the sultanas in hot water, drain, mix with the halved stoned cherries and pour the rum over. Add to the cream when it is about to set, fill into the containers and refrigerate. Decorate each one with a large whirl of whipped cream, sprinkle with chocolate shavings and dust lightly with icing sugar.

Germany

Liqueur soufflé

Proceed as for custard soufflé, adding 2 cl (2 dessertspoons) liqueur.

When about to serve, a few holes may be made in the top of the soufflé and a little liqueur poured into them.

France

Macaroon fancies I

Sandwich two macaroon biscuits (see page 1024) with rum flavoured ganache. Finish with spun chocolate.

Great Britain

Macaroon fancies II

Take larger macaroon biscuits and proceed as above. Cut each in half and dip the cut edge into chocolate and place to set on greaseproof paper. Place a few yellow coralettes in the centre.

Great Britain

Mandarinette cream

25 portions

Ingredients in basic recipe for 20 portions

	12 sponge fingers	
	2 small cans mandarin	
	sections	
1 dl	Curaçao	3 fl oz

To decorate

4 dl	whipped cream	⅔ pt

Drain the mandarin sections and set aside 25 for decoration. Cut the remainder in half, mix with the coarsely crumbled sponge fingers and pour the Curaçao over. Fold into the cream when it begins to set, fill into the containers, smooth the top and refrigerate. Decorate with a whirl of whipped cream topped with a section of mandarin.

The basic cream may be flavoured with grated mandarin or tangerine zest when in season.

Germany

Milk and cream strudel with vanilla sauce

10 portions   Baking time: 40 minutes

Pastry

300 g	flour (strong)	10 oz
	1 large egg	
1 dl (at least)	lukewarm water	$\frac{1}{6}$ pt (or a
	pinch of salt	little more)
	oil	

Filling

	$7\frac{1}{2}$ rolls without crusts	
120 g	butter	4 oz
2 dl	milk	$\frac{1}{3}$ pt
40 g	raisins	1–2 oz
60 g	icing sugar	2 oz
40 g	breadcrumbs	1–2 oz
2 dl	sour cream	$\frac{1}{3}$ pt
	6 eggs	
60 g	granulated sugar	2 oz
	zest of half a lemon	
	$\frac{1}{4}$ vanilla pod, scraped	

Topping

	1 large egg	
70 g	sugar	2 oz
6 dl	milk	1 pt

Cut the rolls into small cubes and moisten with the milk. Cream the butter with the icing sugar and gradually add the egg yolks, vanilla and lemon zest. Now stir in the remaining ingredients for the filling, together with the diced rolls, and lastly fold in the stiffly whisked egg whites.

Prepare the strudel pastry, pull it out until very thin, spread with the filling and roll up. Place in a buttered fireproof dish and bake in an oven with good centre heat. After 20 minutes pour over the topping made by beating the egg very well with the milk and sugar and bake off.

Vanilla sauce

$\frac{1}{2}$ l	milk	1 pt
100 g	sugar	4 oz
	4 egg yolks	
	$\frac{1}{4}$ vanilla pod	
15 g	cornflour	$\frac{1}{2}$ oz

Heat the milk and steep the vanilla pod in it, or use vanilla sugar. Blend the egg yolks thoroughly with the sugar and cornflour, add the milk a little at a time and whisk over a bain-marie to make a thick sauce. Strain and continue whisking for a few minutes while cooling.

Austria

Miss Alder's Kentish cherry pancakes

	pancake batter	
	stock syrup, allowing	
115 g	sugar	4 oz
	to	
$\frac{1}{4}$ l	water	$\frac{1}{2}$ pt
	compôte of cherries	
	raspberry jam	
	cornflour	
	cherry brandy	
	double cream	

Make pancakes in the usual manner. Fill with two-thirds of the cherry compôte and decorate with the remaining cherries. Cover with a sauce made from the stock syrup and raspberry jam, thickened with a little cornflour and flavoured with cherry brandy. Ignite with cherry brandy and flood the dish with a cordon of double cream.

Great Britain

Mohicans

8–10 minutes in a hot oven

> savarin dough
> kirsch buttercream
> pineapple fondant
> pineapple
> chopped pistachio nuts
> kirsch flavoured pineapple syrup

Dice the pineapple finely and squeeze the dice in a cloth to extract the juice. Mix the pineapple with the savarin dough at the rate of 1 part pineapple to 20 parts dough. Half fill well greased small moulds with the mixture. Prove in a warm place until level with the top of the mould, then bake. Soak in the syrup and allow to cool. Make a small hollow in the centre of each one and fill with kirsch buttercream mixed with a little chopped pineapple. Ice with the fondant and sprinkle the top with chopped pistachio nuts.

France

Morello cherry pyramid

Cherry cream

½ l	whipped dairy cream	⅞ pt
100 g	icing sugar	3½ oz
10 g	vanilla sugar	⅓ oz
5 g	cinnamon	⅙ oz
200 g	stoned morello cherries	7 oz
	poached and well drained	
	(canned morellos may be used)	
100 g	roasted ground hazelnuts	3½ oz
20 g	gelatine	¾ oz
	1 sponge base	

Vanilla custard

3 dl	milk	½ pt
	2 eggs	
100 g	sugar	3½ oz
30 g	custard powder	1 oz
	half a vanilla pod	
1 dl	rum	⅙ pt

To decorate

	50 petits choux	
100 g	thickened syrup	3½ oz
100 g	candied cherries	3½ oz
50 g	blanched almonds	1¾ oz
	marzipan flowers	
	chocolate	

Sauce

¼ l	whipped dairy cream	½ pt
250 g	morello pulp	8¾ oz
150 g	sugar	5¼ oz
30 g	custard powder	1 oz
3 g	citric acid	1/10 oz
2 g	almond essence	1/10 oz
2 g	red food colour	1/10 oz

Soak the gelatine, squeeze dry and dissolve in a bain-marie. Add the icing and vanilla sugar to the whipped cream, flavour with cinnamon, mix with the cherries and hazelnuts, then stir in the dissolved gelatine quickly but carefully. Fill into a mould and refrigerate until set. Steep the half vanilla pod in the milk. Mix the eggs with the sugar and custard powder, stir in the milk and cook to a firm custard. Remove the vanilla pod, flavour with rum and allow to cool, stirring from time to time. Fill the petits choux with the custard when it is cold. Place the sponge base in the centre of a round dish and turn out the cherry cream on top. Starting at the bottom, stick on the petits choux with melted chocolate all the way round the cherry cream to the shape of a pyramid. Fill up the spaces with candied cherries cut in half. Glaze the pyramid with thickened syrup and decorate with split blanched almonds and marzipan flowers. Place a chocolate ornament at the top of the pyramid.

To make the sauce, boil up the morello pulp with the sugar and custard powder, add the citric acid and almond essence and a little colour if necessary. When cold, carefully fold in the whipped cream. To serve, pour some of the sauce round the pyramid and decorate the inside edge of the dish with whipped cream. Hand the rest of the sauce separately.

(Illustration, p. 374)   Hungary

Natilla (caramel custard)

6 persons

| ¾ l | milk | 1¼ pt |

100 g	sugar	4 oz
	6 egg yolks	
50 g	flour	1½ oz
	pinch of salt	
	piece of vanilla pod	
100 g	brown sugar ('pieces')	4 oz
	butter	

Steep the vanilla in ½ l (⅞ pt) hot milk. Blend the egg yolks, sugar, flour and remaining milk (cold) to a smooth paste, then gradually pour in the hot milk. Remove the vanilla and cook to a thick custard over low heat, stirring constantly.

Butter dariole moulds thinly, fill with the custard and leave until quite cold. Turn out on to a fireproof dish, sprinkle evenly with the brown sugar and brown slowly under a moderately hot salamander. Allow to cool, then refrigerate for a few hours or overnight. When serving, pour the sauce formed by the caramelised brown sugar round the custards.

USA

New Year's waffles

These waffles are traditionally served at the New Year in some Dutch provinces.

500 g	flour	1 lb
300 g	sugar	10 oz
150 g	butter	5 oz
	2 egg yolks	
5 g	cinnamon	1 large teaspoon
	few spoonfuls of water	

Mix all the ingredients with sufficient water to make a firm paste. To cook these waffles, an old round waffle iron of the type traditional in Holland is required. Shape the paste into little balls the size of a hazelnut. Place a ball of paste on the oiled waffle iron, close the iron and cook the waffle over fierce heat. If desired, the waffles may be rolled round a stick while still hot. In some districts they are served with cane sugar syrup.

Holland

Orange Savigny

Cut off the stalk end of an orange, scoop out the flesh and clean the inside without damaging the shell. Fill with Champagne and orange sherbet and place a marzipan cover and leaves on top. Dish the orange on a glass plate, placing it on a ring of short pastry first to make it stand more firmly.

Germany

Pancakes

Grease the pan by rubbing it with a linen cloth tied in a ball over a small wooden stick, repeatedly dipping the cloth in melted clarified butter. Alternatively, rub the pan with a piece of unsalted pork fat on the end of a fork. As soon as the butter or fat in the pan is hot, pour in a little batter with the right hand. Still holding the handle of the pan in the left hand, tilt the pan with a circular motion so that the batter covers the bottom thinly and evenly. This should be done as quickly as possible. Place the pan over brisk heat. As soon as the edges of the pancake begin to turn golden brown, turn it over and cook the other side. Pile the pancakes one on another on a hot plate, cover with a vegetable dish or any other suitable dish—and keep them hot. A few moments before serving, sprinkle each one with sugar and either fold in four to a fan shape or roll up. Arrange on a serving dish and place in the oven for a few moments. Dust with sugar and serve on hot plates.

France

Pancakes hussar style

2 pancakes   Cooking time: 5–6 minutes

17 g	butter	1 oz
17 g	flour	1 oz
6–7 cl	milk	2 fl oz
	2 egg yolks	
	2 egg whites	
17 g	sugar	1 oz
3 g	vanilla sugar	½ teaspoon
	pinch of salt	
	dash of Cognac	
	zest of ⅛ lemon	
30 g	butter for frying	1 oz
	whipped dairy cream	
	2 tablespoons strawberry purée	
1 dl	strawberry sauce	3 fl oz

Melt the butter, add the flour and cook for a few moments, blend in the milk and stir over gentle heat with a wooden spoon until the mixture comes away from the sides of the pan. Remove from the heat, add the sugar, vanilla sugar, Cognac, salt and lemon zest, then stir in the egg yolks. Just before frying, fold in the stiffly whisked egg whites. Heat the butter in a frying pan, fry each pancake lightly on one side, turn and fry on the other side. Sandwich the pancakes in pairs with a little strawberry purée. Coat one half with thick strawberry sauce and the other with chocolate sauce. Decorate with whipped cream.

Strawberry sauce

To make the strawberry sauce, mix freshly sieved ripe strawberries with a little icing sugar.

Chocolate sauce for pancakes hussar style

60 g	chocolate	2 oz
40 g	sugar	1½ oz
$\frac{1}{16}$ l	water	2 fl oz
	3 tablespoons whipped dairy cream	

Boil the water with the sugar for a few moments, add the softened chocolate, mix to a smooth paste, allow to cool and fold in the whipped cream.

(Illustration, p. 804)   Austria

Pancakes Johann Strauss

2 persons   Cooking time: 5–7 minutes

40 g	butter	2 oz
20 g	flour	1 oz
20 g	cornflour	1 oz
	pinch of salt	
¼ l	milk	½ pt
	3 egg yolks	
	3 egg whites	
20 g	sugar	1 oz
	raspberries	
	orange segments	
	whipped dairy cream	
	chopped pistachio nuts	

Orange sauce

¼ l	fresh orange juice	½ pt
¼ l	water	½ pt
150 g	sugar	5 oz
70 g	cornflour	3 oz
	stock syrup	
	lemon juice	

Melt the butter, stir in the flour, cornflour and salt, cook for a few moments, blend in the milk, bring to the boil and mix to a smooth paste. Remove from the heat, beat in the egg yolks and fold in the egg whites whipped to a stiff snow with the sugar. Cook on both sides in small greased pans until well coloured. Sandwich in pairs with raspberries and orange segments, stack one pair on top of the other, decorate with whipped cream, coat lightly with orange sauce and sprinkle with chopped pistachio nuts.

To make the sauce, bring the orange juice to the boil with the water, the sugar and a few drops of yellow colour. Stir in the cornflour blended with a little water and cook well. Allow to cool, then dilute with stock syrup and flavour to taste with lemon juice.

(Illustration, p. 1104)   Austria

Pancakes Marie Louise

2 persons

40 g	butter	2 oz
20 g	flour	1 oz
20 g	cornflour	1 oz
	pinch of salt	
¼ l	milk	½ pt
	3 egg yolks	
	3 egg whites	
20 g	sugar	1 oz

Filling

	1 tablespoon roasted ground hazelnuts	
	1 teaspoon honey	
	1 tablespoon sponge crumbs	
⅛ l	milk	¼ pt
	pinch of cinnamon	
	chocolate sauce	

Place the hazelnuts, sponge crumbs, honey, milk and cinnamon in a pan and boil for a moment, stirring constantly.

Prepare the pancakes in exactly the same manner as pancakes Johann Strauss, but sandwich with the hazelnut filling and coat with chocolate sauce.

(Illustration, p. 1104)   Austria

Peaches Giannino

6 portions	Baking time: 30–40 minutes	
	6 fresh yellow peaches	
100 g	almond macaroons	4
30 g	ground almonds	1 oz
	1 egg yolk	
	1 egg white	
	1 tablespoon cocoa	
¼ l	good quality red wine	½ pt
	1 tablespoon sugar	
20 g	butter	½ oz

Place the peaches in boiling water for 5 minutes, then remove, skin, cut in half, stone and scoop out a little of the flesh. Butter a fireproof dish of suitable size, stand the peaches in it with the cut side uppermost and fill the hollows with a mixture made as follows: grind the macaroons and amalgamate with the ground almonds, the scooped out peach flesh which has been mashed, the cocoa and egg yolk, then fold in the egg white whipped to a stiff snow. Mix the wine with the sugar and pour into the dish. Bake in a very moderate oven and serve cold.

(Illustration, p. 372)　　　　　　　　　　　　　　　　　　　　　Italy

Peaches Hilda

6 persons

	3 large ripe fragrant peaches	
approx. 250 g	raspberries	8 oz
2 cl	raspberry brandy	2 dessertspoons
	caster sugar	
	1 round wafer base	
	6 small scoops vanilla ice cream	
	1 pulled sugar rose	
	tuft of spun sugar	

Wafer mixing

50 g	flour	2 oz
50 g	sugar	2 oz
5 cl	milk	2 fl oz

Plunge the peaches in boiling water for a moment, remove and peel. Poach in vanilla flavoured stock syrup, cut in half and stone. Arrange the vanilla ice cream in a chilled glass bowl, flatten a little and place the half peaches on top with the hollow side uppermost. Fill the hollows with the raspberries which have been macerated in sugar and raspberry brandy. Cover the bowl with a paper thin wafer base, place a tuft of spun sugar on top and finish off with a pulled sugar rose.

Switzerland

Pears Burgundy style

6 persons

	6 medium pears	
150 g	sugar	5 oz
¾ l	Burgundy	1 bottle
	a small piece of cinnamon quill	
	zest of half an orange	
3 dl	half-whipped dairy cream	½ pt

Peel the pears, which should be choice and juicy. Shorten the stalk a little, but do not remove. Poach in the Burgundy with the sugar, orange zest and cinnamon. Remove, boil down the Burgundy and strain. Allow to cool a little; while still warm, pour into 6 wine glasses, place a pear in each with the stalk uppermost, coat with the half-whipped cream and serve at once.

Switzerland

Pears Mony

12 persons

Parfait

8 cl	water	3 fl oz
100 g	sugar	4 oz
	1 vanilla pod	
	5 egg yolks	
½ l	whipped dairy cream	¾ pt
150 g	red glacé cherries finely diced	5 oz
2 cl	kirsch	2 dessertspoons
	12 cold poached half-pears	
	apricot purée	
	12 red glacé cherries	
2 dl	whipped dairy cream	⅓ pt

Prepare stock syrup at 96°R with the sugar, water and vanilla. Slowly pour on to the egg yolks while beating constantly and continue beating until cold. Remove the vanilla, add the chopped cherries which have been macerated in the kirsch, then fold in the whipped cream lightly. Fill into a 1 l (1¾ pt) brick shaped mould and deep-freeze. After turning out, cut into 12 thick slices. Cover each one with half a pear coated with apricot purée and decorate with a whirl of whipped cream and a glacé cherry.

Switzerland

Pears St. Peter

6 persons

	3 choice fresh pears	
	stock syrup flavoured	
	with vanilla, cinnamon,	
	lemon zest and cloves	
120 g	ginger nougat paste	4 oz
360 g	coffee ice cream	12 oz
200 g	fresh raspberry purée	6 oz
200 g	Romanoff cream	6 oz
	pistachio nuts	

Peel the pears, cut them in half and core them, poach in the stock syrup, keeping them fairly firm, and allow to cool in the syrup. Drain thoroughly, fill the centre with ginger nougat paste and arrange on the coffee ice cream in individual dishes. Mask half of each one with Romanoff cream and the other half with thick raspberry purée. Sprinkle chopped pistachio nuts in between and decorate with fresh leaves. Serve fancy biscuits separately.

(Illustration, p. 1103)

Ginger nougat paste

The paste is made in the following proportions.

1 kg	preserved ginger	2 lb 4 oz
600 g	nougat	1 lb 4 oz
	grated zest of 2 lemons	
	grated zest of 2 oranges	

Sieve the ginger finely and work thoroughly with the nougat and the orange and lemon zest.

Romanoff cream

Sweeten thick sour cream (smetana) or double cream with sugar, flavour well with raspberry brandy and fold in unsweetened whipped cream at the rate of 1 part to 4 parts sweetened cream.

Germany

Pears Swedish style

25 portions

	25 medium sized pears	

Raspberry mousseline cream

$\frac{1}{4}$ l	well drained raspberry pulp	$\frac{1}{2}$ pt
$\frac{1}{4}$ l	vanilla custard	$\frac{1}{2}$ pt
$\frac{1}{4}$ l	whipped cream	$\frac{1}{2}$ pt

Vanilla custard

$\frac{1}{4}$ l	milk	$\frac{1}{2}$ pt
50 g	sugar	$1\frac{3}{4}$ oz
20 g	custard powder	$\frac{3}{4}$ oz
	3 egg yolks	
	1 vanilla pod	

Peel the pears with their stalks, poach in vanilla flavoured stock syrup and leave in the syrup until cold. To make the custard, place the vanilla in the milk and bring to the boil. Mix together the egg yolks, sugar and custard powder, gradually blend in the boiling milk, bring to the boil again, strain through a conical strainer and allow to cool. Mix the custard with the fruit pulp and fold in the whipped cream. Drain the pears well and mask with the mousseline cream. If preferred, the cream may be served separately.

Germany

Pineapple Amphytrion

	1 large fresh pineapple	
50 g	chopped glacé cherries	2 oz
30 g	chopped candied fruit	1 oz
150 g	sugar	5 oz
	3 egg whites	
$6\frac{1}{2}$ dl	whipped dairy cream	1 pt
	few drops lemon juice	
	little yellow colouring	

Soufflé omelette mixture

125 g	icing sugar	4 oz
	2 egg yolks	
	3 large egg whites	
	little vanilla	
	spun sugar	
	Maraschino	

Cut the pineapple in half lengthwise, hollow out carefully without damaging the shell and cut away the core. Cook the flesh with 100 g (3½ oz) sugar until soft, then sieve. Prepare Italian meringue with 3 egg whites and 50 g (1¾ oz) sugar. Allow to cool, then mix with the pineapple flesh, fold in the whipped cream and add the cherries, previously macerated in the Maraschino, and the candied fruit. Fill into the pineapple shells then freeze.

To serve, have ready a block of ice hollowed out to take the two pineapple shells on a rectangular dish. At the last minute pipe the soufflé omelette mixture on to the filled pineapple shells in a decorative pattern, dust with icing sugar, flash in the oven and arrange on the ice with a border of spun sugar.

Switzerland

Pineapple Brazilian style

	fresh pineapple
	vanilla ice cream
	whipped cream
	flaked roasted almonds

Caramel sugar syrup

500 g	sugar	1 lb 2 oz
3 dl	water	½ pt
50 g	glucose	2 oz

To make the syrup, boil the sugar, glucose and 2 dl (⅓ pt) water to the pale caramel degree, add 1 dl (⅙ pt) hot water and allow to cool. Peel and slice the pineapple and remove the cores. For each portion, place a slice of pineapple on a glass plate and cover the centre with a scoop of vanilla ice cream. Coat with caramel sugar syrup, decorate with whipped cream and sprinkle the cream with flaked roasted almonds.

Canned pineapple may be used if the fresh fruit is not available.

Germany

Pineapple custard cream

10 glasses

½ l	milk	¾ pt
100 g	sugar	3 oz
5 g	custard powder	1 teaspoon
	6 egg yolks	
300 g	poached pineapple (fresh or canned)	10 oz
6 dl	sweetened whipped cream	1 pt
	citric acid	
	pineapple essence	

Cook the milk, egg yolks, custard powder and sugar to a thick custard over gentle heat and allow to cool. When cold, blend with 4 dl (⅔ pt) sweetened whipped cream and the pineapple, finely diced, and flavour with citric acid and pineapple essence. Fill into glasses and decorate with the rest of the whipped cream and small pieces of pineapple.

Hungary

Pineapple dessert with Swedish cream

30 persons

300 g	couverture	10 oz
	30 poached pineapple rings	
150 g	large red cherries	5 oz
½ l	whipped cream	¾ pt
50 g	sugar	2 oz
40 g	finely chopped macaroons	2 oz
4 cl	Swedish punch	4 dessertspoons
140 g	pineapple jelly	5 oz
	8 sheets gelatine	

Spread the tempered couverture on greaseproof paper and cut out with a fluted cutter of the same size as the pineapple rings. Prepare a Swedish cream of piping consistency from the whipped cream, the sugar, the macaroons and the gelatine which has been soaked and dissolved. Flavour with the Swedish punch. When almost setting, pipe the Swedish cream in spirals on to the couverture circles and cover at once with a pineapple ring. Glaze the pineapple with pineapple jelly and fill the hollow in the centre with a large red cherry complete with piped couverture stalk.

If desired rum may be used instead of Swedish punch.   Germany

Pineapple surprise

24–25 persons

	3 pineapples	
	10 egg yolks	
$\frac{1}{8}$ l	water	$\frac{1}{4}$ pt
250 g	caster sugar	8 oz
250 g	glacé cherries, coarsely cut up	8 oz
5 cl	kirsch	2 fl oz
100 g	blanched pistachio nuts	3 oz
$1\frac{1}{4}$ l	dairy cream	2 pt
100 g	strawberry purée	3 oz
	praline nougat and couverture flowers	
	strawberry ice cream	
	vanilla ice cream	
	tempered couverture	

Spun sugar veil

1 kg	granulated sugar	$2\frac{1}{4}$ lb
400 g	glucose	14 oz
$\frac{1}{2}$ l	water	$\frac{7}{8}$ pt

Select the best of the 3 pineapples. Cut off the top, with the leaves, and the base, making sure that the underside is level. Set aside. Hollow out all the pineapples, cut away the cores and chop the flesh very finely in the blender. Beat the egg yolks, water and sugar, warm until foamy, then remove from the heat and beat until cold. Using a wire whisk, fold in the cream, whipped until almost stiff, making sure it is smoothly blended in. Amalgamate three-quarters of the mixture with the cherries which have been macerated in half the kirsch, the pistachio nuts, the pineapple flesh and a little pineapple juice (not too much, or the mixture will curdle). Flavour the remaining quarter of the mixture with strawberry purée and kirsch to make strawberry cream. If the colour is too pale, add a little permitted food colour. Fill 8 small bombe moulds with strawberry cream. Fill the pineapple shells with two layers of pineapple/cherry/pistachio cream separated by the remainder of the strawberry cream. Deep-freeze together with the 8 small bombes.

To make the veil of spun sugar, dissolve the granulated sugar in the water, add the glucose and boil to 118°R. Cool slightly, then repeatedly dip a wire whisk with the end evenly cut off in the sugar and move the whisk to and fro with short movements of the hand, preferably over an oiled wooden spoon fixed on the table. This will throw threads of sugar over the spoon. Place oiled paper or an oiled baking sheet on the table to catch the threads. If the sugar becomes too thick, add a little water and boil until the correct degree is reached.

To dish, cut the stuffed pineapples in four or six, depending on size. Using a coarse plain tube, pipe a spiral of strawberry and vanilla ice cream on to the pineapple base which has been set aside, cover with the tuft of pineapple leaves and surround with a veil of spun sugar. Arrange the sections of stuffed pineapple in front, decorating each one with a bulb of whipped cream and a praline nougat flower. Arrange the small bombes in between, placing each one on a slice of pineapple which has been dipped in tempered couverture, and decorate with a couverture flower and whipped cream.

(Illustration, p. 1096)   Austria

Plum or apricot dumplings

10 persons (3 dumplings each)   Cooking time: 5–8 minutes

1 kg	floury potatoes, boiled	2¼ lb
40 g	butter	2 oz
	2 eggs	
250 g	flour	8 oz
	4 tablespoons semolina	
	pinch of salt	
	30 stoned quetsche plums or fairly small apricots	
	30 small lumps of sugar	

Coating for dumplings

250 g	butter	8 oz
250 g	white breadcrumbs	8 oz
	icing sugar	

Peel the boiled potatoes while still hot and press at once through a potato masher or sieve. Work to a dough with the semolina, salt, butter, eggs and flour. Allow to rest for a short time, then pin out to ½ cm (about ¼ in) thick on a floured board and cut into squares. Insert a small lump of sugar into each of the stoned plums or apricots, place one of these on each square of dough, bring the corners up to enclose the fruit and shape into a dumpling, making sure that the joins do not show. Place in lightly salted boiling water, bring to the boil again and poach gently. When cooked, drain in a colander. Meanwhile, fry the breadcrumbs in the butter until golden, then roll the dumplings in them, dish and dust with icing sugar.

(Techniques, p. 135)   Austria

Plum blancmange

10 persons

1 kg	plums	2¼ lb
160 g	sugar	5 oz
	8 sheets gelatine	
65 g	hazelnuts	2 oz
6 dl	whipped cream	1 pt

Roast the hazelnuts in the oven at 200°C and grind them. Scald, skin and stone the plums and cook them with the sugar. Dissolve the gelatine in a bain-marie and add to the fruit. Add the hazelnuts to the whipped cream. Mix with the stewed fruit and fill into a glass bowl or individual dishes or goblets. Serve cold.

Sweden

Plum jam turnovers

10 persons   Baking time: about 12 minutes

300–350 g	puff paste	10–12 oz approx.
approx. 400 g	plum jam	14 oz approx.
	icing sugar	

Pin out the puff paste about 3 mm (⅛ in) thick and cut into 10 cm (4 in) rounds with a plain cutter. Moisten the edges lightly with water. Place a small spoonful of plum jam on one half of each round and fold the other half over to make a half moon shape. Seal the edges tightly, make 2 or 3 small slits in the top and bake at 210°C. Dust with icing sugar on removing from the oven and serve hot.

Finland

Pomponnettes

6–8 minutes in a medium oven

savarin dough
seedless muscatels
kirsch fondant
kirsch flavoured syrup

Place a muscatel in the bottom of well greased pomponnette tins. Half fill with savarin dough and prove in a warm place. Bake, then soak in kirsch flavoured syrup and drain on a wire rack. When cold, dip into kirsch fondant. Place in small paper cases to serve.

France

Port wine jelly

$\frac{1}{8}$ l	port	$\frac{1}{4}$ pt
$\frac{1}{4}$ l	water	$\frac{1}{2}$ pt
30 g	sugar	1 oz
15 g	leaf gelatine	$\frac{1}{2}$ oz
15 ml	red currant jelly	$\frac{1}{2}$ oz
	few drops cochineal	

Dissolve the water, sugar, red currant jelly and gelatine in a saucepan by simmering together. Add half the wine and a few drops of cochineal to improve the colour, strain through muslin or jelly bag. Finally, add the rest of the wine. Pour into a mould and place in the refrigerator to set, then turn out on to a round dish.

Great Britain

Prunes Empress style

50–60 prunes

50–60 prunes three quarters
    cooked in sweetened wine
rice Empress style
(recipe, see page 911)
(the same amount as in the recipe)

Drain the prunes carefully. Make a slit in one side to remove the stone. Drain again on a sieve with the cut side of the prunes underneath. Prepare rice Empress style, place it in the refrigerator, but do not leave it there for more than half an hour so that the rice is not too firm. Fill the inside of each prune with the rice and impale each one on a small stick (a cocktail stick may be used) inserted on the slant. Return to the refrigerator for half an hour. Serve in small paper cases or on a plate covered with a doyley.

France

Rainbow cream

10 glasses

$8\frac{1}{2}$ dl	sweetened whipped cream	$1\frac{1}{2}$ pt
30 g	cocoa powder	1 oz
100 g	roasted ground hazelnuts	
	or almonds	4 oz
60 g	strawberry purée	2 oz
	grated chocolate	

Mix 3½ dl (⅜ pt) sweetened whipped cream with the ground hazelnuts or almonds and 3 dl (½ pt) with the cocoa powder. Mix the rest of the cream with the strawberry purée. Using a savoy bag, pipe into glasses, starting with the nut cream, then the cocoa cream and lastly the strawberry cream. Sprinkle with grated chocolate and serve well chilled.

(Illustration, p. 1106)   Hungary

Rainbow desserts

Prepare two chocolate Swiss rolls and one plain Swiss roll about 4 cm (1½ in) in diameter. Fill one with chocolate cream, the second with strawberry cream and the third with orange cream. Refrigerate until firm, then arrange two of the rolls side by side and the third on top and stick together with chocolate cream. Coat all over with chocolate and stick a strip of pink marzipan on top. When quite cold, cut into slices.

(Illustration, p. 813)   Hungary

Rasgollah

Make curds by warming milk gently with lemon juice. When set, transfer to a cloth, tie into a ball and squeeze out the liquid. Knead well, shape into balls and dip into syrup flavoured with rose essence. Serve with the syrup.

India

Rice Empress style

15–18 small moulds each containing 5 cl (1/12 pt)   18 minutes

125 g	rice	4 oz
½ l	milk	¾ pt
75 g	sugar	2 oz
	half a vanilla pod	
100 g	diced candied fruit macerated in kirsch	3 oz
10 g	butter	3 oz
1 dl	double cream	3 fl oz
1 dl	unboiled milk	3 fl oz
¼ l	custard made with gelatine	½ pt approx.
50 g	angelica	2 oz
	15–18 glacé cherries	

Blanch the rice for 5 minutes, then drain, refresh and drain again. Drop it in the boiling milk containing the vanilla and butter, 25 g (1 oz) sugar and a pinch of salt. Lift the rice with a fork to separate the grains, cover and cook without stirring. Add the remaining sugar after the rice is cooked. Allow to cool until lukewarm, then stir in the custard, which should be cold but not set, together with the macerated candied fruit. Whip the double cream and unboiled milk together and fold into the rice mixture when the latter is beginning to set. Fill into lightly oiled individual moulds and place in the refrigerator for three-quarters of an hour. Stand the moulds in tepid water to turn out. Decorate with angelica and a glacé cherry and serve in small fluted paper cases.

France

Rice porridge

4 persons   Cooking time: 40 minutes

140 g	rice	5 oz
3 dl	water	½ pt
	1 stick cinnamon	
20 g	butter or margarine	1 oz
8 dl	milk	1⅓ pt
5 g	salt	1 teaspoon
15 g	sugar	1 oz
	ground cinnamon	
	granulated sugar	

Bring the water to the boil, add the butter and boil for a moment. Add the rice and the cinnamon stick. Cook over gentle heat until the water has evaporated. Pour in the milk and simmer under cover over gentle heat until the rice is tender, stirring occasionally. Add the sugar and salt.

To serve, sprinkle with ground cinnamon and granulated sugar.

Sweden

Rose Marie

6–8 minutes in a medium oven

savarin dough
well boiled apricot jam
pink fondant flavoured with kirsch

▲ Stuffed quails on chestnut rice, p. 735
▼ Saddle of venison with fruit, p. 710

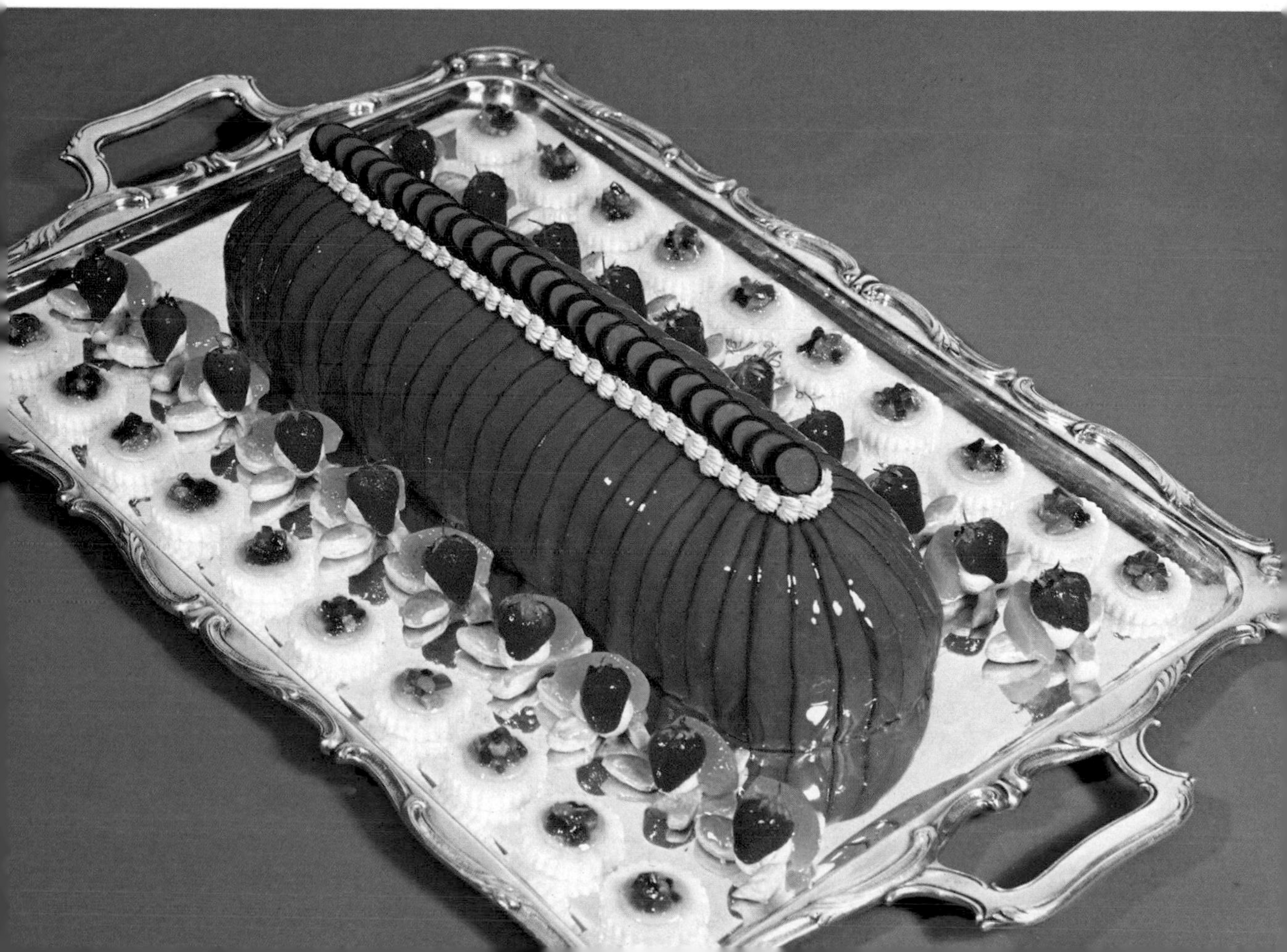

914 ▲ A display of small cold game dishes   ► Cold roast pheasant and partridge, p. 731
     ▼ Stuffed fillet of roe calf, p. 713   ►► Cold rabbit in white wine and tarragon jelly

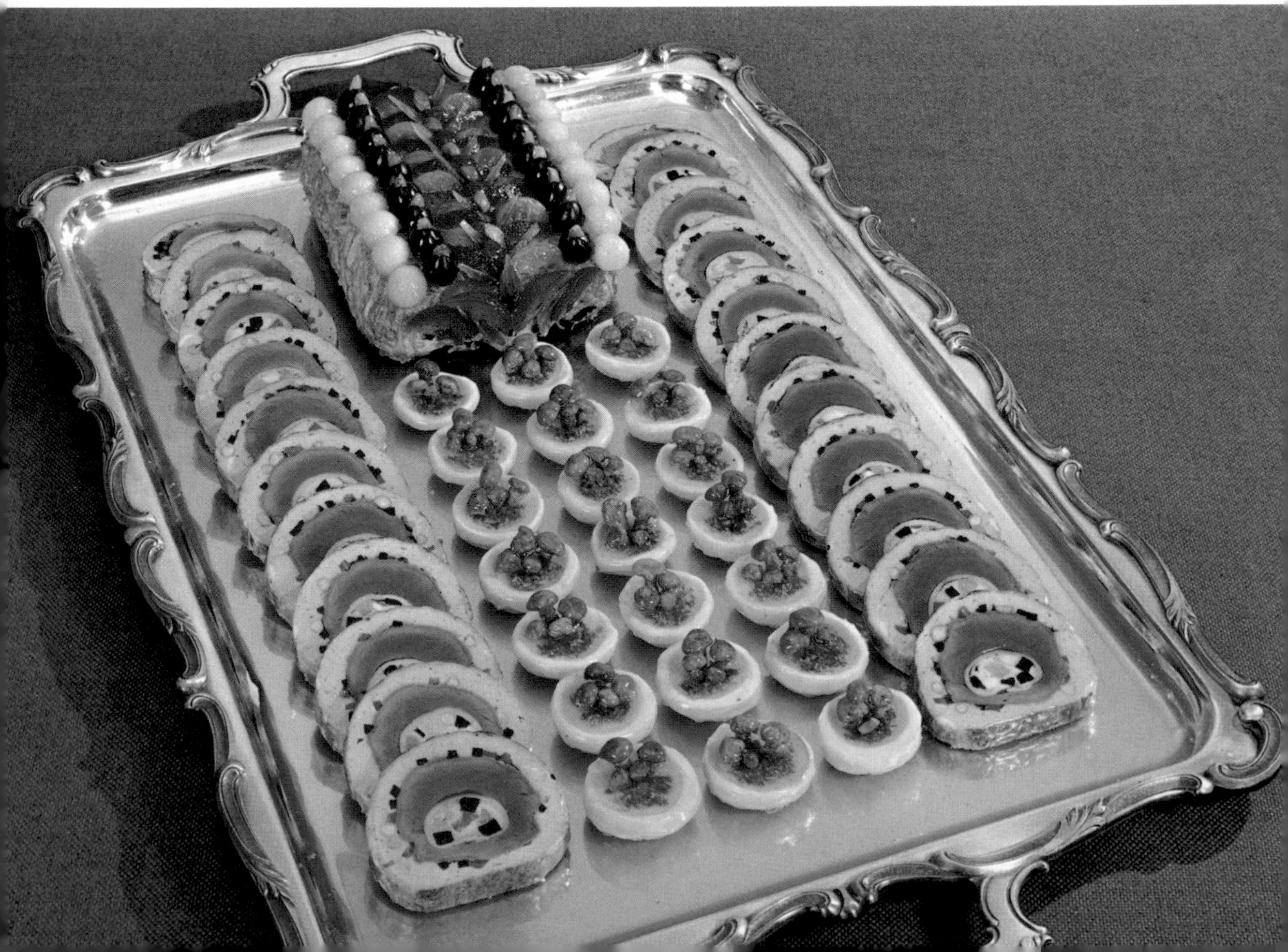

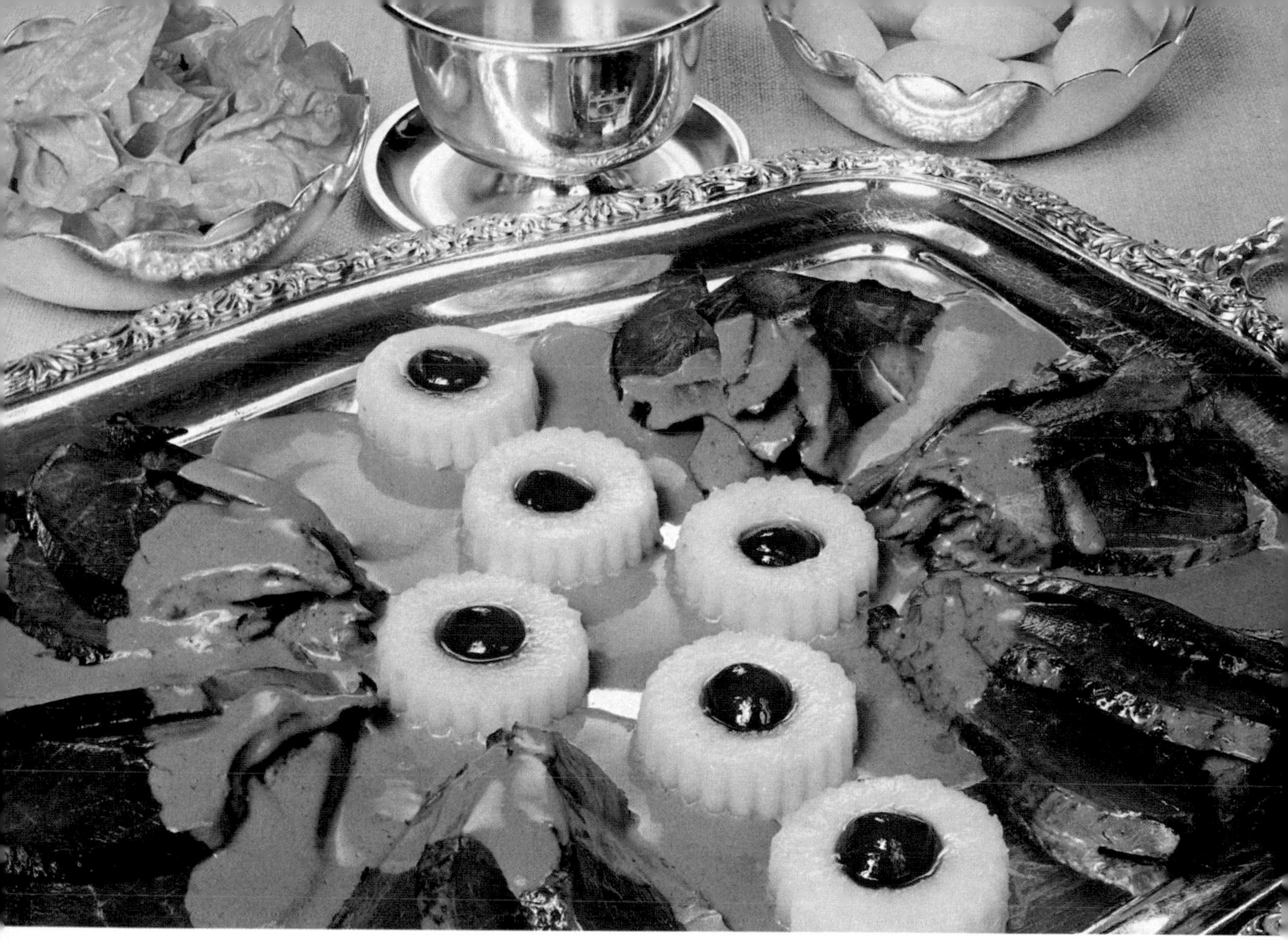

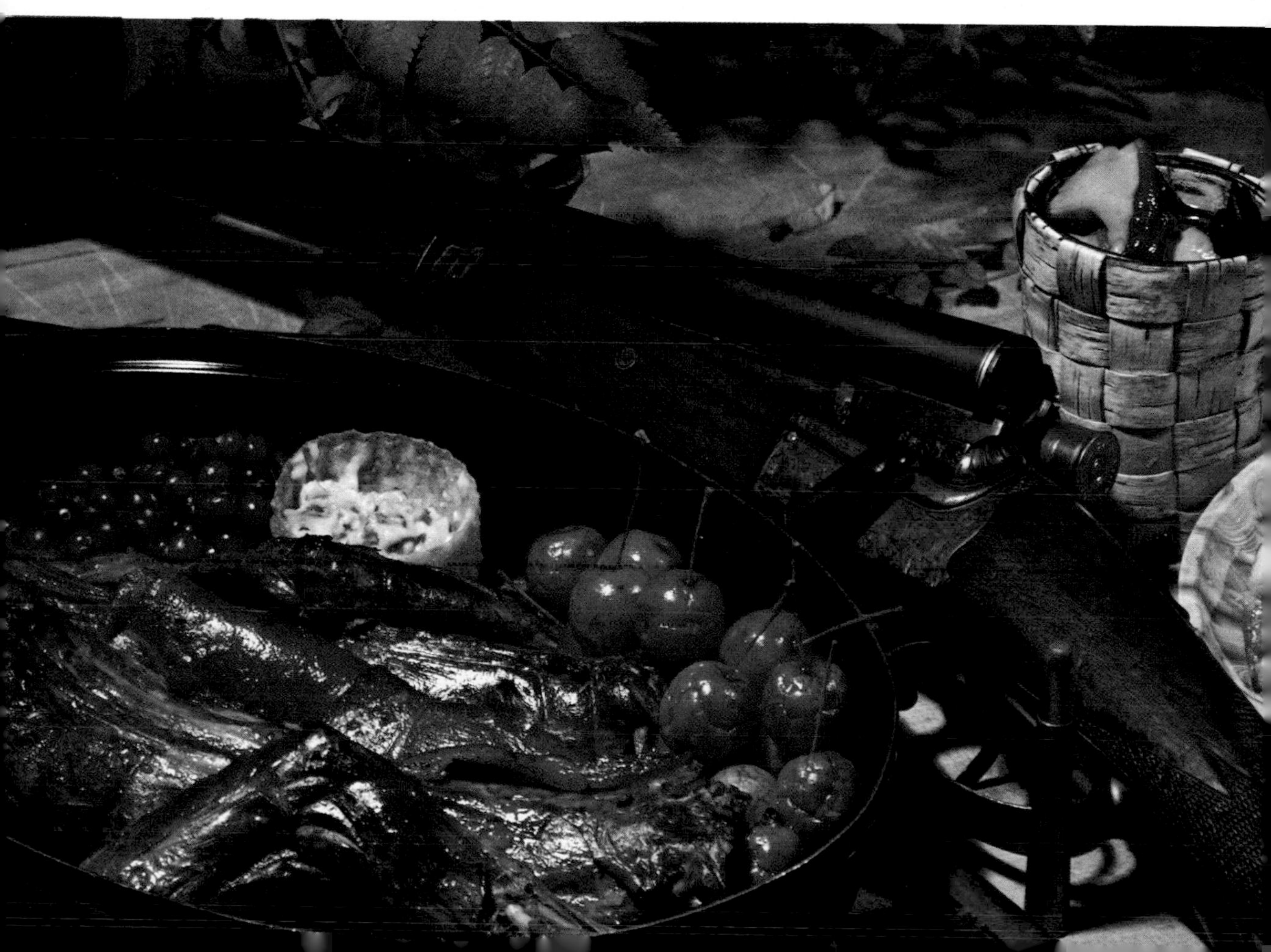

▲ Hungarian style cold pheasants: cover with white chaud-froid sauce and truffles. Garnish as shown

918

◄ Fillet of Reindeer, Christian IV, p. 725

◄ Roast hare, Finnish style, p. 722

▼ Cold saddle of venison, p. 708

▲ Foie gras in aspic, p. 683, Foie gras mousselines, p. 685
▼ Wild duck parfait, p. 735

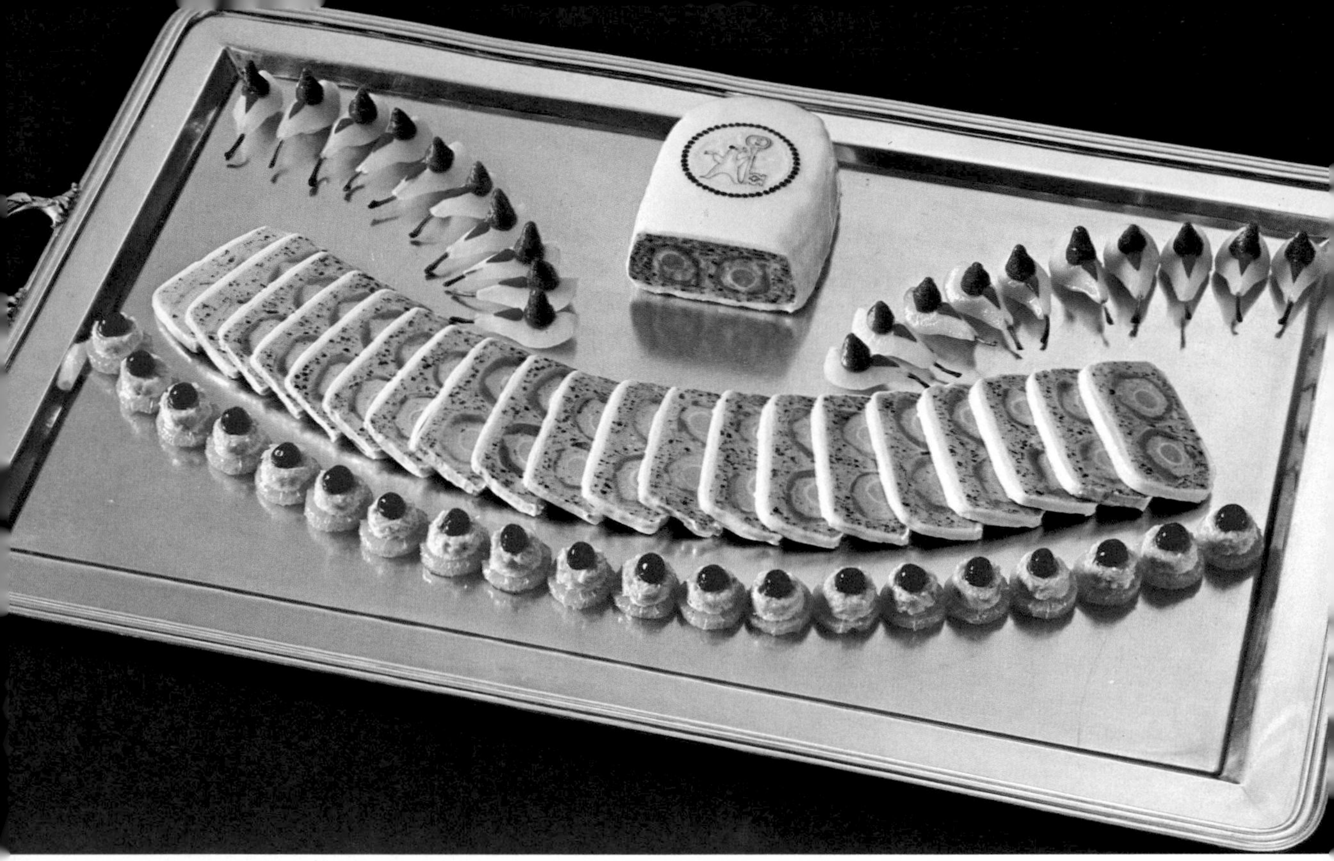

▲ Quail terrine Schweizerhof, p. 745

 ► Chicken liver pâté in brioche, p. 750

▼ Stuffed saddle of venison Père Salice, p. 714

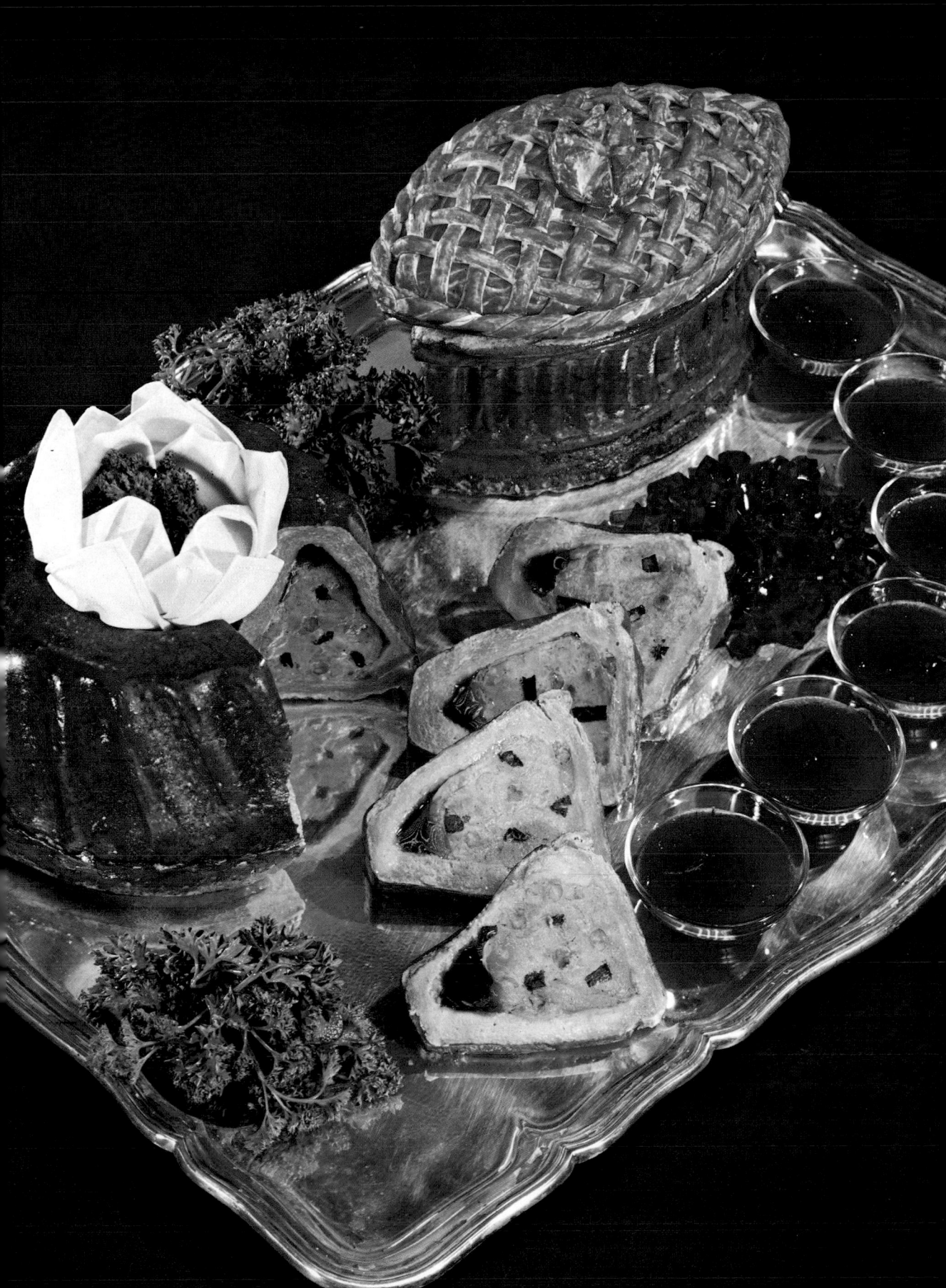

▲ Chicken pâté en croûte, p. 736
▼ Venison pâté en croûte, p. 742

▲ Chaud-froid of duck Stresa: cover the breasts with brown chaud-froid sauce decorated with salted butter. Cover the birds with curried white chaud-froid sauce and place on boiled rice

923

▼ Supreme of turkey and melon

924

◀ Ham American style, p. 636

▼ Chicken galantine, p. 751

▲ Hawaiian Luau, p. 619
▼ Ox tongue in aspic, p. 757

926

◄ Chicken Belle de Mai, p. 668

▼ Viennese fried chicken, p. 665

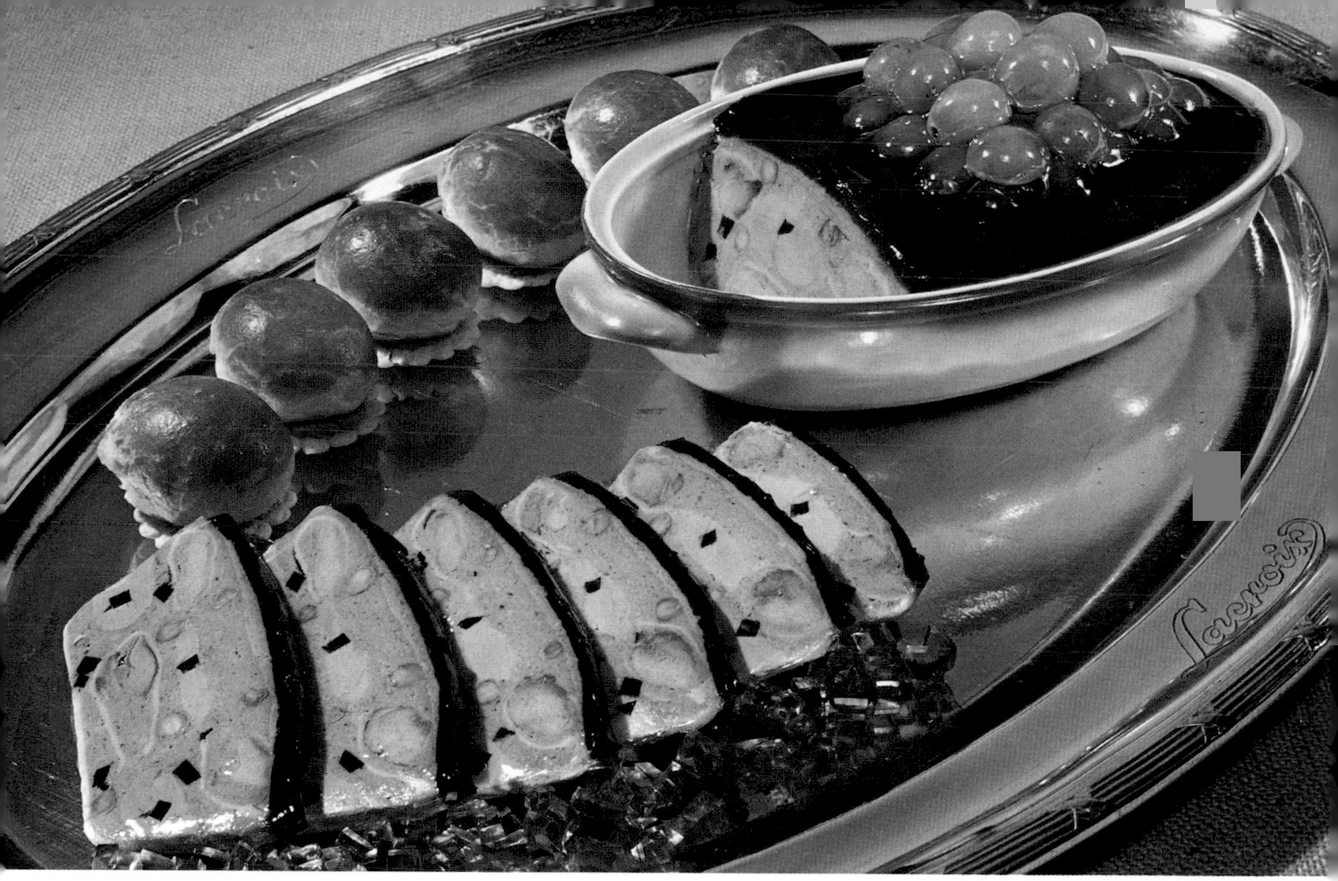

▲ Terrine of pheasant, p. 747
▼ A well presented pâté en croûte

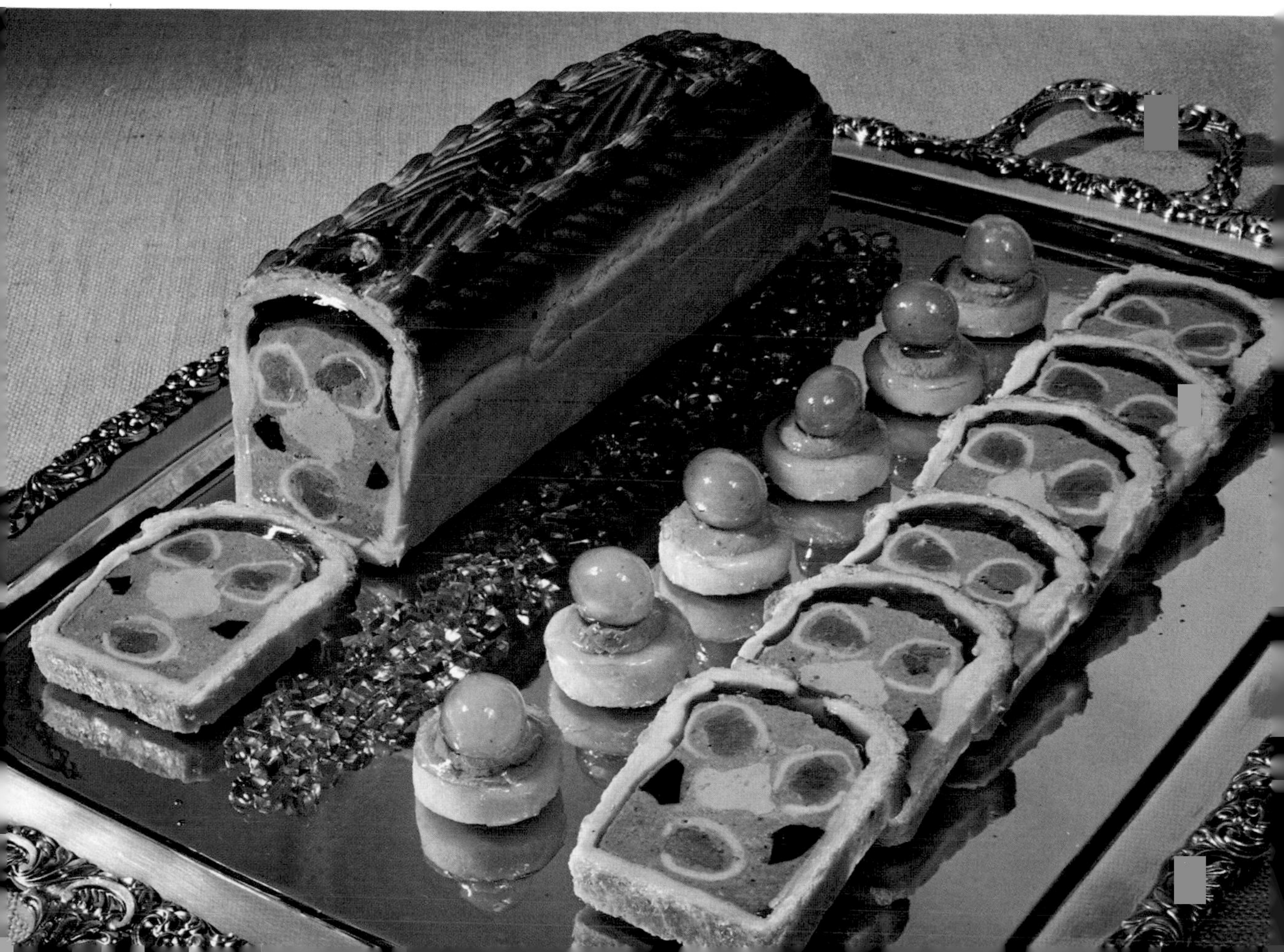

928 ▲ Galantine of chicken, p. 754

▼ Galantine of foie gras

Half fill small greased tartlet tins with savarin dough and prove in a warm place until level with the top of the tins. Bake. Make a slit in the side of each and fill with apricot jam. Splash with syrup, but do not soak. Drain, then drip into the fondant and place in small round paper cases to serve.

France

Rum babas

Prepare baba dough and fill into tiny moulds. Bake, then soak in special syrup for babas and savarins. Place in small paper cases to serve. (A few currants previously macerated in rum and drained may be added to the dough.)

France

Savarin Recreatio

Fill small individual moulds with savarin dough and bake. While still hot, soak in the alcoholic syrup from bilberries Recreatio. Fill the centre with bilberries and pipe on a whirl of whipped cream. Decorate with crystallised violets or mimosa balls and diamond shaped pieces of angelica.

Switzerland

Scotch pancakes

10 pancakes

100 g	self raising flour	4 oz
25 g	butter	1 oz
15 g	sugar	$\frac{1}{2}$ oz
	1 egg	
	pinch of salt	
10 g	syrup	1 dessertspoon
approx. $\frac{1}{8}$ l	milk	$\frac{1}{4}$ pt

Sieve the flour and a pinch of salt, and add the sugar. Rub in the butter and make a bay in the flour. Add the beaten egg, syrup and milk. Mix to a smooth batter. Heat a griddle and brush with lard. Drop a dessertspoonful of the batter on to the hot griddle to spread 6 cm (2½ in) in diameter. Cook until brown underneath, then turn over and cook the second side. Place inside a folded napkin. Serve hot or cold, spread with butter.

Great Britain

Sherry trifle

10 persons

300 g	sponge cake or finger biscuits	12 oz
125 g	raspberry jam	5 oz
1 dl	sherry	3 fl oz
1 l	milk	1¾ pt
125 g	sugar	5 oz
	12 egg yolks	
3 dl	sweetened whipped cream	½ pt
	glacé cherries and	
	angelica	
	vanilla essence	

Split the sponge cake and sandwich with jam; if using finger biscuits, sandwich two together with jam. Cut into 2½ cm (1 in) pieces, place in a large glass bowl or individual coupes and sprinkle with the sherry.

Boil the milk with a few drops of vanilla essence. Whisk the egg yolks and sugar together, gradually add the milk, return to the pan and stir over gentle heat without allowing to boil until the custard thickens. Allow to cool a little, then ladle over the cake or biscuits and leave in the refrigerator until cold. Decorate with whirls of whipped cream, half glacé cherries and diamonds of angelica.

Great Britain

Soufflé fritters

Fine choux paste
liqueur

Flavour the choux paste with liqueur and shape into balls the size of a pigeon's egg. Drop these into fairly hot (160–180°C) frying fat, preferably oil. When they have swelled the fritters will turn over by themselves. As soon as they are golden brown, drain on a cloth and dust with sugar. Arrange in a pyramid shape to serve.

The temperature of the oil should be increased as soon as the fritters have been dropped into it; if there is any heat loss at this point, the fritters will become saturated with oil.

France

Soufflé omelette

10 minutes

125 g	sugar	4 oz
	4 egg yolks	
	6 egg whites	
	pinch of vanilla	

Beat the egg yolks and sugar together in a basin until pale in colour and thick enough to fall like a ribbon from the whisk. Now fold in the egg whites whipped to a very stiff snow. Shape four-fifths of the mixture into an omelette on a greased oven-proof dish. Decorate the top with the rest of the mixture, using a savoy bag fitted with a star pipe. Bake at 150–160°C. Before removing from the oven, dust with icing sugar. Serve quickly.

France

Soufflé pancakes

pancakes
soufflé mixture

Spread each pancake with soufflé mixture and roll up. Place on a greased dish and bake at 180°C. As soon as the pancake is well risen and fluffy (5–6 minutes) dust with icing sugar and serve at once.

France

Strawberry baskets

Yield: 14 baskets

500 g	flour	1¼ lb
150 g	butter	6 oz
40 g	icing sugar	1½ oz
40 g	yeast	1½ oz
⅛ l	milk	¼ pt
	pinch of salt	
	lemon zest	
	small strawberries	
	sieved apricot purée	
	marzipan	
	Parisian nougat flowers	
	beaten egg	

Prepare the dough quickly with the flour, butter, icing sugar, yeast, milk, salt and lemon zest. Place in a bowl covered with a damp cloth, or wrap in the cloth, and leave in the refrigerator, only taking out as much dough as is required at any one time. To make the baskets, weave strips of dough between small metal rods inserted into a perforated wooden base. Support the handles on aluminium foil. Brush all over with beaten egg, bake, then remove the metal rods. When cold, fill the baskets with strawberries, glaze with apricot purée and decorate each with marzipan ribbons and bows and a flower made of Parisian nougat.

Austria

Strawberries Cecil

10 persons

	4 oranges	
	2 small lemons	
175 g	sugar	6 oz
1 kg	strawberries	2¼ lb

Squeeze out the oranges and lemons, strain the juice, pour into a silver or glass dish, add the sugar and stir. Hull the strawberries, wash quickly, drain, place in the dish and leave to macerate in the juice for 5–10 minutes. Stir, chill well and serve.

Great Britain

Strawberry cream

10 glasses

1⅕ l	sweetened whipped cream	2 pt
300 g	fresh strawberry purée	10 oz
	10 choice fresh strawberrie	
	citric acid	

Mix 1 l (1¾ pt) sweetened whipped cream with the strawberry purée and flavour with a little citric acid. Using a paper bag filled with tempered couverture, pipe motifs as desired on to the inside of each glass, then allow to set. Fill into the glasses, decorate with the rest of the cream, using a star pipe, and place a fresh strawberry in the centre of each.

(Illustration, p. 1106)   Hungary

Strawberry purée

1 kg	fresh strawberries	2¼ lb
800 g–1 kg	sugar	1¾–2¼ lb
10 g	citric acid	2 teaspoons

Rub the strawberries through a sieve, add the sugar and citric acid and stir until the sugar is completely dissolved. Will keep for some time in the refrigerator.

Austria

Striped Bavarian cream

Proceed as for either recipe for Bavarian cream, but arrange the Bavarian creams made with different flavourings or fruit in layers one above the other. Allow each layer to set in the mould before adding the next one, and be careful not to let the mixture run down the sides of the mould—this would spoil the appearance of the finished product.

France

Stuffed bananas

bananas
coarsely chopped roasted hazelnuts
melted couverture
whipped dairy cream
marzipan

Cut away the peel from the centre portion of choice ripe bananas on the inner side of the curve, scoop out the flesh in the middle and mash through a sieve. Mix with the chopped hazelnuts, stir in a little melted couverture and fold in the whipped cream. Fill the hollows in the bananas with the mixture, cover with thinly pinned out marzipan and decorate each one with a Mexican modelled in marzipan and palm trees made of piped couverture.

(Illustration, p. 814)

Austria

Sweet fried ravioli

6–8 persons

240 g	flour	10 oz
20 g	butter	1 oz
20 g	icing sugar	1 oz
	2 eggs	
	1 tablespoon aquavit, kirsch or other fruit liqueur	
150 g	quince jam	6 oz
200 g	home-made compôte	8 oz
50 g	blanched bitter almonds	2 oz

Prepare a paste with the flour, butter, icing sugar, eggs and liqueur, shape into a ball, cover and leave in a cool place for an hour. Pin out to 3 mm ($\frac{1}{10}$ in) thick and cut out with a round cutter. Place a teaspoonful of quince jam or of well drained compote mixed with chopped bitter almonds on each round of paste. Moisten the edges lightly, fold over to enclose the filling, press the edges together firmly and fry in hot deep fat, preferably oil. Drain well and dish dusted with vanilla flavoured icing sugar.

Italy

Sweet ravioli from San Provino

Dough

200 g	butter	7 oz
$\frac{1}{4}$ l	water	$\frac{1}{2}$ pt
40 g	sugar	$1\frac{1}{2}$ oz
	pinch of salt	
	flour as required	

Filling

500 g	prunes	1 lb
250 g	macaroons	8 oz
10 g	almonds	$\frac{1}{2}$ oz
10 g	hazelnuts	$\frac{1}{2}$ oz
	zest of 1 lemon	
	liqueur (maraschino or other liqueur according to preference)	
	coconut oil	
	icing sugar	

Pour the water into a pan, add the butter, salt and sugar, heat gently until the butter has melted and the salt and sugar dissolved, then stand aside. Cook the prunes which have been soaked, then drain, stone and chop finely. Mix with the finely crushed macaroons and the ground almonds and hazelnuts. Flavour well with liqueur.

Add sufficient flour to the water/butter mixture to make a dough of medium firmness. Allow to rest for at least 30 minutes, then pin out to a thickness of 3 mm (about $\frac{1}{10}$ in) and cut into 5 cm (2 in) squares. Place a little filling in the centre of half the squares, moisten the edges lightly with water, cover with the rest of the squares, seal the edges well and fry until golden in hot coconut oil. Drain well on absorbent paper, dust with icing sugar and keep hot until required.

(Illustration, p. 372)   Switzerland (Tessin)

Syllabub*

10 persons

1 l	double cream	1½ pt
125 g	sugar	4 oz
¼ l	sweet white wine	½ pt
	3 lemons	
5 cl	brandy	2 measures

Place the cream in a basin, whisk a little and add the wine and lemon juice gradually as the cream thickens. Add the sugar and brandy and mix lightly. Fill into individual dishes and chill well. Serve with finger biscuits.

Great Britain

* Syllabub is frequently served at City of London dinners.

Tea cream

4 persons

	3 teaspoons tea	
¼ l	boiling water	½ pt
	3 egg yolks	
80 g	sugar	3 oz
	zest of half a lemon	
	zest of 1 orange	
	2 small glasses of rum	
	5 leaves gelatine	
⅜ l	whipped cream	¾ pt

Pour the boiling water on the tea leaves and allow to stand for 3–4 minutes. Whisk the egg yolks and sugar until foamy, add the lemon and orange zest and the rum, then stir in the gelatine which has been soaked beforehand. Now strain in the tea and fold in the whipped cream. Fill into glasses and leave to set in the refrigerator. Decorate with whipped cream and flat or curled wafer biscuits.

(Illustration, p. 1095)

Germany

Tippaleipa

30 pancakes

	1 egg yolk	
	9 egg whites	
170 g	sugar	6 oz
170 g	flour	6 oz
	lard	
	icing sugar	

Whisk the egg yolk and 7 egg whites with the sugar until thick and frothy. Lightly fold in the sieved flour, then fold in the remaining 2 egg whites whipped to a stiff snow. Heat the lard in a small sauté pan or other shallow pan no bigger than a small saucer. Pour a tablespoon of the batter into a thin funnel held over the pan with the end dipped into the lard and move the funnel to and fro to make a spun pancake. Alternatively, use a savoy bag fitted with a fine pipe; in this case the outlet has to be closed off each time. If the batter is too thick, dilute with a little dairy cream. When the underside of the pancake is brown, turn and brown on the other side, then curve at once round a stick or rolling pin and drain off the fat. Sprinkle with icing sugar to serve.

Finland

Turkentommerl

4 persons   Baking time: 12 minutes

120 g	maize meal	5 oz
$\frac{1}{2}$ l	milk	$\frac{7}{8}$ pint
	3 tablespoons sugar	
	zest of 1 lemon	
	little vanilla and cinnamon	
	good pinch of salt	
200 g	butter or margarine	7 oz
	3 apples, peeled	
50 g	sultanas	$1\frac{3}{4}$ oz

Stir the maize meal into the boiling milk, and add sugar, lemon zest, salt, vanilla and cinnamon. Whisk all well, using a wire whisk. Heat the butter or margarine (oil may be used if preferred) in a pan large enough for the mixture to cover the bottom to a thickness of about 1 cm (about $\frac{1}{2}$ in), leaving room for it to rise. After pouring in the mixture, shred the apples on top and sprinkle with the sultanas. Bake in an oven with medium bottom heat and good top heat, stirring once at first. Sprinkle with sugar before serving.

Austria

Van Gogh palette

6 persons

Bavarian creams

½ l	milk	¾ pt
125 g	sugar	4 oz
	3 egg yolks	
	1 vanilla bean	
	10 sheets gelatine	
¾ l	whipped cream	1¼ pt
2½ cl	dried jasmine blossom infusion, or, if not available, Nestea extract	2½ dessertspoons
2½ cl	strong fresh mint infusion coloured with spinach mate or, if not available, mint tea	2½ dessertspoons
2½ cl	lemon leaf syrup or, if no leaves available, lemon juice	2½ dessertspoons
	little grated lemon zest	
	little turmeric for colouring	
25 g	sieved red currant jelly	1 oz
25 g	sieved cranberries	1 oz

Kirsch cream

¼ l	whipped cream	½ pt
30 g	sugar	1 oz
	2 sheets gelatine	
5 cl	kirsch	2 fl oz

Decoration

fresh jasmine blossom
fresh mint
lemon leaves, chocolate raspings
blanched orange and lemon zest cut in
    very fine julienne strips
fresh cherries

Prepare the custard for the Bavarian cream and add the soaked gelatine, but do not fold in the whipped cream. Divide the custard into four equal portions. Stir the jasmine blossom infusion into one portion; mix the second with the mint infusion and colour well with spinach mate; mix the third portion with the lemon leaf syrup, lemon zest and a little turmeric to colour; beat the cranberries and the red currant jelly into the fourth portion. Now fold a quarter of the whipped cream into each portion. To make the kirsch cream, mix together the whipped cream and the sugar, flavour with the kirsch and add the gelatine which has been soaked and dissolved.

Fill the five creams into small moulds of suitable shape and refrigerate. When set, arrange on a painter's palette and decorate the jasmine cream with a jasmine blossom, the mint cream with a fresh mint leaf, the lemon cream with a lemon leaf and chocolate raspings, the red cream with the strips of orange and lemon zest, and the kirsch cream with a fresh cherry.

Germany

Various fruit coupes

A great deal of variety is possible in the preparation of fruit coupes, depending on the season and the availability of suitable fresh fruit. The fruit should always be lightly macerated in appropriately flavoured spirits. The whipped cream used should be slightly sweetened. In addition to the fruit and cream, the coupes contain sweetened strawberry purée or chocolate sauce. The decoration consists of piped royal icing, couverture, praline nougat, short pastry or marzipan.

Austria

Vine harvest festival dessert

Total cooking time: 1 hour 20 minutes

3 kg	black grapes	6½ lb
50 g (or more)	flour	2 oz
50 g	candied fruit, finely diced	2 oz

Wash the grapes, remove the stalks, place in a pan and cook for 20 minutes, when the juice should have begun to run out. Transfer the grapes and juice to a large conical strainer or fine mesh wire sieve and extract as much of the juice as possible. Sieve the flour and blend slowly with the grape juice, taking care to avoid the formation of lumps. Cook over moderate heat while stirring constantly until the mixture is of a more or less creamy consistency. Stir in the diced candied fruit, transfer to a soup tureen and serve when cold.

Italy

Waffles

Yields 20–25 waffles   2–3 minutes

250 g	flour	8 oz
125 g	sugar	4 oz
100 g	butter	3½ oz
	2 eggs	
	1 egg white	
	whipped to a snow	
½ l	cold boiled milk	¾ pt
	pinch of vanilla	
	pinch of salt	

Make a pancake batter in a slightly warmed basin. Heat the butter until foamy but not brown, and add to the batter. Allow to stand in a fairly warm place for 1 hour. Just before baking, add the egg white whipped to a snow. Grease the waffle iron with butter or pork fat. As soon as it is hot, spread some batter on it, close the iron and cook on both sides. The iron must be very hot on both sides before it is used. The waffle is ready when it has become golden brown.

The extra egg white is optional.

France

Waffles with maple syrup

6 waffles

	3 eggs (separated)	
½ l	sour milk	¾ pt
250 g	flour	8 oz
	1 teaspoon bicarbonate of soda	
	2 teaspoons baking powder	
	½ teaspoon salt	
100 g	butter	3 oz

Beat the egg yolks and mix with the milk. Sieve the flour, bicarbonate of soda, baking powder and salt together, blend in the egg yolks and milk and beat well in the mixer. Melt the butter, allow to cool and stir lightly into the batter. Lastly fold in the egg whites whipped to a stiff snow. Use a spoon to deposit the batter on the waffle iron, which has been heated and greased. Cook until golden brown. Serve hot with maple syrup, which should be handed separately.

Germany

FROZEN DESSERTS

There are many types of frozen desserts—cream ices, water ices, iced soufflés, etc., and these are always popular both at formal meals or on an à la carte menu. Many excellent frozen desserts can be bought ready to serve, but a greater variety is possible, and as well as being an incentive to a creative chef, many people consider that the flavour of home-made ice cream is superior to that of bought products.

Ice cream can be frozen in several ways. The old-fashioned freezing machine, with a cranked handle which is turned continuously whilst the mixture is frozen by a combination of ice and salt has been largely superseded by modern ice cream makers powered by electricity and designed to fit inside a deep freeze cabinet. Both of these embody the principle of stirring the mixture whilst it is being frozen. This obtains a smoother mixture by preventing the formation of large ice crystals. When neither type of machine is available then the mixture should be removed from the freezer when it is just beginning to set, turned into a well chilled bowl and thoroughly whisked with a rotary whisk and returned to the freezer.

Quick home-made ices

These ices are parfaits made with raw egg yolks. They are frozen in the freezing unit of a refrigerator.

6 persons

Standard recipe

4 dl	double cream	⅔ pt
	and	
2 dl	unboiled milk	⅓ pt
	whipped together to make Chantilly cream	
	or	
½ l	Chantilly cream	1 pt
	3 egg yolks	
125 g	icing sugar (sieved)	4 oz
	pinch of ground vanilla	
	or other flavouring	
	or liqueur	

Whisk the egg yolks, sugar and vanilla together until straw-coloured and thick enough to fall in a ribbon from the whisk. Add the Chantilly cream. Fill into the ice trays of the refrigerator and place in the freezing compartment for 4 hours. If using liqueur, add 2 cl (2 dessertspoons) before blending in the cream. Unmould in hot water.

France

Ice cream with evaporated milk

450 g	1 tin evaporated milk	1 lb
150 g	icing sugar	5¼ oz

Flavouring

Coffee

1 teaspoon coffee essence

Chocolate.
1 teaspoon chocolate powder

Praline.
1 teaspoon crushed sieved praline

Orange-flower.
1 teaspoon orange-flower water

Vanilla.
pinch of ground vanilla
Never flavour with liqueur

Chill the tin of evaporated milk for 2 hours. Pour the contents into a well chilled container. Add the icing sugar and flavouring and surround with ice. Whisk until the volume has doubled. Place in the freezing unit of the refrigerator for 4 or 5 hours.

France

Custard ices

These are made with a custard of

1 l	milk	1¾ pt
	10 egg yolks	
150 g	sugar	12 oz

With ¼ l (approx. ½ pt) of unwhipped double cream added just before freezing.

(Each recipe is sufficient for 10 persons)

Almond ice cream

Proceed as for pistachio ice cream, using freshly blanched, chopped almonds instead of pistachio nuts.

France

Chocolate ice cream

1 l	chocolate custard	1¾ pt

France

Coffee ice cream

1 l	coffee custard	1¾ pt

France

Pistachio ice cream

Steep 150 g (5¼ oz) very finely chopped pistachio nuts in 1 l (1¾ pt) boiling milk. Make a custard with the milk and tint with very little natural green colouring.

France

Plombières ice cream

Prepare 1 l (1¾ pt) vanilla ice cream. Place in the freezer. When half-set, add 250 g (8¾ oz) finely diced candied fruit which has been macerated in ½ dl ($\frac{1}{12}$ pt) kirsch. Churn briskly in the freezer to mix well. Freeze.

France

Praline ice cream

Prepare 1 l (1¾ pt) vanilla custard. Add 150 g (5¼ oz) finely crushed praline. If using praline paste, first blend it with a little custard.

France

Tutti-frutti ice cream

Proceed as for Plombières ice cream, but use maraschino instead of kirsch.

France

Vanilla ice cream

1 l	vanilla custard	1¾ pt

France

FRUIT OR WATER ICES

Basic recipe

Prepare a syrup at 32°B and reduce it to 18–22°B by the addition of fruit pulp and juice. These ices need continuous stirring whilst they are being frozen.

Each recipe is sufficient for 10 persons.

Apricot water ice

½ l	pulp of very ripe apricots	¾ pt
½ l	cold syrup	¾ pt
	juice of 1 lemon	

The density of the mixture should be 18°B.

France

Lemon ice

15–20 persons   Freezing time: 15 minutes

	5 large lemons (unsprayed)	
½ l	white wine	¾ pt
250 g	sugar	8 oz
½ l	water	¾ pt
¼ l	egg white	½ pt
3 dl	*or* whipped cream	½ pt

Prepare stock syrup with the sugar and water. Scrub the lemons, remove the zest, pour over the lukewarm syrup and a little white wine, cover and steep for a few hours. Add the juice from the lemons, the rest of the wine and sufficient cold boiled water, if required, to bring the density to 18°B. Strain through a cloth and freeze in a freezer. Shortly before the ice is ready fold in the stiffly whipped egg white or the whipped cream (1 part egg white or cream to 4 parts lemon ice).

Germany

Lemon water ice

1 l	syrup	1¾ pt
	zest (without white skin) of 3 or 4 lemons	
	juice of 3 or 4 lemons	

Soak the lemon zest in the cold syrup for 2 or 3 hours under cover. Add the juice. Strain through a fine cloth. The mixture should measure 20–22°B.

France

Orange water ice

8 dl	cold syrup	1⅓ pt
	zest of 3 oranges	
	juice of 5 oranges	
	juice of 1 lemon	

Proceed as for lemon water ice. The density of the mixture should be 20–21°B.

France

Pineapple water ice

½ l	pulp of very ripe pineapple	¾ pt
½ l	cold syrup	¾ pt
	juice of 1 orange	
	juice of 1 lemon	

The density of the mixture should be 18°B.

France

Raspberry water ice

Proceed as for strawberry water ice, omitting the orange juice.

France

Strawberry water ice

600 g	strawberries (preferably wild ones)	1 lb 4 oz
½ l	syrup	¾ pt
	juice of half an orange	
	juice of half a lemon	

The density of the mixture should be 18°B. A brighter colour may be achieved by adding a few drops of carmine.

France

Tangerine water ice

8 dl	cold syrup	1¼ pt
	zest of 4 tangerines	
	juice of 8 tangerines	
	juice of 1 lemon	

Proceed as for lemon water ice. The density should be 20°B.

France

PARFAITS

Parfaits are frozen without a churn type freezer, either by burying the mould in ice and salt or in the freezing compartment of the refrigerator. The amount of time required will, of course, depend on the size of the mould. On average, three or four hours should be allowed for a mould containing half a litre (⅞ pt).

Each of the recipes given below is sufficient for 12–15 persons.

Chocolate parfait

4 dl	water	⅔ pt
200 g	chocolate	8 oz
200 g	sugar	8 oz
	16 egg yolks	
½ l	whipped cream	¾ pt
	made with	
	2 dl (⅓ pt) double cream and	
	1 dl (3 fl oz) unboiled milk	

Dissolve the chocolate and sugar in the water and cook for 2 minutes, then proceed as for coffee parfait.

France

Cloudberry parfait

10 persons

	8 egg yolks	
125 g	sugar	4 oz
5 dl	whipped cream	¾ pt
500 g	cloudberries	1 lb

Whisk the egg yolks and sugar over gentle heat in a bain-marie until light and frothy. Remove from the bain-marie and continue whisking. Add the crushed cloudberries and the whipped cream, fill into a mould and freeze.

Sweden

Coffee parfait

4 dl	very strong coffee	⅔ pt
300 g	sugar	10 oz
	16 egg yolks	
½ l	whipped cream	¾ pt
	made with	
	2 dl (⅓ pt) double cream and	
	1 dl (3 fl oz) unboiled milk	

Dissolve the sugar in the coffee without allowing it to boil. Mix the coffee with the egg yolks and cook in the same way as custard. Pass through a fine conical strainer and whisk while cooling. Place the bowl on crushed ice and continue whisking for a short time. Lightly fold in the whipped cream, fill into a mould, then surround with ice and salt or place in the freezing unit of the refrigerator.

France

Liqueur flavoured parfait

Proceed as for vanilla parfait, but replace the vanilla by liqueur, using a maximum of 2 centilitres (2 dessertspoons) for the quantities given in the recipe. As alcohol has a low freezing point, this type of parfait takes longer to freeze.

France

Parfait with candied fruit

Proceed as for vanilla parfait, adding 150 g (5 oz) candied fruit macerated in Cognac, kirsch or maraschino.

France

Parfait 'Désir de Sultane'

Vanilla parfait masked with spun sugar.

France

Parfait Montmorency

This is a parfait with cherry brandy.

France

Parfait aux perles de Soliès-Pont

This is a parfait flavoured with cherry brandy and decorated with cherries macerated in kirsch.

France

Parfait Pompadour

Half-vanilla and half-strawberry parfait, decorated with small whirls of white and pale pink sweetened whipped cream.

France

Praline parfait

Proceed as for vanilla parfait, adding 150 g (5 oz) praline.

France

Praline parfait with rose hip sauce

10–15 persons

	16 egg yolks	
4 dl	stock syrup at 28°B	$\frac{2}{3}$ pt
5 cl	kirsch	2 fl oz
200 g	crushed and sieved praline croquant	7 oz
1 l	whipped cream	1$\frac{3}{4}$ pt

Blend the egg yolks into the cold syrup. Transfer to a bain-marie and beat over gentle heat until thick and frothy, then whisk on ice until cold. Add the kirsch, fold in the whipped cream and the paraline croquant, fill into moulds and freeze.

Turn out and serve with rose hip sauce. To make the sauce, heat rose hip purée and concentrated apple juice together, adding a little sugar if required, and flavour with rum.

Germany

Vanilla parfait

4 dl	water	$\frac{2}{3}$ pt
350 g	sugar	12 oz
	good pinch of ground vanilla	
	16 egg yolks	
$\frac{1}{2}$ l	whipped cream made with	$\frac{3}{4}$ pt
	2 dl ($\frac{1}{3}$ pt) double cream and	
	1 dl (3 fl oz) unboiled milk	

Whisk the egg yolks. Dissolve the sugar in the water and boil up. Allow to cool; when lukewarm, slowly pour the syrup on the yolks. Cook in the same way as custard and proceed as for coffee parfait.

France

COMPOSITE ICES

These consist of ices of different flavours frozen in the same mould and sometimes containing other ingredients, e.g. fruit, meringue, etc. There is an infinite number of different varieties. A few of them are given below.

Aida

Mould lined with tangerine ice and filled with vanilla ice flavoured with kirsch.

France

Alhambra

Mould lined with vanilla ice and filled with a mixture of Chantilly cream and wild strawberries flavoured with kirsch.

France

Archduke

Mould lined with apricot ice and filled with finely chopped, fresh skinned walnuts.

France

Brazilian style

Half coffee parfait, half vanilla parfait.

France

Cardinal

Mould lined with raspberry ice and filled with vanilla praline ice.

France

Havanese style

Coffee parfait with liqueur-filled coffee beans.

France

Hawaiian style

Pineapple ice with diced pineapple macerated in kirsch.

France

Montmorency

Mould lined with kirsch flavoured vanilla ice and filled with cherry brandy ice containing pieces of glacé cherry macerated in kirsch.

France

Nelusko

Mould lined with vanilla ice and filled with chocolate ice.

France

Parisian style

Mould lined with raspberry ice and filled with vanilla ice containing diced apricots and cherries macerated in kirsch.

France

Sultane

Mould lined with chocolate ice and filled with praline ice. Whirls of Chantilly cream are used for decoration.

France

Tosca

Mould lined with apricot ice and filled with maraschino ice containing mixed diced candied fruit macerated in maraschino.

France

White Lady

Mould lined with vanilla ice and filled with almond milk ice.

Ice bombes

A bombe mixture is usually only used as a filling, the mould being first lined with ice cream. After it has been filled with bombe mixture, it is surrounded with ice and salt or placed in the freezing unit of the refrigerator. For a ¾ l (1¼ pt) mould, at least 3½ hours should be allowed for freezing.

Bombe mixture

For approx. 1 l (1¾ pt)

	8 egg yolks	
¼ l	cold syrup at 32°B	½ pt
½ l	whipped cream	¾ pt
	made with	
	2 dl (⅓ pt) double cream and	
	1 dl (3 fl oz) unboiled milk	
3 cl	liqueur as desired	3 dessertspoons

Blend the egg yolks with the syrup and pass through a fine conical strainer. Place over gentle heat, preferably in a bain-marie. Whisk as for a genoese sponge until the mixture has doubled in volume and falls like a ribbon from the whisk. Now remove from the heat and whisk until completely cold. Add the liqueur, then fold in the whipped cream.

100 g (3½ oz) candied fruit may be added to the mixture.

France

Some recipes

Bombe Abricotine

Line mould with chocolate ice and fill with apricot bombe mixture.

France

Bombe Archiduc

Line mould with strawberry ice and fill with paraline bombe mixture.

France

Bombe Cerisette

Line mould with cherry ice and fill with bombe mixture flavoured with cherry brandy.

France

Bombe Diplomate

Line mould with vanilla ice and fill with maraschino flavoured bombe mixture containing candied fruit.

France

Bombe Favorite

Line mould with vanilla ice and fill with coffee mousse. After unmoulding, decorate with sweetened whipped cream.

France

Bombe Francillon

Line mould with coffee ice and fill with bombe mixture flavoured with Fine Champagne liqueur brandy.

France

Bombe Frou-Frou

Line mould with vanilla ice and fill with bombe mixture containing candied fruit.

France

Bombe Monselet

Line mould with tangerine ice and fill with port-flavoured bombe mixture containing finely diced candied orange peel macerated in kirsch.

France

Bombe Tutti-Frutti

Line mould with strawberry ice and fill with vanilla bombe mixture containing candied fruit macerated in kirsch.

France

ICE CREAM COUPES

These consist of various kinds of ice cream and fruit macerated in liqueur, decorated with jam, fruit pulp sprinkled with almonds and/or Chantilly cream.

They are served in silver or glass goblets.

France

Cherry brandy coupe

Place a few tangerine segments in the bottom of a tall ice cream goblet and sprinkle well with cherry brandy. Fill up with half-cherry ice and half-vanilla ice and mask with a spoonful of Melba sauce. Place a few cherry brandy cherries* on top and decorate with tiny bulbs of whipped cream.

Germany

* Cherry brandy cherries are stoned cherries which have been preserved in cherry brandy.

Coupe Aida

Cover the bottom of the coupe with diced peaches. Place a scoop of tea ice on top and surround with a ring of small whole strawberries. Sprinkle well with Grand Marnier, decorate with whipped cream and place a chocolate ornament in the centre.

Germany

Coupe Ambassade

Raspberry ice. A poached half-peach. Mask with kirsch flavoured strawberry pulp. Decorate with Chantilly cream.

France

Coupe Cerisette

Vanilla ice. Stoned cherries macerated in kirsch. Fresh flaked almonds.

France

Coupe Chantilly

Diced mixed fresh fruit macerated in kirsch. Cover with vanilla ice. Decorate with Chantilly cream. Sprinkle with chopped pistachio nuts. Top with half a glacé cherry.

France

Coupe Coral

Dice bananas and strawberries and place in the bottom of the coupe to cover. Fill up with banana and lemon ice and decorate with whipped cream. Place a chocolate ornament in the centre and add half a sponge finger.

Germany

Coupe Créole

Pineapple ice. Decorate with pieces of pineapple and sliced banana. Splash with rum.

France

Coupe First Lady

Cover the bottom of the coupe with small cubes of light butter sponge. Place a scoop of peppermint ice on top and sprinkle with Parisian nougat shavings. Serve with a sand biscuit.

Germany

Coupe Florida

Place a scoop of lemon ice in the coupe and coat with red-currant jelly. Cover with small triangles of pineapple, decorate with whipped cream and place a chocolate ornament in the centre. Sprinkle the edges of the pineapple triangles with chopped pistachio nuts.

Germany

Coupe Geisha

Peel and seed white grapes, poach in white wine, keeping them firm, and leave until cold. Place a spoonful of grapes in the bottom of the coupe and cover with tangerine ice. Pipe four bulbs of whipped cream in the centre and surround with a ring of tangerine segments. Decorate with a chocolate ornament and sprinkle the tangerine segments with chopped pistachio nuts.

Germany

Coupe Grimaldi

Diced pineapple macerated in kirsch. Cover with tangerine ice. Decorate with Chantilly cream and crystallised violet.

France

Coupe Hawaienne

Vanilla ice. Decorate with almonds soaked in kirsch. Top with a glacé cherry.

France

Coupe Héricart

Strawberry ice. Arrange Héricart strawberries round the ice at the bottom of the goblet and pipe a line of Chantilly cream between the strawberries from the base up to the centre.

France

Coupe Jacqueline

Cover the bottom of the coupe with an almond macaroon and line the sides with narrow strips of sponge cake. Top with a spiral of almond ice cream and mask with Cardinal sauce. Pour a tablespoon of orange liqueur over and decorate the ice cream with a zigzag-shaped couverture ornament.

This coupe should be served in a tall glass container.

Germany

Coupe Jacques

Half lemon, half strawberry ice. In the centre, a dome of fresh fruit salad macerated in kirsch.

France

Coupe Jamaica

Cover the bottom of the coupe with rum flavoured chocolate sauce. Place a scoop of rum ice cream on top and cover with half a small poached pear. Splash with rum, decorate with whipped cream and top the half-pear with a small couverture ornament.

Germany

Coupe Jeannette

Vanilla ice surrounded by a border of Chantilly cream. Sprinkle the ice with chocolate granules.

France

Coupe King Edward

Mix vanilla ice cream with a little whipped cream and flavour with white rum and Scotch whisky. Fill into a tall silver ice cream goblet or Champagne glass and decorate with a piped chocolate ornament and an almond biscuit.

Germany

Coupe Melba

Vanilla ice cream. Poached half-peach. Mask with raspberry purée.

France

Coupe Montreuil

Diced peach macerated in kirsch. Cover with peach ice. Decorate with Chantilly cream.

France

Coupe Nesselrode

Pieces of glazed chestnut macerated in kirsch. Cover with vanilla ice. Top with glazed chestnut. Using a star pipe, surround the base with a border of Chantilly cream.

France

Coupe Patrick

Apricot ice. Decorate with a ring of quarter-apricots macerated in rum. Sprinkle chopped pistachio nuts in the centre.

France

Coupe Rêve de Pierrot

Raspberry ice. Rosette of Chantilly cream with half a glacé cherry on top. Surround the half-cherry with a small ring of tiny diamond shaped pieces of angelica inserted into the cream. Lightly sprinkle the base with kirsch.

France

Coupe Romagna

Place three stoned poached cherries in the bottom of the coupe. Line the sides from top to bottom at intervals of 2 cm ($\frac{3}{4}$ in) with strips of filled petitsfours. Fill the spaces between them with chocolate ice cream and place vanilla ice cream in the centre of the coupe. Top with half a poached peach and pipe whipped cream round it. Finish off with two chocolate flower ornaments at the edge.

Coupe Rothschild

Place a small scoop each of vanilla and strawberry ice cream in the coupe and surround with peeled grapes, stoned cherries, tangerine segments and small pieces of pineapple. Pipe on whipped cream lattice fashion and place a glacé cherry and two small chocolate ornaments in the centre.

Germany

Coupe Truffins

Cover the bottom of the coupe with a piece of well-dried meringue. Place a scoop of truffle ice cream on top, surround with a border of whipped cream and decorate with piped couverture. Place a choux paste ornament in the centre.

Germany

Coupe Tutti-Frutti

Fill the bottom of the goblet with diced candied fruit macerated in maraschino. Cover with two layers of ice—one lemon, the other strawberry.

France

Coupe Vienna Woods

Place three small scoops of ice cream (vanilla, strawberry and chocolate) in a glass coupe and cover with a tablespoon of finely diced peaches. Arrange a border of sliced strawberries round the edge of the coupe, decorate with small bulbs of whipped cream and place a large choice strawberry in the centre. Splash with maraschino and sprinkle the cream lightly with chopped pistachio nuts.

Germany

Fresh raspberry and ice cream coupe

8 persons

	8 scoops fine vanilla ice cream	
750 g	fresh raspberries	1¾ lb
2–3 cl	raspberry brandy	2–3 dessertspoons
	8 tablespoons double cream	
	2–3 large macaroons, crumbled	
	rolled wafers	

Place a scoop of vanilla ice cream in the bottom of each coupe and flatten a little. Cover with raspberries and sprinkle with a little raspberry brandy (or macerate the raspberries in the brandy first). Coat the raspberries lightly with double cream, sprinkle with macaroon crumbs and serve with rolled wafers.

Germany

Ice cream coupe Recreatio

Place 2 or 3 small scoops of vanilla ice cream in the coupe. Cover liberally with bilberries Recreatio and a little of the syrup, pipe on small whirls of whipped cream and decorate with crystallised violets.

(Illustration, p. 372)   Switzerland

Meringue coupe

Chop up well-dried meringues finely and place enough in the coupe to cover the bottom. Mask lightly with coffee sauce and fill up with coffee ice cream. Pipe on a ring of whipped cream, using a star pipe, and placed a piped sand biscuit star in the centre.

Germany

SNOWBALLS

These are plain or composite ices covered with Chantilly cream, which is piped on using a savoy bag fitted with a star pipe. They are decorated with angelica, glacé cherries, and crystallised rose petals or violets.

If no deep freeze cabinet is available, or if the freezing unit of the refrigerator is not large enough, the cream is piped on at the last minute.

Snowballs are often named after the ice cream on which they are based.

Chantilly snowball

Based on vanilla ice made with Chantilly cream.

Raspberry snowball

Based on raspberry ice.

Plombières snowball

Based on Plombières ice cream.

Pompadour snowball

Based on strawberry ice, covered with Chantilly cream decorated with rose petals, etc.

France

OTHER FROZEN DESSERTS

Biscuits glacés

These are made up of $\frac{2}{3}$ ice parfait and $\frac{1}{3}$ savoy fingers soaked in liqueur or spirits (maraschino, Curaçao, rum, kirsch, etc.) or sprinkled with candied fruit. All kinds of combinations are possible. Cover the bottom of a brick shaped mould with vanilla parfait to come one-third of the way up. Arrange an even layer of rather tightly packed savoy fingers soaked in liqueur on top. Cover the savoy fingers with parfait mixture flavoured with hazelnuts, praline or chocolate (or other flavouring). Surround with ice and salt or return to the freezing unit of the refrigerator for at least $3\frac{1}{2}$ hours.

France

Biscuit glacé Santiago

12 persons

$3\frac{1}{2}$ dl	chocolate ice cream	$\frac{2}{3}$ pt
$3\frac{1}{2}$ dl	vanilla ice cream	$\frac{2}{3}$ pt
2 dl	cassata filling	$\frac{1}{3}$ pt
	1 sheet genoese sponge 1 cm (about $\frac{1}{2}$ in) thick	
1 dl	kirsch	3 fl oz

Soufflé omelette mixture

	4 egg yolks	
100 g	sugar	4 oz
	zest of 1 orange	
	5 egg whites	

Line the bottom of a 1 l (1$\frac{3}{4}$ pt) brick shaped mould with a layer of chocolate ice cream. Cover with a layer of vanilla ice cream, then a layer of genoese sponge soaked in kirsch, top with the cassata filling and freeze. Turn out and cut into 12 slices. Using a savoy bag and star tube, quickly pipe soufflé omelette mixture on each one, dust with icing sugar, flash in a hot oven and serve at once.

To make soufflé omelette mixture, beat the egg yolks with part of the sugar and the orange zest until foamy and fold in the egg whites whipped to a stiff snow with the rest of the sugar.

Switzerland

Cassatas

Cassatas are ices made up of several outer layers of various sorts of ice cream with a different filling in the centre. There is an infinite variety of possible combinations. Here is a typical recipe. Line a mould with vanilla ice, then cover this with raspberry ice. Finally, fill with parfait mixture containing candied fruit macerated in maraschino. Freeze in ice and salt for at least 4 hours. Unmould and cut in slices.

France

Cream iced mousse

8 persons

	6 egg yolks	
150 g	sugar	5 oz
¼ l	milk	½ pt approx.
½ l	whipped cream	¾ pt
	pinch of vanilla	

Blend the egg yolks with the sugar, then add the milk flavoured with vanilla. Proceed as for custard, then remove from the heat and whisk until quite cold. Lightly fold in the whipped cream, fill into goblets or moulds and freeze.

France

Désir de roi

6–8 persons

250 g	choux paste	8 oz
¾ l	vanilla ice	1¼ pt
¾ l	hot chocolate sauce	1¼ pt
	flavoured with rum	

Make some petits choux. When cold, cut them open with scissors three-quarters of the way up, but do not cut the tops right off. Fill with vanilla ice and arrange in a dome on a serving dish. Pour hot chocolate sauce over and serve quickly. Hand the rest of the chocolate sauce separately in a sauce-boat.

France

Frosted tangerines

8 persons

¾ l	8 tangerines tangerine ice a few orange leaves	1¼ pt

Cut off the tops of the tangerines three-quarters of the way up and set aside. Scoop out the pulp and use to prepare tangerine water ice. Fill the cleaned tangerine shells with the ice and replace the tops. Place in the freezing unit of the refrigerator or in a cooler well packed with ice and salt for at least 2 hours. Remove at the last minute when well frosted and serve on napkins or paper doyleys.

France

Granités

12 persons

½ l ½ l	syrup at 28°B fruit juice juice of 1 lemon	¾ pt ¾ pt

Proceed as for sherbets. The density should be 14°. The mixture should barely be stirred during freezing so that it becomes a little more granular than a sherbet. Any recipe for fruit ice may be used to prepare granités, but the basic syrup should only be at 28°B.

France

Iced chocolate mousse

8 persons

Formula I

	6 egg yolks	
100 g	sugar	3 oz
125 g	chocolate	4 oz
1½ dl	milk	¼ pt
½ l	whipped cream	¾ pt

Dissolve the chocolate in the milk. Prepare custard with the milk, sugar and egg yolks, then proceed as for cream iced mousse.

Formula II

250 g	3 egg yolks	
	chocolate	8 oz
	2 tablespoons fresh cream	
	8 egg whites whipped to	
	a stiff snow	

Break up the chocolate and dissolve in the cream over gentle heat. Remove from the heat and add the 3 egg yolks. Whisk well for 2 or 3 minutes, then leave until lukewarm. Fold in the whipped egg whites. Fill into individual containers and leave in the refrigerator for at least 2 hours before serving. (Do not unmould.) A few flaked almonds and a little rum may be added if desired.

France

Iced coffee mousse

Proceed as for cream iced mousse. Add coffee essence or alternatively roast 125 g (4 oz) coffee and infuse at once in the milk to be used in making the mousse.

France

Iced chocolate soufflé

8–10 persons

200 g	sugar	7 oz
	10 egg yolks	
	6 egg whites	
1 l	whipped dairy cream	1¾ pt
	(unsweetened)	
5–7 cl	Cointreau or Grand Marnier	2–3 measures

Decoration

	whipped sweetened cream
	chocolate powder

Chocolate sauce

3 dl	milk	½ pt
400 g	Velma couverture	14 oz

Boil the sugar and a little water to the thread degree and cool. Whisk the egg yolks and sugar to a stiff sponge, whip the whites to a stiff snow and blend the two together.

29

Fold in the whipped cream and flavour with Cointreau or Grand Marnier. Fasten a strip of cardboard round a soufflé mould so that it projects 2–3 cm (about 1 in) above the top edge of the mould. Fill with the soufflé mixture and place in the freezer. After freezing, remove the strip of cardboard, place a wire rack on top of the soufflé, dust with chocolate powder and remove the rack. Decorate with a border of small bulbs of whipped cream.

To make the sauce, bring the milk to the boil, add the couverture which has been cut into small pieces, allow to melt, stir well and leave until cold.

Switzerland

Ice gâteau caprice

12–15 persons

Parfait

7 cl	water	2½ fl oz
150 g	sugar	5 oz
	1 vanilla pod	
	8 egg yolks	
8 dl	whipped dairy cream	1¼ pt

Chocolate sponge

	5 egg yolks	
	4 egg whites	
90 g	sugar	3 oz
	pinch of salt	
20 g	flour	2½ tablespoons
30 g	cornflour	2½ tablespoons
10 g	cocoa powder	1 tablespoon

Sauce

¼ l	caramel syrup	½ pt
5 g	cornflour	1 teaspoon
5 cl	rum	1½ measures
5 cl	Cognac	1½ measures
200 g	chopped candied fruit	7 oz

To make the chocolate sponge, beat the egg yolks with 40 g (1½ oz) sugar until foamy. Whip the egg whites to a stiff snow, gradually adding the rest of the sugar mixed with the cornflour. Carefully blend the two together and lastly fold in the flour and cocoa powder. Line a baking sheet with paper, spread the sponge on it evenly, bake in a brisk oven, making sure the sponge does not become too dry, and remove from the paper.

To make the parfait, boil the water with the sugar and vanilla to obtain stock syrup at 96°R. Beat up the egg yolks, gradually add the stock syrup and continue beating until cold. Fold in the whipped cream and the candied fruit. Line the bottom and sides of a 30 × 10 cm (12 × 4 in) cake tin with a thin layer of chocolate sponge, fill with the parfait mixture, cover with sponge and deep freeze. Turn out, cut into portions and serve with the following sauce:—blend the cornflour with a little water, add to the thick caramel syrup, boil up, allow to cool and flavour with the rum and Cognac.

Switzerland

Iced mousses

Iced mousses are served in small individual glass or china goblets. In these containers they require one and a half to two hours in the freezing compartment of the refrigerator, unless they are to be unmoulded, in which case at least three hours should be allowed for small containers or four for large ones. If no freezing unit is available, the containers may be packed in ice and salt.

France

Ice soufflés

These are made with the same mixture as ice mousses.

Wrap a strip of greaseproof paper round the mould to come 2 or 3 cm (about 1 in) above the top edge. (To keep the paper in position, wrap a piece of string round it two or three times and tie.) Fill the mould with the mixture so that the latter is level with the top of the paper (i.e. above the top of the mould). Place in the deep freeze or the freezing unit of the refrigerator. Remove the paper when about to serve; the ice soufflé now looks like a baked soufflé. The top may be decorated.

Ice soufflés may be moulded in any kind of soufflé mould or in small ramekin or similar dishes suitable for bringing to the table.

France

Iced pineapple

8 persons

1 kg 500	1 pineapple weighing	3¼ lb
¾ l	pineapple ice	1¼ pt

Cut off the top of the pineapple without damaging the leaves and set aside. Remove a cylinder of flesh from the shell in one piece as follows:—insert a knife vertically into the flesh 1 cm (½ in) away from the shell down to within 2 cm (1 in) of the base. Cut out the cylinder of flesh by running the blade of the knife round the pineapple, keeping it the same distance from the shell all the way round. Take another, smaller knife with a narrow blade and insert it into the pineapple 2 cm (1 in) above the base, holding it flat and almost at right angles to the fruit. Give the blade of the knife a half-turn to detach the bottom of the cylinder of pineapple flesh and remove from the shell. Cut 150 g (5¼ oz) of the flesh in small dice and macerate in kirsch in a cool place, being sure to cover the dish. Leave the pineapple shell in a cool place. Make pineapple ice with the remainder of the flesh. At the last minute, mix the diced pineapple with the ice and fill into the shell. Replace the leaves on top and dish on a napkin.

France

Iced soufflé Nicole Seitz

16 persons

	10 egg whites	
500 g	sugar	1 lb 2 oz
approx. 1 kg	ripe bananas	2¼ lb approx.
½ l	whipped cream	¾ pt
8 cl	Grand Marnier	3 measures

Boil the sugar to the soft ball and carefully stir at once into the stiffly whipped egg whites. Cool in a glazed dish, then blend in 500 g (1 lb 1½ oz) raw banana purée which has been passed through a hair or silk sieve. Add the Grand Marnier and fold in the stiffly whipped cream.

Tie a strip of greaseproof paper or thin white cardboard round the edge of the two silver timbales or soufflé moulds about 6 cm (2½ in) higher than the mould. Fill with soufflé mixture and smooth off level with the top of the paper. Freeze for 2–3 hours.

To serve, remove the paper by running a warm knife round the inside edge. Stand each soufflé on a dish covered with a napkin and surround it with crushed ice. Decorate the top with a rosette arrangement of thin slices of banana cut on the slant and flavoured with Grand Marnier. Serve at once.

N.B.—The natural colour of white, yellow or red fruit can only be preserved by the use of a silk or hair sieve when making purée.

France

Iced wild strawberry gâteau

16 portions   Baking time: 20–25 minutes

100 g	butter	4 oz
100 g	sugar	4 oz
	3 eggs	
100 g	flour	4 oz
50 g	cornflour	2 oz
50 g	cocoa powder	2 oz
	1 teaspoon baking powder	

Filling and decoration

$\frac{3}{4}$ l	dairy cream	$1\frac{1}{4}$ pt
225 g	sugar	8 oz
approx. 400 g	wild strawberries	14 oz approx.
	grated chocolate	

Cream the butter with the sugar and beat in the eggs a little at a time. Sieve the flour with the cornflour, baking powder, cocoa powder and a pinch of salt, and fold into the butter/egg/sugar mixture. Bake at 180°C in a greased and floured tin 26 cm (10½ in) in diameter. Whip ½ l (⅞ pt) cream, add 180 g (6¼ oz) sugar and stir in 300 g (10½ oz) crushed wild strawberries. When the gâteau base is cold, split it once and place the bottom half in a tin lined with greaseproof paper. Cover with the strawberry cream filling, place the other half of the gâteau base on top and leave in the deep freeze cabinet until frozen. Whip the rest of the cream and mix with the remaining sugar. Before serving, thinly coat the top and sides of the gâteau with the whipped cream and mask with grated chocolate. Mark into portions and decorate each one with a whirl of whipped cream and 3 wild strawberries.

Germany

Liqueur sherbet

12 persons

1 l	syrup at 18°B	$1\frac{3}{4}$ pt
1 dl	liqueur	4 measures
	(according to preference)	

Proceed as for wine sherbet. The density should be 14 or 15°.

France

Mystery ice

Mix together equal parts of bombe mixture and vanilla parfait mixture. Fill into a large mould or small individual ones. Insert a piece of meringue (or several, depending on size) into the centre until completely hidden. For large moulds, pack well with ice and salt; for small ones, leave in the freezing compartment of the refrigerator for at least 3 hours. Unmould and roll in crushed praline. Freeze again until ready to serve.

France

Neopolitan slices

Fill a brick shaped mould with layers of different sorts of ice placed one on top of the other. Surround with ice and salt, unmould and cut in slices.

Norwegian omelette (baked Alaska)

5 or 6 persons

	1 genoese base	
$\frac{1}{2}$ l	ice cream (of desired flavour)	$\frac{3}{4}$ pt
	3 egg whites	
150 g	caster sugar	5 oz

Place a genoese sponge base at the bottom of a dish, trimming it to the same shape. Prepare Swiss meringue with the egg whites and sugar. Place the ice cream on the genoese sponge, making it as flat as possible. Cover with meringue, setting a little aside. Smooth with a spatula. Decorate the top with the rest of the meringue, using a savoy bag fitted with a star pipe. Set in a very hot oven (180–200°C) with the dish standing on a pan of cold water. Serve as soon as the meringue is lightly coloured.

It is difficult to specify exactly how long this dish should be left in the oven; this depends on the actual oven temperature. In any case, the maximum time is 4 or 5 minutes. A soufflé omelette mixture may be substituted for the meringue.

France

Peaches cardinal

8 persons   8–10 minutes

	4 very large or 8 medium peaches	
$\frac{1}{2}$ l	vanilla flavoured stock syrup	
	at 15°B	$\frac{3}{4}$ pt
$\frac{3}{4}$ l	vanilla ice cream	$1\frac{1}{4}$ pt
350 g	raspberry purée	12 oz

Plunge the peaches in boiling water for a few moments, then peel and cut in half. Poach in vanilla flavoured syrup and allow to cool in the syrup. Fill a serving bowl with the ice cream moulded to a dome shape, drain the peaches well and arrange them in a ring round the ice cream. Cover the fruit and ice cream with kirsch flavoured raspberry purée and sprinkle with a frew fresh flaked almonds.

France

Tea ice cream

4 persons

	2 heaped tablespoons tea	
½ l	boiling water	¾ pt
	3 egg yolks	
120 g	sugar	4 oz
	juice of 1 orange	
	juice of half a lemon	
½ l	whipped cream	¾ pt

Pour the boiling water on the tea leaves and allow to stand for 4–5 minutes. Now whisk the egg yolks and sugar until foamy, strain in the tea and add the orange and lemon juice. Lastly, fold in the stiffly whipped cream. Fill into ice cream cups and freeze. Decorate with whipped cream and glacé cherries to serve.

(Illustration, p. 1095) Germany

Wine sherbet

12 persons

½ l	white wine	¾ pt
	(according to preference)	
½ l	syrup at 22°B	¾ pt
	juice of 1 orange	
	juice of 1 lemon	

Mix the ingredients together and strain through a fine cloth. Measure the density with a saccharometer; it should register 15°. If the reading is higher, add a little cold water; if lower, add a little sugar. Pour into a churn freezer or other container that can be packed with ice and salt. Serve in 'flute' type or Madeira glasses.

(These sherbets are called after the wines used in making them, e.g. Champagne sherbet, Sauternes sherbet, etc.)

France

SMALL CAKES

Alsatians

7–8 minutes in a medium oven

125 g	flour	5 oz
100 g	icing sugar	4 oz
50 g	butter	2 oz
	3 egg yolks	
1 cl	rum	1 dessertspoon
	pinch of salt	

Mix the sugar with the flour and make a bay. Pour in the egg yolks and the rum in which the salt has been dissolved, and add the softened butter. Draw in the flour and sugar and work to a firm paste. Pin out to a thickness of 3 mm ($\frac{1}{8}$ in) and cut into small sticks 8 cm (about 3 in) long. Wash with egg and decorate with tiny lines, using a fork, then bake.

France

Amandines

Yields 25–30   10 minutes in a hot oven

250 g	sweet paste	10 oz
	and	
75 g	ground almonds	3 oz
	and	
100 g	sugar	4 oz
175–200 g	*or* raw marzipan	7–8 oz
25 g	flour	1 oz
40 g	melted butter	1½ oz
	1 egg	
	1 egg yolk	
	1 tablespoon double cream	
3 cl	kirsch	3 dessertspoons
50 g	chopped pistachio nuts	2 oz
	well-boiled apricot purée	
	glacé cherries	

Line small patty pans with the sweet paste and prick the bottom. Mix the sugar and ground almonds together (raw marzipan may be used instead). Blend in the eggs and add the flour, then the melted butter, the cream and the kirsch. Fill the tartlets with the mixture and sprinkle with chopped pistachio nuts. Bake. On removing from the oven, take the tartlets out of the pans and brush with boiling-hot, well reduced apricot purée. Place a quarter of a glacé cherry in the centre of each one.

France

Amerias

7–8 minutes in a medium oven

100 g	ground almonds	4 oz
150 g	sugar	6 oz
50 g	flour	2 oz
	2 eggs	
	pinch of vanilla	
	thick apricot jam	

Make a softish paste with the ground almonds, sugar, flour, eggs and vanilla. Using a savoy bag, pipe out in small rounds on to a greased baking sheet. Bake, then sandwich base to base in pairs with thick apricot jam.

France

Apple barquettes

250 g	sweet paste	8 oz
250 g	thick apple purée	8 oz
	2 apples	
	apricot jam	

Line small, boat shaped tins with the pastry and prick the bottom with a fork. Fill with apple purée and place small triangles of raw apple on top. Bake, remove from the oven and glaze with apricot jam.

France

Apricot tartlets (with fresh fruit)

Yields 20–25   7–8 minutes in a hot oven

250 g	sweet paste	8¾ oz
	12 medium sized apricots	
	apricot jam	

Line patty pans with the sweet paste, prick the bottom with a fork and sprinkle with a little sugar. Place half an apricot in each one and bake. Glaze with reduced apricot jam and decorate with whipped cream.

France

Apricotines I

Yields 20–25   8–10 minutes in a medium oven

> savarin dough
> 6 lightly cooked apricots
> kirsch flavoured white fondant
> kirsch flavoured syrup for soaking

Grease small pomponnette tins and cover the bottom with savarin dough. Place a well drained quarter apricot in the centre of each and cover with savarin dough so that the tin is two-thirds full. Prove, bake, then soak in kirsch flavoured syrup, drain and coat the top with white fondant flavoured with kirsch.

France

Apricotines II

6–8 minutes in a hot oven

> savarin dough
> well boiled apricot purée
> candied apricots
> rum flavoured syrup

Half fill well greased small boat shaped tins with savarin dough and place a small piece of candied apricot in the centre of each. Prove in a warm place until almost level with the top of the tin, then bake. On removing from the oven, soak in rum flavoured syrup. Drain on a wire rack. Brush with hot well boiled apricot purée. Place in small oblong paper cases to serve.

France

Ariane

4–5 minutes in a hot oven

> sweet paste
> raspberry jelly flavoured with kirsch
> very sound fresh raspberries
> spun sugar

Line small boat shaped tins with thinly pinned out sweet paste. Prick the bottom and bake blind. When cold, cover the bottom with a thin layer of raspberry jelly. Fill the pastry cases with fresh raspberries and cover with jelly level with the top edge. Decorate with a few threads of spun sugar at the last minute.

France

Avocats

Yields 25–30	15 minutes in a slow oven	
250 g	sweet paste	10 oz
125 g	ground almonds	5 oz
200 g	sugar	8 oz
	2 egg whites	
	1 tablespoon kirsch	
100 g	citron peel	4 oz
	well boiled apricot purée	

Pin out the sweet paste to a thickness of 3 mm (about $\frac{1}{8}$ in). Cut into ovals with a fluted cutter. Line small, boat shaped tins with the pastry ovals and prick the bottom with a fork. Brush with apricot purée. Make a softish paste with the sugar, almonds and unbeaten egg whites, adding the latter a little at a time. Flavour with the kirsch. Fill the tins with the paste and place a strip of citron peel on top of each one lengthwise. Set aside uncovered for a moment to dry. Dust with icing sugar and bake. Check from time to time while baking, and cover with paper if necessary.

Alternatively, the pastry cases may be baked blind, the remaining procedure being the same, except that the filled tartlets may then be baked off in a very slow oven.

France

Beaumarchais

genoese sponge
walnut buttercream
chopped walnuts
icing sugar

Sandwich 2 sheets of genoese with walnut buttercream. Cut into 3 cm (about 1 in) squares. Spread the sides thinly with buttercream and mask with chopped walnuts. Dust the top with icing sugar and decorate with straight lines or arabesques, using the point of a knife.

France

Benoitons

8–10 minutes in a hot oven

> baba dough
> rum buttercream
> white fondant flavoured with rum

Half fill well greased small boat shaped tins with baba dough. Prove in a warm place until level with the top of the tin, then bake. Soak in rum flavoured syrup and drain on a wire rack. Decorate with a dome of buttercream and refrigerate until firm. Dip into white fondant flavoured with rum (preferably white). Place in small paper cases to serve.

France

Berlin doughnuts

Yields about 15 doughnuts

375 g	flour	15 oz
20 g	yeast	$\frac{3}{4}$ oz
	1 egg	
	2 egg yolks	
65 g	sugar	$2\frac{1}{2}$ oz
75 g	butter	3 oz
	2 ground bitter almonds	
	zest of half a lemon	
	pinch of salt	
approx. 1$\frac{1}{2}$ dl	lukewarm milk	$\frac{1}{4}$ pt approx.
	jam for filling	
	cinnamon sugar	

Sieve the flour into a warmed bowl and make a bay. Disperse the yeast in half the lukewarm milk and pour into the centre. Make into a soft ferment with the surrounding flour. Cover the bowl with a cloth and leave to rise for 20 minutes. Add the egg, egg yolks, lemon zest, sugar, salt, bitter almonds and sufficient milk to make a dough of medium firmness, neither too slack nor too tight. Beat until the dough comes away from the bowl. Add the butter, which should be liquid or very soft, and work again until smooth. Cover with a cloth again and allow to rise, then transfer to a floured board or marble slab, knock back and roll out to a thickness of about 1 cm ($\frac{1}{2}$ in). Cut into rounds, using a cutter 7–8 cm (3 in) in diameter, and moisten the edges of half of them lightly with a little water. Place a small teaspoonful of plum purée or jam in the centre of each moistened round, cover with an unmoistened one and seal the edges well. If necessary, cut again with a slightly smaller round cutter. Place on a floured board or table, cover with a lightly floured cloth and prove. When well risen, fry a few at a time in deep fat at about 180°C until golden brown on both sides. Drain on a cloth, then roll in cinnamon sugar or dust with icing sugar. The top may be coated with water icing if desired.

Raspberry, strawberry or another type of jam may be used as a filling, but plum purée is the most typical.

Germany

Bigourdanes

10 minutes in a slow oven

> Swiss or Italian meringue
> candied chestnut purée
> flavoured with rum

Pipe small oval meringues on to a greased and floured baking sheet and bake. On removing from the oven, make a small hollow in the underside of each one by pressing with the finger. Allow to cool, then assemble in pairs with a small ball of chestnut purée in between. Place in small paper cases to serve.

France

Blidahs

8–10 minutes in a slow oven

100 g	ground almonds	4 oz
100 g	sugar	4 oz
15 g	flour	½ oz
	3 finely grated orange-flavoured lumps of sugar	
	3 egg whites	
	icing sugar	
	carmine	

Whip the egg whites to a very stiff snow. Sift in the flour mixed with the ground almonds, sugar and orange-flavoured sugar, and fold in gently. Colour with a few drops of carmine. Shape into ovals, using a stencil repeatedly moistened with water, on a greased and floured baking sheet. Dust with icing sugar and bake.

France

Bobes

Pastry

375 g	butter	15 oz
500 g	flour	1¼ lb
200 g	icing sugar	8 oz
20 g	cornflour	1 oz
	3 egg yolks	
	vanilla	
	lemon	

Filling

300 g	marzipan	12 oz
5 cl	arrack	2 fl oz
	little stock syrup	
100 g	chopped candied lemon peel	4 oz
100 g	chopped candied orange peel	4 oz

Butter streusel

250 g	flour	10 oz
125 g	butter	5 oz
125 g	icing sugar	5 oz
	pinch of salt	
	little cinnamon	
	egg wash	

To make the pastry, cream the butter and sugar, add the egg yolks and flavouring, then lightly work in the flour and cornflour. Leave in a cool place. Bring the marzipan to a spreading consistency with the arrack and a little stock syrup. Pin out the pastry about 4 mm (⅛ in) thick, cover with the marzipan filling, sprinkle with the candied peel and roll up. The roll should be about 5 cm (2 in) in diameter. Flatten a little and wash with egg. Prepare coarse butter streusel by rubbing the ingredients together until they resemble breadcrumbs and sprinkle the roll with it. Cut into slices 3 cm (1¼ in) thick, arrange on lightly greased baking sheets, spacing the slices at 3 cm (1¼ in) and bake at 180°C.

Germany

Bohemian cakes (Ceske kolace)

10 portions, 2 cakes each   Baking time: 15–20 minutes

500 g	flour	1¼ lb
40 g	yeast	1½ oz

120 g	sugar	5 oz
¼ l	milk	½ pt
100 g	butter	4 oz
10 g	salt	1 heaped teaspoon
	good pinch of mace	
	zest of half a lemon	

Prepare a dough of medium tightness with the above ingredients, preceeding as for Moravian cakes (page 1035), and knead well. Allow to ferment for 30 minutes, knock back, set aside one-third of the dough, pin out the rest and divide into four. Shape each of these portions into a roll and cut into 30 g (1 oz) pieces. Mould round, arrange on baking sheets, spacing the cakes at about 4 cm (1½ in) and prove for 15 minutes. Make a depression in the centre of each cake (preferably using a small weight from the kitchen scales which has first been floured) and fill with curd cheese, poppy seed or plum jam filling. Pin out the rest of the dough, cut into small strips, place two of these on top of each cake in the shape of a cross and press down firmly at the edges. Egg wash and bake in a moderate oven. After removing from the oven, sprinkle with sugar.

Czechoslovakia

Bombe Eva

Pipe out Othello sponge mixture in bulbs, as for chocolate maces (page 986) and bake. Make a cavity in each base by scooping out a little from the underside and fill with strawberry or morello cherry cream. Place a brandy cherry stuffed with fondant in the middle. Sandwich in pairs and refrigerate until firm. Coat very thinly with chocolate, roll in flaked or coarsely cut roasted almonds and sprinkle a little chopped pistachio nut on top. If desired, brush the top lightly with well boiled apricot purée after rolling in almonds and before sprinkling with pistachio nuts.

(Illustration, p. 1106)

Hungary

Bordelaises

12–15 minutes in a medium oven

150 g	puff paste	6 oz
75 g	ground almonds	3 oz
150 g	sugar	6 oz
	4 egg whites whipped to a	
	stiff snow	
	ground vanilla	
	apricot purée	

Pin out the puff paste to a thickness of 3 mm (about ⅛ in). Line tartlet pans with the paste and prick the bottom. Brush inside with well boiled apricot purée. Mix the ground almonds with the sugar and vanilla. Sift into the stiffly whipped egg whites and fold in lightly. Fill the tartlets with the mixture and sprinkle at once with a little granulated sugar. Bake in medium oven.

France

Bourbon sticks

8–10 minutes in a moderate oven

250 g	almonds	10 oz
200 g	sugar	8 oz
	pinch of ground vanilla	
	1 small teaspoon flour	
	1 tablespoon water	
	icing sugar	
	royal icing	

Grind the almonds and sugar together, gradually adding the cold water. Blend in the flour to a firm paste. Pin out ½ cm (¼ in) thick on a marble slab dusted with icing sugar. Cover with a thin layer of royal icing, then cut into sticks 6 cm (about 2 in) long and 1½ cm (½ in) wide. Place on a greased baking sheet. Bake carefully, making sure the royal icing does not take on too much colour.

France

Brazilian boats

Line boat shaped tartlet pans with good sweet paste and bake blind. Fill with a mixture of sponge or butter sponge trimmings, strong coffee, rum and sugar syrup. Cover with mocha buttercream to form a slight dome shape. Mask the edges with a little crushed meringue. Place a sweet coffee bean in the centre.

Switzerland

Brussels sticks

50–60 biscuits

500 g	butter	1¼ lb
200 g	icing sugar	8 oz
350 g	marzipan	14 oz
	6 egg yolks	
600 g	flour	1 lb 8 oz

> zest of half a lemon
> pinch of salt
> apricot jam
> apricot brandy

Cream the butter and sugar and beat in the marzipan well. Add the egg yolks, lemon zest, salt and two-thirds of the flour, then blend in the rest of the flour. Using a No. 4 star tube, pipe out small ribbed sticks on to a lightly greased baking sheet, and bake at 200°C.

After baking, sandwich in pairs with apricot jam flavoured with apricot brandy. Decorate with three lines of couverture and place a little gold leaf in the middle.

(Techniques, p. 158)   Germany

Bruxelloises

7–8 minutes in a hot oven

250 g	choux paste	10 oz
¼ l	pistachio-flavoured confectioner's custard	½ pt approx.
250 g	green pistachio fondant	10 oz
50 g	chopped pistachio nuts	2 oz

Pipe small bulbs of choux paste on to a baking sheet and bake. Allow to cool, fill with the confectioner's custard and dip into fondant. Sprinkle with chopped pistachio nuts. Place in small paper cases to serve.

France

Buns with filling

10 portions, 2 buns each   Baking time: 20–30 minutes

500 g	flour	1¼ lb
30 g	yeast	1 oz
10 g	salt	2 teaspoons
100 g	sugar	4 oz
	2 egg yolks	
120 g	butter	5 oz
	zest of 1 lemon	
	pinch of salt	
50 g	icing sugar for dusting top of buns	2 oz
200 g	butter for brushing sides of buns	8 oz

Prepare a dough of medium tightness from the flour, the yeast dispersed in luke-warm milk, the sugar, salt, lemon zest, egg yolks and butter, then leave to ferment for about 30 minutes. Knock back and pin out on a floured table to a thickness of 1 cm (about ½ in). Cut into 5 cm (2 in) squares, place a little filling in the centre and fold each square over to make a rectangle. Arrange close together on a buttered baking sheet (or preferably in a frying pan) and brush the sides of the buns with soft butter. Prove for 15 minutes and bake in a moderate oven until golden brown. Turn out on to a board, separate the buns and dust the top with icing sugar. These buns are generally served with white coffee.

Fillings

Curd cheese.

250 g	sieved curd cheese	10 oz
90 g	icing sugar	4 oz
	1 egg yolk	
	1 tablespoon rum	
	little lemon zest	
30 g	raisins	1 oz

Beat the above ingredients together well.

Poppy seed.

100 g	ground poppy seed	4 oz
30 g	chocolate	1 oz
2 dl	milk	⅓ pt
50 g	icing sugar	2 oz
5 g	vanilla sugar	1 teaspoon

Cook the poppy seed and chocolate in the milk for 10 minutes, stirring constantly. Allow to cool, then mix well with the sugar.

Plum jam.

250 g	plum jam	10 oz
	little lemon zest	
	good pinch of cinnamon	
	2 tablespoons rum	

Mix the above ingredients together well.

Czechoslovakia

Butterflies

8–10 minutes in a hot oven

puff paste
caster sugar

Proceed as for palmiers to complete six turns. Pin out the pastry 2 mm (about $\frac{1}{10}$ in) thick to make a strip 20 cm (8 in) wide. Cut up into strips 4–5 cm (about 2 in) wide and place one on top of another. Holding the rolling pin lengthwise, press the strips together firmly down the middle to make a deep trough. Now cut across at intervals of 1 cm ($\frac{3}{8}$ in). Pick up each piece by the ends (holding one end in each hand) and twist half way round in opposite directions. Place on a baking sheet splashed with water, leaving room for spreading and bake.

France

Calvados

Yields 15–18   7–8 minutes in a medium oven

250 g	sweet paste	10 oz
	18 small half apricots	
150 g	royal icing	6 oz
	18 stoned fresh cherries	
	or 18 glacé cherries	

Pin out the sweet paste to a thickness of 2–3 mm (about $\frac{1}{10}$ in). Cut out 30 to 36 rounds to fit the patty pans, using a fluted cutter. Line the pans with half the rounds of pastry and prick the bottom. Place half an apricot in each patty pan and cover with a second round of pastry, after making a small hole in the latter with a small cutter or plain pipe. Egg wash and bake. After baking, pour a little royal icing on top and place a fresh or glacé cherry in the hole in the centre.

France

Carolines

8–10 minutes in a hot oven

choux paste
vanilla flavoured whipped cream
white fondant

Pipe tiny eclairs on to a baking sheet and bake. When cold, make a small slit in the side or end and pipe in some whipped cream. Ice with fondant. Place in small paper cases to serve.

France

Cats' tongues (Langues de chat)

4–5 minutes in a hot oven

125 g	flour	5 oz
125 g	vanilla sugar	5 oz
125 g	butter	5 oz
	4 egg whites	

Cream the butter with the sugar and add the unbeaten egg whites a little at a time, then fold in the flour. Pipe out on to a greased and floured baking sheet in finger shapes as thick as a pencil and 4–5 cm (about 2 in) long, leaving room for spreading. Bake until the edges only are a light golden colour. Remove from the baking sheet immediately.

(Illustration, p. 804)

Cerisettes

genoese sponge
kirsch buttercream
apricot jam
kirsch flavoured fondant
glacé cherries
kirsch

Cut out small rounds of genoese, using a plain cutter 3 cm (about 1 in) in diameter. Split once, splash with a little kirsch, then sandwich with kirsch buttercream. Brush with apricot jam, coat with white fondant and top with half a glacé cherry.

France

Chamonix

10–12 minutes in a slow oven

	Swiss or Italian meringue	
250 g	chestnut purée	10 oz
$\frac{1}{4}$ l	Chantilly cream	$\frac{1}{2}$ pt approx.

Pipe small round meringues resembling macaroons on to a greased and floured baking sheet. Bake and allow to cool. Pipe on a border of chestnut purée. Decorate with a small whirl of Chantilly cream in the centre. Place in small paper cases to serve.

France

Chelsea buns

200 g	flour	8 oz
	½ teaspoon sugar	
13 g	yeast	½ oz
110 ml	milk	4 fl oz
	½ teaspoon salt	
13 g	butter	½ oz
	1 egg	
	melted butter	
75 g	dried fruit	3 oz
25 g	cut mixed peel	1 oz
50 g	soft brown sugar	2 oz
	honey	

In a large bowl blend together 50 g (2 oz) of the flour, the sugar, yeast and milk until smooth. Set aside in a warm place until the batter froths—20–30 minutes. Mix in the remaining flour and the salt; rub in the fat and add the egg to give a faintly soft dough that will leave the side of the bowl clean after beating. Turn the dough on to a lightly floured surface and knead until it is smooth and no longer sticky—about 5 minutes. Put the dough into a lightly greased polythene bag, tie loosely and leave to rise at room temperature—about 1–1½ hours. Knead the dough thoroughly and roll to an oblong 30 cm × 23 cm (12 in × 9 in). Brush with melted butter and cover with a mixture of dried fruit, peel and brown sugar. Roll up from the longest side like a Swiss roll, and seal the edge with water. Cut into 9 equal slices and place these cut side down, in the prepared tin. Place in a greased polythene bag and put to rise in a warm place until the dough feels springy—about 30 minutes. Remove the polythene bag and bake just above the centre of a fairly hot oven 190°C (375°F)—for 30–35 minutes. While buns are still warm brush with a wet brush dipped in honey.

Great Britain

Cherry baskets

Yields 40 croustades

350 g	cherry pulp	14 oz
150 g	icing sugar	6 oz
	juice of 1 lemon	
	15 sheets gelatine	
1 l	unsweetened whipped cream	1½ pt
	little cochineal	
approx. 400 g	short pastry	1 lb approx.
	choux pastry	
	baked choux pastry ornaments	
	200 large cherries	
	(canned or poached)	

Pin out the short pastry about 6 mm ($\frac{1}{4}$ in) thick, cut into rounds with a plain cutter about 5 cm (2 in) in diameter and bake lightly.

Lightly grease the outside of plain round patty pans, stand them upside down on a greased baking sheet, place a round of short pastry on each and pipe on an edging of sieved choux pastry. Bake at about 190°C, remove from the pans while still warm, then leave until cold. Dredge with icing sugar and place four well drained cherries in each one.

Soak the gelatine, squeeze dry and dissolve in a bain-marie. Mix the cherry pulp well with the sugar, flavour with the lemon juice, add a little cochineal to colour and stir in the gelatine. When on the point of setting, fold in the whipped cream and fill into the croustades. Decorate each one with a well drained cherry and a choux pastry ornament.

(Techniques, p. 153)   Germany

Cherry pomponettes

10 minutes in a hot oven

> savarin dough
> glacé cherries macerated in kirsch
> pink fondant flavoured with kirsch
> kirsch flavoured baba syrup

Half fill small tartlet tins with savarin dough. Place a well drained glacé cherry in the centre of each one. Prove in a warm place and bake. Soak in syrup and ice with the fondant.

France

Cherry timbalines

Yields 18   7–8 minutes in a hot oven

250 g	sweet paste	10 oz
	confectioner's custard	
	flavoured with vanilla and kirsch	
	fresh cherries	
	red currant jelly	

Line small timbale moulds with the sweet paste and bake blind. When cold, half fill with confectioner's custard and fill up with stoned cherries. Glaze with kirsch flavoured red currant jelly.

France

Chestnut vermicelli meringues

Meringue

250 g	egg whites	10 oz
500 g	sugar	1¼ lb

Chestnut purée

600 g	chestnuts	1½ lb
150 g	sugar	6 oz
	vanilla	
	milk	
30 g	butter	1 oz

Decoration

vanilla flavoured whipped
cream

Whisk the egg whites with 150 g (5¼ oz) sugar, add a further 150 g (5¼ oz) with the machine still running, then fold in the remaining 200 g (7 oz) sugar by hand. Pipe out this meringue in tiny bulbs on to paper and dry slowly at 160°C with the oven door ajar and vents for steam escape.

Using a special vermicelli-press or a savoy bag fitted with a fine tube, pipe out the chestnut purée on to paper in the form of spaghetti. Place in deep freeze until set, then cut out into small disks with a plain cutter. When the meringues are cold, place them in paper cases, pipe on the whipped cream and top each one with a disk of chestnut purée.

To make the purée, peel and skin the chestnuts, cook in vanilla flavoured milk, drain well and rub through a wire sieve. Boil the sugar to the ball degree with 3 cl (3 dessertspoons) of water. While still hot, stir into the chestnut purée together with the butter.

(Techniques, p. 156)   Switzerland

Children's party fancies

About 50 portions   Baking time: 6–7 minutes

Butter sponge

	8 eggs	
	6 egg yolks	
200 g	sugar	8 oz
160 g	flour	6 oz
50 g	melted butter	2 oz

Almond sponge

	12 egg yolks	
	8 egg whites	
400 g	almond paste (equal amounts of almonds and sugar)	1 lb
250 g	sugar	10 oz
150 g	flour	6 oz
3 cl	water	3 dessertspoons

Decoration

buttercream
apricot jelly or jam
marzipan
fondant

Butter sponge. Beat up the eggs, egg yolks and sugar, warming the mixture, then remove from the heat and continue beating until cool. Blend in the flour and lastly the cold melted butter. Spread on a paper lined baking sheet 40 × 25 cm (16 × 10 in) and bake at 220–230°C.

Almond sponge. Beat the yolks with the almond paste, 100 g (3½ oz) sugar and the water. Whip the egg whites to a stiff snow with the rest of the sugar, blend the two mixtures together and fold in the flour. Spread on the same size baking sheet as the butter sponge and bake at the same temperature.

When cold, sandwich the two sheets of sponge together with buttercream of the desired flavour and coat the top very thinly with the same cream. Place a very thin sheet of marzipan on top and leave in a cool place. Proceed in either of the two following ways:

1. Brush the marzipan with very light apricot jelly and cut into portions.

2. Cut into portions, brush with well boiled apricot jam and coat with fondant as desired.

Decorate each fancy with a small marzipan animal, e.g. a hedgehog dipped in couverture with spines made of royal icing.

(Illustration, p. 814)   Switzerland

Chocolate baskets

Bake Othello bases as for chocolate maces, make a cavity in each, sandwich in pairs with chocolate cream, coat with marzipan, refrigerate until firm and cut in half evenly. Dip the lower half in chocolate and pipe on a border of chocolate buttercream, using a savoy bag and star tube. When the buttercream is firm, fill the baskets with cut-up candied fruit and add a handle made of chocolate. To make the handles, pipe chocolate on to greaseproof paper or plexiglass and allow to dry before use.

(Illustration, p. 813)   Hungary

Chocolate bouchées

These are made with the help of special rings. Cut out small disks from a sheet of genoese, allowing two for each bouchée. Place one disk in each ring, splash with rum and fill up the lower part of the ring with chocolate buttercream, using a palette knife. Make a slight hollow in the centre and fill it with small cubes of pineapple flavoured with rum. Cover with a second disk of genoese and leave in a cold place until firm. To turn out, warm the outside of the ring with the hands; the bouchée can then be pushed out. Spread the sides with the same cream and mask with chocolate vermicelli. Coat the top with chocolate fondant, edge with coffee buttercream and place a crystallized violet in the centre.

(Illustration, p. 1101)   Switzerland

Chocolate croquants

8–10 minutes in a slow oven

125 g	ground almonds	5 oz
375 g	sugar	15 oz
	3 unbeaten egg whites	
100 g	chocolate	4 oz

Mix the almonds with the sugar and gradually work in the egg whites. Soften the chocolate and add to the paste, which should be fairly soft. Moisten the hands and shape into fingers 6–8 cm (2½–3 in) long and as thick as a pencil. Roll in sugar and bake on a greased baking sheet.

France

Chocolate délicieuses

Proceed as for coffee délicieuses, but fill the hollows with coffee buttercream and ice with chocolate fondant.

France

Chocolate maces

Yields 18

Othello sponge mixture

	6 egg yolks	
	6 egg whites	
60 g	sugar	2 oz
120 g	flour	5 oz
2 cl	water	2 dessertspoons

Filling

2 dl	dairy cream	⅓ pt
160 g	sugar	6 oz
100 g	cocoa powder	4 oz
300 g	butter	12 oz
	chocolate for coating	

Whip the egg whites to a stiff snow and blend with the yolks, the sugar, a little flour and the water. Fold in the rest of the flour, pipe on to paper to make 36 bulbs and bake at 180°C.

To make the filling, boil up the dairy cream with the sugar and mix with the cocoa powder and half the butter. Allow to cool, then cream with the rest of the butter.

Sandwich the bases in pairs with this cream. Decorate the top with small spikes of cold filling cream, leave until set, then pour liquid chocolate over or impale each one on a fork and dip into the chocolate (the latter method requires less chocolate).

(Illustration, p. 813)   Hungary

Chocolate meringue biscuits

	10 egg whites	
1 kg	sugar	2¼ lb
½ l	water	¾ pt
150 g	block cocoa	6 oz
	little stock syrup	

Melt the block cocoa in a bain-marie and work to a thick paste with a little stock syrup. Boil the sugar and water to the feather degree and slowly pour into the whites which have been whipped to a stiff snow. When cold, blend in the cocoa paste. Using a star tube, pipe out in small 's' shapes on to waxed baking sheets, place in a warm cupboard for 2 hours to dry, then bake at 160°C for about 40 minutes. If correctly baked, a small projection will have formed at the base of each biscuit.

Germany

Chocolate parfaits

Bake small round sable biscuits, allow to cool, then sandwich in pairs with chocolate buttercream. Spread the tops with the same buttercream, leave until firm, then dip into fairly liquid couverture. Pipe a zig-zag design on top with couverture and sprinkle a little chopped pistachio nut on top.

France

Chocolate rosettes

Othello bases

200 g	8 egg yolks	8 oz
300 g	12 egg whites	12 oz
200 g	sugar	8 oz
150 g	flour	6 oz
150 g	cornflour	6 oz
	grated zest of half a lemon	

Coating

couverture

Filling

vanilla confectioner's custard

Decoration

chocolate buttercream
chocolate or cocoa powder

Whisk the egg yolks with half the sugar. Whisk the egg whites with the other half to a stiff snow, blend one-third of this into the yolk/sugar sponge, stir in the flour and cornflour and lastly fold in the rest of the egg white/sugar snow. Pipe bulbs of the mixture on to paper or special Othello baking sheets and bake at 220–230°C. When cold, dip each base in couverture and allow to set.

Place the Othello bases in paper cases with the cavity uppermost. Fill the cavities with vanilla confectioner's custard. Decorate with a rosette of chocolate buttercream and dust with chocolate or cocoa powder.

Switzerland

Chocolatines I

genoese sponge
chocolate buttercream
roasted chopped almonds

Split a sheet of genoese once and sandwich with chocolate buttercream. Spread the top with the same buttercream and cut into 2 or 3 cm (about 1 in) squares. Coat the sides with the same buttercream and mask with roasted chopped almonds. Decorate the top, using a savoy bag filled with buttercream. Place in small paper cases to serve.

France

Chocolatines II

chocolate sponge
vanilla buttercream
fresh cream
chocolate fondant

Split the chocolate sponge twice and sandwich with a mixture of buttercream and fresh cream (1 tablespoon fresh cream to 250 g (8¾ oz) buttercream). The finished height should not exceed 4 cm (about 1½ in). Coat the top with chocolate fondant. Cut into diamonds, rounds or squares and place in small paper cases to serve.

France

Choux à la crême

Yields 18–20   10–12 minutes in a medium oven

250 g	choux paste	8 oz
¼ l	confectioner's custard flavoured with liqueur	½ pt approx.
250 g	fondant	8 oz

Pipe out bulbs of choux paste the size of a walnut on to a greased baking sheet, using a savoy bag fitted with a plain pipe. Wash with egg, then bake. After baking, leave in the oven for a moment to dry with the door open, then remove and allow to cool. Make a slit in the side of each chou and fill with a little confectioner's custard flavoured with liqueur. Coat the top with coloured fondant, choosing a colour that matches the liqueur used for flavouring, or two different colours. Chocolate granules, silver balls, etc. may be used for final decoration.

(Illustration, p. 804) France

Choux grillés

7–8 minutes in a hot oven

250 g	choux paste	10 oz
100 g	chopped almonds	4 oz
400 g	praline buttercream	1 lb

Pipe very small bulbs of choux paste on to a baking sheet and brush with beaten egg. Sprinkle the tops with chopped almonds and granulated sugar. Bake, then cool on a wire rack. Make a slit three-quarters of the way up and pipe in a little buttercream. Place in small paper cases to serve.

France

Choux à la Necker

Yields 15–20   15 minutes in a slow oven

125 g	choux paste	5 oz
125 g	vanilla flavoured confectioner's custard	5 oz
	caster sugar	

Mix the choux paste and confectioner's custard together. Pipe out bulbs of the mixture the size of a walnut on to a greased baking sheet, using a savoy bag fitted with a plain pipe. Brush over with beaten egg and sprinkle liberally with sugar. Wait until the sugar has dissolved, then bake. Serve without further decoration.

France

Ciboulettes

8–10 minutes in a hot oven

250 g	choux paste	10 oz
500 g	chestnut purée flavoured	
	with rum	1¼ lb
250 g	chocolate fondant	10 oz
25 g	chopped pistachio nuts	1 oz

Proceed as for king bouchées (see recipe, page 985), but fill with chestnut purée and coat with chocolate fondant. Sprinkle a few chopped pistachio nuts on top. Place in small paper cases to serve.

France

Cigarettes

200 g	vanilla sugar	7 oz
	4 egg whites	
100 g	butter	3½ oz
90 g	flour	3 oz

Whisk the egg whites to a stiff snow and lightly fold in the sugar, sieved flour and finally the warm melted butter. Test the mixture by baking off one or two small biscuits on a greased and floured baking sheet. If the biscuit breaks too easily, add a little sieved flour. If too solid, add a little more melted butter. When baked roll up cigarette fashion.

Clairette

well reduced pear purée flavoured
    with maraschino
swiss meringue
genoese sponge

To make the pear purée, peel and core ripe, juicy pears and cook under cover with a little butter and sugar in a moderate oven. Rub through a sieve and boil to thicken if necessary. Flavour with maraschino. Cut the genoese into small pear shapes or ovals 4 cm (about 1½ in) long. Indent the top of each one slightly, splash with maraschino and fill up with the pear purée. Smooth over and cover with a thin layer of meringue. Place in a very slow oven for 3–4 minutes. Insert a small strip or triangle of angelica into one end to represent the stalk.

France

Clémences

7–8 minutes in a hot oven

> berrichon paste
> coffee buttercream
> coffee fondant
> roasted almonds

Pipe out fingers of berrichon paste, using a savoy bag. Bake and allow to cool. Spread with coffee buttercream and refrigerate until firm. Coat with coffee fondant and decorate the centre with roasted chopped almonds.

France

Coconut rocks

125 g	desiccated coconut	5 oz
100 g	sugar	4 oz
	1 egg (separated)	

Beat the egg yolk and sugar with a spatula and add the coconut. Whip the egg white to a stiff snow. Add a little of this to the egg yolk/sugar/coconut mixture to lighten it, then fold in the remainder lightly. Desposit in small rough heaps on a greased baking sheet and bake.

France

Coconut tongues

Pipe out a cats' tongue biscuit mixture in small fingers on to greased and floured baking sheets and sprinkle liberally with fine coconut. Bake, allow to cool and sandwich together with ganache.

France

Coffee délicieuses

7–8 minutes in a hot oven

> berrichon paste
> ganache
> coffee fondant

Pipe out small ovals of paste from a savoy bag and bake. On removing from the oven, press the thumb into the top to make a small hollow. When cold, fill the hollow with ganache. Place in the refrigerator until firm. Ice with coffee fondant and fix a silver ball in the centre.

France

Coffee marquises

10 minutes in a medium oven

> genoese sponge mixture
> coffee flavoured confectioner's custard
> coffee fondant

Three-quarters fill small boat shaped tins with genoese sponge mixture and bake. After baking, cut a piece of sponge out of the top of each one to leave a cone shaped hollow and fill with coffee flavoured confectioner's custard. Put the tops back in place after trimming their base. Ice with fondant and top with a chocolate coffee bean.

France

Coffee sticks

7–8 minutes in a very moderate oven

125 g	ground almonds	5 oz
125 g	sugar	5 oz
	2 egg whites	
50 g	praline	2 oz
	coffee essence	
	royal icing	

Add the egg whites a little at a time to the ground almonds and mix well. Gradually work in the sugar and a few drops of coffee essence. Now add the praline. Pin out to a thickness of $\frac{1}{2}$ cm ($\frac{1}{4}$ in) on a marble slab dusted with icing sugar. Spread with a thin layer of royal icing. Cut into small sticks 8 cm by $1\frac{1}{2}$–2 cm (3 in by about $\frac{3}{4}$ in). Bake on a greased and floured baking sheet.

France

Condés

10 minutes in a hot oven

| 250 g | puff paste | 10 oz |

▲ Asparagus mousse timbale, p. 758
▼ Ham mousse en chaud-froid

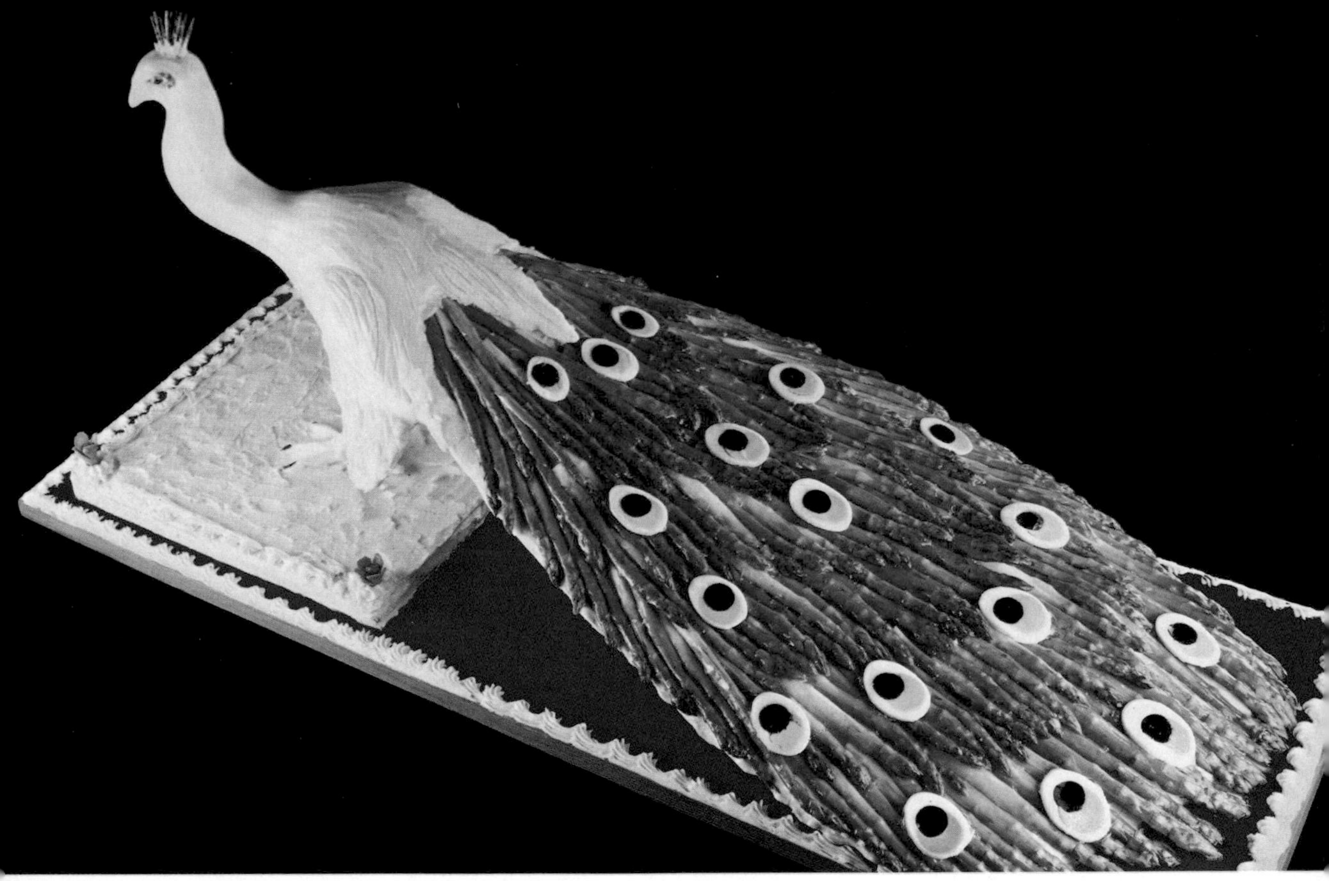

994 ▲ A margarine-sculptured peacock, covered with cold asparagus tips, decorated with egg and truffles
▼ Chicory salad, fennel salad, mixed salad, mushroom salad, pp. 798, 817, 821–2

royal icing
chopped almonds
icing sugar

Pin out the puff paste into a strip 5 cm (2 in) wide and 3–4 mm (about ⅛ in) thick. Cover with royal icing mixed with chopped almonds (1 part almonds to 5 parts icing). Dust with icing sugar. Cut the strip in 2 cm (⅘ in) slices with a knife dipped in water or flour. Place on a lightly moistened baking sheet, cover with a sheet of paper and bake.

France

Conversation tartlets

15–20 minutes in a slow oven

short paste
confectioner's custard
royal icing

Line patty pans with short paste. Fill with cold confectioner's custard, mixed with a small amount of ground almonds if desired. Moisten the edge of each pastry case and place a thin round of short paste on top, pressing it down all round. Using a spatula, spread with a thin layer of royal icing. Place four strips of short paste 1 mm wide (about 1/20 in) on top of each to form a diamond pattern. Cover with paper while baking if necesssary.

France

Cream buns

Prepare in the same way as choux à la crême (see recipe, page 988). Fill with Chantilly cream and dust with icing sugar.

France

Cream horns

10–12 minutes in a hot oven

puff paste
Chantilly cream

Pin out puff paste to a thickness of 2 mm (about 1/10 in). Cut into long, even strips ½ cm (¼ in) wide. Roll each strip round a cream horn tin in a spiral, starting at the

30

pointed end of the tin (if the tins are large, only cover half their length). Place on a baking sheet, brush over with beaten egg and bake. When cold, fill with Chantilly cream.

France

Crumpets

10–12 crumpets

500 g	strong flour	1 lb 2 oz
5 dl	milk	¾ pt
30 g	butter	1 oz
30 g	yeast	1 oz
	pinch of salt and sugar	

Warm the milk with the butter, salt and sugar to 37°C. Add the yeast and mix into the flour to form a smooth paste. Allow to rise for half an hour. Place 10 cm (4 in) greased rings on a hot greased griddle plate and half fill with the batter. Cook until well holed and beginning to bubble, then turn and cook on the other side. The crumpets should be set, but not coloured.

When cold, toast and serve hot.

Great Britain

Curd cheese pastries

15–16 pastries   Baking time: 35 minutes

Danish pastry

250 g	flour	10 oz
40 g	sugar	1½ oz
50 g	butter	2 oz
10 g	yeast	⅓ oz
	1 egg	
	1 egg yolk	
⅛ l	milk	¼ pt
5 g	salt	1 teaspoon
	zest of half a lemon	
100 g	butter (for rolling in)	4 oz

Curd cheese filling

40 g	butter	1½ oz
80 g	icing sugar	3 oz

20 g	cornflour	1 oz
200 g	curd cheese, sieved	8 oz
	juice and zest of half a lemon	
	pinch of salt	
	little vanilla	
50 g	sultanas	2 oz
	beaten egg	

Dissolve the sugar in the cold milk and disperse the yeast in it. Add the flour, butter, egg and extra yolk, salt and lemon zest and work to a smooth dough. Allow to rest for 10–15 minutes and pin out evenly. Cover evenly with the butter for rolling in and fold into three as when making puff pastry. Allow to rest for a further 10 minutes and fold in three again.

To make the filling, cream the butter with the sugar, add the curd cheese, cornflour, salt, vanilla, lemon juice and zest and the sultanas and mix well. Pin out the pastry evenly and cut in 10 cm (4 in) squares. Place equal amounts of filling on each one and brush the ends with egg. Fold the four corners up towards the middle, place a small square of pastry in the centre of the join, brush with egg and bake at 190°C.

Austria

Custard rings

10 portions, 2 rings each   Baking time: about 10 minutes

100 g	butter	4 oz
¼ l	milk	½ pt
250 g	flour	10 oz
	7 eggs	
	pinch of salt	
	custard as for millefeuille	
	slices (see recipe, page 1033)	
	icing sugar or fondant	

Place the butter, milk and salt in a pan and bring to the boil. Add the sieved flour all at once and cook while stirring until the paste leaves the sides of the pan without sticking. Allow to cool a little, then beat in the eggs one at a time. Transfer the paste to a savoy bag fitted with a star tube and pipe out rings 5 cm (2 in) in diameter and 1 cm (about ½ in) high on to a greased baking sheet. Bake in a hot oven, leave until cold, split and sandwich with the custard. Dust with icing sugar or coat the top thinly with fondant.

Czechoslovakia

Cyranos

8–10 minutes in a medium oven

150 g	almonds	6 oz
150 g	sugar	6 oz
	1 egg white	
	1 spoon rum	
	1 spoon flour	
½ dl	royal icing	2 fl oz
100 g	ground almonds	4 oz

Grind the almonds with the sugar, gradually adding the rum and then three-quarters of the egg white. Mix with the flour to a firm but moist paste. If it is too dry, add the rest of the egg white. Grease small boat shaped tins and dust with ground almonds. Fill up to the top with the paste and cover with a thin layer of royal icing. Bake with low top heat to prevent caramelisation of the royal icing. On removing from the oven, loosen with the point of a knife to turn out. Run the knife round the edge of the tins if necessary.

France

Darioles

Yields 10–15   15 minutes in a slow oven

250 g	short paste	10 oz
30 g	flour	1 oz
75 g	sugar	3 oz
	2 eggs	
2 dl	milk	⅓ pt
25 g	butter	1 oz
	finely chopped zest of 1 orange	

Line small baba moulds with short paste. Whisk the eggs and sugar together. Add the flour, orange zest and milk (cold). Whisk again and blend in the cold melted butter. Fill the moulds with the mixture (which is called 'dariole cream') and bake.

Other types of moulds may be used, providing they are rather deep.

France

Dartois

Yields 15–20   15–18 minutes in a hot oven

250 g	puff paste	10 oz
	thick jam	
	icing sugar	

Pin out the puff paste into long strips 6 cm (about 2½ in) wide and 3–4 mm (about ⅛ in) thick. Lay 2 strips on a moistened baking sheet and spread with jam, leaving the edges uncovered. Moisten the edges and cover with 2 further strips of pastry, pressing the sides down a little to seal. Trim and notch the edges with a knife. Wash with egg, score the top with a fork or the point of a knife to decorate, then bake. Shortly before they are baked off, dust with icing sugar. When cold, cut in 2 cm (¾ in) slices.

France

Dauphines

7–8 minutes in a medium oven

250 g	puff paste	10 oz
175 g	choux paste	7 oz
	red currant jelly	

Pin out the puff paste to a thickness of 3 mm (⅛ in). Cut out small rounds with a fluted cutter 3–4 cm (1–1½ in) in diameter. Pipe a ring of choux paste bulbs round the edge of each one, using a savoy bag fitted with a small plain pipe. Place on a baking sheet splashed with water, prick the centre and bake. When cold, fill the centre with red currant jelly.

France

Detitagnan

Cover small oval soft macaroons with glazed chestnut purée and coat with chocolate fondant.

France

Diplomates I

Yields 20–25   12–15 minutes in a slow oven

250 g	short paste	10 oz
125 g	macerated diced candied fruit	5 oz

75 g	sugar	3 oz
	2 eggs	
30 g	flour	1 oz
2 dl	milk	⅓ pt
	finely chopped zest of 1 orange	
25 g	butter	1 oz
	rum fondant	

Line rather deep tartlet tins with short paste and prick the bottom. Cover with a little well drained candied fruit. Prepare dariole cream (see darioles) and fill into the tartlets. Bake, allow to cool and coat with rum fondant.

France

Diplomates II

3–4 minutes in a hot oven

125 g	ground almonds	5 oz
150 g	sugar	6 oz
	1 large egg white	
	pinch of vanilla	
	well boiled apricot purée	

Gradually work the egg white into the almonds and sugar with a spatula to make a softish paste and add the vanilla. Pipe on to greaseproof paper in small fingers 4–5 cm (about 2 in) long, using a savoy bag fitted with a small plain pipe. Bake. On removing from the oven, sandwich in pairs with thick apricot purée.

France

Dobos slices

(Recipe of the Budapest confectioner Vorosmarty)

Sponge

360 g	eggs	15 oz
120 g	sugar	5 oz
120 g	flour	5 oz

Buttercream filling

170 g	butter	7 oz
30 g	cocoa butter	1 oz
30 g	cocoa	1 oz
200 g	sugar	8 oz
240 g	eggs	10 oz

Caramel

| 200 g | sugar | 8 oz |

Decoration

sponge crumbs or chocolate
vermicelli

Whisk the egg yolks and half the sugar to a sponge, whip the whites and the rest of the sugar to a stiff snow and blend the two together, then fold in the flour. Spread about 5 mm ($\frac{1}{4}$ in) thick on a buttered and floured baking sheet. Bake at 200°C, taking care that the sponge does not become dry.

To make the filling, melt the butter and cocoa butter, add the cocoa and stir well. Whisk the eggs and sugar over a little heat, allow to cool and blend with the butter/cocoa mixture.

Cut the sheet of sponge evenly into six strips. Set aside one for the top. Spread the remaining five with buttercream filling and assemble. Boil the sugar to the caramel degree and spread very quickly on the sixth strip of sponge. Mark into portions with a buttered knife, cut through at once and place on the assembled slices. Coat the edges lightly with buttercream and mask with sponge crumbs or chocolate vermicelli.

(Illustration, p. 1101) Hungary

Dobos Torte

Use the same ingredients and method as above recipe—Dobos Slices—but bake in 5 equal sized circles. Then proceed as shown in Techniques, p. 152.

Doughnuts Bohemian Forest style

10 portions, 4–5 doughnuts each   Cooking time: about 10 minutes

1 kg	flour	2$\frac{1}{2}$ lb
200 g	butter	8 oz
40 g	yeast	1$\frac{1}{2}$ oz
150 g	caster sugar	6 oz
	zest of 1 lemon	
15 g	salt	$\frac{1}{2}$ oz
4 dl	milk	$\frac{2}{3}$ pt
300 g	plum jam	12 oz
300 g	hard cottage cheese	12 oz
3 dl	sweetened whipped cream	$\frac{1}{2}$ pt
	oil for frying	

Make a ferment with about 100 g (3½ oz) flour, the yeast, a little sugar and a little lukewarm milk and leave to rise for 30 minutes. Sieve the rest of the flour into a bowl, make a bay, add the butter, salt and lemon zest, the rest of the sugar and, lastly, the ferment and work to a smooth dough with the remaining milk. Leave to rise for about 50 minutes, knock back and pin out to 15 mm (about ½ in) thick on a floured table or marble slab. Cut into rounds with a 6–8 cm (2½ or 3 in) cutter and prove. Make a depression in the centre of each with the thumb and place in hot oil with this side underneath. Fry until the underside is golden brown, then turn and fry on the other side. Remove from the pan, drain well and fill the hollows with plum jam. Sprinkle the filling with grated cottage cheese and decorate with whipped cream.

Czechoslovakia

Duchesses I

560 g	egg whites	1 lb 2 oz
500 g	caster sugar	1 lb
375 g	hazelnuts	12 oz
100 g	flour	3½ oz

Whisk the egg whites with half the sugar until stiff. Grind the hazelnuts and the rest of the sugar and add the flour.

Lightly mix all the ingredients with a spatula. Pipe out small sticks on to a greased baking sheet, sprinkle with finely grated hazelnuts and bake in a slow oven. Sandwich the biscuits together with praline flavoured ganache.

France

Duchesses II

Proceed as for praline duchesses, but omit the ground hazelnuts and replace by ground almonds. Use a little more vanilla and sandwich with well boiled apricot purée.

France

Easter mammi

Baking time: 3 hours

1 kg	rye flour	2¼ lb
250 g	rye malt	9 oz
	6 tablespoons thinly pared orange rind, finely chopped	
approx. 8 dl	water	1⅓ pt
	salt	

Mix together half the rye flour, a quarter of the malt, the orange rind, 6–7 g (about ¼ oz) salt and 2 dl (⅓ pt) warm water. Cover with a thick layer of rye flour and malt and leave in a warm place for an hour. Mix thoroughly, add another 2 dl (⅓ pt) warm water and again sprinkle on a surface layer of flour and malt, then cover with a cloth and leave in a warm place (e.g. by the open oven door) for a further hour. Proceed in the same way until all the flour, malt and water have been used up; the last part of the water is added boiling hot. Bring the mixture to the boil while stirring constantly and beat with a wire whisk or in the mixer until cold. Fill into small birch-bark bowls and bake in a slow oven (150°C). Serve cold with sugar and unwhipped cream.

Finland

Fanchonnettes

8–10 minutes in a hot oven, and a few moments in a slow oven

> sweet paste
> confectioner's custard
> swiss meringue
> red currant jelly

Line patty pans with sweet paste, place a teaspoonful of confectioner's custard in each and bake. On removing from the oven, decorate with meringue, leaving a small cavity in the centre. Dust with icing sugar and place in a slow oven for a few moments until the meringue is crisp. Transfer to a wire rack and fill the cavity in the centre with a little red currant jelly. Serve in small paper cases.

France

Fedoras

7–8 minutes in a slow oven

100 g	ground almonds	4 oz
275 g	sugar	11 oz
	good pinch of vanilla	
	5 egg whites	
150 g	chopped almonds	6 oz
	carmine	

Mix the ground almonds with the sugar and vanilla and sift into the egg whites whipped to a stiff snow. Fold in gently with a spatula. Colour with a few drops of carmine. Pipe out in small rounds on to a greased and floured baking sheet. Sprinkle with chopped almonds and dust with icing sugar. Check while baking to make sure the biscuits remain soft.

France

Festival cakes

1 kg	flour	2½ lb
150 g	melted butter	6 oz
150 g	sugar	6 oz
	2 eggs	
50 g	yeast	2 oz
¼ l	milk	½ pt
	salt	

Make a ferment with part of the flour, the yeast and a little lukewarm milk. Sieve the rest of the flour on to a table, make a bay, place the sugar, the eggs, a little salt and the ferment in the centre and work to a dough of medium tightness with the melted butter and the rest of the milk. Leave to rise, then knock back, pin out, weigh into about 50 g (1¾ oz) pieces and mould into small round cakes. Arrange on a baking sheet, spaced at 3 cm (1¼ in), prove for a short time, then press down in the centre to make a small hollow. Fill this with curd cheese, poppy seed, plum jam or fruit filling, egg wash or brush with melted butter the edges and bake at about 200°C.

Fillings

Curd cheese.

150 g	curd cheese	6 oz
	1 egg yolk	
30 g	sugar	1 oz

Beat the above ingredients together well.

Poppy seed.

150 g	ground poppy seeds	6 oz
30 g	sugar	1 oz
	zest of half a lemon	
1 dl	milk	3 fl oz

Mix the above ingredients together and bring to the boil. Cool before use.

Plum jam.

Flavour plum jam with a little lemon zest, also rum if desired. Any other type of jam may be used instead.

Fruit.

150 g	apples or pears, finely grated	6 oz
30 g	sugar	1 oz
	pinch of cinnamon	
	pinch of ground cloves	

Mix the above ingredients together well.

Czechoslovakia

Filled Florentines

560 g	butter	1 lb 6 oz
560 g	sugar	1 lb 6 oz
180 g	honey	7 oz
2 dl	dairy cream	⅓ pt
200 g	chopped almonds	8 oz
180 g	strip almonds	7 oz
90 g	chopped candied lemon peel	4 oz
135 g	finely chopped candied orange peel	5 oz
350 g	chopped red glacé cherries	14 oz
	3 egg whites	
50 g	flour	2 oz
280 g	flaked almonds	11 oz

Punch marzipan

500 g	marzipan	1 lb 2 oz
1 dl	Swedish punch	3 fl oz
	little stock syrup	
	couverture	

Bring the cream, butter and honey to the boil, add the sugar, almonds, peel and cherries, then the egg whites and lastly the flour. Bake Florentines 5 cm (2 in) in diameter with this mixture. Bring the marzipan to a spreading consistency with the Swedish punch and a little stock syrup. Sandwich the Florentines in pairs with punch marzipan, placing the undersides inside, and decorate with a cross made of couverture.

Germany

Finger biscuits

25–30

120 g	caster sugar	4¼ oz
	5 yolks of egg	
	4 whites of egg	
120 g	flour	4¼ oz

Whisk the yolks and sugar until creamy. Whisk the white until stiff. Fold a quarter of the white into the yolk mixture. Add small amounts of white and flour alternately using a metal spoon to fold it in. Place the mixture into a piping bag with 1 cm (½ in) tube. Pipe on to greaseproof paper on a tray, approx. 9 cm (3½ in) long. Sprinkle with caster sugar, remove surplus. Bake at 200°C for 8–10 minutes. Remove from the paper by turning it upside down and sprinkling with cold water.

Great Britain

Flaky biscuits

8–10 minutes in a hot oven

puff paste
chopped pistachio nuts
granulated sugar

Pin out the puff paste to a thickness of 3 mm (⅛ in) and cut out with a 4–5 cm (1½–2 in) round cutter or a 4 cm (1½ in) square one. Place on a baking sheet splashed with water, wash with egg, mark a criss-cross pattern on top with a fork and sprinkle with a mixture of granulated sugar and chopped pistachio nuts. Bake.

France

Flemish sticks

10 minutes in a slow oven

100 g	flour	4 oz
125 g	sugar	5 oz
50 g	ground almonds	2 oz
	1 egg	
	1 egg yolk	
40 g	chopped almonds	1½ oz
	ground vanilla	

Mix the sugar and eggs together and whisk vigorously to a stiff sponge. Add the flour, ground almonds and vanilla. Using a savoy bag and plain tube, pipe out on a greased baking sheet in sticks 5 cm (2 in) long, the thickness of the little finger. Sprinkle with chopped almonds and dust with icing sugar, then bake.

France

Florentines I

150 g	butter	6 oz
150 g	sugar	6 oz
45 g	honey	2 oz
5 cl	dairy cream	2 fl oz
50 g	flaked almonds	2 oz
50 g	nibbed almonds	2 oz
50 g	strip almonds	2 oz
35 g	candied orange peel, chopped	1½ oz
25 g	candied lemon peel, chopped	1 oz
20 g	flour	1 oz
	half a vanilla pod	
	12–13 red glacé cherries	
	plain couverture	

Put the butter, sugar, honey and cream into a pan and cook over a fire to 107°C. Add all the almonds, the orange and lemon peel, the flour and the scraped vanilla and continue cooking until the mixture leaves the sides of the pan. Deposit in 25 small heaps on a waxed baking sheet and bake in two stages, shaping the florentines with a round cutter and topping each with half a glacé cherry after the first stage. Allow to cool, then coat the undersides with couverture, leave until set, coat again with couverture and make a wavy design with a fork.

(Illustration, p. 804) France

Florentines II

250 g	sugar	10 oz
150 g	butter	6 oz
2½ dl	dairy cream	½ pt
500 g	flaked almonds	1¼ lb
150 g	candied fruit	6 oz
75 g	glucose	3 oz
75 g	honey	3 oz

Place the sugar, butter, honey and glucose in a pan and bring to the boil. Stir in the almonds and candied fruit. Transfer to an oiled baking sheet, spread evenly with the hands which have been rubbed with oil, then smooth off with an oiled spatula. Bake in a slow oven. Chill well, then cut into rounds with a 3 cm (1¼ in) cutter. Spread thinly with tempered milk or plain couverture, leave to set, recoat with couverture and mark with a comb scraper.

Switzerland

Florentines III

15–18 minutes

> Genoa almond cake mixture
> almond paste
> well boiled apricot purée
> roasted chopped almonds

Bake the Genoa almond cake mixture in small round tins or patty pans. Remove from the tins and decorate the centre of each with a rosette of almond paste. Flash in a hot oven. Brush with boiling hot, well reduced apricot purée to glaze. Mask the edges with roasted chopped almonds.

France

Fondant cubes

Sponge

500 g	eggs	1¼ lb
350 g	sugar	14 oz
350 g	flour	14 oz
	grated zest of half a lemon	

Filling

> mocha buttercream

Coating

> coffee coloured and flavoured fondant

Decoration

> crushed croquant, chocolate coffee beans

Mix the eggs and sugar together, warm gently and whip until frothy. Fold in the flour and lemon zest. Spread on to a greased and floured baking sheet 30 cm × 60 cm (12 in × 24 in). Bake at 200–230°C, cool and split twice. Sandwich with mocha buttercream, refrigerate until firm, then coat with coffee coloured and flavoured fondant. When set, cut into even sized cubes. With the aid of a fork, coat the sides of each cube with mocha buttercream and mask them with crushed croquant by rolling or sprinkling, then remove the fork. Decorate with a small rosette of mocha buttercream and a chocolate coffee bean.

Switzerland

Fondants

7–8 minutes in a medium oven

250 g	flour	10 oz
200 g	butter	8 oz
75 g	sugar	3 oz
75 g	ground almonds	3 oz
	pinch of ground vanilla	
	red currant jelly	
	icing sugar	

Prepare in the same way as sable pastry. Allow to rest for 2 or 3 hours. Pin out to a thickness of 2 mm (about $\frac{1}{10}$ in). Using a pastry wheel, cut into rectangles 6–8 cm by 2 cm (about 3 in by $\frac{3}{4}$ in). Bake, then sandwich in pairs with red currant jelly and dust with icing sugar.

France

Fruit buns

15 buns   Baking time: 15 minutes

500 g	flour	1¼ lb
60 g	butter	2 oz
30 g	yeast	1 oz
60 g	sugar	2 oz
¼ l	milk	½ pt
	1 egg	
120 g	mixed fruit (raisins, currants, sultanas, peel)	5 oz
5 g	mixed spice	1 teaspoon
	salt	

Sieve the flour, spice and a pinch of salt into a basin, rub in the butter. Disperse the yeast and dissolve the sugar in the milk at 35°C, add the beaten egg. Add to the flour, mix in gradually and work to a smooth dough, kneading thoroughly. Cover the basin with a floured cloth and allow to rise until doubled in size. Mix in the fruit, divide into equal pieces and mould round. Place on greased baking sheets, prove until doubled in size and bake at about 220°C. Remove from the oven and brush at once with bun wash. To make the bun wash, boil together equal quantities of milk and sugar to a syrupy consistency.

Great Britain

Fruit half moons

Baking time: about 40 minutes

Pastry

1 kg 500	flour	3¼ lb
1 kg	butter	2½ lb
500 g	icing sugar	1¼ lb
50 g	cornflour	2 oz
	3 egg yolks	
	pinch of salt	

Filling

1 kg	marzipan	2½ lb
1¼ dl	arrack	¼ pt
	little stock syrup	
1 kg 500	mixed chopped candied fruit	3½ lb

Egg wash

	2 egg yolks	
20 g	honey	1 oz

Make the sweet paste and pin out half of it to a thickness of about 4 mm (⅙ in). Bring the marzipan to a spreading consistency with the arrack and a little stock syrup, then spread on the rolled out paste. Sprinkle with the chopped fruit. Pin out the rest of the sweet paste to the same size, refrigerate, then place on top of the filling. Brush with the egg yolks whisked with the honey and mark with a decorating comb. Cut into half moons of the desired size and bake at 180°C.

Germany

Galettes

7–8 minutes in a hot oven

125 g	flour	5 oz
50 g	butter	2 oz
60 g	sugar	2 oz
40 g	ground almonds	1½ oz
	2 egg yolks	
	pinch of salt	

Mix the sugar, flour and ground almonds together, make a well in the centre and pour in the egg yolks. Dissolve the salt in these, then add the slightly softened butter. Work to a very smooth paste. Wrap in a damp cloth and allow to rest for 2 hours in a cool place. Pin out to a thickness of 3 mm ($\frac{1}{8}$ in). Cut out with a round cutter 3 or 4 cm (about $1\frac{1}{2}$ in) in diameter. Place on a greased baking sheet. Brush with beaten egg and mark lines on top with a fork to make a criss-cross pattern. Bake.

France

Glazed matchsticks

10 minutes in a medium oven

250 g	puff paste	10 oz
100 g	icing sugar	4 oz
	half a teaspoon cornflour	
	1 egg white	

Pin out the puff paste 3 mm ($\frac{1}{8}$ in) thick to make a strip 10 or 12 cm (4 or 5 in) wide. Mix the icing sugar, cornflour and a little egg white to a paste of the same consistency as royal icing; it should fall like a ribbon from the spatula. Spread on to the puff paste with a metal spatula dipped in water from time to time. Cut into small fingers 2 cm ($\frac{3}{4}$ in) wide with a knife and bake on a baking sheet splashed with water.

France

Grand Marnier parfaits

Proceed as for chocolate bouchées, but splash with Grand Marnier and fill with buttercream containing chopped candied orange peel and flavoured with Grand Marnier. Dip into pale green fondant and decorate with a Grand Marnier chocolate disk.

(Illustration, p. 1101) Switzerland

Guignettes

6–8 minutes in a hot oven

> baba dough
> kirsch fondant
> glacé cherries
> kirsch flavoured syrup

Half fill small pomponnette tins with baba dough. Prove in a warm place, then bake. Soak in kirsch flavoured syrup and drain on a wire rack. Dip into kirsch fondant tinted pale pink. Press a piece of glacé cherry into the centre of each one before the fondant has set.

France

Hazelnut and almond slices

1 kg	good quality sweet paste	2½ lb
300 g	butter	12 oz
400 g	sugar	1 lb
300 g	honey	12 oz
100 g	glucose	4 oz
¼ l	dairy cream	½ pt
1 kg	whole blanched almonds	2½ lb
1 kg	whole blanched hazelnuts	2½ lb

Pin out the sweet paste 4 mm (about ⅙ in) thick to a rectangular shape 30 × 60 cm (12 × 24 in). Bake lightly at 180°C until half cooked. Boil up the butter, sugar, honey, glucose and cream, add the hazelnuts and almonds, stir well and spread evenly on the sweet paste base. Bake off at 180°C until golden, preferably in a sandwich loaf tin. Cut into pieces as desired while still lukewarm.

Germany

Hazelnut boats

Yields 12   4–5 minutes in a hot oven

125 g	sweet paste	5 oz
	apricot purée	
	roasted hazelnuts	

Line small boat shaped tins with the sweet paste and bake blind. Boil the apricot purée until it is no longer liquid and stir in a few roasted hazelnuts. Fill the pastry boats with the mixture.

France

Hazelnut crescents

300 g	yeast dough	12 oz
600 g	sweet paste	1 lb 8 oz

Filling

300 g	ground hazelnuts	12 oz
300 g	marzipan	12 oz
300 g	fine sponge crumbs	12 oz
	rum	

Work the yeast dough and sweet paste together thoroughly and divide into 30 pieces. Pin out each one to an oval shape about 10 cm (4 in) long. To make the filling, moisten the hazelnuts, marzipan and sponge crumbs with rum, amalgamate well and divide into 30 pieces. Cover each piece of dough with a piece of filling, roll up well, taper the ends, arrange on lightly greased baking sheets, moulding the crescents to an oval shape and sealing the ends well. Brush with egg, dry, brush with egg again and press down a little. Bake at 180°C. The pastry will crack here and there while baking as a result of being pressed down.

Germany

Hazelnut slices

Split a sheet of genoese twice and sandwich with hazelnut buttercream. When firm cut into slices. Spread the sides with the same buttercream and mask with roasted chopped hazelnuts. Coat the top with pink fondant and pipe on two diagonal lines of fondant. Place a roasted hazelnut in the centre.

(Illustration, p. 1101) Switzerland

Honey cakes

40 cakes   Baking time: 10–15 minutes

500 g	honey	1¼ lb
2 dl	water	⅓ pt
10 g	carbonate of ammonia	1 heaped teaspoon
	wheat flour	

For 1 kg (2 lb 3 oz) dough

10 g	bicarbonate of soda	1 teaspoon
10 g	ground cloves	1 teaspoon
10 g	ground allspice	1 teaspoon
10 g	cinnamon	1 teaspoon
10 g	aniseed	1 teaspoon
	zest of 1 orange	

1 dl	water	3 fl oz
	beaten egg yolk to egg wash	
100–200 g	blanched almonds	4–8 oz

Bring the honey and water to the boil, strain and work to a smooth dough with flour, sieving the carbonate of ammonia into the first portion of flour added. Allow to rest for at least 24 hours.

Weigh the dough into 1 kg (2 lb 3 oz) pieces, add the bicarbonate of soda, the spices, orange zest and water to each one and work thoroughly. Pin out to a thickness of 5 mm ($\frac{1}{4}$ in) and cut out in various shapes. Arrange on a baking sheet, egg wash and decorate with split or nib almonds. Bake in a moderate oven until the cakes have risen, then increase the heat and bake off to a golden brown colour.

Instead of egg washing, the cakes may be glazed with a sugar solution after baking and cooling.

Czechoslovakia

Horseshoes

300 g	sugar	12 oz
450 g	butter	1 lb 2 oz
600 g	flour	1$\frac{1}{2}$ lb
	4 eggs	
	2 egg whites	
350 g	roasted ground hazelnuts	14 oz
	apricot jam	
	couverture	

Cream the butter with the sugar, eggs, egg whites and a pinch of salt. Mix the flour with the hazelnuts and stir into the creamed mixture. Shape into horseshoes on greased baking sheets and bake at about 200°C. Sandwich in pairs with apricot jam and dip the ends in couverture.

Holland

Indians

15 minutes in a medium oven

125 g	ground almonds	5 oz
125 g	sugar	5 oz
75 g	melted butter	3 oz
50 g	cocoa	2 oz
	1 unbeaten egg white	

2 egg whites whipped to a snow
chocolate fondant
chopped pistachio nuts

Mix the ground almonds with the sugar, rubbing the mixture against the sides of the basin. Gradually add the unbeaten egg white to make a stiffish paste. Add the melted butter and the cocoa dissolved in a few drops of water. Fold in the whipped egg whites lightly. Fill into a greased and floured genoese sponge tin and bake. Turn out on to a wire rack and allow to cool. Cut into rectangles. Sprinkle some chopped pistachio nuts in the centre of each one to decorate.

France

Inseparables

7–8 minutes in a slow oven

125 g	ground almonds	5 oz
125 g	vanilla sugar	5 oz
	2 egg whites	
	red currant jelly	

Sift the ground almonds and sugar into the egg whites and fold in lightly. Pipe out in small rounds on a sheet of white paper, using a savoy bag fitted with a plain pipe. Bake. Detach from the paper on removing from the oven. When cold, sandwich base to base in pairs with red currant jelly, flavoured with kirsch if desired.

France

Italians

genoese sponge
pistachio buttercream
pistachio fondant flavoured with kirsch

Cut a long strip of genoese 4 cm (about $1\frac{1}{2}$ in) wide. Split once and sandwich with the buttercream. Coat the top with the fondant. Cut into $1\frac{1}{2}$ cm ($\frac{1}{2}$ in) slices and place half a pistachio nut on each one.

France

Java

8–10 minutes in a slow oven

125 g	ground almonds	5 oz
125 g	vanilla sugar	5 oz
75 g	cocoa powder	3 oz
	2 egg whites	
100 g	praline paste	4 oz

Mix the ground almonds, sugar and cocoa together and blend in the egg whites a little at a time to make a softish paste. Pipe out in small rounds on paper, using a savoy bag fitted with a plain pipe. Sprinkle a little sugar on each biscuit and bake. Sandwich base to base in pairs with softened praline paste.

France

Jeannettes

6–8 minutes in a medium oven

baba dough
white fondant flavoured with port or Madeira
port or Madeira flavoured syrup
chopped pistachio nuts

Proceed as for benoîtons. After baking, soak in port or Madeira flavoured syrup and drain. When cold, ice with white fondant flavoured with port or Madeira and sprinkle with chopped pistachio nuts. Place in small paper cases to serve.

France

Jésuites

12–15 minutes in a slow oven

250 g	puff paste	10 oz
	almond flavoured confectioner's custard	
	coarsely chopped almonds	
	royal icing	
	icing sugar	

Proceed as for dartois, but spread with confectioner's custard instead of jam. Sprinkle with coarsely chopped almonds coated with royal icing. Cut into small triangles. Dust with icing sugar on removing from the oven.

France

Juliettes

150 g	butter	6 oz
150 g	sugar	6 oz
100 g	strip almonds	4 oz
50 g	nibbed almonds	2 oz
50 g	honey	2 oz
1 dl	dairy cream	3 fl oz
	vanilla	

Mix all the ingredients thoroughly, place in a pan and cook over gentle heat until the mixture leaves the sides of the pan. Spread on a non-stick baking sheet and bake in the same way as florentines (page 1007). Remove from the baking sheet while still warm and cut into oblong strips.

France

Kermesse cakes

1 kg	best flour	2¼ lb
150 g	melted butter	6 oz
150 g	sugar	6 oz
	2 eggs	
50 g	baker's yeast	2 oz
¼ l	milk	½ pt approx.
	¼ teaspoon salt	

Make a ferment with a little of the flour, the yeast, a pinch of sugar and a little warm milk. Sieve the rest of the flour with the salt, make a bay and add the ferment, the melted butter, the eggs and the rest of the lukewarm milk. Work to a fairly stiff dough. Leave to prove and knock back. Divide the dough into 50 g (2 oz) pieces, roll into balls and place on a greased baking sheet, leaving a space between them, to allow them to rise a little. Make a hollow in the centre of each and fill with one of the following fillings. Brush the dough with egg wash (or melted butter) and bake at about 200°C. When cooked, dredge with icing sugar.

Fillings

1. 150 g (6 oz) cream cheese; 30 g (1½ oz) sugar and one egg yolk beaten well together.

2. 150 g (6 oz) ground poppy seeds; 100 ml (4 fl oz) milk; 30 g (1½ oz) sugar; grated zest of half a lemon. Boil the milk and ground poppy seeds together for 10 minutes, stirring continually. Allow to cool, then mix in the sugar and lemon zest.

3. 150 g (6 oz) fruit purée sharpened with lemon juice and liqueur.

4. 150 g (6 oz) finely grated apple or pear; 30 g (1½ oz) sugar and a hint of cinnamon and nutmeg.

Techniques, p. 154   Czechoslovakia

King bouchées

8–10 minutes in a medium oven

250 g	choux paste	10 oz
½ l	apple jelly flavoured with kirsch	¾ pt
250 g	maraschino flavoured white fondant	10 oz

Pipe small bulbs of choux paste on to a baking sheet and bake. Cool on a wire rack. Make a slit in one side of each about three quarters of the way up. Pipe in a little apple jelly and dip the tops in fondant. Place in small paper cases to serve.

France

Kirsch petits fours

Using the same mixture as for chocolate petits fours, bake 3 squares of sheet genoese. When cold, sandwich with kirsch buttercream and cut into rounds. Brush with apricot purée, wrap in a thin sheet of marzipan and pipe on kirsch buttercream. Cover with a ring of marzipan with serrated edges and sprinkle the centre with chopped pistachio nuts.

(Illustration, p. 1102)   Austria

Konigsberg marzipan tea confections

Yield: about 120 confections

1 kg	raw marzipan	2½ lb
200 g	icing sugar	6 oz
	few drops preservative*	
	gum arabic	
	kirsch flavoured fondant	
	glacé fruit	
	angelica	

Work the marzipan well with the sugar and preservative. Pin out between two parallel strips of wood, cut out with a Konigsberg marzipan punch-cutter and dry the cases on a wooden board for 24 hours. Flash in the oven at 250°C or under a salamander and glaze with gum arabic. Fill with kirsch flavoured fondant and decorate with small pieces of angelica and glacé fruits of different colours. (Techniques, p. 160)

*Obtainable commercially.

Lacy tuiles

3–4 minutes in a very hot oven

100 g	vanilla sugar	4 oz
100 g	flaked almonds	4 oz
100 g	butter	4 oz
50 g	flour	2 oz
2½ cl	orange juice	2½ dessertspoons

Cream the butter in a slightly warmed basin, add the orange juice and beat in the almonds and flour. Proceed as for ordinary tuiles.

France

Ladies' croquettes

7–8 minutes in a hot oven

150 g	flour	6 oz
75 g	sugar	3 oz
75 g	chopped almonds	3 oz
75 g	butter	3 oz
	1 large egg	
2 cl	rum	2 dessertspoons

Mix the sugar, almonds and flour and make a bay in the centre. Place the softened butter, the egg, rum and a little salt in the bay and work to a paste. Allow to rest in a cool place for 1 hour. Fashion into small shuttle shapes, brush with beaten egg, roll in sugar and bake on a greased baking sheet.

France

Ladies' fingers (chocolate)

12–15 minutes in a slow oven

	Italian meringue	
40 g	cocoa powder	1½ oz
50 g	icing sugar	1¾ oz

Mix the cocoa powder with the icing sugar and sift into the meringue. Proceed as for coffee ladies' fingers.

France

Ladies' fingers (coffee)

12–15 minutes in a slow oven

Italian meringue
coffee essence

Flavour Italian meringue with coffee essence. Pipe out in fingers 3 or 4 cm (about 1½ in) long and as thick as a pencil on to a greased and floured baking sheet. Bake carefully and remove from the baking sheet immediately. When cold, arrange in a pyramid.

France

Lebrija cakes

550 g	flour	1 lb 6 oz
250 g	caster sugar	10 oz
	4 eggs	
	1 small cup fine oil	
	2 spoons aniseed	
	almonds	
	pine kernels	
	a little sesame	

Sieve 500 g (1 lb 4 oz) flour on to a table in a heap (the rest of the flour will be used to dust the table when shaping the cakes). Make a bay and place the sugar, eggs and oil in the centre together with a little salt. Add a little milk or water if required (this will depend in part on the quality of the flour). Work to a well blended, fairly firm paste, cover with a cloth and leave to recover for 20 minutes. Now work in the aniseed, kneading for a few minutes to mix in thoroughly. Shape the paste into a roll, dust the table lightly with flour, place the roll on it and cut into short lengths. Mould each one to the shape and size of an egg (no larger). Arrange on a lightly oiled baking sheet, press almonds, pine kernels and sesame seeds into the top of each cake and bake in a slow oven.

Spain

Lemons—citrons

Line some round shallow patty pans with Linz paste and bake blind in a medium oven at about 187°C (370°F). As soon as cold, fill with lemon custard. Coat with lemon flavoured and coloured fondant, and write the word 'Citron' or 'Lemon' in chocolate on top of each.

(Illustration, p. 1101)   Switzerland

Lemon rings

Yield: 40

¼ l	water	½ pt
¼ l	milk	½ pt
60 g	butter	2 oz
60 g	lard	2 oz
	pinch of salt	
450 g	sieved flour	1 lb
	pinch of sugar	
	zest of half a lemon	
	9–11 eggs	
	apricot purée	
	lemon flavoured and coloured	
	fondant	

Lemon cream

	juice of 4 lemons	
	4 egg yolks	
300 g	sugar	10 oz
	16 sheets gelatine	
1 l	unsweetened whipped cream	1¾ pt
	whipped cream for decoration	
	couverture ornaments	

Place the water, milk, butter, lard, sugar and salt in a pan and bring to the boil, making sure that the butter and lard are completely melted. Pour in the flour all at once and cook the mixture until it leaves the side of the pan without sticking, while stirring constantly with a spatula. Remove from the heat, allow to cool slightly, then beat in the eggs a little at a time and lastly add the lemon zest. Pipe out in small rings on to lightly greased baking sheets, using a savoy bag fitted with a star pipe. Bake at 210°C. When cold, split the rings, brush the tops with hot, well boiled apricot purée and coat with lemon flavoured and coloured fondant.

To make the lemon cream, place the lemon juice, egg yolks and sugar in a pan, whip up while warming the mixture, add the gelatine which has been soaked and squeezed dry and continue warming until the mixture has reached blood heat, stirring meanwhile. Remove from the heat and fold in the whipped cream.

Fill the bases of the rings with the lemon cream, using a star pipe, cover with the tops and decorate each one with a rosette of whipped cream and a couverture ornament.

Germany

Little men (yeasted fancies)

This is an easily made attractive novelty. Various types of fermented dough may be used—bread or milk roll dough, fermented almond or brioche dough.

To shape the head, mould a small piece of dough into a ball and model it to a slightly elongated shuttle shape. Press raisins into the dough for the eyes and nose and pinch or cut the top of the head to the shape of a cap or hat. If a hat is desired, fix on a rolled strip of dough for the brim.

To make the body, mould a larger piece of dough into a ball, model to an elongated shape and flatten lightly. Cut into the dough with scissors to make the arms and legs, open out, flatten the ends a little and make cuts for the fingers. Twisted or untwisted ropes of dough are used for the beard and any other additions. Where a pointed shape is required, the dough is cut with scissors. A small hollow is made in the top of the body and brushed with a little beaten egg so that the head may be fixed in position.

Egg wash and prove, but do not allow the dough to rise too much. Egg wash again and bake in a medium oven.

(Illustration, p. 1105)   Switzerland

Livances

10 portions

Cooking time: 5–7 minutes each side

1 kg	flour	2½ lb
	4 eggs	
1·3 l	milk	2¼ pt
100 g	sugar	4 oz
30 g	yeast	1 oz
3 g	cinnamon	¼ teaspoon
15 g	salt	1 teaspoon
	zest of 1 lemon	

200 g	hard cottage cheese*	8 oz
300 g	jam	12 oz
200 g	icing sugar	8 oz
¼ l	oil	½ pt

Disperse the yeast in the lukewarm milk, add the sugar, eggs, salt and lemon zest, then gradually work in the flour, while beating with a wire whisk, to make a very slack dough. Strain into a clean bowl, cover with a cloth and leave to ferment for 30 minutes. Grease a special livance pan by brushing its indentations well with oil, heat the pan, drop in a small ladleful of the batter and fry on both sides until golden. When the livances are cooked, spread half of them with jam and sprinkle with grated cottage cheese, and coat the other half on both sides with icing sugar mixed with cinnamon. Livances are always freshly made shortly before they are required.

Czechoslovakia

*'Layer' Cottage Cheese

This is a type of curd cheese made in square moulds. It consists of three layers, the top and bottom one having a low fat content, while the one in between has a high fat content. The latter may be lightly tinted with carotene.

Lombardy carnival fritters

8–10 persons

½ l	water	¾ pt
100 g	butter	4 oz
30 g	sugar	1 oz
350 g	flour	14 oz
	8 eggs	
	pinch of salt	

Place the water in a pan with the butter, sugar and salt and bring to the boil. As soon as the butter is completely melted add the sieved flour all at once. Cook while stirring with a spatula until the mixture is smooth and leaves the side of the pan. Remove from the heat, allow to cool a little, then blend in the eggs one at a time to make a soft choux paste. Shape into fritters with a tablespoon and drop into deep fat, which should not be too hot. When the fritters are lightly coloured, raise the heat a little until they are cooked—they should swell up well. Remove, drain on a cloth, sprinkle with vanilla sugar, dish and serve hot.

Italy

Macaronettes

500 g	ground almonds	1¼ lb
90 g	egg whites	4 oz
275 g	sugar	11 oz
	egg white for glazing	
	ganache	

Mix the almonds and sugar well with 90 g (4 oz) egg whites. Shape into small macaroon biscuits, brush with a little lightly beaten egg white and bake at 230°C. Allow to cool and sandwich together with ganache.

France

Macaroons I

12–15 minutes in a medium oven

150 g	almonds	6 oz
300 g	sugar	300 oz
	2 egg whites	
	pinch of ground vanilla	

Grind the blanched almonds, gradually adding the sugar and vanilla. Pound in the egg whites a little at a time to make a softish paste. Using a savoy bag, pipe out in well spaced large drops on to greaseproof paper. Moisten the tops, using a brush, and sprinkle with icing sugar, then bake.

After baking, turn the paper over and moisten the back to facilitate removal of the macaroons; alternatively, damp a marble slab or baking sheet and slide the paper on to it.

(Illustration, p. 804)

France

Macaroons II

200 g	almonds	8 oz
300 g	icing sugar	12 oz
3 cl	well boiled apricot purée	3 dessertspoons
	3 large egg whites	

Proceed as for classic macaroons, but after grinding the almonds and sugar, add the apricot purée before the egg whites. Continue as for classic macaroons.

France

Macaroons III

7–8 minutes in a medium oven

125 g	ground almonds	5 oz
150 g	sugar	6 oz
30 g	flour	1 oz
	3 large or 4 small egg whites	
	finely chopped zest of 1 orange *or* 3 lumps of orange flavoured sugar	

Whisk the egg whites to a very stiff snow. Mix the ground almonds, sugar and orange zest together and add all at once to the whites. Fold in quickly without working the mixture too much. Pipe out on to greaseproof paper in the same way as classic macaroons.

France

Macaroons IV

8–10 minutes for large macaroons, less for smaller ones

250 g	almonds	10 oz
400 g	sugar	1 lb
120 g	melted chocolate	5 oz
	4 egg whites	

Proceed as for classic macaroons. Add the warm chocolate after grinding the almonds with the sugar. Blend in the egg whites a little at a time. The paste should be firm enough to be moulded by hand. Shape into large or small macaroons on greaseproof paper and flatten with a damp brush.

The macaroons may be given various shapes.

France

Madeleines

7–8 minutes in a hot oven in small tins, 10–15 minutes in standard size tins

120 g	flour	5 oz
120 g	butter	5 oz
120 g	sugar	5 oz
	4 eggs	
	2 pinches of ground vanilla	

Whisk the eggs and sugar until very foamy. Sift in the flour and vanilla and fold in lightly with a spatula. Add the melted, barely lukewarm butter. Grease and flour the tins, deposit the mixture in them and bake.

France

Magalis

4–5 minutes in a hot oven

> sweet paste
> ganache
> chocolate fondant
> roasted ground almonds

Line patty pans, boat shaped tins or any similar small moulds with sweet paste and bake blind. When cold, fill with ganache. Refrigerate for a few moments to set, then coat with fondant. Decorate with a border of ground almonds. Place in small paper cases to serve.

France

Maltese lemon slices

Cut strips of sweet pastry about 2 cm ($\frac{3}{4}$ in) and $7\frac{1}{2}$ cm (3 in) wide and spread them with red currant jelly. With a star tube pipe on the following mixture:

500 g	butter	1 lb
500 g	sugar (caster)	1 lb
500 g	egg	1 lb
1 kg	flour (soft)	2 lb

Bake each strip at 200°C between metal bars. When cool, cut into slices. Cover the top and sides with arrack buttercream. Mask the sides with chocolate vermicelli and sprinkle chocolate shavings on the top. Dust lightly with icing sugar and cut into slices.

Switzerland

Marbled biscuits

250 g	flour	10 oz
175 g	butter	7 oz
75 g	icing sugar	3 oz
	1 egg	
	pinch of salt	
40 g	cocoa powder	$1\frac{1}{2}$ oz

▲ Vegetable aspic
▼ Sliced ham with Gervais cream and vegetable timbale

1027

1028 ▲ A chaud-froid of vegetable salad

Make a short friable paste with the flour, butter, sugar, egg and salt. Take off a third of the paste and work in the cocoa powder. Allow to rest a little, then arrange the light and dark coloured paste in alternate layers and shape by hand into a roll of the desired thickness. Refrigerate until firm, cut into thin slices with a sharp knife and bake at 180°C.

(Techniques, p. 159)   Switzerland

Marignan

10 minutes in a hot oven

> savarin dough
> Chantilly cream
> syrup for soaking savarins
> rum

Half fill well greased boat shaped tins with savarin dough. Prove in a warm place until the dough is almost level with the top of the tins. Bake, then soak in syrup and splash with rum. Make a horizontal slit near the top without cutting right through, lift up the top and pipe in Chantilly cream, using a savoy bag fitted with a star tube.

France

Marinettes

4–5 minutes in a hot oven

> sweet paste
> very thick apple purée blended
>   with a little butter
> rum fondant
> sultanas

Line patty pans with sweet paste and bake blind. On removing from the oven fill each one with a pyramid of very hot apple purée and smooth over with a knife. Leave until quite cold, when a skin will have formed on the purée. Coat with fondant and place a sultana on either side of the pyramid.

France

Mars

12–15 minutes in a hot oven, plus 10 minutes in a slow oven

> sweet or puff paste
> vanilla or almond flavoured
>   confectioner's custard
> Swiss meringue
> chopped almonds
> icing sugar

Pin out a strip of paste to a thickness of 3 mm ($\frac{1}{8}$ in), making it 4–5 cm (about 2 in) wide. Moisten the edges and border on both sides with a strip of paste of the same thickness 2 cm ($\frac{3}{4}$ in) in width. Notch the edges and prick the bottom. Spread with confectioner's custard and bake. Leave until almost cold. Cover the custard with a layer of meringue 2 cm ($\frac{3}{4}$ in) thick. Sprinkle with chopped almonds and dust with icing sugar. Mark the top crosswise with the back of a knife at intervals of 2 cm ($\frac{3}{4}$ in). Place in a slow oven and leave for 10 minutes; the meringue should be crisp but only lightly coloured. When cold, cut along the knife marks.

France

Marzipan candles

Yield: 35

Almond genoese

	9 eggs	
375 g	sugar	15 oz
125 g	ground almonds	5 oz
225 g	flour	9 oz
60 g	cornflour	2 oz
175 g	melted butter	7 oz
	vanilla	
	zest of $\frac{1}{4}$ lemon	
	pinch of salt	

Filling and decoration

	nougat paste	
	red currant jelly	
350 g	short pastry	14 oz
400 g	marzipan	1 lb
180 g	finely chopped roasted almonds	7 oz
150 g	chocolate fondant	6 oz
60 g	pink marzipan	2 oz
	apricot purée	
	vanilla buttercream	

Beat up the eggs and sugar warm, remove from the heat and continue beating. Blend in the flour which has been sieved with the cornflour, together with the vanilla, lemon zest, salt and ground almonds. Lastly fold in the melted butter (without whey). Spread on a paper lined baking sheet and bake at 200°C. Allow to cool, then split twice and sandwich with nougat paste and red currant jelly, keeping the top dry. Weight with a heavy board and chill well. Cut out candles, using a cutter 4 cm (1½ in) in diameter. Coat thinly with vanilla buttercream, then wrap in thinly pinned out marzipan to project about 5 mm (¼ in) over the top. Brush the marzipan thinly with well boiled apricot purée and mask with the chopped roasted almonds. Coat the top of each candle with chocolate fondant inside the marzipan edging and place a small piece of pink marzipan shaped like a flame in the centre. Stand each candle on a small baked short pastry base lightly brushed with apricot purée.

Germany

Meringue rings

1 kg	10 egg whites	
	sugar	2¼ lb
½ l	water	⅞ pt
	coloured sugar	

Boil the sugar and water to the feather degree (94°C). Whip the egg whites to a stiff snow and slowly pour in the sugar solution while whisking slowly. When cold, pipe out in rings on waxed baking sheets, using a star pipe, and sprinkle with coloured sugar. Dry in a warm cupboard for about 2 hours, then bake at 180°C for about 40 minutes.

Germany

Meringuettes

4 hours at 50°C or 10–12 minutes at 100°C

Swiss meringue
buttercream (various flavours)

Pipe out small meringues on to a greased and floured baking sheet. Dry in the oven without baking. Sandwich base to base in pairs with a little buttercream.

The dry meringues may be stored in an airtight tin.

France

Merveilles

	12 egg whites	
200 g	caster sugar	8 oz
500 g	butter	1 lb 4 oz
400 g	icing sugar	1 lb
	zest of 2 lemons	
2 dl	dairy cream	$\frac{1}{3}$ pt
750 g	flour	1 lb 14 oz
	pinch of salt	

Whip the egg whites to a stiff snow with the caster sugar. Beat the butter with the icing sugar, lemon zest, salt and cream, fold in the whites and the flour together, pipe into rounds on buttered baking sheets and bake in a brisk oven.

Switzerland

Mignons

genoese sponge
well boiled apricot purée
    coloured red
granulated sugar
kirsch fondant

Cut disks 3 cm (about 1 in) in diameter from a sheet of genoese 3–4 cm (1–1$\frac{1}{2}$ in) thick. Using an apple-corer 1$\frac{1}{2}$ cm ($\frac{1}{2}$ in) in diameter, make a cavity in the centre of each disk without cutting right through. Dip quickly in boiling hot apricot purée, using a dipping fork. Drain on a wire rack. Roll the sides in granulated sugar, but keep the top free of sugar. Fill the cavity in the centre of each one with fondant.

France

Milanese

7–8 minutes in a hot oven

125 g	flour	5 oz
50 g	butter	2 oz
50 g	ground almonds	2 oz
50 g	sugar	2 oz
	1 egg	
	pinch of salt	
	finely chopped zest of 1 lemon	

Mix the flour, sugar, ground almonds and lemon zest together and make a bay in the centre. Pour in the egg, dissolve the salt in it and add the softened butter. Work into a paste in the same way as short pastry. Wrap in a damp cloth and allow to rest for 2 hours in a cool place. Pin out to a thickness of 3 mm ($\frac{1}{8}$ in). Cut into various shapes, either with a knife or a cutter. Place on a greased baking sheet and brush with beaten egg. Finish off with various kinds of decoration—candied fruit, almonds, pistachio nuts, dried fruit, etc. Bake.

France

Milk or cream sablés

7–8 minutes in a hot oven

125 g	flour	5 oz
100 g	butter	4 oz
50 g	sugar	2 oz
	1 egg yolk	
	pinch of salt	
	pinch of ground vanilla	
	1 tablespoon milk	
	or single cream	

Proceed as for Normandy sablés, adding the milk or cream when working up to a dough.

France

Millefeuille slices

10 portions   Baking time: 7–10 minutes

Puff paste

500 g	flour	1 lb 4 oz
500 g	butter	1 lb 4 oz
$\frac{1}{4}$ l	milk	$\frac{1}{2}$ pt
	1 tablespoon water	
	1 tablespoon lemon juice	
	1 tablespoon rum	
10 g	salt	1 teaspoon
	beaten egg to wash	

Custard

	10 egg yolks	
250 g	sugar	10 oz

120 g	flour	5 oz
1 l	milk	1¾ pt
	half a vanilla pod	
½ l	whipped dairy cream	¾ pt
50 g	red currant jelly	2 oz
	fondant	

Make the puff paste and pin out to a rectangle 4–5 mm (about ¼ in) thick, then cut into strips 4–5 cm (about 2 in) wide. Arrange on a baking sheet, prick well with a fork, egg wash and bake in a hot oven until golden.

To make the custard, mix the egg yolks with the sugar, add the flour, blend in the milk until smooth, add the vanilla and cook for 10 minutes, stirring constantly. The custard should be smooth and thick. Allow to cool, remove the vanilla and fold in the whipped cream. Spread half the strips very thinly with sieved red currant jelly. Cover the other half to a thickness of 2 cm (about ¾ in) with custard, place the jelly coated strips on top and ice with a thin film of fondant. Mask the edges smoothly with custard and cut the strips into slices 3 cm (1¼ in) wide, using a sharp knife.

Mitsukas

Sandwich three sheets of japonaise with hazelnut buttercream. Press down lightly to hold the layers together, coat the top with hazelnut buttercream and make a wavy surface with a comb scraper. Leave in a cold place until firm, then cut into squares and place a chocolate seal on top of each one.

(Illustration, p. 1101)   Switzerland

Mocha parfaits

Cut out disks of sweet paste and bake. Allow to cool, then sandwich in pairs with mocha buttercream. Coat the top with the same buttercream, leave until firm, then dip into coffee coloured and flavoured fondant. Decorate the top as desired.

(Illustration, page 1101)   France/Switzerland

Moors' Heads

Yield: 60 bases

| 150 g | egg yolks | 6 oz |
| 700 g | egg whites | 1 lb 12 oz |

100 g	sugar (caster)	4 oz
100 g	flour	4 oz
200 g	cornflour	8 oz

Whisk the egg yolks, flour and half the sugar. Whisk the egg whites and the rest of the sugar to a stiff snow, blend the two together and lastly add the cornflour. Pipe out on to special Othello baking sheets and bake at 200°C. When cool, sandwich the bases with vanilla flavoured whipped dairy cream or good vanilla custard. Coat with cooked chocolate icing.

Germany

Moravian cakes

10 portions, 2 cakes each   Baking time: 15–20 minutes

500 g	flour	1 lb 4 oz
40 g	yeast	1½ oz
120 g	sugar	5 oz
¼ l	milk	½ pt
100 g	butter	4 oz
	2 eggs	
10 g	salt	1 teaspoon
	zest of a quarter of a lemon	
50 g	icing sugar	2 oz
	beaten egg to wash	

Fruit filling

200 g	apples, peeled, cored and grated	8 oz
	zest of 1 lemon	
50 g	sugar	2 oz
	pinch of cinnamon	
	pinch of ground cloves	
40 g	sultanas	1½ oz

Make a smooth dough from the flour, the yeast dispersed in lukewarm milk, the salt, butter, eggs and lemon zest. Allow to ferment for 30 minutes, then divide into 40 pieces. Pat each one into a round about 5 cm (2 in) thick and press the centre with the finger to make a hollow. Fill this with fruit filling or with one of those used for buns with filling (buchty) and prove for 15 minutes. Egg wash the edges and bake in a moderate oven until golden. Dust with icing sugar and serve. To make the fruit filling, mix the apples well with the lemon zest, sugar and spices, cook for 10 minutes and stir in the sultanas.

Czechoslovakia

Muffins

12 muffins

500 g	strong flour	1 lb 4 oz
3 dl	milk	½ pt
50 g	butter	2 oz
30 g	yeast	1 oz
	pinch of salt and sugar	

Warm the milk with the butter, salt and sugar to 37°C. Add the yeast and mix to a smooth dough with the flour. Allow to rise in a warm place until doubled in size. Knock back, roll out on a floured table to a thickness of about 1 cm (½ in), cover with a floured cloth and allow to prove. Cut out with a 10 cm (4 in) cutter, place on a greased griddle and cook slowly for 10 minutes, turning when cooked under-neath. The finished muffins should be very pale in colour. If preferred, the muffins may be baked at 185°C for 15 minutes.

When cold, split in two and toast.

Great Britain

Mushrooms

10–12 minutes in a slow oven

	Italian meringue	
100 g	chocolate powder	4 oz
	kirsch buttercream	
	(or any other flavour)	

Pipe out small flattish bulbs of meringue (for the mushroom caps) on a greased and floured baking sheet. To make the stalks, pipe out an equal number of small peaked bases. Sprinkle the caps and stalks with chocolate powder, but do not cover completely. Bake. On removing from the oven, make a small hole in the underside of each cap by pressing lightly with the finger. Allow to cool, then fill the holes with buttercream. Insert the stalks into the buttercream. Serve in small paper cases or as they are on small plates covered with a paper doyley.

France

Mutzen almond puffs

Yield: about 100 puffs

500 g	flour	1 lb 4 oz
225 g	sugar	9 oz
	2 eggs	
	2 egg yolks	
100 g	butter	4 oz
75 g	raw marzipan	3 oz
7 g	baking powder	1 teaspoon
3 cl	rum	3 dessertspoons
	little vanilla	
1 g	pinch of cinnamon	
1 g	pinch of salt	
	little milk	

Sift the flour on to the table and make a bay. Beat the eggs, yolks, sugar and baking powder lightly. Work the marzipan to a smooth paste with a little milk. Melt the butter and leave until barely lukewarm. Lightly work the egg mixture, marzipan and flour into a paste with the addition of the rum, vanilla, cinnamon and salt, then mix in the butter. Leave in a cool place for 30 minutes, then pin out between two parallel strips of wood or metal bars to a thickness of about 6 mm ($\frac{1}{4}$ in). Cut out with a 'mutzen almond' cutter and fry in fat at 190°C while agitating with a skimmer to brown the puffs evenly. Remove from the fat, drain well on a sieve and dredge with icing sugar.

Germany

Neros

6–7 minutes in a medium oven

100 g	flour	4 oz
100 g	butter	4 oz
25 g	caster sugar	1 oz
	pinch of ground vanilla	
	3 hard-boiled egg yolks	

Place all the ingredients in a basin and mix to a paste with a spatula. Work with a rolling pin until smooth, then allow to rest for 2 hours. From this paste roll thin sticks 12 cm (5 in) long, fold each one in half and twist the two halves together. Brush with beaten egg, sprinkle with a little sugar and bake on a greased baking sheet.

France

Ninis

7–8 minutes in a hot oven

250 g	choux paste	10 oz
½ l	confectioner's custard mixed with candied fruit macerated in kirsch	⅞ pt
250 g	kirsch flavoured fondant 10 glacé cherries	10 oz

Pipe out eclairs no thicker than a large pencil on to a baking sheet. Bake and allow to cool. Make a slit in the side of each one and pipe in the confectioner's custard. Place a quarter of a glacé cherry on top of each one. Serve in small paper cases.

France

Noisettines

genoese sponge

Hazelnut mousseline buttercream

50 g	roasted hazelnuts	2 oz
50 g	butter	2 oz
50 g	sugar	2 oz
	1 level tablespoon double cream	
	well boiled apricot purée chocolate fondant chopped pistachio nuts	

Cut out oval bases of genoese sponge. To make the mousseline buttercream, grind the hazelnuts and sugar together, add the butter, rub through a sieve and blend in the double cream. Split the bases once and sandwich with the buttercream. Brush with apricot purée and coat with chocolate fondant. Sprinkle the top with chopped pistachio nuts.

France

Normandy sablés

7–8 minutes in a hot oven

125 g	flour	5 oz
100 g	butter	4 oz
50 g	ground almonds	2 oz

75 g	sugar	3 oz
	2 egg yolks (raw)	
	pinch of salt	
	grated zest of 1 lemon	

Proceed as for sablés, but pin out a fraction more thinly and cut into disks with a large round cutter 8–10 cm (3–4 in) in diameter. Cut each disk in quarters with a knife, place on a greased baking sheet, brush with beaten egg, draw lines on top with a knife and bake.

If no suitable cutter is available, use a saucer, inverting it on top of the dough and cutting round with a knife.

France

Nut crescents

About 17 crescents   Baking time: 25 minutes

250 g	flour	10 oz
110 g	butter	4½ oz
10 g	icing sugar	½ oz
10 g	yeast	½ oz
	1 egg yolk	
$\frac{1}{16}$ l	milk	2 fl oz
5 g	salt	1 teaspoon
	zest of a quarter of a lemon	

Filling

300 g	finely ground hazelnuts	12 oz
100 g	sponge crumbs	4 oz
50 g	sugar	2 oz
50 g	honey	2 oz
$\frac{1}{16}$ l	milk	2½ fl oz
	zest of a quarter of a lemon	
	rum	

Make a firm dough with the flour, butter, icing sugar, yeast, egg yolk, milk, lemon zest and salt. Allow to rest for at least 15 minutes. Shape into a long roll, cut in thick slices and pin each one out to an oval shape. To make the filling, mix the hazelnuts with the sponge crumbs, honey, sugar and milk and flavour with the lemon zest and a little rum. Spread the ovals of dough with nut filling, roll up, shape into crescents and arrange on a greased baking sheet. Brush with egg, allow to dry, egg wash again, allow to dry and bake at 190–200°C.

Austria

Orange croquettes

Proceed as for ladies' croquettes, adding a tablespoonful of chopped candied orange peel and a few drops of Curaçao.

France

Orange peel soufflés

250 g	ground almonds	10 oz
250 g	caster sugar	10 oz
	8 egg whites	
50 g	candied orange peel, very finely chopped	2 oz
	orange jelly	

Mix the ground almonds thoroughly with the sugar and fold into the stiffly whipped egg whites, together with the peel. Using a savoy bag fitted with a plain tube, pipe out in ovals on to a waxed baking sheet and bake in a moderate oven. While still hot remove from the baking sheet with a flexible knife and sandwich together with well boiled orange jelly or apricot jam.

France

Orléans or strawberry meringues

12–15 minutes in a slow oven

	3 egg whites whipped to a very stiff snow	
150 g	sugar	6 oz
30 g	glucose (optional)	1 oz
150 g	strawberry purée (preferably Orléans strawberries rubbed through a fine hair sieve)	6 oz

Mix the sugar with the glucose and boil to the crack degree. Add the strawberry purée and cook until the small ball degree is reached. Pour in a thin stream on to the whipped egg whites (as for Italian meringue). Tint pink with a few drops of carmine. Pipe out small meringues on to a greased and floured baking sheet and bake.

All kinds of sieved fruit may be used for this recipe. The fruit purée and sugar may be boiled together to the small ball degree without first boiling the sugar on its own, but there is some risk of the mixture sticking to the pan in this case.

France

Othellos I (Old method)

Yield: 80 bases, 40 finished confections

	15 egg whites	
	13 egg yolks	
$\frac{1}{16}$ l	water	2½ fl oz approx.
250 g	sugar	10 oz
230 g	flour	9 oz
120 g	cornflour	5 oz
	little vanilla	
	pinch of salt	

Whisk the egg yolks, sugar and the water with the salt and vanilla added. Whip the egg whites and the rest of the sugar to a stiff snow and fold into the egg yolk/sugar sponge at the same time as the flour and cornflour which have been sieved together.

Othellos II (New method)

Yield: 90 bases, 45 finished confections

	20 egg whites	
	15 egg yolks	
260 g	sugar	10 oz
250 g	flour	10 oz
110 g	cornflour	4½ oz
	little lemon zest	
	pinch of salt	

Beat the egg yolks and cornflour together with the salt and lemon zest added. Whip the egg whites and sugar to a stiff snow and fold into the egg yolk/cornflour mixture alternately with the flour which has been sieved twice.

Using a savoy bag and large plain tube, pipe out in rounded bulbs on to paper lined baking sheets. A better and more efficient procedure is to pipe the mixture on to special Othello baking sheets studded with metal knobs.

Filling

Vanilla custard.

	5 egg yolks	
	5 egg whites	
180 g	sugar	7 oz
100 g	custard powder	4 oz
	½ scraped vanilla pod	
¾ l	milk	1¼ pt

Prepare a cooked custard with the egg yolks, the milk, half the sugar, the custard powder and the vanilla, and fold in the whites whipped to a stiff snow with the rest of the sugar.

Chocolate icing for coating Othellos.

1 kg 500	sugar	3¼ lb
400 g	block cocoa, cut up finely	1 lb
¾ l	water	1¼ pt

Place the sugar and water in a pan and boil to the thread degree (108°C), repeatedly removing the scum and washing down the sides of the pan. Transfer the sugar solution to another pan and place the finely cut up block cocoa in the first pan. Slowly pour in the sugar solution, stirring constantly, then work the icing in the machine with a spatula or against the edge of the pan with the hand until it has reached coating consistency.

Always brush Othello bases thinly with apricot purée before coating.

Germany

Owis Molis

1 kg	flour	2½ lb
800 g	butter	2 lb
300 g	icing sugar	12 oz
	3 egg yolks	
	little vanilla	
	pinch of salt	

Beat the butter, sugar and egg yolks together well. Place the flour on the table and make a large well, put the remaining ingredients in the centre and work to a smooth dough. Pin out to 5 mm (¼ in) thick, cut out with a 3 cm (1¼ in) cutter and make small holes in each round. Bake at 180°C until lightly coloured, remove from the oven, coat at once with water icing and leave on a rack to dry.

Switzerland

Palets Biarritz

5 minutes in a very hot oven

125 g	ground almonds	5 oz
125 g	sugar	5 oz
	3 egg whites	
	pinch of vanilla	
200 g	couverture	8 oz

Mix the sugar and almonds in a basin with a spatula and gradually work in the unbeaten egg whites to make a very soft paste. (If desired, use 250–300 g (10–11 oz) ready-made raw marzipan and blend in the whites.) Using a stencil with 3 cm (about 1 in) holes, deposit the mixture in thin rounds on a greased baking sheet. Bake. On removing from the oven, transfer the biscuits from the baking sheet to a marble slab or other flat surface. When cold, coat the underside of each biscuit with couverture, using a metal spatula. Stand in a draught until the couverture is cold, to give a glossy finish.

France

Palets des dames

5 minutes in a hot oven

150 g	flour	6 oz
125 g	sugar	5 oz
125 g	butter	5 oz
75 g	currants	3 oz
	2 eggs	
1 cl	rum	1 dessertspoon

Pick and wash the currants and macerate in the rum. Cream the butter and sugar in a warmed basin and whip for 7 or 8 minutes, then beat in the eggs. Fold in the flour and the currants. Pipe small round shapes not too close together on to a greased and floured baking sheet. Bake, then remove at once from the baking sheet.

France

Palets glacés

6 minutes in a hot oven

100 g	butter	4 oz
100 g	sugar	4 oz
	1 egg	
50 g	flour	2 oz
	apricot jam	
	rum fondant	

Proceed as for palets des dames. After baking, allow to cool, then brush the undersides with apricot jam and coat with rum fondant. Leave uncovered to dry.

France

Palmiers

10–12 minutes in a hot oven

puff paste which has
been given 4 turns
caster sugar

Pin out the paste according to the instructions for giving a turn, sprinkle with sugar and complete the turn. Repeat to give the sixth turn and allow to rest for a time. Now pin out 3 mm ($\frac{1}{8}$ in) thick to make a rectangle 10 or 12 cm (4 or 5 in) wide. Dredge with sugar. Roll the two long sides of the rectangle inwards, making two cylinders that meet in the middle. Cut across these with a knife at intervals of 1 cm ($\frac{1}{2}$ in). Lay the slices flat on a baking sheet splashed with water, leaving room for spreading. Bake. Turn over when partly baked and leave in the oven until lightly caramelised.

France

Parisian mirlitons

Yields 20–25   15 minutes in a medium oven

250 g	sweet paste	10 oz
100 g	sugar	4 oz
	2 eggs	
	3 finely crushed macaroons	
30 g	*or* ground almonds	1 oz
	pinch of vanilla	
	apricot jam	
	13 blanched almonds	
	icing sugar	

Line small tartlet tins with sweet paste, raising the edges of the paste slightly. Prick the bottom and spread with apricot jam. Whip the eggs and sugar together until very foamy, then add the crushed macaroons or ground almonds and the vanilla. Fill the tartlets with the mixture. Cut half an almond into three flakes for each one and arrange round the centre on top of the filling. Dust with icing sugar. Bake carefully, covering with paper if necessary.

France

Parisianas

4–5 minutes in a hot oven

> sweet paste
> chestnut purée flavoured with vanilla
> chopped pineapple
> glacé cherries
> chopped pistachio nuts

Line small square tins with sweet paste and bake blind. When cold, cover the bottom with chestnut purée. Arrange a border of chopped pineapple on top. Place half a glacé cherry in the centre and sprinkle chopped pistachio nuts round it. Serve in small paper cases.

France

Pavés Suchard

Sandwich a sheet of chocolate sponge with raspberry jam and cut into squares. Pipe a thick diagonal line of chocolate buttercream on top of each one and leave until firm. Dip in chocolate fondant to coat all over and decorate with a pink ball.

(Illustration, p. 1101)   Switzerland

Pearly tuiles

5–6 minutes in a hot oven

125 g	butter	5 oz
125 g	sugar	5 oz
150 g	flour	6 oz
	2 egg yolks	
	pinch of salt	
	sugar nibs (or coarsely crushed cube sugar)	
	thick apricot jam	

Make a paste with all the ingredients except the sugar nibs and jam and allow to rest for 1 hour. Pin out to a thickness of $1\frac{1}{2}$ mm ($\frac{1}{16}$ in) and cut into rounds with a plain cutter 5 cm (2 in) in diameter. Place on a greased baking sheet and bake. On removing from the oven, given the biscuits a curved shape as described in the recipe for ordinary tuiles. Brush the convex side with apricot jam and sprinkle with sugar nibs.

France

Petticoat tails

Baking time: 20 minutes

400 g	flour		1 lb
50 g	rice flour		2 oz
115 g	sugar		5 oz
	1 egg yolk		
225 g	butter		9 oz

Cream the butter and sugar and add the egg yolk. Sieve the flour and rice flour on to the butter mixture and knead together until smooth. Roll into a rectangular shape, prick the base evenly with a fork and cut into fingers 1 cm ($\frac{1}{2}$ in) thick, 8–10 cm (3–4 in) long and 2 cm ($\frac{3}{4}$ in) wide. Bake lightly in a medium oven.

Caraway seeds may be added to this mixture.

Great Britain

Pineapple 'fritters'

10 minutes in a medium oven

100 g	blanched almonds	4 oz
100 g	caster sugar	4 oz
	half an egg white	
	pinch of ground vanilla	
	1 spoon well boiled apricot purée	
	1 spoon kirsch	
75 g	well drained chopped pineapple	3 oz
	2 egg whites whipped to a stiff snow	

Grind the almonds with the sugar and vanilla and gradually add half an egg white. Blend in the apricot purée and kirsch, mixing well. Fold in the pineapple and the stiffly whipped egg whites. Three quarters fill small round paper cases with the mixture and bake. Top with a small piece of pineapple.

France

Pineapple slices I

Sandwich two sheets of genoese with pineapple buttercream. Refrigerate and cut into strips 7–8 cm (3 in) wide. Spread the sides with the same cream and mask with roasted chopped almonds. Coat the top with white fondant flavoured with pineapple juice and decorate with a piece of pineapple.

(Illustration, p. 1101)

Switzerland

Pineapple slices II

Sandwich two sheets of swiss roll with pineapple buttercream into which chopped pistachio nuts have been mixed. Refrigerate and cut into strips 7–8 cm (3 in) wide. Spread the sides with the same cream and mask with chocolate shavings. Pipe two lines of buttercream along the top so that they are 1 cm (about ½ in) from each edge. Cut into slices and decorate each one with a piece of pineapple and half a glacé cherry.

Switzerland

Pineapple tartlets

Sweet pastry

300 g	sugar	12 oz
200 g	butter	8 oz
500 g	flour	1¼ lb
	little grated lemon zest	

Hollandaise filling

500 g	almond paste	1¼ lb
200 g	butter	8 oz
300 g	6 eggs	12 oz
170 g	flour	7 oz
5 g	baking powder	½ teaspoon
	little grated lemon zest	
	well boiled apricot purée	
	pineapple crush	
	tiny triangles of pineapple	
	halved red cherries	
	water icing	

To make the sweet pastry, mix the eggs and sugar together well, then blend thoroughly with the butter. Work to a paste with the flour and lemon zest and allow to rest in the refrigerator before using.

To make the hollandaise filling, cream the butter with the almond paste and add the eggs a little at a time. Mix in the lemon zest and the flour which has been sieved with the baking powder.

Pin out the sweet pastry thinly, cut out with a round cutter and line patty pans with the pastry. Press down with the back of the cutter. Pipe a little apricot purée into the tartlets and cover with a teaspoonful of pineapple crush. Pipe on hollandaise filling, using a savoy bag, and decorate with a triangle of pineapple and half a cherry. Bake at 180°C. While still hot, brush with apricot purée and coat with water icing.

Switzerland

Pistachio cornets

200 g	blanched almonds	8 oz
250 g	sugar	10 oz
60 g	flour	2 oz
	vanilla	
	egg white	
	milk	
	'fondante' pistachio	
	almond paste	

Grind the almonds and sugar very finely with a little egg white and work down to a pliable paste with milk and egg white in equal amounts. Add the flour and vanilla and mix to a smooth fairly soft consistency. Using a savoy bag, pipe in small disks on to a waxed baking sheet. Bake in a hot oven, remove at once and shape into cones. When cold fill with the pistachio almond paste.

(Illustration, p. 804)   France

Pistachio rolls

400 g	almonds	1 lb
600 g	caster sugar	1½ lb
200 g	flour	8 oz
200 g	egg whites	8 oz
230 ml	milk	8 fl oz

Grind the almonds and sugar without moistening. Add the whites, flour and milk and mix well. Stencil out on to greased and floured baking sheets. Bake at 195°C (380°F) and while still hot fashion into tubes using an oiled rod. When cold, fill with pistachio marzipan softened with kirsch and dip both ends of each roll in couverture.

France

Polkas

Yields 20–50   10–12 minutes in a hot oven

250 g	short paste	10 oz
125 g	choux paste	5 oz
200 g	confectioner's custard	8 oz
	icing sugar	

Pin out the pastry to a thickness of 2–3 mm (about ⅛ in). Cut out with a round fluted cutter 2 or 3 cm (about 1 in) in diameter. Place the rounds of pastry on a greased baking sheet and prick with a fork. Pipe a ring of choux paste round the edge of each one, using a savoy bag fitted with a small plain pipe. Brush with beaten egg. Bake, then fill the centre with vanilla flavoured confectioner's custard. Dust with icing sugar and caramelise with a red hot iron.

France

Pomone

Proceed as for pineapple 'fritters', replacing the pineapple by apricots, peaches, firm cherries, pears or other fruit. Flavour with kirsch or rum.

France

Pompadours

7–8 minutes in a hot oven

250 g	choux paste	10 oz
350 g	chestnut purée	14 oz
250 g	rum flavoured fondant	10 oz
	30 split almonds	

Using a savoy bag fitted with a medium plain tube, pipe out the choux paste into shapes resembling large commas on a baking sheet. Bake and allow to cool. Fill the bulging part of each one with chestnut purée and coat with fondant. Place a split almond on each one. Serve in small oblong paper cases.

France

Pont-Neufs

Yields 20–25   10–12 minutes in a hot oven

250 g	short paste	10 oz

125 g	confectioner's custard	5 oz
125 g	choux paste	5 oz
	icing sugar	
	red currant jelly	

Line patty pans with short paste and prick the bottom with a fork. Fill up to the top with a well blended mixture of confectioner's custard and choux paste. Lay 2 thin strips of short paste on top in the shape of a cross. Bake, then dust with icing sugar. Brush two opposite segments between the crossed strips of pastry with red currant jelly.

France

Praline barquettes

Yields 25–30   10–15 minutes in a hot oven

125 g	flour	5 oz
75 g	ground almonds	3 oz
75 g	butter	3 oz
75 g	sugar	3 oz
	1 egg	
	salt	
200 g	praline buttercream	8 oz
100 g	chocolate fondant	4 oz

Prepare almond short paste and leave overnight. Next day, pin out to a thickness of 2–3 mm (about $\frac{1}{10}$ in). Line small boat shaped tins with the pastry and bake blind. Allow to cool, then fill with the buttercream, making the top slightly dome shaped. Place in the refrigerator for a quarter of an hour to harden the buttercream. Coat the top with chocolate fondant.

France

Praline cakes

Yields 20–25   12–15 minutes in a medium oven

250 g	sweet paste	10 oz
125 g	sugar	5 oz
200 g	unblanched almonds	8 oz
	1 egg white	
	pinch of vanilla	
	apricot jam	

Pin out the sweet paste to a thickness of 2–3 mm (about $\frac{1}{10}$ in). Cut into ovals with a fluted cutter. Line small boat shaped tins with the ovals of pastry, prick the bottom and spread with apricot jam. Chop the unblanched almonds finely. Work them with the sugar in a mortar or basin. Gradually add the unwhisked egg white and the vanilla. Fill the tins with the mixture and bake.

France

Praline duchesses

3–4 minutes in a hot oven

100 g	sugar	4 oz
30 g	ground almonds	1 oz
30 g	roasted ground hazelnuts	1 oz
30 g	flour	1 oz
30 g	butter	1 oz
	3 egg whites whipped to a stiff snow	
	pinch of ground vanilla	
100 g	praline paste	4 oz

Sift the sugar mixed with the ground almonds and hazelnuts, the flour and vanilla into the stiffly whipped egg whites and fold in lightly with a spatula. Add the lukewarm melted butter. Using a stencil, deposit in small ovals on a greased and floured baking sheet and bake. When cold, sandwich in pairs with a little softened praline paste.

France

Puits d'amour

Yields 12–14   10–12 minutes in a very hot oven

250 g	puff paste	10 oz
	well boiled apricot purée	
	or vanilla flavoured	
	confectioner's custard	

Pin out the puff paste to a thickness of 2 mm (about $\frac{1}{10}$ in), cut out with a plain round cutter 3 or 4 cm (about $1\frac{1}{2}$ in) in diameter. Cut out the centre of half the rounds of pastry to make small rings. Place the remaining rounds of pastry on a baking sheet and moisten slightly with water. Place a ring of pastry on each one and press down a little to make it stick. Brush with beaten egg. Bake, then allow to cool on a wire rack. Fill the centres with confectioner's custard (decorating with a hot iron if desired) or well boiled apricot purée. Top with a piece of glacé cherry.

France

Reginas

7–8 minutes in a hot oven

>sweet paste
>strawberry jam
>chopped pistachio nuts
>glacé cherries

Line small tartlet pans with sweet paste, fill with strawberry jam and bake. Allow to cool, then mask the top with chopped pistachio nuts. Place half a glacé cherry in the centre of each one.

France

Réjane

8–10 minutes in a medium oven

>virgin puff paste or puff paste cuttings
>choux paste
>flaked almonds
>well boiled apricot purée

Line small boat shaped tins with puff paste and fill with choux paste. Brush with egg, sprinkle with flaked almonds and bake. Turn out and allow to cool. Using a savoy bag fitted with a small tube, pipe in apricot purée flavoured with kirsch. Dust with icing sugar.

France

Rieuses

8–10 minutes in a hot oven

>berrichon paste
>praline buttercream flavoured with Curaçao
>Curaçao fondant
>stiff apple jelly

Using a savoy bag fitted with a plain pipe, line oval moulds with berrichon paste. Bake, allow to cool, then remove from the moulds. Fill with the buttercream and leave in the refrigerator until firm. Ice with Curaçao fondant. Cut out dots of apple jelly with a round cutter and place one at each end and one in the centre of the petits fours.

France

Rigolettos

Sponge

500 g	10 eggs	1¼ lb
350 g	sugar	14 oz
250 g	flour	10 oz
	grated zest of half a lemon	

Filling

chocolate buttercream

Decoration

chocolate shavings
milk couverture

Mix the eggs and sugar together, warm gently and whip until frothy. Fold in the flour and lemon zest and spread on paper to a thickness of 1 cm (about ½ in). Bake at about 230°C. Allow to cool, then remove the paper and cut into small rounds. Spread tempered milk couverture on greaseproof paper; when almost set, cut out rounds of the same size as the sponge rounds, invert the paper and peel it off.

With the help of a savoy bag, sandwich the sponge rounds in threes with chocolate buttercream. When firm, dip each of the fancies in the same buttercream, using a fork. Smooth off, roll the sides in the chocolate shavings, and place a couverture cut out on top.

Switzerland

Royal sticks

7–8 minutes in a medium oven

150 g	flour	6 oz
150 g	ground almonds	6 oz
150 g	sugar	6 oz
150 g	butter	6 oz
	1 egg	
	good pinch of ground vanilla	

Mix the sugar, flour, almonds and vanilla together and make a bay in the centre. Place the egg and butter in the bay, draw in the dry ingredients and knead. Allow to rest in a cool place for half an hour. To shape into sticks, either pin out the paste and cut to the desired size, or use a savoy bag fitted with a medium star pipe. Bake on a greased baking sheet.

Sablés I

7–8 minutes in a hot oven

125 g	flour	5 oz
90 g	butter	3¼ oz
60 g	sugar	2 oz
	2 hard-boiled egg yolks	
3 g	salt	1/10 oz
	finely chopped zest of 1 lemon	

Rub the hard-boiled egg yolks through a fine sieve. Make a bay in the flour and place all the other ingredients in the centre, mix well and gradually draw in the flour. Allow to rest for at least 2 hours in a cool place (or mould into a ball, wrap in a cloth and leave in a cool place overnight). Pin out to a thickness of 4 mm (about ⅛ in) and cut out with a fluted round or triangular cutter. Mark with a criss-cross patterned roller, dusting it with flour from time to time. Bake.

France

Sablés II

250 g	flour	10 oz
175 g	butter	7 oz
75 g	icing sugar	3 oz
	1 egg	
	pinch of salt	
	zest of 1 lemon	

Make the ingredients into a paste and shape with the hands into a long roll of the desired thickness. Roll the paste in caster sugar to coat all round. Refrigerate until firm. Cut into thin slices with a sharp knife and bake in a medium oven.

Switzerland

Sacristans

6–7 minutes in a hot oven

puff paste
chopped almonds
caster sugar

Pin out the paste 2 mm (about $\frac{1}{10}$ in) thick to make a strip 12 cm (5 in) wide. Wash with egg and sprinkle with a mixture of chopped almonds and caster sugar. Cut across at intervals of 1 cm ($\frac{1}{2}$ in). Hold each piece by both ends and twist. Place on a baking sheet and stick the ends down to prevent the strips of pastry untwisting. Bake.

France

Salambos

7–8 minutes in a hot oven

250 g	choux paste	10 oz
$\frac{1}{2}$ l	Chantilly cream	$\frac{7}{8}$ pt
150 g	chopped pistachio nuts	6 oz
	sugar boiled to the crack degree	

Pipe out small bulbs of choux paste on to a baking sheet. Bake and allow to cool. Make a slit in each one three-quarters of the way up and fill with Chantilly cream. When all the petits choux have been filled, quickly dip the tops in sugar boiled to the crack degree and then lightly press into chopped pistachio nuts. Place in small paper cases to serve.

France

Scottish shortbread

45–50 minutes in a medium oven

150 g	plain flour	6 oz
	pinch of salt	
100 g	butter	4 oz
50 g	caster sugar	2 oz

Sift the flour and salt together, then rub in the butter until the mixture resembles fine breadcrumbs. Add the sugar and knead the mixture until it binds well together. Turn the dough on to a lightly floured board and press into a round shape. Crimp the edges with the finger and thumb. Mark the round into sections with a knife and prick the surface with a fork. Bake towards the bottom of the oven on a greased baking tray until firm and lightly coloured. Divide when cool.

Shuttles

7–8 minutes in a medium oven

125 g	flour	5 oz
50 g	sugar	2 oz
75 g	butter	3 oz
	1 egg yolk	
	small pinch of salt	
10 g	orange flavoured sugar	½ oz
5 cl	milk or water	2 fl oz
	1 egg white	
	granulated sugar	

Proceed as for sweet paste. Wrap in a damp cloth and allow to rest for at least 2 hours in a cool place. Fashion into shuttle shapes 3 cm (about 1 in) thick and 5 cm (2 in) long, place on a greased baking sheet, brush with lightly beaten egg white and sprinkle with granulated sugar. Bake.

France

Small croissants (mignons)

50 croissants

500 g	flour	1¼ lb
8 cl	oil	2½ fl oz
80 g	*or*, if desired butter	2 oz
50 g	yeast	2 oz
30 g	caraway seeds	1 oz
	4 eggs	
approx. 4 dl	milk	⅔ pt approx.
5 g	sugar	1 teaspoon
	zest of 1 lemon	

Disperse the yeast in lukewarm milk and work to a smooth dough with the flour, the oil, 2 eggs, the sugar, a good pinch of salt and lemon zest. Cover with a cloth and leave to ferment. Scale at 150 g (6 oz) divide each piece evenly into eight and shape into croissants. Arrange on a baking sheet, brush with beaten egg and prove. Egg wash again, sprinkle with caraway seeds and salt and bake in a hot oven until golden brown.

If preferred, the dough may be shaped into round rolls. In this case the caraway should be omitted and the rolls sprinkled with salt only.

(Techniques, p. 103)   Czechoslovakia

Snowballs

160 g	flour	5½ oz
60 g	icing sugar	2½ oz
	6 egg yolks	
50 g	butter	2 oz
2 cl	fine rum	2 dessertspoons
	finely chopped peel of ¼ lemon	
	pinch of salt	

Work all the ingredients to a paste on a floured table or marble slab and leave to rest for a short time. Pin out into an oblong 5 mm (¼ in) thick and cut into long strips with a pastry wheel. Shape the strips with the hands into small loose heaps and fry in clarified butter to a good golden brown colour. Drain well at once and sprinkle with vanilla sugar.

Snowballs may be served with fruit juice if desired.

Austria

Soupirs

Yields 20–25   8–10 minutes in a hot oven

250 g	sweet paste	10 oz
150 g	frangipane custard	6 oz
	Italian meringue	
	fondant (various colours and flavours)	

Line patty pans with the sweet paste and prick the bottom with a fork. Fill with frangipane custard and bake. Pipe a pear shaped bulb of Italian meringue in the centre of each one, holding the savoy bag upright. Dry out the meringue for a few minutes in a cool oven. When quite cold, ice with white, pink and green fondant.

France

Souvaroff biscuits

5–6 minutes in a very hot oven

125 g	flour	5 oz
100 g	butter	4 oz
50 g	icing sugar	2 oz
	1 egg yolk	
	pinch of salt	
	red currant or apricot jam	

Place the softened butter, the icing sugar and salt in the centre of a basin with the flour all round. Cream the butter and sugar, then draw in the flour to make a smooth dough. Remove from the basin and allow to rest for at least 2 hours. Pin out to a thickness of 2½ mm (1/10 in). Cut out with an oval cutter 4 cm (1½ in) long and bake. When almost baked, dust with icing sugar (either leaving the baking sheet in the oven or removing it for a moment) and caramelise slightly. When cold, sandwich base to base in pairs with jam.

France

Spiced honey cakes Pardubice style

40–50 cakes   Baking time: 12–15 minutes

600 g	honey	1½ lb
2 dl	stock syrup	⅓ pt
2 dl	water	⅓ pt
250 g	rye flour	10 oz
	wheat flour	

For 1 kg (2 lb 3 oz) dough

100 g	icing sugar	4 oz
	2 egg yolks	
10 g	carbonate of ammonia	1 teaspoon
5 cl	water	2 fl oz
10 g	ground cloves	1 level teaspoon
10 g	ground cinnamon	1 level teaspoon
50 g	ground almonds	2 oz
	zest of 1 orange	
	sugar glaze	

Bring the honey, syrup and water to the boil and allow to cool until lukewarm. Stir in the rye flour and add sufficient wheat flour to work the mixture into a dough of medium firmness. Leave for at least 24 hours, preferably 3–4 days, before using.

Weigh into 1 kg (2 lb 3 oz) pieces, add the icing sugar, egg yolks, spices, carbonate of ammonia, water, orange zest and ground almonds, then work thoroughly, adding a little more wheat flour. Pin out to a thickness of 5 mm (¼ in), cut out in various shapes and arrange on a greased baking sheet. Bake in a moderate oven until the cakes have risen, then increase the heat and bake off, turning the cakes when one side is golden to colour the other side. After removing from the oven, glaze with a sugar solution.

Czechoslovakia

Spitzbuben

150 g	butter	6 oz
200 g	icing sugar	8 oz
400 g	flour	1 lb
	pinch of salt	
	grated lemon zest	
	apricot purée	

Make a paste with the butter, icing sugar, flour, lemon zest and salt, and allow to rest for a time. Pin out to 2 mm ($\frac{1}{10}$ in) thick, cut into 3 cm ($1\frac{1}{4}$ in) rounds and make small holes in half of these. Bake at 200°C. After baking spread the whole rounds with apricot purée and place the perforated rounds on top.

Switzerland

Sponge fingers

	12 egg yolks	
	8 egg whites	
250 g	flour	10 oz
250 g	sugar	10 oz
	zest of 1 lemon	

Whisk the egg yolks and half the sugar to a stiff sponge with the addition of the grated lemon zest. Whip the whites to a stiff snow, add the rest of the sugar and fold into the yolk/sugar sponge. Lastly fold in the flour. Using a plain tube, pipe out finger shapes on greaseproof paper. Dredge with sugar and bake quickly in a hot oven.

Switzerland

Spritz biscuits

500 g	butter	1$\frac{1}{4}$ lb
250 g	icing sugar	10 oz
3$\frac{1}{2}$ dl	dairy cream	$\frac{2}{3}$ pt
800 g	flour	2 lb
	pinch of salt	
	zest of 1 lemon	
	jam	
	couverture	

Cream the butter with the sugar and gradually work in the cream, lemon zest, salt and flour. Using a star tube, pipe out shell shapes on to lightly greased baking sheets and bake at 180°C. Sandwich in pairs with jam and dip the tips in tempered couverture.

Switzerland

Suns

8–10 minutes in a medium oven

> Provence crescent paste
> chopped almonds
> well boiled apricot purée
> candied orange peel
> pistachio nuts

Shape the paste into balls the size of a greengage. Roll in beaten egg, drain, then roll in chopped almonds. Place on greaseproof paper. Make a cavity in each with the end of a spatula handle. Bake. On removing from the oven, fill each cavity with apricot purée and place a disk of orange peel on top. Arrange thin strips of pistachio nut all round, radiating from the centre, to represent the sun's rays.

France

Surprises

7–8 minutes in a hot oven

250 g	choux paste	10 oz
500 g	praline buttercream	1¼ lb
150 g	chopped almonds	6 oz

Pipe out small bulbs of choux paste on to a baking sheet. Brush with beaten egg. Sprinkle the top with a mixture of chopped almonds and granulated sugar. Bake and allow to cool. Slit and fill with buttercream. Dust with icing sugar. Place in small paper cases to serve.

France

Tea scones

20 scones   Baking time: about 15 minutes

240 g	flour	10 oz
15 g	baking powder	½ oz
60 g	butter	2 oz
50 g	sugar	2 oz
	1 egg	
approx. ⅛ l	milk	¼ pt
	egg wash	

Sieve the flour and baking powder. Cream the butter and sugar, add the egg and then half the milk. Add the flour and half mix in. Now add the rest of the milk and mix to a dough. Roll out 1¼ cm (½ in) thick, cut out 5 cm (2 in) rounds and place on a lightly greased baking sheet. Brush with egg wash and bake at 225°C. When cold, split and spread with butter, or sandwich together with jam and cream.

Great Britain

Toscas

4–5 minutes in a hot oven

250 g	sweet paste	10 oz
200 g	vanilla buttercream flavoured with kirsch	8 oz
200 g	white fondant	8 oz
	chopped pistachio nuts	

Cut the sweet paste into rounds with a fluted cutter and line small pomponnette moulds. Bake, allow to cool, and fill up to the top with the buttercream. Coat with fondant and sprinkle the centre lightly with chopped pistachio nuts.

This type of petit four may be varied by using buttercream of different flavours and colours.

France

Triads

7–8 minutes in a moderate oven

choux paste
Chantilly cream
icing sugar
glacé cherries

Using a savoy bag, pipe out small bulbs of choux paste in groups of three arranged in a triangle. Wash with egg and bake. On removing from the oven, snip the tops off each group of three choux with a pair of scissors (set the tops aside). When cold, fill with Chantilly cream and put the tops back into place. Dust with icing sugar and place a glacé cherry in the centre of each triad.

France

Tuiles

4–5 minutes in a very hot oven

100 g	sugar	4 oz
50 g	flour	2 oz
50 g	butter	2 oz
40 g	flaked almonds	2 oz
	2 egg whites	

Whisk the egg whites and sugar until frothy. Using a spatula, blend in the flour, then the almonds and, lastly, the melted butter. Deposit a teaspoonful at a time in well spaced heaps on a greased baking sheet, flatten and bake. On removing from the oven, curl round a rolling pin or similar curved surface and allow to cool. The paste may be tinted pink with a few drops of carmine if desired.

France

Turkish tartlets

	sweet paste	
	apricot jam	

Egg yolk macaroon paste

500 g	marzipan	1¼ lb
100 g	icing sugar	4 oz
	5 egg yolks	
	mixed candied fruit macerated in rum	
	chopped roasted almonds	

Pin out the sweet paste thinly and cut into ovals 8 cm (3 in) long. Bake at 180°C. When cold, sandwich in pairs with apricot jam. Mix the ingredients for the macaroon paste together well, pipe a ring of the paste on to each tartlet and flash. Fill the centre with mixed fruit, glaze all over with hot apricot jam and mask the edges with chopped almonds.

Germany

Tutti

4–5 minutes in a hot oven

	sweet paste	

> sponge or other cake trimmings,
>   broken biscuits, etc.
> rum
> chopped candied fruit
> rum fondant
> small diamond shaped pieces of
>   angelica

Macerate the candied fruit in rum. Line patty pans or small boat shaped tins with sweet paste and bake blind. Allow to cool. Steep the cake trimmings, etc. in rum, then chop up finely with the candied fruit. Fill the pastry cases with the mixture and coat with fondant or butter cream. Decorate with diamonds of angelica.

France

Ursulines

Yields 20–25   8–10 minutes

250 g	sweet paste	10 oz
200 g	raw marzipan	8 oz
	Italian meringue	
	red currant jam	

Line small boat shaped tins with the sweet paste and prick the bottom. Fill with raw marzipan and cover with a dome of Italian meringue. Using a savoy bag fitted with a small tube, pipe a ring of meringue in the centre of the dome. Dry out in a slow oven. When cold, place a little red currant jam in the centre of the ring of meringue.

France

Viennese waffles

Baking time: about 30 minutes

Pastry

400 g	butter	1 lb
250 g	sugar	10 oz
500 g	flour	1¼ lb
100 g	ground almonds	4 oz
	2 egg yolks	
	pinch of salt	
	lemon, vanilla	

Meringue

$\frac{1}{8}$ l	egg white	$\frac{1}{4}$ pint
200 g	sugar	8 oz
	apricot jam	
	raspberry jam	

Make the pastry, allow to rest, then pin out 4 mm (about $\frac{1}{6}$ in) thick to a rectangular shape and bake at 180°C. Divide in half and sandwich the two halves with apricot jam. Pipe meringue on top lattice fashion and flash quickly. Fill in the spaces between the criss-cross lines of meringue with hot raspberry jam. When cold, cut into oblongs about 4 × 6 cm ($1\frac{1}{2}$ × $2\frac{1}{2}$ in) or as desired.

Germany

Visitants

8–10 minutes in a hot oven

150 g	sugar	6 oz
125 g	ground almonds	5 oz
50 g	flour	2 oz
150 g	butter	6 oz
	4 unwhipped egg whites	
	2 egg whites whipped to a stiff snow	
	good pinch of vanilla	

Using a spatula, beat the sugar, the ground almonds and the 4 unwhipped egg whites together in a basin for at least 15 minutes. Add the flour and vanilla. Heat the butter until nut-brown, strain to remove any sediment, leave until cold but still liquid and blend into the mixture. Fold in the 2 stiffly whipped egg whites lightly. Bake in small greased and floured boat shaped tins.

France

Wafer mixture for decoration

About 120 wafers

500 g	raw marzipan	$1\frac{1}{4}$ lb
375 g	icing sugar	15 oz
125 g	flour	5 oz
$\frac{1}{8}$ l	egg whites	$\frac{1}{4}$ pt
$\frac{1}{8}$ l	milk	$\frac{1}{4}$ pt
20 g	melted butter	1 oz
	pinch of cinnamon	

Blend the marzipan, icing sugar, flour and egg whites to a very smooth paste and add just enough milk to give a spreading consistency. Do not whisk, to avoid blistering during baking. Cover and allow to stand overnight to amalgamate the ingredients thoroughly.

Stencil out thinly on to waxed baking sheets, using home made stencils. Bake at 220°C. Before the wafers turn brown, remove from the oven and stand aside until almost cold. Now bake off until evenly brown, then roll the wafers immediately over a rolling pin or roll up.

Germany

Waffles with wine cream

Yield: 50 fancies, 2 waffles each
Waffles

1 kg	flour	2½ lb
	14 egg yolks	
	14 egg whites	
475 g	sugar	1 lb 3 oz
600 g	butter	1½ lb
100 g	ground almonds	4 oz
	1 scraped vanilla pod	
	pinch of salt	

Wine cream

	6 egg yolks	
160 g	sugar	6 oz
¼ l	white wine	½ pt
	juice of half a lemon	
	7 sheets gelatine	
6½ dl	unsweetened whipped cream	1 pt

Cream the butter and sugar together, then add the egg yolks a little at a time. Flavour with the vanilla, add the salt, blend in the flour and almonds and lastly fold in the egg whites whipped to a stiff snow. Bake until crisp in a preheated lightly greased waffle iron.

To make the wine cream, whip up the egg yolks, sugar and white wine over low heat; while still hot, add the gelatine which has been soaked and flavour with the lemon juice. When the custard is cold and about to set, blend in the whipped cream.

Sandwich the waffles in pairs with the wine cream, dredge with icing sugar, decorate with a rosette of whipped cream and place a grape glazed with jelly in the centre.

Any unused waffles should be stored in airtight tins to keep them fresh and crisp.

Germany

Walnut Fancies

Pastry

700 g	flour	1 lb 12 oz
500 g	butter	1¼ lb
150 g	icing sugar	6 oz
	10 sieved hard-boiled egg yolks	

Filling

250 g	lightly roasted ground hazelnuts	10 oz
250 g	ground walnuts	10 oz
500 g	fondant	1¼ lb
	¼ vanilla pod	
1 dl	dairy cream	3 fl oz

Work the icing sugar, egg yolks and butter to a smooth paste and blend in the flour. Allow to rest in a cool place, then pin out 3 mm ($\frac{1}{10}$ in) thick, cut into half moon shapes of the desired size and bake at about 180° until golden. Mix the nuts, fondant and vanilla together and add sufficient cream (about 1 dl) ($\frac{1}{6}$ pt) to bring to a spreading consistency. Sandwich the half moons in pairs with the filling, dust with icing sugar and decorate with a caramelised walnut.

Germany

Walnut pavés

Split a sheet of genoese and sandwich with walnut buttercream. Leave until firm, brush the top with apricot purée and cut evenly into squares. Fix half a walnut on top of each one, then dip into fairly liquid white fondant. Using a paper piping bag, edge the top with a thin line of chocolate icing.

(Illustration, p. 1101)

Switzerland

Walnut tartlets

Line shallow plain tartlet pans with Linz paste and bake blind. Allow to cool, then fill with praline buttercream. When firm, dip into coffee coloured and flavoured fondant. For final decoration, place half a walnut dusted with icing sugar in the centre.

(Illustration, p. 1101)   France

White amaretti

250 g	blanched sweet almonds	10 oz
50 g	blanched bitter almonds	2 oz
900 g	sugar	2¼ lb
	10–12 egg whites	

Grate the almonds and mix with the sugar and half the egg white. Grind 3 or 4 times, setting the rollers as close together as possible the last time. The paste should be smooth and fine, but not oily. Work in the mixer and add the rest of the egg white, using a coarse whisk. Pipe out on to greased and floured baking sheets or silicone paper, using a savoy bag fitted with a 10–12 mm (½ in) plain pipe. As the paste remains somewhat soft, the piped out amaretti spread rather quickly; this should be allowed for to obtain a final diameter of 5–6 cm (about 2 in), which is the correct size for amaretti. Leave for at least 12 hours in a dry, moderately warm place (a prover may be used, but it must be steam-free). It is essential for the surface to crust slightly. With the finger tips lightly squeeze each circle into an almost square or trapezoid shape. There should be cracks both at the edges and in the centre of the amaretti; they are a characteristic feature of these biscuits. Dust well with icing sugar and bake for a few minutes in a fairly hot steam-free oven. The cracks should become golden brown, contrasting with the white icing sugar. Due to the short baking time, the amaretti remain soft in the centre.

Switzerland

Williamine fancies

Split a sheet of genoese twice and sandwich with buttercream flavoured with William pear brandy. Leave until firm, cut into strips, then cut each strip into triangles. Place a small pear made of buttercream on top of each triangle and leave until firm. Dip into white fondant flavoured with William pear brandy. Place a piece of candied angelica on top to make a leaf for the pear showing through the fondant.

(Illustration, p. 1101)   Switzerland

Yo-Yos

5–6 minutes in a medium oven

200 g	cream skimmed from the top of boiled milk	7 oz
150 g	flour	6 oz
200 g	caster sugar lightly flavoured with vanilla	7 oz
	quince butter	

Mix the flour, sugar and cream to a smooth paste. Deposit on a greased baking sheet in small heaps, leaving room for spreading. Bake. On removing from the oven, transfer to a flat surface and allow to cool. Sandwich in pairs with a little quince butter (or any other fruit butter).

Raisins or chopped candied fruit may be added to the paste if desired. Devonshire cream can be used for this dish.

France

Zug kirsch tartlets

Japonaise

250 g	10 egg whites	10 oz
350 g	sugar	14 oz
250 g	ground almonds	10 oz

Whisk the egg whites with 150 g (5¼ oz) sugar, then fold in the rest of the sugar and the almonds. Stencil in circles on to greased baking sheets or silicone paper and bake slowly at about 180°C.

Butter sponge

500 g	10 eggs	1¼ lb
300 g	sugar	12 oz
300 g	flour	12 oz
100 g	melted butter	4 oz

Mix the eggs and sugar together, warm gently and whisk until frothy. Fold in the flour, blend in the melted butter (without whey) and spread on to paper to a thickness of about 1½ cm (½ in). Bake at about 200–220°C, allow to cool and cut out with a round cutter of the same size as the japonaise disks.

Splash the butter sponge bases with kirsch syrup (3 parts stock syrup at about 28°B to 2 parts kirsch) and pipe on kirsch buttercream. Cover each base with a japonaise disk spread with the same buttercream, dredge with icing sugar and mark into lines with an egg slicer.

Switzerland

GÂTEAUX AND TORTEN

Aargau carrot torte

125 g	egg yolks	5 oz
100 g	icing sugar	4 oz
	pinch of salt	
250 g	grated carrots	10 oz
125 g	ground almonds	5 oz
125 g	ground hazelnuts	5 oz
50 g	rusk crumbs	2 oz
30 g	flour	1 oz
10 g	baking powder	1 teaspoon
150 g	egg whites	6 oz
100 g	caster sugar	4 oz
	zest of ½ lemon	
	cinnamon	
	ground cloves	

Whip the egg yolks, icing sugar, zest and salt until foamy. Stir in the carrots, hazelnuts, almonds, rusk crumbs, flour, baking powder and spices and lastly fold in the whites whisked to a stiff snow with the caster sugar. Fill into a greased and floured cake hoop or a deep flan ring and bake for about an hour at 180°C (360°F). The formula yields 1 gâteau 25 cm (10 in) in diameter. After baking, dust with icing sugar if desired. Marzipan carrots may be used for final decoration. If preferred, the gâteau may be enclosed in marzipan. With careful storage the gâteau will remain moist for a long time. It should not be sold before the second day.

Switzerland

Apple tart Rouen style

12 portions

approx. 650 g	short paste	1 lb 10 oz
500 g	apples, peeled, cored and finely sliced	1¼ lb
50 g	granulated sugar	2 oz
2 dl	white wine	⅓ pt
30 g	raisins	1 oz
	a little cinnamon	

Hollandaise filling

250 g	ground almonds	10 oz
250 g	sugar	10 oz
	5 eggs	
250 g	butter	10 oz
	apricot purée	
100 g	roasted flaked almonds	4 oz

Line a 22 cm (9 in) flan hoop with the short pastry, keeping the rim thicker than the base. Cover the base with apricot purée. Stew the apples until soft with the sugar, wine, raisins, flaked almonds and a little cinnamon. Allow to cool, then fill into the pastry case, cover with a thick layer of Hollandaise filling and bake at 200°C. To make the Hollandaise filling place the almonds and sugar in a basin, add the eggs and beat slightly. Melt the butter, make it fairly hot and add, stirring constantly.

Switzerland

Apple tart Tatin

6–8 persons   Baking time: 20–25 minutes

1 kg	apples	2½ lb
400–450 g	unsweetened short paste	1 lb–1 lb 2 oz
200 g	icing sugar	8 oz
125 g	butter	5 oz

This tart is baked either in a round cake tin about 6 cm (2½ in) deep or in a frying pan of corresponding size. Butter the bottom and sides very well; cover the bottom with icing sugar to a thickness of about 1 cm (½ in). Peel and core the apples, cut each one into eight and arrange evenly on the icing sugar. Dot with butter and dust with icing sugar. Pin out the pastry into a round barely 3 mm ($\frac{1}{10}$ in) thick, cover the tin or frying pan with it so that it projects over the edge a little and press down round the edge. Bake at about 200°C. On removing from the oven, turn out so that the apples are on top.

France

Baumkuchen Christmas gâteau

16 portions

250 g	sugar	10 oz
	9 egg yolks	
	7 egg whites	

250 g	butter	10 oz
125 g	flour	5 oz
125 g	cornflour	5 oz
	½ vanilla pod, scraped	
2 cl	arrack	2 dessertspoons
	zest of half a lemon	
	pinch of salt	
	apricot purée	
	arrack flavoured fondant	
	vanilla buttercream	
	couverture	
	icing sugar	
	roasted nibbed almonds	
	marzipan	

Whisk the egg yolks and sugar to a stiff sponge. Cream the butter with the flour, cornflour, vanilla, lemon zest, salt and arrack, blend in the egg yolk/sugar sponge and lastly fold in the egg whites whipped to a stiff snow. Bake on a Baumkuchen machine in 10–12 layers.

When cold, brush thinly with hot apricot purée and coat with the fondant. Mask the bottom edge to a height of 1 cm (½ in) with roasted nibbed almonds and pipe a border of royal icing or vanilla buttercream. Place a pale yellow marzipan star in the centre of the gâteau. Mark into portions with piped chocolate icing, fix small Baumkuchen in position all round with small bulbs of vanilla buttercream and edge with milk couverture. Decorate the centre of the gâteau with finely piped couverture stars of various sizes which have been allowed to set, then assembled to the shape of a Christmas tree and dusted with icing sugar.

Germany

Berlin Napfkuchen

Yield: about 15–18 good sized portions   Baking time: about 1 hour

525 g	butter	1 lb 5 oz
550 g	flour	1 lb 6 oz
500 g	sugar	1 lb 4 oz
	11 eggs, separated	
100 g	chopped or ground almonds	4 oz
	zest of 1 lemon	

Cream the butter and work in the flour a little at a time. Whisk the egg yolks to a stiff sponge with 300 g (10½ oz) sugar and the lemon zest. Whip the whites and the rest of the sugar to a stiff snow. Carefully mix the egg yolk sponge with the butter/flour mixture and fold in the whipped whites very lightly. Butter 'Napfkuchen' tins and sprinkle with chopped or ground almonds. Three-quarters fill with the mixture and bake at 190–200°C. Cover with greased paper after a time to prevent excessive browning of the top. Leave in the tins until cold, then turn out and dust with icing sugar.

Germany

Birthday torte

14–16 persons   Baking time: about 35 minutes

Base

200 g	butter	8 oz
	7 egg yolks	
	8 egg whites	
160 g	sugar	6 oz
125 g	crushed finely sieved croquant	5 oz
150 g	flour	6 oz
	vanilla	
	pinch of salt	
	pinch of cinnamon	

Vanilla buttercream

500 g	butter	1¼ lb
100 g	icing sugar	4 oz
¾ l	vanilla confectioner's custard	1¼ pt

Croquant buttercream

300 g	vanilla buttercream	12 oz
50 g	crushed sieved croquant	1 oz
2 cl	arrack or kirsch	2 dessertspoons
	marzipan candles and flowers	
	stock syrup flavoured with arrack or kirsch	
	marzipan	

To make the base, cream the butter with a third of the sugar and gradually beat in the egg yolks with the addition of the vanilla, cinnamon and salt. Whip the egg whites to a stiff snow with the rest of the sugar and fold into the yolk/butter/sugar mixture, together with the flour which has been mixed with the croquant. Deposit in a heart-shaped cake tin and bake at 200°C. Allow to cool, split three times, splash with arrack or kirsch syrup and sandwich with croquant buttercream. Cover the torte with a thin layer of marzipan and coat and decorate with croquant butter-cream. Finish off with an arrangement of marzipan candles in flower shaped marzipan holders.

Germany

Bolognese rice torta

10 portions approx.   Baking time: 20 minutes

1 l	milk	1¾ pt
	zest of ⅓ lemon	
150 g	rice	6 oz
300 g	sugar	12 oz
150 g	citron peel, finely diced	6 oz
150 g	roasted strip almonds	6 oz
150 g	almond macaroons	6 oz
2 dl	maraschino	⅓ pt
	8 eggs	
	butter, icing sugar	

Heat the milk, add the lemon zest and the rice and cook until the rice is tender. Meanwhile caramelise the sugar lightly. Add the cooked rice and allow to cool. Stir in the almonds, the citron peel, the crumbled macaroons and the lightly beaten eggs. Lastly add a third of the maraschino. Fill into a buttered shallow round tin lined with buttered aluminium foil or waxed paper and bake at 180°C. While still hot, soak with the rest of the maraschino. Dust with icing sugar before serving.

Italy

Chocolate almond gâteau

12 portions

140 g	couverture	5½ oz
140 g	butter	5½ oz
160 g	sugar	6½ oz
	3 egg yolks	
	3 egg whites	
80 g	finely ground almonds	3 oz
80 g	rye or wheat flour	3 oz

To decorate

100 g	raw marzipan	4 oz.
40 g	icing sugar	1½ oz
	1 small pot soft chocolate icing	
	split almonds	

Dissolve the couverture in a bain-marie and allow to cool a little. Cream the butter with half the sugar, pour in the couverture, then beat in the egg yolks a little at a time. Add the ground almonds and beat well. Whip the egg whites and remaining sugar to a stiff snow, fold into the mixture and lastly fold in the sieved flour lightly. Bake at 180°C in a mould 24–26 cm (about 10 in) in diameter which has been greased and dusted with flour or cake crumbs. Allow to cool, then turn out. Knead the marzipan with the icing sugar and roll out thinly. Soften the chocolate icing in a bain-marie and spread over the top and sides of the gâteau thinly to hold the marzipan in place. Cover firmly with the marzipan and coat with the rest of the chocolate icing. Decorate with split almonds if desired.

Germany

Chocolate torte

360 g	icing sugar	14 oz
	10 egg yolks	
	5 eggs	
	10 egg whites	
130 g	ground almonds	5 oz
140 g	cocoa paste	6 oz
110 g	melted butter	4 oz
130 g	cake crumbs	5 oz
	vanilla	

Place the butter and cocoa in a bowl and melt over a bain-marie, then temper. Whisk the egg yolks and eggs with two-thirds of the sugar, warming the mixture, remove from the heat and continue whisking until cool (as for genoese). Whip the egg whites to a stiff snow with the rest of the sugar and fold lightly into the egg/sugar sponge. Now carefully fold in the ground almonds, the cake crumbs and, lastly, the butter/cocoa mixture and the vanilla. Bake at 180°C. Split and sandwich as desired. Coat with chocolate icing.

Austria

Chocolate gâteau (fatless)

105 g	sugar	4 oz
105 g	ground almonds	4 oz
	6 egg yolks	
	3 eggs	
	6 egg whites	
35 g	flour	1½ oz
105 g	chocolate	4 oz
	a little vanilla	

Whip the egg yolks and whole eggs with two-thirds of the sugar until very light and frothy. Meanwhile melt the chocolate and work to a smooth, slightly liquid paste with hot water. Whip the egg whites and the rest of the sugar to a half-stiff snow. Blend the chocolate and the vanilla into the egg/yolk/egg/sugar sponge, then fold in the whipped egg whites, the ground almonds and the flour. Fill into two hoops or circular tins and bake at 180°C. Sandwich with well boiled apricot jam and coat with chocolate icing.

Austria

Christmas gâteau

This gâteau consists of three layers of puff pastry sandwiched with Italian confectioner's custard flavoured with Grand Marnier.

Italian confectioner's custard

1 l	milk	1¾ pt
500 g	sugar	1¼ lb
450 g	egg yolks	1 lb 2 oz
50 g	egg	2 oz
50 g	flour	2 oz
	1 vanilla pod	
25 g	butter	1 oz

Whip up the egg yolks, whole egg and sugar and add the sieved flour. Boil the milk with the vanilla pod and stir into the egg/sugar/flour mixture. Return to the heat and bring to the boil while whisking. Remove from the heat at once, add the butter and cool quickly.

To prepare the gâteau for assembly, it is helpful to pipe a thin strip of chestnut purée along the edges of each layer of puff pastry, using a savoy bag fitted with a plain pipe. This will provide a frame for the filling. Spread each layer of puff pastry with a thin film of red currant jelly and cover with confectioner's custard. Assemble the gâteau, brush the top with apricot purée and coat the top and sides with pink fondant. Mask the sides with chopped roasted hazelnuts.

Decoration

The 'ribbon' across the centre, bearing the inscription, is made of pink almond paste. The little stars are made of yellow almond paste. Royal icing is used for the white lines marking off the portions and also for the cords on which the red balls are hung. The decorative motif symbolising little fir branches is made out of well boiled coloured apricot purée. Spread the purée on a moistened tray to a thickness of 4–5 mm (about ¼ in). When cold, and set, remove from the tray and cut out with a fluted cutter. Alternatively, use pistachio nuts cut to a wedge shape to symbolise the fir branches. The balls are cut out of well boiled red currant or raspberry jelly. They may be made with the aid of the special funnel used for preparing powdered fruit jellies.

The Santa Claus heads are made of royal icing only. The actual head is first modelled to a pear shape; when quite dry, the beard is piped on with a star pipe and the eyes, hair, etc. with a paper bag.

The red balls may be made out of fruit cheese, which can be bought ready-made, instead of fruit jelly.

Diced candied fruit, macerated in Grand Marnier if desired, may be added to the Italian confectioner's custard. Diplomat cream may be used instead of the custard.

Switzerland

Christmas Star

This is made up of two separate gâteau one on top of another.

Chocolate gâteau (base).

Linz pastry

400 g	flour	1 lb
300 g	finely ground hazelnuts	12 oz
400 g	sieved sponge crumbs	1 lb
500 g	butter	1¼ lb
500 g	sugar	1¼ lb
600 g	eggs	1½ lb
	grated zest of 1 lemon	
1 g	pinch of cinnamon	
1 g	pinch of ground cloves	
	little vanilla	

Work into a paste, proceeding as for sweet short pastry. Pin out to a round shape and bake.

Hazel butter sponge

500 g	eggs	1¼ lb
400 g	sugar	1 lb
300 g	flour	12 oz
150 g	ground lightly roasted hazelnuts	6 oz
70 g	melted butter	3 oz

Whisk the eggs and sugar to a stiff sponge, warming the mixture. Remove from the heat and continue whisking. Fold in the flour mixed with the ground hazelnuts and lastly blend in the melted butter. Bake in a sandwich tin.

Ganache

500 g	dairy cream	1¼ lb
1 kg	vanilla couverture	2½ lb

Bring the cream to the boil and add the finely cut couverture. Mix carefully, allow to cool and beat until light.

To assemble the chocolate gâteau, spread the Linz pastry base thinly with ganache. Cover with the hazelnut sponge which has been split, soaked with rum and sand-wiched with ganache. Mask the top and sides thinly with ganache, then cover with dark gianduja (see basic preparations) and coat with chocolate fondant.

Lemon gâteau (star).

Butter sponge

500 g	eggs	1¼ lb
400 g	sugar	1 lb
350 g	flour	14 oz
100 g	cornflour	4 oz
150 g	melted butter	6 oz

Whisk the eggs and sugar to a stiff sponge, warming the mixture. Remove from the heat and continue whisking. Fold in the flour which has been sieved with the corn-flour and lastly blend in the melted butter. Bake in a star shaped or round tin and allow to cool. If a round tin is used, cut the butter sponge to a star shape when quite cold.

Lemon buttercream

750 g	sugar	1 lb 14 oz
300 g	butter	12 oz
375 g	eggs	15 oz
	juice of 8 lemons	
	grated zest of 4 lemons	

Cream the butter and sugar. Add the eggs and the lemon juice and zest and whisk over a little heat to a smooth creamy consistency. Remove from the heat, strain and allow to cool, stirring frequently.

Split the star-shaped butter sponge twice, sandwich with lemon buttercream and cover with yellow almond paste.

Finally, place the star in the centre of the chocolate gâteau. Surround the base with a rope of ganache covered with couverture and sprinkled with milk chocolate vermicelli. Place couverture stars sprinkled with chocolate vermicelli on the chocolate gâteau between the points of the star and stand a yellow marzipan candle on each. Pipe small bulbs of royal icing all round the base of the star and decorate the top with royal icing piped on in a snow crystal design.

Alternatively, this gâteau may be made as an iced dessert.

(Illustration, p. 1097)   Switzerland

Date torte

Prepare the same mixture as for Viennese hazelnut torte, adding 100 g (3½ oz) finely sliced dates before folding in the egg whites. Bake, allow to cool, split, sandwich with well boiled apricot jam and coat with rum flavoured fondant.

                                                                              Austria

(See Viennese hazelnut torte, p. 1162)

Dundee cake

100 g	currants	4 oz
100 g	raisins	4 oz
100 g	sultanas	4 oz
100 g	cut mixed peel	4 oz
50 g	almonds	2 oz
	1 lemon	
	1 orange	
250 g	plain flour	10 oz
200 g	butter	8 oz
200 g	soft brown sugar	8 oz
	4 eggs	

Oven temperature 163° C (325°F)

Clean the fruit and chop the peel and nuts, leaving a few nuts for decorating the cake top; split these in half lengthwise. Grate the lemon and orange peel. Mix these ingredients with the flour. Cream the butter and sugar until pale and fluffy, then beat in the eggs gradually; lastly fold in the dry ingredients. Put the mixture into a greased 20 cm (8 in) tin and arrange the split almonds on top. Bake in the centre of the oven for 2½–3 hours. When the cake is quite firm to the touch, remove from the tin and cool on a rack.

Great Britain

Emperor gâteau

Bake a chocolate cake mixture (Sacher formula) in a rectangular tin. Split, soak in pear brandy and sandwich with caramel flavoured ganache. Coat first with fondant, then with vanilla couverture and make a wavy design with a comb scraper while the couverture is still soft.

Marzipan motifs are used for decoration; these have to be made in advance. To fix them in position, brush them with couverture before placing on the gâteau. The oak leaves are dried on a rolling pin to give them a curved shape.

Engadine nut torte

450 g	granulated sugar	1 lb 2 oz
300 g	single dairy cream	12 oz
30 g	honey	1 oz
375 g	walnuts (coarsely chopped)	15 oz

Line two 22 cm (9 in) flan rings with sweet pastry. The depth of the rings should be 3 cm (1¼ in). Boil the sugar until caramelised and dissolve in the single dairy cream after which the honey and walnuts are stirred in. When cold, fill into the lined rings and cover each with a sweet pastry top. Brush with egg, make a design with a fork and lightly dock. Bake for about 25 minutes at 220°C (425°F). This torte remains moist for a long time.

Switzerland

Fan torte

65 g	egg yolks	2¼ oz
190 g	egg whites	7½ oz
220 g	marzipan	9 oz
125 g	caster sugar	5 oz
125 g	flour	5 oz
125 g	butter (hot)	5 oz
150 g	sweet paste	6 oz
650 g	buttercream	1 lb 10 oz
100 g	nougat paste	4 oz
	chocolate couverture	

Beat the egg yolks, 100 g (3½ oz) marzipan and half the sugar until frothy. Whip the egg whites and remaining sugar to a stiff snow, add to the egg yolk mixture, blend in the flour and lastly fold in the butter. Spread on to paper to make a genoese 35 × 25 cm (14 in by 10 in) and approximately 1 cm (½ in) thick, and bake at 200°C (392°F) for 20 minutes.

Pin out the sweet paste into a round 25 cm (10 in) in diameter and after baking and cooling, spread with part of the nougat buttercream (made by adding the nougat to the buttercream). Spread the rest of the buttercream on to the genoese, smooth off, cut into strips 4 cm (1½ in) wide and arrange on the cream covered sweet paste base in a spiral. Coat the whole torte with cream and place roasted almonds round the sides. Mark the top into 16 portions and pipe a whirl of cream on each. Pin out the rest of marzipan into a disc 25 cm (10 in) in diameter and coat with couverture. After impressing with the fluted roller and cutting into 16 sections, dust 8 of them with icing sugar and place the dusted and undusted marzipan triangles alternately on top of the torte.

Germany

Fine chocolate torte

105 g	butter	4 oz
105 g	icing sugar	4 oz
105 g	ground almonds	4 oz
	6 egg yolks	
	3 eggs	
	6 egg whites	
200 g	chocolate	8 oz
35 g	flour	1½ oz

Melt the chocolate and work to a smooth, slightly liquid paste with hot water. Cream the butter with two-thirds of the sugar and gradually beat in the egg yolks and whole eggs, together with the almonds a little at a time. When the mixture is light and frothy, add the melted chocolate. Now whip the egg whites and the rest of the sugar to a stiff snow and fold very lightly into the butter/egg/sugar/chocolate mixture, together with the flour. Bake in two hoops or circular tins. When cool, split twice, sandwich with light chocolate buttercream and mask completely with bands of Selva paste.

Austria

Grand Marnier gâteau

	2 chocolate génoese bases	
	vanilla buttercream with finely crushed praline	
	chocolate buttercream	
	chocolate shells made with Selva and shavings	
1 dl	Grand Marnier	3 fl oz

Selva

500 g	plain couverture	1 lb 2 oz
500 g	milk couverture	1 lb 2 oz
100 g	glucose	3½ oz
100 g	water	3½ oz

Soak the génoese bases in Grand Marnier and sandwich together with butter-cream. Mask the top and sides with chocolate buttercream flavoured with Grand Marnier. Cover the sides with chocolate shavings and decorate the top with shells.

France

Melt the chocolate. Bring the glucose and water to the boil and add to the chocolate. When well mixed, place in the refrigerator for 5–6 hours, then pass through the refiner. Mould into one piece and return to the refrigerator. Cut off pieces as required and make into a thin ribbon by passing through the refiner.

(Illustration, p. 1097)

Italy

Fruit bread

Baking time: 1 kg (2 lb 3 oz)—45 minutes; 500 g (1 lb 1½ oz)—40 minutes; 250 g (8¾ oz)—35 minutes

2 kg 500	flour	6 lb 4 oz
125 g	yeast	5 oz
700 g	hazelnuts (unblanched)	1 lb 12 oz
1 kg 500	figs	3 lb 12 oz
1 kg	sultanas	2 lb 8 oz
1 kg	prunes	2 lb 8 oz
400 g	diced candied orange peel	1 lb
400 g	diced candied lemon peel	1 lb
2 kg	dried pears	5 lb
500 g	dried apricots	1 lb 4 oz
30 g	cinnamon	1 oz
10 g	aniseed	1 teaspoon
15 g	fennel seeds	1 teaspoon
10 g	cloves	1 teaspoon
10 g	coriander	1 teaspoon
30 g	salt	1 oz
600 g	sugar	1 lb 8 oz
	zest of 3 lemons	
⅜ l	rum	¾ pt

Prepare a ferment with half the flour, the yeast and lukewarm water. Cut up the fruit and the nuts, mix well and warm in the oven. As soon as the ferment has risen fully, stir in the sugar and the rest of the flour, then the fruit and nuts, the spices, salt, lemon zest and rum. Mix thoroughly and allow to ferment for a few hours. Scale off into pieces at 1 kg (2 lb 3 oz), 500 g (1 lb 1½ oz) and 250 g (8¾ oz) and mould into loaves. Leave to prove, then bake at 190°C. After baking, glaze with hot apricot purée and ice with fondant. Candied fruit may be used for additional decoration if desired.

Germany

Fruit cake I

7 minutes in a hot oven +45–50 minutes in a moderate oven

250 g	flour	10 oz
200 g	butter	8 oz
200 g	caster sugar	8 oz
	6 eggs	
300 g	mixed raisins and candied fruit	12 oz
5 cl	rum	2 fl oz
	baking powder	¼ teaspoon

Soften the butter without overheating it, then cream with the sugar until pale and fluffy. Beat in the eggs one at a time, then mix in the flour very lightly. Add a pinch of salt, then the fruit which has been cut up, macerated in the rum and well drained. Add the baking powder last of all as lightly as possible. Deposit in a cake tin that has been lined with buttered paper extending 2 or 3 cm (about 1 in) above the top edge. The tin should be only two-thirds filled with the mixture. Set in a hot oven (200–220°C) for 7 to 8 minutes so that the cake becomes firm enough to prevent the fruit sinking to the bottom, then make a cut right along the top of the cake, cover with buttered paper and reduce the oven temperature to 160–180°C.

N.B.—The mixture may appear to curdle while the eggs are being beaten in; this does not matter, as the addition of the flour will restore its smooth consistency.

Fruit cake II

65–75 minutes

200 g flour	flour	8 oz

65 g	cornflour	2½ oz
250 g	butter	10 oz
250 g	sugar	10 oz
	3 eggs	
	pinch of ground vanilla	
	grated zest of half a lemon	
40 g	chopped almonds	2 oz
125 g	currants	5 oz

Mix the flour and cornflour together, and proceed as for Fruit cake I.

Fruit cake III

65–75 minutes

225 g	flour	9 oz
250 g	butter	10 oz
250 g	sugar	10 oz
	4 egg yolks	
	4 egg whites	
	pinch of salt	
100 g	ground almonds	4 oz
	grated zest of half a lemon	
	or pinch of vanilla	
75 g	stoned Malaga muscatels	3 oz
	2 tablespoons rum	
	½ teaspoon baking powder	

Cream the butter and sugar together, then beat in the egg yolks one at a time. Stir in the muscatels, lemon zest and rum. Whisk the egg whites to a snow and add to the mixture, together with the flour mixed with the baking powder.

France

Fudge layer cake with chocolate

8–10 persons   Baking time: about 30 minutes

Cake

150 g	chocolate	6 oz
⅛ l	water	¼ pt
300 g	sugar	6 oz

300 g	flour	6 oz
	1 teaspoon baking powder	
	½ teaspoon salt	
100 g	butter	4 oz
	3 eggs	
⅛ l	milk	¼ pt
	1 tablespoon vanilla sugar	

Filling

	3 egg whites	
	3 tablespoons light corn syrup	
	1 teaspoon vanilla	
	2 tablespoons water	
	pinch of sugar	

Coating

250 g	icing sugar	10 oz
100 g	cocoa powder	4 oz
	1 teaspoon vanilla	
5 cl	hot strong brewed coffee	2 fl oz
60 g	butter	2½ oz
200 g	chopped hazelnuts	8 oz

Melt the chocolate in a bain-marie, mix well with the water and 100 g (4 oz) sugar and cool slightly. Cream the butter with 200 g (8 oz) sugar and the vanilla sugar, then beat in the eggs one at a time. Slowly blend in the flour, sieved with the baking powder and the salt, and the milk a little at a time until the mixture is smooth. Draw in the melted chocolate at the last minute, deposit in two sandwich tins or hoops lined with greased and floured paper, and bake at about 180°C.

Slowly whisk the ingredients for the filling in a bain-marie until the mixture resembles an Italian meringue. Sandwich the cake bases with this filling and stand aside for 20–30 minutes. Meanwhile mix together the cocoa powder, icing sugar, coffee, vanilla and butter until smooth and creamy. Spread over the top and sides of the cake and sprinkle the top with the chopped hazelnuts.

USA

Gâteau 'Bon Voyage' (young people's party, surprise party, etc.)

Bake a sponge or genoese mixture in a chromium plated bowl to make a dome shaped cake. (Sponge mixture should be enriched with melted butter for greater stability.) After baking, place the cake on a base of almond or sweet short pastry 3½ mm (about ⅛ in) thick. Split the butter sponge 4 times, soak with rum syrup and sandwich with 4 different buttercreams—e.g. chocolate, pistachio, vanilla, and hazelnut. Mask the whole dome with hazelnut buttercream. Working from the bottom upwards, cover with strips of almond paste in different colours.

The semicircles representing the meridians, the parallels and the band round the base are made of nougatine brushed with vanilla couverture. The aeroplane, the sailing boat and the plaque bearing the inscription are made of white couverture. The flowers (optional) are made of almond paste.

Switzerland

Gâteau 'Felicita'

Genoese

500 g	eggs	1¼ lb
400 g	sugar	1 lb
350 g	flour	14 oz
100 g	cornflour	4 oz
80 g	melted butter	3 oz

Orange buttercream

½ l	milk	⅞ pint
50 g	vanilla sugar	2 oz
450 g	sugar	2 oz
200 g	eggs	8 oz
875 g	butter	2 lb 3 oz
	juice of 8 oranges	
	grated zest of 2 oranges	
	grated zest of 1 lemon	

To make the genoese, whisk the eggs with the sugar, warming the mixture. Remove from the heat and continue whisking until cool. Fold in the flour and cornflour which have been sieved together and lastly add the melted butter. Bake and leave until completely cold. Split, soak with orange liqueur and sandwich with the orange buttercream.

To make the buttercream, whisk the eggs with the sugar and add the milk, orange juice and orange and lemon zest. Bring to the boil and cook until thick enough to coat the spatula. Strain, allow to cool and gradually beat in the creamed butter.

To decorate the gâteau, pin out pure white almond paste to a thickness of 2 mm (1/10 in) and yellow almond paste to a thickness of 1½ mm (1/15 in). Using small plain cutters 4 mm (1/6 in) and 6 mm (1/4 in) in diameter, cut out tiny disks of yellow almond paste. Place these on the white almond paste in a flower petal arrangement. Now pin out the decorated almond paste to a thickness of 1·3–1·4 mm (about 1/20 in) and cover the gâteau with it. Using a small knife, draw lines between the petals to make them stand out more clearly. Mark the centre of each flower with a small plain cutter.

The floral decoration on the strip of green almond paste bearing the inscription is made out of royal icing in advance.

(Illustration, p. 803)   Switzerland

Genoa almond cake

34–40 minutes

100 g	butter	4 oz
100 g	almonds	4 oz
150 g	sugar	6 oz
50 g	flour	2 oz
	3 eggs	
	1 liqueur glass kirsch	
	pinch of salt	
	half a bitter almond (optional)	

Grind the almonds with the sugar, add the well softened butter and beat for 5 or 6 minutes. Add the eggs one at a time and continue beating for a moment, then stir in the flour, salt and liqueur. Bake in a buttered mould, the bottom of which has been lined with buttered paper.

N.B.—If using ground almonds, start by beating the almonds, sugar and well softened butter together.

France

Gooseberry gâteau

14 portions

	1 sponge base 26 cm (10½ in) in diameter	
150 g	raw marzipan	6 oz
4 cl	rum	2 tablespoons
	2 tablespoons icing sugar	
	3–4 tablespoons water	
350 g	green gooseberries	14 oz
	stock syrup	
	4 egg whites	
170 g	sugar	7 oz
	half a vanilla pod	
	roasted flaked almonds	

Split the sponge base once. Mix the marzipan, icing sugar, rum and water to a smooth paste and use to sandwich the sponge and coat the top. Cover the top with the gooseberries which have been poached in the syrup, allowed to cool and well drained. Set aside a few large ones for final decoration. Whip the egg whites and sugar to a stiff snow and flavour with vanilla from inside the pod. Mask the gooseberries and the sides of the gâteau with the snow, keeping some for decoration. Fill this into a savoy bag fitted with a star tube and pipe on to the top of the gâteau. Mask the sides with flaked almonds. Brown in the oven with good top heat, remove and mark into portions by placing a large poached gooseberry on each one.

(Illustration, p. 1102)   Germany

Harvest festival gâteau

8 persons

Butter sponge

	3 eggs	
	4 egg yolks	
125 g	sugar	5 oz
125 g	flour	5 oz
	zest of 1 lemon	
	pinch of salt	
60 g	butter	2½ oz

Short paste

90 g	flour	3½ oz
60 g	butter	2½ oz
20 g	sugar	1 oz
	1 egg yolk	
	little lemon zest	
	pinch of salt	

French maraschino buttercream

	3 eggs	
125 g	sugar	5 oz
350 g	butter	14 oz
	little vanilla	
	pinch of salt	
	maraschino	
	roasted chopped almonds	
	beaten egg	

Prepare the butter sponge mixture in the usual manner and bake 4 thin bases. For the decoration on top of the gâteau, shape the short pastry into 12 ears of wheat and a ring of wheat ears and egg wash before baking. Also bake 4 pretzels sprinkled with sugar to caramelise the top. To make the buttercream, whisk the eggs and sugar warm, remove from the heat, add a little vanilla and a pinch of salt and continue beating until cold. Cream the butter, flavour well with maraschino and blend in the beaten eggs and sugar.

Sandwich the sponge base with maraschino buttercream and coat the top and sides with the same cream. Mask the bottom edge with roasted chopped almonds. Arrange the wheat ears, ring and pretzels on top and finish off with piped buttercream.

Germany

Hazelnut tourte Solothurn

This tourte consists of 2 hazelnut meringue bases with a layer of sponge in between, sandwiched with hazelnut buttercream.

Yield: 1 tourte about 22 cm (9 in) in diameter

Hazelnut meringue

	3 egg whites	
100 g	sugar	4 oz
100 g	finely grated hazelnuts	4 oz
10 g	cornflour	$\frac{1}{2}$ oz

Sponge

	3 egg yolks	
100 g	sugar	4 oz
50 g	flour	2 oz
50 g	cornflour	2 oz
50 g	finely grated hazelnuts	2 oz
	3 egg whites	

Hazelnut buttercream

150 g	butter	6 oz
120 g	icing sugar	5 oz
50 g	roasted ground hazelnuts	2 oz

To make the meringue, whip the egg whites to a stiff snow, gradually blending in the sugar, then add the hazelnuts mixed with the cornflour. Mark out the size required on a greased and floured baking sheet and pipe on the meringue in a spiral, using a savoy bag fitted with a plain pipe. Bake at 190°C for 10–15 minutes. Remove at once from the baking sheet with the help of a palette knife and cool on a wire rack.

To make the sponge, whisk the egg yolks and sugar until stiff and frothy, add the hazelnuts alternately with the flour which has been sieved with the cornflour, and lastly fold in the whites whipped to a stiff snow. Deposit in a buttered and floured sponge tin and bake at 180°C for 30–40 minutes.

To make the buttercream, cream the butter with the icing sugar and work in the hazelnuts.

To assemble the tourte, spread one of the meringue bases with part of the butter-cream, place the sponge on top, spread with the rest of the buttercream and cover with the second meringue base, smooth side downwards. If desired, the sides of the tourte may be masked with buttercream and sprinkled with roasted chopped hazelnuts. In this case, the quantities given for the buttercream should be increased.

Switzerland

Italian curd cheese tart

10–12 persons   Baking time: about 40 minutes

750 g	flour	1 lb 14 oz
400 g	butter	1 lb
350 g	sugar	14 oz
	3 eggs	
500 g	ricotta (curd cheese made from ewe's milk)	1¼ lb
50 g	candied lemon peel, finely diced	2 oz
	3 tablespoons dairy cream	
25 g	bitter chocolate, finely diced	1 oz

Prepare a paste with the flour, the softened butter, 100 g (3½ oz) sugar and the eggs, but do not work it too much. Shape into a ball, wrap in a cloth or aluminium foil and leave in a cool place for at least an hour. Sieve the curd cheese or mash well and beat with the rest of the sugar (caster) and the cream until soft and light. Stir in the diced candied peel and chocolate. Pin out the pastry to about 4 mm (⅛ in) thick, cut a round base out of three-quarters of it and line a thinly buttered 25 cm (10 in) flan ring with this base, pressing it down well. Cut the pastry level with the edge, fill with the cheese mixture and smooth the top. Cut the rest of the pastry into strips 2 cm (¾ in) wide, arrange on the tart lattice fashion and press the ends firmly on to the edge of the pastry case. Bake in a moderate oven until golden. The tart is cooked when a needle or toothpick inserted into it remains dry.

N.B.—If ricotta is not obtainable, use curd cheese softened with cream.

Italy

Key West Florida lime chiffon pie

8–10 persons　　　Baking time (pastry case): 5–10 minutes

Pastry case

150 g	flour	6 oz
50 g	lard or vegetable fat	2 oz
	and	
25 g	butter	1 oz
	or	
75 g	butter	3 oz
10 g	sugar	1 heaped teaspoon
	pinch of salt	
	4 tablespoons iced water	

Filling

	3 egg yolks	
	3 egg whites	
100 g	sugar	4 oz
	pinch of salt	
	4 sheets gelatine	
	juice of 3 limes or 2 lemons	
4 dl	sweetened whipped cream	⅔ pt
	18 triangles of candied	
	lime or lemon	

Rub the lard and butter, or butter alone, into the flour, salt and sugar. Pour in the water, quickly mould into a ball, cover and allow to rest for 1 hour. Pin out thinly, line a fluted shallow tin 24 cm (10 in) in diameter and bake blind. Soak the gelatine, squeeze dry and heat with the lemon or lime juice in a bain-marie. Whisk the egg yolks with half the sugar in a bain-marie, add the gelatine dissolved in the lime or lemon juice and allow to cool a little. Meanwhile whip the egg whites to a stiff snow with the rest of the sugar, fold into the mixture and pour at once into the baked pastry case. Leave in a cool place for a few hours until the pie is firm enough to cut. Pipe on whipped cream, using a star tube, and decorate with the candied lime or lemon triangles.

USA

Lemon chiffon pie I

210 g	sugar	7 oz
	5 egg yolks	
	3 egg whites	
2 cl	white wine	2 dessertspoons
	juice and grated zest of 1 lemon	
	1 short pastry flan case, baked blind	

Whisk together the egg yolks, wine and 120 g (4¼ oz) sugar in a bain-marie until thick and smooth, then add the lemon zest and gradually stir in the lemon juice. Allow to cool, fill into the pastry case and smooth the top. Whip the egg whites to a stiff snow with the rest of the sugar, pipe on top, using a savoy bag fitted with a star pipe, and decorate as desired. Flash at about 250°C for 5 minutes or so. Candied lemon slices or glacé cherries may be used for final decoration.

USA

Lemon chiffon pie II

	4 egg yolks	
	3 egg whites	
225 g	sugar	9 oz
1 dl	water	3 fl oz
	juice of 2 large lemons	
	grated zest of 1 lemon	
	3 sheets gelatine	
	1 short pastry flan case, baked blind	
	whipped cream (optional)	

Whisk together the egg yolks, water, 125 g (4½ oz) sugar, lemon juice and zest in a bain-marie until thick and smooth. Stir in the gelatine which has been soaked and squeezed dry, then allow to cool. When about to set, fold in the egg whites whipped to a stiff snow with the rest of the sugar. Fill into the pastry case, keeping a little back for decoration. Smooth the top and pipe on the rest of the filling, using a savoy bag fitted with a star pipe. A more popular way of decorating the pie is to cover the filling with whipped cream.

USA

Lemon chiffon pie III

130 g	sugar	5 oz

	5 egg yolks	
	3 egg whites	
2 cl	white wine	2 dessertspoons
	juice and zest of 1 lemon	
	1 shortcrust pastry case	
	with a raised rim	

Whisk the egg yolks with half the sugar and the wine in a bain-marie. When thick, slowly stir in the lemon juice and zest. Allow to cool, then fill the pastry case with the mixture. Whip the egg whites to a stiff snow with the rest of the sugar and pipe on top, using a savoy bag fitted with star tube. Place in a preheated oven at about 250°C and leave for about 5 minutes. Decorate with candied lemon peel or glacé cherries if desired.

Germany

Lemon cream torte

16–20 portions

	1 sweet short paste base	
	25 cm (10 in) in diameter	
	2 thin Viennese bases	
	25 cm (10 in) in diameter	
	juice and zest of 2 lemons	
50 g	sugar	2 oz
	3 egg yolks	
	8 sheets gelatine	
2 dl	white wine	$\frac{1}{3}$ pt
6 dl	whipped dairy cream	1 pt
	mixed fresh or stewed fruit	
	red currant jelly	
1 dl	port	3 fl oz
1 dl	raspberry juice	3 fl oz

To decorate

sweetened vanilla flavoured
whipped cream
half glacé cherries
chocolate cut-outs
roasted chopped almonds

Prepare a custard with the lemon juice and zest, 1 dl ($\frac{1}{6}$ pt) white wine, the sugar and the egg yolks. While still hot, add the gelatine which has been soaked and squeezed dry, stir until dissolved and strain. Meanwhile, spread the short paste base with red currant jelly, place a thin Viennese base on top and surround with a

▲ Fructidor dessert, p. 882
▼ Grapefruit lido, p. 888

1093

▲   Fantasie glacé leda, fantasie glacé Hawaii
1094   ▶   Tea cream, iced tea cocktail, tea flip, tea ice cream, tea confections, pp. 935, 967, 1157, 1189, 1190
▼   Pears Bordaloue

E x 1
FIRST FLUS
DARJEELIN
F.O.P.

1096 ▲ Small petits fours displayed in a Dutch Street scene, p. 1138
▼ Pineapple surprise, p. 907

▲ Grand Marnier gâteau, p. 1080
▼ Christmas gateau, p. 1076

1098

▲ A summertime tea table
◄ Fresh fruits and fruit salads
◄ Apple salad, p. 861
▼ Charlotte Old Salzburg, p. 869

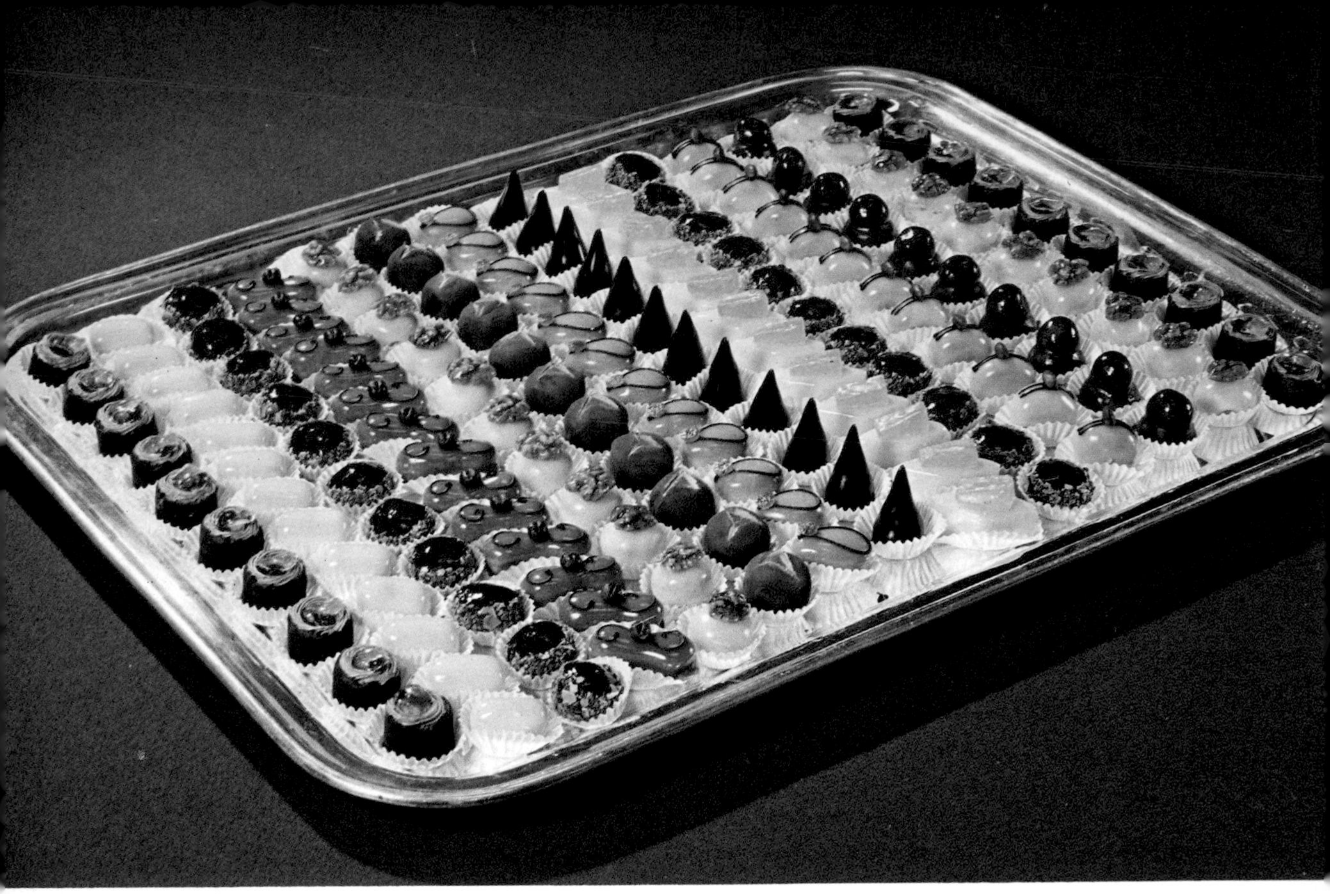

▲ A selection of glazed petits fours, p. 1150

▼ Fruit desserts, pp. 885–7

▲ Afternoon tea fancies from the Confiserie Ryser, Berne, pp. 985, 1001, 1011, 1013, 1020, 1034,
▼ 1045, 1046, 1066–7

1102　　▲　Salzburg petits fours, pp. 1018, 1131, 1133, 1134, 1144, 1147, 1149, 1153
　　　　▼　Gooseberry gateau, p. 1086

1103

► Sabayon with red wine
▼ Pears St. Peter, p. 903

▲ Pancakes Johann Strauss, pancakes Marie Louise, pp. 899, 900
► Yeasted fancies for St. Nicolas, p. 1022
▼ Strawberry baskets, p. 931

1106 ▲ A buffet of sweets and tea fancies at the Confiserie Vörösmarty, Budapest, p. 975

▼ Strawberry cream, chestnut cream, pineapple custard cream, rainbow cream, pp. 871, 910, 932

▲ Witches dance carnival gateau, p. 1163

▼ Hungarian wedding cake, p. 1164

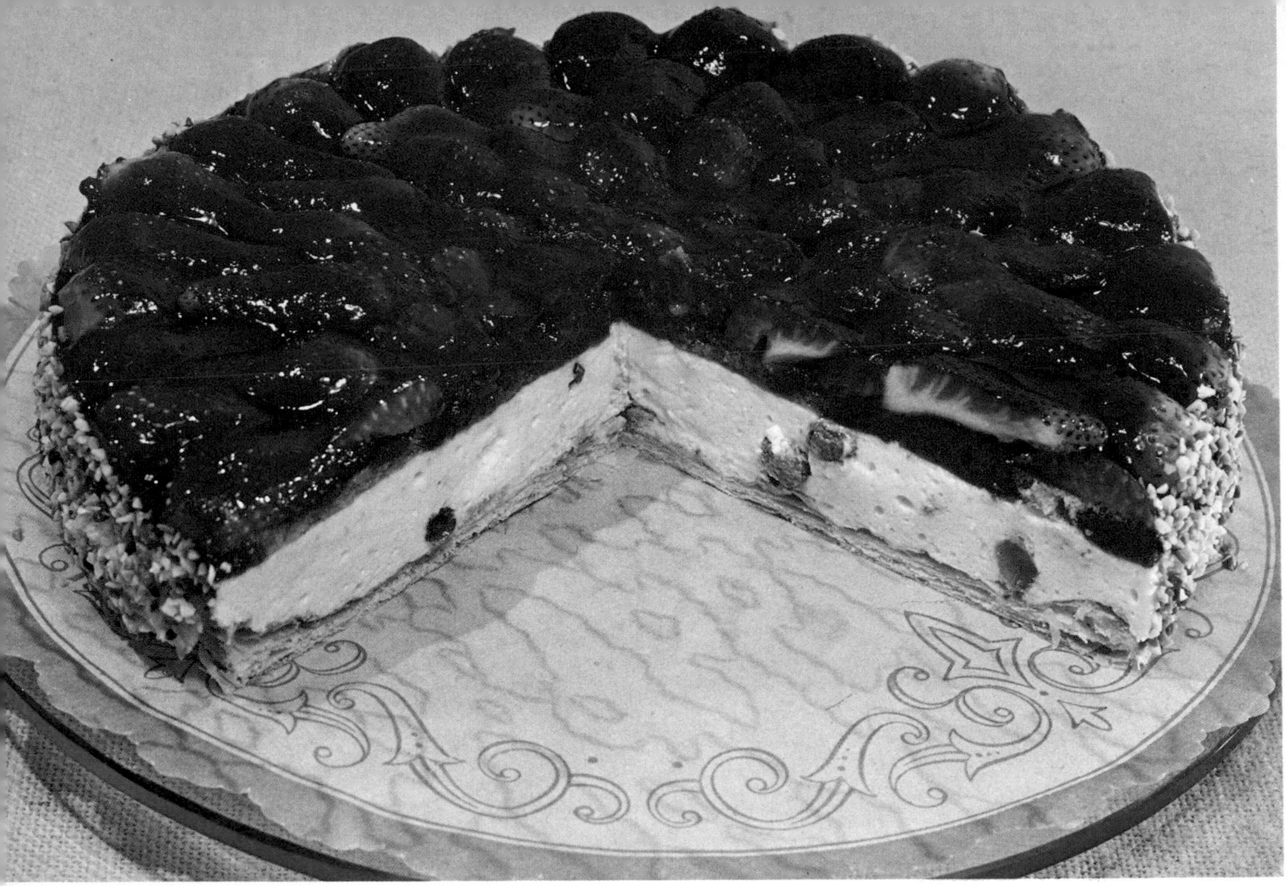

▲ Parisian strawberry tart: flaky pastry base with filling of cream cheese, currants and whipped cream. Cover with genoese and halved strawberries, p. 1129

▼ Silesian poppy seed cake, p. 1123

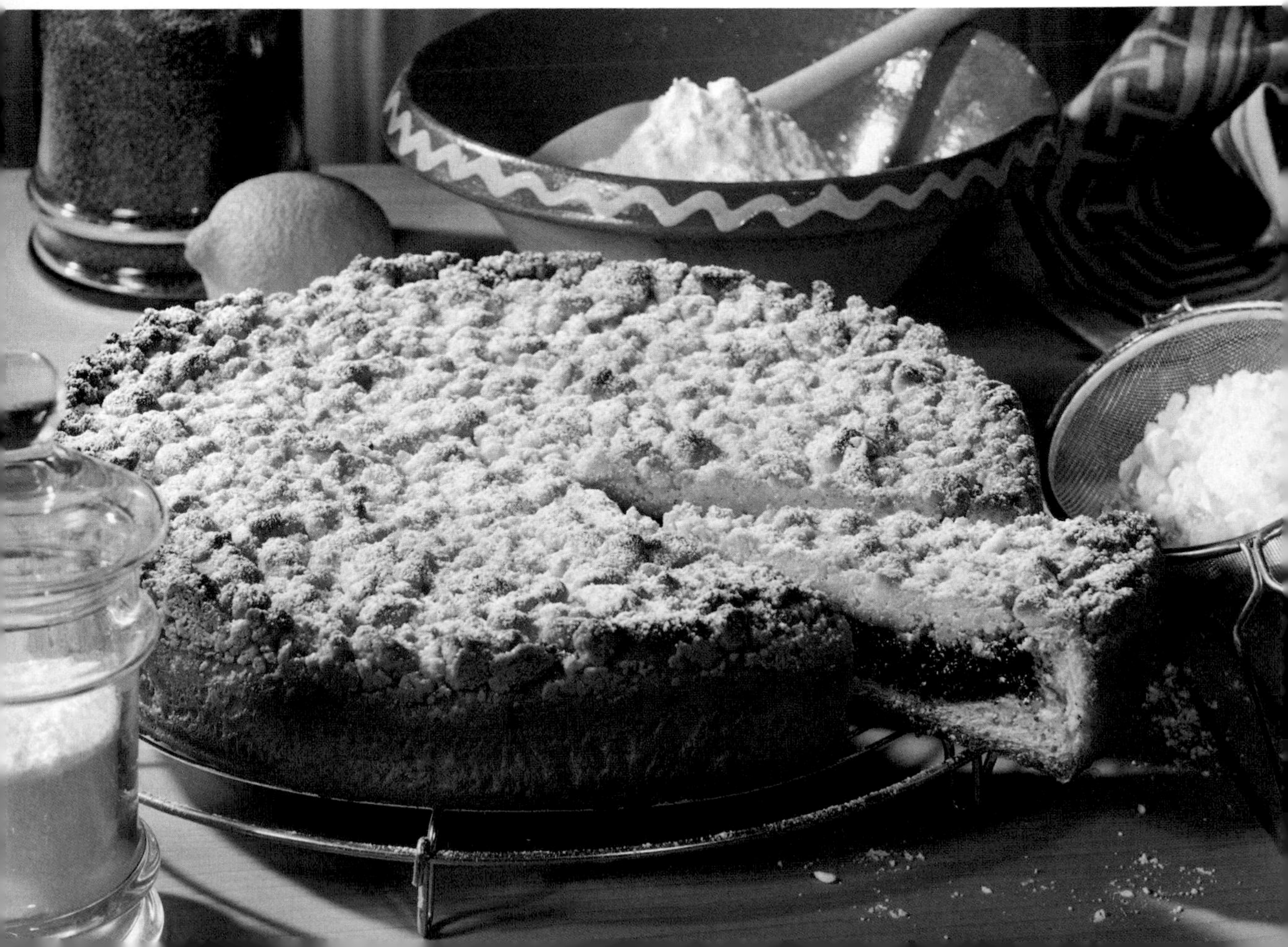

cake hoop 4 cm (1½ in) deep. Soak the second Viennese base in the rest of the white wine mixed with the port and raspberry juice. Fold 6 dl (1 pt) whipped dairy cream into the lemon custard which has been allowed to set. Arrange the mixed fruit on the Viennese base inside the hoop and cover with half the lemon custard cream. Place the Viennese base which has been soaked in the wine and raspberry juice on top, cover with the rest of the custard cream, smooth the top and refrigerate until firm. Remove the hoop and mask the top and sides with sweetened vanilla flavoured whipped cream. Decorate the top with dairy cream rosettes, half glacé cherries and small chocolate cut-outs. Sprinkle the centre lightly with roasted chopped almonds.

Germany

Lemon meringue pie

2 short or puff pastry cases baked blind

Lemon cream

	5 eggs	
250 g	sugar	10 oz
200 g	butter	8 oz
2 dl	lemon juice	⅓ pt

Custard

250 ml	milk	10 fl oz
25 g	sugar	1 oz
25 g	custard powder	1 oz
125 ml	whipped cream	¼ pt

Meringue

	4 egg whites	
150 g	sugar	6 oz
	grated zest of 1 lemon	

To make the lemon cream, beat the eggs and sugar together, mix with the softened butter and the lemon juice, bring to the boil, stir until smooth and refrigerate. Prepare a cooked custard with the milk, sugar and custard powder, allow to cool and blend in the shipped cream. Mix well with the lemon cream and fill into the two pastry cases.

To make the meringue, whip the egg whites and sugar to a stiff snow with the addition of the lemon zest. Cover the pies with this meringue and decorate as desired. Flash in an oven with good top heat.

Switzerland

Lemon rolls

15 portions

Swiss roll mixture

	5 eggs	
100 g	caster sugar	4 oz
100 g	flour	4 oz
	zest of half a lemon	

Filling

300 g	butter	12 oz
200 g	fondant or icing sugar	8 oz
	2 lemons	
	citric acid	
	sponge cake crumbs	

Whip the egg yolks and half the sugar to a stiff sponge. Whisk the whites to a stiff snow with the rest of the sugar. Stir the lemon zest into the egg yolk/sugar sponge and fold in the whites and the flour at the same time. Spread thinly on a paper lined baking sheet and bake in a hot oven.

To make the filling, cream the butter with the fondant or icing sugar and a little lemon zest, and flavour to taste with lemon juice and citric acid. Remove the Swiss roll from the paper, spread with the buttercream, roll up, spread the outside thinly with the buttercream and set aside until firm. Roll the sides in sponge crumbs and decorate the top with thin slices of lemon, skinned, seeded and cut into quarters.

Hungary

Lubeck nut cream torte

16 portions

125 g	sweet paste	5 oz
	raspberry jam	
	2 mushroom bases	
approx. 200 g	vanilla buttercream	8 oz approx.
½ l	whipped sweetened cream	¾ pt
30 g	praline nougat (chopped)	1 oz
30 g	roasted ground hazelnuts	1 oz
30 g	chopped walnuts	1 oz

	4 sheets gelatine	
	16 half walnuts	
200 g	raw marzipan	8 oz
150 g	almond paste	6 oz
125 g	sugar	5 oz
	whipped cream to decorate	

Pin out the sweet paste thinly to a round base 25 cm (10 in) in diameter and bake until golden. Spread with raspberry jam and cover with the two mushroom bases which have been sandwiched with vanilla buttercream. Mix the whipped sweetened cream with the praline nougat, hazelnuts and chopped walnuts and stiffen with the dissolved gelatine. Spread the top mushroom base with this cream, smooth the top and sides and refrigerate until firm. Cover with a thin disk of marzipan. Work the sugar into the almond paste, shape into small macaroons, bake and arrange round the edge of the torte, spacing them evenly. Mark the torte into 16 portions and decorate each one with a rosette of whipped cream and half a walnut.

Mushroom bases

	10 large eggs	
375 g	sugar	15 oz
375 g	flour	15 oz
375 g	butter	15 oz
75 g	nougat (chocolate praline) paste	3 oz

Separate the eggs. Whisk the yolks with half the sugar and add the nougat paste. Whip the whites to a stiff snow with the rest of the sugar. Blend the two mixtures carefully, fold in the flour and then draw in the melted butter. Spread into circular shapes on greaseproof paper and bake briskly.

Germany

Madeira cake

150 g	butter	6 oz
150 g	sugar	6 oz
75 g	eggs	3 oz
	½ lemon	
200 g	flour	8 oz
	4 tablespoons milk	
	citron peel to decorate	

Cream the butter and sugar until pale and fluffy. Beat in the eggs with the flavouring, adding a little of the flour if it begins to curdle. Fold in the sifted flour, with sufficient milk to give a dropping consistency. Put into a 18 cm (7 in) round cake tin lined with greaseproof paper. Bake in the centre of the oven at 177°C (350°F) for ½ hour. Put the peel across the cake and continue to bake for a further 1 hour.   Great Britain

Mille-feuilles gâteau

8–10 persons

	puff paste	
	icing sugar	

Filling

	4 egg yolks	
15 cl	stock syrup at 30°B	¼ pt
7 dl	whipped cream (unsweetened)	1¼ pt
75 g	chocolate powder	3 oz
150 g	milk couverture, coarsely grated	6 oz
	beaten egg to egg wash	

Pin out puff paste about 4 mm (⅛ in) thick and cut out 3 disks 25 cm (10 in) in diameter. Dock, bake on a damp baking sheet and caramelise lightly. Cut out small half-moons and diamonds of puff paste, egg wash, bake on a damp baking sheet, dust with icing sugar and caramelise.

To make the filling, beat up the egg yolks and stock syrup warm, remove from the heat and continue beating until cold. Mix with the chocolate powder and blend in the whipped cream. Set aside a little of the mixture to coat the gâteau and mix the rest with the grated milk couverture. Place one puff paste base in a metal or cardboard hoop about 24 cm (9¾ in) in diameter. Spread with half the filling and cover with the second puff paste base. Spread this with the rest of the filling and cover with the third base, flat side uppermost. Freeze before removing the hoop. Spread the top and sides with the chocolate cream which was set aside. Mask the sides with chopped roasted almonds and decorate round the top edge with the puff paste half-moons and diamonds.   Switzerland

Napfkuchen with nut or poppy seed filling

1 kg	flour	2½ lb

250 g	butter	10 oz
140 g	icing sugar	6 oz
	5 egg yolks	
	grated zest of 1 lemon	
30 g	yeast	1¼ oz
	milk	
200 g	raisins	8 oz
3 cl	rum	3 dessertspoons

Nut filling

750 g	blanched hazelnuts	1 lb 14 oz
750 g	sugar	1 lb 14 oz
	1 small stick vanilla	
2 dl	water	⅓ pt

Poppy seed filling

750 g	poppy seed	1 lb 14 oz
750 g	sugar	1 lb 14 oz
	finely chopped peel of	
	half a lemon	
	ground cinnamon	

Soak the raisins in warm water. Drain well and macerate in the rum under cover for a few hours before use.

Make a ferment from the yeast, 250 g (10 oz) flour and a little lukewarm milk. Leave to rise in a warm, but not hot place. Make a bay in the rest of the flour and place in it the butter, which should be fairly soft, the sugar, egg yolks and lemon zest, a good pinch of salt and the ferment. Mix well with as much milk as required to make a smooth, fairly slack dough. Pin out into a long rectangle about 5 cm (2 in) thick, spread with the desired filling, sprinkle with the raisins and roll up. Join up the ends to make a ring and fill into a greased chimney mould with the seam uppermost. Prove and bake in a medium oven.

Fillings

Nut filling. Grind the nuts finely. Make a stock syrup from the sugar, water and vanilla, skim well and stir in the nuts while still hot.

Poppy seed filling. Grind the poppy seed very finely. Make stock syrup as above, omitting the vanilla, skim and mix with the poppy seed while still hot. Work well, flavouring with the lemon peel and a little ground cinnamon.

Austria

Neapolitan Easter gâteau

8–10 persons   Baking time: about 40 minutes

200 g	wheat grains	8 oz
400 g	flour	1 lb
200 g	butter	8 oz
350 g	sugar	14 oz
	5 eggs	
$\frac{1}{2}$ l	milk	$\frac{7}{8}$ pt
	zest of half an orange	
	$\frac{1}{3}$ vanilla pod	
350 g	curd cheese	14 oz
5 cl	orange flower water	2 fl oz
200 g	candied fruit, finely diced	8 oz
	pinch of cinnamon	

Leave the wheat grains in cold water for 5–6 days to swell, changing the water daily; this will prevent the grains from cracking. Prepare a fine paste with the flour, 175 g (6¼ oz) sugar, the butter and 3 eggs, shape into a ball, wrap in a cloth or aluminium foil and leave in a cold place for at least an hour. Place the milk in a pan with the orange zest, the vanilla and the rest of the sugar and bring to the boil. Add the wheat grains and simmer for 4 hours, when the wheat grains will have split open and the liquid will be of a creamy consistency. Remove the orange zest and the vanilla pod.

Sieve the curd cheese, beat well with a wooden spoon, add the orange flower water, 2 beaten eggs and the cinnamon, then beat vigorously. As soon as the mixture is foamy, carefully stir in the candied fruit and the wheat grains together with the cooking liquid. Pin out the pastry to about 3 mm ($\frac{1}{10}$ in) thick and use two-thirds of it to line a 25 cm (10 in) cake tin. Fill with the curd cheese mixture, smooth the top and cover lattice fashion with the rest of the pastry cut into strips 2 cm (¾ in) wide. Press the ends firmly on to the edge of the pastry case and bake at 190°C. Serve cold—the gâteau tastes best when a day old.

The wheat grains may be replaced by hard grained rice cooked 'al dente' with the orange zest. In this case the sugar is not added until the end of the cooking time. The rice is allowed to cool before being mixed with the curd cheese. If necessary, the orange flower water may be replaced by equal parts of Grand Marnier and water.

Italy

Nut stollen

Baking time: about 50 minutes

Almond stollen dough

3 kg 300	flour	7¼ lb
1 l	milk	1¾ pt
200 g	yeast	8 oz
400 g	sugar	14 oz
1 kg	butter	2¼ lb
30 g	salt	1 oz
1 kg 700	chopped almonds	3¾ lb
1 kg 700	chopped candied orange and lemon peel	3¾ lb

Filling

1 kg	roasted ground hazelnuts	2¼ lb
500 g	sugar	1 lb 2 oz
	5 eggs	
500 g	marzipan	1 lb 2 oz
250 g	fine sponge crumbs	9 oz
250 g	hot butter	9 oz
	vanilla	
	lemon	

Make a ferment with half the flour, the milk and the yeast, then add the remaining ingredients and knead into a smooth firm dough. Weigh into 1 kg 200 (2 lb 10 oz) pieces and pin out to measure 40×30 cm (16×12 in).

To make the filling, work the marzipan, eggs and sugar to a smooth paste, add the hazelnuts and sponge crumbs and lastly draw in the hot butter. Spread on to the rectangles of dough and roll up from both ends as shown in the illustration. Prove for a short time, then bake at 190°C. After baking, spread with hot butter and sprinkle with vanilla sugar.

Germany

Orange cream torte

12 portions

250 g	sweet short paste 1 thin Viennese (butter sponge) base	10 oz

500 g	stewed morello cherries, slightly thickened	1¼ lb
	red currant jelly	
	juice and zest of 2 large oranges	
	3 egg yolks	
80 g	sugar	3 oz
	juice of a quarter of a lemon	
6 dl	whipped dairy cream (unsweetened)	1 pt
	12 orange segments	
	6 red glacé cherries	
	12 quarter pistachio nuts	
	flaked roasted almonds	
	pectin jelly	
	8 sheets gelatine	

Bake a short pastry case 25 cm (10 in) in diameter. When cold, spread thinly with red currant jelly, lay the Viennese base on top and cover with the cold stewed cherries.

Beat up the orange juice and zest, the sugar and the egg yolks over gentle heat, remove from the heat as soon as the mixture has thickened and add the gelatine which has been soaked and squeezed dry. Strain, allow to cool, add the lemon juice and blend into the whipped cream. Cover the cherries with the orange cream, keeping back a little for decoration, and shape so that the sides are slightly sloping. Decorate with the rest of the orange cream and with the orange segments, previously glazed, the glacé cherries cut in half and the quarter pistachio nuts, spacing these evenly round the top. Mask the sides with the flaked almonds.

Germany

Orange gâteau

About 50 portions

250 g	sugar	10 oz
250 g	flour	10 oz
	18 egg yolks	
	18 egg whites	
1 l	dairy cream	1¾ pt

Sabayon

	juice of 8 oranges	
	zest of 4 oranges	
	12 eggs (whole)	
600 g	butter	1½ lb

1 kg 200	sugar	3½ lb
	cornflour	
	white wine	

Caramel

1 kg	sugar	2½ lb
½ l	water	⅞ pt
	juice of 1 large orange	

Blend the egg yolks with the sugar, cream and flour and fold in the stiffly whipped whites. Bake in the oven in medium size omelette pans without turning; each pancake should be about 5 mm (¼ in) thick. Sandwich 5 or 6 together with a thin layer of sabayon, prepared as follows. Mix the orange juice and zest, sugar, butter and eggs in a pan and cook over gentle heat until the mixture comes to the boil. Thicken slightly with a little cornflour blended with white wine.

After sandwiching the pancakes, prepare light amber caramel with the sugar and water, finish off with the orange juice and quickly coat the top with this solution.

If desired, the sabayon may be made with lemon juice, using 2–3 lemons instead of the oranges.

France

Party gâteau

2 gâteaux, 25 cm (10 in) in diameter (10–12 portions each)

	15 egg yolks	
200 g	ground almonds	8 oz
350 g	sugar	14 oz
	12 egg whites	
70 g	cocoa powder	3 oz
130 g	flour	5 oz

Filling and decoration

1 l	whipped dairy cream (unsweetened)	1¾ pt
	4 egg yolks	
150 g	stock syrup at 30°B	6 oz
3 cl	rum	3 dessertspoons
400 g	Velma couverture	1 lb
75 g	glacé cherries	3 oz
	grated and flaked couverture	
¼ l	sweetened whipped dairy cream for coating	½ pt

Whisk the egg yolks and 200 g (7 oz) sugar to a sponge. Whip the whites and the rest of the sugar to a stiff snow. Sieve the flour with the cocoa powder. Stir the almonds into the egg yolk/sugar sponge, then fold in the whipped whites together with the flour and cocoa. Fill into 2 cake tins or 6–8 hoops 25 cm (10 in) in diameter and bake at 220°C.

To make the filling, beat up the egg yolks and stock syrup warm, remove from the heat and continue beating until cold. Mix with the unsweetened whipped cream and divide in half. Stir the liquid Velma couverture and the rum into one half, and mix the other with the cut-up cherries. Split each gâteau twice and place the bottom layer in a cardboard or metal hoop of the same diameter. Spread with the chocolate rum filling and cover with the second layer. Spread this with the cherry cream filling and top with the third layer. To prevent drying out, spread the top with a little whipped cream. Freeze for 5 hours. When about to serve, remove the hoop, coat the top and sides with sweetened whipped cream, mask the sides with grated couverture and cover the top with flaked couverture. Finish off with a dusting of icing sugar if desired.

Switzerland

Peach tart

14–16 portions

	1 baked short pastry base 26 cm (10½ in) in diameter	
275 g	weighing	11 oz
	1 Viennese base 26 cm (10½ in) in diameter and 1 cm (½ in) thick	
50 g	red currant jelly	2 oz
75 g	large cherries, stoned	3 oz
	7–8 choice even sized peaches	
150 g	peach jelly	6 oz
150 g	marzipan	6 oz
	white wine	
	sugar	
	arrack or Cointreau	

Poach the peaches in sweetened white wine and allow to cool in the wine. To prevent discoloration, do not skin until required for the tart.

Spread the short pastry base with the red currant jelly and place the Viennese base on top. Cover with the peaches which have been very well drained, skinned, cut in half and stoned. Fill up the spaces in between with the cherries flavoured with arrack of Cointreau. Glaze with peach jelly.

Germany

Pineapple dairy cream gâteau

10 gâteaux

Butter sponge bases

	25 eggs	
500 g	sugar	1¼ lb
500 g	flour	1¼ lb
100 g	butter	4 oz
	zest of 1 lemon	
20 g	vanilla sugar	1 oz

Filling

1³⁄₁₀ l	sweetened whipped cream	2¼ pt
400 g	well drained poached	1 lb
	pineapple (fresh or canned)	
2 g	2 sheets of gelatine	
60 g	sponge cake crumbs	2 oz
	citric acid	
	pineapple essence	

Prepare and bake the butter sponge bases in the same way as for royal chocolate gâteau. When cold, split each base twice. Mix 1 l (1¾ pt) sweetened whipped cream with finely diced pineapple, a few drops of citric acid and pineapple essence, and the gelatine which has been soaked and dissolved. Sandwich the bases with this filling. Spread the sides thinly with sweetened whipped cream and mask with the sponge cake crumbs. Decorate the top with the rest of the whipped cream and with triangles of pineapple.

Hungary

Poppy seed stollen

Baking time: about 50 minutes

Stollen dough as for nut stollen

Filling

800 g	ground poppy seeds	2 lb
1 l	milk	2 pt

300 g	butter	12 oz
540 g	sugar	1 lb 6 oz
	6 eggs	
450 g	ground unblanched almonds	1 lb 2 oz
200 g	finely chopped candied lemon peel	8 oz
360 g	sultanas	14 oz
	little cinnamon	

Blanch the poppy seeds in the hot milk, then strain and allow to cool. Cream the butter with the sugar, then gradually add the eggs (unseparated), almonds, lemon peel and sultanas, a little cinnamon and the poppy seeds. Weigh the stollen dough into 1 kg 200 (3 lb) pieces, pin out, spread with the filling, roll up from both ends, place in an oblong cake tin and prick over lightly with a needle. Prove for a short time, then bake at 190°C. After baking, turn out, brush with hot butter and sprinkle with vanilla sugar.

Germany

Revellers' carnival gâteau

170 g	butter	7 oz
100 g	icing sugar	4 oz
	10 egg yolks	
	10 egg whites	
120 g	caster sugar	4 oz
	lemon zest	
150 g	lightly roasted ground hazelnuts	6 oz
100 g	sponge crumbs	4 oz
100 g	flour	4 oz
	a little cinnamon	
	hazelnut buttercream	
	marzipan	
	coffee fondant	

Beat the butter, icing sugar, egg yolks and lemon zest until foamy. Whip the egg whites to a stiff snow with the caster sugar, fold into the butter/egg yolk/sugar mixture and carefully blend in the hazelnuts, sponge crumbs, flour and cinnamon. Bake at 180–200°C in a greased and floured gâteau tin lined with paper. When cold, sandwich with hazelnut buttercream and coat with coffee fondant. Model the figures and the edging round the base of the gâteau in marzipan.

Austria

Royal chocolate gâteau

10 gâteaux

Butter sponge bases

	25 eggs	
500 g	sugar	1¼ lb
450 g	sugar	1 lb 2 oz
60 g	cocoa	2 oz
100 g	butter	4 oz
	zest of half a lemon	
20 g	vanilla sugar	1 oz

Filling

1 3/10 l	sweetened whipped cream	2¼ pt
100 g	cocoa	4 oz
150 g	raisins	6 oz
1 dl	rum	3 fl oz
2 g	2 sheets of gelatine	
60 g	chocolate sponge crumbs	2 oz
	grated chocolate	

To make the bases, whip the egg yolks and half the sugar to a stiff sponge and whisk the whites with the rest of the sugar until stiff. Blend the two carefully with the flour, the melted butter, the lemon zest and the vanilla sugar. Line a baking sheet with greaseproof paper. Stand 10 cake hoops 11 cm (4½ in) in diameter and 4 cm (1½ in) deep on the baking sheet, divide the sponge mixture between them and bake at about 180°C. After removing from the oven, leave the bases in the hoops until cold, then run a knife round to release them from the hoops, invert, split each base twice and sandwich with the following filling.

Mix 1 l (1¾ pt) sweetened whipped cream with the raisins which have been macerated in the rum, the cocoa powder, and the gelatine dissolved in a few drops of water.

Spread the sides thinly with sweetened whipped cream and mask with the sponge crumbs. Decorate the top with the rest of the whipped cream and sprinkle with grated chocolate.

Hungary

Sacher torte

Baking time: 1 hour–1 hour 20 minutes

140 g	butter	5½ oz
150 g	icing sugar	6 oz
150 g	chocolate	6 oz
50 g	potato flour	2 oz
50 g	flour	2 oz
	7 egg yolks	
	9 egg whites	
	apricot purée	
	chocolate icing	
	whipped dairy cream	

Warm the chocolate until soft, then cream with the butter and about 100 g (4 oz) sugar. Beat in the egg yolks well a little at a time. Add the egg whites whipped to a stiff snow with the rest of the sugar, then fold in the flour and potato flour very carefully. Fill into a cake hoop, smooth the top and bake slowly in a medium oven, leaving the oven door ajar at first. After baking, invert on a wire rack and leave until cold. Remove the hoop and mask the top and sides with apricot purée (but do not split and sandwich). Coat with chocolate icing and mark into portions with a decoration of whipped cream.

Austria

Sand cake

60–70 minutes in a hot oven

250 g	butter	10 oz
250 g	sugar	10 oz
200 g	cornflour	8 oz
	1 tablespoon flour	
	3 eggs	
	pinch of ground vanilla	
	or grated zest of 1 lemon	
1 cl	rum	1 dessertspoon
	good pinch of baking powder	
	small pinch of salt	

Soften the butter and cream it with the sugar. Beat in the eggs one at a time. Fold in the cornflour, flour, lemon zest or vanilla, baking powder and, lastly, the rum. Deposit in a well greased tin and bake at once.

France

Seed cake

150 g	flour	6 oz
	pinch of salt	
	2 teaspoons caraway seeds	
100 g	butter	4 oz
	2 eggs	
	a little milk	

Grease a 18 cm (7 in) cake tin and line the base with greased greaseproof paper.

Sift the flour and salt together and add the caraway seeds. Cream the butter and sugar until pale and fluffy and gradually beat in the eggs. Fold in the sifted flour adding a little milk to make the mixture of a dropping consistency. Put into the tin and bake in the centre of the oven at 177°C (350°F) for about 1 hour.

Great Britain

Silesian poppy seed cake

12 portions

Dough

500 g	flour	1¼ lb
30 g	yeast	1 oz
¼ l	milk	½ pt approx.
60 g	sugar	2 oz
80 g	butter	3 oz
	1 egg	
	grated zest of 1 lemon	
	pinch of salt	

Filling

150 g	freshly ground poppy seeds	6 oz
¼ l	milk	½ pt approx.
100 g	sugar	4 oz
	1 egg	
	small knob of butter	
	zest of 1 lemon	
	small amount of fine breadcrumbs if required	

Butter streusel topping

250 g	flour	10 oz
150 g	sugar	6 oz
170 g	butter	7 oz
	icing sugar	

Sieve the flour into a basin, make a bay, pour in the lukewarm milk in which the yeast has been dispersed, dust with a little flour and leave to ferment in a warm place for 15 minutes. Now add the sugar, the egg, the softened butter, the lemon zest and a pinch of salt and work to a dry dough. Set aside to rise again, then roll out and line a cake mould with the dough. Meanwhile soak the poppy seeds in the milk for the filling over gentle heat, remove from the heat, add the sugar, grated lemon zest and a little butter, and allow to cool. Fill the mould with the mixture and cover evenly with the butter streusel. To make this topping, mix the butter and sugar well, add the flour and crumble between the finger-tips. Bake at 180°C. When cold, dredge with icing sugar.

(Illustration, p. 1108)   Germany

Smaland cheese cake

10 persons

12 l	milk	21 pt
200 g	flour	8 oz
	1 tablespoon rennet	
1 l	dairy cream	1¾ pt
260 g	sugar	9 oz
	6 eggs	
130 g	chopped almonds	5 oz
	10 chopped bitter almonds	
	Chantilly cream	
	thick raspberry jam	

Warm the milk to 35°C. Stir in the flour and rennet vigorously, then continue stirring until thick. Stand aside until a curd has formed, then stir until the curd separates from the whey. Drain the curd well, pass through a sieve, then beat in the cream, sugar, eggs and chopped almonds. Fill into two buttered moulds and bake at 175°C for 1–2 hours. Do not unmould. Serve in portions with Chantilly cream and thick raspberry jam.

                                                                           Sweden

Springtime gâteau

Almond sponge

500 g	eggs	1¼ lb
400 g	sugar	1 lb
300 g	flour	12 oz
300 g	ground almonds (unblanched)	12 oz

Praline buttercream

500 g	plain buttercream	1¼ lb
250 g	finely chopped praline croquant (made with 2 parts sugar to 1 part flaked almonds)	10 oz

This gâteau is particularly suitable for birthdays or similar occasions. The decoration in the centre may be replaced by a heart or by a small plaque bearing an appropriate inscription.

To make the almond sponge, whisk the eggs with the sugar, warming the mixture, then remove from the heat and continue whisking until cool. Add the sieved flour mixed with the ground almonds. Bake in a hexagonal mould; alternatively, use an ordinary round tin and cut to a hexagonal shape after baking. Split, soak with stock syrup well flavoured with maraschino and sandwich with the praline buttercream. Coat the top and sides with hazelnut buttercream and mask the sides with milk chocolate vermicelli.

Spread milk couverture on to thick paper, make a wavy design with a comb scraper, cut out 6 rectangles and then cut each of these into 2 triangles. Decorate with green almond paste to simulate leaves and flower stems and with white flowers made out of white couverture.

Arrange 12 half-truffles in pairs on top of the gâteau. Pipe on a dot of ganache or gianduja and place the couverture triangles on top with their apex pointing towards the centre and slightly on a slant. For final decoration, place white couverture hearts at the points of the hexagon and at the apex of the triangles.

Switzerland

Suvretta cake

10 persons   Baking time: 1 hour at 180–200°C

200 g	butter	8 oz
200 g	sugar	8 oz
	2 eggs	
200 g	flour	8 oz
50 g	raisins	2 oz
50 g	currants	2 oz
50 g	candied fruit	2 oz
25 g	blanched pistachio nuts	1 oz
25 g	blanched almonds	1 oz
	rum	
	good pinch of salt	
	grated zest of 1 lemon	

Finely dice the candied fruit and the nuts. Macerate the diced fruit and the raisins and currants in the rum.

Cream the butter and sugar and whisk in the eggs vigorously until light. Drain the macerated fruit and stir it in, together with the lemon zest and the nuts. Work well, but keep the mixture light. Fold in the flour and, lastly, the salt. Fill into a buttered cake tin lined with buttered greaseproof paper. Bake slowly at 180–200°C for 1 hour. On removing from the oven, splash the top with rum. Repeat when the cake is quite cold and has been turned out.

Switzerland

St. Gallen Monastery tart

150 g	butter	6 oz
100 g	ground almonds	4 oz
100 g	sugar	4 oz
	2 tablespoons cocoa	
	1 teaspoon cinnamon	
	1 teaspoon baking powder	
300 g	flour	12 oz
5 cl	milk	2 fl oz
	1 egg	

Cream the butter and sugar, then add the flour, ground almonds and remaining ingredients. Mix well and allow the pastry to rest for 1 hour. Pin out to the thickness of half a finger. Line the bottom of a buttered spring-form pan with pastry and cover with apricot jam. Edge with a 2 cm (¾ in) rim of pastry and cover with strips of pastry lattice fashion. Shape the rest of the pastry into 2 ropes, plait them together and place on the rim which has been egg washed. Bake in a medium oven for 45 minutes.

Switzerland

Schellmann gâteau

Baking time: 35 minutes

	15 egg whites	
300 g	sugar	12 oz
300 g	ground hazelnuts	12 oz
50 g	cake crumbs	2 oz
50 g	grated chocolate	2 oz
	red currant jam	
	chocolate icing	

Whip the egg whites to a stiff snow with the sugar and lightly fold in the hazelnuts, cake crumbs and chocolate. Bake in a hot oven in a lightly greased round cake tin, the bottom of which has been lined with paper. Allow to cool, then split carefully with a sharp knife, sandwich with red currant jam and coat with chocolate icing.

Austria

Strawberry shortcake

10–15 persons	Baking time: 15–20 minutes	
1 kg	strawberries	2¼ lb
75 g	sugar	3 oz
100 g	strawberry jam	4 oz

Shortcake

400 g	flour	1 lb
100 g	sugar	4 oz
	2 teaspoons baking powder	
100 g	butter	4 oz
	pinch of grated nutmeg	
	pinch of salt	

Decoration

¼ l	sweetened whipped cream	½ pt

Set aside 8–10 large choice strawberries. Hull the fruit, wash quickly and drain well, then place in a bowl, divide into small pieces with the help of a knife and fork, sprinkle with the sugar, mix with the jam and set aside.

To make the shortcake, sieve the flour with the baking powder, salt and nutmeg, rub in the butter, mix with the sugar, work to a fairly dry dough with a little milk and allow to rest for a short time. Pin out to a thickness of 1½ cm (about ½ in) and cut to a round shape. Bake at 220°C and allow to cool. Split, place one half on a glass dish and cover with half the strawberries. Place the other half on top, cover with the rest of the strawberries and decorate with the whipped cream, using a savoy bag fitted with a star tube. Finish off the decoration with the whole strawberries which have been set aside.

USA

Swiss roll

Bake a thin sheet of sponge, remove from the oven at once, cover with a sheet of paper of the same size and invert quickly on to a table. Remove the paper on which it was baked (this is now on top) spread the sponge while still hot with a thin layer of red currant jelly and roll up with the aid of the paper on which it is lying. When cold, brush with hot apricot jam and mask with roasted flaked almonds. Alternatively, dust with icing sugar.

Other suitable fillings are jam, vanilla or chocolate cream.

For a delicious, quickly made sweet, serve a slice of Swiss roll in vanilla custard or Sabayon sauce on a glass plate.

Germany

Variations of Swiss roll

Simple, but very attractive sweets, which are particularly suitable for entertaining on a small scale, may be made with a fresh Swiss roll filled with red currant or raspberry jelly but left plain on the outside. Cut the roll in $1\frac{1}{2}$–2 cm ($\frac{3}{4}$ in) slices, place on individual glass plates, allowing 1 slice per portion, and decorate in one of the following ways:

1. Pipe a large whirl of whipped cream on each slice, decorate with 2 tangerine segments and surround with a little cold vanilla custard sauce.

2. Place a small poached well drained half-apricot on each slice and pipe a border of whipped cream round it, using a star tube. Coat the apricot very lightly with thick cold apricot sauce and sprinkle a few roasted almond nibs on top.

3. Pipe a whirl of whipped cream on each slice and top with two-eighths of a slice of pineapple and a red glacé cherry. Pour a little cold vanilla custard sauce all round.

4. Coat each slice very thinly with couverture. Pipe a large whirl of whipped cream on top, sprinkle with chocolate shavings and dust lightly with icing sugar. The shavings may be scraped off a block of chocolate on to the Swiss roll with a knife.

5. Pipe a whirl of whipped cream mixed with a little instant coffee powder on each slice, sprinkle with a little cocoa powder and dust with icing sugar.

Germany

Teziutlan gâteau

16 portions   Baking time: about 25 minutes

	6 egg yolks	
	2 eggs	
200 g	sugar	8 oz
200 g	flour	8 oz
	1 teaspoon baking powder	
	6 egg whites	
100 g	melted butter	4 oz

Filling

500 g	desiccated coconut	1¼ lb
1 l	milk	1¾ pt
	pinch of bicarbonate of soda	
	3 eggs	
approx. 100 g	icing sugar	3½ oz approx.

Whisk the egg yolks, eggs and 150 g (5¼ oz) sugar to a stiff sponge. Blend in the flour which has been sieved with the baking powder, then lightly fold in the egg whites whipped to a stiff snow with the rest of the sugar. Lastly, stir in the melted butter carefully. Bake at 180°C in a greased and paper lined cake tin 25 cm (10 in) in diameter. Cool on a wire rack.

To make the filling, cook the coconut in the milk with the bicarbonate of soda until the mixture is thick. Add the beaten eggs, cook to a spreading consistency while stirring constantly, then allow to cool. Split the gâteau twice, sandwich evenly with the coconut filling and dust very liberally with icing sugar—about 100 g (3½ oz). Caramelise with a red-hot iron or skewer to make a diamond pattern, or as desired.

Mexico

Parisian strawberry tart

Layer of flaky pastry 25 cm in diameter
Thin layer of génoese (same size)
Strawberries
Strawberry jelly
Chopped toasted almonds

Filling

½ l	milk	½ pint
	2 egg yolks	
90 g	sugar	3 oz
	½ vanilla pod	
250 g	cream cheese	8 oz
40 g	currants	2 oz
2 dl	cream	⅓ pint
	5 sheets gelatine	
	grated zest of ½ lemon	
	pinch of salt	

Infuse ½ vanilla pod in tepid milk. Beat egg yolks, sugar and lemon zest. Add the milk and cook until thickened stirring continuously. Take out vanilla pod. Remove pan from fire, add the soaked gelatine. Let it cool. Add the cream cheese, the softened currants and the cream, whipped beforehand. Spread the mixture on the pastry base. Cover with a layer of génoese and top with halved strawberries. Glazed with strawberry jelly and cover the sides with chopped, roasted almonds.

(Illustration, p. 1108)   France

CONFISERIE

Almonds Aboukir

Tint fondante almond paste pale green with natural colour and shape into almonds with their shells. Insert a blanched almond lengthwise into each imitation almond so that the real almond remains visible. Dip into sugar cooked to the crack degree. Leave on an oiled baking sheet or marble slab until cold. Place in small paper cases to serve.

France

Almond crescents

8–10 minutes in a medium oven

125 g	ground almonds	5 oz
200 g	sugar	8 oz
	2 unbeaten egg whites	
	pinch of ground vanilla	
150 g	flaked almonds	6 oz

Beat the ground almonds with part of the egg whites, using a spatula, add the sugar and vanilla and mix well to a fairly stiff paste. If it is not smooth enough, add a little egg white. Moisten the hands and shape the paste into sticks the thickness of the little finger. Taper the ends by rolling on a marble slab. Beat the rest of the egg white lightly, dip the sticks of paste in it and drain. Roll in flaked almonds, exerting a little pressure to make them stick. Fashion into crescents and place on a greased baking sheet or paper. Wash with egg and bake. On removing from the oven, brush with well sweetened milk to glaze.

Commercially available raw marzipan may be used for this recipe. The proportions are 2 unbeaten egg whites to 400 g (14 oz) marzipan.

France

Almond dainties

1 kg	blanched almonds	2½ lb

1 kg 300	sugar	3¼ lb
50 g	glucose	2 oz
150 g	candied orange peel	6 oz
	rind of 2 lemons	
8 dl	egg whites	1½ pt
	glacé fruit	
	gum arabic	

Grind the almonds with the sugar, orange peel, glucose, lemon rind and enough egg white to make a fairly firm paste. Pipe on to paper in various shapes, using a star pipe, and decorate with glacé fruit. Allow to dry overnight, bake at 250°C, glaze with gum arabic while still hot, moisten the paper and remove.

Switzerland

Almond petits fours

	7 egg whites	
280 g	caster sugar	11 oz
220 g	ground almonds	9 oz
	little cinnamon	
	little lemon zest	
	almond buttercream	
	marzipan	
	chocolate marzipan	

Gradually whisk the egg whites and caster sugar to a stiff snow and fold in the ground almonds, cinnamon and lemon zest. Spread on a greased and floured baking sheet to make 5 or 6 sheets of equal size and bake at about 150°C. When cold, sandwich with almond buttercream, cut into rounds, cover the top with a disk of chocolate marzipan with a cut out flower design in the centre and wrap in a thin sheet of white marzipan. Lastly fill the cut out flower with fondant.

(Illustration, p. 1102)   Austria

Almond rocks

10–12 minutes in a slow oven

	2 egg whites	
125 g	icing sugar	5 oz
60 g	flaked almonds	2½ oz
	pinch of ground vanilla	

Whisk the 2 egg whites with the sugar and vanilla. Place over very gentle heat and continue whisking until the mixture is firm enough to stick to the whisk. Stir in the flaked almonds. Deposit with a tablespoon on a greased and floured baking sheet, dropping the meringue in small heaps, then bake without further shaping.

France

Andalouses

10–12 minutes in a slow oven

100 g	ground almonds	4 oz
	2 egg whites	
35 g	icing sugar	1½ oz
	currants	

Gradually mix the unwhipped egg whites with the ground almonds. Beat in the icing sugar with a spatula to make a fairly firm paste. Shape into small balls and press currants into them. Bake on a greased and floured baking sheet. The balls will split while baking, showing the currants.

France

Berrichons

7–8 minutes in a hot oven

200 g	ground almonds	8 oz
200 g	sugar	8 oz
80 g	flour	3 oz
	6 egg whites	
	pinch of vanilla	

Whip the egg whites to a very stiff snow. Mix the almonds well with the flour and vanilla. Sift into the egg whites, folding in with a spatula and working the mixture as little as possible. Pipe out on to a greased and floured baking sheet, using a savoy bag fitted with a plain or star pipe, depending on the shapes desired. Bake.

This is a basic paste for many different kinds of petits fours.

France

Caramel cherries

Take well drained brandy cherries and wipe them over lightly to dry. Hold them by their stalks and dip them in light brown caramel sugar. Leave on an oiled baking sheet or marble slab until cold. Place in small paper cases to serve.

France

Chocolate petits fours

Yield: about 30

140 g	butter	5½ oz
120 g	icing sugar	5 oz
	7 egg yolks	
130 g	melted couverture	5 oz
	7 egg whites	
120 g	caster sugar	5 oz
140 g	flour	5½ oz
30 g	ground blanched almonds	1 oz

Ganache

¼ l	dairy cream	½ pt
250 g	couverture	10 oz

Icing for piping

	2–3 egg whites	
350 g	icing sugar	14 oz
	few drops citric acid	
	marzipan	
	apricot purée	
	chocolate fondant	

Cream the butter and icing sugar, beat in the egg yolks and mix with the couverture. Fold in the egg whites whipped to a stiff snow with the caster sugar and stir in the flour and ground almonds. Spread on to paper to a square shape, bake, allow to cool, then split once, sandwich with ganache and brush the top with apricot purée. Cut out with a round cutter, wrap a thin layer of marzipan round each one, coat the top with chocolate fondant and top with a piped icing flower.

To make the ganache, bring the cream to the boil, break up the couverture and stir it in, and beat thoroughly before use. To make the icing, stir the egg whites, icing sugar and citric acid together until stiff. Using a paper bag, pipe out flowers on to oiled paper. It is advisable to oil the paper on the previous day; if it is too oily, the flowers may slip off or become discoloured. A sheet of plexiglass may be used with advantage.

(Illustration, p. 1102)   Austria

Chocolate shells

500 g	butter	1¼ lb
250 g	icing sugar	10 oz
3½ dl	dairy cream	⅔ pt
750 g	flour	1 lb 14 oz
50 g	cocoa powder	2 oz
	pinch of salt	
	apricot jam	
	couverture	
	chocolate granules	

Cream the butter with the sugar. Gradually work in the flour, cream and cocoa powder. Using a star tube, pipe out in shell shapes on to lightly greased baking sheets and bake at 180°C. Sandwich in pairs with apricot jam, dip the tips in couverture and cover these with chocolate granules.

Switzerland

Chocolate sticks

	8 egg whites	
400 g	sugar	1 lb
275 g	ground almonds	11 oz
250 g	cocoa powder	10 oz

Make Italian meringue with the egg whites and sugar. Carefully blend in the almonds and cocoa powder. Pipe out in small sticks on to paper, using a plain pipe, bake at 160°C and remove from the paper while still hot.

Switzerland

Coffee petits fours

Yield: about 25

500 g	short paste	1¼ lb
	couverture	
	marzipan	
	diced sponge cake	
	coffee buttercream	
	glacé cherries	

Pin out the short paste thinly, wrap round the end of tiny metal cylinders, brush with egg and place a ring of pastry, which has been cut out formerly, in position at the top of each one. Allow 20 g ($\frac{3}{4}$ oz) pastry for each petit four. Leave to rest for at least 30 minutes and bake slowly at about 150°C. Remove from the cylinders and leave until cold. Spread the inside thinly with couverture, fill with diced marzipan and sponge cake, pipe on a spiral of coffee buttercream and place a small round piece of glacé cherry in the centre.

(Illustration, p. 1102)   Austria

Colettes

| 250 g | couverture | 10 oz |
| 2 dl | ganache | $\frac{1}{3}$ pt |

Melt the couverture. When it is lukewarm and sufficiently liquid, coat the inside of small round paper cases with it thickly, making it thicker at the top. Refrigerate for 40 minutes to harden the couverture completely. Remove the paper cases and fill the couverture cases with ganache, using a savoy bag fitted with a star tube.

France

Créoles

Pin out Parisian nougat and press into small moulds, trimming the edges evenly. Fill the nougat cases with chestnut purée and cover with chocolate fondant. Place a silver ball in the centre.

France

Date petits fours

6–8 minutes in a medium oven

sweet paste
dates
rum

Macerate the dates in rum for at least half an hour. Pin out the sweet paste 2 mm ($\frac{1}{10}$ in) thick and cut into rounds 3 cm (about 1 in) in diameter. Place a stoned date in the centre of each one. Fold the pastry over the date edge to edge, leaving the ends of the date uncovered. Brush with beaten egg, mark with a palm-leaf design, using the point of a knife, then bake.

France

Délicieux

These are different versions of Colettes. Make small couverture cases as above and fill with buttercream of various flavours—coffee, vanilla, rum, praline, etc., decorate the top with a little royal icing in a contrasting colour.

France

Disguised apricots

Cut very small apricots in half and remove the stones. (Apricots cut in four may also be used.) Replace each stone by a knob of fondante almond paste the size of a hazelnut and put the apricot halves together to their original shape. Dip into sugar boiled to the crack degree or light brown caramel sugar. Drain, then leave on an oiled baking sheet until cold. Place in small paper cases to serve.

France

Disguised cherries

Carefully dry brandy cherries. Dip some of them in white fondant and the remainder in pink fondant flavoured with kirsch. Leave on a baking-sheet sprinkled with icing sugar until cold. Place in small paper cases to serve.

France

Disguised chestnuts I

500 g	chestnuts	1¼ lb
650 g	sugar	1 lb 10 oz
50 g	glucose	2 oz
125 g	chocolate	5 oz
	good pinch of vanilla	

Skin the chestnuts and cook in water containing a little sugar and vanilla. Drain and rub through a fine metal sieve. Transfer to a basin. Boil 300 g (10½ oz) sugar to the small crack degree, remove from the heat and mix with the chestnut purée, stirring with a spatula until quite cold. Shape into chestnuts, dusting with icing sugar while working to facilitate moulding. Boil 350 g (12½ oz) sugar with the glucose. When the large crack degree has been reached add the chocolate, dissolved in very little water, and mix, using a perfectly clean fork. Continue boiling for 3 or 4 minutes until the large crack degree has been reached again. Insert a small stick into the base of each chestnut (or impale them on a dipping fork or trussing needle one after the other) and dip into the chocolate syrup which should be kept warm. Do not coat the base of the chestnuts, so that they look as much like real chestnuts as possible. Drain for a moment. If the chestnuts have been impaled on sticks, fix the free ends of these into the holes of a strainer until the chestnuts have cooled. If a fork has been used to dip them, place them on an oiled baking sheet or marble slab. Serve in small paper cases.

Disguised chestnuts II

400 g	broken glazed chestnuts	1 lb
1 dl	syrup at 32°B	¼ pt
350 g	sugar	14 oz
50 g	glucose	2 oz
125 g	chocolate	5 oz

Pound the glazed chestnuts with the syrup, adding the latter gradually. Shape the paste into chestnuts, then proceed as for formula I.

Disguised chestnuts III (home style)

500 g	chestnuts	1¼ lb
100 g	butter	4 oz
	little syrup at 32°B	
500 g	couverture	1¼ lb
	good pinch of vanilla	

Skin the chestnuts and cook in sweetened milk flavoured with vanilla, drain and rub through a fine metal sieve. Place over very gentle heat and add the butter a little at a time, while mixing with a spatula. If the purée does not hold together, bind with a little syrup. Allow to cool. Shape the paste into chestnuts and leave in a cool place. Melt the couverture over gentle heat. Dip the chestnuts into it one by one and drain. Leave until cold on an oiled baking sheet or marble slab. Place in small paper cases to serve.

France

Disguised strawberries

Use medium sized varieties of strawberries, preferably 'Sovereign', 'Surprise des Halles' or 'Orleans'. The fruit should be sound and freshly picked. Do not wash, but wipe over. Holding each strawberry by its hull, dip into kirsh-flavoured pink fondant. Place on a baking sheet sprinkled with icing sugar and flatten the hulls. Leave until cold. Serve in small paper cases.

France

Dolorès

	Parisian nougat	
250 g	chopped pineapple mixed with a little kirsh-flavoured apricot jam	10 oz
200 g	orange fondant	8 oz
	20 small diamond shaped pieces of pineapple	

Mould the nougat in tiny boat-shaped tins. Fill with chopped pineapple and coat with orange fondant. Decorate with the pineapple diamonds and place in oblong paper cases to serve.

France

Dutch street scene

500 g	icing sugar	1¼ lb
	gelatine, soaked and dissolved	

Add sufficient dissolved gelatine to the sugar to make a firm paste. Cover with cloth to keep fresh.

First cut the stencils out of cardboard. Pin out the paste to 1 cm (about ½ in) thick and cut out with the aid of the stencils. Allow to dry for 24 hours before assembling with royal icing of piping consistency. Decorate with the same royal icing and stick red paper on the internal house walls. Use stencils to make the barrow. Model the man and flowers for the barrow with marzipan.

(Illustration, p. 1096)   Switzerland

Eugènias

fondant almond paste
rum
chocolate fondant
chocolate granules

Add rum to the almond paste (a few drops for 150 g (5¼ oz)). Shape by hand into rather large balls and dip in the chocolate fondant. Drain well and roll in chocolate granules. When cold, place in small paper cases to serve.

France

FROSTED FRUITS

Either fruit preserved in brandy or fresh fruit may be used.

Frosted cherries, black currants, red currants and Mirabelle plums (brandy fruit) I

Drain the fruit well and dry gently. Dip in cold gum arabic solution (cover 50 g (1¾ oz) gum arabic with water and dissolve in a bain-marie). Drain off the surplus gum arabic and roll in granulated sugar. Stand aside uncovered to dry. Place in small paper cases to serve.

Frosted cherries, black currants, red currants and Mirabelle plums (brandy fruit) II

Dip the fruit in syrup at 36°B. Drain, then roll in granulated sugar.

France

Frosted cherries, black currants, red currants and grapes

(Fresh fruit—cherries: leave part of the stalks on the fruit;
          black currants and red currants: keep these in clusters;
          grapes: use in tiny clusters.)

Lightly beat up 1 egg white and dip the fruit in it. Drain off the surplus. Roll in granulated sugar. Place on a baking sheet covered with white paper and dry over very gentle heat or in any warm place. Serve in small paper cases.

France

Frosted Muscat and Malaga grapes

Pick the grapes off the bunches, leaving a little of the stalk. Dip each grape in beaten white of egg. Drain, then roll in granulated sugar. Place on white paper and leave in a warm place to dry. Place in small paper cases in pairs, with one Muscat and one Malaga grape in each one.

France

Frosted strawberries

Use sound, barely ripe strawberries. Leave them unhulled. Do not wash them, but wipe carefully if dirty, making sure not to damage them in any way. Dip one by one in beaten egg white. Drain, then roll in granulated sugar. Allow to dry. Place in small paper cases to serve.

France

Ganaches

400 g	good cooking chocolate	1 lb
1½ dl	custard	6 fl oz
200 g	couverture	8 oz

Warm the chocolate to the consistency of a paste. Warm the custard and beat into the chocolate with a spatula. Leave in a cool place until completely cold (overnight if necessary). Shape into large olives and dip in lukewarm melted couverture. Drain on a wire rack. When quite dry, place in small paper cases to serve.

France

Grape truffles

Macerate large Muscat grapes in very good quality spirits for at least 1 month. Drain and leave to dry uncovered. Dip one by one in white fondant, allow to dry, then dip one by one in lukewarm couverture. Now roll them in a mixture of chocolate powder and chocolate granules. Place in small paper cases to serve.

France

Harlequin dates

	30 dates	
2 dl	pistachio buttercream	⅓ pt
	chocolate fondant	
	pistachio fondant	

Stone the dates and stuff with buttercream. Dip half of them in chocolate fondant and the other half in pistachio fondant. Place in small paper cases to serve.

France

Harlequins

fondant almond paste
kirsch or Cognac
cherry brandy
granulated sugar

Tint one-third of the almond paste pale green and flavour with kirsch, colour one-third pale pink and flavour with cherry brandy, and leave the rest white and flavour with kirsch. Pin out into strips 7–8 cm (3 in) wide and place one on top of the other. Roll up together like a sausage. Cut into small rounds and roll each one into a ball in granulated sugar. Place in small paper cases to serve.

France

▶ Waltzing peach, p. 1190

1142

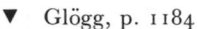
◀ Coffee time in Ankara
▼ Glögg, p. 1184

Horn of plenty

Horn

100 g	raw marzipan	4 oz
500 g	sugar	1¼ lb
100 g	fresh egg white	4 oz
	caramel sugar	
	chocolate	
	praline paste	

Macaroon biscuits

1 kg	raw marzipan	2½ lb
600 g	sugar	1½ lb
200 g	egg white	8 oz
	couverture	
	royal icing for piping	
	glacé cherries	

To make the horn, mix the marzipan with the sugar and gradually work in the egg white. Pipe into ring moulds 15 mm (about ½ in) wide, similar to savarin moulds, and bake at 220–230°C. When cold, stick the rings together with hot caramel sugar to the shape of a cornucopia and decorate with chocolate and praline paste.

To make the biscuits, prepare macaroon paste with the marzipan, sugar and egg white, pipe out in various shapes and bake, keeping the biscuits moist. When cold, decorate with piped royal icing, couverture, buttercream, half-glacé cherries, etc. Fill the horn with macaroons until brimming over.

Norway

Impératrices

200 g	glazed chestnut purée	8 oz
200 g	praline	8 oz
100 g	chocolate	4 oz
	chocolate fondant	

Soften the chocolate to the consistency of a paste. Mix with the praline and the chestnut purée (broken glazed chestnuts rubbed through a fine sieve). Work with a spatula, then shape by hand into little balls and coat with fondant. Drain on a wire rack. When quite dry, place in small paper cases to serve.

France

Italian petits fours

Yield: about 30

200 g	butter	8 oz
100 g	icing sugar	4 oz
	7 egg yolks	
	lemon zest	
	7 egg whites	
100 g	caster sugar	4 oz
300 g	flour	12 oz
150 g	chopped candied fruit	6 oz
	apricot purée	
	marzipan	

Meringue

	5 egg whites	
200 g	caster sugar	8 oz
50 g	icing sugar	2 oz

Cream the butter with the icing sugar, beat in the egg yolks and lemon zest and whisk until foamy. Fold in the egg whites whipped to a stiff snow with the caster sugar and carefully draw in the flour and the candied fruit. Spread on paper to make a 20 cm (8 in) square and bake. When cold, split once and sandwich with apricot purée, cut out with a round cutter and cover the sides very thinly with marzipan. To make the meringue, whip the egg whites stiffly with the caster sugar, then stir in the icing sugar. Pipe on to the petits fours and flash.

(Illustration, p. 1102)   Austria

Jocondes

	Parisian nougat	
2 dl	pistachio buttercream	⅓ pt
50 g	chopped almonds and	2 oz
	pistachio nuts	

Pin out the nougat into a thin rectangle and quickly cut into rounds with a plain cutter 3·5 cm (about 1½ in) in diameter. Using a savoy bag fitted with a star tube, pipe a peaked whirl of buttercream in the centre of each one. Sprinkle the buttercream with chopped almonds and pistachio nuts. Place on a paper doyley to serve.

France

Maltais

> fondante almond paste
> kirsch
> finely chopped candied
> orange peel

Mix the almond paste with 1 small teaspoon kirsch and 1 level spoon finely chopped candied orange peel to 150 g (5¼ oz) paste. Shape into large balls and flatten with a metal spatula to make rounds 3 cm (about 1 in) in diameter and 1½ cm (about ½ in) thick. Ice with orange fondant and decorate with candied orange peel. (No baking required.)

France

Marzipan fondant centre

Basic recipe I

300 g	almonds, blanched and dried	12 oz
600 g	granulated sugar	1½ lb
400 g	icing sugar	1 lb
3 dl	water	½ pt
	fondant, etc.	

Boil up the water and the granulated sugar and mix with the almonds and the icing sugar. Pour on to a marble slab, allow to cool and grind to a paste.

Divide into 10 equal portions and proceed as indicated in 1–10 below.

Basic recipe II

650 g	raw marzipan	1 lb 10 oz
650 g	icing sugar	1 lb 10 oz
	glucose	
	fondant, etc.	

Mix the raw marzipan thoroughly with the icing sugar. The total sugar content may include 3·5% glucose; this will make the paste more pliable.

Divide into 10 equal portions and proceed as directed under Basic recipe I.

1. *Hazelnut.* Work 20 g (1 oz) finely ground roasted hazelnuts into 100 g (4 oz)

of the above almond paste and shape into 10 small balls. Dip in light brown fondant, decorate with half a hazelnut and leave to dry on oiled paper.

2. *Pineapple*. Flavour 100 g (4 oz) of the almond paste with pineapple essence. Shape into 10 small sticks, sprinkle liberally with finely cut pineapple and dip the bottom half in white fondant.

3. *Chocolate*. Work 10 g ($\frac{1}{3}$ oz) cocoa powder into 100 g (4 oz) of the almond paste, shape into 10 balls and dip in chocolate fondant.

4. *Strawberry or raspberry*. Flavour 100 g (4 oz) of the almond paste with strawberry or raspberry essence, shape into balls and dip in pink fondant.

5. *Cherry*. Flavour almond paste well with kirsch and fill into 10 sugared cherries. Fix the cherries upside down on to nails and surround each one with a calyx of white fondant piped through a paper bag.

6. *Coffee*. Work 10 g ($\frac{1}{3}$ oz) instant coffee into 100 g (4 oz) of the almond paste. Shape into balls and dip in coffee fondant.

7. *Lemon*. Flavour 100 g (4 oz) of the almond paste with citric acid and dip in yellow fondant.

8. *Walnut*. Work 20 g (1 oz) ground walnuts into 100 g (4 oz) of the almond paste and shape into balls. Dip in light brown fondant and decorate with a quarter of a walnut.

9. *Pistachio nut*. Work 20 g (1 oz) ground very green pistachio nuts into 100 g (4 oz) of the almond paste, shape into balls and dip in light green fondant.

10. *Orange*. Flavour 100 g (4 oz) of the almond paste with orange essence, shape into small ovals and dip in orange fondant.

After dipping in fondant, deposit all the above on oiled paper to dry and to facilitate handling. When dry, place in small paper cases.

Hungary

Masked hazelnuts

Roast some choice hazelnuts, remove from the oven and rub in a cloth to remove the skin. As soon as they are cold dip them in hot couverture one by one. Drain on a rack.

Imitation leaves are available commercially which may be inserted into the couverture immediately after dipping the nuts.

France

Miniature eggs

	Parisian nougat	
250 g	praline buttercream	10 oz

Pin out the nougat into a thin sheet. Cut with an oval cutter a little larger than a teaspoon. Mould quickly to resemble half-eggshells, using a teaspoon or, preferably, an egg mould. Trim the edges very evenly. When cold, fill half of them with a dome of the buttercream and place the other half on top, edge to edge, to make up small whole eggs. Serve in small paper cases, either without further decoration or coated with fondant of various colours and flavours.

France

Morello petits fours

Prepare sheet genoese as for pineapple petits fours and sandwich with morello cherry buttercream. Thicken the cherry purée a little with cornflour if necessary and flavour the buttercream with kirsch. Cut into rounds, brush with apricot purée, then wrap in a thin sheet of marzipan. Coat the top with pink fondant and decorate with piped couverture flower.

(Illustration, p. 1102)

Austria

Nougat cups

	Parisian nougat	
$\frac{1}{2}$ l	Chantilly cream	$\frac{7}{8}$ pt
	glacé cherries	

Place a piece of hot nougat the size of a walnut in the bottom of a cylindrical mould, first wrapping the mould in a cloth to avoid burning the hands. Spread the nougat round the inside of the mould to a thickness of 2 mm (about $\frac{1}{10}$ in) with a moistened stick or wooden handle. If any holes develop in the nougat while moulding, fill in with a little fresh nougat. Using a knife, trim the top edges evenly. Keep the nougat warm while working; each little cup has to be moulded individually and left until cold before unmoulding. Pin out the rest of the nougat. Cut small sticks and shape them into cup handles. Dip the ends in a little sugar boiled to the crack degree and fix on to the nougat cups. Fill with Chantilly cream, using a savoy bag fitted with a star pipe. Top with half a glacé cherry or some other suitable decoration.

France

Nougat horns

	Parisian nougat	
50 g	buttercream (any flavour desired)	2 oz

First cut a triangular paper pattern corresponding in size to the inside of the pipe which will be used to mould the horns. Pin out the nougat into strips of the same width as the height of the paper pattern. To cut out, place the pattern on the pinned-out nougat and cut to size with the apex of the triangle alternately at the top and at the bottom. Keep the cut-out nougat warm. Shape each triangle into a horn by inserting it apex first into the wider end of the pipe and pressing it against the wall with the finger. Allow to cool. Decorate with chopped pistachio nuts, glacé cherries, angelica or silver balls, etc., depending on the flavour of the buttercream used for filling the horns. Place in small paper cases to serve.

France

Nougat sticks

	Parisian nougat	
250 g	vanilla buttercream	10 oz
100 g	chopped almonds	4 oz
100 g	chopped pistachio nuts	4 oz

Pin out the nougat into a strip of 5–6 cm (about 2 in) wide and cut across at intervals of 3 cm (about 1 in) to make small oblongs. Roll these up quickly to make tubes, either by hand or round an oiled metal rod. When cold, fill with the buttercream, using a savoy bag fitted with a small plain pipe. Brush with gum arabic and roll in a mixture of chopped almonds and pistachio nuts. Place on white paper and leave uncovered to dry for some time. To serve, pile the sticks on top of one another criss-cross fashion, either on their own or in the centre of a plate of assorted petits fours.

France

Nougatins

Cut a sheet of nougat into rectangles 4 cm by 2 cm ($1\frac{1}{2}$ in by $\frac{3}{4}$ in). Sandwich in pairs with hot, well-reduced apricot jam flavoured with rum. Cool quickly. Decorate by sticking half a pistachio nut in the centre with a little jam.

France

Nut desserts

Shape a thin sheet of sponge into a cylinder with the help of a rolling pin and fill with nut cream. Refrigerate until the filling is firm, then wrap in a thin sheet of white marzipan and cut into 5–6 cm (about 2 in) lengths. Dip both ends of each piece in chocolate, allow to set, then stand upright in paper cases. Place a quarter walnut dusted with icing sugar in the centre.

Hungary

Oranges

Use neatly cut, undamaged orange segments. Stand them upright and leave them uncovered to dry for a short time. Dip in sugar boiled to the crack degree or light brown caramel sugar. Drain, then leave on an oiled baking sheet until cold. Place in small paper cases to serve.

France

Orange petits fours

Yield: about 30

160 g	marzipan	6 oz
	7 egg yolks	
	lemon zest	
	vanilla	
	pinch of salt	
	7 egg whites	
130 g	sugar	5 oz
90 g	flour	3½ oz
100 g	finely chopped arancini (candied bitter oranges)	4 oz
100 g	finely chopped candied fruit	4 oz
50 g	melted butter	2 oz
	small strawberries	
	apricot purée	

Work the marzipan, egg yolks, lemon zest, vanilla and salt to a smooth paste. Fold in the egg whites whipped to a stiff snow with the sugar, stir in the flour, arancini and candied fruit and lastly blend in the melted butter. Spread on paper to make a 20 cm (8 in) square and bake. When cold, cut into rounds or ovals, place a strawberry on each one and glaze with apricot purée.

(Illustration, p. 1102)

Austria

Parisian baskets

	Parisian nougat	
200 g	buttercream	8 oz

Pin out Parisian nougat into a thin sheet. Cut out small disks, turn up the edges and shape into baskets. Cut out small handles from the rest of the nougat and fix them to the baskets with a little sugar boiled to the crack degree. Fill with buttercream and sprinkle the latter with chopped pistachio nuts.

France

Petits fours glacés

Yield: about 50 petits fours

Almond genoese

	9 eggs	
350 g	sugar	12¼ oz
150 g	ground almonds	5¼ oz
225 g	flour	8 oz
90 g	cornflour	3¼ oz
225 g	melted butter	8 oz
	vanilla	
	zest of half a lemon	
	pinch of salt	

Filling and decoration

500 g	arrack buttercream	1 lb 1½ oz
150 g	red currant jelly	5¼ oz
500 g	white fondant	1 lb 1½ oz
200 g	marzipan	7 oz
30 g	piping chocolate	1 oz
10 g	mimosa balls	⅓ oz
	angelica	

Beat the eggs and sugar warm, remove from the heat and continue beating. Sieve the flour and cornflour together, mix with the almonds and blend into the egg/sugar mixture. Lastly add the melted butter, the vanilla, lemon zest and salt. Spread on a prepared baking sheet and bake at 200°C, then allow to cool and peel off the paper. Split the genoese once, spread with red currant jelly and sandwich the buttercream, cover with a thin sheet of marzipan, invert, weight with a board and refrigerate until firm. Cut into fancy shapes with a number of different cutters and place on a wire rack. Fill the prepared and flavoured fondant into a wide-lipped jug, pour over the petits fours and allow to dry. Decorate with piping chocolate, mimosa balls and lozenges of angelica.

(Illustration, p. 1100)

(Techniques, p. 160)

Germany

Petits fours glacés Kranzler

Macaroon paste for petits fours

500 g	raw marzipan	1¼ lb
375 g	sugar	15 oz
	zest of half a lemon	
	approx. 4 egg whites	

Beat all the ingredients together to make a paste of piping consistency. Using a savoy bag and plain tube, pipe out macaroons 2 cm (¾ in) in diameter on sheets of paper. Bake at about 180°C and remove from the paper while still warm.

Buttercream for macaroon petits fours

	10 eggs	
300 g	sugar	12 oz
600 g	butter	1½ lb
100 g	white vegetable fat	4 oz
	(optional)	
	half a vanilla pod	
	(scraped out)	

Whisk the eggs and sugar warm, add the vanilla, remove from the heat and continue beating until cold. Add the creamed butter, together with the desired flavouring. As a rather firm buttercream is required for these petits fours, a little white vegetable fat may be added to stiffen it.

Fondant

It is advisable to mix a little butter with the fondant to be used for coating these petits fours.

1. Spread macaroons 2 cm (¾ in) in diameter with apricot jam. Pipe on a bulb of arrack buttercream and coat with white arrack flavoured fondant. Decorate with four tiny bows made of yellow fondant and 2 quarter pistachio nuts.

2. Spread macaroons of the same size with orange marmalade. Pipe on a bulb of milk ganache and place a thin disk of candied orange peel on top. Coat with milk couverture, decorate with spun couverture, using a paper bag, and top with a little gold leaf.

3. Spread the macaroons with apricot jam and pipe on a bulb of maraschino-flavoured buttercream. Place a tiny piece of candied pineapple on top, coat with white vanilla flavoured fondant and insert two tiny pieces of pistachio nut.

4. Spread the macaroons with pineapple jam and pipe on a bulb of plain ganache. Insert four half-almonds, coat with plain couverture and decorate with milk couverture and gold leaf.

5. Spread the macaroons with raspberry jam and pipe on a bulb of arrack buttercream. Top with a small piece of candied greengage, red pear and yellow cherry and coat with arrack-flavoured fondant. Decorate the fruit with little bows of fondant and place a small piece of rose petal in the centre.

6. Soak the macaroons in a little kirsch and pipe on a small dome of mocha buttercream. Coat with coffee fondant, pipe on a whirl of the same fondant and place a chocolate coffee bean in the centre.

7. Pipe a bulb of kirsch buttercream on to the macaroons and place half a glacé cherry on top. Coat with kirsch-flavoured fondant tinted pale pink, surround the cherry with a ring of the same fondant and decorate with a mimosa ball and a small piece of pistachio nut.

8. Pipe a bulb of orange-flavoured milk ganache on to the macaroons. Coat with milk couverture, sprinkle the top with chocolate shavings and dust with icing sugar.

Germany

Pierrots

250 g	Parisian nougat buttercream mixed with chopped candied fruit macerated in kirsch	10 oz
1 dl	royal icing	4 fl oz
	6 glacé cherries	
	40 small diamond shaped pieces of angelica	

Shape the nougat in small pomponnette moulds and allow to cool. Fill with the buttercream and coat as lightly as possible with royal icing. Cut each glacé cherry into eight and decorate each of the petits fours with two pieces of cherry and two angelica diamonds.

France

Pineapple petits fours

Yield: about 30

	6 eggs	
	4 egg yolks	
250 g	caster sugar	10 oz
150 g	flour	6 oz
100 g	cornflour	4 oz
90 g	melted butter	3½ oz
	pineapple buttercream	
	apricot purée	
	pineapple fondant	

Sugar roses

500 g	granulated sugar	1¼ lb
180 g	glucose	7 oz
	pinch of cream of tartar	

Beat the whole eggs, egg yolks and sugar together over gentle heat, remove from the heat and continue beating. Fold in the flour and cornflour and lastly blend in the melted butter. Spread on greaseproof paper to make three 20 cm (8 in) squares and bake briskly, keeping the sponge moist. When cold, sandwich with well flavoured pineapple buttercream and brush with apricot purée. Cut into rounds, wrap in a thin layer of marzipan and coat the top with pineapple fondant (made by adding reduced pineapple juice to fondant). Decorate each petit four with a small rose. To make the roses, place the sugar, the glucose and the cream of tartar, dissolved in water, in a clean pan and boil to 116°R, constantly washing down the sides of the pan and skimming the solution. Pour on to a lightly oiled slab. Warm again in the oven, colour lightly, pull, fold and fashion into small roses in the usual manner, making a small green leaf for each one.

(Illustration, p. 1102)   Austria

Pistachio balls

Japonaise bases

250 g	about 10 egg whites	10 oz
450 g	sugar	4 oz
100 g	ground almonds	4 oz

Filling

	pistachio buttercream	
	flavoured with a little kirsch	

Coating

plain couverture

Decoration

milk couverture

Whisk the egg whites to a stiff snow with 100 g (4 oz) sugar, then whisk in a further 100 g (4 oz) sugar and fold in the rest of the sugar mixed with the almonds. Pipe the mixture out in large bulbs on to greased baking sheets or silicone paper and bake slowly at about 160°C. When firm enough to handle, press the thumb into the underside of each base to make a cavity, then bake off. Allow to cool, place half the bases in small paper cases and fill with the pistachio buttercream. Coat the rest of the bases with tempered plain couverture and pipe on lines of milk couverture. Wait until the couverture has set completely before placing on top of the filled bases.

Switzerland

Praline petits fours

Yield: about 30

160 g	butter	6 oz
100 g	icing sugar	4 oz
	10 egg yolks	
100 g	crushed finely sieved praline	4 oz
	10 egg whites	
120 g	caster sugar	5 oz
100 g	flour	4 oz
100 g	sponge crumbs	4 oz
150 g	roasted ground hazelnuts	6 oz
	little cinnamon	
	praline buttercream	
	marzipan	
	marzipan flowers	
	Parisian nougat	
	cut-out disks	

Cream the butter with the icing sugar, beat in the egg yolks and a little lemon zest and add the sieved praline. Fold in the egg whites whipped to a stiff snow with the caster sugar and stir in the flour, sponge crumbs, hazelnuts and cinnamon. Spread on paper to make a 20 cm (8 in) square and bake, but do not allow to become too dry. When cold, split once and sandwich with praline buttercream, cut into rounds, brush with apricot purée and wrap in a thin sheet of marzipan. Coat the top with praline buttercream, place a fancy disk of Parisian nougat on top and decorate with a marzipan flower.

(Illustration, p. 1102)   Austria

Sans-façon

250 g	praline paste	10 oz
75 g	finely chopped candied fruit macerated in kirsch and well drained	3 oz
250 g	green pistachio-flavoured fondant	10 oz
50 g	chopped pistachio nuts	2 oz

Enclose a little chopped candied fruit (no larger than a pea) in a ball of praline paste the size of a large cherry. Coat with fondant and sprinkle with chopped pistachio nuts. Make a small notch in each ball with the back of a knife. Place in small paper cases to serve.

France

Snowballs

10 minutes in a medium oven

125 g	mixed almonds and hazelnuts	5 oz
250 g	icing sugar	10 oz
	pinch of ground vanilla *or* a few drops of coffee essence	
	1 egg white	

Grind the nuts with the sugar and vanilla or coffee essence, gradually blending in the egg white. The paste should be firm enough to roll in the hands. Shape into balls the size of a cherry. Place in small round paper cases and bake. Serve in the paper cases.

France

Spirals

7–8 minutes in a medium oven

250 g	ground almonds	10 oz
200 g	vanilla fondant	8 oz
	3 egg whites	
	glacé cherries	

Knead the ground almonds into the fondant with the palm of the hand. Add the unbeaten egg whites a little at a time to make a fairly soft paste. Pipe out in spirals on sheets of paper, using a savoy bag fitted with a star pipe. Place the paper on a baking sheet. Top each spiral with a piece of glacé cherry. Set aside for at least 5 or 6 hours until the surface has hardened, then bake. On removing from the oven, brush lightly with gum arabic or well sweetened milk.

France

'Piped petits fours'

The recipe for spirals is used to make a variety of petits fours which only differ from one another in shape and type of decoration, and which are known as 'piped petits fours'. They are fashioned in drops, rosettes, bows, plaits, etc. and decorated with split almonds, cherries, angelica, citron peel, dried fruit, etc. If desired, they may be made with ready-made raw marzipan, blended with sufficient egg white to give a softish paste (the amount of egg white will vary, depending on the quality of the marzipan).

France

Stuffed cherries

Split glacé cherries in half. Shape fondant almond paste into little balls and insert one into each split cherry, pressing it down a little. Dip the stuffed cherries one by one into sugar boiled to the crack degree. Drain, then leave on an oiled baking sheet or marble slab until cold. Place in small paper cases to serve.

France

Stuffed dates

Split some dates open lengthwise and remove the stones. Replace these by fondant almond paste moulded to the size and shape of an olive. (Use pink almond paste flavoured with kirsch and green almond paste flavoured with Chartreuse.) Dip the stuffed dates one by one in sugar boiled to the crack degree. Drain, then leave on an oiled baking sheet or marble slab until cold. Place in small paper cases to serve.

France

Stuffed muscatels

Slit open some large Malaga muscatels and remove the pips. Fill with fondant almond paste. Dip into sugar boiled to the crack degree and drain. Leave on an oiled baking sheet or marble slab until cold. Place in small paper cases to serve.

France

Stuffed prunes

Proceed as for stuffed dates.

France

Stuffed walnuts

Choose good, perfectly sound green walnuts. Shape fondant almond paste flavoured with Armagnac into balls the size of large hazelnuts. Sandwich the walnuts in pairs with a ball of almond paste in between, exerting slight pressure. Dip one by one in sugar boiled to the crack degree and drain. Leave until cold on an oiled baking sheet or marble slab. Place in small paper cases to serve.

France

Tangerines

Proceed as for oranges, p. 1149

France

Tea confections

50 g	butter	2 oz
	2 egg yolks	
100 g	icing sugar	4 oz
	3 heaped tablespoons tea	
	1 cup water (boiling)	
	zest of half an orange	
300 g	couverture	12 oz

Whisk the butter, egg yolks and sugar together until frothy. Pour the boiling water on the tea leaves, allow to stand for 5–6 minutes and strain the very strong tea into the butter/egg yolk/sugar mixture. Lastly, add the orange zest and the melted couverture. Spread on to aluminium foil or greaseproof paper to a thickness of 1 cm (about ½ in), allow to set, then cut in squares and roll in cocoa powder.

(Illustration, p. 1095)

Germany

Truffettes

250 g	chocolate	10 oz
75 g	butter	3 oz
3 cl	milk	3 dessertspoons
	2 egg yolks	
100 g	chocolate granules	4 oz
75 g	*or* chocolate powder	3 oz

Warm the chocolate in the milk over very gentle heat and mix to a smooth paste. Remove from the heat. Add the egg yolks, then the butter a little at a time, while beating with a spatula. Refrigerate until the mixture has set hard (overnight, if necessary). Shape into balls the size of a walnut. Roll them in chocolate powder or granules, or a mixture of the two. Place in small paper cases to serve.

France

Truffles

praline paste flavoured
with rum if desired
couverture
chocolate powder
currants

Shape the praline paste into small balls and dip in barely lukewarm melted couverture. Drain a little and roll in chocolate powder. Press a few currants into each ball here and there to represent holes. Place in small paper cases to serve.

(Illustration, p. 804)

France

Variations of chocolate truffles

The centres for truffles may be made of different sorts of ganache in various flavours. For large quantities, beat up the mixture in the mixer, pipe into ropes, using a plain pipe, and cut with a caramel cutter. Leave to harden and shape into balls which are rolled in the hand with a little couverture and placed on greaseproof paper. Small quantities may be beaten by hand.

Here are some popular varieties:

Kirsch truffles

$\frac{1}{4}$ l	kirsch	$\frac{1}{2}$ pt
$\frac{1}{4}$ l	dairy cream	$\frac{1}{2}$ pt
5 cl	96% alcohol	2 fl oz
50 g	butter	2 oz
1 kg	milk couverture	$2\frac{1}{2}$ lb

Cognac truffles

$\frac{1}{4}$ l	Cognac	$\frac{1}{2}$ pt
$\frac{1}{4}$ l	dairy cream	$\frac{1}{2}$ pt
5 cl	96% alcohol	2 fl oz
50 g	butter	2 oz
1 kg 400	milk couverture	$3\frac{1}{2}$ lb

Cherry brandy truffles

2 dl	cherry brandy	⅓ pt
¼ l	dairy cream	½ pt
5 cl	96% alcohol	2 fl oz
50 g	butter	2 oz
1 kg	plain couverture	2½ lb

Honey truffles

600 g	honey	1½ lb
375 g	butter	15 oz
4½ dl	dairy cream	¾ pt
1 kg	milk couverture	2½ lb
1 kg	fondant	2½ lb

Plain truffles

½ l	dairy cream	⅞ pt
50 g	butter	2 oz
1 kg 100	plain couverture	2¾ lb

Milk truffles

¾ l	dairy cream	1¼ pt
75 g	butter	3 oz
2 kg 100	milk couverture	5¼ lb

Plum truffles

¼ l	Pflumliwasser (or other plum brandy)	½ pt
¼ l	dairy cream	½ pt
5 cl	96% alcohol	2 fl oz
50 g	butter	2 oz
600 g	plain couverture	1½ lb
750 g	milk couverture	1¾ lb

Rum truffles

¼ l	rum	½ pt
¼ l	dairy cream	½ pt
5 cl	96% alcohol	2 fl oz
50 g	butter	2 oz
1 kg 500	milk couverture	3¾ lb

White truffles

¾ l	dairy cream	1¾ pt
75 g	butter	3 oz
2 kg 100	white couverture	¼ lb

Boil up the dairy cream with the butter, add the chopped couverture and the desired liqueur, and mix until smooth. Allow to stand for a time, then beat well, shape into balls and roll in the hand with a little couverture to coat lightly. Dip in thickened couverture and roll on a truffle rack. If desired, the truffles may be rolled in chocolate granules, cocoa powder or chocolate shavings, roughened on a grater when they are firm, and deposited on paper.

Switzerland

Twelfth cake

25 minutes in a medium oven

250 g	flour	10 oz
125 g	butter	5 oz
100 g	sugar	4 oz
	2 eggs	
100 g	citron peel	4 oz
50 g	granulated sugar	2 oz
5–6 cl	water	2 fl oz approx.
5 g	salt	1 teaspoon
12 g	yeast	$\frac{1}{2}$ oz

Proceed as for brioche dough (see p. 828). Shape the dough into a hollow ring on a floured marble slab, then place on a baking sheet lined with well buttered paper. Insert thin strips of citron peel into the dough and prove. Egg wash and sprinkle with granulated sugar. Avoid excessive top heat when baking; cover with paper if necessary. This cake is traditionally served on Twelfth Night, that is 6th January and has a 'bean' (which may be a coffee bean or a small gold or silver charm) hidden in it. Whoever receives the slice of cake containing the 'bean' is King (or Queen) for the night.

France

Velma gâteau

Yield: 5–6 sponges 24 cm ($9\frac{3}{4}$ in) in diameter, or 1 sheet genoese 44×35 cm (18×14 in).

Sponge mixture

	18 egg yolks	
	9 eggs	
375 g	sugar	15 oz
100 g	cocoa powder	4 oz
150 g	flour	6 oz
90 g	warm melted butter	$3\frac{1}{2}$ oz

Filling

I.	pistachio buttercream	
II.	2 parts whipped dairy cream	
	1 part Velma couverture	

Coating

milk or plain couverture
or chocolate fondant

Whip up the egg yolks, eggs and sugar over gentle heat, then continue beating until cold. Gradually blend in the cocoa powder, the flour and the warm butter. Fill into round tins or spread on a paper-lined baking sheet and bake at about 220°C. When cold, split twice, making the middle layer thinner than the other two.

Carefully mix the cream with the Velma couverture which has been melted and tempered, making sure the couverture is not too warm, otherwise the cream will be too liquid.

Invert the top layer of sponge, spread thinly with pistachio buttercream and cover with a second, thin layer of sponge. Spread with chocolate cream to a thickness of about 3 cm ($1\frac{1}{4}$ in) and cover with the remaining layer of sponge. Refrigerate until firm. Coat with couverture or chocolate fondant before cutting.

Switzerland

Viennese apple strudel

10 persons   Baking time: 25–30 minutes

250 g	strong flour	10 oz
	1 egg	
30 g	oil	1 oz
	pinch of salt	
	dash of vinegar	
	little lukewarm water	
	oil for brushing pastry	

Filling

120 g	butter	5 oz
80 g	white breadcrumbs	3 oz
1 kg 500	cooking apples, peeled and cored	$3\frac{3}{4}$ lb
50 g	sultanas	2 oz
150 g	caster sugar	6 oz

pinch of cinnamon
pinch of ground cloves
juice of half a lemon
a little rum
icing sugar

Work the flour, egg, oil, salt, vinegar and a little lukewarm water to a softish dough which does not stick to the board or the hands. Lay it on a floured part of the board, brush with oil and allow to rest for 20 minutes. Now place it on a large floured cloth, roll out a little with a rolling pin and brush with oil to prevent sticking when the dough is pulled out. Slip the floured hands under the ends of the paste and pull and stretch the paste until the ends are hanging over the edge of the table and the centre is paper thin. Cut off the thick ends which are hanging down. Brush the paste thinly with butter and sprinkle one half lengthwise lightly with breadcrumbs toasted in butter. Cover with the sliced apples, sprinkle with the sultanas and finish off with the spices, rum, caster sugar and lemon juice. Roll up tightly, starting with the side covered with filling, and place on a greased baking sheet or tin. Bake in a medium oven, brushing with butter from time to time. Serve hot or cold, dusted with icing sugar.

(Techniques, p. 137)   Austria

Viennese hazelnut torte

175 g	sugar	7 oz
140 g	hazelnuts	$5\frac{1}{2}$ oz
	10 egg yolks	
	2 eggs	
	7 egg whites	
70 g	cake crumbs	3 oz
70 g	flour	3 oz
	vanilla	
	2–3 spoons water	

Roast, skin and grind the hazelnuts. Place two-thirds of the sugar in a pan and stir over the heat until lightly coloured. Add 2–3 spoonfuls of water drop by drop. When the sugar is completely dissolved boil to the thick thread degree. Allow to cool. When quite cold, mix with the egg yolks, whole eggs, vanilla and hazelnuts and whip until very frothy. Whisk the egg whites and the rest of the sugar to a stiff snow and fold in. Lastly, fold in the flour and the cake crumbs. Fill into two hoops or circular tins and bake in a medium oven. When cold, split each base once and sandwich with hazelnut buttercream. Coat the whole torte with vanilla or maraschino-flavoured fondant and decorate the top with a ring of caramelised roasted hazelnuts.

Austria

Wacheau gâteau

Almond sponge

	10 egg yolks	
250 g	sugar	10 oz
	juice and zest of 1 lemon	
	10 egg whites	
250 g	unblanched almonds, finely ground	10 oz
100 g	streusel (butter crumble)	4 oz

Buttercream

200 g	butter	8 oz
200 g	sugar	8 oz
	3 egg yolks	
	vanilla sugar	
	lemon juice	
	1 tablespoon rum	
	almond oil	
100 g	melted chocolate	4 oz

To make the almond sponge mixture, whisk the egg yolks with half the sugar. Whip the egg whites to a stiff snow with the rest of the sugar. Mix the almonds with the streusel and carefully blend all the ingredients together. Fill into a lightly buttered gâteau tin which has been lined with buttered and floured paper and bake for about 1 hour at 190–200°C.

To make the buttercream, cream the butter with the sugar and work in the egg yolks a little at a time. Flavour with vanilla sugar, a little lemon juice, rum and a few drops of almond oil. Lastly, stir in the melted chocolate.

When the sponge is cold, split once and sandwich with part of the buttercream. Coat the top and sides with the rest of the buttercream, splash with rum, mask with ground almonds and decorate with split blanched almonds.

Austria

Witches' dance carnival gâteau

170 g	butter	7 oz
150 g	icing sugar	6 oz
	8 egg yolks	
	8 egg whites	
160 g	couverture	6½ oz
150 g	caster sugar	6 oz

170 g	flour	7 oz
	ganache	
	marzipan	
	royal icing	
	chocolate fondant	

Cream the butter with the icing sugar, beat in the egg yolks and stir in the melted couverture. Fold in the egg whites whipped to a stiff snow with the caster sugar and lastly stir in the flour. Bake at 180°C in a greased gâteau tin lined with greased and floured paper. When cold, split once, sandwich with ganache and coat with chocolate fondant. Make the witches with marzipan and their brooms with royal icing brought to a piping consistency. Fix an edging of marzipan round the base of the gâteau.

(Illustration, p. 1107)   Austria

Wedding cake

40 persons

Butter sponge

	10 egg yolks	
	10 egg whites	
200 g	sugar	8 oz
	a little caramel colour	
	a little grated lemon zest	
180 g	flour	7 oz
50 g	cocoa powder	2 oz
50 g	melted butter	2 oz

Chocolate cream

350 g	butter	14 oz
300 g	sugar	12 oz
150 g	cocoa powder	6 oz
50 g	chocolate	2 oz
15 g	dairy cream	$\frac{1}{2}$ oz
300 g	brandied cherries	12 oz

Decoration

400 g	fondant almond paste	1 lb

Spray of flowers

1 kg	cube sugar	2$\frac{1}{2}$ lb
	1 tablespoon vinegar (20%)	
	a little green colour	

To make the butter sponge, place the sugar and egg yolks in a basin together with a little caramel colour and grated lemon zest. Whisk until light and frothy, then fold in the stiffly-whipped egg whites, the flour and cocoa and lastly the melted butter. Deposit in an oval tin and bake at 180–200°C. When cold, split twice, sandwich with chocolate cream and leave in a cool place until firm.

To make the chocolate cream, bring the cream and sugar to the boil, add the cocoa powder and chocolate and allow to cool. Beat in the softened butter until light and frothy and stir in the finely-cut brandied cherries.

Cover the assembled gâteau with a sheet of white almond paste which has been marked with a fluted roller. Surround the base with an edging of pale green almond paste. Place the spray of flowers on top.

To make the spray of flowers, boil the cube sugar with the vinegar and 2–3 dl (about ½ pt) water to the hard crack degree. Pour on to an oiled marble slab and divide into two. Pull one half between the hands until satiny and use to make the arum lilies and ribbon.

Tint the other half pale green and shape into stems and leaves without pulling. Assemble the bouquet on the marble slab before placing on the gâteau.

(Illustration, p. 1107)   Hungary

BEVERAGES

POPULAR COCKTAILS

Adonis

⅔ dry sherry
⅓ vermouth rouge
1 dash orange bitter
mixing glass

Affinity

½ Scotch whisky
¼ dry vermouth
¼ vermouth rouge
1 dash orange bitter
mixing glass

Alaska

¾ gin
¼ chartreuse yellow
shaker

Alexander

⅓ brandy
⅓ creme de caçao
⅓ fresh cream
shaker

Americano

in a tumbler:
small piece of ice
little soda water
twist of lemon peel
1 part Campari
2 parts Italian vermouth

Angel face

⅓ dry gin
⅓ apricot brandy
⅓ calvados
shaker

Bacardi

⅔ Bacardi rum
⅓ lime juice or lemon juice
1 teaspoon grenadine
shaker

Bamboo

½ dry sherry
½ dry vermouth
1 dash orange bitter
mixing glass

Bentley

½ Calvados
½ Dubonnet
shaker

Between the sheets

⅓ brandy
⅓ Cointreau
⅓ Bacardi rum
1 dash lemon juice
shaker

Block and fall

$\frac{1}{3}$ brandy
$\frac{1}{3}$ Cointreau
$\frac{1}{6}$ Calvados
$\frac{1}{6}$ absinthe
shaker

Bloody Mary

1 liqueur glass vodka
2 dashes Worcestershire sauce
iced tomato juice
into smaller tumbler glass
stir well

Bobby Burns

$\frac{1}{2}$ Scotch whisky
$\frac{1}{2}$ sweet vermouth
2 dashes benedictine
twist lemon peel
mixing glass

Bombay

$\frac{1}{2}$ brandy
$\frac{1}{4}$ dry vermouth
$\frac{1}{4}$ vermouth rouge
1 dash absinthe
2 dashes curaçao
shaker

Bronx

$\frac{1}{2}$ dry gin
$\frac{1}{6}$ fresh orange juice
$\frac{1}{6}$ dry vermouth
$\frac{1}{6}$ sweet vermouth
shaker

Brooklyn

> ⅔ rye whisky
> ⅓ vermouth rouge
> 1 dash maraschino
> 1 dash Amer Picon
> mixing glass

Caruso

> ⅓ dry gin
> ⅓ dry vermouth
> ⅓ green creme de menthe
> shaker

Casino

> ¾ dry gin
> 1/12 maraschino
> 1/12 orange bitter
> 1/12 lemon juice
> shaker
> add cherry

Claridge

> ⅓ dry gin
> ⅓ dry vermouth
> ⅙ apricot brandy
> ⅙ cointreau
> mixing glass

Clover Club

> ⅔ dry gin
> ⅓ grenadine
> juice of ½ lemon
> ½ white of 1 egg
> shake and strain into a
>   double cocktail glass

Czarine

$\frac{1}{2}$ vodka
$\frac{1}{4}$ dry vermouth
$\frac{1}{4}$ apricot brandy
1 dash Angostura bitter
mixing glass

Daiquiri

$\frac{3}{4}$ white Cuba rum
$\frac{1}{4}$ lemon juice
3 dashes syrup nat.
shaker

Derby

2 dashes peach bitter
2 sprigs fresh mint
1 glass dry gin
shaker

Diki-Diki

$\frac{2}{3}$ calvados
$\frac{1}{6}$ Swedish punch
$\frac{1}{6}$ grapefruit juice
shaker

Duchess

$\frac{1}{3}$ vermouth rouge
$\frac{1}{3}$ dry vermouth
$\frac{1}{3}$ absinthe
mixing glass

East-India

$\frac{3}{4}$ brandy
$\frac{1}{8}$ curaçao
$\frac{1}{8}$ pineapple juice
2 dashes angostura bitter
add cherry
shaker

Eden Rock

in a champagne glass:
1 part kirsch
3 drops raspberry syrup
9 parts champagne or similar
  dry sparkling wine
1 slice of orange to decorate

Gibson

$\frac{1}{6}$ dry vermouth
$\frac{5}{6}$ dry gin
add pearl onion
mixing glass

Gin and It. (Gin and Italian)

$\frac{1}{2}$ dry gin
$\frac{1}{2}$ sweet vermouth
to be prepared directly
  in the cocktail glass

Grand Slam

$\frac{1}{2}$ Swedish punch
$\frac{1}{4}$ vermouth rouge
$\frac{1}{4}$ dry vermouth
shaker

Grasshopper

$\frac{1}{3}$ green creme de menthe
$\frac{1}{3}$ white creme de cacao
$\frac{1}{3}$ heavy cream
serve in a double cocktail glass

Luisito special

in a mixing glass:
6 parts vodka
3½ parts dry vermouth
½ part creme de cacao
curl of orange rind to decorate

Manhattan

⅔ rye whisky or bourbon
⅓ sweet vermouth
1 dash angostura bitter
1 cherry maraschino
mixing glass

Martini Dry

¾ dry gin
¼ dry vermouth
twist of lemon peel
mixing glass

(Illustration, p. 1176)

Martini Sweet

⅔ dry gin
⅓ sweet vermouth
add 1 cherry
mixing glass

Mary Pickford

½ white rum
½ pineapple juice
1 teaspoonful grenadine
6 drops maraschino
shaker

Mikado

$\frac{1}{2}$ glass brandy
2 dashes angostura bitter
2 dashes creme de Noyau
2 dashes orgeat sirup
2 dashes curaçao
shaker

Mimosa (short drink)

60% vodka
30% galliano liqueur
5% kirsch
5% dry vermouth
1 small cherry

Monkey Gland

$\frac{3}{5}$ dry gin
$\frac{2}{5}$ orange juice
2 dashes granadine
2 dashes absinthe
shaker

Negroni

$\frac{1}{3}$ dry gin
$\frac{1}{3}$ sweet vermouth
$\frac{1}{3}$ bitter campari
$\frac{1}{2}$ slice orange
large cube of ice
to be prepared in a
    small tumbler glass

Old Fashioned

1 lump of sugar with
2 dashes of Angostura bitter
$\frac{1}{2}$ slice orange
$\frac{1}{2}$ slice lemon
1 Maraschino cherry
1 glass bourbon whisky
large piece of ice
to be prepared in the
    old fashioned glass

Old Pal

$\frac{1}{2}$ Dubonnet
$\frac{1}{2}$ dry gin
1 dash angostura bitter
shaker

Orange Blossom

$\frac{1}{2}$ dry gin
$\frac{1}{2}$ orange juice
shaker

Oriental

$\frac{1}{2}$ Canadian whisky
$\frac{1}{4}$ sweet vermouth
$\frac{1}{4}$ white curaçao
juice of $\frac{1}{2}$ lemon
shaker

Paradise

$\frac{1}{2}$ dry gin
$\frac{1}{4}$ apricot brandy
$\frac{1}{4}$ orange juice
shaker

Parisian

$\frac{2}{5}$ dry gin
$\frac{2}{5}$ dry vermouth
$\frac{1}{5}$ creme de cassis
mixing glass

Planters

$\frac{1}{2}$ Jamaica rum
$\frac{1}{2}$ orange juice
few dashes lemon juice
shaker

▶ Tea punch, p. 1183

Princeton

$\frac{2}{3}$ dry gin
$\frac{1}{3}$ Porto wine
2 dashes orange bitter
twist of lemon peel
mixing glass

Recreatio

juice of $\frac{1}{2}$ orange
10 cc   1 small glass cognac $\frac{1}{3}$ fl oz
$\frac{1}{2}$ glass champagne
1 cocktail cherry on a
    cocktail stick to decorate
1 slice of orange

Red whortleberry cocktail

1 part red
    whortleberry juice
1 part vodka
place some ice in the
    shaker, pour in the juice
    and the vodka,
    shake well and strain
    into cocktail glasses

Finland

Rob-Roy

$\frac{1}{2}$ Scotch Whisky
$\frac{1}{2}$ sweet Vermouth
1 dash Angostura bitter
add one cherry
mixing glass

Rose

$\frac{3}{4}$ dry Vermouth
$\frac{1}{4}$ Kirsch
2 dashes sirop de framboise

◄   Cocktails at the Gritti Palace Hotel, Venice, pp. 1171–2, 1179, 1180–81
35

Sidecar

½ brandy
¼ Cointreau or Curaçao triple sec
¼ lemon juice
shaker

Stinger

⅔ old brandy
⅓ white Creme de Menthe
shaker

Symphonie in Blue

60% Vodka
30% blue Curaçao
5% Kirsch
5% dry Vermouth
orange peel
lemon peel
1 cherry

The New Eden Special

50% white rum
40% dry Vermouth
10% Grand Marnier
3 drops of lemon juice
orange peel

White Lady

½ dry gin
¼ Cointreau or Curaçao triple sec
¼ lemon juice
shaker

(Illustration, p. 1176)

Zaza

½ Dubonnet
½ dry gin
1 dash Angostura bitter
shaker

LONG DRINKS

Exotic

In a tall glass:

small ice cubes to come halfway up
4 parts sweet sherry
5 parts gin
good quality lemonade to fill up

Decoration

half a slice orange
half a slice lemon
1 pineapple cube
1 slice banana
sprig of mint
2 striped straws

Exotic 71

60% gin
40% Bristol Cream Sherry
slice of lemon
slice of orange
slice of banana
slice of pineapple
cherry
fill up with lemonade
fresh mint

El Petiso

Use tumblers:
50% Vodka
20% Galliano liqueur
15% Grenadine
15% lemon juice
fill up with orange juice
ice
garnish with 2 slices of lemon and
    2 small cherries

Fior di Loto

10% Cointreau
10% Cognac
20% orange juice
60% champagne Brut
slice of pineapple
slice of orange
1 small cherry

Galante

In a tall glass:
small ice cubes to come halfway up
2 parts peach brandy
5 parts white rum
3 parts dry sherry
good quality lemonade to fill up

Decoration

1 slice orange
1 slice lemon
1 cocktail cherry
2 striped straws

Gin Fizz

In a shaker:
1 small teaspoon caster sugar
juice of half a lemon
1 small glass gin
shake well, pour into a tumbler and
fill up with soda water

Pool side special

50% white rum
50% orange juice
drops of lime juice
drops of almonds liqueur
1 cherry
slice of pineapple
ice

Summertime

1 part orange liqueur
1 part gin
2 parts orange juice
1 cocktail cherry to decorate

HOT DRINKS WITH ALCOHOL

Bishop's wine

The origin of this traditional name is probably to be found in the best known of all bishops, St. Nicolas, the most popular saint in Holland.

2 bottles of red wine
(preferably Bordeaux)
1 orange
1 lemon
16–20 cloves
piece of cinnamon quill
sugar to taste

In the past this hot wine was prepared in a china kettle, the spout being plugged with cotton-wool to retain the full aroma.

Stud the orange and lemon with the cloves, so that they resemble a porcupine. Place them in a kettle or pan, add the cinnamon and pour the wine over. Leave to steep over very gentle heat until the wine has reached a temperature of about 80°. Remove the cinnamon and fruit, add sugar to taste and serve as hot as possible.

Holland

Dutch chocolate punch

	2 tablespoons grated chocolate	
	1 level tablespoon sugar	
	1 level teaspoon instant	
	coffee powder	
⅛ l	hot milk	¼ pt approx.
	2 small glasses rum	

Mix the chocolate, sugar and coffee powder together, dissolve in the hot milk, stir in the rum and reheat.

Germany

Egg grog

1 egg yolk
tea
sugar
2 small glasses rum or arrack

Whip the egg yolk with a little tea and sugar until frothy, preferably using a small wire whisk. Pour in the rum or arrack a glassful at a time while stirring constantly. If too strong, fill up with a little hot water.

Germany

Egg toddy

	1 egg yolk	
	2 tablespoons sugar	
5 cl	Cognac, port, sherry	1/12 pt
	or Marsala (or other alcohol)	
	boiling water	

Place the egg yolk and sugar in the glass in which the toddy is to be served and whip with a fork or a small whisk until light and foamy. Add the Cognac, wine of other alcohol and fill up with boiling water.

Fire-tongs tea punch

24 glasses approx.	12 teaspoons tea	
	(or equivalent number of tea-bags)	
1 l	water	1¾ pt
	2 bottles red wine	
	½ bottle rum (at least 45%)	
	cinnamon quills	
	cloves	
	2 lemons	
	1 sugar loaf	

Make the tea, allow to stand for 5 minutes, then strain off. Heat the wine without boiling, add the tea and flavour with cinnamon, cloves and lemon juice. Pour into the punch bowl, place the tongs on the bowl with the sugar loaf on top, pour the rum over and set alight.

Germany

(Illustration, p. 1175)

Fischerhaus coffee

1 person

	2 small teaspoons brown sugar	
3 cl	kirsch	3 dessertspoons
2 dl	very strong black coffee	⅓ pt
	1 tablespoon lightly	
	whipped dairy cream	

Place the sugar and kirsch in a glass of suitable size and pour in very hot coffee almost to the top. Stir, cover with the cream and serve at once.

Germany

(Illustration, p. 247)

Gaelic coffee

Pre-heat the stemmed glasses in which it should be served. Over 2 lumps of sugar and a jigger of Irish pot still whiskey pour really hot black coffee. Stir vigorously and top off with a layer of fresh cream poured gently over a spoon poised near the surface. Do not stir or let the spoon into the glass.

Glögg

	7 cardamom seeds	
	20 cloves	
	4 sticks cinnamon	
	1 crushed vanilla pod	
250 g	cube sugar	8¾ oz
7 dl	2 bottles red wine each	1¼ pt
¼ l	aquavit or colourless fruit brandy	½ pt

Accompaniments

100 g	currants	3½ oz
100 g	blanched almonds	3½ oz

Place the spices, vanilla and sugar in a serving pot (e.g. one with a handle) or punch bowl. Pour in the wine and heat, then add the aquavit or brandy and ignite. Serve in suitable glasses or mugs. Place the almonds and currants on small plates as accompaniments.

(Illustration, p. 1142)   Sweden

Grape juice punch

1 l	red grape juice	1¾ pt
	juice and zest of 1 lemon	
	2 oranges	
	1 heaped tablespoon brown sugar	
¼ l	arrack	½ pt

Pour the grape juice into a pan and add the lemon juice and zest. Wash the oranges and clean the skin thoroughly, cut into sections and add to the grape juice. Sweeten with the brown sugar and lastly pour in the arrack. Heat until almost boiling and and serve hot.

Germany

Hawaii grog

Place a few pineapple cubes in a glass with a few small brown sugar pieces and a teaspoonful of lemon juice. Pour in hot water to come three-quarters of the way up, then fill up the glass with arrack.

Germany

Milk Pott

1 person

1 large glass milk
1 tablespoon honey
2 tablespoons rum

Dissolve the honey in the hot milk, pour into a glass and add the rum. The milk should be drunk hot.

Germany

Old Berlin punch
4 persons

$\frac{1}{4}$ l

2 bottles red wine
hot tea
juice of 1 lemon
sugar to taste
1 bottle rum

$\frac{1}{2}$ pt

Heat the wine to boiling point, then add the hot tea, the lemon juice and sugar to taste. Lastly, stir in the rum and serve at once. Any punch left over may be kept if well covered; it tastes just as good cold.

Germany

Orange punch

125 g

$\frac{1}{4}$ l

juice and zest of 2 oranges
juice and zest of 2 lemons
sugar
1 bottle light white wine
water
$\frac{1}{2}$ bottle rum or arrack

$4\frac{1}{2}$ oz

$\frac{1}{2}$ pint

Mix the orange and lemon juice and zest with the sugar. Pour in the wine mixed with the water, cover and set aside for at least 2 hours. Before serving, heat and filter, mix with the rum or arrack and pour into glasses while still hot. Decorate with a strip of orange peel.

Germany

Raspberry punch

1 l	strong tea	1¾ pt
	juice of 1 lemon	
½ l	sweetened raspberry	⅞ pt
	syrup	
¼ l	arrack	½ pt approx.

Add the lemon juice and syrup to the hot tea, bring to the boil, pour in the arrack and serve.

Germany

Red sand

1 person

2 tablespoons rum (54%)
1 tablespoon sugar
1 tablespoon dairy cream
hot strong tea

Warm a cup, pour in the rum, stir in the sugar, ignite, then fill almost to the top with tea. Lastly stir in the cream.

Germany

Red wine punch

2 parts red wine
1 part strong tea
brown sugar
lemon juice
rum or arrack to taste

Heat the wine and tea together, sweeten with the sugar and add a little lemon juice. Reheat and flavour with rum or arrack to taste.

Germany

Royal Mocha

1 person

        2 tablespoons rum (54%)
        2 lumps sugar
        hot strong black coffee
        1 tablespoon whipped cream

Warm a cup, pour in the rum, add the sugar and ignite. When the sugar begins to dissolve, fill up with the coffee and top with the cream.

                                    Germany

COLD ALCOHOLIC DRINKS

Apple toddy

4 persons

        4 apples
        ½ bottle rum
        ½ bottle brandy
        4 lumps sugar
¾ l   boiling water   1¼ pt

Core the apples, but do not peel. Bake in an oven-proof dish, then place in a bowl and add the rum, brandy, sugar and boiling water. Cover and allow to stand for 2 hours.

                                    Germany

Grape juice frappe

1 person

Place 2 cubes of vanilla ice cream in a glass goblet, pour over half a small glass of brandy, fill up with grape juice, decorate with a small whirl of whipped cream and sprinkle with chopped almonds or pistachio nuts.

                                    Germany

Grape juice milk drink

4 glasses

¾ l	white grape juice	1¼ pt
¼ l	milk	½ pt
	3 egg yolks	
50 g	sugar	1¾ oz
	2 small glasses rum	
	whipped cream	
	2 teaspoons cocoa powder	

Mix the grape juice with the milk, egg yolks, sugar and rum, chill well and pour into glasses. Decorate with a small whirl of whipped cream and sprinkle half a teaspoon cocoa powder on top of each one.

Germany

'Good morning' hang-over fizz

Mix 1 glass Scotch whisky with an egg yolk, a pinch of sugar and a pinch of pepper. Add the juice of 1 lemon, mix well on ice, pour into a large champagne glass or lemonade glass and serve with a few slices of cucumber.

Germany

Swedish Mead

7 l	water	12 pt
500 g	sugar	1 lb
500 g	brown sugar	1 lb
	1 lemon	
35 g	hops	1¼ oz
	¼ teaspoon yeast	
	currants, sugar	

Bring the water to the boil, add the sugar and boil until the sugar has dissolved. Peel and slice the lemon. Rinse the hops in hot water, then add to the boiling sugar solution together with the lemon. Allow to cool, then whisk in the yeast which has been dispersed in lukewarm water. Leave to ferment overnight. Wash the currants and place a few in each bottle with a spoonful of sugar. Fill up with the mead and seal hermetically or cork and tie the corks down. Store in a cool place. Serve after 10 days.

Sweden

Iced tea cocktail

1 person

Make a fairly strong tea and allow to cool. Pour one small glass Cognac and half a small glass orange liqueur into a tall glass, add one teaspoon icing sugar, 2 or 3 ice cubes and a piece of orange peel, and fill up with tea. Chill well before serving.

Germany

(Illustration, p. 1095)

Kvass

1 kg	dry rye bread with crust	2 lb
200 g	sugar	6 oz
20 g	yeast	½ oz
50 g	raisins	1½ oz
3 l	water	5 pt

Break the bread into small pieces, pour on the boiling water and leave until quite cold, then strain off the liquid. Add the sugar to it, stir well, then disperse the yeast in the liquid and leave to ferment in a warm place for 12 hours. Pour into bottles, adding a few raisins to each one, and store in a cool place. The kvass will be ready for use in two days.

Russia

Maraschino grape juice drink

4 glasses

3 cups grape juice
2 tablespoons honey
juice of 1 grapefruit
dash of maraschino
2 egg whites
1 heaped tablespoon sugar
2 cups soda water

Mix the grape juice with the honey and grapefruit juice and add a dash of maraschino. Stir in the egg whites whipped to a snow with the sugar and add the soda water. Place a few ice cubes in each glass and fill up with the mixture. The whipped whites will quickly rise to the top, making a pleasant drink.

Germany

Sangria

	1 lemon	
	1 orange	
	2 glasses Cointreau	
¼ l	brandy	½ pt
	1 bottle red wine	
	1 bottle lemonade	
	fresh mint	

Wash the lemon and orange and slice thinly without peeling. Steep these in the liqueur and brandy. Place all the ingredients into a well-chilled earthenware jug with plenty of ice.

Spain

Tea flip

2 persons

	milk	
¼ l	2 teaspoons tea	½ pt
	2 teaspoons honey	
	1 egg yolk	
	2 small glasses rum	
	whipped cream and	
	chocolate shavings to decorate	

Boil up the milk and pour on the tea-leaves. Sweeten with the honey and stir in the egg yolk. Lastly, add the rum. Decorate with a topping of whipped cream and chocolate shavings.

Germany

(Illustration, p. 1095)

Waltzing peach

Brush, wash and drain ripe peaches. Prick them with a fork, place each one in a balloon glass and pour in sparkling wine or champagne. After a moment the peach begins to turn as the carbon dioxide bubbles up to the top. The wine takes on the delicate fragrance of the fruit.

Germany

(Illustration p. 1141)

NON-ALCOHOLIC DRINKS

Créole coffee

1 dl	water	4 fl oz
120 g	brown sugar	4 oz
60 g	cocoa powder	2 oz
	very strong coffee	
	Chantilly cream	

Place the sugar and cocoa in a pan, add the water and bring to the boil while whisking. Remove from the heat when the mixture is smooth and thick (after about 5 minutes). Make very strong coffee. Place 2–3 teaspoons of the sugar/cocoa mixture in each cup, pour in the coffee and stir. Pipe Chantilly cream on top.

Sweden

Grape, orange and lemon fruit drink

4 glasses

½ l	grape juice	⅞ pt
	2 tablespoons lemon juice	
	2 tablespoons orange juice	
	1 tablespoon sugar	
	½ cup rolled oats	

Mix all the ingredients together thoroughly and serve well chilled.

Germany

Grape juice and pineapple cocktail

4 glasses

4 slices pineapple
2 tablespoons honey
juice of half a lemon
3 cups white grape juice

Reduce the pineapple to a purée in the liquidiser. Mix with the honey, lemon juice and grape juice. Serve with a curl of lemon peel and ice cubes.

Germany

Grape juice and yoghourt drink

4 glasses

½ l	2 pots yoghourt red grape juice 2 egg yolks juice and zest of half a lemon	¾ pt

Mix the yoghourt with the grape juice, and add the egg yolks, lemon juice and zest. Serve with drinking straws.

Germany

Vitamin yoghourt drink

⅛ l ⅛ l	1 pot yoghourt spinach juice or purée tomato juice juice of 1 lemon salt and white pepper pinch of sugar	¼ pt ¼ pt

Mix the yoghourt well with the spinach juice or purée and the tomato juice. Add the lemon juice, season with salt and a little white pepper, add a pinch of sugar and serve with a curl of lemon rind and a slice of tomato.

Germany

Sima

6 persons

2 l	water	3½ pt
500 g	light brown pieces sugar	1 lb 2 oz
500 g	granulated sugar	
	juice of 2 lemons	
	thinly pared rind of 2 lemons	
25 g	hops	1 oz
5 g	yeast	⅙ oz

Bring the water to the boil, add the lemon rind and all the sugar. Stir until the sugar is dissolved, then add the lemon juice and the hops which have been rinsed in hot water. Cool to 37°C then disperse the crumbled yeast in the liquid. Leave to ferment at room temperature for the whole of the next day. The sima can be drawn off as soon as the lemon rind has risen to the surface. Strain into bottles through a sieve lined with filter paper and store in a cool place. The drink will be ready in 3–5 days.

Finland

ALPHABETICAL
INDEX

INDEX

Page numbers in **bold** type refer to illustrations

NATIONAL
DISHES

INDEX — NATIONAL DISHES